Law Bookstore
thelawbookstore.com
New & Used

D1790441

West's Law School
Advisory Board

JESSE H. CHOPER
Professor of Law and Dean Emeritus,
University of California, Berkeley

JOSHUA DRESSLER
Professor of Law, Michael E. Moritz College of Law,
The Ohio State University

YALE KAMISAR
Professor of Law, University of San Diego
Professor of Law Emeritus, University of Michigan

MARY KAY KANE
Professor of Law, Chancellor and Dean Emeritus,
University of California,
Hastings College of the Law

LARRY D. KRAMER
Dean and Professor of Law, Stanford Law School

JONATHAN R. MACEY
Professor of Law, Yale Law School

ARTHUR R. MILLER
University Professor, New York University
Formerly Bruce Bromley Professor of Law, Harvard University

GRANT S. NELSON
Professor of Law, Pepperdine University
Professor of Law Emeritus, University of California, Los Angeles

A. BENJAMIN SPENCER
Professor of Law,
Washington & Lee University School of Law

JAMES J. WHITE
Professor of Law, University of Michigan

EVIDENCE: THE CALIFORNIA CODE AND THE FEDERAL RULES

A PROBLEM APPROACH

Fifth Edition

∎ ∎ ∎

By

Miguel A. Méndez

Member, California State Bar
Professor of Law and Martin Luther King, Jr. Scholar
University of California Davis School of Law
Adelbert H. Sweet, Jr. Professor of Law Emeritus
Stanford University

AMERICAN CASEBOOK SERIES®

WEST®

A Thomson Reuters business

Mat #41176427

Thomson Reuters created this publication to provide you with accurate and authoritative information concerning the subject matter covered. However, this publication was not necessarily prepared by persons licensed to practice law in a particular jurisdiction. Thomson Reuters does not render legal or other professional advice, and this publication is not a substitute for the advice of an attorney. If you require legal or other expert advice, you should seek the services of a competent attorney or other professional.

American Casebook Series is a trademark registered in the U.S. Patent and Trademark Office.

COPYRIGHT © 1995 WEST PUBLISHING CO.
© West, a Thomson business, 1999, 2004, 2008
© 2012 Thomson Reuters

    610 Opperman Drive
    St. Paul, MN 55123
    1–800–313–9378

Printed in the United States of America

ISBN: 978–0–314–27685–8

To Gabriela and Arabela Méndez

PREFACE TO THE FIFTH EDITION

Like many evidence professors, I too have experimented with different methods for teaching evidence. I began by using a casebook which had an excellent collection of cases but found the process of having the students recall and describe the issues raised by the cases unduly time-consuming. Using cases presented another problem. Opinions focus almost exclusively on the concerns of appellate judges and often fail to convey a feel for the problems facing the trial judge and trial counsel. For a number of years, I tried to compensate for these deficiencies by preparing a handbook that students used in conjunction with the casebook and that presented most of the cases in the book in a problem or witness examination form.

The student response to the handbook was very positive. The difficulty of trying to recall the "facts" of a case was eliminated, and using transcripts of witness examinations gave students an opportunity to visualize the process of presenting and objecting to evidence. In turn viewing evidence in action helped them understand the rules in practice as well as in theory, and enabled them to ask important questions about the relationship of the rules to principles of trial advocacy.

Because of my interest in different teaching methods, I was asked by my dean at Stanford to develop materials to be used in an evidence course emphasizing self-study. One decision was easy: reading appellate cases was not the best way to teach this course. I decided to combine the problem and witness examination approach with text—not cases—that sets out the law of evidence in a clear and concise manner. The goal was to help the students learn the rules by having them read about evidence and then having them apply their knowledge to discrete problems. Class time was to be devoted to reviewing their "rulings" and answering their questions.

The challenge was to find a text that would work well with the problems and witness examinations. Eventually, I opted for adapting the text from an evidence treatise which I had prepared for lawyers who practice primarily in California state and federal courts. Although derived from my treatise, the text of this book is not merely a black letter law distillation of the rules of evidence. Much of the discussion is devoted to the policies and concepts underlying the rules. As a teacher and former trial lawyer, I believe that students will attain a better understanding of the rules by examining the concerns that initially drove judges and then legislators to place limits on the evidence parties can offer.

The book's thirty chapters are organized by sections. "**Questions and Problems**" following most sections contain the problems and witness examinations. The examinations are designed to raise significant evidentiary issues; they are not intended as model interrogations. Indeed, most of the objections are "late" and in real life would require follow-up motions to strike and admonish if sustained. But by using this approach, the student becomes aware of the nature of the contested evidence without the distraction required by offers of proof.

The book focuses on the California Evidence Code as well as the Federal Rules of Evidence. California was among the first jurisdictions to replace the Common Law rules of evidence with a comprehensive code. The influence of the California Evidence Code in shaping the Federal Rules has been substantial and can be measured in part by the number of times the framers of the Rules cite the Code as a model. Over the years, many evidence professors have found that students can gain valuable insights into problems of proof by comparing the approach of the Code and with that of the Rules in those instances where the two depart. The book follows this tradition by providing a systematic comparison of the California and federal approaches to admissibility.

Because the Common Law rules of evidence have been replaced largely by codes, today's study of evidence necessarily involves statutory interpretation. To help students with this task, Thomson–West has prepared a separate statutory supplement that includes the California Evidence Code and the Federal Rules of Evidence, as well as the comments and notes prepared by their drafters. Because of space limitations, only those provisions of the Evidence Code and the Federal Rules discussed in a chapter are set out at the end of that chapter.

The fifth edition includes recent amendments to the Evidence Code and the Federal Rules, and discusses important new cases. The most extensive changes can be found in the discussion of the Confrontation Clause. In previous editions, the impact of the Sixth Amendment was limited to one section in Chapter 6. As a result of the United States Supreme Court's decision in Crawford v. Washington,[1] that section has grown to eight. The Court's confrontation jurisprudence is still evolving, and instructors and students should check other sources for the latest developments.

The fifth edition replaces the original Federal Rules of Evidence with the restyled Rules. These went into effect on December 1, 2011. According to the Advisory Committee Note to Rule 101, the Rules were rewritten:

> to make them more easily understood and to make style and terminology consistent throughout the rules. These changes are intended to be stylistic only. There is no intent to change any result in any ruling on evidence admissibility.

The language of the restyled Rules replaces the language of the original Rules where I quoted the original Rules in the text. However, where courts quoted the original rules, the quotations have remained unchanged.

I am grateful for the invaluable feed-back instructors who adopted earlier editions have provided to me. I have incorporated many of their suggestions into this edition. I am especially indebted to my research assistants; their help

---

1.   541 U.S. 36 (2004).

and encouragement were indispensable to the completion of this project. I alone, however, am responsible for errors and omissions in this work.

MIGUEL A. MÉNDEZ
Professor of Law and Martin
Luther King, Jr. Scholar
U.C. Davis School of Law
Adelbert H. Sweet, Jr.
Professor of Law, Emeritus
Stanford Law School

December 2011

SUMMARY OF CONTENTS

TABLE OF CONTENTS

CHAPTER 4. OTHER EVIDENCE EXCLUDED BY EXTRINSIC POLICIES—SUBSEQUENT PRECAUTIONS, PLEAS, COMPROMISE OFFERS, AND LIABILITY INSURANCE

CHAPTER 5. THE HEARSAY RULE

CHAPTER 6. EXCEPTIONS TO THE HEARSAY RULE: GENERAL CONSIDERATIONS

CHAPTER 7. EXCEPTIONS TO THE HEARSAY RULE: ADMISSIONS

CHAPTER 8. EXCEPTIONS TO THE HEARSAY RULE: PRIOR STATEMENTS OF WITNESSES AND PRIOR RECOLLECTION RECORDED

CHAPTER 9. EXCEPTIONS TO THE HEARSAY RULE: DECLARATIONS AGAINST INTEREST, DYING DECLARATIONS, EXCITED UTTERANCES, CONTEMPORANEOUS STATEMENTS, AND STATE OF MIND DECLARATIONS

CHAPTER 10. EXCEPTIONS TO THE HEARSAY RULE: BUSINESS AND OFFICIAL RECORDS

CHAPTER 11. EXCEPTIONS TO THE HEARSAY RULE: FORMER TESTIMONY

CHAPTER 12. EXCEPTIONS TO THE HEARSAY RULE: LEARNED TREATISES, COMMERCIAL LISTS, AND JUDGMENTS

CHAPTER 13. AUTHENTICATION AND THE BEST AND SECONDARY EVIDENCE RULES

CHAPTER 30. THE HUMAN TRAFFICKING
CASEWORKER–VICTIM PRIVILEGE

EVIDENCE:
THE CALIFORNIA
CODE AND THE
FEDERAL RULES

A PROBLEM APPROACH

Fifth Edition

CHAPTER 1

EVIDENCE IN PERSPECTIVE

■ ■ ■

Table of Sections

§ 1.01 INTRODUCTION

As a law student, I was perplexed by the ease with which individual rules of evidence could be understood and by the difficulty of imagining their application. There seemed to be no principle around which the mass of rules could be organized. It was only after I practiced law and began to teach evidence that I was able to provide my students with insights that would enable them to appreciate the rules of evidence in theory as well as in practice.

Three points about the rules should help the practitioner as well as the student of evidence. First, the rules are designed to limit the kinds of information lawyers can offer to the trier of fact. Second, the rules are used principally to help the trier of fact reconstruct an historical event whose contours are contested by the parties. If the parties do not disagree about who ran the light and the resulting damages, for example, there is no need for a proceeding affording them an opportunity to provide the trier of fact with information that is subject to the limitations and prohibitions contained in the rules of evidence.

Third, the rules operate mainly in an adversarial environment. As in the case of procedural rules, whether a particular rule is applied depends initially on whether its application is invoked by a party. This aspect of party initiative can perhaps be seen most clearly by reference to one of my professor's introductory remarks: "All evidence is admissible unless excluded." What he meant is that generally all evidence offered by a party will be admitted unless it is objected to by the opposing party and the objection is sustained.[1]

The third point is what makes mastery of the rules of evidence crucial to the trial lawyer. In adversarial proceedings, it is prudential to assume that most of what the opposing party is attempting to do will in some way be harmful to your case. When the attempt consists of information that your opponent is presenting to the trier of fact, effective advocacy calls for defensive action, which in a trial usually will take the form of an objection to the introduction of the information. Preventing unfavorable information from reaching the trier of fact is a cardinal goal of good trial lawyers.

Focusing on the relationship between advocacy and the rules of evidence helps put the rules in perspective. Adversarial proceedings assume that all relevant information that is necessary to resolve the case will be produced because each party can be depended upon to present all information that is helpful to its case. The rules of evidence advance this goal by permitting each party to assume generally that its evidence will be admitted unless successfully objected to by the opposing party. To ensure that factual controversies are decided on the basis of admissible information, the rules permit the opposing party to make objections that cluster around five broad limitations on the information that can be presented.

Assume a simple personal injury action in which the principal issue is whether the plaintiff or the defendant ran the light giving rise to the plaintiff's injuries. The fundamental limitation on the information that the parties can present to the jury is that the evidence must be relevant. In the words of Evidence Code § 350, "No evidence is admissible except relevant evidence."[2] Evidence, for example, that the defendant belongs to the Communist Party would be irrelevant in determining fault in the collision. It is difficult to see how a party's political inclinations have anything to do with whether the party ran the light. Yet, during the Red Scare days of the nineteen fifties, that kind of information might have caused some jurors to find against a party. Thus, information that may be helpful from an advocate's perspective may nonetheless be inadmissible if it is irrelevant. In Chapter 2, the meaning of relevance is explored.

Helpful information may also be excluded if it is presumed by the rules to be unduly prejudicial. Evidence that the defendant ran a light one month before the accident would be relevant. Yet, for policy reasons that are discussed in the chapter on character evidence, both the California Evidence Code and the Federal Rules exclude this information if offered to prove that the defendant ran the light because he is the kind of person who runs lights.[3]

---

1. Trial judges have no general duty to exclude evidence on their own motion. People v. Carpenter, 15 Cal.4th 312, 411, 63 Cal.Rptr.2d 1, 60, 935 P.2d 708, 767 (1997), cert. denied, 522 U.S. 1078, 118 S.Ct. 858, 139 L.Ed.2d 757 (1998).

2. West's Ann. California Evidence Code § 350. Federal Rule of Evidence 402 is the analogous federal provision.

3. West's Ann.California Evidence Code § 1101(a); Federal Rule of Evidence 404(a).

Relevant information may be excluded if the trial judge concludes that its probative value is substantially outweighed by countervailing concerns. Evidence that the defendant had been cited for running the light in question one week before the accident might be offered to show that the defendant was aware of the presence of the light on the date of the accident. Such evidence would help prove that the defendant was aware of his duty to obey the light as well as his disregard of that duty the day of the accident. The evidence thus would be relevant, as it would be probative of a proposition that is properly provable in the case. The evidence might nonetheless be excluded if the judge concludes that its value as proof of this proposition would be seriously outweighed by the risk that the jury might misuse the information as proof that the defendant ran the light because he is the kind of person who runs lights. Judicial power to exclude relevant evidence meeting all other tests of admissibility is considered in Chapter 2.

Information may also be excluded if the rules deem it to be unreliable. Assume, for example, that to prove the defendant's negligence the plaintiff calls a witness to testify as follows: "My wife told me that the defendant ran the light." The value of the testimony would depend on the credibility, not of the witness, but of the spouse. The defendant would be vitally interested in the wife's ability to perceive and remember the collision accurately and to tell the truth about what she saw. The defendant can best explore these matters if the wife is produced for cross-examination. The hearsay rule attempts to achieve this result by excluding the husband's proffered testimony and compelling the plaintiff to call the wife. Thus, the hearsay rule, which is examined in detail in Chapter 5, can be viewed as a rule designed to exclude evidence whose reliability cannot be tested through cross-examination.

Finally, information that is obviously relevant may be excluded if its introduction undermines some other goal considered by the rules to be more important. The plaintiff in our hypothetical case might want to call the defendant to the stand to have him tell the jury what the defendant told his lawyer about the collision. It would, of course, be fatal to the defendant to have to disclose that he told his lawyer that he indeed ran the light. Fortunately, the attorney-client privilege would protect the defendant from having to answer the plaintiff's question. Indeed, the plaintiff's lawyer could risk a mistrial and face ethical sanctions by asking for an answer that she should know is privileged. Privileges—rules that bar disclosure of relevant evidence—are explored in subsequent chapters.

§ 1.02 THE PROCESS OF PROOF AND THE ADVERSARIAL SYSTEM

Thus far, we have been considering the rules of evidence defensively, as a means of preventing the opposing party from offering evidence that is harmful to your case. Effective advocates, however, must also know how to use the rules affirmatively, to overcome their opponent's efforts to invoke the rules to keep them from offering evidence favorable to their case. A brief description of how a case should be prepared for trial will underscore the importance of using the rules affirmatively.

The typical trial consists of thirteen distinct phases: (1) jury selection or voir dire, (2) opening statements, (3) the plaintiff's or prosecution's case-in-chief, (4) the defendant's motion for a directed verdict, (5) the defendant's case-in-chief, (6) the plaintiff's motion for a directed verdict, (7) the plaintiff's or prosecution's rebuttal, (8) the defendant's rebuttal, (9) in civil cases, cross motions for directed verdicts, (10) closing arguments, (11) jury instructions, (12) jury deliberations, and (13) verdict. In planning a trial, an advocate will usually focus first on the role she will last play in the trial, delivering the closing argument. Although this may appear to a novice as approaching the planning process from the wrong end, a number of considerations will confirm the soundness of this approach.

One is the function of the closing argument. It is designed to give opposing lawyers an opportunity to explain to the jury why their client should prevail given the evidence presented and the substantive law that applies to the dispute. In our hypothetical case, the plaintiff's theory may be that she should win because, despite the defendant's denial on the stand, the only impartial witness, a bystander, corroborated the plaintiff's account that it was the defendant who ran the light. If that is indeed the plaintiff's theory, then, in addition to testifying on her own behalf, it will be indispensable for the plaintiff to call the bystander to render his account of the accident and to establish the bystander's impartiality. The reason is quite simple: as a general rule, all factual assertions made in the closing argument must be supported by the evidence.[1] This limitation is found not in the Code or the Rules but in the case law[2] as well as in the

---

1. It is not misconduct, however, for an attorney to argue matters before the jury which have not been the subject of proof, provided those matters are within the common knowledge of the jurors. Jurors, collectively, bring a common fund of information to the jury box which does not have to be proved or disproved by the parties. For a discussion of this point, see § 19.03 infra.

2. See, e.g., People v. Kirkes, 39 Cal.2d 719, 249 P.2d 1 (1952). Arguments by prosecutors of factual assertions not supported by the evidence are tantamount to offering the fact finder "unsworn testimony violative of the [accused's] Sixth Amendment right to confrontation and to his right to effective assistance of counsel." People v. Herring, 20 Cal.App.4th 1066, 1076, 25 Cal.Rptr.2d 213, 219 (1993).

It is also misconduct for a party to argue irrelevant matter to a jury, especially where the matter is likely to invite the jurors to return a verdict on an improper basis. See, e.g., Du Jardin v. City of Oxnard, 38 Cal.App.4th 174, 179–180, 45 Cal.Rptr.2d 48, 51 (1995) and cases cited therein (Counsel for the city improperly urged jurors to return a verdict for the city on the ground that a contrary verdict could result in the curtailment of public services.). In arguing damages in a personal injury case, it is improper for the plaintiff to ask the jurors how much they would charge to undergo equivalent pain and suffering. See, e.g., Loth v. Truck–A–Way Corp., 60 Cal.App.4th 757, 765, 70 Cal.Rptr.2d 571, 576 (1998). Such "Golden Rule" appeals invite the jurors to return a verdict on an emotional basis rather than on detached consideration of all of the evidence. Id.

In the guilt phase of a criminal case, it is misconduct for the prosecutor to appeal to the passions of the jurors by asking them to consider the crime from the victim's perspective. Closing arguments asking jurors to sympathize with the victim are "out of place during an objective determination of guilt," People v. Stansbury, 4 Cal.4th 1017, 1057, 17 Cal.Rptr.2d 174, 198, 846 P.2d 756, 780 (1993), "since the guilt jury is not to balance the defendant's right to a fair trial

rules of professional conduct.[3]

The effect of this limitation on the closing argument is to force the parties to isolate the factual assertions and to identify the evidentiary sources needed to produce evidence supporting the assertions. Good lawyers must go further, however. They must be satisfied that over the opposing party's objections they can produce the needed evidence from the desired evidentiary source. This assessment requires as firm a grasp of the rules of evidence as is needed to ensure that your objections will preclude your opponent from producing evidence favorable to her side. Just as your defensive use of the rules will aid you in precluding your opponent from producing the evidence needed to support the factual assertions of her closing argument, so, too, will your affirmative use of the rules help you produce the evidence needed to support the factual assertions of your closing argument.

In addition to helping define the content of the witness examinations, approaching trial planning in this manner will assist in determining the content of the opening statement. Opening statements provide the parties with an opportunity to inform the trier of fact of what they think the evidence will show.[4] Opening statements differ from closing arguments in that in the former no argument is permitted. In closing arguments, lawyers are free to tell the jury why they should disregard some evidence, accept other evidence, and bring back a particular verdict. In essence, the lawyers are free to review and comment on the evidence, as well as on the law governing the case. In contrast, in opening statements the attorneys are limited to giving the jury a preview of what they expect the evidence will show.[5]

Applying this limitation to our hypothetical case, the plaintiff's lawyer would know that in her opening statement she should tell the jury a number of things. Setting aside the question of damages, she needs to inform the jury about what the plaintiff will say regarding the circumstances surrounding the accident. She also needs to tell them about what the bystander will say about the accident and acquaint them with the evidence that will allow the jury to conclude that the bystander is an impartial witness.

---

against the victim's right to life or safety." People v. Arias, 13 Cal.4th 92, 161, 51 Cal.Rptr.2d 770, 814, 913 P.2d 980, 1024 (1996), cert. denied, 520 U.S. 1251, 117 S.Ct. 2408, 138 L.Ed.2d 175 (1997).

3. See, e.g., California Rule of Professional Responsibility Disciplinary Rule 5–200(E).

4. Lawyers must take care not to include inadmissible matter in their opening statements. For example, it is error for a lawyer to include inadmissible hearsay. People v. Hinton, 37 Cal.4th 839, 863, 38 Cal.Rptr.3d 149, 174, 126 P.3d 981, 1001, cert. denied, 549 U.S. 1033, 127 S.Ct. 581, 166 L.Ed.2d 434 (2006). The better course is to refrain from referring to the inadmissible matter until after the issue of admissibility has been resolved. Id.

5. In civil cases the failure to state a cause of action in the opening statement can result in a nonsuit. See West's Ann. Civil Procedure Code § 581c. Because granting a nonsuit at this stage of the proceedings is disfavored, the order will be upheld "only where it is clear plaintiff's counsel has stated all facts he expects to prove and such facts do not constitute a cause of action" even if the court accepts as true all facts asserted in the opening statement. Sturgeon v. Curnutt, 29 Cal.App.4th 301, 305, 34 Cal.Rptr.2d 498, 501 (1994).

Thinking about what to say in closing argument can provide a lawyer with some clues about the kind of jury to select. At a minimum, one must select a jury that is at least willing to consider one's closing argument. In civil cases, focusing on the closing argument at an early stage can also help frame amendments to the pleadings. The pleadings, after all, must be sufficiently broad to support the kind of discovery needed to identify evidentiary sources that are essential to support the kind of closing argument that should be made. These and other concerns fall properly within the realm of trial advocacy and procedure, and are beyond the scope of this work. The point they make, however, is that effective advocacy is inseparable from a firm grasp of the rules of evidence. Imaginative lawyering goes hand in hand with confidence in the use of the rules.

QUESTIONS AND PROBLEMS

1. In her closing argument, may the plaintiff's attorney tell the jury that she would not have agreed to represent the plaintiff unless she believed that the plaintiff was telling the truth?

2. In his summation in a criminal case, the defendant's attorney tells the jurors that they ought to ignore the defendant's confession because he was pressured into confessing. (At the trial the defendant testified that he confessed only because an officer told him that no case would be brought against him if he confessed. The officer testified that he made no such promise to the defendant and that the defendant confessed only after having been given his *Miranda* rights. The judge ruled the confession admissible and allowed the jury to hear the confession, including the defendant's and the officer's testimony regarding the circumstances attending the confession.) In support of his argument, the attorney tells the jurors about how U.S. servicemen taken prisoner by the North Koreans recanted their confessions once they had been released. The prosecutor objects to the argument on the ground that the defendant did not offer evidence of the behavior of U.S. servicemen after they had been released. The defendant's attorney counters that stories of how they recanted their confessions appeared in the media and are part of the common knowledge which the jurors bring to the case. Should the judge sustain the prosecutor's objection?

3. In a personal injury action, it is proper for the plaintiff's attorney in closing argument to ask the jurors to ask themselves how much they would charge to give up a leg, since a good way to help jurors assess the loss of a leg is by placing them in the position of the plaintiff. Such practice, after all, is rooted in the "Golden Rule" to do unto others what you would have others do unto you. True or false?

§ 1.03 MAKING AND MEETING OBJECTIONS

A key feature of the adversarial system is that it imposes upon the opposing party the obligation of objecting to inadmissible evidence. The failure to object carries a penalty: it waives the right to complain about the use of erroneously admitted evidence. Section 353 of the Code provides that a "verdict or finding shall not be set aside, nor shall the judgment or decision based thereon be reversed, by reason of the erroneous admission of evidence unless: (a) There appears of record an objection to or a motion to exclude or to strike the evidence that was timely made and so stated as to make clear the specific ground of the objection or motion * * *."[1] Waiver is imposed in order to encourage litigants to bring errors to the attention of the trial judge, so that they may be corrected and a fair trial held.[2]

Timeliness. In order to preserve the error, the objection must be timely.[3] Usually, this means that a party must object prior to the receipt of the inadmissible evidence. If a question calls for hearsay, for example, the opponent should object on that ground at the conclusion of the question and not after the witness's answer containing the inadmissible hearsay has been received.

Sometimes, timely objections are impossible. Assume, for example, that the plaintiff calls a witness to establish that the color of the light facing the defendant was red. If in response to the question, "What was the color of the light facing the defendant?" the witness answers "Red," it may not be readily apparent that the witness may not be testifying on the basis of first-hand knowledge.[4] But voir dire[5] or cross-examination may reveal that the witness based his answer on what his spouse told him about the light's color. If that is the case, then the opponent should move to strike the witness's answer upon uncovering the witness's lack of first-hand knowledge. But a motion to strike improperly admitted evidence will not preserve the error for appellate review if the party opposing the evidence had an opportunity to object on the proper grounds at the time the evidence was offered.[6]

---

1. West's Ann.California Evidence Code § 353 (comment). The federal rules are generally to the same effect. See Federal Rule of Evidence 103(a).

2. People v. Saunders, 5 Cal.4th 580, 590, 20 Cal.Rptr.2d 638, 642, 853 P.2d 1093, 1097 (1993), cert. denied, 510 U.S. 1131, 114 S.Ct. 1101, 127 L.Ed.2d 413 (1994).

3. West's Ann. California Evidence Code § 353(a); Federal Rule of Evidence 103(a). The timeliness requirement affords the judge an opportunity "to remedy the situation before any prejudice accrues." People v. Taylor, 31 Cal.3d 488, 496, 183 Cal.Rptr. 64, 69, 645 P.2d 115, 120 (1982).

4. A witness's testimony is inadmissible unless the witness has personal knowledge of the subject matter of the testimony. West's Ann.California Evidence Code § 702; Federal Rule of Evidence 702. For an extended discussion of this requirement, see § 14.02 infra.

5. Voir dire refers to an examination the judge may permit a party to undertake in support of an objection. If, upon hearing the witness's answer on direct, the opponent suspects that the witness was not testifying on the basis of personal knowledge, the opponent could object on that ground and ask the court for permission to question the witness to establish the witness's lack of first-hand knowledge of the light's color. Some judges might deny the request for voir dire and, instead, ask the proponent to establish the witness's personal knowledge. The Code and the Rules provide that, against objection, the proponent must establish the witness's personal knowledge before the witness may continue with his testimony. West's Ann.California Evidence Code § 702; Federal Rule of Evidence 602.

6. People v. Demetrulias, 39 Cal.4th 1, 21, 45 Cal.Rptr.3d 407, 424, 137 P.3d 229, 244 (2006) (holding that a motion to strike inadmissible character evidence did not preserve error in the admission of the evidence).

Occasionally, a judge may allow evidence to be received subject to a motion to strike. Where the opposing party fails to move to strike, the objection to the evidence is waived.[7]

Parties often use motions in limine to exclude matter which they believe should be inadmissible at the trial.[8] Motions in limine are usually made at hearings held immediately before the trial. If a judge denies a motion to exclude, in California the opponent of the evidence should renew the objection at the time the evidence is offered. The failure to renew the objection can preclude appellate review of the use of the evidence.[9] Although this result seems surprising, renewing the objection gives the trial judge an opportunity to reconsider the earlier ruling in light of the evidence adduced at the trial.[10] It is unnecessary, however, for the objecting party to renew the in limine objection if the evidence presented at trial is substantially similar to the evidence presented at the in limine hearing.[11]

In federal courts, an amendment to Federal Rule of Evidence 103 dispenses with the need to renew the objection at trial if the in limine ruling was definitive. The amended rule provides that "[o]nce the court rules definitively on the record—either before or at trial—a party need not renew an objection or offer proof to preserve a claim of error for appeal."[12] Nothing in the amendment, however, prohibits the judge from revisiting the in limine ruling denying the motion to exclude when the evidence is offered at the trial.[13]

In California the in limine objection does not have to be renewed in two circumstances: (1) when the parties stipulate on the record that the in limine ruling will be binding at the trial,[14] and (2) when the judge overrules an objection that is specific, is directed to a particular, identifiable body of evidence, and gives the judge an opportunity to rule on the objection in its appropriate context.[15] In People v. Rowland,[16] for example, the accused objected in limine to the prosecution's anticipated use of a hearsay declaration. The trial judge overruled the objection and allowed the prosecution to offer the declaration at the trial. The reviewing court held that the accused did not have to object to the introduction of the declaration to preserve his objection: the in limine objection was specific

---

7. People v. Benenato, 77 Cal.App.2d 350, 360–363, 175 P.2d 296, 302 (1946), overruled on other grounds, In re Wright, 65 Cal.2d 650, 654, 56 Cal.Rptr. 110, 112, 422 P.2d 998, 1000 (1967).

8. For a discussion of the rules pertaining to motions in limine, see generally Kelly v. New West Federal Sav., 49 Cal.App.4th 659, 56 Cal.Rptr.2d 803 (1996).

9. People v. Jennings, 46 Cal.3d 963, 975, note 3, 251 Cal.Rptr. 278, 284, note 3, 760 P.2d 475, 481, note 3 (1988), cert. denied, 489 U.S. 1091, 109 S.Ct. 1559, 103 L.Ed.2d 862 (1989).

10. Id.

11. Summers v. A.L. Gilbert Co., 69 Cal.App.4th 1155, 1184, 82 Cal.Rptr.2d 162, 179 (1999).

12. Federal Rule of Evidence 103.

13. Id. (Advisory Committee Note).

14. Id.

15. People v. Morris, 53 Cal.3d 152, 190, 279 Cal.Rptr. 720, 740, 807 P.2d 949, 969 (1991), cert. denied, 502 U.S. 959, 112 S.Ct. 421, 116 L.Ed.2d 441 (1991), disapproved on other grounds, People v. Stansbury, 9 Cal.4th 824, 889 P.2d 588, 38 Cal.Rptr.2d 394 (1995).

16. 4 Cal.4th 238, 14 Cal.Rptr.2d 377, 841 P.2d 897 (1992).

and directed to an identifiable body of evidence, and nothing occurred at the trial that would have affected the judge's ruling.[17]

Specific grounds. Neither the Code nor the Rules specifies the precise form in which an objection must be made.[18] A general objection, however, will not preserve the error for appellate review.[19] Good lawyers always specify the grounds of their objections. The object, after all, is to give the judge the information needed to sustain the objection. The specificity requirement also affords the proponent an opportunity to establish the admissibility of proffered evidence.[20] Accordingly, an objection must be specific, that is, the objecting party must specify the grounds on which the objection is based.[21] Objecting on the wrong grounds will not preserve the right to complain on appeal about the admission of evidence that should have been excluded on another ground.[22] For example, objecting to expert testimony on vagueness grounds will not preserve an objection that the testimony is beyond the witness's expertise.[23] Similarly, objecting to evidence of uncharged misdeeds on irrelevance grounds will not preserve an objection that the evidence is inadmissible character evidence.[24] Moreover, failing to include a pertinent ground will preclude appellate review of the claimed error. Accordingly, objecting to expert testimony on the ground that the scientific principle involved has not been generally accepted by the relevant scientific community will not preserve an objection that the expert failed to follow correct procedures in arriving at the results;[25] objecting on state grounds will not preserve a claim that the erroneously admitted evidence also violated such federal constitutional guarantees as the rights to due process and to confront witnesses.[26]

17.   Id. at 264, note 3, 14 Cal.Rptr.2d at 393, note 3, 841 P.2d at 913, note 3.

18.   West's Ann.California Evidence Code § 353 (comment). Federal Rule of Evidence 103(a)(1).

19.   West's Ann.California Evidence Code § 353 (comment). Federal Rule of Evidence 103(a)(1).

20.   People v. Clark, 3 Cal.4th 41, 126, 10 Cal.Rptr.2d 554, 599, 833 P.2d 561, 599 (1992), cert. denied, 507 U.S. 993, 113 S.Ct. 1604, 123 L.Ed.2d 166 (1993). See also People v. Hayes, 21 Cal.4th 1211, 1261, 91 Cal.Rptr.2d 211, 245, 989 P.2d 645, 676 (1999), cert. denied, 531 U.S. 980, 121 S.Ct. 431, 148 L.Ed.2d 438 (2000) ("The objection must be made in such a way as to alert the trial court to the nature of the anticipated evidence and the basis on which exclusion is sought, and to afford the [opposing party] an opportunity to establish its admissibility.") (quoting People v. Williams, 44 Cal.3d 883, 906, 245 Cal.Rptr. 336, 351, 751 P.2d 395, 409–10 (1988)).

21.   Id. Complaining about the inability to "cross-examine" a witness will not preserve a federal or state confrontation objection. People v. Waidla, 22 Cal.4th 690, 726, note 8, 94 Cal.Rptr.2d 396, 419, note 8, 996 P.2d 46, 67, note 8 (2000), cert. denied, 531 U.S. 1018, 121 S.Ct. 580, 148 L.Ed.2d 497 (2000). Neither will a bare reference to the "confrontation rule." People v. Alvarez, 14 Cal.4th 155, 186, 58 Cal.Rptr.2d 385, 403, 926 P.2d 365, 383 (1996), cert. denied, 522 U.S. 829, 118 S.Ct. 94, 139 L.Ed.2d 50 (1997).

22.   People v. Green, 27 Cal.3d 1, 22, note 8, 164 Cal.Rptr. 1, 12, note 8, 609 P.2d 468, 479, note 8 (1980).

23.   People v. Gutierrez, 14 Cal.App.4th 1425, 1433, 18 Cal.Rptr.2d 371, 376 (1993).

24.   People v. Escobar, 48 Cal.App.4th 999, 55 Cal.Rptr.2d 883, 896 (1996) and cases cited therein.

25.   People v. Riel, 22 Cal.4th 1153, 1193, 96 Cal.Rptr.2d 1, 32, 998 P.2d 969, 997 (2000), cert. denied, 531 U.S. 1087, 121 S.Ct. 803, 148 L.Ed.2d 690 (2001).

26.   People v. Carpenter, 15 Cal.4th 312, 385, 63 Cal.Rptr.2d 1, 42, 935 P.2d 708, 749 (1997), cert. denied 522 U.S. 1078, 118 S.Ct. 858, 139 L.Ed.2d 757 (1998) and cases cited therein. In state

A distinction, however, is drawn between failing to object to the introduction of evidence on federal grounds and claiming on appeal that the introduction of the evidence over a valid state ground objection nonetheless violated the accused's due process right to a fair trial. In People v. Partida[27] the accused claimed that the judge erroneously overruled his objection that evidence of his gang involvement was more prejudicial than probative. On appeal from his conviction, the accused claimed that the judge's erroneous ruling had the effect of depriving him of a fair trial. Even though he had not included this ground in his objection, the California Supreme Court held that he was not precluded from urging reversal on the federal ground:

> To the extent, if any, that defendant may be understood to argue that due process required exclusion of the evidence for a reason different from his trial objection, that claim is forfeited. Defendant could have apprised, but did not apprise, the trial court of such a claim. But defendant primarily makes a two-step argument on appeal: (1) the trial court erred in overruling the trial objection, and (2) the error was so serious as to violate due process. To consider this narrow due process argument on appeal "entails no unfairness to the parties," who had the full opportunity at trial to litigate whether the court should overrule or sustain the trial objection. (People v. Yeoman, supra, 31 Cal.4th at p. 118, 2 Cal.Rptr.3d 186, 72 P.3d 1166.) Defendant's limited due process claim "merely invites us to draw an alternative legal conclusion [i.e., that erroneously admitting the evidence violated due process] from the same information he presented to the trial court [i.e., that the evidence was more prejudicial than probative]. We may therefore properly consider the claim on appeal." (Id. at p. 133, 2 Cal.Rptr.3d 186, 72 P.3d 1166.)[28]

When a judge overrules a specific objection on the wrong ground and admits the contested evidence, a reviewing court will nonetheless sustain the judge's ruling if the evidence could have been received on a proper ground. In People v. Smithey[29] the trial judge overruled the accused's

---

criminal cases it is not unusual for the defense to object to evidence on both state and federal grounds. For example, a criminal defendant might object to autopsy photographs on the state ground of undue prejudice as well as on the federal ground that their introduction would violate his right to a fair trial. Unless the defendant includes the federal ground in the objection, the federal claim will not be preserved for appellate review. People v. Bolin, 18 Cal.4th 297, 319, 75 Cal.Rptr.2d 412, 428, 956 P.2d 374, 390 (1998) and cases cited therein. See also People v. Chaney, 148 Cal.App.4th 772, 777–779, 56 Cal.Rptr.3d 128, 132–134 (2007) (holding that objecting merely on hearsay grounds, including the inability to cross examine the hearsay declarant, does not preserve a confrontation objection). But see People v. Partida, 37 Cal.4th 428, 35 Cal.Rptr.3d 644, 122 P.3d 765 (2005), which draws a distinction between objecting to the introduction of evidence on federal constitutional grounds and claiming on appeal that the erroneous introduction of the evidence on state grounds had the effect of depriving the objecting party of the right to a fair trial. The latter claim does not prevent the objecting party from asking for a reversal on federal due process grounds, even though the objecting party failed to include this ground at the trial. For a discussion of this point, see text at note 27, infra.

27.   37 Cal.4th 428, 35 Cal.Rptr.3d 644, 122 P.3d 765 (2005).

28.   Id. at 436, 35 Cal.Rptr.3d at 649, 122 P.3d at 770.

29.   20 Cal.4th 936, 86 Cal.Rptr.2d 243, 978 P.2d 1171 (1999), cert. denied, 529 U.S. 1026, 120 S.Ct. 1435, 146 L.Ed.2d 324 (2000).

hearsay objection and allowed a witness on redirect to relate the victim's suspicions that the accused had been stealing from her. The trial judge ruled that the testimony was proper because the accused had opened the door by having allowed the witness to mention the victim's beliefs on cross-examination. On appeal the prosecution conceded that the ground stated by the judge was incorrect. Notwithstanding the judge's error, the reviewing court upheld the judge's ruling since the evidence was admissible over a hearsay objection to prove the victim's state of mind.[30] The opposite problem is posed when a judge excludes evidence on the wrong ground. The rule in California is that the exclusion will be upheld if the evidence was nonetheless excludable on a proper basis.[31] Thus a judge's erroneous ruling excluding evidence as irrelevant should be sustained on appeal if the evidence was properly excludable as inadmissible character evidence.

In one species of cases—death penalty appeals—California courts will relax the requirement that the appealing party must have objected properly in order to preserve the objection. In such cases, when the objection is merely technically insufficient, "the form of an objection will be disregarded and the entire record will be examined to determine if a miscarriage of justice resulted."[32]

The Federal Rules also require the making of specific objections.[33] But no ground need be specified if the ground is apparent from the context in which the objection is made.[34]

A continuing objection to a line of questioning is proper so long as the objecting party makes the ground clear.[35]

Meeting objections. A party is entitled to meet the opponent's objections. That means that a party is entitled to be heard on why the objection should not be sustained before the judge rules. For example, if the opponent objects on hearsay grounds, the proponent should be given an opportunity to state why the evidence is not hearsay or, if hearsay, explain why it falls within an exception. Failing to raise the correct arguments in support of admissibility carries a penalty: the complaining party may not raise those arguments on appeal to attack the trial judge's

---

30. Id. at 971–72, 86 Cal.Rptr.2d at 266, 978 P.2d at 1172. For a discussion of hearsay and nonhearsay, see § 5.04 infra.

31. See Davey v. Southern Pacific Co., 116 Cal. 325, 330, 48 P. 117, 118 (1897).

32. People v. Frank, 38 Cal.3d 711, 729, note 3, 214 Cal.Rptr. 801, 810, note 3, 700 P.2d 415, 424 note 3 (1985), appeal after remand, 51 Cal.3d 718, 274 Cal.Rptr. 372, 798 P.2d 1215 (1990), cert. denied, 501 U.S. 1213, 111 S.Ct. 2816, 115 L.Ed.2d 988 (1991), reh'g denied, 501 U.S. 1270, 112 S.Ct. 15, 115 L.Ed.2d 1099 (1991). Although the California Supreme Court has not overruled *Frank*, neither has it embraced it wholeheartedly. "We previously have noted that '[t]he lead opinion in *Frank* was not signed by a majority of the court, and although later cases from this court have never disapproved its language, they have cited it only for the purpose of distinguishing it.' " People v. Williams, 16 Cal.4th 153, 209, 66 Cal.Rptr.2d 123, 161, 940 P.2d 710, 748 (1997), cert. denied 522 U.S. 1150, 118 S.Ct. 1169, 140 L.Ed.2d 179 (1998) (citing People v. Diaz, 3 Cal.4th 495, 527, 11 Cal.Rptr.2d 353, 365, 834 P.2d 1171, 1183 (1992)).

33. Federal Rule of Evidence 103(a)(1).

34. Id.

35. West's Ann.California Evidence Code § 353 (comment).

ruling excluding the evidence. For example, a party may not complain on appeal of a judge's ruling excluding evidence as hearsay when at the trial the party failed to argue that the evidence was nonetheless admissible for a nonhearsay purpose.[36]

Offers of proof. Just as errors in the admission of evidence can result in reversible error, so can errors in the exclusion of evidence. As in the case of errors in the admission of evidence, errors in the exclusion of evidence are waived unless the complaining party takes specific action. In the case of the erroneous exclusion of evidence, the proponent must make the substance, purpose, and relevance of the excluded evidence known to the judge.[37] The requirement has two purposes: it enables the reviewing court to determine whether the exclusion of the evidence was prejudicial;[38] it also affords the trial judge an opportunity to re-evaluate the ruling excluding the evidence.

An offer of proof is the usual way of making the substance of the excluded evidence known to the judge. The offer can take several forms. In the case of testimony, an oral summary by counsel of what the witness would say if permitted to testify may suffice. If the excluded testimony is lengthy, counsel may request the court for permission to make the offer by having the witness answer the questions to which objections have been sustained. Of course, the offer must take place out of the presence or hearing of the jury in order to prevent the jurors from hearing evidence that has been ruled inadmissible.[39]

If the excluded evidence consists of a document or demonstrative or real evidence,[40] the proponent may request the judge to designate the evidence an exhibit to be appended to the record. While such an exhibit will be part of the record in the event an appeal is taken, it will not form part of the evidence which the jury is entitled to consider in reaching a verdict.

An offer of proof is not required when an objection is improperly sustained to a question on cross-examination or recross-examination.[41]

---

36. People v. Fauber, 2 Cal.4th 792, 854, 9 Cal.Rptr.2d 24, 62, 831 P.2d 249, 286 (1992).

37. West's Ann.California Evidence Code § 354. Federal Rule of Evidence 103(a)(2). "The substance of evidence in a valid offer of proof must be attributed to the testimony of specific witnesses, writings, material objects, or other things presented to the senses * * *." People v. Eid, 31 Cal.App.4th 114, 126, 36 Cal.Rptr.2d 835, 841 (1994).

38. See People v. Foss, 155 Cal.App.4th 113, 127, 65 Cal.Rptr.3d 790, 800 (2007). A reviewing court, however, will dispense with the requirement of an offer of proof whenever the trial judge declares an entire class of evidence inadmissible. For example, in Castaneda v. Bornstein, 36 Cal.App.4th 1818, 43 Cal.Rptr.2d 10 (1995), the reviewing court excused the requirement where the trial judge precluded the plaintiff from offering any expert evidence on causation. Id. at 1826, 43 Cal.Rptr.2d at 16.

39. The Federal Rules require that offers of proof be held outside the hearing of the jury to the "extent practicable." Federal Rule of Evidence 103(c).

40. Demonstrative evidence refers to such items as maps and drawings used to illustrate other evidence, such as the testimony of a witness. Real evidence usually refers to items that played a part in the event litigated, such as the weapon used to commit the offense. For an extended discussion of the admissibility of demonstrative and real evidence, see § 13.05 infra.

41. West's Ann.California Evidence Code § 354(c).

The cross examiner should not be forced to reveal his strategy to the witness or guess what the witness's answer would have been had the witness been permitted to answer.[42]

Plain error doctrine. The Federal Rules permit a court to consider not "a plain error affecting a substantial right, even if the claim of error was properly preserved."[43] Parties to federal proceedings should not permit this doctrine to excuse making specific objections. It is impossible to forecast when a reviewing court may decide that the circumstances of a particular case warrant applying the plain error doctrine.

The Evidence Code does not contain a plain error rule. In one circumstance, however, California courts will allow a party to complain on appeal about the opponent's misconduct even if the party failed to object during the trial: where the appealing party can show that an objection and admonition would have failed to cure the effect of the misconduct.[44] As in the case of the federal plain error doctrine, reliance on this exception is risky. One simply does not know when a reviewing court will apply the exception.[45]

Rulings on objections. To obtain appellate review of rulings erroneously admitting or excluding evidence, it is not enough for the objecting party to show a timely and specific objection. In addition, the appealing party must show that the trial judge ruled on the objection. The failure of counsel to secure a ruling waives the objection.[46]

QUESTIONS AND PROBLEMS

1. The judge sustains your opponent's hearsay objection without giving you an opportunity to explain why the answer sought was not hearsay or, if hearsay, fell within an exception. Should you accept the judge's ruling without

---

42. In California, however, an offer of proof will be required if the cross examiner seeks to elicit evidence outside the scope of direct examination. See People v. Foss, 155 Cal.App.4th 113, 127, 65 Cal.Rptr.3d 790, 800 (2007) (holding that the accused was obligated to make an offer of proof when the trial judge sustained the prosecution's objection to a question about whether the witness—the mother of the complaining witness in a sexual assault prosecution—had a morbid fear of sex).

43. Federal Rule of Evidence 103(e).

44. People v. Green, 27 Cal.3d 1, 27, 164 Cal.Rptr. 1, 16, 609 P.2d 468, 483 (1980).

45. In California criminal cases, the accused does not need to object to erroneous jury instructions in order to preserve the error if the substantial rights of the accused were affected by the error. West's Ann. California Penal Code § 1259. "Substantial rights are affected if the error 'result[s] in a miscarriage of justice, [i.e.,] making it reasonably probable defendant would have obtained a more favorable result in the absence of error.' " People v. Elsey, 81 Cal.App.4th 948, 953, note 2, 97 Cal.Rptr.2d 269, 273, note 2 (2000) (quoting from People v. Andersen, 26 Cal.App.4th 1241, 1249, 32 Cal.Rptr.2d 442, 446 (1994)). But despite the plain intent of this provision, some appellate courts still insist, as a general rule, that the accused must show that he unsuccessfully requested the trial judge for language curing the error before the court will review an incorrect instruction. See, e.g., People v. O'Connell, 39 Cal.App.4th 1182, 1190, 46 Cal.Rptr.2d 379, 383 (1995) and cases cited therein.

46. See Haskell v. Carli, 195 Cal.App.3d 124, 129, 240 Cal.Rptr. 439, 442 (1987) (Appealing party failed to secure a ruling on an objection that the evidence admitted at the hearing was barred by the parol evidence rule.). See also People v. Samayoa, 15 Cal.4th 795, 827, 64 Cal.Rptr.2d 400, 422, 938 P.2d 2, 24 (1997), cert. denied, 522 U.S. 1125, 118 S.Ct. 1071, 140 L.Ed.2d 131 (1998) (Judge's "provisional ruling" that counsel were not to mention certain evidence during jury voir dire because it might "very well not be allowable" was not a ruling excluding the evidence at trial, and thus the appealing party's belief that the evidence could not be elicited during cross-examination would not be reviewed on appeal.).

objection rather than upset the judge? Should you demand an opportunity to be heard? Should you join to your demand your willingness to make an offer of proof should the judge insist on upholding her ruling?

2.   You object to your opponent's question on the ground that it calls for hearsay. The judge responds that your objection is "noted." Should you accept this ruling?

3.   Because all that is required with respect to specificity is that an objection be specific, in California objecting on the wrong grounds will preserve the right to complain on appeal about the admission of evidence that should have been excluded on some other ground. For example, incorrectly objecting to expert testimony on the ground that the scientific principle involved has not been generally accepted by the relevant scientific community will preserve a proper objection raised on appeal for the first time that the expert failed to follow correct procedures in arriving at the results. The appealing party, after all, put the trial judge and the opponent on notice that the expert testimony was inadmissible. True or false?

4.   Similarly, in California when a judge erroneously excludes evidence on the wrong ground, the exclusion will be upheld on appeal if the evidence was nonetheless excludable on a proper basis. Accordingly, a judge's ruling erroneously excluding evidence as irrelevant will be sustained on appeal if the evidence was properly excludable as inadmissible character evidence. True or false?

§ 1.04   COMMON OBJECTIONS

Neither the Code nor the Rules contains a list of objections. Most objections, however, are derived from the rules of evidence themselves. For example, the presence of a hearsay rule gives rise to a hearsay objection. Likewise, the rule banning the use of character evidence permits a party to object on character evidence grounds. Some objections are not rooted in specific evidentiary rules but are the product of lessons learned over decades of litigation. Examples include objections to compound questions and to questions that assume facts not in evidence. Only the most common objections are summarized here.

Leading. As a rule, leading questions are inappropriate on direct examination.[1] A leading question is one that suggests the answer to the witness.[2] Even in the absence of the prohibition, a good lawyer would avoid leading questions on direct examination. Leading questions prevent a witness from doing most of the testifying, as the question is designed principally to get the witness to agree with the propositions in the examiner's question. Agreement usually takes the form of a simple yes or no. If you have a good witness, give the witness a chance to impress the jury with his testimony by asking non-leading, open-ended questions.

---

1.   West's Ann.California Evidence Code § 767(a)(1); Federal Rule of Evidence 611(c).

2.   West's Ann.California Evidence Code § 764.

In some circumstances, leading questions are permitted on direct. These include preliminary matters, refreshing recollection, and examining handicapped witnesses (e.g., children and the mentally impaired), experts, and hostile witnesses.[3] Preliminary matters usually refer to answers to questions designed to introduce a witness or a subject area. They can also embrace foundational matters. Leading questions can be asked of experts on the theory that experts cannot be led to give answers that are inconsistent with their fields of expertise.[4]

Leading questions are expressly permitted on cross-examination.[5] They provide an effective means for controlling the witness while challenging the witness's testimony on direct examination. But they may not be asked of a witness who is allied with or biased in favor of the cross examiner.[6] Such a witness can be led.

Calls for a narrative. To give the opposing party an opportunity to object to inappropriate questions or answers, witnesses are examined in the form of questions and answers. A question that simply asks a witness to relate all that witness may know about a specific event defeats this purpose. Such questions cannot put the opponent on notice of inadmissible matter until it is too late, i.e., after the witness has divulged the matter. Consequently, such questions are objectionable on the ground that they call for a "narrative." Good lawyers avoid these questions for another reason: they prevent the lawyer from focusing the witness's and the jury's attention on truly important matters.

As in the case of all interrogations, the judge ultimately controls the mode in which witnesses are examined.[7] Accordingly, a judge may allow a witness to testify in a narrative form if that is the best way to elicit a particular witness's testimony.

Irrelevant. The question calls for matter that is not germane to the issues being tried.[8] An old New York case, People v. Caruso,[9] case illustrates this objection. Caruso, an Italian immigrant, was on trial for murder. On cross-examination, the prosecutor asked Caruso whether he "was a citizen or had applied for naturalization."[10] As the reviewing court

---

3. West's Ann.California Evidence Code § 767 (comment). A child under ten can be asked leading questions on direct in prosecutions for child endangerment and cruelty, as well as for lewd and lascivious conduct, if the judge finds that such questions are in the interests of justice. Id. Trial judges have broad discretion in determining when special circumstances justify the use of leading questions. People v. Augustin, 112 Cal.App.4th 444, 449, 5 Cal.Rptr.3d 171, 176 (2003). Among the circumstances justifying their use are the witness's age and physical disabilities, such as deafness, paralysis, and the effects of diseases, such as cerebral palsy. Id. and cases cited therein.

4. See West's Ann.California Evidence Code § 767 (comment).

5. West's Ann.California Evidence Code § 767(a)(2); Federal Rule of Evidence 611(b).

6. West's Ann.California Evidence Code § 767 (comment).

7. West's Ann.California Evidence Code § 765; Federal Rule of Evidence 611(a).

8. For an extended discussion of what constitutes relevant matter, see § 2.01 infra.

9. 246 N.Y. 437, 159 N.E. 390 (1927).

10. Id. at 444, 159 N.E. 390 at 392.

noted, these questions "were so plainly incompetent, it cannot be believed they were asked in good faith."[11]

Occasionally, only part of an answer contains irrelevant matter. When that occurs, the opponent should move to strike the irrelevant portion.

Asked and answered. Ordinarily, the examiner is not entitled to impress the jury by asking the witness to repeat an answer. If the examiner does so, the opponent can object on the ground that the witness has already answered the examiner's question. But an examiner, especially a cross examiner, does not have to accept the answer a witness gives to a particular question. If she can, the examiner is entitled to try to get the witness to change the answer. If this is the examiner's goal, then the judge should overrule the objection.[12]

The objection that the question has been asked and answered does not apply when a cross examiner asks a question the calling party asked and the witness answered on direct. The objection is appropriate only when your opponent has asked and the witness has answered the question in the opponent's current examination of the witness.

Assumes facts not in evidence. Unless the examining lawyer is on the stand under oath, a question is not evidence. Accordingly, questions which assume facts not in evidence are objectionable because they permit the examining lawyer to testify. If you want to ask the witness if she saw the victim with the accused on the night of the killing, ask her first if she saw the victim that evening. Then ask her if the victim was alone.

Questions, however, that assume facts about preliminary matters are not objectionable. You can ask a witness where she works without first asking her if she works. You can ask a witness for her name without first asking if she has a name.

Argumentative. On direct examination the witness testifies that she saw your client bite the victim's nose. On cross, the witness concedes that the encounter took place on a dark night. If you then ask the witness just how it is that she was able to see your client bite the victim's nose, your question is argumentative. Questions that ask a witness to reconcile conflicting positions are argumentative.

Good lawyers usually do not ask argumentative questions. Such questions are dangerous, as the witness might reconcile the conflict. In the example, the witness might say, "I saw him spit it out."[13] That prevents you from exploiting the inconsistency in summation, when the proponent no longer has the option of recalling the witness to explain the apparent conflict. As the opponent, resist the argumentative question and, instead, save the conflict for argument. If you are the proponent, clear it up if you

---

11. Id.

12. See People v. Riel, 22 Cal.4th 1153, 1197, 96 Cal.Rptr.2d 1, 35, 998 P.2d 969, 1000 (2000), cert. denied, 531 U.S. 1087, 121 S.Ct. 803, 148 L.Ed.2d 690 (2001).

13. I am indebted to a great teacher, Judge Irving Younger, for this example, which he includes in his lectures on trial advocacy.

can. On redirect, for example, ask the witness about the lighting conditions.

An argumentative question can also include a speech to the jury masquerading as a question:

> The questioner is not seeking to elicit relevant testimony. Often it is apparent that the questioner does not even expect an answer. The question may, indeed, be unanswerable. The prosecutor's question whether "the safe [was] lying" is an example. An inanimate object cannot "lie." * * *An argumentative question that essentially talks past the witness, and makes an argument to the jury, is improper because it does not seek to elicit relevant, competent testimony, or often any testimony at all. Defendant had already explained he had no explanation for the safe being open. Asking whether the safe was "lying" could add nothing to this testimony.[14]

Compound question. Did the accused hit and kick the victim? The witness may say no because the witness saw the accused only hit *or* only kick the victim. The witness may also say no because the witness did not see the accused hit or kick the victim. In either case, the jury would not know which of the questions the witness was answering. Accordingly, compound questions are objectionable.

Lack of personal knowledge. You call a witness to establish that the light facing your client, who was in a blue car, was green. After preliminary matters, your first substantive question is, "What was the color of the light facing the blue car?" If other evidence has been received showing that your client drove a blue car on the street with the light on the day of the accident, the question would not be objectionable on the ground that it assumes facts not in evidence. But with respect to the witness on the stand, the question would be objectionable on the ground that you have not established that the witness was in a position to see the color of the light facing the blue car.

Under the Code and the Federal Rules, a witness may not testify to a matter unless the witness has first-hand knowledge of the subject matter of the testimony.[15] Against objection, a witness may not testify unless the proponent shows that the witness has the requisite personal knowledge.[16] To avoid the objection, ask the witness if she saw the color of the light facing the blue car. If she answers in the affirmative, then ask her to describe the light's color.

Calls for inadmissible opinion. As a rule, a lay witness can testify in the form of an opinion only if the opinion is based on the perception of the witness and is helpful to a clear understanding of the witness's testimony.[17] Examples include such conclusionary statements as "it was

---

14. People v. Chatman, 38 Cal.4th 344, 384, 42 Cal.Rptr.3d 621, 656 133 P.3d 534, 563 (2006).

15. West's Ann.California Evidence Code § 702; Federal Rule of Evidence 602.

16. Id.

17. West's Ann.California Evidence Code § 800; Federal Rule of Evidence 701.

raining," "the car was going fast," "he looked drunk," and the like. A question that calls for a lay witness to give an opinion that is beyond his common understanding and experience is objectionable on the grounds that the witness is not qualified to provide the opinion. Some lawyers object to such questions on the equivalent ground that they call for speculation.

Experts, of course, may testify in the form of an opinion.[18] But even their opinions are objectionable if the fact finder does not need the opinion or if the expert is not qualified to provide it.[19]

Unresponsive. Under the Code, a witness must give answers that respond to the question.[20] Answers that are unresponsive must be stricken on the motion of any party.[21] Since all parties are entitled to responsive answers, it is immaterial that the party moving to strike is not the examining party.

The Federal Rules do not contain an equivalent provision. Some federal judges will allow the examining party to strike answers that are not responsive. Others will not permit the nonexamining party to strike answers unless the answers are also irrelevant or otherwise inadmissible.

The California rule is a good one. It allows the parties to control the witness. It is especially helpful in controlling witnesses who are more interested in telling their version of the story than in responding to the questions asked. In the case of such witnesses, it is advisable to request the judge to admonish the witness to answer only the questions that are asked after the judge has granted a motion to strike an unresponsive answer. Of course, the moving party should also ask the judge to instruct the jury to disregard the stricken matter.

Other objections. Objections can be predicated on any rule that limits or bans the use of evidence. Examples include any question calling for matter that violates the hearsay rule, a privilege, the ban on character evidence, the limits on evidence that is unfairly prejudicial, the restrictions on attacking or supporting the credibility of witnesses, the Best Evidence Rule, as well as rules that promote policies that encourage subsequent repairs and settlements. These and other rules are examined in detail in subsequent chapters.

Sometimes a witness will include inadmissible matter in response to an appropriate question. When that occurs, the opponent should move to strike the inadmissible matter from the answer and, if the motion is granted, to have the court admonish the jury to disregard the inadmissible matter.[22]

---

18. West's Ann.California Evidence Code § 801; Federal Rule of Evidence 702.

19. Id.

20. West's Ann.California Evidence Code § 766.

21. Id.

22. One disadvantage of the admonition is the risk that it will impress the inadmissible matter upon the jurors even more.

Objections to errors made in closing arguments. In California, errors made by a party or counsel in closing arguments are termed "misconduct." It is not necessary, however, for the opponent to use this term when objecting to such errors. "Objection" will do. However, as in the case of objections to evidence, objections to improper arguments must be specific if the error is to be preserved on appeal.[23] Moreover, if the charge of misconduct is sustained, the objecting party must request the trial judge to instruct the jurors to disregard the error in order to preserve the misconduct for appellate review.[24]

QUESTIONS AND PROBLEMS

1. Most of us tell stories to convey information. Sometimes, we do this on our own; often it is in response to requests for information. For example, someone who wants to know what we saw at the law school when the faculty confronted the dean over his working hours, typically might ask, "Tell us what happened." The rules of evidence capitalize on this human tendency by encouraging the direct examiner to ask such questions as, "Tell the jury what you saw" or "Tell us what you know about this case." True or false?

2. On direct examination a witness called by the plaintiff testifies that the light facing the plaintiff was green. On cross-examination, the defendant asks the witness to describe the color of the light facing the plaintiff. The plaintiff objects on the ground that the question has been asked and answered. How should the judge rule?

§ 1.05 THE ORIGINS OF THE CALIFORNIA EVIDENCE CODE AND THE FEDERAL RULES OF EVIDENCE

Until the middle of the Twentieth Century, few American jurisdictions had evidence codes. In the Common Law tradition, the rules of evidence had to be gleaned from the case law and a few statutes. In California, the statutory references were treated as an adjunct to procedure.[1] These references, though intended as a comprehensive statement of the law of evidence, did not resemble a contemporary code. Some of the provisions were contradictory, others were redundant, and, worst of all, many accepted rules were omitted.[2]

Early efforts to reform California's law of evidence proved unsuccessful. But the restatement and codification movements that took place in the first part of the Twentieth Century gave new impetus to the reform efforts. Of special importance was the American Law Institute's 1942

---

23. See § 1.03 supra.

24. People v. Bryden, 63 Cal.App.4th 159, 182, 73 Cal.Rptr.2d 554, 568–569 (1998) and cases cited therein.

1. West's Ann.California Evidence Code 24 (Recommendation of the California Law Revision Commission Proposing an Evidence Code).

2. Id.

Model Code of Evidence. The Model Code was the first to codify the Common Law rules of evidence. Unfortunately, the Model Code contained some provisions that departed sharply from conventional evidentiary practices and was rejected by every jurisdiction that considered it for adoption.[3] Nonetheless, the Model Code had an important and lasting effect. Under the leadership of Professor Edmund Morgan, the framers opted for a concise statement of evidentiary principles of general applicability and rejected Dean John Wigmore's call for detailed rules of the kind found in his multi-volume treatise on evidence.

Professor Morgan's concept of what an evidence code should be shaped not only the Model Code, but also all subsequent codes, including the California Evidence Code and the Federal Rules of Evidence. As he explained in his foreword to the Model Code:

> A code of evidence should concern itself primarily with admissibility, and in this respect it should be complete in itself. Consequently it should begin with a sweeping declaration that all relevant evidence is admissible, that no person is incompetent as a witness and that there is no privilege to refuse to be a witness or to disclose relevant matter or to prevent another from disclosing it. Then it should set up specific exceptions to this fundamental rule.[4]

As will become evident in subsequent chapters, both the California Evidence Code and the Federal Rules of Evidence begin with this fundamental rule.

In 1953, the National Conference of Commissioners on Uniform State Laws approved the Uniform Rules of Evidence.[5] The Uniform Rules eliminated many of the objections raised to the Model Code. The Uniform Rules were cited by courts and approved by the American Bar Association.[6] In 1956, the California Legislature asked the California Law Revision Commission to study the feasibility of having the state adopt the Uniform Rules. In 1965, the Commission presented its recommendations to the Legislature in the form of a proposed code, which after modifications by the Legislature, was adopted as the Evidence Code.[7] It became effective on January 1, 1967.

On July 1, 1975, the Federal Rules of Evidence went into effect.[8] Like the Evidence Code, they were the product of a detailed study by a commission (the Advisory Committee appointed by the United States Supreme Court) and legislative modifications (Congressional amendments).[9] Though the Rules and the Code differ in important respects, their structure is remarkably similar. Both draw heavily from their

---

3. Id.

4. American Law Institute, Model Code of Evidence 11 (1942).

5. Id.

6. Id.

7. Id.

8. Federal Rules of Evidence for United States Courts and Magistrates III.

9. Id.

predecessors, the Model Code and the Uniform Rules, in presenting concise rules of general applicability. Indeed, the similarities between the Code and the Rules are far greater than their differences, a feature undoubtedly attractive to lawyers who practice in federal and California courts.

§ 1.06   APPLICABILITY OF THE CODE AND THE FEDERAL RULES OF EVIDENCE

Unless otherwise provided by statute, the Evidence Code applies in every civil and criminal action before any California court, including proceedings before referees, court commissioners, and similar officers.[1] Although grand jury proceedings are part of a criminal action, they are exempted from the Code's application.[2] Under the Penal Code, however, an indictment can be set aside if it is not supported by sufficient legally admissible evidence.[3] The Code applies to preliminary hearings, since they too are a criminal action, but a 1990 amendment permits the use of hearsay in support of the probable cause finding.[4]

Proceedings that do not take place in California courts are not subject to the Code. Accordingly, the Code does not apply to legislative hearings, administrative proceedings, and other proceedings unless some statute so provides or the agency concerned chooses to apply the Code.[5]

The Federal Rules of Evidence apply in all civil and criminal actions brought in the federal courts.[6] Grand jury proceedings, preliminary examinations in criminal cases, and bail, sentencing, and probation revocation hearings are exempted from the Rules other than those governing privileges.[7]

CALIFORNIA EVIDENCE CODE

§ 300.   Applicability of code

Except as otherwise provided by statute, this code applies in every action before the Supreme Court or a court of appeal, superior court, municipal court, or, including proceedings in such actions conducted by a referee, court commissioner, or similar officer, but does not apply in grand jury proceedings.

---

1.   West's Ann.California Evidence Code § 300.

2.   Id.

3.   West's Ann.California Penal Code § 939.6.

4.   West's Ann.California Evidence Code § 1203.1.

5.   West's Ann.California Evidence Code § 300 (comment).

6.   Federal Rule of Evidence 1101.

7.   Id. Other proceedings exempted in part or in whole are enumerated in Federal Rule of Evidence 1101(d)–(e).

§ 353. Effect of erroneous admission of evidence

A verdict or finding shall not be set aside, nor shall the judgment or decision based thereon be reversed, by reason of the erroneous admission of evidence unless:

(a) There appears of record an objection to or a motion to exclude or to strike the evidence that was timely made and so stated as to make clear the specific ground of the objection or motion; and

(b) The court which passes upon the effect of the error or errors is of the opinion that the admitted evidence should have been excluded on the ground stated and that the error or errors complained of resulted in a miscarriage of justice.

§ 354. Effect of erroneous exclusion of evidence

A verdict or finding shall not be set aside, nor shall the judgment or decision based thereon be reversed, by reason of the erroneous exclusion of evidence unless the court which passes upon the effect of the error or errors is of the opinion that the error or errors complained of resulted in a miscarriage of justice and it appears of record that:

(a) The substance, purpose, and relevance of the excluded evidence was made known to the court by the questions asked, an offer of proof, or by any other means;

(b) The rulings of the court made compliance with subdivision (a) futile; or

(c) The evidence was sought by questions asked during cross-examination or recross-examination.

FEDERAL RULES OF EVIDENCE

Rule 101. Scope; Definitions

(a) Scope. These rules apply to proceedings in United States courts. The specific courts and proceedings to which the rules apply, along with exceptions, are set out in Rule 1101.

Rule 1101. Applicability of the Rules

(a) To Courts and Judges. These rules apply to proceedings before:

- United States district courts;
- United States bankruptcy and magistrate judges;
- United States courts of appeals;
- the United States Court of Federal Claims; and
- the district courts of Guam, the Virgin Islands, and the Northern Mariana Islands.

(b) To Cases and Proceedings. These rules apply in:

- civil cases and proceedings, including bankruptcy, admiralty, and maritime cases;

- criminal cases and proceedings; and

- contempt proceedings, except those in which the court may act summarily.

(c) Rules on Privilege. The rules on privilege apply to all stages of a case or proceeding.

(d) Exceptions. These rules—except for those on privilege—do not apply to the following:

(1) the court's determination, under Rule 104(a), on a preliminary question of fact governing admissibility;

(2) grand-jury proceedings; and

(3) miscellaneous proceedings such as:

- extradition or rendition;

- issuing an arrest warrant, criminal summons, or search warrant;

- a preliminary examination in a criminal case;

- sentencing;

- granting or revoking probation or supervised release; and considering whether to release on bail or otherwise.

(e) Other Statutes and Rules. A federal statute or a rule prescribed by the Supreme Court may provide for admitting or excluding evidence independently from these rules.

Rule 103.   Rulings on Evidence

(a) Preserving a Claim of Error. A party may claim error in a ruling to admit or exclude evidence only if the error affects a substantial right of the party and:

(1) if the ruling admits evidence, a party, on the record:

(A) timely objects or moves to strike; and

(B) states the specific ground, unless it was apparent from the context; or

(2) if the ruling excludes evidence, a party informs the court of its substance by an offer of proof, unless the substance was apparent from the context.

(b) Not Needing to Renew an Objection or Offer of Proof. Once the court rules definitively on the record—either before or at trial—a party need not renew an objection or offer of proof to preserve a claim of error for appeal.

(c) Court's Statement About the Ruling; Directing an Offer of Proof. The court may make any statement about the character or form of the evidence, the objection made, and the ruling. The court may direct that an offer of proof be made in question-and-answer form.

(d) Preventing the Jury from Hearing Inadmissible Evidence. To the extent practicable, the court must conduct a jury trial so that inadmissible evidence is not suggested to the jury by any means.

(e) Taking Notice of Plain Error. A court may take notice of a plain error affecting a substantial right, even if the claim of error was not properly preserved.

CALIFORNIA EVIDENCE CODE

§ 765. Court to control mode of interrogation

(a) The court shall exercise reasonable control over the mode of interrogation of a witness so as to make such interrogation as rapid, as distinct, and as effective for the ascertainment of the truth, as may be, and to protect the witness from undue harassment or embarrassment.

(b) With a witness under the age of 14 is a dependent person with a substantial cognitive impairment, the court shall take special care to protect him or her from undue harassment or embarrassment, and to restrict the unnecessary repetition of questions. The court shall also take special care to insure that questions are stated in a form which is appropriate to the age or cognitive level of the witness. The court may in the interests of justice, on objection by a party, forbid the asking of a question which is in a form that is not reasonably likely to be understood by a person of the age or cognitive level of the witness.

§ 766. Responsive answers

A witness must give responsive answers to questions, and answers that are not responsive shall be stricken on motion of any party.

§ 767. Leading questions

(a) Except under special circumstances where the interests of justice otherwise require:

(1) A leading question may not be asked of a witness on direct or redirect examination.

(2) A leading question may be asked of a witness on cross-examination or recross-examination.

(b) The court may in the interests of justice permit a leading question to be asked of a child under 10 years of age or a dependent person with a substantial cognitive impairment in a case involving a prosecution under Section 273a, 273d, 288.5 368, or any of the acts described in Section 11165.1 or 11165.2 of the Penal Code.

§ 772.   Order of examination

(a) The examination of a witness shall proceed in the following phases: direct examination, cross-examination, redirect examination, re-cross-examination, and continuing thereafter by redirect and recross-examination.

(b) Unless for good cause the court otherwise directs, each phase of the examination of a witness must be concluded before the succeeding phase begins.

(c) Subject to subdivision (d), a party may, in the discretion of the court, interrupt his cross-examination, redirect examination, or recross-examination of a witness, in order to examine the witness upon a matter not within the scope of a previous examination of the witness.

(d) If the witness is the defendant in a criminal action, the witness may not, without his consent, be examined under direct examination by another party.

§ 773.   Cross-examination

(a) A witness examined by one party may be cross-examined upon any matter within the scope of the direct examination by each other party to the action in such order as the court directs.

(b) The cross-examination of a witness by any party whose interest is not adverse to the party calling him is subject to the same rules that are applicable to the direct examination.

§ 774.   Re-examination

A witness once examined cannot be reexamined as to the same matter without leave of the court, but he may be reexamined as to any new matter upon which he has been examined by another party to the action. Leave may be granted or withheld in the court's discretion.

§ 775.   Court may call witnesses

The court, on its own motion or on the motion of any party, may call witnesses and interrogate them the same as if they had been produced by a party to the action, and the parties may object to the questions asked and the evidence adduced the same as if such witnesses were called and examined by an adverse party. Such witnesses may be cross-examined by all parties to the action in such order as the court directs.

§ 776.   Examination of adverse party or witness

(a) A party to the record of any civil action, or a person identified with such a party, may be called and examined as if under cross-examination by any adverse party at any time during the presentation of evidence by the party calling the witness.

(b) A witness examined by a party under this section may be cross-examined by all other parties to the action in such order as the court directs; but, subject to subdivision (e), the witness may be examined only as if under redirect examination by:

(1) In the case of a witness who is a party, his own counsel and counsel for a party who is not adverse to the witness.

(2) In the case of a witness who is not a party, counsel for the party with whom the witness is identified and counsel for a party who is not adverse to the party with whom the witness is identified.

(c) For the purpose of this section, parties represented by the same counsel are deemed to be a single party.

(d) For the purpose of this section, a person is identified with a party if he is:

(1) A person for whose immediate benefit the action is prosecuted or defended by the party.

(2) A director, officer, superintendent, member, agent, employee, or managing agent of the party or of a person specified in paragraph (1), or any public employee of a public entity when such public entity is the party.

(3) A person who was in any of the relationships specified in paragraph (2) at the time of the act or omission giving rise to the cause of action.

(4) A person who was in any of the relationships specified in paragraph (2) at the time he obtained knowledge of the matter concerning which he is sought to be examined under this section.

(e) Paragraph (2) of subdivision (b) does not require counsel for the party with whom the witness is identified and counsel for a party who is not adverse to the party with whom the witness is identified to examine the witness as if under redirect examination if the party who called the witness for examination under this section:

(1) Is also a person identified with the same party with whom the witness is identified.

(2) Is the personal representative, heir, successor, or assignee of a person identified with the same party with whom the witness is identified.

§ 777. Exclusion of witness

(a) Subject to subdivisions (b) and (c), the court may exclude from the courtroom any witness not at the time under examination so that such witness cannot hear the testimony of other witnesses.

(b) A party to the action cannot be excluded under this section.

(c) If a person other than a natural person is a party to the action, an officer or employee designated by its attorney is entitled to be present.

§ 778. Recall of witness

After a witness has been excused from giving further testimony in the action, he cannot be recalled without leave of the court. Leave may be granted or withheld in the court's discretion.

FEDERAL RULES OF EVIDENCE

Rule 611.   Mode and Order of Examining Witnesses and Presenting Evidence

(a) Control by the Court; Purposes. The court should exercise reasonable control over the mode and order of examining witnesses and presenting evidence so as to:

    (1) make those procedures effective for determining the truth;

    (2) avoid wasting time; and

    (3) protect witnesses from harassment or undue embarrassment.

(b) Scope of Cross–Examination. Cross-examination should not go beyond the subject matter of the direct examination and matters affecting the witness's credibility. The court may allow inquiry into additional matters as if on direct examination.

(c) Leading Questions. Leading questions should not be used on direct examination except as necessary to develop the witness's testimony. Ordinarily, the court should allow leading questions:

    (1) on cross-examination; and

    (2) when a party calls a hostile witness, an adverse party, or a witness identified with an adverse party.

Rule 614.   Calling and Interrogation of Witnesses by Court

(a) Calling by Court. The court may, on its own motion or at the suggestion of a party, call witnesses, and all parties are entitled to cross-examine witnesses thus called.

(b) Interrogation by Court. The court may interrogate witnesses, whether called by itself or by a party.

(c) Objections. Objections to the calling of witnesses by the court or to interrogation by it may be made at the time or at the next available opportunity when the jury is not present.

Rule 615.   Excluding Witnesses

At a party's request, the court must order witnesses excluded so that they cannot hear other witnesses' testimony. Or the court may do so on its own. But this rule does not authorize excluding:

(a) a party who is a natural person;

(b) an officer or employee of a party that is not a natural person, after being designated as the party's representative by its attorney;

(c) a person whose presence a party shows to be essential to presenting the party's claim or defense; or

(d) a person authorized by statute to be present.

CHAPTER 2

RELEVANCE

■ ■ ■

Table of Sections

§ 2.01 INTRODUCTION

This chapter examines the basic concept of relevance—its components and the idea that evidence that meets all conditions of admissibility can still be excluded by the trial judge under certain circumstances. Other chapters, notably 3 and 4, explore rules that ban or limit relevant evidence out of concern that its unrestrained admission would endanger interests the rules of evidence seek to protect. Chapter 2 should be viewed only as an introduction to the concept of relevance.

Materiality. Section 350 of the Code sets out the fundamental condition that all evidence must satisfy if it is to be admitted: "No evidence is admissible except relevant evidence."[1] Building on § 350, § 351 then postulates the general rule of admissibility: "Except as otherwise provided by statute, all relevant evidence is admissible."[2] Since these two sections form the cornerstone upon which the entire evidence struc-

---

1. West's Ann.California Evidence Code § 350. Federal Rule of Evidence 402 is to the same effect. See § 2.05 infra.

2. West's Ann.California Evidence Code § 351. Federal Rule of Evidence 402 is to the same effect. See § 2.05 infra.

ture is constructed, it is indispensable to know what is meant by "relevance."

The definition of relevance is contained in § 210: " 'Relevant evidence' means evidence, including evidence relevant to the credibility of a witness or hearsay declarant, having any tendency in reason to prove or disprove any disputed fact that is of consequence to the determination of the action."[3] This section defines relevance in terms of two components. One refers to the proving or disproving quality of an item of evidence. This aspect is known as the probative value of an item of evidence. The other focuses on the relationship between an item of evidence and disputed facts that are of consequence to the determination of the action. This relationship is known as materiality.

To be material, an item of evidence must be directed at a proposition that is properly provable in the action being tried. Typically, that determination can be made by referring to the pleadings and the substantive law that governs the action. If the proffered evidence is beyond the definition of the action as defined by the substantive law, it is immaterial. The crime of murder, for example, does not include whether the victim was pregnant.[4] Accordingly, in an attempted murder prosecution, evidence that the victim was pregnant should be excluded.[5] Moreover, as a rule, evidence regarding punishment is irrelevant in California criminal cases. The issue in the guilt phase is the accused's guilt and not his or her punishment.[6]

If the item of evidence is offered to settle a factual question raised by the pleadings, then the item will be material.[7] Fuentes v. Tucker[8] provides a good illustration of this concept. *Fuentes* was a wrongful death action brought by the parents of children who were killed when the defendant struck them with his car. On the day of the trial the defendant filed an amended answer in which he admitted liability for the deaths of the children. Over the defendant's objection, the plaintiffs were permitted to introduce evidence that the defendant was intoxicated at the time of the accident and that the children were thrown eighty feet by the force of the impact. Since in his amended answer the defendant had removed the issue of liability from the case, the California Supreme Court held that it was error for the trial judge to admit the evidence. Although the evidence was probative of the defendant's negligence and other aspects of his liability, it

---

3. West's Ann.California Evidence Code § 210. Federal Rule of Evidence 401 is to the same effect. See § 2.05 infra.

4. See West's Ann.California Penal Code § 187.

5. People v. Cash, 28 Cal.4th 703, 729, 122 Cal.Rptr.2d 545, 562, 50 P.3d 332, 347 (2002), cert. denied, 537 U.S. 1199, 123 S.Ct. 1270, 154 L.Ed.2d 1039 (2003). For the victim's pregnancy to be admissible, it must be probative of some proposition that is properly provable in the action. For example, if the identity of the assailant is contested, it would be relevant to prove the victim's pregnancy if her condition is what motivated the defendant to attack her.

6. People v. Rains, 75 Cal.App.4th 1165, 1170, 89 Cal.Rptr.2d 737, 739 (1999) (citing § 351 of the Evidence Code and People v. Alvarez, 49 Cal.App.4th 679, 687, 56 Cal.Rptr.2d 814, 818 (1996)).

7. As the definition makes clear, evidence that is directed to attacking or supporting the credibility of witnesses is likewise material.

8. 31 Cal.2d 1, 187 P.2d 752 (1947).

was directed at a proposition that no longer was properly provable in the action.[9] Accordingly, the evidence was immaterial and therefore was irrelevant and inadmissible.

QUESTIONS AND PROBLEMS

1. According to the Old Testament's First Book of Kings, King Solomon was called upon to decide a dispute between two women, each of whom claimed that a certain child was hers. To resolve the conflicting claims, King Solomon proposed that the child be divided in two and that each of the women receive one-half. One woman protested, asking the king to award the child to the other woman rather than slay the child. The other woman asked the king to divide the child. King Solomon then awarded the child to the woman who protested, saying, "She is the mother thereof."

With which proposition was the king concerned: which woman was the biological mother or which woman was the "better" mother?

2. Would evidence that the protesting woman offered to give up the child rather than have it slain be relevant in an action to establish the biological mother? The better mother?

3. If the evidence is relevant to establish both propositions, should the judge exclude it in an action in which only one of the propositions can properly be proved?

§ 2.02 STIPULATIONS

Admissions in pleadings are not the only way to remove an issue from a case. Parties may enter into stipulations. In *Fuentes*,[1] for example, the defendant could have stipulated to liability. Unlike an admission, a stipulation is essentially an offer to admit to a fact or set of facts. As an offer, it can be rejected by the opposing party, although judges generally encourage their acceptance because of the time saved by dispensing with the need to prove the stipulated facts. Stipulations of this type are as binding on the trier of fact as are admissions in pleadings.[2]

Stipulations, however, do not bar the introduction of evidence of relevant matters that are outside the scope of the stipulation.[3] Nor do they preclude a judge from rejecting a stipulation where its effect would drain the opposing party's evidence of its legitimate effect.[4] In People v. Poon,[5]

---

9. Under California law, the parents were not entitled to recover for the pain and suffering experienced by the children. Id. at 5, 187 P.2d at 755. Accordingly, the evidence could not be directed at this proposition. This outcome illustrates the other aspect of the rule: materiality is determined also by referring to the substantive law that governs the action.

1. Fuentes v. Tucker, 31 Cal.2d 1, 187 P.2d 752 (1947). For a discussion of *Fuentes*, see § 2.01 supra.

2. Smith v. Walter E. Heller & Co., Inc., 82 Cal.App.3d 259, 269, 147 Cal.Rptr. 1, 7 (1978).

3. People v. Poon, 125 Cal.App.3d 55, 78–79, 178 Cal.Rptr. 375, 389–390 (1981).

4. See, e.g., People v. Edelbacher, 47 Cal.3d 983, 1007, 254 Cal.Rptr. 586, 599–600, 766 P.2d 1, 14 (1989) (The prosecution "cannot be compelled to accept a stipulation if the effect would be to deprive the state's case of its persuasiveness and forcefulness.").

for example, the accused offered to stipulate that the victim in a rape prosecution had been raped. Because acceptance of the stipulation would have drained the state's evidence of its value on the question of who committed the rape, the appellate court upheld the trial judge's refusal to require the prosecution to accept the stipulation. By rejecting the stipulation, the trial judge permitted the prosecution to offer medical testimony that corroborated the victim's account about the manner in which she was raped.[6] Such corroboration in turn helped the prosecution persuade the jury to accept the victim's testimony about the identity of her assailant.[7]

Stipulations offering to admit to facts must be distinguished from stipulations regarding evidence. To save time and prevent inconvenience to witnesses, sometimes a party is willing to stipulate to the contents of testimony or a document. Assume, for example, that in *Fuentes* the plaintiff was prepared to call the bartender of the local tavern to testify that he had served the defendant beer on the morning of the accident. Assume further that the defendant offered to stipulate that, if called, the bartender would have so testified, and that the plaintiff accepted the stipulation. Such a stipulation would not be binding on the trier of fact or on the defendant. The defendant would still be free to offer evidence contradicting the stipulated testimony, and the jury would be free to disregard it. The stipulated testimony would have the same status as the testimony of the bartender had he appeared and testified as stipulated, and the jury would so be instructed.[8]

Since the decision to stipulate is a tactical matter, counsel generally have discretion to stipulate to facts in both civil and criminal cases with or without the express authority of the client.[9] But since these stipulations are binding on the trier of fact, in criminal cases some stipulations are invalid unless the accused personally and intelligently waives his constitutional rights to confront his accusers, to refuse to incriminate himself, and to have the prosecution prove and the jury find the stipulated facts beyond a reasonable doubt.[10] Stipulations that are "destructive of the accused's position at trial" require an intelligent waiver.[11] An example is a stipulation in which the accused admits suffering prior convictions when such an admission leads to enhanced penalties upon conviction of the offense charged.[12] But stipulations that do not admit all of the evidentiary facts

---

5. 125 Cal.App.3d 55, 78–79, 178 Cal.Rptr. 375, 389–390 (1981).

6. Id.

7. Although parties generally have a right to reject stipulations proposed by their opponents, in People v. Hall, 28 Cal.3d 143, 616 P.2d 826, 167 Cal.Rptr. 844 (1980), the California Supreme Court held that the accused has the right over the prosecution's objection to admit or stipulate to allegations in the charging instrument. Id. at 155–156, 616 P.2d at 832–833, 167 Cal.Rptr. at 850–851. For a discussion of state constitutional limitations on this right, see § 7.09 infra.

8. See BAJI 2.09, Stipulated Testimony (Fall 2007 Edition).

9. People v. Adams, 6 Cal.4th 570, 578, 24 Cal.Rptr.2d 831, 836, 862 P.2d 831, 836 (1993).

10. Id. at 577, 24 Cal.Rptr.2d at 837, 862 P.2d at 835.

11. Id. at 579, 24 Cal.Rptr.2d at 836–837, 862 P.2d at 836, citing People v. Chasco, 276 Cal.App.2d 271, 80 Cal.Rptr. 667 (1969).

12. In re Yurko, 10 Cal.3d 857, 860, 112 Cal.Rptr. 513, 514, 519 P.2d 561, 562 (1974). In charging the accused with burglary, the prosecution also alleged that he had been previously

that are necessary to conviction of an offense or to the imposition of additional punishment on a finding that an enhancement is true do not require a waiver.[13] Examples include: stipulating to kidnaping and killing the victim in a prosecution for murder with a kidnaping special circumstance,[14] to having suffered prior convictions where the convictions are simply penalty phase aggravating evidence,[15] to the narcotic content of capsules seized from the accused[16] or of balloons the accused sold to an informant,[17] to having been on bail where the prosecution seeks to enhance the punishment for the offenses charged by alleging and proving that the accused committed them while on bail,[18] to having been convicted of a felony where the prosecution has charged the accused with being a felon in possession of a firearm.[19]

The task of determining when a waiver is necessary would be eased substantially if the courts simply adopted a rule requiring a waiver whenever a stipulation has the effect of admitting an element of the offense, irrespective of whether the element is designated as part of the definition of the offense or simply as a penalty enhancement. A plea of not guilty puts in issue all elements of the offense charged; a denial of the facts asserted in any enhancement clause likewise puts those facts in issue. Since the prosecution must then prove these elements and facts beyond a reasonable doubt, clearly those stipulations which admit these elements and facts should require the accused's waiver.[20]

---

convicted on three occasions of other offenses. At the time of Yurko's conviction, proof of the underlying offense (burglary) and of the prior convictions led to a finding that the accused was an habitual offender subject to life imprisonment. Id. A jury convicted Yurko of the underlying offense. Id.

13. People v. Adams, 6 Cal.4th 570, 580, 24 Cal.Rptr.2d 831, 838, 862 P.2d 831, 837 (1993).

14. People v. Hovey, 44 Cal.3d 543, 567, 244 Cal.Rptr. 121, 134, 749 P.2d 776, 780 (1988).

15. People v. Ramirez, 50 Cal.3d 1158, 1184, 270 Cal.Rptr. 286, 302, 791 P.2d 965, 981 (1990).

16. People v. McCoy, 40 Cal.App.3d 854, 859, 115 Cal.Rptr. 559, 562 (1974).

17. People v. Chasco, 276 Cal.App.2d 271, 274–276, 80 Cal.Rptr. 667, 669–671 (1969).

18. People v. Adams, 6 Cal.4th 570, 580, 24 Cal.Rptr.2d 831, 838, 862 P.2d 831, 838 (1993). The court sought to distinguish *Yurko* on the ground that in *Adams* the accused still had the right to be tried of the offenses he was charged with committing while on bail. Id. In *Yurko*, however, the accused still had the right to be tried of the underlying offense (burglary). Since in neither case the accused would be subject to an enhanced penalty unless convicted of the underlying offenses, the basis for the court's distinction in *Adams* is unclear.

19. People v. Newman, 21 Cal.4th 413, 422, 87 Cal.Rptr.2d 474, 480, 981 P.2d 98, 103 (1999).

20. "Other than the fact of a prior conviction, any fact that increases the penalty for a crime beyond the prescribed statutory maximum must be submitted to a jury, and proved beyond a reasonable doubt" as a federal constitutional matter. Apprendi v. New Jersey, 530 U.S. 466, 490, 120 S.Ct. 2348, 2362–2363, 147 L.Ed.2d 435 (2000). But as a statutory matter, a California criminal defendant is entitled to a jury determination of whether he has suffered a prior conviction even if the conviction is not an element of the offense. West's Ann. California Penal Code § 1025.

Stipulations regarding the content of testimony can also raise waiver issues. When, for example, the accused submits the issue of guilt on the basis of the preliminary hearing transcript and the accused does not dispute his guilt, such a procedure is tantamount to a "slow plea" requiring a waiver. People v. Stone, 27 Cal.App.4th 276, 281–282, 32 Cal.Rptr.2d 494, 497 (1994). But where the accused does not concede guilt, merely stipulating to the use of the victim's former testimony will not require a waiver. Id.

Sometimes, for tactical reasons, an attorney will concede the accused's guilt of some charges or other wrongdoing in summation. Those concessions, even in a capital trial, do not require the

QUESTIONS AND PROBLEMS

1. The plaintiff sues the defendant for negligent entrustment on the theory that the defendant negligently lent his car to a driver the defendant knew or should have known was an unsafe driver. The defendant offers to stipulate that he is the owner of the car that struck the plaintiff and that he lent his car to the driver. The plaintiff accepts the stipulation. The defendant then takes the stand and testifies that he never lent his car to the driver. The plaintiff moves to strike the answer on the ground that the defendant is bound by the stipulation. Should the judge grant the motion to strike?

2. The defendant also offers to stipulate that if the defendant's spouse appeared as a witness, she would testify that the plaintiff had the green light. The plaintiff accepts this stipulation. During his direct examination, the defendant testifies that the plaintiff had the red light. The plaintiff moves to strike the answer on the ground that the defendant is bound by his stipulation. Should the judge grant the motion to strike?

3. In the same action, in response to the plaintiff's pretrial request for admissions, the defendant responds that on the day of the accident he was not wearing his glasses. At the trial the defendant takes the stand and testifies that he was wearing his glasses. The plaintiff moves to strike the answer on the ground that the defendant is bound by his response to the request for admissions. Should the judge grant the motion to strike?

§ 2.03   CREDIBILITY

Materiality also encompasses the credibility of witnesses. Section 210 expressly includes "evidence relevant to the credibility of a witness or hearsay declarant" within the definition of "relevant evidence."[1] This is not surprising, as often a trial's outcome will depend on which of two conflicting versions of an event a jury believes. Accordingly, evidence of the veracity or mendacity of the witnesses may be of special consequence to the determination of the action. To underscore the importance of evidence relating to credibility, the seminal rule on credibility, § 780, provides that in determining the credibility of a witness the trier of fact may consider "any matter that has any tendency in reason to prove or disprove the truthfulness of his testimony * * *."[2]

The Code contains numerous limitations on the manner and the circumstances in which the credibility of a witness may be assailed or supported.[3] Unless evidence of credibility is excluded by one of these limitations, such evidence, being material, is relevant and, hence, admissible.

Whether a ruling that violates one of these limitations should result in reversal of the verdict depends on the test the reviewing court employs.

---

accused's express waiver. See People v. Lucas, 12 Cal.4th 415, 446, 48 Cal.Rptr.2d 525, 544, 907 P.2d 373, 392 (1995) and cases cited therein.

1. West's Ann.California Evidence Code § 350.

2. West's Ann.California Evidence Code § 780.

3. See § 15.01 infra.

Ordinarily, the appellant has the burden of persuading the reviewing court that a ruling erroneously admitting evidence was prejudicial.[4] But where the record discloses judicial bias against the appealing party, the appellate court will dispense with the harmless error standard and reverse on grounds of unfairness.

Hernandez v. Paicius,[5] a medical malpractice case, illustrates this distinction. Under the Code, a witness may not be impeached by evidence that the witness has engaged in "bad acts" that may be probative of the witness's predisposition to lie under oath.[6] A party, for example, may not offer evidence that a witness cheats on his taxes as proof of the witness's predisposition to be untruthful under oath.[7] Despite this prohibition, the trial judge denied the plaintiff's motion to exclude all references to his alienage if his illegal status was offered to attack his credibility. Accordingly, defense counsel in his opening argument informed the jurors that the plaintiff was in the United States illegally. In denying the plaintiff's motion, the judge made statements the appellate court found evinced bias against the plaintiff on the basis of his alienage.[8] The reviewing court reversed the judgment for the defendant, holding that a special standard, not the customary harmless error standard, would apply where, "as here, the appearance of judicial bias and unfairness colors the entire record * * *. The test is not whether plaintiff has proved harm, but whether the court's comments would cause a reasonable person to doubt the impartiality of the judge or would cause us to lack confidence in the fairness of the proceedings such as would necessitate reversal. The record here inspires no confidence in either case."[9]

When does the credibility of a witness become an issue? In the case of a witness who appears, the moment the witness takes the stand; in the

---

4. See West's Ann. California Evidence Code § 353(b).

5. 109 Cal.App.4th 452, 134 Cal.Rptr.2d 756 (2003).

6. West's Ann. California Evidence Code § 787.

7. See § 15.06 infra.

8. In response to the plaintiff's argument in favor of the motion, the judge stated, "I understand your argument, but you missed my point. I'm alerting you to the realities of life. It's not the reality [of] life as you conveniently make the jump where someone is from and their ethnicity to a malpractice doctor and getting injured. You missed something there. You jumped right over the illegality portion, the lying portion, the credibility portion. [¶] So if this jury is going to hear a story about a guy who's been damaged, can't work, and they're going to have to believe him about—and I noticed he dropped some of the claims so he might have been fudging on those—faking it as it were, that if he's here claiming this hoarseness has impacted his life so much he's entitled [to] a ton of money from this good doctor they have to believe him. If they don't believe him he gets nada." Id. at 458, 134 Cal.Rptr.2d at 759.

9. Id. at 460, 134 Cal.Rptr.2d at 762. In its order reversing the judgment and remanding the case for a new trial, the reviewing court ordered the presiding judge of the Superior Court to assign the case to different judge.

Attacking parties or witnesses on the basis of their alienage is not new. In People v. Caruso, 246 N.Y. 437, 159 N.E. 390 (1927), the prosecutor, in his cross-examination, attempted to ask the defendant, an Italian immigrant, whether he was a citizen or had applied for naturalization. Although reversing the defendant's conviction on other grounds, New York's highest court noted that the prosecutor's appeal to the prejudices of the jury would have also warranted reversal. Id. at 445, 159 N.E. at 392.

case of a hearsay declarant who does not appear, when the declarant's hearsay declaration is received in evidence.

QUESTIONS AND PROBLEMS

In a prosecution for murdering an officer who was attempting to arrest the defendant, the defendant testified that the reason he killed the officer was that he was afraid that the officer might kill him. When asked "why" by his attorney, the defendant testified that he had heard that the officer had killed an old man, Frank Smith, while arresting him. The prosecutor in rebuttal called the county coroner who testified that Frank Smith died of natural causes. The defendant moves to strike on the ground that the coroner's testimony is irrelevant. Should the judge grant the motion to strike?

§ 2.04   PROBATIVE VALUE

In addition to materiality, relevance has another aspect known as probative value. This term refers to the proving or disproving quality of an item of evidence and is captured by the language of § 210 which defines relevant evidence as evidence "having any tendency in reason to prove or disprove any disputed fact * * *."[1] Thus, to be relevant, an item of evidence not only must be directed at a proposition that is properly provable in the action, the item must also be probative of that proposition. How strong must its "tendency" be in terms of proving or disproving the proposition? If the item of evidence renders the existence of the proposition more likely or less likely than it would be without the item, then the item possesses the requisite probative value and is relevant.[2]

The test does not require the proponent to persuade the judge that the proffered evidence will move the trier of fact to accept the proposition. It simply requires the proponent to convince the judge that the item of evidence renders the existence of the proposition more likely or less likely than the proposition would be *without* the evidence.

The difference in the burdens can be illustrated by returning to the *Fuentes* case.[3] Assume that the defendant had not admitted liability. Under these circumstances, the plaintiffs would have been entitled to prove that the defendant was negligent in the operation of his car because he was intoxicated. Would evidence that he had one beer on the morning of the accident be probative of this proposition? The answer would be yes, not because the jury would have been moved by the evidence to believe that the defendant was intoxicated—this would be unlikely—but because the proposition that the defendant was intoxicated is rendered more likely by the evidence that he had one beer than the proposition would be without the evidence.

---

1.   West's Ann.California Evidence Code § 210.

2.   See C. McCormick, Handbook of the Law of Evidence § 185 (E. Cleary 2d ed. 1972).

3.   Fuentes v. Tucker, 31 Cal.2d 1, 187 P.2d 752 (1947). For a discussion of *Fuentes*, see § 2.01 supra.

Dean Charles McCormick explained, in memorable words, the difference in the burdens. If one imagines the proposition that the defendant was intoxicated to be a wall, then evidence that he had one beer on the morning of the accident would constitute only one brick. To the objection that proof of one beer is not proof of intoxication, Dean McCormick would retort, "A brick is not a wall."[4]

Although all evidence is probative of some proposition in the sense contemplated by § 210, not all evidence has the same probative force or persuasive effect. Relevant evidence, depending on its nature, may or may not persuade the trier of fact to find the proposition desired by the proponent. In the *Fuentes* case, for example, evidence that the defendant had been arrested on three separate occasions for speeding and driving while intoxicated would have been more persuasive of his negligence when he struck the children than evidence that he had only one beer the morning of the accident. Both items of evidence, however, would be probative of a material proposition and, hence, would be relevant.

QUESTIONS AND PROBLEMS

1. The plaintiff sues the defendant for the price of an unopened drum of Navajo white paint, claiming that the paint is defective. At the trial, the judge sustains the defendant's irrelevance objection to the plaintiff's proffered testimony that Navajo white paint from a drum he purchased one month earlier from the defendant ruined his walls after drying. Both drums of paint were made by the defendant. Was the judge's ruling correct?

2. On irrelevance grounds, should the defendant be precluded from offering evidence that other Navajo white paint produced by the defendant did not ruin surfaces after drying?

§ 2.05 RELEVANCE UNDER THE FEDERAL RULES

The Federal Rules of Evidence follow the California approach to relevance. Like §§ 350 and 351, Federal Rule of Evidence 402 provides that "[i]rrelevant evidence is not admissible" and then declares that, except as otherwise provided, "[r]elevant evidence is admissible."[1]

Federal Rule of Evidence 401 defines relevant evidence as evidence "having any tendency to make a fact more probable or less probable than it would be without the evidence" and "the fact is of consequence in determining the action."[2] Although the rule makes no express reference to credibility, evidence relating to credibility is embraced in the definition, since, as discussed, the outcome of an action is often determined by the jurors' assessment of the credibility of the witnesses.

---

4. C. McCormick, Handbook of the Law of Evidence § 185 (E. Cleary 2d ed. 1972).

1. Federal Rule of Evidence 402.

2. Federal Rule of Evidence 401.

prob = logically relevant
mat = legally relevant

Rule 401 makes clearer than § 210 the burden the proponent must discharge when confronted by an irrelevance objection. The proponent need only convince the judge that the proffered evidence makes the existence of any consequential fact more or less probable than the fact would be without the evidence. Though the language of Rule 401 is superior in this respect, both rules impose the same burden on the proponent of the evidence.

§ 2.06　RELEVANCE AND INFERENCE

Neither the Code nor the Rules establishes a preference between direct and circumstantial evidence. Section 410 of the Code defines direct evidence as "evidence that directly proves a fact, without an inference or presumption, and which in itself, if true, conclusively establishes that fact."[1] This section, however, does not favor direct evidence over circumstantial evidence.

From a relevance perspective, the distinction between direct and circumstantial evidence is without significance. Either can satisfy the tests of materiality and probative value, and both are acceptable means of proof in civil and criminal matters.[2] In California criminal cases, however, before an inference essential to establish guilt may be found to have been proved beyond a reasonable doubt, each fact or circumstance upon which such an inference necessarily rests must also be proved beyond a reasonable doubt.[3]

Circumstantial evidence may not be as convincing as direct evidence because of the additional reasoning required to reach the proposition to which it is directed.[4] If the proposition to be proved is that the defendant had six beers, then testimony by the bartender that he served and saw the defendant consume six beers would have greater probative worth than testimony by the arresting officer that the defendant smelled of an alcoholic beverage or that the defendant had bloodshot eyes. The fact, however, that the probative value of the officer's testimony depends on inferential reasoning and that, among the various inferences that can be drawn from his testimony, the one most favorable to the proponent is only that the defendant may have drunk an intoxicating liquor, does not detract from the evidence's relevance. Moreover, the fact that the officer's testimony may be probative of other, inconsistent propositions does not render the testimony irrelevant.[5] It simply places upon the fact finder the

---

1. West's Ann.California Evidence Code § 410. The Federal Rules do not contain an analogous provision.

2. Jurors are routinely told that both direct and circumstantial evidence are acceptable means of proof and that neither is entitled to greater weight as a matter of law. See CALJIC 2.00 (Fall 2006 Edition) and BAJI 2.00 (Fall 2007 Edition).

3. CALJIC 2.01, Sufficiency of Circumstantial Evidence—Generally (Fall 2006 Edition).

4. See C. McCormick, McCormick on Evidence § 185 (E. Cleary 3d ed. 1984).

5. Id.

burden of determining, for example, whether the bloodshot eyes are evidence of intoxication or lack of sleep.

Questions and Problems

In a drunk-driving prosecution, the defendant moves to strike on irrelevance grounds testimony by the arresting officer that the defendant's car wove in and out of its lane three times in a space of one mile. In support of her objection, the defendant offers to call a mechanic who will testify that he examined the defendant's car shortly after her arrest for drunk-driving and that his inspection revealed that the front end was misaligned, a condition which would cause the car to veer to the left and which would require a hard turn to the right to keep the car from veering off the road. Should the judge grant the motion to strike? Would you change your ruling if the defendant moved to strike after the mechanic had testified?

§ 2.07 CONDITIONAL ADMISSIBILITY

Sometimes the relevance of an item of evidence depends on proof of other facts. For example, in an action for breach of a written contract, the relevance of a contract tendered by the plaintiff will depend on whether it was the contract entered into by the defendant. If the contract was signed by someone other than the defendant, then the relevance of the contract will depend on whether the person signing was authorized to do so by the defendant.[1] Absent evidence that the defendant entered into the contract or that it was signed by an agent authorized to do so, the contract would be irrelevant. It would be wholly unconnected with the defendant and, therefore, immaterial.

Section 403 of the Evidence Code places upon the proponent of the evidence (the plaintiff in our example) the burden of producing evidence of the facts connecting the contract with the defendant.[2] Against the objection of the opposing party, the proponent of the proffered evidence (the contract) must usually produce the evidence of the preliminary facts (the connecting evidence) before the proffered evidence can be received in evidence.[3] But the trial judge may admit the proffered evidence on the condition that the proponent supply the evidence of the preliminary or connecting facts before the close of the evidence.[4]

If the proffered evidence is received, the judge may, and upon request of the opposing party must, instruct the jury to disregard the proffered

---

1. Brown v. Spencer, 163 Cal. 589, 126 P. 493 (1912).

2. West's Ann.California Evidence Code § 403.

3. West's Ann.California Evidence Code § 403(a).

4. West's Ann.California Evidence Code § 403(b). No such discretion exists when the opposing party objects to evidence on the ground that the witness does not possess the requisite personal knowledge. Against such an objection, the proponent must show that the witness possesses the required personal knowledge before the witness may continue with his testimony. West's Ann.California Evidence Code § 702.

evidence unless the jury first finds the preliminary facts.[5] The instruction helps insure that the judge's conclusion about the existence of the preliminary facts will not deprive the opponent of a jury determination of those issues.

By what standard must the proponent persuade the judge of the existence of the preliminary facts? By a sufficiency standard, one requiring the proponent to produce "evidence sufficient to sustain a finding of the existence of the preliminary fact * * *."[6] This standard limits the fact finding role of the judge: in determining whether the preliminary facts exist, the judge must look at the evidence in the light most favorable to the proponent. This requires the judge to assume the credibility of the witnesses called by the proponent to establish the preliminary facts, to disregard contradicting evidence offered by the opponent, and to draw only those inferences most favorable to the proponent.[7] If, after viewing the evidence in this light, the judge concludes that a reasonable jury *could* find the preliminary facts, then the judge must rule the proffered evidence admissible.[8]

Questions and Problems

1.   The defendant is prosecuted for assaulting the victim with a deadly weapon. As his first witness, the prosecutor calls a police officer. The prosecutor hands the officer a bat and asks the officer if she can identify it. She testifies that it is the bat which the victim told her the defendant used in attacking him. The defendant objects and moves to strike on hearsay grounds that portion of the answer relating what the victim said to the officer about the bat. The judge sustains the objection and grants the motion. The prosecutor then moves the bat in evidence. The defendant objects on the ground of irrelevance, arguing that no evidence has been adduced connecting him with bat. Should the judge sustain or overrule the defendant's objection?

Suppose the prosecutor responds that the "connecting" evidence will be supplied when the victim is called to testify. May the judge admit the bat subject to a motion to strike?

2.   Assume that the judge declines to receive the bat. As his second witness, the prosecutor calls the victim. The victim testifies that the defendant hit him with a baseball bat. The prosecutor hands the victim a bat and asks the victim if he can identify it. The victim replies that the bat looks just like the one the defendant hit him with but that the bat he is holding is a different color. The prosecutor offers the bat in evidence as an example of the kind of bat the defendant used to hit the victim. The defendant objects on grounds of irrelevance. Should the judge sustain the objection?

3.   If the judge admits the bat, what limiting instruction, if any, should the defendant request?

---

5. West's Ann.California Evidence Code § 403(c)(1).

6. West's Ann.California Evidence Code § 403(a).

7. The sole question for the judge is whether a reasonable jury *could* find the preliminary fact if the proponent's evidence is believed. For an extended discussion of this point, see § 17.01 infra.

8. Id.

§ 2.08 CONDITIONAL RELEVANCE AND THE FEDERAL RULES

Federal Rule of Evidence 104(b) adopts an approach quite similar to that of § 403, including the test the judge should employ in determining the existence of the preliminary facts. Rule 104(b) provides that "[w]hen the relevance of evidence depends on whether a fact exists, proof must be introduced sufficient to support a finding that the fact does exist."[1]

§ 2.09 PROBABILISTIC EVIDENCE

Any item of evidence is probative of a proposition in the sense that it renders the existence of the proposition more likely or less likely than the proposition would be without the item. The probative aspect of evidence, focusing as it does on the existence or nonexistence of a proposition, fits in with probability theories concerned with the likelihood of events occurring or not occurring. Accordingly, probabilistic evidence can meet the relevance requirements of the Code and the Federal Rules.

A more difficult question is whether courts should admit such evidence. In California, the prevailing view is that probabilistic evidence is admissible if it otherwise meets the standards governing the use of expert testimony and scientific evidence,[1] and if the evidence passes the tests of § 352. Section 352 empowers trial judges to exclude relevant evidence whenever its probative value is substantially outweighed by such concerns as unfair prejudice to the opposing party.[2]

The use, as well as the misuse, of probabilistic evidence was examined critically by the California Supreme Court in People v. Collins.[3] In that case the prosecution sought to prove the guilt of a couple accused of robbery by offering the testimony of a mathematician. On the basis of the mathematician's testimony, the prosecution argued that there was but one chance in 12 million (later changed to one in a billion) that a couple other than the defendants committed the robbery. In reversing, the court stressed that the inferences drawn by the prosecutor were not based on

1. Federal Rule of Evidence 104(b). For an extended discussion of the federal approach to "conditional relevancy," see § 17.06 infra. Like West's Ann.California Evidence Code § 702, against the objection of the opposing party, Federal Rule of Evidence 602 requires the proponent to establish the personal knowledge of a witness before the witness may continue testifying. See note 4, § 2.07 supra.

1. People v. Brown, 40 Cal.3d 512, 535, note 6, 230 Cal.Rptr. 834, 845, note 6, 726 P.2d 516, 527 (1985) ("[B]oth California and the majority of other jurisdictions have traditionally admitted statistical blood-group evidence * * *."). See also People v. Axell, 235 Cal.App.3d 836, 865, 1 Cal.Rptr.2d 411, 429 (1991) (Evidence of the statistical probabilities underlying DNA fingerprinting is admissible if the statistical methods used are generally accepted by the pertinent scientific community.); Bell v. Farmers Ins. Exchange, 115 Cal.App.4th 715, 747, 9 Cal.Rptr.3d 544, 571 (2004) (Statistically accepted sampling and extrapolation methods may be used to calculate aggregate damages in class actions brought by employees against their employer.).

2. For an extended discussion of § 352, see § 2.10 infra.

3. 68 Cal.2d 319, 66 Cal.Rptr. 497, 438 P.2d 33 (1968).

accepted statistical theory.[4] In California, evidence based on scientific principles is inadmissible unless the principles have been generally accepted by the relevant scientific community.[5]

The court went further, however, and expressed reservations about the use of even proper statistical techniques, especially in criminal cases. In the court's view, the use of probabilistic evidence must be "critically examined" because of the risk that a jury might be unable to weigh the evidence properly as well as the difficulties the accused might face in meeting the evidence.[6] The risk that the fact finder might attach unwarranted weight to probabilistic evidence is a concern which a trial judge can consider in deciding whether to admit the evidence under § 352.[7]

Most California decisions have rejected the use of probabilistic evidence at least in criminal cases.[8] In this respect, the federal courts have been more generous.[9] But the emergence of new forensic tools, such as DNA fingerprinting, has led some California courts to reconsider and approve the use of statistical evidence in criminal cases, especially where the proponent establishes that the statistical methods used have been generally accepted by the relevant scientific community.[10]

---

4. Id. at 327–328, 66 Cal.Rptr. at 502–503, 438 P.2d at 38–39.

5. People v. Kelly, 17 Cal.3d 24, 30, 130 Cal.Rptr. 144, 148, 549 P.2d 1240, 1244 (1976). For an extended discussion of the admissibility of scientific evidence, see § 16.04 infra.

6. People v. Collins, 68 Cal.2d 319, 332, 66 Cal.Rptr. 497, 505, 438 P.2d 33, 40 (1968).

7. See § 2.10 infra. Whether jurors will make sound use of statistical evidence is unclear. Some scholars have found that lay people often will ignore base rates in making predictions even when those rates are available. See Tversky & Kahnemann, Judgment under Uncertainty: Heuristics and Biases 4–5, as reported in D. Kahneman, P.Slovic & A. Tversky, et al., Judgment Under Uncertainty: Heuristics and Biases (1982).

8. See, e.g., People v. Louie, 158 Cal.App.3d Supp. 28, 205 Cal.Rptr. 247 (1984); People v. Cella, 139 Cal.App.3d 391, 188 Cal.Rptr. 675 (1983). But see People v. Marx, 54 Cal.App.3d 100, 112, 126 Cal.Rptr. 350, 357 (1975) (An expert properly used probability theory to confirm his view that the accused's dentition was unusual enough to point to him as the person who had left his teeth marks on the victim's nose.).

9. See, e.g., United States v. Hickey, 596 F.2d 1082 (1st Cir.1979), cert. denied, 444 U.S. 853, 100 S.Ct. 107, 62 L.Ed.2d 70 (1979) (approving of evidence that hairs found on a ski mask and a sweater "could have" been the defendant's); Oi Lan Lee v. District Director of Immigration and Naturalization Service, 573 F.2d 592 (9th Cir.1978) (holding that although evidence was admissible to show that a blood test did not conclusively rule out the parents as the biological parents, that possibility did not preclude a finding that the parents were not the biological parents); Contemporary Mission, Inc. v. Famous Music Corp., 557 F.2d 918 (2d Cir.1977) (approving the use of statistics to calculate the damages suffered by the plaintiff if the defendant had not discontinued promoting the plaintiff's record). See, generally, J. Weinstein and M. Berger, Weinstein's Evidence Manual ¶ 6.01[04][a] (1987).

10. See, e.g., People v. Axell, 235 Cal.App.3d 836, 844, 1 Cal.Rptr.2d 411, 431 (1991). "Simply put, Cellmark's analysis meant that the chance that anyone but appellant left the unknown hairs at the scene of the crime is 6 billion to 1." Id. at 844, 1 Cal.Rptr.2d at 415. See also People v. Peneda, 32 Cal.App.4th 1022, 1027, 38 Cal.Rptr.2d 312, 315 (1995) (On the basis of applying statistical theory to samples taken from a stash of cocaine, a criminalist was allowed to testify that there was but one chance in "300 million" that the stash did not contain at least 100 pounds of cocaine.).

For an analysis of key cases involving the use of different forms of statistical evidence, see J. Conley & J. Moriarity, Scientific and Expert Evidence, Chapter 3 (Aspen Publishers 2007).

§ 2.10 PROBATIVE VALUE v. PREJUDICIAL EFFECT

Section 352 embodies the principle that a judge may exclude otherwise admissible evidence if its probative value on contested issues is substantially outweighed by enumerated concerns.[1] These include the dangers that the evidence may prejudice a party unduly, confuse the issues to be decided, mislead the jury, or consume too much time.[2] A key feature is that the section does not come into play at all if another rule excludes the evidence. Only if the evidence is otherwise admissible can the judge's discretion be invoked as a last resort by the objecting party.

Section 1155, for example, bans the use of evidence of insurance to prove the insured's negligence or other wrongdoing.[3] Such evidence is excluded because it may not be probative of negligence or other wrongdoing[4] and invites the fact finder to return a verdict on an improper basis (against the party insured). Appeals to § 352 will not render the evidence admissible. But if the evidence is offered for some other purpose that is relevant to the case, then the evidence will be admitted unless excluded under § 352.

Hrnjak v. Graymar, Inc.[5] illustrates this point. The plaintiff was injured when struck by a truck owned by the defendant. To prove that the plaintiff had a motive for feigning injury and refusing to resume employment, the defendant offered evidence that the plaintiff had received payments from his automobile and disability insurance policies. The evidence was outside the ban of § 1155, as it was not offered to prove that the plaintiff was negligent at the time of the accident. The California Supreme Court nonetheless held that the trial judge should have excluded the evidence under § 352. Its probative value on the issue of the plaintiff's malingering was outweighed by the risk that the jury might render a verdict on an improper basis: the evidence invited the jurors to view the plaintiff simply as a "grasping person" who was not entitled to a detached consideration of his claims.[6]

Though the court can exclude evidence under § 352 on its own motion,[7] the party opposing the evidence should ask the court to exercise its discretion on the record.[8] On-the-record weighing is required in order to furnish the reviewing court with an adequate record for meaningful

---

1. West's Ann.California Evidence Code § 352.

2. Id.

3. West's Ann.California Evidence Code § 1155.

4. Id. (comment).

5. 4 Cal.3d 725, 94 Cal.Rptr. 623, 484 P.2d 599 (1971).

6. Id. at 732, 94 Cal.Rptr. at 628, 484 P.2d at 604. On the other hand, a ruling precluding a plaintiff from offering evidence that he personally paid for the medical expenses arising from an accident can result in reversal, especially where the defendant offers evidence that the plaintiff was "malingering." See Smalley v. Baty, 128 Cal.App.4th 977, 987, 27 Cal.Rptr.3d 575, 582 (2005).

7. Gherman v. Colburn, 72 Cal.App.3d 544, 140 Cal.Rptr. 330 (1977).

8. People v. Quaintance, 86 Cal.App.3d 594, 150 Cal.Rptr. 281 (1978).

review of claims of abuse of discretion.[9] It also helps ensure that the trial judge's ruling is the product of mature and careful reflection.[10] The record's failure to disclose the court's reasons for excluding the evidence can result in a reversal for abuse of discretion,[11] unless the ruling, its context, and the arguments of counsel show that the court engaged in the required weighing.[12]

Weighing requires the judge to balance the probative value of the evidence against the harms enumerated in § 352. The principal harm—undue prejudice—is not synonymous with damage; rather, it refers to the risk that the fact finder will be tempted to reach a verdict on the basis of emotional bias against a party rather than on the evidence.[13] In determining the value of the evidence, the court should also take into account the proponent's need for the evidence,[14] the availability of less harmful evidence,[15] and the effectiveness of an instruction advising the jury of the limited purpose of the offer.[16]

Assessing the probative value of the evidence obviously requires the judge to be aware of the nature of the evidence offered by the proponent. In People v. Filson[17] the accused claimed that he was too intoxicated to form the mens rea of the offense charged. An officer testified that though the accused was intoxicated when arrested, he was able to follow commands and seemed to be oriented to his surroundings. The defense then sought the production of a tape recording which the officer made of the accused shortly after his arrest. The trial judge denied the request in part because he considered the recording to be cumulative. The reviewing court reversed, holding that by "ruling without knowing what was on the tape, the trial court could not make an intelligent evaluation of any probative value of the tape, could not assess any prejudice it might pose, and therefore could not undertake the weighing of these factors required for

---

9.   People v. Green, 27 Cal.3d 1, 25, 164 Cal.Rptr. 1, 15, 609 P.2d 468, 482 (1980).

10.   Id.

11.   Hrnjak v. Graymar, 4 Cal.3d 725, 732, 94 Cal.Rptr. 623, 628, 484 P.2d 599, 604 (1971).

12.   People v. Johnson, 193 Cal.App.3d 1570, 239 Cal.Rptr. 190 (1987). See also People v. Triplett, 16 Cal.App.4th 624, 628, 20 Cal.Rptr.2d 225, 228 (1993) (The record need not expressly reflect the judge's weighing of probative value against prejudicial effects so long as it discloses that the judge understood and undertook the weighing required by § 352.). Accord: People v. Mendoza, 24 Cal.4th 130, 178, 99 Cal.Rptr.2d 485, 516–517, 6 P.3d 150, 179 (2000), cert. denied, 532 U.S. 1040, 121 S.Ct. 2004, 149 L.Ed.2d 1006 (2001) and cases cited therein; People v. Hinton, 37 Cal.4th 839, 892, 38 Cal.Rptr.3d 149, 197, 126 P.3d 981, 1021 (2006).

13.   People v. Yu, 143 Cal.App.3d 358, 191 Cal.Rptr. 859 (1983), cert. denied, 464 U.S. 1072, 104 S.Ct. 981, 79 L.Ed.2d 218 (1984). See also Vorse v. Sarasy, 53 Cal.App.4th 998, 1009, 62 Cal.Rptr.2d 164, 170 (1997): "[E]vidence should be excluded as unduly prejudicial when it is of such nature as to inflame the emotions of the jury, motivating them to use the information, not to logically evaluate the point upon which it is relevant, but to reward or punish one side because of the jurors' emotional reaction. In such a circumstance, the evidence is unduly prejudicial because of the substantial likelihood the jury will use it for an illegitimate purpose."

14.   Kessler v. Gray, 77 Cal.App.3d 284, 143 Cal.Rptr. 496 (1978).

15.   Federal Rule of Evidence 403 (Advisory Committee Note).

16.   Id.

17.   22 Cal.App.4th 1841, 28 Cal.Rptr.2d 335 (1994).

an informed exercise of the discretion granted by section 352."[18]

In weighing the harm to the objecting party, the court may take into account benefits conferred upon that party by law. In *Hrnjak*, for example, the California Supreme Court said that the trial judge should have considered the value to the plaintiff of the collateral source rule.[19] Under this substantive law rule, a California tort defendant is not entitled to have the jury deduct from the damages any amounts which the plaintiff may have received from his insurance policies for the injuries suffered.[20] The purpose of the rule is to prevent tort defendants from benefitting from their victims' foresight.[21] For the same reason, evidence that a plaintiff is receiving disability payments or that such payments are tax free may not be offered to show that the plaintiff is malingering. The probative value of the evidence on malingering is substantially outweighed by the damage to the policy that "tortfeasors should not recover a windfall from the thrift and foresight of persons who have actively or constructively secured insurance, pension, or disability benefits to provide for themselves and their families."[22]

Trial rulings under § 352 will not be disturbed by an appellate court unless the trial court abused its discretion.[23] Since such rulings often involve trial assessments that cannot be replicated on appeal, appellate courts are generally unwilling to overturn a trial judge's discretionary rulings unless they resulted from "palpable abuse."[24] This standard requires the complaining party to show that the trial judge exercised his discretion in an "arbitrary, capricious, or patently absurd manner that resulted in a manifest miscarriage of justice."[25]

---

18. Id. at 1849, 28 Cal.Rptr.2d at 338.

19. Hrnjak v. Graymar, Inc., 4 Cal.3d 725, 732, 94 Cal.Rptr. 623, 626, 484 P.2d 599, 602 (1971).

20. Id. at 732, 94 Cal.Rptr. at 628, 484 P.2d at 604.

21. Cox v. Superior Court, 98 Cal.App.4th 670, 673, 120 Cal.Rptr.2d 45, 46 (2002). In medical malpractice actions, however, § 3333.1 of the Medical Injury Compensation Reform Act of 1975 creates an exception to the collateral source rule by allowing the introduction of the value of benefits received. It is up to the trier of fact to decide how such evidence should affect the assessment of damages. Cox v. Superior Court, supra at 674, 120 Cal.Rptr.2d at 47. But even under § 3333.1, the defendant may not offer evidence that the benefits were received tax-free. Id. at 676, 120 Cal.Rptr.2d at 49.

22. Id. (citing Arambula v. Wells, 72 Cal.App.4th 1006, 1009, 85 Cal.Rptr.2d 584, 586 (1999)).

23. People v. Rollo, 20 Cal.3d 109, 117–120, 141 Cal.Rptr. 177, 180, 182, 569 P.2d 771, 774–776 (1977).

24. People v. Demond, 59 Cal.App.3d 574, 587, 130 Cal.Rptr. 590, 597 (1976).

25. People v. Rodrigues, 8 Cal.4th 1060, 1124, 36 Cal.Rptr.2d 235, 267, 885 P.2d 1, 33 (1994), cert. denied, 516 U.S. 851, 116 S.Ct. 147, 133 L.Ed.2d 93 (1995) (quoting People v. Jordan, 42 Cal.3d 308, 228 Cal.Rptr. 197, 721 P.2d 79 (1986)). Although the abuse of discretion standard is designed to protect trial judges in their discretionary rulings, occasionally appellate courts do find abuse. In People v. Basuta, 94 Cal.App.4th 370, 114 Cal.Rptr.2d 285 (2001), the defendant, the operator of a day care facility for children, was convicted of violating West's Ann. California Penal Code § 273ab, assaulting a child with force likely to produce great bodily injury resulting in death. The prosecution's evidence was that the child died when the defendant shook the child violently. The defense countered with evidence that the child died as a result of a minor injury following a "rebleed" of an earlier hematoma. The trial judge, however, prevented the defense from offering evidence that the earlier hematoma might have been the result of violent shaking by the child's mother. The appellate court found the exclusion of the evidence especially egregious

Since trial judges are charged with the responsibility of determining the admissibility of evidence, § 352 would seem to be limited to describing their discretion in discharging this function in the case before them. At times, however, the California Supreme Court has used § 352 to lay down guidelines for trial judges to follow in determining the admissibility of classes of evidence. In People v. Beagle,[26] for example, the court construed § 352 as authority for formulating appellate guidelines governing the use of convictions to impeach witnesses under § 788. Such a pronouncement is not surprising since presumably the court has the inherent power to assure a uniform approach to evidence that may be so prejudicial or unreliable as to threaten the integrity of the fact finding process. But, as we shall see in § 2.12, in criminal cases the court's authority to formulate general rules may be more limited than in civil cases as a result of an initiative approved by the voters in 1982 known as Proposition 8.

Federal Rule of Evidence 403 vests federal judges with similar authority to exclude relevant evidence whenever its probative value is substantially outweighed by the danger of unfair prejudice, confusion of the issues, misleading the jurors, or by considerations of undue delay, waste of time, or needless presentation of cumulative evidence.[27] As in the case of § 352, unfair prejudice is not synonymous with damage, since presumably most everything the opposing party does is damaging to the other party. Rather, unfair prejudice means "an undue tendency to suggest decision on an improper basis, commonly, though not necessarily, an emotional one."[28]

QUESTIONS AND PROBLEMS

1. Section 352 of the Evidence Code and Federal Rule of Evidence 403 can be seen as the last card to be played by the opponent of an item of evidence. Only if no other rules call for the exclusion of the evidence, may the opponent invoke § 352 or Rule 403. True or false?

2. When a party asks the judge to exclude evidence on the grounds that it is "unduly prejudicial," what argument is the party attempting to make?

3. The plaintiff sued the defendant to recover for injuries which the plaintiff claimed she suffered when the defendant struck her while running a red light. To prove that the defendant was negligent in driving the car, the plaintiff offered the results of a blood test taken shortly after the accident which showed that the defendant had a high level of alcohol in his blood. The defendant objected on the ground that the evidence was unduly prejudicial and in support of his argument cited the fact that the county in which the case was being tried had voted to remain "dry" after the repeal of Prohibition. How should the judge rule?

---

because the evidence admitted at the trial and prosecutor's summation suggested that the child's home life was "happy, safe and unremarkable." Id. at 388, 114 Cal.Rptr.2d at 298.

26. 6 Cal.3d 441, 447, 99 Cal.Rptr. 313, 316, 492 P.2d 1, 4 (1972).

27. Federal Rule of Evidence 403.

28. Id. (advisory committee note).

4. In addition, the defendant offered to call a witness who would testify that she had been with the defendant shortly before the accident and that she did not detect an odor of alcoholic beverage about his person. In determining the probative value of the blood test, should the judge take the proffered testimony into account? What right, if any, would be violated if the judge is permitted to take the witness's credibility into account?

§ 2.11 CONSTITUTIONAL CONSTRAINTS ON THE EXCLUSION OF RELEVANT DEFENSE EVIDENCE

Although state and federal rule-makers have broad latitude to establish rules excluding evidence from criminal trials,[1] the Federal Constitution places some limits on the exclusion of defense evidence. The Due Process Clause of the Fourteenth Amendment and the Compulsory Process and Confrontation Clauses of the Sixth Amendment guarantee criminal defendants "a meaningful opportunity to present a complete defense."[2] This right can be infringed by exclusionary rules that are "arbitrary" or "disproportionate to the purposes they are designed to serve."[3] Examples of rules that exclude important defense evidence but do not serve any legitimate state interests include the following:

Rules barring a witness who has been charged as a participant in a crime from testifying in defense of another alleged participant unless the witness has been acquitted. This rule precluded a Texas defendant from calling as a witness an individual who had been previously convicted of committing the crime the defendant was accused of committing. In Washington v. Texas[4] the United States Supreme Court held that the exclusion of the witness's testimony violated the defendant's right to present a defense.[5]

Rules barring defendants from impeaching their witnesses or excluding reliable statements by declarants admitting committing the crime for which the defendant is on trial. These rules prevented a Mississippi defendant from impeaching a defense witness with statements in which the witness admitted committing the offense with which the defendant was charged and prevented the defense from calling other witnesses who overheard the witness admit responsibility for the offense. In Chambers v. Mississippi[6] the United States Supreme Court held that the effect of the two rules was to deny the defendant "a trial in accord

---

1. United States v. Scheffer, 523 U.S. 303, 308, 118 S.Ct. 1261, 140 L.Ed.2d 413 (1998).

2. Holmes v. South Carolina, 547 U.S. 319, 126 S.Ct. 1727, 1730, 164 L.Ed.2d 503 (2006) (quoting from Crane v. Kentucky, 476 U.S. 683, 690, 106 S.Ct. 2142, 90 L.Ed.2d 636 (1986)).

3. United States v. Scheffer, 523 U.S. 303, 308, 118 S.Ct. 1261, 140 L.Ed.2d 413 (1998) (quoting from Rock v. Arkansas, 483 U.S. 44, 58, 107 S.Ct. 2704, 97 L.Ed.2d 37 (1987)).

4. 388 U.S. 14, 87 S.Ct. 1920, 18 L.Ed.2d 1019 (1967).

5. Id. at 22–23.

6. 410 U.S. 284, 93 S.Ct. 1038, 35 L.Ed.2d 297 (1973).

with traditional and fundamental standards of due process."[7]

Rules barring defendants from offering evidence of their confessions' unreliability. This rule was stricken by the U.S. Supreme Court in Crane v. Kentucky.[8] Prior to the trial, the defendant sought to suppress his confession on the grounds that it was involuntary. The judge presiding at the pretrial hearing ruled the confession voluntary. "At trial, petitioner sought to introduce testimony about the physical and psychological environment in which the confession was obtained. His objective in so doing was to suggest that the statement was unworthy of belief. The trial court ruled that the testimony pertained solely to the issue of voluntariness and was therefore inadmissible."[9] The Court reversed the order of the Kentucky Supreme Court affirming the defendant's conviction. Under the Due Process Clause of the Fourteenth Amendment the defendant was denied the right to offer "competent, reliable evidence bearing on the credibility of a confession when such evidence [was] central to the defendant's claim of innocence."[10]

Rules barring all hypnotically refreshed testimony, including that of defendants. In Rock v. Arkansas[11] the United States Supreme Court held that such rules violate a defendant's right to present evidence in his or her own defense in the absence of clear evidence by the state demonstrating the unreliability of such testimony in the case at hand.[12]

Rules barring defendants from offering evidence showing that a third party committed the offense charged "where there is strong evidence of [the defendant's] guilt, especially where there is strong forensic evidence."[13] In Holmes v. South Carolina[14] the United States Supreme Court struck down this rule because it precluded the fact finder from considering the defense evidence if the judge found that the state's evidence was strong.[15] Excluding evidence of third party guilt is constitutional only if after comparing the prosecution's evidence with the defense evidence the judge concludes that the defense evidence "has only a very weak logical connection to the central issues."[16]

In People v. Hall[17] the California Supreme Court defined the test to be applied by California judges in determining the admissibility of evidence of third party guilt:

---

7. Id. at 302.

8. 476 U.S. 683, 106 S.Ct. 2142, 90 L.Ed.2d 636 (1986).

9. Id. At 684, 106 S.Ct. at 2143.

10. Id. at 690, 106 S.Ct. at 2147.

11. 483 U.S. 44, 107 S.Ct. 2704, 97 L.Ed.2d 37 (1987).

12. Id. at 61. For additional discussion of this point, see § 14.04 infra.

13. Holmes v. South Carolina, 547 U.S. 319, 126 S.Ct. 1727, 1734, 164 L.Ed.2d 503 (2006) (quoting from State v. Holmes, 361 S.C. 333, 342, 605 S.E.2d 19, 24 (2004)).

14. Id.

15. Id. at 1734.

16. Id. at 1734.

17. 41 Cal.3d 826, 226 Cal.Rptr. 112, 718 P.2d 99 (1986).

To be admissible, the third party evidence need not show "substantial proof of a probability" that the third person committed the act; it need only be capable of raising a reasonable doubt of defendant's guilt. At the same time, we do not require that any evidence, however remote, must be admitted to show a third party's possible culpability. As this court observed in *Mendez*, evidence of mere motive or opportunity to commit the crime in another person, without more, will not suffice to raise a reasonable doubt about a defendant's guilt: there must be direct or circumstantial evidence linking the third person to the actual perpetration of the crime.[18]

Because the California test requires the trial judge to consider the probative value of the third party evidence before ruling on its admissibility, a proper application of the test is unlikely to run afoul of *Holmes*.[19]

The United States Supreme Court decisions are generally in accord with the California Constitution's approach to relevant evidence offered by the defense. As is discussed in the next section, under the Right to Truth-in-Evidence provision of Proposition 8, California criminal defendants have a state constitutional right not to have otherwise admissible relevant evidence excluded.[20] Accordingly, a California judge may not exclude such defense evidence unless the judge finds that "its probative value is substantially outweighed by the probability that its admission will (a) necessitate undue consumption of time or (b) create substantial danger of undue prejudice, of confusing the issues, or misleading the jury."[21]

§ 2.12 PROPOSITION 8 AND § 352

In June 1982, the California electorate approved Proposition 8, an initiative entitled "The Victims' Bill of Rights." One of its provisions, "The Right to Truth-in-Evidence," transformed the rules of evidence applicable to criminal proceedings by amending the constitution to give parties a right *not* to have relevant evidence excluded. Section 3 amended the state constitution by adding Section 28(f)(2) which reads as follows:

> Except as provided by statute hereafter enacted by a two-thirds vote of the membership in each house of the Legislature, relevant evidence shall not be excluded in any criminal proceeding, including pretrial and post conviction motions and hearings, or in any trial or hearing of a juvenile for a criminal offense, whether heard in juvenile or adult court. Nothing in this section shall affect any existing statutory rule of evidence relating to privilege or hearsay, or Evidence Code Sections 352, 782, or 1103. Nothing in this section shall affect any existing

---

18. Id. at 833, 226 Cal.Rptr. at 117, 718 P.2d at 104.

19. See, e.g., People v. Prince, 40 Cal.4th 1179, 1242, 156 P.3d 1015, 1061, 57 Cal.Rptr.3d 543, 597 (2007).

20. West's Ann. California Constitution Article I § 28(f)(2).

21. West's Ann. California Evidence Code § 352. For an extended discussion of the effects of Proposition 8, see §§ 2.11, supra, and 15.01, infra.

statutory or constitutional right of the press.[1]

Construed literally, this provision would repeal any statute and over-turn any case banning or limiting the admission of relevant evidence, unless the prohibition or limitation is expressly exempted from the opera-tion of Proposition 8.[2] Since § 352 is one of the provisions exempted, the effect of the proposition is to commit to the trial judge's discretion the admissibility of much evidence formerly banned or limited by specific rules.[3]

The continued availability of § 352 under Proposition 8 could be construed as retaining the appellate bench's authority to use the section to lay down rules of general applicability in criminal cases. That construc-tion, however, overlooks the fact that one of the principal targets of the proponents of Proposition 8 was the set of evidentiary restrictions created by the appellate bench, especially under the aegis of § 352.[4]

The California Supreme Court has given Proposition 8 its plain meaning on occasion.[5] On others, it has upheld limitations, both statutory and judicially created, on the use of relevant evidence. For example, in People v. Harris[6] the court held that proponents of evidence based on novel scientific principles must still show that the principle has been generally accepted by the pertinent scientific community. Similarly, in People v. Castro[7] the court held that felony convictions offered to impeach a witness are still subject to discretionary exclusion under § 352 despite another Proposition 8 provision making such convictions admissible "without limitation."[8] That the court was willing to impose conditions on

---

1. West's Ann.California Constitution Article I § 28(f)(2).

2. Five provisions are expressly exempted from Proposition 8. These are the provisions relating to privileges and hearsay, and the limitations codified in California Evidence Code §§ 352, 782, and 1103. Section 1103(b) generally prohibits the use of a rape victim's past sexual conduct with others to prove the victim's predisposition to consent to sexual transactions with the accused. West's Ann. California Evidence Code § 1103(b). Section 782 limits the use of similar evidence to impeach the credibility of rape victims. Id. at § 782.

3. West's Ann.California Constitution Article I § 28(f)(2).

4. People v. Castro, 38 Cal.3d 301, 322–323, 211 Cal.Rptr. 719, 723, 696 P.2d 111, 125 (1985) (Lucas, J., concurring and dissenting).

5. People v. Harris, 47 Cal.3d 1047, 1080–1082, 255 Cal.Rptr. 352, 373, 767 P.2d 619, 640 (1989) (The Right to Truth–in–Evidence provision repeals West's Ann.California Evidence Code § 787 which prohibits the use of evidence of specific instances of conduct to attack or support the credibility of a witness.); id. at 1090, note 22, 255 Cal.Rptr. at 380, note 22, 767 P.2d at 647, note 22 (The same provision repeals California Evidence Code § 788 which limits impeachment by conviction to felony convictions.).

6. Id. at 1094–95, 255 Cal.Rptr. at 382–83, 767 P.2d at 649–650. The rule that evidence based on novel scientific principles is inadmissible unless the principles have been generally accepted by the relevant scientific community was imposed by the California Supreme Court in People v. Kelly, 17 Cal.3d 24, 30, 130 Cal.Rptr. 144, 148, 549 P.2d 1240, 1244 (1976). Despite *Harris*, the court's continued adherence to the *Kelly* rule is not unqualified. In People v. Stoll, the court held that the effect of Proposition 8 on the rule was still an open question, at least with regard to the scientific evidence involved in that case. 49 Cal.3d 1136, note 16, 265 Cal.Rptr. 111, 120, note 16, 783 P.2d 698, 707, note 16 (1989). See generally § 3.08 infra.

7. 38 Cal.3d 301, 211 Cal.Rptr. 719, 696 P.2d 111 (1985).

8. Id. at 312–13, 211 Cal.Rptr. at 724, 696 P.2d at 117. The court laid down the general rule that to be admissible such convictions must entail moral turpitude. Id. at 314, 211 Cal.Rptr. at 726, 696 P.2d at 119.

the admissibility on scientific evidence and felony convictions suggests that the court is still prepared to use § 352 to lay down general rules protecting the fact finding process despite Proposition 8.

Civil cases are unaffected by Proposition 8. Accordingly, in these cases the Supreme Court has greater latitude in relying on § 352 to justify the continued application of judicially created limitations on the admissibility of relevant evidence.

Because there is no federal equivalent of Proposition 8, the federal appellate bench does not distinguish between civil and criminal cases in using Federal Rule of Evidence 403 to lay down general rules of admissibility. Rule 403 is the equivalent of § 352. The federal trend, however, is to limit Rule 403 to excluding evidence on a case by case rather than on a categorical basis.[9]

QUESTIONS AND PROBLEMS

1. In the Civil Law (as opposed to the Common Law) tradition, judges are given broad discretion in determining the admissibility of evidence. The myriad Common Law restrictions on the use of relevant evidence are virtually unknown. Do you agree that the Right to Truth–in–Evidence provision grants to California judges the type of discretion enjoyed by Civil Law judges?

2. Much of the justification for the Common Law rules is the need to protect jurors from unreliable information. Civil Law jurists do not have this concern because lay jurors are usually not used as fact finders. Judges trained in the law sit as the fact finders. In light of this procedural difference between Common Law and Civil Law trials, does it make sense to adopt a Civil Law model in American criminal trials?

3. Trial planning is facilitated by Proposition 8. Parties to California criminal proceedings no longer have to worry about the myriad rules banning or limiting evidence. Instead, they can focus their energies on finding and offering evidence that is relevant to the case being tried. True or false?

ARTICLE 1 OF THE CALIFORNIA CONSTITUTION

§ 28. Findings and declarations; rights of victims; enforcement

* * *

(f) In addition to the enumerated rights provided in subdivision (b) that are personally enforceable by victims as provided in subdivision (c), victims of crime have additional rights that are shared with all of the People of the State of California. These collectively held rights include, but are not limited to, the following:

---

9. See generally Mengler, *The Theory of Discretion in the Federal Rules of Evidence*, 74 Iowa L. Rev. 413 (1989).

* * *

(2) Except as provided ~~...~~ y a two-thirds vote of the membership i~~...~~ ant evidence shall not be excluded ~~...~~ retrial and post conviction ~~...~~ ring of a juvenile for a ~~...~~ t court. Nothing in this ~~...~~ idence relating to privi~~...~~ ?, or 1103. Nothing in t~~...~~ ti-tutional right of the ~~...~~

[handwritten note on pink sticky: "— yes, it should be allowed to use discretion — yes, not as re motion, swayed b/c are bias alct → TRUE, but still w/ held some exceptions"]

CALIFO...

§ 210. "Relevant evidence"

"Relevant evidence" means e~~...~~ ncluding evidence relevant to the credibility of a witness or hears~~...~~ declarant, having any tendency in reason to prove or disprove any disputed fact that is of consequence to the determination of the action.

§ 350. Only relevant evidence admissible

No evidence is admissible except relevant evidence.

§ 351. Admissibility of relevant evidence

Except as otherwise provided by statute, all relevant evidence is admissible.

§ 352. Discretion of court to exclude evidence

The court in its discretion may exclude evidence if its probative value is substantially outweighed by the probability that its admission will (a) necessitate undue consumption of time or (b) create substantial danger of undue prejudice, of confusing the issues, or of misleading the jury.

FEDERAL RULES OF EVIDENCE

Rule 401. Test for Relevant Evidence

Evidence is relevant if:

(a) it has any tendency to make a fact more or less probable than it would be without the evidence; and

(b) the fact is of consequence in determining the action.

Rule 402. General Admissibility of Relevant Evidence

Relevant evidence is admissible unless any of the following provides otherwise:

- the United States Constitution;
- a federal statute;
- these rules; or
- other rules prescribed by the Supreme Court.

Irrelevant evidence is not admissible.

Rule 403. Excluding Relevant Evidence for Prejudice, Confusion, Waste of Time, or Other Reasons

The court may exclude relevant evidence if its probative value is substantially outweighed by a danger of one or more of the following: unfair prejudice, confusing the issues, misleading the jury, undue delay, wasting time, or needlessly presenting cumulative evidence.

CHAPTER 3

EVIDENCE AFFECTED OR EXCLUDED BY EXTRINSIC POLICIES—CHARACTER, HABIT, AND SIMILAR OCCURRENCES

■ ■ ■

Table of Sections

---

§ 3.01   INTRODUCTION

Chapter 3 reviews rules that ban or limit relevant evidence largely as a result of policies that are rooted in the substantive law as well as in the law of evidence. Most of the chapter is devoted to "character evidence," a species of evidence often misunderstood by students, lawyers, and judges. Because of their importance, the character evidence rules are examined first, beginning with a definition of character evidence. The rules governing the admissibility of habit and custom evidence follow because of their close relationship to character evidence. The chapter closes with an examination of the rules governing the admissibility of evidence of similar occurrences. This evidence easily can be confused with character evidence, and much of the discussion focuses on ways in which this evidence can be used without violating the character evidence rules.

The evidence discussed in this chapter is not restricted because it is irrelevant. Rather, the evidence is usually banned or limited because its unrestrained admission would endanger some interest which the law protects at the cost of excluding relevant evidence.

§ 3.02   THE MEANING OF CHARACTER EVIDENCE

One reason why character evidence is misunderstood is its name. The name fails to convey clearly the kind of evidence which the rules for a variety of reasons exclude. In the abstract, it is difficult to imagine evidence as having "character." But, as we shall see, the term is not about evidence in the abstract. Rather, "character evidence" refers to the use of evidence of a person's character traits to prove that on a given occasion that person acted in conformity with his or her character.

An example helps illustrate this point. Assume that you are thinking of buying a used car from Fred. If prior to the purchase your best friend tells you that a used car she bought from Fred turned out to a lemon, you will be less likely to buy the car, at least without having the car carefully checked out. If another friend tells you that a used car he bought from Fred also turned out to be a lemon, then you may decide not to buy the car at all. In either case, your decision to have the car checked out or not to buy the car is based on your prediction of how likely the car Fred is offering you will be free of major problems.

All of us engage in this kind of reasoning in everyday life. We consider a person's past conduct in trying to predict that person's future behavior. If Fred assured your two friends that the cars he sold them were free of defects, you would be much less likely to believe Fred's statements about the condition of the car he is trying to sell you. Indeed, your conclusion not to buy the car would appear to most observers to be well-grounded. The problem is not necessarily with the car but with Fred's trustworthiness. In light of your friends' experiences with him, most people would not rely on his assurances. Thus, a defect in Fred's "character" would cause most people to refrain from doing business with him.

In evidentiary terms, this kind of everyday reasoning is captured by the concept of relevance. The proposition that Fred would sell you a defective car is rendered more likely by the evidence that he sold defective cars to your friends than the proposition would be without the evidence.[1] If we assume an action in which you are trying to prove that Fred misrepresented the condition of the car he sold you, then evidence that Fred misrepresented the condition of the cars he sold to your friends would likewise be relevant.

Further examination reveals why this kind of evidence is relevant. Jurors may conclude that Fred misrepresented the condition of the car he sold to you because they believe that he is the kind of person who misrepresents the condition of cars he sells. After all, his "character" or "predisposition" to behave in this manner is evidenced by his having misrepresented the condition of the cars he has sold to others. Because we engage in this kind of reasoning in everyday life, character evidence can be pretty persuasive. In part for this reason, the rules of evidence generally disfavor this kind of evidence. But before exploring this somewhat startling position, we need to understand the kinds of character evidence that might be offered in any action.

character evidence disfavored

§ 3.03   THE KINDS OF CHARACTER EVIDENCE

The California Evidence Code and the Federal Rules identify three kinds of character evidence.[1] One consists of specific instances of a person's conduct that are offered to prove a person's character or character trait. Evidence that Fred misrepresented the condition of the cars he sold to your two friends illustrates this kind of character evidence.[2] The evidence would be offered to show that Fred has a trait for misrepresenting the condition of cars he sells and, because he has that trait, that he misrepresented the condition of the car he sold you.

One aspect of this evidence is especially noteworthy. The evidence of Fred's character is used circumstantially. In our hypothetical case, the proposition to be proved is that Fred misrepresented the condition of the car he sold you. That proposition is precisely the inference you want the fact finder to draw from the evidence that Fred is the kind of person who misrepresents the condition of the cars he sells.

inference from the circumstantial evidence

The other two kinds of character evidence consist of opinion and reputation evidence.[3] Opinion evidence consists of the testimony of someone who knows Fred well and who can say under oath that in his opinion

---

1.   See § 2.04 supra.
1.   West's Ann.California Evidence Code § 1100; Federal Rules of Evidence 404–405.
2.   See the example expounded in § 3.02 supra.
3.   West's Ann.California Evidence Code § 1100.

Fred is the kind of person who misrepresents the condition of cars he sells. Reputation evidence consists of the testimony of someone who knows Fred's reputation well in the community in which Fred resides and who can say under oath that Fred has a reputation for misrepresenting the cars he sells.[4] In either case, the evidence is again being used circumstantially. The fact finder is being asked to draw the inference that Fred misrepresented the condition of the car he sold you from the opinion or reputation evidence regarding Fred's character.

§ 3.04   THE REASONS FOR EXCLUDING CHARACTER EVIDENCE

California Evidence Code § 1100 states that, except as provided by statute, any otherwise admissible evidence can be used to prove a person's character or character trait.[1] That generous grant, however, is immediately limited by § 1101(a) which bans the use of character evidence—whether in the form of opinion or reputation evidence, or evidence of specific instances of conduct—to prove a person's conduct on a specified occasion.[2] In other words, evidence that Fred misrepresented the condition of cars he sold to others, his reputation that he does so, and an opinion that he would do so, would all be inadmissible to prove that he is the kind of person who would misrepresent the condition of the car he sold to you.[3] Why does the law of evidence take such an unfriendly and counter-intuitive stance toward this kind of evidence? Imagining what could occur if the evidence were admissible provides some answers.

Assume first that in your suit against Fred you are allowed to call your two friends to testify that Fred misrepresented the condition of the cars he sold to them. If your two friends are allowed to testify, then Fred must be given an opportunity to disprove their contentions. He could take the position that your two friends are deliberately fabricating their claim or that your friends, though honest, are simply mistaken about what he said about the cars. In either case, just as your friends must tell their stories in the form of admissible evidence, so must Fred tell his side of what may have occurred. The requirement that each side comply with the rules of evidence means that what was originally a trial on what Fred told you about the condition of the car he sold to you, has now become three trials, each concerning what Fred said or did not say about the condition of cars he sold to three different persons on three separate occasions.

One trial would turn into 3 trials

The disadvantages of converting one trial into three separate trials to be heard in the same proceeding are fairly obvious. First, there is the risk that the character evidence and its counter evidence will consume too

---

4. For a discussion of the qualifications of opinion and reputation witnesses, see People v. Felix, 70 Cal.App.4th 426, 430, 82 Cal.Rptr.2d 701, 703 (1999).

1. West's Ann.California Evidence Code § 1100.

2. West's Ann.California Evidence Code § 1101(a). The analogous federal provision is Federal Rule of Evidence 404(a).

3. See the hypothetical expounded in § 3.02 supra.

much time and too many judicial resources.[4] Second, there is the danger that the fact finder may become confused about the issues to be decided.[5] Third, and perhaps of greatest importance, there is the risk that the jury may unjustifiably return a verdict against the party against whom the character evidence has been offered.[6]

The last risk is predicated on two assumptions. One is the belief that the fact finder will overestimate the probative value of character evidence: if jurors learn that the party on other occasions engaged in the misconduct charged, they may jump to the unwarranted conclusion that the party must be guilty of the misconduct charged.[7] The other is the belief that character evidence will invite jurors to return verdicts against "bad" persons. Especially in criminal cases, a major concern is that character evidence will tempt jurors to apply a theory of culpability that is based on character rather than on the commission of a punishable act. Having heard evidence of the accused's bad character, jurors may conclude that the accused is a bad person deserving of punishment, irrespective of whether the other evidence convinces them of the accused's guilt.[8]

The principle that individuals are accountable only "for what they do and not for what they are"[9] is central to the law's concept of criminal blameworthiness. The principle has been elevated to constitutional status by the United States Supreme Court.[10] And though no comparable principle applies in civil matters, § 1101(a)'s ban on the use of character evidence to prove conduct applies to civil cases as well.[11]

The application of § 1101(a) is not discretionary. Though one can imagine a judge using § 352 to exclude character evidence for the reasons listed, the fact is that, if § 1101(a) applies, the judge must exclude the evidence irrespective of its probative value. The reason is clear: in enacting § 1101(a) the California Legislature weighed the probative value of character evidence as a class against its prejudicial effects and concluded that the latter outweighed the former in all cases. Congress reached the same conclusion in enacting Federal Rule of Evidence 404(a) which, like

---

4. C. McCormick, Handbook of the Law of Evidence § 185 (E. Cleary 2d ed. 1972).

5. Id.

6. Id. Dean Charles McCormick cited a fourth reason for excluding character evidence: the fear that if the accused has no reason to anticipate the prosecution's character evidence, the accused will be unfairly surprised and be unprepared to meet the evidence. Id.

7. 1 J. Wigmore, Evidence § 194 (3d ed. 1940).

8. Id. Bad character evidence also presents the risk that the jurors might convict for crimes other than those charged. United States v. Moccia, 681 F.2d 61, 63 (1st Cir.1982).

9. H. Packer, The Limits of the Criminal Sanction 73–74 (1968).

10. Robinson v. California, 370 U.S. 660, 667, 82 S.Ct. 1417, 1420, 8 L.Ed.2d 758 (1962), reh'g denied, 371 U.S. 905, 83 S.Ct. 202, 9 L.Ed.2d 166 (1962) (The Eighth Amendment's prohibition of cruel and unusual punishments prohibits punishing an addict on account of his narcotics addiction.).

11. So does Federal Rule of Evidence 404(a), the federal analogue to § 1101(a). A 2006 amendment to Federal Rule of Evidence 404 removes any uncertainty about this matter by making it clear that character evidence is not admissible in civil cases to prove conduct in conformity therewith.

§ 1101(a), bans the use of character evidence to prove conduct in conformity therewith.[12]

Character trait for care or skill. Section 1104 provides that, except as otherwise provided by §§ 1102 and 1103, character evidence with respect to care or skill is inadmissible to prove the quality of an act on a given occasion.[13] Since §§ 1102 and 1103 deal with criminal cases, § 1104 applies principally in civil cases involving negligence.[14] An example is Hinson v. Clairemont Community Hospital,[15] in which the plaintiff attempted to prove that a physician was negligent when he performed facial surgery on the plaintiff. The court refused to permit the plaintiff to offer evidence that the physician had been terminated from two residency programs as well as from a job after only one day, and had also had his hospital privileges suspended.[16] His incompetence on other occasions was not admissible to prove that he was the kind of doctor who was incompetent on the occasion in question.

Section 1104 is not necessary. Section 1101(a) would in any event bar the use of character evidence of care or skill to prove conduct on a given occasion. The Federal Rules of Evidence do not contain a rule equivalent to § 1104, presumably on the theory that the general ban on the use of character evidence bars the use of such evidence. Perhaps the purpose of § 1104 is to alert the parties and the court to the inadmissibility of such evidence, especially in negligence actions.

QUESTIONS AND PROBLEMS

Over an inadmissible character evidence objection, determine the admissibility of the following evidence under the California Evidence Code and the Federal Rules of Evidence:

In an action to recover damages from the defendant for fraudulently misrepresenting the condition of a car the defendant sold the plaintiff, the defendant denies that he misrepresented the condition of the car:

> 1.   In her case-in-chief the plaintiff testifies that she bought a car from the defendant in September 1990, that the defendant told her that the car was in good running condition, and that the following day the transmission broke.

---

12.   Federal Rule of Evidence 404(b).

13.   West's Ann.California Evidence Code § 1104.

14.   For a discussion of § 1102, see § 3.06 infra; of § 1103, see § 3.12 infra. In a criminal case, however, a literal application of the Right to Truth-in-Evidence provision of Proposition 8 would repeal § 1104. See § 3.07 infra. The admissibility of evidence governed by the section would then depend on the exercise of the judge's discretion under § 352. As discussed in § 3.07, a post initiative amendment to § 1101(b) had the effect of reenacting § 1101(a), the general rule prohibiting the use of character evidence to prove conduct. Because reenacted § 1101(a) does not expressly refer to § 1104, under a literal interpretation of the initiative, the section may not be applied in criminal cases.

15.   218 Cal.App.3d 1110, 267 Cal.Rptr. 503 (1990).

16.   Id. at 1122, 267 Cal.Rptr. at 510.

2. In his case-in-chief the defendant testifies that he sold the car to the plaintiff but that he never told her that the car was in good running condition.

3. In rebuttal, over the defendant's objection, the plaintiff calls a witness to testify that in June 1990 he bought a car from the defendant, that the defendant told him that the car was in top condition, and that a week later the clutch had to be replaced.

4. In rebuttal, over the defendant's objection, the plaintiff also calls a witness to testify that she knows the defendant's reputation for fair dealing in the community in which the defendant resides and that his reputation in that respect is bad.

5. In rebuttal, over the defendant's objection, the plaintiff calls a final witness to testify that she is familiar with the defendant's business dealings and that in her opinion the defendant is the kind of person who would misrepresent the condition of property he sells.

§ 3.05   THE ADMISSIBILITY OF CHARACTER EVIDENCE WHERE CHARACTER IS AN ISSUE

In a few cases, the existence or nonexistence of a particular character trait may be an issue under the law governing the action. In these instances, § 1100, not § 1101(a), applies and all three types of character evidence are admissible.[1]

Such evidence is admissible in defamation actions where the issue is the existence or nonexistence of the trait attributed by the defendant to the plaintiff,[2] in defamation actions to mitigate damages by showing that the plaintiff's reputation was so bad as not to be harmed by the defendant's untruthful statements,[3] in wrongful death actions to show the deceased's predisposition to provide support and other benefits to the survivors,[4] in negligent entrustment actions to show the operator's unfitness to operate a particular instrumentality,[5] in wrongful discharge actions to show an employee's unfitness for a particular job,[6] in child custody proceedings to determine the fitness of a parent to have custody,[7] in juvenile court dependency proceedings to determine the fitness of a

---

1. West's Ann.California Evidence Code § 1101 (comment). Federal Rule of Evidence 405(a)–(b), like § 1100, authorizes the use of character evidence whenever it is admissible.

2. Pierson v. Robert Griffin Investigations, 92 Nev. 605, 605–607, 555 P.2d 843, 843–844 (1976) (Evidence of plaintiff's crimes occurring ten years prior to the alleged defamation was admissible to prove that the defendant's statements about the plaintiff were true.). See also cases cited in C. McCormick, McCormick on Evidence § 187 (E. Cleary 3d ed. 1984).

3. F. L. Wellman, The Art of Cross–Examination 170–171 (3d ed. 1923).

4. Carr v. Pacific Tel. Co., 26 Cal.App.3d 537, 545–546, 103 Cal.Rptr. 120, 126 (1972).

5. Allen v. Toledo, 109 Cal.App.3d 415, 167 Cal.Rptr. 270, 273 (1980).

6. Pugh v. See's Candies, Inc., 203 Cal.App.3d 743, 756–757, 250 Cal.Rptr. 195, 204 (1988).

7. Feist v. Feist, 236 Cal.App.2d 433, 436, 46 Cal.Rptr. 93, 95 (1965).

parent to retain custody,[8] and in actions for malicious prosecution to show the defendant's lack of probable cause to believe that the plaintiff committed a crime, especially where the defendant knew of the plaintiff's good character.[9]

Some penal statutes expressly make uncharged offenses a material element to be proved by the prosecution. For example, in determining whether to impose the death penalty California jurors may take into account whether the accused has engaged in criminal activity (in addition to the crime charged) involving the use or attempted use of force or violence or the express or implied threat to use force or violence.[10] Since the jurors' role is to determine the accused's fitness to be put to death, the evidence of the uncharged offenses can properly be classified as character evidence.

Other statutes explicitly make a character trait an element of the cause of action. For example, under California's Sexually Violent Predators Act (SVPA), the state may seek to commit civilly someone who (1) suffers from "a diagnosed mental disorder that makes the person a danger to the health and safety of others in that it is likely that he or she will engage in sexually violent criminal behavior" and (2) has been "convicted of a sexually violent offense against two or more victims."[11] Evidence of the defendant's history of sexual offenses is admissible to prove the defendant's propensity to engage in sexually violent criminal behavior.[12]

Even where character evidence is admissible, judges may exclude it under their discretionary power to exclude relevant evidence when its probative value is outweighed by enumerated concerns, such as undue prejudice.[13]

§ 3.06 EXCEPTIONS TO THE CHARACTER EVIDENCE BAN—CALIFORNIA CRIMINAL CASES AND THE MERCY RULE

California Evidence Code § 1102 adopts the Common Law Mercy Rule, which allows the accused to dispute his guilt by offering character evidence to show that he is not the kind of person who would commit the offense charged.[1] Because life and liberty are at stake, the accused is given the option, not available to civil litigants, to offer evidence of a character trait that is inconsistent with committing the offense charged.[2] But the

---

8. In re Dorothy I., 162 Cal.App.3d 1154, 1158, 209 Cal.Rptr. 5, 7–8 (1984).

9. Murphy v. Davids, 181 Cal. 706, 717, 186 P. 143, 148 (1919).

10. See West's Ann. California Penal Code § 190.3.

11. See West's Ann. California Welfare & Institutions Code §§ 6600 et seq.

12. See People v. Hubbart, 88 Cal.App.4th 1202, 1234–1235, 106 Cal.Rptr.2d 490, 513–514 (2001), cert. denied, 534 U.S. 1143, 122 S.Ct. 1097, 151 L.Ed.2d 994 (2002).

13. See Carr v. Pacific Tel. Co., 26 Cal.App.3d 537, 545–546, 103 Cal.Rptr. 120, 126 (1972) (applying West's Ann. California Evidence Code § 352); see also Federal Rule of Evidence 403.

1. West's Ann.California Evidence Code § 1102.

2. Id. (comment).

option is of limited value because § 1102 limits the accused to proving the relevant trait by reputation or opinion evidence.[3] If the accused exercises the option, the prosecution may rebut the good character evidence with bad character evidence of the accused.[4] The prosecution is also limited to using reputation or opinion testimony.[5]

If the accused does call good character witnesses in the case-in-chief, the prosecution is entitled to discredit the witnesses by inquiring on cross-examination about specific instances of the accused's conduct that are inconsistent with the witnesses' opinion or reputation testimony. For example, if in a homicide prosecution a witness for the accused testifies that in her opinion the accused is a peaceable person, the prosecution may ask the witness if she has heard that the accused committed an assault.[6] If the witness denies having heard about the assault, the prosecution can then ask whether the witness would change her testimony now that she has heard about it.[7]

The prosecution must ask the questions about the assault in good faith.[8] To avoid harming the accused with baseless information, the cross-examiner must "have in his possession information that reasonably leads him to believe that the acts of conduct by the defendant have in fact been committed or the reports of their commission have been generally circulated."[9]

If the witness denies knowing or having heard about the assault, the prosecution may not prove it extrinsically.[10] The prosecution, for example, may not call the victim of the assault or offer documentary evidence, such as a judgment of conviction, of the assault. Extrinsic evidence not only would waste time and distract the jury, but would also be irrelevant.[11] The

---

3.　West's Ann.California Evidence Code § 1102. The opinion witnesses may include an expert. In prosecutions for sex offenses against children, for example, the accused may call an expert to testify that, based on standardized tests and personal interviews, the accused's personality profile does not include the capacity for deviant behavior with children. See People v. Brodit, 61 Cal.App.4th 1312, 1334, 72 Cal.Rptr.2d 154, 167 (1998) and cases cited therein. See also People v. Guerra, 37 Cal.4th 1067, 1119, 40 Cal.Rptr.3d 118, 165, 129 P.3d 321, 361 (2006) (holding that in a homicide prosecution, the accused was entitled to call an expert to testify that the accused had a nonviolent personality).Whether or not the testimony may be received over objection depends on whether the expert's opinion meets the requirements of expert testimony. For a discussion of these requirements, see Chapter 16 infra.

4.　West's Ann.California Evidence Code § 1102. If the accused offers bad character evidence of the *victim*, the prosecution is entitled to offer bad character evidence of the accused. See § 3.12 infra. Such evidence may include specific acts of the accused in addition to reputation and opinion evidence. Id.

5.　West's Ann.California Evidence Code § 1102.

6.　People v. Hurd, 5 Cal.App.3d 865, 880, 85 Cal.Rptr. 718, 727–728 (1970). Accord: People v. Lopez, 129 Cal.App.4th 1508, 1528, 29 Cal.Rptr.3d 586, 601 (2005). In California, the opinion witness may be asked on cross-examination whether he knows or has heard of instances that are inconsistent with the opinion the witness gave on direct examination. See People v. Hurd, supra.

7.　People v. McKenna, 11 Cal.2d 327, 335–336, 79 P.2d 1065, 1069 (1938).

8.　People v. Pic'l, 114 Cal.App.3d 824, 891, 171 Cal.Rptr. 106, 145 (1981), rev'd on other grounds, 31 Cal.3d 731, 183 Cal.Rptr. 685, 646 P.2d 847 (1982).

9.　Id. at 891, 171 Cal.Rptr. at 145.

10.　People v. Aguilar, 32 Cal.App.3d 478, 483, 108 Cal.Rptr. 179, 182 (1973).

11.　Id.

issue is not whether the accused committed the assault but whether the character witness knew or had heard about it. Since the inquiry is designed to test the qualifications of the character witness,[12] the accused is likewise precluded from disproving the assault or explaining the circumstances surrounding it.[13] The most that the accused can hope for is a limiting instruction telling the jurors to use the evidence of the accused's assault only to assess the weight they should give to the character witness's testimony and not to determine the character of the accused.[14]

A number of factors should cause defense lawyers to consider the wisdom of calling character witnesses on behalf of their clients. One is the improbability that friends and acquaintances of the accused are likely to be taken seriously by the fact finder when providing favorable opinion or reputation testimony. Their potential for impeachment for bias is obvious.[15] Moreover, the constraints on their testimony are likely to deprive the evidence of much convincing force. The witnesses are not permitted on direct examination to relate specific instances which led them to conclude that the accused is not the kind of person who would commit the offense charged. They are limited to stating the relevant opinion or reputation and their qualifications for giving such testimony. Perhaps most disquieting is that calling such witnesses opens them to the type of cross-examination that has been described. This risk can be mitigated by limiting the character witnesses to a trait that is narrowly inconsistent with the offense charged. Consider a case in which the accused is prosecuted for assault. The cross of a witness who states that the accused is a peaceable person will be more restricted than the cross of a witness who states that the accused is a law-abiding person. The latter witness can be asked about any instance in which the accused engaged in behavior that violates any law, civil or penal.[16]

§ 3.07 THE CHARACTER EVIDENCE RULES AND PROPOSITION 8

In June 1982, California voters approved Proposition 8, an initiative billed by its supporters as the "Victims' Bill of Rights." Proposition 8 introduced a wide range of changes in criminal procedure, including major changes in the rules of evidence that apply to criminal proceedings. The

---

12. Id.

13. Id.

14. See CALJIC 2.42, Cross-Examination of a Character Witness (Fall 2006 Edition).

15. Unlike the opinion witness, the reputation witness need not know the accused personally. Rios v. Chand, 130 Cal.App.2d 833–840, 280 P.2d 47, 50–51 (1955). The theory is that the witness need only know the accused's reputation regarding the pertinent character trait.

16. Irrespective of whether the good character evidence offered by the accused is in the form of an opinion or reputation, it is important to underscore that the purpose of the testimony is to establish a character trait that is inconsistent with the crime charged. A good character witness is not called to give an opinion on whether the accused is guilty of the offense charged. People v. Honig, 48 Cal.App.4th 289, 349, 55 Cal.Rptr.2d 555, 591 (1996). Such an opinion is barred by the opinion rule and the limitations on expert testimony, as the jurors simply do not need it to determine the accused's guilt or innocence. See § 16.01 infra.

most radical can be traced to one provision which strongly favors the admissibility of relevant evidence. This provision, labeled the "Right to Truth–in–Evidence," amends the state constitution to give parties to a criminal proceeding a *constitutional* right not to have relevant evidence excluded. In pertinent part, the new provision reads as follows:

> SEC.28(f)(2) *Right to Truth–in–Evidence.* Except as provided by statute hereafter enacted by two-thirds vote of the membership in each house of the Legislature, relevant evidence shall not be excluded in any criminal proceeding * * *. Nothing in this section shall affect any existing statutory rule of evidence relating to privilege or hearsay, or Evidence Code Sections 352, 782, or 1103 * * *.[1]

If construed literally, this provision would create two systems of evidence: one to govern civil proceedings and a new one to govern criminal proceedings. The former would be subject to the Evidence Code. The new one would consist of a highly modified version of the Code in which all sections banning or limiting the admissibility of relevant evidence are repealed unless expressly saved by the provision. If construed literally, the admissibility of evidence banned or limited by statutes predating the proposition would now be decided by judges applying their discretionary powers under California Evidence Code § 352. Section 352 is one of the few sections exempted from the operation of the Right to Truth–in–Evidence provision.

If the Right to Truth–in–Evidence provision is construed literally, the rules governing the admissibility of character evidence in criminal cases would be transformed in the following ways:

1. Section 1101(a)'s ban on the use of character evidence to prove conduct on a specified occasion would be repealed. This means that the prosecution could offer all three kinds of character evidence[2] in its case-in-chief to prove that the accused is guilty of the offense charged because he is the kind of person who would commit such an offense. It would also authorize the accused to offer similar evidence to prove that he is not guilty of the offense charged.

2. Section 1102's limitations on the Mercy Rule[3] would be repealed. Neither the accused nor the prosecution would be limited to opinion or reputation character evidence in showing that the accused did or did not commit the offense charged. Both sides could offer evidence of specific instances of conduct. Moreover, since repeal of § 1101(a) would permit the prosecution to offer bad character evidence about the accused in its case-in-chief, § 1102's provision limiting the prosecution's right to offer such evidence only in rebuttal would be repealed.

3. The case law limitations on discrediting character witnesses would be overturned. Cross examiners would no longer be bound by the

---

1.   West's Ann.California Constitution Article I § 28(f)(2).

2.   See § 3.03, supra, for a discussion of the three kinds of character evidence.

3.   See § 3.06, supra, for a discussion of the Mercy Rule.

witnesses' answers when inquiring into specific instances of conduct that are inconsistent with the reputation or opinion testimony given by the witnesses on direct examination. Though such cross-examination may still have a discrediting effect on the witnesses, under the Right to Truth–in–Evidence provision the prosecution could offer the specific instances for the additional purpose of proving that the accused is guilty of the offense charged. Similarly, in crossing prosecution bad character witnesses the defense could offer specific instances of conduct that are inconsistent with the opinion or reputation evidence as proof that the accused is not guilty of the offense charged.

For over thirteen years the California Supreme Court declined to rule on the effects a literal construction of Proposition 8 would have on the character evidence rules.[4] When it finally confronted the question in *People v. Ewoldt*,[5] the court held that amendments to the character evidence rules enacted after the initiative had been approved rendered it unnecessary to answer the question. By amending § 1101(b), the court held that the Legislature reenacted § 1101, including subsection (a), in its entirety.[6] Since the reenactment was by more than the two-thirds vote required by Proposition 8 for amendments to the initiative, the court ruled that the reenactment superseded any repealing effects which the initiative may have had on § 1101(a).[7] *Ewoldt* thus dispelled some of the uncertainties surrounding the admissibility of character evidence created by Proposition 8 for over a decade. After *Ewoldt*, the limitations on the Mercy Rule and on discrediting character witnesses have been restored,[8] and prosecutors and defense counsel know once more that, as a rule, they may not offer evidence of a person's character to prove conduct in conformity therewith on a given occasion.[9]

§ 3.08 PROPOSITION 8 AND § 352

Section 352 empowers judges to exclude relevant evidence whenever its probative value on contested issues is substantially outweighed by enumerated concerns, including undue prejudice to the objecting party.[1]

---

4. People v. Sully, 53 Cal.3d 1195, 1225–1226, 283 Cal.Rptr. 144, 162, 812 P.2d 163, 180–181 (1991), cert. denied, 503 U.S. 944, 112 S.Ct. 1494, 117 L.Ed.2d 634 (1992); People v. Harris, 47 Cal.3d 1047, 1081, 255 Cal.Rptr. 352, 373, 767 P.2d 619, 640 (1989).

5. 7 Cal.4th 380, 27 Cal.Rptr.2d 646, 867 P.2d 757 (1994).

6. Id. at 391, 27 Cal.Rptr.2d at 651, 867 P.2d at 762.

7. Id. at 392, 27 Cal.Rptr.2d at 652, 867 P.2d at 763.

8. Section 1101(a), which was reenacted as part of the amendment to § 1101(b), specifically refers to the exception provided by § 1102. Section 1102 allows criminal defendants to offer good character evidence as proof they did not commit the offenses charged. But § 1102 limits them to offering reputation and opinion evidence. Thus an effect of the amendment to § 1101(b) was to resurrect the limitations of § 1102.

9. The reenactment of § 1101 does not, however, affect the impact of Proposition 8 on rules governing evidence to support or attack the credibility of witnesses. For an extended discussion of this point, see § 3.08 infra.

1. California Evidence Code § 352 (West 1966). For a general discussion of § 352, see § 2.10 supra.

So long as the California Supreme Court declined to rule on the effect of Proposition 8 on § 1101(a), § 352, which is expressly exempted from the operation of the initiative, took on added importance. Since the use of character evidence can be extremely prejudicial to the objecting party for the reasons discussed in § 3.04, a trial judge could rely on § 352 to exclude character evidence previously barred by § 1101. After People v. Ewoldt,[2] it is no longer necessary for trial judges to rely on § 352. *Ewoldt* holds that by amending § 1101(b), the Legislature reenacted § 1101 in its entirety.[3] Since the reenactment satisfied Proposition 8's voting requirements for amendments to the initiative, *Ewoldt* holds that whatever repealing effects the initiative may have had on § 1101(a) have been superseded by the reenactment. Thus, the restoration of § 1101(a) has led to a decline in the importance of § 352 in the administration of the character evidence rules.

It should be noted, however, that § 352 retains its pre-initiative vitality. As is discussed in subsequent sections, the Code permits the use of character evidence in some circumstances. Section 1103, for example, allows the accused to offer evidence of the crime victim's character to prove that the victim engaged in behavior which under the substantive criminal law excuses the accused's conduct.[4] The accused, for example, might offer evidence that the victim engaged in unprovoked attacks in order to prove that the victim was the first aggressor in the altercation with the accused. In these instances, trial judges still retain the discretion to exclude the evidence on the grounds enumerated in § 352.[5] The Code also allows parties to use what seems to be inadmissible character evidence if offered for a noncharacter purpose.[6] For example, to prove that the accused committed the offense charged, the prosecution may attempt to offer evidence that the accused has committed similar offenses. The evidence is not offered to prove that the accused is guilty because he is the kind of person who would commit the offense. Rather, the theory of admissibility is that the accused is guilty because the method used to commit the offenses is so unique as to suggest that only the accused committed the offense charged. Since jurors may be unable to grasp this subtle distinction, trial judges retain the power to exclude the evidence if they conclude that the risk is too great that the jurors will misuse it as character evidence.

Moreover, as is discussed in Chapter 15, a literal interpretation of Proposition 8 also repeals those Code sections which restrict the use of character evidence to attack or support the credibility of witnesses. The reenactment of § 1101 leaves these effects of the initiative untouched.

---

2. 7 Cal.4th 380, 27 Cal.Rptr.2d 646, 867 P.2d 757 (1994).

3. For an extended discussion of this point, see § 3.07 supra.

4. See § 3.12 infra.

5. Similarly, trial judges retain discretion under § 352 to exclude bad character evidence offered under § 1108 to prove the accused's guilt in prosecutions of sexual offenses. For an extended discussion of § 1108, see § 3.14 supra.

6. See § 3.14 infra.

Section 1101 expressly provides that "[n]othing in the section affects the admissibility of evidence offered to support or attack the credibility of a witness."[7] Consequently, judges who wish to curb the effects of Proposition 8 on witness credibility will have to rely on § 352.[8]

§ 3.09 CHARACTER EVIDENCE AND SCIENTIFIC STUDIES

The character evidence rules are premised on two assumptions. One is that character evidence is probative of conduct; the other is that its probative value in predicting conduct is outweighed by its potential to bias the fact finder against the person or party against whom the character evidence is offered. Recent scientific studies have cast doubts on the validity of the former assumption and have confirmed the latter.

Prejudicial effect. Psychological studies confirm the law's intuitive belief that character evidence can be highly prejudicial. One reason for the prejudice is the setting—the courtroom—in which the character evidence is heard. Gustav Ichheiser found that, in classifying others, people are motivated by two factors: "by the attitude of the person performing the classificatory act and by the situation in which this act is being performed. However, as a general rule, the situation seems to be the dominant factor."[1] Because an accused is tried in a setting where wrongdoing is explored, Ichheiser's findings suggest that jurors are more likely to be receptive to character evidence suggesting guilt than to character evidence suggesting innocence.

Psychologists have also found that people give greater weight to unfavorable, unpleasant, or socially derogatory information about a person than to information of equal intensity but of a positive nature.[2] This finding suggests that jurors are likely to give greater weight to bad character than to good character evidence, especially given the setting where the evidence is heard.[3]

---

7. West's Ann. California Evidence Code § 1101(c).

8. For an extended discussion of the role of § 352 in this context, see § 15.03 infra.

1. Ichheiser, *Misunderstandings in Human Relations—A Study in False Social Perception*, 55 Am. J. Soc. 24 (Supp. 1949).

2. See, e.g., Hamilton and Huffman, *Generality of Impression–Formation Processes for Evaluative and Nonevaluative Judgments*, 20 J. Personality & Soc. Psychology 200, 201, 204 (1971); Schneider, *Implicit Personality Theory: A Review*, 79 Psychological Bull. 294 (1973). But see Weinstein & Crowdus, *The Effects of Positive and Negative Information on Person Perception*, 21 Hum. Rel. 383, 389 (1963) ("The basic hypothesis that negative information has greater saliency than positive information for person perception was generally not supported [by the study].").

3. Psychologists Felicia Pratto of Stanford University and Oliver P. John of the University of California at Berkeley believe that unconscious mental categorization of people as good or bad accounts in part for negative judgments about people. Their research suggests that people unconsciously remember the negative and the bad because the bias toward the negative is an evolutionary adaptation to protect individuals from immediate threats. *Stanford University Campus Report*, "Negative Judgments May Be Automatic, Unconscious, Psychologists' Studies Find," page 6, October 21, 1992. Some fears may be "hardwired" into the brain, enabling us to escape danger before we even understand what the menace is. Newborn monkeys, for example, have been observed freezing at their first sight of a snake even though they had not encountered

But perhaps the factor that most induces jurors to overestimate the probative value of character evidence is what psychologists call the "halo effect."[4] The term refers to the propensity of people to judge others on the basis of one outstanding "good" or "bad" quality.[5] Combined with the tendencies to see others as simple people whose behavior is easily predictable[6] and to give greater weight to negative information, bad character evidence can induce jurors to reach unfavorable conclusions about a person's behavior which the evidence simply cannot support.

To be sure, the psychological studies did not test the prejudicial effects of bad character evidence directly. Nonetheless, they support the law's intuitive judgment that character evidence is unduly prejudicial.

Probative value. The probative worth of character evidence is predicated on the belief that character traits exert sufficient influence over time and across different situations as to tell us something about a person's behavior on a specified occasion. As is discussed at the beginning of this chapter, "common sense" tells us that if someone misrepresented the condition of cars he sold to others that information helps us determine whether he misrepresented the condition of the car he sold us. Even though we engage in this kind of reasoning in everyday affairs, recent psychological studies question its predictive validity.

In particular, the work of Walter Mischel has undermined the assumptions of trait theorists. These theorists hold that behavior is governed by personality traits that exert sufficient influence to produce generally consistent behavior in widely divergent situations.[7] Mischel's empirical work did not bear this claim out. Instead, he found that behavior is largely shaped by specific situational determinants that do not lend themselves easily to predictions about individual behavior.[8] The reasons, explains Mischel, are as follows:

> First, behavior depends on stimulus situations and is specific to the situation: response patterns even in highly similar situations often fail to be strongly related. Individuals show far less cross-situational consistency in their behavior than has been assumed by trait-state theories. The more dissimilar the evoking situations, the less likely they are to lead to similar or consistent responses from the *same*

one before. See *The Wall Street Journal*, "Panic Pathway: Study of Fear Shows Emotion can alter 'Wiring' of the Brain," page 1, September 29, 1993.

4. G. Allport, Personality—A Psychological Interpretation 1, 521 (1937).

5. Id.

6. Ichheiser, Ichheiser, *Misunderstandings in Human Relations—A Study in False Social Perception*, 55 Am. J. Soc. 24, 27–28 (Supp. 1949).

7. See G. Allport, Personality—A Psychological Interpretation 1, 289 (1937); H. Eysenck, *The Structure of Human Personality* 3 (1970).

8. W. Mischel, Personality And Assessment 122 (1968). More recent research confirms many of Mischel's findings. According to Stanford University psychologist Lee Ross, predicting behavior is risky business because most people underestimate the power of the situation to influence behavior and overestimate the power of personality traits or past behavior. *Stanford University Campus Report*, "Predicting Behavior of Friends, Even Self, is Risky Business, Social Psychologist Says," page 1, January 6, 1993.

individual. *Even seemingly trivial situational differences may reduce correlations to zero.*[9]

If even seemingly trivial situational differences can render behavioral predictions invalid, character evidence may possess little or no probative value. Added to its potential to prejudice unduly, the scientific findings confirm the law's intuitive position disfavoring the use of character evidence in most circumstances.[10]

§ 3.10 CHARACTER EVIDENCE AND DUE PROCESS

Evidence offered against the accused is most likely to offend due process whenever its probative value on guilt is low and its prejudicial effect is great. Evidence that sheds little or no light on the issues to be decided but that moves the trier of fact to convict the accused on improper grounds can hardly be said to comport with the fairness requirements of the Due Process Clause.[1] Though neither the United States Supreme Court[2] nor the California Supreme Court[3] has held that the unrestricted

---

9. W. Mischel, Personality And Assessment 122, 177 (1968) (emphasis added).

10. In 1995, with the help of Yuichi Shoda, Mischel undertook further work which demonstrates that under some circumstances a person's behavioral tendencies can be used to predict behavior across a broad range of situations. Mischel and Shoda, *A Cognitive–Affective System Theory of Personality: Reconceptualizing Situations, Dispositions, Dynamics, and Invariance in Personality Structure*, 102 Psychological Review 246, 248 (1995). Making a prediction for a given individual, however, requires extensive testing for the behavioral tendency in question. Thus, their findings cannot serve at this time as a basis for lifting the categorical ban on the use of character evidence. For an assessment of Mischel's and Shoda's work from a legal perspective, see Méndez, *The Law of Evidence and the Search for a Stable Personality*, 45 Emory Law Journal 221 (1996).

1. Even where amendments to the California Evidence Code permit the use of bad character evidence to prove the accused's propensity to commit the crime charged (see, e.g., West's Ann. California Evidence Code §§ 1108–1109), the California appellate courts recognize that "[a] careful weighing of prejudice against probative value under that section [§ 352] is essential to protect a defendant's due process right to a fundamentally fair trial." People v. Jennings, 81 Cal.App.4th 1301, 1314, 97 Cal.Rptr.2d 727, 737 (2000).

2. In Estelle v. McGuire, 502 U.S. 62, 112 S.Ct. 475, 116 L.Ed.2d 385 (1991), on remand, 956 F.2d 923 (9th Cir.1992), the accused claimed that the use of character evidence against him violated his due process rights. Because the Court did not reach the issue, the Court expressed no opinion "on whether state law would violate the Due Process Clause if it permitted the use of 'prior crimes' evidence to show propensity to commit a charged crime." Id. at 75, note 5, 112 S.Ct. at 484, note 5.

The following year, the Court granted certiorari in a Ninth Circuit case in which the accused claimed that the use of character evidence against him violated due process. United States v. Hadley, 918 F.2d 848 (9th Cir.1990), cert. granted, 503 U.S. 905, 112 S.Ct. 1261, 117 L.Ed.2d 491 (1992). But the Court subsequently dismissed certiorari as improvidently granted. 506 U.S. 19, 113 S.Ct. 486, 121 L.Ed.2d 324 (1992).

The Ninth Circuit maintains that the use of character evidence against the accused can violate due process where it is "highly prejudicial." Henry v. Estelle, 993 F.2d 1423 (9th Cir.1993), reversed on other grounds, Duncan v. Henry, 513 U.S. 364, 115 S.Ct. 887, 130 L.Ed.2d 865 (1995). In determining whether the use of the evidence was prejudicial, the Ninth Circuit will consider the strength of the prosecution's case. The weaker the case, the more likely that the use of the evidence prejudiced the accused. Id.

3. The California Supreme Court has acknowledged that the use of character evidence against the accused may violate due process if it lightens the prosecution's burden of proof. People v. Garceau, 6 Cal.4th 140, 186, 24 Cal.Rptr.2d 664, 691, 862 P.2d 664, 691 (1993).

use of character evidence against an accused violates due process, the California court has held that one species of character evidence must meet a threshold requirement of relevance to satisfy due process.

In People v. Castro[4] the court was asked whether felony convictions used to impeach a witness in criminal cases were subject to discretionary exclusion under § 352 when a provision of Proposition 8 made such convictions admissible "without limitation."[5] Despite the clear meaning of the proposition, the court held that the use of felony convictions was still subject to § 352.[6] The court was moved in part by concern that the unrestricted use of convictions might offend due process.[7] To comply with the demands of the Fourteenth Amendment, the court held that convictions used to impeach the accused at a minimum must entail moral turpitude.[8]

The use of convictions lacking moral turpitude offends due process because in the court's view they say nothing about whether the accused should be disbelieved as a witness.[9] To the court, truth-telling is a moral function, unlikely to be discharged by individuals who engage in immoral acts.[10] Accordingly, only convictions entailing moral turpitude can be used to impeach the accused, because only these convictions allow the trier of fact to draw logical inferences about the accused's veracity as a witness.

Convictions to impeach a witness are a species of character evidence. A specific instance of conduct—the misconduct giving rise to the conviction—is offered as circumstantial evidence that the witness should not be believed because the witness is unworthy of belief. In this respect, evidence of convictions does not differ from evidence of other misdeeds offered to prove conduct. But the use of convictions does differ from the use of the character evidence considered in this chapter in one important respect: the use of convictions is predicated on the *existence* of a conviction. The conviction is either the product of a guilty plea by the accused admitting the misdeed or of a verdict finding the accused guilty of committing the misdeed beyond a reasonable doubt.

The character evidence considered in this chapter is bereft of this degree of reliability. It need not consist of hard evidence of a misdeed but can be as ephemeral as the testimony of an opinion or reputation witness. Even evidence of specific uncharged misdeeds fails to rise to a high degree of reliability; when admissible, the prosecution needs to satisfy only a

---

4. 38 Cal.3d 301, 211 Cal.Rptr. 719, 696 P.2d 111 (1985).

5. This provision of Proposition 8 should not be confused with § 28(f)(2) which gives parties to a criminal proceeding the right not to have relevant evidence excluded. See § 3.07 supra. The provision on convictions is § 28(f)(4). Like § 28(f)(2), it too is an amendment to the California Constitution. See Article I, § 28 of West's Ann.California Constitution.

6. People v. Castro, 38 Cal.3d 301, 312–313, 211 Cal.Rptr. 719, 725, 696 P.2d 111, 117–118 (1985).

7. Id.

8. Id. at 314, 211 Cal.Rptr. at 727, 696 P.2d at 119.

9. Id.

10. Id.

sufficiency standard with respect to their occurrence,[11] a far cry from the certainty required by conviction evidence.

Social scientists have cast serious doubts on the probative value of character evidence.[12] Their studies suggest that, like convictions lacking moral turpitude, character evidence may be devoid of any value in predicting conduct.[13] Moreover, social scientists have confirmed the law's intuitive fear that character evidence may be inherently prejudicial.[14] In light of their findings and the California Supreme Court's due process concerns over the use of irrelevant evidence, the unfettered use of character evidence against the accused raises troubling fairness questions.

QUESTIONS AND PROBLEMS

1. Why is due process implicated when evidence offered against the accused is low in probative value but high in prejudice?

2. Why are convictions a more reliable form of character evidence than the testimony of a reputation or opinion witness? Would you be more inclined to disbelieve a witness who has been convicted of perjury or a witness, who according to his enemies, has a poor reputation for honesty and veracity?

§ 3.11 EXCEPTIONS TO THE CHARACTER EVIDENCE BAN—FEDERAL CRIMINAL CASES AND THE MERCY RULE

Federal Rule of Evidence 404(a), like California Evidence Code § 1101(a), bans the use of character evidence to prove "that on a particular occasion the person acted in accordance with the character or trait."[1] The ban applies to civil and criminal proceedings, unless the existence of the character trait is an ultimate issue under the substantive law governing the action or unless an exception applies.[2]

A major exception in criminal cases is the Mercy Rule embodied in Federal Rule of Evidence 404(a)(1).[3] Like the California Mercy Rule, the federal exception allows criminal defendants to offer evidence of character traits that are inconsistent with committing the offenses charged.[4] If the

---

11. West's Ann.California Evidence Code § 403(a)(4). See also Huddleston v. United States, 485 U.S. 681, 108 S.Ct. 1496, 99 L.Ed.2d 771 (1988).

12. See § 3.09 supra.

13. Id.

14. Id.

1. Federal Rule of Evidence 404(a).

2. Federal Rule of Evidence 405(b) and Advisory Committee Note. Accord: West's Ann.California Evidence Code § 1100. In 2006, Federal Rule 404(a) was amended to make clear that character evidence is not admissible in civil or criminal cases to prove conduct in conformity therewith unless an exception applies. Rule 404(a)'s exceptions apply only to criminal cases. See Federal Rule of Evidence 404(a)(1)–(2).

3. Federal Rule of Evidence 404(a)(1). For discussion of the Mercy Rule, see § 3.06 supra.

4. Federal Rule of Evidence 404(a)(1).

accused takes advantage of the exception, the prosecution is permitted to rebut with bad evidence of the accused's character.[5] Like its California counterpart, Federal Rule of Evidence 405(a) limits the parties to opinion or reputation evidence.[6] Unlike the Code, however, Rule 405 expressly allows the cross-examiner to test the qualifications of the defense good character witnesses by inquiring into specific instances of conduct by the accused that are inconsistent with the witnesses' good character testimony.[7] In California, this result is achieved by applying the Code's general relevance sections.

QUESTIONS AND PROBLEMS

1. Plaintiff brings an action against Driver to recover for personal injuries which Plaintiff claims she suffered when Driver hit her with his car at 11 a.m. on June 1. Over an inadmissible character evidence objection, determine the admissibility of the following evidence in a California or federal court:

civil action negligence

Plaintiff's Case–in–Chief

To prove that Driver was negligent, Plaintiff offers the following evidence:

   a.   Bartender: Between eight and nine in the morning of June 1, I saw Driver consume ten beers.

   b.   Arresting Officer: I followed Driver for two minutes before the accident. He was driving erratically. I spoke to him after the accident. His speech was slurred and he smelled of an alcoholic beverage.

   c.   Second Officer: Last year I arrested Driver three times for driving while intoxicated.

   d.   Court Records: Driver has been convicted three times for violating Vehicle Code § 23152 (driving while intoxicated).

   e.   Driver's Ex–Lover: In my opinion Driver is a drunk. His reputation for sobriety is terrible in the community in which he resides.

Driver's Case–in–Chief

To counter Plaintiff's evidence, Driver offers the following evidence in his case-in-chief:

   f.   Driver: On the morning of June 1, I only had two beers.

   g.   Driver's Drinking Buddy: Driver only had two beers on that morning.

   h.   Driver's Current Lover: Every time we go out, Driver only has two beers. In my opinion Driver is a sober person. Moreover, his reputation for sobriety in the community in which he resides is excellent.

---

5.   Federal Rule of Evidence 404(a)(1).

6.   Federal Rule of Evidence 405(a).

7.   Id.

Plaintiff's Rebuttal

In rebuttal Plaintiff offers the kinds of evidence described in Plaintiff's case-in-chief. Over an inadmissible character objection, determine its admissibility in a California or federal court.

2. Plaintiff also sues Owner for negligently entrusting his car to Driver. The essence of Plaintiff's claim is that Owner was negligent because he lent his car to someone he knew or should have known was an unfit driver. Over an inadmissible character evidence objection, determine whether the parties may offer the following evidence against each other:

Plaintiff's Case–in–Chief

To prove that Owner was negligent, Plaintiff offers the following evidence:

    a. Second Officer: Last year I arrested Driver three times for driving while intoxicated.

    b. Court Records: Driver has been convicted three times for violating Vehicle Code § 23152 (driving while intoxicated).

    c. Driver's Ex–Lover: In my opinion Driver is a drunk. His reputation for sobriety is terrible in the community in which he resides.

Owner's Case–in–Chief

To counter Plaintiff's evidence, Owner offers the following evidence:

    d. Driver's Current Lover: Every time we go out, Driver only has two beers. In my opinion Driver is a sober person. Moreover, his reputation for sobriety in the community in which he resides is excellent.

3. Driver is prosecuted by California for driving while intoxicated on June 1. Over an inadmissible character evidence objection, determine the admissibility of the following evidence in a California court:

Prosecution's Case–in–Chief

To prove that Driver was under the influence, the prosecution offers the following evidence:

    a. Bartender: Between eight and nine in the morning of June 1, I saw Driver consume ten beers.

    b. Arresting Officer: I followed Driver for two minutes before the accident. He was driving erratically. I spoke to him after the accident. His speech was slurred and he smelled of an alcoholic beverage.

    c. Second Officer: Last year I arrested Driver three times for driving while intoxicated.

    d. Court Records: Driver has been convicted three times for violating Vehicle Code § 23152 (driving while intoxicated).

    e. Driver's Ex–Lover: In my opinion Driver is a drunk. His reputation for sobriety is terrible in the community in which he resides.

specific instances 2. opinion 3. reputation

Driver's Case–in–Chief

To counter the prosecution's evidence, Driver offers the following evidence in his case-in-chief:

f.   Driver: On the morning of June 1, I only had two beers.

g.   Driver's Drinking Buddy: Driver only had two beers on that morning.

h.   Driver's Current Lover: Every time we go out, Driver only has two beers. In my opinion Driver is a sober person. Moreover, his reputation for sobriety in the community in which he resides is excellent.

Prosecution's Rebuttal

c.   Second Officer: Last year I arrested Driver three times for driving while intoxicated.

d.   Court Records: Driver has been convicted three times for violating Vehicle Code § 23152 (driving while intoxicated).

e.   Driver's Ex–Lover: In my opinion Driver is a drunk. His reputation for sobriety is terrible in the community in which he resides.

If the prosecution had taken place in California *after* the enactment of Proposition 8 but *prior* to the California Supreme Court's *Ewoldt* decision, would you change any of your rulings in the prosecution's and defendant's cases-in-chief? If so, how?

4.   Assume that the accident took place on a federal enclave located in California. The United States Attorney prosecutes Driver in federal court for driving while intoxicated. Over an inadmissible character evidence objection:

a.   Determine whether the prosecution can offer in its case-in-chief the kinds of evidence the California prosecutor offered against Driver in its case-in-chief.

b.   Determine whether Driver can offer in his case-in-chief the kinds of evidence which Driver offered against the California prosecutor.

c.   Determine whether the prosecution can offer in rebuttal the kinds of evidence which the California prosecutor offered in its rebuttal.

5.   Consider the following cross-examination of Driver's Current Lover, who in the California Vehicle Code § 23152 prosecution testified on direct that Driver's reputation for sobriety was excellent:

Prosecutor: In ascertaining Driver's reputation for sobriety, did you hear that he had been arrested three times for driving while intoxicated?

Driver's Counsel: Objection. Inadmissible character evidence.

Judge: ?

6.   Assume that the objection was overruled. Consider the continuation of the cross-examination:

Current Lover: No, I did not hear that he had been arrested three times for driving while under the influence.

Prosecutor: Having now heard that he was arrested for driving while under the influence, would that change what you told the jury about Driver's reputation for sobriety?

If you were Driver's lawyer, what limiting instruction, if any, would ask the judge to give the jurors?

§ 3.12 EXCEPTIONS TO THE CHARACTER EVIDENCE BAN—CALIFORNIA CRIMINAL CASES AND CRIME VICTIMS

1101-bans.
1103 - allows for defendant.

As originally enacted, California Evidence Code § 1103 allowed the accused to offer all three kinds of character evidence to prove that the victim engaged in conduct which, under the law applicable to the prosecution, gave rise to a defense or otherwise exculpated the accused.[1] The crime of murder serves as an example. Under the principles of self-defense, one is entitled to take life to preserve his or her own life. Accordingly, under the Code as originally enacted, a defendant was entitled to prove that the victim was the first aggressor by opinion, reputation, and specific instance evidence showing that the victim was the kind of person who would engage in unprovoked attacks. Like § 1102's Mercy Rule, § 1103 is an exception to § 1101's ban on the use of character evidence. Both sections reflect the policy that an accused should be permitted to offer such evidence because life and liberty are at stake.[2] Unlike § 1102, § 1103 is expressly exempted from the operation of the Right to Truth–in–Evidence provision of Proposition 8.[3]

If the accused impugns the victim's character, then the prosecution is entitled to rebut with good character evidence.[4] Unless the accused first offers the bad character evidence, the prosecution, for example, may not offer good character evidence of the victim to show that the accused was the first aggressor and, therefore, not entitled to act in self-defense.

1990 and 1991 Amendments. Since its enactment in 1965, § 1103 has been amended in a number of significant ways. In 1990 § 1103(a) was amended to restrict the evidence of the victim's character to reputation and opinion evidence.[5] A 1991 amendment restored the use of specific instances of conduct and added a new provision. Today, § 1103(b) provides that if the accused impugns the victim's character for peacefulness, in addition to rebutting with evidence of the victim's good character for that

---

1. West's Ann.California Evidence Code § 1103(a).

2. Id. (comment).

3. See § 3.07 supra.

4. West's Ann.California Evidence Code § 1103(a)(2).

5. West's Ann.California Evidence Code § 1103 (historical and statutory notes). Though the amendment barred the use of unquestionably relevant evidence, that amendment was not affected by Proposition 8. Section 1103 is specifically exempted from the operation of the initiative. See § 3.07 supra. Moreover, the 1990 amendment passed by the super majority required by Proposition 8 for amendments to the Right to Truth–in–Evidence Provision. See Assembly Final History, 1989–90, AB 2615, at 1719.

ceuse
im's peacefulness)
ecution can
ugn peacefulness.

trait, the prosecution may also impugn the <u>accused's character for peace-</u>fulness.[6] Thus, the accused can open the door to evidence of his bad character for peacefulness in one of two ways: (1) by offering evidence of his good character for peacefulness under § 1102(a), or (2) by offering evidence of the victim's bad character for violence under § 1103(a)(2).

Section 1103(b) differs from § 1102 in one significant respect: the latter section limits the prosecution to reputation and opinion evidence in proving the accused's bad character while the former permits the prosecution to use evidence of specific instances of conduct as well. Section 1103(b) represents a minority position.[7] Only one other jurisdiction—Missouri—appears to have a similar rule.[8] Nonetheless, the section has withstood the claim that its use against criminal defendants violates due process.[9]

Under the Code, it is immaterial that the accused was unaware of the specific instances of conduct offered to establish the victim's bad character under § 1103(a). The use of the evidence for this purpose must be distinguished from evidence the accused may offer to explain why he took defensive action. For example, in a murder prosecution in which the accused claims self-defense, the accused is entitled to offer the reasons that moved him to kill. These can include the immediate circumstances that led him to conclude that he had to act (e.g., "The victim came at me with a knife.") as well as other factors that convinced him of the victim's deadly intentions (e.g., "A month earlier, I saw the victim stab a bar patron without provocation.").[10] But as originally enacted in 1965 and as amended in 1991, § 1103(a) allows the accused to offer specific instances of conduct to show that the victim was the kind of person who would engage in conduct justifying the accused's actions even if the accused was unaware of those instances. This position departs from the Common Law which limits the accused to reputation and opinion evidence in proving the victim's character.[11] But the departure is not as sharp as it appears: the Common Law permits the use of reputation and opinion evidence even if at the time the accused acted he was unaware of the victim's reputation or of the opinion in which others held the victim. Thus, in a murder prosecution it is immaterial that at the time the accused acted he was unaware, say, that the victim had attacked someone else on a third

---

6. West's Ann.California Evidence Code § 1103(b).

7. People v. Blanco, 10 Cal.App.4th 1167, 1173, 13 Cal.Rptr.2d 176, 180 (1992).

8. Id. at 1175, 13 Cal.Rptr.2d at 180–181.

9. Id.

10. Some courts, however, fail to grasp this distinction and erroneously treat past attacks by the victim upon third persons in the accused's presence as evidence of the victim's predisposition toward violence. See, e.g., People v. Walton, 42 Cal.App.4th 1004, 1014–1015, 49 Cal.Rptr.2d 917, 923–924 (1996) and cases cited therein.

The factors convincing the accused of the victim's deadly intentions can include third-party threats directed at the accused by persons the accused associates with the victim. People v. Minifie, 13 Cal.4th 1055, 1068–1069, 56 Cal.Rptr.2d 133, 140, 920 P.2d 1337, 1344–1345 (1996). Whether or not the accused acts reasonably in taking such threats into account is a question for the jurors. Id. at 1069, 56 Cal.Rptr.2d at 140, 920 P.2d at 1345.

11. See, e.g., Federal Rules of Evidence 404–405.

occasion, or that the victim had a reputation for violence, or that those who knew the victim believed the victim to be a violent person.[12]

The California Rape Shield Law. In 1974 § 1103 was amended to include a rape shield provision.[13] Since to convict of forcible rape the prosecution must prove that the victim did not consent to the act,[14] prior to the amendment the accused could rely on § 1103 to offer evidence of the victim's relations with him as well as with others to prove the victim's predisposition to consent on the occasion being tried. Now, § 1103(c)(3) limits the accused to evidence of the victim's sexual conduct with him.[15] The accused may not offer evidence of the victim's sexual conduct with others unless the prosecution "introduces evidence * * * or the complaining witness * * * gives testimony" relating "to the complaining witness's sexual conduct."[16] If that occurs, the accused may offer evidence "limited specifically" to rebutting the evidence introduced by the prosecution or given by the complaining witness.[17] The use of the victim's character to attack credibility is governed by § 782, not § 1103.[18]

Although § 1103(c)(3) preserves the right of the accused to offer instances of the victim's sexual conduct with him to prove her consent to the act in question, that right is not limitless. To begin with, a judge may exclude the evidence of the past relations if the judge concludes that its probative value on the issue of consent is outweighed by its prejudicial effects.[19] Also, in proving the victim's consent to the act in question, the accused may not offer evidence of the manner in which the victim was dressed. That evidence is admissible only if, after a hearing outside the presence of the jury, the judge determines that it is "relevant and admissible in the interests of justice."[20]

Because § 1103(c) bars some relevant evidence that may be probative of consent, its constitutionality has been questioned. People v. Black-

12. People v. Smith, 249 Cal.App.2d 395, 404–405, 57 Cal.Rptr. 508, 514 (1967). Some courts, however, do not appreciate the significance of a victim's misdeeds when the accused was unaware of them. For example, in People v. Cash, 28 Cal.4th 703, 122 Cal.Rptr.2d 545, 50 P.3d 332 (2002), cert. denied, 537 U.S. 1199, 123 S.Ct. 1270, 154 L.Ed.2d 1039 (2003), the defendant was prosecuted for murdering his creditor. He attempted to prove the victim's propensity for inflicting violence on his debtors by evidence that he inflicted violence on some debtors. The California Supreme Court held that the victim's debt collection practices were irrelevant unless the defendant knew about them. Id. at 726, 122 Cal.Rptr.2d at 560–561, 50 P.3d at 344–345. Perhaps the court's confusion can be justified because the accused also offered evidence that he was present at the time the victim had evicted another creditor "with force." Id. at 726, 122 Cal.Rptr.2d at 560, 50 P.3d at 345. In any event, both classes of evidence should have been admissible to prove that, at the time he was killed, the victim engaged in misconduct that precluded the defendant from premeditating the killing.

13. West's Ann.California Evidence Code § 1103 (historical and statutory notes).

14. See West's Ann.California Penal Code §§ 261(a)(2) and 261.6.

15. West's Ann.California Evidence Code § 1103(c)(3).

16. West's Ann.California Evidence Code § 1103(c)(4).

17. Id.

18. West's Ann.California Evidence Code § 782. For an extended discussion of the right of the accused to impeach the complaining witness, see § 15.12 infra.

19. West's Ann.California Evidence Code § 352.

20. West's Ann.California Evidence Code § 1103(c)(2).

burn[21] holds that prohibiting the accused from offering evidence of the victim's sexual conduct with others does not violate the accused's right to a fair trial or to confront the witnesses against him.[22]

Since the due process right to a fair trial does not require that all relevant evidence that may tend to exonerate a defendant be received and since the evidence barred by subsection [c] of Evidence Code section 1103 is of limited probative value at best, subsection [c] does not deprive the defendant charged with rape of a fair trial. Since subsection [c] does not bar evidence of sexual conduct of the victim or her cross-examination concerning that conduct to attack her credibility, the right of confrontation encompassed in due process is not impinged.[23]

Character evidence and sexual harassment lawsuits. The same concerns that prompted the Legislature to enact the rape shield laws moved it to pass legislation protecting plaintiffs in sexual harassment, battery, and assault lawsuits.[24] California Evidence Code § 1106 prohibits the defendant in such actions from offering character evidence of the plaintiff's sexual conduct with others to prove consent or the absence of injury, unless the plaintiff claims loss of consortium.[25] Accordingly, § 1106 prevents the defendant from eliciting evidence that the plaintiff had sex with others to prove her predisposition to have sex with him on the occasion in question. But if the plaintiff claims loss of consortium, § 1106 entitles the defendant to disprove that claim by evidence that the plaintiff had sex with others following the alleged assault. As in the case of the rape shield laws, § 1106 allows the defendant to offer evidence of the plaintiff's sexual conduct with him to prove her predisposition to consent to having sex with him on the occasion in question.[26] Moreover, if the plaintiff introduces evidence making his or her sexual conduct an issue, the defendant is entitled to offer rebutting evidence.[27]

Section 1106 is limited to actions in which the plaintiff alleges a cause of action for sexual harassment, assault, or battery.[28] The section's prohibitions do not apply to an action for medical malpractice and infliction of emotional distress even though the basis for the action is the defendant's alleged sexual contact with the plaintiff.[29]

---

21. 56 Cal.App.3d 685, 128 Cal.Rptr. 864 (1976).

22. Id. at 690–691, 128 Cal.Rptr. at 866–867.

23. Id. at 691, 128 Cal.Rptr. at 867.

24. See West's Ann.California Civil Procedure Code § 2036.1 (legislative history). See also West's Ann.California Evidence Code § 783 (legislative history).

25. West's Ann.California Evidence Code § 1106.

26. Id.

27. Id.

28. Patricia C. v. Mark D., 12 Cal.App.4th 1211, 1217–1218, 16 Cal.Rptr.2d 71, 74–75 (1993). For a discussion of how § 1106 applies in cases alleging a hostile work environment, see Rieger v. Arnold, 104 Cal.App.4th 451, 128 Cal.Rptr.2d 295 (2002).

29. See Patricia C. v. Mark D., supra note 28.

The use of character evidence to attack the credibility of the plaintiff is governed by § 783, not § 1106.

§ 3.13 EXCEPTIONS TO THE CHARACTER EVIDENCE BAN—FEDERAL CRIMINAL CASES AND CRIME VICTIMS

Federal Rule of Evidence 404(a)(2), like California Evidence Code § 1103, allows the accused to offer character evidence of the victim if, under the law governing the offense, the evidence exculpates the accused.[1] If the accused offers such evidence, then the prosecution may rebut with good character evidence. Moreover, as is the case in California, an amendment to Rule 404(a)(1) now provides that if evidence of a trait of character of the alleged victim of the crime is offered by the accused and admitted under the rule, evidence of the same trait of character of the accused may be offered by the prosecution.[2]

> The amendment makes clear that the accused cannot attack the alleged victim's character and yet remain shielded from the disclosure of equally relevant evidence concerning the same character trait of the accused. For example, in a murder case with a claim of self-defense, the accused, to bolster this defense, might offer evidence of the alleged victim's violent disposition. If the government has evidence that the accused has a violent character, but is not allowed to offer this evidence as part of its rebuttal, the jury has only part of the information it needs for an informed assessment of the probabilities as to who was the initial aggressor. * * * Thus, the amendment is designed to permit a more balanced presentation of character evidence when an accused chooses to attack the character of the alleged victim.[3]

Rule 404(a)(1) is broader than the California provision. The Federal Rule opens the accused to evidence of the same bad trait the accused offered against the victim. Under Evidence Code § 113(b), however, the only trait that can be proved under this method is the trait for violence. Only if the accused first impugns the victim's bad character for violence may a California prosecutor offer evidence of the accused's trait for violence.[4] The difference between the rules may not be significant in practice, however. Other than rape prosecutions which are governed by separate rules, criminal defendants are most likely to raise the victim's character in homicide and assault prosecutions in which they claim that the victim was the first aggressor.

Federal Rule 404(a)(2) differs from § 1103 in another respect. In a federal homicide case, the prosecution may offer evidence of the victim's

---

1. Federal Rule of Evidence 404(a)(2).

2. Federal Rule of Evidence 404(a)(1).

3. Id. (Advisory Committee Note).

4. West's Ann. California Evidence Code § 113(b).

trait for peacefulness to rebut noncharacter evidence that the victim was the first aggressor.[5] In California, the prosecution would have this right only if the accused first offered bad character evidence showing that the victim was the first aggressor. In federal homicide cases, evidence describing only the victim's conduct at the time of the homicidal act is sufficient if it gives rise to an inference that the victim attacked first. This rule makes sense when the accused is the only eyewitness to the homicide, and the fact finder has access only to the accused's version of what occurred. But the rule applies in federal homicide cases irrespective of the number of eyewitnesses.

Under the Federal Rules, neither the accused nor the prosecution may offer specific instances of victim's conduct to prove the desired character trait. Specific instances are admissible only when the substantive law governing the case makes the trait an ultimate issue.[6] Since in most prosecutions the character evidence is offered as circumstantial evidence of the victim's conduct on a given occasion, both sides are limited to reputation or opinion evidence.

Federal Rape Shield Law. *Criminal Cases.* Like the Code, the Federal Rules have a rape shield law. It is embodied in Federal Rule of Evidence 412, which bars the use of evidence offered to prove that the victim engaged "in other sexual behavior" or to prove the victim's sexual predisposition in cases involving sexual misconduct, whether offered as substantive evidence or for impeachment.[7]

> The rule aims to safeguard the alleged victim against invasion of privacy, potential embarrassment and sexual stereotyping that is associated with public disclosure of intimate sexual details and the infusion of sexual innuendo into the factfinding process. By affording victims protection in most instances, the rule also encourages victims of sexual misconduct to institute and to participate in legal proceedings against alleged offenders.[8]

As amended in 1994, the prohibition is to be read broadly and excludes such evidence as the victim's mode of dress, speech, and lifestyle.[9] Rule 412, not Rule 404, governs the use of character evidence to prove consent in criminal cases involving sexual misconduct.[10] The rule permits the accused to offer evidence of specific instances of his own sexual conduct with the victim to prove consent, unless the judge concludes that the probative value of the evidence is substantially outweighed by the prejudicial concerns enumerated in Rule 403.[11] In proving consent,

---

5. Federal Rule of Evidence 404(a)(2).

6. Federal Rule of Evidence 405(b) and Advisory Committee Note.

7. Federal Rule of Evidence 412 (Advisory Committee Note).

8. Id.

9. Id.

10. Id.

11. In its Note, the Advisory Committee expressly states that evidence that is admissible under Rule 412 is subject to exclusion under Rule 403. Rule 403 is the federal equivalent of California Evidence Code § 352.

the accused is not limited to evidence of prior instances of sexual activity between the victim and the accused. The accused may also offer other evidence that is probative of the victim's predisposition to engage in consensual activities with the accused, including statements in which the victim expressed an interest in engaging in sexual activities with the accused or voiced sexual fantasies involving the accused.[12] The rule also allows the accused to offer evidence of specific instances of the victim's sexual conduct with others to prove that someone other than the accused is responsible for the assault charged.[13]

Civil Actions. The 1994 amendment makes it clear that Rule 412's rape shield law applies as well in civil cases involving sexual misconduct, such as sexual harassment claims.[14] Rather than spell out the limited purposes for which evidence of a victim's sexual behavior or predisposition can be received in civil cases, Rule 412(b)(2) commits the admissibility of the evidence to the court's discretion. If the evidence is admissible under the Rules, it may be received only if the court finds that its probative value on contested issues substantially outweighs the danger of harm to the victim and of unfair prejudice to any party.[15] In contrast, California Evidence Code § 1106 places strict limits on the admissibility of the victim's sexual conduct with others in suits involving sexual harassment, battery, or assault.[16]

Under Rule 403, the objecting party has the burden of persuading the judge that the probative value of the contested evidence is substantially outweighed by the countervailing concerns enumerated in the Rule.[17] Under Rule 412(b)(2), however, the burdens are reversed, and it is the proponent who in civil cases has to persuade the judge that the probative value of the evidence substantially outweighs the danger of harm to the victim and of unfair prejudice to the opposing party.[18]

Is evidence offered in civil actions under Rule 412(b)(2) subject to exclusion under Rule 404(a) which generally prohibits the use of character evidence to prove that a person acted in accordance with a character trait? If so, over objection, the proponent must convince the judge that the evidence is being offered for a noncharacter purpose. An example can be found in Judd v. Rodman,[19] where the defendant was allowed to introduce the plaintiff's sexual history in a suit for damages in which the plaintiff claimed that the defendant had infected her with genital herpes. The evidence was not admitted as proof of the plaintiff's promiscuity but as proof that someone other than the defendant might have infected the

---

12. Federal Rule of Evidence 412 (Advisory Committee Note).

13. Id.

14. Id. and Advisory Committee Note.

15. Federal Rule of Evidence 412 and Advisory Committee Note.

16. See § 3.12 supra.

17. Federal Rule of Evidence 403.

18. Federal Rule of Evidence 412(b)(2).

19. 105 F.3d 1339 (11th Cir. 1997).

plaintiff.[20] *Judd*, however, was decided before the restyled Rules went into effect on December 1, 2011. Under former Rule 412(b)(2), the evidence had to be "otherwise admissible" under the rules, thus suggesting that the evidence could be excluded under Rule 404(a). Restyled Rule 412(b)(2) eliminated the "otherwise admissible" language, thereby suggesting that the admission of evidence under Rule 412(b)(2) is subject now only to the limitations specified in the rule. But militating against this construction is the directive that the Restyled Rules not make any substantive changes to the rules they replaced.[21]

Whether offered in a criminal or civil case, evidence offered under Rule 412 must first be screened by the judge.[22] Before admitting evidence under Rule 412, the judge must, upon motion by the offering party, hold an in camera hearing at which the alleged victim and all parties are entitled to be heard. The motion must be filed at least fourteen days before the trial, unless the judge for good cause requires a different time or permits filing during trial.[23]

QUESTIONS AND PROBLEMS

1. Over an inadmissible character evidence objection, determine the admissibility in a California and a federal court of the following evidence in a murder prosecution:

Defendant's Case-in-Chief

a. Defendant: Yes, it is true that I hit the victim, but I did so because the victim hit me first.

b. Defendant: Also, I had heard that the victim sometimes killed people he arrested, and I was afraid that he would kill me too.

c. Defendant's Sister: The victim's reputation for violence in the community in which he resided was terrible.

d. Defendant's Mother: I knew the victim well. In my opinion he was a violent person who would attack for no good reason.

e. Stranger: Two years ago the victim attacked me and almost killed me while arresting me. I wasn't resisting arrest. I don't know the defendant and have never spoken with him.

Prosecution's Rebuttal

f. Victim's Best Friend: I knew the victim well. In my opinion he was a peaceful person.

g. Victim's Lover: The victim's reputation for peacefulness in the community in which he resided was excellent.

---

20. Id. at 1343.

21. See Federal Rule of Evidence 101 (Advisory Committee Note).

22. Federal Rule of Evidence 412(c).

23. Id.

h. Victim's Clergyman: Because of his peace-loving nature, the victim refused to serve in Vietnam. Instead, he joined the Peace Corps.

i. Defendant's Ex–Lover: I remember a time when an officer approached us to ask if he could help us find our car. The defendant proceeded to beat him for no apparent reason.

j. Defendant's Ex–Lover: In my opinion, the defendant is the kind of person who engages in unprovoked attacks.

2. Suppose that in his case-in-chief the defendant had limited himself to testifying that the victim hit him first and refrained from offering any evidence relating to the victim's bad character. In a California or federal court, could the prosecution offer any of the evidence described under the Prosecution's Rebuttal?

3. Determine the admissibility in a California and a federal court of the following evidence in a rape prosecution:

Prosecution's Case–in–Chief

a. Victim: The defendant had intercourse with me against my will on January 1.

b. Defense Counsel: Before January 1, you had sexual intercourse with the defendant?

Victim: Yes.

Defense Counsel: You didn't resist on those occasions?

Victim: No.

c. Defense Counsel: Before having intercourse with the defendant, you had intercourse with Harry on numerous occasions?

Victim: Yes.

Defense Counsel: You didn't resist on those occasions?

Victim: No.

Defendant's Case–in–Chief

d. Defendant: On January 1, I had intercourse with the victim; she did not resist.

e. Defendant: Before January 1, I had intercourse with the victim on numerous occasions; she never resisted; it was usually her idea.

f. Harry: Prior to January 1, I had intercourse with the victim on numerous occasions; it was always her idea.

g. Defendant's Lover: I know the victim well. In my opinion she is the kind of person who would engage in consensual intercourse.

h. Defendant's Sister: I know the victim's reputation for chastity in the community in which she resides. It is not a good reputation.

§ 3.14   EMERGING EXCEPTIONS TO THE CHARACTER EVIDENCE BAN

California—§ 1108. In 1995, the California Legislature amended the Evidence Code by adding § 1108. This section provides that "[i]n a criminal action in which the defendant is accused of a sexual offense, evidence of the defendant's commission of another sexual offense or offenses is not made inadmissible by Section 1101, if the evidence is not inadmissible pursuant to Section 352."[1] Because the accused's propensity to commit such offenses is not an issue under the governing substantive law governing the criminal case, § 1108 is an exception to § 1101's ban on the use of bad character evidence to prove the accused's predisposition to engage in the misconduct charged.[2]

By its terms, § 1008 does not authorize the use of evidence of sexual misdeeds committed by a third party to prove the third party's predisposition to commit the sexual misdeed charged. Section 1108 is limited to evidence of "the defendant's commission of another sexual offense or offenses."[3]

Section 1108 is California's response to the Congressional enactment in 1994 of Federal Rules of Evidence 413–415. These rules allow the use of uncharged sexual misdeeds against a defendant in prosecutions for sexual assault and child molestation, and in civil cases in which the plaintiff seeks compensation for having been sexually assaulted or molested.[4] Section 1108 differs from the federal rules in one important respect. Under the California provision, the bad character evidence is limited to prosecutions[5] and is not admissible in civil actions for damages.[6] Like Federal Rules 413–414, § 1108 requires the prosecution to notify the accused of its intention to offer the bad character evidence prior to the start of the trial.[7]

Section 1108 expressly empowers trial judges to exclude the evidence of uncharged sexual misdeeds if its probative value is substantially outweighed by its prejudicial effects.[8] In assessing the probative value of the evidence, the judge should consider the dissimilarities between the uncharged and charged misdeeds, the remoteness of the uncharged misdeed,

---

1. West's Ann. California Evidence Code § 1108.

2. See West's Ann. California Evidence Code § 1101.

3. West's Ann. California Evidence Code § 1108.

4. See text accompanying note 56.

5. West's Ann. California Evidence Code § 1108.

6. Federal Rule of Evidence 415 allows the use of the evidence in civil cases for damages or other relief.

7. Section 1108 and Federal Rules of Evidence 413–414 also require the prosecution to provide the defense with the statements of witnesses or a summary of the substance of any testimony that is expected to be offered under the rules. Police reports containing the statements of the witnesses can satisfy the requirement of § 1108. People v. Soto, 64 Cal.App.4th 966, 981–82, 75 Cal.Rptr.2d 605, 614 (1998).

8. By its terms, evidence offered under § 1108 is subject to exclusion under § 352.

the amount of time needed to receive evidence proving and disproving the uncharged misdeed, and the probability that the evidence of the uncharged misdeed might confuse the jurors.[9] Special attention should be given to the inflammatory nature of the evidence; evidence of a violent sexual assault upon a stranger may be extremely prejudicial when offered in a prosecution for a nonviolent sexual battery committed against victims known by the accused.[10] If the trial judge admits the evidence of the uncharged sexual misdeeds, then the jurors must be told not to consider the evidence against the accused unless they first find by a preponderance of the evidence that the accused committed the misdeeds.[11]

The range of prosecutions in which the evidence is admissible in California is broad. Crimes qualifying as "sexual offenses" under § 1108 include not only various forms of sexual assaults on minors and adults but also such offenses as possessing pornographic materials depicting minors, employing minors for sexual depictions, and distributing obscene material to minors[12]. In addition, even murder qualifies as a crime involving a sexual offense if the prosecution is based on the felony murder doctrine and the underlying felony is rape.[13] Moreover, under § 1108 a sexual offense can include any crime that involves "[d]eriving sexual pleasure or gratification from the infliction of death, bodily injury, or physical pain on another person."[14] The trial judge's role in determining whether the offense charged meets this definition was considered in People v. Walker.[15] Walker was tried for murdering a prostitute. Over the accused's objection, the prosecution was allowed to offer evidence of three un-

---

9. People v. Harris, 60 Cal.App.4th 727, 737–741, 70 Cal.Rptr.2d 689, 695–696 (1998) (It was an abuse of discretion for the trial judge to admit evidence of an extremely violent assault occurring 23 years prior to the charged offenses where it was unclear whether a sexual offense took place.). Compare People v. Soto, 64 Cal.App.4th 966, 991, 75 Cal.Rptr.2d 605, 621 (1998) (Evidence of sexual misdeeds occurring many years before the charged offense was not remote since the evidence was offered to show the accused's propensity to molest children of similar age.). See also People v. Branch, 91 Cal.App.4th 274, 284–285, 109 Cal.Rptr.2d 870, 877–878 (2001) (Uncharged offenses similar to the charged offenses have greater probative value as proof of the defendant's propensity to commit the charged offenses and may overcome claims of remoteness.).

10. People v. Harris, 60 Cal.App.4th 727, 737–741, 70 Cal.Rptr.2d 689, 695–696 (1998).

11. For a discussion of this requirement, see § 3.18 infra. An early form of this instruction gave rise to a split among the districts of the Court of Appeal over whether it misled jurors into convicting the accused of the sexual misdeed charged by a preponderance of the evidence. See People v. Orellano, 79 Cal.App.4th 179, 181, 93 Cal.Rptr.2d 866, 866–67 (2000) and cases cited therein. The standard jury instruction now warns jurors that a finding by a preponderance of the evidence that the accused committed the uncharged sexual misdeed is not sufficient by itself to prove beyond a reasonable doubt that the accused committed the sexual misdeed charged. CALJIC 2.50.1 (Fall 2006 Edition). Previously, the instruction told the jurors that if they found that the accused was predisposed to commit sexual misdeeds on the basis of the uncharged misdeeds, they could "infer that he was likely to commit and did commit [the sexual misdeed charged]." See People v. Orellano, supra.

12. West's Ann. California Evidence Code § 1108(d).

13. See People v. Story, 45 Cal.4th 1282, 1285, 204 P.3d 306, 309, 91 Cal.Rptr.3d 709, 712 (2009). In addition, a charge of murder with the special circumstance that it was committed during the commission of a lewd and lascivious act on a child under the age of fourteen, allows the prosecution to rely on § 1108 to offer evidence of the defendant's commission of other sexual offenses. See People v. Loy, 52 Cal.4th 46, 60, 127 Cal.Rptr.3d 679, 693, 254 P.3d 980, 991 (2011).

14. West's Ann. California Evidence Code § 1108(d)(1)(E).

15. 139 Cal.App.4th 782, 43 Cal.Rptr.3d 257 (2006).

charged sexual assaults Walker had committed against other prostitutes. Since murder is not among the specific crimes enumerated by § 1108 as a sexual offense, the prosecution argued that murder nonetheless qualified as a sexual offense because "Walker had a history of inflicting bodily injury and physical pain while engaged in sexual encounters with prostitutes or women he perceived to be prostitutes" and he acted with this motivation when he murdered the victim.[16]

> [The question presented is] whether section 1108, subdivision (d)(1)(E)'s inclusion in the definition of sexual offense of crimes that involve "deriving sexual pleasure or gratification from the infliction of death, bodily injury, or physical pain on another person" authorizes use of evidence of other sexual offenses when the circumstances under which a violent crime has been committed suggests the defendant derived sexual pleasure or gratification from the victim's pain, even though sexual pleasure or gratification is neither a necessary element of the charged offense nor alleged in the information as an enhancement or aggravating factor.[17]

The reviewing court answered the question in the negative. It held that the deriving pleasure provision is limited "to crimes in which sexual misconduct is an element of the charged offense (and of the offenses offered as evidence of the defendant's predisposition to commit the charged offense)."[18] Because the elements of murder do not include sexual misconduct, the court held that the trial judge erred in admitting the evidence of the uncharged sexual assaults.[19]

The reviewing court cited the legislative history of § 1108 in support of its holding. Because sexual offenses often occur in seclusion, the "ensuing trial often presents conflicting versions of the event and requires the trier of fact to make difficult credibility determinations."[20] The legislature enacted § 1108 to assist the fact finders resolve the credibility questions by giving them "an opportunity to learn of the defendant's possible disposition to commit sex crimes."[21]

If under § 1108 evidence of uncharged sexual misdeeds is received to prove the accused's propensity to commit the sexual misdeed charged, the accused is entitled to disprove the propensity with good character evidence.[22] In People v. Callahan[23] the accused was charged with committing

---

16.   Id. at 798, 43 Cal.Rptr.3d at 268.

17.   Id. at 799, 43 Cal.Rptr.3d at 269.

18.   Id. at 801, 43 Cal.Rptr.3d at 271.

19.   Id.

20.   Id.

21.   Id.

22.   By its terms, § 1108 would appear to allow only the prosecution to offer evidence of the defendant's predisposition to commit the sexual offense charged. But since § 1108 makes such evidence admissible, then under § 1100 the defendant is entitled to offer countervailing character evidence in rebuttal. Section 1100 governs the use character evidence when it is admissible to prove or disprove a character trait. See West's Ann. California Evidence Code § 1100.

23.   74 Cal.App.4th 356, 87 Cal.Rptr.2d 838 (1999).

a lewd act upon a child under the age of 14. To prove his propensity to commit the offense, the prosecution was allowed to call a witness who testified that the accused had committed a lewd act upon her when she was under 14. In rebuttal, the accused was allowed to call a number of witnesses to testify that he had treated them well while babysitting them. The trial judge, however, prevented one of the witnesses from answering whether the accused had ever touched her in an inappropriate manner. The reviewing court held that the trial judge's ruling was erroneous. A criminal defendant is entitled to offer good character evidence to rebut the prosecution's bad character evidence and may do so by offering it in the form of specific instances.[24]

Section 1108 limits the prosecution to offering evidence of specific instances of sexual misconduct in establishing the accused's propensity to commit the sexual misdeed charged.[25] Opinion evidence that the accused is the kind of person who would commit the sexual misdeed charged is not admissible, even if the opinion is offered by a qualified expert.[26] Neither is expert testimony that the accused matches the profile of a rapist.[27] But as *Callahan* notes, the defendant's right of rebuttal is not so limited.[28] The defendant's greater rights stem from the fact that the rebuttal evidence is governed by § 1100 which provides that, when character evidence is admissible, the pertinent trait may be proved by evidence of reputation, opinion, or specific instances of conduct.[29]

That the accused was acquitted of the sexual misdeed offered under § 1108 to prove his propensity to commit the sexual misdeed charged is immaterial. An acquittal is not a finding of innocence; it is simply an adjudication that in the earlier proceeding the evidence was not sufficient to overcome all reasonable doubts about the accused's guilt.[30] But to help the jury assess the significance of the uncharged misdeed evidence, the trial judge must inform the jury that the accused was acquitted of the

---

24. Id. at 378–79, 87 Cal.Rptr.2d at 855. The right to rebut with good character evidence, including evidence of specific instances, is independent of the accused's right under the Mercy Rule to tender by opinion and reputation evidence a character trait that is inconsistent with the offense charged. For a discussion of the Mercy Rule, see § 3.06 supra.

25. Section 1108 speaks in terms of "another sexual offense or offenses." As People v. McFarland notes, the language precludes the prosecution from offering bad character evidence in the form of an expert opinion against the accused under § 1108. 78 Cal.App.4th 489, 493–495, 92 Cal.Rptr.2d 884, 888–889 (2000). Nor may the prosecution offer such expert evidence under § 1101(b) to prove some fact other than the accused's predisposition to commit the offense charged. Id. That section speaks in terms of "wrongs" or "acts." The prosecution, however, may offer a certified official record of conviction as proof of the sexual misconduct underlying the conviction. See People v. Wesson, 138 Cal.App.4th 959, 968, 41 Cal.Rptr.3d 883, 889 (2006). For a discussion of the hearsay difficulties inherent in offering convictions as proof of the underlying misconduct, see § 12.03 infra.

26. People v. McFarland, 78 Cal.App.4th 489, 495, 92 Cal.Rptr.2d 884, 889 (2000).

27. People v. Robbie, 92 Cal.App.4th 1075, 1085, 112 Cal.Rptr.2d 479, 485 (2001).

28. People v. Callahan, 74 Cal.App.4th 356, 379, 87 Cal.Rptr.2d 838, 855 (1999).

29. West's Ann. California Evidence Code § 1100.

30. Dowling v. United States, 493 U.S. 342, 349, 110 S.Ct. 668, 672, 107 L.Ed.2d 708 (1990); People v. Tatum, 209 Cal.App.2d 179, 186, note 2, 25 Cal.Rptr. 832, 836, note 2 (1962).

sexual misdeed offered under § 1108.[31] The failure to inform the jury constitutes error.[32]

The California Supreme Court has upheld the constitutionality of § 1108.[33] In upholding the section, the court assumed that an accused's predisposition to commit sexual misdeeds is probative of whether he committed the sexual misdeed charged.[34] While that may be true as a matter of legal relevance,[35] scientific studies have cast serious doubts on the assumed probative value of character evidence, especially when presented in the form of specific misdeeds.[36]

The probative value of character evidence is predicated on the belief that character "traits" exert sufficient influence over time and across different situations as to tell us something about a person's behavior on a specified occasion. To trait theorists, committing other rapes manifests a "trait" or predisposition to commit such misdeeds, and a person with such a trait is more likely than those without it to commit a rape. But empirical research has not only failed to validate trait theory, it has generally rejected it.[37] Despite its lack of predictive value, the scientific studies suggest that jurors nonetheless are likely to give bad character evidence much undeserved weight.[38] Clearly, evidence offered against the accused is most likely to offend due process whenever its probative value on guilt is low and its potential to prejudice the fact finder is great. This is precisely the scientific case against the use of character evidence, but it is a case that will remain unheard, unless appellate judges begin to take into account what the social scientists have to say.

California—§ 1109. Section 1108 is not the only recent exception to the rule banning the use of character evidence to prove conduct. Section 1109 allows prosecutors to offer evidence of an accused's acts of domestic violence, elder or dependent person abuse, or child abuse as proof of the accused's propensity to commit such violence or abuse if offered in an action in which the accused is charged with an offense involving domestic violence, elder or dependent person abuse, or child abuse.[39]

---

31. People v. Mullens, 119 Cal.App.4th 648, 666, 14 Cal.Rptr.3d 534, 546–547 (2004). This requirement is not limited to § 1008 prosecutions. It applies to all prosecutions where the state offers evidence of uncharged offenses against the accused: "[People v. Griffin, 66 Cal.2d 459, 464–466, 58 Cal.Rptr. 107, 110, 426 P.2d 507, 511 (1967),] and its progeny * * * stand for the proposition * * * that if a trial court permits the prosecution to present evidence that the defendant committed one or more similar offenses for which he or she is not charged in the current prosecution, the trial court must allow the defense to present evidence of the defendant's acquittal, if any, of such crimes, and failure to allow such acquittal evidence constitutes error." Id. at 665, 14 Cal.Rptr.3d at 546.

32. Id.

33. People v. Falsetta, 21 Cal.4th 903, 922, 89 Cal.Rptr.2d 847, 859, 986 P.2d 182, 193 (1999), cert. denied, 529 U.S. 1089, 120 S.Ct. 1723, 146 L.Ed.2d 645 (2000).

34. Id. at 916, 89 Cal.Rptr.2d at 855, 986 P.2d at 189.

35. See §§ 2.02–2.04 supra.

36. See § 3.09 supra.

37. Id.

38. Id.

39. West's Ann. California Evidence Code § 1109. As in the case of § 1108, § 1109 appears to restrict the prosecution to offering only evidence of specific instances of domestic violence. The

As in the case of § 1108, § 1109 does not authorize the use of specific acts of domestic violence committed by a third party to prove that party's predisposition to commit the offense charged against the accused. By its terms, § 1109 limits the use of the uncharged acts to proving only the accused's predisposition to commit the domestic violence act involved in the offense charged.

Victims of "domestic violence" include:

[A]n adult or a minor who is a spouse, former spouse, cohabitant, former cohabitant, or person with whom the suspect has had a child or is having or has had a dating or engagement relationship. For purposes of this subdivision, "cohabitant" means two unrelated adult persons living together for a substantial period of time, resulting in some permanency of relationship. Factors that may determine whether persons are cohabiting include, but are not limited to, (1) sexual relations between the parties while sharing the same living quarters, (2) sharing of income or expenses, (3) joint use or ownership of property, (4) whether the parties hold themselves out as husband and wife, (5) the continuity of the relationship, and (6) the length of the relationship.[40]

"Domestic violence" is defined as "intentionally or recklessly causing or attempting to cause bodily injury, or placing another person in reasonable apprehension of imminent serious bodily injury to himself or herself, or another."[41]

Elder or dependent person abuse means "physical or sexual abuse, neglect, financial abuse, abandonment, isolation, abduction, or other treatment that results in physical harm, pain, or mental suffering, the deprivation of care by a caregiver, or other deprivation by a custodian or provider of goods or services that are necessary to avoid physical harm or mental suffering."[42]

Child abuse means "any cruel or inhuman corporal punishment or an injury resulting in a traumatic condition."[43]

In the case of domestic abuse, the accused does not need to be charged with "domestic violence" for the other acts of domestic violence to be admissible. The section is triggered if the offense charged involves such

---

section refers to the "defendant's commission of other domestic violence." In rebuttal, however, the defendant is not limited to evidence of specific instances. The rebuttal is governed by § 1100 which allows the use of opinion, reputation, and specific instance evidence to prove or disprove the pertinent character trait. West's Ann. California Evidence Code § 1100.

40. West's Ann. California Penal Code § 13700. In addition, victims of domestic violence include the individuals specified in Family Code § 6211. See West's Ann. California Evidence Code § 1109. Section 6211 defines domestic violence in terms of its victims. Among the persons who qualify as victims are a spouse or former spouse, a cohabitant or former cohabitant, a person with whom the accused is having or had a dating relationship, a person with whom the accused has had a child, any other person related by consanguinity or affinity within the second degree. Id.

41. West's Ann. California Penal Code § 13700(a).

42. West's Ann. California Evidence Code § 1109(d)(1).

43. West's Ann. California Penal Code § 273d.

acts. For example, forcibly raping a girlfriend[44] or a spouse[45] can be viewed as a form of domestic violence. Accordingly, forcible rape can open the door to other acts of domestic violence even if the other acts did not involve sexual misconduct.[46] Moreover, the prosecution is not limited to offering only acts of domestic violence with the victim of the offense charged. In proving the accused's propensity to engage in acts of domestic violence, the prosecution may call as witnesses other victims of the accused's violence.[47]

It is not essential for the prosecution to prove that the uncharged acts of domestic violence or abuse resulted in a conviction.[48] However, before the jurors may consider the other acts of domestic violence or abuse, they must first find by a preponderance of the evidence that the accused committed those acts.[49] California courts impose this limitation on the use of the misdeed evidence, whether or not offered to prove conduct in conformity with a character trait.[50]

Like § 1108, § 1109 requires the prosecution to inform the accused prior to the trial of its intention to offer the uncharged acts.[51] And, as in the case of § 1108, the judge is empowered under § 1109 to exclude the uncharged acts evidence if its probative value is substantially outweighed by its prejudicial effects.[52] Factors a judge should consider include whether the uncharged misconduct is more inflammatory than the misconduct charged, the risk jurors might confuse the uncharged misconduct with the misconduct charged, the remoteness of the uncharged misconduct, and whether the accused was convicted and punished for the uncharged

---

44. People v. Poplar, 70 Cal.App.4th 1129, 1139, 83 Cal.Rptr.2d 320, 326 (1999).

45. People v. Garcia, 89 Cal.App.4th 1321, 1332–1333, 107 Cal.Rptr.2d 889, 897 (2001).

46. Id. In *Garcia* the evidence of other acts of domestic violence included warnings that the victim would be sorry if she failed to take the accused back, chasing the victim, and attempting to contact the victim in violation of a restraining order.

47. People v. Poplar, 70 Cal.App.4th 1129, 1139, 83 Cal.Rptr.2d 320, 326 (1999).

48. People v. Escobar, 82 Cal.App.4th 1085, 1095–1096, 98 Cal.Rptr.2d 696, 703–704 (2000), cert. denied, 532 U.S. 1053, 121 S.Ct. 2195, 149 L.Ed.2d 1026 (2001).

49. The standard jury instruction also warns jurors that finding that the accused committed the prior misdeeds by a preponderance of the evidence is not sufficient by itself to prove beyond a reasonable doubt that the accused committed the charged misdeed. See CALJIC 2.50.1 (Fall 2006 Edition). The failure to give this warning can result in reversible error. See People v. Younger, 84 Cal.App.4th 1360, 1383–1384, 101 Cal.Rptr.2d 624, 641 (2000). Indeed, instructing the jurors that they can infer from the accused's predisposition that the accused was likely to commit, and did commit, the offense charged is a due process violation: the prosecution's obligation to prove each element of an offense beyond a reasonable doubt "is substantially eroded by instructions suggesting that a defendant's prior offenses may be sufficient to convict him of the charged crime." People v. James, 81 Cal.App.4th 1343, 1353, 96 Cal.Rptr.2d 823, 830 (2000).

50. See § 3.18 infra.

51. West's Ann. California Evidence Code § 1109. Since § 1109 specifically empowers the trial judge to exclude other acts of domestic violence when their probative value is substantially outweighed by their prejudicial effects, it follows that a prosecutor may not use as predisposition evidence, acts of domestic violence that are the basis of other charges brought against the accused. Acts of domestic violence that are charged must be proved and cannot be excluded under § 352. See People v. Quintanilla, 132 Cal.App.4th 572, 579, 33 Cal.Rptr.3d 782, 787 (2005), cert. granted and judgment vacated on other grounds by Quintanilla v. California, 549 U.S. 1191, 127 S.Ct. 1215, 167 L.Ed.2d 40 (2007).

52. Id.

misconduct.[53] Evidence of uncharged acts occurring more than ten years before the charged act is generally inadmissible unless the judge determines that its admission is "in the interest of justice."[54] As in the case of § 1108, § 1109 has been upheld against the claim that use of predisposition evidence violates the accused's right to a fair trial[55] or to equal protection of the laws.[56]

Federal Rules. The Violent Crime Control and Law Enforcement Act approved by Congress in 1994 creates three exceptions to Rule 404(a)'s ban of the use of character evidence to prove conduct in conformity therewith. Rules 413–415 allow the use of character evidence in prosecutions in which the accused is charged with sexual assault or child molestation, or in civil cases in which the victim seeks compensation for having been sexually assaulted or molested.[57] The new rules authorize the use of evidence of the defendant's commission of other sexual assaults or molestations to prove any relevant matter, including the defendant's predisposition to commit the misdeed charged.[58] Under the Act, the Judicial Conference was to provide Congress with a report containing the Conference's recommendations on the new rules. In its report, the Conference concurred with the views of the Advisory Committees on the Evidence Rules and on the Criminal and Civil Rules that adopting the new rules was undesirable. Of the more than 40 judges, practicing lawyers, and academicians asked to review the new rules, only the representatives of the Department of Justice favored adopting them. Among the reasons cited by the Judicial Conference for its opposition were (1) the lack of empirical evidence to support the proposition that evidence of past acts is predictive of future acts, (2) the danger of convicting the accused on account of his "bad" character, (3) the undue consumption of time and potential for confusion of issues that could emanate from the mini-trials required to prove or disprove that the defendant engaged in the uncharged misconduct, and (4) concerns that the uncharged misconduct evidence would have to be received if relevant.[59] Despite this strong opposition, Congress did not modify or reject the new rules, and they went into effect in 1995.

The Eighth, Ninth, and Tenth Circuits have construed the Federal Rules as authorizing federal judges to employ Rule 403 to exclude propensity evidence offered under Rules 413–415 whenever its probative value on

---

53. People v. Rucker, 126 Cal.App.4th 1107, 1119, 25 Cal.Rptr.3d 62, 71 (2005). The fact that the defendant was acquitted of the uncharged offense does not necessarily require exclusion of the uncharged offense. But the judge must inform the jurors of the acquittal in order to help them assess the probative value of the uncharged offense. See text accompanying note 30 supra.

54. Id.

55. People v. Johnson, 77 Cal.App.4th 410, 420, 91 Cal.Rptr.2d 596, 602 (2000).

56. People v. Jennings, 81 Cal.App.4th 1301, 1312, 97 Cal.Rptr.2d 727, 736 (2000).

57. Federal Rules of Evidence 413–415.

58. Id.

59. Report of the Judicial Conference of the United States on the Admission of Character Evidence in Certain Sexual Misconduct Cases, February 1996.

contested issues is substantially outweighed by it prejudicial effects.[60] Rules 413–415 are silent on the applicability of Rule 403. Among the factors Ninth Circuit judges should consider in admitting the evidence are the similarity of the uncharged misdeeds to the charged misdeed, the need for the evidence of the uncharged misdeed in light of other evidence presented, and the proximity in time between the commission of the uncharged and the charged misdeeds.[61]

Rules 413 and 414 authorize the prosecution to offer evidence that the accused engaged in other sexual misdeeds or molestations to prove his or her predisposition to commit the sexual misdeed or molestation charged. The Rules are silent on the defendant's right to offer countervailing evidence to prove the opposite character traits. But a defendant should have such a right. Rules 413 and 414 in effect make the accused's predisposition to commit the offense charged a material issue. Accordingly, evidence having any tendency to prove or *disprove* the pertinent character trait would be admissible as a matter of relevance under the Federal Rules.[62] The same principle applies to the bad character evidence offered under Rule 415 in civil cases for damages for sexual assault or child molestation. If the plaintiff offers evidence that the defendant committed other sexual assaults or molestations as proof of his predisposition to commit the assault or molestation alleged in the complaint, the defendant should be entitled to dispute that trait by evidence that he possesses the opposite character traits.

QUESTIONS AND PROBLEMS

Determine the admissibility of the following evidence in a California and federal court:

1.   In a prosecution for committing a lewd act upon a child in June, the prosecutor calls another child to testify that in May the defendant committed a similar act upon the child witness.

2.   In the same prosecution, the defendant calls a child to testify that the defendant serves as the child's babysitter and that the defendant has never touched him improperly.

3.   The child victim in the previous prosecution brings an action against the defendant to recover damages for sexual assault. The child plaintiff calls the child who testified for the prosecution to testify that the defendant committed a lewd act upon her in May.

4.   The defendant is prosecuted for committing a nonsexual battery upon his wife. The prosecution calls the defendant's ex-spouse to testify that he inflicted a nonsexual battery against her on three occasions.

60. United States v. Sumner, 119 F.3d 658, 661 (8th Cir.1997); Doe ex rel. Rudy–Glanzer v. Glanzer, 232 F.3d 1258, 1269 (9th Cir.2000); United States v. Guardia, 135 F.3d 1326, 1330 (10th Cir.1998).

61. See Doe ex rel. Rudy–Glanzer v. Glanzer, 232 F.3d 1258, 1269 (9th Cir.2000).

62. See Federal Rule of Evidence 401.

5. The defendant is prosecuted for forcibly raping his girlfriend. The prosecution calls the defendant's ex-spouse to testify that he inflicted a nonsexual battery against her on three occasions.

6. In a rape prosecution, the prosecutor calls a duly qualified expert to testify that the conduct of the accused, as described by the victim, matches the profile of the most common type of rapist.

7. In a rape prosecution tried in a California court, the judge must exclude evidence of other rapes committed by the defendant, unless the judge is convinced by a preponderance of the evidence that the defendant committed the other rapes. True or false?

§ 3.15   THE USE OF SPECIFIC ACTS TO PROVE PROPOSITIONS OTHER THAN THE PROPENSITY TO ENGAGE IN SUCH ACTS ON A GIVEN OCCASION

Just as California Evidence Code § 1101(a) bans the use of character evidence to prove conduct, § 1101(b) recognizes the admissibility of evidence of crimes, civil wrongs, and other acts when offered to prove a proposition *other* than a person's predisposition to engage in such acts.[1]

Subsection (b) is not necessary. Under California's relevance concept, evidence of such acts would be admissible in any event since it is not being offered for the purpose prohibited by § 1101(a). So long as the evidence is not barred by § 1101(a) or another rule and is probative of some other proposition that is properly provable in the action, the evidence is admissible.[2]

Though § 1101(b) is not a creature of necessity, it is a "measure of precaution."[3] It signals to the parties and the judge that seemingly inadmissible character evidence is being offered for a proper purpose. Section 1101(b) even includes a helpful, nonexclusive list of propositions to which such evidence may be directed in a given case: to prove motive, opportunity, intent, preparation, plan, knowledge, identity, absence of mistake or accident, or whether a defendant in a prosecution for an unlawful sexual act did not reasonably and in good faith believe that the victim consented.[4]

---

1. West's Ann.California Evidence Code § 1101. Federal Rule of Evidence 404(b) is the federal analogue to § 1101(b). Evidence offered under § 1101(b) should consist of specific instances of misconduct. Section 1101(b) speaks in terms of "a crime, civil wrong or other act" and Rule 404(b) about evidence of "other crimes, wrongs, or acts." Accordingly, under § 1101(b) evidence in the form of an expert opinion is not admissible. See People v. McFarland, 78 Cal.App.4th 489, 493–495, 92 Cal.Rptr.2d 884, 888–889 (2000).

Section 1101(b) reflects the principle of § 355 that evidence that is inadmissible for one purpose but admissible for another may be admitted for the proper purpose. West's Ann.California Evidence Code § 355.

2. See §§ 2.01 and 2.04 supra. The same outcome would obtain under the Federal Rules. See Federal Rules of Evidence 105 and 401–402.

3. 6 California Law Revision Commission, Reports, Recommendations, and Studies 669 (1964).

4. West's Ann.California Evidence Code § 1101(b). Federal Rule of Evidence 404(b) contains an almost identical list.

This list is remarkably similar to one compiled by Dean Charles McCormick. His list is especially useful because he explains how evidence of specific acts is admissible to prove a relevant proposition other than the actor's predisposition to engage in such acts. In compiling his list, Dean McCormick drew from cases from many jurisdictions. As we shall see, California cases cite many of the propositions which he identified. In reviewing Dean McCormick's list, two cautionary notes are in order. First, most of his examples are taken from criminal cases. But § 1101(b) applies to civil cases as well,[5] and examples of how courts have applied this subsection in civil cases can be found in § 3.18. Second, a trial judge's ruling admitting evidence of specific acts for a proper purpose is unlikely to be disturbed by an appellate court. An appellate court should not declare a trial judge's discretionary rulings to be erroneous unless the trial judge abused his or her discretion in admitting the evidence.[6] Since such rulings often involve trial assessments that cannot be replicated on appeal, appellate courts are generally unwilling to overturn a trial judge's discretionary rulings unless they resulted from "palpable abuse."[7]

Dean McCormick came up with the following list:

1. "To complete the story of the crime on trial by placing it in the context of nearby and nearly contemporaneous happenings."[8] In People v. Fritts[9] the accused was prosecuted for having intercourse with his minor stepdaughter. A witness, who described an act of intercourse between the accused and the stepdaughter, was allowed to testify about the accused's attempts to have intercourse with the witness.[10] Both the act of intercourse and attempted intercourse occurred on the same occasion, and "it would have been impossible to testify about one without referring to the other."[11]

However, where disclosure of the other misdeed is not essential, a trial judge should exclude it. For example, in People v. Medina[12] the prosecution called a witness who had been raped by the accused to identify a gun and car used by the accused. Her testimony tied the accused to a homicide for which he was on trial. The reviewing court held that, although the prosecution was entitled to call the witness for the limited purpose of identifying the gun and car, the trial judge properly excluded any testimony about the rape.[13]

---

5. West's Ann. California Evidence Code § 1101(b). The analogous federal provision, Federal Rule of Evidence 404(b), applies also to civil cases.

6. People v. Gray, 37 Cal.4th 168, 202, 118 P.3d 496, 520, 33 Cal.Rptr.3d 451, 479 (2005), cert. denied, 549 U.S. 827, 127 S.Ct. 38, 166 L.Ed.2d 45 (2006).

7. People v. Demond, 59 Cal.App.3d 574, 587, 130 Cal.Rptr. 590, 597 (1976).

8. C. McCormick, McCormick on Evidence § 190 (J. Strong 4th ed. 1992) (footnotes omitted).

9. 72 Cal.App.3d 319, 140 Cal.Rptr. 94 (1977).

10. Id. at 324, 140 Cal.Rptr. at 96. Amendments to the Code and the Rules now allow prosecutors to offer bad character evidence to prove the accused's propensity to commit enumerated sexual offenses. For a discussion of these provisions, see § 3.14 supra.

11. People v. Fritts, 72 Cal.App.3d 319, 324, 140 Cal.Rptr. 94, 96 (1977).

12. 11 Cal.4th 694, 47 Cal.Rptr.2d 165, 906 P.2d 2 (1995).

13. Id. at 750, 47 Cal.Rptr.2d at 196, 906 P.2d at 34.

2. "To prove the existence of a larger plan, scheme, or conspiracy, of which the crime on trial is a part. Each crime should be an integral part of an over-arching plan explicitly conceived and executed by the defendant or his confederates. This will be relevant as showing motive, and hence the doing of the criminal act, the identity of the actor, or his intention."[14] The accused is prosecuted for purchasing a stolen bicycle from Harry. The accused admits buying the bicycle but denies knowing that it was stolen. To prove that the accused knew that the bicycle was stolen, the prosecution calls Harry who testifies that the sale of the bicycle was part of an agreement between Harry and the accused calling for Harry to sell to the accused bicycles that Harry would steal from the Stanford campus. Harry also testifies that, pursuant to the plan, he sold the accused five stolen bicycles prior to the sale in question.

The evidence is not inadmissible character evidence. It is not being offered to show that the accused is guilty because he is the kind of man who would knowingly purchase stolen bicycles. Rather, the evidence is being offered to show that the accused knew the bicycle in question to be stolen because he purchased it as part of a plan or scheme to buy stolen bicycles.[15]

The use of "common plan or scheme" to justify the admission of uncharged misdeeds can be troubling when the offering party does not have access to direct evidence of the plan but relies instead on other misdeeds to prove the plan. In these circumstances, the risk is greater that the jurors might treat the misdeed evidence as proof, not of a common plan, but of the accused's propensity to commit the charged misdeed. In People v. Miller[16] a man and a woman were charged with theft by false pretenses. The prosecution's evidence showed that the defendants induced two elderly men who lived alone to give them money by falsely claiming that their children were in need of medical care and clothing. The defendants claimed that they did not falsely induce the two men to part with their money. To prove their wrongful intent, the prosecution was allowed to call three other elderly men who lived alone and who also gave money to the defendants to pay for their children's medical care and other

---

14. C. McCormick, McCormick on Evidence § 190 (J. Strong 4th ed. 1992) (footnotes omitted).

15. Cf. People v. Carter, 19 Cal.App.4th 1236, 23 Cal.Rptr.2d 888 (1993). The accused was prosecuted for murdering a gay man the accused claimed was attempting to kill him. To prove that the accused did not kill in self-defense, the prosecution offered evidence that the accused had killed another gay man two weeks before the killing in question. The reviewing court upheld the use of the evidence: it was not offered as evidence that the accused was guilty because he was the kind of person who killed gay men but as evidence of his intent to kill the victim. The killing, the court reasoned, was part of the accused's scheme to rob and kill gay men. Id. at 1246–1247, 23 Cal.Rptr.2d at 894–895. See also People v. Carter, 36 Cal.4th 1114, 1149, 32 Cal.Rptr.3d 759, 786, 117 P.3d 476, 499 (2005), cert. denied, 547 U.S. 1099, 126 S.Ct. 1881, 164 L.Ed.2d 570 (2006) (holding that evidence of two uncharged murders was admissible to show that the defendant committed the charged murders as part of a common plan to kill and rob the victims of the charged and uncharged murders).

When evidence of uncharged offenses is used to prove intent, the similarities between the charged and uncharged offenses must be substantial but need not reach the degree of similarity required when the uncharged offense is offered to prove the identity of the perpetrator of the offense charged. People v. Carter, supra, at 1245, 23 Cal.Rptr.2d at 894.

16. 81 Cal.App.4th 1427, 97 Cal.Rptr.2d 684 (2000).

expenses. As the reviewing court emphasized, the testimony of the three other men was not offered to prove the defendants' predisposition to commit the charged offenses. It was offered instead as circumstantial proof that the defendants committed the charged and uncharged offenses as part of a common plan or scheme to defraud single elderly men of their money.[17] Although evidence of the other crimes was admissible for this purpose, a trial judge nonetheless should consider whether the jurors can be expected to abide by the limiting instruction. The increased risk that the jurors might treat the misdeed evidence as bad character evidence despite the limiting instruction is a ground for excluding the evidence under § 352.

As will be discussed, the use of the "common plan or scheme" doctrine has proven to be controversial in California, especially in prosecutions for sex offenses.

3. "To prove other crimes by the accused so nearly identical in method as to earmark them as the handiwork of the accused."[18] The evidence of other crimes is used to prove that the accused committed the crime for which he is being tried. Since it goes to the identity of the perpetrator, Dean McCormick believed that the charged and uncharged offenses should "be so unusual and distinctive as to be like a signature."[19]

The California courts use Dean McCormick's test, although they express it in different terms. "[T]he inference of identity arises when the marks common to the charged and uncharged offenses, considered singly or in combination, logically operate to set the charged and uncharged offenses apart from other crimes of the same general variety and, in so doing, tend to suggest that the perpetrator of the uncharged offenses was the perpetrator of the charged offenses."[20] In the words of Justice Kaus, the modus operandi connecting the offenses must be so distinctive as to amount to "the criminal's calling card."[21] In making this determination, the judge should consider the uniqueness of the shared marks as well as their number.[22]

Though evidence of a unique modus operandi is used principally by the prosecution to prove that the accused was the perpetrator of the offense charged, the same evidence sometimes may be available to the

---

17. Id. at 1447–1448, 97 Cal.Rptr.2d at 698. See also People v. Catlin, 26 Cal.4th 81, 120–121, 109 Cal.Rptr.2d 31, 60–61, 26 P.3d 357, 381–383 (2001). Catlin was prosecuted for murdering his fourth wife and her mother. The prosecution's theory was that the accused poisoned them with the toxic chemical paraquat for financial gain. To prove that he poisoned them as part of a common plan to kill women closely related to him for financial gain, the prosecution was permitted to offer evidence that the accused also killed his fifth wife by administering paraquat and that following her death he collected the proceeds from a life insurance policy in which the deceased was the insured and he was the beneficiary.

18. C. McCormick, McCormick on Evidence § 190 (J. Strong 4th ed. 1992) (footnotes omitted).

19. Id.

20. People v. Haston, 69 Cal.2d 233, 246, 70 Cal.Rptr. 419, 428, 444 P.2d 91, 100 (1968). See also People v. Matson, 13 Cal.3d 35, 117 Cal.Rptr. 664, 528 P.2d 752 (1974).

21. People v. Tassell, 36 Cal.3d 77, 86, 201 Cal.Rptr. 567, 572, 679 P.2d 1, 6 (1984).

22. People v. Carter, 36 Cal.4th 1114, 1148, 117 P.3d 476, 498, 32 Cal.Rptr.3d 759, 785 (2005), cert. denied, 547 U.S. 1099, 126 S.Ct. 1881, 164 L.Ed.2d 570 (2006).

defense to show that a third party is guilty of the offense. State v. Bock[23] is a good example. Bock was prosecuted for forgery. In its case-in-chief the prosecution was permitted to offer evidence connecting the accused with another forgery on the theory that the similarities between the uncharged and charged forgeries suggested that the accused committed the charged offense. The accused, however, was precluded from offering evidence showing distinctive similarities between the charged forgery and forgeries committed by a third party. The reviewing court reversed the accused's conviction, holding that the exclusion of the evidence was particularly egregious since the similarities between these forgeries were even greater than the similarities between the forgeries offered by the prosecution and the charged offense.[24]

When evidence of prior misdeeds is offered against the accused to prove his identity as the perpetrator of the charged offense, the accused is entitled to offer countervailing evidence. For example, to prove that the accused was the codefendant's accomplice in burning a residence, the prosecution in People v. Robinson[25] was allowed to offer evidence that the accused and the codefendant had been seen burning a car. To rebut the inference that because he and the codefendant had been seen burning a car he was an accomplice to the burning of the residence, the accused was entitled to offer evidence that on other occasions the codefendant had been seen setting fires alone.[26]

4. "To prove a passion or propensity for unusual and abnormal sexual relations."[27] In People v. Clark[28] the accused was prosecuted for murdering six prostitutes. To prove that the accused was the killer, the prosecution was allowed, over objection, to offer evidence that the accused had hired a prostitute to dance for the accused and a female friend and to have three-way sex with them.[29] According to the California Supreme Court, the evidence was admissible "to show the defendant's fondness for hiring prostitutes, which was relevant on the question of identity and motive."[30] However, as will be demonstrated, if one's fondness or predisposition to engage in certain activities is admissible to prove conduct in conformity with such a trait or inclination, then the ban on the use of character to prove conduct is effectively repealed.[31]

---

23. 229 Minn. 449, 39 N.W.2d 887 (1949). *Bock* illustrates another point. The ban on the use of character evidence to prove the commission of an act extends to any person, not just the accused, and applies in civil as well as criminal cases. See People v. Davis, 10 Cal.4th 463, 41 Cal.Rptr.2d 826, 844, 896 P.2d 119, 137 (1995).

24. State v. Bock, 229 Minn. 449, 458, 39 N.W.2d 887, 892 (1949).

25. 31 Cal.App.4th 494, 37 Cal.Rptr.2d 183 (1995).

26. Id. at 503, 37 Cal.Rptr.2d at 188.

27. C. McCormick, McCormick on Evidence § 190 (J. Strong 4th ed. 1992) (footnotes omitted).

28. 3 Cal.4th 41, 10 Cal.Rptr.2d 554, 833 P.2d 561 (1992), cert. denied, 507 U.S. 993, 113 S.Ct. 1604, 123 L.Ed.2d 166 (1993).

29. Id. at 125, 10 Cal.Rptr.2d at 599, 833 P.2d at 606.

30. Id.

31. See § 3.16 infra.

5. "To show, by similar acts or incidents, that the act in question was not performed inadvertently, accidentally, involuntarily, or without guilty knowledge."[32] In People v. Goodall[33] the accused was charged with possessing PCP for sale. Prior to the trial, the accused told the police that she would not recognize PCP if she saw it.[34] To prove that the accused was aware that contraband seized at her residence was PCP, the prosecution was permitted to offer evidence that on an earlier occasion a PCP lab had been found in a residence connected with the accused.[35]

Defendants charged with lewd conduct sometimes claim that the improper touching of the minor was accidental. Prosecutors attempt to undermine this claim by calling other minors who also testify to having been improperly touched by the accused. The testimony of the other minors is not inadmissible character evidence; the evidence is not offered to show that the accused committed the offense charged because he is the kind of person who molests children. Rather, the evidence is offered as proof that the accused touched the minor with the required mens rea because of the improbability that he touched all of the testifying minors accidentally.[36] As Professor Mark Cammack points out, "The probative value of the similar act evidence in disproving the claim of innocence rests on the improbability of non-recurrent similar events recurring by chance."[37]

---

32. C. McCormick, McCormick on Evidence § 190 (J. Strong 4th ed. 1992) (footnotes omitted).

33. 131 Cal.App.3d 129, 182 Cal.Rptr. 243 (1982).

34. Id. at 138, 182 Cal.Rptr. at 250.

35. Id. at 139–140, 182 Cal.Rptr. at 250–251. See also People v. Terry, 2 Cal.3d 362, 396, 85 Cal.Rptr. 409, 430–431, 466 P.2d 961, 982–983 (1970), cert. dism'd, 406 U.S. 912, 92 S.Ct. 1619, 32 L.Ed.2d 112 (1972) (Evidence that the accused was present at two robberies committed by a co-defendant was admissible to show that the accused was his accomplice at the robbery in issue, where the accused claimed that she was unaware that the co-defendant intended to commit the robbery.). Accord: People v. Garcia, 115 Cal.App.3d 85, 106–108, 171 Cal.Rptr. 169, 182–183 (1981) (Evidence that the accused was present when an accomplice committed a number of crimes was admissible to prove that the accused was not an innocent bystander when the accomplice killed a robbery victim.); People v. Westek, 31 Cal.2d 469, 480–481, 190 P.2d 9, 13–14 (1948) (Evidence that the accused performed lewd acts on other boys was admissible to show that the touching of the young boys in question was lustful and done without innocent intent.); People v. Honaker, 205 Cal.App.2d 243, 244–45, 22 Cal.Rptr. 829, 829–830 (1962) (Evidence that the accused improperly touched other girls was admissible to show that touching of the girl in question was not accidental.). See also People v. Thornton, 85 Cal.App.4th 44, 47, 101 Cal.Rptr.2d 825, 827 (2000) (In a prosecution for possessing heroin, evidence that the defendant admitted to police officers that he had used heroin on other occasions was admissible to prove his knowledge that the substance in a baggie found in his car was heroin.).

36. Where certain sexual offenses are charged, amendments to the Evidence Code and the Federal Rules of Evidence have mooted the prosecutors' need to establish a noncharacter use for the evidence of other sexual misdeeds by the accused. Prosecutors now may offer evidence of the accused's predisposition to engage in sexual misdeeds as proof that the accused committed enumerated sexual offenses. See § 3.14 supra.

37. Cammack, *Using the Doctrine of Chances to Prove Actus Reus in Child Abuse and Acquaintance Rape: People v. Ewoldt Reconsidered*, 29 U.C. Davis L. Rev. 355, 380 (1996). The California courts have relied on the doctrine of chances to uphold the use of prior misdeeds. See, e.g., People v. Carpenter, 15 Cal.4th 312, 379, 63 Cal.Rptr.2d 1, 38–39, 935 P.2d 708 (1997), cert. denied, 522 U.S. 1078, 118 S.Ct. 858, 139 L.Ed.2d 757 (1998) and cases cited therein. See also People v. Steele, 27 Cal.4th 1230, 1244, 120 Cal.Rptr.2d 432, 443, 47 P.3d 225, 234 (2002), cert. denied, 537 U.S. 1115, 123 S.Ct. 874, 154 L.Ed.2d 791 (2003) ("[T]he doctrine of chances teaches that the more often one does something, the more likely that something was intended, and even premeditated, rather than accidental or spontaneous."). Still, one must wonder whether the

The doctrine of chances has not been limited to cases involving child molestation. It has also been applied in homicide prosecutions to prove that the defendant did not kill the victim accidentally or in self-defense. In People v. Demetrulias,[38] for example, the prosecution offered evidence that the accused killed an elderly man named Wissel while robbing him, to rebut evidence by the defendant that he had killed the victim in self-defense. Both Wissel's and the victim's homicides occurred the same evening. In upholding the use of the evidence at the accused's murder trial, the court observed:

> The jury could rationally find it unlikely that defendant had the extremely bad luck to be attacked within a short period of time by two older solitary men in ways that required him to use potentially deadly force against the older men to repel the attacks. Especially given the evidence that defendant's assault on Wissel went far beyond any conceivable need for self-defense and that defendant then ransacked Wissel's house and stole from him, the jury could rationally infer instead that defendant probably attacked both men with the same criminal intent-robbery.[39]

6. "To establish motive."[40] Motive in turn may be used to prove the identity of the perpetrator or the mens rea of the offense charged. In People v. Linkenauger[41] the accused was charged with murdering his wife. To prove that the accused was the perpetrator, the court upheld the prosecution's use of evidence that on a number of occasions the accused had beaten his wife and accused her of engaging in extra-marital affairs. The evidence was not admitted to show that the accused was guilty of murder because he was the kind of man who would commit such an offense. Instead, it was admitted to show that the accused was the perpetrator because he had a motive to plan and carry out the premeditated murder of his wife. The court conceded that the circumstances attending the fatal attack and the prior attacks were insufficiently identical to earmark them as the work of the accused. Nonetheless, the court found that the evidence of marital discord was admissible to identify the accused as the perpetrator because "the prior misconduct and the charged offense

---

conclusion that it was improbable that the accused touched the victim accidentally isn't driven by the assumption that this must be the case because of the accused's propensity to engage in lewd acts, a character flaw which in light of the uncharged misdeed evidence the accused finds difficult or impossible to overcome. In this respect, the California Supreme Court's admonition is especially pertinent: "The inference of a criminal disposition may not be used to establish any link in the chain of logic connecting the uncharged offense with a material fact." People v. Thompson, 27 Cal.3d 303, 317, 165 Cal.Rptr. 289, 295, 611 P.2d 883, 889 (1980).

The doctrine of chances has not been limited to proving the mens rea but has been used also to prove the identity of the perpetrator of the offense charged. See, e.g., People v. Erving, 63 Cal.App.4th 652, 661–62, 73 Cal.Rptr.2d 815, 821 (1998), where evidence of 40 other fires occurring in neighborhoods where the accused lived was used to prove that the accused was the person who set the fires charged at her arson trial.

38. 39 Cal.4th 1, 137 P.3d 229, 45 Cal.Rptr.3d 407 (2006), cert. denied, 549 U.S. 1222, 127 S.Ct. 1282, 167 L.Ed.2d 102 (2007).

39. Id. at 16, 137 P.3d at 240, 45 Cal.Rptr.3d at 420.

40. C. McCormick, McCormick on Evidence § 190 (J. Strong 4th ed. 1992) (footnotes omitted).

41. 32 Cal.App.4th 1603, 38 Cal.Rptr.2d 868 (1995).

involve[d] the identical perpetrator and victim."[42] Similarly, in the survival action brought by the personal representative of Nicole Simpson against O. J. Simpson, evidence of O. J.'s prior abuse of Nicole was admissible to prove that he had a motive (jealousy) to kill Nicole, even though the circumstances attending the instances of prior abuse were not similar to those surrounding the fatal attack.[43]

Just as *Linkenauger* shows how evidence of motive can help identify the perpetrator of an offense, People v. Hill[44] illustrates how such evidence can help establish the mens rea of the offense charged. Hill was charged, among other offenses, with attempting to kill a convenience store clerk with a gun. Hill admitted shooting at the clerk but claimed that the gun discharged accidentally as he was backing out the store door. To prove that Hill fired the gun to eliminate the clerk as a witness, the prosecution was permitted to offer evidence that after his arrest Hill asked a friend to have the clerk killed: "the evidence permitted the inference that the defendant had a consciousness of guilt regarding his criminal state of mind and thus tended to prove defendant shot [the clerk] with an intent to kill."[45]

Racial or religious animus can likewise be offered to prove the mens rea of the offense charged. For example, racial epithets can be used to prove that the killing of a victim was premeditated and deliberate on account of his race.[46] Similarly, anti-religious statements can be used to show that the killing of a victim was premeditated and deliberate on account of her religious beliefs.[47] In People v. Nicolaus,[48] for example, the prosecution was allowed to prove the accused's intent to murder the victim by a written entry in which the accused confessed his hope "to live long enough to see the end of religion" and identified his victim as one of the "gang of four" Christians who had "been his downfall, my worst enemies."[49]

Gang affiliation and activity may also supply a motive linking the accused with a crime. In People v. Funes[50] the accused was prosecuted for murder. To prove that the accused committed the killing, the prosecution was allowed to offer evidence that the accused killed the victim in retaliation for the victim's gang's attacks on the accused's gang. To

---

42. Id. at 1613, 38 Cal.Rptr.2d at 874. When the accused's prior misdeeds are offered to link the accused with the charged offense by showing that he had a motive to commit the charged offense, the modus operandi or signature doctrine simply does not apply.

43. Rufo v. Simpson, 86 Cal.App.4th 573, 586, 103 Cal.Rptr.2d 492, 500 (2001).

44. 34 Cal.App.4th 727, 41 Cal.Rptr.2d 39 (1995).

45. Id. at 737, 41 Cal.Rptr.2d at 44.

46. People v. Quartermain, 16 Cal.4th 600, 627, 66 Cal.Rptr.2d 609, 625, 941 P.2d 788, 804 (1997) (The accused used racial epithets to describe the murder victim as well as members of the victim's race.).

47. See, e. g., People v. Nicolaus, 54 Cal.3d 551, 577–578, 286 Cal.Rptr. 628, 641–642, 817 P.2d 893, 906–907 (1991).

48. Id.

49. Id.

50. 23 Cal.App.4th 1506, 28 Cal.Rptr.2d 758 (1994).

establish the accused's motive for killing the victim, the prosecution was permitted to introduce evidence showing the accused's and victim's membership in rival gangs, and tracing the gangs' attacks on each other's members for a year.[51] But because gang membership, even when relevant, "may have a highly inflammatory impact on the jury, trial courts should carefully scrutinize such evidence before admitting it."[52] As a rule, trial judges should not admit evidence of gang membership and activity unless "it is logically relevant to some material issue in the case, other than character evidence, is not more prejudicial than probative, and is not cumulative."[53]

The accused's need for money may link him with the crime charged by showing that the accused had a motive for committing the offense.[54] But in California, evidence of the accused's "poverty or indebtedness generally is inadmissible to establish motive to commit robbery or theft, because reliance on poverty alone as evidence of motive is considered to be unfair to the defendant, and the probative value of such evidence is considered outweighed by the risk of prejudice."[55] The evidence, however, may be admitted for a limited purpose, to refute, for example, the accused's claim that he did not commit the robbery because he did not need money.[56]

Evidence that the accused is addicted to narcotics is probative of the proposition that the accused committed such offenses as robbery, burgla-

---

51. Id. at 1518, 28 Cal.Rptr.2d at 766. See also People v. Champion, 9 Cal.4th 879, 921–923, 39 Cal.Rptr.2d 547, 570, 891 P.2d 93, 115–117 (1995) (In a homicide prosecution, the accused's gang affiliation was admissible to show why the accused may have been concerned about whether a fellow gang member may have disclosed the accused's role in the killing.). Gang activity and affiliation may also be admissible when the prosecution requests an enhanced penalty on the theory that the accused committed the offense charged to promote a gang's criminal conduct. The evidence is not offered to prove the accused's predisposition to commit the offense charged but to prove the activities giving rise to the enhancement. People v. Martin, 23 Cal.App.4th 76, 82, 28 Cal.Rptr.2d 660, 664 (1994). Accord: People v. Sengpadychith, 26 Cal.4th 316, 324, 109 Cal. Rptr.2d 851, 857, 27 P.3d 739, 744 (2001) (California's Street Terrorism Enforcement and Prevention [enhancement] Act justifies admission of evidence of a gang's past and present offenses to prove that the group's primary activities include the commission of enumerated felonies.).

For a discussion of how gang affiliation may be used to impeach a witness for bias, see § 15.11 infra.

52. People v. Williams, 16 Cal.4th 153, 193, 66 Cal.Rptr.2d 123, 151, 940 P.2d 710, 738 (1997), cert. denied, 522 U.S. 1150, 118 S.Ct. 1169, 140 L.Ed.2d 179 (1998).

53. People v. Albarran, 149 Cal.App.4th 214, 223, 57 Cal.Rptr.3d 92, 100 (2007).

54. People v. Martin, 17 Cal.App.3d 661, 95 Cal.Rptr. 250 (1971) (sale of narcotics); People v. Gorgol, 122 Cal.App.2d 281, 265 P.2d 69 (1953) (theft); People v. Orloff, 65 Cal.App.2d 614, 151 P.2d 288 (1944) (also theft).

55. People v. Wilson, 3 Cal.4th 926, 939, 13 Cal.Rptr.2d 259, 266, 838 P.2d 1212, 1219 (1992), cert. denied, 507 U.S. 1006, 113 S.Ct. 1648, 123 L.Ed.2d 269 (1993). See also People v. Carrillo, 119 Cal.App.4th 94, 102, 13 Cal.Rptr.3d 878, 883 (2004): "As the court explained in United States v. Mitchell (9th Cir.1999) 172 F.3d 1104, 'Lack of money gives a person an interest in having more. But so does desire for money, without poverty. A rich man's greed is as much a motive to steal as a poor man's poverty. Proof of either, without more, is likely to amount to a great deal of unfair prejudice with little probative value.' (Id. at pp. 1108–1109 [reversing robbery conviction because the prosecutor introduced evidence of defendant's 'impecunious financial circumstances'].)"

56. Id.

ry, and theft in order to obtain funds to satisfy his addiction. But because of its potential to prejudice the jurors, the evidence is limited. The evidence may be offered to prove a motive for obtaining narcotics, but not for committing such offenses as robbery or burglary,[57] unless the accused gave his addiction as the reason for committing the offense.[58]

Evidence of an accused's parole status may furnish a motive connecting the accused with a crime. In People v. Powell[59] the prosecution was allowed to prove the accused's parole status as evidence of a motive to kill a police officer who had stopped the accused for a minor traffic violation. The evidence, according to the court, showed that the accused was the officer's killer, since the accused had a reason for killing the officer, i.e., a desire to avoid being returned to prison on an outstanding parole violation.[60]

Evidence that the accused had a reason for exacting revenge from the victims may also connect the accused with crimes committed against the victims. In People v. Daniels[61] the accused was prosecuted for murdering two police officers who came to his home to arrest him after he failed to appear at a hearing following the affirmance of a robbery conviction. The accused denied that he was the killer. To prove that he was the killer, the prosecution was permitted to show that a year earlier the accused had engaged in a shootout with the police officers who had responded to the robbery. Since the exchange of fire left the accused a paraplegic, the shootout evidence showed that the accused had a reason for killing the arresting officers: to avenge his own injuries.[62]

7.   "To establish opportunity, in the sense of access to or presence at the scene of the crime or in the sense of possessing distinctive or unusual skills or abilities employed in the commission of the crime charged."[63] Evidence, for example, that the accused bypassed alarm systems in committing burglaries would be admissible for the limited purpose of showing

57.   People v. Cardenas, 31 Cal.3d 897, 906, 184 Cal.Rptr. 165, 171–172, 647 P.2d 569, 575–576 (1982).

58.   People v. Felix, 23 Cal.App.4th 1385, 1392–1393, 28 Cal.Rptr.2d 860, 864 (1994) (The accused gave his narcotics addiction as the reason for committing the burglary with which he was charged.).

59.   40 Cal.App.3d 107, 115 Cal.Rptr. 109 (1974), cert. denied, 420 U.S. 994, 95 S.Ct. 1435, 43 L.Ed.2d 677 (1975).

60.   Id. at 154–155, 115 Cal.Rptr. at 139–140.

61.   52 Cal.3d 815, 277 Cal.Rptr. 122, 802 P.2d 906 (1991), cert. denied, 502 U.S. 846, 112 S.Ct. 145, 116 L.Ed.2d 111 (1991).

62.   Id. at 858, 277 Cal.Rptr. at 141, 802 P.2d at 925. Sometimes, it is unnecessary for the prosecution to offer evidence proving that the accused in fact committed the uncharged misdeed. In People v. Barnett, 17 Cal.4th 1044, 74 Cal.Rptr.2d 121, 954 P.2d 384 (1998), the prosecution offered evidence showing that a murder victim had complained to the police that the accused had vandalized his Jeep. The reviewing court held that it was unnecessary to connect the accused with the vandalism. The evidence was not offered to prove that the accused had in fact vandalized the Jeep but instead to show that he had a motive to seek revenge against the victim because of the victim's report to the police. On the day of the murder, the accused had complained that the victim had "turned him in" for vandalizing the Jeep. Id. at 1120, 74 Cal.Rptr.2d at 170, 954 P.2d at 433.

63.   C. McCormick, McCormick on Evidence § 190 (J. Strong 4th ed. 1992) (footnotes omitted).

that the accused had the knowledge needed to bypass the alarm in the burglary charged.[64] This kind of evidence, however, should not be confused with "profile" evidence, which is excludable as inadmissible character evidence.[65] Like motive, evidence of opportunity is probative of the perpetrator's identity and is listed in § 1101(b) as an example of evidence of misconduct used to show a fact other than character.[66]

Evidence that the accused possessed special knowledge required to commit the offense or had access to the weapons used must be treated with care. In People v. Archer[67] the prosecution sought to connect the accused with a stabbing by evidence that he owned seven knives. Only one of the knives tested presumptively for blood and only one other knife was identified by a witness as resembling the knife used to stab the victim. Admission of the other five knives was held to be error: their only relevance was to establish the accused as the kind of person who surrounds himself with deadly weapons.[68] Such bad character evidence is inadmissible to prove guilt.

Over the accused's objection, the prosecution also introduced several videotapes, books, and catalogs seized from the accused's home and storage locker. As the reviewing court explained, the materials constituted inadmissible bad character evidence:

> Some sections of the materials dealt with the use or purchase of knives. But the prosecutor did not limit the evidence to those materials. He included numerous other items with no relevance whatsoever to the issues at trial. We are unable to ascertain the probative value of these materials. There was no indication that the murder was performed in an unusual manner which required special training. Nor was there any indication that an exotic or unusual knife was used for the murder, which might have been ordered from a specialized catalogue such as the ones seized from appellant. All that can be shown from this large amount of reading and videotape material is that appellant had an interest in weapons and methods of using them. This interest has little or no probative value as to whether appellant murdered John Pate. But given the large amount of materials and their inflammatory nature, there is a strong possibility that the jury could infer that appellant had a propensity to act in accordance with his interests.[69]

By contrast, in People v. Gibson[70] the reviewing court approved the admission of two manuscripts from the defendant's home which described

---

64. Compare United States v. Barrett, 539 F.2d 244, 246 (1st Cir.1976).

65. For a discussion of "profile" evidence, see § 16.03 infra.

66. West's Ann.California Evidence Code § 1101(b). The federal analogue, Federal Rule of Evidence 404(b), also lists opportunity.

67. 82 Cal.App.4th 1380, 99 Cal.Rptr.2d 230 (2000).

68. Id. at 1392–1393, 99 Cal.Rptr.2d at 238.

69. Id. at 1394, 99 Cal.Rptr.2d at 238–239.

70. 90 Cal.App.4th 371, 108 Cal.Rptr.2d 809 (2001).

how to operate a prostitution enterprise. The defendant was prosecuted for pimping, and the manuscripts showed how she could have obtained the knowledge needed to run such an enterprise.[71]

8. "To show, without considering motive, that defendant acted with malice, deliberation, or the requisite specific intent."[72] In People v. Brogna[73] an issue was whether the accused harbored the malice aforethought required for murder at the time he struck and killed a bystander while driving under the influence. To prove that the accused was aware that drinking and driving posed a substantial risk to life, the prosecution offered evidence that the accused had previously been convicted of driving under the influence and, as a condition of probation, had attended meetings of Alcoholics Anonymous and participated in drinking driver education programs.[74] Since the evidence was not offered to prove the accused's propensity to commit the offense charged but instead to prove that he possessed the mental state of the offense, the court held that the evidence was admissible under § 1101(b).[75]

In People v. Ortiz[76] the court reached a similar conclusion but in somewhat different circumstances. Like Brogna, Ortiz was was charged with murder when as a result of a head-on collision some of the occupants of the oncoming car were killed. To prove that Ortiz was aware of the homicidal risk crossing a double yellow line posed to others, the prosecution was allowed to offer evidence that, as a result of a previous drunk driving conviction, Ortiz was required to attend a class in which the dangers of drunk driving were presented. Ortiz objected to the introduction of the evidence because the prosecution offered no evidence showing that he had consumed any alcoholic beverages on the day of the collision. The reviewing court upheld the use of the evidence: proof that Ortiz was presented with the dangers of drunk driving was probative of the proposi-

---

71. Id. at 382–383, 108 Cal.Rptr.2d at 816–817.

72. C. McCormick, McCormick on Evidence § 190 (J. Strong 4th ed. 1992) (footnotes omitted). Dean McCormick listed two additional purposes. One, identity, is subsumed by other purposes, such as motive, common scheme, opportunity, and distinctive characteristics. The other, impeaching the accused with past convictions, is discussed in § 15.07 infra.

73. 202 Cal.App.3d 700, 248 Cal.Rptr. 761 (1988).

74. Id. at 705, 248 Cal.Rptr. at 764.

75. Id. at 709–710, 248 Cal.Rptr. at 766. The court acknowledged that the convictions were not as probative of the accused's mental state as the drinking driver programs, which informed the accused of the physical and mental impairments produced by alcohol. Id. Whether misdemeanor convictions can be received over a hearsay objection to prove the underlying conduct giving rise to the conviction or conduct subsequent to the conviction is problematical, see § 12.03 infra, although courts and parties often miss the issue. See, e.g., People v. Johnson, 30 Cal.App.4th 286, 291–292, 36 Cal.Rptr.2d 4, 8 (1994) and cases cited therein.

See also People v. Evers, 10 Cal.App.4th 588, 598–599, 12 Cal.Rptr.2d 637, 643–644 (1992) (In a murder prosecution, evidence that the accused shook a child so violently as to render her a quadriplegic was admissible to show that the accused was aware that severely shaking the victim was likely to cause serious injury or death.); People v. Klvana, 11 Cal.App.4th 1679, 1685, 1700, 15 Cal.Rptr.2d 512, 515, 525 (1992) (In a murder prosecution, evidence that the accused had been denied hospital privileges because of mismanaging obstetric patients was admissible to prove that the accused was aware that the methods he used for delivering babies at issue exposed the babies to a substantial risk of death.).

76. 109 Cal.App.4th 104, 134 Cal.Rptr.2d 467 (2003).

tion that he must have been aware of the dangers posed by other forms of risky driving, including the dangers posed to oncoming traffic by crossing a double yellow line.[77] Although the evidence of attending a drunk driving class as a result of a drunk driving conviction was less probative of Ortiz's state of mind than of Brogna's, the reviewing court nonetheless held that the trial judge did not abuse his discretion under § 352 in admitting the evidence.[78]

California law requires a plaintiff to prove that a defendant acted with malice in order to recover punitive damages.[79] Malice is not confined to intentional conduct but embraces also "conduct which is carried on by the defendant with a willful and conscious disregard of the rights or safety of others."[80] To prove that a defendant acted in conscious disregard of her rights, a plaintiff in a sexual harassment suit is entitled to offer evidence that the defendant had been reprimanded for engaging in similar misconduct with others.[81]

Evidence of the accused's misdeeds may also be admissible to prove the victim's state of mind when that is relevant. In People v. Solis[82] the accused was charged with rape. Since under the California Penal Code consent is not a defense unless freely and voluntarily given,[83] the victim was allowed to tell the jury that she submitted because the accused warned her that he had killed his own brother.[84] In People v. Garrett[85] the accused was charged with threatening his wife with immediate bodily injury. Since that offense requires the prosecution to prove that, as a result of the threat, the victim experienced a sustained state of fear, the wife was permitted to explain why the accused's statements had that effect on her. Her explanation included knowing that the accused had been convicted of voluntary manslaughter after shooting a man and knowing that he had obtained a gun which he kept in their apartment following a skirmish with another man. In addition, the wife was allowed to tell the jury that the accused's threats induced fear because of the number of times he had beaten her in the past.[86]

Other crimes requiring proof of a victim's state of mind include making terrorist threats[87] and stalking.[88] Each of these offenses requires

---

77. Id. at 116, 134 Cal.Rptr.2d at 476.

78. Id. at 117, 134 Cal.Rptr.2d at 477.

79. West's Ann. California Civil Code § 3294(a).

80. Id.

81. Weeks v. Baker & McKenzie, 63 Cal.App.4th 1128, 1162, 74 Cal.Rptr.2d 510, 532 (1998).

82. 172 Cal.App.3d 877, 218 Cal.Rptr. 469 (1985).

83. West's Ann.California Penal Code § 261(a)(2) and (6). Consent is not, strictly speaking, a defense. Since in a rape case the prosecution must prove that the rape was accomplished against a person's will, West's Ann.California Penal Code § 261(a)(2) and (6), evidence that the victim consented simply casts doubts on this element.

84. People v. Solis, 172 Cal.App.3d 877, 884–887, 218 Cal.Rptr. 469, 472–474 (1985).

85. 30 Cal.App.4th 962, 36 Cal.Rptr.2d 33 (1994).

86. Id. at 965, 36 Cal.Rptr.2d at 36.

87. West's Ann. California Penal Code § 422.

the prosecution to prove that the accused's actions reasonably caused the victim to fear for her safety or suffer emotional distress.[89] Evidence of past domestic abuse is therefore admissible to show why the accused's actions caused the victim to fear for her safety or to suffer emotional distress.[90]

Sometimes, the accused's uncharged misdeeds may be relevant to a witness's state of mind. In People v. Hawkins[91] a prosecution witness testified that the accused had confessed committing the crimes for which he was on trial. On cross-examination, the defense impeached the witness with his preliminary hearing testimony in which the witness denied having heard the accused admit committing the crimes. Over objection, the witness testified on redirect that he lied at the preliminary hearing because he feared for his safety: when he appeared at the preliminary hearing he was in the same jail as the accused, who had stabbed the witness at the time of the confession. The reviewing court upheld the trial judge's ruling allowing the jury to hear about stabbing; the uncharged conduct was essential to explain why the witness made the statement used by the defense to impugn the witness's credibility.[92]

A codefendant's specific misdeeds may also be relevant to a defendant's state of mind. In People v. Escobar,[93] Escobar and Medina were tried for murder and kidnaping. To prove that he acted out of fear of Medina rather than with the intent to commit the offenses charged, Escobar was permitted to offer evidence that on several occasions Medina had been seen carrying a firearm.[94]

The reliability of opinions by mental health experts on the mental state of a patient depends in part on the accuracy and completeness of the information imparted by the patient. For example, the value of an expert's opinion that the accused was insane at the time he committed the offense will depend on whether the accused furnished the expert with complete and accurate information. Accordingly, a defense mental expert may be asked on cross-examination whether in relating his history the accused informed the expert that he had committed a violent act if committing

---

88. West's Ann. California Penal Code § 646.9(a).

89. People v. McCray, 58 Cal.App.4th 159, 172, 67 Cal.Rptr.2d 872, 881 (1997).

90. Id. Accord: People v. Zavala, 130 Cal.App.4th 758, 770, 30 Cal.Rptr.3d 398, 406 (2005).

91. 10 Cal.4th 920, 42 Cal.Rptr.2d 636, 897 P.2d 574 (1995).

92. Id. at 950–951, 42 Cal.Rptr.2d at 653, 897 P.2d at 591. Compare People v. Garcia, 89 Cal.App.4th 1321, 1335–1336, 107 Cal.Rptr.2d 889, 899 (2001) (holding that in a prosecution for spousal rape, the prosecution was entitled to offer evidence that the accused assaulted the victim a year after the rape to explain why the victim delayed reporting the rape for more than 15 months).

93. 48 Cal.App.4th 999, 55 Cal.Rptr.2d 883 (1996).

94. Id. at 1023, 55 Cal.Rptr.2d at 897. Of course, to be relevant to his state of mind, Escobar would have had to offer evidence that he was aware that Medina carried the firearm. See also People v. Alvarez, 14 Cal.4th 155, 216, 58 Cal.Rptr.2d 385, 422, 926 P.2d 365, 402 (1996), cert. denied, 522 U.S. 829, 118 S.Ct. 94, 139 L.Ed.2d 50 (1997) (To prove that she acted out of fear of Codefendant Alvarez rather than with the intent to commit the crimes charged against her, Codefendant Ross was entitled to tell the jury that her fear stemmed from having seen Alvarez assault a woman shortly before the commission of the offenses charged against her.).

such an act would affect the diagnosis.[95] The inquiry does not violate the ban on the use of character evidence. The violent act is not offered to prove the accused's propensity to commit the offense charged but to test the reliability of the expert's opinion.[96]

Questions regarding the reliability of testimony are not limited to expert evidence. They extend as well to lay testimony. One way lawyers try to persuade jurors to accept their witnesses' testimony is by offering evidence that corroborates some aspect of their testimony. In People v. Stern,[97] for example, the defendant was charged with attempted murder and using threats of physical injury to dissuade a witness from testifying. The witness testified that in the course of attempting to dissuade him from testifying, the defendant told him about assaulting another person. Over the defendant's objection, the trial judge allowed the prosecution to offer evidence regarding the assault. The reviewing court upheld the admission of the evidence. It was not offered to prove the defendant's propensity to inflict injury upon the witness but to support the witness's credibility by corroborating an aspect of his testimony.[98] Of course, the trial judge took the precaution of instructing the jurors not to consider the evidence of the uncharged assault as proof of the defendant's propensity to commit the crimes charged.

Despite the seeming ease with which the courts have applied § 1101(b), the subsection has been a source of difficulties. A number of factors account for the problems parties and courts have encountered in applying § 1101(b). One is misunderstanding the principle underlying the subsection. Another is the failure of courts to engage in the proper analysis in determining the admissibility of evidence offered under the subsection. A third is the failure of some courts to distinguish clearly between the kind of character evidence banned by § 1101(a) and the kind sanctioned by § 1101(b). Each of these factors bears examination.

Understanding § 1101(b). Section 1101(b) should not be confused with §§ 1102, 1103, 1108, and 1109. The latter are true exceptions to § 1101(a)'s ban on the use of character evidence to prove that the actor conformed his or her conduct with a character trait on a given occasion.[99] Section 1102 allows the accused to offer character evidence to show that he is not the kind of person who would commit the offense charged.[100] Similarly, § 1103 allows the accused to offer evidence of the victim's

---

95. People v. Coddington, 23 Cal.4th 529, 595, 97 Cal.Rptr.2d 528, 605, 2 P.3d 1081, 1142 (2000), cert. denied, 531 U.S. 1195, 121 S.Ct. 1199, 149 L.Ed.2d 113, overruled on other grounds, Price v. Superior Court, 25 Cal.4th 1046, 108 Cal.Rptr.2d 409, 25 P.3d 618 (2001).

96. Id.

97. 111 Cal.App.4th 283, 3 Cal.Rptr.3d 479 (2003).

98. 111 Cal.App.4th 283, 296, 3 Cal.Rptr.3d 479, 488.

99. Other sections creating exceptions to the character evidence ban include §§ 1108–1109. Section 1108 allows the prosecution to offer evidence of sexual misdeeds to prove the accused's predisposition to commit the sexual misdeed charged. § 1109 allows the prosecution to offer evidence of acts of domestic violence to prove the defendant's predisposition to commit an offense involving domestic violence.

100. West's Ann.California Evidence Code § 1102.

character to prove that the victim is the kind of person would engage in conduct that under the criminal law excuses or mitigates the misconduct charged against the defendant.[101] Section 1108 allows the prosecution to offer evidence of uncharged sexual offenses to prove the defendant's predisposition to commit the sexual offense charged.[102] Similarly, § 1109 allows the prosecution to offer evidence of uncharged acts of domestic violence to prove the accused's predisposition to commit such acts when charged with an offense involving domestic violence.[103] But § 1101(b) is not an exception to § 1101(a). Subsection (b) merely authorizes the use of specific act evidence when offered to prove a relevant proposition other than the actor's predisposition to conform his or her conduct to his or her character.

Analyzing § 1101(b) evidence. The fact that the use of proffered evidence may be authorized by § 1101(b) does not mean that the trial judge must admit it. A proper analysis of evidence authorized by § 1101(b) requires the judge to apply a three part test. First, the judge must resolve whether the evidence is being offered to prove a proposition within the ban of § 1101(a) or to prove the kind of proposition contemplated by § 1101(b). If the former, the evidence is inadmissible unless it falls within an exception.[104] If the evidence falls within § 1101(b), then the judge must determine whether the evidence is material, i.e., probative of a proposition that is properly provable in the action.[105] If it is not, the evidence must be excluded on grounds of irrelevance. If the evidence is material and therefore relevant, the judge must finally decide whether its probative value is substantially outweighed by its prejudicial effects.[106]

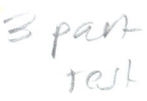

---

101.   West's Ann.California Evidence Code § 1103.

102.   West's Ann. California Evidence Code § 1108.

103.   West's Ann. California Evidence Code § 1109. Section 1109 also allows the prosecution to offer evidence of the accused's predisposition to abuse an elder or dependent adult in a case in which the accused is charged with committing an act of elder or dependent adult abuse. Id.

104.   Such evidence may be admissible if character is in issue, see § 3.05 supra, or under an exception to the character evidence ban.

105.   For a discussion of materiality as a component of relevance, see § 2.01 supra. In assessing the probative value of the proffered evidence, the judge is not limited to considering its value in proving only a single proper proposition. The specific bad act evidence may be offered to prove more than one such proposition. For example, evidence that the accused was involved in robbing victims attending other swap meets might be offered to prove his identity as the robber of the victim at the swap meet in the case being tried as well as his motive for robbing the victim. See, e.g., People v. Roldan, 35 Cal.4th 646, 705, 27 Cal.Rptr.3d 360, 407, 110 P.3d 289, 328, cert. denied, 546 U.S. 986, 126 S.Ct. 570, 163 L.Ed.2d 477 (2005).

106.   West's Ann.California Evidence Code § 352. For a discussion of a trial judge's functions under § 352, see § 2.10 supra.

Evidence of uncharged misdeeds that is weak can be easily outweighed by the countervailing concern that the jurors, despite limiting instructions, might consider the misdeeds as evidence of the accused's predisposition to commit the misdeed charged. That would be a good reason for excluding the evidence. In a curious reversal of this analysis, the California Supreme Court held that the uncharged misdeed evidence was properly admitted precisely because it was not highly probative of the proposition for which it was offered. In People v. Carpenter, 15 Cal.4th 312, 63 Cal.Rptr.2d 1, 935 P.2d 708 (1997), cert. denied 522 U.S. 1078, 118 S.Ct. 858, 139 L.Ed.2d 757 (1998), the accused was charged, among other offenses, with murder and attempted murder of two hikers in Santa Cruz County. To prove that he killed and attempted to kill the hikers with the mens rea of murder, the trial judge allowed the prosecution to offer evidence that on an earlier occasion the accused killed other hikers in Marin County. The California Supreme Court

In making the decision, the judge must weigh the need for the evidence against the risk that the jury might disregard instructions limiting their consideration of the evidence to the admissible purpose.[107] Other prejudicial effects the judge should consider include the sensational nature of the evidence[108] and its remoteness.[109] The need for the evidence, moreover, will be lessened if the evidence is merely cumulative[110] or if the purpose for which it is offered can be proved by other available evidence that is less prejudicial.[111]

The three part test is the product of applying the California Evidence Code sections on relevance and discretionary exclusion to § 1101(b). But it was not until People v. Thompson[112] that the California Supreme Court required trial judges to use the test in ruling on the admissibility of evidence offered under § 1101(b).[113]

One aspect of *Thompson* warrants elaborating. The court underscored that evidence offered under § 1101(b) should be excluded unless relevant to an ultimate fact actually in dispute or to an intermediate fact from

concurred with the trial judge's finding that so little evidence connected the accused with the Marin County killings that the jurors could find that the accused committed these killings only if they first found that he committed the Santa Cruz County killings. Instead of viewing the weakness of the Marin County killings as a reason for excluding those killings, the court approved their use as not being unduly prejudicial: "There was no danger the jury might doubt that he committed the charged offenses but convict anyway because of a belief he committed the uncharged crimes." Id. at 380, 63 Cal.Rptr.2d at 39, 935 P.2d at 746. But if that was the case, there was no need for evidence of doubtful probative value but that nonetheless carried the risk of misuse as character evidence. As the *Carpenter* court itself noted, because "[e]vidence of uncharged crimes is inherently prejudicial," it should be excluded unless "it has substantial probative effect." Id.

107. Although trial judges should give limiting instructions on their own motion, they generally do not have a sua sponte duty to do so. Accordingly, the party opposing the evidence should request the judge to give the appropriate limiting instruction. See People v. Hernandez, 33 Cal.4th 1040, 1051, 16 Cal.Rptr.3d 880, 889, 94 P.3d 1080, 1087 (2004).

108. People v. Anderson, 43 Cal.3d 1104, 1137, 240 Cal.Rptr. 585, 604, 742 P.2d 1306, 1324 (1987) (In a murder prosecution it was not error to admit evidence that the accused had earlier proposed robbing a gasoline station because the evidence was not sensational or inflammatory.).

109. Compare People v. Douglas, 50 Cal.3d 468, 788 P.2d 640, 268 Cal.Rptr. 126 (1990), cert. denied, 498 U.S. 1110, 111 S.Ct. 1023, 112 L.Ed.2d 1105 (1991) (Three years is not remote.) with People v. Thomas, 20 Cal.3d 457, 143 Cal.Rptr. 215, 573 P.2d 433 (1978) (Ten years is too remote.).

110. People v. Schader, 71 Cal.2d 761, 775, 80 Cal.Rptr. 1, 9, 457 P.2d 841, 849 (1969).

111. See, e.g., Federal Rule of Evidence 403 (Advisory Committee Note).

112. 27 Cal.3d 303, 165 Cal.Rptr. 289, 611 P.2d 883 (1980). Despite occasional pronouncements to the contrary, see, e.g., People v. Thornton, 85 Cal.App.4th 44, 48–49, 101 Cal.Rptr.2d 825, 828 (2000), *Thompson* is still good law for the points cited. For additional discussion of this point, see § 3.18 infra.

113. People v. Thompson, 27 Cal.3d 303, 315, 165 Cal.Rptr. 289, 294, 611 P.2d 883, 888 (1980). Defense lawyers, not just judges, have a responsibility to guard against the unjustified admission of evidence of prior misdeeds. "One of the principal tasks of a defense attorney is to attempt to protect his or her client from the admission of evidence that is more prejudicial than probative, and that obligation clearly applies to efforts made by the prosecution to introduce evidence of prior crimes or acts of violence alleged to have been committed by a defendant when such crimes are unrelated to the charged offense." In re Jones, 13 Cal.4th 552, 581–582, 54 Cal.Rptr.2d 52, 68, 917 P.2d 1175, 1191 (1996). The failure by defense counsel to object to such evidence can constitute ineffective assistance of counsel. Id. at 582–583, 54 Cal.Rptr.2d at 69, 917 P.2d at 1192.

which an ultimate fact can be inferred.[114] Obviously, the court had more in mind than just materiality, for evidence is material if it is probative of any proposition that is properly provable in the action, not just intermediate or ultimate propositions.[115] Two concerns account for the court's limitations on § 1101(b) evidence. One is the danger that the evidence may be misused by jurors for a character purpose condemned by § 1101(a).[116] The other is the risk that the evidence is most harmful when offered against a criminal defendant.[117] Accordingly, the court held that a judge should exclude § 1101(b) evidence in a criminal case unless it is substantially probative of an important, contested proposition.[118]

Evidence of other misdeeds and the Federal Rules. Like the Code, the Federal Rules allow evidence of other crimes, wrongs, and acts when offered to prove a relevant proposition other than that a person acted in accordance with his or her character on a particular occasion.[119] The Federal Rules, however, add a condition to the use of such evidence in criminal cases: upon request by the accused, the prosecution must provide reasonable notice in advance of trial, or during trial if the court excuses pretrial notice on good cause shown, of the general nature of any such evidence it intends to introduce at trial.[120]

The purpose of the notice requirement is to reduce surprise and promote early resolution of issues of admissibility.[121] The prosecution is required to provide the notice, regardless of whether it intends to use the evidence in its case-in-chief, in impeaching witnesses, or in rebuttal.[122] Failure to comply with the notice requirements can result in the exclusion of the evidence.[123]

§ 3.16   LINGERING DIFFICULTIES: THE COMMON PLAN CONUNDRUM, CORROBORATION, AND INTERMEDIATE PROPOSITIONS

The common plan conundrum. At times it is difficult to distinguish between evidence banned under § 1101(a) as inadmissible character evidence and evidence offered under § 1101(b) as proof of some relevant

---

114. People v. Thompson, 27 Cal.3d 303, 315, 165 Cal.Rptr. 289, 294, 611 P.2d 883, 888 (1980).

115. See § 2.01 supra.

116. People v. Thompson, 27 Cal.3d 303, 316–317, 165 Cal.Rptr. 289, 294, 611 P.2d 883, 888 (1980).

117. *Thompson* is a criminal case. Although § 1101(b) applies to civil cases as well, the prejudicing potential of Subsection (b) evidence is likely to be highest in criminal cases when the misdeeds offered against the accused are similar to the misdeed for which the accused is on trial.

118. People v. Thompson, 27 Cal.3d 303, 318, 165 Cal.Rptr. 289, 294, 611 P.2d 883, 888 (1980).

119. Federal Rule of Evidence 404(b).

120. Id.

121. Id. (Advisory Committee Note).

122. Id.

123. Id.

proposition other than the actor's predisposition to engage in such conduct. The problem is often most acute in sex prosecutions when the theory of admissibility is common design or common scheme.

The Tassell approach. Tassell was prosecuted for rape and oral copulation.[1] As part of its case-in-chief the prosecution called two other women who testified that they too had been raped by Tassell under circumstances similar to those described by the complaining witness.[2] The prosecution's theory was that the evidence was admissible to show "common design or plan."[3] The California Supreme Court held that it was error to admit the evidence of the uncharged offenses on such a theory. Merely invoking the common plan or scheme incantation will not supply the foundation required for the use of evidence of past misdeeds under this theory. To use this theory, the prosecution must first identify the noncharacter proposition to which the evidence of common plan or scheme is directed. According to the court, the uncharged offenses could not have been offered to prove the perpetrator's identity since Tassell had conceded that he had had sex with the victim but claimed only that the act was consensual.[4] Moreover, the uncharged offenses could not have been offered to prove the defendant's intent to rape the victim because in the court's view "[n]o rational argument would [have] support[ed] a contention that the three sets of sex crimes were part of one larger plan."[5] Accordingly, the court concluded that the uncharged offense evidence was probative only of the accused's predisposition to commit the sexual offenses charged.[6] In reaching this result, the court disapproved of cases ignoring the requirement that evidence of misdeeds offered under common plan or design must be probative of an issue other than the accused's predisposition to commit the offense charged.[7]

---

1. People v. Tassell, 36 Cal.3d 77, 201 Cal.Rptr. 567, 679 P.2d 1 (1984).

2. Id. at 82–83, 201 Cal.Rptr. at 569–570, 679 P.2d at 3–4.

3. Id. The prosecution also claimed that the evidence was admissible to corroborate the testimony of the complaining witness. Id. The use of the evidence for this purpose has been disapproved. People v. Thomas, 20 Cal.3d 457, 143 Cal.Rptr. 215, 573 P.2d 433 (1978).

4. 36 Cal.3d at 81, 201 Cal.Rptr. at 568, 679 P.2d at 2.

5. Id. at 88–89, 201 Cal.Rptr. at 574, 679 P.2d at 8.

6. Id.

7. Id. at 88–89, note 8, 201 Cal.Rptr. at 574, note 8, 679 P.2d at 8, note 8.

In his dissent, Justice Reynoso took the position that the evidence of the other rapes was admissible on the issue of whether the accused reasonably and in good faith believed that the victim had consented. Id. at 92–96, 201 Cal.Rptr. at 576–579, 679 P.2d at 10–13. In California, rape is a negligence offense. People v. Mayberry, 15 Cal.3d 143, 125 Cal.Rptr. 745, 542 P.2d 1337 (1975). Where the accused claims consent, the prosecution must prove beyond a reasonable doubt that the victim did not consent and that a reasonable person in the accused's situation would not have concluded that the victim had consented. Id. at 153–158, 125 Cal.Rptr. at 752–755, 542 P.2d at 1344–1347. In 1986 the Legislature amended § 1101(b) to add that subsection (a) does not prohibit the use of uncharged offenses in sex offense cases to prove that the accused did not reasonably and in good faith believe that the victim consented. West's Ann.California Evidence Code § 1101 (Historical and Statutory Notes).

Although aspects of *Tassell* are still good law, the need to offer evidence of the accused's sexual misdeeds on a noncharacter theory has been virtually eliminated by amendments to the Evidence Code. As of 1996, California prosecutors may offer the accused's sexual misdeeds as evidence of

Tassell's central teaching—that the proponent first identify the non-character purpose to which evidence of common scheme is directed—has not been fully appreciated. In People v. Stark,[8] for example, neither the proponent nor the reviewing court identified such a proposition, even though the court acknowledged *Tassell's* applicability.

Stark, a Scoutmaster, was convicted of engaging in lewd and lascivious conduct with a child who was a Scout Troop member. Four other Scouts were permitted to describe acts by Stark that were similar to those described by the victim. In upholding the use of the evidence, the court said:

> Here, the evidence demonstrates a common scheme and plan of Stark's to (1) use his position of authority to meet boys about age 12, and (2) obtain their trust, then (3) initiate physical contact which (4) became sexual in nature during night time periods sleeping near the children, with (5) the type of sex act (fondling of penis followed by Stark's oral copulation) and (6) the location of the activity (Stark's home, car, and campouts) being remarkably similar in all cases. Thus, as we have seen, in this case the evidence of Stark's other offenses had much material value here in resolving the issues in dispute.[9]

Undoubtedly, the testimony of the other Scouts was probative of the proposition that Stark committed the offenses against the victim. But that was not the issue raised by the accused. Rather, the question was whether the evidence was *improperly* received to prove that Stark was guilty because he was the kind of man who would molest the victim or whether the evidence was *properly* received to prove a noncharacter proposition that was nonetheless relevant in establishing Stark's guilt. As *Tassell* emphasized, merely invoking the "common scheme or plan" incantation is insufficient: unless explicitly aimed at proving some other relevant proposition, evidence of common plan or scheme is probative of the very proposition condemned by § 1101(a).[10]

That point has eluded some federal judges as well. As the Seventh Circuit has warned, unless aimed at a clearly identified noncharacter proposition, evidence that the accused engaged in similar misdeeds on other occasions is proof that the accused committed the misdeed charged precisely because he is the kind of person who would commit such a misdeed:

---

the accused's predisposition to commit the sexual misdeed charged. For a discussion of the amendment, see § 3.14 supra.

8. 4 Cal.App.4th 1407, 6 Cal.Rptr.2d 408 (1992), opinion vac'd 13 Cal.App.4th 1357, 11 Cal.Rptr.2d 207 (1992), review granted and opinion superseded 13 Cal.Rptr.2d 510, 839 P.2d 1018 (1992).

9. Id. at 1426, 6 Cal.Rptr.2d at 417–18.

10. Amendments to the Evidence Code have mooted the issue raised by Mr. Stark. As of 1996, prosecutors may offer evidence of other sexual misdeeds to prove the accused's predisposition to commit the sexual misdeed charged. For a discussion of these changes to the Code, see § 3.14 supra.

Some language in the government's brief suggests that any commission of similar crimes is the sort of "pattern" that permits the evidence to come in. * * * A rule that a judge may admit all evidence that the defendant committed crimes of similar varieties produces the gravest risk of offending the central prohibition of Rule 404(b): "Evidence of other crimes, wrongs, or acts is not admissible to prove the character of a person in order to show that he acted in conformity therewith." The inference from "pattern" by itself is *exactly* the forbidden inference that one who violated the drug laws on one occasion must have violated them on the occasion charged in the indictment. Unless something more than a pattern and temporal proximity is required, the fundamental rule is gone. * * * Patterns of acts may *show* identity, intent, plan, absence of mistake, or one of the other listed grounds, but a pattern is not itself a reason to admit the evidence.[11]

The Ewoldt approach. In People v. Ewoldt[12] the California Supreme Court attempted once more to clarify the use of the plan doctrine as a noncharacter theory of admissibility. Ewoldt, like Stark, was prosecuted for engaging in lewd and lascivious conduct with a child. The victim's sister was permitted to describe acts which Ewoldt committed with her and which were similar to the acts described by the victim. The accused denied engaging in lewd and lascivious conduct with the victim. But to prevent the prosecution from offering the sister's testimony on the issue of his intent with the victim, the accused offered to stipulate to the requisite intent if the jurors found that he had committed the acts charged. The California Court of Appeal reversed Ewoldt's conviction, holding that the trial judge erred in admitting the sister's testimony in the absence of evidence that the accused committed the charged and uncharged offenses as part of a single plan. The California Supreme Court in turn reversed and announced a new test for determining the admissibility of uncharged misdeeds when offered under the plan doctrine.

Before focusing on *Ewoldt*'s new test, it is important to identify those aspects of *Tassell* that survived *Ewoldt*. *Ewoldt* left undisturbed *Tassell*'s central teaching that plan evidence is inadmissible unless the prosecution first identifies the noncharacter proposition to which the evidence is directed. *Ewoldt* also left untouched the principle that unconnected misdeeds do not support a plan theory of admissibility. On the contrary, *Ewoldt* stresses that the plan theory requires the prosecution to offer evidence of a common plan that goes beyond mere proof that the charged and uncharged misdeeds produced similar results.[13] Thus, *Ewoldt*, like *Tassell*, rejects the concept that spontaneous or unconnected misdeeds can be the product of a plan.[14] Finally, *Ewoldt* does not quarrel with the proposition that, unless offered under an identifiable noncharacter theory,

---

11.   United States v. Beasley, 809 F.2d 1273, 1277–1278 (1987) (emphasis in the original).

12.   7 Cal.4th 380, 27 Cal.Rptr.2d 646, 867 P.2d 757 (1994).

13.   Id.

14.   Id.

unconnected misdeeds give rise only to the inference that the accused committed the misdeed charged because of a predisposition to commit such an offense.[15]

Ewoldt took issue primarily with that portion of *Tassell* which requires the prosecution to prove that the charged and uncharged offenses are "part of a single, continuing conception or plot" and disapproved of *Tassell* and its progeny to that extent.[16] *Ewoldt*, instead, holds that the prosecution can establish the foundation for using the common plan doctrine by evidence that the "uncharged misconduct and the charged offense are sufficiently similar to support the inference that they are manifestations of a common design or plan."[17] Because *Ewoldt*'s test is less stringent than *Tassell*'s single plot test, *Ewoldt* raises a serious question about whether its test will prove to be as effective as *Tassell*'s in preventing the misuse of plan evidence as character evidence.

Assessing *Ewoldt*'s efficacy in this regard requires a review of how the law of evidence defines relevance in the context of character evidence claims. Assume that D is prosecuted for killing B. To prove that D killed B, the prosecution calls W who testifies that D told W that he killed B as part of a plan to kill A and B. W, who was not present when D allegedly killed B, also testifies that he saw D kill A. May W's testimony that he saw D kill A be received without violating the ban on the use of character evidence?

The answer is yes. The jury is not being asked to find that D killed B on the basis that, because he killed A, D is the kind of man who kills. That, as we have seen, is precisely the inference which the ban on the use of character evidence condemns. Rather, the jury is being asked to find that D killed B because he killed him as part of a plan to kill A and B. To protect D against the misuse of the evidence as character evidence, D is entitled to have the jurors instructed to consider the evidence only for its admissible, noncharacter purpose.[18]

The judge, however, may still exclude W's testimony that he saw D

---

15. People v. Scheer, 68 Cal.App.4th 1009, 80 Cal.Rptr.2d 676 (1998), provides an example of the insufficiency of unconnected misdeeds as proof of a common plan. Scheer was charged with felony hit and run. To counter evidence that his departure from the accident scene resulted from a concussion rather than from a desire to leave the scene, the prosecution was allowed to offer evidence that on an earlier occasion the defendant fled from police officers after committing a traffic infraction. "We * * * conclude the prior flight evidence was not admissible to prove a common plan or design. Although the prior flight offense and charged crime were committed in a similar manner, i.e., appellant drove through residential areas recklessly with flagrant disregard for the safety of others, and shared the same general purpose of avoiding capture and accountability for his misdeeds, such characteristics are insufficiently probative to constitute evidence of a common plan or design. Instead, the only reasonable inference is that the prior flight and the charged crime were spontaneous events. * * * Neither flight was a planned event. Instead, each was a spur of the moment response to an unexpected event, i.e., the sudden appearance of the police in the prior instance and the attempt by volunteer bystanders to detain him after the accidental collision in the other." Id. at 1021, 80 Cal.Rptr.2d at 682.

16. Id. at 401, 27 Cal.Rptr.2d at 658, 867 P.2d at 769.

17. Id.

18. West's Ann. California Evidence Code § 403.

kill A. Under Evidence Code § 352,[19] a judge may exclude relevant evidence whenever its probative value on contested issues outweighs its prejudicial effects on the adverse party. Because this portion of W's testimony is also probative of the proposition that D killed B because of his predisposition to kill (as evidenced by his killing A), a judge could conclude that the risk is simply too great that the jurors would be unable to abide by the limiting instruction.

A review of the principles relating to relevance confirms the validity of this analysis. An item of evidence is relevant if it is probative of a material proposition.[20] A material proposition in this case is that D killed B. Evidence that D killed B as part of a plan to kill A and B is probative of that proposition because the evidence renders the proposition that D killed B more likely than it would be without the evidence.[21] But the same evidence is also probative of D's predisposition to kill. The proposition that D is predisposed to kill is rendered more likely by evidence that he killed A (whether or not pursuant to a plan) than that proposition would be without the evidence. Evidence that D is predisposed to kill in turn is probative of the material proposition that he killed B, because that proposition is rendered more likely by evidence of D's inclination to kill than the proposition would be without the evidence. That evidence may be susceptible to two interpretations, one which is admissible while the other is not, is not a new dilemma to the rules of evidence. The rules resolve this conflict by providing that evidence which is inadmissible for one purpose may nonetheless be received for an admissible purpose.[22] Thus, judges who allow W to testify that he saw D kill A would be invoking this principle and would instruct the jurors to consider the evidence only for the admissible noncharacter purpose.

The type of testimony that W would provide does not pose unusually severe evidentiary problems. D's admission to W (which the judge, for purposes of admissibility, must assume to be true) that he killed B as part of a plan to kill A and B provides persuasive evidence that D may have killed B as a result of the plan. Though the evidence is susceptible to a character interpretation, W's testimony does provide a basis for a non-character finding that D may have killed B pursuant to a plan.

Serious problems, however, arise when the prosecution, as in *Tassell* and *Ewoldt*, relies only on circumstantial evidence to prove the plan. Suppose that the only evidence of a plan consists of W's testimony that he saw D kill A. Should a judge exclude the evidence on the ground that it is probative solely of D's character? The most powerful argument against exclusion is that the evidence is also probative of the proposition that D killed B as part of a plan to kill A and B. As a matter of relevance, the proposition that D killed B pursuant to the plan is rendered more likely by

---

19.   West's Ann. California Evidence Code § 352.

20.   West's Ann. California Evidence Code § 210; Federal Rule of Evidence 401.

21.   See West's Ann. California Evidence Code § 210; Federal Rule of Evidence 401.

22.   West's Ann. California Evidence Code § 355; Federal Rule of Evidence 105.

evidence that D killed A than the proposition would be without the evidence.

The strongest argument against admission is that the evidence is equally probative of the opposite proposition, namely that the killings of A and B were unconnected. If in fact they were unconnected, then in the absence of some other noncharacter justification, evidence that D killed A would be probative *only* of the proposition that D is the kind of person who kills, and the ban on the use of character evidence would prohibit using W's testimony as a basis for inferring that D killed B.

The validity of this analysis is confirmed when W's testimony is viewed from D's perspective. If D's objective is to show that the two killings are unconnected or spontaneous, D could do so simply by offering evidence that A was killed on one day and B on another. From a relevance perspective, the proposition that the killings are unconnected is rendered more likely by evidence that the killings occurred on different days than the proposition would be without the evidence. The problem with the circumstantial use of past misdeeds to prove a common plan, then, is that in many cases the evidence is equally probative of the proposition that the accused committed the charged misdeed because of his predisposition (or character) to commit such misdeeds.

How serious is the risk that the jurors will be unable to abide by an appropriate limiting instruction? As is pointed out in § 3.09, social scientists have found that people routinely use character-type reasoning in making everyday decisions. Three aspects of their research are especially troubling in a court setting. First, people tend to remember the bad about others rather than the good. Thus, jurors hearing about the accused's uncharged misdeeds are likely to remember them in reaching their verdict and may well ignore countervailing evidence about the accused's good deeds. Second, social scientists have found that past behavior is generally a poor basis for predicting future behavior. Just because D may have killed A does not mean that he may have killed B. Whether or not the first killing tells us anything about the second one depends on the similarity of the circumstances attending the two killings. Even trivial differences in the two settings can reduce the value of the prediction to zero. Third, people not only use past behavior to predict future behavior, but tend to overestimate the effect of past behavior on future behavior. If the jurors hear that D killed A, they are likely to jump to the unwarranted conclusion that he killed B.

To be sure, neither the California courts nor the Legislature has relied on the social science studies in restricting the admissibility of character evidence. But the legal limitations on the use of character evidence nonetheless reflect the law's abiding suspicion about the dangerousness of this kind of evidence. That is why, as a rule, character evidence is inadmissible to prove that a person conformed his conduct to his "character." Moreover, even when aspects of a person's past behavior are offered for a noncharacter purpose, judges retain the authority to exclude the evidence if the risks are nonetheless too great that the jurors, despite limiting instructions, might misuse the evidence as character evidence.

Tassell's analysis reflects these concerns about the common plan doctrine. First, *Tassell* reaffirms *Thompson*'s holding[23] that prosecutors should be precluded from offering plan evidence unless it is probative of important, contested issues.[24] Second, *Tassell* requires prosecutors to offer evidence that the charged and uncharged misdeeds are indeed the product of a single plan.[25] Only then can the probative value of the evidence on contested issues justify the risk of misuse by the jurors. Thus, under *Tassell*, evidence that the charged and uncharged misdeeds gave rise to similar results would be insufficient to justify the admissibility of the uncharged misdeeds as evidence of a common plan. Evidence in addition to testimony that D killed A and that B was found dead would be required for the prosecution to get the killing of A before the jury.

Ewoldt does not ignore these concerns. But *Ewoldt* parts company with *Tassell* by relaxing *Tassell*'s requirement that judges should exclude plan evidence unless the prosecution offers substantial evidence that the charged and uncharged misdeeds were the product of a single plan. Instead, *Ewoldt* requires the prosecution to show only "such a concurrence of common features [between the charged and uncharged misdeeds] that the various acts are naturally to be explained as caused by a general plan of which they are the individual manifestations."[26] Whether this lower standard undermines the protection which *Tassell* afforded to the accused has now become the overriding policy question. Consideration of another noncharacter theory of relevance sheds important light on the answer.

It is settled that prosecutors may offer evidence of uncharged misdeeds by the accused to prove that the accused committed the charged misdeed if the unique circumstances attending the commission of the uncharged and charged misdeeds are so distinctive as to suggest that only one person—the accused—committed the charged misdeed.[27] Though this evidence is also susceptible to a character interpretation (the accused committed the charged misdeed because, given his past misdeeds, he is the kind of person who would commit the charged misdeed), the risk that the evidence may be misused for a character purpose is believed to be outweighed by its substantial value as proof that the accused was the perpetrator of the crime charged. To assure that the evidence possesses that high degree of probative value, courts prohibit prosecutors from using this route to get evidence of the accused's uncharged misdeeds before the jury unless they are convinced that the similarities between the charged

---

23. People v. Thompson, 27 Cal.3d 303, 318, 165 Cal.Rptr. 289, 294, 611 P.2d 883, 888 (1980).

24. People v. Tassell, 36 Cal.3d 77, 88–89, note 8, 201 Cal.Rptr. 567, 574, note 8, 679 P.2d 1, 8, note 8 (1984).

25. Id.

26. People v. Ewoldt, 7 Cal.4th 380, 401, 27 Cal.Rptr.2d 646, 658, 867 P.2d 757, 769 (1994).

27. See People v. Tassell, 36 Cal.3d 77, 86, 201 Cal.Rptr. 567, 572, 679 P.2d 1, 6 (1984).

and uncharged misdeeds are so great as to warrant a finding that only the accused could have committed the charged misdeed.

Prosecutors, however, do not always have access to that kind of evidence. Prosecutors, therefore, may look for alternative theories of admissibility which do not impose such rigorous requirements. *Tassell* can be read as forestalling the use of the plan theory as an alternative by requiring prosecutors to offer compelling evidence that the charged and uncharged misdeeds were the product of a single plan. But by disapproving this aspect of *Tassell*, *Ewoldt* threatens to undermine the protection that *Tassell* afforded to criminal defendants.

The magnitude of the threat can be estimated by considering *Ewoldt*'s specification of the sufficiency of the evidence the prosecution must produce to invoke the plan theory. In specifying the foundational requirements, *Ewoldt* distinguished "the nature and degree of similarity (between uncharged misconduct and the charged offense) required * * * to establish a common design or plan, from the degree of similarity required to prove intent or identity."[28] According to the court, the least degree of similarity is required when the evidence of uncharged offenses is offered to prove intent.[29] The highest degree is required when the evidence of the uncharged misdeeds is offered to identify the accused as the perpetrator of the misdeed charged.[30] But only an intermediate degree of similarity is required when the uncharged misdeeds are offered in support of a claim that the accused committed the charged misdeed as part of a plan to commit the charged and uncharged misdeeds.[31] Thus, it is apparent from the court's own analysis that when prosecutors lack the evidence to satisfy the identity test they can use the same evidence to try to satisfy the plan test. *Tassell*'s single plan test can be viewed as the functional equivalent of the similarity test of the modus operandi doctrine. Both are designed to withhold evidence of uncharged offenses from the jurors unless the commission of the charged and uncharged offenses is highly similar. Though *Ewoldt* requires prosecutors to offer more evidence than just similarity of results to invoke the plan doctrine, its rejection of the *Tassell* test signals the court's unwillingness to allow *Tassell* to continue to play the same prophylactic role as does the modus operandi doctrine. Consequently, under *Ewoldt*, more evidence of uncharged misdeeds will be received against the accused.

In fairness to the *Ewoldt* court, requiring a high degree of similarity in the commission of the charged and uncharged misdeeds will not dispel entirely the risk that the jurors will misuse the evidence as proof of character. Obviously, the greater the similarity in the manner in which the charged and uncharged misdeeds is committed, the greater is the likelihood that only the accused committed the charged misdeed (modus

---

28. People v. Ewoldt, 7 Cal.4th 380, 402, 27 Cal.Rptr.2d 646, 658, 867 P.2d 757, 769 (1994).

29. Id.

30. Id.

31. Id.

operandi theory) or that he committed the misdeed charged as part of single plan to commit the charged and uncharged misdeeds (*Tassell*'s plan theory). But so is the likelihood that the accused committed the charged misdeed precisely because the accused is the kind of person who would commit such a misdeed. The uncharged misdeeds, after all, would be convincing evidence that the accused is indeed predisposed to commit such offenses.[32] The fact is that any noncharacter theory of admissibility relying on the similarity between the charged and uncharged misdeeds carries a heightened risk that the jurors will misuse the evidence as proof of the accused's character to commit the offense charged. But, as has been noted, the law of evidence resolves this dilemma—not by banning the use of other crimes evidence—but by balancing its value as proof of a noncharacter proposition against the risk that it might be misused as proof of character. *Tassell* and the modus operandi theory at least reduce that risk by limiting the circumstances in which evidence of uncharged misdeeds can be received as proof of a noncharacter purpose.

Ewoldt poses problems for jurors as well as criminal defendants. *Ewoldt* holds that "evidence of a common design or plan is admitted not to prove the defendant['s] intent or identity, but to prove that the defendant engaged in the conduct alleged to constitute the charged offense."[33] It may be that the court was attempting to prevent prosecutors who cannot meet the rigorous modus operandi test from falling back on the plan doctrine to prove that the accused was the perpetrator of the offense charged. But that goal, commendable as it may be, creates a serious problem for the jurors. Applied to *Ewoldt*, evidence that Ewoldt molested the victim's sister would be admissible to prove only that he engaged in acts of molestation with the victim as part of a plan to molest both sisters *but not to prove that he was the one who engaged in such acts with the victim*. How jurors are expected to abide by such a conflicting instruction is left unexplained by the court.[34]

Without repealing the plan doctrine, the risk that jurors may misuse evidence in support of a plan as character evidence can be eliminated in only one way: judges could require the prosecution to offer only direct evidence of the plan. But unless the accused has in some manner divulged his plans prior to the trial, such helpful admissions are simply unavailable to prosecutors in most cases. The risks associated with the doctrine can be

---

32. "[I]f the prior offenses are very similar in nature to the charged offenses, the prior offenses have greater probative value in proving propensity to commit the charged offenses." People v. Branch, 91 Cal.App.4th 274, 285, 109 Cal.Rptr.2d 870, 878 (2001). Although the court made this observation in connection with California Evidence Code § 1108, which allows evidence of other sexual misconduct to be used to prove the accused's predisposition to commit the sexual misconduct charged, the observation applies as well to all bad acts evidence regardless of the type of prosecution in which the evidence is offered.

33. People v. Ewoldt, 7 Cal.4th 380, 399, 27 Cal.Rptr.2d 646, 657, 867 P.2d 757, 768 (1994).

34. Although *Ewoldt* is not limited to sexual offense prosecutions, its holding has been rendered moot in the prosecution of certain sexual offenses. Amendments to the Code now allow prosecutors to offer evidence of other sexual misdeeds by the accused as proof of the accused's predisposition to commit the sexual misdeed charged. See § 3.14 supra. Thus, in these prosecutions the trial judge can avoid the conflicting instruction by simply admitting the other misdeeds as bad character evidence.

ameliorated, though not eliminated, by returning to the *Tassell* test. When the evidence of the plan consists only of circumstantial evidence, prosecutors should be precluded from offering the uncharged misdeeds unless the evidence warrants a finding that the charged and uncharged misdeeds were indeed the product of a single plan. The need to assure that criminal defendants be convicted only for what they do and not for who they are, as well as the undesirability of placing jurors in untenable positions, argue for a return to the *Tassell* test.

Character evidence and corroboration. As we have seen, evidence that the accused is predisposed to commit the offense charged is probative of the proposition that he committed the offense. Thus, evidence that the accused molested B would be relevant in proving that he molested A. For reasons that have been examined, however, until the mid–1990's both the Code and the Federal Rules prohibited the use of this kind of predisposition evidence to convict the accused.[35] But even before the changes in the rules, if the evidence was offered for a relevant purpose other than to prove the accused's predisposition to commit the molestation charged, the evidence of the other molestations could be received. Some early cases used this rationale to admit the accused's sexual misconduct with others. The evidence was not offered to prove that the accused was the kind of person who would commit the offense charged but to "corroborate" the testimony of the complaining witness.

It may well be that jurors will be more disposed to accept the complaining witness's testimony about the accused's sexual misconduct if they hear other victims testify about similar misconduct by the accused. But upon closer analysis the jurors may find the complaining witness's testimony more credible for the wrong legal reasons: the jurors may be more likely to accept the victim's story because they are less likely to accept the accused's; they are less likely to accept the accused's story because, having heard of his misconduct with others, they believe that he is the kind of person who would commit the acts described by the victim. In short, the jurors may base their decision on their assessment of the accused's character. Given the kind of person they think he is, the jurors may conclude that the victim must be telling the truth. Thus, it becomes apparent that offering evidence of other acts of misconduct merely "to corroborate" the complaining witness's testimony may still run afoul of the rule banning the use of character evidence to prove conduct. The California Supreme Court acknowledged as much in People v. Thomas,[36] where it held that prosecutors could no longer rely on the corroboration route to escape the strictures of § 1101(a).[37]

---

35. As discussed in prior sections, there are exceptions to this rule.

36. 20 Cal.3d 457, 143 Cal.Rptr. 215, 573 P.2d 433 (1978).

37. Section 1101 itself does not purport to govern the admissibility of character evidence to attack or support the credibility of witnesses. West's Ann. California Evidence Code § 1101(c). According to the Law Revision Commission, the admissibility of that evidence is determined by §§ 786–790. Id. (comment). Section 786 limits the use of character evidence to proving only a witness's traits for veracity or lack of veracity. West's Ann. California Evidence Code § 786. Section 787 prohibits the use of specific instances of conduct to establish a witness's character for

Despite the California Supreme Court's reaffirmation of *Thomas* in People v. Tassell,[38] some lower courts continue to disregard *Thomas*. In part, their disregard can be traced to the difficulty the courts and bar have in understanding character evidence. People v. O'Connor[39] is illustrative. In that case the accused was prosecuted for molesting a number of boys. Some of the boys testified that the accused had them "play Indians."[40] Over the accused's objection, the prosecution was allowed to introduce sketches found at the accused's house which depicted boys engaged in sexual conduct with at least one boy dressed like an Indian. The reviewing court upheld the use of the sketches, holding that they were "not opinion evidence, evidence of reputation, or evidence of specific instances of conduct."[41]

That holding, however, failed to address the accused's complaint. His theory was that the sketches constituted inadmissible character evidence because they were offered to prove that he was the kind of man who would commit the offenses described by the complaining witnesses: men who keep sketches of boys engaging in sex are the kind of men who engage in sex with boys. From the accused's perspective, the sketches thus comprised evidence of specific instances of conduct offered to show his predisposition to commit the offenses charged. But in the court's view, the evidence was nonetheless admissible to corroborate the boys' testimony.[42]

Testimony by other boys accusing the defendant of molesting them would have had the same corroborative effect, especially if the other boys, like the victims, also testified that the accused had them play Indians. But *Thomas* bars the use of evidence of specific acts for that purpose at least in sex offense prosecutions.[43] Although the evidence in *O'Connor* did not

veracity or lack of veracity. West's Ann. California Evidence Code § 787. Thus combined, these sections limit a party to reputation or opinion testimony in establishing a witness's trait for truthfulness or untruthfulness. See generally § 15.08 infra.

In sexual offense prosecutions, *Thomas* has been superseded by amendments to the Evidence Code. As of 1996, prosecutors may offer evidence of other sexual misdeeds by the accused as proof of the accused's predisposition to commit the sexual misdeed charged. See § 3.14 supra. Accordingly, in such cases prosecutors do not need to reach for a "corroboration" rationale to offer the evidence of the other sexual misdeeds.

38. 36 Cal.3d 77, 88, note 8, 201 Cal.Rptr. 567, 574, note 8, 679 P.2d 1, 8, note 8 (1984).

39. 8 Cal.App.4th 941, 10 Cal.Rptr.2d 530 (1992).

40. Id. at 945, 10 Cal.Rptr.2d at 532.

41. Id. at 949, 10 Cal.Rptr.2d at 534.

42. Id. at 949, 10 Cal.Rptr.2d at 535. In contrast, the court in People v. Archer, 82 Cal.App.4th 1380, 99 Cal.Rptr.2d 230 (2000), correctly analyzed the kind of evidence offered in *O'Connor*.

Archer was convicted of first degree murder with a true finding that he personally used a knife in the commission of the killing. Over his objection, the prosecution introduced several videotapes, books, and catalogs seized from his home and storage locker. The materials were not limited to the purchase or use of knives but included information on silencers, explosives, and other weapons. Since the prosecution introduced no evidence that the murder required special training or the use of a special knife, the reviewing court held the material constituted inadmissible character evidence of Archer's propensity to engage in violent acts such as murder. Id. at 1394, 99 Cal.Rptr.2d at 239.

43. Amendments to the Evidence Code may now preclude applying the *Thomas* limitation in certain sexual offense prosecutions, including child molestation cases. As of 1996, California

constitute a gross violation of the character evidence rule, its use nonetheless violated the ban. Paradoxically, the court cited *Tassell*;[44] obviously, it failed to appreciate its teaching.[45]

O'Connor would have presented a different situation if the prosecution had offered the Indian headdress which the victims claimed was the one they wore. Evidence of the existence of facts testified to by witnesses can be offered to support their credibility.[46] For purposes of "corroborating" the victims, the prosecution could have also offered a sketch of such a headdress recovered from the accused's home. Even the sketches offered in *O'Connor* could have fallen in this category if the boys had testified that the accused had used the sketches in connection with the acts of molestation. But as the reviewing court conceded, the prosecution produced no evidence showing that the boys had ever seen the sketches.[47]

Character evidence and intermediate propositions. People v. Clark[48] illustrates the difficulties courts can encounter in identifying inadmissible character evidence when the evidence is offered to prove intermediate propositions from which the fact finder can infer ultimate propositions. In *Clark*, the accused was prosecuted for murdering six women, all of whom were prostitutes. To prove that the accused was the killer, the prosecution was permitted to offer the following evidence: (1) evidence that the accused had hired a prostitute to dance for the accused and a female friend, and to have three-way sex with them, (2) evidence that the accused collected and at times wore the underwear of his old girlfriends, and (3) evidence that the accused picked up prostitutes.

According to the California Supreme Court, the evidence that the accused hired a prostitute to entertain him and a friend and to have three-way sex with them was admissible "to show the defendant's fondness for hiring prostitutes, which was relevant on the question of identity and motive."[49] The evidence was indeed relevant: people who use prostitutes were more likely to have come in contact with the victims than people who

---

prosecutors may offer other sexual misdeeds by the accused as evidence of the accused's predisposition to commit the sexual offense charged. See § 3.14 supra. Since *Thomas*'s concern is with the risk that jurors might misuse evidence of corroboration as inadmissible bad character evidence, that concern disappears when the prosecution is allowed to offer the sexual misdeeds as evidence of the accused's propensity to commit the sexual misdeed charged. Thus, evidence of sexual misdeeds may be offered under the new amendments to prove the accused's predisposition to commit the sexual misdeed charged as well as any other proper purpose, including bolstering the credibility of the victim. See People v. Falsetta, 21 Cal.4th 903, 922, 89 Cal.Rptr.2d 847, 860, 986 P.2d 182, 193 (1999), cert. denied, 529 U.S. 1089, 120 S.Ct. 1723, 146 L.Ed.2d 645 (2000).

44. See People v. O'Connor, 8 Cal.App.4th 941, 945, 10 Cal.Rptr.2d 530, 532 (1992).

45. Other courts, however, have taken *Tassell* and *Thomas* to heart and used these cases to prevent the prosecution from relying on § 1101(b) to justify the use of uncharged offenses to support the credibility not just of the complaining witness in sex offense prosecutions but of any witness in any kind of prosecution. See People v. Brown, 17 Cal.App.4th 1389, 1397, 22 Cal.Rptr.2d 14, 19 (1993) and cases cited therein.

46. West's Ann.California Evidence Code § 780(i).

47. People v. O'Connor, 8 Cal.App.4th 941, 949, 10 Cal.Rptr.2d 530, 535 (1992).

48. 3 Cal.4th 41, 10 Cal.Rptr.2d 554, 833 P.2d 561 (1992), cert. denied, 507 U.S. 993, 113 S.Ct. 1604, 123 L.Ed.2d 166 (1993).

49. Id. at 125, 10 Cal.Rptr.2d at 599, 833 P.2d at 606.

avoid prostitutes. The problem with this reasoning, however, is that it contravenes the ban on the use of character evidence. The violation becomes apparent if the offense is changed. Assume that instead of killing prostitutes the defendant was accused of using the services of prostitutes on a specified occasion. Evidence that he used a prostitute on a different occasion would thus be offered to convict the accused on the basis of his predisposition to use prostitutes. That is precisely the type of reasoning the character evidence rules seek to ban.

The court's choice of words, moreover, was singularly unfortunate. If one's "fondness" for certain activities can be received in evidence, the ban on the use of character evidence is effectively repealed, at least in some cases.[50] Such evidence would be especially useful in proving the accused's guilt in cases involving sex offenses. Evidence, for example, that the accused molested other children would be admissible to prove that the accused molested the victim because the evidence would establish the accused's fondness or predisposition to commit such an offense. Impermissible character evidence reasoning cannot be avoided: the accused is guilty of molesting the victim because he is the kind of person who is fond of molesting children.[51]

At the trial the evidence showed that, except in the case of one of the victims, no underwear was recovered from the site of any of the killings. According to the court, this circumstance showed that the killer collected and kept as trophies some items of the victims' clothing.[52] Therefore, evidence that the accused collected and wore the underwear of old girlfriends was "relevant to the issue of identity",[53] to prove that the accused was the killer of the prostitutes. Again, the evidence was relevant: the proposition that the accused was the killer was rendered more probable by the evidence that he collected and wore his girlfriends' underwear than the proposition would be without the evidence. But, again, impermissible character reasoning is involved. The jury was asked to find that the accused was the killer because people with a predisposition to collect women's underwear are more likely to remove the underwear of women with whom they come into contact.

As in the case of the evidence of hiring prostitutes, the character nature of the evidence of collecting women's underwear becomes apparent if the offense is changed. If instead of being accused of killing prostitutes

---

50. The California Supreme Court, however, still does not appreciate this point. In People v. Memro, 11 Cal.4th 786, 47 Cal.Rptr.2d 219, 905 P.2d 1305 (1995), the court approved of the prosecution's use of sexually explicit photographs owned by the accused as probative of his "attraction" for young boys, an attraction which in turn was probative of his motive to molest a young boy, one of the offenses charged against the accused. Id. at 865, 47 Cal.Rptr.2d at 262, 905 P.2d at 1348. The court failed to see that "attraction" like "fondness" is simply another term for predisposition.

51. A 1996 amendment to the Evidence Code now permits prosecutors to offer other instances of child molestation by the accused as evidence of the accused's predisposition to commit the molestation charged. See § 3.14 supra.

52. People v. Clark, 3 Cal.4th 41, 124, 10 Cal.Rptr.2d 554, 598, 833 P.2d 561, 605 (1992), cert. denied, 507 U.S. 993, 113 S.Ct. 1604, 123 L.Ed.2d 166 (1993).

53. Id.

the defendant had been accused of taking their underwear, evidence that he collected the underwear of other women would invite jurors to convict the accused on the basis of his predisposition to commit the offense.[54]

The court declined to rule on the admissibility of the evidence that the accused "liked to pick up prostitutes" because he failed to make a timely and specific objection to its introduction.[55] In light of the court's other rulings, however, it is likely that the court would have upheld the use of the evidence on the ground that it was relevant to prove the identity of the killer. People who like to pick up prostitutes, after all, are more likely than others to have had contact with the victims. But, as in the instance of hiring a prostitute, the accused's character—his fondness for associating with prostitutes—is being used to convict him. Had the accused been prosecuted for picking up, instead of killing, the six victims, the character nature of evidence that he liked to pick up prostitutes would have been apparent.

Cases like *Clark* are difficult because the character evidence is used to prove an intermediate, instead of an ultimate, proposition. As was seen by changing the offense, the character nature of evidence is easier to discern when the evidence is offered to prove an ultimate issue directly. The fact, however, that character evidence is limited to proving intermediate propositions from which the fact finder can infer the existence of ultimate propositions is immaterial. Section 1101(a) prohibits the use of a person's predisposition to behave in a particular manner to prove that he behaved in that manner on a given occasion.[56] Therefore, the accused's predisposition to associate with prostitutes could no more be offered to prove that he associated with the six prostitutes who were killed than it could be offered to prove that he hired prostitutes.

QUESTIONS AND PROBLEMS

1. Over an inadmissible character evidence objection, determine the admissibility of the following evidence under the California Evidence Code and the Federal Rules of Evidence; in making your rulings, ignore Code § 1108 and Rules 413–414:

Case 1. Consider the admissibility of the following evidence in a prosecution charging the defendant with receiving (buying) stolen property (a bicycle).

---

54. The evidence could have been offered for the noncharacter purpose of proving that the accused was the killer of the prostitutes on the theory that the marks common to the charged and uncharged offenses (removing women's underwear) suggested that only one person—the accused—could have committed the offenses. But neither the prosecution nor the court identified this purpose as the one to which the evidence was directed. Confusion over the admissibility of the evidence could have been avoided if the prosecution had complied with *Tassell*'s requirement that the prosecution identify the noncharacter purpose to which the evidence of specific acts is directed.

55. People v. Clark, 3 Cal.4th 41, 125, 10 Cal.Rptr.2d 554, 599, 833 P.2d 561, 606 (1992), cert. denied, 507 U.S. 993, 113 S.Ct. 1604, 123 L.Ed.2d 166 (1993).

56. West's Ann.California Evidence Code § 1101(a) and comment.

DA Witness One: I stole a bicycle from the Stanford campus and sold it to the defendant for $50 on June 1. I told him that I had stolen the bicycle.

Defendant: I bought the bicycle from Witness One for $50. I never would have bought it from him if I had known it was stolen.

DA Witness Two: I am the defendant's ex-lover. Before we broke up, he told me that he bought bicycles from Witness One, which Witness One would steal from the Stanford campus. He would then resell the bicycles at UC Berkeley.

Defendant: Objection, inadmissible bad character evidence. Move to strike.

Judge: ?

Compare with:

DA Witness One: I stole a bicycle from the Stanford campus and sold it to the defendant for $50 on June 1. I told him that I had stolen the bicycle.

Defendant: I bought the bicycle from Witness One for $50. I never would have bought it from him if I had known it was stolen.

DA Witness Two: On May 1, I stole a bicycle from the Stanford campus and sold it to the defendant for $40. I told him that I had stolen the bicycle.

Defendant: Objection, inadmissible bad character evidence. Move to strike.

Judge: ?

DA Witness Three: On April 1, I stole a bicycle from the Stanford campus and sold it to the defendant for $30. I told him that I had stolen the bicycle.

Defendant: Objection, inadmissible bad character evidence. Move to strike.

Judge: ?

DA Witness Four: On March 1, I stole a bicycle from the Santa Clara campus and sold it to the defendant for $20. I told him that I had stolen the bicycle.

Defendant: Objection, inadmissible bad character evidence. Move to strike.

Judge: ?

Suppose that the goal of the proponent is to show that the defendant did *not* engage in a common plan to buy stolen bicycles (i.e., that each of the acts is unconnected to the others). Setting aside trial advocacy considerations, would the testimony of witnesses Two through Four be probative of this proposition?

Assume that the instances of misconduct described by each witness are unconnected. If that is so, they may not be offered by the prosecution as circumstantial proof of the defendant's common plan or scheme to buy stolen bicycles. If that is case, then the four instances of misconduct are most likely probative of only one proposition. What proposition is that?

Case 2. In a prosecution for rape, the accused admits that he had intercourse with the victim but claims that she consented. In his case-in-chief, may the prosecutor call two women to testify that the accused had intercourse with them against their will?

Assume that the accused claims that the evidence would constitute inadmissible character evidence. Would the prosecutor's claim that the evidence was being offered to show a "common design or plan" affect your ruling?

Case 3. In a prosecution for engaging in lewd and lascivious conduct with a Scout Troop member, the accused, the Scoutmaster, denies engaging in any such conduct. May the prosecution call four other Scouts to testify that the accused also engaged in lewd and lascivious conduct with them?

In upholding the use of the evidence, the appellate court said:

Here, the evidence demonstrates a common scheme and plan of Stark's to (1) use his position of authority to meet boys about age 12, and (2) obtain their trust, and (3) initiate physical contact which (4) became sexual in nature during night time periods sleeping near the children, with (5) the type of sex act (fondling of penis followed by Stark's oral copulation) and (6) the location of the activity (Stark's home, car, and campouts) being remarkably similar in all cases. Thus, as we have seen, in this case the evidence of Stark's other offenses had much material value here in resolving the issues in dispute.

Do you agree with the appellate court that receiving the evidence to prove a "common scheme or plan" overcame the accused's claim that the evidence was improperly received to show that he was the kind of man who would commit the offense charged?

If not, what additional claims or arguments would you require the prosecutor to make before letting the jury hear from the other boys? In considering the question, disregard the judge's discretionary power to exclude relevant evidence.

Case 4. In a prosecution for engaging in lewd and lascivious conduct with a minor, would you admit the following evidence offered by the prosecution?

a. To corroborate the minor's claim that the accused had him play Indians during the acts, an Indian headdress, recovered from the accused's home, which the minor identifies as the headdress the accused had him wear.

b. For the same purpose, a photograph of an Indian headdress which the minor identifies as a fair and accurate depiction of the headdress the accused had him wear.

c. For the same purpose, the testimony of other boys describing how the accused had them wear an Indian headdress while engaging in lewd and lascivious acts with them.

d. For the same purpose, drawings recovered from the accused's home showing boys engaged in sex acts while a boy wore an Indian headdress. In making your ruling, would it make any difference that the prosecutor was unable to show that the victim had seen the drawings while in the accused's home? That the headdress in the drawings did not resemble the headdress the minor claims he was asked to wear?

e. To corroborate the victim's testimony, testimony by other boys that the accused had also molested them.

Case 5. In a prosecution for murdering six prostitutes, over the accused's character evidence objection, would you admit the following evidence?

a. To prove that the accused was the killer, evidence that the accused had hired a prostitute to dance for him and to have three-way sex with him and a female friend. Would you be more inclined to admit the evidence if the prosecutor argued that the evidence was offered to prove the accused's "fondness" for hiring prostitutes, a proposition that in turn would help prove that the accused was the killer?

Assume, instead, that the accused is prosecuted for using the services of a prostitute. Over the accused's character evidence objection, would you allow the prosecutor to offer the evidence to show the accused's "fondness" for using prostitutes?

b. To prove that the accused was the killer of the six prostitutes, evidence that the accused collected and wore underwear belonging to old girlfriends, where other evidence showed that none of the six prostitutes was found with underwear.

Assume, instead, that the accused is prosecuted for taking the prostitutes' underwear. Over the accused's character evidence objection, would you allow the prosecutor to offer evidence that he collected and wore underwear belonging to old girlfriends to be received to show that the accused was the one who took the prostitutes' underwear? To show that the accused's "fondness" for taking women's underwear?

c. To prove that the accused was the killer of the six prostitutes, evidence that the accused "liked to pick up prostitutes."

Assume, instead, that the accused is prosecuted for using the services of a prostitute. Over the accused's character evidence objection, would you allow the prosecution to offer evidence that the accused "liked to pick up prostitutes"? In ruling on the objection, disregard the rules dealing with habit evidence.

2. California Evidence Code § 1108 and Federal Rules of Evidence 413–414 create new exceptions to the ban on the use of character evidence. These rules allow the use of uncharged sexual assaults and molestations by the accused as proof of the accused's propensity to commit the sexual assault or molestation charged. How would these rules change your rulings in the preceding cases?

§ 3.17   PROPOSITION 8 AND § 1101(b)

Until the California Supreme Court dispelled the uncertainties surrounding the impact of Proposition 8 on the character evidence rules, the status of § 1101(b) remained unclear. If, as some feared, the proposition repealed § 1101(a)'s ban on the use of character evidence to prove conduct in criminal cases,[1] then § 1101(b) likewise was repealed.[2] Since the evidence would be admissible in the first place to prove conduct, the need to find a noncharacter purpose for the evidence would be lessened considerably.

With its *Ewoldt*[3] decision, the California Supreme Court removed these uncertainties. By holding that the Legislature had restored § 1101 to its pre-initiative status,[4] the court revived subsection (b). Unless an exception applies, parties to criminal proceedings may now use evidence of prior acts only to prove some relevant proposition other than a person's predisposition to engage in such acts. Accordingly, the noncharacter purposes delineated in subsection (b) have become important once more.

§ 3.18   OBJECTING TO § 1101(b) EVIDENCE

A judge does not have a *sua sponte* duty to instruct a jury on the limited purpose of evidence received under § 1101(b).[1] Accordingly, the party opposing the evidence should urge not only its exclusion on § 352 grounds, but if the party loses the motion, should request the judge to give the jury the appropriate limiting instruction.[2] The standard jury instruction given in California criminal cases provides directions that apply to most situations;[3] it is up to the opposing party, however, to make sure that the judge gives the jurors the instruction appropriate to the case.[4]

A difference of opinion exists on whether the opposing party can object to § 1101(b) evidence on the ground that the misdeeds have not been proved by a preponderance of the evidence. Courts concerned with the potential harm such evidence can cause apply this standard,[5] while those focusing on the relevance provisions of the Code apply a sufficiency standard.[6] After Proposition 8, the appropriate test in criminal cases ought to be a sufficiency test. Since the Right to Truth-in-Evidence provision gives parties to criminal proceedings the constitutional right not

---

1. See § 3.07 supra.

2. In People v. Tassell, 36 Cal.3d 77, 201 Cal.Rptr. 567, 679 P.2d 1 (1984), the California Supreme Court expressly reserved the question whether Proposition 8 repealed California Evidence Code § 1101(b). Id. at 82, note 1, 201 Cal.Rptr. at 569, note 1, 679 P.2d at 3, note 1. *Ewoldt* dispenses with the need for the court to answer this question.

3. People v. Ewoldt, 7 Cal.4th 380, 27 Cal.Rptr.2d 646, 867 P.2d 757 (1994).

4. See § 3.08 supra.

1. People v. Milner, 45 Cal.3d 227, 252, 246 Cal.Rptr. 713, 729, 753 P.2d 669, 685 (1988). See also People v. Collie, 30 Cal.3d 43, 63–64, 177 Cal.Rptr. 458, 469–470, 634 P.2d 534, 545–546 (1981).

2. Upon request, the opposing party is entitled to such an instruction. West's Ann. California Evidence Code § 355.

3. See CALJIC 2.50 (Fall 2006 Edition).

4. People v. Bruce, 208 Cal.App.3d 1099, 1106, 256 Cal.Rptr. 647, 651 (1989).

5. People v. Simon, 184 Cal.App.3d 125, 134, 228 Cal.Rptr. 855, 861 (1986); People v. Donnell, 52 Cal.App.3d 762, 777, 125 Cal.Rptr. 310, 320 (1975). See also CALJIC 2.50.1 (Fall 2006 Edition).

6. People v. Terry, 2 Cal.3d 362, 396, 85 Cal.Rptr. 409, 430–431, 466 P.2d 961, 982–83 (1970), cert. dism'd, 406 U.S. 912, 92 S.Ct. 1619, 32 L.Ed.2d 112 (1972). Although the court seemingly applied a sufficiency test, it found that the test was satisfied by clear and convincing evidence. Id.

to have relevant evidence excluded,[7] evidence offered under § 1101(b) meeting the relevance requirements of § 210[8] and the sufficiency test of § 403(a)(4)[9] should be admitted unless excluded under § 352. Of course, the judge can take the convincing force of the evidence into account in determining whether its probative value is outweighed by its potential to prejudice the objecting party. If the judge finds the evidence to be weak, the judge can exclude the evidence. Thus, the effect of Proposition 8 is to shift the controversy from one over standards of proof to one concerning the probative value and prejudicial effect of the evidence.

Once the misdeed evidence has been admitted, however, courts may impose conditions on its use by the jury beyond those contained in the usual limiting instruction. In California, for example, judges must inform the jurors not to consider the misdeed evidence for the purpose admitted unless they first find by a preponderance of the evidence that the misdeed was in fact committed.[10]

In federal courts, the United States Supreme Court ended the controversy over standards by holding that under the Federal Rules of Evidence the admissibility of uncharged offenses calls initially for a relevance analysis and the application of a sufficiency test.[11] But because of the

---

7. See § 3.07 supra.

8. Section 210 defines relevant evidence. West's Ann.California Evidence Code § 210. For a discussion of this definition, see § 2.04 supra.

9. Section 403 requires the judge to apply a sufficiency standard in determining the relevance of evidence of the conduct of a person when the question is whether the person so conducted himself. West's Ann.California Evidence Code § 403(a)(4).

10. See People v. Carpenter, 15 Cal.4th 312, 380, 63 Cal.Rptr.2d 1, 39–40, 935 P.2d 708, 746 (1997), cert. denied 522 U.S. 1078, 118 S.Ct. 858, 139 L.Ed.2d 757 (1998). Where the evidence of the uncharged misdeeds is offered in the penalty phase of a California capital case, the jurors should be instructed to disregard the uncharged misdeeds, unless they first find that the misdeeds were committed beyond a reasonable doubt. A higher standard is called for because the evidence of the uncharged misdeeds may move the jurors to vote for death. Id.

California jurors are routinely instructed not to convict on the basis of circumstantial evidence unless they find each link in the chain of reasoning to be true beyond a reasonable doubt. See California Jury Instructions, Criminal 2.01 (CALJIC) (Fall 2006 Edition). But some California cases suggest that facts found and used by jurors in a chain of reasoning leading to a guilty verdict can be found by a preponderance of the evidence. As noted, California jurors are routinely told to disregard evidence of uncharged misdeeds unless they first find by a preponderance of the evidence that the misdeed was committed. See People v. Carpenter, supra; see also California Jury Instructions, Criminal 2.50.1 (CALJIC) (Fall 2006 Edition). In its note, the Committee on Standard Jury Instructions, Criminal, acknowledges a conceivable conflict between 2.01 and 2.50.1. Id. Other cases hold that in screening the evidence under § 403, a judge should withhold the evidence from the jury unless the judge finds that a reasonable jury could find the preliminary fact in issue by a preponderance of the evidence. Under this standard a judge would withhold a co-conspirator's declaration from the jury unless the proponent proffers "sufficient evidence to allow the trier of fact to determine that the conspiracy exists by a preponderance of the evidence." See People v. Herrera, 83 Cal.App.4th 46, 64, 98 Cal.Rptr.2d 911, 922 (2000) and cases cited therein. This is the approach followed by the Federal Rules of Evidence as construed. See Huddleston v. United States, 485 U.S. 681, 687, 108 S.Ct. 1496, 1500, 99 L.Ed.2d 771, 780 (1988). For purposes of admissibility, the question for the trial judge would appear to be whether a reasonable juror could find that a conspiracy existed if the proponent's evidence is believed. Whether jurors should be instructed to disregard the evidence *after* it has been admitted unless they find the conspiracy or other preliminary fact by some higher standard is a separate question.

11. Huddleston v. United States, 485 U.S. 681, 687, 108 S.Ct. 1496, 1500, 99 L.Ed.2d 771, 780 (1988). The question for the federal trial judge is whether a reasonable jury could find by a preponderance of the evidence that the uncharged misdeed was committed if the proponent's

potential prejudice such evidence poses, the Court emphasized a judge's discretion to exclude the evidence under Federal Rule of Evidence 403.[12] Rule 403 is the federal equivalent of California Evidence Code § 352.

A related question is whether the accused can object to § 1101(b) evidence on the grounds that a plea of not guilty does not render such evidence admissible until after the accused offers evidence disputing such elements as the identity or intent of the perpetrator. This question was answered in People v. Daniels,[13] where the accused was prosecuted for murdering two police officers who were attempting to take the accused to prison after his conviction for bank robbery had been affirmed on appeal. To prove that the accused intended to kill the officers, the prosecution offered evidence that the accused had been become disabled by the fire of police officers who were attempting to apprehend the accused after the robbery. The prosecution's theory was that the accused intended to kill the officers attempting to take him to prison because the accused had a motive for killing them—revenge for having been left disabled by other officers.[14] The accused objected on the grounds that he was contesting only the "identity" of the perpetrator and not the perpetrator's "intent."[15] The court upheld the use of the bank robbery evidence to prove the perpetrator's intent: "when a defendant [does] not isolate the issue of identity until after the prosecutor [has] completed his case-in-chief, the court [does] not err in permitting the prosecutor to present evidence [in his case-in-chief] of prior criminal conduct to prove premeditation, willfulness, and malice aforethought. [Thus an accused's plea of not guilty puts] the elements of the crime in issue for the purpose of deciding the admissibility of evidence under Evidence Code section 1101, unless the accused takes some action to narrow the prosecution's burden of proof."[16] Admitting the element to which the § 1101(b) evidence is directed should in most instances preclude the use of the evidence. The element having been admitted, the § 1101(b) evidence would be immaterial and, hence, inadmissible as irrelevant.[17]

Because § 1101(b) evidence of uncharged offenses is offered to prove some proposition other than the accused's predisposition to commit the

---

evidence is believed. The addition of the more likely than not standard probably adds little to the traditional sufficiency test since the test remains heavily tilted toward admissibility. *Huddleston* specifically rejected the claim that the proponent must convince the judge of the existence of the uncharged misdeed by a preponderance of the evidence. Id.

12. Id. at 692, 108 S.Ct. at 1502.

13. 52 Cal.3d 815, 277 Cal.Rptr. 122, 802 P.2d 906 (1991), cert. denied, 502 U.S. 846, 112 S.Ct. 145, 116 L.Ed.2d 111 (1991).

14. Id. at 856, 277 Cal.Rptr. at 140, 802 P.2d at 924.

15. Id. at 857, 277 Cal.Rptr. at 141, 802 P.2d at 924 (footnotes omitted).

16. Id. at 857–858, 277 Cal.Rptr. at 141, 802 P.2d at 924–925 (footnotes omitted). In People v. Thompson the California Supreme Court held that the "fact that an accused has pleaded not guilty is not sufficient to place the elements of the crimes charged against him 'in issue.' " 27 Cal.3d 303, 315, 165 Cal.Rptr. 289, 294, 611 P.2d 883, 888 (1980). But in People v. Rowland, the court disapproved of this language, 4 Cal.4th 238, 260, 14 Cal.Rptr.2d 377, 391, 841 P.2d 897, 911 (1992), cert. denied, 510 U.S. 846, 114 S.Ct. 138, 126 L.Ed.2d 101 (1993), thereby resolving the conflict between this aspect of *Thompson* and *Daniels*.

17. See § 2.01 supra.

offense charged, the evidence is admissible even though the accused was not prosecuted for the uncharged offense[18] or, if prosecuted, even though the accused was acquitted of the offense.[19] But the fact that the accused was not prosecuted or, if prosecuted, was acquitted may be offered to help the jury determine the weight, if any, to give to the evidence of the uncharged offense.[20] Indeed, the judge's failure to inform the jurors of an acquittal constitutes error in California.[21] Perhaps of greater importance to the accused is the right to offer evidence disproving the commission of the uncharged offense. As pointed out in § 3.04, the requirement that the prosecution prove the uncharged offense through admissible evidence gives the accused the right to offer admissible evidence to disprove participating in the offense.[22] This right embraces attacking the prosecution's witnesses as well as calling witnesses who can exonerate the accused.

QUESTIONS AND PROBLEMS

1. Given the dangers posed by the prosecution's use of character evidence, judges should not allow prosecutors to use evidence of uncharged misdeeds against the accused in the prosecution's case-in-chief. Judges should restrain prosecutors from using such evidence until such time as the accused has raised an issue to which the evidence properly may be directed.

     a.   Must California judges follow this advice after *Daniels*?

     b.   What Rule may federal judges invoke in support of this advice?

2. The defendant is prosecuted for knowingly buying a bicycle stolen from the Stanford campus on January 1. The prosecution calls Harry who testifies that on that date he sold the defendant a bicycle after telling him that he stole it from the Stanford campus. The prosecution also calls Bob who testifies that on December 1 he sold the defendant a bicycle after telling him that he had stolen it from the Stanford campus. The defendant objects and moves to strike Bob's testimony on the ground that he was acquitted of buying a stolen bicycle from Bob on December 1. Should the judge grant the motion to strike?

3. Assume that the judge overrules the defendant's objection and denies the motion to strike. On cross-examination by the defense, Bob admits that in the last year he has been convicted of perjury, a felony. The defendant now moves to strike Bob's testimony on direct on the ground that the prosecution

---

18.   People v. Jenkins, 3 Cal.App.3d 529, 534, 83 Cal.Rptr. 525, 528–529 (1970).

19.   People v. Griffin, 66 Cal.2d 459, 466, 58 Cal.Rptr. 107, 110, 426 P.2d 507, 511 (1967). "[A]n acquittal in a criminal case does not preclude the government from relitigating an issue when it is presented in a subsequent action governed by a lower standard of proof." Dowling v. United States, 493 U.S. 342, 348, 110 S.Ct. 668, 672, 107 L.Ed.2d 708 (1990). Accordingly, the use of uncharged offense evidence does not violate due process even if the accused was acquitted of the uncharged offense. Id. at 351–52, 110 S.Ct. at 674–675.

20.   People v. Griffin, 66 Cal.2d 459, 466, 58 Cal.Rptr. 107, 110, 426 P.2d 507, 511 (1967); see also People v. Jenkins, 3 Cal.App.3d 529, 534, 83 Cal.Rptr. 525, 528–529 (1970).

21.   People v. Griffin, 66 Cal.2d 459, 466, 58 Cal.Rptr. 107, 110, 426 P.2d 507, 511 (1967).

22.   See § 3.04 supra.

has failed to prove the illegal sale described by Bob by a preponderance of the evidence. How should the judge rule?

4. Assume that the judge overrules the defendant's objection and denies the motion to strike. In California, what limiting instruction, if any, should the defendant request?

§ 3.19   SECTION 1101(b) AND CIVIL CASES

Though most opinions construing § 1101(b) involve criminal cases, the subsection applies to civil cases as well. For example, in the Estate of Zalud[1] the principal issue was whether a will had been signed by the testatrix, as contended by the beneficiary, or had been forged, as claimed by the contestants. To disprove the beneficiary's testimony that he had no knowledge regarding the circumstances surrounding the signing of the will, the contestants offered two wills disposing of different estates.[2] The other wills, like the contested will, had been typed on printed forms and named the contested will's beneficiary or his brother as beneficiaries.[3] Neither the contested will's beneficiary nor his brother was related to any of the testatrixes, all of whom were elderly women.[4] Though the court did not say so, it would appear that the method employed in preparing the three wills was so unique as to earmark them as the handiwork of the beneficiary.

In upholding the introduction of the other wills, the court stressed that the beneficiary's "connection with each will supported the inference that he had knowledge of the availability of the [printed] forms which could readily be used in the preparation of a will without recourse to the services of a lawyer."[5] The court also emphasized the

> unusual circumstance that in three instances [the beneficiary] would have some relationship to a will which was prepared on such a form, the named testator in each instance not being related to the principal beneficiary and provisions having been inserted in each form which contain striking similarities to provisions so inserted in one or both of the other will forms. Neither the industry of counsel nor the research of this court has uncovered a will contest proceeding presenting a closely similar factual situation.[6]

In Cobian v. Ordonez[7] the plaintiff sued the defendant for fraud and punitive damages in connection with the purchase of a car.[8] The plaintiff was allowed to call a witness to testify that the defendant had misrepre-

---

1. 27 Cal.App.3d 945, 104 Cal.Rptr. 329 (1972).

2. Id. at 955, 104 Cal.Rptr. at 335.

3. Id. at 955–956, 104 Cal.Rptr. at 335–336.

4. Id.

5. Id. at 956–957, 104 Cal.Rptr. at 336–337.

6. Id.

7. 103 Cal.App.3d Supp. 22, 163 Cal.Rptr. 126 (1980).

8. Id. at 28–29, 163 Cal.Rptr. at 129–130.

sented the condition of a car he sold to the witness.[9] The evidence, according to the court, was admissible to prove the defendant's "interest, common plan and absence of mistake or accident" in his dealings with the plaintiff.[10]

In Nelson v. Gaunt[11] the plaintiff sued a doctor for malpractice for injecting her with silicone to augment her breasts.[12] To prove that the doctor was aware that silicone was a dangerous substance at the time he injected the plaintiff, the plaintiff was permitted to offer evidence that previously the doctor had been arrested for and convicted of injecting silicone without a permit.[13]

In Bihun v. AT & T Information Systems, Inc.[14] an employee sued her employer for sexual harassment allegedly perpetrated by the employee's supervisor. To prove the employer's knowledge and opportunity to learn of the supervisor's misconduct, the employee was permitted to offer evidence of other instances of the supervisor's sexual misconduct that had been communicated to the employer.[15]

In Hassoldt v. Patrick Media Group, Inc.[16] the owner of a tree sued the owner of a billboard, claiming that the billboard owner without permission had trimmed the tree to better expose the billboard. To prove that the billboard owner was responsible for the trimming, the tree owner, over objection, called a former employee of the billboard owner. The employee testified that, while employed by the billboard owner, he often trimmed trees without first obtaining the tree owner's consent. The reviewing court held that it was error to receive the employee's testimony. Holding that the *Ewoldt*[17] principles apply to civil cases as well as to criminal cases, the court held that the employee's testimony was inadmissible in the absence of evidence that the circumstances attending the trimming of the tree in issue and of the trees trimmed by the employee were so distinctive as to suggest that only the billboard owner or his agents trimmed the plaintiff's tree.[18]

---

9. Id. at 30, 163 Cal.Rptr. at 130.

10. Id. *Cobian* must be read in light of the California Supreme Court's admonitions in People v. Tassell. It is no longer sufficient for the proponent to claim that the evidence is offered to prove a common scheme, plan, or design. See text accompanying note 108 at § 3.15 supra. The scheme, plan, or design must itself be probative of some contested proposition other than the predisposition to commit the conduct complained of. Id.

11. 125 Cal.App.3d 623, 178 Cal.Rptr. 167 (1981).

12. Id. at 628–629, 178 Cal.Rptr. at 169.

13. Id. at 640, 178 Cal.Rptr. at 176.

14. 13 Cal.App.4th 976, 16 Cal.Rptr.2d 787 (1993).

15. Id. at 990, 16 Cal.Rptr.2d at 794.

16. 84 Cal.App.4th 153, 100 Cal.Rptr.2d 662, 670 (2000).

17. See § 3.15 supra.

18. Hassoldt v. Patrick Media Group, Inc., 84 Cal.App.4th 153, 165, 100 Cal.Rptr.2d 662, 670, 671 (2000).

Under California law, two categories of sexual harassment are recognized.[19] The first is quid pro quo harassment where a term of employment is conditioned upon submission to unwelcome sexual advances.[20] The second category consists of subjecting an employee to a hostile work environment.[21] In proving the existence of a hostile work environment, a plaintiff may offer evidence of sexually harassing conduct directed at other employees, provided the plaintiff was aware of the conduct.[22] The use of the evidence for this purpose does not run afoul of the character evidence ban. The evidence is not offered to prove the employer's predisposition to engage in the sexual harassment directed at the plaintiff; it is offered to show that the plaintiff's knowledge of the harassing conduct directed at others contributed to her perception of a hostile work environment.[23]

California law prohibits discrimination on the basis of age.[24] To prove that an employee was terminated for reasons unrelated to age, an employer is entitled to offer the reasons for the termination. These may consist of evidence of the employee's inability to learn new skills, to undertake new responsibilities, or to perform at required levels.[25] Receiving the evidence of the employee's inadequacies does not violate the ban on the use of character evidence. It is not received to prove the employee's bad "character" as an employee but to explain why the employer terminated the employee.

As discussed in the preceding section, a party cannot object to the introduction of evidence of uncharged misdeeds on the ground that the proponent has failed to prove the misdeeds by a preponderance of the evidence. A proper construction of the Evidence Code does not require the proponent to prove the misdeeds by that standard. Section 1101(b) merely requires that the evidence be probative of some proposition other than the actor's predisposition to commit the misdeed.[26] Whether the evidence satisfies this requirement depends on § 210 which defines relevant evidence.[27] If the misdeed is relevant, then § 403(a)(4) specifies the standard of proof that must be satisfied, and that standard is a sufficiency one.[28] But, as noted in the preceding section, a trial judge may nonetheless exclude § 1101(b) evidence that satisfies this standard if its probative value is substantially outweighed by the risk of undue prejudice to the objecting party.[29]

---

19. Beyda v. City of Los Angeles, 65 Cal.App.4th 511, 516–17, 76 Cal.Rptr.2d 547, 550 (1998). Title VII of the federal Civil Rights Act also prohibits gender discrimination. 42 U.S.C.A. § 2000e et seq.

20. Beyda v. City of Los Angeles, 65 Cal.App.4th 511, 516–17, 76 Cal.Rptr.2d 547, 550 (1998).

21. Id.

22. Id. at 518–19, 76 Cal.Rptr.2d at 551.

23. Id.

24. West's Ann.California Government Code §§ 12900 et seq.

25. Muzquiz v. City of Emeryville, 79 Cal.App.4th 1106, 1124, 94 Cal.Rptr.2d 579, 593 (2000).

26. West's Ann.California Evidence Code § 1101(b).

27. West's Ann.California Evidence Code § 210.

28. West's Ann.California Evidence Code § 403(a)(4).

29. Because of its potentially prejudicial nature, California judges presiding over criminal cases must instruct the jurors not to consider the misdeed evidence for the purpose received, unless they first find by a preponderance of the evidence that the misdeed was in fact committed. See § 3.18 supra. Presumably, the same concerns should prompt judges presiding over civil trials to issue a similar limiting instruction.

The Federal Rules, like the Code, also prohibit the use of character to prove action in conformity therewith in civil cases as well as in criminal cases.[30]

QUESTIONS AND PROBLEMS

1.   Plaintiff sues Defendant for denying her a salary increase on account of her gender. Plaintiff calls the Defendant's supervisor who testifies that in the three years preceding Plaintiff's suit Defendant employed ten employees, five of whom were women, and that only the five men were given salary increases. The supervisor also testifies that all ten employees were started at the same salary. Defendant moves to strike the testimony on the grounds that it constitutes inadmissible character evidence. In the absence of special employment discrimination rules, how should the judge rule?

2.   Suppose that in response to Defendant's objection, Plaintiff argues that the evidence is being offered to show that Defendant engaged in a "pattern" of favoring men over women. In the absence of special employment discrimination rules, should that argument affect the judge's ruling?

3.   Suppose that, instead, Plaintiff argues that the evidence is being offered to show that Defendant discriminated against Plaintiff as part of plan or scheme to discriminate against women. Should that argument affect the judge's ruling?

4.   Plaintiff sues Employer for maintaining a hostile work environment. At the trial Plaintiff testifies that her immediate supervisor told her on several occasions that he would not raise her salary unless she dated him. Plaintiff also calls Betty, a co-worker, who testifies that she and Plaintiff have the same supervisor and that the supervisor also told her (Betty) that he would not raise her salary unless she dated him. Betty also testifies that she informed Plaintiff about the supervisor's statement. Employer moves to strike Betty's testimony on the ground that it constitutes inadmissible character evidence. How should the judge rule?

§ 3.20 HABIT AND CUSTOM

If evidence that would be inadmissible as character evidence can be offered as evidence of habit or custom, it will be admissible. California Evidence Code § 1105 and Federal Rule of Evidence 406 provide that evidence of a habit may be admitted to prove that on a specified occasion a person conducted himself or herself in conformity with the habit.[1] Moreover, both provide that evidence of custom may likewise be admitted to prove that on a given occasion an organization conformed its operations to the custom.[2]

---

30.   Federal Rule of Evidence 404(a). A 2006 amendment to Rule 404 makes clear that character evidence is not admissible in civil cases to prove conduct in conformity therewith. Advisory Committee Note.

  1.   West's Ann.California Evidence Code § 1105; Federal Rule of Evidence 406.

  2.   West's Ann.California Evidence Code § 1105; Federal Rule of Evidence 406.

Since evidence of habit or custom is beyond the ban on the use of character evidence to prove conduct, it is important for the parties and the court to distinguish between character evidence and evidence of habit and custom. A clue to the difference can be found in the definition of a habit. It is a "regular response to a repeated specific situation."[3]

This definition was taken from Dean Charles McCormick's treatise on evidence. He distinguished character evidence from habit and custom evidence in the following way:

> Character is a generalized description of a person's disposition * * * in respect to a general trait, such as honesty, temperance or peacefulness. Habit * * * is more specific. It denotes one's regular response to a repeated situation. If we speak of a character for care, we think of the person's tendency to act prudently in all the varying situations of life—in business, at home, in handling automobiles and in walking across the street. A habit, on the other hand, is the person's regular practice of responding to a particular kind of situation with a specific type of conduct. Thus, a person may be in the habit of bounding down a certain stairway two or three steps at a time, of patronizing a particular pub after each day's work, or of driving his automobile without using a seatbelt. The doing of the habitual act may become semi-automatic, as with a driver who invariably signals before changing lanes.[4]

Dean McCormick's reference to "semi-automatic" acts provides another clue. Because habits are regular responses to repeated situations, their execution does not require much thought. They are more probative of conduct than character because as semi-automatic, consistent responses to a specific stimulus they say much about a person's conduct when encountering the stimulus.[5]

Habit evidence, moreover, is not as likely as character evidence to prejudice the objecting party. Proof that the plaintiff does not wear a seatbelt to prove that she was not wearing her seatbelt on the occasion in question simply will not prejudice the plaintiff in the same way as evidence that she is a careless driver. Since proof of the latter proposition could include evidence of specific instances in which the plaintiff was seen driving carelessly, a single trial on the issue of the plaintiff's conduct on one occasion could become multiple trials involving aspects of her conduct on different occasions. The dangers inherent in such an eventuality have been described and include confusing the fact finder about the issues to be decided as well as inviting the fact finder to return a verdict on an improper basis.[6]

---

3. West's Ann. California Evidence Code § 1105 (comment); Federal Rule of Evidence 406 (advisory committee note).

4. C. McCormick, McCormick on Evidence § 195 (E. Cleary 3d ed. 1984).

5. Studies by social scientists, especially Walter Mischel, support the law's assumptions about the predictive value of habit evidence. See § 3.09 supra.

6. See § 3.04 supra.

How is a habit or a custom established? They can be proved by evidence of reputation, opinion, or specific instances of conduct.[7] But since evidence of specific instances is the most persuasive, the proponent should offer sufficient instances to warrant a finding that the habit existed or the custom was routine.[8] Applying a sufficiency test is appropriate because the issue is whether a person or an organization conducted themselves in a fashion giving rise to a habit or custom.[9] Thus, the evidence should come in subject to a motion to strike in the event the proponent fails to persuade the court that a reasonable jury could find the desired habit or custom from the proffered evidence. Moreover, even if the motion is denied, the opponent, upon request, is entitled to an instruction directing the jury to disregard the evidence unless the jurors first find the desired habit or custom.[10]

Receiving evidence of custom or routine practice can be justified on the grounds of need. It would be unrealistic, for example, for a large business to prove through knowledgeable witnesses that one customer out of many was mailed a particular bill. Human memory simply cannot help. Accordingly, evidence of routine billing practices has been admitted to prove that a particular party received a bill.[11] The opposing party, of course, may deny receiving the bill[12] and may also offer evidence showing that the practice lacks the routine quality required of a habit or custom.[13] Ordinarily, however, the court may not take the countervailing evidence into account in determining the existence of the habit or custom.[14] But the jury may consider that evidence in deciding whether the desired habit or custom exists.

The use of evidence of habit and custom has been approved by the California courts in a variety of circumstances. In Marshall v. Brown,[15] to prove that the defendant had interfered with the plaintiff's prospective employment, the defendant's manager was allowed to testify that at the defendant's request he gave former employees bad recommendations.[16] In

---

7. Since evidence of habit and custom is not within the ban of § 1101, habit and custom can be proved by any otherwise admissible relevant evidence. See West's Ann.California Evidence Code §§ 210, 351; Federal Rule of Evidence 402.

8. People v. Memro, 38 Cal.3d 658, 681, 214 Cal.Rptr. 832, 847–48, 700 P.2d 446, 461–62 (1985).

9. West's Ann.California Evidence Code § 403(a)(4).

10. West's Ann.California Evidence Code § 403(c)(1).

11. Lucas v. Hesperia Golf and Country Club, 255 Cal.App.2d 241, 247, 63 Cal.Rptr. 189, 193 (1967).

12. Id.

13. Just as the relevance provisions of the Code allow the proponent to offer otherwise admissible evidence to prove the habit or custom, so do the same provisions permit the opponent to prove their nonexistence.

14. The sufficiency test requires the judge to view the evidence in the light most favorable to the proponent. This requires the judge to resolve credibility issues in favor of the proponent and to draw only those inferences from the evidence favoring the proponent. In essence, the test forces the judge to disregard the opponent's countervailing evidence. See § 17.01 infra.

15. 141 Cal.App.3d 408, 190 Cal.Rptr. 392 (1983).

16. Id. at 416, 190 Cal.Rptr. at 397–398.

People v. Cabral,[17] to prove that the accused, a chiropractor, did not advise a patient to cease taking anticonvulsant medication, it was reversible error to preclude other patients from testifying that the chiropractor did not interfere with medication prescribed to them by their doctors.[18] In In re Charles G.[19] a burglary victim was allowed to testify about his habit of locking his car doors to prove that his car was locked on the day the accused was found inside the car.[20] In Romeo v. Jumbo Market[21] the defendant was permitted to offer evidence of the procedures used to clean the store's floors to show the condition of the floors on the day the plaintiff fell.[22] In People v. Webb,[23] to prove that the accused took money the victim stored in baby food jars, the prosecution was allowed to offer evidence about the victim's habit of storing money in the jars.[24] In Alvarez v. State of California[25] the state was allowed to offer testimony regarding the state's custom and practice in providing discretionary approval of roadway designs to prove that the state followed those practices in approving the design of a roadway on which the plaintiff was injured.[26]

In one unusual case, habit evidence was held admissible to discredit a witness. In People v. Humphries[27] it was error to exclude evidence that a prosecution witness was an habitual drug user when offered to prove that, contrary to his testimony, the witness ingested PCP on the day of the crime.[28] The habit evidence was admissible because the Code does not prohibit the use of habit evidence to support or attack the credibility of a witness.[29]

QUESTIONS AND PROBLEMS

1. In a prosecution for breaking and entering into a dwelling, to prove that the vandalized store was locked on the occasion in question, over an inadmissible character evidence objection the owner may testify that it was her policy to have the store locked at all times after business hours. True or false?

2. Over the same objection, the store manager may testify that periodically he informed the employees on the last shift to make sure that all doors were locked after business hours. True or false?

---

17. 141 Cal.App.3d 148, 190 Cal.Rptr. 194 (1983).
18. Id. at 154, 190 Cal.Rptr. at 198.
19. 95 Cal.App.3d 62, 156 Cal.Rptr. 832 (1979).
20. Id. at 66, 156 Cal.Rptr. at 834.
21. 247 Cal.App.2d 817, 56 Cal.Rptr. 26 (1967).
22. Id. at 822–824, 56 Cal.Rptr. at 31–32.
23. 6 Cal.4th 494, 24 Cal.Rptr.2d 779, 862 P.2d 779 (1993).
24. Id. at 529, 24 Cal.Rptr.2d at 801, 862 P.2d at 801.
25. 79 Cal.App.4th 720, 95 Cal.Rptr.2d 719 (1999).
26. Id. at 732, 95 Cal.Rptr.2d at 728.
27. 185 Cal.App.3d 1315, 230 Cal.Rptr. 536 (1986).
28. Id. at 1338–1339, 230 Cal.Rptr. at 548–549.
29. West's Ann.California Evidence Code § 787 prohibits only the use of specific instances of conduct to prove a witness's *character* to support or attack the witness's credibility.

3.   Over the same objection, the employees on the last shift may testify that it was their practice to lock all doors after business hours. True or false?

4.   The judge should allow the jurors to consider the above testimony only if the judge is persuaded by a preponderance of the evidence that it was the store's custom to lock all doors after business hours. True or false?

5.   Assume that on cross-examination, the employees on the last shift concede that they cannot remember whether they locked the doors after business hours on the occasion in question. Should such a concession cause the judge to withhold from the jurors the evidence regarding the store's policy and practice of locking all doors after business hours?

§ 3.21   EVIDENCE OF SIMILAR OCCURRENCES

Of the evidence considered in this chapter, only evidence relating to similar occurrences is not regulated by a specific Evidence Code section or Federal Rule. The use of this kind of evidence is governed by a number of principles derived from cases decided both before and after the adoption of the Evidence Code and the Federal Rules. As will be seen, however, the principles can be justified by Code's and Rules' provisions on relevancy and the exclusion of unduly prejudicial evidence.

Evidence of similar occurrences is somewhat akin to character evidence in that conduct not directly related to the action being tried is offered to prove some disputed fact. For example, earlier we saw that evidence that the defendant misrepresented the condition of a car to a third party is inadmissible to prove that he misrepresented the condition of the car he sold to the plaintiff.[1] The evidence would be barred by the character evidence rules.[2] The plaintiff would be asking the fact finder to find that the defendant misrepresented the condition of the car he sold the plaintiff because, having misrepresented the condition of a car on another occasion, the defendant is the kind of person who misrepresents the condition of cars. That is precisely the type of reasoning condemned by the character evidence rules.[3] The same rules would prevent a grocer in a tort action from offering evidence that the plaintiff had previously fallen in his store to prove that she was negligent when she fell on the occasion being litigated.

Evidence of similar occurrences is not made inadmissible by the ban on the use of character evidence because the evidence is offered to prove a proposition *other* than a person's predisposition to act in a particular way on a given occasion. Take the slip and fall case. The plaintiff may call as witnesses other persons who have fallen in the grocer's store, provided that the plaintiff satisfies two conditions. The first is that the plaintiff offer the evidence for a noncharacter reason, such as to prove the

1.   See §§ 3.02–3.04 supra.

2.   See § 3.04 supra.

3.   Id.

existence of a dangerous condition or the grocer's awareness of such a condition. The second is that the plaintiff satisfy the judge that the circumstances surrounding her fall and that of the other witnesses are substantially similar.[4] Each of these conditions merits discussion.

With respect to the first, note should be taken that the evidence is not being offered for a character purpose, even though the plaintiff may hope that the fact finder will use it as bad character evidence of the grocer's negligence on the occasion of her fall. Assume that the plaintiff's theory of recovery is that the grocer was negligent because he failed to remove vegetable matter from the floor in the produce area and failed to warn the plaintiff of the condition. If on earlier occasions the plaintiff's witnesses encountered the same conditions and informed the grocer about them, then the evidence would be admissible to prove that the grocer was aware of the existence of the dangerous condition at the time the plaintiff fell. Though such evidence is designed to prove that the grocer was negligent on that occasion, the evidence is not being used in a character manner. The fact finder is not being asked to find the grocer negligent at the time of the plaintiff's fall because he may have been negligent when others also fell. Rather, the fact finder is being asked to find the grocer negligent on the occasion of the plaintiff's fall because he was or should have been aware of the dangerous condition and failed either to remedy the condition or warn the plaintiff of its existence. The grocer, of course, would be entitled to an instruction admonishing the fact finder to consider the evidence only for the permissible purpose.[5]

From a defendant's perspective, any evidence of carelessness on other occasions is dangerous: the fact finder might be tempted to use the evidence in a character manner, and the defendant must defend against more than one suit. The prejudicial nature of such evidence accounts for the second condition which the plaintiff must satisfy. The judge should not allow the plaintiff to offer evidence of other occurrences unless the circumstances attending the occurrence in question and the other occurrences are substantially similar.[6] If the plaintiff's theory is that the defendant was negligent in its maintenance of the produce area, then the plaintiff should be limited to offering evidence of the conditions in that area on other occasions and should not, for example, be permitted to offer evidence about the conditions of the parking lots. The conditions of the lots are less likely to put the defendant on notice about the conditions prevailing in the produce area. If a party is to be confronted with evidence that is potentially quite prejudicial, the least the law can do is ensure that the evidence bears directly on important contested issues.

The circumstances attending the two occurrences do not have to be identical, however. In Gilbert v. Pessin Grocery Co.[7] the plaintiff sued a

---

4.   Gilbert v. Pessin Grocery Co., 132 Cal.App.2d 212, 216–217, 282 P.2d 148, 153–154 (1955).

5.   West's Ann. California Evidence Code § 355; Federal Rule of Evidence 105. See also BAJI 2.05 (Fall 2007 Edition) and CALJIC 2.09 (Fall 2006 Edition).

6.   Gilbert v. Pessin Grocery Co., 132 Cal.App.2d 212, 216–217, 282 P.2d 148, 153–154 (1955).

7.   132 Cal.App.2d 212, 282 P.2d 148 (1955).

grocery store for injuries she suffered when she tripped and fell in the parking lot at night. The trial judge precluded the plaintiff from offering evidence showing that on an earlier occasion another customer had fallen in the lot at night when some of the floodlights were burned out.[8] Since the plaintiff's theory was that the none of the lights were on the night she fell, the appellate court held that it was error for the trial judge to exclude the evidence. If the lot presented a dangerous condition with some lights on, then it posed an even greater danger without any lights.[9] But if the litigated accident had been the one occurring with some lights, then the trial judge would have been correct in excluding the one occurring without lights.

These opposing results provide insight into the substantial similarity requirement. That in the first case accidents could occur while the lot was partially lighted tells us much about the dangerous condition of the lot when it was unlighted and also about the defendant's awareness of the danger the condition of the lot presented to nighttime customers. In the second case, that accidents could occur when the lot was unlighted tells us little about the dangers the lot presented when partially lighted and about the defendant's awareness of these dangers. In evidentiary terms, in the first case the evidence of the prior accident was highly probative of the dangerousness of the lot and the defendant's awareness of the dangers. In the second case, the probative value of the prior accident on these two questions would be very slight. Since evidence of prior carelessness could in any event be quite prejudicial to the defendant, a trial judge would be justified under Evidence Code § 352 or Federal Rule 403 in admitting the evidence in the first case while excluding it in the second. In applying these rules, trial judges must weigh the probative value of the proffered evidence against its prejudicial effects.[10]

The probative value of other occurrences may vary with the proposition sought to be proved. When offered to prove a dangerous or defective condition, greater similarity may be required. Evidence, for example, that others had fallen in a stairwell was held inadmissible to prove that the step the plaintiff fell on was defective.[11] Although this result has been criticized as unduly restrictive,[12] it is clear that, if the defendant was informed about the falls, then the evidence would be admissible today to prove that the defendant was or should have been aware of the dangerous condition of the stairs, including the step the plaintiff claims was defective.[13]

---

8. Id. at 218, 282 P.2d at 154.

9. Id.

10. West's Ann.California Evidence Code § 352; Federal Rule of Evidence 403. See also § 2.10 supra.

11. Thompson v. Buffums' Inc., 17 Cal.App.2d 401, 404–405, 62 P.2d 171, 173 (1936).

12. Laird v. T.W. Mather, 51 Cal.2d 210, 220, 331 P.2d 617, 623 (1958).

13. Id. " '[T]he requirement of similarity may vary in strictness according to the purpose for which the evidence is introduced. Thus if offered to show a dangerous condition of a particular thing . . . the other accident must be connected in some way with that thing; but if offered only to show knowledge or notice of the dangerous condition, an accident at the place—a broader area—

QUESTIONS AND PROBLEMS

1. Determine the admissibility of the following evidence offered in a slip and fall case tried in a California or federal court:

Plaintiff: About 10 AM on June 6, I fell when I slipped on a piece of lettuce in front of the defendant's produce section.

Plaintiff's Witness One: About 9 AM on June 5 I fell when I slipped on a piece of lettuce in front of the defendant's produce section.

Defendant: Objection. Inadmissible character evidence offered to prove that I am the kind of the shop keeper who fails to remove debris from the area in front of the produce section.

Plaintiff: Offered to prove the existence of a dangerous condition.

Judge: ?

Assume the same testimony except that the Plaintiff in addition testifies that only some of the lights were on at the time she fell and that Witness One testifies that all of the lights were on when he fell. If the store owner objects and moves to strike Witness One's testimony on the ground that the lighting conditions attending the two accidents were not similar, how should the plaintiff respond?

How should the judge rule?

2. Suppose that the accident took place on a sidewalk maintained by the Defendant. After the Plaintiff testifies that around noon he tripped on a crack in the sidewalk, he calls Store Owner as a witness. In ruling on the admissibility of Store Owner's testimony, assume that the Plaintiff fell within six months of the date of the trial.

Store Owner: For the last two years, I have operated a business across the street where the plaintiff says he fell.

Plaintiff: In that period of time, have you seen other people trip and fall in that area of the sidewalk around noon time?

Store Owner: Yes, I've seen at least three people trip and fall in that area.

Defendant: Objection. Move to strike. No proof that the conditions encountered by others were similar to the those encountered by Plaintiff.

Judge: Motion to strike granted. The answer will be stricken and the jurors admonished to disregard it.

Plaintiff: During the time you have operated your store, have any changes been made to that portion of the sidewalk where I said I fell?

Store Owner: No.

Plaintiff: During the time you have operated your store, have you seen other people trip and fall in that portion of the sidewalk around noon time?

---

may be shown.' " Sambrano v. City of San Diego, 94 Cal.App.4th 225, 237, 114 Cal.Rptr.2d 151, 161 (2001) (quoting from 1 Witkin, Evidence, Circumstantial Evidence § 104 (4th ed. 2000)).

Defendant: Same objection.

Judge: ?

If the judge admits the evidence, upon request by the defendant should the judge limit the jury's consideration of the evidence to show (1) the existence of a dangerous condition, (2) the cause of the plaintiff's accident, or (3) notice to the defendant of the existence of dangerous condition? [Answer after reviewing the next section.]

3. *Compare with:*

Tavern Owner: I have operated the tavern across the street from Store Owner's business for ten years. From my tavern I can see the sidewalk where plaintiff claims she fell. The sidewalk has not been changed from the time it was constructed.

Defendant: In that time, have you seen anyone fall on the sidewalk?

Tavern Owner: No.

Defendant: In that time, has anyone complained to you about the condition of the sidewalk?

Tavern Owner: No.

Plaintiff: Objection. Hearsay.

Judge: ? [Refrain from ruling until after the chapter on hearsay.]

4. *Compare with:*

Plaintiff: Mr. Store Owner, in the time that you've operated your business in front of the sidewalk, has anyone complained to you about the condition of the sidewalk?

Store Owner: Yes, three people told me that it was uneven.

Defendant: Objection. Hearsay.

Judge: ? [Refrain from ruling until after the chapter on hearsay.]

§ 3.22   PERMISSIBLE USES OF EVIDENCE OF SIMILAR OCCURRENCES

To be material, an item of evidence must be directed at a proposition that is properly provable in the action being tried.[1] In the case of similar occurrences, this means that the evidence must not be offered for a character or other prohibited purpose. Since the issue of similar occurrences has arisen principally in personal injury actions, most cases speak in terms of the permissible purposes for which evidence of prior and subsequent accidents may be offered.[2]

Prior accidents may be offered to prove the existence of a dangerous condition, notice to the defendant of the existence of such a condition, and

---

1. See § 2.01 supra.

2. See Gilbert v. Pessin Grocery Co., 132 Cal.App.2d 212, 282 P.2d 148 (1955) and cases cited therein.

the cause of the accident in dispute.[3] Subsequent accidents, of course, may not be offered to prove notice to the defendant.

These purposes presuppose their use by a plaintiff in a personal injury action. A defendant, however, may have access to evidence that may be viewed as the flip-side of the similar occurrences coin. In a slip and fall case, for example, the defendant might call the parking lot attendant to state that in the years he has been in charge of the lot he has seen no one fall. He might also state that in those years no one has complained to him about the condition of the lot.[4] Such evidence would be admissible to show the nonexistence of a dangerous condition or the defendant's reasons for not anticipating the condition harming the plaintiff.[5]

As in the case of similar occurrences, evidence of the lack of accidents or the absence of complaints must relate to conditions or circumstances that are similar to the ones in dispute. In Beauchamp v. Los Gatos Golf Course[6] the defendant's golf course operator was permitted to tell the jury that, other than the plaintiff, no one had complained to him about the condition of a cement veranda where the plaintiff fell and that between 3500 and 4000 persons used the veranda each month. The fact that so many others had used the same veranda for considerable time without complaint was relevant to show the safe condition of the veranda on the day the plaintiff fell.

When evidence of lack of complaints is offered to prove that the defendant was not on notice of the claimed defect, some courts require the proponent to show that users of the product could readily complain about the defect and that a reliable system for recording complaints was in place. The foundation can be established through a witness who is familiar with the complaint process and safety records of the product in issue. In Benson v. Honda Motor Co., Ltd.,[7] after laying the necessary foundation, Honda was allowed to have its claims history expert testify that purchasers of 913,000 cars similar to plaintiff's had not complained of the defect the plaintiff claimed gave rise to her injuries.[8]

---

3. Id. Some cases mention the "negligence" of the parties as one of the propositions to which evidence of prior and subsequent accidents may be directed. See, e.g., Jaehne v. Pacific Tel. & Tel. Co., 105 Cal.App.2d 683, 689, 234 P.2d 165, 169 (1951); Westman v. Clifton's Brookdale, Inc., 89 Cal.App.2d 307, 312, 200 P.2d 814, 817 (1948). But as discussed in § 3.20 supra, the purpose of the evidence in personal injury cases is usually to prove negligence *without* violating the ban on the use of character evidence. Hence the use of "negligence" can be misleading.

4. See Beauchamp v. Los Gatos Golf Course, 273 Cal.App.2d 20, 36–38, 77 Cal.Rptr. 914, 925–926 (1969) and cases cited therein. Though testimony regarding the absence of complaints may seem to violate the hearsay rule, it does not do so. Not complaining is not the equivalent of telling the parking lot attendant that the lot is in good condition. Accordingly, the act of not complaining generally does not constitute the kind of assertive nonverbal conduct contemplated by the hearsay rule. See West's Ann.California Evidence Code §§ 225 and 1200; Federal Rule of Evidence 801(a); see also § 5.05 infra.

5. Beauchamp v. Los Gatos Golf Course, 273 Cal.App.2d 20, 36–38, 77 Cal.Rptr. 914, 925–926 (1969) and cases cited therein.

6. Id.

7. 26 Cal.App.4th 1337, 32 Cal.Rptr.2d 322 (1994).

8. at 1343, 32 Cal.Rptr.2d at 324.

§ 3.23 SIMILAR OCCURRENCES AND MANUFACTURING AND DESIGN DEFECTS

The requirement that the circumstances attending the occurrence in dispute and other occurrences be similar is relaxed in cases involving manufacturing and design defects. In Ault v. International Harvester Co.[1] the plaintiff was injured while riding in a Scout vehicle which plunged 500 feet to the bottom of a canyon in rural California.[2] The plaintiff's theory was that the failure of the gearbox caused the Scout to go out of control, while the defendant claimed that the accident was caused by the driver's negligence, the gearbox having broken upon impact.[3] Over the defendant's objection, the plaintiff was permitted to introduce evidence of other accidents involving Scouts with failed gearboxes without satisfying the substantial similarity requirement.[4] The reviewing court upheld the trial judge's ruling, holding that where the focus is on a common design or manufacturing defect and not on the accidents themselves, no reason exists for applying the substantial similarity test.[5]

The court was unquestionably right. In cases involving design or manufacturing defects, the *differences* in the circumstances attending the disputed occurrence and the other occurrences are precisely what give the evidence its added probative value. Take the *Ault* situation. Evidence that Scout gearboxes failed and caused loss of control on different roads and at different speeds would say much about whether the plaintiff's injuries were caused by a defective gearbox or the driver's negligence. What matters is that the instrumentality (the gearbox in this case) be the same in all occurrences. An example can be found in Buell–Wilson v. Ford Motor Co.,[6] where the reviewing court approved the use of evidence of the instability of Ford Bronco II vehicles to prove that Ford was on notice of the instability of Ford Explorer vehicles.[7] The evidence was received after the plaintiff offered evidence that both vehicles shared the same design characteristics that gave rise to the instability.[8]

The same principle applies to evidence of absence of complaints regarding manufacturing or design defects. Unlike the evidence considered by the *Beauchamp* court,[9] in this instance the evidence of the absence of

1. 13 Cal.3d 113, 117 Cal.Rptr. 812, 528 P.2d 1148 (1974).

2. Id. at 117, 117 Cal.Rptr. at 814, 528 P.2d at 1150.

3. Id.

4. Id.

5. Id. at 122, 117 Cal.Rptr. at 817, 528 P.2d at 1153.

6. 141 Cal.App.4th 525, 46 Cal.Rptr.3d 147 (2006), cert. granted and judgment vacated on other grounds, Ford Motor Co. v. Buell–Wilson, 550 U.S. 931, 127 S.Ct. 2250, 167 L.Ed.2d 1087 (2007).

7. Id. at 161, 546 Cal. Rptr.3d at 543.

8. Id.

9. See § 3.21 supra.

complaints derives its added probative value from the fact that the instrumentality at issue may have been used in diverse circumstances over a considerable period of time without a mishap or complaint occurring.

QUESTIONS AND PROBLEMS

Rule on the admissibility of the following evidence offered in a personal injury action in which the plaintiff claimed that a design or manufacturing defect caused the accident:

Plaintiff: I own a Scout jeep. I was injured when it veered off the road and landed in a gully. At the time, I was driving on a one lane, unpaved mountain road.

Plaintiff's Expert: I examined the plaintiff's Scout. In my opinion, the cause of the accident was a defective transmission.

Plaintiff's Witness: I own a Scout jeep. One day it veered off the road and landed in a gully. At the time, I was in the center lane of US 280, on the way to Palo Alto from San Francisco.

Plaintiff's Expert: I examined the witness's Scout. In my opinion, the cause of the accident on US 280 was a defective transmission.

Defendant's Counsel: Move to strike the testimony of the last two witnesses on the ground that plaintiff failed to comply with the substantial similarity test.

Judge: ?

§ 3.24   SIMILAR SUITS AND ACCUSATIONS

To prove that the present claim is false, Dean Charles McCormick would admit evidence that a party has made previous similar claims if the evidence also shows that the previous claims were fraudulent.[1] Although more troubled by it, he would also admit evidence that a witness has made similar, false accusations about others to prove that the witness's present accusations are false.[2] He would justify the use of such evidence on two grounds: the need to expose fraudulent claims and false testimony, and the availability of rather convincing evidence.[3]

The difficulty with this evidence, as Dean McCormick admits, is that its use could violate the rules banning character evidence. In the first situation, the proponent may be asking the fact finder to find the present claim false because, having filed similar false claims, the opposing party is

---

1. C. McCormick, McCormick on Evidence § 196 (J. Strong 4th ed. 1992).

2. Id.

3. Id. "It would seem that the judge, balancing probative value against prejudice, should admit the evidence only if the probability of coincidence seems negligible or if the proponent has distinct evidence of fraud." Id. (footnotes omitted).

The reference to "coincidence" may be an appeal to the doctrine of chances. Evidence offered under this doctrine is not considered to be character evidence. For a discussion of this doctrine, see § 3.15, note 32, supra.

the kind of person who files false claims, including the present one. The second situation may involve similar reasoning: the fact finder should disbelieve the witness's accusation because, having made similar false accusations, the witness is the kind of person who makes false accusations, including the present one. This is precisely the kind of reasoning condemned by the character evidence rules.[4]

Absent persuasive due process claims, California Evidence Code § 1101(a) and Federal Rule of Evidence 404(a) would bar the use of such evidence for these purposes.[5] Moreover, in California civil cases, it would not help the proponent to claim that she is offering the evidence only to attack the credibility of the opposing party or the witness. Though such evidence is relevant on that issue, § 787 prohibits a party from offering evidence of specific instances of a witness's conduct to prove that the witness is the kind of person who ought to be disbelieved.[6]

Evidence of similar suits may be admissible if offered to prove some contested fact other than a person's predisposition to act in a particular way on a given occasion. In Brown v. Affonso[7] the plaintiff sued the defendant for head injuries he claimed to have suffered in an automobile accident.[8] The defendant was permitted to elicit evidence that the plaintiff had claimed similar injuries on previous occasions.[9] The evidence was not admitted to show that the plaintiff had filed a false claim; rather, it was received to show that the defendant was not the cause of the plaintiff's injuries.[10]

Likewise, evidence of similar accusations may be admitted if offered to prove some relevant proposition other than a person's propensity to act in a particular way on a given occasion. In re Malone[11] is illustrative. In this case, a key prosecution witness related incriminatory statements which the witness claimed the accused had made while they were inmates. To attack the credibility of the witness, the accused was allowed to offer evidence that on other occasions the witness had offered law enforcement officials false incriminating information about fellow inmates in the hope that he would receive favorable treatment in his pending cases. The evidence did not violate the ban on the use of character evidence. It was not received as proof that the witness fabricated his testimony against the accused because the witness was the kind of person who made false accusations. Rather, the evidence was received to prove that the witness made false accusations against the accused as part of a common plan or

---

4. See §§ 3.02 and 3.04 supra.

5. West's Ann.California Evidence Code § 1101(a); Federal Rule of Evidence 404(b). See also §§ 3.02 and 3.04 supra.

6. West's Ann.California Evidence Code § 787. See also § 15.06 infra. This limitation, however, no longer applies to criminal cases. See §§ 15.01 and 15.06 infra.

7. 185 Cal.App.2d 235, 8 Cal.Rptr. 156 (1960).

8. Id. at 238, 8 Cal.Rptr. at 158–159.

9. Id.

10. Id.

11. 12 Cal.4th 935, 50 Cal.Rptr.2d 281, 911 P.2d 468 (1996).

scheme to curry favor with the authorities by offering false evidence against inmates.[12]

Obviously, if admitted over a § 352 or Rule 403 objection, such evidence should come in with the appropriate limiting instruction. But where the probative value of such evidence is not strong, then the trial judge should exclude the evidence because of the danger that the fact finder may treat it as character evidence.[13]

QUESTIONS AND PROBLEMS

1. To prove that the defendant filed a false medical claim with the plaintiff, an insurance company, the plaintiff may offer evidence that the defendant filed similar false claims with other insurance companies as part of a common scheme to defraud insurers. True or false?

2. Suppose that the defendant claims that he filed the false claim with the plaintiff by accident. May the plaintiff offer the evidence of the other false filings to disprove the defendant's claim?

3. A professor sues her dean, claiming that the dean denied the professor a salary increase on account of her gender. The dean testifies that he denied the professor a raise because of her low scholarly output. The professor calls the associate dean who testifies that the dean granted salary increases to male professors with the same or less scholarly output of the professor. The dean moves to strike on the ground that the testimony is inadmissible character evidence.

    a. How should the judge rule? *Denies*

    b. If the judge denies the motion to strike, what protection should the dean seek?   *Jury instruction limiting.*

§ 3.25 SIMILAR CONTRACTS

As a matter of relevance, evidence of other transactions between the same parties can be received to determine the meaning the parties intended to attach to disputed terms of a contract.[1] The evidence is clearly relevant: evidence that in the past the parties have given a special meaning to a term renders more likely the proposition that they intended to give the same meaning to the disputed term than the proposition would be without the evidence.[2] Whether the evidence runs afoul of the rule banning the use of character evidence is problematical, however. To the extent that the manner in which the opposing party treated the disputed term in past transactions gives rise to a habit or custom, the issue

---

12. Id. at 947, 50 Cal.Rptr.2d at 289, 911 P.2d at 476.

13. See, e.g., Lowenthal v. Mortimer, 125 Cal.App.2d 636, 643, 270 P.2d 942, 945 (1954), a pre-Code case discussing the prejudicial effects of admitting such evidence even for a noncharacter purpose.

1. C. McCormick, McCormick on Evidence § 198 (J. Strong 4th ed. 1992).

2. For a discussion of relevance, see §§ 2.01 and 2.04 supra.

disappears. Evidence of a habit or custom is admissible to show that a person or an organization conforms its practices with a habit or custom.[3]

If the evidence of the other transactions fails to qualify as a habit or custom, then the character evidence concerns are revived. If, for example, the proponent is asking the fact finder to find that the opposing party extended a warranty because having extended warranties in the past he is the kind of person who extends warranties, then the character evidence ban is violated.[4] The California cases, however, have not focused on this aspect of evidence of similar transactions but on its relevance.[5]

With regard to relevance, the principal concern has been whether a party's transactions with others should be admitted to prove some aspect of the party's transactions with the proponent of the evidence. For example, in Moody v. Peirano[6] the issue was whether evidence that the defendant warranted wheat he sold to third persons could be received to prove that he warranted the wheat he sold the plaintiff;[7] in Firlotte v. Jessee[8] it was whether evidence that the defendant had failed to reserve grazing rights in land he offered to lease to another could be received to prove that he failed to reserve such rights in the land he leased to the plaintiff.[9] In both instances, the court upheld the receipt of the evidence. In contemporary terms, the holdings could be described as follows: the evidence was relevant because it rendered the proposition to be proved more likely than the proposition would have been without the evidence;[10] moreover, given the similarities between the transaction in dispute and the transactions with the third parties, the value of the evidence in proving the proposition was sufficiently great as to outweigh such countervailing concerns as confusion of the issues and undue consumption of time.[11]

Neither case, however, addressed the question whether the use of the evidence violated the character evidence rules. A later case, Lande v. Southern Cal. Freight Lines,[12] defended *Moody* and *Peirano* on the ground that the evidence admitted in those cases amounted to a habit or custom, or common plan.[13] Although the court at least reached for terms that begin to address the character concerns raised by the evidence,[14] the

---

3. See § 3.19 supra.

4. See §§ 3.02 and 3.04 supra.

5. See, e.g., Firlotte v. Jessee, 76 Cal.App.2d 207, 211, 172 P.2d 710, 711–712 (1946); Moody v. Peirano, 4 Cal.App. 411, 416–417, 88 P. 380, 382–383 (1906).

6. 4 Cal.App. 411, 88 P. 380 (1906).

7. Id. at 415–416, 88 P. at 382–383.

8. 76 Cal.App.2d 207, 172 P.2d 710 (1946).

9. Id. at 209, 172 P.2d at 711.

10. For a discussion of the meaning of relevance, see §§ 2.01 and 2.04 supra.

11. For a discussion of the probative value and prejudicial effects of evidence, see § 2.10 supra.

12. 85 Cal.App.2d 416, 193 P.2d 144 (1948).

13. Id. at 423, 193 P.2d at 148.

14. See §§ 3.15 and 3.19 supra.

discussion, as in the earlier cases, centered on relevance.[15]

If confronted with an inadmissible character evidence objection, the proponent of evidence of similar transactions must satisfy the court that the evidence is being offered to prove a relevant noncharacter purpose.

ARTICLE 1 OF THE CALIFORNIA CONSTITUTION

§ 28. Findings and declarations; rights of victims; enforcement

* * *

(f) In addition to the enumerated rights provided in subdivision (b) that are personally enforceable by victims as provided in subdivision (c), victims of crime have additional rights that are shared with all of the People of the State of California. These collectively held rights include, but are not limited to, the following:

* * *

(2) Except as provided by statute hereafter enacted by a two-thirds vote of the membership in each house of the Legislature, relevant evidence shall not be excluded in any criminal proceeding, including pretrial and post conviction motions and hearings, or in any trial or hearing of a juvenile for a criminal offense, whether heard in juvenile or adult court. Nothing in this section shall affect any existing statutory rule of evidence relating to privilege or hearsay, or Evidence Code Sections 352, 782, or 1103. Nothing in this section shall affect any existing statutory or constitutional right of the press.

CALIFORNIA EVIDENCE CODE

§ 1100. Manner of proof of character

Except as otherwise provided by statute, any otherwise admissible evidence (including evidence in the form of an opinion, evidence of reputation, and evidence of specific instances of such person's conduct) is admissible to prove a person's character or a trait of his character.

§ 1101. Evidence of character to prove conduct

(a) Except as provided in this section and in Sections 1102 and 1103, 1108, and 1109, evidence of a person's character or a trait of his or her character (whether in the form of an opinion, evidence of reputation, or evidence of specific instances of his or her conduct) is inadmissible when offered to prove his or her conduct on a specified occasion.

---

15. Lande v. Southern Cal. Freight Lines, 85 Cal.App.2d 416, 423, 193 P.2d 144, 148 (1948).

(b) Nothing in this section prohibits the admission of evidence that a person committed a crime, civil wrong, or other act when relevant to prove some fact (such as motive, opportunity, intent, preparation, plan, knowledge, identity, absence of mistake or accident, or whether a defendant in a prosecution for an unlawful sexual act or attempted unlawful sexual act did not reasonably and in good faith believe that the victim consented) other than his or her disposition to commit such an act.

(c) Nothing in this section affects the admissibility of evidence offered to support or attack the credibility of a witness.

§ 1102. Opinion and reputation evidence of character of criminal defendant to prove conduct

In a criminal action, evidence of the defendant's character or a trait of his character in the form of an opinion or evidence of his reputation is not made inadmissible by Section 1101 if such evidence is:

(a) Offered by the defendant to prove his conduct in conformity with such character or trait of character.

(b) Offered by the prosecution to rebut evidence adduced by the defendant under subdivision (a).

§ 1103. Character evidence of crime victim to prove conduct; evidence of defendant's character or trait for violence; evidence of manner of dress of victim; evidence of complaining witness' sexual conduct

(a) In a criminal action, evidence of the character or a trait of character (in the form of an opinion, evidence of reputation, or evidence of specific instances of conduct) of the victim of the crime for which the defendant is being prosecuted is not made inadmissible by Section 1101 if the evidence is:

(1) Offered by the defendant to prove conduct of the victim in conformity with the character or trait of character.

(2) Offered by the prosecution to rebut evidence adduced by the defendant under paragraph (1).

(b) In a criminal action, evidence of the defendant's character for violence or trait of character for violence (in the form of an opinion, evidence of reputation, or evidence of specific instances of conduct) is not made inadmissible by Section 1101 if the evidence is offered by the prosecution to prove conduct of the defendant in conformity with the character or trait of character and is offered after evidence that the victim had a character for violence or a trait of character tending to show violence has been adduced by the defendant under paragraph (1) of subdivision (a).

(c)(1) Notwithstanding any other provision of this code to the contrary, and except as provided in this subdivision, in any prosecution under Section 261, 262 or 264.1 of the Penal Code, or under Section 286, 288a, or 289 of the Penal Code, or for assault with intent to commit, attempt to commit, or conspiracy to commit a crime defined in any of those sections, except where the crime is alleged to have occurred in a local detention facility, as defined in Section 6031.4, or in a state prison, as defined in Section 4504, opinion evidence, reputation evidence, and evidence of specific instances of the complaining witness' sexual conduct, or any of that evidence, is not admissible by the defendant in order to prove consent by the complaining witness.

(2) Notwithstanding paragraph (3), evidence of the manner in which the victim was dressed at the time of the commission of the offense shall not be admissible when offered by either party on the issue of consent in any prosecution for an offense specified in paragraph (1), unless the evidence is determined by the court to be relevant and admissible in the interests of justice. The proponent of the evidence shall make an offer of proof outside the hearing of the jury. The court shall then make its determination and at that time, state the reasons for its ruling on the record. For the purposes of this paragraph, "manner of dress" does not include the condition of the victim's clothing before, during, or after the commission of the offense.

(3) Paragraph (1) shall not be applicable to evidence of the complaining witness' sexual conduct with the defendant.

(4) If the prosecutor introduces evidence, including testimony of a witness, or the complaining witness as a witness gives testimony, and that evidence or testimony relates to the complaining witness' sexual conduct, the defendant may cross-examine the witness who gives the testimony and offer relevant evidence limited specifically to the rebuttal of the evidence introduced by the prosecutor or given by the complaining witness.

(5) Nothing in this subdivision shall be construed to make inadmissible any evidence offered to attack the credibility of the complaining witness as provided in Section 782.

(6) As used in this section, "complaining witness" means the alleged victim of the crime charged, the prosecution of which is subject to this subdivision.

§ 1104. Character trait for care or skill

Except as provided in Sections 1102 and 1103, evidence of a trait of a person's character with respect to care or skill is inadmissible to prove the quality of his conduct on a specified occasion.

§ 1105. Habit or custom to prove specific behavior

Any otherwise admissible evidence of habit or custom is admissible to prove conduct on a specified occasion in conformity with the habit or custom.

§ 1106. Sexual harassment, sexual assault, or sexual battery cases; opinion or reputation evidence of plaintiff's sexual conduct; inadmissibility; exception; cross-examination

(a) In any civil action alleging conduct which constitutes sexual harassment, sexual assault, or sexual battery, opinion evidence, reputation evidence, and evidence of specific instances of plaintiff's sexual conduct, or any of such evidence, is not admissible by the defendant in order to prove consent by the plaintiff or the absence of injury to the plaintiff, unless the injury alleged by the plaintiff is in the nature of loss of consortium.

(b) Subdivision (a) shall not be applicable to evidence of the plaintiff's sexual conduct with the alleged perpetrator.

(c) If the plaintiff introduces evidence, including testimony of a witness, or the plaintiff as a witness gives testimony, and the evidence or testimony relates to the plaintiff's sexual conduct, the defendant may cross-examine the witness who gives the testimony and offer relevant evidence limited specifically to the rebuttal of the evidence introduced by the plaintiff or given by the plaintiff.

(d) Nothing in this section shall be construed to make inadmissible any evidence offered to attack the credibility of the plaintiff as provided in Section 783.

§ 1107. Intimate partner battering and its effects; expert testimony in criminal actions; sufficiency of foundation; abuse and domestic violence; applicability to Penal Code; impact on decisional law

(a) In a criminal action, expert testimony is admissible by either the prosecution or the defense regarding intimate partner battering and its effects, including the nature and effect of physical, emotional, or mental abuse on the beliefs, perceptions, or behavior of victims of domestic violence, except when offered against a criminal defendant to prove the occurrence of the act or acts of abuse which form the basis of the criminal charge.

(b) The foundation shall be sufficient for admission of this expert testimony if the proponent of the evidence establishes its relevancy and the proper qualifications of the expert witness. Expert opinion testimony on intimate partner battering and its effects shall not be considered a new scientific technique whose reliability is unproven.

(c) For purposes of this section, "abuse" is defined in Section 6203 of the Family Code and "domestic violence" is defined in Section 6211 of the Family Code and may include acts defined in Section 242, subdivision (e) of Section 243, Section 262, 273.5, 273.6, 422 or 653m of the Penal Code.

(d) This section is intended as a rule of evidence only and no substantive change affecting the Penal Code is intended.

(e) This section shall be known, and may be cited as, the Expert Witness Testimony on Intimate Partner Battering and its Effects Section of the Evidence Code.

(f) The changes in this section that become effective on January 1, 2005, are not intended to impact any existing decisional law regarding this section, and that decisional law should apply equally to this section as it refers to "intimate partner battering and its effects" in place of "battered women's syndrome."

§ 1108. Evidence of another sexual offense

(a) In a criminal action in which the defendant is accused of a sexual offense, evidence of the defendant's commission of another sexual offense or offenses is not made inadmissible by Section 1101, if the evidence is not inadmissible pursuant to Section 352.

(b) In an action in which evidence is to be offered under this section, the people shall disclose the evidence to the defendant, including statements of witnesses or a summary of the substance of any testimony that is expected to be offered, in compliance with the provisions of Section 1054.7 of the Penal Code.

(c) This section shall not be construed to limit the admission or consideration of evidence under any other section of this code.

(d) As used in this section, the following definitions shall apply:

(1) "Sexual offense" means a crime under the law of a state or of the United States that involved any of the following:

(A) Any conduct proscribed by Section 243.4, 261, 261.5, 262, 264.1, 266c, 269, 286, 288, 288a, 288.2, 288.5, or 289, or subdivision (b), (c), or (d) of Section 311.2 or Section 311.3, 311.4, 311.10, 311.11, 314, or 647.6, of the Penal Code.

(B) Any conduct proscribed by Section 220 of the Penal Code, except assault with intent to commit mayhem.

(C) Contact, without consent, between any part of the defendant's body or an object and the genitals or anus of any person.

(D) Contact, without consent, between the genitals or anus of the defendant and part of another person's body.

(E) Deriving sexual pleasure or gratification from the infliction of death, bodily injury, or physical pain on another person.

(F) An attempt or conspiracy to engage in conduct described in this paragraph.

(2) "Consent" shall have the same meaning as provided in Section 261.6 of the Penal Code except that it does not include consent which is legally ineffective because of the age, mental disorder, or developmental or physical disability of the victim.

§ 1109. Evidence of an offense involving domestic violence

(a)(1) Except as provided in subdivision (e) or (f), in a criminal action in which the defendant is accused of an offense involving domestic violence, evidence of the defendant's commission of other domestic violence is not made inadmissible by Section 1101 if the evidence is not inadmissible pursuant to Section 352.

(2) Except as provided in subdivision (e) or (f), in a criminal action in which the defendant is accused of an offense involving abuse of an elder or dependent person, evidence of the defendant's commission of other abuse of an elder or dependent person is not made inadmissible by Section 1101 if the evidence is not inadmissible pursuant to Section 352.

(3) Except as provided in subdivision (e) or (f) and subject to a hearing conducted pursuant to Section 352, which shall include consideration of any corroboration and remoteness in time, in a criminal action in which the defendant is accused of an offense involving child abuse, evidence of the defendant's commission of child abuse is not made inadmissible by Section 1101 if the evidence is not inadmissible pursuant to Section 352. Nothing in this paragraph prohibits or limits the admission of evidence pursuant to subdivision (b) of Section 1101.

(b) In an action in which evidence is to be offered under this section, the people shall disclose the evidence to the defendant, including statements of witnesses or a summary of the substance of any testimony that is expected to be offered, in compliance with the provisions of Section 1054.7 of the Penal Code.

(c) This section shall not be construed to limit or preclude the admission or consideration of evidence under any other statute or case law.

(d) As used in this section:

(1) "Abuse of an elder or dependent person" means physical or sexual abuse, neglect, financial abuse, abandonment, isolation, abduction, or other treatment that results in physical harm, pain, or mental suffering, the deprivation of care by a caregiver, or other deprivation by a custodian or provider of goods or services that are necessary to avoid physical harm or mental suffering.

(2) "Child abuse" means an act proscribed by Section 273d of the Penal Code.

(3) "Domestic violence" has the meaning set forth in Section 13700 of the Penal Code. Subject to a hearing conducted pursuant to Section 352, which shall include consideration of any corroboration and remoteness in time, "domestic violence" has the further meaning as set forth in Section 6211 of the Family Code, if the act occurred no more than five years before the charged offense.

(e) Evidence of acts occurring more than 10 years before the charged offense is inadmissible under this section, unless the court determines that the admission of this evidence is in the interest of justice.

(f) Evidence of the findings and determinations of administrative agencies regulating the conduct of health facilities licensed under Section 1250 of the Health and Safety Code is inadmissible under this section.

———————

FEDERAL RULES OF EVIDENCE

Rule 404. Character Evidence; Crimes or Other Acts

(a) Character Evidence.

(1) *Prohibited Uses.* Evidence of a person's character or character trait is not admissible to prove that on a particular occasion the person acted in accordance with the character or trait.

(2) *Exceptions for a Defendant or Victim in a Criminal Case.* The following exceptions apply in a criminal case:

(A) a defendant may offer evidence of the defendant's pertinent trait, and if the evidence is admitted, the prosecutor may offer evidence to rebut it;

(B) subject to the limitations in Rule 412, a defendant may offer evidence of an alleged victim's pertinent trait, and if the evidence is admitted, the prosecutor may:

(i) offer evidence to rebut it; and

(ii) offer evidence of the defendant's same trait; and

(C) in a homicide case, the prosecutor may offer evidence of the alleged victim's trait of peacefulness to rebut evidence that the victim was the first aggressor.

(3) *Exceptions for a Witness.* Evidence of a witness's character may be admitted under Rules 607, 608, and 609.

(b) Crimes, Wrongs, or Other Acts.

(1) *Prohibited Uses.* Evidence of a crime, wrong, or other act is not admissible to prove a person's character in order to show that on a particular occasion the person acted in accordance with the character.

(2) *Permitted Uses; Notice in a Criminal Case.* This evidence may be admissible for another purpose, such as proving motive, opportunity, intent, preparation, plan, knowledge, identity, absence of mistake, or lack of accident. On request by a defendant in a criminal case, the prosecutor must:

(A) provide reasonable notice of the general nature of any such evidence that the prosecutor intends to offer at trial; and

(B) do so before trial—or during trial if the court, for good cause, excuses lack of pretrial notice.

Rule 405. Methods of Proving Character

(a) By Reputation or Opinion. When evidence of a person's character or character trait is admissible, it may be proved by testimony about the person's reputation or by testimony in the form of an opinion. On cross-examination of the character witness, the court may allow an inquiry into relevant specific instances of the person's conduct.

(b) By Specific Instances of Conduct. When a person's character or character trait is an essential element of a charge, claim, or defense, the character or trait may also be proved by relevant specific instances of the person's conduct.

Rule 406.   Habit; Routine Practice

Evidence of a person's habit or an organization's routine practice may be admitted to prove that on a particular occasion the person or organization acted in accordance with the habit or routine practice. The court may admit this evidence regardless of whether it is corroborated or whether there was an eyewitness.

Rule 412.   Sex–Offense Cases: The Victim's Sexual Behavior or Predisposition

(a) Prohibited Uses. The following evidence is not admissible in a civil or criminal proceeding involving alleged sexual misconduct:

> **(1)** evidence offered to prove that a victim engaged in other sexual behavior; or

> **(2)** evidence offered to prove a victim's sexual predisposition.

(b) Exceptions.

> **(1)** *Criminal Cases.* The court may admit the following evidence in a criminal case:

>> **(A)** evidence of specific instances of a victim's sexual behavior, if offered to prove that someone other than the defendant was the source of semen, injury, or other physical evidence;

>> **(B)** evidence of specific instances of a victim's sexual behavior with respect to the person accused of the sexual misconduct, if offered by the defendant to prove consent or if offered by the prosecutor; and

>> **(C)** evidence whose exclusion would violate the defendant's constitutional rights.

> **(2)** *Civil Cases.* In a civil case, the court may admit evidence offered to prove a victim's sexual behavior or sexual predisposition if its probative value substantially outweighs the danger of harm to any victim and of unfair prejudice to any party. The court may admit evidence of a victim's reputation only if the victim has placed it in controversy.

(c) Procedure to Determine Admissibility.

> **(1)** *Motion.* If a party intends to offer evidence under Rule 412(b), the party must:

>> **(A)** file a motion that specifically describes the evidence and states the purpose for which it is to be offered;

>> **(B)** do so at least 14 days before trial unless the court, for good cause, sets a different time;

(C) serve the motion on all parties; and

(D) notify the victim or, when appropriate, the victim's guardian or representative.

(2) *Hearing.* Before admitting evidence under this rule, the court must conduct an in camera hearing and give the victim and parties a right to attend and be heard. Unless the court orders otherwise, the motion, related materials, and the record of the hearing must be and remain sealed.

(d) Definition of "Victim." In this rule, "victim" includes an alleged victim.

Rule 413.   Similar Crimes in Sexual–Assault Cases

(a) Permitted Uses. In a criminal case in which a defendant is accused of a sexual assault, the court may admit evidence that the defendant committed any other sexual assault. The evidence may be considered on any matter to which it is relevant.

(b) Disclosure to the Defendant. If the prosecutor intends to offer this evidence, the prosecutor must disclose it to the defendant, including witnesses' statements or a summary of the expected testimony. The prosecutor must do so at least 15 days before trial or at a later time that the court allows for good cause.

(c) Effect on Other Rules. This rule does not limit the admission or consideration of evidence under any other rule.

(d) Definition of "Sexual Assault." In this rule and Rule 415, "sexual assault" means a crime under federal law or under state law (as "state" is defined in 18 U.S.C. § 513) involving:

(1) any conduct prohibited by 18 U.S.C. chapter 109A;

(2) contact, without consent, between any part of the defendant's body—or an object—and another person's genitals or anus;

(3) contact, without consent, between the defendant's genitals or anus and any part of another person's body;

(4) deriving sexual pleasure or gratification from inflicting death, bodily injury, or physical pain on another person; or

(5) an attempt or conspiracy to engage in conduct described in subparagraphs (1)–(4).

Rule 414.   Similar Crimes in Child–Molestation Cases

(a) Permitted Uses. In a criminal case in which a defendant is accused of child molestation, the court may admit evidence that the defendant committed any other child molestation. The evidence may be considered on any matter to which it is relevant.

(b) Disclosure to the Defendant. If the prosecutor intends to offer this evidence, the prosecutor must disclose it to the defendant, including witnesses' statements or a summary of the expected testimony. The prosecutor must do so at least 15 days before trial or at a later time that the court allows for good cause.

(c) Effect on Other Rules. This rule does not limit the admission or consideration of evidence under any other rule.

(d) Definition of "Child" and "Child Molestation."

In this rule and Rule 415:

> **(1)** "child" means a person below the age of 14; and

> **(2)** "child molestation" means a crime under federal law or under state law (as "state" is defined in 18 U.S.C. § 513) involving:

>> **(A)** any conduct prohibited by 18 U.S.C. chapter 109A and committed with a child;

>> **(B)** any conduct prohibited by 18 U.S.C. chapter 110;

>> **(C)** contact between any part of the defendant's body—or an object—and a child's genitals or anus;

>> **(D)** contact between the defendant's genitals or anus and any part of a child's body;

>> **(E)** deriving sexual pleasure or gratification from inflicting death, bodily injury, or physical pain on a child; or

>> **(F)** an attempt or conspiracy to engage in conduct described in subparagraphs (A)–(E).

Rule 415. Similar Acts in Civil Cases Involving Sexual Assault or Child Molestation

(a) Permitted Uses. In a civil case involving a claim for relief based on a party's alleged sexual assault or child molestation, the court may admit evidence that the party committed any other sexual assault or child molestation. The evidence may be considered as provided in Rules 413 and 414.

(b) Disclosure to the Opponent. If a party intends to offer this evidence, the party must disclose it to the party against whom it will be offered, including witnesses' statements or a summary of the expected testimony. The party must do so at least 15 days before trial or at a later time that the court allows for good cause.

(c) Effect on Other Rules. This rule does not limit the admission or consideration of evidence under any other rule.

CHAPTER 4

OTHER EVIDENCE EXCLUDED BY EXTRINSIC POLICIES—SUBSEQUENT PRECAUTIONS, PLEAS, COMPROMISE OFFERS, AND LIABILITY INSURANCE

■ ■ ■

Table of Sections

§ 4.01 INTRODUCTION

Chapter 4, like Chapter 3, reviews rules that ban or limit the use of evidence for certain purposes. Examples include the rules regarding the use of evidence of subsequent remedial measures, of pleas and related statements in criminal cases, of statements made in settling civil cases, and of statements referring to liability insurance.

With the possible exception of evidence referring to liability insurance, the evidence discussed in this chapter is not restricted because it is irrelevant; rather, limits are placed on its admissibility because its unrestrained admission would harm some interest the law protects at the cost of excluding relevant evidence.

§ 4.02 SUBSEQUENT PRECAUTIONS

Personal injury lawyers can appreciate the value of presenting the fact finder with evidence of the steps the defendant took to remedy the condition or instrumentality which harmed the plaintiff. They know that the fact finder would consider such steps as an admission by the defendant of wrongdoing, whether inadvertent or otherwise. Unfortunately for the plaintiffs' bar, evidence of subsequent remedial measures is inadmissible if offered to prove negligence or culpable conduct. As stated in California Evidence Code § 1151, "When, after the occurrence of an event, remedial or precautionary measures are taken, which if taken previously, would have tended to make the event less likely to occur, evidence of such subsequent measures is inadmissible to prove negligence or culpable conduct in connection with the event."[1] Federal Rule of Evidence 407 is to the same effect.

The evidence is not excluded because it is irrelevant. Rather, it is excluded because of the belief that its use to prove negligence or other culpable conduct would discourage defendants from making repairs after an accident.[2] Only evidence of *subsequent* remedial measures is barred by the rule. The doctrine does not apply to evidence of remedial measures undertaken by the defendant *prior* to the plaintiff's accident and offered to prove that the defendant was aware of the dangerous condition giving rise to the plaintiff's injuries.[3]

Section 1151 does not apply to strict liability actions.[4] In Ault v. International Harvester Co.[5] the California Supreme Court held that the term "culpable conduct" does not embrace strict liability. In a strict liability action against a manufacturer, "negligence or culpability is not a necessary ingredient. The plaintiff may recover if he establishes that the product was defective, and he need not show that the defendants breached a duty of due care."[6]

In holding that § 1151 does not apply to strict liability actions, the court did not rely exclusively on the language of the statute. The court

---

1. West's Ann.California Evidence Code § 1151.

2. West's Ann.California Evidence Code § 1151 (comment). The Advisory Committee that drafted the Federal Rules of Evidence takes the position that evidence of subsequent remedial measures is excluded also because it may be irrelevant. "The conduct is not in fact an admission, since the conduct is equally consistent with injury by mere accident or through contributory negligence." Federal Rule of Evidence 407 (Advisory Committee Note). The committee concedes, however, that under "a liberal theory of relevancy" evidence of remedial measures does operate as an admission. Id.

3. See Alpert v. Villa Romano Homeowners Assn., 81 Cal.App.4th 1320, 1339–1342, 96 Cal.Rptr.2d 364, 380–382 (2000). See also Federal Rule of Evidence 407.

4. See Brisbois, *California Products Liability* §§ 324 and 327 (West 1985).

5. 13 Cal.3d 113, 117 Cal.Rptr. 812, 528 P.2d 1148 (1974).

6. Id. at 118, 117 Cal.Rptr. at 814, 528 P.2d at 1150. How is evidence of subsequent repairs relevant in a strict liability action in which culpable conduct presumably is not an issue? As a concession that it was indeed the defendant's instrumentality which caused the harm complained of. Causation remains an issue even in strict liability actions. Moreover, evidence that a manufacturer changed a product can be probative of the proposition that the product was designed defectively.

stressed that the policy of encouraging repairs does not apply to the mass manufacturer. "[I]t is manifestly unrealistic to suggest that such a producer will forego making improvements in its product, and risk innumerable additional lawsuits and the attendant adverse effect upon its public image, simply because evidence of adoption of such improvement may be admitted in an action founded on strict liability for recovery on an injury that preceded the improvement."[7]

The federal circuits split on whether the subsequent repair doctrine of Federal Rule of Evidence 407 as originally enacted applied to strict liability cases. The Eighth and Tenth Circuits adopted the *Ault* approach,[8] while the Second, Fifth, Sixth, Seventh, and Ninth Circuits rejected it.[9] The proper construction of Rule 407 is no longer an issue, however. A 1997 amendment provides that evidence of subsequent remedial measures is not admissible to prove "a defect in a product or its design."[10]

However, the question in federal courts is not simply one of construing Rule 407. *Erie*[11] concerns are implicated in diversity cases. If the *Ault* construction of state rules such as § 1151 is deemed to imbue the state rule with a substantive purpose, then a federal court may have to apply the state rule in a diversity case irrespective of the construction given to Rule 407 in federal question cases.[12] On the other hand, Rule 407's extension of the subsequent repair doctrine to strict liability cases necessarily embodies a policy designed to protect all defendants. That policy clashes with state policies adopting the *Ault* approach. The federal circuits disagree on whether in such circumstances Federal Rule 407 must yield to state rules like § 1151.[13]

The 1997 amendment also makes clear that Rule 407 applies only to remedial measures made after the occurrence that produced the damages giving rise to the action.[14] The amendment, however, does not resolve the controversy of whether a federal judge should apply the federal rule or a contrary state rule, such as California Evidence Code § 1151, when presiding over a diversity case.

---

7. Id. at 120, 117 Cal.Rptr. at 816, 528 P.2d at 1152.

8. Roth v. Black & Decker, 737 F.2d 779, 782 (8th Cir.1984); Herndon v. Seven Bar Flying Service, Inc., 716 F.2d 1322, 1326–1329 (10th Cir.1983), cert. denied, 466 U.S. 958, 104 S.Ct. 2170, 80 L.Ed.2d 553 (1984).

9. Cann v. Ford Motor Co., 658 F.2d 54, 60 (2d Cir.1981), cert. denied, 456 U.S. 960, 102 S.Ct. 2036, 72 L.Ed.2d 484 (1982); Alexander v. Conveyors & Dumpers, Inc., 731 F.2d 1221, 1229 (5th Cir.1984); Hall v. American Steamship Co., 688 F.2d 1062, 1066 (6th Cir.1982); Flaminio v. Honda Motor Co., 733 F.2d 463, 468–472 (7th Cir.1984); Gauthier v. AMF, Inc., 788 F.2d 634, 636–637 (9th Cir.1986), opinion amended, reh'g denied, 805 F.2d 337 (1986).

10. Federal Rule of Evidence 407.

11. Erie Railroad v. Tompkins, 304 U.S. 64, 58 S.Ct. 817, 82 L.Ed. 1188 (1938).

12. Hanna v. Plumer, 380 U.S. 460, 85 S.Ct. 1136, 14 L.Ed.2d 8 (1965).

13. Compare Flaminio v. Honda Motor Co., 733 F.2d 463, 470–473 (7th Cir.1984) (applying Federal Rule of Evidence 407) with Moe v. Avions Marcel Dassault–Breguet Aviation, 727 F.2d 917, 932 (10th Cir.1984), cert. denied, 469 U.S. 853, 105 S.Ct. 176, 83 L.Ed.2d 110 (1984) (applying state rule). See also Fasanaro v. Mooney Aircraft Corp., 687 F.Supp. 482, 485 (N.D. Cal. 1988) (applying Rule 407 after comparing *Flaminio* with *Moe*).

14. Federal Rule of Evidence 407 (Advisory Committee Note).

so in admissible.

section 1151 doesn't apply to S.L.

but FRE 407 supersedes above.

FRE 407 vs. 1151 unclear

Adm. ∵ prior

QUESTIONS AND PROBLEMS

1. The plaintiff is injured in California while driving a "Scout" sports utility vehicle manufactured in California. The plaintiff brings a strict liability action in a California court against the manufacturer, claiming that he was injured in a crash when the Scout's transmission failed as a result of a design or manufacturing defect. The manufacturer denies liability, claiming that the crash was the result of the plaintiff's negligence.

At the trial the plaintiff calls an engineer who works for the manufacturer and who testifies that, shortly after the plaintiff's accident, the manufacturer began to build the transmissions in Scouts like the plaintiff's out of malleable iron instead of aluminum. The manufacturer objects and moves to strike on the ground that the engineer's testimony is barred under the subsequent repair doctrine. How should the judge rule?

2. Suppose that the plaintiff is a citizen of Texas. Because of the diversity of the parties' citizenship, the plaintiff brings a strict liability action against the manufacturer in a federal district court located in California. The manufacturer objects to the engineer's testimony and moves to strike on the ground that under Federal Rule 407, as amended, the engineer's testimony is inadmissible in a strict liability action. The plaintiff counters that under *Erie* the federal judge must apply the California subsequent repair doctrine as construed by the California Supreme Court in *Ault*. How should the judge rule?

3. The plaintiff sues the defendant, a store owner, for damages the plaintiff alleges she sustained when she fell on the defendant's stairs. At the trial, the plaintiff calls the store manager who testifies that shortly before the plaintiff fell, he ordered signs warning customers that the stairs were slippery. The signs, however, had not yet been posted by the date of the plaintiff's fall. The store owner objects on the ground of the subsequent repair doctrine and moves to strike. How should the judge rule?

§ 4.03 THE KINDS OF PRECAUTIONARY MEASURES AFFECTED BY § 1151 AND RULE 407

Many kinds of remedial measures have been held to be within the kind of protection afforded by the subsequent doctrine. They include replacing a sewer line in an area where collapsing pavement injured the plaintiff,[1] replacing the knives of a planing machine which the plaintiff claimed caused his injuries,[2] installing handrails where the plaintiff fell,[3] substituting pins in railroad cars with safer ones,[4] and terminating the

---

1. Maddern v. City and County of San Francisco, 74 Cal.App.2d 742, 169 P.2d 425 (1946).
2. Helling v. Schindler, 145 Cal. 303, 78 P. 710 (1904).
3. Morehouse v. Taubman Co., 5 Cal.App.3d 548, 85 Cal.Rptr. 308 (1970).
4. Sappenfield v. Main St. & A. P. R. Co., 91 Cal. 48, 27 P. 590 (1891).

employees involved in the occurrence causing the plaintiff's injuries.[5]

The sending of warning or recall notices to owners of products may be viewed as a remedial measure. But consistent with *Ault*'s[6] holding that § 1151 does not apply in strict liability actions, notices alerting consumers to take safety measures are admissible against a manufacturer in a California strict liability case. Under Federal Rule of Evidence 407, as amended in 1997, such notices may not be offered to prove a design or manufacturing defect.[7] Subsequent remedial measures may not be offered in federal court to prove a design or manufacturing defect.

Dismissing an employee after an accident is inadmissible as a subsequent remedial measure if offered to prove negligence or other culpable conduct, but is the investigation leading to the dismissal likewise inadmissible? Admitting such investigations could frustrate the policy of promoting remedial measures by discouraging potential defendants from undertaking the very investigations needed to determine the necessity for such measures. On the other hand, excluding the investigations could deprive injured claimants of one of the best and most accurate sources of information. The Ninth Circuit holds that such investigations are inadmissible under Federal Rule of Evidence 407.[8] The California Supreme Court disagrees. Section 1151 includes "only *subsequent actions taken to repair or correct* a problem identified by an investigation—not the factual inquiries undertaken to determine whether such repair or correction was necessary."[9]

QUESTIONS AND PROBLEMS

1. Federal courts, unlike California courts, do not permit the use of recall notices alerting consumers to take safety measures against manufacturers in strict liability cases. True or false?

2. If following an accident a manufacturer redesigns a helicopter, the plaintiff may not offer evidence of the redesign in a negligence action in the Ninth Circuit or a California court to prove negligence or other culpable conduct. However, in either court the plaintiff may offer the investigation leading to the redesign, as both the Federal Rules and the Evidence Code protect only those remedial measures taken to remedy a flaw and not the investigation that led to the discovery of the flaw. True or false?

---

5. Turner v. Hearst, 115 Cal. 394, 47 P. 129 (1896).

6. Ault v. International Harvester Co., 13 Cal.3d 113, 117 Cal.Rptr. 812, 528 P.2d 1148 (1974). See § 4.02, supra.

7. Prior to the amendment, the federal courts were split on whether the subsequent repair doctrine of Rule 407 barred the use of such notices to prove a design or manufacturing defect. Compare Rozier v. Ford Motor Co., 573 F.2d 1332, 1343 (5th Cir.1978), reh'g denied, 578 F.2d 871 (1978) (recall notice admitted) with Vockie v. General Motors Corp., Chevrolet Division, 66 F.R.D. 57, 61 (E.D.Pa.1975), aff'd mem., 523 F.2d 1052 (3d Cir.1975) (recall notice excluded but action based on *negligent* design).

8. Maddox v. City of Los Angeles, 792 F.2d 1408, 1417 (9th Cir.1986); contra: Rocky Mountain Helicopters v. Bell Helicopters, 805 F.2d 907, 918–919 (10th Cir.1986).

9. Fox v. Kramer, 22 Cal.4th 531, 544, 93 Cal.Rptr.2d 497, 506, 994 P.2d 343, 351 (2000) (emphases in the original).

§ 4.04 EVIDENCE OF SUBSEQUENT PRECAUTIONS AS PROOF OF PROPOSITIONS OTHER THAN NEGLIGENCE OR CULPABLE CONDUCT

As *Ault* illustrates, evidence of remedial measures may be admissible if relevant to some contested issue other than the defendant's negligence or culpable conduct.[1] In the words of original Federal Rule of Evidence 407, evidence of subsequent remedial measures need not be excluded "when offered for another purpose, such as proving ownership, control, or feasibility of precautionary measures, if controverted, or impeachment."[2]

Alcaraz v. Vece[3] is illustrative. The plaintiff sued his landlords for injuries he suffered when he stepped on a water meter embedded in the lawn next to the sidewalk of the building in which his apartment was located. The landlords moved for summary judgment on the ground that the meter was located on land owned by the city. Following the plaintiff's injuries, the landlords constructed a fence around the building's yard that included the area on which the meter was located. The landlords objected to the evidence of the fence's construction on the basis of the subsequent repair doctrine. The trial court sustained the objection and granted the landlords' summary judgment motion on the ground they did not own or exercise control over the meter box. The California Supreme Court reversed: though the evidence was inadmissible to prove the landlords' negligence, it was admissible to show that they exercised control over the meter and thus owed a duty of care to the plaintiff.[4]

The use of evidence of remedial measures for impeachment purposes requires a word of caution: the impeaching party must show that the witness to be impeached "authorized, recommended, approved, directed, or supervised the making, or himself made the subsequent repair, alteration or change of procedure."[5] Otherwise, whenever a defendant offers evidence about the safety of his premises at the time of the accident, the door would automatically be opened to the plaintiff "to prove (by way of impeachment) every subsequent repair or precaution taken."[6] In Pierce v.

---

1. Ault v. International Harvester Co., 13 Cal.3d 113, 117 Cal.Rptr. 812, 528 P.2d 1148 (1974). See § 4.02, supra.

2. See original Federal Rule of Evidence 407. The restyled rule has eliminated this language, but the evidence would still admissible when offered to prove some other pertinent proposition under the relevance provisions of the Federal Rules. See Federal Rule of Evidence 401.

3. 14 Cal.4th 1149, 60 Cal.Rptr.2d 448, 929 P.2d 1239 (1997).

4. Id. at 1169–1170, 60 Cal.Rptr.2d at 461, 929 P.2d at 1232–1253.

5. Pierce v. J. C. Penney Co., 167 Cal.App.2d 3, 8, 334 P.2d 117, 120 (1959).

6. Id. at 11, 334 P.2d at 122. Although the holding in *Pierce* predates the adoption of the Evidence Code, presumably a court today could reach the same result by applying California Evidence Code § 352. In the absence of the kind of authorization or approval described in *Pierce*, the probative value of the impeaching evidence would be very slight when compared with its potential to prejudice the opposing party unduly. For a discussion on the need to balance the probative value of evidence with its prejudicial effects, see § 2.10 supra.

J.C. Penney Co.[7] the plaintiff sued for injuries she claimed to have suffered when she slipped and fell on the stairs in the defendant's store. The store manager testified that immediately after the accident he inspected the stairs and found that they were not slippery. Over the defendant's objection, the plaintiff was allowed to elicit testimony from the manager that adhesive strips had been added to the stairs shortly after the accident. Although the answer was limited to impeachment, the reviewing court nonetheless held that it was error to receive the answer for that purpose in the absence of evidence showing that the witness had something to do with the installation of the strips.

The reviewing court distinguished the manager's testimony about the condition of the stairs from claims by expert witnesses that a particular instrumentality, such as a railroad signal, is of the "safest type."[8] Such claims open the proponent to evidence disproving them; they are akin to claims that it was not feasible to undertake changes to protect against the risk that harmed the plaintiff. As Federal Rule of Evidence 407 expressly recognizes, such claims can be disproved even if the evidence of feasibility consists of a subsequent remedial measure undertaken by the defendant. However, to prevent misuse of this ground of admissibility, Rule 407 requires that the feasibility of precautionary measures first be controverted.[9]

In one interesting case, the *failure* to undertake remedial measures was held to be admissible to prove punitive damages. In Hilliard v. A. H. Robins Co.[10] the plaintiff sued the defendant for injuries stemming from use of the defendant's intrauterine device.[11] The plaintiff's claim for punitive damages was based on the allegation that the defendant in designing, manufacturing, and marketing the device consciously disregarded the rights of others by continuing to market the device after becoming aware of the probable dangers it posed.[12] In proving this claim, the court held that the plaintiff was entitled to offer evidence of the defendant's conduct occurring after the plaintiff last used the device.[13] In the court's view, § 1151 did not bar the use of the evidence; § 1151 "was not intended to exclude evidence of the failure to make changes in a defective product or the failure to withdraw a dangerous product from the market."[14] Receiving the evidence, moreover, would promote the policy of § 1151 by encouraging manufacturers to remedy or withdraw defective products.[15]

---

7.   Pierce v. J. C. Penney Co., 167 Cal.App.2d 3, 8, 334 P.2d 117, 120 (1959).

8.   Id. at 12, 334 P.2d at 123.

9.   Federal Rule of Evidence 407.

10.   148 Cal.App.3d 374, 196 Cal.Rptr. 117 (1983).

11.   Id. at 385, 196 Cal.Rptr. at 123.

12.   Id. at 397, 196 Cal.Rptr. at 132.

13.   Id. at 401, 196 Cal.Rptr. at 134–135.

14.   Id.

15.   Id. at 401–402, 196 Cal.Rptr. at 135.

Evidence of remedial measures undertaken by third parties independently of the defendant is not barred by the subsequent repair doctrine.[16] For example, in Magnante v. Pettibone–Wood Mfg. Co.,[17] a boom which became disengaged from its base struck the plaintiff. To prove that the manufacturer had defectively designed the boom, the plaintiff was permitted to show the remedial measures his employer undertook after the accident to prevent the boom from disengaging.[18] It is immaterial whether the evidence is offered to prove a defective condition in a strict liability case,[19] as in *Ault*,[20] or to prove negligence or other culpable conduct.[21] In the latter case, the policy of encouraging repairs is not undermined " 'as liability is not sought against the person taking the remedial action.' "[22]

QUESTIONS AND PROBLEMS

1. In a personal injury action in which the plaintiff claims that he was injured as a result of the malfunction of the defendant's backhoe, the defendant calls one of its engineers to testify that, as designed and manufactured, the backhoe could not have caused the plaintiff's injuries. On cross-examination, the plaintiff offers a letter admittedly signed by the engineer warning owners of the backhoe of the danger plaintiff claims caused his injuries. The defendant objects to the introduction of the letter on the grounds that it violates the subsequent repair doctrine. How should the judge rule? In ruling, assume that the suit is in a jurisdiction that does not follow *Ault*.

2. Assume that the judge overrules the objection. What protection should the defendant seek?

3. Suppose that the engineer had merely testified that it was not feasible to undertake changes in the backhoe to protect against the risk that harmed the plaintiff. Over an objection that the evidence would violate the subsequent repair doctrine, could the plaintiff offer the testimony of another engineer that such changes were in fact made by the defendant after the plaintiff's accident?

4. Suppose that instead of calling the engineer the plaintiff called a fellow employee to testify that, after the plaintiff's accident, on his own he modified the backhoe so as to prevent similar accidents from occurring. Over a subsequent remedial measures objection, could the testimony be received to prove that the backhoe had been negligently designed? Does it matter whether the suit is being tried in a California or federal court?

16. Magnante v. Pettibone–Wood Mfg. Co., 183 Cal.App.3d 764, 767–769, 228 Cal.Rptr. 420, 422–423 (1986).

17. Id.

18. Id.

19. Id.

20. Ault v. International Harvester Co., 13 Cal.3d 113, 117 Cal.Rptr. 812, 528 P.2d 1148 (1974). For a discussion of *Ault*, see § 4.02, supra.

21. Magnante v. Pettibone–Wood Mfg. Co., 183 Cal.App.3d 764, 767–769, 228 Cal.Rptr. 420, 422–423 (1986).

22. Id. (quoting from Denolf v. Frank L. Jursik Co., 395 Mich. 661, 238 N.W.2d 1, 4 (1976)).

§ 4.05 PLEAS AND RELATED STATEMENTS UNDER THE EVIDENCE CODE

Prosecutors would have an easier time obtaining convictions if they could offer the jury evidence that prior to the trial the accused offered to plead guilty to the offense charged or to some lesser offense. Though such evidence would constitute a relevant admission, it is nonetheless excluded in order to encourage plea bargains. California Evidence Code § 1153 prohibits the use of such evidence in "any action or in any proceeding of any nature, including proceedings before agencies, commissions, boards, and tribunals."[1] Moreover, evidence of a plea of guilty, later withdrawn, is also made inadmissible by § 1153[2] and, in the case of some felonies, by § 1192.4 of the Penal Code.[3]

A key question is whether the protection extends to the statements made in connection with the offer to plead guilty or the withdrawn plea. If only the words constituting an offer were protected, then knowledgeable defendants would refrain from engaging in plea bargaining since admissions made in the course of negotiations would be admissible in the event no bargain was struck. To give effect to § 1153's purpose of facilitating plea bargains, statements made in the course of plea negotiations are as inadmissible as the offer to plead guilty.[4]

In the event that the plea negotiations fail and the accused testifies inconsistently with his negotiation statements, may the prosecution use the statements to impeach the accused? Despite § 1153's broad command that evidence of an offer to plead guilty is "inadmissible in any action,"[5] People v. Crow[6] holds that § 1153, as construed, does not prohibit the prosecution from using the statements "for the limited purpose of impeaching the defendant regarding testimony which was elicited either during the direct examination of the defendant or during cross-examination which is plainly within the scope of the defendant's direct examination."[7] In effect, Crow construed § 1153 as prohibiting only the use of negotiation statements as admissions. While Crow's construction might discourage plea bargaining, the decision is nevertheless consistent with the principle that evidence that may be inadmissible for one purpose (e.g., admissions) may nonetheless be received as proof of some other relevant, admissible purpose (e.g., impeachment).

---

1. West's Ann.California Evidence Code § 1153.

2. Id.

3. West's Ann.California Penal Code § 1192.4 provides that if an accused's plea of guilty to certain felonies is rejected by the prosecuting attorney and the court, the plea is deemed withdrawn, and the "pleas so withdrawn may not be received in evidence in any criminal, civil, or special action or proceeding of any nature, including proceedings before agencies, commissions, boards, and tribunals." West's Ann.California Penal Code § 1192.4.

4. People v. Tanner, 45 Cal.App.3d 345, 348–352, 119 Cal.Rptr. 407, 410–411 (1975).

5. West's Ann. California Evidence Code § 1153.

6. 28 Cal.App.4th 440, 33 Cal.Rptr.2d 624 (1994).

7. Id. at 452, 33 Cal.Rptr.2d at 631.

However, only statements made in the course of bona fide plea negotiations are protected.[8] Unsolicited offers to plead guilty, without any expectation that they will not be used against the accused, are not protected.[9] Neither are statements by the accused to friends about the type of offer he would be willing to accept, since friends are not participants in the plea bargaining process.[10]

Section 1153 does not expressly limit bona fide plea negotiations to discussions with attorneys employed by the county district attorney or the California Attorney General. The California courts are divided on whether police officers and other law enforcement personnel qualify as plea bargain participants. People v. Posten[11] assumes that police officers qualify so long as the accused made the statements to them in the course of bona fide plea negotiations.[12] People v. Magana[13] limits law enforcement participants to prosecutors on the assumption that defense lawyers negotiate only with prosecutors.[14] While that assumption might be warranted in the case of criminal defense attorneys, *Posten* implicitly recognizes that unrepresented defendants occasionally engage in plea negotiations with police officers and other law enforcement personnel.

Admissions of guilt made in the absence of plea negotiations are unprotected and may be offered as party admissions. An example can be found in People v. Leonard,[15] where the defendant, while the court was in session, exclaimed, "I am guilty." As the reviewing court noted, "[T]he defendant's in-court outburst declaring that he was guilty was not a 'bona fide offer to plead guilty * * * but simply an unsolicited admission.' "[16]

Pleas and related statements and Proposition 8. The Right to Truth–in–Evidence provision of Proposition 8 amended the state constitution to give each party to criminal proceedings the right not to have relevant evidence excluded.[17] Since offers to plead guilty and guilty pleas later withdrawn and their related statements are relevant as admissions, they should be admissible under Proposition 8 unless excluded by the court under § 352.[18] No case, however, has so held.[19]

---

8.   People v. Posten, 108 Cal.App.3d 633, 647–648, 166 Cal.Rptr. 661, 669 (1980).

9.   Id.

10.   People v. Magana, 17 Cal.App.4th 1371, 1377, 22 Cal.Rptr.2d 59, 62 (1993).

11.   108 Cal.App.3d 633, 166 Cal.Rptr. 661 (1980).

12.   Id. at 647–648, 166 Cal.Rptr. at 669.

13.   17 Cal.App.4th 1371, 22 Cal.Rptr.2d 59 (1993).

14.   Id. at 1377, 22 Cal.Rptr.2d 62.

15.   40 Cal.4th 1370, 157 P.3d 973, 58 Cal.Rptr.3d 368, cert. denied, 552 U.S. 1013, 128 S.Ct. 539, 169 L.Ed.2d 378 (2007).

16.   Id. at 1404, 157 P.3d at 999, 58 Cal.Rptr.3d at 399.

17.   For an extended discussion of the effects of the Right to Truth–in–Evidence provision of Proposition 8, see § 3.07 supra.

18.   For a discussion of the role of § 352 under Proposition 8, see § 3.08 supra.

19.   In People v. Cummings, 4 Cal.4th 1233, 1319, note 59, 18 Cal.Rptr.2d 796, 851, note 59, 850 P.2d 1, 56, note 59 (1993), cert. denied, 511 U.S. 1046, 114 S.Ct. 1576, 128 L.Ed.2d 219 (1994), the California Supreme Court declined ruling on whether Proposition 8 repealed the ban on the use of statements made during plea negotiations.

At least two reasons may account for the absence of reported cases. First, prosecutors may not have pressed the issue, since a ruling that § 1153 has been repealed by Proposition 8 would seriously undermine the plea bargaining process. Defendants would not engage in the kind of open discussions that often lead to a negotiated plea. Second, Proposition 8 expressly exempts any "statutory rule of evidence relating to privilege" from the operation of the Right to Truth–in–Evidence provision.[20] Since the negotiations and other statements contemplated by § 1153 are protected from disclosure, an argument could be made that the section creates a privilege even though § 1153 is not found in the division of the Code dealing with privileges. Section 1153, however, only prohibits the use of offers and related statements when offered against the accused as *admissions*. The section does not provide the broad protection offered by most privileges. Generally, privileges prevent the disclosure of the protected information irrespective of the purpose for which the information is sought.[21] Consequently, the kinds of privileges exempted from the operation of Proposition 8 may not embrace the statements protected by § 1153.

QUESTIONS AND PROBLEMS

1.   In California only offers to plead guilty and guilty pleas later withdrawn are inadmissible as admissions at a subsequent criminal trial. But the statements accompanying such offers are admissible. Accordingly, this rule prevents prosecutors from offering evidence that the accused offered to plead guilty in exchange for a deal. The rule, however, does not prevent prosecutors in a theft trial from offering evidence that at the plea negotiation session the accused said, "Ok, I am willing to come through clean in order to get a deal; I'm the one who stole the cell phone." True or false?

2.   Suppose that at the theft trial the accused takes the stand and on direct testifies as follows: "No, I did not steal the cell phone." May the prosecution offer his statement at the failed negotiations to prove that the accused stole the cell phone? To impeach the accused?

3.   Assume that the judge prevents the prosecutor from offering the accused's statement as an admission that he stole the cell phone. As proof that the accused stole the cell phone, may the prosecutor call the accused's best friend to testify as follows: "The accused said to me, 'I took the phone and am willing to say so to the prosecutor if necessary to get a deal.'"

4.   The California Supreme Court has construed Proposition 8 as repealing § 1153. True or false?

§ 4.06   PLEAS AND RELATED STATEMENTS UNDER THE FEDERAL RULES

In one respect, Federal Rule of Evidence 410 is superior to § 1153. The federal rule makes it clear that the protection afforded by the

---

20.   See § 3.07 supra.

21.   See § 20.01 infra.

provision embraces "a statement made during plea discussions" as well as the offer to plead guilty.[1] In another respect, the federal rule is not as protective as § 1153 as construed. In the plea bargain context, the federal rule protects only those statements made by the accused or his lawyer to "an attorney for the prosecuting authority."[2] This limitation resulted from a 1980 amendment to the Federal Rules designed to reverse United States v. Herman.[3] In that case, the Fifth Circuit held that the rule as then worded extended to incriminating statements made by an in-custody defendant to postal inspectors.[4] So long as the defendant made the statements in an effort to obtain concessions for a guilty plea and so long as the defendant believed that the persons with whom he was dealing had the authority to negotiate, the statements were protected under the rule.[5]

Under Rule 410, as amended, defendants who unwittingly attempt to negotiate with agents other than an attorney for the prosecuting authority lose the rule's protection. But, according to the Advisory Committee, the amendment "does not compel the conclusion that statements made to law enforcement agents, especially when the agents purport to have authority to bargain, are inevitably admissible."[6] Whether such statements are now admissible is to be "resolved by that body of law dealing with police interrogations."[7]

If the accused testifies inconsistently with his statements at the plea negotiations, may the statements be used for the limited purpose of impeaching his credibility? The expansive language of the Federal Rules of Evidence appears to preclude such a use.[8] As the United States Supreme Court has acknowledged, "[T]he Rules give a defendant the right not to be impeached by statements made during plea discussions * * *."[9] This concession is not surprising since Congress specifically rejected a rule that would have allowed such statements to be used for impeachment.[10] May the prosecution nonetheless compel the accused to waive the use of the statements for impeachment purposes as a plea bargaining condition? Despite concerns that such compulsion might impair the plea bargaining process, in United States v. Mezzanatto the United States Supreme Court held that the Rules do not prohibit the voluntary relinquishment of the

---

1. Federal Rule of Evidence 410(4).

2. Id.

3. 544 F.2d 791 (5th Cir.1977), reh'g denied, 549 F.2d 204 (5th Cir.1977).

4. Id. at 797.

5. Id. at 798.

6. Federal Rule of Evidence 410 (Advisory Committee Note).

7. Id.

8. Rule 410 provides that evidence of any statement made in the course of plea discussions which do not result in a plea of guilty is not admissible against the defendant who participated in the plea discussions. Federal Rule of Evidence 410.

9. United States v. Mezzanatto, 513 U.S. 196, 200, note 2, 115 S.Ct. 797, 801, note 2, 130 L.Ed.2d 697, 703, note 2 (1995).

10. United States v. Mezzanatto, 998 F.2d 1452, 1454 (9th Cir.1993), reversed, 513 U.S. 196, 115 S.Ct. 797, 130 L.Ed.2d 697 (1995).

right not to be impeached by statements made during plea discussions.[11]

QUESTIONS AND PROBLEMS

1. While being transported to the jail after his arrest, the accused makes the following statement to the arresting officers with the expectation that the statement will not be used against him: "Look, I'm willing to identify the person who helped me rob the store in exchange for your recommendation to the DA that I be charged only with petty theft." The officers reject the offer, and the defendant is prosecuted for robbery. Over his objection, may the prosecutor offer the accused's statement as an admission in a California court? In answering this question, assume that the accused has not raised any *Miranda* claims.

2. May the Assistant U.S. Attorney offer the statement for the same purpose in a federal court? In answering this question, assume that the accused has not raised any *Miranda* claims.

3. The accused is charged with burglary. Prior to the trial, the accused and the assistant district attorney assigned to the case engage in plea negotiations. At the negotiations, the accused admits having entered the store with the intent to steal a bottle of wine. The parties are unable to strike a bargain, and at the trial, the accused takes the stand and testifies that he entered the store to buy a bottle of wine and simply forgot to pay for the bottle that was found in a paper bag that was taken from the him after he was arrested outside the store. May a California prosecutor use the accused's admission at the plea negotiations to "impeach" the accused?

4. May a federal prosecutor use the accused's admission for the same purpose?

5. If you were a federal prosecutor, what protective steps would you take to ensure the use of such admissions for impeachment purposes? Would you agree to such steps if you were defense counsel?

§ 4.07   PLEAS OF NOLO CONTENDERE

Guilty pleas, unlike offers to plead guilty and guilty pleas later withdrawn, are not protected from disclosure. Thus, if a defendant pleads guilty to a speeding violation, that plea can then be offered against the defendant as an admission by any plaintiff injured by the defendant's driving. Because that prospect may discourage criminal defendants from negotiating a plea to charges stemming from occurrences which injure others, California Penal Code § 1016(3) permits a plea of nolo contendere.[1] That "plea and any admissions required by the court during any inquiry it makes as to the voluntariness of, and factual basis for, the plea may not be used against the defendant as an admission in any civil suit based upon or growing out of the act upon which the criminal prosecution

---

11. United States v. Mezzanatto, 513 U.S. 196, 210, 115 S.Ct. 797, 806, 130 L.Ed.2d 697, 709 (1995).

1. West's Ann.California Penal Code § 1016(3).

is based."[2] In 1982, however, that protection was limited to "cases other than those punishable as felonies"[3] in order to "assist the efforts of victims of crime to obtain compensation for their injuries from the criminals who inflicted those injuries."[4]

Federal Rule of Evidence 410, on the other hand, continues the traditional approach. It prohibits the use of a plea of nolo contendere in any civil or criminal proceeding regardless of the grade of the offense.[5]

QUESTIONS AND PROBLEMS

1. California Penal Code § 1016(3), like Federal Rule of Evidence 410, is designed to encourage persons accused of committing misdemeanors and felonies to admit their wrongdoing without the need for a trial by ensuring that a plea of nolo contendere will not be admitted at a subsequent civil trial as an admission. True of false?

2. A literal interpretation of the Right to Truth–in–Evidence provision of Proposition 8 would repeal California Penal Code § 1016(3). True or false?

Should the California Supreme Court's *Ewoldt* opinion regarding Proposition 8 affect your ruling?

§ 4.08   COMPROMISE OFFERS AND THE EVIDENCE CODE

Life would be easier for plaintiffs if they could show that defendants offered to settle their claims. But to promote the public policy of compromising and settling disputes, § 1152 prohibits the use of settlement offers to prove the validity of a claim.[1] Section 1152, moreover, applies to settlement conference statements and conduct as well as the offers themselves to ensure a candid exchange of views.[2]

To invoke the protection of § 1152, the objecting party must show that the statement was made in an effort to compromise an actual dispute over the validity of a claim or its amount.[3] For example, a party's offer to

---

2. Id. But a plea of nolo contendere will operate as an admission in an action by an insurer against the insured for a declaratory judgment that, as a result of such a plea, the insurer is not liable under the policy for injuries inflicted by the insured. Century–National Ins. Co. v. Glenn, 86 Cal.App.4th 1392, 1397, 104 Cal.Rptr.2d 73, 76 (2001).

3. West's Ann. California Penal Code § 1016(3).

4. Id. (legislative history).

5. Federal Rule of Evidence 410(2).

1. West's Ann.California Evidence Code § 1152. In pertinent part, § 1152 provides that "[e]vidence that a person has, in compromise or from humanitarian motives, furnished or offered or promised to furnish money or any other thing, act, or service to another who has sustained or will sustain or claims that he or she has sustained or will sustain loss or damage, as well as any conduct or statements made in negotiation thereof, is inadmissible to prove his or her liability for the loss or damage or any part of it."

2. Id.

3. This is apparent from the use of the term "compromise" in § 1152. Id. See also C. McCormick, McCormick on Evidence § 266 (J. Strong 4th ed. 1992).

buy an interest in land is not excludable, unless the party made the offer in an effort to settle a dispute over the ownership of the land.[4] Section 1152, however, is not limited to statements made in an effort to compromise only claims known to exist at the time the statement was made. Section 1152 also protects from disclosure offers to compromise unknown claims and liabilities arising out of the dispute. Mangano v. Verity, Inc.[5] illustrates this point. Mangano sued his employer (Verity) for disability discrimination. Verity subsequently terminated Mangano's employment. At the time it did so, Verity offered Mangano a lump sum in exchange for a release of all claims, "both known or unknown," arising out of the employment dispute.[6] Mangano rejected the offer and filed a second action against Verity claiming that Verity had terminated him in retaliation for filing and prosecuting the disability discrimination suit. At the retaliation trial, the judge excluded the evidence of the lump sum offer. The reviewing court upheld the trial judge's ruling. In its offer, Verity was attempting to settle all potential claims arising out of the employment dispute, including those raised in the retaliation suit.[7]

Section 1152, however, does not embrace offers to pay claims that are undisputed as to validity or amount. As Dean Charles McCormick underscores, "[T]here is no policy of encouraging compromises of undisputed claims. They should be paid in full."[8] This position is reflected in those provisions of § 1152 which provide that the section does not affect the admissibility of evidence of "(1) [p]artial satisfaction of an asserted claim or demand without questioning its validity when such evidence is offered to prove the validity of the claim [and] (2) [a] debtor's payment or promise to pay all or a part of his or her preexisting debt when such evidence is offered to prove the creation of a new duty on his or her part or a revival of his or her preexisting duty."[9]

In one instance, however, the objecting party does not have to show that the statements were made or the conduct undertaken in an attempt to compromise a claim or its amount. Statements made and conduct undertaken for humanitarian purposes are afforded the same protection as statements made or conduct undertaken to compromise disputed claims.[10]

Recognizing that many personal suits are prompted by anger at the defendant's failure to apologize for the injury, the Legislature in 2000 amended the Code to reduce suits by encouraging defendants to apologize without fear their apologies might be considered admissions. The Code now provides that the "portion of statements, writings, or benevolent

---

4. Preciado v. Wilde, 139 Cal.App.4th 321, 326, 42 Cal.Rptr.3d 792, 795 (2006).

5. 179 Cal.App.4th 217, 101 Cal.Rptr.3d 555 (2009).

6. Id. at 218, 101 Cal.Rptr.3d at 557.

7. Id. at 223, 101 Cal.Rptr.3d at 560.

8. See also C. McCormick, McCormick on Evidence § 266 (J. Strong 4th ed. 1992).

9. West's Ann.California Evidence Code § 1152(c).

10. West's Ann.California Evidence Code § 1152(a).

gestures expressing sympathy or a general sense of benevolence relating to the pain, suffering, or death of a person involved in an accident and made to that person or to the family of that person shall be inadmissible as evidence of an admission of liability in a civil action."[11] Statements of fault, however, remain admissible even if part of protected statements, writings, and benevolent gestures.[12] Accordingly, "I didn't see you coming because I was using my cell phone" would be admissible, but not the preamble, "I'm sorry you were hurt."[13]

Section 1152 is most likely to be invoked by a defendant who objects to the use of compromise offers to prove the validity of the plaintiff's claim. But the section can also be used by plaintiffs to preclude defendants from using compromise offers made by third parties to prove that the third party is liable for the plaintiff's injuries. In Granville v. Parsons[14] the plaintiff was injured in a multi-car freeway collision.[15] Before the jury was impaneled, the plaintiff accepted a settlement from one of the defendants, who was then dismissed.[16] In his closing argument, the non-settling defendant claimed that the settlement was evidence that the dismissed defendant was responsible for the plaintiff's injuries.[17] The court held the argument to be improper: the non-settling defendant violated § 1152 by using the third party's settlement offer to prove the third party's liability for the plaintiff's injuries.[18]

If the evidence of settlement is not offered to prove liability, but for some other relevant purpose, then the evidence can be admitted.[19] For example, if a defendant settles with one of several plaintiffs and then calls the dismissed plaintiff as a witness, the remaining plaintiffs may elicit the fact of settlement on cross to show the bias of the witness. But whether the question and answer will be permitted in a given case rests with the trial judge's discretion.[20] The danger to the objecting party is obvious: the jury might not abide by the instruction limiting their consideration of the evidence to its impeachment value. Moreover, the probative value of the evidence may not be great: "The former plaintiff may have been forced by economic circumstances to take a paltry sum[;] the former defendant may

---

11. West's Ann. California Evidence Code § 1160. "Benevolent gestures" are defined as "actions that convey a sense of compassion or commiseration emanating from humane impulses." Id.

12. Id.

13. Id. (comment).

14. 259 Cal.App.2d 298, 66 Cal.Rptr. 149 (1968).

15. Id. at 300, 66 Cal.Rptr. at 150.

16. Id.

17. Id.

18. Id. at 304, 66 Cal.Rptr. at 153–154. *Granville* was a pre-Code case, but the court made it clear that § 1152 would require the same ruling with respect to the closing argument. Id. Under the Code, eliciting the fact of settlement on cross to prove liability would also be improper.

19. Id. See also West's Ann.California Evidence Code § 355 (Evidence which is inadmissible for one purpose but is admissible for another may be admitted by the court for the admissible purpose with an appropriate limiting instruction.).

20. Granville v. Parsons, 259 Cal.App.2d 298, 304, 66 Cal.Rptr. 149, 153–154 (1968).

have been coerced into an excessive payment by considerations foreign to the litigation."[21]

In addition to impeachment for bias, evidence of settlement offers has been received to prove the intention of the parties in a contract dispute,[22] to prove the falsity of statements in a defamation action,[23] to prove the breach of the covenant of good faith and fair dealing in an insurance dispute,[24] and to determine the source of funds to pay off a judgment in a judgment debtor's examination.[25]

The protection afforded by § 1152 does not extend to criminal cases. In People v. Muniz[26] the accused sought to exclude evidence that he had offered to pay for the victim's medical expenses in a sex offense prosecution.[27] The court upheld the admission of the evidence, holding that § 1152 is limited to civil cases.[28] The court refused to construe "liability" as used in the section to include criminal matters.[29]

The same question has arisen in federal courts. Some courts have held that Rule 408's protection does not extend to criminal cases.[30] A 2006 amendment to Rule 408 now allows the use of statements or conduct made during compromise negotiations "when offered in a criminal case and when the negotiations related to a claim by a public office or agency in the exercise of regulatory, investigative, or enforcement authority."[31] By way of justification, the Advisory Committee Note emphasizes that "[w]here an individual makes a statement in the presence of government agents, its subsequent admission in a criminal case should not be unexpected."[32]

---

21. Id.

22. Fieldson Associates, Inc. v. Whitecliff Laboratories, Inc., 276 Cal.App.2d 770, 771–772, 81 Cal.Rptr. 332, 333–334 (1969).

23. Carney v. Santa Cruz Women Against Rape, 221 Cal.App.3d 1009, 1023–1024, 271 Cal.Rptr. 30, 38–39 (1990).

24. Shade Foods, Inc. v. Innovative Products Sales & Marketing, Inc., 78 Cal.App.4th 847, 915, 93 Cal.Rptr.2d 364, 411 (2000); White v. Western Title Ins. Co., 40 Cal.3d 870, 885–889, 221 Cal.Rptr. 509, 516–519, 710 P.2d 309, 317–319 (1985). In 1987, § 1152 was amended to read as follows: "(b) In the event that evidence of an offer to compromise is admitted in an action for breach of the covenant of good faith and fair dealing or violation of subdivision (h) of Section 790.03 of the Insurance Code, then at the request of the party against whom the evidence is admitted, or at the request of the party who made the offer to compromise that was admitted, evidence relating to any other offer or counteroffer to compromise the same or substantially the same claimed loss or damage shall also be admissible for the same purpose as the initial evidence regarding settlement. Other than as may be admitted in an action for breach of the covenant of good faith and fair dealing or violation of subdivision (h) of Section 790.03 of the Insurance Code, evidence of settlement offers shall not be admitted in a motion for a new trial, in any proceeding involving an additur or remittitur, or on appeal."

25. Young v. Keele, 188 Cal.App.3d 1090, 1092–1094, 233 Cal.Rptr. 850, 851–852 (1987).

26. 213 Cal.App.3d 1508, 262 Cal.Rptr. 743 (1989).

27. Id. at 1515–1516, 262 Cal.Rptr. at 746.

28. Id.

29. Id.

30. See, e.g., United States v. Prewitt, 34 F.3d 436, 439 (7th Cir. 1994), where the court held that admissions of fault made while compromising a civil securities enforcement action were admissible against the defendant in a later criminal action for mail fraud.

31. Federal Rule of Evidence 408.

32. Id. (Advisory Committee Note).

Accordingly, where a defendant in a civil proceeding brought by the IRS makes damaging admissions in an effort to compromise the claim, the amendment would allow the government to offer those admissions in a subsequent prosecution for tax evasion. The judge, however, would still be empowered to exclude the admissions under Federal Rule of Evidence 403 if their probative value is substantially outweighed by their prejudicial effects. As an example, the Advisory Committee cites the statements an unrepresented individual makes in a civil enforcement proceeding.[33]

Rule 408, as amended, distinguishes between evidence of statements and conduct made during compromise negotiations, and evidence that the accused offered or agreed to settle the claim.[34] Only the former are admissible. Accordingly, in a tax evasion prosecution, the government may not offer evidence that the accused offered to compromise the tax claim as proof of its validity but may offer may offer the accused's settlement statement, "I concede that I owe the back taxes," as a party opponent admission. In the Committee's view, an offer or an acceptance of a compromise, unlike a direct statement of liability, says little about the accused's guilt.

Another Evidence Code provision, § 1153.5, applies to criminal as well as civil cases. This section bans the use of an offer for a civil resolution of a complaint alleging a crime against property if the offer is made with the assistance of the prosecutor.[35] Both the offer as well as the admissions made in the course of the negotiations are protected from disclosure in any subsequent proceeding.[36]

Section 1152 is limited to the inadmissibility of settlement conference statements and conduct to prove the *validity* of a claim. A different provision, § 1154, bans the use of settlement conference statements and conduct to prove the *invalidity* of a claim. It provides that "[e]vidence that a person has accepted or offered or promised to accept a sum of money or any other thing, act, or service in satisfaction of a claim, as well as any conduct or statements made in negotiation thereof, is inadmissible to prove the invalidity of the claim or any part of it."[37] Accordingly, a defendant may not prove the invalidity of the plaintiff's trial claims by evidence that the plaintiff was prepared to accept a lower amount.

Compromise Offers and Mediation. Recognizing the increasing role of mediation in resolving disputes, the Legislature added a chapter to the Evidence Code that protects from disclosure information that is exchanged in the course of mediation. Mediation is defined as "a process in which a neutral person or persons facilitate communication between

---

33. Id.

34. Id.

35. West's Ann.California Evidence Code § 1153.5. This section implements the policy of West's Ann.California Code of Civil Procedure § 33, which vests prosecutors with the discretion to assist in the civil resolution of crimes against property in lieu of filing a criminal complaint. West's Ann.California Code of Civil Procedure § 33.

36. West's Ann.California Evidence Code § 1153.5.

37. West's Ann.California Evidence Code § 1154.

the disputants to assist them in reaching a mutually acceptable agreement."[38] The chapter applies to all mediations except settlement conferences in civil cases and those undertaken pursuant to the Family Code.[39]

Unless all of the participants otherwise agree,[40] "[n]o evidence of anything said or any admission made for the purpose of, in the course of, or pursuant to, a mediation or a mediation consultation is admissible or subject to discovery, and disclosure of the evidence shall not be compelled, in any arbitration, administrative adjudication, civil action, or other noncriminal proceeding in which, pursuant to law, testimony can be compelled to be given."[41] Identical protection from disclosure is given to writings that are prepared for the purpose of, in the course of, or pursuant to, a mediation or a mediation consultation.[42] All communications, negotiations, or settlement discussions by the participants are to remain confidential.[43]

Unless the parties to the mediation otherwise agree, a mediator may not submit any report, assessment, evaluation, recommendation, or finding to a court or other adjudicative body concerning the mediation.[44] So unless the parties otherwise agree, a mediator may not report to a court a party's failure to comply with the mediator's orders or to participate in good faith in the mediation.[45] A mediator, however, is generally competent to testify about statements or conduct that could give rise to civil or criminal contempt or constitute a crime.[46]

As in the case of the attorney-client privilege, evidence that is otherwise admissible or subject to discovery outside the mediation or mediation consultation may not be immunized from disclosure solely by reason of its introduction or use in the mediation or mediation consultation.[47] Moreover, as has been noted, even communications protected by the mediation privilege can be disclosed if all the persons who participated in the

---

38. West's Ann. California Evidence Code § 1115. A proceeding may be a mediation, even though it is denominated differently. Id. (comment). An attorney or other representative of a party is not a neutral person and does not qualify as a mediator. Id.

39. Id. § 1117. Special rules apply to family and custody conciliation proceedings. Settlement conferences are conducted under special court rules. Id. (comment).

40. Id. § 1122(a)(1). The agreement may be oral or in writing. Id.

41. Id. § 1119(a).

42. Id. § 1119(b).

43. Id. § 1119(c). The protection accorded to mediation statements must yield to a criminal defendant's confrontation right to impeach a witness. Rinaker v. Superior Court, 62 Cal.App.4th 155, 167, 74 Cal.Rptr.2d 464, 470 (1998). However, mediation statements should not be used for impeachment purposes, unless the accused first convinces the trial judge at an in camera hearing that the statements are trustworthy and noncumulative. Id. at 169–171, 74 Cal.Rptr.2d at 472–473.

44. West's Ann. California Evidence Code § 1121. A report that is mandated by court rule and that states only whether an agreement was reached is exempted from the prohibition. Id.

45. See Foxgate Homeowners' Assoc. v. Bramalea, 26 Cal.4th 1, 4, 108 Cal.Rptr.2d 642, 645, 25 P.3d 1117, 1119 (2001).

46. West's Ann. California Evidence Code § 703.5.

47. Id. § 1120(a). For a discussion of the attorney-client privilege, see § 21.01 infra.

mediation agree to do so in writing or orally.[48] "Participants" include the parties, the mediator, and other nonparties, such as accountants, spouses, and employees of the parties, attending the mediation.[49]

The power to override the protection accorded mediations is pivotal in actions to enforce mediation agreements. In Ryan v. Garcia[50] the parties settled their dispute in the course of mediation but failed to agree in writing at the outset that any such agreements could be offered in the event one of the parties subsequently refused to abide by the terms of the mediation agreement. After the mediation was concluded, the parties disagreed about the terms of the agreement. In a subsequent suit to enforce the agreement, the plaintiff was precluded from proving its terms by evidence of the statements made in the course of the mediation. As the court pointed out, the parties should have agreed at the outset of the mediation to the admissibility of any agreements subsequently reached.[51] Today, a written settlement agreement may be admitted or otherwise disclosed if the agreement provides that it is admissible or subject to disclosure, or that it is enforceable or binding.[52] The parties, of course, can always agree to disclose the agreement.[53] Moreover, a settlement agreement can always be used to show fraud, duress, or illegality.[54]

Only matters disclosed during the mediation are protected from disclosure. Matters disclosed after the mediation ends are not entitled to protection.[55]

The mediation provisions do not diminish in any way the protection afforded by §§ 1152 and 1154 or other statutory provisions. Thus, if a communication is not protected by the mediation provisions but is within § 1152, it remains protected under this section. In addition, such a communication may also be protected from disclosure by the right of privacy embodied in Article I, § 1 of the California Constitution.[56]

§ 4.09 COMPROMISE OFFERS AND THE FEDERAL RULES

The Federal Rules of Evidence follow an approach similar to that of the Code in preventing the use of compromise negotiations as admissions.[1]

---

48. Id. § 1122(a)(1). Oral agreements to disclose are valid only if they meet a number of requirements. See id. § 1118. An agreement to disclose may be made at any time, not only just before the mediation begins. See id. § 1121 (comment).

49. See id. § 1122 (comment).

50. 27 Cal.App.4th 1006, 33 Cal.Rptr.2d 158 (1994).

51. Id. at 1012, 33 Cal.Rptr.2d at 162. See also Regents of the University of California v. Sumner, 42 Cal.App.4th 1209, 1213, 50 Cal.Rptr.2d 200, 202 (1996) (Where the document memorializing the mediation agreement is prepared after the mediation session has been concluded, the mediation provisions do not bar the use of the document to prove the terms of the agreement.).

52. West's Ann. California Evidence Code § 1123.

53. Id.

54. Id.

55. West's Ann.California Evidence Code § 1126. See id. for a list of the ways in which a mediation can be terminated.

56. Garstang v. Superior Court, 39 Cal.App.4th 526, 532 46 Cal.Rptr.2d 84, 87 (1995).

1. See Federal Rules of Evidence 408–409.

Federal Rule of Evidence 408, however, differs from California Evidence Code §§ 1152 and 1154 in several respects.

First, the rule itself makes it clear that exclusion is not required when the evidence is offered for another purpose, such as proving "a witness's bias or prejudice, negating a contention of undue delay, or proving an effort to obstruct a criminal investigation or prosecution."[2] This result is obtained in California by applying the section that provides that when evidence is inadmissible for one purpose but admissible for another, the court may admit it for the proper purpose with the appropriate limiting instruction.[3]

Second, Rule 408 excludes impeachment by contradiction or self-contradiction among the permissible purposes for which settlement conference statements can be offered. Whether statements made in compromise negotiations should be admitted as prior inconsistent statements to impeach a party has been controversial. Opponents point out that the value of impeaching a party through inconsistent statements made in compromise negotiations is outweighed by the negative effect impeachment would have on the candor required for successful settlement discussions. As amended in 2006, Federal Rule 408 adopts this view. It prohibits the use of statements made in settlement negotiations if offered to impeach as a prior inconsistent statement or as evidence of contradiction.[4] California decisions only indirectly support the position taken in the federal amendment. No California appellate court has approved the use of settlement conference statements to impeach a party.

Prior to the 2006 amendment, Federal Rule 408 was also explicit in another important respect: exclusion was not required of "any evidence otherwise discoverable merely because it is presented in compromise negotiations."[5] The 2006 amendment deleted this language as unnecessary.[6] Accordingly, even after the amendment, a party cannot immunize information that is germane to the case by raising it in the settlement negotiations. Thus, if the defendant admits at the settlement conference that his mechanic warned him that his brakes needed to be replaced, the plaintiff would be precluded merely from offering the defendant's admission to prove the mechanic's warning. The plaintiff, however, would be free to discover the mechanic's statement and to call the mechanic to the stand to repeat the warning he gave to the defendant.

The deletion of the language is unfortunate. Not all judges and parties are aware that a party cannot immunize information that is germane to the case simply by raising it in the settlement negotiations. The California provisions do not include the proviso deleted from the Federal Rule. But like his federal counterpart, a California plaintiff would also be free to

2. Federal Rule of Evidence 408(b).

3. West's Ann. California Evidence Code § 355.

4. Federal Rule of Evidence 408(a).

5. Id. (Advisory Committee Note).

6. Id.

discover the mechanic's statement and to call the mechanic to the stand to repeat the warning he gave to the defendant. Neither §§ 1152 nor 1154 purports to immunize the subject matter of evidence presented at the settlement conference.

Third, the Federal Rules do not provide a separate rule on admissions made in the course of mediation or in the civil resolution of complaints alleging crimes against property.

Fourth, the Federal Rules, like the Code, protect the statements and conduct of persons who offer or furnish humanitarian aid. Federal Rule of Evidence 409 provides that "[e]vidence of furnishing, promising to pay, or offering to pay medical, hospital, or similar expenses resulting from an injury is not admissible to prove liability for the injury."[7] The Federal Rules, however, do not contain a provision exempting apologies and other benevolent gestures from being used as admissions of liability in civil actions.

QUESTIONS AND PROBLEMS

1. Determine the admissibility of the following evidence in a California and federal court over an objection that its use violates the rule protecting the sanctity of statements made in the course of compromise negotiations:

a. Immediately following the collision giving rise to the suit, the defendant says to the plaintiff, "Look, I am really sorry; it was my all my fault."

b. At the settlement conference, the defendant says to the plaintiff, "Look, I'll settle if you reduce your pain and suffering by one-half."

c. At the settlement conference, the defendant says to the plaintiff, "Look, it was my fault; I'll settle if you reduce your pain and suffering by one-half."

d. At the settlement conference, the defendant says to the plaintiff, "Look, I admit I wasn't wearing my glasses; I'll settle if you reduce your pain and suffering by one-half."

2. Suppose that no settlement is reached and at the trial the defendant testifies that at the time of the accident he was wearing his glasses. May the plaintiff use the defendant's settlement conference statement to impeach his credibility in a California or federal personal injury trial?

3. Suppose that as a result of the defendant's admissions at the settlement conference the plaintiff learns for the first time that the defendant was not wearing his glasses at the time of the accident. Over the defendant's objection, at the trial may the plaintiff ask the defendant whether he was wearing his glasses at the time of the accident?

4. a. In a California or federal personal injury case, evidence that the defendant offered to pay the medical bills incurred by the plaintiff is admissi-

---

7. Federal Rule of Evidence 409.

ble to prove the validity of the plaintiff's claims, unless the offer is made in an attempt to compromise the plaintiff's claims. True or false?

F. excluded

    b.   In a California prosecution, evidence that the accused offered to pay the medical bills incurred by the person he is accused of assaulting is inadmissible as evidence that the accused committed the assault. True or false?

Adm.

    c.   In a federal prosecution for tax evasion, the prosecutor may offer evidence that at a meeting with IRS officials the defendant offered to enter into negotiations to settle the amount of taxes the government claims the defendant owes. True or false?

F

    d.   In the same prosecution, the prosecution may call an IRS agent to testify that at a meeting with the defendant, the defendant said, "I admit I owe the government back taxes." True or false?

T. Adm.

    5.   Since the rules banning the use of compromise offers seek to protect defendants, a defendant in a personal injury action is entitled to offer evidence (a) that the plaintiff offered to accept one-half of the amount the plaintiff is claiming at the trial to prove the invalidity of the plaintiff's claim; (b) that the plaintiff accepted a settlement offered by a third party to prove that the third party is liable for the damages the plaintiff is seeking from the defendant. True or false?

F

F

    6.   In a California or federal personal injury trial, the defendant may offer, over the plaintiff's objection, evidence that during an unsuccessful effort to mediate the dispute arising from the accident, the plaintiff said to the defendant, "To tell the truth, I wasn't watching where I was going." True or false?

F

In a California court, would it matter whether the defendant was offering the evidence only to contradict the plaintiff's testimony at the trial that the plaintiff was paying attention to where he was going?

§ 4.10   LIABILITY INSURANCE

California Evidence Code § 1155 provides that "[e]vidence that a person was, at the time a harm was suffered by another, insured wholly or partially against loss arising from liability for that harm is inadmissible to prove negligence or other wrongdoing."[1] Two concerns account for the rule: one is that the evidence may be irrelevant because possessing liability insurance simply does not make one more or less careful on a given occasion.[2] The other is the risk that the fact finder will be tempted to return a verdict against an insured defendant, regardless of the strength or weakness of the evidence of fault, because of the belief that the defendant will not have to pay the judgment from his own resources.[3]

If in fact evidence of liability insurance is not probative of fault, then the evidence should be inadmissible in any event. But since the mere

---

1.   West's Ann.California Evidence Code § 1155. Federal Rule of Evidence 411 is to the same effect.

2.   C. McCormick, McCormick on Evidence § 201 (J. Strong 4th ed. 1992).

3.   Id.

mention of liability insurance may create the very risk the rule seeks to avoid, modern codes do not rely on relevance principles but on special rules, such as § 1155 and Federal Rule of Evidence 411.

If possessing liability insurance is not probative of fault, then *not* possessing such insurance is likewise not probative of care. Rule 411 proceeds on this assumption. It provides that "[e]vidence that a person was or *was not* insured against liability is not admissible to prove whether the person acted negligently or otherwise wrongfully."[4] Section 1155 does not contain a similar provision. Accordingly, in California courts the party opposing evidence of the lack of liability insurance must object on irrelevance grounds.[5]

Evidence of liability insurance may be admissible if offered to prove a purpose other than negligence or other wrongdoing. In the words of Federal Rule of Evidence 411, exclusion is not required when the evidence is offered for another purpose, "such as proving a witness's bias or prejudice or proving agency, ownership, or control."[6] Even when offered for such a purpose, the trial judge may nonetheless exclude the evidence if its probative value is outweighed by the risk that the jury might misuse the evidence.[7] If the evidence is received, upon request the opposing party is entitled to an instruction limiting the jury's consideration of the evidence to the purpose for which it was received.[8]

The California courts have dealt with a number of recurring problems when evidence of liability insurance has been offered for a purpose other than proving negligence or other wrongdoing. One that has diminished in importance arises when a plaintiff joins the defendant's insurer on the theory that the insurer violated its duty to refrain from unfair settlement practices. Where such joinder has taken place, the suit against the insurer should be stayed until the action between the plaintiff and the defendant has been concluded.[9] Otherwise, a joint trial would violate the spirit of § 1155, even though the evidence of insurance is not offered to prove the defendant's negligence or other wrongdoing.[10] Section 1155, however, does

---

4. Federal Rule of Evidence 411 (emphasis supplied).

5. As a matter of relevance, is the Advisory Committee's assumption correct? Especially in jurisdictions that punish driving without liability insurance, isn't evidence that the driver was especially careful to avoid being fined probative of care the driver exercised? In some jurisdictions, the cost of insurance goes up if the driver is involved in an accident. Isn't evidence that the driver was especially careful to avoid increased insurance costs probative of the care the driver exercised? Of course, even if the evidence is probative, the legislature can still exclude the evidence on a categorical basis because of concerns that the jurors might misuse it.

6. Id.

7. For a discussion of the trial judge's discretionary power to exclude relevant evidence on grounds of prejudice, see § 2.10 supra.

8. West's Ann.California Evidence Code § 355.

9. Royal Globe Ins. Co. v. Superior Court of Butte County, 23 Cal.3d 880, 891–892, 153 Cal.Rptr. 842, 849–850, 592 P.2d 329, 336–337 (1979), overruled on other grounds, Moradi–Shalal v. Fireman's Fund Ins. Companies, 46 Cal.3d 287, 303, 250 Cal.Rptr. 116, 126, 758 P.2d 58, 68–69 (1988).

10. Id.

not preclude a plaintiff from suing the insurer directly, where that right is created by contract or by another state's direct action statute.[11]

A related problem arises when the insured sues his insurer for breach of the insurance contract as well as for the tort of refusing in bad faith to honor the contract. If the insurer offers to settle both claims and the plaintiff rejects the offer, the plaintiff will be precluded from offering the insurer's offer as evidence of the validity of the contract and tort claims. In this case, however, § 1155 is not really implicated; there is no risk that the jurors may improperly consider insurance, since the plaintiff does not seek to recover for an injury against which the defendant may have insured. Rather, the plaintiff seeks to recover for the insured's failure to honor the insurance contract. Thus, the offer is excluded under the rule which precludes the use of settlement offers to prove the validity of claims.[12]

Another recurring problem is whether references to liability insurance by a party or its agents should be admitted as part of a party admission offered to prove fault. Where the reference to the insurance is the admission, then the statement cannot be received without violating § 1155. An example of such a statement can be found in Menefee v. Williams,[13] where the plaintiff sued the defendant for injuries he claimed he suffered when the defendant shot him in a hunting accident.[14] The court upheld the exclusion of a statement in which the defendant purportedly said to the plaintiff, "Don't worry, if your insurance doesn't cover this, mine will."[15]

A different situation would have been presented if the defendant had said, "Look, it's all my fault; don't worry, if your insurance doesn't cover this, mine will." Should the admission be excluded even if the reference to insurance is not offered to prove fault? In applying § 352, a trial judge would have several choices. One would be to admit the entire statement with the admonition that the jurors not consider the reference to insurance as proof of fault. Another would be to rule the entire statement inadmissible because of the prejudicial effect of the reference to insurance even with a limiting instruction. Finally, the court could redact the statement, allowing the jurors to hear only the admission but not the reference to the insurance.

If a statement referring to insurance is offered for a purpose other than to prove negligence or other wrongdoing, then that purpose must be relevant. In Brainard v. Cotner[16] the plaintiff sued the defendant for injuries he received while a passenger in the defendant's car.[17] Prior to

---

11. Roberts v. Home Ins. Indem. Co., 48 Cal.App.3d 313, 321, 121 Cal.Rptr. 862, 867 (1975).

12. See § 4.08 supra.

13. 259 Cal.App.2d 56, 66 Cal.Rptr. 108 (1968).

14. Id. at 58–59, 66 Cal.Rptr. at 111.

15. Id.

16. 59 Cal.App.3d 790, 130 Cal.Rptr. 915 (1976).

17. Id. at 792–793, 130 Cal.Rptr. at 916–917.

the trial, the plaintiff learned that the defendant had told the police that the accident had been caused by the plaintiff's unzipping of the defendant's dress.[18] When the plaintiff confronted the defendant with this statement, the defendant allegedly responded, "Well, I did it because I was fearful of my insurance."[19] The appellate court held that the statement should have been admitted. Properly limited, its probative value on the defendant's credibility substantially outweighed any concerns that the jury would misuse it for the purposes condemned in § 1155.[20]

Given the widespread use of liability insurance, jurors today may assume that the parties are insured. Even if no insurance is mentioned in the course of the trial, should the jurors nonetheless be told to refrain from discussing insurance in their deliberations? In California, the question has been answered in the affirmative. A party may request the court to instruct the jurors that whether or not insurance exists has no bearing on the case and that the jurors "must refrain from any inference, speculation or discussion" on the subject.[21]

QUESTIONS AND PROBLEMS

No   1. You represent a plaintiff who claims that she was injured when the defendant hit her while running a red light. Do you want the jurors to know that the defendant is insured against such accidents? Why?

No   2. Is such evidence admissible in a California or federal court to prove the defendant's negligence or other wrongdoing?

Adm.   3. A statute makes it a misdemeanor to leave the scene of an accident without leaving a note on the damaged vehicle with your name, address, and telephone number. The defendant is prosecuted under this statute. At the trial the defendant testifies that he didn't leave the required note because he was not aware that his car struck the victim's car. He testifies that at the time of the accident he had nothing to fear by leaving the note because he was insured. The prosecution moves to strike the last part of his testimony. How should the judge rule?

yes   4. You represent the defendant in a personal injury action. During the course of the trial no mention is made of insurance. Should you ask the judge to instruct the jurors that the existence or nonexistence of insurance has no bearing on the case and that they should refrain from discussing the subject?

§ 4.11   OTHER EVIDENCE EXCLUDED BY EXTRINSIC POLICIES

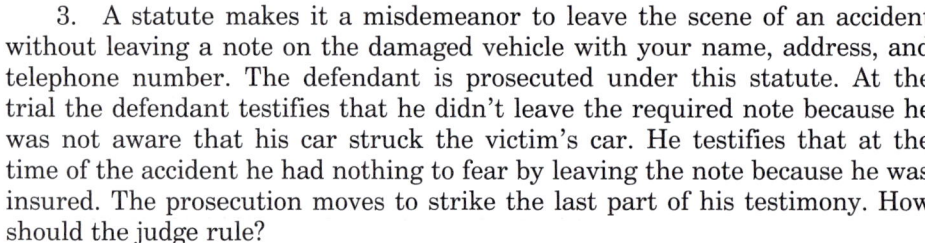

The Evidence Code has a number of additional provisions calling for the exclusion of relevant evidence on policy grounds. The Federal Rules do not have counterparts.

18.   Id. at 794, 130 Cal.Rptr. at 917.

19.   Id.

20.   Id. at 795–796, 130 Cal.Rptr. at 918.

21.   BAJI 1.04 (Fall 2007 Edition).

Section 1156 promotes research to reduce morbidity and mortality by in-hospital medical or medical-dental staff committees of licensed hospitals by limiting the admissibility of the written records of the interviews, reports, statements and memoranda connected with the research.[1]

Section 1156.1 promotes research to reduce morbidity and mortality by committees established to undertake medical or psychiatric study by limiting the admissibility of the written records of the interviews, reports, statements and memoranda connected with the research.[2]

Section 1157(a) applies to the proceedings and records of committees charged with evaluating and improving the quality of care rendered by a variety of health professionals, including medical doctors, dentists, and therapists.[3] In addition to exempting the proceedings and records from discovery, subject to certain exceptions § 1157(b) provides that "no person in attendance at a meeting of any of those committees shall be required to testify as to what transpired at that meeting."[4]

Section 1157.6 extends § 1157's prohibitions on discovery and testimony to the proceedings and records of committees charged with evaluating and improving the quality of mental health rendered in county operated and contracted mental health facilities.[5]

Section 1157.7 extends § 1157's prohibitions on discovery and testimony to the proceedings and records of any committee established by a local governmental agency to monitor, evaluate, and report on the necessity, quality, and level of specialty care provided by a general acute care hospital which has been designated or recognized by the local governmental agency as qualified to render specialty care services, including trauma care.[6]

Section 1159 prohibits the use of evidence pertaining to live animal experimentation in any product liability action involving a motor vehicle.[7]

§ 4.12 MAJOR DIFFERENCES BETWEEN THE FEDERAL RULES AND THE EVIDENCE CODE

The breadth of topics covered in Chapters 3 and 4 makes generalizations difficult. Nonetheless, when it comes to relevance and its limits, the conceptual overlap between the Rules and the Code is striking. Both define relevance in almost identical terms and vest judges with discretion to exclude otherwise admissible evidence when its probative value is substantially outweighed by similar enumerated concerns.

---

1. West's Ann. California Evidence Code § 1156.
2. West's Ann. California Evidence Code § 1156.1.
3. West's Ann. California Evidence Code § 1157(a).
4. West's Ann. California Evidence Code § 1157(b).
5. West's Ann. California Evidence Code § 1157.6.
6. West's Ann. California Evidence Code § 1157.7.
7. West's Ann. California Evidence Code § 1159.

In addition, the Rules and the Code have similar provisions for excluding categories of relevant evidence in order to advance important policies. Subsequent remedial measures are excluded to encourage the making of repairs; offers to plead guilty and related statements are banned to promote plea bargaining; pleas of nolo contendere are excluded to encourage defendants to settle criminal cases; humanitarian gestures are promoted by eliminating the risk that they might be used as admissions; and the settlement of civil claims is encouraged by banning the use of settlement conference statements to prove the validity or invalidity of the claims.

The Rules and the Code take similar, though not identical, approaches to the admissibility of character evidence. When character is not an element of the cause of action, both posit a general rule disfavoring the use of character evidence to prove that on a given occasion a person conformed his or her conduct to a particular character trait. Both build on the Common Law exceptions that allow criminal defendants to offer evidence of their good character to counter evidence of guilt and of their victims' bad character to disprove or diminish their culpability for the crime charged. In addition, the Rules and the Code have come to recognize new exceptions which disfavor the accused. In sexual assault cases, for example, federal and California prosecutors may now offer evidence of uncharged sexual misdeeds as proof of the accused's propensity to commit the sexual misdeed charged.

The Rules and the Code seek to protect the victims of sexual assaults through rape shield laws that limit the kind of evidence the accused may offer to prove consent or to discredit the victim as a witness. In addition, both permit the use of evidence of habit and routine practices because the evidence does not raise the concerns associated with character evidence.

But despite the overlap, some significant differences between the Rules and the Code remain. In some instances, one set of rules has provisions the other set does not. The Code provisions on mediation are a good example. Because of the importance of mediation as a conflict resolution tool, the Code devotes an entire chapter to rules promoting mediation. The Rules are silent on mediation. In other instances, the approach of one set of rules is superior to the other set's approach. The Rules, for example, expressly prohibit the use of a statement made in settlement negotiations if offered as a prior inconsistent statement or as evidence of contradiction. The Code says nothing about this important matter. Other differences worth highlighting include the following:

(1) Rule 401 makes clearer than Code § 210 the burden the proponent must discharge when confronted by an irrelevance objection. The proponent need only convince the judge that the proffered evidence makes the existence of any consequential fact more or less probable than the fact would be without the evidence. Though both provisions impose the same burden on the proponent of the evidence, the language of Rule 401 is superior in this respect.

(2) Neither the Code nor the Rules establishes a preference between direct and circumstantial evidence. In § 410, however, the Code at least defines direct evidence. The Rules do not have an analogous provision.

(3) Under Rule 404(a)(2), the government may, in a homicide prosecution, offer evidence of the victim's trait of peacefulness even if the accused did not first offer evidence of the victim's predisposition to engage in unprovoked attacks. So long as the accused offers evidence that the victim was the first aggressor on the occasion in question, the prosecution may offer evidence of the victim's trait of peacefulness in the form of opinion and reputation evidence. Rule 404(a)(2) applies, however, even if other eyewitnesses testify to the fatal attack. The Code does not contain a similar provision.

(4) Rule 404(b) and Code § 1101(b) provide similar, though not identical, non-exclusive lists of permissible propositions that may be proved by seemingly inadmissible character evidence. Rule 404(b) differs from the Code in that it requires the prosecution in a criminal case to provide notice in advance of trial of its intention to offer evidence under the Rule. Pretrial notice is included to reduce surprise and promote early resolution of the issue of admissibility.

(5) Code § 1104 bans the use of evidence of a trait of a person's character with respect to care or skill to prove the quality of his or her conduct on a specified occasion. The California provision is a specific application of the general prohibition on the use of character evidence. Its value is putting the parties and the court on notice that the prohibition applies to traits of care and skill as well, especially in personal injury cases. The Federal Rules do not contain an equivalent provision.

(6) With regard to subsequent repairs, the California rule differs from the federal provision in that the state's subsequent repair doctrine does not apply in strict liability actions.

(7) Rule 408 does not include impeachment among the permissible purposes for which settlement conference statements may be offered. Whether statements made in compromise negotiations should be admitted as prior inconsistent statements to impeach a party has been controversial. Opponents point out that the value of impeaching a party through inconsistent statements made in compromise negotiations is outweighed by the negative effect such impeachment would have on the candor required for successful settlement negotiations. As amended in 2006, Rule 408 adopts this view. It prohibits the use of a statement made in settlement negotiations if offered as a prior inconsistent statement or as evidence of contradiction. The Code is silent on this point.

(8) As noted, the Code devotes an entire chapter to the admissibility of statements made in the course of mediation. There are no equivalent provisions under the Federal Rules.

(9) California has an additional provision relating to the policy of excluding evidence of humanitarian gestures. Recognizing that many

personal suits are prompted by anger at the defendant's failure to apologize for the injury, the California Legislature in 2000 amended Code § 1160 to reduce suits by encouraging defendants to apologize without fear their apologies might be considered admissions.

(10) An important question is whether the protection afforded to an offer to plead guilty or a withdrawn guilty plea extends also to the statements made in connection with the offer or the withdrawn plea. Rule 410 answers this question in the affirmative by extending the protection to any statement made in the course of plea discussions as well as the offer to plead guilty. Section 1153 of the Code is silent on this point but has been construed as extending to the statements made in the course of plea negotiations as well as to the offers to plead guilty.

(11) Whether the accused should be impeached by statements made in plea discussions presents difficult choices between promoting plea bargains, on the one hand, and discouraging criminal defendants from testifying inconsistently with their prior statements, on the other. Rule 410 strikes the balance in favor of plea bargaining by prohibiting the use of plea discussion statements for impeachment unless the accused relinquishes the Rule's protection as a condition to entering into plea negotiations. Code § 1153 appears to be as broad as Rule 410 but has been construed as applying only when statements made in plea discussions are offered as admissions, and not to impeach the defendant.

(12) Code § 1153 does not define the participants in plea negotiations. Offers and related statements made to prosecuting attorneys qualify for protection, but it is less clear whether plea participants include police officers and others who participate in bona fide plea negotiations on behalf of the prosecution. Unlike Federal Rule 410, Code § 1153 does not expressly limit bona fide plea discussions to discussions with prosecutors, such as attorneys employed by the county district attorney or the California Attorney General. Police officers and other law enforcement personnel sometimes participate in plea negotiations. The California courts, however, disagree whether police officers and others who do not represent the district attorney qualify as plea participants.

(13) Rule 410, following the traditional approach, prohibits the use of a plea of nolo contendere in any civil or criminal proceeding regardless of the grade of the offense. Section 1016(3) of the California Penal Code excludes felonies from the protection afforded to nolo contendere pleas in civil actions.

(14) If possessing liability insurance is not probative of fault, then not possessing such insurance is likewise not probative of care. Rule 411 proceeds on this assumption. It provides that evidence that a person was or was not insured against liability is not admissible upon the issue of whether the person acted negligently or otherwise wrongfully. Code § 1155 does not contain a similar provision. Accordingly, in California courts the party opposing evidence of the lack of liability insurance must object on irrelevance grounds.

(15) Code § 1153.5 bans the use of an offer for a civil resolution of a complaint alleging a crime against property if the offer is made with the assistance of the prosecutor. Both the offer as well as the admissions made in the course of the negotiations are protected from disclosure in any subsequent proceeding. The Rules do not have an equivalent provision.

CALIFORNIA EVIDENCE CODE

§ 1115. Definitions

For purposes of this chapter:

(a) "Mediation" means a process in which a neutral person or persons facilitate communication between the disputants to assist them in reaching a mutually acceptable agreement.

(b) "Mediator" means a neutral person who conducts a mediation. "Mediator" includes any person designated by a mediator either to assist in the mediation or to communicate with the participants in preparation for a mediation.

(c) "Mediation consultation" means a communication between a person and a mediator for the purpose of initiating, considering, or reconvening a mediation or retaining the mediator.

§ 1116. Effect of chapter

(a) Nothing in this chapter expands or limits a court's authority to order participation in a dispute resolution proceeding. Nothing in this chapter authorizes or affects the enforceability of a contract clause in which parties agree to the use of mediation.

(b) Nothing in this chapter makes admissible evidence that is inadmissible under Section 1152 or any other statute.

§ 1117. Application of chapter

(a) Except as provided in subdivision (b), this chapter applies to a mediation as defined in Section 1115.

(b) This chapter does not apply to either of the following:

(1) A proceeding under Part 1 (commencing with Section 1800) of Division 5 of the Family Code or Chapter 11 (commencing with Section 3160) of Part 2 of Division 8 of the Family Code.

(2) A settlement conference pursuant to Rule 3.1380 of the California Rules of Court.

§ 1118. Oral agreements

An oral agreement "in accordance with Section 1118" means an oral agreement that satisfies all of the following conditions:

(a) The oral agreement is recorded by a court reporter or reliable means of audio recording.

(b) The terms of the oral agreement are recited on the record in the presence of the parties and the mediator, and the parties express on the record that they agree to the terms recited.

(c) The parties to the oral agreement expressly state on the record that the agreement is enforceable or binding or words to that effect.

(d) The recording is reduced to writing and the writing is signed by the parties within 72 hours after it is recorded.

§ 1119. Written or oral communications during mediation process; admissibility

Except as otherwise provided in this chapter:

(a) No evidence of anything said or any admission made for the purpose of, in the course of, or pursuant to, a mediation or a mediation consultation is admissible or subject to discovery, and disclosure of the evidence shall not be compelled, in any arbitration, administrative adjudication, civil action, or other noncriminal proceeding in which, pursuant to law, testimony can be compelled to be given.

(b) No writing, as defined in Section 250, that is prepared for the purpose of, in the course of, or pursuant to, a mediation or a mediation consultation, is admissible or subject to discovery, and disclosure of the writing shall not be compelled, in any arbitration, administrative adjudication, civil action, or other noncriminal proceeding in which, pursuant to law, testimony can be compelled to be given.

(c) All communications, negotiations, or settlement discussions by and between participants in the course of a mediation or a mediation consultation shall remain confidential.

§ 1120. Evidence otherwise admissible

(a) Evidence otherwise admissible or subject to discovery outside of a mediation or a mediation consultation shall not be or become inadmissible or protected from disclosure solely by reason of its introduction or use in a mediation or a mediation consultation.

(b) This chapter does not limit any of the following:

(1) The admissibility of an agreement to mediate a dispute.

(2) The effect of an agreement not to take a default or an agreement to extend the time within which to act or refrain from acting in a pending civil action.

(3) Disclosure of the mere fact that a mediator has served, is serving, will serve, or was contacted about serving as a mediator in a dispute.

§ 1121. Mediator's reports and findings

Neither a mediator nor anyone else may submit to a court or other adjudicative body, and a court or other adjudicative body may not consider, any report, assessment, evaluation, recommendation, or finding of any kind by the mediator concerning a mediation conducted by the mediator, other than a report that is mandated by court rule or other law and that states only whether an agreement was reached, unless all parties to the mediation expressly agree otherwise in writing, or orally in accordance with Section 1118.

§ 1122.   Communications or writings; conditions to admissibility

(a) A communication or a writing, as defined in Section 250, that is made or prepared for the purpose of, or in the course of, or pursuant to, a mediation or a mediation consultation, is not made inadmissible, or protected from disclosure, by provisions of this chapter if either of the following conditions is satisfied:

(1) All persons who conduct or otherwise participate in the mediation expressly agree in writing, or orally in accordance with Section 1118, to disclosure of the communication, document, or writing.

(2) The communication, document, or writing was prepared by or on behalf of fewer than all the mediation participants, those participants expressly agree in writing, or orally in accordance with Section 1118, to its disclosure, and the communication, document, or writing does not disclose anything said or done or any admission made in the course of the mediation.

(b) For purposes of subdivision (a), if the neutral person who conducts a mediation expressly agrees to disclosure, that agreement also binds any other person described in subdivision (b) of Section 1115.

§ 1123.   Written settlement agreements; conditions to admissibility

A written settlement agreement prepared in the course of, or pursuant to, a mediation, is not made inadmissible, or protected from disclosure, by provisions of this chapter if the agreement is signed by the settling parties and any of the following conditions are satisfied:

(a) The agreement provides that it is admissible or subject to disclosure, or words to that effect.

(b) The agreement provides that it is enforceable or binding or words to that effect.

(c) All parties to the agreement expressly agree in writing, or orally in accordance with Section 1118, to its disclosure.

(d) The agreement is used to show fraud, duress, or illegality that is relevant to an issue in dispute.

§ 1124.   Oral agreements; conditions to admissibility

An oral agreement made in the course of, or pursuant to, a mediation is not made inadmissible, or protected from disclosure, by the provisions of this chapter if any of the following conditions are satisfied:

(a) The agreement is in accordance with Section 1118.

(b) The agreement is in accordance with subdivisions (a), (b), and (d) of Section 1118, and all parties to the agreement expressly agree, in writing or orally in accordance with Section 1118, to disclosure of the agreement.

(c) The agreement is in accordance with subdivisions (a), (b), and (d) of Section 1118, and the agreement is used to show fraud, duress, or illegality that is relevant to an issue in dispute.

§ 1125. End of mediation; satisfaction of conditions

(a) For purposes of confidentiality under this chapter, a mediation ends when any one of the following conditions is satisfied:

(1) The parties execute a written settlement agreement that fully resolves the dispute.

(2) An oral agreement that fully resolves the dispute is reached in accordance with Section 1118.

(3) The mediator provides the mediation participants with a writing signed by the mediator that states that the mediation is terminated, or words to that effect, which shall be consistent with Section 1121.

(4) A party provides the mediator and the other mediation participants with a writing stating that the mediation is terminated, or words to that effect, which shall be consistent with Section 1121. In a mediation involving more than two parties, the mediation may continue as to the remaining parties or be terminated in accordance with this section.

(5) For 10 calendar days, there is no communication between the mediator and any of the parties to the mediation relating to the dispute. The mediator and the parties may shorten or extend this time by agreement.

(b) For purposes of confidentiality under this chapter, if a mediation partially resolves a dispute, mediation ends when either of the following conditions is satisfied:

(1) The parties execute a written settlement agreement that partially resolves the dispute.

(2) An oral agreement that partially resolves the dispute is reached in accordance with Section 1118.

(c) This section does not preclude a party from ending a mediation without reaching an agreement. This section does not otherwise affect the extent to which a party may terminate a mediation.

§ 1126. Protections before and after mediation ends

Anything said, any admission made, or any writing that is inadmissible, protected from disclosure, and confidential under this chapter before a mediation ends, shall remain inadmissible, protected from disclosure, and confidential to the same extent after the mediation ends.

§ 1127. Attorney's fees and costs

If a person subpoenas or otherwise seeks to compel a mediator to testify or produce a writing, as defined in Section 250, and the court or other adjudicative body determines that the testimony or writing is inadmissible under this chapter, or protected from disclosure under this chapter, the court or adjudicative body making the determination shall award reasonable attorney's fees and costs to the mediator against the person seeking the testimony or writing.

§ 1128. Subsequent trials; references to mediation

Any reference to a mediation during any subsequent trial is an irregularity in the proceedings of the trial for the purposes of Section 657 of the Code of Civil Procedure. Any reference to a mediation during any other subsequent noncriminal proceeding is grounds for vacating or modifying the decision in that proceeding, in whole or in part, and granting a new or further hearing on all or part of the issues, if the reference materially affected the substantial rights of the party requesting relief.

§ 1151. Subsequent remedial conduct

When, after the occurrence of an event, remedial or precautionary measures are taken, which, if taken previously, would have tended to make the event less likely to occur, evidence of such subsequent measures is inadmissible to prove negligence or culpable conduct in connection with the event.

§ 1152. Offer to compromise and the like

(a) Evidence that a person has, in compromise or from humanitarian motives, furnished or offered or promised to furnish money or any other thing, act, or service to another who has sustained or will sustain or claims that he or she has sustained or will sustain loss or damage, as well as any conduct or statements made in negotiation thereof, is inadmissible to prove his or her liability for the loss or damage or any part of it.

(b) In the event that evidence of an offer to compromise is admitted in an action for breach of the covenant of good faith and fair dealing or violation of subdivision (h) of Section 790.03 of the Insurance Code, then at the request of the party against whom the evidence is admitted, or at the request of the party who made the offer to compromise that was admitted, evidence relating to any other offer or counteroffer to compromise the same or substantially the same claimed loss or damage shall also be admissible for the same purpose as the initial evidence regarding settlement. Other than as may be admitted in an action for breach of the covenant of good faith and fair dealing or violation of subdivision (h) of Section 790.03 of the Insurance Code, evidence of settlement offers shall not be admitted in a motion for a new trial, in any proceeding involving an additur or remittitur, or on appeal.

(c) This section does not affect the admissibility of evidence of any of the following:

(1) Partial satisfaction of an asserted claim or demand without questioning its validity when such evidence is offered to prove the validity of the claim.

(2) A debtor's payment or promise to pay all or a part of his or her preexisting debt when such evidence is offered to prove the creation of a new duty on his or her part or a revival of his or her preexisting duty.

§ 1153. Offer to plead guilty or withdraw plea of guilty by criminal defendant

Evidence of a plea of guilty, later withdrawn, or of an offer to plead guilty to the crime charged or to any other crime, made by the defendant in a criminal action is inadmissible in any action or in any proceeding of any nature, including proceedings before agencies, commissions, boards, and tribunals.

§ 1153.5. Offer for civil resolution of crimes against property

Evidence of an offer for civil resolution of a criminal matter pursuant to the provisions of Section 33 of the Code of Civil Procedure, or admissions made in the course of or negotiations for the offer shall not be admissible in any action.

§ 1154. Offer to discount a claim

Evidence that a person has accepted or offered or promised to accept a sum of money or any other thing, act, or service in satisfaction of a claim, as well as any conduct or statements made in negotiation thereof, is inadmissible to prove the invalidity of the claim or any part of it.

§ 1155. Liability insurance

Evidence that a person was, at the time a harm was suffered by another, insured wholly or partially against loss arising from liability for that harm is inadmissible to prove negligence or other wrongdoing.

§ 1156. Records of medical or dental study of in-hospital staff committee

(a) In-hospital medical or medical-dental staff committees of a licensed hospital may engage in research and medical or dental study for the purpose of reducing morbidity or mortality, and may make findings and recommendations relating to such purpose. Except as provided in subdivision (b), the written records of interviews, reports, statements, or memoranda of such in-hospital medical or medical-dental staff committees relating to such medical or dental studies are subject to Title 4 (commencing with Section 2016.010) of Part 4 of the Code of Civil Procedure (relating to discovery proceedings) but, subject to subdivisions (c) and (d), shall not be admitted as evidence in any action or before any administrative body, agency, or person.

(b) The disclosure, with or without the consent of the patient, of information concerning him to such in-hospital medical or medical-dental staff committee does not make unprivileged any information that would otherwise be privileged under Section 994 or 1014; but, notwithstanding

Sections 994 and 1014, such information is subject to discovery under subdivision (a) except that the identity of any patient may not be discovered under subdivision (a) unless the patient consents to such disclosure.

(c) This section does not affect the admissibility in evidence of the original medical or dental records of any patient.

(d) This section does not exclude evidence which is relevant evidence in a criminal action.

§ 1156.1. Records of medical or psychiatric studies of quality assurance committees

(a) A committee established in compliance with Sections 4070 and 5624 of the Welfare and Institutions Code may engage in research and medical or psychiatric study for the purpose of reducing morbidity or mortality, and may make findings and recommendations to the county and state relating to such purpose. Except as provided in subdivision (b), the written records of interviews, reports, statements, or memoranda of such committees relating to such medical or psychiatric studies are subject to Title 4 (commencing with Section 2016.010) of Part 4 of the Code of Civil Procedure but, subject to subdivisions (c) and (d), shall not be admitted as evidence in any action or before any administrative body, agency, or person.

(b) The disclosure, with or without the consent of the patient, of information concerning him or her to such committee does not make unprivileged any information that would otherwise be privileged under Section 994 or 1014. However, notwithstanding Sections 994 and 1014, such information is subject to discovery under subdivision (a) except that the identity of any patient may not be discovered under subdivision (a) unless the patient consents to such disclosure.

(c) This section does not affect the admissibility in evidence of the original medical or psychiatric records of any patient.

(d) This section does not exclude evidence which is relevant evidence in a criminal action.

§ 1157. Proceedings and records of organized committees having responsibility of evaluation and improvement of quality of care; exceptions

(a) Neither the proceedings nor the records of organized committees of medical, medical-dental, podiatric, registered dietitian, psychological, marriage and family therapist, licensed clinical social worker, professional clinical counselor, or veterinary staffs in hospitals, or of a peer review body, as defined in Section 805 of the Business and Professions Code, having the responsibility of evaluation and improvement of the quality of care rendered in the hospital, or for that peer review body, or medical or dental review or dental hygienist review or chiropractic review or podiatric review or registered dietitian review or veterinary review or acupuncturist review committees of local medical, dental, dental hygienist, podiatric, dietetic, veterinary, acupuncture, or chiropractic societies, marriage and family therapist, licensed clinical social worker, professional clinical counselor, or psychological review committees of state or local marriage and family therapist, state or local licensed clinical social worker, professional clinical counselor, state or local psychological associations or societies having the responsibility of evaluation and improvement of the quality of care, shall be subject to discovery.

(b) Except as hereinafter provided, no person in attendance at a meeting of any of those committees shall be required to testify as to what transpired at that meeting.

(c) The prohibition relating to discovery or testimony does not apply to the statements made by any person in attendance at a meeting of any of those committees who is a party to an action or proceeding the subject matter of which was reviewed at that meeting, or to any person requesting hospital staff privileges, or in any action against an insurance carrier alleging bad faith by the carrier in refusing to accept a settlement offer within the policy limits.

(d) The prohibitions in this section do not apply to medical, dental, dental hygienist, podiatric, dietetic, psychological, marriage and family therapist, licensed clinical social worker, professional clinical counselor, veterinary, acupuncture, or chiropractic society committees that exceed 10 percent of the membership of the society, nor to any of those committees if any person serves upon the committee when his or her own conduct or practice is being reviewed.

(e) The amendments made to this section by Chapter 1081 of the Statutes of 1983, or at the 1985 portion of the 1985–86 Regular Session of the Legislature, at the 1990 portion of the 1989–90 Regular Session of the Legislature, at the 2000 portion of the 1999–2000 Regular Session of the Legislature, or at the 2011 portion of the 2011–12 Regular Session of the Legislature, do not exclude the discovery or use of relevant evidence in a criminal action.

§ 1157.5. Organized committee of nonprofit medical care foundation or professional standards review organization; proceedings and records

Except in actions involving a claim of a provider of health care services for payment for such services, the prohibition relating to discovery or testimony provided by Section 1157 shall be applicable to the proceedings or records of an organized committee of any nonprofit medical care foundation or professional standards review organization which is organized in a manner which makes available professional competence to review health care services with respect to medical necessity, quality of care, or economic justification of charges or level of care.

§ 1157.6. Proceedings and records of quality assurance committees for county health facilities

Neither the proceedings nor the records of a committee established in compliance with Sections 4070 and 5624 of the Welfare and Institutions

Code having the responsibility of evaluation and improvement of the quality of mental health care rendered in county operated and contracted mental health facilities shall be subject to discovery. Except as provided in this section, no person in attendance at a meeting of any such committee · shall be required to testify as to what transpired thereat. The prohibition relating to discovery or testimony shall not apply to the statements made by any person in attendance at such a meeting who is a party to an action or proceeding the subject matter of which was reviewed at such meeting, or to any person requesting facility staff privileges.

§ 1157.7. Application of Section 1157 discovery or testimony prohibitions; application of public records and meetings provisions

The prohibition relating to discovery or testimony provided in Section 1157 shall be applicable to proceedings and records of any committee established by a local governmental agency to monitor, evaluate, and report on the necessity, quality, and level of specialty health services, including, but not limited to, trauma care services, provided by a general acute care hospital which has been designated or recognized by that governmental agency as qualified to render specialty health care services. The provisions of Chapter 3.5 (commencing with Section 6250) of Division 7 of Title 1 of the Government Code and Chapter 9 (commencing with Section 54950) of Division 2 of Title 5 of the Government Code shall not be applicable to the committee records and proceedings.

§ 1158. Inspection and copying of patient's records; authorization; failure to comply; costs

Whenever, prior to the filing of any action or the appearance of a defendant in an action, an attorney at law or his or her representative presents a written authorization therefor signed by an adult patient, by the guardian or conservator of his or her person or estate, or, in the case of a minor, by a parent or guardian of the minor, or by the personal representative or an heir of a deceased patient, or a copy thereof, a physician and surgeon, dentist, registered nurse, dispensing optician, registered physical therapist, podiatrist, licensed psychologist, osteopathic physician and surgeon, chiropractor, clinical laboratory bioanalyst, clinical laboratory technologist, or pharmacist or pharmacy, duly licensed as such under the laws of the state, or a licensed hospital, shall make all of the patient's records under his, hers or its custody or control available for inspection and copying by the attorney at law or his, or her, representative, promptly upon the presentation of the written authorization.

No copying may be performed by any medical provider or employer enumerated above, or by an agent thereof, when the requesting attorney has employed a professional photocopier or anyone identified in Section 22451 of the Business and Professions Code as his or her representative to obtain or review the records on his or her behalf. The presentation of the authorization by the agent on behalf of the attorney shall be sufficient proof that the agent is the attorney's representative.

Failure to make the records available, during business hours, within five days after the presentation of the written authorization, may subject the person or entity having custody or control of the records to liability for all reasonable expenses, including attorney's fees, incurred in any proceeding to enforce this section.

All reasonable costs incurred by any person or entity enumerated above in making patient records available pursuant to this section may be charged against the person whose written authorization required the availability of the records.

"Reasonable cost," as used in this section, shall include, but not be limited to, the following specific costs: ten cents ($0.10) per page for standard reproduction of documents of a size 8½ by 14 inches or less; twenty cents ($0.20) per page for copying of documents from microfilm; actual costs for the reproduction of oversize documents or the reproduction of documents requiring special processing which are made in response to an authorization; reasonable clerical costs incurred in locating and making the records available to be billed at the maximum rate of sixteen dollars ($16) per hour per person, computed on the basis of four dollars ($4) per quarter hour or fraction thereof; actual postage charges; and actual costs, if any, charged to the witness by a third person for the retrieval and return of records held by that third person.

Where the records are delivered to the attorney or the attorney's representative for inspection or photocopying at the record custodian's place of business, the only fee for complying with the authorization shall not exceed fifteen dollars ($15), plus actual costs, if any, charged to the record custodian by a third person for retrieval and return of records held offsite by the third person.

§ 1159. Animal experimentation in product liability actions

(a) No evidence pertaining to live animal experimentation, including, but not limited to, injury, impact, or crash experimentation, shall be admissible in any product liability action involving a motor vehicle or vehicles.

(b) This section shall apply to cases for which a trial has not actually commenced, as described in paragraph (6) of subdivision (a) of Section 581 of the Code of Civil Procedure, on January 1, 1993.

§ 1160. Evidence of expressions of sympathy; statements of fault

(a) The portion of statements, writings, or benevolent gestures expressing sympathy or a general sense of benevolence relating to the pain, suffering, or death of a person involved in an accident and made to that person or to the family of that person shall be inadmissible as evidence of an admission of liability in a civil action. A statement of fault, however, which is part of, or in addition to, any of the above shall not be inadmissible pursuant to this section.

(b) For purposes of this section:

(1) "Accident" means an occurrence resulting in injury or death to one or more persons which is not the result of willful action by a party.

(2) "Benevolent gestures" means actions which convey a sense of compassion or commiseration emanating from humane impulses.

(3) "Family" means the spouse, parent, grandparent, stepmother, stepfather, child, grandchild, brother, sister, half brother, half sister, adopted children of parent, or spouse's parents of an injured party.

FEDERAL RULES OF EVIDENCE

Rule 407. Subsequent Remedial Measures

When measures are taken that would have made an earlier injury or harm less likely to occur, evidence of the subsequent measures is not admissible to prove:

- negligence;

- culpable conduct;

- a defect in a product or its design; or

- a need for a warning or instruction. But the court may admit this evidence for another purpose, such as impeachment or—if disputed—proving ownership, control, or the feasibility of precautionary measures.

Rule 408. Compromise Offers and Negotiations

(a) Prohibited Uses. Evidence of the following is not admissible—on behalf of any party—either to prove or disprove the validity or amount of a disputed claim or to impeach by a prior inconsistent statement or a contradiction:

(1) furnishing, promising, or offering—or accepting, promising to accept, or offering to accept—a valuable consideration in compromising or attempting to compromise the claim; and

(2) conduct or a statement made during compromise negotiations about the claim—except when offered in a criminal case and when the negotiations related to a claim by a public office in the exercise of its regulatory, investigative, or enforcement authority.

(b) Exceptions. The court may admit this evidence for another purpose, such as proving a witness's bias or prejudice, negating a contention of undue delay, or proving an effort to obstruct a criminal investigation or prosecution.

Rule 409.   Offers to Pay Medical and Similar Expenses

Evidence of furnishing, promising to pay, or offering to pay medical, hospital, or similar expenses resulting from an injury is not admissible to prove liability for the injury.

Rule 410.   Pleas, Plea Discussions, and Related Statements

(a) Prohibited Uses. In a civil or criminal case, evidence of the following is not admissible against the defendant who made the plea or participated in the plea discussions:

> **(1)** a guilty plea that was later withdrawn;

> **(2)** a nolo contendere plea;

> **(3)** a statement made during a proceeding on either of those pleas under Federal Rule of Criminal Procedure 11 or a comparable state procedure; or

> **(4)** a statement made during plea discussions with an attorney for the prosecuting authority if the discussions did not result in a guilty plea or they resulted in a later-withdrawn guilty plea.

(b) Exceptions. The court may admit a statement described in Rule 410(a)(3) or (4):

> **(1)** in any proceeding in which another statement made during the same plea or plea discussions has been introduced, if in fairness the statements ought to be considered together; or

> **(2)** in a criminal proceeding for perjury or false statement, if the defendant made the statement under oath, on the record, and with counsel present.

Rule 411.   Liability Insurance

Evidence that a person was or was not insured against liability is not admissible to prove whether the person acted negligently or otherwise wrongfully. But the court may admit this evidence for another purpose, such as proving a witness's bias or prejudice or proving agency, ownership, or control.

CHAPTER 5

THE HEARSAY RULE

■ ■ ■

Table of Sections

§ 5.01 DEFINITION AND RATIONALE

Assume that the plaintiff sues the defendant for injuries the plaintiff claims she suffered when the defendant ran a red light and struck her car. The plaintiff testifies that, as she entered the intersection, the light facing her was green and that moments later the defendant's car struck her on the driver's side. The plaintiff also calls a motorist who testifies that he and his spouse were parked at the intersection facing the defendant and that at the time of the collision the spouse told the motorist that the light facing them was red.

Setting aside the issue of damages, the plaintiff's testimony alone would make out a prima facie case and allow the plaintiff to get to the jury on the issue of fault. With the motorist's testimony, her chances of persuading the jury to return a favorable verdict are enhanced significantly. But if the defendant contradicts the plaintiff's testimony ("I, not the plaintiff, had the green light.") and precludes the motorist from testifying, the outcome is cast into doubt. Indeed, if under these circumstances the jury cannot decide whether to believe the plaintiff or the defendant, they would be bound to return a defense verdict under the rule that the plaintiff, as the complaining party, must establish her claim by a preponderance of the evidence. To the defendant, then, preventing the motorist from testifying is crucial.

Over a hearsay objection, should the motorist be allowed to testify that his spouse told him that the light facing them was red? No, if the evidence is being offered to establish the color of the light facing them. In the words of California Evidence Code § 1200, the motorist's testimony is hearsay because it consists of a "statement that was made other than by a witness while testifying at the hearing" (what the spouse told the motorist about the color of the light prior to the trial) and "that is offered to prove the truth of the matter stated" (that the color of the light facing the motorist and his spouse was red shortly before the collision).[1]

Why should the hearsay rule disfavor the use of the spouse's statement? One reason is that receiving hearsay through a witness other than the declarant deprives the party opposing the hearsay from cross examining the declarant. Cross examiners generally have one of two goals: (1) to persuade a witness to recant the testimony on direct and, instead, affirm the cross examiner's theory of the case or (2) failing that, to discredit the witness's account on direct by impeaching the witness's credibility.

An example of the former would be a concession by the spouse on cross that, indeed, the color of the light facing her was really green. That doesn't happen often. More likely, she might concede that, although she thinks the light was red, she can't be absolutely sure because the sun was in her eyes. But regardless of which goal the cross examiner pursues, one matter is clear: the cross examiner cannot pursue either unless the motorist's spouse is produced for cross-examination under oath in the presence of the fact finder. It is her ability to perceive and recall the color of the light accurately, as well as her willingness to tell the truth about what she saw, that matters to the cross examiner. The motorist's abilities in these respects are much less important, since he did not see the light. Put another way, even if the motorist correctly heard what his spouse said about the color of the light and even if he recalls her statement correctly and relates it accurately to the jury, none of that would matter if his spouse either lied or was mistaken about the color of the light. The hearsay rule thus forces parties to focus on evidence about what people saw and heard, and not about what they heard others *say* they saw or heard.[2]

Some authorities link the hearsay rule to goals that go beyond the concessions that might be obtained on cross-examination. In their view, the use of hearsay violates the ideal conditions under which testimony should be received: witnesses should testify under oath in the fact finder's presence and subject to cross-examination.[3] The oath is believed to impress witnesses with the importance of testifying truthfully.[4] Having

---

1. West's Ann.California Evidence Code § 1200. Federal Rule of Evidence 801(c) is to the same effect: " 'Hearsay' means a statement that: (1) the declarant does not make while testifying at the current trial or hearing; and (2) a party offers in evidence to prove the truth of the matter asserted in the statement."

2. One, of course, can acquire information through senses other than sight or sound. One can also perceive by touching, smelling, and tasting. The Evidence Code recognizes that all five senses are involved in the acquisition of knowledge. See West's Ann.California Evidence Code § 170.

3. See Advisory Committee Note, Article VIII, Federal Rules of Evidence, and authorities cited therein.

4. Id.

witnesses testify before the fact finders enables them to take the witnesses' demeanor into account in assessing their credibility.[5] And subjecting witnesses to a searching cross-examination helps the opposing party expose inadvertent as well as conscious inaccuracies in perception, recollection, and narration.[6]

Sometimes hearsay is described as "inherently untrustworthy." What is meant is that hearsay should not be relied upon to reach factual decisions in the absence of the kind of cross-examination that has been described. The hearsay rule, however, does not proceed on the assumption that the hearsay declaration (in our example, what the spouse told the motorist) should be received in evidence so long as the opposing party is given a chance to call and cross examine the hearsay declarant (the spouse); on the contrary, the rule makes the declaration inadmissible. If the plaintiff wants to establish the color of the light facing the motorist's spouse at the time of the collision, then, in the absence of hearsay exceptions, she must do so by offering the spouse as a witness on that point and not by offering the spouse's statement to her husband or anyone else.

§ 5.02 PRIOR STATEMENTS OF WITNESSES AND THE HEARSAY RULE

Focusing on cross-examination as the principal justification for the hearsay rule has led some to question whether statements made prior to the trial by declarants who appear as witnesses should be excluded from the definition of hearsay. In particular, Professor Edmund Morgan and others proposed a rule, first found in the Model Code of Evidence[1] and later in the 1953 version of the Uniform Rules of Evidence,[2] that would make admissible any hearsay declaration if the judge found that the declarant was present and subject to cross-examination. Such a rule would have permitted the motorist in our example to repeat his spouse's statement about the color of the light facing him if she appeared at the hearing and could be called by the defendant as an adverse witness. Moreover, the rule would have permitted the plaintiff to call the spouse to testify not only about the color of the light facing them but also to repeat her statement to her spouse about the color of the light.

From a cross-examination perspective, the rule can be justified. After all, the opposing party's concerns can be satisfied by guaranteeing the examiner an opportunity to cross examine the hearsay declarant under oath in the presence of the fact finder. The framers of the California Evidence Code rejected this position, however. They feared that such a

---

5. Id.

6. Id.

1. Model Code of Evidence Rule 503 (1942).

2. Uniform Rule of Evidence 63(1) (1953). The Uniform Rule added a further condition: the prior statement could be admitted only if it would have been admissible if made by the declarant while testifying as a witness. Id.

rule "would permit a party to put in his case through statements carefully prepared in his attorney's office, thus enabling him to present a smoothly coherent story which could often not be duplicated on direct examination of the declarant."[3] They were also concerned that such a rule would undermine the rule prohibiting the use of leading questions on direct examination and the requirement that in most instances testimony be given under oath.[4]

Perhaps, though, the reason for rejecting the Model Code's position is simpler. In recreating an historical event, we are much more interested in what the witnesses remember about the event than in what they told others about it. Whatever the reason, in California prior statements of witnesses are hearsay if offered for the truth of the matter asserted. Their admissibility in most instances depends on the rules creating exceptions to the hearsay rule and governing the impeachment and accreditation of witnesses.[5]

§ 5.03 PRIOR STATEMENTS OF WITNESSES AND THE FEDERAL RULES

Although the Federal Rules define hearsay in much the same way as the Evidence Code,[1] the Rules take a different approach to the classification of prior statements of witnesses. Under the Rules, many prior statements of witnesses are exempted from the definition of hearsay even though they fall squarely within the definition.[2] The justification for the exemption is similar to the one offered by Professor Morgan: since in each instance the hearsay declarant must testify as a witness, the party opposing the hearsay declaration will have an opportunity to cross examine the declarant about the statement under oath in the presence of the fact finder.[3] In short, the conditions of the hearsay rule are satisfied.

Not all prior statements of witnesses are admissible, however, to prove the truth of the matter asserted. Federal Rule of Evidence 801(d)(1) divides them into three kinds—inconsistent statements, consistent statements, and statements of identification—and attaches different conditions of admissibility to each.[4] The admissibility of each kind of prior statement is discussed in later sections.[5]

One type of prior statement, party admissions, is treated separately under the Federal Rules. For party admissions to be admissible, it is not

---

3. 6 California Law Revision Commission, Reports, Recommendations, and Studies, Appendix 313 (1964).

4. Id.

5. See §§ 7.13 and 7.16 infra.

1. Compare Federal Rule 801(a)–(c) with West's Ann.California Evidence Code §§ 225 and 1200.

2. See Federal Rule of Evidence 801 and Advisory Committee Note.

3. Federal Rule of Evidence 801(d) (Advisory Committee Note).

4. Federal Rule of Evidence 801(d)(1).

5. See §§ 7.12 and 7.18 infra.

essential that the party testify as a witness.[6] The federal justification for exempting admissions from the definition of hearsay and California's treatment of admissions as exceptions to the hearsay rule are discussed in § 6.03.

The Federal Rules' treatment of prior statements as nonhearsay calls for a special response whenever the opponent objects on hearsay grounds. In California, if the opposing party believes that the proponent is offering hearsay, the opponent will object on hearsay grounds. If the proponent is merely offering the evidence for a relevant nonhearsay purpose—that is, not for the truth of the matter stated—that is the end of the matter as far as hearsay is concerned. If, on the other hand, the proponent is offering the evidence for a hearsay purpose and an exception applies, then that too is the end of the matter under the hearsay rule. But in federal courts, if the proponent is offering a prior statement for a hearsay purpose—that is, for the truth of the matter stated—then the response to the opponent's hearsay objection must be that the evidence is admissible for that purpose not because the statement falls within an exception but because it is "exempted" or "excluded" from the federal definition of hearsay.

§ 5.04　HEARSAY AND NONHEARSAY

A statement made prior to the hearing and offered at the hearing is hearsay only if offered to prove the truth of the matter stated.[1] If the evidence is offered for a relevant nonhearsay purpose—that is, *not* to prove the truth of the matter stated—then the hearsay objection must be overruled. Though the distinction is easily stated, it can be difficult to make in practice. Cases from California and other jurisdictions illustrate the distinction between statements offered for a hearsay and a nonhearsay purpose.[2]

To prove that the declarant was conscious or otherwise alive. Because of the paucity of good cases on point, Kaplan and Waltz created the following case for their casebook. In the Estate of Murdock[3] Arthur Murdock left his entire estate to his second wife, Sarah Hayes, if she survived him, but if she should not, then to his children by his first marriage. Sarah in turn left her entire estate to Arthur if he survived her, but if he should not, then to her children by her first marriage. Both Arthur and Sarah were killed in the same aircraft accident. As a result, it became crucial to determine who died last: if Arthur, his children would take; if Sarah, then her children would. To prove that Arthur died last, his children called a deputy sheriff who investigated the accident scene to testify that, after ascertaining that Sarah was dead, he then heard Arthur say, "I'm still alive." Although the statement would be hearsay if offered

---

6. Compare Federal Rule of Evidence 801(d)(1) with (d)(2).

1. See West's Ann. California Evidence Code § 1200; Federal Rule of Evidence 801(c).

2. Many of the best cases are collected in evidence casebooks. An especially good collection is provided by Kaplan and Waltz in Cases and Materials on Evidence (6th ed. 1987).

3. Kaplan and Waltz, Cases and Materials on Evidence 91 (6th ed. 1987).

to prove the truth of the matter stated—that the declarant was still alive—the reviewing court correctly held that the statement was admissible as relevant nonhearsay. Arthur engaged in conduct—uttering a phrase—from which the fact finder could conclude that he was alive. As the reviewing court noted, it would have made no difference if Arthur had said, "I am dead." That statement would have been as admissible as his actual statement to prove that he was at that moment alive.

To explain why a particular course of action was taken. In People v. Duran[4] the defendant was prosecuted for assaulting a fellow inmate with a deadly weapon. To prove that the defendant was the perpetrator, the prosecution offered evidence that he was seen fleeing from the crime scene. The defendant attempted to counter this evidence by testifying that he fled the scene because he feared administrative reprisals and not because he was the perpetrator. Over the prosecution's hearsay objection, the trial judge, prevented the defendant from testifying that a correctional officer had previously warned him to avoid further difficulties while in custody. The reviewing court held that the judge's ruling was in error. The defendant did not offer the correctional officer's out of court statement to prove as true the matters the officer asserted but to explain why in light of the statement the defendant fled from the scene of the stabbing.[5]

In Holland v. Union Pacific R. Co.[6] the trial judge dismissed the plaintiff's employment discrimination complaint because he failed to file it a timely manner. The reviewing court reversed the dismissal. The plaintiff was entitled to prove that his delay was occasioned by statements made by employees of the Department of Fair Employment and Housing. Receiving the employees' statements did not violate the hearsay rule; they were not offered to prove the "truth" of the matters asserted but to explain why the plaintiff delayed in filing his complaint.[7]

In People v. Sanders[8] the manager of a fast food restaurant identified the accused as one of the persons who had robbed the restaurant employees. He testified that he paid particular attention to the physical characteristics of the robber because he was following written instructions he had received on witness identification from his employer. Over a hearsay objection, the prosecution was allowed to offer the written instructions in evidence. The reviewing court upheld the receipt of the instructions. They were not offered to prove the "truth" of the matters they stated but as proof of the very instructions the manager attempted to follow. As such, they were nonhearsay and were probative of the manager's credibility.[9]

---

4. 16 Cal.3d 282, 545 P.2d 1322, 127 Cal.Rptr. 618 (1976).

5. Id. at 298, 545 P.2d at 1333, 127 Cal.Rptr. at 629.

6. 154 Cal.App.4th 940, 65 Cal.Rptr.3d 145 (2007).

7. Id. at 947, 65 Cal.Rptr. at 150.

8. 11 Cal.4th 475, 46 Cal.Rptr.2d 751, 905 P.2d 420 (1995).

9. Id. at 512, 46 Cal.Rptr.2d at 768, 905 P.2d at 437.

Consider the following evidence in a prosecution for driving under the influence:

Prosecutor: Why did you follow the white BMW?

Arresting Officer: Because communications told us to be on the lookout for a drunk driver in a white BMW.

The evidence is not hearsay if offered only to show why the officer followed the car. But because the significance of the evidence of the officer's conduct is slight when compared with the risk that the fact finder may misuse the evidence as proof that the driver was under the influence, defense lawyers should move to exclude it as unduly prejudicial.[10]

To prove that a warning was given. In Safeway Stores, Inc. v. Combs[11] the plaintiff sued the defendant for injuries she suffered when she slipped on spilt ketchup while shopping at the defendant's store. To prove that the defendant's agents had warned the plaintiff about the presence of the ketchup, the store's manager was permitted to testify that he had said, "Please don't step in that ketchup."[12] Because his statement was not offered to prove that ketchup was on the floor, but to prove that he warned the plaintiff about its presence, the evidence did not violate the hearsay rule.[13]

The manager's wife was in the store at the time the plaintiff fell. She, too, was called as a witness to repeat the statement her husband made to the plaintiff.[14] Again, receiving the statement did not violate the hearsay rule, since the evidence was offered to prove that a warning had been given. The wife's actual testimony was also relevant to prove another nonhearsay purpose. The fact that the manager's wife heard his warning was circumstantial evidence that the plaintiff also heard it.

Compare the warnings given in *Combs* with the following evidence:

Defendant: What, if anything did your husband tell you about the accident in the store?

Wife: He said, "I told the lady, 'Please don't step in that ketchup.' "

Her testimony would now violate the hearsay rule. The manager's out of court statement would be received to prove the truth of the matter stated, namely that he had warned the plaintiff about the ketchup's presence.

Depending on the theory of recovery, plaintiffs as well as defendants can benefit from evidence that a warning was given. In Hickman v. Arons[15] the plaintiffs sued for wrongful death when a wall fell and killed the decedent. To prove that the defendant knew or should have known of the danger posed by the wall, they were permitted to offer a notice a

---

10. Some courts take the view that this kind of nonhearsay evidence is irrelevant and therefore inadmissible because it has no tendency to prove or disprove any disputed issues. See, e.g., People v. Lucero, 64 Cal.App.4th 1107, 1109, 75 Cal.Rptr.2d 806, 808 (1998).

11. 273 F.2d 295 (5th Cir.1960).

12. Id.

13. Id.

14. Id.

15. 187 Cal.App.2d 167, 9 Cal.Rptr. 379 (1960).

building inspector sent to the defendant warning about the dangerous condition of the wall.[16] As in *Combs*, the warning was not offered to prove the existence of a dangerous condition but only that a warning had been given.[17]

To prove that information requiring further investigation was available. In Johnson v. Misericordia Community Hospital[18] the plaintiff sued a hospital for hiring and permitting an incompetent doctor to perform surgery on the plaintiff. The defendant objected to documents stating that, prior to the defendant's hiring of the doctor, one hospital had suspended the doctor's privilege to see patients and another had refused the doctor's request to serve on its staff.[19] Since the plaintiff's theory was that the defendant had been negligent in failing to investigate the doctor's background adequately before hiring him, the evidence was admissible to show the ease with which the defendant could have obtained information about the doctor's incompetence.[20] The evidence did not violate the hearsay rule because it was not offered to prove the doctor's incompetence.

To prove verbal acts that are material under the substantive law governing the action. Contracts are among the best examples of evidence received for this purpose. Because the law of contracts gives special legal significance to some utterances, it is sometimes crucial to show that such utterances were made. For example, to prove the existence of a contract, it is necessary to prove that an offer and an acceptance were made. Consequently, evidence that a party uttered or wrote words constituting an offer or an acceptance is admissible where the existence of a contract is disputed.[21] Or take an auction. Evidence that the defendant raised his hand in response to the plaintiff's question, "Who will give me $10.00 for this book?", is not hearsay. The evidence is not offered to prove that by raising his hand the defendant intended to say, "I will." Rather, the evidence is offered to prove that by his conduct (raising his hand) the defendant accepted the plaintiff's offer; under the legal rules pertaining to auctions, the raising of hands signals acceptance of the offer.

The use of evidence for this purpose is sometimes called the verbal acts doctrine.[22] The name is intended to convey the idea that certain utterances ("I accept") should be viewed as acts, such as the defendant's raising his hand at an auction. Thus, when the doctrine applies, evidence describing what someone said ("I accept your offer") is analytically the

---

16. Id. at 171, 9 Cal.Rptr. at 381–382.

17. See also Caro v. Smith, 59 Cal.App.4th 725, 733, 69 Cal.Rptr.2d 306, 311 (1997) (holding that evidence that the defendant told an arbitrator that she understood that the award would be binding did not violate the hearsay rule when offered only as proof that she had been warned about the binding effects of the arbitration proceeding).

18. 97 Wis.2d 521, 294 N.W.2d 501 (1980), aff'd, 99 Wis.2d 708, 301 N.W.2d 156 (1981).

19. Id. at 546–548, 294 N.W.2d at 514–515.

20. Id.

21. Bank of America Nat. Trust & Sav. Ass'n v. Taliaferro, 144 Cal.App.2d 578, 301 P.2d 393 (1956).

22. C. McCormick, McCormick on Evidence § 249 (J. Strong 4th ed. 1992).

same as evidence describing what someone did ("The defendant raised his hand").

Statements which constitute an element of any cause of action, whether civil or criminal, can be viewed as verbal acts.[23] In addition to statements evidencing contracts, examples include words constituting an offer or an acceptance of a bribe, creating a conspiracy,[24] encouraging persons to become prostitutes (pandering),[25] soliciting prostitution and other crimes,[26] threatening others with great bodily injury or death,[27] constituting a bet,[28] evincing consent in rape cases,[29] giving a warning as in *Combs*, and embracing defamatory matter.[30] In these cases, the statement is not offered to prove the truth of the matter asserted but only the fact that the statement was made.[31] Defamation actions make the point clear. Obviously, the plaintiff in such an action would not offer the defamatory statement for the truth, as that would defeat the plaintiff's action.[32] Rather, the statement ("The defendant said to me, 'You are a liar' ") is offered to prove only that it was made[33] or published.[34]

---

23. In a California wrongful employment termination action, an employer may offer evidence that the employee was terminated after "an investigation that was appropriate under the circumstance." Silva v. Lucky Stores, Inc., 65 Cal.App.4th 256, 264, 76 Cal.Rptr.2d 382, 387 (1998). Accordingly, an employer is entitled to offer evidence describing the investigation that was undertaken. An objection to the reports and other statements gathered in the course of the investigation is not objectionable on hearsay grounds so long as the evidence is not offered to prove the truth of the matters stated. Id. at 265, 76 Cal.Rptr.2d at 388.

24. People v. Collier, 111 Cal.App. 215, 295 P. 898 (1931). See also People v. Han, 78 Cal.App.4th 797, 93 Cal.Rptr.2d 139 (2000), where the reviewing court held that in a conspiracy prosecution, it is proper for the prosecution to offer the statement soliciting the commission of the offense as proof of the formation of the conspiratorial agreement. Receiving the statement for this purpose does not implicate the hearsay rule. But if the statement is offered also as proof of the declarant's intention to engage in conduct achieving the conspiratorial goal, then it may be offered under the state of mind exception of the hearsay rule. Id. at 802–804, 93 Cal.Rptr.2d at 143–144. For a discussion of this hearsay exception, see § 9.07 infra.

25. People v. Patton, 63 Cal.App.3d 211, 133 Cal.Rptr. 533 (1976).

26. C. McCormick, McCormick on Evidence § 247 (J. Strong 4th ed. 1992).

27. West's Ann. California Evidence Code § 422 makes it a crime to threaten another with great bodily injury or death with the specific intent that the threat be taken seriously even if there is no intent to carry out the threat. To obtain a conviction, the prosecution must also prove that the threat would have induced in a reasonable person in the victim's position a sustained fear for his or her own safety or immediate family's safety. See People v. Felix, 92 Cal.App.4th 905, 911, 112 Cal.Rptr.2d 311, 317 (2001).

28. People v. Reyes, 62 Cal.App.3d 53, 132 Cal.Rptr. 848 (1976).

29. People v. Burnham, 176 Cal.App.3d 1134, 1144, note 10, 222 Cal.Rptr. 630, 638, note 10 (1986).

30. See generally Russell v. Geis, 251 Cal.App.2d 560, 59 Cal.Rptr. 569 (1967).

31. The fact that some crimes have an element consisting of a statement should not be confused with the mens rea of the crime. Solicitation, for example, requires proof that the accused solicited the crime as well as proof that he did so with the purpose of promoting or facilitating the commission of the crime. See, e.g., Model Penal Code § 5.02 (1962). Evidence that the accused said, "I want you to rob the bank" does not violate the hearsay rule if offered only to prove that the accused made the statement. But if offered to prove the accused's desire to bring about the commission of the crime, the evidence must fall within a hearsay exception, most likely the one for party admissions or declarations of mental state.

32. Truth is a defense.

33. Russell v. Geis, 251 Cal.App.2d 560, 59 Cal.Rptr. 569 (1967).

34. Stoneking v. Briggs, 254 Cal.App.2d 563, 62 Cal.Rptr. 249 (1967).

To prove the nature of a place or business. In Los Robles Motor Lodge v. Department of Alcoholic Beverage Control[35] the plaintiff's liquor license was suspended because prostitution was permitted on the premises. To prove that prostitution was allowed, the department called several undercover officers who testified about solicitations directed at them to engage in sexual activities within the premises for a fee.[36] The court held that the evidence disclosing the solicitations did not violate the hearsay rule. The evidence was not offered to prove that for a price certain sexual favors would be performed but to prove that such offers were made at the lodge.[37]

Compare the evidence of solicitations in *Los Robles* with the following evidence:

Plaintiff: What did the undercover officer tell you?

Witness: That a woman walked up to him and said, "For $100 you can have me for one hour."

Whether offered to prove that a woman approached the undercover officer or the making of the solicitation, the evidence would be hearsay. In each instance, the plaintiff would be offering the out of court statement of the officer to prove the truth of the matter asserted. But if the officer were the witness, he could describe the woman's approach to him as well as what she said to him. The officer would have personal knowledge of the woman's approach as well as of what she said to him.

• In People v. Barnhart[38] the accused was prosecuted for keeping a gambling house. A police officer who was at the house answered the telephone several times.[39] To prove that the house was used for gambling purposes, the officer described conversations in which the callers attempted to place bets.[40] As in *Los Robles*, the court held that repeating the callers' conversations did not violate the hearsay rule.[41] The evidence was

---

35. 246 Cal.App.2d 198, 54 Cal.Rptr. 547 (1966).

36. Id. at 201, 54 Cal.Rptr. at 548.

37. Id. at 205, 54 Cal.Rptr. at 551. Accord: People v. Jones, 205 Cal.App.2d 460, 23 Cal.Rptr. 418 (1962) (holding that the use of statements constituting solicitations does not violate the hearsay rule where the statements are offered to prove the making of solicitations). Note that under the verbal acts doctrine described in the preceding paragraphs, evidence of an offer to engage in sexual activities for a fee would not violate the hearsay rule.

38. 66 Cal.App.2d 714, 153 P.2d 214 (1944).

39. Id. at 716–719, 153 P.2d at 215–217.

40. Id.

41. Id. at 721–722, 153 P.2d at 218. But see People v. Morgan, 125 Cal.App.4th 935, 23 Cal.Rptr.3d 224 (2005), a case affirming the defendants' convictions of possessing methamphetamine and possessing it for sale. While the police were conducting a search of one of the defendant's home, a police officer answered the telephone. The caller said he wanted to buy drugs. The court approved the use of the evidence, holding that "that under the provisions of California's Evidence Code the caller's oral expressions [were] hearsay, but that case law, recognized and accepted when the Evidence Code was adopted and continuing thereafter, has created an exception to the hearsay rule for this reliable type of evidence." Id. at 937, 23 Cal.Rptr.3d at 225. In concluding that the caller's call constituted hearsay (because the caller's statement was tantamount to offering his belief that methamphetamine could be obtained at the number called), the court adopted the "implied assertion" view of hearsay.

In California, however, the declarant's underlying belief is not considered hearsay unless the declarant intends his statement as a substitute for the underlying belief. In *Morgan* that would

not offered to prove the terms of a particular bet but to prove that bets were placed at the house.[42]

Compare the bets placed in *Barnhart* with the following evidence:

Prosecutor: What did the caller say?

Officer: She said, "The place you are at is a gambling establishment."

The evidence violates the hearsay rule. The caller's out of court statement is being offered to prove the truth of the caller's assertion, namely that the premises are used for gambling.

To prove the possession of relevant knowledge. Consider the following evidence:

Witness 1: The house had two bedrooms, one bath, and a kitchen, dining room and living room.

If offered to prove the layout of the house, the evidence is not hearsay as no out of court statement is being offered.

Witness 2: Witness 1 said to me, "The house had two bedrooms, one bath, and a kitchen, dining room and living room."

If offered to prove the layout of the house, the evidence is hearsay as Witness 1's out of court statement is being offered to prove the matters asserted in the statement, namely the layout of the house. But if the evidence is being offered to prove that Witness 1 has knowledge of the layout of the house, then some authorities would admit the evidence as nonhearsay.[43] Of course, the value of the evidence would depend on its coinciding with the actual layout of the house, which must be proved from a nonhearsay source. Moreover, the better view is that such evidence should be excluded unless the proponent convinces the trial judge that the declarant acquired his knowledge first hand and not from information supplied by others.[44]

A similar issue can arise in child molestation prosecutions. To rebut the inference that the victim must have learned of the sexual acts through the accused, the accused is entitled to show that the victim may have learned about the acts from some other source. For example, evidence that the victim accused others of committing similar acts with the victim may be offered for this purpose without violating the hearsay rule. The evidence is not offered to prove the truth of the matters asserted—that

---

have required proof that the caller intended his statement evincing a desire to buy drugs as a substitute for the direct assertion, "The place I am calling is a place where drugs can be purchased." The reviewing court, however, did not engage in this kind of analysis. For a discussion of the "implied assertion" doctrine, see infra § 5.05.

42. As in *Los Robles*, 246 Cal.App.2d 198, 54 Cal.Rptr. 547 (1966), repeating a caller's conversation to prove the terms of the caller's bet would not violate the hearsay rule if offered to prove the terms of the caller's betting offer. The use of the conversation in this fashion would fall within the verbal acts doctrine.

43. See United States v. Muscato, 534 F.Supp. 969 (E.D.N.Y.1982) and authorities cited therein.

44. Id.

others also molested the victim—but the victim's knowledge of sexual acts similar to those allegedly committed by the accused.[45]

Witness 2: Witness 1 said to me, "I know the layout of the house."

Even authorities who believe that Witness 2's previous statement is not hearsay will agree that the second is hearsay if offered to prove Witness 1's knowledge. Witness 1's out of court statement is being offered to prove the matters stated, namely that Witness 1 knows the layout of the house.

An interesting variation of the nonhearsay use of out of court statements to prove knowledge occurred in People v. Roberson.[46] Roberson was prosecuted for selling heroin to an undercover agent.[47] He denied making the sale. To prove that he would not have made the sale, he called a witness to testify that before the alleged sale, the witness told him that the alleged buyer was an undercover agent.[48] The reviewing court held that the prosecution's hearsay objection should have been overruled.[49] The witness's statement was not offered to prove that the alleged buyer was in fact an undercover agent. Rather, it was offered to prove that the accused would not have sold heroin to someone he had reason to believe was an undercover agent.

The witness's statement in *Roberson* also could have been offered for another nonhearsay purpose, namely, to show its effect on the accused. This theory is often invoked to justify the admission of out of court statements for a nonhearsay purpose. In People v. Bolin[50] the accused was prosecuted for first degree murder. To show that the accused engaged in the premeditation required for first degree murder, the prosecution offered statements the victim made urging the accused to spare his life. As the reviewing court noted, the victim's statements were not offered to prove as true any assertions they may have contained; they were offered to prove the accused's callousness in killing the victim after having heard his pleas for mercy.[51]

To impeach a witness by disproving assertions testified to by the witness. In Tennessee v. Street[52] the accused testified that his confession had been coerced by an officer who compelled him to say the same things as an accomplice who had confessed earlier. To disprove the accused's claim, the officer was permitted to read the accomplice's confession to the jury and to point out differences between that confession and the accused's.[53] Reading the accomplice's confession did not constitute

---

45. For limitations on the use of such evidence to impeach the credibility of victims of sexual offenses, see § 15.12 infra.

46. 167 Cal.App.2d 429, 334 P.2d 666 (1959).

47. Id. at 431, 334 P.2d at 667.

48. Id.

49. Id.

50. 18 Cal.4th 297, 75 Cal.Rptr.2d 412, 956 P.2d 374 (1998).

51. Id. at 320, 75 Cal.Rptr.2d at 429, 956 P.2d at 391.

52. 471 U.S. 409, 105 S.Ct. 2078, 85 L.Ed.2d 425 (1985).

53. Id. at 410–411, 105 S.Ct. at 2080–2081.

hearsay because the confession was not offered to prove as true what the accomplice had said, but to discredit the accused's claim by showing the differences between that confession and the accused's.[54]

A declarant who testifies can be impeached with his own out of court statement without violating the hearsay rule. In People v. Thomas[55] the accused testified that at the time the crime was committed he was visiting friends in another part of town. To impeach the accused, a police officer was permitted to testify that the accused had told him that he had been attending night school at that time.[56] The prosecution did not offer the accused's statement to the police officer for the truth of the matter stated; the statement would have provided the accused with an additional alibi. Rather, the prosecution offered the statement for impeachment purposes only. The theory, an old one, is that people who tell different stories about the same event are unworthy of belief.[57]

When the out of court declarant is a party, it is not essential that the party testify as a witness in order for the out of court declaration to be admitted. In People v. Mendoza[58] the accused told arresting officers that he could not have committed the crime of false imprisonment because at the time the crime was committed he had been washing a truck. At the trial, the prosecution was permitted to offer the accused's statement, as well as evidence that the truck was dusty.[59] Use of the accused's statement did not offend the hearsay rule because the statement was not offered to prove that he had been washing the truck at the time of the crime. Combined with the evidence of the dusty condition of the truck, it was offered, instead, to prove that the accused had made a false statement

---

54. In People v. Millwee, 18 Cal.4th 96, 74 Cal.Rptr.2d 418, 954 P.2d 990 (1998), the accused, who was prosecuted for murder, testified that he killed his mother accidentally when a rifle he was holding suddenly discharged. To impeach the accused, the prosecution was allowed to introduce a transcript from an unrelated prosecution in which the accused testified that he shot a man accidentally when the same rifle discharged unexpectedly. The reviewing court sustained the use of the evidence. It was not offered to prove as true the accused's claims at the second trial but to show the implausibility of the accused's claims. Id. at 131, 74 Cal.Rptr.2d at 439, 954 P.2d at 1010. The evidence showed that the second shooting occurred within two days of the mother's death.

Implicit in the court's holding is the doctrine of chances—the improbability of non-recurrent similar events recurring by chance. For a discussion of this doctrine, see § 3.15 supra.

55. 96 Cal.App.3d 507, 158 Cal.Rptr. 120 (1979).

56. Id. at 510–511, 158 Cal.Rptr. at 122.

57. At Common Law, prior inconsistent statements were admissible only to discredit the witness. West's Ann.California Evidence Code § 1235 (comment). Under the Code, such statements are now admissible also for the truth of the matter stated. West's Ann.California Evidence Code § 1235. But the fact that a hearsay exception has been created does not compel the proponent to offer such statements for the truth of the matter stated.

Under the Federal Rules of Evidence, Thomas' statement would be admissible only to impeach his testimony on direct. His statement could be received for the truth only if he had made it under "oath". Federal Rule of Evidence 801(d)(1)(A). For an extended discussion of prior inconsistent statements as an exception to the hearsay rule in California and federal courts, see §§ 802–804 infra.

58. 192 Cal.App.3d 667, 238 Cal.Rptr. 1 (1987).

59. Id. at 671, 238 Cal.Rptr. at 3.

regarding a material element of the offense—his whereabouts at the time the crime was committed.[60]

To prove the declarant's state of mind. Often, what a person thinks is a material issue. In criminal cases, for example, what an accused thought at a given time may help prove or disprove the mens rea of the offense charged. The intoxicated driver who is aware of the extreme danger he poses to others may be guilty of murder if he kills a pedestrian but only of negligent homicide if he is unaware of the danger. In civil cases, the issue may arise in a variety of circumstances, ranging from a testator's competency to form a will in inheritance disputes to a conservatee's ability to take care of herself and not endanger herself or others in conservatorship proceedings.

Typically, what a person was thinking on a given occasion is proved in one of two ways. It can be proved directly by that person's statements regarding her state of mind or indirectly by things that person says or does that reflect her state of mind. For example, an issue in conservatorship proceedings is whether by reason of a mental disorder a respondent is a danger to herself or to others. A respondent's statements that she is "mentally disordered" would be direct evidence of the mental state essential to establishing a conservatorship. Since such statements would be offered to prove the truth of the matter stated, they would constitute hearsay.[61] If, on the other hand, the respondent had said, "I am the Pope," then under one view that statement would not be hearsay. It is not being offered to prove that the respondent is the Pope but as circumstantial or indirect evidence of her disability. If she truly thinks that she is the Pope, then she must be mentally disabled.

Under a different view, however, even the latter statement is hearsay.[62] The declarant who sincerely but erroneously maintains that she is the Pope obviously believes that she is the Pope. Thus, her statement is the equivalent of saying, "I believe that I am the Pope." If her out of court statement regarding her belief is then offered to prove the existence of her belief, the hearsay rule is violated.

---

60. Id. at 672–673, 238 Cal.Rptr. at 4. Accord: People v. Cain, 10 Cal.4th 1, 31–32, 40 Cal.Rptr.2d 481, 499, 892 P.2d 1224, 1242 (1995) (holding that the accused's statement to a television reporter denying any knowledge of the murders of his neighbors was admissible as a false statement that was inconsistent with his police interview statement admitting that he had been present during the crimes but that others had committed the killings); People v. Hughes, 27 Cal.4th 287, 335, 116 Cal.Rptr.2d 401, 437, 39 P.3d 432, 462–463 (2002) (holding that the defendant's false statement that he did not know the murder victim and had never been in her apartment was admissible to demonstrate his consciousness of guilt, where other evidence showed the defendant's fingerprints inside the victim's apartment.). See also People v. Kimble, 44 Cal.3d 480, 498, 244 Cal.Rptr. 148, 159, 749 P.2d 803, 813 (1988), cert. denied, 488 U.S. 871, 109 S.Ct. 188, 102 L.Ed.2d 157 (1988) (overruling cases limiting the use of a party's statements for the nonhearsay purpose of discrediting the party's claims only if the party testifies).

Although most cases involving false statements are prosecutions, the nonhearsay impeachment theory applies in civil cases as well. See, e.g., Donchin v. Guerrero, 34 Cal.App.4th 1832, 1840, 41 Cal.Rptr.2d 192, 197 (1995).

61. These statements would nonetheless be admissible as party admissions, an exception to the hearsay rule, see § 7.01 infra, or as declarations of then existing state of mind, also an exception to the hearsay rule. See § 8.06 infra.

62. E. Morgan, Basic Problems of Evidence 248–250 (1961).

The California Supreme Court appears to have opted for the nonhearsay theory of declarations offered as circumstantial proof of a declarant's state of mind. In People v. Green[63] the accused was charged with kidnapping, among other crimes. To prove that the victim accompanied the accused against her will, the prosecution called a friend of the victim who testified that on the morning of the kidnapping the victim told her that the accused had threatened to kill the victim if she left him.[64] To the court, the evidence did not violate the hearsay rule. It was not offered to prove that the accused had threatened to kill the victim. Rather, it was used to prove that the victim accompanied the accused against her will because she would not have voluntarily accompanied someone she believed (rightly or wrongly) might kill her.[65] Similarly, in Rufo v. Simpson[66] Nicole Simpson's telephone call to a battered women's shelter was not admitted to prove that O. J. Simpson had threatened to kill Nicole if he caught her with another man. Rather, Nicole's call was received as circumstantial proof of her negative feelings toward O. J., feelings that would help explain why she ended her relationship with him. The plaintiffs' theory was that the sense of rejection and rage unleashed by the rupture provoked O. J. into killing his ex-spouse.[67]

Green is in accord with the view taken by the framers of the Evidence Code. According to the Assembly Committee,

> Statements of a decedent narrating threats or brutal conduct by some other person may * * * be used as circumstantial evidence of the decedent's fear—his state of mind—when that fear is itself in issue or when it is relevant to prove or explain the decedent's subsequent conduct; and for that purpose, the evidence is not subject to a hearsay objection because it is not offered to prove the truth of the matter stated. * * *[68]

Fortunately, whether the use of statements such as the one in *Green* violates the hearsay rule is often insignificant. In *Green*, for example, even if the victim's statement is viewed as hearsay (a direct statement of her fear), it would nonetheless be admissible to prove her fear under the exception for state of mind declarations.[69]

---

63. 27 Cal.3d 1, 164 Cal.Rptr. 1, 609 P.2d 468 (1980).

64. Id. at 23, 164 Cal.Rptr. at 13, 609 P.2d at 480.

65. Id. at 23, note 9, 164 Cal.Rptr. at 13, note 9, 609 P.2d at 480, note 9. See also In re Dorinda A., 10 Cal.App.4th 1657, 1662, 13 Cal.Rptr.2d 653, 656 (1992) (holding that statements by a minor that her father molested her were admissible as nonhearsay evidence to prove the child's dislike and fear of her father in a juvenile court proceeding in which the father's fitness to retain custody of the child was an issue).

66. 86 Cal.App.4th 573, 103 Cal.Rptr.2d 492 (2001).

67. Id. at 591–595, 103 Cal.Rptr.2d at 504–506. *Rufo* was a wrongful death action brought by the parents of Ronald Goldman and a survival action brought by the personal representatives of Ronald Goldman and Nicole Brown Simpson against O. J. Simpson following O. J.'s acquittal of murdering Ronald and Nicole. The jury found for the plaintiffs.

68. West's Ann.California Evidence Code § 1250 (comment).

69. See § 8.07 infra.

In determining whether an out of court statement should be received over a hearsay objection for a nonhearsay purpose, the trial judge should keep two factors in mind. First, the judge should require the proponent to specify how receiving the statement for a nonhearsay purpose would be relevant to the issues to be determined. Since in many instances the only relevant purpose is the hearsay purpose, the judge should exclude the statement on relevance grounds in those cases. Second, even if the nonhearsay purpose identified by the proponent is relevant, the judge should consider whether the statement should nonetheless be excluded under § 352 or Federal Rule of Evidence 403.[70] In making this determination, the judge must assess whether the jurors can abide by an instruction limiting their consideration of the statement to its nonhearsay purpose.

§ 5.05 ASSERTIVE v. NONASSERTIVE CONDUCT

Suppose that in a case an issue is whether a ship lost at sea was seaworthy. Is evidence that the captain inspected his ship and then placed his family on it hearsay if offered to prove that the ship was seaworthy? Under the California Evidence Code and the Federal Rules the answer is no, unless the captain intended his acts of inspecting the ship and placing his family on it to substitute for the statement, "The ship is seaworthy."[1]

The fact that an inference can be drawn from the ship captain's conduct that he believed the ship to be seaworthy does not make his conduct hearsay. Both the Code and the Rules reject the "implied assertion" view of hearsay.[2] Unless the captain intended his conduct as a substitute for an oral or written assertion about the ship's seaworthiness, his conduct is not hearsay.

Why should nonassertive conduct be exempted from the definition of hearsay? Had the sea captain said, "The ship is seaworthy," the opposing party would have wanted an opportunity to cross examine the captain under oath and in the presence of the fact finder about the basis of his opinion. But where the value of the evidence depends not on what a person says but on what he does, then in the words of the framers of the Evidence Code, "[A]ctions speak louder than words."[3] The captain's acts are an apt illustration, since one can assume that the captain was unlikely to place his family on a ship he considered to be unseaworthy. As the Advisory Committee Note to the Federal Rule explains, "No class of evidence is free of the possibility of fabrication, but the likelihood is less with nonverbal conduct than assertive conduct. The situations giving rise

---

70. For an extended discussion of a judge's discretionary power to exclude relevant evidence, see § 2.10 supra.

1. West's Ann.California Evidence Code §§ 225 and 1200; Federal Rule of Evidence 801(a).

2. 6 California Law Revision Commission, Reports, Recommendations and Studies, Appendix 416–420 (1964); Federal Rule of Evidence 801(a) (Advisory Committee Note).

3. West's Ann.California Evidence Code § 1200 (comment).

to the nonverbal conduct are such as virtually to eliminate questions of sincerity."[4]

The ship captain's case should be contrasted with that of the witness who points out the accused as the guilty party. Evidence by a police officer that a witness at the scene pointed to the accused in response to the question, "Who killed the victim?", is clearly hearsay. By pointing to the accused, the witness intends his conduct to substitute for the statement, "He did."[5]

Inferring the intentions of the ship captain and the crime witness is relatively easy. Harder to fathom is the motivation of the accused who is seen fleeing from the crime scene. By taking flight, does the accused simply intend to get away or does he intend also to state that he is the guilty party? Since under the Code the question presented is whether the accused's conduct is hearsay, the proponent would have the burden of persuading the trial judge that the accused did not intend to state his guilt.[6] The Rules take a different approach. Because the Rules favor admissibility, the burden is on the party objecting on hearsay grounds to show that the "declarant" intended his conduct as an assertion of guilt.[7]

Who bears the burden of proving the declarant's intention is sometimes unimportant. For example, if the trial judge agrees that taking flight is hearsay because assertive, the evidence of the accused's flight would nonetheless be admissible under the hearsay exception for party admissions.[8] A more difficult situation is posed when the conduct, if hearsay, does not fall within an exception. People v. Clark[9] is illustrative. In this case, witnesses described a murder suspect as wearing a jacket with a fur collar. An officer testified that, when he arrested the accused, he asked him whether he owned such a jacket.[10] The accused objected on hearsay grounds to evidence that his wife fainted when in response to the officer's question, the accused asked his wife, "I don't have one like that, do I dear?"[11] The court upheld the overruling of the objection; by fainting, the wife did not intend to say, "Yes, you do."[12]

---

4. Federal Rule of Evidence 801(a) (Advisory Committee Note).

5. See, e.g., People v. Mayfield, 23 Cal.App.3d 236, 100 Cal.Rptr. 104 (1972). Under the Federal Rules, however, assertive conduct is not hearsay (and, therefore, can be received for the truth) if it is the equivalent of a prior statement and certain conditions on the admissibility of prior statements are met. See § 5.03 supra.

6. West's Ann.California Evidence Code § 405 and comment. The preliminary fact to be decided by the judge is whether the accused intended his flight as a substitute for the statement, "I am the guilty one." Because hearsay generally is deemed too unreliable for consideration by the jury, the judge should withhold the statement from the jury unless persuaded by the proponent that the statement is not hearsay.

7. Federal Rule of Evidence 801(a) (Advisory Committee Note).

8. See § 7.01 infra.

9. 6 Cal.App.3d 658, 86 Cal.Rptr. 106 (1970).

10. Id. at 662, 86 Cal.Rptr. at 108.

11. Id. at 668, 86 Cal.Rptr. at 112.

12. Id.

A similar problem is presented when evidence of how a child manipulates an anatomically correct doll is offered in child abuse cases. If a child manipulates a doll in response to questions designed to demonstrate sexual abuse ("Show me how he touched you"), the manipulation is assertive and therefore hearsay. But if the evidence consists of how a child manipulates the doll in the absence of questions or directions, then the manipulation is nonassertive. Such evidence should be admissible over a hearsay objection for the light it casts on the case.[13]

Earlier, we saw that the absence of complaints may be offered to prove the nonexistence of a dangerous condition or the defendant's reasons for not anticipating a condition that harmed the plaintiff.[14] In Beauchamp v. Los Gatos Golf Course,[15] for example, evidence that no patrons complained to a club operator about the condition of a veranda was admitted to show that the condition of the veranda was safe on the day the plaintiff fell. Evidence that others have complained about a condition is hearsay if offered to prove the existence of the condition. For this reason, some have argued that evidence that others have not complained about a condition is likewise hearsay if offered to prove the nonexistence of the condition.[16] In the case of complaints about a condition, the opposing party would be vitally interested in cross examining, not the person transmitting the reports in court, but the persons who made the complaints. Similarly, with regard to the absence of complaints the opposing party would want to cross examine those who failed to complain and not the person claiming that no one has complained. Under the approach taken by the Code and Rules, however, failing to complain is probably not assertive conduct. Most likely, people fail to complain because they have nothing to complain about, and not because they intend their silence to substitute for a statement approving the conditions the plaintiff claims caused the harm.

In an unusual case, the prosecution used the accused's silence as evidence of his guilt. In People v. Snow[17] the accused was prosecuted for murdering the only witness who could identify him as the perpetrator of a robbery. To prove that the accused was the murderer, the prosecutor offered evidence that, when the accused first heard of the death of the witness, he remained silent and did not otherwise evince any reaction to the news.[18] Whether the accused's conduct offers much help in identifying the murderer may be debatable. But that his conduct was nonassertive is not. Clearly, he did not intend his response (or nonresponse) to substitute for an admission that he was the guilty party. Accordingly, receiving the

---

13. In re Cheryl H., 153 Cal.App.3d 1098, 200 Cal.Rptr. 789 (1984); accord: People v. Roberto V., 93 Cal.App.4th 1350, 1365, note 9, 113 Cal.Rptr.2d 804, 815, note 9 (2001). Such evidence may be offered to prove the child's knowledge of sexual matters, for example. See § 5.04 supra.

14. See §§ 3.21–3.22 supra.

15. 273 Cal.App.2d 20, 77 Cal.Rptr. 914 (1969). See § 3.20 supra.

16. Menard v. Cashman, 94 N.H. 428, 55 A.2d 156 (1947).

17. 44 Cal.3d 216, 242 Cal.Rptr. 477, 746 P.2d 452 (1987).

18. Id. at 227, 746 P.2d at 458, 242 Cal.Rptr. at 483.

evidence of his response to the death of the witness did not violate the hearsay rule.[19]

Statements and the implied assertion doctrine. Both the California Evidence Code and the Federal Rules also reject the doctrine of implied assertions when an out of court statement is offered, not for the truth of the matter stated, but as circumstantial evidence of the declarant's belief underlying the statement. In Wright v. Doe D. Tatham[20] an heir at law sought to set aside the testator's will on the ground that the testator was mentally incompetent at the time he made the will. At the trial, the beneficiary attempted to prove the testator's competency by offering several letters written to the testator. In one of the letters, the writer described a voyage to Virginia and the conditions he encountered there.[21]

Under the Code and the Federal Rules, receiving the letters would not violate the hearsay rule. The letters were not offered to prove the truth of the matters stated (for example, the conditions the writer encountered in Virginia), but as circumstantial evidence of the writers' belief in the testator's competency: none of the writers would have bothered to communicate with the testator unless they believed that he was sufficiently possessed of his faculties to understand the subject matter of their letters.

Critics of the Federal Rules and the Code emphasize that the writer's belief is equivalent to the writer's direct assertion that the testator was competent. Offering such an assertion to prove the testator's competence is hearsay under the Rules and Code as well as under the Common Law. In the absence of hearsay exceptions, the direct assertion would have to be excluded because receiving it through a witness other than the declarant would deny the opposing party an opportunity to test its reliability by crossing the declarant. Since the value of the assertion would depend on the declarant's powers to perceive, recall, and narrate accurately, critics and supporters of the Rules and the Code would favor giving the opposing party an opportunity to probe for flaws in these powers by subjecting the declarant to cross-examination under oath in the presence of the fact finder.

Partisans of the implied assertion doctrine maintain that the same concerns apply whenever an out of court declarant's statements are offered as circumstantial evidence of the declarant's beliefs. In their view,

---

19.   Id. at 227–228, 746 P.2d at 458, 242 Cal.Rptr. at 483.

20.   7 Ad. & El. 313 (Exchequer Chamber 1837).

21.   Id. at 317–321, Similarly, in People v. Price, 1 Cal.4th 324, 437, 3 Cal.Rptr.2d 106, 171, 821 P.2d 610, 675 (1991), the court over a hearsay objection upheld the admission of a letter between two prison inmates; the letter was not offered as proof of the various assertions contained in the letter but as evidence of a relationship (a writing one, in this case) between the inmates. See also People v. Fields, 61 Cal.App.4th 1063, 1069, 72 Cal.Rptr.2d 255, 259 (1998), a case in which the accused objected on hearsay grounds to evidence that his pager contained a number which other evidence showed was assigned to a telephone used by a buyer to place a drug order. The reviewing court upheld the use of the evidence, holding that it was admissible to show a relationship between the accused and the buyer as well as the accused's use of the pager to facilitate drug sales.

the value of the belief depends, as in the case of direct assertions of belief, on the declarant's powers of perception, recollection, and narration. Accordingly, they would sustain a hearsay objection to the introduction of the letter, even though it was not offered to prove the truth of the matters asserted but only as circumstantial evidence of the writer's belief in the competency of the testator.

On the other hand, the supporters of the position taken by the Code and the Rules believe that there is a crucial difference in the reliability of the letter writer's direct assertion that the testator is competent and the writer's belief or assumption that the testator is sufficiently competent to understand a letter describing Virginia:

> A man does not lie to himself. Put otherwise, if in doing what he does a man has no intention of asserting the existence or non-existence of a fact, it would appear that the trustworthiness of evidence of his conduct is the same whether he is an egregious liar or a paragon of veracity. Accordingly, the lack of opportunity for cross-examination in relation to his veracity or lack of it, would seem to be of no substantial importance. Accordingly, the usual judicial disposition to equate the "implied" to the "express" assertion is very questionable.[22]

The Code and the Rules assume that the hearsay rule is "assertion" centered.[23] If the proffered statement is not offered to prove the various propositions expressly contained in the statement, then a hearsay objection should be overruled, since the statement is obviously not being offered for the truth of the matters asserted.

Advocates of the implied assertion doctrine, on the other hand, view the hearsay rule as "declarant" centered. The question for them is whether the value of the evidence depends on the declarant's perceptual, recall, and narrative powers, including the declarant's sincerity. Since they believe that the value of implied assertions depends on some of these powers, they insist on producing the hearsay declarant for cross-examination.[24]

---

22. Falknor, *The "Hear–Say" Rule as a "See–Do" Rule: Evidence of Conduct*, 33 Rocky Mt. L. Rev. 133, 136 (1961).

23. Park, *Two Definitions of Hearsay*, J. Kaplan, J. Waltz & R. Park, Evidence 90 (7th ed. 1991).

24. In the alternative, advocates of the implied assertion doctrine will permit the statement to be received for the "truth" under an exception to the hearsay rule. In People v. Morgan, 125 Cal.App.4th 935, 937, 23 Cal.Rptr.3d 224 (2005), the defendants were convicted of possessing methamphetamine and possessing it for sale. While the police were conducting a search of one of the defendant's home, a police officer answered the telephone. The caller said he wanted to buy drugs. The court approved the use of the evidence, holding that "that under the provisions of California's Evidence Code the caller's oral expressions [were] hearsay, but that case law, recognized and accepted when the Evidence Code was adopted and continuing thereafter, has created an exception to the hearsay rule for this reliable type of evidence." Id. at 937, 23 Cal.Rptr.3d at 225. In concluding that the caller's call constituted hearsay (because the caller's statement was tantamount to offering his belief that methamphetamine could be obtained at the number called), the court adopted the "implied assertion" view of hearsay. In California, however, the declarant's underlying belief is not considered hearsay unless the declarant intends his statement as substitute for the underlying belief. In *Morgan* that would have required proof that the caller intended his statement evincing a desire to buy drugs as a substitute for the direct

Although the position taken by the Code and the Rules has come to dominate the debate, some out of court declarations can still prove troublesome. An example is provided in United States v. Zenni.[25] Suppose that a security guard at an airport, after running a metal detector over a passenger, says, "Go on through." Over a hearsay objection, may the declaration be received in a California or federal court to prove that the passenger was not armed at the time? The guard's statement, obviously is not offered for the truth of the matter stated, as it is bereft of direct assertions. Moreover, his belief that the passenger is not armed cannot be barred under the implied assertion doctrine, since the Code and the Rules reject the doctrine. But a California or federal judge can nonetheless sustain the hearsay objection if the judge concludes that the guard intended his statement as a substitute for the assertion, "You are not armed."

Whether the judge sustains the hearsay objection depends on who has the burden of proving that the guard intended his statement as a substitute for the assertion. Under the Code, the proponent would have the burden of persuading the judge that the guard did *not* intend his statement to substitute for the assertion.[26] Because the Rules favor admissibility, the objecting party would have the burden of persuading the judge that the guard *intended* his statement as a substitute for the assertion.[27] Who bears the burden is crucial, since the guard's intentions are not likely to be known by anyone other than the guard. Presumably, the proponent is offering the guard's statement because the guard is not available to testify.

The fact that part of a course of conduct may be assertive does not make the conduct hearsay if the assertive part is not offered for the truth. The letters offered in *Wright* are a good example. The fact that in their letters the writers made assertions did not bring the letters within the hearsay rule. The letter describing Virginia, though assertive in that respect, was not offered to prove that Virginia was as the writer described. What mattered was that the writers wrote the testator letters. In this respect, the writers' conduct was nonassertive and, hence, not hearsay.

§ 5.06 MACHINE AND OTHER NONHUMAN EVIDENCE

In the preceding section we saw that the hearsay rule is implicated by evidence that a witness at the crime scene pointed to the accused in

---

assertion, "The place I am calling is a drug establishment." The reviewing court, however, did not engage in this kind of analysis.

25. 492 F.Supp. 464, 468, note 19 (E.D.Ky.1980).

26. West's Ann.California Evidence Code § 405 and comment. The preliminary fact to be decided by the judge is whether the guard intended his statement as a substitute for the statement, "You are not armed." Because hearsay generally is deemed too unreliable for consideration by the jury, under § 405 the judge should withhold the statement from the jury unless persuaded by the proponent that the statement is not hearsay.

27. Federal Rule of Evidence 801(a) and Advisory Committee Note.

response to the question, "Who killed the victim?". By pointing to the accused, the witness intends his act to substitute for the statement, "He did." Is the hearsay rule likewise implicated if, instead of a human, a bloodhound "picks" the accused by jumping on him? As a statutory matter, the answer is "no" under the Evidence Code as well as under the Federal Rules. Both define a declarant as "a person who makes a statement",[1] and persons do not include animals.[2]

Substantive considerations should lead to the same result. Hearsay is suspect because its use deprives the opposing party from cross examining the person who possesses the knowledge that matters. To test the reliability of that knowledge, the cross examiner needs to probe for flaws in that person's ability to perceive, remember, and relate events accurately. A dog cannot be cross-examined, but his reliability can be tested by examining the dog's trainers and handlers about the dog's training and past reliability.[3]

Machine evidence presents a similar issue. It is one matter for an officer to testify that another officer told him that the accused was speeding. That would call for hearsay. But it is quite another for the officer to testify that the accused was speeding because the radar gun indicated that the accused was doing 40 in a 30 mile per hour zone.[4] In the first instance, the accused would want to cross examine the officer who claims to have seen the accused speeding; the officer, after all, could be mistaken. In the second, the accused is concerned with probing the reliability of the instrument used to measure her speed. She can do that by challenging the witnesses who claim that the instrument is designed to measure speed accurately, that the instrument was properly calibrated on the day used against the accused, and that the officer using the instru-

---

1. West's Ann.California Evidence Code § 135; Federal Rule of Evidence 801(b).

2. West's Ann.California Evidence Code § 175.

3. See, e.g., People v. Malgren, 139 Cal.App.3d 234, 237–238, 188 Cal.Rptr. 569, 571 (1983). "We conclude that the following must be shown before dog trailing evidence is admissible: (1) the dog's handler was qualified by training and experience to use the dog; (2) the dog was adequately trained in tracking humans; (3) the dog has been found to be reliable in tracking humans; (4) the dog was placed on the track where circumstances indicated the guilty party to have been; and (5) the trail had not become stale or contaminated." Id.

A distinction, however, is drawn between using a dog to track a suspect and using a dog to trace a scent from an object a person of interest may have touched. In California, the foundation for admitting scent evidence is more stringent. The proponent must lay a foundation "from academic or scientific sources regarding (a) how long scent remains on an object or at a location; (b) whether every person has a scent that is so unique that it provides an accurate basis for scent identification, such that it can be analogized to human DNA; (c) whether a particular breed of dog is characterized by acute powers of scent and discrimination; and (d) the adequacy of the certification procedures for scent identifications." People v. Willis, 115 Cal.App.4th 379, 385–386, 9 Cal.Rptr.3d 235, 240–241 (2004). In addition, the proponent must demonstrate that the relevant scientific community has generally accepted as reliable the means for capturing and preserving scents. Id. For an extended discussion of this point, see § 16.04 infra.

4. See, e.g., City of Webster Groves v. Quick, 323 S.W.2d 386 (Mo.App.1959) (rejecting defense claim that the use of machine evidence violated the hearsay rule). Accord: People v. Hawkins, 98 Cal.App.4th 1428, 1448–1451, 121 Cal.Rptr.2d 627, 642–643 (2002), cert. denied, 537 U.S. 1189, 123 S.Ct. 1256, 154 L.Ed.2d 1021 (2003) (rejecting claim that receiving a computer printout indicating the times the computer had been accessed was hearsay).

ment followed the operating instructions.[5] Moreover, the accused would be entitled in her own case to offer evidence challenging the accuracy of the instrument as well as the operating procedures.

Of course, the fact that information stored in a computer is retrieved through a printout does not convert the information into "machine evidence" for purposes of the hearsay rule. A police officer, for example, may use a computer to store his observation that the defendant was speeding. If the printout is offered to prove that the defendant was speeding, it is still subject to a hearsay objection even though two "machines" (the computer and a printer) provided the printout. There is a difference between offering information generated by a "machine" (a radar gun, for example) and information merely stored in a "machine" (the speed information the officer entered into his computer).[6]

§ 5.07   THE HEARSAY RULE AND THE PERSONAL KNOWLEDGE REQUIREMENT

The testimony of a witness is inadmissible unless the witness has personal knowledge of the subject matter of the testimony.[1] " 'Personal knowledge' means a present recollection of an impression derived from the exercise of the witness's own senses."[2]

Because a witness must have first hand knowledge of the subject matter, the personal knowledge requirement is sometimes confused with the hearsay rule. Examples can help illustrate the similarities and differences between the two rules.

If my goal is to prove that a defendant accused of running a red light had the red light, then under the personal knowledge requirement I must do so through witnesses who saw the color of the light facing the defendant. I could also do so inferentially through witnesses who saw the light facing the plaintiff. If these witnesses testify that the light facing the

---

5. Generally, the proponent must convince the judge of the reliability of scientific evidence by a preponderance of the evidence. People v. Sangani, 22 Cal.App.4th 1120, 1137, 28 Cal.Rptr.2d 158, 167 (1994). For an extended discussion of the limitations on expert witnesses and scientific evidence, see § 16.04 infra. Of course, the hearsay rule applies to out of court statements vouching for the reliability of the instrument involved. For example, over a hearsay objection, the proponent may not offer a letter from a stopwatch's manufacturer asserting that the stopwatch in question is accurate, unless the assertion falls within an exception. See People v. Zunis, 134 Cal.App.4th Supp. 1, 5, 36 Cal.Rptr.3d 489, 492 (2005).

6. See People v. Hawkins, 98 Cal.App.4th 1428, 1449, 121 Cal.Rptr.2d 627, 642 (2002), cert. denied, 537 U.S. 1189, 123 S.Ct. 1256, 154 L.Ed.2d 1021 (2003) ("A computer can be used to store documents and information entered by human operators. A computer can also be programmed to generate information on its own, such as a record of its internal operations. Some jurisdictions have recognized that the latter type of computer-generated information is not hearsay because it is not a statement by a person.").

1. West's Ann.California Evidence Code § 702. Federal Rule of Evidence 602. An exception, however, is made for experts who may base opinions on matters made known to them at or before the hearing. West's Ann.California Evidence Code § 801; Federal Rule of Evidence 703.

2. West's Ann.California Evidence Code § 702 (comment).

plaintiff was green, then I can argue to the jury that they ought to conclude that the light facing the defendant was red.

Assume that the plaintiff calls a witness who testifies that shortly before the collision he was parked next to the defendant and the light facing the witness was red. On cross-examination the witness concedes that his testimony on direct was based on what his spouse told him about the color of the light facing the witness. Should the defendant object on grounds of hearsay or lack of personal knowledge? Some authorities would say lack of personal knowledge.[3] The witness was asked about the color of the light, not about what someone told him about the color of the light. Since he did not see the color of the light, the witness has no first hand knowledge of the light's color, and his testimony on direct should be stricken.[4] But if the witness had been asked about what his wife told him about the color of the light, then the appropriate objection would be hearsay. A lack of personal knowledge objection would be inappropriate because the witness has first hand knowledge, not about the color of the light, but about what his wife said about the color of the light.

A similar analysis can be made when a hearsay objection applies. Assume that the wife saw the defendant run the light. As she saw him running the light, she exclaimed, "Look, the green car is running the light!" If her statement is received to prove that the green car ran the light, its use violates the hearsay rule. It is an out of court statement used to prove the truth of the matters stated. Under the exception for excited utterances, however, it would be admissible to prove that the green car ran the light.[5] If the wife's excited utterance were offered through her husband, would its receipt violate the personal knowledge requirement? The answer is "no." Anyone who heard what she said about the color of the light has first hand knowledge of what she said and can repeat the utterance in court. Moreover, since the utterance falls within a hearsay exception, it can be received for the truth of the matter stated even if the utterance is offered through the husband.

Assume that several hours after the accident the wife tells her cousin, "As I saw the green car go through the light, I said, 'Look, the green car is running the light!'" If the cousin is now called to prove the wife's excited utterance, the appropriate objection is lack of personal knowledge. The cousin was not present at the time the wife made the statement while watching the car run the light. The cousin has first hand knowledge only of what the wife told him she said and not of what the wife said at the time the defendant ran the light.

If the wife is called to report the statement she made while seeing the green car run the light, a personal knowledge objection would have to be overruled, since she has first hand knowledge of what she said. A hearsay objection would also have to be overruled, since the statement falls within

---

3. C. McCormick, McCormick on Evidence § 247 (J. Strong 4th ed. 1992).

4. West's Ann.California Evidence Code § 702 (comment).

5. For a detailed discussion of excited utterances, see § 9.04 infra.

the hearsay exception for excited utterances. But if in addition to reporting her out of court statement the wife is also asked to report the statement she made to her cousin ("I said to my cousin, 'As I saw the green car go through the light, I said, "Look, the green car is running the light!" ' "), then the appropriate objection is hearsay. The wife has personal knowledge both of what she said to her cousin as well as of what she said when she saw the green car run the light. But now, she is attempting to prove what she said when she saw the green car run the light, not by repeating what she said, but by repeating what she said to her cousin.

Are such fine distinctions between hearsay and the personal knowledge requirement important? Probably not, as either objection most likely preserves the correct ground. As Dean McCormick has noted, "[W]hen it appears, either from the phrasing of his testimony or from other sources, that the witness is testifying on the basis of reports from others, though he does not in terms testify to their statements, the distinction loses much of its significance, and courts simply apply the label 'hearsay.' "[6]

QUESTIONS AND PROBLEMS

1. Determine whether a California or federal judge should sustain a hearsay objection to the following evidence; in answering the questions, assume there are no hearsay exceptions: *beg. of H is rule.*

a. On the issue of whether Lord Raleigh conspired with Lord Cobham to overthrow the monarchy, testimony by Lord Cobham that Raleigh said to him, "I agree to help you overthrow the monarchy."

On the same issue, testimony by Lady Cobhan that Lord Cobham said to her, "Raleigh said to me, 'I agree to help you overthrow the monarchy.' "

b. On the issue of whether the accused committed the murder, testimony by a police officer that one Jones, who has disappeared, said to him, "I killed the victim."

c. On the issue of whether the defendant had the red light, testimony by W, "The defendant had the red light."

d. On same issue, testimony by W that B told W, "The defendant had the red light."

e. On the same issue, testimony by W that he told B, "The defendant had the red light."

f. On the issue of whether the testator was alive when found after an aircraft accident, testimony by a rescue worker that the testator said, "I am alive."

g. On the same issue, testimony by another rescue worker that the testator said, "I am dead."

h. On the issue of whether the accused was coerced into stealing money from a bank, testimony by the accused that her kidnappers said, "We will kill you unless you help us rob the bank."

---

6. C. McCormick, McCormick on Evidence § 247 (J. Strong 4th ed. 1992).

i. On the issue of whether the defendant was on notice of whether the area in front of the produce section was wet, testimony by W that prior to the plaintiff's falling she told the defendant, "The area in front of the produce section is wet."

 j. On the same issue, testimony by X that she heard W tell the defendant, "The area in front of the produce section is wet."

 k. On the issue of whether the defendant was negligent in hiring an unfit taxi driver named Joe, testimony by W that she heard many taxi drivers say, "Joe is an unfit driver."

 l. On the same issue, a letter from the Department of Motor Vehicles saying, "Joe, your driver's license has been suspended because you are an unfit driver," where other evidence shows the letter can be obtained by anyone seeking to employ taxi drivers.

 m. On the issue of whether the defendant breached his promise to sell the plaintiff evidence notes for $10, testimony by the plaintiff that the plaintiff said, "I'll give you $10 for your evidence notes," and the defendant said, "I accept your offer."

 n. On the same issue, testimony by the plaintiff's boyfriend that the plaintiff said to him, "The defendant said to me, 'I accept your offer.' "

 o. On the issue of the layout of a gambling establishment, testimony by an undercover agent, "It has two rooms and five card tables."

p. On the same issue, testimony by another undercover agent that a patron told him, "It has two rooms and five card tables."

? ✗ q. To prove that the patron had knowledge of the layout of the gambling establishment, testimony by the second undercover agent that the patron said, "It has two rooms and five card tables," where other evidence showed that it did have two rooms and five card tables.

implied
assertion
doctrine

r. To prove that the house was a gambling establishment, testimony by an officer that while he was raiding the house, he picked up the phone and the caller said, "$100 on the Forty–Niners and seven points."

s. On the same issue, testimony by the same officer that when he picked up the phone the second time the caller said, "The place you are in is a gambling establishment."

t. In a drunk driving prosecution, testimony by the arresting officer that the reason he stopped the defendant was that "Communications said, 'We have a report of a drunk driver in a white VW in your area. Be on the lookout for it.'" imperative

u. On the issue of whether a BART car was too cold as claimed by the plaintiff, testimony by the plaintiff's friend that two other passengers said to her, "This car sure is cold."

v. On the same issue, testimony by the friend, "I saw two other passengers shivering."

On the same issue, testimony the conductor, "None of the other thirty passengers in the car complained to me about the temperature in the car,'' where other evidence showed that the conductor was on board the car the entire time the plaintiff was in the car.

w. In a tax prosecution, a duly qualified expert testifies on direct examination that the defendant, an accountant, overstated the itemized deductions on ten returns. On cross, the expert testifies that he determined the overstatement by comparing the amounts in each return with the amounts the taxpayers told the expert that they had provided to the defendant. The defendant moves to strike the testimony on direct on hearsay grounds. Should the judge grant the motion?

x. On the issue of the identity of the killer, testimony by a witness that he told the investigating officer, ''The defendant killed the victim.''

y. On the same issue, testimony by the investigating officer that when he asked, ''Who killed the victim?,'' a man in a green coat pointed at the defendant.

z. On the same issue, testimony by the officer that the defendant then ran away.

aa. On the same issue, testimony by another officer that his bloodhound sniffed the knife still lodged in the victim, that his hound then set off in the direction of some trees, and that when the hound reached the trees, she jumped on the defendant and wagged her tail.

bb. On the issue of whether the defendant was intoxicated, testimony by a technician that when she had the defendant blow into an intoxilyzer a light turned green, meaning that the defendant had consumed intoxicating liquors.

cc. On the issue of the time when the intoxilyzer test was administered, a document printed out by the intoxilyzer immediately after the test, stating: ''Test administered at 6 PM.''

dd. On the same issue, testimony by a witness that the intoxilyzer technician said to her, ''I administered the test at 6 PM.''

ee. On the same issue, testimony by the intoxilyzer technician that prior to administering the test, he ''calibrated'' the time indicated on the intoxilyzer's clock by changing it to reflect the time stated by a radio announcer who said, ''The correct time is 5:50 PM.''

ff. On the issue of whether the decedent, a law professor, was competent to execute a will, testimony by a witness stating, ''In my opinion the law professor was competent to execute a will.''

gg. On the same issue, testimony by a law student that at about the time the decedent executed the will she left the decedent a Voice Mail message stating, ''In my opinion you [the law professor] are competent to execute a will.''

hh. On the same issue, testimony by another law student that he left the decedent a Voice Mail message stating, ''You're so smart and possess such good judgment that I really value your comments.''

ii. On the same issue, testimony by a third law student that at about the time the decedent executed the will she left the decedent a

Interrogative sent.

Voice Mail message stating, "Please tell me why the following evidence does not violate the hearsay rule: testimony by a witness that she saw the sea captain inspect the ship, then put his family on the ship, and then sail away, when offered to prove that the ship was seaworthy."

jj. On the issue of whether The Three Mile Island nuclear facility had been properly decontaminated following a radiation leak, testimony by an engineer, "I saw the head engineer inspect the facility; then he had his family join him for a brown bag lunch inside the facility; and none of the participants wore protective clothing."

In ruling, would it matter if at the request of the head engineer the press was present during his inspection and brown bag lunch?

kk. On the issue of whether the conservatee's is suffering from a mental disorder (delusions), testimony by a witness that she overheard the conservatee say, "I am suffering from a mental disorder."

ll. On the same issue, testimony that the conservatee also said, "I am the Pope."

mm. On the same issue, testimony that the conservatee also said, "I believe I am the Pope."

CALIFORNIA EVIDENCE CODE

§ 135. Declarant

"Declarant" is a person who makes a statement.

§ 145. The hearing

"The hearing" means the hearing at which a question under this code arises, and not some earlier or later hearing.

§ 225. Statement

"Statement" means (a) oral or written verbal expression or (b) nonverbal conduct of a person intended by him as a substitute for oral or written verbal expression.

§ 1200. The hearsay rule

(a) "Hearsay evidence" is evidence of a statement that was made other than by a witness while testifying at the hearing and that is offered to prove the truth of the matter stated.

(b) Except as provided by law, hearsay evidence is inadmissible.

(c) This section shall be known and may be cited as the hearsay rule.

FEDERAL RULES OF EVIDENCE

Rule 801. Definitions That Apply to This Article; Exclusions from Hearsay

(a) Statement. "Statement" means a person's oral assertion, written assertion, or nonverbal conduct, if the person intended it as an assertion.

(b) Declarant. "Declarant" means the person who made the statement.

(c) Hearsay. "Hearsay" means a statement that:

  (1) the declarant does not make while testifying at the current trial or hearing; and

  (2) a party offers in evidence to prove the truth of the matter asserted in the statement.

(d) Statements That Are Not Hearsay. A statement that meets the following conditions is not hearsay:

  (1) *A Declarant–Witness's Prior Statement.* The declarant testifies and is subject to cross-examination about a prior statement, and the statement:

    (A) is inconsistent with the declarant's testimony and was given under penalty of perjury at a trial, hearing, or other proceeding or in a deposition;

    (B) is consistent with the declarant's testimony and is offered to rebut an express or implied charge that the declarant recently fabricated it or acted from a recent improper influence or motive in so testifying; or

    (C) identifies a person as someone the declarant perceived earlier.

  (2) *An Opposing Party's Statement.* The statement is offered against an opposing party and:

    (A) was made by the party in an individual or representative capacity;

    (B) is one the party manifested that it adopted or believed to be true;

    (C) was made by a person whom the party authorized to make a statement on the subject;

    (D) was made by the party's agent or employee on a matter within the scope of that relationship and while it existed; or

    (E) was made by the party's coconspirator during and in furtherance of the conspiracy. The statement must be considered but does not by itself establish the declarant's authority under (C);

the existence or scope of the relationship under (D); or the existence of the conspiracy or participation in it under (E).

Rule 802. The Rule Against Hearsay

Hearsay is not admissible unless any of the following provides otherwise:

- a federal statute;
- these rules; or
- other rules prescribed by the Supreme Court.

CHAPTER 6

EXCEPTIONS TO THE HEARSAY RULE: GENERAL CONSIDERATIONS

■ ■ ■

Table of Sections

§ 6.01 INTRODUCTION

One of the most recent studies of hearsay was conducted by the Advisory Committee appointed by the United States Supreme Court in 1965 to draft the Federal Rules of Evidence. In its study, the Advisory Committee acknowledged the central role the hearsay rule plays in preserving a party's right to cross examine the witnesses called by the adverse party.[1] The best way to preserve this right is simply by excluding all hearsay. But as the Advisory Committee conceded:

> No one advocates this position. Common sense tells that much evidence which is not given under the three [ideal] conditions [that is, under oath and subject to cross-examination in the presence of the fact finder] may be inherently superior to much that is. Moreover, when the choice is between evidence which is less than best and no evidence at all, only clear folly would dictate an across-the-board policy of doing without. The problem thus resolves itself into effecting a sensible accommodation between these considerations and the desirability of giving testimony under the ideal conditions.[2]

---

1. See Advisory Committee Note, reprinted in Federal Rules of Evidence for United States Courts and Magistrates, Article VIII. Hearsay, Introductory Note: the Hearsay Problem.

If the choice is between excluding all hearsay or admitting some evidence "which is less than best," a rule favoring some evidence rather than none would call for abolishing the hearsay rule and allowing the use of hearsay. But as the Advisory Committee noted, abolishing the rule would not necessarily result in placing before the fact finders testimony that has not been subjected to cross-examination.[3]

> If the declarant were available [to testify], compliance with the ideal conditions would be optional with either party. Thus the proponent could call the declarant as a witness as a form of presentation more impressive than his hearsay statement. Or the opponent could call the declarant to be cross-examined upon his statement.[4]

The Advisory Committee rejected this option.[5] Abolition of the hearsay rule could also result in the admission of hearsay by declarants who are unavailable to testify. Their out of court statements would be admitted without giving the fact finders the benefits that might accrue from cross-examination. The Advisory Committee thus rejected the position at each end of the spectrum: a rule excluding all hearsay and a rule admitting all hearsay. Instead, the Committee opted for a rule favoring the use of reliable hearsay.

In the Committee's view, such a rule could take one of two forms. The trial judge could be given the task of excluding unreliable hearsay whenever in the judge's discretion its probative value would be outweighed by the possibility of prejudice, waste of time, or the availability of more satisfactory evidence.[6] Or the judge could be charged with excluding hearsay upon objection, unless the proponent convinces the judge that the hearsay falls within an a statutory exception that is believed to exclude unreliable hearsay.[7] The Committee rejected the first form as "involving too great a measure of judicial discretion, minimizing the predictability of rulings, enhancing the difficulties of preparation for trial, adding a further element to the already over-complicated congeries of pretrial procedures, and requiring substantially different rules for civil and criminal cases."[8]

Of all the reasons the Advisory Committee advanced, enhancing the difficulties of preparation for trial is the most persuasive. Because in the United States the lawyers—not the trial judge—play the key role in determining how a trial unfolds, in planning their trials the lawyers need to know whether the judge will admit or exclude evidence. A rule that commits the admissibility of hearsay to the trial judge's discretion ignores this reality and cannot work in the American style adversarial system.

---

2. Id.

3. Id.

4. Id.

5. Id.

6. Id.

7. Id.

8. Id.

If asked, most first year law students will respond that the judge is the most important person in a trial. The judge, after all, is dressed differently from all others—whether lawyers, parties, jurors, or spectators—attending the trial. Judges are the only ones dressed in a black robe. Moreover, they sit at a special place (the bench) which is usually elevated. Whenever a judge enters the court room, an armed guard (the bailiff) orders all others to stand. No one can sit until after the judge sits. No one can speak until after the judge formally opens the proceedings, usually by announcing the case to be heard that day.

The reality is otherwise, however. In jury trials, it is the lawyers who are the most important persons. In criminal trials, for example, it is the prosecutor and defense counsel who are responsible for the manner in which the trial unfolds. It is the lawyers who decide which witnesses to call and the order in which they will testify. It is the lawyers who decide whether non-testimonial evidence will be offered and when it will be offered. It is the lawyers who decide what the witnesses will say, since witnesses are expected to respond only to the questions put to them. It is the lawyers who formulate these questions and who put them to the witnesses. Even though the presiding judge is free to ask questions of witnesses, most judges leave this task almost exclusively to the lawyers.[9]

Other than ministerial duties such as opening trials and informing the jurors of the law that applies to the case, a judge's principal role in a jury trial is to rule on objections to the introduction of evidence offered by a party. But even this role is circumscribed. The rules of evidence operate in an adversarial environment. As in the case of procedural rules, whether a particular rule of evidence will be applied will depend initially on whether its application is invoked by a party. If a party fails to object to evidence offered by the opponent, as a rule the party loses the right to complain on appeal about the introduction of inadmissible evidence. The California Evidence Code is illustrative. It provides that a "verdict or finding shall not be set aside, nor shall the judgment or decision based thereon be reversed, by reason of the erroneous admission of evidence unless: (a) There appears of record an objection to or motion to exclude or strike the evidence that was timely made and so stated as to make clear the specific ground of objection or motion * * *."[10]

In the end, the Advisory Committee opted to retain the common law approach to hearsay: a general rule of exclusion with exceptions.[11] As the Committee explained, the exceptions listed in the Federal Rules "are designed to take full advantage of the accumulated wisdom and experience of the past in dealing with hearsay. It would, however, be presumptuous

---

9. The degree to which the lawyers control the interrogation of witnesses is evidenced by the virtual disuse of a procedure available in California and some other states. Jurors, under certain circumstances, can ask questions of witnesses. See infra § 17.12. It is the rare case where jurors exercise this right, mainly because they are not apprised of their right to ask questions.

10. See West's Ann. California Evidence Code § 353.

11. See Advisory Committee Note, reprinted in Federal Rules of Evidence for United States Courts and Magistrates, Article VIII. Hearsay, Introductory Note: the Hearsay Problem.

to assume that all possible desirable exceptions to the hearsay rule have catalogued and to pass the hearsay rule to oncoming generations as a closed system."[12]

Not passing "a closed system" to future generations of lawyers and judges may be commendable. But the soundness of uncritically accepting "the accumulated wisdom and experience of the past" is contestable. Enacting a general rule of exclusion necessarily invites the question of exceptions. The approach taken by the Advisory Committee is revealing. In identifying the exceptions that should be included in the Federal Rules, the Committee did not undertake research that draws on the social sciences. The Committee did not ask, for example, whether empirical research justifies the legal assumption that most exceptions allow the use of only reliable evidence. Consider the hearsay exception for declarations against interest.[13] Intuitively, it may be true that most people do not say things that are against their interest unless they believe the things they are saying are true. But in the absence of solid social science research, we simply do not know as a scientific matter whether this proposition is accurate. Consider also the exception for excited utterances.[14] Their reliability is said to derive from the spontaneity (and consequent lack of reflection) induced by the stress associated with the startling event giving rise to the declaration.[15] Some social science studies, however, suggest that stress can distort perception.[16] But in their search for reliable hearsay, neither the Common Law judges who first confronted the question of exceptions nor their successors who were charged with codifying the exceptions appear to have considered systematically the role of the social sciences.

An examination of the hearsay exceptions discloses that proponents have generally advanced two grounds to justify their creation. One is the need for the evidence. In the case of dying declarations, for example, the dead victim may be the only person who identified the killer. If the declaration is not admitted, the killer may go free. The other is the belief that the circumstances under which the declaration was made suggest that the declaration is reliable for proving the truth of the matter stated. These circumstances are believed to furnish an adequate substitute for the benefits that would accrue if the declarant were cross examined under oath in the presence of the fact finder. Take an excited utterance in which the declarant exclaims that the green car had the red light. The exception for these declarations requires that they be made spontaneously while the declarant while was under the stress of the exciting event giving rise to the statement.[17] Since the declarant has no opportunity to reflect on and

---

12. Id.

13. See West's Ann. California Evidence Code § 1230; Federal Rule of Evidence 804(b)(3).

14. See West's Ann. California Evidence Code § 1240; Federal Rule of Evidence 803(2).

15. See, e.g., West's Ann. California Evidence Code § 1240 (comment).

16. See the studies cited in C. McCormick, Mccormick on Evidence § 272 (4th ed. 1992).

17. West's Ann. California Evidence Code § 1240; Federal Rule of Evidence 803(3).

thereby fabricate his statement, his declaration is believed to be as reliable as would be his testimony about who had the red light.[18]

The Federal Rules of Evidence classify the hearsay exceptions by whether the proponent must demonstrate the unavailability of the hearsay declarant as a witness. Rule 803 lists those exceptions where the availability of the hearsay declarant is immaterial.[19] Under these exceptions, the hearsay is admissible even if the declarant can be produced by the proponent. Indeed, in some instances the proponent may offer the hearsay declaration through the declarant.

The major exceptions under this classification include excited utterances, state of mind declarations, statements made for medical diagnosis or treatment, statements in learned treatises, and entries in business and official records. Since hearsay is admissible under these exceptions even if the declarant is available as a witness, their status as exceptions necessarily rests on the notion that the out of court statement is as reliable as the declarant's in court testimony.[20] Consequently, the hearsay declarant's availability to testify is immaterial.

Rule 804 lists those exceptions which apply only if the hearsay declarant is unavailable.[21] Unlike Rule 803, Rule 804 evinces a clear preference for producing the hearsay declarant. Only if the declarant cannot be produced will the hearsay declaration be received. Major exceptions under this classification include former testimony, dying declarations, and declarations against interest.

Unlike the Federal Rules, the California Evidence Code does not classify the hearsay exceptions by whether the proponent must demonstrate the unavailability of the hearsay declarant. Instead, the Code lists first those exceptions in which the statement is most likely to be oral (admissions, prior statements of witnesses, declarations against interest, dying declarations, excited utterances, and state of mind declarations) and then those in which the statement is offered in a writing (business and official entries, former testimony, learned treatises, and judgments). This division is neither perfect[22] nor intended to be so. But it does provide a convenient way for analyzing the exceptions and is followed here.

Not all hearsay exceptions are discussed. The focus is on the major exceptions, especially those requiring detailed explanation.

Beyond organizational differences, the Evidence Code and the Federal Rules differ in two significant respects in their approach to the hearsay exceptions. The Code, following the Common Law tradition, treats admis-

---

18. West's Ann. California Evidence Code § 1240 (comment).

19. Federal Rule of Evidence 803.

20. See C. McCormick, McCormick on Evidence § 253 (J. Strong 4th ed. 1992).

21. Federal Rule of Evidence 804.

22. For example, prior recollection recorded is grouped with prior statements of witnesses even though the exception contemplates a writing; moreover, though former testimony is usually proved by the transcript of the former hearing, it can in theory be proved by the testimony of a witness who was present at the former hearing.

sions and prior statements of witnesses as exceptions to the hearsay rule. By definition, statements falling within the two exceptions are hearsay since these out of court statements are offered for the truth of the matter stated.[23] The Federal Rules deviate from this practice and, instead, permit the use of the statements for their truth on the theory that they should be exempted from the definition of hearsay, despite the unquestioned applicability of the federal hearsay rule. The justification for the federal treatment of these statements is explored in §§ 5.02 (prior statements of witnesses) and 7.11 (admissions).

The Rules depart from the Code in another way. They empower the trial judge to fashion new hearsay exceptions for statements not covered by the Rules but having "equivalent circumstantial guarantees of trustworthiness" if the proponent meets certain conditions.[24] These include the requirements that the statement be probative of a material fact, be more probative of the point for which it is offered than any other available evidence which the proponent can obtain through reasonable efforts, and best serve the interests of justice.[25] This innovative approach to the hearsay exceptions was prompted by an unwillingness "to assume that all possible desirable exceptions to the hearsay rule have been catalogued and to pass the hearsay rule to oncoming generations as a closed system."[26]

The Code does not create a closed system either. Under the Code, exceptions to the hearsay rule may be found either in statutes or in decisional law.[27] But, unlike the Federal Rules, the Code does not expressly empower trial judges to craft an exception for evidence offered in the case being tried. Instead, consistent with the Common Law tradition, it authorizes especially appellate judges to create new exceptions only for classes of evidence for which there is a substantial need and which possess such an intrinsic reliability as to enable the exceptions to surmount constitutional and other objections that generally apply to hearsay.[28]

§ 6.02 UNAVAILABILITY OF THE HEARSAY DECLARANT

Some exceptions to the hearsay rule require the proponent to demonstrate the unavailability of the hearsay declarant as a witness. These include the exceptions for former testimony and statements against interest. Under the Federal Rules, the proponent of a dying declaration must

---

23. For an extended discussion of this point see infra §§ 7.01 (admissions) and 8.01 (prior statements of witnesses).

24. Federal Rule of Evidence 807.

25. Id.

26. Federal Rule of Evidence 803(24) (Advisory Committee Note).

27. West's Ann.California Evidence Code § 1200 (comment). For a discussion of how California appellate judges can use § 1200(b) in crafting new hearsay exceptions, see Kandis Scott, *California's Dormant Hearsay Exception: Section 1200(b) of the Evidence Code*, 23 Santa Clara Law Review 157 (1983).

28. In re Cindy L., 17 Cal.4th 15, 28, 69 Cal.Rptr.2d 803, 811, 947 P.2d 1340, 1348 (1997).

also show the unavailability of the declarant.[1] The Code, on the other hand, does not impose this condition.[2] Because these exceptions are not discussed as a group, the unavailability requirement is examined here.

Evidence Code § 240 sets out the grounds for determining the unavailability of witnesses. It defines as unavailable declarants who are (1) exempted or precluded from testifying on the grounds of privilege, (2) disqualified from testifying, (3) dead or unable to testify on account of mental or physical illness, (4) absent from the hearing and beyond the court's process to compel attendance, (5) absent from the hearing despite the proponent's reasonable efforts to compel attendance through the court's process, or (6) persistent in refusing to testify concerning the subject matter of the declarant's statement despite having been found in contempt for refusal to testify.[3] Under the Code, the proponent has the burden of persuading the judge of the declarant's unavailability by a preponderance of the evidence.[4]

Whether a declarant is "unavailable" despite the proponent's efforts to compel his attendance through the court's process is a question that turns on the circumstances of each case.[5] As a general rule, however, in criminal cases the prosecution must take special precautions to prevent a witness from disappearing if the testimony is vital to the People's case.[6] Where a witness is a known flight risk, the failure by the People to keep the witness under surveillance will preclude a finding of the witness's unavailability. In People v. Louis,[7] for example, the witness who failed to show up at the trial was facing a felony theft charge and was awaiting sentencing in another case. He was released from jail on his own recognizance to spend the weekend before sentencing with a friend and disappeared. The court held that no due diligence was shown, as the People failed even to obtain the name or address of the friend.[8] But where the record fails to reflect any reason for the prosecution to suspect that a

1. Federal Rule of Evidence 804(b)(2).

2. West's Ann.California Evidence Code § 1242. See also § 9.03 infra.

3. West's Ann. California Evidence Code § 240(a).

4. West's Ann.California Evidence Code § 405 (comment).

5. People v. Wise, 25 Cal.App.4th 339, 343, 30 Cal.Rptr.2d 413, 415 (1994), citing People v. Cummings, 4 Cal.4th 1233, 18 Cal.Rptr.2d 796, 850 P.2d 1, cert. denied, 511 U.S. 1046, 114 S.Ct. 1576, 128 L.Ed.2d 219 (1993). In determining whether the proponent has exercised due diligence in procuring the attendance of a witness, a court should compare those steps the proponent took with those the proponent failed to take. People v. Walton, 42 Cal.App.4th 1004, 1010–1011, 49 Cal.Rptr.2d 917, 921 (1996), disapproved on other grounds by People v. Cromer, 24 Cal.4th 889, 901, note 3, 103 Cal.Rptr.2d 23, 30, note 3, 15 P.3d 243, 250, note 3 (2001). But the Code does not require the proponent to take all conceivable steps; it requires only "reasonable efforts, not prescient perfection." People v. McElroy, 208 Cal.App.3d 1415, 1428, 256 Cal.Rptr. 853, 860 (1989), disapproved on other grounds by People v. Cromer, 24 Cal.4th 889, 901, note 3, 103 Cal.Rptr.2d 23, 30, note 3, 15 P.3d 243, 250, note 3 (2001). The proper standard for reviewing a trial court's due diligence ruling is independent review rather than abuse of discretion. People v. Cromer, supra, at 892–893, 103 Cal.Rptr.2d at 24–25, 15 P.3d at 244–245.

6. People v. Hovey, 44 Cal.3d 543, 564, 244 Cal.Rptr. 121, 132, 749 P.2d 776, 787 (1988).

7. 42 Cal.3d 969, 232 Cal.Rptr. 110, 728 P.2d 180 (1986).

8. Id. at 992, 232 Cal.Rptr. at 123, 728 P.2d at 193.

material witness might disappear, the prosecution has no obligation to keep periodic tabs on the witness.[9]

At one time, witnesses who were beyond the court's process because they resided outside of California were deemed to be unavailable. Today, the party seeking to establish their unavailability must in addition show a good faith effort to secure their attendance at the trial in order to have the judge declare them unavailable.[10] Where the witness resides in another state, the party seeking to establish the witness's unavailability must show that securing the witness's attendance through agreements between California and other states to obtain the attendance of witnesses proved unavailing.[11] In the case of a witness who resides in a foreign country, the party must show that agreements between the United States and that country calling for mutual assistance in obtaining witnesses failed to produce the witness.[12] Resort to agreements between states and treaties between the United States and other countries may nonetheless be insufficient to establish a witness's unavailability. Where the party seeking to show a witness's unavailability is the prosecution, the Confrontation Clause requires the prosecution to show that other reasonable measures would not have produced the witness.[13] In People v. Sandoval,[14] in addition to showing that an effort was made to secure the witness's attendance under agreements between the United States and Mexico, this demand required the prosecution to offer a witness a modest amount of funds to enable the witness to attend the trial.[15]

A declarant is not unavailable if his unavailability was procured by the proponent for the purpose of preventing the declarant from testifying.[16] In this case, however, it is the opponent who has the burden. She must persuade the judge by a preponderance of the evidence that this is the reason for the declarant's unavailability.[17]

As originally enacted, California Evidence Code § 240 did not explicitly render unavailable the contumacious witness—the witness who refuses to testify despite a court order to do so. A 2010 amendment now includes as unavailable, declarants who persist "in refusing to testify concerning the subject matters of the declarant's statement despite having been found

---

9. People v. Wise, 25 Cal.App.4th 339, 344, 30 Cal.Rptr.2d 413, 415 (1994). Cases raising questions of due diligence do not always involve the steps taken unsuccessfully to locate and produce a witness. Sometimes the complaint centers around the time when the steps were taken. For a review of the cases discussing whether the search for a witness was begun in a timely manner, see People v. Saucedo, 33 Cal.App.4th 1230, 1238, 40 Cal.Rptr.2d 153, 158 (1995).

10. People v. Sandoval, 87 Cal.App.4th 1425, 1440, 105 Cal.Rptr.2d 504, 515 (2001).

11. Id. at 1436–1437, 105 Cal.Rptr.2d at 512–513. California is a party to the Uniform Act to Secure the Attendance of Witnesses. See West's Ann. California Penal Code § 1334 et seq.

12. People v. Sandoval, 87 Cal.App.4th 1425, 1441, 105 Cal.Rptr.2d 504, 515 (2001).

13. Id. at 1443–1444, 105 Cal.Rptr.2d at 517.

14. Id. at 1440, 105 Cal.Rptr.2d at 515.

15. Id. at 1442, 105 Cal.Rptr.2d at 516.

16. West's Ann. California Evidence Code § 240(b).

17. West's Ann. California Evidence Code § 405 (comment).

in contempt for refusal to testify."[18] The 2010 amendment aligns the Code with the Federal Rules which recognize that a contumacious witness is as unavailable to testify as is a declarant who does not attend the hearing.[19]

Prior to the 2010 amendment, California courts had interpreted another provision of § 240 to include some contumacious witnesses. A witness who refused to testify because of fear for his safety or that of his family was unavailable under § 240(a)(3) by reason of "mental illness or infirmity" due to a "defect of personality or will."[20] Mere inconvenience, however, including the anguish and physical discomfort that can be produced by testifying, was insufficient to render the witness unavailable.[21] But if expert testimony established that the physical or mental trauma suffered by a crime witness had caused such harm that the witness could not testify or could do so only by enduring additional substantial trauma, the witness could be declared unavailable.[22]

The expert testimony requirement was codified in Code § 240(c) prior to the enactment of the contumacious witness provision, and it was not repealed by the new provision. Accordingly, a party who requests the court to declare as unavailable a witness who refuses to testify despite a court order to do so may also have to comply with the expert witness requirement if the witness's reason for refusing to testify is fear for his or her safety, or that of his or her family.

California judges should not find a contumacious witness to be unavailable unless the witness has first rejected reasonable inducements to testify.[23] Finding a witness in contempt and sending him to jail may not serve as the basis for an unavailability finding if other steps might have persuaded the witness to testify.[24] In People v. Sul, for example, a witness said that he might testify if his attorney were present.[25] The reviewing court held that the trial judge should have pursued this alternative before holding the witness in contempt and declaring him to be unavailable.[26]

The Federal Rules differ from the Code in three important respects. Only two are examined here.[27] First, unlike the Code, the Rules do not

---

18. See West's Ann. California Evidence Code § 240(a)(6).

19. Federal Rule of Evidence 804(a)(2).

20. People v. Rojas, 15 Cal.3d 540, 550–551, 125 Cal.Rptr. 357, 363–364, 542 P.2d 229, 235–236 (1975) (Webster's definition of "infirmity," when considered with the wide discretion given judges to determine necessity in a particular case, "permits the trial court to consider whether a mental state induced by fear of personal or family harm is a 'mental infirmity' that renders the person harboring the fear unavailable as a witness.").

21. People v. Williams, 93 Cal.App.3d 40, 54, 155 Cal.Rptr. 414, 421 (1979).

22. Id.

23. People v. Sul, 122 Cal.App.3d 355, 364, 175 Cal.Rptr. 893, 899 (1981). Such steps need not be taken if they would prove unavailing, however. Id.

24. Id.

25. Id. at 365, 175 Cal.Rptr. at 899.

26. Id.

27. The Federal Rules take a more stringent approach to the admissibility of some hearsay statements when the declarant is unavailable to testify. In addition to the usual grounds of

have a provision declaring as unavailable declarants who have been disqualified from testifying. Second, the Rules acknowledge that a witness who cannot testify because of a failure of recollection is unavailable.[28] Although the Code does not have an equivalent provision, California cases recognize that a witness's memory loss can constitute a mental or physical illness that renders the witness unavailable. In People v. Alcala[29] the prosecution was allowed to offer a witness's former testimony after eliciting evidence from the witness that she could not recall any matters connected with the case as a result of a stress related disability. In upholding the trial judge's ruling, the California Supreme Court noted that total memory loss can constitute a "mental infirmity" within the meaning of § 240.[30] Expert testimony is unnecessary to establish that the loss constitutes a mental infirmity. The witness's own testimony, if believed by the trial judge, can support a finding of unavailability on this basis.[31]

QUESTIONS AND PROBLEMS

1. Because of the need to give the opposing party an opportunity to cross-examine the hearsay declarant under oath and in the presence of the fact finder, the Code and the Rules require the hearsay proponent to demonstrate the unavailability of the hearsay declarant before invoking a hearsay exception. True or false?

2. The Federal Rules have a provision recognizing that a witness who is unable to testify on account of failure of recollection is unavailable as a witness. True or false? The Code does not have an analogous provision, but other unavailability provisions of Section 240 have been construed to embrace a witness whose memory loss results from a mental or physical illness. True or false? Both the Rules and the Code recognize as unavailable a witness who refuses to testify despite a court order to answer the questions put to the witness. True or false? Only the Code, however, has a provision declaring as unavailable witnesses who are exempted or precluded from testifying on account of a privilege. True or false?

§ 6.03 HEARSAY AND CONFRONTATION

The hearsay rule and cross-examination. Earlier, we saw that the chief goal of the hearsay rule is to enhance the fact finding process by excluding certain declarations whenever the declarants cannot be subjected to cross-examination.[1] The rule achieves this goal by permitting the opposing party to object to the use of out of court statements that are

---

unavailability, in some cases the proponent must show that an attempt was made to depose the declarant. See § 9.02 infra.

28. Federal Rule of Evidence 804(a)(3).

29. 4 Cal.4th 742, 15 Cal.Rptr.2d 432, 842 P.2d 1192 (1992).

30. Id. at 778–779, 15 Cal.Rptr.2d at 452–453, 842 P.2d at 1212–1213.

31. Id. at 780, 15 Cal.Rptr.2d at 454, 842 P.2d at 1214.

1. See § 5.01 supra.

offered to prove the truth of the matter stated. Since the use of hearsay could deprive the opponent of an opportunity to challenge the credibility of the hearsay declarant, the rule proceeds on the assumption that cross-examination is vital to assuring the reliability of evidence.

The nature of testimony supports this assumption. In evaluating the testimony of witnesses, the fact finder should take into account the witnesses' abilities to perceive the subject matter of their testimony, to recall those perceptions, and to narrate them accurately at the hearing.[2] Flaws in these abilities need to be exposed, a task that falls upon the party opposing the witness. That party is given a powerful tool—the right to cross examine the witness under oath in the presence of the fact finder. The hearsay rule gives substance to that right by allowing the opposing party to object whenever an out of court statement is offered for the truth of the matter stated. In the absence of exceptions, the rule forces the proponent of the statement to produce the testimonial sources for cross-examination under oath in the presence of the fact finder.[3]

Cross-examination and confrontation. The Sixth Amendment guarantees the accused the right to confront the witnesses called against him. In California v. Green[4] the United States Supreme Court recognized that the hearsay rule and the Confrontation Clause protect similar values: insuring that witnesses adverse to the accused will testify under oath, subject to cross-examination, and in the presence of the fact finder.[5] The Court, however, rejected the proposition that "the Confrontation Clause is nothing more or less than a codification"[6] of the hearsay rule and its exceptions:

> Our decisions have never established such a congruence; indeed, we have more than once found a violation of confrontation values even though the statements in issue were admitted under an arguably recognized hearsay exception. * * * The converse is equally true: merely because evidence is admitted in violation of a long-established hearsay rule does not lead to the automatic conclusion that confrontation rights have been denied.[7]

---

2. See Federal Rules of Evidence for United States Courts and Magistrates, Article VIII at 105–106 (Advisory Committee Note) (West 1992).

3. When a witness refuses to submit to cross-examination, the conventional remedy is for the trial judge to strike the testimony the witness gave on direct examination. Fost v. Superior Court, 80 Cal.App.4th 724, 735–736, 95 Cal.Rptr.2d 620, 627 (2000).

4. 399 U.S. 149, 90 S.Ct. 1930, 26 L.Ed.2d 489 (1970), on remand, 3 Cal.3d 981, 92 Cal.Rptr. 494, 479 P.2d 998 (1971).

5. Id. at 157, 90 S.Ct. at 1934. "[T]he Clause envisions 'a personal examination and cross-examination of the witness, in which the accused has an opportunity, not only of testing the recollection and sifting the conscience of the witness, but of compelling him to stand face to face with the jury in order that they may look at him, and judge by his demeanor upon the stand and the manner in which he gives his testimony whether he is worthy of belief.'" Ohio v. Roberts, 448 U.S. 56, 63–64, 100 S.Ct. 2531, 2537–2538, 65 L.Ed.2d 597 (1980), quoting from Mattox v. United States, 156 U.S. 237, 242–243, 15 S.Ct. 337, 339, 39 L.Ed. 409 (1895).

6. California v. Green, 399 U.S. 149, 155–156, 90 S.Ct. 1930, 1933, 26 L.Ed.2d 489 (1970), on remand, 3 Cal.3d 981, 92 Cal.Rptr. 494, 479 P.2d 998 (1971).

7. Id. (footnotes omitted).

The Court's unwillingness to equate confrontation with hearsay, as well as its case-by-case approach, make it difficult to generalize about the status of the hearsay exceptions under the Sixth Amendment. But until 2004, two matters were fairly clear: a majority of the Court was disinclined to find a confrontation violation where the hearsay offered against the accused was received under an accepted exception; moreover, even where the prosecution relied on a novel exception, the Court was willing to dispense with cross-examination if the prosecution showed that the circumstances attending the making of the hearsay rendered the declaration trustworthy.

§ 6.04 HEARSAY AND CONFRONTATION: THE EVOLUTION OF THE *ROBERTS* RULE

In California v. Green[1] the defendant was prosecuted for furnishing marihuana to a minor. At the preliminary hearing, the minor identified the accused as his supplier. At the trial, the minor claimed that he was unable to recall who supplied him with the marihuana because at the time he received it he was on LSD.

The prosecution then offered the minor's preliminary hearing testimony. The minor's former testimony was admitted under the theory that it constituted a prior statement that was inconsistent with his trial testimony. Under the California Evidence Code, the testimony was admissible to impeach the minor as well as to prove the truth of what he had stated. The Court rejected a confrontation claim to the use of the evidence: at the trial, the accused was given an opportunity to cross examine the minor about his earlier statement while the minor was under oath and in the presence of the fact finder.[2] Accordingly, the defendant had an opportunity to provide the fact finder with an adequate basis for evaluating the witness's testimony.

Though the issue was not before the it, the Court noted that the minor's preliminary hearing testimony identifying the accused as his supplier would have been admissible if the minor had been unable to testify at the trial.[3] That position was confirmed in Ohio v. Roberts,[4] where the Court upheld the use against the accused of the preliminary hearing testimony of a witness who was unavailable to testify at the trial. Emphasizing that "the prosecution must either produce, or demonstrate the unavailability, of the [hearsay] declarant,"[5] the Court held that the statement of an unavailable declarant is admissible "if it bears adequate 'indicia of reliability.' "[6] That reliability "can be inferred without more in

---

1. 399 U.S. 149, 90 S.Ct. 1930, 26 L.Ed.2d 489 (1970), on remand, 3 Cal.3d 981, 92 Cal.Rptr. 494, 479 P.2d 998 (1971).

2. Id. at 164, 90 S.Ct. at 1938.

3. Id. at 165, 90 S.Ct. at 1938–1939.

4. 448 U.S. 56, 100 S.Ct. 2531, 65 L.Ed.2d 597 (1980).

5. Id. at 65, 100 S.Ct. at 2538.

6. Id. at 66, 100 S.Ct. at 2539 (footnotes omitted).

a case where the evidence falls within a firmly rooted hearsay exception."[7]

Notions that the Confrontation Clause required the prosecution to produce or show the unavailability of the hearsay declarant in all cases were dispelled in United States v. Inadi.[8] In that case, the accused was prosecuted for manufacturing and distributing a controlled substance. The accused objected on confrontation grounds to the introduction of a coconspirator's declaration implicating the accused that satisfied the evidentiary foundation for coconspirator's statements under the Federal Rules of Evidence. In light of *Roberts*, the accused claimed that the statement was inadmissible absent a showing by the prosecution of the declarant's unavailability to testify. The Court rejected this reading of *Roberts*.[9] In the Court's view, coconspirators' declarations derive much of their value from the fact that they are made while the conspiracy is in progress. They "provide evidence of the conspiracy's context that cannot be replicated, even if the declarant testifies to the same matters in court."[10] Because of their presumed reliability, their use does not violate the Sixth Amendment even if the hearsay declarant is not produced for cross-examination. Indeed, their use, according to the Court, is consistent with "the 'Confrontation Clause's very mission'" which is to "'advance the accuracy of the truth-determining process in criminal trials.'"[11]

In White v. Illinois[12] the Court reaffirmed the limited reach of *Roberts*: "*Roberts* stands for the proposition that unavailability analysis is a necessary part of the Confrontation Clause inquiry only when the challenged out-of-court statements were made in the course of a prior judicial proceeding."[13] The Court, moreover, reiterated what it said in *Roberts*: That reliability "can be inferred without more in a case where the evidence falls within a firmly rooted hearsay exception."[14] Excited

---

7. Id. That was the case in *Roberts*, where the evidence fell within the former testimony exception to the hearsay rule.

8. 475 U.S. 387, 106 S.Ct. 1121, 89 L.Ed.2d 390 (1986), on remand, 790 F.2d 383 (3d Cir.1986).

9. Id. at 394, 106 S.Ct. at 1125.

10. Id. at 396, 106 S.Ct. at 1126.

11. Id. (quoting Dutton v. Evans, 400 U.S. 74, 89, 91 S.Ct. 210, 27 L.Ed.2d 213 (1970), on remand, 441 F.2d 657 (5th Cir.1971)). Prior to *Inadi*, the Court had held that the use of dying declarations against the accused did not offend the Confrontation Clause. See § 9.03 infra. Nor does the use of personal admissions offend the Sixth Amendment; the accused can hardly complain of an inability to cross examine himself.

12. 502 U.S. 346, 112 S.Ct. 736, 116 L.Ed.2d 848 (1992).

13. Id. at 354, 112 S.Ct. at 741. Accord: People v. Sandoval, 87 Cal.App.4th 1425, 1443–1444, 105 Cal.Rptr.2d 504, 517 (2001) (The accused's right to confront his accuser was violated where the prosecution was permitted to use a Mexican witness's preliminary hearing testimony without first showing that it attempted to secure the cooperation of Mexican authorities in obtaining the witness's attendance under a treaty calling for such cooperation in criminal matters; under the circumstances, merely showing that the witness was beyond the court's subpoena power did not satisfy the Confrontation Clause). In California, whether the prosecution exercised the required "due diligence" in attempting to secure the witness's attendance is subject to de novo review by the appellate courts. People v. Cromer, 24 Cal.4th 889, 901, 103 Cal.Rptr.2d 23, 30, 15 P.3d 243, 250 (2001).

14. Ohio v. Roberts, 448 U.S. 56, 66, 100 S.Ct. 2531, 2539, 65 L.Ed.2d 597 (1980) (footnotes omitted).

utterances and statements made in the course of receiving medical care, in the Court's view, met this test.[15]

Only where the prosecution relied on a comparatively novel exception did the Court require the prosecution to offer evidence showing that the hearsay offered was reliable. In Idaho v. Wright[16] the question was the admissibility over a confrontation objection of statements which a child made to a doctor claiming that the defendant had abused her. Because the child was incompetent to testify under state law, the statements were admitted pursuant to a "residual exception" to the Idaho hearsay rule. This innovative approach permits the use of hearsay not specifically allowed by established exceptions but having "equivalent circumstantial guarantees of trustworthiness."[17] The Court held that the use of the statements violated the accused's confrontation rights.[18] The residual exception, according to the Court, was not a firmly rooted exception to the hearsay rule. Consequently, such evidence could be used only upon a showing of particularized guarantees of trustworthiness.[19] In making this showing, the prosecution could rely on the circumstances "that surround the making of the statement and that render the declarant particularly worthy of belief."[20] But the prosecution could not rely on other evidence that corroborated the truth of the hearsay statement: "To be admissible under the Confrontation Clause, hearsay evidence used to convict a defendant must possess indicia of reliability by virtue of its inherent trustworthiness, not by reference to other evidence at trial."[21]

In sum, then, until 2004 the Court was willing to dispense with cross-examination whenever the evidence against the accused was received under a firmly rooted exception to the hearsay rule. Only where the prosecution did not rely on an established exception would the state be required to show that the statement was worthy of belief. Thus, despite the Court's protestations, the Court's opinions did evince a substantial, though not perfect, congruence between the Confrontation Clause and the hearsay rule and its exceptions.

---

15. Id. at 355–356, 112 S.Ct. at 742. The California Supreme Court has held that the hearsay exception for declarations concerning future plans also qualifies as a firmly rooted exception. People v. Majors, 18 Cal.4th 385, 405, 75 Cal.Rptr.2d 684, 697, 956 P.2d 1137, 1150 (1998). The Federal Court for the Central District of California has held that the California hearsay exception for official records is likewise a firmly rooted exception. See Lacy v. Lewis, 123 F. Supp.2d 533, 553 (2000) (approving the admission of a chemist's report against the accused).

16. 497 U.S. 805, 110 S.Ct. 3139, 111 L.Ed.2d 638 (1990).

17. Id. at 811–812, 110 S.Ct. at 3144–3145.

18. Id. at 818, 110 S.Ct. at 3148.

19. Id. at 816, 100 S.Ct. at 3147.

20. Id. at 817, 110 S.Ct. at 3149.

21. Id. at 822, 110 S.Ct. at 3150.

§ 6.05 HEARSAY AND CONFRONTATION: THE *CRAWFORD* RULE

That congruence no longer exists. In Crawford v. Washington[1] the Court announced a new test to determine the constitutionality under the Confrontation Clause of hearsay offered against the accused. Crawford was convicted of assault and attempted murder. Over his confrontation objection, the prosecution was allowed to offer a recorded statement his wife made to the police in which she appeared to contradict Crawford's claim that he attacked the victim in self-defense. The wife's statement was admitted for the truth under Washington's hearsay exception for declarations against penal interest.[2] Since this exception required the prosecution to show that the declarant was unavailable to testify,[3] Crawford did not have an opportunity to cross examine his wife about her out of court statement. The Court reversed Crawford's conviction.

Under *Crawford*, when the prosecution offers "testimonial statements" against the accused, the accused's confrontation rights are violated unless the out of court declarant is produced for cross-examination under oath before the fact finder.[4] If the out of court declarant is produced, then the Confrontation Clause "places no constraints at all on the use of his prior testimonial statements."[5] But if the out of court declarant is not produced, a confrontation violation will occur unless (1) the declarant was unavailable to testify and (2) the accused had "a prior opportunity" to cross examine the out of court declarant.[6] Since prior to the trial Crawford had not been afforded an opportunity to cross examine his wife about her statement to the police, the Court upheld his confrontation claim.

Crawford changes the Court's previous confrontation analysis in a number of ways. First, *Crawford* overrules *Roberts* to the extent that *Roberts* approved of the use against the accused of testimonial statements falling within a "firmly rooted" exception to the hearsay rule or bearing "particularlized guarantees of trustworthiness" if offered under a novel exception.[7] That testimonial statements offered against the accused fall within a firmly rooted hearsay exception or a novel exception meeting *Wright*'s reliability requirements are no longer the dispositive considerations in ruling on a confrontation claim.[8]

---

1. 541 U.S. 36, 124 S.Ct. 1354, 158 L.Ed.2d 177 (2004).

2. Id. at 1358.

3. Id. Under the Washington rules of evidence, the wife could not testify without Crawford's consent. He refused to consent to her testifying. Id. at 1357.

4. Id. at 1369, note 9.

5. Id.

6. Id. at 1370. "Where testimonial evidence is at issue, however, the Sixth Amendment demands what the common law required: unavailability and a prior opportunity for cross-examination." Id.

7. Id. at 1369–1372.

8. Indeed, to the Court it was immaterial that the Washington Supreme Court had found that the use of the wife's statement satisfied the *Roberts* and *Wright* test for admitting hearsay against a defendant under a novel hearsay exception. Id. at 1373.

Second, *Crawford* governs confrontation claims only in cases in which the prosecution offers "testimonial statements" against the accused. According to the Court, in adopting the Confrontation Clause the Framers were concerned with excluding from the trial the kind of ex parte witness statements often taken by magistrates and offered against the accused in Civil Law jurisdictions.[9] Although the Court declined to provide a comprehensive definition of "testimonial statements," the Court held that at a minimum the term applies "to prior testimony at a preliminary hearing, before a grand jury, or at a former trial; and to police interrogations."[10] "Involvement of government officers in the production of testimony with an eye toward trial * * * presents [a] unique potential for prosecutorial abuse," a concern that justifies scrutinizing the evidence under Confrontation Clause.[11] But, according to the Court, statements in business records and in furtherance of a conspiracy do not ordinarily fall within the definition of "testimonial statements."[12]

Third, where the hearsay offered against the accused is nontestimonial, the Confrontation Clause may not be implicated. The Court reserved for another day the question whether nontestimonial hearsay is subject to confrontation scrutiny.[13] "[I]t is wholly consistent with the Framers' design to afford the States flexibility in their development of hearsay law—as does *Roberts*, and as would an approach that exempted such statements from Confrontation Clause scrutiny altogether."[14]

Fourth, *Crawford* does not bar the use of testimonial statements if offered for a purpose other than establishing the truth of the matter stated or asserted.[15] In California, for example, experts may base their opinions on data, including hearsay, that are inadmissible, so long as the data are of the type reasonably relied upon by experts in the field.[16] A mental health expert is thus entitled to base his or her diagnosis on statements provided by the patient that might qualify as "testimonial" so long as the statements are not offered for the truth of the matter asserted.[17] The Confrontation Clause applies only to out of court statements offered for a hearsay purpose.

9. Id. at 1363–1364.

10. Id. at 1374. The Court declined to decide whether "testimonial dying declarations" fall within an exception to the Confrontation Clause. Id. at 1367, note 6.

11. Id. at 1367, note 7.

12. Id. at 1367. Subsequently, the Court acknowledged that some hearsay statements in business and official records can qualify as testimonial. See § 6.07 infra.

13. Id. at 1369–1370.

14. Id. at 1374. Subsequently, the Court held that the Confrontation Clause applies only to testimonial hearsay. For an extended discussion of this point, see § 6.09 infra.

15. Id. at 1369, note 9.

16. See § 16.03, infra.

17. See People v. Cooper, 148 Cal.App.4th 731, 746, 56 Cal.Rptr.3d 6, 18 (2007). In *Cooper* the mental health expert may have relied on information supplied by the patient in a police interview which the court found to be testimonial. However, the portions relied upon by the expert were offered only to explain the basis of his opinion and not for the truth of the matter asserted. Id.

***Crawford*'s effects on the court's confrontation jurisprudence.**
Although *Crawford* is a marked departure from the Court's previous
confrontation approach, *Crawford* would not change the result in most of
the leading confrontation cases. The result in *Green* would remain unchanged since in that case the hearsay declarant appeared at the trial and
was subject to cross-examination under oath before the jury about his out
of court statements. Neither would *Crawford* appear to change the outcome in *Roberts*. Although the hearsay declarant did not appear at the
trial, the prosecution demonstrated her unavailability as a witness and the
accused had been afforded an opportunity at the preliminary hearing to
cross examine her under oath about the statements offered at the trial.

Significantly, *Crawford* would not affect *Inadi*. A coconspirator's
declaration in furtherance of the conspiracy is not the kind of "testimonial
statement" contemplated by the Confrontation Clause, at least in the
absence of proof that the government was somehow involved in its
production with an eye toward using the declaration at trial.[18]

Crawford, however, might overrule White v. Illinois.[19] Among other
crimes, White was convicted of sexually assaulting a four year-old girl. He
appealed on the ground that the trial judge overruled his confrontation
objections to statements identifying White as her assailant which the
victim made to her babysitter, her mother, a police officer, a nurse, and a
doctor. The statements to the babysitter, mother, and officer were admitted under the Illinois hearsay exception for excited utterances; the statements to the nurse and the doctor, under the Illinois hearsay exception for
statements made to medical personnel for purposes of medical diagnosis or
treatment insofar as reasonably pertinent to diagnosis or treatment.[20]
Because the prosecution did not produce the victim, the accused was
unable to cross examine her about her out of court statements. The Court
nonetheless affirmed the accused's convictions, holding that the Confrontation Clause was satisfied where the proffered hearsay, as in *White*, had
sufficient guarantees of reliability to come within firmly rooted exceptions
to the hearsay rule.[21]

Of the statements admitted in *White*, the one most likely to qualify as
a "testimonial statement" under *Crawford* was the victim's statement to
the police officer. Indeed, in *Crawford* the Court singled out this statement in characterizing *White* as the "[o]ne case arguably in tension with
the rule requiring a prior opportunity for cross-examination when the

---

18. Although not involving coconspirators' declarations, People v. Vargas, 178 Cal.App.4th
647, 100 Cal.Rptr.3d 578 (2009), contains an interesting example of the creation of an out of court
statement in which the government was impermissively involved. Vargas was prosecuted for rape.
At the trial, the prosecution, over objection, offered the victim's description of the attack through
a nurse who was required under state law to complete a form designed to elicit the description.
According to the court, "[The nurse] acted as agent of law enforcement." Id. at 660, 100 Cal.Rptr.
at 588. This finding enabled the court to determine that the victim's responses to the nurse
constituted testimonial hearsay under the Sixth Amendment. Id. at 661–662, 100 Cal.Rptr.3d at
588–589.

19. 502 U.S. 346, 112 S.Ct. 736, 116 L.Ed.2d 848 (1992).

20. Id. at 349–350.

21. Id. at 356 and note 8.

proffered statement is testimonial * * *."[22] The victim made the statement to the officer approximately 45 minutes after the attack while the officer was questioning her alone in the kitchen of her home.[23] Although the Court declined to rule whether *Crawford* overruled *White*,[24] as is explained in § 6.06, subsequent decisions by the Court suggest that the statement to the officer may qualify as testimonial.

The Federal Rules of Evidence, like the Illinois rules, provide a hearsay exception for statements made for purposes of medical diagnosis or treatment and describing medical history, including the cause of a medical condition, if the statements are reasonably pertinent to diagnosis or treatment.[25] California's exception is narrower. It applies only if in addition the statements were made by declarants under age twelve describing an act or attempted act of child abuse or neglect.[26] Both exceptions, however, have been used to identify the accused as the perpetrator in child abuse prosecutions.[27] Whether statements offered under these exceptions qualify as testimonial depends in part on whether the United States Supreme Court takes a categorical or case by case approach in determining whether the hearsay offered against the accused qualifies as a testimonial statement. If the Court takes a case by case approach, then whether the statements qualify as testimonial statements may depend on such factors as whether the dominant purpose for giving or taking the statement was to diagnose or treat the patient, or to gather evidence with an eye toward possible use at trial. In Davis v. Washington[28] the Court signaled its willingness to take a case by case approach in some instances.

§ 6.06 CONFRONTATION AND POLICE INTERROGATIONS: THE *DAVIS* RULE

In *Davis*[1] the Court considered two consolidated cases to determine when statements made to law enforcement personnel during a 911 call or at a crime scene qualify as testimonial statements under the Confrontation Clause. The 911 call was taken up in Davis v. Washington and the crime scene statements in Hammon v. Indiana.

---

22. Crawford v. Washington, 541 U.S. 36, 124 S.Ct. 1354, 1368, note 8, 158 L.Ed.2d 177 (2004).

23. White v. Illinois, 502 U.S. 346, 349–350, 112 S.Ct. 736, 116 L.Ed.2d 848 (1992).

24. Crawford v. Washington, 541 U.S. 36, 124 S.Ct. 1354, 1368, note 8, 158 L.Ed.2d 177 (2004).

25. Federal Rule of Evidence 803(3).

26. West's Ann. California Evidence Code § 1253.

27. See, e.g., People of the Territory of Guam v. Ignacio, 10 F.3d 608, 612 (9th Cir. 1993) (upholding the use of a child's statement to a doctor identifying her assailant); People v. Brodit, 61 Cal.App.4th 1312, 1331, 72 Cal.Rptr.2d 154, 165 (1998) (upholding the use of a child's statement to a nurse identifying the accused as her assailant).

28. 547 U.S. 813, 126 S.Ct. 2266, 165 L.Ed.2d 224 (2006).

1. Id.

Davis was charged with a felony violation of a domestic no-contact order. To prove that Davis contacted a former girlfriend in violation of the order, the prosecution offered the tape recording of a 911 exchange between the girlfriend and the operator. In that call, the girlfriend, in response to questions by the operator, identified Davis as the person who was hitting her. The tape was received under Washington's hearsay exception for excited utterances. Because the former girlfriend did not testify at his trial, Davis claimed that his inability to cross examine her about the statements she made to the 911 operator deprived him of his right to confront his accuser. The Washington Supreme Court rejected his claim, concluding that the portion of the 911 tape admitted in evidence did not qualify as testimonial. The United States Supreme Court agreed.[2]

As in *Crawford*, the Court declined to provide a comprehensive definition of testimonial statements. Instead, the Court offered only that definition which it deemed necessary to decide the cases before it:

> Statements are nontestimonial when made in the course of police interrogation under circumstances objectively indicating that the primary purpose of the interrogation is to enable police assistance to meet an ongoing emergency. They are testimonial when the circumstances objectively indicate that there is no such ongoing emergency, and that the primary purpose of the interrogation is to establish or prove past events potentially relevant to later criminal prosecution.[3]

Applying this definition, the Court concluded that the portion of the 911 interrogation at issue did not produce testimonial statements. "[I]ts primary purpose was to enable police assistance to meet an ongoing emergency. [The girlfriend] simply was not acting as a *witness*; she was not *testifying*."[4] The Court, however, acknowledged that a conversation which begins as an interrogation to determine the need for emergency assistance can evolve into testimonial statements once that purpose has been achieved.[5] The Court charged trial judges with the task of redacting or excluding at in limine hearings those portions of statements that have become testimonial.[6]

In *Hammon* the police responded to a domestic disturbance at the home of Hershel and Amy Hammon. The police found Amy alone on the front porch, and she told them that nothing had happened. She gave them permission to enter the house, and the police saw a gas heater emitting flames from a broken front glass and pieces of glass on the floor in front of the heater. Herschel, who was in the kitchen, admitted that he and Amy had been in an argument but that "everything was fine now." One officer remained with Hershel while another asked Amy in the living room "what had occurred." Although Hershel made several attempts to participate in

---

2. Id. at 2277.

3. Id. at 2273 (footnotes omitted).

4. Id. at 2277 (emphasis in the original).

5. Id.

6. Id.

Amy's conversation with the officer, the officers insisted that he remain separate from Amy so they could "investigate what had happened." After hearing Amy's account, the officer had her complete an affidavit in which she stated that Hershel had broken the heater, pushed her onto the broken glass, and hit her.

Hershel was prosecuted for domestic battery and violating the terms of his probation. Although Amy was subpoenaed, she did not appear at the trial. The state called the investigating officer and had him relate Amy's oral statements which the judge admitted under Indiana's hearsay exception for excited utterances.[7] The state also offered Amy's affidavit which the judge admitted under Indiana's hearsay exception for present sense impressions.[8] The Indiana Supreme Court affirmed Herschel's conviction. It found that Amy's oral statements to the investigating officer were not testimonial for Confrontation purposes; it did find that Amy's affidavit was testimonial but that its admission was harmless beyond a reasonable doubt.[9]

The United States Supreme Court reversed. "It is entirely clear from the circumstances that the interrogation was part of an investigation into possibly criminal past conduct. * * * There was no emergency in progress * * *. When the officer questioned Amy for the second time, and elicited the challenged statements, he was not seeking to determine (as in *Davis*) 'what is happening,' but rather 'what has happened.' "[10]

Amy's statements, according to the Court, were much closer to the testimonial statements in *Crawford* than to the nontestimonial statements in *Davis*.

> Both declarants were actively separated from the defendant * * *. Both statements deliberately recounted, in response to police questioning, how potentially criminal past events began and progressed. And both took place some time after the events described were over. Such statements under official interrogation are an obvious substitute for live testimony, because they do precisely *what a witness does* on direct examination; they are inherently testimonial.[11]

In *Davis* the Court also considered the question whether responses to initial inquiries by police at a crime scene can result in testimonial statements. The answer, according to the Court, depends on the circumstances. Exigencies such as the need by police to know who they are dealing with in order to assess the situation, the threat to their own safety, and possible danger to the potential victim "*often* mean that 'initial inquiries' produce nontestimonial statements. But in cases like [*Hammon*], where Amy's statements were neither a cry for help nor the provision of information enabling officers immediately to end a threaten-

---

7. Id. at 2272.

8. Id.

9. Id. at 2273.

10. Id. at 2278.

11. Id. (emphasis in the original) (footnotes omitted).

ing situation, the fact that they were given at an alleged crime scene and were 'initial inquiries' is immaterial."[12]

Davis left unanswered an important question: in determining whether the declarant's statements are testimonial, may judges can take into account the interrogating officers' motive in asking questions and the declarant's motive in answering them?[13] In Michigan v. Bryant,[14] the Court said no:

> An objective analysis of the circumstances of an encounter and the statements and actions of the parties to it provides the most accurate assessment of the "primary purpose of the interrogation." The circumstances in which an encounter occurs—*e.g.,* at or near the scene of the crime versus at a police station, during an ongoing emergency or afterwards—are clearly matters of objective fact. The statements and actions of the parties must also be objectively evaluated. That is, the relevant inquiry is not the subjective or actual purpose of the individuals involved in a particular encounter, but rather the purpose that reasonable participants would have had, as ascertained from the individuals' statements and actions and the circumstances in which the encounter occurred.[15]

The Court's unwillingness to allow judges to consider the participants' actual purpose is surprising. The officers' motivation would be probative of whether they were responding to the exigencies of an emergency or investigating a past crime; similarly, the declarant's motivation would be probative of whether she was crying for help or providing a statement for possible use at a future trial. Although the Court does not explain why such evidence would be irrelevant, its concern must be with limiting extended inquiry into the officers' and the declarants' state of mind.

To help California judges apply *Davis,* the California Supreme Court in People v. Cage[16] formulated six guidelines:

---

12. Id. (emphasis in the original).

13. On one hand, the Court's use of the term "objectively" suggests that neither the declarant's nor the investigating officer's subjective thoughts should count. On the other hand, the Court's emphasis on whether the primary purpose of the interrogation is to enable the police to render emergency aid or prove a past crime suggests that the officer's motive in interrogating the hearsay declarant should matter. Indeed, in finding that the interrogation in *Hammon* gave rise to testimonial statements, the Court emphasized the interrogating officer's testimony that he was seeking to determine "what [had] happened," as opposed to "what [was] happening" as in *Davis.* Id. at 2278. But in the footnote accompanying the definition, the Court seems to shift its focus to the declarant's state of mind. The Court states that even when the statements are the product of police interrogation, "it is in the final analysis the declarant's statements, not the interrogator's questions, that the Confrontation Clause requires us to evaluate." Id. at 2274, note 1. That inquiry appears to make the declarant's motive material. Moreover, in the same footnote, the Court warns that the opinion's emphasis on police interrogations should not imply "that statements made in the absence of any interrogation are necessarily nontestimonial." Id. Since in those circumstances the declarant's motive would seem to be dispositive, the Court suggests once again that the declarant's state of mind should count, at least in some cases.

14. ___ U.S. ___, 131 S.Ct. 1143, 179 L.Ed.2d 93 (2011).

15. Id. at 1156 (footnotes omitted).

16. 40 Cal.4th 965, 155 P.3d 205, 56 Cal.Rptr.3d 789 (2007).

First, * * * the confrontation clause is concerned solely with hearsay statements that are testimonial, in that they are out-of-court analogs, in purpose and in form, of the testimony given by witnesses at trial. Second, though a statement need not be sworn under oath to be testimonial, it must have occurred under circumstances that imparted, to some degree, the formality and solemnity characteristic of testimony. Third, the statement must have been given and taken *primarily* for the *purpose* ascribed to testimony—to establish or prove some past fact for possible use in a criminal trial. Fourth, the primary purpose for which a statement was given and taken is to be determined "objectively," considering all of the circumstances that might reasonably bear on the intent of the participants in the conversation. Fifth, sufficient formality and solemnity are present when, in the nonemergency situation, one responds to questioning by law enforcement officials, where deliberate falsehoods might be criminal offenses. Sixth, statements elicited by law enforcement officials are not testimonial if the primary purpose in giving and receiving them is to deal with a contemporaneous emergency, rather than to produce evidence about past events for possible use at a criminal trial.[17]

Applying these guidelines, the court held the answers which a crime victim had given to a law enforcement officer in a hospital emergency room were testimonial. In response to the officer's questions, the victim identified the defendant as the person who had assaulted him. At the time of the interrogation, the incident that had given rise to the assault had been over for more than an hour, and the victim was no longer in danger of further violence. "[The officer's] clear purpose in coming to speak with [the victim] at this juncture was not to deal with a *present emergency*, but to obtain a fresh account of *past events involving defendant* as part of an inquiry into possible criminal activity. * * * [T]he requisite solemnity was imparted by the potentially criminal consequences of lying to a peace officer."[18]

Applying the same guidelines, the court held that the victim's answer to a doctor's question given in the hospital emergency room was nontestimonial. When the victim arrived at emergency room, the attending doctor asked him, "What happened?" In response, the victim stated that the defendant had cut him.[19] "Objectively viewed, the primary purpose of the question, and the answer, was not to establish or prove past facts for possible criminal use, but to help [the doctor] deal with the immediate medical situation he faced. It was thus akin to the 911 operator's emergency questioning of [the victim] in *Davis*."[20]

---

17. Id. at 984, 155 P.3d at 216, 56 Cal.Rptr.3d at 802 (footnotes omitted; emphasis in the original).

18. Id. at 986, 155 P.3d at 218, 56 Cal.Rptr.3d at 804 (emphasis in the original). In California, it is a misdemeanor to report to a sworn peace officer that a felony or misdemeanor has been committed, knowing the report to be false. See West's Ann. California Penal Code § 148.5.

19. People v. Cage, 40 Cal.4th 965, 986, 155 P.3d 205, 218, 56 Cal.Rptr.3d 789, 805 (2007).

20. Id.

§ 6.07   FORENSIC EVIDENCE AND CONFRONTATION

Crawford raises the question whether the prosecution's use of documentary forensic evidence violates the accused's confrontation rights. The issue arises whenever the prosecution offers fingerprint, autopsy, serology, drug, DNA, and similar reports to link the accused with the crime charged or to prove some other element of the offense. The classic example is the drug analysis report which is offered to prove that the substance taken from the accused is an illegal drug. Establishing that the substance is an illegal drug is one of the elements which the prosecution must prove in order to obtain a conviction. If the technician who performed the drug analysis is not produced at the trial for cross-examination and instead his report is offered in evidence, is the accused deprived of the opportunity to confront a key prosecution witness?

The answer, according to the United States Supreme Court, is yes. In Melendez–Diaz v. Massachusetts,[1] the Court held that the prosecution's use of affidavits by drug analysts to establish that material seized by the police and connected to the defendant was cocaine violated the defendant's confrontation rights.[2] Since the drug analysts' statements amounted to the kind of testimony they would have given against the defendant if called by the prosecution at the drug trial, the Court found that the affidavits comprised testimonial hearsay under *Crawford*. "Absent a showing that the analysts were unavailable to testify at trial *and* that petitioner had a prior opportunity to cross-examine them, petitioner was entitled to 'be confronted with' the analysts at trial."[3]

Prior to *Melendez–Diaz*, the lower courts, both state and federal, were divided over whether the use of forensic reports violated the accused's confrontation rights.[4] Some held that these reports were testimonial, since the reports are prepared for possible use against the accused at the trial.[5] Others, including California's, did not consider these types of reports to be testimonial. These courts emphasized that reports that merely convey a scientific conclusion ("the substance tested turned out to be cocaine") and describe the steps taken to reach the conclusion are not the type of testimonial statements that concerned the Court in *Crawford*.[6] Some of these courts underscored that the preparer of the report is a neutral party who analyzes evidence but is not actively engaged in gathering evidence; these courts also pointed out that forensic reports can exonerate as well as

---

1. 557 U.S. 305, 129 S.Ct. 2527, 174 L.Ed.2d 314 (2009).

2. Id. at 2540.

3. Id. at 2532 (emphasis in the original).

4. See cases cited in People v. Geier, 41 Cal.4th 555, 598, 161 P.3d 104, 134, 61 Cal.Rptr.3d 580, 615 (2007).

5. Id.

6. See Commonwealth v. Verde, 444 Mass. 279, 827 N.E.2d 701 (2005), as recounted in People v. Geier, supra note 4.

incriminate the accused.[7] Some courts favoring admissibility worried about the practicable difficulties that would result if the forensic reports could be excluded on confrontation grounds. The prosecution would be forced to call as witnesses the person or persons who prepared the reports.[8]

In People v. Geier[9] the California Supreme Court aligned itself with those courts favoring the admissibility of forensic reports. At issue was the admissibility of the testimony of a DNA expert who testified that based on the genetic profiles generated by one of her firm's technicians, DNA samples extracted from the victim's vagina matched a sample of the defendant's DNA. The defendant was on trial for the rape and murder of the victim. In describing the procedures used to make the DNA match, the expert "relied entirely on [the technician's] forms, notes and report and at points quoted or paraphrased statements [the technician] had made in those written records, thus introducing them into evidence. * * * The prosecution thus introduced, through [the expert], hearsay statements of a declarant—[the technician]—who was not present at the trial and whom defendant had no prior opportunity to cross-examine."[10]

In holding that the technician's report was not testimonial, the court said that the report did not describe "a past fact related to criminal activity * * * for possible use at a later trial."[11]

> [The technician's observations constituted] a contemporaneous recordation of observable events rather than the documentation of past events. That is, she recorded her observations regarding the receipt of the DNA samples, her preparation of the samples for analysis, and the results of that analysis as she was actually performing those tasks. "Therefore, when [she] made those observations, [she]—like the declarant reporting an emergency in *Davis*—[was] 'not acting as [a] witness; and [was] not testifying.' "[12]

This holding is unlikely to withstand analysis under *Melendez–Diaz*. The United States Supreme Court rejected the dissent's claim that forensic analysts are disinterested unconventional witnesses who are not subject to confrontation.[13] Instead, the Court emphasized the need for the defense to cross examine seemingly neutral forensic experts.

> * * * Forensic evidence is not uniquely immune from the risk of manipulation. According to a recent study conducted under the auspices of the National Academy of Sciences, "[t]he majority of [labora-

---

7. See State v. Forte, 360 N.C. 427, 629 S.E.2d 137 (2006), as recounted in People v. Geier, supra note 4.

8. See State v. Lackey, 280 Kan. 190, 120 P.3d 332 (2005), as recounted in People v. Geier, supra note 4.

9. 41 Cal.4th 555, 598, 161 P.3d 104, 134, 61 Cal.Rptr.3d 580, 615 (2007).

10. Id. at 621, 161 P.3d at 150, 61 Cal.Rptr.3d at 633 (Werdegar concurring opinion).

11. Id. at 605, 161 P.3d at 138, 61 Cal.Rptr.3d at 620.

12. Id.

13. Melendez–Diaz v. Massachusetts, 557 U.S. 305, 129 S.Ct. 2527, 174 L.Ed.2d 314 (2009).

tories producing forensic evidence] are administered by law enforcement agencies, such as police departments, where the laboratory administrator reports to the head of the agency.'' National Research Council of the National Academies, Strengthening Forensic Science in the United States: A Path Forward 6–1 (Prepublication Copy Feb. 2009) (hereinafter National Academy Report). And ''[b]ecause forensic scientists often are driven in their work by a need to answer a particular question related to the issues of a particular case, they sometimes face pressure to sacrifice appropriate methodology for the sake of expediency.'' *Id.*, at S–17. A forensic analyst responding to a request from a law enforcement official may feel pressure—or have an incentive—to alter the evidence in a manner favorable to the prosecution. Confrontation is one means of assuring accurate forensic analysis. While it is true, as the dissent notes, that an honest analyst will not alter his testimony when forced to confront the defendant, *post,* at 10, the same cannot be said of the fraudulent analyst. See Brief for National Innocence Network as *Amicus Curiae* 15–17 (discussing cases of documented ''drylabbing'' where forensic analysts report results of tests that were never performed); National Academy Report 1–8 to 1–10 (discussing documented cases of fraud and error involving the use of forensic evidence). Like the eyewitness who has fabricated his account to the police, the analyst who provides false results may, under oath in open court, reconsider his false testimony. See *Coy* v. *Iowa,* 487 U.S. 1012, 1019 (1988). And, of course, the prospect of confrontation will deter fraudulent analysis in the first place.

Confrontation is designed to weed out not only the fraudulent analyst, but the incompetent one as well.[14]

Significantly, in *Grier* the California Supreme Court observed that merely because a document qualifies as business record does not render it ''nontestimonial since conceivably some such document could contain historical facts.''[15] This view accords with that of the United States Supreme Court in *Melendez–Diaz.* The fact that documentary evidence offered by the prosecution qualifies under the forum's evidence rules as a business or official record does not foreclose an inquiry into whether the evidence constitutes testimonial hearsay under the Sixth Amendment.[16]

In *Melendez–Diaz* the Court also rejected the claim that no confrontation violation occurs where the defendant has the ability to subpoena the hearsay declarant.

[T]hat power—whether pursuant to state law or the Compulsory Process Clause—is no substitute for the right of confrontation. Unlike the Confrontation Clause, those provisions are of no use to the

---

14. Id. at 2536–2537.

15. Id. at 606, note 12, 161 P.3d at 140, note 12, 61 Cal.Rptr.3d at 621, note 12.

16. ''Whether or not they qualify as business or official records, the analysts' statements here—prepared specifically for use at petitioner's trial—were testimony against petitioner, and the analysts were subject to confrontation under the Sixth Amendment.'' Melendez–Diaz v. Massachusetts, 557 U.S. 305, 129 S.Ct. 2527, 2540, 174 L.Ed.2d 314 (2009).

defendant when the witness is unavailable or simply refuses to appear. See, *e.g.*, *Davis*, 547 U.S., at 820 ("[The witness] was subpoenaed, but she did not appear at . . . trial"). Converting the prosecution's duty under the Confrontation Clause into the defendant's privilege under state law or the Compulsory Process Clause shifts the consequences of adverse-witness no-shows from the State to the accused. More fundamentally, the Confrontation Clause imposes a burden on the prosecution to present its witnesses, not on the defendant to bring those adverse witnesses into court. Its value to the defendant is not replaced by a system in which the prosecution presents its evidence via *ex parte* affidavits and waits for the defendant to subpoena the affiants if he chooses.[17]

In Bullcoming v. New Mexico,[18] the Court was faced with the question whether receiving a forensic report through an expert who did not prepare the report or observe the analyst who prepared the report violated the accused's confrontation rights. Bullcoming was prosecuted for driving under the influence of an intoxicating liquor. At the trial, the prosecution offered a report in which the analyst concluded that Bullcoming's blood alcohol level exceeded state limits. The prosecution did not call the analyst; instead, it called the analyst's supervisor and offered the analyst's report as a business record. The Court held that the prosecution's failure to call the analyst deprived the accused of the right to confront his accuser.[19] When an expert opinion is offered, the opposing party should be given the opportunity to assess, among other matters, the expert's qualifications and to determine whether the expert followed appropriate protocols and drew valid conclusions. As the Court observed, without the analyst on the stand, the cross-examiner could not "expose any lapses or lies on the certifying analyst's part."[20]

§ 6.08   FORFEITURE OF CONFRONTATION RIGHTS

In *Davis* the Court acknowledged that domestic violence cases pose special problems because the victims are especially susceptible to intimidation or coercion to discourage their presence at the trial. Although *Davis* would appear to give defendants in these cases a "windfall," the Court emphasized that "one who obtains the absence of a witness by wrongdoing forfeits the constitutional right to confrontation."[1] The Court, however, declined to specify the standard of persuasion that should govern a forfeiture hearing or the kind of evidence the judge can consider in making the forfeiture finding. Instead, the Court simply noted that federal

---

17.   Id. at 2540.

18.   ___ U.S. ___, 131 S.Ct. 2705, 180 L.Ed.2d 610 (2011).

19.   Id. at 2719.

20.   Id. at 2715.

1.   Davis v. Washington, 547 U.S. 813, 833, 126 S.Ct. 2266, 165 L.Ed.2d 224 (2006).

courts and some state courts require the prosecution to prove forfeiture by a preponderance of the evidence.[2] The Court also noted that at least one state court allows the use of hearsay, including the hearsay declarant's statements, at the forfeiture hearing.[3]

In People v. Giles[4] the California Supreme Court was asked to answer the questions which the U.S. Supreme Court declined to answer. Giles was convicted of murdering his former girlfriend. At the trial, the judge admitted a statement the victim had made to a police officer. The officer testified that the victim told him that Giles had said, "If I catch you fucking around I'll kill you."[5] The hearsay was admitted under California Evidence Code § 1370, which establishes an exception for out of court statements relating a threat of physical injury upon the declarant if the judge, among other matters, finds that the declarant is unavailable under § 240 to testify and the statement is trustworthy.[6]

The California Supreme Court affirmed Giles' conviction. Even though the court conceded that the victim's statement was "testimonial" under the Sixth Amendment,[7] it held that Giles had forfeited his right to object to its introduction on confrontation grounds.[8] In reaching its holding, the court laid down important guidelines to help California judges in applying the Sixth Amendment's forfeiture doctrine.

First, a judge should not find that the accused has forfeited his or her right to object on Sixth Amendment grounds unless the prosecution persuades the judge by a preponderance of the evidence that "the witness [is] genuinely unavailable to testify and the unavailability for cross-examination [was] caused by the defendant's intentional criminal act."[9]

Second, in determining whether the prosecution has carried its persuasion burden, the judge may consider the hearsay declarant's statement. But the judge's forfeiture finding may not be based "solely on the unavailable witness's unconfronted testimony; there must be independent corroborative evidence that supports the forfeiture finding."[10]

Third, although relevant, the prosecution does not have to prove that the accused's purpose was to prevent the hearsay declarant from testifying. It is enough for the prosecution to show that the accused's criminal act had the effect of preventing the hearsay declarant from testifying.[11] In this regard, it is immaterial that the criminal act giving rise to the

---

2. Id.

3. Id.

4. 40 Cal.4th 833, 152 P.3d 433, 55 Cal.Rptr.3d 133 (2007).

5. Id. at 839, 152 P.3d at 437, 55 Cal.Rptr.3d at 136.

6. West's Ann. California Evidence Code § 1370.

7. Id. at 841, 152 P.3d at 438, 55 Cal.Rptr.3d at 138.

8. Id. at 855, 152 P.3d at 447, 55 Cal.Rptr.3d at 149.

9. Id. at 854, 152 P.3d at 446, 55 Cal.Rptr.3d at 148.

10. Id.

11. Id. at 849, 152 P.3d at 443, 55 Cal.Rptr.3d at 144.

witness's unavailability at the trial is also the criminal act for which the accused is being tried.[12]

In Giles v. California[13] the United States Supreme Court reversed this aspect of the California court's opinion. The Court held that the Sixth Amendment's forfeiture doctrine requires the prosecution to persuade the judge that the accused's purpose was to prevent the hearsay declarant from testifying.[14] The Court, however, did not specify the standard of persuasion that should govern a forfeiture hearing or the kind of evidence the judge can consider in making the forfeiture finding. Until the Court does so, California judges may continue to apply the more likely than not standard of persuasion and may consider the hearsay declarant's statement in determining whether the prosecution has met its burden.

Where the accused is on trial for murdering the hearsay declarant, additional evidence may enable the prosecution to persuade the judge that the accused did so for the purpose of preventing the victim from testifying. Evidence that the accused had an abusive relationship with the victim might supply the additional proof. As the United States Supreme Court observed:

> Acts of domestic violence often are intended to dissuade a victim from resorting to outside help, and include conduct designed to prevent testimony to police officers or cooperation in criminal prosecutions. Where such an abusive relationship culminates in murder, the evidence may support a finding that the crime expressed the intent to isolate the victim and to stop her from reporting abuse to the authorities or cooperating with a criminal prosecution—rendering her prior statements admissible under the forfeiture doctrine. Earlier abuse, or threats of abuse, intended to dissuade the victim from resorting to outside help would be highly relevant to this inquiry, as would evidence of ongoing criminal proceedings at which the victim would have been expected to testify.[15]

The accused, of course, is still entitled to object on state grounds, including hearsay, to the introduction of the victim's out of court state-

---

12. Id. at 851, 152 P.3d at 445, 55 Cal.Rptr.3d at 146.

13. 554 U.S. 353, 128 S.Ct. 2678, 171 L.Ed.2d 488 (2008).

14. Id. at 367.

15. Id. at 377. In People v. Banos, 178 Cal.App.4th 483, 100 Cal.Rptr.3d 476 (2009), the California Court of Appeal noted that the language employed by the United States Supreme Court allows judges to base their forfeiture finding on one of two distinct grounds: on the basis of evidence showing that the accused intended (1) to prevent the hearsay declarant from reporting the abuse to the authorities or (2) to prevent the declarant from testifying in a criminal proceeding. Id. at 501–502, 100 Cal.Rptr.3d at 491. Either ground would support an inference that the accused's goal was to prevent the declarant from testifying against him.

In *Banos* the court also considered whether the prosecution must prove that the accused's sole motive for his misconduct toward the victim was his desire to prevent her from testifying. The evidence showed that in murdering the victim the accused may have also been moved by his belief that she had been unfaithful to him. The court held that the accused's other motives were immaterial so long as the evidence supported a finding that he also killed the victim to prevent her from testifying against him at a hearing to determine whether he had violated a restraining order directing him to stay away from her. Id. 504, 100 Cal.Rptr.3d at 493.

ment. If the hearsay is inadmissible under the forum's law, the *Giles* forfeiture doctrine cannot be invoked by the prosecution. The doctrine applies only where the accused claims that testimonial hearsay admitted against him under a forum's hearsay exception deprived him of his right under the Sixth Amendment to confront the hearsay declarant. As noted, in People v. Giles, the defendant's hearsay objection was properly overruled because the prosecution offered his former girlfriend's statement under the exception created by § 1370 of the California Evidence Code.

§ 6.09   CONFRONTATION AND NONTESTIMONIAL HEARSAY STATEMENTS

In *Crawford* the Court left open the question whether nontestimonial hearsay offered against the accused is subject to confrontation scrutiny. Although not free of all doubt, *Davis* appears to answer this question in the negative.

> We must decide, therefore, whether the Confrontation Clause applies only to testimonial hearsay; and, if so, whether the recording of a 911 call qualifies. [¶] The answer to the first question was suggested in *Crawford*, even if not explicitly held: "The text of the Confrontation Clause reflects this focus [on testimonial hearsay]. It applies to 'witnesses' against the accused—in other words, those who 'bear testimony.' " * * * [¶] A limitation so clearly reflected in the text of the constitutional provision must fairly be said to mark out not merely its "core" but its perimeter.[1]

The California Supreme Court has interpreted *Davis* as limiting the Confrontation Clause only to testimonial statements.[2] If indeed the reach of the Confrontation Clause is limited to testimonial hearsay, then it will be up to the states to determine whether nontestimonial hearsay should be admissible under their evidence or constitutional rules. The California Constitution[3] and the California Penal Code[4] give the accused the right to confront the witnesses called against them. The California Supreme Court has held that California courts are not bound by federal precedents in

---

1. Davis v. Washington, 547 U.S. 813, 823, 126 S.Ct. 2266, 165 L.Ed.2d 224 (2006). In Whorton v. Bockting, 549 U.S. 406, 127 S.Ct. 1173, 167 L.Ed.2d 1 (2007), the United States Supreme Court noted without limitation that *Crawford* overruled *Roberts*. Id. at 413. Such an unqualified outcome makes it unlikely that the Court would employ a *Roberts*-type analysis in determining the constitutionality of nontestimonial hearsay offered by the prosecution against the accused. Accordingly, the accused may be left with due process as the only federal ground for challenging such evidence. In Michigan v. Bryant, ___ U.S. ___, 131 S.Ct. 1143, 179 L.Ed.2d 93 (2011), the United States Supreme Court acknowledged that the Due Process Clauses of the Fifth and Fourteenth Amendments, not just the Confrontation Clause, can bar some hearsay evidence. Id. at 1162, note 13.

2. People v. Cage, 40 Cal.4th 965, 981, note 10, 155 P.3d 205, 215, note 10, 56 Cal.Rptr.3d 789, 801, note 10 (2007).

3. West's Ann. Cal. Const., Art.1, § 15.

4. West's Ann. Cal. Penal Code § 686(3).

defining the scope of an analogous state constitutional provision.[5] So unless the California courts extend the state constitutional provision to encompass nontestimonial hearsay offered against the accused, *Davis* may have defined the outer limits of the right of confrontation in California prosecutions.[6]

§ 6.10 CONFRONTATION AND MULTIPLE DEFENDANTS

In Bruton v. United States[1] the Court reversed the robbery conviction of a defendant who had been implicated in the crime by his codefendant's extrajudicial confession. Because the codefendant did not take the stand at the joint trial and thus could not be cross examined, the Court held that the admission of the codefendant's confession deprived the defendant of his confrontation rights.[2]

Aranda[3] is California's equivalent of *Bruton*. Until 1990, the California courts held that *Aranda* was violated even if the confessing defendant testified at the joint trial.[4] That year, however, the California Court of Appeal held that the Right to Truth–in–Evidence provision of Proposition

---

5. "[J]ust as the United States Supreme Court bears the ultimate judicial responsibility for determining matters of federal law, this court bears the ultimate judicial responsibility for resolving questions of state law, including the proper interpretation of provisions of the state Constitution." People v. Chavez, 26 Cal.3d 334, 352, 605 P.2d 401, 412, 161 Cal.Rptr. 762, 773 (1980).

6. Extending the state provisions to embrace nontestimonial hearsay would require considering the effect of the Right to Truth-in-Evidence provision of Proposition 8, the Victim's Bill of Rights. Subject to enumerated exceptions, this provision gives parties to California criminal proceedings the state constitutional right not to have relevant evidence excluded. See West's Ann. Cal. Const. Art. I, § 28. The courts have construed the initiative as overriding some California cases affording state criminal defendants rights greater than those provided by the Federal Constitution. See generally § 8.03 infra.

1. 391 U.S. 123, 88 S.Ct. 1620, 20 L.Ed.2d 476 (1968), appeal after remand, 416 F.2d 310 (8th Cir.1969), cert. denied, 397 U.S. 1014, 90 S.Ct. 1248, 25 L.Ed.2d 428 (1970).

2. Id. at 135, 88 S.Ct. at 1628. No *Bruton* error is committed, however, where the confessing codefendant takes the stand and testifies favorably to the accused; in these circumstances, the use of the codefendant's confession does not deny the accused his confrontation rights. Nelson v. O'Neil, 402 U.S. 622, 629–630, 91 S.Ct. 1723, 1727, 29 L.Ed.2d 222 (1971). In addition, no *Bruton* error is committed where the nontestifying codefendant's confession or admissions do not implicate the defendant in the offenses charged. People v. Olguin, 31 Cal.App.4th 1355, 1374–1375, 37 Cal.Rptr.2d 596, 605 (1994).

Because *Bruton* is believed to apply only to trials, *Bruton* is inapplicable to California preliminary hearings held to determine whether probable cause exists to bind the accused over for trial. Hearsay may be offered against the accused at California preliminary hearings. Accordingly, a declarant's confession implicating a nondeclarant may be offered against the nondeclarant at the preliminary hearing even if the declarant does not take the stand. People v. Miranda, 23 Cal.4th 340, 349, 96 Cal.Rptr.2d 758, 764, 1 P.3d 73, 78 (2000).

But where *Bruton* error is committed, it is immaterial that the jury was instructed to consider the confession only against the confessing defendant. Jurors cannot be expected to abide by such an instruction. Bruton v. United States, supra at 135–136, 88 S.Ct. at 1628.

3. People v. Aranda, 63 Cal.2d 518, 47 Cal.Rptr. 353, 407 P.2d 265 (1965).

4. People v. Boyd, 222 Cal.App.3d 541, 561, 271 Cal.Rptr. 738, 751 (1990) and cases cited therein.

8 abrogated *Aranda*.[5] Proposition 8, an initiative approved by the California electorate in June 1982, gives parties to a criminal proceeding a state constitutional right to introduce relevant evidence.[6] Since the testifying codefendant's confession is relevant, its use is mandated by the initiative unless barred by the Federal Constitution. Accordingly, the admissibility of a codefendant's confession at a joint trial in now governed by *Bruton* and not by *Aranda*.[7]

Bruton does not require the exclusion of a nontestifying codefendant's confession when all references to the accused have been redacted and the jury warned to use the confession only against the confessing defendant.[8] Nor does *Bruton* require exclusion of the nontestifying codefendant's confession in bench trials when offered only against the confessing defendant.[9] Unlike jurors, judges are presumed capable of disregarding those portions of the nontestifying codefendant's confession implicating the defendant.[10] Such confessions are therefore admissible in California bench trials.[11] Moreover, *Bruton* error can be avoided even in a joint trial by

---

5. Id. at 562, 271 Cal.Rptr. at 751. The California Supreme Court, however, has not determined the extent to which Proposition 8 may have abrogated *Aranda*. People v. Mitcham, 1 Cal.4th 1027, 1045, note 6, 5 Cal.Rptr.2d 230, 242, note 6, 824 P.2d 1277, 1289, note 6 (1992), cert. denied, 506 U.S. 925, 113 S.Ct. 349, 121 L.Ed.2d 263 (1992).

6. For a discussion of Proposition 8 and its impact on California criminal evidence, see § 3.07 supra.

7. People v. Boyd, 222 Cal.App.3d 541, 562, 271 Cal.Rptr. 738, 751 (1990).

8. Richardson v. Marsh, 481 U.S. 200, 211, 107 S.Ct. 1702, 1709, 95 L.Ed.2d 176, 188 (1987). But "[r]edactions that simply replace a name with an obvious blank space or a word such as 'deleted' or a symbol or other similarly obvious indications of alteration * * * leave statements that, considered as a class, so closely resemble *Bruton*'s unredacted statements that, in our view, the law must require the same result." Gray v. Maryland, 523 U.S. 185, 118 S.Ct. 1151, 1155, 140 L.Ed.2d 294 (1998).

Moreover, even substituting a symbol or a neutral pronoun for the nonconfessing defendant's name does not necessarily satisfy the Confrontation Clause. Though such substitution "will make the confession less directly incriminating, * * * it does not invariably provide sufficient assurance that the average reasonable juror will be able to obey an instruction to disregard the confession when considering the guilt of the nondeclarant." People v. Fletcher, 13 Cal.4th 451, 465, 53 Cal.Rptr.2d 572, 580, 917 P.2d 187, 195 (1996). "Rather, the efficacy of this form of editing must be determined on a case by case basis in light of the other evidence to be presented at the trial. This editing will be deemed insufficient to avoid a confrontation violation if, despite the editing, reasonable jurors could not avoid drawing the inference that the defendant was the coparticipant designated by symbol or neutral pronoun." Id. at 456, 53 Cal.Rptr.2d at 574, 917 P.2d at 189.

Applying this test, the *Fletcher* court held that the use of a neutral pronoun ("another person") and a limiting instruction did not prevent a confrontation violation. "Because [a witness] placed Moord in Fletcher's company moments after the fatal shooting, reasonable jurors could not avoid drawing the inference that Moord was the unnamed person mention in Fletcher's [confession]." Id. at 469, 53 Cal.Rptr.2d at 582–583, 917 P.2d at 197–198. See also People v. Archer, 82 Cal.App.4th 1380, 1389–1390, 99 Cal.Rptr.2d 230, 236 (2000) (Omitting any mention of the nonconfessing defendant will not prevent a confrontation violation where the redacted confession nonetheless establishes that the confessing defendant was assisted in committing the crime by the nonconfessing defendant.).

See also People v. Hampton, 73 Cal.App.4th 710, 86 Cal.Rptr.2d 665 (1999), cert. denied, 529 U.S. 1042, 120 S.Ct. 1541, 146 L.Ed.2d 354 (2000), where the appellate court rejected the accused's claims that the redactions in his codefendant's confession failed to meet the requirements of Richardson v. Marsh: "As redacted. [the codefendant's] confession nowhere states that he participated in the robbery with any other person." Id. at 720, 86 Cal.Rptr.2d at 672.

9. See, e.g., Rogers v. McMackin, 884 F.2d 252, 256–257 (6th Cir.1989), cert. denied Rogers v. Hills, 493 U.S. 1061, 110 S.Ct. 877, 107 L.Ed.2d 960 (1990); Cockrell v. Oberhauser, 413 F.2d 256, 258 (9th Cir.1969).

10. People v. Walkkein, 14 Cal.App.4th 1401, 1408, 18 Cal.Rptr.2d 383, 387 (1993).

11. Id. at 1408, 18 Cal.Rptr.2d at 387. Because juvenile jurisdictional hearings are tried to the court, *Bruton* does not require the exclusion of confessions by nontestifying codefendants offered in these proceedings. In re Jose, 21 Cal.App.4th 1470, 1479, 27 Cal.Rptr.2d 55, 60 (1994).

according the codefendants separate juries, with each jury being excused when necessary to avoid exposure to the inadmissible evidence.[12]

Crawford[13] is consistent with some aspects of *Bruton*. Confessions resulting from police interrogations can qualify as "testimonial statements."[14] Accordingly, admitting a codefendant's confession to the police implicating the accused in the crime charged can violate *Crawford* as well as *Bruton*, unless the confessing codefendant takes the stand and is subject to cross-examination by the accused.[15] A codefendant, who claims the privilege against self-incrimination and declines to take the stand, is by definition unavailable as a witness.[16] If the codefendant exercises the privilege, then *Bruton* would preclude the use of the codefendant's confession against the accused. *Crawford*, however, would allow the prosecution to use the confession if the accused had previously been afforded an opportunity to cross examine the codefendant under oath about the statements offered at the trial. Since such opportunities are rare, this conflict between *Bruton* and *Crawford* is unlikely to arise.

A different situation is presented if the codefendant confesses not to the police but to a friend and implicates the accused. Such a confession is unlikely to be testimonial under *Crawford*. If the codefendant and the accused are tried jointly, *Crawford* would not bar the use of the confession against the codefendant and the accused if the confessing codefendant does not testify. *Bruton*, however, would bar its use against the accused, unless *Bruton*'s application to these circumstances has not survived *Crawford*.

The example assumes that under the forum's hearsay rules the prosecution can offer the confession against both the codefendant and the accused. If the confession is admissible only against the codefendant, then it would be received with an instruction directing the jurors to consider the confession only against the codefendant. Since the confession would not be received against the accused, *Crawford* should not be implicated in the first place. Accordingly, *Bruton* should apply and the judge should prevent the use of the confession even against the confessing codefendant, unless the judge deletes all references to the accused.

Because judges are presumed capable of disregarding those portions of the nontestifying codefendant's confession implicating the accused in the

---

12. People v. Harris, 47 Cal.3d 1047, 1070–1076, 255 Cal.Rptr. 352, 365–370, 767 P.2d 619, 632–637 (1989).

13. 541 U.S. 36, 124 S.Ct. 1354, 158 L.Ed.2d 177 (2004).

14. Id. at 1364. Where the nontestifying codefendant's confession is "testimonial," its use against the nontestifying codefendant with an instruction directing the jurors not to consider the confession against the accused will not cure the violation of the accused's *Bruton* and *Crawford* rights. See People v. Song, 124 Cal.App.4th 973, 981, 22 Cal.Rptr.3d 118, 124 (2004).

15. Where the nontestifying codefendant's confession is stripped of all references to the accused, its use does not implicate the accused's confrontation rights under *Bruton* or *Crawford*. See People v. Stevens, 41 Cal.4th 182, 199, 158 P.3d 763, 775, 59 Cal.Rptr.3d 196, 210 (2007), cert. denied, 552 U.S. 1118, 128 S.Ct. 921, 169 L.Ed.2d 762 (2008).

16. See, e.g., West's Ann. California Evidence Code § 240(a)(1); Federal Rule of Evidence 804(a)(1).

crime charged, *Bruton* does not require exclusion of a nontestifying codefendant's confession in California bench trials. *Crawford*, however, does not distinguish between bench and jury trials. Still, *Crawford* should not be implicated in bench trials when the confession is offered not against the accused, but only against the confessing codefendant. In contrast, in jury trials a limiting instruction directing jurors to consider the confession only against the confessing codefendant will not prevent *Bruton* error. Jurors, as the the Court acknowledged in *Bruton*, cannot be expected to abide by such an instruction.[17] As long as the Court continues to adhere to this view of jurors, *Crawford* should not reverse this aspect of *Bruton*.

Declarations against interest. Would characterizing a nontestifying codefendant's confession as a declaration against penal interest avoid *Bruton*'s limitations? In Lilly v. Virginia[18] the accused was charged with a number of offenses, including robbery and murder. An accomplice called by the state declined to testify on Fifth Amendment grounds. The state then offered the accomplice's confession in which he admitted participating in the robbery but claimed that the accused was the one who committed the killing. The confession was received against the accused as a declaration by the accomplice against penal interest under Virginia's evidence rules.

The accused appealed his convictions on the ground that admitting the confession violated his confrontation rights. The United States Supreme Court agreed. Noting that the question whether out of court statements fall within a firmly rooted exception for Confrontation Clause purposes is a federal question, a plurality held that accomplices' confessions that inculpate a criminal defendant are not within a firmly rooted exception to the hearsay rule.[19] The admissibility of these confessions according to *Lilly* depends on whether the prosecution can demonstrate that they contain such "particularized guarantees of trustworthiness" that adversarial testing through cross-examination would add little, if anything, to their reliability.[20]

Lilly did not implicate *Bruton* directly because the accused and the accomplice were tried separately. Still, *Lilly* is not of much help to federal prosecutors in joint trials. In Williamson v. United States[21] the United States Supreme Court held that only those statements that are disserving of the declarant's interest are admissible under the federal hearsay exception for statements against interest.[22] Accordingly, a codefendant's statement, "I am taking the cocaine to Atlanta for Williamson," could not be offered in a federal prosecution against Williamson, even if it qualifies

---

17.　391 U.S. 123, 135–136, 88 S.Ct. 1620, 20 L.Ed.2d 476 (1968).

18.　527 U.S. 116, 119 S.Ct. 1887, 144 L.Ed.2d 117 (1999).

19.　Id. at 134, 119 S.Ct. at 1899.

20.　Id. at 136, 119 S.Ct. at 1900.

21.　512 U.S. 594, 114 S.Ct. 2431, 129 L.Ed.2d 476 (1994).

22.　Id. at 599, 114 S.Ct. at 2435.

as a declaration against the declarant's penal interest.[23] Neither could such a declaration be offered against Williamson in a California prosecution. In People v. Leach[24] the California Supreme Court, like the United States Supreme Court, limited California's hearsay exception for declarations against interest to those statements disserving only of the declarant's interest.[25]

Given these statutory limitations, federal and California criminal defendants should not have to rely on *Crawford* to exclude declarations against penal interest that implicate them in the crime charged. But some divisions of the California Court of Appeal have ignored *Leach* and set out the kinds of factors trial judges should consider in determining the admissibility of such declarations. In People v. Greenberger,[26] for example, the California Court of Appeal held that in determining whether the declarations were made under circumstances that render them particularly worthy of belief, the trial judge must look to the totality of the circumstances in which the declarations were made, including whether the declarant spoke from personal knowledge, the declarant's motivation in making the statements, and the words actually used by the declarant.[27]

> [T]he least reliable circumstance is one in which the declarant has been arrested and attempts to improve his situation by deflecting criminal responsibility onto others. * * * [T]he most reliable circumstance is one in which the conversation occurs between friends in a noncoercive setting that fosters uninhibited disclosures. * * * When examining what was actually said by the declarant special attention must be paid to any statements that tend to inculpate the nondeclarant. This is so because a statement's content is most reliable in that portion which inculpates the declarant * * * and least reliable in that portion that shifts responsibility. * * * This is not to say that a statement that incriminates the declarant and also inculpates the nondeclarant cannot be specifically disserving of the declarant's penal interest. Such a determination necessarily depends upon a careful analysis of what was said and the totality of the circumstances.[28]

Lilly's and *Greenberger*'s approach should not have survived *Crawford*. To the extent that the declarations against interest offered in those

---

23. For further discussion of this point, see § 9.02 infra.

24. 15 Cal.3d 419, 124 Cal.Rptr. 752, 541 P.2d 296 (1975), cert. denied, 414 U.S. 926, 94 S.Ct. 224, 38 L.Ed.2d 160 (1973).

25. Id. at 441, 124 Cal.Rptr. at 766, 541 P.2d at 310.

26. 58 Cal.App.4th 298, 68 Cal.Rptr.2d 61 (1997).

27. Id. at 329, 68 Cal.Rptr.2d at 77.

28. Id. at 335, 68 Cal.Rptr.2d at 81. See also People v. Duke, 74 Cal.App.4th 23, 87 Cal.Rptr.2d 547 (1999), where the reviewing court upheld the admission against the accused of a declaration against penal interest in which the declarant implicated himself as well as the accused in the crime for which the accused was on trial. The reviewing court held that the accused's confrontation rights had not been violated because the circumstances attending the making of the declaration satisfied the particularized guarantees of trustworthiness required by *Lilly*. Id. at 32, 87 Cal.Rptr.2d at 553. The court, however, failed to consider the declaration's inadmissibility as a statutory matter under *Leach*. Perhaps, the accused failed to object to the use of the declaration on this ground.

cases would qualify as "testimonial statements" under *Crawford*, they would be inadmissible over a confrontation objection unless (1) the prosecution produces the hearsay declarant for cross-examination by the accused or (2) the prosecution establishes the declarant's unavailability as a witness and shows that the accused had a prior opportunity to cross examine the declarant about the statement offered at the trial. Of course, if the hearsay declarant is available to testify, a California prosecutor cannot rely on the hearsay exception for declarations against interest in the first place. The unavailability of the declarant as a witness is required by the California exception.[29]

Some California cases hold that the *Leach* limitation can be circumvented where the portion of the declaration against interest inculpating the accused itself falls within another hearsay exception, for example, the exception for party admissions.[30] But these cases may not have survived *Crawford* if the declarations qualify as "testimonial evidence." Although party admissions do not implicate the Confrontation Clause, their use by the prosecution in this instance still depends on the admissibility over a confrontation objection of the out of court declaration of which they are a part. If the declaration as a whole qualifies as a "testimonial statement," the fact that the part incriminating the accused falls within a firmly rooted exception should no longer be determinative of whether the accused's confrontation rights have been violated.

Adoptive admissions. Suppose that in A's presence, B in response to police questioning states, "Yes, I was involved in the robbery, but A was the mastermind." Upon hearing B's answer, A says, "Yes, that's true." A and B are then tried jointly for robbery. The prosecution calls the police officer who questioned B, and he repeats B's answer and A's response. A moves to strike B's out of court statement on hearsay grounds, but the judge overrules the objection, ruling that the statement falls within the hearsay exception for adoptive admissions. B does not take the stand, and A then moves to strike the officer's testimony on *Bruton* and *Crawford* grounds. Should the judge grant these motions?

In People v. Castille[31] the California Court of Appeal held that even if B's statement qualifies as "testimonial" under *Crawford*, the motion to strike on *Crawford* grounds should be denied. Citing California Supreme Court precedent, the lower court held that *Crawford* was not triggered because B's out of court statement implicating A in the crime was not offered for the truth but only to "supply meaning" to A's conduct in the face of B's accusation.[32] This analysis is plainly wrong; the point of the adoptive admissions exception to the hearsay rule is to allow the fact

---

29. West's Ann. California Evidence Code § 1230.

30. See, e.g., People v. Wilson, 17 Cal.App.4th 271, 275, 21 Cal.Rptr.2d 420, 422 (1993); see also § 9.01 infra.

31. 129 Cal.App.4th 863, 29 Cal.Rptr.3d 71 (2005), cert. denied, 546 U.S. 1192, 126 S.Ct. 1380, 164 L.Ed.2d 86 (2006).

32. Id. at 878, 29 Cal.Rptr.3d at 82–83.

finder to consider the out of the court statement for the truth of the matter stated.[33]

The court compounded its error by extending this flawed analysis to the *Bruton* objection. In holding that A's motion to strike should be denied, the court observed: "[Appellant misapplies] the law. In such a situation, the statement of defendant [B] implicating defendant [A] is admitted not for its truth, but to supply meaning to [A]'s response adopting [B]'s statement as his own."[34] Since in the court's mistaken view B's confession implicating A was not admitted for the truth, *Bruton* was inapplicable.

Spontaneous statements. Suppose that, instead of confessing to the police, A tells his girlfriend that he and B committed a crime. At their joint trial, the prosecutor calls the girlfriend and offers A's statement as an excited utterance. A does not testify. Should the judge sustain B's *Bruton* objection? In People v. Smith[35] the reviewing court held that the trial judge did not err in failing to exclude the statement. Finding that the trial judge did not abuse his discretion in receiving A's statement as an excited utterance, the court held that B's confrontation rights were not violated: A's statement to his girlfriend did not qualify as a testimonial statement because A did not make his statement in a "formal proceeding" or in response to "structured police questioning."[36]

QUESTIONS AND PROBLEMS

1. To be meaningful, confrontation must mean the right to cross examine one's accusers under oath in the presence of the fact finder. Therefore, in determining whether the use of hearsay exceptions against the accused violates the Right of Confrontation, the United States Supreme Court starts with the presumption of a violation. Discuss.

2. To vouchsafe the Right of Confrontation, the United States Supreme Court requires the prosecution either to produce the hearsay declarant for cross-examination or to show the declarant's unavailability. True or false?

3. Prior to *Crawford*, hearsay offered against the accused did not offend the Confrontation Clause when offered under a "firmly rooted" exception even if the hearsay declarant did not testify at the trial. True or false?

4. Prior to *Crawford*, hearsay offered against the accused under a novel hearsay exception did not offend the Confrontation Clause if the prosecution showed that the hearsay was particularly trustworthy. True or false?

5. In demonstrating that hearsay offered against the accused under a novel exception was particularly trustworthy, the prosecution could point to

---

33. For an extended critique of the court's analysis of adoptive admissions, see § 7.02 infra.

34. 129 Cal.App.4th 863, 878, 29 Cal.Rptr.3d 71, 82–83 (2005), cert. denied, 546 U.S. 1192, 126 S.Ct. 1380, 164 L.Ed.2d 86 (2006).

35. 135 Cal.App.4th 914, 38 Cal.Rptr.3d 1 (2005).

36. Id. at 924, 38 Cal.Rptr.3d at 8.

other evidence received at the trial that corroborated the hearsay. True or false?

6. Under *Crawford*, hearsay offered against the accused at the trial will require a confrontation analysis only if the hearsay qualifies as a "testimonial statement." True or false?

7. In *Crawford* the U.S. Supreme Court declined to offer a comprehensive definition of "testimonial statements." At a minimum, however, the Court said that testimony given at a preliminary hearing, before a grand jury, or at a former trial qualifies as a "testimonial statement," as may a statement given in the course of a police interrogation. True or false?

8. "Testimonial statements" do not embrace personal admissions. Neither do coconspirators' declarations qualify as testimonial statements in the absence of evidence that government agents were involved in their production. True or false?

9. Testimonial statements do not include out of court statements that are not offered for the truth of the matter asserted. True or false?

10. Testimonial statements offered by the prosecution against the accused will not violate the Confrontation Clause if the out of court declarant is produced for cross-examination by the accused under oath before the fact finder. True or false?

11. If the maker of an out of court testimonial statement is not produced for cross-examination by the accused, over a confrontation objection the prosecution can nonetheless offer the statement against the accused for the truth of the matter stated if the prosecution persuades the judge of the maker's unavailability to testify and shows that the accused had been afforded a prior opportunity to cross examine the maker about the statement offered at the trial. True or false?

12. (a) California Evidence Code § 1370 creates a hearsay exception for statements by crime victims describing the infliction or the threat of infliction of physical injuries upon the victim if the victim is unavailable to testify, the statement was made at or near the time of the infliction or the threat of infliction of the physical injuries, and the statement was made in writing or electronically recorded or was made to a physician, nurse, paramedic, or law enforcement officer. At Jones' trial for murder, the prosecution relies on § 1370 in offering a 911 recording in which the victim says, "A couple of days ago, Jones said to me, 'I will kill you if I catch you with another man.'" Would receiving the statement violate the Confrontation Clause?

(b) At the same trial, the prosecution calls a doctor who testifies that the victim was brought to the emergency room with a serious knife wound and that when he asked the victim, "What happened?", she said, "Jones stabbed me when he caught me with another man." Would receiving the statement under § 1370 violate the Confrontation Clause?

13. A prosecutor who claims that the defendant has forfeited her right to object to hearsay on Sixth Amendment grounds must persuade the judge that the declarant's unavailability to testify at the trial is the result of wrongdoing undertaken by defendant for the purpose of silencing the declarant. True or false?

14. The defendant is prosecuted for possessing cocaine. To prove that the substance taken from the defendant was cocaine, the prosecution offers in evidence a report prepared by a qualified government chemist in which the chemist states that the substance brought to the laboratory "tested positive for cocaine". The prosecution offers the report as an official record. The defendant does not contest the report's admissibility under the official records exception to the hearsay rule but objects on the ground that the report should be excluded as constituting inadmissible testimonial hearsay under the Sixth Amendment. The judge should overrule the defendant's objection. True or false?

15. Assume the same facts as in Question 14. The prosecution offers the report as an official record during its direct examination of the chemist's supervisor. In response to the prosecutor's questions, the supervisor testifies that the chemist is qualified to do the test and is required to follow the protocol printed on the report. In addition, the supervisor testifies that the protocol, if followed, will yield valid results. The defendant objects on confrontation grounds and is given permission to take the supervisor on voir dire in aid of his objection. On voir dire, the supervisor testifies that he was not present when the analyst conducted the test. The judge should overrule the defendant's confrontation objection. True or false?

16. *Bruton* error is committed if A and B are tried jointly for robbery and the prosecution offers against A a confession in which A said, "B and I committed the robbery," and A fails to take the stand in his case-in-chief. True or false?

17. *Bruton* error can be avoided if the trial judge instructs the jurors to consider the confession only in determining the guilt of A, the confessing defendant. True or false?

18. No *Bruton* error is committed if A takes the stand and can be cross examined by B. True or false?

19. No *Bruton* error is committed if the confession does not implicate B directly or indirectly. True or false?

CALIFORNIA EVIDENCE CODE

§ 240. "Unavailable as a witness"

(a) Except as otherwise provided in subdivision (b), "unavailable as a witness" means that the declarant is any of the following:

(1) Exempted or precluded on the ground of privilege from testifying concerning the matter to which his or her statement is relevant.

(2) Disqualified from testifying to the matter.

(3) Dead or unable to attend or to testify at the hearing because of then existing physical or mental illness or infirmity.

(4) Absent from the hearing and the court is unable to compel his or her attendance by its process.

(5) Absent from the hearing and the proponent of his or her statement has exercised reasonable diligence but has been unable to procure his or her attendance by the court's process.

(6) Persistent in refusing to testify concerning the subject matter of the declarant's statement despite having been found in contempt for refusal to testify.

(b) A declarant is not unavailable as a witness if the exemption, preclusion, disqualification, death, inability, or absence of the declarant was brought about by the procurement or wrongdoing of the proponent of his or her statement for the purpose of preventing the declarant from attending or testifying.

(c) Expert testimony which establishes that physical or mental trauma resulting from an alleged crime has caused harm to a witness of sufficient severity that the witness is physically unable to testify or is unable to testify without suffering substantial trauma may constitute a sufficient showing of unavailability pursuant to paragraph (3) of subdivision (a). As used in this section, the term "expert" means a physician and surgeon, including a psychiatrist, or any person described by subdivision (b), (c), or (e) of Section 1010.

The introduction of evidence to establish the unavailability of a witness under this subdivision shall not be deemed procurement of unavailability, in absence of proof to the contrary.

FEDERAL RULES OF EVIDENCE

Rule 804. Exceptions to the Rule Against Hearsay—When the Declarant Is Unavailable as a Witness

(a) Criteria for Being Unavailable. A declarant is considered to be unavailable as a witness if the declarant:

(1) is exempted from testifying about the subject matter of the declarant's statement because the court rules that a privilege applies;

(2) refuses to testify about the subject matter despite a court order to do so;

(3) testifies to not remembering the subject matter;

(4) cannot be present or testify at the trial or hearing because of death or a then-existing infirmity, physical illness, or mental illness; or

(5) is absent from the trial or hearing and the statement's proponent has not been able, by process or other reasonable means, to procure:

(A) the declarant's attendance, in the case of a hearsay exception under Rule 804(b)(1) or (6); or

(B) the declarant's attendance or testimony, in the case of a hearsay exception under Rule 804(b)(2), (3), or (4).

But this subdivision (a) does not apply if the statement's proponent procured or wrongfully caused the declarant's unavailability as a witness in order to prevent the declarant from attending or testifying.

(b) The Exceptions. The following are not excluded by the rule against hearsay if the declarant is unavailable as a witness:

(1) *Former Testimony.* Testimony that:

(A) was given as a witness at a trial, hearing, or lawful deposition, whether given during the current proceeding or a different one; and

(B) is now offered against a party who had—or, in a civil case, whose predecessor in interest had—an opportunity and similar motive to develop it by direct, cross-, or redirect examination.

(2) *Statement Under the Belief of Imminent Death.* In a prosecution for homicide or in a civil case, a statement that the declarant, while believing the declarant's death to be imminent, made about its cause or circumstances.

(3) *Statement Against Interest.* A statement that:

(A) a reasonable person in the declarant's position would have made only if the person believed it to be true because, when made, it was so contrary to the declarant's proprietary or pecuniary interest or had so great a tendency to invalidate the declarant's claim against someone else or to expose the declarant to civil or criminal liability; and

(B) is supported by corroborating circumstances that clearly indicate its trustworthiness, if it is offered in a criminal case as one that tends to expose the declarant to criminal liability.

(4) *Statement of Personal or Family History.* A statement about:

(A) the declarant's own birth, adoption, legitimacy, ancestry, marriage, divorce, relationship by blood, adoption, or marriage, or similar facts of personal or family history, even though the declarant had no way of acquiring personal knowledge about that fact; or

(B) another person concerning any of these facts, as well as death, if the declarant was related to the person by blood, adoption, or marriage or was so intimately associated with the person's family that the declarant's information is likely to be accurate.

(5) [*Other Exceptions.*] [Transferred to Rule 807.]

(6) *Statement Offered Against a Party That Wrongfully Caused the Declarant's Unavailability.* A statement offered against a party that wrongfully caused—or acquiesced in wrongfully causing—the declarant's unavailability as a witness, and did so intending that result.

Rule 807.   Residual Exception

(a) In General. Under the following circumstances, a hearsay statement is not excluded by the rule against hearsay even if the statement is not specifically covered by a hearsay exception in Rule 803 or 804:

(1) the statement has equivalent circumstantial guarantees of trustworthiness;

(2) it is offered as evidence of a material fact;

(3) it is more probative on the point for which it is offered than any other evidence that the proponent can obtain through reasonable efforts; and

(4) admitting it will best serve the purposes of these rules and the interests of justice.

(b) Notice. The statement is admissible only if, before the trial or hearing, the proponent gives an adverse party reasonable notice of the intent to offer the statement and its particulars, including the declarant's name and address, so that the party has a fair opportunity to meet it.

CHAPTER 7

EXCEPTIONS TO THE HEARSAY RULE: ADMISSIONS

■ ■ ■

Table of Sections

---

§ 7.01   ADMISSIONS IN GENERAL

A party's out of court statements may be offered by the opposing party for the truth of the matter stated as an exception to the hearsay rule.[1] Known as admissions by the party opponent, these statements implicate the hearsay rule because the matters they assert are offered to prove some aspect of the proponent's case or to disprove some aspect of the declarant's case.[2] For example, in Estate of Anderson[3] the petitioner moved a probate court for an order entitling him to one-half of the decedent's estate on the theory that he was the decedent's spouse. To disprove this claim, the estate was entitled to offer a declaration previously made by the petitioner in which he had stated that he had never been married.[4]

---

1.   West's Ann.California Evidence Code § 1220. For the federal treatment of admissions as evidence of the matter asserted, see § 7.11 infra.

2.   The admission must be probative of some proposition that is properly provable in the case. Otherwise, it would not be relevant. See West's Ann. California Evidence Code § 210; Federal Rule of Evidence 401.

3.   60 Cal.App.4th 436, 70 Cal.Rptr.2d 266 (1997).

4.   Id. at 441, 70 Cal.Rptr.2d at 269.

Some courts miss this point and assume that any statement made by a party is admissible under the exception, even if it is not offered for the truth.[5] Section 1220, however, is inapplicable unless the statement is offered for the truth of the matters stated.[6]

Admissions are received for the truth for historical reasons. At Common Law, a party's statements were admissible against the party before the crystallization of the hearsay rule.[7] Moreover, the usual justification for excluding hearsay—to insure the opponent an opportunity to cross examine the hearsay declarant under oath in the presence of the fact finder—does not apply in the case of personal admissions. Since the objecting party is the hearsay declarant, he can hardly complain about the lack of an opportunity to cross examine himself.[8] The fact that a party opponent's statements can be offered through any witness having first hand knowledge of the statements does not affect this analysis. The party opponent can always cross examine that witness as well as take the stand to explain or deny the statements.[9] Thus, the dangers posed by the unrestrained use of hearsay are simply not present when the proponent offers the party opponent's own statements or admissions.[10]

The absence of these dangers probably accounts for a related rule: party admissions are admissible as an exception to the hearsay rule even if the statements would be inadmissible if made for the first time at the hearing.[11] In particular, neither the personal knowledge requirement nor the opinion rule applies to admissions.[12] A party's statement admitting the cause of an accident is admissible against that party even if the party learned about the cause from an employee.[13] A party's opinion conceding

---

5. See, e.g., People v. Guerra, 37 Cal.4th 1067, 1123, 129 P.3d 321, 363, 40 Cal.Rptr.3d 118, 168 (2006), cert. denied, 549 U.S. 1182, 127 S.Ct. 1149, 166 L.Ed.2d 998 (2007) and cases cited therein.

6. See West's Ann. California Evidence Code § 1220.

7. See § 7.11 infra.

8. West's Ann. California Evidence Code § 1220 (comment).

9. Id.

10. The Code overlooks the fact that admissions can embrace statements made by persons other than the party. Where an admission consists of a statement made, say, by a coconspirator who is not produced as a witness, the opposing party is denied the opportunity to cross examine the declarant under oath and in the presence of the fact finder. In these circumstances the justification for receiving admissions for the truth of the matter stated must rest on other grounds. For a discussion of these grounds, see § 7.11 infra.

11. West's Ann.California Evidence Code § 1220 (comment) ("The statement need not be one which would be admissible if made at the hearing."). See also the Advisory Committee Note to Federal Rule of Evidence 801(d)(2) in which the committee stresses that admissions have traditionally been free from the "restrictive influences of the opinion rule and the rule requiring firsthand knowledge * * *."

12. 6 California Law Revision Commission, Reports, Recommendations, and Studies, Appendix 484 (1964). Federal Rule of Evidence 801(d)(2) (Advisory Committee Note).

13. See, e.g., Reed v. McCord, 160 N.Y. 330, 54 N.E. 737 (1899); see also Abbett Elec. Corp. v. Sullwold, 193 Cal.App.3d 708, 714, note 8, 238 Cal.Rptr. 496, 500, note 8 (1987) ("[A]dmissions by a party are admissible over foundational [such as lack of personal knowledge] and hearsay objections."). Presumably, a party will not make statements based on information furnished by others unless the party has good reason for believing that the information is reliable.

liability for an accident is admissible even if the proponent makes no effort to comply with the requirements of the opinion rule.[14]

Another important feature of admissions is that the admitting party need not have known that the statement was against interest when made. In Krajewski v. Western & Southern Life Ins. Co.[15] the beneficiary of a life insurance company sued the insurer to compel payment of death benefits. The company resisted payment on the ground that the insured had falsely claimed that he did not abuse alcohol at the time he applied for the life insurance policy. To prove this allegation, the company offered statements which the beneficiary made in divorce proceedings and in which she described the insured's heavy drinking habits. The beneficiary's declarations in the divorce proceedings were held to be admissions even though those declarations, being in support of her divorce action, were in her interest at the time she made them.[16]

QUESTIONS AND PROBLEMS

1. Wife sues Husband for divorce. At the hearing to determine the division of community property, she testifies that Husband said to her, "The cars are yours." Husband objects on the ground of hearsay. Should the judge sustain the objection?

2. In 2000, in completing a loan application in which he pledged the family home as collateral, Husband placed a $500,000 value on the home. In 2010, Wife offered the loan application in evidence at divorce proceedings as an "admission" by Husband of the value of the home. Husband objected on the ground that at the time he completed the loan application it was in his interest to inflate the value of the home. Should the judge sustain the objection?

3. Husband also objects on the ground that he was not "qualified" to place a fair market value on the home. Should the judge sustain this objection?

Whether the person supplying the information to the admitting party must have first hand knowledge of the subject matter is controversial. Weinstein would construe the Federal Rules of Evidence to include such a requirement. Weinstein & Berger, Weinstein's Evidence Manual ¶ 15.02[04] (1987). Contra: Mahlandt v. Wild Canid Survival & Research Center, Inc., 588 F.2d 626 (8th Cir.1978). Under the Code, such a requirement can be inferred from the section governing the admissibility of multiple hearsay. If the person supplying the information learned of it from someone else, then the section would require the proponent to show that the statement containing the information also falls within a hearsay exception. See West's Ann.California Evidence Code § 1201.

14. See, e.g., Shields v. Oxnard Harbor Dist., 46 Cal.App.2d 477, 116 P.2d 121 (1941). But opinions by an insurer's employees that an insurance contract insures against a particular risk do not operate as authorized admissions. "It is well settled that the interpretation of an insurance policy is a *legal* rather than a *factual* determination * * *. Consistent therewith, it has been held that opinion evidence is completely irrelevant to interpret an insurance contract." Chatton v. National Union Fire Ins. Co., 10 Cal.App.4th 846, 865, 13 Cal.Rptr.2d 318, 331 (1992) (emphasis in the original). See also Quan v. Truck Ins. Exchange, 67 Cal.App.4th 583, 602, 79 Cal.Rptr.2d 134, 145 (1998) (Insurer's employees' memos stating that the insurer had a duty to defend could not constitute authorized admissions; whether or not the insurer had a duty to defend was question of law calling for a legal determination.).

15. 241 Mich. 396, 217 N.W. 62 (1928).

16. Id. at 400, 217 N.W. at 63.

§ 7.02 ADOPTIVE ADMISSIONS

Admissions made by others can be offered against a party for the truth of the matter asserted if the proponent satisfies the judge that the opponent adopted the admissions as his own statements.[1] No problem is encountered when the party expressly adopts the statement as his own. An example is the defendant's response to the plaintiff's accusation in Shields v. Oxnard Harbor Dist.[2] that it looked as though the defendant was "in the wrong."[3] In reply, the defendant said, "Yes, I guess it does."[4]

Difficulties arise, however, when the proponent relies on conduct other than the opposing party's words to prove the opposing party's adoption of statements made by others. If in *Shields* the defendant had remained silent, would his silence have manifested his adoption or his belief in the truth of the plaintiff's accusation? Under the Code, a judge should not allow the jurors to consider the statement unless the proponent satisfies the judge that a reasonable juror could find that it was the opponent's intention to adopt the statement as his own.[5] Where silence is relied upon, the judge may consider whether under the circumstances the opposing party would have protested if the accusation were untrue.[6] This is an invitation to apply a negligence standard, since judges are likely to ask whether a reasonable person in the opponent's position would have protested if the accusation was false.[7] If the judge answers the question in the affirmative, the jurors may consider the accusation and the opponent's response.[8] But the opponent is entitled to an instruction directing the jurors to disregard the out of court declaration unless they first find that the opponent adopted the accusation as his own.[9]

---

1. West's Ann. California Evidence Code § 1221; Federal Rule of Evidence 801(d)(2)(B).

2. 46 Cal.App.2d 477, 116 P.2d 121 (1941).

3. Quoted in Johnson v. Bimini Hot Springs, 56 Cal.App.2d 892, 903, 133 P.2d 650, 655 (1943).

4. Id.

5. West's Ann.California Evidence Code § 403 (comment). See also People v. Davis, 36 Cal.4th 510, 535, 31 Cal.Rptr.3d 96, 116, 115 P.3d 417, 435 (2005): "In determining whether a statement is admissible as an adoptive admission, a trial court must first decide whether there is evidence sufficient to sustain a finding that: (a) the defendant heard and understood the statement under circumstances that normally would call for a response; and (b) by words or conduct, the defendant adopted the statement as true."

6. Baldarachi v. Leach, 44 Cal.App. 603, 610, 186 P. 1060, 1061–1062 (1919). See also Federal Rule of Evidence 801(d)(2) (Advisory Committee Note). The circumstances include whether the party heard the accusation. The failure to protest an accusation is irrelevant unless the accusation was heard. See People v. Mayfield, 14 Cal.4th 668, 741, 60 Cal.Rptr.2d 1, 42, 928 P.2d 485, 526 (1997), cert. denied, 522 U.S. 839, 118 S.Ct. 116, 139 L.Ed.2d 68 (1997).

7. See, e.g., People v. Pic'l, 114 Cal.App.3d, 824, 858–859, 171 Cal.Rptr. 106, 125 (1981), disapproved on other grounds, People v. Kimble, 44 Cal.3d 480, 244 Cal.Rptr. 148, 749 P.2d 803 (1988), and cases cited therein. See also People v. Riel, 22 Cal.4th 1153, 1189, 96 Cal.Rptr.2d 1, 29, 998 P.2d 969, 995 (2000) (" 'When a person makes a statement in the presence of a party to an action under circumstances that would normally call for a response if the statement were untrue, the statement is admissible for the limited purpose of showing the party's reaction to it. [Citations.] His silence, evasion, or equivocation may be considered as a tacit admission of the statements made in his presence.' " Id. (quoting from Estate of Neilson, 57 Cal.2d 733, 746, 22 Cal.Rptr. 1, 9, 371 P.2d 745, 753 (1962))).

8. See BAJI 2.26, Admissions Implied from Silence or Evasion (Fall 2007 Edition); CALJIC 2.71.5, Adoptive Admission—Silence, False or Evasive Reply to Accusation (Fall 2006 Edition).

In criminal cases, the accused's silence in the face of official accusations can be problematical. Is the accused manifesting an intention to adopt the accusation or is the accused asserting the right to remain silent? Deference to the accused's privilege against self-incrimination has led some courts to construe the accused's silence as invoking the privilege and to prevent prosecutors from using the accused's silence as adoptive admissions.[10] Prosecutors, however, might seek to use the accused's silence in other ways. For example, to discredit the accused's story on direct examination, a prosecutor might attempt on cross to show that the accused failed to give the police the same explanation even though afforded an opportunity to do so.[11] Prosecutors, however, cannot pose such questions of defendants who failed to give the police any explanation because they asserted their *Miranda* rights.[12] If the judge erroneously overrules the defense objection to such a question, *Doyle* error is committed.[13] No such error occurs, however, where the prosecution uses only the accused's pre-*Miranda* silence.[14]

A party who challenges the accusation obviously does not adopt it, and the accusation and the party's response cannot be received for the truth of the matter stated.[15] Where the party's response is equivocal, some authorities maintain that the response should not be viewed as adopting the accusation unless the response is more probative of assent than of

---

9. West's Ann. California Evidence Code § 403(c). For the adoptive admission exception to apply, a direct accusation is not essential. People v. Fauber, 2 Cal.4th 792, 851, 9 Cal.Rptr.2d 24, 60, 831 P.2d 249, 285 (1992), cert. denied, 507 U.S. 1007, 113 S.Ct. 1651, 123 L.Ed.2d 272 (1993). It is enough for the accused to remain silent or respond evasively after hearing conversations implicating him in criminal activity. Id.

10. See People v. Savala, 10 Cal.App.3d 958, 89 Cal.Rptr. 475 (1970), and cases cited therein. See also People v. Riel, 22 Cal.4th 1153, 1189–1190, 96 Cal.Rptr.2d 1, 29, 998 P.2d 969 (2000).

11. Cf. People v. Champion, 134 Cal.App.4th 1440, 1451, 37 Cal.Rptr.3d 122, 130 (2005) (holding that to rebut the defendant's claim on direct examination that he had never been given the opportunity to tell his side of the story, the prosecution may offer evidence showing that during the defendant's custodial interrogation a police officer afforded the defendant such an opportunity).

12. Doyle v. Ohio, 426 U.S. 610, 617, 96 S.Ct. 2240, 2244, 49 L.Ed.2d 91 (1976). The rationale appears to be that the evidentiary use of the accused's silence violates due process because the state through the *Miranda* warnings has implicitly assured the accused that no penalty will be exacted if he exercises his privilege to remain silent.

13. People v. Evans, 25 Cal.App.4th 358, 367–368, 31 Cal.Rptr.2d 20, 24 (1994). See also Wainwright v. Greenfield, 474 U.S. 284, 292, 106 S.Ct. 634, 639, 88 L.Ed.2d 623 (1986) (holding that the prosecution may not attempt to disprove the accused's claim that he was insane at the time of the offense by evidence that the accused, following his arrest, understood the *Miranda* warnings and invoked the rights to remain silent and to counsel). But see People v. Jones, 15 Cal.4th 119, 172, 61 Cal.Rptr.2d 386, 419, 931 P.2d 960, 993 (1997), cert. denied, 118 S.Ct. (1997) (holding that where in support of an insanity defense the accused offered evidence of his inability to communicate while in jail, the prosecutor was entitled to rebut with evidence that when first placed in custody the accused understood and asserted his *Miranda* rights).

14. Jenkins v. Anderson, 447 U.S. 231, 100 S.Ct. 2124, 65 L.Ed.2d 86 (1980).

15. In some circumstances, however, a party's statement that is inadmissible for the truth of the matter stated may still be used to impeach or otherwise discredit the party's claims. See § 5.04 supra.

dissent.[16] But if assent is one of the inferences that reasonably can be drawn from the circumstances surrounding the accusation and the response, then the proponent should be entitled to have the fact finder resolve the controversy regarding the party's intent. The issue whether a party intends to adopt an accusation presents only a sufficiency question.[17]

Adoptive admissions and confrontation. The exception for adoptive admissions allows the proponent to offer the declarant's out of court statement for the truth of the matter asserted. Some courts, however, miss this point and hold that the use of adoptive admissions against the accused does not raise confrontation issues. People v. Combs[18] is illustrative. The prosecution offered a confession in which the declarant, in the presence of the accused, said that the accused had instructed her to strike the victim. Because the accused remained silent, the trial judge instructed the jurors not to consider the declarant's out of court statement against the accused unless they first found that the accused had adopted the declarant's accusation. In holding that the declarant's statement had been properly received as an adoptive admission, the California Supreme Court noted that the declarant's out of court statement had been received for a nonhearsay purpose:

> Having concluded that Purcell's statements were admissible under the adoptive admissions rule, the trial court submitted to the jury the question whether defendant's conduct actually constituted an adoptive admission. The jury was instructed how to consider the evidence, including that "[e]vidence of such an accusatory statement is not received for the purpose of proving its truth, but only as it supplies meaning to the silence and conduct of the accused in the face of it. Unless you should find that the defendant's silence and conduct at the time indicated an admission that the accusatory statement was true, you should entirely disregard the statement." (CALJIC No. 2.71.5.).[19]

But if that had been the case, there would have been no need to resort to the adoptive admissions exception to the hearsay rule. More likely what the court meant was that under the Evidence Code the jurors were precluded from considering the out of court statement for the truth (that the accused instructed the declarant to strike the victim) unless they first found that the accused had adopted the declarant's statement as his own. And in deciding whether the accused's silence amounted to a tacit admission of the truth of the accusation, the jurors could consider the circumstances surrounding the making of the declaration, including the accused's failure to respond to the accusation.

---

16. See Pawlowski v. Eskofski, 209 Wis. 189, 244 N.W. 611 (1932) and authorities cited therein.

17. See People v. Davis, 36 Cal.4th 510, 535, 31 Cal.Rptr.3d 96, 116, 115 P.3d 417, 435 (2005). Whether or not the response adopts the accusation presents a preliminary question that should be resolved under the standard described in § 403 of the California Evidence Code and Federal Rule 104(b). These rules set out a sufficiency standard. West's Ann. California Evidence Code § 403(a); Federal Rule of Evidence 104(b).

18. 34 Cal.4th 821, 22 Cal.Rptr.3d 61, 101 P.3d 1007 (2004), cert. denied, 545 U.S. 1107, 125 S.Ct. 2549, 162 L.Ed.2d 281 (2005).

19. Id. at 844, 22 Cal.Rptr.3d at 80, 101 P.3d at 1022.

Because the out of court declarant (Purcell) was not called as a witness by the prosecution, the accused claimed that he was deprived of his Sixth Amendment right to confront his accuser. But the court's mistaken observation that the accusation was not offered for the truth but only for the limited purpose of supplying meaning to the accused's silence allowed the court to reject the accused's confrontation claim: "Thus, because Purcell's statements were admitted for a nonhearsay purpose, defendant's Sixth Amendment right was not implicated."[20]

The hearsay issue in *Combs* would have been clearer if instead of saying that the accused ordered her to strike the victim, the declarant had said, "You killed the victim." Then the hearsay use of the out of court declaration would have been obvious. The jurors could have considered the declaration as an adoptive admission only if they found that by his silence the accused meant to say, "Yes, I did." The Sixth Amendment's implications also would have been clearer. The prosecution's failure to produce the declarant meant that the accused was not afforded an opportunity to cross examine his accuser about the statement accusing him of killing the victim.

Taking their lead from *Combs*, some lower courts hold that the use of adoptive admissions against the accused does not violate the accused's confrontation rights when the out of declarant is not produced at the trial for cross-examination. No Sixth Amendment violation occurs because of the mistaken view that the declaration is not offered to prove the truth of the matter stated (e.g., that the accused killed the victim) but only to "supply meaning" to the defendant's response.[21]

Defendants, of course, cannot object on Sixth Amendment grounds to their own statements when offered by the prosecution for the truth. Defendants cannot complain about an inability to cross examine themselves. They can always take the stand and deny or explain statements attributed to them. When a defendant adopts statements made by others as his own, those statements occupy the same status as personal admissions insofar as the hearsay rule is concerned. Adopting someone's statement as your own is the equivalent of making the statement. Seizing on this aspect of adoptive admissions, the California Supreme Court in People v. Roldan[22] offered an alternative ground for holding that the use of adoptive admissions against the accused does not violate the Confrontation Clause:

> Because the statements were adopted by defendant, they become, in effect, his statements, and, "[b]eing deemed the defendant's own admissions, we are no longer concerned with the veracity or credibility of the original declarant." (People v. Silva (1988) 45 Cal.3d 604,

---

20. Id.

21. See, e.g., People v. Castille, 129 Cal.App.4th 863, 878, 29 Cal.Rptr.3d 71, 82–83 (2005), cert. denied, 546 U.S. 1192, 126 S.Ct. 1380, 164 L.Ed.2d 86 (2006). For an extended discussion of "testimonial statements" and the Confrontation Clause, see § 6.03 et seq. supra.

22. 35 Cal.4th 646, 110 P.3d 289, 27 Cal.Rptr.3d 360, cert. denied, 546 U.S. 986, 126 S.Ct. 570, 163 L.Ed.2d 477 (2005).

624, 247 Cal.Rptr. 573, 754 P.2d 1070; see People v. Combs (2004) 34 Cal.4th 821, 842–843, 22 Cal.Rptr.3d 61, 101 P.3d 1007.) In sum, admission of defendant's adoptive admissions did not violate the confrontation clause as interpreted in Crawford v. Washington.[23]

Whether or not this rationale satisfies *Crawford*'s concerns is contestable. Adoptive admissions differ from personal admissions in that someone other than the accused made the statement. Unless the prosecution produces the hearsay declarant for cross-examination, the accused is deprived of the opportunity to cross examine the declarant. Affording the accused an opportunity to take the stand to explain why he didn't "adopt" the accusation will not confer the same benefits as cross examining the hearsay declarant before the jurors. But unlike *Combs'* explanation, at least *Roldan*'s rationale acknowledges the unquestioned hearsay aspects of adoptive admissions.

QUESTIONS AND PROBLEMS

1.   Plaintiff sued Defendant for injuries Plaintiff claimed to have suffered while walking on Defendant's dock. Plaintiff called Defendant's supervisor who testified as follows:

> Plaintiff: Were you present at the time the dock collapsed under me?
>
> Supervisor: Yes, I was.
>
> Plaintiff: Who else was present?
>
> Supervisor: My employer, Defendant.
>
> Plaintiff: What did you do after the dock collapsed?
>
> Supervisor: I checked the area where the dock collapsed.
>
> Plaintiff: What did you find?
>
> Supervisor: That rotten boards had given way under your weight.
>
> Plaintiff: Did you tell anyone about this?
>
> Supervisor: Yes, I turned toward you and Defendant and said, "It looks as though those rotten boards finally gave way."
>
> Plaintiff: Did Defendant say anything?
>
> Supervisor: Yes, he said, "Yes it does."
>
> Defendant: Move to strike on grounds of hearsay.
>
> Plaintiff: Adoptive admission, your Honor.
>
> Judge: ?

2.   Compare with:

> Plaintiff: Did you tell anyone about this?
>
> Supervisor: Yes, I turned toward you and Defendant and said, "It looks as though those rotten boards finally gave way."
>
> Plaintiff: Did Defendant say anything?

---

23.   Id. at 711, note 25 110 P.3d at 332, note 25, 27 Cal.Rptr.3d at 412, note 25.

Supervisor: Yes, he said, "No, it doesn't."

Defendant: Move to strike on grounds of hearsay.

Plaintiff: Adoptive admission, your Honor.

Judge: ?

3. Compare with:

Plaintiff: Did you tell anyone about this?

Supervisor: Yes, I turned toward you and Defendant and said, "It looks as though those rotten boards finally gave way."

Plaintiff: Did Defendant say anything?

Supervisor: No, he just looked at me.

Defendant: Move to strike on grounds of hearsay.

Plaintiff: Adoptive admission, your Honor.

Defendant: There's no evidence of adoption. Plaintiff cannot prove by a preponderance of the evidence that I adopted my supervisor's statement.

Judge: ?

4. Do you agree with the California courts that the use of adoptive admissions against the accused poses no hearsay problem and, therefore, no confrontation problems even when the out of court declarant is not produced for cross-examination? In answering these questions, assume that the accused is on trial for murder and the prosecution calls a witness who testifies that the accused remained silent after being confronted by a man in a blue shirt who yelled at the accused, "You killed the victim!" Assume that the prosecution does not call the man in the blue shirt to testify.

§ 7.03 AUTHORIZED ADMISSIONS

Admissions made by others can be offered against a party if the proponent satisfies the judge that the opponent authorized the declarant to make the damaging statement.[1] Though the question of authorization is only one of sufficiency,[2] the absence of direct evidence showing that a party expressly authorized the declarant to make the admission accounts for many decisions denying admissibility.[3] Luman v. Golden Ancient

---

1. West's Ann.California Evidence Code § 1222; Federal Rule of Evidence 801(d)(2)(C).

2. West's Ann.California Evidence Code § 403 and comment; Federal Rule of Evidence 104(b).

3. See, e.g., Kimic v. San Jose–Los Gatos Interurban Ry., 156 Cal. 379, 104 P. 986 (1909); Luman v. Golden Ancient Channel Mining Co., 140 Cal. 700, 74 P. 307 (1903); Durkee v. Central Pac. R.R., 69 Cal. 533, 11 P. 130 (1886); Shaver v. United Parcel Service, 90 Cal.App. 764, 266 P. 606 (1928); Baker v. Western Auto Stage Co., 48 Cal.App. 283, 192 P. 73 (1920); Morgan v. Regents of the University of Cal., 88 Cal.App.4th 52, 70, 105 Cal.Rptr.2d 652, 666 (2000). However, the courts do not insist on evidence of an express authorization in the case of attorneys and their clients. Presumably, because an attorney is authorized to speak for her client, some courts hold that, in the absence of fraud, the admissions of an attorney in open court are binding on the client. See In re Rebekah R., 27 Cal.App.4th 1638, 1649, 33 Cal.Rptr.2d 265, 271 (1994) and cases cited therein. Moreover, an attorney's admissions do not have to be made in open court. Even concessions made by an attorney in a letter written on a client's behalf can constitute an authorized admission. See, e.g., Nissel v. Subscribing Underwriters at Lloyd's of London, 62

Channel M. Co.[4] is illustrative. In holding that an agent's statement was not admissible against his employer, the court noted:

> Haskins, the superintendent of the mine, had no power to bind his employer * * * by admissions as to the cause of the accident than had Smith, the man operating the lever and brake. He was not the defendant corporation, and did not represent it for the purpose of making admissions as to the cause of the accident that had already occurred. If he made an admission as to such cause, he was not in doing so performing on behalf of the defendant corporation any duty by law imposed upon it, and was not, as to such admission, the representative of his employer.[5]

A few decisions circumvent the need to produce direct evidence of authority to make the admission by finding the agent's statement to be admissible as an excited utterance.[6] Others find the needed authorization from evidence that the declarant had been authorized to speak on matters embracing the admission. In W.T. Grant Co. v. Superior Court[7] a retailer was prosecuted for selling used television sets as new. The retailer objected to evidence that one of its managers had stated that selling used sets as new was "company policy."[8] In upholding the use of the statement against the retailer, the court said that the manager's statement amounted to "an admission by an agent made while acting within the scope of his employment."[9] As a manager, the agent had the authority to fix the terms of the merchandise offered for sale. That authority, in the court's view, included the manager's statements regarding the policy governing the sale of used sets.[10]

Grant's approach is intriguing. The California Law Revision Commission acknowledged that the courts' insistence on proof that a party had expressly authorized a declarant to make an admission deprived the

---

Cal.App.4th 1103, 1108, note 7, 73 Cal.Rptr.2d 174, 177, note 7 (1998) (In a letter to the insurer, the insured's attorney conceded that the insured's agent left a car containing the insured property—jewels—unattended, a circumstance precluding coverage under the insurance policy.).

4. 140 Cal. 700, 74 P. 307 (1903).

5. Id. at 709–710, 74 P. at 311. See also Thompson v. County of Los Angeles, 142 Cal.App.4th 154, 169, 47 Cal.Rptr.3d 702, 713 (2006) (upholding the trial judge's ruling that the plaintiff had failed to produce any evidence that the defendant county had authorized a consultant to speak on its behalf: " 'The fact that the County hires someone to be a consultant as to making an analysis, an investigation, and let's say also making recommendations regarding a variety of police practices, including canine practices, doesn't make that person authorized to make an admission.' Reiterating its conclusion, the trial court further stated: '[The consultant] is authorized to give us the results of his analysis and investigation, including recommendations to us, and to tell the public at the same time. That isn't the same as saying he is authorized to speak for us which is what an authorized admission is.' "). See also O'Neill v. Novartis Consumer Health, Inc., 147 Cal.App.4th 1388, 1403, 55 Cal.Rptr.3d 551, 563 (2007) (holding that mere fact that an employee had been authorized to prepare and sign minutes containing admissions did not support an inference that the employer had authorized the employee to make the admissions).

6. See, e.g., Dillon v. Wallace, 148 Cal.App.2d 447, 306 P.2d 1044 (1957), and cases cited therein.

7. 23 Cal.App.3d 284, 100 Cal.Rptr. 179 (1972).

8. Id. at 286–287, 100 Cal.Rptr. at 180.

9. Id.

10. Id.

exception of much of its usefulness.[11] The Commission noted that similar limitations in other jurisdictions had moved the framers of the Model Code of Evidence and the Uniform Rules of Evidence to adopt a provision admitting statements concerning matters within the scope of the declarant's agency and made before the termination of the agency relationship.[12] But this approach, which seems to be the one used by the *Grant* court, was not enacted by the California Legislature.

Under the Code, however, the authority of the declarant to make the admission does not need to be express; it can be implied.[13] Indeed, under the Code the question of the declarant's authority to speak is to be determined by reference to the law of agency.[14] To the extent, then, that agency principles permit inferring the declarant's authority to speak from the circumstances attending the declaration, including the declarant's position, *Grant* is not necessarily inconsistent with the Code.[15] This issue, however, does not have to be reached in federal courts, for Congress enacted the provision which the Legislature rejected. The Federal Rules also define an admission as a statement that "was made by the party's agent or employee on a matter within the scope of that relationship and while it existed".[16]

The California Legislature did adopt a provision, § 1224, that can help some parties who do not have much evidence of the declarant's authority to speak for the opponent. If, under the substantive law that

---

11. 6 California Law Revision Commission, Reports, Recommendations and Studies, Appendix 485–489 (1964).

12. Id. at 489.

13. West's Ann.California Evidence Code § 1222 and comment.

14. Whether the declarant had the authority to make the statement "is to be determined in each case under the substantive law of agency." West's Ann.California Evidence Code § 1222 (comment). Accord: O'Mary v. Mitsubishi Electronics America, Inc., 59 Cal.App.4th 563, 571, 69 Cal.Rptr.2d 389, 395 (1997).

15. Other cases recognize that an employee's authority to speak can be inferred from the employee's position as well as from the subject matter of the employee's declaration. See O'Mary v. Mitsubishi Electronics America, 59 Cal.App.4th 563, 574, 69 Cal.Rptr.2d 389, 396 (1997) (In an age discrimination suit, a vice-president had the implied authority to inform his managers that the person responsible for the defendant's U.S. operations made a statement "about getting rid of managers who were over 40 and replacing them with younger, more aggressive managers.") and cases cited therein. An employee, however, loses whatever authority he had to speak for his principal once his employment is terminated. Admissions by an ex-employee do not bind the employer. Myricks v. Lynwood Unified School Dist., 74 Cal.App.4th 231, 239 note 12, 87 Cal.Rptr.2d 734, 740 note 12 (1999).

16. Federal Rule of Evidence 801(d)(2)(D). As the Advisory Committee noted, "Since few principals employ agents for the purpose of making damaging statements, the usual result [is] exclusion of the evidence." Id. (Advisory Committee Note). Accordingly, the drafters opted for the generous treatment accorded to agent's statements under the Federal Rules. Id.

A federal judge, moreover, may take the agent's out of court declaration into account in determining whether the agent was authorized to make the statement or whether the agent's statement concerned a matter within his or her scope of employment and was made during the existence of the relationship. Id. Although using the declaration for these purposes violates the hearsay rule, federal judges are permitted to consider inadmissible, unprivileged evidence in determining the existence of preliminary facts. See Federal Rule of Evidence 104(a). On the other hand, a federal judge may not rely on the out of court statement alone to determine the existence of the preliminary facts. Federal Rule of Evidence 801(d)(2) requires some independent evidence to establish the agent's authority or the employment relationship and its scope.

applies to the action, the liability of the opponent depends in whole or in part upon the liability of the declarant, then evidence of a statement made by the declarant is as admissible against the opponent as it would be if offered against the declarant in an action involving that liability.[17]

Labis v. Stopper[18] illustrates how § 1224 can be used. The plaintiff sued a painting contractor for injuries she received when one of the contractor's painters moved a drop cloth while the plaintiff was walking on it. To prove that the painter moved the drop cloth without first looking, she offered a statement in which the painter told an investigating police officer that he was not aware that anyone was on the drop cloth when he moved it.[19] The contractor's liability depended in part on the painter's breach of the duty of care he owed the plaintiff; consequently, since the painter's statement would have been admissible against him as an admission, it was admissible against the contractor under § 1224 for the truth of the matter stated.[20]

In some instances, § 1224 can confer a benefit on the plaintiff without according the defendant a similar advantage. Suppose that in *Labis* the plaintiff had died of her injuries and the action had been brought by her survivor as a wrongful death action. Suppose further that prior to her death the plaintiff had said that she had walked around a sawhorse designed to keep pedestrians off the drop cloth. The statement would not be admissible against the survivor as an admission by the party opponent, since the decedent is not a party in the wrongful death action. Nor would the statement be admissible under § 1224, since the section contemplates the use of the statement against defendants, not plaintiffs. To help rectify this imbalance, the Code includes a hearsay exception for some statements made by the deceased in wrongful death actions. Under § 1227, statements made by the deceased are as admissible against the survivor as they would have been against the deceased in an action brought by the deceased.[21] Similarly, in actions brought by parents to recover for injuries to their children, the children's statements are as admissible against the parents as they would have been against the children in an action brought by the children.[22] These sections permit the

---

17. West's Ann.California Evidence Code § 1224.

18. 11 Cal.App.3d 1003, 89 Cal.Rptr. 926 (1970). Although § 1224 would appear to apply to any case involving the liability of an employer under the doctrine of respondeat superior, 6 California Revision Commission, Reports, Recommendations, and Studies, Appendix 495 (1964), the California Supreme Court, citing lack of precedent, refused to give that construction to § 1224. Markley v. Beagle, 66 Cal.2d 951, 59 Cal.Rptr. 809, 429 P.2d 129 (1967). The *Labis* court in turn declined to follow *Markley,* holding that "it would be an unfair extension of the true rule of *Markley* to broaden its language beyond its holding * * *." Labis v. Stopper, supra, at 1005, 89 Cal.Rptr. at 927.

19. 11 Cal.App.3d at 1004–1005, 89 Cal.Rptr. at 926, 927.

20. Id. Section 1224 would not have helped the prosecution in the *Grant* case. The provision is limited to civil actions. West's Ann.California Evidence Code § 1224.

21. West's Ann.California Evidence Code § 1227.

22. West's Ann.California Evidence Code § 1226. For a similar provision permitting the declarations of predecessors in interest of property to be admitted against the successors, see West's Ann.California Evidence Code § 1225.

In some instances, hearsay statements by children who have been abused sexually may be offered for the truth of the matter stated in order to comply with the foundational requirements

use of the statements even though the parties against whom they are offered in no way authorized the declarants to make the statements.

QUESTIONS AND PROBLEMS

1. The major obstacle to using the authorized admissions exception to the hearsay rule has been the courts' insistence on evidence that the party opponent expressly authorized the declarant to speak on the subject of the declaration. True or false?

2. The Rules overcome the limitations on the admissibility of authorized admissions by creating a hearsay exemption for statements made by an employee of the opponent if the statements concern a matter within the scope of the declarant's employment and were made during the employment relationship. True or false?

3. The *Grant* case can be read as an attempt by the California courts to adopt the federal approach to the admissibility of an employee's extra judicial declarations by dispensing with the need of having the proponent establish the employee's express authority to speak on the subject matter of the declarations. Discuss.

4. In some circumstances, the limitations of the authorized admissions exception to the hearsay rule can be overcome in California by applying § 1224. Under this section, an out of court declarant's statements can be offered against the party opponent if the liability of the opponent depends in whole or in part upon the liability of the declarant and the declaration would be admissible against the declarant as an admission in an action against her. True or false?

When § 1224 applies, the admissibility of the out of court statement does not depend on whether the party against whom offered authorized the hearsay declarant to make the statement. True or false?

5. Plaintiff sues Defendant for personal injuries Plaintiff claims she suffered when one of Defendant's trucks struck her. Plaintiff calls the truck driver who testifies in a California court as follows:

> Plaintiff: Why didn't you stop the truck?
>
> Truck Driver: Because the brakes failed.
>
> Plaintiff: Prior to the accident, were you aware that your truck had a brake problem?
>
> Truck Driver: Yes.
>
> Plaintiff: Did you tell anyone at the company about the brake problem?
>
> Truck Driver: Yes, I said to Defendant, "My truck has a brake problem."
>
> Defendant: Hearsay. Move to strike.

---

for the introduction of the confessions of the persons accused of abusing the children. See West's Ann.California Evidence Code § 1228 for a list of the conditions that must be satisfied for the children's hearsay statements to be received.

Plaintiff: Authorized admission.

Defendant: He made the statement to me, not "for" me.

Judge: ?

6. Would your ruling be different if the trial were held in a federal court?

§ 7.04　COCONSPIRATORS' DECLARATIONS

In stark contrast with authorized admissions, neither the Code nor the Federal Rules requires the proponent to show that the opposing party authorized a coconspirator to make damaging statements on his behalf. Such authorization is presumed for purposes of admitting the coconspirator's declaration if certain conditions are met. These conditions relate principally to the circumstances attending the making of the declaration.

In California, the proponent must show that the coconspirator made the declaration while participating in a conspiracy to commit a crime or civil wrong and in furtherance of the conspiracy.[1] The proponent must also show that the coconspirator made the declaration prior to or during the time that the opponent was participating in the conspiracy.[2] Similarly, the Federal Rules require the proponent to show that the declaration was made by the coconspirator during the course and in furtherance of the conspiracy. And though the Rules seemingly require the proponent to show that at the time the declaration was made the declarant was a coconspirator of the party opponent,[3] case law holds that, as in California, declarations made prior to the time the party joined the conspiracy are admissible against the party.[4] In neither jurisdiction are the declarations of a conspirator made after the conspiracy has ended binding on the other conspirators.[5]

The major differences between the California and federal approaches to coconspirators' declarations concern the standard that must be met in

---

1. West's Ann.California Evidence Code § 1223. Statements not in furtherance of the conspiracy are outside the exception because they are not the acts "of the conspiracy for which the party, as a coconspirator, is legally responsible." Id. (comment). Underlying this concept is the notion that conspirators act as agents for each other only with respect to acts and statements that promote the agreed upon criminal enterprise. See Federal Rule of Evidence 801(d)(2)(E) (Advisory Committee Note). Accordingly, where a coconspirator's explanation of check kiting to a bank lawyer was not in furtherance of the conspiracy to convert bank funds, the explanation did not fall within the hearsay exception for coconspirators' declarations. Bank of California, N.A. v. Pan American Tire Corp., 132 Cal.App.3d 843, 183 Cal.Rptr. 470 (1982).

2. West's Ann.California Evidence Code § 1223.

3. Federal Rule of Evidence 801(d)(2)(D).

4. United States v. United States Gypsum Co., 333 U.S. 364, 68 S.Ct. 525, 92 L.Ed. 746 (1948), reh'g denied, 333 U.S. 869, 68 S.Ct. 788, 92 L.Ed. 1147 (1948).

5. See People v. Leach, 15 Cal.3d 419, 124 Cal.Rptr. 752, 541 P.2d 296 (1975), cert. denied, 424 U.S. 926, 96 S.Ct. 1137, 47 L.Ed.2d 335 (1976); Federal Rule of Evidence 801(d)(2)(D) (Advisory Committee Note). Compare People v. Saling, 7 Cal.3d 844, 103 Cal.Rptr. 698, 500 P.2d 610 (1972) (holding that a coconspirator's declaration was inadmissible when made three and one-half weeks after the charged murder) with People v. Dominguez, 121 Cal.App.3d 481, 175 Cal.Rptr. 445 (1981) (holding that a coconspirator's declaration made after the charged murder was nonetheless admissible where the evidence showed that the declaration was made while other goals of the conspiracy remained unattained).

proving the preliminary or foundational facts and the kind of evidence that can be offered to satisfy the standard. In California, a sufficiency standard applies.[6] Viewing the evidence in the light most favorable to the proponent, the judge must be convinced that a reasonable fact finder could find the foundational facts.[7] In making this showing, however, the proponent is limited to offering admissible evidence.[8] This rule precludes bootstrapping. The proponent may not offer the hearsay declaration as evidence of the foundational requirements.[9]

Assume, for example, that A, the accused, is being prosecuted for robbing a bank and that the prosecution wishes to offer the following declaration by B under the hearsay exception for coconspirator's declarations: "C, lend me your car; A and I plan to rob the bank but don't want to use our cars." Since B made the declaration to facilitate the commission of the crime, it appears to satisfy the foundational requirement that it further the conspiracy. The prosecution can offer the declaration for this purpose without violating the hearsay rule, since the prosecution is merely offering the declaration to show the judge that it is the kind of utterance contemplated by the exception. In this respect, the offer is akin to the type of evidence received under the verbal acts doctrine discussed earlier.[10] The prosecution, however, may not offer the declaration to prove the existence of the conspiracy or A's participation in it. The use of the declaration for these purposes would violate the hearsay rule, as the out of court statement would then be offered to prove as true the matters asserted by B.

To comply with the foundational requirements under the Code, the prosecution must offer other, admissible evidence to prove the existence of

---

6. West's Ann.California Evidence Code § 1223(c).

7. See § 17.01 infra. Some reviewing courts impose a stricter sufficiency test in determining the existence of preliminary facts under a prima facie standard. For example, some courts hold that for a co-conspirator's declaration to be admissible the proponent has to "proffer sufficient evidence to allow the trier of fact to determine that the conspiracy exists by a preponderance of the evidence." See People v. Herrera, 83 Cal.App.4th 46, 63, 98 Cal.Rptr.2d 911, 922 (2000) and cases cited therein. The addition of the more likely than not standard probably adds little to the traditional sufficiency test, since the modified test is still heavily tilted in favor of admissibility. For purposes of admissibility, however, the question for the trial judge under Proposition 8 would appear to be merely whether a reasonable juror could find that a conspiracy existed if the proponent's evidence is believed. Subject to certain limitations, Proposition 8 requires the admission of relevant evidence as a matter of constitutional right in California criminal cases. See West's Ann. Cal. Const. Art. I, § 28. Whether jurors should be instructed to disregard the evidence *after* it has been admitted unless they find the conspiracy by some higher standard is a separate question and one apparently beyond the reach of Proposition 8. In California, for example, jurors are routinely told to disregard evidence of uncharged misdeeds unless they first find by a preponderance of the evidence that the misdeed was committed. See § 3.17 supra. CALJIC 6.24 (Fall 2006 Edition) warns jurors not to consider a coconspirator's declaration unless they first find the foundational facts, including the conspiracy, by a preponderance of the evidence.

8. The California Law Revision Commission recommended a rule on preliminary fact determinations that would have permitted the judge to consider inadmissible evidence in some instances. 6 California Law Revision Commission, Reports, Recommendations, and Studies 19–21 (1964). The proposed rule, however, was not enacted by the Legislature which instead retained the practice of requiring the use of admissible evidence. See West's Ann.California Evidence Code §§ 400–406.

9. See People v. Longines, 34 Cal.App.4th 621, 626, 40 Cal.Rptr.2d 356, 359 (1995).

10. See § 5.04 supra. See also People v. Curtis, 106 Cal.App.2d 321, 326, 235 P.2d 51, 54 (1951).

the conspiracy and A's participation. Under the Code, however, the prosecution need not satisfy the foundational requirements before offering the hearsay declaration. The judge may permit the prosecution to satisfy the foundational requirements after the declaration has been received.[11] But if the prosecution fails to supply the foundational requirements before the evidence is closed, then upon motion the accused can have the declaration stricken from the evidence. Moreover, even if the declaration remains in evidence, the accused is entitled to have the jurors instructed to disregard the declaration unless they first find that the foundational requirements have been satisfied. Such a limiting instruction is proper because under the Code a sufficiency standard governs the proof of the foundational facts.[12]

If in the example we assume that A was also charged with conspiracy, it becomes apparent that the prosecution must prove the existence of the conspiracy and A's participation twice: once by a sufficiency standard to satisfy the foundational requirements for admitting B's declaration; then a second time, by proof beyond a reasonable doubt, to persuade the fact finder to convict A of conspiracy. Though proof beyond a reasonable doubt is a much higher standard than sufficiency, the second time the prosecution can use the declaration to convict A of conspiracy if the prosecution meets the foundational requirements for receiving the declaration.

The Federal Rules are seemingly more protective of the accused than is the Code. The United States Supreme Court has construed the Rules to require the prosecution to prove the foundational facts by a preponderance of the evidence.[13] This added protection, however, is undercut by the Rules' position permitting the proponent to offer the hearsay declaration as evidence of the existence of the conspiracy and of the accused's participation.[14] Thus, where the accused is charged with conspiracy, a federal prosecutor too has to prove the conspiracy twice: once by a preponderance of the evidence to make use of the hearsay declaration and then again beyond a reasonable doubt to convict the accused. But the prosecutor's initial burden can be lightened considerably by the Federal Rule allowing the use of the declaration to satisfy the foundational requirements. In enacting Federal Rule 104, Congress adopted the approach rejected by the California Legislature: in making preliminary fact determinations, the judge is not bound by the rules of evidence except those regarding privileges.[15] Consequently, the judge can consider the

---

11.   West's Ann.California Evidence Code § 1223(c).

12.   West's Ann.California Evidence Code § 403(c). Although a sufficiency standard governs the question of admissibility, once a coconspirator's declaration has been received, the judge may impose additional limitations on its use by the jury. For example, California judges should instruct the jurors to disregard a coconspirator's declaration unless they first find by a preponderance of the evidence that a conspiracy existed at the time the statement was made, that the statement was made by a person who was a member of the conspiracy, that the statement was made in furtherance of the conspiracy, and that the statement is offered against a person who was a member of the conspiracy. See CALJIC 6.24 (Fall 2007).

13.   Bourjaily v. United States, 483 U.S. 171, 175, 107 S.Ct. 2775, 2778, 97 L.Ed.2d 144 (1987).

14.   See Federal Rule of Evidence 104(a); see also Federal Rule of Evidence 1101(d)(1).

15.   See Federal Rule of Evidence 104(a); see also Federal Rule of Evidence 1101(d)(1).

coconspirator's declaration in determining whether the prosecution has proved the conspiracy and the accused's participation by a preponderance of the evidence, even though the use of the declaration for these purposes violates the hearsay rule.[16]

A federal judge, however, may not rely on the coconspirator's statement alone to find the preliminary facts. A 1997 amendment to Federal Rule 801 provides that the statement does not by itself establish the existence of the conspiracy or participation in it.[17] The judge, in addition, must consider "the circumstances surrounding the statement, such as the identity of the speaker, the context in which the statement was made, or evidence corroborating the contents of the statement in making its determination as to each preliminary question."[18]

Like the California Evidence Code, the Rules empower the judge to receive the coconspirator's hearsay declaration subject to the proponent's satisfaction of the foundational requirements.[19] The United States Supreme Court, however, has declined to rule on whether federal judges should be allowed by the Rules to admit the declaration subject to a motion to strike.[20]

Unlike California judges, federal judges should not instruct the jurors to disregard the coconspirator's declaration unless they first find the foundational facts. In view of the United States Supreme Court's holding that the preliminary facts must be proved by a preponderance of the evidence, the judge's determination of the existence of the preliminary facts should be final. Under these circumstances, the role of the jury should be to determine only the weight, if any, to be given to the evidence of the coconspirator's declaration.[21]

Neither the Code nor the Rules requires that the crime of conspiracy be charged before declarations of coconspirators can be offered against the party opponent. If the declarations are admissible under the exception, they can be received if relevant to proving or disproving a contested factual issue.[22]

QUESTIONS AND PROBLEMS

1. Consider the admissibility of the following evidence in a prosecution in which A has been charged with robbing a bank:

---

16. See Federal Rule of Evidence 801(d)(2) as amended in 1997 and Advisory Committee Note.

17. Federal Rule of Evidence 801(d)(2).

18. Id. (Advisory Committee Note).

19. Federal Rule of Evidence 104(b).

20. Bourjaily v. United States, 483 U.S. 171, 176, note 1, 107 S.Ct. 2775, 2779, note 1, 97 L.Ed.2d 144 (1987).

21. See generally Lego v. Twomey, 404 U.S. 477, 489–490, 92 S.Ct. 619, 627, 30 L.Ed.2d 618 (1972). See also West's Ann.California Evidence Code § 403 and comment.

22. People v. Morales, 263 Cal.App.2d 368, 374, 69 Cal.Rptr. 402, 406 (1968), cert. denied, 393 U.S. 1104, 89 S.Ct. 907, 21 L.Ed.2d 798 (1969) ("The admissibility of the declaration of a coconspirator is not affected by the fact that the indictment or information fails to charge conspiracy.").

DA: What, if anything, did B say to you at that time?

Witness C: B said to me, "C, lend me your car. A and I plan to rob the bank but don't want to use our cars. We will reward your cooperation."

Defense Counsel: Objection. Hearsay. Move to strike.

DA: Authorized admission.

Judge: ?

2. Suppose that A is also charged with conspiring with B to rob the bank. The DA now claims that B's statement to C qualifies as a coconspirator's declaration. Would that affect your ruling? *CA vs. FRE*

3. Assume that the prosecution has established the foundation for admitting B's statement to C under the hearsay exception for coconspirators' declarations. That being so, if the case is being tried in California, the prosecution is required to prove the conspiracy and A's participation in it twice: once by a sufficiency standard to satisfy the foundational requirements for admitting B's declaration and then a second time by proof beyond a reasonable doubt to persuade the fact finder to convict A of conspiracy. True or false?

4. If the case is being tried in federal court, the prosecutor would also have to prove the conspiracy and A's participation twice: once by a preponderance of the evidence to satisfy the foundational facts for admitting B's declaration and then a second time by proof beyond a reasonable doubt to persuade the fact finder to convict A of conspiracy. True or false?

5. Assume that the answer to Questions 3 and 4 is True. In California, upon the defendant's request may the judge instruct the jurors to disregard the conspiracy evidence unless they first find that B made the statement while a member of the conspiracy and in furtherance of the conspiracy?

In federal court, may the judge give a similar instruction?

6. The Code precludes the prosecution from offering a coconspirator's statement as proof of the foundational facts required for admission of the statement. The Federal Rules, on the other hand, permit such bootstrapping. True or false?

§ 7.05 COCONSPIRATORS' DECLARATIONS AND CONFRONTATION

If the Sixth Amendment's right to confront one's accusers means an opportunity to cross examine one's accusers under oath and in the presence of the fact finder, then the use of a coconspirator's declaration against the accused without producing the coconspirator for cross-examination would appear to violate the right. In United States v. Inadi[1] the United States Supreme Court reached the opposite conclusion, however. The Court held that the use of such a declaration under the Federal Rules

---

1. 475 U.S. 387, 106 S.Ct. 1121, 89 L.Ed.2d 390 (1986), on remand, 790 F.2d 383 (3d Cir.1986).

does not violate the Sixth Amendment. Indeed, the Court went further, holding that to use the declaration the prosecution does not even have to show the coconspirator's unavailability as a witness.[2] In the Court's view, the circumstantial guarantees of trustworthiness attending coconspirators' declarations are an adequate substitute for the benefits that the accused might derive from cross examining the hearsay declarant.[3]

Although the Court has revised its confrontation analysis since *Inadi*, the Court's new approach does not appear to affect the admissibility of coconspirators' declarations. In Crawford v. Washington[4] the Court held that only the use of "testimonial statements" against the accused would violate the accused's confrontation rights unless the accused was afforded an opportunity to cross examine the declarant or, if the declarant was unavailable to testify, unless the accused had been accorded an opportunity prior to the trial to cross examine the declarant. Although the Court declined to provide a comprehensive definition of "testimonial statements," the Court expressly held that statements made in furtherance of a conspiracy would not generally qualify as testimonial.[5]

§ 7.06 THE OPPOSING PARTY'S CONDUCT AND ADMISSIONS

We have seen that nonverbal conduct intended as a substitute for a verbal assertion is hearsay.[1] Thus, if in response to the question, "Who killed the victim?" the accused raises his hand, his conduct would be tantamount to saying, "I did." Evidence that in response to the question the accused raised his hand would be hearsay but admissible as a party admission for the truth of the matter asserted under the Code and the Rules.

An opposing party's nonverbal conduct, however, may be offered against the party even if it fails to qualify as an admission. Indeed, often such conduct is quite damaging even though it is not assertive and, hence, not hearsay. For example, the accused who flees from the crime scene does not intend for his flight to substitute for the statement, "I am guilty." Quite to the contrary, he is fleeing in the hope that he will not be linked to the crime. Yet, the nonhearsay evidence of his flight can be almost as damaging to his cause as confessing the crime and is admissible as circumstantial evidence of the accused's consciousness of guilt.[2] Other nonassertive conduct by a party evidencing a consciousness of guilt includes attempts to persuade witnesses to testify falsely, to dissuade

---

2. Id. at 394–396, 106 S.Ct. at 1126.

3. For an extended discussion of whether receiving hearsay against the accused violates the accused's right to confront his accusers, see § 6.03 supra.

4. 541 U.S. 36, 124 S.Ct. 1354, 158 L.Ed.2d 177 (2004).

5. Id. at 1367. For a detailed discussion of hearsay and confrontation, see § 6.03 supra.

1. See § 5.05 supra.

2. People v. Sanchez, 35 Cal.App.2d 231, 95 P.2d 169 (1939).

witnesses from testifying, and to destroy or conceal evidence.[3] A party's refusal to remove his sunglasses so that a witness can better identify him[4] or to provide hair and blood samples can also be offered as nonassertive conduct of the party's consciousness of guilt.[5]

Similarly, a third person's nonassertive acts undertaken on behalf of a party may be offered against the party even if the acts do not qualify as authorized admissions. For example, evidence that a third person attempted to intimidate the witnesses into finding for a party is nonassertive. The party probably did not intend her request to the third person or the third person's acts to substitute for a statement confessing the weakness of her case and admitting the strength of the opponent's. Accordingly, receiving such evidence will not violate the hearsay rule. The evidence is nonetheless admissible, as circumstantial evidence of the party's consciousness of guilt or belief in the weakness of her case. But, as in the case of authorized admissions, such evidence should not be received in the absence of proof that the party authorized the third person to act on her behalf.[6]

Declarations by witnesses prevented from testifying. Occasionally, parties try to win their cases by preventing adverse witnesses from testifying. To dissuade parties from profiting from this type of misconduct, the Federal Rules provide an exception for a statement offered against a party who "has wrongfully caused—or acquiesced in wrongfully causing—the declarant's unavailability as a witness, and did so intending that result."[7] A party who engages in this kind of misconduct forfeits the right to object on hearsay grounds. Under the Rules, the statement may be offered against any party (including the government) in a criminal or civil proceeding, so long as the proponent proves the foundational facts by a preponderance of the evidence.[8]

California has two provisions. Section 1390(a), enacted in 2010, is similar to the Federal Rule. It provides that "[e]vidence of a statement is not made inadmissible by the hearsay rule if the statement is offered against a party that has engaged or aided and abetted in the wrongdoing that was intended to, and did, procure the unavailability of the declarant as a witness."[9] Like the Federal Rule, § 1390 can be offered against any party, including the prosecution, in both civil and criminal cases,[10] and the

---

3. People v. Coffman, 34 Cal.4th 1, 102, 96 P.3d 30, 107, 17 Cal.Rptr.3d 710, 802 (2004).

4. People v. Ramirez, 39 Cal.4th 398, 456, 139 P.3d 64, 103, 46 Cal.Rptr.3d 677, 723 (2006), cert. denied, 550 U.S. 970, 127 S.Ct. 2877, 167 L.Ed.2d 1155 (2007).

5. People v. Farnam, 28 Cal.4th 107, 153, 47 P.3d 988, 1022, 121 Cal.Rptr.2d 106, 147 (2002), cert. denied, 537 U.S. 1124, 123 S.Ct. 861, 154 L.Ed.2d 806 (2003).

6. See People v. Brooks, 88 Cal.App.3d 180, 151 Cal.Rptr. 606 (1979) and cases cited therein. See also CALJIC 2.05, Efforts Other than by Defendant to Fabricate Evidence (Fall 2006 Edition).

Evidence that a witness is afraid to testify is probative of the witness's credibility and is therefore relevant. For a discussion of this point, see § 15.11 infra.

7. Federal Rule of Evidence 804(b)(6).

8. Id. (Advisory Committee Note).

9. West's Ann. California Evidence Code § 1390.

10. Id. § 1390(c).

wrongdoing behind the declarant's unavailability does not have to amount to a criminal act.[11]

Section 1390 differs from the Federal Rule in two respects. Section 1390 vests the judge with discretion to exclude the declaration if the judge deems it untrustworthy and unreliable.[12] Moreover, while the new section allows the proponent to offer the hearsay declaration as proof of the exception's foundation, § 1390 prohibits the judge from finding that the foundational elements have been met "solely on the unconfronted hearsay statement".[13] The judge must in addition find that the declaration is "supported by independent corroborative evidence."[14]

An older provision, § 1350, places more restrictions on the use of these declarations. They are admissible only in prosecutions charging a serious felony if the proponent proves by clear and convincing evidence that the declarant's unavailability was "knowingly caused by, aided by, or solicited by the party against whom the statement is offered for the purpose of preventing the arrest or prosecution" of that party.[15] In addition, the proponent must also prove by clear and convincing evidence that the declarant's unavailability is the result of death by homicide or of kidnaping.[16]

Other limitations include proof by a preponderance of the evidence that the statement was made under circumstances which indicate that it is trustworthy and not the result of promise, inducement, threat, or coercion.[17] Corroboration is also required. The proponent must corroborate the statement by evidence tending to connect the party against whom the statement is offered with the commission of the serious felony with which the party is charged.[18] Proof that shows merely the commission of the offense or its circumstances is insufficient.[19]

The proponent must also show that the statement was memorialized in a tape recording made by a law enforcement official or in a statement prepared by a law enforcement official and signed and notarized by the declarant in the presence of the law enforcement official.[20]

Procedural safeguards include a requirement that the prosecution serve a written notice upon the accused of its intent to use the statement at least 10 days prior to the hearing or trial at which the statement is to be offered, unless the prosecution shows good cause for the failure to

---

11. Id. § 1390(a).

12. Id. § 1390(b)(4).

13. Id. § 1390(b)(2).

14. Id.

15. West's Ann. California Evidence Code § 1350.

16. Id.

17. Id.

18. Id.

19. Id.

20. Id.

provide the notice.[21] If good cause is shown, the accused is entitled to a reasonable continuance of the hearing or trial.[22]

If the statement is offered during the trial, the judge must determine its admissibility at a hearing out of the presence of the jury. If the accused testifies at the hearing, the judge must exclude all persons, except for the clerk, the court reporter, the bailiff, the prosecutor, the investigating officer, the accused, and defense counsel.[23] The accused's testimony is not admissible in any other proceeding, and if a transcript is made, it must be sealed and transmitted to the clerk of the court in which the action is pending.[24]

Hearsay declarations by others included in the statement admitted are inadmissible unless they fall within an exception to the hearsay rule.[25]

Section 1350's numerous limitations evince an abundance of caution when abolishing the right of criminal defendants to object to hearsay even when they have been charged with causing the hearsay declarant's unavailability as a witness. But because of its limitations, it is doubtful that a California prosecutor today would rely on § 1350 given the ease of applying § 1390.

California has an additional, though limited, hearsay exception allowing the use of sworn statements by dead declarants regarding gang related crimes.[26] The purpose of the exception is to discourage gang members from eliminating potential witnesses in prosecutions for gang crimes. California makes it a separate offense for a gang member to promote or assist any felonious criminal activity by members of gangs.[27] The statements may be used only in anti-gang prosecutions and are subject to numerous restrictions.[28]

QUESTIONS AND PROBLEMS

1. The accused was arrested and jailed on a complaint charging him with committing a burglary in San Francisco. At the trial the prosecutor calls Cellmate, who testifies that he shares a cell with the accused. He also testifies that the accused asked him to say that the accused was visiting him in San Jose on the day of the burglary. The accused objects and moves to strike on the grounds that Cellmate's testimony about what he said violates the hearsay rule. The judge should sustain the objection and grant the motion to strike. True or false?

2. Both the Code and the Rules allow hearsay to be received against a party whose wrongdoing prevented the declarant from appearing at the trial

---

21. Id.

22. Id.

23. Id.

24. Id.

25. Id.

26. West's Ann. California Evidence Code § 1231.

27. West's Ann. Penal Code § 186.22.

28. See § 9.03 infra.

to testify. If certain requirements are met, the Rules allow the use of the hearsay in both civil and criminal cases. Under the Code, however, the hearsay declarations are admissible only in criminal cases in which a serious felony is charged. True or false?

§ 7.07 JUDICIAL ADMISSIONS IN CIVIL CASES

Thus far, we have been considering evidentiary admissions. These differ from judicial admissions in an important respect: they bind neither the party nor the fact finder. In a personal injury action, for example, a party's statement that he ran the light, though admissible as an admission against the party, would not preclude the party from offering evidence that he did not run the light. Nor would the admission prevent the fact finder from finding that the party did not run the light. It would be up to the fact finder to determine the weight, if any, to give to the admission as well as to contrary evidence that the party did not run the light.

Judicial admissions, on the other hand, are binding on both the admitting party and the fact finder. In Fuentes v. Tucker[1] the parents of children killed by the defendant brought a wrongful death action on the theory that the defendant's negligent operation of a car caused the children's death. On the day of the trial, the defendant filed an amended answer in which he admitted liability.[2] Since the amended answer removed the issue of liability from the case, the California Supreme Court held that it was error for the trial judge to have admitted evidence that the defendant had been intoxicated at the time he struck the children.[3]

Had the defendant attempted to offer evidence of the care he exercised while driving the car, his offer too would have been subject to objection. His admission of liability also precluded him from offering evidence contradicting the admission.[4] Moreover, since the defendant's concession in the amended answer removed the issue of liability from the jury's consideration, the jury was precluded from finding in the defendant's favor on that issue.

Not all admissions in pleadings constitute judicial admissions, however. As a matter of policy, some superseded pleadings should be inadmissible even as evidentiary admissions. Suppose that in Fuentes v. Tucker the defendant had admitted liability in the original answer and then had obtained leave of the court to file an amended answer in which he denied liability. Obviously, the original answer, having been superseded by the amended answer, could not operate as a judicial admission. But could the plaintiffs offer the original answer as an evidentiary admission? Dean Charles McCormick says no for the sensible reason that allowing the use of the superseded pleading would undermine the policy of the rules of civil

---

1. 31 Cal.2d 1, 187 P.2d 752 (1947).

2. Id. at 3, 187 P.2d at 754.

3. Id. at 5, 187 P.2d at 755.

4. Technically, the defendant's offer would be irrelevant. Because admissions in pleadings remove issues from the case, the offer would be immaterial and hence irrelevant. For a discussion of this point, see § 2.01 supra.

procedure favoring amendments to pleadings.[5] The California Supreme Court agrees. In Meyer v. State Bd. of Equalization[6] the court held that a superseded pleading could not be used as an evidentiary admission in the pending action. At most, the proponent could use the pleading only to impeach the pleader but not to prove the truth of the matter admitted in the pleading.[7] The same can be said of inconsistent claims or defenses. If the opposing party were permitted to offer a party's inconsistent claims or defenses, the policy of permitting parties to use pleadings primarily for giving notice would be defeated.[8]

A different approach, however, is taken where the pleadings taken in one action are offered in another action. In Dolinar v. Pedone[9] the plaintiff sued Universal Film Exchange for injuries she sustained in a multiple car collision. To prove that one of the drivers of the cars was Universal's agent at the time of the collision, the plaintiff offered the pleadings in another case then pending in which another person injured in the same collision had sued Universal.[10] In those pleadings, Universal had admitted that the driver of one of the cars was its agent.[11] The reviewing court upheld the use of the admission in the pleadings.[12] But having been made in pleadings filed in a different case, the admission was received only as an evidentiary admission.[13] Accordingly, Universal was free to offer evidence contradicting the admission, and the jury was entitled to give whatever weight it chose to the admission as well as to the contradicting evidence.[14]

---

5. See C. McCormick, McCormick on Evidence § 265 (J. Strong 4th ed. 1992).

6. 42 Cal.2d 376, 267 P.2d 257 (1954).

7. Id. at 385, 267 P.2d at 263. *Meyer* was decided before the adoption of the Evidence Code. Prior to the Code, inconsistent statements were admissible only to impeach a witness and could not be received for the truth of the matter stated. West's Ann.California Evidence Code § 1235 and comment. Now, they can be received for the truth. Id. That difference, however, does not necessarily change *Meyer*. Permitting the superseded pleading to operate as an admission would undermine the policy favoring amendments to pleadings. Protecting policies extrinsic to the law of evidence may be taken into account by the judge in determining whether the prejudicial effects of evidence outweigh its probative value. See § 2.10 supra.

8. See C. McCormick, McCormick on Evidence § 265 (J. Strong 4th ed. 1992). But see Beatty v. Pacific States Savings & Loan, 4 Cal.App.2d 692, 41 P.2d 378 (1935), where the court held that contradictions in pleadings could be used as judicial admissions against the pleader if the pleader verified the pleadings. In these circumstances, "the averment which bears most strongly against the party so pleading will be taken as true upon the trial." Id. at 697–698, 41 P.2d at 380. By verifying a pleading, the pleader swears that he has reviewed the pleading and that the factual assertions are true. West's Ann.California Civil Procedure Code § 446. Therefore, in the case of verified pleadings, the rule permitting the pleading of inconsistent claims and defenses does not allow "the pleader to blow both hot and cold in the same complaint on the subject of facts of which he purports to speak with knowledge under oath." Beatty v. Pacific States Savings & Loan, supra.

9. 63 Cal.App.2d 169, 146 P.2d 237 (1944).

10. Id. at 176, 146 P.2d at 240.

11. Id.

12. Id. at 177–178, 146 P.2d at 241.

13. Id.

14. In addition to offering evidence contradicting the admission made in the prior pleading, the party opposing the admission is entitled to show that the admission was inadvertently made,

Judicial admissions do not have to take the form of concessions in pleadings or stipulations. "Oral statements of counsel may be treated as judicial admissions if they were intended to be such or reasonably construed by the court or the other party as such. * * * This rule, however, does not apply 'to admissions which are improvidently or unguardedly made, or which are in any degree ambiguous.' "[15] An example of the former can be found in Fassberg Const. Co. v. Housing Authority of City of Los Angeles.[16] During closing argument, counsel for the defendant conceded that the amount of damages the defendant suffered was lower than the amount claimed on its cross-complaint. The court held that the concession amounted to a judicial admission.[17]

QUESTIONS AND PROBLEMS

1. Under modern codes, the distinction between "judicial" and "evidentiary" admissions has lost all significance. Admissions in pleadings are simply treated in the same way as ordinary admissions even when offered in the case in which the "judicial" admissions were made. True or false?

2. According to Dean McCormick, superseded pleadings do not lose all value and should be treated as evidentiary admissions when offered in the action arising from the superseded pleadings. Therefore, Dean McCormick would allow the plaintiff to offer as an evidentiary admission an answer in which the defendant originally admitted liability but which has been superseded by an amended answer in which the defendant denies liability. True or false?

3. Admissions in pleadings operate only as evidentiary admissions when offered in an action which does not arise from those pleadings. Accordingly, a defendant's admission of agency in the pleadings in another action may be offered to prove the agency in the present action but the admission is not binding on the fact finder or the parties. True or false?

§ 7.08 ADMISSIONS AS STIPULATIONS

Admissions in pleadings are not the only way to remove issues from a case. Earlier, we saw that stipulations may have the same effect as judicial

---

unauthorized, or made under a mistake of fact. Magnolia Square Homeowners v. Safeco Ins. Co., 221 Cal.App.3d 1049, 1061, 271 Cal.Rptr. 1, 7 (1990). Some courts, however, have erroneously concluded that the opponent is entitled to offer only the latter evidence. See, e.g., Barr v. ACandS, 57 Cal.App.4th 1038, 1056, 67 Cal.Rptr.2d 494, 506 (1997).

Where the party signs the pleadings filed in the other action, the pleadings can be offered in the present action as an evidentiary admission only if the proponent produces evidence sufficient to sustain a finding that the signature is the party's. See West's Ann. California Evidence Code § 403(a)(3); Federal Rules of Evidence 104(b) and 901(a). Where the pleadings are signed by the attorney for the party, the proponent must show that the party authorized the attorney to speak for the party. Dolinar v. Pedone, 63 Cal.App.2d 169, 177–178, 146 P.2d 237, 241 (1944). Whether the attorney had the authority to speak for the party presents a sufficiency question under West's Ann.California Evidence Code § 1222 and Federal Rule of Evidence 104(b).

15. People v. Jackson, 129 Cal.App.4th 129, 160, 28 Cal.Rptr.3d 136, 160 (2005) (quoting from Scafidi v. Western Loan & Bldg. Co., 72 Cal.App.2d 550, 562, 165 P.2d 260 (1946)).

16. 152 Cal.App.4th 720, 60 Cal.Rptr.3d 375 (2007).

17. Id. at 751, 60 Cal.Rptr.3d at 402.

admissions.[1] If in *Dolinar*[2] Universal had stipulated that one of the drivers of the cars involved in the collision was its agent, that stipulation would have been as binding on Universal and the fact finder as an admission to that effect in the pleadings.[3] In this respect, stipulations and judicial admissions are like the responses parties make to pretrial requests for admissions in civil matters. Under the California Code of Civil Procedure and the Federal Rules of Civil Procedure, any matter so admitted under the rules is conclusively established for purposes of the pending action unless the court permits the admitting party to withdraw or amend the admission.[4]

QUESTIONS AND PROBLEMS

1. In an action for personal injuries, the plaintiff accepted the defendant's stipulation that if Bartender were called as a witness, he would testify that the defendant had three beers on the morning of the accident.

    a. This stipulation binds the jurors to find that the defendant had three beers, and the judge should so instruct them. True or false?

    b. This stipulation precludes the defendant from having his drinking buddy testify that the defendant only had two beers that morning. True or false?

2. Would you change your rulings if instead the plaintiff had accepted the defendant's stipulation that he had at least three beers on the morning of the accident?

3. If instead of stipulating to Bartender's testimony the defendant had admitted in a request for admissions that he had had three beers, would that admission preclude the defendant from proving that he had only two beers? Would it preclude the plaintiff from proving that the defendant had four beers?

§ 7.09 JUDICIAL ADMISSIONS IN CRIMINAL CASES

The pleadings in criminal cases do not lend themselves to the kind of judicial admissions associated with pleadings in civil cases. The rules of

---

1. See § 2.02 supra.

2. Dolinar v. Pedone, 63 Cal.App.2d 169, 146 P.2d 237 (1944), discussed in § 7.07 supra.

3. See Gonzales v. Pacific Greyhound Lines, 34 Cal.2d 749, 214 P.2d 809 (1950). Stipulations made in one proceeding may be used as evidentiary admissions against the stipulating party in subsequent proceedings. Nungaray v. Pleasant Valley Lima Bean Growers & Warehouse Ass'n, 142 Cal.App.2d 653, 300 P.2d 285 (1956). "The fact that in the stipulation in the [earlier] action the parties agreed neither of them would be bound thereby in any other action did not preclude plaintiff from using it as an admission. Plaintiff was not a party to the stipulation, nor a party in that action, and was not bound by the agreement." Id. at 668, 300 P.2d at 294. See also Knowles v. Tehachapi Valley Hospital Dist., 49 Cal.App.4th 1083, 57 Cal.Rptr.2d 192 (1996). Plaintiffs sued a doctor for malpractice and the hospital where he rendered the services for negligence in allowing the doctor to practice there. On the day the trial was to begin, the plaintiffs accepted the doctor's stipulation that he had been negligent in his treatment, and judgment was entered against the doctor. The reviewing court held that the stipulation did not preclude the hospital from offering evidence, including the doctor's testimony, that it had not been negligent in allowing the doctor to use its facilities. Id. at 1093, 57 Cal.Rptr.2d at 198.

4. See West's Ann.California Civil Procedure Code § 2033; Federal Rule of Civil Procedure 36. Under the Code and the Federal Rules, an admission made in response to a request is binding only in the pending action and cannot be used against the admitting party in another action. Id.

criminal procedure do not require a written answer to the allegations in the complaint. Instead, arraignment procedures generally contemplate that the accused will enter either a guilty or not guilty plea.[1] If the latter plea is entered, it operates as a general denial forcing the prosecution to prove each of the elements of the offense beyond a reasonable doubt.

Prior to June 1982, a California criminal defendant could admit as true allegations in the complaint, information, or indictment. If the accused did so, the admission would operate as a judicial admission and would preclude the prosecution from proving the admitted allegation at the trial. Such preclusion stemmed from the Code's requirement that only relevant evidence is admissible.[2] Since the accused's admission would have the effect of removing the admitted allegation from the case, evidence proving or disproving such an allegation would be immaterial and, hence, irrelevant and inadmissible.[3] But this simple, direct approach to judicial admissions in criminal cases has become quite complicated in California principally as a result of a provision of Proposition 8 which, as a matter of state constitutional law, requires proof in open court of any felony conviction whenever the conviction is an element of the felony charged.[4]

Penalty enhancement and status clauses. Both California law and federal law contain anti-recidivist provisions that call for increased punishment upon conviction of the current offense if the accused previously had been convicted of enumerated offenses. In addition, other penal provisions predicate punishment on such factors as the status of the accused. A classic example is the offense that punishes felons convicted of violent crimes for possessing weapons. Defendants prosecuted under these statutes do not want jurors to learn about their previous criminal activity out of fear that the jurors might be tempted to punish them for their predisposition to violate the law, rather than upon the evidence that they committed the current offense. Defendants facing these charges may seek to eliminate this risk by removing the issue of their previous criminal activity from the jurors' consideration. As a matter of evidence law, they can do so by admitting as true those allegations in the enhancement clauses charging them, for example, with the previous convictions or alleging their status as felons.

California. In People v. Hall[5] the California Supreme Court held that the accused had the right to admit or stipulate to allegations in the charging instrument over the prosecution's objection.[6] That right, howev-

---

1. See West's Ann.California Penal Code § 1016. The accused can also enter other pleas, such as not guilty by reason of insanity and once in jeopardy. Id.

2. West's Ann.California Evidence Code § 350.

3. For an extended discussion of materiality and relevance, see § 2.01 supra.

4. West's Ann.California Constitution Article I, § 28(f)(4).

5. 28 Cal.3d 143, 167 Cal.Rptr. 844, 616 P.2d 826 (1980).

6. Id. at 155–156, 167 Cal.Rptr. at 850–851, 616 P.2d at 832–833.

er, was subsequently limited by Proposition 8, which in 1982 amended the California Constitution to provide that "[w]hen a prior felony conviction is an element of any felony offense, it shall be proven to the trier of fact in open court."[7]

The response by the California courts to the constitutional provision has been twofold: (1) to allow the trial judge to withhold the *nature* of the prior conviction from the jury if the accused admits having committed the felony, and (2) to declare those portions of some penal statutes enhancing punishment on the basis of prior convictions to be a "sentencing matter" and not an "element" of the felony charged requiring trial by jury.[8]

People v. Valentine[9] is illustrative of the first response. The accused was charged with several offenses arising from a robbery. One count charged him with the crime of being an ex-felon in possession of a concealable firearm. To prevent the jury from learning about the offenses giving rise to his status as an ex-felon, the accused offered to stipulate to those offenses. Relying on Proposition 8, the trial judge ruled that the prosecution was entitled to prove those convictions. The California Supreme Court reversed, holding that, while the initiative entitles the prosecution to prove the accused's convictions to the fact finder, it limits the prosecution to proving only that the accused has been convicted of a felony where the accused admits the convictions. The initiative "does not require the nature of [the] prior convictions to go to the jury in such a case, since that information is utterly irrelevant to the charge."[10]

---

7. West's Ann.California Constitution Article I, § 28(f)(4).

8. As a statutory matter, a California criminal defendant is entitled to a jury determination of whether he has suffered a prior conviction even if the conviction is not an element of the offense. West's Ann. California Penal Code § 1025. The right is not plenary, however. The question whether the accused suffered the prior conviction is to be determined by the jury that decides the issue of guilt but the question whether the accused is the person who suffered the conviction is to be determined by the court. Id. How a jury can determine whether the accused suffered a prior conviction without necessarily determining that it was the accused who suffered the conviction is unclear. This mystery, a product of legislative compromise, has been acknowledged by the California Supreme Court. People v. Kelii, 21 Cal.4th 452, 458–459, 87 Cal.Rptr.2d 674, 678–679, 981 P.2d 518, 521–522 (1999). See also People v. Epps, 25 Cal.4th 19, 28, 104 Cal.Rptr.2d 572, 577, 18 P.3d 2, 7(2001), where the California Supreme Court invites the Legislature to revisit the role jurors should play in the proof of prior convictions.

9. 42 Cal.3d 170, 228 Cal.Rptr. 25, 720 P.2d 913 (1986).

10. Id. at 181–182, 228 Cal.Rptr. at 32, 720 P.2d at 920. What matters is that the accused was an ex-felon at the time he committed the offense charged; the offense giving rise to that status is immaterial.

A related statute makes it a crime for an ex-felon who has been convicted of a violent crime to possess a weapon. West's Ann. California Penal Code § 12021.1. If the accused charged under this section admits the prior crime, the prosecution cannot inform the jury of its violent nature or even that the conviction is for a violent crime. People v. Hopkins, 10 Cal.App.4th 1699, 1704, 13 Cal.Rptr.2d 451, 454 (1992). The prosecution is limited to offering evidence that the accused was convicted of violating the code section or sections alleged in the information or indictment. Id.

The same statute makes it an offense for a person who has been convicted of specified misdemeanors to possess a firearm. A person charged under this section may withhold the nature, but not the fact, of the misdemeanor convictions from the jury by admitting them. People v. Wade, 48 Cal.App.4th 460, 467, 55 Cal.Rptr.2d 855, 859 (1996).

Proposition 8 does not apply to misdemeanor convictions. Accordingly, one would expect the rules of evidence to govern the effect of admitting such convictions. Under the rules pertaining to materiality, admitting the conviction would take away from the jury the question of whether the

The other response of the California courts to Proposition 8 has been to declare those portions of some penal statutes enhancing punishment on the basis of prior convictions to be a "sentencing matter" and not an "element" of the felony charged.[11] Under the California Penal Code, persons who commit misdemeanor petty theft can charged with felony theft if at the time they committed the petty theft they had previously been convicted of and served time for enumerated misdemeanors and felonies.[12] In People v. Bouzas[13] the trial judge, relying on Proposition 8, refused to allow the accused to withhold his prior felony conviction and incarceration from the jury by admitting these allegations prior to the trial. The California Supreme Court reversed the accused's conviction, holding that "the prior conviction requirement of section 666 is a sentencing matter for the trial court and not an 'element' of a section 666 'offense' that must be determined by a jury."[14] Accordingly, an accused charged with a felony under § 666 can admit the prior conviction and incarceration and thereby preclude the jury from learning about the conviction.[15]

accused has suffered the conviction. The *Wade* court was concerned that asking jurors to find the accused merely guilty or not guilty of possessing a firearm might cause them to exercise their power of nullification and acquit, unless they were informed about the accused's status as a misdemeanant. Id. But the *Wade* court's concern may have been misplaced. Nothing in the Code would have precluded the trial judge from informing the jurors in such a case of the elements of the offense and of the fact that the accused had admitted his misdemeanant status.

11. The question whether the accused has suffered a prior conviction does not have to be submitted to the jury under the Due Process Clause of the Fourteenth Amendment. "Other than the fact of a prior conviction, any fact that increases the penalty for a crime beyond the prescribed statutory maximum must be submitted to a jury, and proved beyond a reasonable doubt." Apprendi v. New Jersey, 530 U.S. 466, 490, 120 S.Ct. 2348, 2362–2363, 147 L.Ed.2d 435 (2000). In *Apprendi* the Court struck down a New Jersey hate crime enhancement statute that allowed the judge to impose a penalty above the statutory maximum for the charged offense, if after the jury convicted the accused of charged offense the judge found by preponderance of the evidence that the accused's purpose in committing the offense was to intimidate the victim on account of race, color, gender, handicap, sexual orientation, or ethnicity. Id. The Court, however, declined to overrule McMillan v. Pennsylvania, 477 U.S. 79, 106 S.Ct. 2411, 91 L.Ed.2d 67 (1986). In that case the Court sustained a Pennsylvania statute that allowed a judge to impose a mandatory minimum sentence within the prescribed statutory range, if after conviction of enumerated felonies the judge found by a preponderance of the evidence that the accused "visibly possessed a firearm" in the course of committing one of the enumerated felonies. Apprendi v. New Jersey, supra. According to the Court, *McMillan* is limited to those cases "that do not involve the imposition of a sentence more severe than the statutory maximum for the offense established by the jury's verdict." Id. at 487 note 13, 120 S.Ct. at 2361 note 13.

12. West's Ann. California Penal Code § 666.

13. 53 Cal.3d 467, 279 Cal.Rptr. 847, 807 P.2d 1076 (1991).

14. Id. at 478, 279 Cal.Rptr. at 854, 807 P.2d at 1083.

15. Id. at 480, 279 Cal.Rptr. at 856, 807 P.2d at 1085. Section 314 of the California Penal Code makes indecent exposure a misdemeanor. However, a second conviction is punished as a felony. West's Ann. California Penal Code § 314. People v. Merkley, 51 Cal.App.4th 472, 476, 58 Cal.Rptr.2d 21, 23 (1996), holds that the prior conviction allegation in a § 314 charge is a "sentencing factor" permitting a defendant to stipulate to the conviction in order to prevent the jury from learning about it. For a review of the cases holding certain elements to be sentencing factors, see People v. Hall, 67 Cal.App.4th 128, 135, 79 Cal.Rptr.2d 690 (1998).

If the accused denies the truth of the allegation charging him with committing the prior conviction, the accused may move to have the allegation bifurcated from the jury's determination of the truth of the offense charged. Whether the motion should be granted is committed to the judge's discretion. People v. Calderon, 9 Cal.4th 69, 72, 36 Cal.Rptr.2d 333, 335, 885 P.2d 83, 86

Federal cases. The California courts have not been alone in having to resolve the problems caused when criminal defendants are charged with prior convictions or with possessing the status of a felon, and they attempt to prevent jurors from learning about their prior criminal activity. Although there is no federal equivalent to Proposition 8's mandate that prior convictions be proved in open court whenever they are an element of the offense charged, similar problems arise whenever a federal prosecutor charges an offense alleging a prior conviction. Old Chief v. United States[16] is illustrative.

Federal law makes it unlawful for anyone "who has been convicted in any court of a crime punishable by imprisonment for a term exceeding one year" to "possess * * * any firearm * * *."[17] Old Chief was charged with violating this prohibition as well as other federal statutes. To prevent the jurors from learning about the nature of the crime underlying the conviction, Old Chief offered to stipulate to the conviction and to have the trial judge instruct the jurors that he had been previously convicted of a felony. The prosecution refused to join in the stipulation, and the judge allowed the prosecution to prove the conviction through a conviction record which informed the jurors that Old Chief previously had been sentenced to five years' imprisonment for committing an assault resulting in serious bodily injury. In addition to finding Old Chief guilty of being a felon in possession of a firearm, the jurors convicted him of assault with a dangerous weapon and using a firearm in connection with a crime of violence.

Holding that the trial judge abused his discretion in allowing the prosecution to prove the prior conviction through the conviction record, the United States Supreme Court reversed the Ninth Circuit's affirmance of the conviction.[18] In light of Old Chief's proffered stipulation, the Court concluded that the trial judge should have excluded the conviction record as unduly prejudicial under Federal Rule of Evidence 403. Rule 403 is the federal equivalent of California Evidence Code § 352. It empowers a federal judge to exclude relevant evidence whenever its probative value is substantially outweighed by its prejudicial effect.[19] In the Court's view, Old Chief's stipulation was at least as probative of the accused's status as a felon as was the conviction record.[20] But, unlike the conviction record, the stipulation did not carry the risk that the jurors might misuse the

---

(1994). The judge may deny the motion if the accused will not be unduly prejudiced by having the jury determine the truth of the allegation charging the prior conviction in a unitary trial. Id.

IP the accused demands a jury trial on the truth of the allegation charging the commission of a prior conviction, the accused is entitled to a jury determination of all elements of the conviction except the identity of the perpetrator. In California that element is for the judge's determination. West's Ann. California Penal Code § 1025.

16. 519 U.S. 172, 117 S.Ct. 644, 136 L.Ed.2d 574 (1997).

17. 18 U.S.C.A. § 922(g)(1).

18. Old Chief v. United States, 519 U.S. 172, 192, 117 S.Ct. 644, 656, 136 L.Ed.2d 574 (1997).

19. Federal Rule of Evidence 403; see generally § 2.10 supra.

20. Indeed, if accepted, the stipulation would have been more probative of the point in question than the conviction record. Stipulations, if accepted by the opposing party, operate as judicial admissions and are binding on the jurors. See § 2.02 supra.

information in the conviction record as evidence of Old Chief's propensity to commit the other assaults charged against him. This risk was exceptionally high because of the similarities between the prior conviction and the offenses charged against Old Chief.

Special recidivist statutes. Some recidivist statutes require proof of the nature of the prior felony as a condition of imposing additional punishment. Under California Penal Code § 667, a person convicted of a "serious felony" who previously has been convicted of a serious felony shall have his sentence enhanced by five years.[21] If the accused denies having been convicted of the previous felony, the prosecution must prove that allegation beyond a reasonable doubt. No unusual difficulties are encountered when the documentary evidence offered by the prosecution identifies the previous felony among the discrete crimes listed under § 1192.7 as a "serious felony." Murder, for example, is among the discrete offenses listed in the section. But § 1192.7 also lists generic injuries among the serious felonies. For example, a serious felony can include "any * * * felony in which the defendant personally inflicts great bodily harm upon any person * * *."[22] Over a hearsay objection, may the prosecution offer portions of the record of conviction, including transcripts of testimony, to prove that the accused inflicted great bodily harm? If the portion offered consists of the accused's admissions, then the hearsay rule would not be violated since those admissions would be admissible against the accused at the current trial as part of an official record.[23] But if the portion instead consists of the testimony of other witnesses—the victim's, for example—describing the injuries inflicted by the accused, then a serious hearsay problem is presented in the absence of exceptions.

To avoid the costs of relitigating aspects of the misconduct giving rise to the prior conviction, People v. Guerrero[24] holds that to find "the substance of a prior conviction the trier of fact may look [only] to the entire record of the conviction."[25] But reliance on the conviction record is subject to the Evidence Code. Over a hearsay objection, the prosecution may offer only those portions of the conviction record that fall within a hearsay exception in proving the serious nature of the prior felony.[26]

In People v. Reed[27] the prosecution sought to establish that the accused had previously committed a serious felony by evidence that he had attacked the victim of that felony with a cane. Since *Guerrero* precluded calling the witnesses to the attack in the current trial, the prosecution

---

21. West's Ann. California Penal Code § 1192.7.

22. West's Ann. California Penal Code § 1192.7(c)(8).

23. People v. Abarca, 233 Cal.App.3d 1347, 1349, 285 Cal.Rptr. 213, 214 (1991).

24. 44 Cal.3d 343, 243 Cal.Rptr. 688, 748 P.2d 1150 (1988).

25. Id. at 355, 243 Cal.Rptr. at 695, 748 P.2d at 1157. What constitutes the "record of conviction" remains undefined. Transcripts of preliminary hearings are part of the record of conviction in cases involving guilty pleas but not in cases involving guilty verdicts. People v. Houck, 66 Cal.App.4th 350, 355–357, 77 Cal.Rptr.2d 837, 840–841 (1998).

26. People v. Reed, 13 Cal.4th 217, 224, 52 Cal.Rptr.2d 106, 110, 914 P.2d 184, 188 (1996).

27. Id.

offered the transcript of the testimony of witnesses who at the preliminary hearing held in connection with the prior felony identified the accused as the person who struck the victim with a cane. The California Supreme Court upheld the use of the former testimony exception to the hearsay rule to admit the witnesses' preliminary hearing testimony. Even though the prosecution made no effort to establish the unavailability of the witnesses as required by the former testimony exception to the hearsay rule, the court held that no such effort was necessary in view of its earlier holding in *Guerrero* prohibiting the prosecution from going beyond the conviction record in proving the serious nature of the prior felony.[28] Since *Guerrero* barred the prosecution from calling the witnesses at the current trial, the witnesses were as unavailable as witnesses found to be unavailable under the Evidence Code.[29]

Reed works both ways. The accused also is entitled to offer a portion of the conviction record to contest the serious nature of a prior felony conviction.[30] Like the prosecution, the accused over objection must rely on a hearsay exception in making the offer. But since defendants, like prosecutors, are precluded by *Guerrero* from calling witnesses, defendants may rely on the prohibition to establish their witnesses' unavailability if using hearsay exceptions, such as former testimony or declarations against interest, that require such a showing.[31]

---

28. Id. at 226–227, 52 Cal.Rptr.2d at 111–112, 914 P.2d at 189–190.

29. Id. at 228, 52 Cal.Rptr.2d at 113, 914 P.2d at 191. The court declined to determine whether a probation report prepared in connection with the prior felony is a part of the conviction record that can be offered by the prosecution to prove the serious nature of the felony. Id.

In 1996 the Legislature amended the Evidence Code by adding § 452.5. This section provides that an "official record of conviction certified in accordance with subdivision (a) of Section 1530 is admissible pursuant to Section 1280 to prove the commission, attempted commission, or solicitation of a criminal offense, service of a prison term, or other act, condition or event recorded by the record." West's Ann. California Evidence Code § 452.5. Section 1280 creates a hearsay exception for official records, and § 1530 permits copies of records in the custody of a public entity to be offered without the need to call a custodian to authenticate the copy if attested or certified as a correct copy of the original record by a public employee having the legal custody of the record. See West's Ann. California Evidence Code §§ 1280 and 1530.

It is unclear whether § 452.5 can be used to offer a conviction record as proof that the accused committed a serious felony as required by Penal Code § 667. Though the section does state that the record may be offered to prove an "act" or "event" recorded in the record, this provision presupposes that the acts qualifying the felony as a serious felony will be recorded in the record. Accordingly, if the prosecution's theory is that the accused committed a serious felony because he inflicted great bodily harm in committing the felony, an entry that the accused was convicted merely of violating a particular Penal Code provision may still be insufficient to support a finding that the accused was convicted of committing a serious felony.

30. People v. Bartow, 46 Cal.App.4th 1573, 1582, 54 Cal.Rptr.2d 482, 487 (1996).

31. Id. at 1582, 54 Cal.Rptr.2d at 487–488. California's Three Strikes law raises similar issues. It mandates enhanced sentences upon conviction of defendants who "have two or more prior felony convictions" which qualify as "violent" or "serious" felonies. West's Ann. Cal. Penal Code §§ 667(d) and (e)(2)(A). Where the convicted offenses are not among the discrete offenses listed in the statute, the prosecution, over a hearsay objection, must prove the serious or violent nature of the felonies by resort only to the record of conviction. That record may include the appellate record, including the appellate court's opinion. People v. Woodell, 17 Cal.4th 448, 458, 71 Cal.Rptr.2d 241, 247, 950 P.2d 85, 91 (1998). However, as pointed out by Justice Mosk in his dissent, appellate findings which are based on inadmissible hearsay may not, over objection, be used to prove the nature of the violent or serious offense. Id. at 467, 71 Cal.Rptr.2d at 253, 950 P.2d at 97.

QUESTIONS AND PROBLEMS

1. In the absence of special statutes such as Proposition 8, whether or not admissions to allegations in charging instruments operate as judicial admissions depends on the principles relating to materiality. Accordingly, prior to Proposition 8 if the prosecution charged the accused with a felony and under a penalty enhancement clause alleged that the accused previously had been convicted of an enumerated felony, the accused could prevent the jurors from learning about the previous felony by admitting as true that portion of the accusatory pleading alleging the previous conviction. True or false?

2. A California defendant is charged with the felony of possessing a gun after having been convicted of committing a violent felony. Prior to Proposition 8, the defendant could preclude the prosecution from proving the conviction of the violent felony by admitting as true that portion of the accusatory pleading alleging his conviction. True or false?

3. Proposition 8 requires California prosecutors to prove a "prior felony conviction" to the fact finder in open court whenever the conviction is an element of a felony offense. Accordingly, if after Proposition 8 the defendant is charged with the felony of being a felon in possession of a gun, one would expect the prosecution to prove to the jurors the felony conviction giving rise to his felon status even if the defendant offers to admit the conviction. True or false?

4. The California Supreme Court, however, holds that if the defendant admits the underlying conviction, the prosecution may prove only that the defendant has been convicted of a felony. Why?

5. Under California Penal Code § 666, a defendant who commits petty theft, a misdemeanor, can nonetheless be charged with felony theft if at the time he committed the petty theft he had previously been convicted of and served time for enumerated felonies. Accordingly, a defendant charged with felony theft under this section may not withhold his felony conviction and incarceration under Proposition 8 by admitting these allegations prior to the trial. True of false?

In Apprendi v. New Jersey, 530 U.S. 466, 120 S.Ct. 2348, 147 L.Ed.2d 435 (2000), the United States Supreme Court held that prior convictions that enhance a sentence do not have to be proved to a jury as a federal due process matter. Consequently, whether California defendants are entitled to have a jury determine whether they been convicted of offenses that qualify as strikes under the Three Strikes Law is a state law question. Section 1025(b) of the California Penal Code provides that the "question of whether or not the defendant has suffered the prior conviction shall be tried by the jury that tries the issue upon a plea of not guilty * * *." But whether the offenses found by the jury qualify as strikes under the Three Strikes Law is question for the court, not the jury, even if a factual inquiry is required to make this determination. People v. Kelii, 21 Cal.4th 452, 456, 87 Cal.Rptr.2d 674, 677, 981 P.2d 518, 520(1999).

The United States Supreme Court, however, has placed some limits on the amount of fact finding a judge may undertake in determining whether the accused has been convicted of a prior conviction that qualifies as a predicate crime for enhancing the sentence. In making the determination, the judge may consider the statute defining the offense, the charging instrument, and the judgment of conviction. Where the accused pleaded guilty to the predicate offense, the judge may also consider the terms of the plea agreement and whatever colloquy took place at the time the plea was accepted. But the judge may not take into account such information as a police report without risking an *Apprendi* violation. See Shepard v. United States, 544 U.S. 13, 125 S.Ct. 1254, 161 L.Ed.2d 205 (2005).

6.   Under California Penal Code § 666, a defendant who commits petty theft, a misdemeanor, can nonetheless be charged with felony theft if at the time he committed the petty theft he had previously been convicted of and served time for petty theft. A defendant charged with felony theft under this section may withhold his misdemeanor conviction and incarceration by admitting these allegations prior to the trial since Proposition 8 is limited to "prior felony" convictions. True or false?

7.   Your client is charged with the federal offenses of being an ex-felon in possession of a gun and of assaulting a federal officer. The conviction giving rise to your client's status as an ex-felon was for assault. You offer to admit the assault conviction to prevent the prosecution from proving it as part of its proof that your client is an ex-felon. Because Proposition 8 does not apply to federal proceedings, a federal judge is free to accept or reject your offer and allow the prosecution to prove the underlying assault conviction. True or false?

§ 7.10   INADMISSIBLE ADMISSIONS

Earlier we encountered several types of admissions which for policy reasons may not be offered against the admitting party. Evidence of subsequent remedial measures may not be offered to prove negligence or other wrongdoing so as not to discourage defendants from undertaking repairs after an accident.[1] To encourage settling disputes, evidence that a party offered to settle the dispute is inadmissible to prove the validity or invalidity of the disputed claim.[2] Similarly, to encourage plea bargaining, evidence that the accused offered to plead to the offense charged or to some lesser offense is inadmissible to prove that the accused is guilty of the offense charged.[3] Evidence that the accused pled guilty but was subsequently permitted to withdraw his plea and enter a not guilty plea is also inadmissible to prove that the accused is guilty of the offense charged.[4] Since ordinarily the accused is not permitted to withdraw a plea of guilty except for good cause,[5] the policies favoring the withdrawal of the plea in a given case would be defeated if the prosecution were permitted to use the withdrawn guilty plea against the accused at the trial.

A guilty plea that is not withdrawn may be used as an admission, however. Thus, if a defendant pleads guilty to a speeding violation, that plea can be offered against the defendant as an admission in a subsequent action brought by a plaintiff injured by the defendant's driving. To encourage pleas, the California Penal Code permits defendants to plead nolo contendere to some criminal charges.[6] That "plea and any admissions required by the court during any inquiry it makes as to the voluntariness

I do not wish to contend

1.   See § 4.02 supra.

2.   See § 4.08 supra.

3.   See § 4.05 supra.

4.   Id.

5.   See West's Ann.California Penal Code § 1018.

6.   West's Ann.California Penal Code § 1016(3).

of, and factual basis for, the plea may not be used against the defendant as an admission in any civil suit based upon or growing out of the act upon which the criminal prosecution is based."[7] In 1982, that protection was limited to "cases other than those punishable as felonies"[8] in order to "assist the efforts of victims of crime to obtain compensation for their injuries from the criminals who inflicted those injuries."[9]

The Federal Rules of Evidence continue the traditional approach. They prohibit the use of a plea of nolo contendere in any civil or criminal proceeding regardless of the grade of the offense.[10]

Admissions made by parties to lawyers, spouses, physicians, psychotherapists, clergymen, counselors, and others are protected under certain circumstances from disclosure by privileges. These admissions are considered in the chapters relating to privileges.[11]

Confessions are admissions. Confessions taken in violation of *Miranda* and other limitations imposed by the Bill of Rights generally may not be used as admissions.[12]

QUESTIONS AND PROBLEMS

1.   Both the California Evidence Code and the Federal Rules of Evidence continue the Common Law policy of precluding the use of a plea of nolo contendere in a civil action regardless of the grade of the offense. True or false?

2.   To avoid unnecessary costs, it is good practice for California and federal defendants to plead guilty to such petty offenses as misdemeanors and infractions, especially where guilt is not contested. True or false?

3.   Among the hearsay exceptions, admissions are the least regulated by the Code and the Federal Rules. Accordingly, admissions made by a party under other circumstances that otherwise would constitute protected settings are still admissible over objection. For example, admissions made in plea negotiations and settlement conferences in civil cases may still be offered by the opponent against the admitting party. True or false?

§ 7.11 ADMISSIONS UNDER
THE FEDERAL RULES

Earlier, we saw that although the California and federal definitions of hearsay are almost identical, the Federal Rules depart from traditional treatment and classify prior statements of witnesses as nonhearsay even

---

7.   Id.

8.   Id.

9.   Id. (legislative history).

10.   Federal Rule of Evidence 410(2).

11.   See the sections beginning with Chapter 20 infra.

12.   Consideration of these admissions is beyond the scope of this work. For a more complete treatment, see LaFave, Search and Seizure § 11.4(b) and (c) (2d ed. 1987); LaFave and Israel, Criminal Procedure §§ 6.1 et seq., 9.4 (1984).

though they fall squarely within the federal definition of hearsay.[1] Since by definition these out of court statements may not be offered for the truth unless the witness testifies, the concerns of the hearsay rule are satisfied: the party opposing the statements is given an opportunity to cross examine the declarant under oath and in the presence of the fact finder.

The Federal Rules also classify admissions of party opponents as nonhearsay despite the unquestioned application of the federal definition of hearsay.[2] In support of the federal position, the Advisory Committee emphasizes that the exclusion of admissions from "the category of hearsay is the result of the adversary system rather than satisfaction of the conditions of the hearsay rule."[3] This signals acceptance of the view that instances of a party's conduct (including his statements) that are inconsistent with his trial claims should be admissible against him. It is also a concession to historical fact. Since admissions were admissible before the crystallization of the hearsay rule, tradition, rather than satisfaction of the rule, also dictates their continued admissibility.[4]

The federal position has merit. The fact that the opposing party can take the stand to explain or deny a personal admission is not of much help when the admission offered was made not by the party but by a nontestifying agent or servant or coconspirator. Thus, the Advisory Committee is right in urging that the admissibility of party admissions must rest on grounds other than satisfying the concerns of the hearsay rule.

QUESTIONS AND PROBLEMS

1.   Because the Federal Rules do not treat admissions as an exception to the hearsay rule, they may be received only to impeach the party but not for the truth of the matter stated. True or false?

2.   Admissions are not hearsay under the Rules because the federal definition of hearsay does not embrace admissions. True or false?

ARTICLE 1 OF THE CALIFORNIA CONSTITUTION

§ 28.   Findings and declarations; rights of victims; enforcement

* * *

(f) In addition to the enumerated rights provided in subdivision (b) that are personally enforceable by victims as provided in subdivision (c), victims of crime have additional rights that are shared with all of the

---

1.   See § 5.03 supra.

2.   Federal Rule of Evidence 801(d)(2).

3.   Id. (Advisory Committee Note).

4.   Weinstein and Berger, Weinstein's Evidence Manual ¶ 15.02[01] (1987).

People of the State of California. These collectively held rights include, but are not limited to, the following:

* * *

(4) Use of Prior Convictions. Any prior felony conviction of any person in any criminal proceeding, whether adult or juvenile, shall subsequently be used without limitation for purposes of impeachment or enhancement of sentence in any criminal proceeding. When a prior felony conviction is an element of any felony offense, it shall be proven to the trier of fact in open court.

CALIFORNIA EVIDENCE CODE

§ 1220. Admission of party

Evidence of a statement is not made inadmissible by the hearsay rule when offered against the declarant in an action to which he is a party in either his individual or representative capacity, regardless of whether the statement was made in his individual or representative capacity.

§ 1221. Adoptive admission

Evidence of a statement offered against a party is not made inadmissible by the hearsay rule if the statement is one of which the party, with knowledge of the content thereof, has by words or other conduct manifested his adoption or his belief in its truth.

§ 1222. Authorized admission

Evidence of a statement offered against a party is not made inadmissible by the hearsay rule if:

(a) The statement was made by a person authorized by the party to make a statement or statements for him concerning the subject matter of the statement; and

(b) The evidence is offered either after admission of evidence sufficient to sustain a finding of such authority or, in the court's discretion as to the order of proof, subject to the admission of such evidence.

§ 1223. Admission of co-conspirator

Evidence of a statement offered against a party is not made inadmissible by the hearsay rule if:

(a) The statement was made by the declarant while participating in a conspiracy to commit a crime or civil wrong and in furtherance of the objective of that conspiracy;

(b) The statement was made prior to or during the time that the party was participating in that conspiracy; and

(c) The evidence is offered either after admission of evidence sufficient to sustain a finding of the facts specified in subdivisions (a) and (b) or, in the court's discretion as to the order of proof, subject to the admission of such evidence.

§ 1224. Statement of declarant whose liability or breach of duty is in issue

When the liability, obligation, or duty of a party to a civil action is based in whole or in part upon the liability, obligation, or duty of the declarant, or when the claim or right asserted by a party to a civil action is barred or diminished by a breach of duty by the declarant, evidence of a statement made by the declarant is as admissible against the party as it would be if offered against the declarant in an action involving that liability, obligation, duty, or breach of duty.

§ 1225. Statement of declarant whose right or title is in issue

When a right, title, or interest in any property or claim asserted by a party to a civil action requires a determination that a right, title, or interest exists or existed in the declarant, evidence of a statement made by the declarant during the time the party now claims the declarant was the holder of the right, title, or interest is as admissible against the party as it would be if offered against the declarant in an action involving that right, title, or interest.

§ 1226. Statement of minor child in parent's action for child's injury

Evidence of a statement by a minor child is not made inadmissible by the hearsay rule if offered against the plaintiff in an action brought under Section 376 of the Code of Civil Procedure for injury to such minor child.

§ 1227. Statement of declarant in action for his wrongful death

Evidence of a statement by the deceased is not made inadmissible by the hearsay rule if offered against the plaintiff in an action for wrongful death brought under Section 377 of the Code of Civil Procedure.

§ 1350. Unavailable declarant; hearsay rule

(a) In a criminal proceeding charging a serious felony, evidence of a statement made by a declarant is not made inadmissible by the hearsay rule if the declarant is unavailable as a witness, and all of the following are true:

(1) There is clear and convincing evidence that the declarant's unavailability was knowingly caused by, aided by, or solicited by the party against whom the statement is offered for the purpose of preventing the arrest or prosecution of the party and is the result of the death by homicide or the kidnapping of the declarant.

(2) There is no evidence that the unavailability of the declarant was caused by, aided by, solicited by, or procured on behalf of, the party who is offering the statement.

(3) The statement has been memorialized in a tape recording made by a law enforcement official, or in a written statement prepared by a law enforcement official and signed by the declarant and notarized in the

presence of the law enforcement official, prior to the death or kidnapping of the declarant.

(4) The statement was made under circumstances which indicate its trustworthiness and was not the result of promise, inducement, threat, or coercion.

(5) The statement is relevant to the issues to be tried.

(6) The statement is corroborated by other evidence which tends to connect the party against whom the statement is offered with the commission of the serious felony with which the party is charged. The corroboration is not sufficient if it merely shows the commission of the offense or the circumstances thereof.

(b) If the prosecution intends to offer a statement pursuant to this section, the prosecution shall serve a written notice upon the defendant at least 10 days prior to the hearing or trial at which the prosecution intends to offer the statement, unless the prosecution shows good cause for the failure to provide that notice. In the event that good cause is shown, the defendant shall be entitled to a reasonable continuance of the hearing or trial.

(c) If the statement is offered during trial, the court's determination shall be made out of the presence of the jury. If the defendant elects to testify at the hearing on a motion brought pursuant to this section, the court shall exclude from the examination every person except the clerk, the court reporter, the bailiff, the prosecutor, the investigating officer, the defendant and his or her counsel, an investigator for the defendant, and the officer having custody of the defendant. Notwithstanding any other provision of law, the defendant's testimony at the hearing shall not be admissible in any other proceeding except the hearing brought on the motion pursuant to this section. If a transcript is made of the defendant's testimony, it shall be sealed and transmitted to the clerk of the court in which the action is pending.

(d) As used in this section, "serious felony" means any of the felonies listed in subdivision (c) of Section 1192.7 of the Penal Code or any violation of Section 11351, 11352, 11378, or 11379 of the Health and Safety Code.

(e) If a statement to be admitted pursuant to this section includes hearsay statements made by anyone other than the declarant who is unavailable pursuant to subdivision (a), those hearsay statements are inadmissible unless they meet the requirements of an exception to the hearsay rule.

§ 1390. Statements against parties involved in causing unavailability of declarant as witness

(a) Evidence of a statement is not made inadmissible by the hearsay rule if the statement is offered against a party that has engaged or aided and abetted in the wrongdoing that was intended to, and did, procure the unavailability of the declarant as a witness.

(b)(1) The party seeking to introduce a statement pursuant to subdivision (a) shall establish, by a preponderance of the evidence, that the elements of subdivision (a) have been met at a foundational hearing.

(2) The hearsay evidence that is the subject of the foundational hearing is admissible at the foundational hearing. However, a finding that the elements of subdivision (a) have been met shall not be based solely on the unconfronted hearsay statement of the unavailable declarant, and shall be supported by independent corroborative evidence.

(3) The foundational hearing shall be conducted outside the presence of the jury. However, if the hearing is conducted after a jury trial has begun, the judge presiding at the hearing may consider evidence already presented to the jury in deciding whether the elements of subdivision (a) have been met.

(4) In deciding whether or not to admit the statement, the judge may take into account whether it is trustworthy and reliable.

(c) This section shall apply to any civil, criminal, or juvenile case or proceeding initiated or pending as of January 1, 2011.

(d) This section shall remain in effect only until January 1, 2016, and as of that date is repealed, unless a later enacted statute, that is enacted before January 1, 2016, deletes or extends that date. If this section is repealed, the fact that it is repealed should it occur, shall not be deemed to give rise to any ground for an appeal or a postverdict challenge based on its use in a criminal or juvenile case or proceeding before January 1, 2016.

FEDERAL RULES OF EVIDENCE

Rule 801. Definitions That Apply to This Article; Exclusions from Hearsay

(a) Statement. "Statement" means a person's oral assertion, written assertion, or nonverbal conduct, if the person intended it as an assertion.

(b) Declarant. "Declarant" means the person who made the statement.

(c) Hearsay. "Hearsay" means a statement that:

(1) the declarant does not make while testifying at the current trial or hearing; and

(2) a party offers in evidence to prove the truth of the matter asserted in the statement.

(d) Statements That Are Not Hearsay. A statement that meets the following conditions is not hearsay:

* * *

(2) *An Opposing Party's Statement.* The statement is offered against an opposing party and:

(A) was made by the party in an individual or representative capacity;

(B) is one the party manifested that it adopted or believed to be true;

(C) was made by a person whom the party authorized to make a statement on the subject;

(D) was made by the party's agent or employee on a matter within the scope of that relationship and while it existed; or

(E) was made by the party's coconspirator during and in furtherance of the conspiracy. The statement must be considered but does not by itself establish the declarant's authority under (C); the existence or scope of the relationship under (D); or the existence of the conspiracy or participation in it under (E).

Rule 804. Exceptions to the Rule Against Hearsay—When the Declarant Is Unavailable as a Witness

* * *

(b) The Exceptions. The following are not excluded by the rule against hearsay if the declarant is unavailable as a witness:

     * * *

     (6) *Statement Offered Against a Party That Wrongfully Caused the Declarant's Unavailability.* A statement offered against a party that wrongfully caused—or acquiesced in wrongfully causing—the declarant's unavailability as a witness, and did so intending that result.

CHAPTER 8

EXCEPTIONS TO THE HEARSAY RULE: PRIOR STATEMENTS OF WITNESSES AND PRIOR RECOLLECTION RECORDED

∎ ∎ ∎

Table of Sections

§ 8.01 PRIOR STATEMENTS OF WITNESSES IN GENERAL

We have seen that party admissions can be made vicariously, for example, by an agent[1] or coconspirator[2] of the party. If in these circumstances the agent or coconspirator does not testify, then the party opposing the statement is denied an opportunity to cross examine the hearsay declarant under oath in the presence of the fact finder. Accordingly, the justification for treating vicarious admissions as an exception to the hearsay rule must rest on grounds other than satisfying the concerns of the rule.[3]

In the case of prior statements of witnesses, the exceptions contemplate that the declarant will take the stand before the evidence is closed.[4]

---

1. See § 7.03 supra.

2. See § 7.04 supra.

3. For a discussion of the additional grounds, see § 7.11 supra.

4. See West's Ann.California Evidence Code §§ 791, 1235–1238; see also Federal Rule of Evidence 801(d)(1).

The party opposing the declaration is thus afforded an opportunity to cross examine the declarant under oath before the fact finder. Thus, there is no need to determine whether prior statements in the abstract possess such circumstantial guarantees of reliability as to justify an exception to the hearsay rule. By cross examining the hearsay declarant, the party opposing the declaration can expose reasons why the fact finder should not rely on the declaration.

Precisely because the opposing party is given an opportunity to cross examine the declarant, the Federal Rules exempt prior statements of witnesses from the definition of hearsay and allow these statements to be received for the truth if certain conditions are satisfied.[5] The Code, on the other hand, classifies prior statements as hearsay but creates an exception for them.[6] As out of court statements offered for the truth of the matter stated, prior statements fall squarely within the Code's definition of hearsay.[7]

QUESTIONS AND PROBLEMS

Under the Federal Rules, prior statements of witnesses may not be received for the truth of the matter asserted because, unlike the Code, the Rules do not create an exception to the hearsay rule for such statements. True or false?

§ 8.02 PRIOR INCONSISTENT STATEMENTS UNDER THE EVIDENCE CODE

Under the Common Law, the use of prior inconsistent statements to impeach the credibility of nonparty witnesses did not violate the hearsay rule.[1] The statements were not received for the truth of the matter stated but only to discredit the witness. The jurors, of course, had to be alerted to this distinction, and the judge, upon request of the party opposing the statement, had to admonish them to consider it only for its impeachment value. Concern that jurors might not be able to perform the mental gymnastics required by the instruction prompted some jurisdictions to create an exception to the hearsay rule for the prior statements of witnesses. California Evidence Code § 1235 provides that "[e]vidence of a statement made by a witness is not made inadmissible by the hearsay rule if the statement is inconsistent with his testimony at the hearing and is offered in compliance with Section 770."[2]

More than mental difficulties account for the exception. As pointed out by the California Law Revision Commission:

---

5. Federal Rule of Evidence 801(d)(1).

6. See West's Ann.California Evidence Code §§ 1235–1238.

7. For an extended discussion of the consequences of the Federal Rules' treatment of prior statements of witnesses as nonhearsay, see § 5.03 supra.

1. West's Ann.California Evidence Code § 1235 (comment).

2. West's Ann.California Evidence Code § 1235.

[T]he dangers against which the hearsay rule is designed to protect are largely nonexistent. The declarant is in court and may be examined and cross-examined in regard to his statements and their subject matter. In many cases, the inconsistent statement is more likely to be true than the testimony of the witness at the trial because it was made nearer in time to the matter to which it relates and is less likely to be influenced by the controversy that gave rise to the litigation. The trier of fact has the declarant before it and can observe his demeanor and the nature of his testimony as he denies or tries to explain away the inconsistency. Hence, it is in as good a position to determine the truth or falsity of the inconsistent testimony given in court.[3]

Although strategic concerns may prompt advocates to confront witnesses with their prior inconsistent statements, § 770 does not require such confrontation.[4] As the Law Revision Commission noted, "Permitting a witness to explain or deny an alleged inconsistent statement is desirable, but there is no compelling reason to provide the opportunity for explanation *before* the inconsistent statement is introduced in evidence. Accordingly, unless the interests of justice otherwise require, Section 770 permits the judge to exclude evidence of an inconsistent statement only if the witness during his examination was not given an opportunity to explain or deny the statement *and* he has been unconditionally excused and is not subject to being recalled as a witness."[5]

Section 770 notwithstanding, most lawyers will confront a witness with his prior inconsistent statements. Faced with his prior statement, the witness may disavow his testimony and, instead, affirm the prior statement as reflecting the truth of the matter in controversy. If the witness declines the invitation to affirm his prior statement, the attorney can always use the statement to discredit the witness.

If the witness refuses to concede having made the prior statement, the impeaching party can prove it extrinsically. Section 770 sets out the circumstances that must exist before a prior inconsistent statement can be received in evidence. It provides that "extrinsic evidence of a statement made by a witness that is inconsistent with any part of his testimony at the hearing shall be excluded unless: (a) the witness was so examined while testifying as to give him an opportunity to explain or to deny the statement; or (b) the witness has not been excused from giving further testimony in the action."[6]

---

3. Id. (comment).

4. Even if a party chooses to confront a witness with a prior inconsistent statement, the party need not "disclose to the witness any information concerning the statement * * *." West's Ann.California Evidence Code § 769.

5. California Evidence Code § 1235 (comment) (emphasis in the original). Moreover, § 770 permits "more effective cross-examination and impeachment of several collusive witnesses, since there need be no disclosure of prior inconsistency before all such witnesses have been examined." Id.

6. West's Ann.California Evidence Code § 770.

Determining whether the prior statement is inconsistent with some part of the witness's testimony sometimes can be problematical. In most instances, the impeaching party will have no difficulty satisfying the judge that a prior statement possesses the requisite inconsistency. If on direct the witness states that the light was green, the witness can be impeached by an earlier statement in which the witness stated that the light was red. But what should the judge do if on direct the witness claims no memory of the light's color? Is saying "I don't remember" sufficiently contradictory of a prior statement as to qualify the statement as an inconsistent one? If the witness cannot recall because of a mental impairment such as amnesia, the fact that the witness made an earlier statement about the matter does not make the statement inconsistent with the claimed failure of recollection.[7] Similarly, where there is no reason to disbelieve the witness's claim of forgetfulness, the witness's earlier statements do not qualify as inconsistent statements.[8] But the fact that the witness previously made a statement about the matter can be brought out. Even though the witness's earlier statement about the color of the light remains inadmissible to prove the light's color, the fact finder, in assessing the witness's credibility, is entitled to know that the witness possessed the very knowledge which he now professes an inability to recall.

"Inconsistency in effect, rather than contradiction in express terms, is the test for admitting a witness' prior statement," including those of the forgetful witness.[9] Thus, where a witness's claimed inability to remember who supplied him with marihuana is a "deliberate evasion", the impeaching party is entitled to offer a prior statement by the witness in which he identified his supplier.[10] In effect, the witness's claimed forgetfulness is treated as a denial of the proposition the examiner is seeking to establish, a proposition that is consistent with the one asserted by the witness in his earlier statement. A witness's refusal to answer all questions, however, does not render the witness's extra-judicial statements inconsistent.[11] Such statements do not qualify as prior inconsistent statements.

Prior inconsistent statements and the multiple hearsay rule. Suppose that in a theft prosecution the People call Witness A to testify that the accused told A, "I took the victim's ring." If Witness A repeats the accused's statement to prove that the accused took the ring, a hearsay objection would have to be overruled; the accused's statement would fall

---

7. People v. Simmons, 123 Cal.App.3d 677, 681–682, 177 Cal.Rptr. 17, 20 (1981).

8. People v. Sam, 71 Cal.2d 194, 208–210, 77 Cal.Rptr. 804, 812–813, 454 P.2d 700, 708–709 (1969).

9. People v. Green, 3 Cal.3d 981, 988, 92 Cal.Rptr. 494, 498, 479 P.2d 998, 1002 (1971).

10. Id. Accord: People v. Ervin, 22 Cal.4th 48, 83–85, 91 Cal.Rptr.2d 623, 644–645, 990 P.2d 506, 524–525, cert. denied, 531 U.S. 842, 121 S.Ct. 107, 148 L.Ed.2d 65 (2000); People v. Coffman, 34 Cal.4th 1, 78, 17 Cal.Rptr.3d 710, 782, 96 P.3d 30, 90, cert. denied, 544 U.S. 1063, 125 S.Ct. 2517, 161 L.Ed.2d 1114 (2004). For a discussion of whether the accused's inability to cross examine the forgetful witness deprives the accused of the right to confront witness, see People v. O'Quinn, 109 Cal.App.3d 219, 226–228, 167 Cal.Rptr. 141, 144–146 (1980), cert. denied, 450 U.S. 928, 101 S.Ct. 1384, 67 L.Ed.2d 359 (1981).

11. People v. Rios, 163 Cal.App.3d 852, 864, 210 Cal.Rptr. 271, 278 (1985).

within the hearsay exception for party admissions.[12] Suppose, however, that Witness A surprises the prosecution and on direct examination testifies that he did not hear the accused say that he took the ring. If the prosecution then calls Witness B to testify that she heard Witness A say, "I heard the accused say, 'I took the victim's ring'", multiple hearsay would be involved. What the accused told Witness A is hearsay, since the accused's out of court statement is being offered to prove that he took the ring. What Witness A told Witness B is also hearsay, since Witness A's out of court statement (incorporating the accused's out of court statement) is being offered to prove that Witness A heard the accused make the statement.

Both the Code and the Federal Rules provide that hearsay included within hearsay may be admitted over a hearsay objection if each hearsay statement meets the requirements of an exception to the hearsay rule.[13] Witness A's statement to Witness B is admissible for the truth of the matter stated because it falls within the prior inconsistent statement exception to the hearsay rule. The portion of Witness A's statement relating what the accused said is admissible for the truth of the matter stated because it falls within the party admission exception. Thus, a hearsay objection to Witness B's testimony would have to be overruled.

Suppose that Witness B also surprises the prosecution and on the stand denies having heard Witness A's statement. May the prosecution call Witness C to testify that Witness B said that Witness A said that the accused admitted taking the ring? Since Witness C is reporting Witness B's prior inconsistent statement and the statements by Witness A and the accused also fall within hearsay exceptions, the hearsay objection to Witness C's testimony must be overruled.[14] Nonetheless, the use of multiple hearsay increases the risk of faulty reproduction. The purpose of Witness C's testimony, after all, is to prove that the accused took the ring, and a chain of declarants is required to reproduce the accused's statement. The risk of faulty reproduction of multiple hearsay, however, goes to its credibility and not to its admissibility.[15] It is up to the fact finder to decide what weight, if any, to give to such hearsay.

Prior inconsistent statements and confrontation. In *Crawford v. Washington*[16] the United States Supreme Court laid down a new test to determine when "testimonial" hearsay offered by the prosecution offends a defendant's Sixth Amendment right to confront his accusers. The Court held that no violation occurs, unless the defendant is denied an opportunity to cross-examine the hearsay declarant at the trial or, if the declarant does not testify, unless the defendant was denied an opportunity to cross examine the declarant prior to the trial.[17] The California hearsay excep-

---

12. West's Ann.California Evidence Code § 1220.

13. West's Ann.California Evidence Code § 1201; Federal Rule of Evidence 805.

14. People v. Zapien, 4 Cal.4th 929, 17 Cal.Rptr.2d 122, 132, 846 P.2d 704 (1993).

15. Id. at 956, 17 Cal.Rptr.2d at 135, 846 P.2d at 717.

16. 541 U.S. 36, 124 S.Ct. 1354, 158 L.Ed.2d 177 (2004).

17. Id. at 1374.

tion for prior inconsistent statements assumes that the hearsay declarant will appear at the trial as a witness. Section 1235 creates a hearsay exception for statements by witnesses which are inconsistent with their testimony.[18] Accordingly, the state's use of the exception to offer hearsay against the accused would not ordinarily violate the accused's confrontation rights.[19]

Occasionally, however, a witness may claim no recall of the event she has been called to relate to the jury. A witness, for example, who informed the police that she saw the accused commit the crime charged may be called by the prosecution to relate that observation to the jury. If the witness surprises the prosecution by claiming not to remember seeing the accused commit the offense, offering the witness's statement to the police as an inconsistent statement poses foundational difficulties. Saying "I don't remember whether I saw the accused commit the offense" is not the same as saying "I did not see the accused commit the offense." Where the witness's claim of failure of recollection is genuine, the Code does not authorize the prosecution to offer the witness's prior statement for the truth under the hearsay exception for prior inconsistent statements. The witness's testimony that she does not recall seeing who committed the offense is insufficiently contradictory of what she related to the police. But where the witness's claim of failure of recollection is feigned, the prosecution may offer the prior statement to impeach the witness as well as for the truth.[20] In these circumstances, saying "I don't remember whether I saw the accused commit the crime" is the equivalent of saying "I did not see the accused commit the crime."[21] Offering the prior statement against the accused under these circumstances will not offend the accused's confrontation rights. Even if the prior statement qualifies as "testimonial" hearsay, the fact that the accused can cross examine the witness about the prior statement, including his failure of recollection, has been held by the California courts to satisfy the cross-examination requirements of the Confrontation Clause.[22]

QUESTIONS AND PROBLEMS

1. In her case-in-chief, the plaintiff calls W who, appearing under a subpoena, testifies that the defendant had the red light. The defendant declines to cross examine W. In response to the judge's question whether W should be excused, the defendant says, "No." In his case-in-chief, the defendant calls X who testifies that just five days earlier W said to him, "The defendant had the green light." The plaintiff objects and moves to strike X's testimony on the ground that the defendant failed to give W a chance to deny or explain her statement to X. Under the Code and the Federal Rules, the judge should grant the motion to strike. ~~True or false?~~ *Overrule*

---

18. See West's Ann. California Evidence Code § 1235.

19. See People v. Butler, 127 Cal.App.4th 49, 59, 25 Cal.Rptr.3d 154, 162 (2005).

20. See § 8.02 supra.

21. Id.

22. See, e.g., People v. Gunder, 151 Cal.App.4th 412, 419, 59 Cal.Rptr.3d 817, 823 (2007).

review now used for truth

2. In a murder prosecution, the prosecutor calls X to testify that the accused told X that she had committed the killing. On the stand, X surprises the prosecution by testifying as follows:

Q: Did you have a conversation with the accused on December 1?

A: Yes.

Q: What, if anything, did the accused say to you?

A: The accused said to me, "I did not commit the killing."

Q: Isn't it a fact that on December 1 you heard the accused say, "I committed the killing"?

A: No, I did not hear the accused make such a statement.

Q: Isn't it a fact that on December 15 you said to Officer Jones, "I heard the accused say, 'I committed the killing.' "?

A: No, I never made such a statement to Officer Jones.

* * *

ofr Jones

Q: Officer Jones, did you have a conversation with X on December 15?

A: Yes.

Q: What, if anything, did X say to you? *one : FRE - Not under oath*   *inconsistent*   *two : party opp.*

A: X said to me, "I heard the accused say, 'I committed the killing.' "

The accused moves to strike on the grounds of multiple hearsay for which there are insufficient exceptions. Should a California judge sustain the objection?

3.   The accused is charged with selling marihuana. At the preliminary hearing, a witness for the prosecution testifies that the accused supplied him with the marihuana. At the trial, the witness surprises the prosecution and in response to the question of who supplied him with the marihuana the witness says that he does not remember. May the prosecution offer the witness's preliminary hearing testimony for the truth of the matter stated? May the prosecution impeach the witness with the statement the witness made at the preliminary hearing? *Yes for IMPEACH / for truth of matter } CA ok (2x) / FRE only impeach*

§ 8.03   PRIOR INCONSISTENT STATEMENTS AND PROPOSITION 8

In June 1982, the California voters approved Proposition 8, an initiative that made marked changes in the evidentiary rules that apply to criminal proceedings.[1] One provision of Proposition 8 gives parties to criminal proceedings the constitutional right not to have relevant evidence excluded.[2]

This provision permits the use of some prior inconsistent statements that had been excluded prior to the enactment of the initiative. In Harris

---

1.   See discussion in § 3.07 supra.

2.   West's Ann.California Constitution Article I, § 28(f)(2).

v. New York[3] the United States Supreme Court held that inconsistent statements that are inadmissible as admissions in the prosecution's case-in-chief because of failure to comply with *Miranda* can nonetheless be used to impeach the accused, as long as the statements are not coerced or involuntary.[4] According to the Court, the "shield provided by *Miranda* cannot be perverted into a license to use perjury by way of a defense, free from the risk of confrontation with prior inconsistent utterances."[5]

In People v. Disbrow[6] the California Supreme Court declined to follow *Harris* on the ground that such evidence, even if limited to impeachment, violated the accused's state constitutional privilege against self-incrimination.[7] Although a number of factors induced the court to reach this conclusion, the principal one was the perceived ineffectiveness of the limiting instruction directing the jurors to consider the accused's prior statement only on the question of the accused's credibility. "[F]aced with the prospect of the jury hearing his admittedly illegally obtained confession if he testifies in his own behalf [the defendant] will be under considerable pressure to forego this most basic right of an accused."[8]

As a matter of relevance, however, prior inconsistent statements are probative of a witness's lack of veracity. Consequently, *Disbrow* conflicts with Proposition 8. In People v. May[9] the California Supreme Court resolved the conflict in favor of the initiative by holding that Proposition 8 overturned *Disbrow*.[10]

The impeachment value of extrajudicial statements offered under *Harris* stems from their self-contradictory nature; the theory is that people who say inconsistent things about the same matter ought not be believed. Accordingly, *Harris* does not require that extrajudicial statements inadmissible under *Miranda* be truthful in order to qualify as impeachment evidence.[11] Thus, a defendant's false statement to a detective that he had rented a van was admissible to impeach the defendant's trial testimony that he merely found the van in a parking lot.[12]

---

3.   401 U.S. 222, 91 S.Ct. 643, 28 L.Ed.2d 1 (1971).

4.   Id. at 224–226, 91 S.Ct. at 645–646.

5.   Id.

6.   16 Cal.3d 101, 127 Cal.Rptr. 360, 545 P.2d 272 (1976).

7.   Id. at 113, 127 Cal.Rptr. at 368, 545 P.2d at 280.

8.   Id. at 112, 127 Cal.Rptr. at 367, 545 P.2d at 279.

9.   44 Cal.3d 309, 243 Cal.Rptr. 369, 748 P.2d 307 (1988).

10.   Id. at 314–315, 243 Cal.Rptr. at 374–375, 748 P.2d at 309–310. In California courts, so long as the statements taken in violation of *Miranda* are reliable under *Harris*, it is immaterial that the interrogating officer deliberately violated *Miranda* in order to secure the statements for impeachment purposes. People v. Peevy, 17 Cal.4th 1184, 1202, 73 Cal.Rptr.2d 865, 877, 953 P.2d 1212 (1998). Whether the systematic violation of *Miranda* by police departments to obtain impeachment evidence is unconstitutional has not been decided, however. See People v. Neal, 31 Cal.4th 63, 78, note 4, 1 Cal.Rptr.3d 650, 661, note 4, 72 P.3d 280, 289, note 4 (2003).

11.   People v. Gutierrez, 28 Cal.4th 1083, 1132, 124 Cal.Rptr.2d 373, 408, 52 P.3d 572, 601 (2002), cert. denied, 538 U.S. 1001, 123 S.Ct. 1899, 155 L.Ed.2d 829 (2003).

12.   Id. The van turned out to contain the body of a woman the defendant was accused of murdering.

Proposition 8 also modifies People v. Belleci,[13] which prohibits the use in subsequent proceedings of any evidence that has been suppressed pursuant to Penal Code § 1538.5.[14] Since the United States Supreme Court has approved the use of evidence seized in violation of the Fourth Amendment to impeach the accused,[15] after Proposition 8 a criminal defendant can be impeached with written prior inconsistent statements that had been previously suppressed under the Fourth Amendment.[16] Moreover, since the United States Supreme Court has also upheld impeaching the accused with statements taken in violation of the Sixth Amendment's right to counsel,[17] such statements should also be admissible in California for this purpose.[18]

Proposition 8 leaves undisturbed the holdings of other cases which limit the use of some statements by criminal defendants to their impeachment value. In Simmons v. United States[19] the United States Supreme Court held that statements made by the accused at a hearing to suppress evidence under the Fourth Amendment could not be used against the accused at the trial. To permit the use of the statements as admissions would discourage defendants from asserting their constitutional rights.[20] But in People v. Douglas[21] the California Court of Appeal held that such statements could nonetheless be used as prior inconsistent statements to impeach the accused.[22] Since such statements are probative of the accused's credibility, their use for this purpose is consistent with Proposition 8.

Douglas relied on People v. Coleman,[23] which in turn held that statements made by the accused at a probation revocation hearing, while inadmissible as admissions at the subsequent trial, can nonetheless be used to impeach should the accused testify inconsistently at the trial.[24] Again, since such statements are probative of the accused's lack of

If the accused offers in exculpation a statement taken by the police in violation of *Miranda,* the prosecution may seek to impeach the accused by evidence that the statement was false. See People v. Williams, 79 Cal.App.4th 1157, 1169, 94 Cal.Rptr.2d 727, 735 (2000).

13.   24 Cal.3d 879, 157 Cal.Rptr. 503, 598 P.2d 473 (1979).

14.   Id. at 887–888, 157 Cal.Rptr. at 508–510, 598 P.2d at 479–480.

15.   United States v. Havens, 446 U.S. 620, 100 S.Ct. 1912, 64 L.Ed.2d 559 (1980), reh'g denied, 448 U.S. 911, 101 S.Ct. 25, 65 L.Ed.2d 1172 (1980).

16.   People v. Moore, 201 Cal.App.3d 877, 884, 247 Cal.Rptr. 353, 358 (1988).

17.   Michigan v. Harvey, 494 U.S. 344, 351, 110 S.Ct. 1176, 1181, 108 L.Ed.2d 293 (1990).

18.   Proposition 8, however, does not affect the law pertaining to privileges. See West's Ann. California Constitution Article I, § 28(f)(2). Evidence taken in violation of the Sixth Amendment's right to counsel may still be excluded in California if it falls within the protection of the California privilege for confidential communications between the accused and their counsel. For a discussion of the California attorney-client privilege, see Chapter 21 infra.

19.   390 U.S. 377, 88 S.Ct. 967, 19 L.Ed.2d 1247 (1968).

20.   Id. at 394, 88 S.Ct. at 976. The Federal Rules provide that the "accused does not, by testifying upon a preliminary matter, become subject to cross-examination as to other issues in the case." Federal Rule of Evidence 104(d).

21.   66 Cal.App.3d 998, 136 Cal.Rptr. 358 (1977).

22.   Id. at 1003, 136 Cal.Rptr. at 361.

23.   13 Cal.3d 867, 120 Cal.Rptr. 384, 533 P.2d 1024 (1975).

24.   Id. at 889, 120 Cal.Rptr. at 402, 533 P.2d at 1042.

veracity, their use for impeachment purposes is consistent with Proposition 8.[25] For the same reason Proposition 8 leaves untouched those cases which hold that a minor's statements to a probation officer or to a juvenile court at a fitness hearing may be used only to impeach the minor's credibility should the minor testify inconsistently with his statements at a subsequent hearing.[26]

QUESTIONS AND PROBLEMS

1. While in custody, the police interrogate the accused without first giving him the *Miranda* warnings. In response to their questions, the accused admits that he committed the offense subsequently charged against him. Over the accused's *Miranda* objection, may the state offer the accused's admission to prove that he was the perpetrator?

2. Assume the answer to the preceding question is "no". If the accused on direct examination testifies that he did not commit the offense, may the state offer his admission to impeach his credibility in a federal court?

3. Would the evidence be admissible for this purpose in a California court before Proposition 8? After Proposition 8?

§ 8.04 INCONSISTENT STATEMENTS UNDER THE FEDERAL RULES

As originally drafted, Federal Rule of Evidence 801(d)(1)(A) would have followed the Code in permitting prior inconsistent statements to be used substantively as well as to impeach the witness.[1] But because of Congressional concerns about their reliability, only those statements "given under penalty of perjury at a trial, hearing, or other proceeding, or in a deposition" can be admitted for the truth of the matter stated.[2] Statements not made under these circumstances can be used only to impeach the witness. Upon the motion of the opposing party, the judge must instruct the jurors to consider such statements only for their impeachment value.

Statements that can be received for the truth of the matters asserted include those made at depositions, prior court hearings, and before grand juries. Statements made to law enforcement authorities, even if given under oath, are outside the definition of "other proceeding" and cannot be received for the truth.[3]

---

25. But *Coleman*'s holding was the result of a "judicial rule of evidence" and was not compelled by the Federal Constitution. Id. Since incriminating statements made by the accused at a revocation hearing are relevant admissions at the subsequent trial, an argument can be made that the judicially created limitation barring the use of such statements as admissions is overturned by Proposition 8. See note 6, § 11.02 infra.

26. People v. Humiston, 20 Cal.App.4th 460, 475, 24 Cal.Rptr.2d 515, 524 (1993).

1. Federal Rule of Evidence 801(d)(1)(A) (Report of House Committee on the Judiciary).

2. Id. (Conference Report).

3. See, e.g., United States v. Day, 789 F.2d 1217, 1222 (6th Cir.1986).

Federal Rule 613, like California Evidence Code § 770, limits the use of extrinsic evidence of a prior inconsistent statement when the impeaching party declines to confront the witness with the statement. Unless the interests of justice otherwise require, a federal judge must exclude the extrinsic proof unless the opposing party is afforded an opportunity to examine the witness about the statement before the close of the evidence.[4]

QUESTIONS AND PROBLEMS

1.   To prove that the accused committed the theft, the prosecutor calls X to testify that the accused told X that she had committed the theft. On the stand, X surprises the prosecution by testifying as follows:

Q: On December 1 did the accused say anything to you?

A: No, he did not.

Q: Isn't it a fact that on December 1 the accused said to you, "I committed the theft"?

A: No, I did not hear the accused make such a statement.

Q: Isn't it a fact that on December 15 you said to Officer Jones, "The accused said to me, 'I committed the theft.' "?

A: No, I never made such a statement to Officer Jones.

* * *

Q: Officer Jones, did you have a conversation with X on December 15?

A: Yes.

Q: What, if anything, did X say to you?

A: X said to me, "The accused said to me, 'I committed the theft.' "

The accused moves to strike on the grounds of hearsay. How should a federal judge rule?

2.   Suppose that Y was the court reporter at the grand jury hearing to determine whether the accused should be indicted. Y testifies that X appeared as a witness and under oath said, "The accused said to me, 'I committed the theft.' " Should a federal judge grant the accused's motion to strike on grounds of hearsay?

§ 8.05   PRIOR CONSISTENT STATEMENTS UNDER THE EVIDENCE CODE

When a witness has been impeached by the suggestion that his testimony on direct is a lie, the proponent might on redirect show that the witness has previously told the same story under circumstances in which he was likely to be truthful. Subject to certain limitations, a party is allowed to rehabilitate the witness by having him relate out of court statements that are consistent with his testimony.

---

4.   Federal Rule of Evidence 613.

Under § 791, the rehabilitating party can offer the witness's consistent statements to support his credibility in two circumstances. If the witness has been impeached by a prior inconsistent statement, the rehabilitating party can offer statements made by the witness that are consistent with his testimony if the witness made those statements before the inconsistent one.[1] In addition, if the impeaching party has implicitly or expressly charged the witness with bias, recent fabrication, or other improper motive, the rehabilitating party can offer statements by the witness that are consistent with his testimony if the witness made those statements before the motive to fabricate or other improper influence arose.[2] If either of these conditions is satisfied, then the witness's consistent statement may be received to rehabilitate the witness as well as for the truth of the matter stated.[3]

In criminal cases, a literal interpretation of the Right to Truth–in–Evidence provision of Proposition 8 would repeal these limitations on the use of consistent statements.[4] Since the credibility of a witness becomes an issue the moment the witness takes the stand, parties to a criminal proceeding would have a state constitutional right to offer a witness's consistent statements even though the witness has not been impeached. Such statements would be relevant to the witness's credibility as well as to prove the truth of the matters asserted and would have to be admitted unless the trial judge excludes them under § 352.[5]

Unlike the Civil Law jurisdictions, Common Law countries have developed a number of rules, such as § 791, to govern the impeachment and accreditation of witnesses. These rules are designed primarily to afford witnesses an opportunity to respond to attacks on their credibility, to safeguard them from abuse, to save time, and, most importantly, to protect the jurors from distraction and confusion.[6] These rules seek to focus the fact finder's attention on the disputed issues by preventing extended inquiry into the credibility of witnesses. In contrast, the Civil Law tradition generally commits the admissibility of evidence on credibility to the discretion of the judge.[7] The justification for this approach stems

---

1. West's Ann.California Evidence Code § 791.

2. Id.

3. West's Ann.California Evidence Code § 1236. The justification for treating prior consistent statements as an exception to the hearsay rule is essentially the same as that advanced for prior inconsistent statements. The maker can be cross examined about the statement under oath and in the presence of the jury. Moreover, the instruction limiting the jurors' consideration of the statement to impeachment is of doubtful value. Id. (comment).

4. An analogous provision, § 790, prohibits the introduction of good character evidence to support a witness's credibility unless the witness's credibility has first been attacked. West's Ann.California Evidence Code § 790. People v. Taylor held that § 790 was repealed by Proposition 8, since evidence supporting the credibility of a witness is relevant. People v. Taylor, 180 Cal.App.3d 622, 631–632, 225 Cal.Rptr. 733, 737–738 (1986). For an extended discussion of the effects of Proposition 8, see § 3.07 supra.

5. For a discussion of the judge's discretionary power to exclude relevant evidence after Proposition 8, see § 2.11 supra.

6. C. McCormick, McCormick on Evidence §§ 37, 42 (E. Cleary 2d ed. 1972).

7. See generally, Méndez, *The Civil Law and Common Law: Differing Approaches to Some Aspects of Credibility*, 20 Stanford Journal of International Law 1, 15 (1985).

from the fact that jurors, as we understand them, play little or no role in Civil Law trials.[8]

In California criminal cases, Proposition 8 threatens to establish a regime similar to that found in Civil Law jurisdictions, where bench, not jury, trials predominate. By repealing specific prescriptions, such as § 791, Proposition 8 commits the admissibility of evidence bearing on credibility to the discretionary powers vested in the trial judge by § 352.

Whether such a radical departure from accepted practice makes sense is unclear. In the absence of appellate guidelines on the use of prior statements, no one can predict how trial judges will exercise their discretion under § 352 in a given case. Section 352, after all, empowers trial judges to micro-manage matters pertaining to admissibility. It requires them to weigh the probative value of an item of evidence against its prejudicial effects in determining the item's admissibility in a particular case.[9] In the absence of appellate guidelines, Proposition 8 replaces the certainty provided by such rules as § 791 with the necessarily imprecise standards of § 352.

QUESTIONS AND PROBLEMS

1. In an action to recover damages for injuries stemming from an assault, the plaintiff calls as his first witness, Bystander, who testifies as follows:

> By the plaintiff's lawyer: After the defendant left the bar, did you see him again that evening?

> Bystander: Yes, he returned to the bar ten minutes later, walked up to the victim, and struck him twice with a billiard cue.

> By the plaintiff's lawyer: Did you mention this incident to anyone?

> Bystander: Yes, when I got home I told my wife, "The defendant returned to the bar ten minutes later, walked up to the victim, and struck him twice with a billiard cue."

> Defendant: Move to strike on grounds of hearsay and improper accreditation. ～ *improperly bolstering cred. of witness*
> Judge?

2. In a prosecution for assault, the prosecutor calls as his first witness, Bystander, who testifies as follows:

> Prosecutor: After the defendant left the bar, did you see him again that evening?

> Bystander: Yes, he returned to the bar ten minutes later, walked up to the victim, and struck him twice with a billiard cue.

> Prosecutor: Did you mention this incident to anyone?

---

8.   J. Merryman, The Civil Law Tradition 122–123 (1969).

9.   For an extended discussion of the effects of Proposition 8 on § 352, see § 2.11 supra.

Bystander: Yes, when I got home I told my wife, "The defendant returned to the bar ten minutes later, walked up to the victim, and struck him twice with a billiard cue."

Defendant: Move to strike on grounds of hearsay and improper accreditation.

Prosecutor: Admissible under Proposition 8.

Judge?

3. If the judge declines to apply Proposition 8, may the statement nonetheless be received only on "credibility?"

§ 8.06   PRIOR CONSISTENT STATEMENTS UNDER THE FEDERAL RULES

Under the Federal Rules, prior consistent statements are admissible to rehabilitate a witness if the impeaching party has charged the witness with recent fabrication, improper motive, or other improper influence.[1] Unlike the Code, the Rules do not expressly require the witness to have made the statement before the motive to fabricate or other improper influence arose.[2] One would expect such a limitation to be read into the Federal Rules, since the rehabilitative value of a prior consistent statement stems from having been made before a motive to fabricate arose. The lower federal courts, however, split on this point. In Tome v. United States[3] the United States Supreme Court settled the controversy by holding that the language of the federal rule and the Advisory Committee Note requires the proponent to show that the declarant made the consistent statement before the alleged fabrication or other improper influence arose.[4]

Congress' distrust of prior inconsistent statements did not extend to prior consistent ones. Under the Rules, prior inconsistent statements can be received for the truth of the matter asserted only if the witness made the statements under oath and subject to the penalty of perjury in some kind of formal proceeding.[5] Prior consistent statements, however, can be received for the truth if they are otherwise admissible to support the credibility of the witness.[6] Congress' differential treatment of prior statements can lead to odd results and put jurors in difficult situations. If a witness is impeached with a prior inconsistent statement that was not made under oath and subject to the penalty of perjury, then under the Federal Rules the statement can be received only to impeach the witness and not for the truth of the matter stated. Where impeachment through a prior inconsistent statement is tantamount to an implied charge that the

---

1. Federal Rule of Evidence 801(d)(1)(B).

2. See § 8.05 supra.

3. 513 U.S. 150, 115 S.Ct. 696, 130 L.Ed.2d 574 (1995).

4. Id. at 159–160, 115 S.Ct. at 702.

5. Federal Rule of Evidence 801(d)(1)(A).

6. Federal Rule of Evidence 801(d)(1)(B).

witness has fabricated his testimony since the time he made the inconsistent statement, the calling party may rehabilitate the witness with a prior consistent statement. This statement can be received for its rehabilitative value as well as the truth of the matter asserted. Upon request of the party opposing the inconsistent statement, the jury must be told, to consider the statement only for its value on the witness's credibility. Of course, no such limiting instruction can be given with respect to the consistent statement.

QUESTIONS AND PROBLEMS

In a federal prosecution for violating the victim's civil rights, the prosecutor calls Fellow Officer and Bystander who testify as follows:

Prosecutor: What did the defendant do after he arrested and handcuffed the victim?

Fellow Officer: He proceeded to beat him with his night stick for ten minutes.

* * *

Defense Attorney: You too were charged with beating the victim?

Fellow Officer: Yes.

Defense Attorney: But in exchange for your testimony here today the prosecutor promised to dismiss the charges against you?

Fellow Officer: Yes.

* * *

Prosecutor: Prior to initiating plea negotiations with me, did you tell anyone about what you saw on the night of the beating?

Fellow Officer: Yes, the day after the beating I said to my spouse, "The defendant proceeded to beat the victim with his night stick for ten minutes."

Defense Lawyer: Objection. Hearsay. Move to strike.

Judge: ?

Compare with:

Prosecutor: What did the defendant do after he arrested and handcuffed the victim?

Bystander: He proceeded to beat him with his night stick for ten minutes.

* * *

Defense Lawyer: Isn't it true that two days after the incident you told your drinking buddy, "The defendant only beat the victim once to keep him from kicking bystanders."?

Bystander: Yes.

Prosecutor: Move to strike on grounds of hearsay.

Judge: ?

* * *

Prosecutor: The day following the beating, did you tell anyone about it?

Bystander: Yes, I told my wife, "After the officer arrested and handcuffed the defendant, he proceeded to beat him with his night stick for ten minutes."

Defendant: Move to strike on grounds of hearsay.

Judge: ?

§ 8.07 STATEMENTS OF IDENTIFICATION

Sometimes a witness called by the prosecution to identify the perpetrator of a crime is unable or unwilling to do so for a variety reasons, ranging from loss of memory to fear of retaliation. If the witness identified the perpetrator prior to the trial and appears at the trial as a witness, under some circumstances the prosecution can offer her out of court statement as an exception to the hearsay rule. Although this exception is especially useful in the case of witnesses who may no longer remember the identity of the perpetrator, the exception is available even if the witnesses can identify the perpetrator at the trial. California Evidence Code § 1238 creates an exception for out of court statements in which witnesses identify participants in a crime or other occurrence.[1] To be admissible, the witness must first testify that she made the statement and that it was a true reflection of the events perceived.[2] In addition, the proponent must satisfy the judge that the witness made the statement at a time when the crime or other occurrence was fresh in the witness's memory.[3]

Statements of identification are presumed to be reliable because the witness is required to vouch for the accuracy of the statement and because the opposing party is given an opportunity to cross examine the witness on the statement.[4] But where the witness claims an inability to recall the identity of the perpetrator at the hearing, the value of cross-examination is questionable. The most that the cross examiner can accomplish is to disclose the witness's bad memory. Such limited cross-examination would appear to deprive the accused of the right to confront her accusers. In *United States v. Owens*,[5] however, the United States Supreme Court disagreed, holding that the requirements of the Confrontation Clause were

---

1. West's Ann.California Evidence Code § 1238.

2. Id.

3. Id. These preliminary facts must be proved by a preponderance of the evidence. The determination of the existence or nonexistence of these preliminary facts is governed by § 405. West's Ann.California Evidence Code § 405 and comment.

4. Additionally, "the generally unsatisfactory and inconclusive nature of courtroom identifications as compared with those made at an earlier time under less suggestive conditions" provides reliability. Federal Rule of Evidence 801(d)(1)(C) (Advisory Committee Note). The California courts agree with this observation. See People v. Cuevas, 12 Cal.4th 252, 265, 906 P.2d 1290, 1298, 48 Cal.Rptr.2d 135, 143 (1995) and cases cited therein.

5. 484 U.S. 554, 108 S.Ct. 838, 98 L.Ed.2d 951 (1988), on remand, 844 F.2d 701 (9th Cir.1988), aff'd, 889 F.2d 913 (9th Cir.1989).

satisfied by the opportunity given to the opponent to cross examine the witness on her memory.[6]

Prior statements of identification are most useful to the proponent whenever the witness claims memory loss. But the failure to recall the identity of the perpetrator is not a condition precedent to the admissibility of the statements. A witness who can identify the perpetrator can nonetheless be asked to relate her out of court statement identifying the perpetrator. Such statements can be used to bolster the credibility of the witness as well as to prove the matters asserted.

The witness does not have to be the sole testimonial source of the statement. Anyone with firsthand knowledge of the witness's statement of identification can repeat the statement in court so long as the foundational requirements are met.

In People v. Gould[7] the California Supreme Court held that an extrajudicial identification that cannot be confirmed by identification at the trial is insufficient as a matter of law to support a conviction in the absence of other evidence connecting the accused with crime charged.[8] Although *Gould* preceded the adoption of the Code, the framers limited themselves to creating a hearsay exception for statements of identification and left this aspect of the opinion undisturbed.[9] In People v. Cuevas[10] the Supreme Court reversed *Gould.* The court held that extrajudicial statements of identification are sufficient to support a conviction even in the absence of corroborating evidence, so long as the hearsay declarant is produced for cross-examination by the accused.[11]

The Federal Rules are generally in accord with the Code. Federal Rule of Evidence 801(d)(1)(C) provides that statements of identification may be received for the truth of the matter stated if the declarant testifies at the trial or hearing and is subject to cross-examination concerning the statement.[12]

QUESTIONS AND PROBLEMS

1.   Consider the admissibility of the following testimony in a prosecution for assault:

> Prosecutor: Can you identify the man who hit you with a pipe on the head?
>
> Victim: Yes, I can; it was the defendant.
>
> Prosecutor: Did you tell anyone that the defendant was the one who hit you?

---

6.   Id. at 559, 108 S.Ct. at 843.

7.   54 Cal.2d 621, 7 Cal.Rptr. 273, 354 P.2d 865 (1960).

8.   Id. at 631, 7 Cal.Rptr. at 278, 354 P.2d at 870.

9.   West's Ann. California Evidence Code § 1238 (comment).

10.   12 Cal.4th 252, 48 Cal.Rptr.2d 135, 906 P.2d 1290 (1995).

11.   Id. at 274–275, 48 Cal.Rptr.2d at 149, 906 P.2d at 1304.

12.   Federal Rule of Evidence 801(d)(1)(C).

Victim: Yes, I told the doctor who examined me at the hospital.

Prosecutor: At the time you told the doctor, was there any question in your mind about who had hit you?

Victim: No.

Prosecutor: Did you tell the doctor the truth?

Victim: Yes.

Prosecutor: What did you tell the doctor?

Victim: "The defendant hit me on the head with a pipe."

Defendant: Move to strike on the grounds of hearsay. Also on the grounds that a prior consistent statement cannot be offered unless the credibility of the witness has first been assailed.

Judge: ?

2. Suppose the victim had testified as follows:

Prosecutor: Can you identify the man who hit you with a pipe on the head?

Victim: No, I can't.

Prosecutor: At one time were you able to identify your assailant?

Victim: I know that I told the investigating officer who it was who hit me.

Prosecutor: At the time you told the investigating officer, was there any question in your mind about who it was who hit you?

Victim: No.

Prosecutor: Did you tell the officer the truth?

Victim: Yes, I did.

Prosecutor: What did you tell the officer?

Victim: "The defendant hit me on the head with a pipe."

Defendant: Move to strike on grounds of hearsay and confrontation. There is no way that I can cross examine a witness who claims no present memory of the events in question.

Judge: ?

§ 8.08 FRESH COMPLAINTS

Neither the Code nor the Rules provides a hearsay exception for complaints by crime victims relating details of the crime, including the identity of the perpetrator. Prior to the adoption of the Code, the case law was in conflict over whether such complaints constituted hearsay. The matter was resolved by the California Supreme Court in People v. Burton.[1] In that case, the court held such statements, though inadmissible hearsay if offered for the truth of the matter stated, could nonetheless be received for a nonhearsay purpose:

---

1. 55 Cal.2d 328, 11 Cal.Rptr. 65, 359 P.2d 433 (1961).

In a case such as the present one, where the nonconsenting victim of a sex offense testifies to its commission, the theory of admissibility of evidence of a complaint which is consistent with her testimony * * * is this: It is natural to expect that the victim of such a crime would complain of it, and the prosecution can show the fact of complaint to forestall the assumption that none was made and that therefore the offense did not occur.[2]

Since the failure to report the offense would tend to discredit the victim's claim that the offense took place, in effect the court held that a victim's extrajudicial statement that is consistent with her testimony is admissible to support the victim's credibility even though no credibility attack has taken place. In this respect, complaints are analytically closer to statements of identification[3] than to prior consistent statements.[4] Prior consistent statements, it will be recalled, cannot be used to rehabilitate a witness under the Code, unless the witness's credibility has first been assailed.[5]

Receiving a complaint to prove the fact that a complaint was made carries the danger that the jury will improperly consider the complaint for the truth of the matter stated. In *Burton* the court emphasized that, while the prosecution may offer those portions of the victim's statement regarding the "nature of the offense and the identity of the asserted offender," it must do so without recounting the "details" surrounding the alleged offense.[6]

Examples of admissible complaints include: that the accused "made me play with his peter,"[7] that the accused had "ruined her,"[8] "that she had had sexual intercourse with her father,"[9] that "the man was sucking his thing,"[10] and that the accused "had taken her zipper down and put his right index finger into her 'front bottom' [vaginal area]."[11]

---

2. Id. at 350, 11 Cal.Rptr. at 75–76, 359 P.2d at 443–444. Despite *Burton's* nonhearsay rationale, some courts mistakenly assume that the court created a hearsay exception for complaint evidence. See, e.g., People v. Rich, 45 Cal.3d 1036, 1105, 248 Cal.Rptr. 510, 554, 755 P.2d 960, 1004 (1988), cert. denied, 488 U.S. 1051, 109 S.Ct. 884, 102 L.Ed.2d 1006 (1989); Matter of Marianne R., 113 Cal.App.3d 423, 427, 169 Cal.Rptr. 848, 850 (1980).

3. See § 8.07 supra.

4. See § 8.06 supra.

5. People v. Burton, 55 Cal.2d 328, 350, 11 Cal.Rptr. 65, 75–76, 359 P.2d 433, 443–444 (1961). *Burton* was decided before the Code was adopted. An argument can thus be made that the Code repealed the fresh complaint doctrine, since complaints offered to support the credibility of the declarant who testifies are prior consistent statements. Accordingly, the limitations of § 791 on the use of such statements to rehabilitate a witness should apply to complaints. But, as has been noted, Proposition 8 may have eliminated these limitations in criminal cases. Id. If this is the proper construction of the Code and the initiative, then Proposition 8 has revived the fresh complaint doctrine in criminal cases.

6. People v. Burton, supra note 5, at 350, 11 Cal.Rptr. at 76, 359 P.2d at 444.

7. Id. at 337, 11 Cal.Rptr. at 67, 359 P.2d at 434.

8. People v. Adams, 92 Cal.App. 6, 16, 267 P. 906, 909 (1928).

9. People v. Lopez, 33 Cal.App. 530, 534, 165 P. 722, 724 (1917).

10. People v. Butler, 249 Cal.App.2d 799, 804, 57 Cal.Rptr. 798, 801 (1967).

11. Matter of Marianne R., 113 Cal.App.3d 423, 425, 169 Cal.Rptr. 848, 849 (1980).

The admissibility of complaints for the nonhearsay purpose of proving that a complaint was made is committed to the judge's discretion under § 352. In weighing the probative value of the complaint evidence against its prejudicial effects, the judge should consider the need for the evidence. It is not happenstance that each of the examples listed is taken from cases in which the victim was a child and the offense involved a sex act. The need to support the credibility of children in these circumstances may be greater than in the case of adult victims.[12] The judge should also consider whether the prejudicial effects of the evidence can be diminished by having the child witness merely relate when and to whom she complained after describing the misconduct on the stand.

At one time to be admissible, complaints had to be "fresh"[13] and volunteered and not the product of questioning[14] or intimidation or fear.[15] In People v. Brown[16] the California Supreme Court eliminated these limitations. Relying on empirical studies showing that it is not normal for victims of a sexual assault to complain promptly, the court held that evidence of delayed complaints may be offered for the nonhearsay purpose of reducing the "risk that the jury, perhaps influenced by outmoded myths regarding the 'usual' or 'natural' response of victims of sexual offenses, will arrive at an erroneous conclusion with regard to whether the offense occurred."[17] Under *Brown*, the admissibility of the complaint "does not turn invariably upon whether the victim's complaint was made immediately following the alleged assault or was preceded by some delay, nor upon whether the complaint was volunteered spontaneously by the victim or instead was prompted by some inquiry or questioning from another person. Rather, these factors simply are to be considered among the circumstances of the victim's report or disclosure that are relevant in assisting the trier of fact in assessing the significance of the victim's statements in conjunction with all of the other evidence presented."[18] In short, the limitations now go to weight, not admissibility, but the "specific

---

12. In federal courts, statements made by sexually abused children to examining doctors are admissible for the truth of the matter stated by virtue of Federal Rule of Evidence 803(4). This rule creates a hearsay exception for statements made for purposes of medical diagnosis or treatment insofar as reasonably pertinent to such diagnosis or treatment. Federal Rule of Evidence 803(4). See United States v. George, 960 F.2d 97 (9th Cir.1992). The California Evidence Code does not have an equivalent provision. In California statements by minors to doctors, even if falling within the complaint doctrine, are inadmissible for the truth of the matter stated unless the statements fall within a hearsay exception. See, e.g., People v. Fair, 203 Cal.App.3d 1303, 1309–1313, 250 Cal.Rptr. 486, 490–491 (1988). See also § 8.13 infra. In 1995 the California Legislature amended the Code to provide such a limited exception. See § 9.13 infra.

13. In re Cheryl H., 153 Cal.App.3d 1098, 1129, 200 Cal.Rptr. 789, 808 (1984), disapproved on other grounds, People v. Raley, 2 Cal.4th 870, 891–895, 8 Cal.Rptr.2d 678, 691–693, 830 P.2d 712, 726–727 (1992).

14. Id.

15. People v. Snyder, 14 Cal.App.4th 1166, 18 Cal.Rptr.2d 496, 500 (1993), citing People v. Fair, 203 Cal.App.3d 1303, 250 Cal.Rptr. 486 (1988).

16. 8 Cal.4th 746, 35 Cal.Rptr.2d 407, 883 P.2d 949 (1994).

17. Id. at 761–762, 35 Cal.Rptr.2d at 416, 883 P.2d at 958.

18. Id. at 763, 35 Cal.Rptr.2d at 417, 883 P.2d at 959.

relevance of the extra-judicial-complaint evidence * * * must [still] be shown in every case."[19]

The complaint doctrine applies both to criminal and civil cases.[20] But the doctrine is limited only to statements made by the victim and does not include statements made by others who may have been present when the misconduct occurred.[21]

Child witnesses. The rise in child abuse prosecutions has led to special provisions creating hearsay exceptions for statements by children complaining of sexual abuse. One provision allows the use against the accused of the preliminary hearing testimony of a child under some circumstances without a showing of the child's unavailability to testify at the trial.[22] Others permit the use of social studies reports prepared by social workers reciting the child's complaints when offered in dependency proceedings.[23] Still others create a hearsay exception for such complaints in dependency hearings even if they are not included in the social studies reports, provided that the complaints are first ruled reliable.[24] The last two exceptions in effect permit some fresh complaints to be received for the truth of the matters asserted in dependency hearings.[25]

QUESTIONS AND PROBLEMS

1. The fresh complaint doctrine creates a hearsay exception for the complaints of victims of wrongdoing in the California courts. True or false?

2. The fresh complaint doctrine merely allows a California party to support the credibility of the victim with her complaint even though the victim's credibility as a witness has not been assailed. True or false?

3. In California, complaints by victims are inadmissible to support their credibility unless the proponent first shows that the complaints were fresh and volunteered, and not delayed or the product of questioning. True or false?

§ 8.09 PRIOR RECOLLECTION RECORDED

Sometimes a witness is unable to answer a question or to answer it fully because of poor recollection. Whenever that occurs, the examining

---

19. Id.

20. Matter of Marianne R., 113 Cal.App.3d 423, 427, 169 Cal.Rptr. 848, 850 (1980).

21. People v. Butler, 249 Cal.App.2d 799, 806, 57 Cal.Rptr. 798, 803 (1967). The fresh complaint doctrine should not be confused with § 1228. This section creates a hearsay exception for statements of minors who have been sexually abused in order to establish the foundation for receiving the confession of the person accused of the sexual abuse. See West's Ann.California Evidence Code § 1228.

22. See § 11.08 infra.

23. See § 14.05 infra.

24. Id.

25. Whether receiving the complaints for the truth of the matters stated is a violation of the accused's Sixth Amendment right to confront his accusers depends on whether the child witness is produced for cross-examination or, if not produced, whether the accused had been afforded an opportunity prior to the hearing to cross examine the child about the complaint. For a discussion of this point, see § 6.03 et seq., supra.

lawyer is allowed to try to refresh the witness's recollection of the matters inquired. If the lawyer succeeds in refreshing the witness's recollection, the lawyer is entitled to have the witness answer the question she left unanswered.

When a witness answers a question from a refreshed recollection, the hearsay rule is not implicated. The witness is testifying from her recollection and is not repeating any out of court statements. But if the lawyer fails to refresh the witness's recollection, then the lawyer will lose the answer unless he can resort to an out of court statement by the witness which contains the desired information. Prior recollection recorded is one of the hearsay exceptions lawyers turn to whenever they are unable to refresh a witness's recollection.

Present recollection refreshed. The Code and the Federal Rules are quite liberal with respect to the sources that can be used to refresh a witness's recollection: anything, including a writing, can be used.[1] If a writing is used, the lawyer must not ask the witness to read the writing to the fact finder. Otherwise, both the hearsay and Best and Secondary Evidence Rules will be violated.[2] Instead, the lawyer should ask the witness to read the writing to herself. Once the witness has done that, then the lawyer should ask the witness whether her recollection has been refreshed with respect to the subject matter about which the witness claimed insufficient recall. If the witness answers in the affirmative, the lawyer may then ask the witness to answer the question that was pending.

Before the witness may be asked any questions about the writing, the opposing party is entitled to examine it.[3] If the witness's recollection is in fact refreshed by the writing, the opposing party may use the writing in cross examining the witness and may introduce such parts as are pertinent to the witness's testimony.[4]

If a witness uses a writing to refresh her recollection *prior* to testifying, then the writing must be produced at the hearing at the request of the opposing party.[5] If the writing is not produced, then a California judge must strike the witness's testimony unless the writing is not in the possession or control of the witness or the party eliciting the testimony, and was not reasonably procurable by the party through the use of the court's process or other available means.[6] The Federal Rules provide the judge greater latitude. If the writing is not produced, the court may issue any appropriate order, except that in criminal cases when the prosecution elects not to comply, "the court must strike the witness's testimony or—if justice so requires—declare a mistrial."[7] In civil cases,

---

1.   West's Ann.California Evidence Code § 771; Federal Rule of Evidence 612.

2.   For a discussion of the Federal Best Evidence Rule and the California Secondary Evidence Rule, see § 13.06 infra.

3.   West's Ann.California Evidence Code § 768(b).

4.   West's Ann.California Evidence Code § 771(b); Federal Rule of Evidence 612.

5.   West's Ann.California Evidence Code § 771; Federal Rule of Evidence 612.

6.   West's Ann.California Evidence Code § 771.

7.   Federal Rule of Evidence 612.

the federal judge may in addition impose such remedies as contempt and finding issues against the offender.[8]

Prior recollection recorded. The Code and Federal Rules create a hearsay exception for statements by witnesses who no longer can recall the subject matter of their statements.[9] For such out of court statements to be admissible, the proponent must meet a number of conditions. First, the proponent must show that the witness no longer possesses sufficient recollection to enable her to testify fully and accurately.[10] Second, the proponent must persuade the judge that the witness's statement would have been admissible through the witness if she had been able to recall the subject matter of the statement.[11] Finally, the proponent must show that the witness's perceptions were reduced to writing at a time when the information recorded was fresh in the witness's memory and that the writing accurately reflects the witness's recollection.[12]

The third condition merits elaboration. It is not necessary for the witness to be the person who recorded the information; the statement can be prepared by the witness or at the witness's direction "or by some other person for the purpose of recording the witness's statement at the time it was made".[13] But whether the witness or someone else prepared the statement, the proponent may not offer the statement until after the witness testifies that the statement she made was a correct reflection of what she perceived and evidence is received that the written statement is "an accurate record" of her statement.[14] The rule is thus worded to allow the person who recorded the statement to testify that the writing is a correct record of what the witness stated. "Sufficient assurance of the trustworthiness of the statement is provided if the declarant is available to testify that he made a true statement and if the person who recorded the statement is available to testify that he accurately recorded the statement."[15]

From a doctrinal perspective, the exception's requirements seem to be in conflict. On the one hand, the proponent must show that the witness no longer has sufficient recollection of the subject matter of the written record as to testify fully and accurately. This means that the proponent did not succeed in refreshing the witness's recollection even with the written statement. At the same time, the witness must testify that her statement was an accurate reflection of her perceptions even though she no longer recalls those perceptions. Where the witness was the one who prepared the written statement, such a claim taxes credulity.

---

8. Id. (Advisory Committee Note).

9. West's Ann.California Evidence Code § 1237(a); Federal Rule of Evidence 803(5).

10. Id. Whether the witness possesses the requisite lack of recollection is a question for the court, not the jury. See West's Ann.California Evidence Code § 405 and comment.

11. West's Ann.California Evidence Code § 1237(a).

12. West's Ann.California Evidence Code § 1237(a); Federal Rule 803(5).

13. West's Ann.California Evidence Code § 1237(a). Federal Rule 803(5) is to the same effect.

14. Id.

15. West's Ann.California Evidence Code § 1237 (comment).

Two factors help mitigate this concern. Witnesses are not likely to prepare records of their observations with the view of escaping cross-examination through a convenient loss of memory on the stand. As a rule, advocates prefer the live testimony of witnesses to their notes. Testimony is generally more persuasive. Moreover, the rule prohibits impressing the written statement with undue status. "The writing may be read into evidence, but the writing itself may not be received in evidence unless offered by an adverse party."[16] This is consistent with trial practice. Parties are not permitted to move in evidence transcripts of the choicest parts of a witness's testimony.

Another factor lessens concerns about the strategic creation of recorded recollections: in most instances, the witness whose perceptions are recorded is not just an ordinary witness who happens to have been present when events that occur are subsequently litigated. People who record occurrences that are litigated are usually traffic officers, emergency medics, housing inspectors, and the like. They have no stake in the outcome. The routine nature of their work makes it difficult for them to differentiate one set of observations from among the many they make. The need for their written statements is thus evident. Still, the opponent is left with the unhappy chore of cross examining a witness who has little or no recollection of perceptions that are now before the fact finder. In criminal cases, the fact that such cross-examination is of questionable value has been held not to deprive the accused of the right to confront the witnesses against him.[17]

QUESTIONS AND PROBLEMS

1.   The dean of the law school informs the district attorney that he saw Professor Méndez leave the Bookstore without paying for a book. Professor Méndez is then prosecuted for theft. Consider the admissibility of the following evidence:

> Prosecutor: Did you see someone leave the Bookstore?
>
> Dean: Yes.
>
> Prosecutor: Was this person carrying anything?
>
> Dean: Yes, a book.
>
> Prosecutor: Did you see this person pay for the book before leaving the Bookstore?
>
> Dean: No.
>
> Prosecutor: Can you tell us who this person was?
>
> Dean: No, I don't remember.
>
> Prosecutor: Do you have anything that would help you remember?
>
> Dean: Yes, a candy wrapper.

---

16. Id. Federal Rule of Evidence 803(5).

17. See People v. Gentry, 270 Cal.App.2d 462, 472, 76 Cal.Rptr. 336, 342 (1969) and cases cited therein.

Correct process

Prosecutor: May we have this wrapper marked as People's Exhibit Number 1 for identification?

Judge: Yes.

Prosecutor: May the record reflect that I am showing opposing counsel People's Exhibit Number 1 for identification?

Judge: Yes.

Prosecutor: May I approach the witness?

Judge: Yes.

Prosecutor: Would you please read People's Exhibit Number 1 to yourself.

Dean: Yes.

Prosecutor: Does it refresh your recollection about the identity of the person you saw leave the Bookstore without paying for the book?

Dean: Yes.

Prosecutor: Can you tell us who this person was?

Dean: Miguel Méndez.

Defendant: Move to strike on grounds of hearsay.

Judge: ?

2.   Compare with the following examination:

Prosecutor: Does the exhibit refresh your recollection about the identity of the person you saw leave the Bookstore without paying for the book?

Dean: No, it does not.

Prosecutor: Did you write the name of the person you saw leave the Bookstore without paying for the book on People's Exhibit Number 1 for identification?

Dean: Yes, I did so on the same day.

Prosecutor: At the time you did so, was your memory of who took the book fresh on your mind?

Dean: Yes.

Prosecutor: Was the name you wrote on People's Exhibit Number 1 for identification the name of the person you saw remove the book without paying for it?

Dean: Yes.

Prosecutor: Request the court's permission to read People's Number 1 for identification into evidence.

Judge: Any objection?

Defendant: Yes, hearsay.

Judge: ? *Overruled - all they do is read it but not into evidence*

CALIFORNIA EVIDENCE CODE

§ 769.   Inconsistent statement or conduct

In examining a witness concerning a statement or other conduct by him that is inconsistent with any part of his testimony at the hearing, it is not necessary to disclose to him any information concerning the statement or other conduct.

§ 770.   Evidence of inconsistent statement of witness

Unless the interests of justice otherwise require, extrinsic evidence of a statement made by a witness that is inconsistent with any part of his testimony at the hearing shall be excluded unless:

(a) The witness was so examined while testifying as to give him an opportunity to explain or to deny the statement; or

(b) The witness has not been excused from giving further testimony in the action.

§ 771.   Production of writing used to refresh memory

(a) Subject to subdivision (c), if a witness, either while testifying or prior thereto, uses a writing to refresh his memory with respect to any matter about which he testifies, such writing must be produced at the hearing at the request of an adverse party and, unless the writing is so produced, the testimony of the witness concerning such matter shall be stricken.

(b) If the writing is produced at the hearing, the adverse party may, if he chooses, inspect the writing, cross-examine the witness concerning it, and introduce in evidence such portion of it as may be pertinent to the testimony of the witness.

(c) Production of the writing is excused, and the testimony of the witness shall not be stricken, if the writing:

(1) Is not in the possession or control of the witness or the party who produced his testimony concerning the matter; and

(2) Was not reasonably procurable by such party through the use of the court's process or other available means.

§ 791.   Prior consistent statement of witness

Evidence of a statement previously made by a witness that is consistent with his testimony at the hearing is inadmissible to support his credibility unless it is offered after:

(a) Evidence of a statement made by him that is inconsistent with any part of his testimony at the hearing has been admitted for the purpose of attacking his credibility, and the statement was made before the alleged inconsistent statement; or

(b) An express or implied charge has been made that his testimony at the hearing is recently fabricated or is influenced by bias or other improper motive, and the statement was made before the bias, motive for fabrication, or other improper motive is alleged to have arisen.

§ 1201. Multiple hearsay

A statement within the scope of an exception to the hearsay rule is not inadmissible on the ground that the evidence of such statement is hearsay evidence if such hearsay evidence consists of one or more statements each of which meets the requirements of an exception to the hearsay rule.

§ 1235. Inconsistent statement

Evidence of a statement made by a witness is not made inadmissible by the hearsay rule if the statement is inconsistent with his testimony at the hearing and is offered in compliance with Section 770.

§ 1236. Prior consistent statement

Evidence of a statement previously made by a witness is not made inadmissible by the hearsay rule if the statement is consistent with his testimony at the hearing and is offered in compliance with Section 791.

§ 1237. Past recollection recorded

(a) Evidence of a statement previously made by a witness is not made inadmissible by the hearsay rule if the statement would have been admissible if made by him while testifying, the statement concerns a matter as to which the witness has insufficient present recollection to enable him to testify fully and accurately, and the statement is contained in a writing which:

(1) Was made at a time when the fact recorded in the writing actually occurred or was fresh in the witness' memory;

(2) Was made (i) by the witness himself or under his direction or (ii) by some other person for the purpose of recording the witness' statement at the time it was made;

(3) Is offered after the witness testifies that the statement he made was a true statement of such fact; and

(4) Is offered after the writing is authenticated as an accurate record of the statement.

(b) The writing may be read into evidence, but the writing itself may not be received in evidence unless offered by an adverse party.

§ 1238. Prior identification

Evidence of a statement previously made by a witness is not made inadmissible by the hearsay rule if the statement would have been admissible if made by him while testifying and:

(a) The statement is an identification of a party or another as a person who participated in a crime or other occurrence;

(b) The statement was made at a time when the crime or other occurrence was fresh in the witness' memory; and

(c) The evidence of the statement is offered after the witness testifies that he made the identification and that it was a true reflection of his opinion at that time.

FEDERAL RULES OF EVIDENCE

Rule 612. Writing Used to Refresh a Witness's Memory

(a) Scope. This rule gives an adverse party certain options when a witness uses a writing to refresh memory:

(1) while testifying; or

(2) before testifying, if the court decides that justice requires the party to have those options.

(b) Adverse Party's Options; Deleting Unrelated Matter. Unless 18 U.S.C. § 3500 provides otherwise in a criminal case, an adverse party is entitled to have the writing produced at the hearing, to inspect it, to cross-examine the witness about it, and to introduce in evidence any portion that relates to the witness's testimony. If the producing party claims that the writing includes unrelated matter, the court must examine the writing in camera, delete any unrelated portion, and order that the rest be delivered to the adverse party. Any portion deleted over objection must be preserved for the record.

(c) Failure to Produce or Deliver the Writing. If a writing is not produced or is not delivered as ordered, the court may issue any appropriate order. But if the prosecution does not comply in a criminal case, the court must strike the witness's testimony or—if justice so requires—declare a mistrial.

Rule 613. Witness's Prior Statement

(a) Showing or Disclosing the Statement During Examination. When examining a witness about the witness's prior statement, a party need not show it or disclose its contents to the witness. But the party must, on request, show it or disclose its contents to an adverse party's attorney.

(b) Extrinsic Evidence of a Prior Inconsistent Statement. Extrinsic evidence of a witness's prior inconsistent statement is admissible only if the witness is given an opportunity to explain or deny the statement and an adverse party is given an opportunity to examine the witness about it, or if justice so requires. This subdivision (b) does not apply to an opposing party's statement under Rule 801(d)(2).

Rule 801. Definitions That Apply to This Article; Exclusions from Hearsay

(a) Statement. "Statement" means a person's oral assertion, written assertion, or nonverbal conduct, if the person intended it as an assertion.

(b) Declarant. "Declarant" means the person who made the statement.

(c) Hearsay. "Hearsay" means a statement that:

(1) the declarant does not make while testifying at the current trial or hearing; and

(2) a party offers in evidence to prove the truth of the matter asserted in the statement.

(d) Statements That Are Not Hearsay. A statement that meets the following conditions is not hearsay:

(1) *A Declarant–Witness's Prior Statement.* The declarant testifies and is subject to crossexamination about a prior statement, and the statement:

(A) is inconsistent with the declarant's testimony and was given under penalty of perjury at a trial, hearing, or other proceeding or in a deposition;

(B) is consistent with the declarant's testimony and is offered to rebut an express or implied charge that the declarant recently fabricated it or acted from a recent improper influence or motive in so testifying; or

(C) identifies a person as someone the declarant perceived earlier.

Rule 803. Exceptions to the Rule Against Hearsay—Regardless of Whether the Declarant Is Available as a Witness

The following are not excluded by the rule against hearsay, regardless of whether the declarant is available as a witness:

* * *

(5) *Recorded Recollection.* A record that:

(A) is on a matter the witness once knew about but now cannot recall well enough to testify fully and accurately;

(B) was made or adopted by the witness when the matter was fresh in the witness's memory; and

(C) accurately reflects the witness's knowledge.

If admitted, the record may be read into evidence but may be received as an exhibit only if offered by an adverse party.

Rule 805. Hearsay Within Hearsay

Hearsay within hearsay is not excluded by the rule against hearsay if each part of the combined statements conforms with an exception to the rule.

CHAPTER 9

EXCEPTIONS TO THE HEARSAY RULE: DECLARATIONS AGAINST INTEREST, DYING DECLARATIONS, EXCITED UTTERANCES, CONTEMPORANEOUS STATEMENTS, AND STATE OF MIND DECLARATIONS

■ ■ ■

Table of Sections

§ 9.01 DECLARATIONS AGAINST INTEREST UNDER THE EVIDENCE CODE

In any trial in which liability is contested, nothing helps defendants more than the testimony of a witness who admits liability for the wrong at issue. If the witness cannot be called because he is unavailable, the next best thing is for defendants to offer an out of court statement in which the witness admits responsibility. California Evidence Code § 1230 creates a hearsay exception for such statements, which are known as declarations against interest.[1] To be admissible, the proponent must show that the declarant is unavailable to testify and that it was against the declarant's interest to have made the declaration.[2]

Declarations against interest are considered to be trustworthy because of the belief that people do not say things disserving of their interests unless they believe their statements to be true. However, this commonplace assumption has not been tested empirically. Moreover, the exception does not require the proponent to show that the declarant was aware of the disserving effects of the statement. Since by definition the declarant must be shown to be unavailable to testify, such a requirement most likely would eviscerate the exception. Instead, the proponent need show only that "the statement, when made, was so far contrary to the declarant's * * * interest * * * that a reasonable man in his position would not have made the statement unless he believed it to be true."[3] Thus, in applying the exception, the court needs to employ only an objective standard; it need not concern itself with whether the declarant subjectively believed the statement to be against interest when made. Indeed, if the objective test is satisfied, some cases hold that the declaration can qualify under the exception even if the declarant thought that it was in his interest to make the statement.[4] Other cases, however, maintain that in determining whether to admit the declaration, the trial judge should consider the declarant's motivation.[5]

It is unclear whether the objective test precludes judges from considering the declarant's or the reporting witness's motivation in assessing the trustworthiness of the declaration. If it does not, statements seemingly against interest under the objective test might nonetheless be excluded if the judge finds that the reporting witness or the hearsay declarant had

---

1.   West's Ann.California Evidence Code § 1230.

2.   For the grounds of unavailability, see § 6.02 supra. Where the hearsay declarant is a party, that party may not establish his or her unavailability to testify by claiming the privilege against self-incrimination. See People v. Elliot, 37 Cal.4th 453, 483, 122 P.3d 968, 988, 35 Cal.Rptr.3d 759, 782 (2005), cert. denied, 549 U.S. 853, 127 S.Ct. 121, 166 L.Ed.2d 91 (2006). Elliot, who was prosecuted for murder, attempted to introduce a letter in which he admitted killing the victim but claimed that he was intoxicated. To establish his unavailability, Elliot claimed the Fifth. The reviewing court upheld the trial judge's ruling excluding the letter.

3.   West's Ann.California Evidence Code § 1230.

4.   See, e.g., United States v. Lang, 589 F.2d 92, 97 (2d Cir.1978) (holding that the declarant's statement to an undercover agent that he supplied counterfeit money to the accused was against interest under the objective test even if the declarant believed that it was in his interest to make such a statement to someone he mistakenly believed to be a confederate).

5.   See, e.g., People v. Hayes, 21 Cal.4th 1211, 1257, note 8, 91 Cal.Rptr.2d 211, 242, note 8, 989 P.2d 645, 673, note 8 (1999), cert. denied, 531 U.S. 980, 121 S.Ct. 431, 148 L.Ed.2d 438 (2000) (holding that the offering party must show that at the time the declarant made her declaration she was aware that it was against her penal interest to do so). See also People v. Lawley, 27 Cal.4th 102, 155, 115 Cal.Rptr.2d 614, 658, 38 P.3d 461, 498 (2002), cert. denied, 537 U.S. 1073, 123 S.Ct. 671, 154 L.Ed.2d 567 (2002) (holding that a convicted felon's declaration that he had been hired by the Aryan Brotherhood to commit a murder did not qualify as a declaration against social interest where the party opposing the declaration offered evidence that the declarant was seeking full membership in the Brotherhood and the party offering the declaration offered no evidence that the declaration exposed the declarant to the risk of hatred, ridicule, or social disgrace in the declarant's community).

reason to fabricate the declaration. People v. Blankenship[6] upheld the exclusion of a declaration in which the declarant confessed committing the offenses for which the accused was on trial. The reporting witness was the accused, who the court found had a motive to fabricate the declaration and who, knowing the circumstances attending the offenses, could supply the declaration with seemingly accurate detail.[7] But Vorse v. Sarasy[8] which overruled *Blankenship,* holds that it is error for a judge to withhold hearsay admissible under an exception on the ground that the reporting witness is not credible; the credibility of any witness who takes the stand is to be determined by the jury.[9] In this regard the California Supreme Court has underscored that the only question for the trial judge is "whether there is evidence sufficient to sustain a finding that the statement was made. * * * As with other facts, the direct testimony of a single witness is sufficient to support a finding unless the testimony is physically impossible or its falsity is apparent 'without resorting to inferences or deductions.' "[10]

With regard to the hearsay declarant's credibility, the Code expressly authorizes trial judges to consider the hearsay declarant's motivation in ruling on the admissibility of hearsay offered under some exceptions. These include the exceptions for state of mind declarations,[11] statements relating to wills[12] and to claims against estates,[13] and business and official records.[14] The Code section relating to declarations against interest does not expressly grant judges this authority.[15] But perhaps the authority can be derived from § 405, which gives trial judges the power to withhold evidence from the jury when it is too unreliable to be evaluated properly or because public policy requires its exclusion.[16] In the case of hearsay, questions regarding "the existence of those circumstances that make the hearsay sufficiently trustworthy to be received in evidence" are committed to the judge.[17] Conceivably, one of those circumstances is the motivation of the hearsay declarant. Although not expressly citing this provision, the

---

6.   167 Cal.App.3d 840, 213 Cal.Rptr. 666 (1985), rejected by Vorse v. Sarasy, 53 Cal.App.4th 998, 62 Cal.Rptr.2d 164 (1997).

7.   Id. at 849, 213 Cal.Rptr. at 671.

8.   53 Cal.App.4th 998, 62 Cal.Rptr.2d 164 (1997).

9.   Id. at 1009, 62 Cal.Rptr.2d at 171.

10.   People v. Cudjo, 6 Cal.4th 585, 607–608, 25 Cal.Rptr.2d 390, 404–405, 863 P.2d 635, 649–650 (1993) (quoting from People v. Huston, 21 Cal.2d 690, 693, 134 P.2d 758, 759 (1943)). The Federal Rules are in accord. In its note to the exception for declarations against penal interest, the Advisory Committee makes clear that federal judges should not consider the reporting witness's credibility in ruling on the admissibility of the declaration. See Federal Rule of Evidence 804(b)(3) (Advisory Committee Note).

11.   West's Ann.California Evidence Code §§ 1251–1252.

12.   West's Ann.California Evidence Code § 1260.

13.   West's Ann.California Evidence Code § 1261.

14.   West's Ann.California Evidence Code §§ 1271, 1280.

15.   West's Ann.California Evidence Code § 1230.

16.   West's Ann.California Evidence Code § 405 and comment.

17.   Id.

California Supreme Court is in agreement. In People v. Duarte[18] the court held that the declarant's statements minimizing his own involvement in a shooting and shifting blame to others justified excluding, as unreliable, his declaration against penal interest.[19] Similarly, in People v. Geier[20] the court held that the hearsay's declarant's inconsistent statement warranted excluding, as unreliable, her declaration against penal interest.[21]

The teaching of these cases seems to be that the objective test should govern where the opponent offers no evidence to prove that the declarant believed that it was in his or her interest to make the declaration. But if the opponent offers such evidence, the trial judge should take it into account in determining whether the declaration is so unreliable as to justify withholding it from the jury.

Under the Common Law, only statements against the declarant's pecuniary or proprietary interests qualified under the exception. Omitted were statements against the declarant's penal interest. The omission gave rise to a bitter dissent by Justice Oliver Wendell Holmes in Donnelly v. United States.[22] In this famous case, the Court affirmed the life sentence of a defendant, who over the prosecution's hearsay objection, was not permitted to introduce a statement by a declarant who was unavailable to testify and in which the declarant confessed killing the victim.[23] Unlike the Common Law, the Code adopts an expansive approach. In addition to statements against pecuniary and proprietary interests, § 1230 includes statements against the declarant's civil, penal, and social interests as well as declarations tending to invalidate claims the declarant has against others.[24]

One aspect of declarations against interest has been especially troubling to judges and scholars. If a declaration is disserving of the declarant's interests and also of the interests of a party mentioned in the declaration, may the declaration be received against that party? The California Supreme Court resolved this question in People v. Leach.[25] It held that as a matter of statutory construction § 1230 is limited to those

---

18. 24 Cal.4th 603, 101 Cal.Rptr.2d 701, 12 P.3d 1110 (2000).

19. Id. at 614–615, 101 Cal.Rptr.2d at 709, 12 P.3d at 1117–1118.

20. 41 Cal.4th 555, 61 Cal.Rptr.3d 580, 161 P.3d 104 (2007).

21. 41 Cal.4th at 585, 61 Cal.Rptr.3d at 604, 161 P.3d at 125. The trial judge also took into account the self-serving nature of the declarant's declaration. Id. The accused was on trial for murder. In the event of a prosecution against the declarant for murder, the facts recited in the declaration could have provided the basis for an instruction on self-defense or a lesser homicide. Id.

22. 228 U.S. 243, 33 S.Ct. 449, 57 L.Ed. 820 (1913), reh'g denied, 228 U.S. 708, 33 S.Ct. 1024, 57 L.Ed. 1035 (1913).

23. Id. at 272–276, 33 S.Ct. at 459–461.

24. West's Ann.California Evidence Code § 1230. For a discussion of the kinds of statements that qualify as being against social interest, see People v. Wheeler, 105 Cal.App.4th 1423, 1426, 129 Cal.Rptr.2d 916, 918 (2003). Examples include admissions of illegitimacy, impotency, adultery, and, in the case of a single woman, pregnancy. Id.

25. 15 Cal.3d 419, 124 Cal.Rptr. 752, 541 P.2d 296 (1975), cert. denied, 424 U.S. 926, 96 S.Ct. 1137, 47 L.Ed.2d 335 (1976).

statements disserving only of the declarant's interest.[26]

In *Leach*, Lorraine Kramer and Donald Leach were prosecuted for murdering Kramer's father. Leach's cellmate testified that Leach told him that he had killed Kramer's father and that Kramer had agreed to pay Leach for killing him. The court held that it was error for the trial judge to have admitted that portion of Leach's declaration in which he incriminated Kramer,[27] even though Leach did not testify and, hence, was unavailable as a witness.[28]

---

26. Id. at 441, 124 Cal.Rptr. at 766, 541 P.2d at 310. *Leach*'s holding was reaffirmed by the California Supreme Court in People v. Duarte, 24 Cal.4th 603, 611, 101 Cal.Rptr.2d 701, 707, 12 P.3d 1110, 1115 (2000), and People v. Lawley, 27 Cal.4th 102, 153, 115 Cal.Rptr.2d 614, 657, 38 P.3d 461, 497 (2002), cert. denied, 537 U.S. 1073, 123 S.Ct. 671, 154 L.Ed.2d 567 (2002). Accord: People v. Smith, 135 Cal.App.4th 914, 922, 38 Cal.Rptr.3d 1, 6 (2005).

27. People v. Leach, 15 Cal.3d 419, 442, 124 Cal.Rptr. 752, 768, 541 P.2d 296, 312 (1975), cert. denied, 424 U.S. 926, 96 S.Ct. 1137, 47 L.Ed.2d 335 (1976). Accord: People v. Lawley, 27 Cal.4th 102, 153, 115 Cal.Rptr.2d 614, 657, 38 P.3d 461, 497 (2002), cert. denied, 537 U.S. 1073, 123 S.Ct. 671, 154 L.Ed.2d 567 (2002) (holding that the exception for declarations against penal interest did not embrace the declarant's statement that he had been hired to kill the victim by the "Aryan Brotherhood" or the statement that an "innocent man" was in jail for his crime).

But see People v. Samuels, 36 Cal.4th 96, 113 P.3d 1125, 30 Cal.Rptr.3d 105 (2005), cert. denied, 547 U.S. 1073, 126 S.Ct. 1771, 164 L.Ed.2d 522 (2006), where the California Supreme Court, while citing *Lawley*, nonetheless approved the use of a declaration in which the declarant not only admitted killing the victim but doing so because the accused paid him to do so: "Defendant argues that Bernstein's assertion 'that [defendant] had paid him' for the killing was either collateral to his statement against penal interest, or an attempt to shift blame. We disagree. This admission, volunteered to an acquaintance, was specifically disserving to Bernstein's interests in that it intimated he had participated in a contract killing—a particularly heinous type of murder—and in a conspiracy to commit murder. Under the totality of the circumstances presented here, we do not regard the reference to defendant incorporated within this admission as itself constituting a collateral assertion that should have been purged from Navarro's recollection of Bernstein's precise comments to him. Instead, the reference was inextricably tied to and part of a specific statement against penal interest." Id. at 120, 113 P.3d at 1141, 30 Cal.Rptr.3d at 125.

28. People v. Greenberger, 58 Cal.App.4th 298, 335, 68 Cal.Rptr.2d 61, 81 (1997), holds that a portion of a declaration against interest incriminating a nondeclarant can be offered against the nondeclarant without the need for an additional hearsay exception if the trial judge finds that both the portions inculpating the declarant and nondeclarant are especially worthy of belief. Apparently, such a finding of trustworthiness with regard to both portions of the declaration satisfies the exception for declarations against interest as well as the nondeclarant's confrontation rights. Id. But whether the declaration offered in *Greenberger* would withstand a confrontation challenge under Crawford v. Washington, 541 U.S. 36, 124 S.Ct. 1354, 158 L.Ed.2d 177 (2004), is another matter and is discussed in § 6.03 et seq., supra. *Greenberger* relied on People v. Gordon, 50 Cal.3d 1223, 270 Cal.Rptr. 451, 792 P.2d 251 (1990) and People v. Wilson, 17 Cal.App.4th 271, 21 Cal.Rptr.2d 420 (1993), for the proposition that there is no need to find a hearsay exception for that portion of the declaration inculpating the nondeclarant. People v. Greenberger supra at 328, 68 Cal.Rptr.2d at 76–77.

Greenberger's reliance on *Gordon* is misplaced, however, since the *Gordon* court did not reach that issue. So is its reliance on *Wilson*, since the *Wilson* court justified its holding on the availability of a separate hearsay exception for that portion of the declaration inculpating the nondeclarant. *Greenberger*, moreover, ignores *Leach* which limits the California exception only to those declarations that are disserving of the declarant's interests. Some decisions relying on *Greenberger* also ignore *Leach*. See, e.g., People v. Cervantes, 118 Cal.App.4th 162, 177, 12 Cal.Rptr.3d 774, 785 (2004).

Leach does not apply to preliminary hearings. The admissibility of hearsay in these proceedings is governed by Proposition 115 which creates a broad hearsay exception for evidence offered by the prosecution. Accordingly, a crime partner's confession implicating other partners can be admitted against the other partners at the hearing. See People v. Miranda, 23 Cal.4th 340, 353, 96 Cal.Rptr.2d 758, 767, 1 P.3d 73, 81 (2000), cert. denied, 531 U.S. 997, 121 S.Ct. 493, 148 L.Ed.2d 464 (2000).

Leach works both ways. Just as a declaration against penal interest may not be received to inculpate a nondeclarant, neither may such a declaration be received to exculpate the nondeclarant where the declaration expressly does so. In People v. Dixon,[29] for example, the reviewing court upheld the trial court's redaction of that portion of a declaration against penal interest in which the declarant expressly stated that the accused had nothing to do with the crime for which he was on trial.[30] Only the portion in which the declarant admitted responsibility for the crime was admissible under the exception.[31]

Leach, however, does not alter the rule permitting the use of hearsay within hearsay if each part satisfies a hearsay exception. For example, a statement by an unavailable declarant that she removed a gun which her husband told her was the weapon he used to commit a crime qualifies as a declaration against penal interest because it subjects the declarant to liability as an accessory.[32] The crime of being an accessory requires the prosecution to prove, among other matters, that the accused was aware that a principal had committed an offense.[33] Thus, that portion of the declarant's statement repeating the husband's statement would be admissible for this purpose. In a trial against the husband for the crime he purportedly admitted to his wife, his statement would be admissible against him as a party admission which, in turn, would be admissible as part of the wife's statement against interest. Under the Code and the Federal Rules, a party may use admissible hearsay to prove another statement that is also admissible hearsay.[34]

Declarations against interest should not be confused with party admissions. Unlike declarations against interest, to be admissible a party's statements need not be against interest when made, can be in the form of an opinion, and do not have to be based on the party's personal knowledge.[35] Declarations against interest, on the other hand, require the proponent to show that the declarant had "sufficient knowledge" of the subject of his statement.[36]

QUESTIONS AND PROBLEMS

1.   Consider the admissibility of the following evidence offered by the defendant (Donnelly) in a murder prosecution tried in a California court (assume the unavailability of the out of court declarant):

---

29.   153 Cal.App.4th 985, 63 Cal.Rptr.3d 637 (2007).

30.   Id. at 997, 63 Cal.Rptr.3d at 647 (2007).

31.   Id.

32.   People v. Wilson, 17 Cal.App.4th 271, 275, 21 Cal.Rptr.2d 420, 423 (1993).

33.   West's Ann. California Penal Code § 32.

34.   West's Ann. California Evidence Code § 1201; Federal Rule of Evidence 805. Whether the declaration offered in *Wilson* would survive a confrontation challenge under Crawford v. Washington, 541 U.S. 36, 124 S.Ct. 1354, 158 L.Ed.2d 177 (2004), is discussed in § 6.03 et seq., supra.

35.   See § 7.01 supra.

36.   West's Ann.California Evidence Code § 1230.

Defense Counsel: Officer, did you ask Jack Green about the killing?

Officer: Yes.

Defense Counsel: What did he say?

Officer: Jack Green said, "I killed the victim."

District Attorney: Objection. Hearsay.

Judge: ?

2. Compare with:

Officer: Jack Green said, "Donnelly did not kill the victim."

District Attorney: Objection. What Green said about Donnelly's lack of involvement is not against Green's interest.

Judge: ?

3. Compare with:

Officer: Jack Green said, "I, not Donnelly, killed the victim."

District Attorney: Objection. What Green said about Donnelly's lack of involvement is not against Green's interest.

Judge: ?

4. Compare with:

District Attorney: You told Green, did you not, that it would be in his interest to confess to the killing?

Officer: Yes.

District Attorney: And you said this to him before he confessed?

Officer: Yes.

District Attorney: Move to strike the confession on the ground that the declarant thought that it was in his interest to confess.

Judge: ?

§ 9.02 DECLARATIONS AGAINST INTEREST UNDER THE FEDERAL RULES

The treatment of declarations against interest under the Federal Rules of Evidence differs from that under the Code in several respects. First, Congress deleted the provision permitting the use of declarations against the declarant's social interest "as lacking sufficient guarantees of reliability."[1] Second, under Federal Rule of Evidence 804(b)(3)(B), a statement tending to expose the declarant to criminal liability is not admissible unless "supported by corroborating circumstances that clearly indicate its trustworthiness."[2] Originally, the restriction applied only when the accused offered the statement. The restriction reflected a fear that such statements might be falsely contrived to aid the accused.[3] A

---

1. Federal Rule of Evidence 804(b)(3) (Report of House Committee on the Judiciary).

2. Id.

3. Id.

2010 amendment rectified this imbalance. Amended Rule 804(b)(3)(B) applies the corroboration requirement to the government as well as to the accused.[4] As the Advisory Committee explains, "A unitary approach to declarations against penal interest assures both the prosecution and the accused that the Rule will not be abused and that only reliable hearsay statements will be adopted under the exception."[5]

The Federal Rules also take a different, more stringent, approach to unavailability. In addition to such usual grounds of unavailability as death or illness, in the case of declarations against interest the proponent must also show that he has been unable to procure the declarant's testimony by process or other reasonable means.[6] According to the House, which added this requirement, the "amendment is designed primarily to require that an attempt be made to depose a witness (as well as to seek his attendance) as a precondition to the witness being deemed unavailable."[7]

Like § 1230, Federal Rule of Evidence 804(b)(3) has been limited only to those statements that are disserving of the declarant's interests.[8] A statement, for example, that is disserving of the declarant's as well as a party's penal interests may not be offered against the party as a declaration against penal interest. Thus, the statement, "I am taking the cocaine to Atlanta for Williamson," though against the declarant's penal interests, may not be offered against Williamson in a drug prosecution. Limiting the exception to those statements disserving of the declarant's interests minimizes the risk of offending the accused's confrontation rights.[9]

QUESTIONS AND PROBLEMS

1.   Plaintiff sues his insurer to recover amounts which Plaintiff claims an employee wrongfully took. Plaintiff calls a witness who testifies that the employee told her that he, the employee, took the money without permission.

---

4. See Federal Rule of Evidence 804(b)(3) (Advisory Committee Note). The Advisory Committee also makes clear that in assessing the corroborating circumstances, federal judges may not take into account the credibility of the witness who relates the hearsay declaration in court. "To base admission or exclusion of a hearsay statement on the witness's credibility would usurp the jury's role of determining the credibility of the testifying witnesses." Id.

5. Even if it meets the corroboration requirement, a declaration offered by the government against a criminal defendant may nonetheless be excludable on confrontation grounds. By definition, the hearsay declarant must be shown to be unavailable to testify. If the declaration qualifies as "testimonial," the judge should exclude it unless the government can demonstrate that the defendant was accorded an opportunity prior to the trial to cross examine the hearsay declarant or that the defendant has forfeited his or her right to object on confrontation rights. For a discussion of this requirement, see §§ 6.03 et seq., supra.

6. Federal Rule of Evidence 804(a)(5).

7. Id. (Report of House Committee on the Judiciary).

8. Williamson v. United States, 512 U.S. 594, 599, 114 S.Ct. 2431, 2435, 129 L.Ed.2d 476 (1994) ("In our view, the most faithful reading of Rule 804(b)(3) is that it does not allow admission of non-self-inculpatory statements, even if they are made within a broader narrative that is generally self-inculpatory. The district court may not just assume for purposes of Rule 804(b)(3) that a statement is self-inculpatory because it is part of a fuller confession, and this is especially true when the statement implicates someone else.") Id. at 601, 114 S.Ct. at 2425. In some jurisdictions, however, declarations against penal interest implicating a nondeclarant defendant in a crime are admissible. For a discussion of whether such declarations can be admitted over a confrontation objection, see §§ 6.03 et seq. supra.

9. For an extended discussion of the confrontation problems raised by the use of hearsay against the accused, see § 6.03 supra.

To establish the employee's unavailability, the plaintiff offers evidence that he was unable to procure the employee's attendance by process. The insurer objects on the ground that the Plaintiff has not satisfied the federal standards for establishing the unavailability of the employee. How should the judge rule?

2.   In a federal homicide prosecution, the defendant, after establishing the declarant's unavailability, offers the declarant's statement in which the declarant confessed stabbing the victim. What else must the defendant offer in order to persuade the judge to overrule the prosecutor's hearsay objections?

3.   In a California or federal prosecution against Williams for possessing illegal drugs, over a hearsay objection may the government offer the following declaration by Jones who is unavailable to testify: "I am taking the cocaine to Atlanta for Williams."?

§ 9.03   DYING DECLARATIONS

As Dean Charles McCormick points out, the advent of the hearsay rule necessarily gave rise to an exception for deathbed statements.[1] When the only witness to a killing is the victim, excluding an out of court statement in which the victim identifies his killer might in many instances result in the loss of the only evidence directly connecting the accused with the crime. Under the Code, statements regarding the cause and circumstances of the declarant's death are not made inadmissible by the hearsay rule if the declarant made the statements on the basis of personal knowledge and under a sense of immediately impending death.[2]

If the declarant in fact dies, the party opposing the statement is deprived of the opportunity to cross examine the declarant under oath and in the presence of the fact finder. But because deathbed statements are believed to be reliable, the need for cross-examination is not indispensable. People about to die, it is assumed, do not want to meet their Maker with a lie on their lips.[3] Accordingly, circumstantial guarantees of trustworthiness, not just need, justify the exception.

Confronting accusers is of the greatest importance in capital cases. Yet, in criminal cases Congress limited the use of dying declarations to homicide prosecutions.[4] Congress's reason is curious: its belief that dying

---

1.   C. McCormick, McCormick on Evidence § 309 (4th ed. J. Strong 1992).

2.   West's Ann.California Evidence Code § 1242. Federal Rule of Evidence 804(b)(2) is generally to the same effect.

The circumstances attending the declarant's death can include the declarant's belief that the accused was engaged in committing another offense at the time the fatal blow was delivered. See People v. Gatson, 60 Cal.App.4th 1020, 1025, 70 Cal.Rptr.2d 729, 732 (1998), where the court upheld the admission of a dying declaration in which the declarant stated that the accused was robbing her when that he shot her. The portion of the declaration describing the robbery was material because the accused was on trial for felony murder.

3.   Regina v. Osman, 15 Cox C.C. 1, 3 (1881). If the declarant is not religious, then the assumption is that individuals facing the prospect of immediate death have no motive to lie.

4.   Federal Rule of Evidence 804(b)(2).

declarations are not "among the most reliable forms of hearsay."[5] So sometimes need can trump trustworthiness.

Under the Code, dying declarations are admissible in all civil and criminal actions, such as wrongful death actions and homicide prosecutions, so long as they are probative of the declarant's cause or circumstances of death.[6] Under the Federal Rules, dying declarations may also be offered in civil as well as criminal actions.[7]

In assessing the admissibility of a dying declaration, the judge plays two distinct functions. If the question is whether the declarant made the statement or made the statement upon personal knowledge, the judge merely determines whether the proponent's evidence, if believed, will permit a reasonable fact finder to resolve the question in the proponent's favor.[8] The judge is not allowed to weigh the evidence, including evidence bearing on credibility. It is the jury's duty to determine the effect and value of this evidence.[9] The opposing party, however, is entitled to a limiting instruction directing the jurors to disregard the dying declaration unless they first find these foundational facts.[10]

If, on the other hand, the question is whether the declarant made the statement while under an impending sense of death or whether the declaration relates to the cause or circumstances of death, then the judge plays a greater role. Since these issues go to the reliability of the evidence, the judge may consider both the proponent's as well as the opponent's evidence and take credibility into account.[11] If the judge, for example, disbelieves the proponent's evidence of the declarant's state of mind, the judge will exclude the declaration. If the judge disbelieves the opponent's evidence, the judge will let the fact finder hear the declaration. In this case, however, the judge will not instruct the jurors to disregard the declaration unless they first find that the declarant made it while under an impending sense of doom. The judge's decision either way is final, and the jury is not given an opportunity to redetermine the issue.[12]

If the judge allows the jury to hear the declaration, the opponent may attack the reliability of the declaration. "Thus, a party may present evidence of the circumstances under which a * * * dying declaration * * *

---

5. Id. (Report of the House Committee on the Judiciary).

6. West's Ann.California Evidence Code § 1242 (comment).

7. Id.

8. West's Ann.California Evidence Code § 403 and comment.

9. Id.

10. Id.

11. West's Ann.California Evidence Code § 405. "To be admissible in evidence as dying declarations, the statements of the decedent must have been made at a time when he had abandoned all hope of life so that he believed that death inevitably must follow. This sense of impending death may be shown in any satisfactory mode, by the express language of the declarant, or be inspired from his evident danger, or the opinions of medical or other attendants stated to him, or from his conduct, or other circumstances in the case, all of which are resorted to in order to ascertain the state of the declarant's mind." People v. Gonzales, 87 Cal.App.2d 867, 878, 198 P.2d 81, 89 (1948).

12. Id. and comment.

was made where such evidence is relevant to the credibility of the statement, even though such evidence may duplicate to some degree the evidence presented to the court on the issue of admissibility. But the jury's sole concern is the truth or falsity of the facts stated, not the admissibility of the statement."[13] In summation, the lawyers may, of course, tell the jurors why they should accept or reject the dying declaration.

Where the judge allows the jury to hear the dying declaration, the judge must exercise caution in commenting on the declaration. The judge must not suggest that the law considers such declarations to be especially trustworthy and, therefore, worthy of belief.[14] It is up to the jury, not the court, to determine what weight, if any, to give to such declarations.[15]

Must the declarant in fact die? The Federal Rules group dying declarations with other hearsay exceptions requiring the hearsay declarant to be unavailable.[16] "Since unavailability is not limited to death, * * * if the declarant is in fact unavailable [for some other reason], an unexpected recovery does not bar admission of the statement made under belief of impending death."[17] This position is justified, as it is the declarant's belief that he or she is about to die that infuses the deathbed declaration with reliability. The Code, on the other hand, does not expressly condition the use of dying declarations on the unavailability of the declarant. Therefore, whether the declarant must die depends on whether the Code merely codified the Common Law definition of dying declarations. Under the Common Law, the proponent had to offer evidence that the declarant had died.[18] But in its Comment the California Law Revision Commission states that the Code's provision is not intended to codify its Common Law predecessor. Among the changes effected by the Code is eliminating the Common Law limitation that dying declarations be offered only in "criminal homicide actions."[19] Moreover, the Commission emphasizes that for "the purpose of the *admissibility* of dying declarations, there is no rational basis for differentiating between civil and criminal actions or among the various types of criminal actions."[20] Various types of criminal actions, of course, include prosecutions not just for homicides but also attempted homicides. Although the issue is not free of all ambiguity, it appears that in California dying declarations should be admissible even if the declarant unexpectedly survives.

---

13. Id. (comment).

14. People v. Smith, 214 Cal.App.3d 904, 913, 263 Cal.Rptr. 155, 160 (1989).

15. Id.

16. Federal Rule of Evidence 804.

17. M. Graham, Handbook of Federal Evidence § 804.2 (3d ed. 1991). In a federal criminal case, however, the declarant must in fact die. In federal criminal cases, dying declarations are admissible only in homicide prosecutions. See Federal Rule of Evidence 804(b)(2).

18. See C. McCormick, McCormick on Evidence § 309 (4th ed. J. Strong 1992).

19. See West's Ann. California Evidence Code § 1242 (comment).

20. Id. (emphasis in the original).

Dying declarations and confrontation. When a dying declaration is offered against the accused in a homicide prosecution, the accused is deprived of the opportunity to confront his accuser. But in light of their presumed reliability, the United States Supreme Court sanctioned their use against criminal defendants over one-hundred years ago.[21] The Court, however, will have to reconsider its position in light of Crawford v. Washington.[22] *Crawford* holds that, over a confrontation objection, testimonial hearsay may not be offered against the accused unless (1) the hearsay declarant is produced for cross-examination by the accused or (2) if not produced, unless the accused was given an opportunity prior to the trial to cross examine the hearsay declarant.[23]

The Court might invoke the forfeiture doctrine to sustain the use of dying declarations against the accused. Although the Court has yet to specify the precise contours of this doctrine, the Court has acknowledged that defendants can forfeit their right to object to hearsay on Sixth Amendment grounds when they engaged in wrongdoing designed to prevent the declarant from testifying at the trial.[24] The Court could also invoke the history of the Sixth Amendment. Apparently, the Founders were aware of the dying declaration exception at the time the Sixth Amendment was adopted and intended the Sixth Amendment to incorporate existing exceptions.[25] Although the Court has not decided this point, the California Supreme Court has held that this was indeed the Founders' intent with regard to dying declarations.[26]

Sworn statements by dead declarants regarding gang related activities. The rise in gang related crime led the California Legislature to enact a new hearsay exception for statements by dead declarants regarding gang related activity. To deter gang related crimes, California makes it a separate offense for a gang member to promote or assist any felonious criminal activity by members of the gang.[27] To discourage gang members from eliminating potential witnesses, § 1231 of the Code allows the use of statements by dead declarants relating to events that are relevant in anti-gang prosecutions.[28] To be admissible, the statement must satisfy a number of conditions: (1) the statement must be a verbatim rendition and a copy of it must exist; (2) the events related in the statement were within the personal knowledge of the declarant; (3) the statement was made under oath; (4) the declarant died from "other than natural causes"; and

---

21. Pointer v. Texas, 380 U.S. 400, 406, 85 S.Ct. 1065, 1069, 13 L.Ed.2d 923 (1965), citing Mattox v. United States, 146 U.S. 140, 13 S.Ct. 50, 36 L.Ed. 917 (1892), where the Court stated that dying declarations are admissible "in favor of the defendant as well as against him." Id. at 151, 13 S.Ct. at 54.

22. 541 U.S. 36, 124 S.Ct. 1354, 158 L.Ed.2d 177 (2004).

23. Id. at 68.

24. See Giles v. California, 554 U.S. 353, 368, 128 S.Ct. 2678, 171 L.Ed.2d 488 (2008).

25. Crawford v. Washington, 541 U.S. 36, 56 note 6, 124 S.Ct. 1354, 158 L.Ed.2d 177 (2004).

26. People v. Monterroso, 34 Cal.4th 743, 763, 101 P.3d 956, 971, 22 Cal.Rptr.3d 1, 19 (2004), cert. denied, 546 U.S. 834, 126 S.Ct. 61, 163 L.Ed.2d 89 (2005).

27. West's Ann. California Penal Code § 186.22.

28. West's Ann. California Evidence Code § 1231.

(5) the statement was made under circumstances indicating its trustworthiness.[29]

Among the factors the court may consider in determining the statement's trustworthiness are whether the declarant had a bias or motive for fabricating the statement and whether the statement is corroborated by other evidence and was against the declarant's interest when made.[30] A statement may not be offered under the exception unless the proponent gives sufficient notice of the intention to use the statement as to afford the opponent a fair opportunity to meet the statement.[31] If the statement is received, the jurors may not be told that the declarant died from other than natural causes; they may be told only that the declarant is unavailable to testify.[32]

QUESTIONS AND PROBLEMS

1. Consider the admissibility of the following evidence in a homicide prosecution tried in a California or federal court:

District Attorney: Mr. Robinson, what happened next?

Mr. Robinson: Cliff Long and I were sitting in the car. I heard a shot somewhere in front of us, and the bullet hit Cliff in the head.

* * *

District Attorney: Mr. Long, what if anything did Cliff say to you when he was brought to your home?

Mr. Long: Cliff said, "Daddy, Carl Soles shot me with a .22 rifle. I am afraid that I am about to die."

Defense Counsel: Objection. Move to strike the first statement as hearsay.

District Attorney: Dying declaration.

Judge: ?

Assume that the judge overrules the objection. Defense counsel then moves to strike the second statement on hearsay grounds. How should the judge rule?

2. If the judge overrules the objections, should she grant the defendant's motion to instruct the jurors to disregard the declaration unless they first find that Cliff made it while under an impending sense of death?

3. Assume that the defense calls the following witness:

Defense Counsel: Did you hear Mr. Long testify that Cliff told him that my client, Carl Soles, shot him with a .22 rifle?

Eyewitness: Yes.

---

29. Id.

30. Id.

31. Id. § 1231.1.

32. Id. § 1231.4.

Defense Counsel: Were you present at Mr. Long's home from the time Cliff was brought home and until Cliff died?

Eyewitness: Yes.

Defense Counsel: In that time did you hear Cliff make the statement which Mr. Long claims he made?

Eyewitness: No, Cliff never once spoke up.

Defense Counsel: Move to strike Mr. Long's testimony about what Cliff said about my client.

Judge: ?

§ 9.04   EXCITED UTTERANCES

People who witness startling events are sometimes moved to describe them. The bystander watching a car run a light may well remark, "Look, the blue car just ran the light!" The spontaneity associated with such statements and the consequent lack of opportunity for reflection and deliberate fabrication justify the creation of a hearsay exception.[1] Under the Code, an excited utterance is admissible over a hearsay objection if the proponent persuades the judge that the statement was "made spontaneously while the declarant was under the stress of excitement caused by such perception."[2]

Under § 1240, the proponent must also show that the utterance "[p]urports to narrate, describe, or explain an act, condition, or event perceived by the declarant".[3] Federal Rule of Evidence 803(2) is broader: the statement need only *relate* to a startling event or condition.[4] The difference between the Code and the Rules can be illustrated by Murphy Auto Parts Co., Inc. v. Ball.[5] To prove that the driver of a vehicle was on company business at the time of the accident, the plaintiff offered the driver's utterance following the accident that he "had to call on a customer".[6] While that utterance may have related to the startling event (the accident), it did not narrate, describe, or explain it. The driver did not say, for example, "I am running the light." or even "I just ran the light." Under a strict reading of the Code, the statement might not qualify as an excited utterance,[7] although it would under the Federal Rules.[8]

---

1. West's Ann.California Evidence Code § 1240 (comment).

2. West's Ann.California Evidence Code § 1240(b).

3. West's Ann.California Evidence Code § 1240(a).

4. Federal Rule of Evidence 803(2). The California Supreme Court has used the term "relate" in explaining the excited utterance exception in California. See People v. Poggi, 45 Cal.3d 306, 318, 246 Cal.Rptr. 886, 893, 753 P.2d 1082, 1089 (1988), cert. denied, 492 U.S. 925, 109 S.Ct. 3261, 106 L.Ed.2d 606 (1989), reh'g denied, 492 U.S. 938, 110 S.Ct. 25, 106 L.Ed.2d 637 (1989). In *Poggi*, however, the scope of the exception was not in issue. Id.

5. 249 F.2d 508 (D.C.Cir.1957), cert. denied, 355 U.S. 932, 78 S.Ct. 413, 2 L.Ed.2d 415 (1958).

6. Id. at 509.

7. Pre–Code cases, however, took a more generous approach to the admissibility of excited utterances. See, e.g., Dillon v. Wallace, 148 Cal.App.2d 447, 449, 306 P.2d 1044, 1045 (1957) (Store manager's statement, upon finding the plaintiff at the scene of the fall, "Don't you worry about this * * * we are insured and will pay your bills," was properly admitted as an excited utterance.)

The California Supreme Court, however, has construed § 1240 liberally. In People v. Farmer[9] the court upheld the use of statements by the victim in which he described his wounds and his assailant to a police dispatcher. The accused objected to a portion of the statement in which the victim described the assailant as an acquaintance and drug customer of his roommate. This portion, the accused claimed, did not narrate, describe, or explain the shooting. The court disagreed: "Although not independently admissible under this exception for their truth, these statements help describe the event by identifying the perpetrator. The claim that the assailant was one of [the roommate's] customers not only helped identify him, but also aided in explaining the event as potentially drug-related."[10]

The court also rejected the accused's claim that the victim's statements were not spontaneous because they had been the product of police questioning. While conceding that extensive questioning may deprive statements of the required spontaneity, the court stressed that in this case the victim was still

> excited, or perhaps more accurately, distraught and in severe pain. * * * His responses were not self serving. * * * Nor were the questions suggestive. * * * While he was being questioned, the intense pain of his gunshot wounds and the concern he rightfully had about his survival no doubt preoccupied him so that he could not have contemplated spinning a false tale. In sum, he had so little opportunity and incentive to deliberate that under these unusual circumstances we can dispense with the testimonial requirements of an oath and cross-examination.[11]

---

8. Federal Rule of Evidence 803(2) (Advisory Committee Note).

9. 47 Cal.3d 888, 254 Cal.Rptr. 508, 765 P.2d 940 (1989), cert. denied, 490 U.S. 1107, 109 S.Ct. 3158, 104 L.Ed.2d 1021 (1989).

10. Id. at 904–905, 254 Cal.Rptr. at 517–518, 765 P.2d at 950. In People v. Arias, 13 Cal.4th 92, 51 Cal.Rptr.2d 770, 913 P.2d 980 (1996), cert. denied, 520 U.S. 1251, 117 S.Ct. 2408, 138 L.Ed.2d 175 (1997), the California Supreme Court construed the hearsay exception for excited utterances even more liberally than in *Farmer*. Arias was prosecuted for murder and rape. The rape took place 13 days after the murder. Shortly after the rape, the victim was overheard saying that during the course of the rape the accused told her that he was the man who committed the murder. Though the rape victim may have been under the stress occasioned by the rape when she repeated the accused's statement, the accused objected that the statement did not narrate, describe, or explain the rape. The court disagreed, holding that "[o]ne may infer that defendant's boast was used to threaten and control [the victim] during her ordeal." Id. at 150, 51 Cal.Rptr.2d at 808, 913 P.2d at 1017. Having determined that the victim's statement qualified as an excited utterance and was relevant because it was probative of the effect that the defendant's statement had on her willingness to resist the rape, the court then held that the defendant's statement could also be considered for the truth of the matter asserted as a party admission. Under the Code, hearsay within hearsay is admissible if each hearsay statement falls within an exception to the hearsay rule. See West's Ann.Cal. Evid. Code § 1202.

11. People v. Farmer, 47 Cal.3d 888, 904–905, 254 Cal.Rptr. 508, 765 P.2d 940, 948 (1989), cert. denied, 490 U.S. 1107, 109 S.Ct. 3158, 104 L.Ed.2d 1021 (1989). See also Rufo v. Simpson, 86 Cal.App.4th 573, 588, 103 Cal.Rptr.2d 492, 501–503 (2001) (Nicole Simpson's statements in response to police questioning that O. J. Simpson had "hit her, kicked her, slapped her, and pulled her hair" were admissible as excited utterances where other evidence showed that she was frightened and exhausted.).

The court likewise rejected a construction of § 1240 limiting stress to psychic distress:

> The statute speaks of excitement caused by the perception of an event. A literal reading of this language conceivably might limit spontaneous declarations to psychic stress caused by *observing* an event, excluding the physical stress or pain experienced by participants. This is plainly not what was meant; spontaneous statements have traditionally included both types of excitement.[12]

Another difference between the Code and the Rules concerns the evidence the proponent may offer to establish the foundation for the exception. Over objection, a California judge may consider only admissible evidence in determining whether the foundational requirements have been satisfied.[13] A federal judge, on the other hand, may consider inadmissible nonprivileged matter.[14] A federal judge may therefore consider the excited utterance as evidence of the exciting event.[15] A California judge may not. Accordingly, where the proponent has no evidence of the exciting event other than the excited utterance, a California judge should exclude the utterance for lack of foundation.[16]

Only those statements made by the declarant while under the stress of excitement qualify under the exception.[17] Since lapses between the time the declarant perceives the exciting event and the time he makes the declaration afford an opportunity for reflection and fabrication, the judge may take such lapses into account in determining the admissibility of the declaration. But even substantial time lapses should not result in exclusion if the declarant's reflective powers had not returned when he made the utterance. Where the time lapses are due to unconsciousness brought on by the exciting event, the reflective powers are in abeyance and the declaration is made under the required stress. In People v. Washington,[18] for example, the victim arrived unconscious at a hospital after a robbery and beating. When he regained consciousness about twenty minutes later,

---

12. People v. Farmer, 47 Cal.3d 888, 901, note 1, 254 Cal.Rptr. 508, note 1, 765 P.2d 940, 948, note 1 (1989), cert. denied, 490 U.S. 1107, 109 S.Ct. 3158, 104 L.Ed.2d 1021 (1989) (emphasis in the original).

13. The California Law Revision Commission recommended a rule permitting judges to consider inadmissible evidence in some circumstances in determining the existence of preliminary facts. 6 California Law Revision Commission, Reports, Recommendations, and Studies 19–21 (1964). The Legislature, however, did not enact the recommended rule and, instead, retained the practice of requiring the use of admissible evidence to establish preliminary facts. See West's Ann.California Evidence Code §§ 400–406.

14. Federal Rule of Evidence 104(a).

15. Federal Rule of Evidence 803(2) (Advisory Committee Note). See also M. Graham, Handbook of Federal Evidence § 803.2 (3d ed. 1991).

16. Compare People v. Pearch, 229 Cal.App.3d 1282, 1289–1291, 280 Cal.Rptr. 584, 586–588 (1991) (There was no evidence that the declarant's statement to his brother over the phone that he was being hurt was made under the stress caused by an exciting event.) with People v. Garcia, 178 Cal.App.3d 814, 821, 224 Cal.Rptr. 198, 203 (1986) (In addition to the victim's statement over the phone that the accused had "gone crazy," there was independent evidence of yelling before the phone went dead.).

17. West's Ann.California Evidence Code § 1240(b).

18. 71 Cal.2d 1170, 81 Cal.Rptr. 5, 459 P.2d 259 (1969).

he stated that he had been "robbed" by "two or three" persons.[19] The court upheld the trial court's finding that the declarant did not have "power to reflect on his answers".[20]

Unconsciousness is not the only justification for time lapses. Persistent shock can also suffice. In People v. Jones[21] the declarant walked into a hospital emergency room about thirty minutes after he was set on fire. The doctor who treated him was permitted to testify that, within five to ten minutes of the onset of treatment, the declarant identified the accused as the person who "threw gasoline" at him.[22] Given the seriousness of his injuries, the court held that the trial judge did not abuse his discretion in finding that the declarant was still under the required stress when he identified the accused as his assailant.[23]

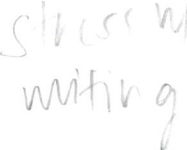

In People v. Gutierrez[24] the accused was convicted of robbery. He claimed that the trial judge should have excluded as hearsay a piece of paper a bystander gave to the victim shortly after the robbery with the license plate numbers of the car in which the robbers had fled. Other evidence showed that the license plate numbers had been issued to the accused. The accused objected to the introduction of the piece of paper on the ground that a written statement could not qualify as a spontaneous statement because the time needed to reduce the observations to writing meant that the declarant was no longer under the stress of the exciting event. The reviewing court rejected this claim, holding that the prosecution had introduced sufficient evidence showing that the declarant was still under the stress occasioned by witnessing the robbery at the time he wrote the down the license plate numbers.[25]

The fact that the declarations may have been elicited by questioning will not deprive them of the required spontaneity if the judge concludes that the declarations were nevertheless made under the stress of excitement while the reflective powers were still in abeyance. In People v. Trimble,[26] for example, a child's declarations describing her father as the person who attacked her mother were admitted although the child's statements in part were elicited by questions posed by her aunt. At the time the child made the statements she was still in an excited stage even though the attack she described had occurred two days earlier.[27]

19.   Id. at 1175, 81 Cal.Rptr. at 9, 459 P.2d at 263.

20.   Id.

21.   155 Cal.App.3d 653, 202 Cal.Rptr. 289 (1984).

22.   Id. at 658, 202 Cal.Rptr. at 292.

23.   Id.

24.   78 Cal.App.4th 170, 92 Cal.Rptr.2d 626 (2000).

25.   Id. at 180–181, 92 Cal.Rptr.2d at 633–634. The trial court correctly excluded evidence that the at the time he handed the piece of paper to the victim, the declarant stated that he had taken down the license plate numbers of the car in which the robbers fled. That statement was simply a recollection of what the declarant had witnessed and presumably was made after the declarant was no longer under the stress occasioned by witnessing the robbery.

26.   5 Cal.App.4th 1225, 7 Cal.Rptr.2d 450 (1992).

27.   Id. at 1235, 7 Cal.Rptr.2d at 456. The outer limits of the California excited utterance exception may have been reached (or crossed) in People v. Panky, 82 Cal.App.3d 772, 147

Excited utterances should narrate, describe, or explain only those acts, conditions, or events perceived by the declarant.[28] Statements by declarants with no personal knowledge of the events narrated, described, or explained do not qualify as excited utterances.[29] Neither do statements that fail to narrate, describe or explain the exciting event. Those portions should be redacted. For example, in People v. Corella[30] the accused was prosecuted for inflicting corporal punishment upon his wife. The prosecution was allowed to offer as an excited utterance a statement the wife made to a police officer shortly after the assault describing the attack. Although the reviewing court approved the use of the statement, it held that the trial judge should have redacted a portion of the statement in which the spouse admonished the defendant not to smoke marihuana.[31] Moreover, opinions and other matters that would be inadmissible if offered through the declarant as a witness are not made admissible by the exception. In People v. Miron,[32] for example, the accused claimed that he acted in self-defense when he shot the victim. In support of his claim, he offered an excited utterance in which the declarant, while describing the attack by the victim ("he busted in, he went past me, * * * and Paul shot him"), said, "This man was trying to kill us."[33] The appellate court upheld the exclusion of the second statement. Since the declarant's conclusion that the assailant was trying to kill them would have been an inadmissible opinion if she had testified, the same conclusion could not be offered as part of an excited utterance.[34] The fact, however, that the declarant would be incompetent to testify does not render her excited utterance inadmissible.[35]

Scientific studies suggest that stress distorts perception.[36] These studies, however, have not resulted in the repeal of the exception for excited utterances. Nor do such studies affect admissibility. But expert evidence about the effects of stress may be considered by the fact finder in

---

Cal.Rptr. 341 (1978). At the defendant's rape trial, the prosecution was allowed to play a tape made during a phone call in which the victim told the police that she had just spotted her assailant. The rape took place three weeks before the victim made the call. The reviewing court upheld the use of the tape as a spontaneous declaration. Id. at 779, 147 Cal.Rptr. at 345.

28. West's Ann.California Evidence Code § 1240(b). See also People v. Jones, 155 Cal.App.3d 653, 661, 202 Cal.Rptr. 289, 294 (1984) (holding that the declarant could have perceived the exciting event—being doused with gasoline and then set on fire).

29. See Ungefug v. D'Ambrosia, 250 Cal.App.2d 61, 67, 58 Cal.Rptr. 223, 228 (1967) (holding that because the hearsay declarant had no personal knowledge of the exciting event, it was error to receive his excited utterance). Accord: People v. Phillips, 22 Cal.4th 226, 236–237, 92 Cal.Rptr.2d 58, 64–65, 991 P.2d 145, 151 (2000).

30. 122 Cal.App.4th 461, 18 Cal.Rptr.3d 770 (2004).

31. Id. at 466, 18 Cal.Rptr.3d at 774.

32. 210 Cal.App.3d 580, 258 Cal.Rptr. 494 (1989).

33. Id. at 582, 258 Cal.Rptr. at 495.

34. Id. at 583–584, 258 Cal.Rptr. at 495.

35. People v. Butler, 249 Cal.App.2d 799, 806, 57 Cal.Rptr. 798, 802–803 (1967) (Fact that the declarant, a five year-old girl, was incompetent to testify did not render her spontaneous statement inadmissible.).

36. See the studies cited in C. McCormick, McCormick on Evidence § 272 (J. Strong 4th ed. 1992).

determining the weight to be given to the utterance.[37] The admissibility of such evidence is committed to the judge's discretion.[38]

A spontaneous utterance made by the accused while in custody will not be barred by *Miranda* if the police remark eliciting the utterance was not designed to elicit an incriminating response.[39]

Excited utterances and confrontation. Spontaneous statements by victims who are not produced by the prosecution have been received against criminal defendants in a number of California cases.[40] Although in these circumstances the accused is deprived of the opportunity to cross examine his accusers under oath and in the presence of the fact finder, the courts have held that the use of excited utterances does not violate the accused's right of confrontation.[41] Prior to the United States Supreme Court's decision in Crawford v. Washington,[42] these statements were believed as a category to be sufficiently reliable to dispense with cross-examination of the declarant: "Where the declarant is truly excited and makes a statement about a concurrently or recently perceived event before having the opportunity to think through the possible consequences of his utterance, it is likely to be a reliable statement."[43]

The holdings of these cases, however, must be reconsidered in light of *Crawford*. *Crawford* holds that, over a confrontation objection, testimonial hearsay may not be offered against the accused unless (1) the hearsay declarant is produced for cross-examination by the accused or (2) if not produced, unless the accused was given an opportunity prior to the trial to cross examine the hearsay declarant.[44] Although the United States Supreme Court has not decided whether an excited utterance qualifies as a testimonial statement, the California Court of Appeal has passed on the question. In People v. Chaney[45] the accused claimed that a spontaneous statement made by a victim to a police officer qualified as testimonial. In her statement, the victim described a number of crimes committed by the accused. Because the prosecution offered the statement through the officer, the accused was deprived of an opportunity to cross examine the victim. The court nonetheless rejected the accused's confrontation claim

---

37. People v. McDonald, 37 Cal.3d 351, 371, 208 Cal.Rptr. 236, 249, 690 P.2d 709, 722 (1984), appeal after remand, 203 Cal.App.3d 925, 237 Cal.Rptr. 597 (1987) (It was an abuse of discretion for the trial court to exclude expert testimony of the factors, including stress, affecting eyewitness identification.).

38. Id. at 373, 208 Cal.Rptr. at 251, 690 at 724.

39. People v. O'Sullivan, 217 Cal.App.3d 237, 241, 265 Cal.Rptr. 784, 785 (1990) (In response to a deputy's remark, "I believe I have something here," upon discovering two clear plastic bags containing a white powdery substance in a deodorant container, the accused said, "Oh, oh.").

40. People v. Farmer, 47 Cal.3d 888, 905, 254 Cal.Rptr. 508, 519, 765 P.2d 940, 951 (1989), cert. denied, 490 U.S. 1107, 109 S.Ct. 3158, 104 L.Ed.2d 1021 (1989), and cases cited therein.

41. Id.

42. 541 U.S. 36, 124 S.Ct. 1354, 158 L.Ed.2d 177 (2004).

43. People v. Farmer, 47 Cal.3d 888, 905, 254 Cal.Rptr. 508, 519, 765 P.2d 940, 951 (1989), cert. denied, 490 U.S. 1107, 109 S.Ct. 3158, 104 L.Ed.2d 1021 (1989).

44. People v. Crawford, supra note 42, at 68.

45. 148 Cal.App.4th 772, 56 Cal.Rptr.3d 128 (2007).

on the ground that the statement did not qualify as testimonial.[46] In reaching this conclusion, the court considered the circumstances surrounding the making of the statement. Because the victim made the statement to the officer at a time when the officer was attempting to determine the nature of an ongoing emergency, the court held that the statement was nontestimonial under the criteria the United States Supreme Court laid down in Davis v. Washington.[47] In *Davis*, the Court held that:

> Statements are nontestimonial when made in the course of police interrogation under circumstances objectively indicating that the primary purpose of the interrogation is to enable police assistance to meet an ongoing emergency. They are testimonial when the circumstances objectively indicate that there is no such ongoing emergency, and that the primary purpose of the interrogation is to establish or prove past events potentially relevant to later criminal prosecution.[48]

QUESTIONS AND PROBLEMS

1. Determine the admissibility of the following evidence in a personal injury accident brought in a California or federal court:

Plaintiff's Counsel: Were you present at the site of the collision?

Witness: Yes, I was.

Plaintiff's Counsel: Immediately before the collision, did you hear anyone say anything?

Witness: Yes, my boyfriend said, "Look, the blue car is running the red light!"

Over.
Adm.

Defense Counsel: Objection, hearsay.

Plaintiff's Counsel: Excited utterance.

Judge: ?

Plaintiff's Counsel: Officer, did you respond to the site of a collision at the intersection of University and Main?

Officer: Yes, I found two cars stopped in the middle of the intersection.

Plaintiff's Counsel: What color were the two cars?

Officer: One was red and the other was blue.

Plaintiff's Counsel: Did you interview the driver of the blue car?

---

46. Id. at 780, 56 Cal.Rptr.3d at 134.

47. Id. Accord: People v. Saracoglu, 152 Cal.App.4th 1584, 1596, 62 Cal.Rptr.3d 418, 426 (2007) (holding that a crime victim's spontaneous statements to police officers at a police station describing her attacker were not testimonial); People v. Brenn, 152 Cal.App.4th 166, 178, 60 Cal.Rptr.3d 830, 838 (2007) (holding that a crime victim's spontaneous statements to a 911 operator were not testimonial); People v. Pedroza, 147 Cal.App.4th 784, 793, 54 Cal.Rptr.3d 636, 642 (2007) (holding that a crime victim's spontaneous statements to police officers regarding the cause of her injuries were not testimonial).

48. Davis v. Washington, 547 U.S. 813, 126 S.Ct. 2266, 2273, 165 L.Ed.2d 224 (2006) (footnotes omitted).

Officer: Yes.

Plaintiff's Counsel: What did he say to you?

Officer: Yes, immediately upon my arrival he jumped out of his car and said, "I was making a pizza delivery at the time of the collision."

Defense Counsel: Objection, hearsay.

Plaintiff's Counsel: Excited utterance.

Judge: ?

2. Determine the admissibility of the following evidence in a wrongful death action brought by the surviving spouse in federal court:

Plaintiff's Counsel: Were you and the decedent co-workers?

Witness: Yes, we were working together at the job site.

Plaintiff's Counsel: Were you the one who first discovered his body?

Witness: Yes, when I didn't hear from him over the two-way radio for over an hour, I decided to hike over the hill to check things out and found him lying on the ground. I checked but couldn't find a pulse.

Plaintiff's Counsel: Did you hear him say anything as you were climbing the hill?

Witness: Yes, I heard him say, "Help! The bulldozer is slipping!"

Defense Counsel: Objection. Hearsay.

Plaintiff's Counsel: Excited utterance.

Judge: ?

3. Would you change your ruling if the case were tried in a California court?

4. Determine the admissibility of the following evidence in a California or federal prosecution in which the defendant is charged with rape; in ruling assume that the prosecution has offered other admissible evidence that the victim had been raped and that victim is unavailable to testify.

Prosecutor: Did the victim say anything to you immediately upon your arrival at the scene?

Police Officer: Yes, she said to me, "Not only did the defendant just rape me but while raping me he said, 'I am the one who killed Joe 13 days ago!'"

5. Would the evidence be admissible in a California or federal prosecution charging the defendant with murdering Joe?

§ 9.05 CONTEMPORANEOUS STATEMENTS

Section 1241 creates a hearsay exception for statements which are "offered to explain, qualify, or make understandable conduct of the declarant" and which were "made while the declarant was engaged in such conduct."[1] Trustworthiness is derived from the requirement that the

---

1. West's Ann.California Evidence Code § 1241.

declaration be contemporaneous with the conduct that is being explained, qualified, or made understandable.

The Assembly Committee questioned the need for this exception, noting that some commentators do not regard the kinds of the statements contemplated by § 1241 to be hearsay.[2] For example, under the laws relating to personal property, merely lending a pen to someone does not strip the lender of ownership of the pen; it creates only a bailment. But giving the pen to another can transfer ownership by creating an inter vivos gift. Whether a bailment or inter vivos gift was created depends on the intention of the owner. Thus, if in the act of handing the pen the owner says, "Use my pen", only a bailment is created. But if the owner says, "I want you to have this pen", then an inter vivos transfer is effected.

Section 1241 is designed to remove any hearsay barriers to these kinds of statements. Depending on which statement the owner made, the declarations will clarify whether a bailment or inter vivos gift was intended. But closer analysis discloses that no hearsay is involved. These statements are verbal acts. As has been discussed, when the substantive law governing the action invests certain utterances with legal significance, then proof of those utterances does not violate the hearsay rule.[3]

The Federal Rules do not contain a hearsay exception for contemporaneous statements. Instead, Federal Rule of Evidence 803(1) creates an exception for statements "describing or explaining an event or condition, made while or immediately after the declarant perceived it."[4] The Code looks inwardly, creating an exception for statements reflecting the declarant's state of mind regarding his own conduct.[5] The Rules focus outwardly, providing an exception for statements by the declarant describing external phenomena. The present sense impressions contemplated by Rule 803(1) are much closer to excited utterances.

People v. Hines[6] illustrates the difference between the California exception for contemporary statements and the federal exception for present sense impressions. Hines was prosecuted for murdering Donna Roberts. To prove that the defendant was the killer, the prosecution sought to introduce a telephone conversation which Jiy Williams had with Donna on the day of the killing. In response to Williams' question about

---

2. Id. (comment).

3. See § 5.04 supra.

4. Federal Rule of Evidence 803(1).

5. Though the Law Revision Commission recommended the adoption of an exception for present sense impressions, see 6 California Law Revision Commission, Reports, Recommendations, and Studies, Appendix 471 (1964), the Legislature rejected the recommendation and adopted only the exception for contemporaneous statements. See West's Ann.California Evidence Code § 1241. In 2007 the Commission invited public comments on a recommendation that would amend the Evidence Code by adopting the Federal Rule of Evidence creating an exception for present sense impressions. Hearings on the proposed rule were held in early 2008. For more information on the Commission's recommendation, see <www.clrc.ca.gov/>.

6. 15 Cal.4th 997, 64 Cal.Rptr.2d 594, 938 P.2d 388 (1997), cert. denied, 522 U.S. 1077, 118 S.Ct. 855, 139 L.Ed.2d 755 (1998).

who was in the house with Donna, Donna replied that Hines was there. Donna's statement did not qualify as a contemporaneous statement because it was offered to explain Hines' conduct and not her own.[7] But Donna's statement would have qualified as a present sense impression since her statement placing Hines' in her home was contemporaneous with her observations of Hines.

Present sense impressions differ from excited utterances under the Federal Rules in two significant respects. First, while excited utterances can be made at any time during the excited state, present sense impressions must be made while the declarant is perceiving the event or shortly thereafter.[8] Moreover, excited utterances under the Rules need only relate to the startling event giving rise to the declaration; present sense impressions are limited to statements describing or explaining the event or condition.[9] "[In] the absence of a startling event, [they] may extend no farther."[10]

QUESTIONS AND PROBLEMS

1. Plaintiff brings an action to determine the ownership of a diamond ring. The defendant concedes that the ring originally belonged to the plaintiff but claims that the plaintiff gave her the ring as inter vivos gift. The plaintiff maintains that he intended only for the defendant to use the ring. At the trial, the plaintiff testifies that when he handed the ring to the defendant, he said: "You may use my ring." The defendant objects on the ground of hearsay. How should the judge rule in a California or federal court?

In her case-in-chief, the defendant testifies that when the plaintiff handed her the ring, he said, "You may have my ring." The plaintiff objects on hearsay grounds. How should a California or federal judge rule?

2. To establish that the defendant was speeding at the time of the collision, the plaintiff called the following witness in a case being tried in federal court:

> Plaintiff's Counsel: You said that one of the cars involved in the collision was yellow. Had you seen that car before?
>
> Eyewitness: Yes, about five minutes before we came upon the collision.
>
> Plaintiff's Counsel: What was the car doing?
>
> Eyewitness: Overtaking us.
>
> Plaintiff's Counsel: Did anyone in your car say anything?
>
> Eyewitness: Yes, my wife said, "That yellow car is going quite fast."
>
> Defense Counsel: Objection. Hearsay.
>
> Plaintiff's Counsel: Excited utterance.

---

7. Id. at 1034, note 4, 64 Cal.Rptr.2d at 621, note 4, 938 P.2d at 415, note 4.

8. Federal Rule of Evidence 803(1) (Advisory Committee Note).

9. Id.

10. Id.

Defense Counsel: No proof of a startling event.

Plaintiff's Counsel: In that case, present sense impression.

Judge: ?

3. Would you change your ruling if the case were being tried in a California court?

§ 9.06   STATE OF MIND DECLARATIONS IN GENERAL

Of all the hearsay exceptions, students encounter the greatest difficulties in grasping the exception for state of mind declarations. The problems can be traced to three factors, each of which will be considered separately. One relates to the difficulty distinguishing between state of mind declarations that violate the hearsay rule and those that do not. Another is understanding that state of mind declarations can be relevant even if the declarant's state of mind is not an ultimate issue in the litigation. Finally, the term—state of mind—is so nebulous as not to provide adequate clues about the kind of evidence that falls within the exception.

§ 9.07   STATE OF MIND DECLARATIONS AND THE HEARSAY RULE

Often what a person thought at a given time is a material issue. For example, in criminal cases, what the accused thought in the course of committing an injury will help prove or disprove the mens rea of an offense. In civil cases, the issue may arise in a variety of circumstances, ranging from a testator's intentions in inheritance disputes, to whether a defendant's thoughts rendered him negligent, to whether an individual is a fit subject for the imposition of a conservatorship. In short, the relevance of what a person thinks is determined by the substantive law governing the action being tried. If, under the substantive law, those thoughts are material, then the thinker's state of mind is relevant.[1]

What a person thought on a given occasion typically can be proved in one of two ways. It can be proved directly by that person's statements describing his state of mind. It can also be proved indirectly by things that person says or does that reflect his state of mind. For example, an issue in conservatorship proceedings is usually whether by reason of a mental disorder a respondent is a danger to himself or others. A respondent's statements that he is "mentally disordered" would be direct evidence of the mental state essential to establishing a conservatorship. Since such statements would be offered for the truth of the matter stated, they would constitute hearsay. They would nonetheless be admissible under the exception for statements of mental state provided by § 1250 of the Code and Federal Rule of Evidence 803(3).[2]

---

1. For a discussion of the meaning of relevance, see § 2.01 supra.

2. West's Ann.California Evidence Code § 1250; Federal Rule of Evidence 803(3). See also § 9.08 infra. The statement would also be admissible as an admission, since the declarant is a party to the action and the opposing party is the party offering the statement. See § 7.01 supra.

Suppose, however, that the respondent also said at a pertinent time, "I am the Pope." Under one view, receiving the statement in evidence would not violate the hearsay rule. Clearly, the evidence is not being offered to prove the matter stated, that the respondent is the Pope. Rather, it is being offered on the theory that people who go around claiming they are the Pope must be mentally disordered. The statement is not directly assertive of the declarant's state of mind; it merely reflects the declarant's mental state.[3]

Under another view, receiving the respondent's statement that she is the Pope violates the hearsay rule.[4] The declarant who sincerely but erroneously maintains that she is the Pope obviously believes that she is the Pope. Her statement is thus the equivalent of saying, "I believe I am the Pope." If her out of court statement about her belief is then offered to prove the existence of her belief, the hearsay rule is violated. Her statement is being offered to prove the truth of the matter stated, namely her belief that she is the Pope.

The California Supreme Court seems to have opted for the former treatment of declarations offered to prove the declarant's state of mind circumstantially. In People v. Green[5] the accused was charged with kidnaping, among other crimes. To prove that the victim accompanied the accused against her will, the prosecution called a friend of the victim who testified that on the morning of the kidnaping the victim told her that the accused had threatened to kill the victim if she left him. To the court, the victim's statement did not violate the hearsay rule. It was not offered to prove that the accused had threatened the victim. Rather, it was offered to prove that the victim accompanied the accused against her will because she would not have voluntarily accompanied someone she believed might kill her.[6]

The court's position accords with that of the framers of the Code. According to the Assembly Committee on the Judiciary,

> Statements of a decedent narrating threats or brutal conduct by some other person may * * * be used as circumstantial evidence of the decedent's fear—his state of mind—when that fear is itself in issue or when it is relevant to prove or explain the decedent's subsequent conduct; and for that purpose, the evidence is not subject to a hearsay objection because it is not offered to prove the truth of the matter stated. * * *[7]

As a practical matter, whether the circumstantial use of such statements as the one in *Green* violates the hearsay rule often makes no

---

3. The fact that the statement is being used circumstantially—i.e., as a circumstance evincing the declarant's state of mind—is not especially useful. State of mind statements that violate the hearsay rule can also be used to prove a proposition indirectly. See §§ 8.08 and 8.10 supra.

4. See E. Morgan, Basic Problems of Evidence 248–250 (1961).

5. 27 Cal.3d 1, 164 Cal.Rptr. 1, 609 P.2d 468 (1980).

6. Id. at 23, note 9, 164 Cal.Rptr. at 13, note 9, 609 P.2d at 480, note 9.

7. West's Ann.California Evidence Code § 1250 (comment).

difference with respect to ultimate admissibility. In *Green,* for example, even if the victim's statement is viewed as hearsay, it would nonetheless be admissible to prove her belief under the exception for state of mind declarations.

QUESTIONS AND PROBLEMS

1.   Determine whether the following evidence constitutes hearsay in a California or federal court:

a.   To prove a child's feelings toward her father in a custody dispute, the mother calls a foster parent who testifies that she overheard the child say, "My father killed my brother; he will kill me too."

b.   In the same case, testimony by the foster parent that she also overheard the child say, "I dislike my father."

2.   In an unfair competition action, to prove that Rogers unfairly imitated the plaintiff's Zippo lighter, Rogers objects to the following evidence offered by Zippo:

prove "likelihood of confusion"

Plaintiff: Did you show her the lighter?

Survey Worker: Yes, the Rogers lighter.

Plaintiff: Did you tell her that it was a Rogers' lighter?

Survey Worker: No, I didn't identify it.

Plaintiff: Did you ask her what kind of a lighter it was?

Survey Worker: Yes, she said, "It's a Zippo lighter."

Defendant: Objection. Hearsay.

Judge: ? *circum. evid. of confusion*

3.   Suppose that instead the survey worker had testified: Yes, she said, "I believe that it's a Zippo lighter." Would you change your ruling?

§ 9.08   DECLARATIONS RELATING A THEN-EXISTING STATE OF MIND

California Evidence Code § 1250 and Federal Rule of Evidence 803(3) provide a hearsay exception only for statements in which the declarant's describes a *then-existing* state of mind.[1] This means that to be admissible the declarant's description of his feelings should be contemporaneous with the feelings experienced. But, as will be seen, the insistence on contemporaneity does not mean that the declaration cannot be used as circumstantial evidence to prove the declarant's state of mind at a time prior or subsequent to the statement.[2]

The insistence on contemporaneity furnishes the exception with trustworthiness. Expressions of existing feelings and discomforts—as opposed

---

1.   West's Ann.California Evidence Code § 1250. Federal Rule of Evidence 803(3).

2.   West's Ann.California Evidence Code § 1250 (comment).

to narratives of past feelings and miseries—are likely to be sincere and spontaneous.[3] The need for this kind of evidence also justifies the exception, since it is difficult to discern what people are thinking unless they tell us. Nonetheless, reservations about the reliability of these expressions caused the Code framers to include a provision empowering trial judges to exclude them if they find that the declarations "were made under circumstances such as to indicate [their] lack of trustworthiness."[4] In a homicide prosecution, for example, the accused's warm feelings for the victim are relevant, since, as a general matter, people do not kill individuals they like. But a judge may nonetheless exclude such declarations if the judge concludes that their self-serving nature deprives them of trustworthiness.[5]

Examples taken from *Adkins v. Brett*[6] help illustrate the scope of § 1250 as well as of Rule 803(3). In *Adkins*, the plaintiff husband sued for alienation of affections, claiming that the defendant had caused the plaintiff's wife to fall in love with the defendant. To prove the transfer of the feelings, the plaintiff offered statements by his wife in which she acknowledged her affections for the defendant.[7] Since these statements expressed her then-existing feelings for the defendant, they were admissible under the exception.[8] Statements expressing the opposite state of mind, such as "I dislike my husband", likewise would have been admissible to prove the wife's then-existing feelings toward the plaintiff.

The transfer of affections from one person to another takes time. Accordingly, statements by the wife about how she felt about her husband prior to meeting the defendant would be relevant. Equally relevant would be statements about how she felt about her husband and the defendant after meeting the latter. The statements need not embrace a particular period of time, so long as they are probative of the wife's feelings during the time in which the alienation took place. This is why § 1250 provides that the declarations are admissible to prove the declarant's state of mind "at that time" or "at any other time when it is itself an issue in the action."[9] In other words, declarations of then-existing states of mind can

---

3. 6 California Law Revision Commission, Reports, Recommendations, and Studies, Appendix at 505 (1964).

4. West's Ann.California Evidence Code § 1252. The Federal Rules do not contain an equivalent provision.

5. See, e.g., People v. Cruz, 264 Cal.App.2d 350, 356–358, 70 Cal.Rptr. 603, 607–608 (1968); People v. Farr, 255 Cal.App.2d 679, 688, 63 Cal.Rptr. 477, 483 (1967) (holding that judges have discretion to take self-serving nature of state of mind declarations into account in determining their admissibility); People v. Jurado, 38 Cal.4th 72, 129, 131 P.3d 400, 439, 41 Cal.Rptr.3d 319, 365, cert. denied, 549 U.S. 956, 127 S.Ct. 383, 166 L.Ed.2d 276 (2006): "As the trial court correctly determined, the circumstance that defendant made his statements during a postarrest police interrogation, when he had a compelling motive to minimize his culpability for the murder and to play on the sympathies of his interrogators, indicated a lack of trustworthiness."

6. 184 Cal. 252, 193 P. 251 (1920).

7. Id. at 254, 193 P. at 252.

8. Id. at 255, 193 P. at 252.

9. West's Ann.California Evidence Code § 1250(a)(1). The Federal Rules do not have an equivalent provision, but one would expect the same outcome in federal court on account of the federal definition of relevance. Evidence, for example, that the declarant harbored certain feelings

be used circumstantially to prove the declarant's state of mind at a time prior or subsequent to the declaration if that state of mind is relevant under the substantive law governing the action.

The circumstantial use of state of mind declarations can extend even further. People v. Lew,[10] for example, involved a homicide in which the accused claimed that the gun which killed the victim went off accidentally while the victim was handling it. Evidence that the victim would not have handled a gun voluntarily was relevant, since it would help disprove the defense claim. Accordingly, the victim's statement that she had a "fear of guns" was admissible under § 1250 to prove the victim's then-existing attitude toward guns.[11] The circumstantial use of this declaration differs from that in *Adkins* in that it involves two reasoning steps. The victim's statement is used first as a basis for inferring a continuing aversion to guns on the day of the shooting; this inference in turn is used to conclude that the victim did not handle the gun voluntarily at the time of the shooting.

QUESTIONS AND PROBLEMS

Plaintiff brings an alienation of affections action against defendant on the ground that the defendant caused the plaintiff's wife to transfer her feelings of affection from the plaintiff to the defendant. Plaintiff alleges that the alienation took place between January 1 and July 1, 1990. Determine whether the following declarations would be admissible under the exception for statements of then-existing states of mind.

    a. Plaintiff: On December 1, 1989, my wife said to me, "I love you so much I could die."

    b. Plaintiff: On March 1, 1990, my wife said to me, "I feel that my love for you is ebbing."

    c. Plaintiff: On June 1, 1990, my wife said to me, "I loved you last year; I no longer love you."

    d. Plaintiff: On July 1, 1990, my wife said to me, "You disgust me."

§ 9.09 STATE OF MIND DECLARATIONS AND STATEMENTS OF REMEMBERED FACTS

A major issue in Adkins v. Brett was whether the defendant caused the wife's alienation from her husband. Among the wife's declarations were statements that she felt good about the defendant because he bought her flowers, dined with her, and took her for car rides.[1] Although the

---

on a particular occasion would be probative of harboring similar feelings on a prior or subsequent occasion.

10. 68 Cal.2d 774, 69 Cal.Rptr. 102, 441 P.2d 942 (1968).

11. Id. at 779, note 2, 69 Cal.Rptr. at 105, note 2, 441 P.2d at 945, note 2. The court nonetheless excluded the statements because they were replete with references to acts by the accused. Id. For a discussion of the inadmissibility of such references, see § 9.09 infra.

1. Adkins v. Brett, 184 Cal. 252, 254, 193 P. 251, 252 (1920).

references to what the defendant did were relevant to the issue of causation, the court properly held that they were inadmissible under the exception for state of mind declarations.[2] As is explained by the Assembly Committee on the Judiciary,

> Section 1250(b) does not permit a statement of memory or belief to be used to prove the fact remembered or believed. This limitation is necessary to preserve the hearsay rule. Any statement of a past event is, of course, a statement of the declarant's then existing state of mind—his memory or belief—concerning the past event. If the evidence of that state of mind—the statement of memory—were admissible to show that the fact remembered or believed actually occurred, any statement narrating a past event would be, by a process of circuitous reasoning, admissible to prove that the event occurred.[3]

In determining the admissibility of declarations containing inadmissible statements of remembered facts, the court should consider the effectiveness of limiting instructions directing jurors to disregard the inadmissible matter, the possibility of redacting the inadmissible matter, as well as the availability of other admissible evidence.[4]

The Federal Rules contain a similar limitation. Statements of then existing state of mind do not include statements of memory or belief to prove the fact remembered or believed.[5] Statements that look "backward", such as "Dr. Shepard has poisoned me,"[6] are simply statements of memory or belief and are inadmissible under the exception.

QUESTIONS AND PROBLEMS

Over a hearsay objection, determine the admissibility of the following evidence in a California or federal court:

a. In a murder prosecution, testimony that the victim was overheard to say, "I am glad that I am alive."

b. In the same prosecution, testimony that the victim was overheard to say, "I am tired of living."

c. In the same prosecution, testimony that the victim was overheard to say, "I am tired of living because my wife [the defendant] refuses to jog with me."

d. In the same prosecution, testimony that the victim was overheard to say, "I am glad that I am alive because my wife [the defendant] buys me flowers."

---

2. Id. at 256, 193 P. at 252.

3. West's Ann.California Evidence Code § 1250 (comment).

4. Adkins v. Brett, 184 Cal. 252, 258, 193 P. 251, 253 (1920).

5. Federal Rule of Evidence 803(3).

6. The example is taken from Shepard v. United States, 290 U.S. 96, 54 S.Ct. 22, 78 L.Ed. 196 (1933).

§ 9.10 DECLARATIONS CONCERNING FUTURE PLANS

In a famous case, Mutual Life Ins. Co. v. Hillmon,[1] the United States Supreme Court had to rule on the admissibility of a declaration regarding a declarant's future plans. In *Hillmon* the plaintiff sued two insurance companies to recover the proceeds of policies on the life of her husband. The key issue was whether a body found at Crooked Creek, Kansas was that of the insured or of a companion named Walters. To prove that the body was that of Walters, the insurance companies offered letters from Walters to his fiancé in which Walters stated that he intended to go to Crooked Creek. The Court held that it was error to exclude the letters:

> The letters in question were competent, not as narratives of facts communicated to the writer by others, nor yet as proof that he actually went away from Wichita, but as evidence that, shortly before the time when other evidence tended to show that he went away, he had the intention of going, and of going with Hillmon, which made it more probable both that he did go and that he went with Hillmon, than if there had been no proof of such intention.[2]

In contemporary terms, the Court is saying that Walters' declarations regarding his future plans were relevant: the proposition that he went to Crooked Creek was rendered more likely by the evidence that he intended to go there than the proposition would be without the evidence. But such declarations violate the hearsay rule when offered to prove the declarant's future plans. Section 1250 creates an exception: statements of the declarant's then existing plans may be received for the truth of the matter stated if "offered to prove or explain acts or conduct of the declarant."[3] Federal Rule of Evidence 803(3) is to the same effect.[4]

Statements regarding future plans do not necessarily have to prove the declarant's conduct. Sometimes having such future plans is an issue under the substantive law governing the action. In a wrongful death action, for example, plans by the decedent to continue working after retirement are relevant to the issue of damages.[5] The plaintiffs are entitled to a greater recovery than if the decedent planned to stopped

---

1. 145 U.S. 285, 12 S.Ct. 909, 36 L.Ed. 706 (1892).

2. Id. at 296, 12 S.Ct. at 912–913.

3. West's Ann.California Evidence Code § 1250(a)(2). Accord: People v. Griffin, 33 Cal.4th 536, 578, 93 P.3d 344, 371, 15 Cal.Rptr.3d 743, 775 (2004).

The declarations contemplated by this hearsay exception should not be confused with declarations explaining the declarant's conduct. A police officer, for example, may testify that he followed a particular car because "communications told him to be on the lookout for a drunk driver in a white VW." The latter declarations do not implicate the hearsay rule because they are not offered to prove the truth of the matter stated (that a drunk was driving a white VW), but to explain why the witness took certain action. But such declarations raise the danger that the fact finder may misuse them for the truth irrespective of limiting instructions. For a discussion of these declarations, see § 5.04 supra.

4. See Federal Rule of Evidence 803(3).

5. Foss v. Anthony Industries, 139 Cal.App.3d 794, 800, 189 Cal.Rptr. 31, 35 (1983).

working upon reaching retirement. Accordingly, statements by the decedent evincing an intention to work after retirement are admissible.[6]

Statements by declarants concerning their future plans sometimes implicate the future plans of others. In People v. Alcalde[7] the accused was tried for murdering a woman he had been seeing socially. At issue was the admissibility of a declaration made by the victim on the day of the killing in which she stated that she was "going out with Frank" that evening.[8] "Frank" was the accused's first name. The accused objected that the declaration was inadmissible to prove *his* future plans to see the victim. The California Supreme Court upheld the use of the declaration, noting that in overruling the objection the trial judge had taken "the precaution to state in the presence of the jury that the evidence was admitted for the limited purpose of showing the decedent's intention."[9] The Code, which was enacted after *Alcalde*, underscores the point: the hearsay exception is only for declarations "offered to prove or explain acts or conduct of the *declarant*."[10]

---

6. Id. Some would contend that a statement by the decedent that he planned to work after retiring would not violate the hearsay rule if offered to prove that the decedent had such plans. The statement is not offered to prove that the decedent planned to work after retiring but simply to prove that the decedent had such plans. But even this use of the declaration violates the hearsay rule. That the decedent had plans to work is proved by the decedent's out of court statement that he had such plans.

7. 24 Cal.2d 177, 148 P.2d 627 (1944).

8. Id. at 185, 148 P.2d at 630.

9. Id.

10. West's Ann. California Evidence Code § 1250(a)(2) (emphasis added). The California Supreme Court, however, has declined to rule on whether the Evidence Code limits *Alcalde* to proving only the declarant's future plans. People v. Melton, 44 Cal.3d 713, 739, 244 Cal.Rptr. 867, 881, 750 P.2d 741, 755 (1988), cert. denied, 488 U.S. 934, 109 S.Ct. 329, 102 L.Ed.2d 346 (1988).

In People v. Morales, 48 Cal.3d 527, 257 Cal.Rptr. 64, 770 P.2d 244 (1989), the accused was prosecuted for murder. The prosecution's theory was that the accused had killed the victim as part of a conspiracy. Over a defense hearsay objection, a witness was allowed to testify to overhearing Ortega state that he intended to kill the victim and would enlist the accused's aid. The California Supreme Court approved the use of the declaration. Ortega's declaration concerning his plan to kill the victim with the accused's aid fell within the exception for state of mind declarations regarding future plans. The declaration was probative of his soliciting the accused to help him kill the victim, and in the court's view, such a solicitation in turn was probative of a conspiracy between the accused and Ortega to kill the victim. Id. at 552, 257 Cal.Rptr. at 77, 770 P.2d at 257.

While this relevance analysis is correct (see Chapter 2 supra), it still raises disturbing questions. If Ortega had said that he intended to conspire with the accused to kill the victim, then under *Alcalde* and the plain language of the Code, the statement would have been admissible to prove only Ortega's participation in such a conspiracy but not the accused's. *Morales* makes no mention of *Melton*. Nonetheless, some lower courts have construed *Morales* as authorizing the use of state of mind declarations concerning future plans to prove the conduct, not just of the declarant, but of someone else. See, e.g., People v. Han, 78 Cal.App.4th 797, 805–806, 93 Cal.Rptr.2d 139, 145–146 (2000) (The declarant's statement that she wanted to arrange her sister's murder was admissible to prove that the declarant and the accused conspired to murder the sister.). See also People v. Majors, 18 Cal.4th 385, 75 Cal.Rptr.2d 684, 956 P.2d 1137 (1998), cert. denied, 526 U.S. 1007, 119 S.Ct. 1148, 143 L.Ed.2d 214 (1999), in which the court approved the hearsay use of a statement made by the victim on the night he was killed that he planned to conduct a drug deal with people from Arizona. Other evidence showed that the accused, who was on trial for murdering the victim, was from Arizona. In approving the use of the statement under the state of mind exception to the hearsay rule for future plans, the court does not mention *Melton* and cites *Morales* only the for the proposition that the use of the statement did not violate

The House Committee on the Judiciary agrees with this limitation. In its report the committee states that its intent is that Federal Rule of Evidence 803(3) "be construed to limit the doctrine of Mutual Life Insurance Co. v. Hillmon * * * so as to render statements of intent by a declarant admissible only to prove his future conduct, not the future conduct of another person."[11] But some federal courts of appeal, including the Ninth Circuit, have not abided by this admonition.[12]

QUESTIONS AND PROBLEMS

Over a hearsay objection, determine the admissibility of the following evidence in a California and federal court:

　　1.　To prove that the body found at Crooked Creek was that of Walters, testimony by Walters' girlfriend that Walters had said to her, "Hillmon and I are going to Crook Creek."

　　2.　To prove that the body found at Crooked Creek was that of Hillmon, testimony by Walters' girlfriend that Walters had said to her, "Hillmon and I are going to Crooked Creek."

　　3.　To prove that Angelo killed Larry, testimony by Larry's friend that Larry said to him, "I'm going to the parking lot to meet Angelo."

§ 9.11　DECLARATIONS OF PAST STATE OF MIND

Both the Code and the Rules prohibit the use of statements of memory or belief to prove the fact remembered or believed because such use would threaten to repeal the hearsay rule.[1] Thus, we saw in Adkins v. Brett that only those declarations of the wife describing her then-existing feelings toward her husband and the defendant were admissible.[2] Only the portion of the declarations in which she stated that she felt good about the defendant was admissible. Other portions in which she attributed her feelings to actions by the defendant were not. Her statement that the defendant bought her flowers was simply a statement of remembered fact and not an expression of then-existing feelings.[3]

Section 1251 permits a statement of memory or belief of a past mental or physical state to be used to prove the previous mental or physical state but only when the previous mental or physical state is itself an issue in

the accused's confrontation rights. Id. at 403–405, 75 Cal.Rptr.2d at 696–697, 956 P.2d at 1149–1150.

11.　Federal Rule of Evidence 803(3) (Report of House Committee on the Judiciary).

12.　See, e.g., United States v. Stanchich, 550 F.2d 1294 (2d Cir.1977); United States v. Pheaster, 544 F.2d 353 (9th Cir.1976), cert. denied, 429 U.S. 1099, 97 S.Ct. 1118, 51 L.Ed.2d 546 (1977).

1.　See § 9.09 supra.

2.　184 Cal. 252, 193 P. 251 (1920). See § 9.09 supra.

3.　See § 9.09 supra.

the case.[4] Assume a personal injury action in which the plaintiff sues a trucking company for injuries the plaintiff sustained when the company's truck struck the plaintiff on U.S. 101. The company denies liability on the ground that the driver was not on company business at the time of the accident. May the plaintiff offer a declaration made by the driver after the accident in which the driver stated that he took U.S. 101 to "save time"? If under agency principles the driver's reasons (i.e., state of mind) for taking U.S. 101 are determinative of whether he was acting on behalf of his principal, then the statement would be admissible notwithstanding the fact that it is a statement of memory or remembered fact. In the words of the Code, the driver's state of mind would "itself [be] an issue in the action and [would] not [be] offered to prove any fact other than such state of mind * * *."[5]

Declarations describing a then-existing state of mind derive their trustworthiness from the requirement that the description be contemporaneous with the feelings experienced.[6] Such contemporaneity is by definition lacking in declarations narrating a past state of mind. As backward looking declarations, they raise questions about the declarant's memory as well as his motive to fabricate. These declarations are therefore admissible only when a special need requires their use: when the hearsay declarant is unavailable to testify.[7]

The Federal Rules of Evidence do not contain a general exception for declarations of past state of mind. But Rule 803(4) creates a broad exception for statements made for purposes of medical diagnosis or treatment, including statements relating past symptoms. This rule is considered in the section on declarations describing physical conditions.[8]

QUESTIONS AND PROBLEMS

Over a hearsay objection, determine the admissibility of the following evidence in a California court:

    a. In Adkins v. Brett, testimony by the wife's best friend, that in December Mrs. Adkins said to her, "By last January, I had concluded that I no longer loved my husband. That was six months before I met Mr. Brett." In ruling on the objection, assume that the wife is unavailable to testify.

    b. In an action to recover for injuries the plaintiff suffered when struck by the defendant's truck on U.S. 280, testimony by the investigat-

---

4. West's Ann.California Evidence Code § 1251 and comment.

5. West's Ann.California Evidence Code § 1251(b). Pre–Code cases do not always distinguish between declarations concerning future plans and declarations describing past mental states. Nor do they focus specifically on whether the declarant must be unavailable in the case of declarations describing past mental states. See, e.g., Katz v. Enos, 68 Cal.App.2d 266, 275, 156 P.2d 461, 466 (1945).

6. See § 9.08 supra.

7. West's Ann.California Evidence Code § 1251(a).

8. See § 9.13 infra.

ing officer that the truck driver said to him, "I took U.S. 280 to save time." Assume that the driver is unavailable to testify and that the defendant instructed the driver to take U.S. 101.

What body of law must the judge turn to in order to rule on the objection?

§ 9.12 DECLARATIONS BY CRIME VICTIMS

Evidence regarding a crime victim's state of mind should not be received unless the victim's mental state is relevant.[1] Some offenses expressly make the victim's state of mind a material issue. Rape, for example, requires the prosecution to prove that the victim did not consent to the sex act;[2] kidnaping requires the prosecution to prove that the victim did not willingly accompany the accused;[3] robbery requires the prosecution to prove that the victim did not part voluntarily with the property taken.[4] Because kidnaping requires the prosecution to prove that the victim accompanied the accused against her will, evidence that the victim feared the accused would be relevant to prove this element of the offense.[5] Similarly, because forcible rape requires the prosecution to prove that the victim did not consent to the sex act, evidence that the victim feared the accused would likewise be relevant to prove this element of the offense.[6] Accordingly, in both cases a an out of court statement by the victim expressing a then existing fear of the accused would be relevant and thus admissible over a hearsay objection under the exception for statements regarding then existing mental states.

Declarations by crime victims require extended discussion because of special dangers they can present to the accused. Often these declarations contain references to past misdeeds by the accused. In a kidnaping case, for example, a declarant may describe not merely a mental state ("I am afraid of the accused.") but also the reasons for that state of mind ("I am afraid of the accused because he has threatened to harm me."). Analytically, the declarant's reason for fearing the defendant is no different than

---

1. People v. Ruiz, 44 Cal.3d 589, 607–608, 244 Cal.Rptr. 200, 209, 749 P.2d 854, 863 (1988), cert. denied, 488 U.S. 871, 109 S.Ct. 186, 102 L.Ed.2d 155 (1988), reh'g denied, 493 U.S. 948, 110 S.Ct. 355, 107 L.Ed.2d 343 (1989); People v. Jablonski, 37 Cal.4th 774, 819, 126 P.3d 938, 968, 38 Cal.Rptr.3d 98, 134, cert. denied, 549 U.S. 863, 127 S.Ct. 150, 166 L.Ed.2d 110 (2006).

2. West's Ann.California Penal Code §§ 261(a)(2) and 261.6.

3. West's Ann.California Penal Code § 207(a).

4. People v. Sakarias, 22 Cal.4th 596, 628–629, 94 Cal.Rptr.2d 17, 39, 995 P.2d 152, 171–172 (2000), cert. denied, 531 U.S. 947, 121 S.Ct. 347, 148 L.Ed.2d 279 (2000) (approving the use of the robbery victim's statement that she feared the accused). Accord: People v. Waidla, 22 Cal.4th 690, 723, 94 Cal.Rptr.2d 396, 417, 996 P.2d 46, 65 (2000), cert. denied, 531 U.S. 1018, 121 S.Ct. 580, 148 L.Ed.2d 497 (2000) (approving the use of the victim's statement that she feared the accused as relevant to proving that the taking in the robbery was by force or fear and that the entry in the burglary was without the victim's consent).

5. See People v. Green, 27 Cal.3d 1, 23, note 9, 164 Cal.Rptr. 1, 13, note 9, 609 P.2d 468, 480, note 9 (1980).

6. See People v. Guerra, 37 Cal.4th 1067, 1114, 129 P.3d 321, 358, 40 Cal.Rptr.3d 118, 161 (2006), cert. denied, 549 U.S. 1182, 127 S.Ct. 1149, 166 L.Ed.2d 998 (2007).

Mrs. Adkins' reason for liking the defendant in Adkins v. Brett.[7] In each instance, the reason given is a statement of remembered fact and may not be offered to prove the fact remembered under the exception for statements of then existing state of mind.[8] In weighing the admissibility of the declaration under § 352 and Federal Rule of Evidence 403, the court should consider (1) the effectiveness of an instruction directing the jury to disregard the portion relating to the threat, (2) the feasibility of redacting that portion, and (3) the availability of other evidence on the same point.[9] If the court concludes that the probative value of the admissible portion is substantially outweighed by the prejudicial effects of the inadmissible portion, the court should exclude the declaration.[10]

The availability of out of court statements for a nonhearsay purpose does not diminish the dangers to the accused. Assume that, instead of expressing her fear of the accused directly, the declarant had merely said, "The accused has threatened to harm me." The use of such a declaration would not violate the hearsay rule if offered, not as proof that the accused threatened the declarant, but only as circumstantial evidence of the declarant's fear of the accused.[11] The dilemma for the accused is the same, however. Upon request, the court must instruct the jury of the limited purpose for which the declaration is received. In this instance, however, the court does not have the option of redacting the declaration, since the fact remembered comprises the entire declaration. Accordingly, the pressures for excluding the declaration are greater. Where " 'it is impossible for the jury to separate the state of mind of the declarant from the truth of the facts contained in the declarations' ", the court should exclude the declarations.[12]

Where the victim's state of mind is not a material issue under the law defining the offense, courts should exclude the evidence unless it is probative of some other proposition that is properly provable in the action. Rufo v. Simpson[13] was a survival action brought by the personal representative of Nicole Simpson against her former husband, O.J. Simpson. The plaintiff's theory was that Nicole's termination of her relationship with

---

7.   184 Cal. 252, 193 P. 251 (1920). See § 9.09 supra.

8.   See § 9.09 supra.

9.   Id.

10.   West's Ann.California Evidence Code § 352; Federal Rule of Evidence 403.

11.   See § 9.07 supra.

12.   People v. Coleman, 38 Cal.3d 69, 85, 211 Cal.Rptr. 102, 112, 695 P.2d 189, 199 (1985), quoting from People v. Hamilton, 55 Cal.2d 881, 13 Cal.Rptr. 649, 362 P.2d 473 (1961). The Law Revision Commission disapproved of *Hamilton* to the extent that it approved the victim's recital of past threats by the accused to prove the accused's past conduct. West's Ann.California Evidence Code § 1252 (comment).

People v. Ortiz, 38 Cal.App.4th 377, 388, 44 Cal.Rptr.2d 914, 921 (1995), disapproves of that aspect of *Hamilton* banning the nonhearsay use of a statement in which the victim recites only a misdeed committed by the accused. Thus, if it otherwise satisfies the tests of § 352, a judge may allow a jury to hear the victim's complaint that the accused intruded on her while she was showering as nonhearsay evidence reflecting her unwillingness to engage in consensual sex with the accused. Id.

13.   86 Cal.App.4th 573, 103 Cal.Rptr.2d 492 (2001).

O.J. provoked him to kill her. To prove that Nicole's feelings toward O.J. prompted the breakup, the plaintiff was allowed to call the director of a battered women's shelter to testify that Nicole had told her that O.J. had been stalking her, had beaten her, and had threatened to kill her if he caught Nicole with another man. The reviewing court upheld the use of the evidence; it was received, not to prove as true the assertions about O.J.'s mistreatment of Nicole, but as circumstantial evidence of Nicole's negative feelings toward O.J. This evidence in turn helped explain why she terminated her relationship with O.J. five days before her murder.[14] In approving the use of the evidence, the reviewing court emphasized the care the trial judge took in ensuring that the jurors understood the limited purpose of the evidence.[15]

Sometimes the accused's claims at trial make the victim's state of mind relevant. If in a homicide prosecution, for example, the accused claims that the victim accidentally shot herself while examining a gun, the prosecution is entitled to disprove that claim by evidence that the victim had an aversion to weapons.[16] If in a murder prosecution the accused claims that the victim invited him into her home, the prosecution is entitled to disprove that claim by statements by the victim that she feared and mistrusted the accused.[17] If the accused claims self-defense, the prosecution may disprove that claim by statements by the victim that he feared the accused.[18] Evidence that the victim feared the accused makes it less likely that the victim was the first aggressor.[19] If in a rape case the accused claims consent, the prosecution may disprove that claim by statements by the victim expressing her sexual preference for men of a different color.[20] Evidence that the victim preferred men of another color makes it less likely that she consented to have sex with the accused.[21]

On some occasions, it is the accused who wishes to offer declarations by a crime victim. Where the accused claims self-defense, for example, the victim's declarations of intent to harm the accused would be relevant to show that the victim was the first aggressor. Such declarations would be

---

14. Id. at 591, 103 Cal.Rptr.2d at 504. Other statements by Nicole describing her then feelings toward O.J. (e.g., that she no longer loved him) were admitted for the truth of the matter stated under the hearsay exception for statements regarding then existing feelings. Id. Their relevance was the same, however.

15. Id.

16. See, e.g., People v. Lew, 68 Cal.2d 774, 69 Cal.Rptr. 102, 441 P.2d 942 (1968).

17. See, e.g., People v. Millwee, 18 Cal.4th 96, 128, 74 Cal.Rptr.2d 418, 437, 954 P.2d 990,1008 (1998). Accord: People v. Escobar, 82 Cal.App.4th 1085, 1103–1104, 98 Cal.Rptr.2d 696, 709 (2000), cert. denied, 532 U.S. 1053, 121 S.Ct. 2195, 149 L.Ed.2d 1026 (2001) (In a murder prosecution, where the accused testified that the victim attacked him and insulted him in a very provocative way, the prosecution was entitled to disprove the accused's claim by statements by the victim that she was afraid of the accused and wanted a divorce.).

18. People v. Romero, 149 Cal.App.4th 29, 37, 56 Cal.Rptr.3d 678, 684 (2007).

19. Id.

20. People v. Geier, 41 Cal.4th 555, 586, 161 P.3d 104, 126, 61 Cal.Rptr.3d 580, 605 (2007), cert. denied, ___ U.S. ___, 129 S.Ct. 2856, 174 L.Ed.2d 600 (2009). Although Geier was prosecuted for murder, the prosecution relied on the felony murder theory in which rape served as the predicate crime. Geier was white; the victim expressed a preference for muscular black men.

21. Id.

admissible under the hearsay exception for declarations concerning future plans.[22]

Emerging exceptions. Following the acquittal of O.J. Simpson on charges of murdering his ex-wife and her companion, the California Legislature created a hearsay exception for some victim statements.[23] Section 1370 of the Evidence Code provides that a victim's hearsay statement may be received for the truth if the following conditions are satisfied: (1) the victim is unavailable to testify; (2) the statement purports to narrate, describe, or explain the infliction or *threat* of physical injury upon the victim;[24] (3) the statement was made at or near the time of the infliction or threat of physical injury; (4) the statement was made in writing, was electronically recorded, or was made to a law enforcement official, physician, nurse, or paramedic; (5) the statement was made under circumstances indicating its trustworthiness; and (6) the proponent makes known to the opposing party the intention to offer the statement and the particulars of the statement sufficiently in advance of proceedings so as to provide the opposing party with a fair opportunity to prepare to meet the statement.[25]

In determining whether the statement was made under circumstances indicating trustworthiness, the trial judge may take into account the following factors, among others: (1) whether the statement was made in contemplation of pending or anticipated litigation in which the declarant was interested; (2) whether the declarant had a bias or motive for fabricating the statement, and the extent of any bias or motive; and (3) whether the statement is corroborated by evidence other than the statements that are admissible under the new hearsay exception.[26] In People v. Quitiquit[27] the reviewing court excluded the victim's statement as untrustworthy where the victim made the statement two months after the assault charged against the accused, her version of the assault was uncorroborated, and she had ample time to fabricate the assault.[28]

Section 1370 and confrontation. At least two kinds of statements useful to prosecutors may be admissible under § 1370 if the other conditions of the exception are satisfied. One consists of statements in which the victim narrates events that are directly probative of the elements of the offense charged. For example, in a prosecution for assault, prosecutors would benefit from the victim's out of court declaration describing the assault and identifying the defendant as the culprit. The other kind of statement useful to prosecutors consists of declarations made by the accused to the victim. In a prosecution for assault, for example, prosecu-

---

22. See § 9.10 supra.

23. West's Ann. California Evidence Code § 1370.

24. Emphasis added. Statements made more than five years before the filing of the action or proceeding in which offered are inadmissible. Id.

25. Id.

26. Id.

27. 155 Cal.App.4th 1, 65 Cal.Rptr.3d 674 (2007).

28. Id. at 9, 65 Cal.Rptr.3d at 680.

tors would benefit from a victim's statement reciting a declaration by the defendant in which he threatened to assault the victim. In this situation, a defendant's statement threatening an assault would be admissible under the hearsay exceptions for declarations concerning future plans or as party admissions. To overcome a hearsay objection to the victim's statement, a prosecutor could invoke § 1370.

Because of its unavailability requirement, evidence offered against the accused under § 1370 raises a number of confrontation questions. In Crawford v. Washington[29] the United States Supreme Court held that over a confrontation objection "testimonial hearsay" may not be offered against the accused unless (1) the hearsay declarant is produced for cross-examination by the accused or (2) if not produced, unless the accused was given an opportunity prior to the trial to cross examine the hearsay declarant.[30] In Davis v. Washington,[31] the Court held that whether statements made by witnesses to police officers are testimonial depends on whether the primary purpose of the police questioning was to enable the police to meet an ongoing emergency or to establish or prove past events potentially relevant to a later criminal prosecution.[32] If the former, then the statements are nontestimonial; if the latter, then the statements are testimonial.[33]

In People v. Cage[34] the California Supreme Court considered whether statements offered against the accused under § 1370 violated his confrontation rights. To help California judges apply *Davis* to California's hearsay exceptions, including § 1370, the court formulated six guidelines:

> First, * * * the confrontation clause is concerned solely with hearsay statements that are testimonial, in that they are out-of-court analogs, in purpose and in form, of the testimony given by witnesses at trial. Second, though a statement need not be sworn under oath to be testimonial, it must have occurred under circumstances that imparted, to some degree, the formality and solemnity characteristic of testimony. Third, the statement must have been given and taken *primarily* for the *purpose* ascribed to testimony—to establish or prove some past fact for possible use in a criminal trial. Fourth, the primary purpose for which a statement was given and taken is to be determined "objectively," considering all of the circumstances that might reasonably bear on the intent of the participants in the conversation. Fifth, sufficient formality and solemnity are present when, in the nonemergency situation, one responds to questioning by law enforcement officials, where deliberate falsehoods might be criminal offenses. Sixth, statements elicited by law enforcement officials are not testimo-

---

29. 541 U.S. 36, 124 S.Ct. 1354, 158 L.Ed.2d 177 (2004).

30. Id. at 68.

31. 547 U.S. 813, 126 S.Ct. 2266, 165 L.Ed.2d 224 (2006).

32. Id. at 2273 (footnotes omitted).

33. Id.

34. 40 Cal.4th 965, 155 P.3d 205, 56 Cal.Rptr.3d 789 (2007).

nial if the primary purpose in giving and receiving them is to deal with a contemporaneous emergency, rather than to produce evidence about past events for possible use at a criminal trial.[35]

Applying these guidelines, the court held the answers which a crime victim had given to a law enforcement officer in a hospital emergency room were testimonial. In response to the officer's questions, the victim identified the defendant as the person who had assaulted him. At the time of the interrogation, the incident that had given rise to the assault had been over for more than an hour, and the victim was no longer in danger of further violence. "[The officer's] clear purpose in coming to speak with [the victim] at this juncture was not to deal with a *present emergency*, but to obtain a fresh account of *past events involving defendant* as part of an inquiry into possible criminal activity. * * * [T]he requisite solemnity was imparted by the potentially criminal consequences of lying to a peace officer."[36]

Applying the same guidelines, the court held that the victim's answer to a doctor's question given in the hospital emergency room was nontestimonial. When the victim arrived at emergency room, the attending doctor asked him, "What happened?" In response, the victim stated that the defendant had cut him.[37] "Objectively viewed, the primary purpose of the question, and the answer, was not to establish or prove past facts for possible criminal use, but to help [the doctor] deal with the immediate medical situation he faced. It was thus akin to the 911 operator's emergency questioning of [the victim] in *Davis*."[38]

If the victim's statement does not qualify as a testimonial statement, then it is unlikely that it can be excluded on confrontation grounds. Although *Crawford* reserved for another day whether nontestimonial statements should be subject to Sixth Amendment scrutiny,[39] *Davis* appears to limit the Sixth Amendment only to testimonial statements.[40] If in the unlikely event the U.S. Supreme Court decides to test nontestimonial statements under the *Roberts*[41] pre-*Crawford* standards, then attention must be given to that provision of § 1370 conditioning admissibility on

---

35. Id. at 984, 155 P.3d at 216, 56 Cal.Rptr.3d at 802 (footnotes omitted; emphasis in the original).

36. Id. at 986, 155 P.3d at 218, 56 Cal.Rptr.3d at 804 (emphasis in the original). In California, it is a misdemeanor to report to a sworn peace officer that a felony or misdemeanor has been committed, knowing the report to be false. See West's Ann. California Penal Code § 148.5.

37. People v. Cage, 40 Cal.4th 965, 986, 155 P.3d 205, 218, 56 Cal.Rptr.3d 789, 805 (2007).

38. Id.

39. Crawford v. Washington, 541 U.S. 36, 124 S.Ct. 1354, 1369–1370, 158 L.Ed.2d 177 (2004).

40. Davis v. Washington, 547 U.S. 813, 126 S.Ct. 2266, 2274, 165 L.Ed.2d 224 (2006). "We must decide, therefore, whether the Confrontation Clause applies only to testimonial hearsay; and, if so, whether the recording of a 911 call qualifies. [¶] The answer to the first question was suggested in *Crawford*, even if not explicitly held: 'The text of the Confrontation Clause reflects this focus [on testimonial hearsay]. It applies to "witnesses" against the accused—in other words, those who "bear testimony." ' * * * [¶] A limitation so clearly reflected in the text of the constitutional provision must fairly be said to mark out not merely its 'core' but its perimeter."

41. For an extended discussion of Ohio v. Roberts, 448 U.S. 56, 100 S.Ct. 2531, 65 L.Ed.2d 597 (1980), see § 6.03 et seq. supra.

whether the statement is corroborated by evidence other than the statements that are admissible under the new hearsay exception. In Idaho v. Wright[42] the Court held that determining whether the use of a newly minted exception to the hearsay rule violates the accused's confrontation rights depends on whether the prosecution can demonstrate that the out of court statement meets particularized guarantees of trustworthiness. In making this showing, the prosecution can rely on circumstances "that surround the making of the statement and that render the declarant particularly worthy of belief."[43] But the prosecution may not rely on other evidence that corroborates the truth of the hearsay statement.[44] This mandate conflicts with § 1370. Accordingly, if the Court retains *Roberts* to scrutinize nontestimonial statements, California prosecutors using § 1370 must take care to comply with *Wright*'s mandate in addition to the requirements of the section.[45]

Section 1370 illustrates some of the dilemmas created by *Crawford*. It is sometimes impossible to determine on a categorical basis whether the hearsay offered against the accused under a particular exception qualifies as a testimonial statement. As *Cage* demonstrates, a single statute like § 1370 may call for the exclusion of some hearsay that qualifies as a testimonial statement but the admission of other hearsay that does not. Moreover, even a categorical approach will not always resolve the definitional problem. A witness's statement elicited by police officers while investigating a past crime should count as testimonial statement even if offered under the business or official records exception.[46] Furthermore, determining whether the person taking the statement is responding to exigencies attending an emergency or is gathering evidence may require an evidentiary hearing to determine whether a doctor, for example, was

---

42. 497 U.S. 805, 110 S.Ct. 3139, 111 L.Ed.2d 638 (1990).

43. Id. at 817.

44. Id. at 822.

45. In People v. Hernandez, 67 Cal.App.4th 397, 78 Cal.Rptr.2d 909 (1998), the trial judge found that a statement met the particularized guarantees of trustworthiness mandated by *Wright*. In making that finding, the judge considered some of the circumstances surrounding the making of the statement. At the time the victim made her statement to the police, she was in a long-term relationship with the accused (and, hence, had no "motive" to fabricate her accusations of violence against the accused) and was upset and crying (and therefore was seeking help rather than "connive" against the accused). Id. at 404, 78 Cal.Rptr.2d at 913. Accordingly, the reviewing court rejected the accused's claim that the use of the victim's statement under § 1370 violated his confrontation rights. Id. However, in contravention of *Wright* both the trial judge and the reviewing court appear to have considered other evidence offered at the trial to corroborate the reliability of the victim's statement. This evidence included a 911 call made by the victim and admissions made by the accused. See id. The California Supreme Court granted review and remanded the case to the Court of Appeal with instructions to vacate its decision and reconsider the case in light of *Wright*. People v. Hernandez, 71 Cal.App.4th 417, 83 Cal.Rptr.2d 747 (1999). On reconsideration, the Court of Appeal acknowledged that *Wright* precluded the use of the other evidence to determine the statement's reliability. But the Court of Appeal nonetheless affirmed the conviction on the ground that the statement was sufficiently reliable to satisfy confrontation concerns even without the corroborating evidence. Id. at 424–425 83 Cal.Rptr.2d at 752.

46. In *Crawford*, the Court stated that statements in business records should not ordinarily qualify as testimonial statements subject to exclusion under the Confrontation Clause. Crawford v. Washington, 541 U.S. 36, 56, 124 S.Ct. 1354, 158 L.Ed.2d 177 (2004).

treating the patient or gathering evidence for possible use in a criminal trial.

Section 1370 and civil cases. Section 1370 is not limited to criminal cases. Following his acquittal, O. J. Simpson sought to terminate the guardianship that was established for his children after he was arrested on the charge of murdering the children's mother, Nicole Brown Simpson.[47] Because a guardianship termination proceeding raises a parent's fitness to care for the children, the Court of Appeal held that it was error for the trial judge to exclude the mother's diaries relating threats of violence upon her by Mr. Simpson.[48] Under § 1370, the diaries could be received to establish that Mr. Simpson had threatened to inflict violence upon the children's mother, and that evidence in turn could be used to determine his propensity for violence, a relevant consideration in determining his fitness to care for the children.[49]

Hearsay declarations by other crime victims. In addition to § 1370, other provisions of the Evidence Code create exceptions for hearsay statements made by crime victims. Section § 1360 creates an exception for statements by children describing acts of abuse or neglect when offered in criminal prosecutions.[50] Section 1380 creates an exception for statements by victims when offered in prosecutions for elder or dependent adult abuse.[51] Under the California Penal Code, it is a crime to inflict enumerated physical or mental injuries upon the elderly or dependent adults.[52] Section 1380, however, has been held to be unconstitutional on its face, as it deprives the accused of the opportunity to cross examine the hearsay declarant.[53] Statements offered under § 1380 are inadmissible unless the declarant is unavailable to testify at the trial.[54]

QUESTIONS AND PROBLEMS

Determine whether the following statements are true or false. To prove that Jones killed the victim, the prosecutor may offer the following evidence:

---

47. In Guardianship of Simpson, 67 Cal.App.4th 914, 79 Cal.Rptr.2d 389 (1998).

48. Id. at 938, 79 Cal.Rptr.2d at 403–404.

49. Id.

50. West's Ann. California Evidence Code § 1360. For an extended discussion of this hearsay exception, see § 14.05 infra.

51. West's Ann. California Evidence Code § 1380.

52. "(b)(1) Any person who knows or reasonably should know that a person is an elder or dependent adult and who, under circumstances or conditions likely to produce great bodily harm or death, willfully causes or permits any elder or dependent adult to suffer, or inflicts thereon unjustifiable physical pain or mental suffering, or having the care or custody of any elder or dependent adult, willfully causes or permits the person or health of the elder or dependent adult to be injured, or willfully causes or permits the elder or dependent adult to be placed in a situation in which his or her person or health is endangered, is punishable by imprisonment in a county jail not exceeding one year, or by a fine not to exceed six thousand dollars ($6,000), or by both that fine and imprisonment, or by imprisonment in the state prison for two, three, or four years." West's Ann. California Evidence Code § 368(b)(1).

53. See People v. Pirwani, 119 Cal.App.4th 770, 786, 14 Cal.Rptr.3d 673, 684 (2004). For an extended discussion of hearsay and confrontation, see § 6.03 et seq., supra.

54. West's Ann. California Evidence Code § 1380(a).

a. Testimony by the victim's best friend that on the morning of the killing the victim said, "I believe that Jones wants to kill me."

b. Testimony by the victim's best friend that on the morning of the killing the victim said, "I am afraid of Jones."

c. Testimony by the victim's best friend that on the morning of the killing the victim said, " 'Jones has threatened me.' "

d. An entry in the victim's diary in which she stated, "Last night, Jones said to me, 'If I catch you with another man, I will beat you to a pulp.' " Another entry in which the victim stated, "This morning, Jones almost beat me to a pulp."

e. Suppose that Jones offers evidence in his case-in-chief that he killed the victim in self-defense. In rebuttal may the prosecutor offer evidence of a statement by the victim in which she said, "I am afraid of Jones"?

f. Suppose that in his case-in-chief Jones testifies that the victim invited him into her home on the night of the killing. In rebuttal may the prosecutor offer evidence by the victim that previously she had said, "I don't trust Jones"?

g. Suppose that instead Jones is being prosecuted for kidnaping. Would that change your rulings in (a)–(c)?

§ 9.13 DECLARATIONS DESCRIBING PHYSICAL CONDITIONS

The Code does not distinguish between declarations describing physical conditions and declarations describing other states of mind. Both § 1250, defining declarations of then existing mental states, and § 1251, defining declarations of prior mental states, speak in terms of a declarant's "state of mind, emotion, or physical sensation (including a statement of intent, plan, motive, design, mental feeling, pain, or bodily health)".[1] The distinction is made here to ease the analysis of these declarations.

Federal Rule of Evidence 803(3) also refrains from distinguishing declarations describing physical conditions from declarations describing other mental states. But the Rules take a more expansive approach by including a special hearsay exception for state of mind declarations describing symptoms when made for purposes of medical diagnosis or treatment.[2]

An example will illustrate the way in which the Code and the Rules treat declarations narrating physical conditions. Assume a case in which the plaintiff sues the defendant for injuries the plaintiff claims she sustained when the defendant struck her with his car. Prior to trial, the plaintiff made the following declarations to her doctor:

1. Doctor, my back hurts.

---

1. West's Ann.California Evidence Code §§ 1250–1251.

2. Federal Rule of Evidence 803(4).

Under the Code, this declaration would be admissible for the truth of the matter stated as it is a statement in which the plaintiff is describing a then-existing physical condition or sensation.[3] In some Common Law jurisdictions, such a statement would have been inadmissible unless made to a treating physician. Declarations made to physicians in anticipation of litigation were suspect. Under § 1252, a California judge can still take this distinction into account in determining the admissibility of the declaration. Section 1252 empowers the judge to exclude statements that satisfy the conditions of the hearsay exception if the judge nonetheless concludes that "the statement was made under circumstances such as to indicate its lack of trustworthiness."[4] As is explained by the Law Revision Commission, "If a statement of mental or physical state was made with a motive to misrepresent or to manufacture evidence, the statement is not sufficiently reliable to warrant its receipt in evidence."[5]

Under Federal Rule of Evidence 803(3), the plaintiff's narration would likewise be admissible to prove that her back hurt at the time she made the declaration. The statement describes the plaintiff's then-existing feelings of pain. Since the plaintiff ostensibly made the statement for purposes of medical diagnosis or treatment, the declaration also would be admissible under the special rule creating an exception for such statements. Unlike § 1252, Rule 803(3) does not empower the judge to exclude the statement if made under circumstances indicating lack of trustworthiness. Accordingly, the fact that the statement was made to a physician in anticipation of litigation goes to weight and not admissibility.

2. Doctor, my back hurt last week.

Under § 1250, this declaration would be inadmissible as the statement is simply a narrative of a past condition.[6] It would also be inadmissible under § 1251 unless under the tort law the plaintiff's previous physical condition was itself an issue in the case and the plaintiff was unavailable as a witness.[7]

Under Federal Rule of Evidence 803(3), the declaration likewise would be inadmissible. The federal rule does not recognize declarations of past mental states or symptoms.[8] The declaration, however, would be admissible under Federal Rule of Evidence 803(4). This rule creates a hearsay exception for a "statement that: (A) is made for—and is reasonably pertinent to—medical diagnosis or treatment; and (B) describes medical history; *past* or present symptoms or sensations; their inception; or their general cause."[9]

---

3. West's Ann.California Evidence Code § 1250.

4. West's Ann.California Evidence Code § 1252.

5. Id. (comment).

6. West's Ann.California Evidence Code § 1250(b).

7. West's Ann.California Evidence Code § 1252.

8. Federal Rule of Evidence 803(3).

9. Federal Rule of Evidence 803(4) (emphasis added).

Rule 803(4) is a marked and generous departure from the Common Law. It includes present as well as past symptoms, and it is immaterial whether the physician was consulted for treatment or for the purpose of enabling the doctor to testify. The declarant's motive goes to weight, not admissibility.[10] Moreover, it is not indispensable for the statement to be made to a doctor. "Statements to hospital attendants, ambulance drivers, or even members of the family" can be included if reasonably pertinent to diagnosis or treatment.[11]

3.   Doctor, my back has been hurting me since a car hit me.

Even though the first part of the declaration can be construed as expressing a then-existing physical symptom, the part relating to causation is simply a statement of memory or remembered fact. Under § 1250, such statements are inadmissible to prove the truth of the matter stated.[12] Under Rule 803(4), however, statements of causation are admissible if reasonably pertinent to diagnosis or treatment.[13] Knowing what caused an injury can assist a doctor in making the proper diagnosis or formulating the appropriate treatment. Thus, even a child's statement to a doctor about the identity of the person who molested her is admissible if made for purposes of medical diagnosis or treatment.[14] The fact that the statement may embrace the identity of the perpetrator does not detract from its reliability: a "patient can be expected to tell the truth about her injury because she will want to be diagnosed correctly and treated appropriately."[15] But even under the Federal Rule, statements relating to fault do not generally qualify. "Thus a patient's statement that he was struck by an automobile would qualify but not his statement that the car was driven through a red light."[16]

California's hearsay exception for statements made for medical diagnosis or treatment, although derived from the federal rule, is much more limited. California Evidence Code § 1253 embraces the kinds of statements contemplated by the federal rule, but the exception applies only "to a statement made when the victim was under the age of 12 describing any act, or attempted act, of child abuse or neglect."[17] Still, the exception has proved useful in prosecutions for sex offenses against children. A child's statement to a nurse identifying the accused as her assailant has been

---

10.   Id. (Advisory Committee Note).

11.   Id.

12.   West's Ann.California Evidence Code § 1250(b).

13.   Federal Rule of Evidence 803(4) (Advisory Committee Note).

14.   People of the Territory of Guam v. Ignacio, 10 F.3d 608 (9th Cir.1993).

15.   Id. at 612. If the statement, however, was not made for the purposes of diagnosis or treatment, then it is not admissible under the Federal Rule. In *Ignacio*, for example, the victim's statement to the doctor was admissible because made for these purposes but not her statement to a social worker who was simply trying to ensure the victim's safety. Id. The record was devoid of any evidence indicating that the child made the statements to the social worker for medical purposes. Id.

16.   Federal Rule of Evidence 803(4) (Advisory Committee Note).

17.   West's Ann. California Evidence Code § 1253.

admitted under this exception.[18] Moreover, the exception, like the federal rule, is not limited to statements made to medical personnel but includes statements made to psychotherapists.[19]

If the child is not called as a witness but the child's statement is received to prove the abuse as well as the defendant's identity as the perpetrator, confrontation concerns are raised.[20] In Crawford v. Washington[21] the United States Supreme Court held that, over a confrontation objection, "testimonial" hearsay may not be offered against the accused unless (1) the hearsay declarant is produced for cross-examination by the accused or (2) if not produced, unless the accused was given an opportunity prior to the trial to cross examine the hearsay declarant.[22] Whether statements offered under the medical exceptions qualify as "testimonial" statements is unclear. Their admissibility may turn on such factors as whether the dominant purpose for taking the statement was to diagnose or treat the patient, or to gather evidence with an eye toward possible use at trial.[23]

The Code allows California trial judges to assess the reliability of the child's statement and to exclude it if the circumstances attending its making indicate lack of trustworthiness.[24] Among the factors a judge should take into account in assessing the reliability of the statement is its spontaneity and consistency, the use of terms indicating a knowledge of sexual matters beyond the level expected of children of the declarant's age, the child's mental state at the time the statements were made, and a motive, if any, to fabricate.[25]

QUESTIONS AND PROBLEMS

1. Both the Code and the Federal Rules depart from the Common Law by authorizing the use of present state of mind statements made by patients to non-treating physicians. Discuss.

2. Because the Federal Rules generally do not allow the use of past mental states as an exception to the hearsay rule, the Rules are more restrictive than the Code with regard to the admissibility of statements by patients to doctors describing past physical conditions. True or false?

---

18. People v. Brodit, 61 Cal.App.4th 1312, 1331, 72 Cal.Rptr.2d 154, 165 (1998) (Where the abuser is a member of the household, the treating physician must know the identity of the abuser in order to render proper treatment.).

19. Id. See also United States v. Yellow, 18 F.3d 1438, 1442 (8th Cir.1994) and cases cited therein.

20. Both exceptions have been used to identify the accused as the perpetrator in child abuse prosecutions. See, e.g., People of the Territory of Guam v. Ignacio, 10 F.3d 608, 612 (9th Cir. 1993) (upholding the use of a child's statement to a doctor identifying her assailant); People v. Brodit, 61 Cal.App.4th 1312, 1331, 72 Cal.Rptr.2d 154, 165 (1998) (upholding the use of a child's statement to a nurse identifying the accused as her assailant).

21. 541 U.S. 36, 124 S.Ct. 1354, 158 L.Ed.2d 177 (2004).

22. Id. at 68.

23. For an extended discussion of confrontation concerns when hearsay is offered against the accused, see § 6.03 et seq., supra.

24. West's Ann. Evidence Code § 1252.

25. People v. Brodit, 61 Cal.App.4th 1312, 1332, 72 Cal.Rptr.2d 154, 165 (1998).

3. Determine the admissibility of the following statements under the Code as well as under the Rules. Assume that the statements are being offered through the doctor.

     a. Doctor, my head hurts.

     b. Doctor, my head hurt last week.

     c. Doctor, my head has been hurting me since the dean hit me with his car. *[handwritten: to grable / Med/Diagnosis / Pertinent to diagnosis]*

     d. Doctor, my head has been hurting me since the dean hit me with his car when he ran a light. *[handwritten: maybe relevant to treatment → could be irrelevant DEAN]*

§ 9.14   DECLARATIONS RELATING TO WILLS AND CLAIMS AGAINST ESTATES

Statements by a declarant that he has or has not made a will or established or amended a revocable trust, or has or has not revoked a will, revocable trust, or an amendment to a revocable trust are hearsay if offered to prove the past acts. These statements do not qualify under the exception for state of mind expressions as they narrate facts remembered or believed.[1] Expediency and necessity, rather than logic, however, dictate an exception.[2] Both the Code[3] and the Rules[4] provide an exception for such declarations, including statements identifying a will. The major difference is that under the Code the hearsay declarant must be unavailable.[5] Moreover, the Code empowers the court to exclude such declarations if the court finds that they were made under circumstances such as to indicate lack of trustworthiness.[6]

The Code also repeals the dead man statute which prohibited a party who sued on a claim against an estate from testifying to any fact occurring prior to the decedent's death.[7] The theory underlying the statute was that it would be unfair to permit the surviving claimant to testify to such facts when the decedent was precluded by his death from doing so.[8] To balance the position of the parties, the living were not allowed to speak because the dead could not.[9]

"Repeal of the dead man statute permits the claimant to testify without restriction. To balance this advantage, Section 1261 permits hearsay evidence of the decedent's statements to be admitted."[10]

---

1. See § 8.09 supra.
2. Federal Rule of Evidence 803(3) (Advisory Committee Note).
3. West's Ann.California Evidence Code § 1260(a).
4. Federal Rule of Evidence 803(3).
5. West's Ann.California Evidence Code § 1260(a).
6. West's Ann.California Evidence Code § 1260(b).
7. West's Ann.California Evidence Code § 1261 (comment).
8. Id.
9. Id.
10. Id.

The decedent's statement, however, must have been made upon his personal knowledge and at a time when the matter narrated had been recently perceived by him and while his recollection was clear.[11] As in the case of statements relating to wills, the court is empowered to exclude the decedent's statements if the court finds that they were made under circumstances indicating a lack of trustworthiness.[12]

§ 9.15 DECLARATIONS BY WITNESSES PREVENTED FROM TESTIFYING

Both the Code and the Rules recognize the need for a hearsay exception for damaging statements made by declarants who are prevented by a party from testifying. The Federal Rules provide an exception for a statement offered against a party who "wrongfully caused—or acquiesced in wrongfully causing—the declarant's unavailability as a witness, and did so intending that result."[1] Under the Federal Rules, the statement may be offered against any party in a criminal or civil proceeding, so long as the proponent proves the foundational facts by a preponderance of the evidence.[2]

California has two provisions. Section 1390(a), enacted in 2010, is similar to the Federal Rule. It provides that "[e]vidence of a statement is not made inadmissible by the hearsay rule if the statement is offered against a party that has engaged or aided and abetted in the wrongdoing that was intended to, and did, procure the unavailability of the declarant as a witness."[3] It differs from the Federal Rule in that § 1390 vests the judge with discretion to exclude the declaration if the judge deems it untrustworthy and unreliable.[4]

An older provision, Evidence Code § 1350, places more restrictions on the use of these declarations. They are admissible only in prosecutions charging a serious felony if, among other matters, the proponent proves by clear and convincing evidence that the declarant's unavailability was "knowingly caused by, aided by, or solicited by the party against whom the statement is offered for the purpose of preventing the arrest or prosecution" of that party.[5] In addition, the proponent must prove by clear and convincing evidence that the declarant's unavailability is the

---

11. West's Ann.California Evidence Code § 1261(a). See also Estate of Luke, 194 Cal.App.3d 1006, 1017, 240 Cal.Rptr. 84, 90 (1987) (The decedent's statement, describing a 40 year old transaction, did not narrate an event recently perceived by him and while his recollection of the event was clear.).

12. West's Ann.California Evidence Code § 1261(b).

1. Federal Rule of Evidence 804(b)(6).

2. Id. (Advisory Committee Note).

3. West's Ann. California Evidence Code § 1390.

4. West's Ann. California Evidence Code § 1390(a)(4).

5. West's Ann. California Evidence Code § 1350. For an example of the application of § 1350, see People v. Zambrano, 41 Cal.4th 1082, 1143, 163 P.3d 4, 47, 63 Cal.Rptr.3d 297, 349 (2007), cert. filed, No. 07–8509 (2008).

result of death by homicide or of kidnaping.[6]

Other limitations include proof that the statement was made under circumstances which indicate it is trustworthy and not the result of promise, inducement, threat, or coercion.[7] Corroboration is also required. The proponent must corroborate the statement by evidence tending to connect the party against whom the statement is offered with the commission of the serious felony with which the party is charged.[8] Proof that merely shows the commission of the offense or its circumstances is insufficient.[9] The proponent must also show that the statement was memorialized in a tape recording made by a law enforcement official or in a statement prepared by a law enforcement official and signed and notarized by the declarant in the presence of the law enforcement official.[10]

Procedural safeguards include a requirement that the prosecution serve a written notice upon the accused of its intent to use the statement at least 10 days prior to the hearing or trial at which the statement is to be offered, unless the prosecution shows good cause for the failure to provide the notice.[11] If good cause is shown, the accused is entitled to a reasonable continuance of the hearing or trial.[12]

If the statement is offered during the trial, the judge must determine its admissibility at a hearing out of the presence of the jury. If the accused testifies at the hearing, the judge must exclude all persons, except for the clerk, the court reporter, the bailiff, the prosecutor, the investigating officer, the accused, and defense counsel.[13] The accused's testimony is not admissible in any other proceeding, and if a transcript is made, it must be sealed and transmitted to the clerk of the court in which the action is pending.[14]

A final limitation is that hearsay declarations by others included in the statement admitted are inadmissible unless they fall within an exception to the hearsay rule.[15]

Because of its numerous limitations, it is doubtful that a prosecutor today would rely on § 1350 given the ease of applying § 1390. Moreover, unlike § 1350, § 1390 can be applied against any party, including the prosecution, in both civil and criminal cases.[16] Also unlike § 1350, under

---

6. West's Ann. California Evidence Code § 1350.

7. Id.

8. Id.

9. Id.

10. Id.

11. Id.

12. Id.

13. Id.

14. Id.

15. Id.

16. West's Ann. California Evidence Code § 1390; this is also true of Federal Rule of Evidence 804(b)(6).

§ 1390 the wrongdoing behind the declarant's unavailability does not have to amount to a criminal act.[17]

Statements by dead declarants regarding gang activities. As noted in § 9.03, California has a limited hearsay exception for sworn statements by dead declarants regarding gang related crimes.[18] The purpose of the exception is to discourage gang members from eliminating potential witnesses in prosecutions for gang crimes. California makes it a separate offense for a gang member to promote or assist any felonious criminal activity by members of gangs.[19]

The statements may be used only in anti-gang prosecutions and are subject to numerous restrictions. Chief among these are that the declarant die from other than natural causes, that the statement relate to acts or events within the personal knowledge of the declarant, that the statement be made under oath or affirmation in an affidavit or at a deposition, preliminary hearing, grand jury hearing, or other hearing under penalty of perjury, and that a verbatim transcript or copy, or record of the statement exists.[20]

In addition, the exception requires the proponent to notify the opponent of the intent to use the statement in advance of the hearing in which the statement will be offered.[21] The proponent must also persuade the judge that the statement was made under circumstances that indicate its trustworthiness and render the declarant's statement particularly worthy of belief.[22] Among the circumstances the judge can take into account are whether the statement was made in contemplation of a pending or anticipated criminal or civil matter in which the declarant had an interest other than as a witness, whether the declarant had a bias or motive to fabricate the statement, whether the statement is corroborated by evidence other than the statements that are admissible under the exception, and whether the statement was a declaration against the declarant's interest.[23]

The Federal Rules do not contain an equivalent exception. But the general federal hearsay exception for statements by declarants who are prevented by a party from testifying can be invoked in this situation.

---

17. West's Ann. California Evidence Code § 1390; this is also true of Federal Rule of Evidence 804(b)(6) (see Rule and Advisory Committee Note).

18. California Evidence Code § 1231.

19. California Penal Code § 186.22.

20. California Evidence Code § 1231.

21. California Evidence Code § 1231.1.

22. California Evidence Code § 1231.

23. California Evidence Code § 1231. For additional limitations on the use of the statements offered under § 1231, see §§ 1231.2–1231.4.

CALIFORNIA EVIDENCE CODE

§ 1230. Declarations against interest

Evidence of a statement by a declarant having sufficient knowledge of the subject is not made inadmissible by the hearsay rule if the declarant is unavailable as a witness and the statement, when made, was so far contrary to the declarant's pecuniary or proprietary interest, or so far subjected him to the risk of civil or criminal liability, or so far tended to render invalid a claim by him against another, or created such a risk of making him an object of hatred, ridicule, or social disgrace in the community, that a reasonable man in his position would not have made the statement unless he believed it to be true.

§ 1231. Prior statements of deceased declarant; hearsay exception

Evidence of a prior statement made by a declarant is not made inadmissible by the hearsay rule if the declarant is deceased and the proponent of introducing the statement establishes each of the following:

(a) The statement relates to acts or events relevant to a criminal prosecution under provisions of the California Street Terrorism Enforcement and Prevention Act (Chapter 11 (commencing with Section 186.20) of Title 7 of Part 1 of the Penal Code).

(b) A verbatim transcript, copy, or record of the statement exists. A record may include a statement preserved by means of audio or video recording or equivalent technology.

(c) The statement relates to acts or events within the personal knowledge of the declarant.

(d) The statement was made under oath or affirmation in an affidavit; or was made at a deposition, preliminary hearing, grand jury hearing, or other proceeding in compliance with law, and was made under penalty of perjury.

(e) The declarant died from other than natural causes.

(f) The statement was made under circumstances that would indicate its trustworthiness and render the declarant's statement particularly worthy of belief. For purposes of this subdivision, circumstances relevant to the issue of trustworthiness include, but are not limited to, all of the following:

(1) Whether the statement was made in contemplation of a pending or anticipated criminal or civil matter, in which the declarant had an interest, other than as a witness.

(2) Whether the declarant had a bias or motive for fabricating the statement, and the extent of any bias or motive.

(3) Whether the statement is corroborated by evidence other than statements that are admissible only pursuant to this section.

(4) Whether the statement was a statement against the declarant's interest.

§ 1231.1 Statements made by deceased declarant; admissibility; notice of statement to adverse party

A statement is admissible pursuant to Section 1231 only if the proponent of the statement makes known to the adverse party the intention to offer the statement and the particulars of the statement sufficiently in advance of the proceedings to provide the adverse party with a fair opportunity to prepare to meet the statement.

§ 1231.2 Administer and certify oaths

A peace officer may administer and certify oaths for purposes of this article.

§ 1231.3 Testimony of law enforcement officer; hearsay

Any law enforcement officer testifying as to any hearsay statement pursuant to this article shall either have five years of law enforcement experience or have completed a training course certified by the Commission on Peace Officer Standards and Training which includes training in the investigation and reporting of cases and testifying at preliminary hearings and trials.

§ 1231.4 Cause of death; deceased declarant

If evidence of a prior statement is introduced pursuant to this article, the jury may not be told that the declarant died from other than natural causes, but shall merely be told that the declarant is unavailable.

§ 1240. Spontaneous statement

Evidence of a statement is not made inadmissible by the hearsay rule if the statement:

(a) Purports to narrate, describe, or explain an act, condition, or event perceived by the declarant; and

(b) Was made spontaneously while the declarant was under the stress of excitement caused by such perception.

§ 1241. Contemporaneous statement

Evidence of a statement is not made inadmissible by the hearsay rule if the statement:

(a) Is offered to explain, qualify, or make understandable conduct of the declarant; and

(b) Was made while the declarant was engaged in such conduct.

§ 1242. Dying declaration

Evidence of a statement made by a dying person respecting the cause and circumstances of his death is not made inadmissible by the hearsay rule if the statement was made upon his personal knowledge and under a sense of immediately impending death.

§ 1250. Statement of declarant's then existing mental or physical state

(a) Subject to Section 1252, evidence of a statement of the declarant's then existing state of mind, emotion, or physical sensation (including a statement of intent, plan, motive, design, mental feeling, pain, or bodily health) is not made inadmissible by the hearsay rule when:

(1) The evidence is offered to prove the declarant's state of mind, emotion, or physical sensation at that time or at any other time when it is itself an issue in the action; or

(2) The evidence is offered to prove or explain acts or conduct of the declarant.

(b) This section does not make admissible evidence of a statement of memory or belief to prove the fact remembered or believed.

§ 1251. Statement of declarant's previously existing mental or physical state

Subject to Section 1252, evidence of a statement of the declarant's state of mind, emotion, or physical sensation (including a statement of intent, plan, motive, design, mental feeling, pain, or bodily health) at a time prior to the statement is not made inadmissible by the hearsay rule if:

(a) The declarant is unavailable as a witness; and

(b) The evidence is offered to prove such prior state of mind, emotion, or physical sensation when it is itself an issue in the action and the evidence is not offered to prove any fact other than such state of mind, emotion, or physical sensation.

§ 1252. Restriction on admissibility of statement of mental or physical state

Evidence of a statement is inadmissible under this article if the statement was made under circumstances such as to indicate its lack of trustworthiness.

§ 1253. Statements for purposes of medical diagnosis or treatment; contents of statement; child abuse or neglect; age limitations

Subject to Section 1252, evidence of a statement is not made inadmissible by the hearsay rule if the statement was made for purposes of medical diagnosis or treatment and describes medical history, or past or present symptoms, pain, or sensations, or the inception or general character of the cause or external source thereof insofar as reasonably pertinent to diagnosis or treatment. This section applies only to a statement made by a victim who is a minor at the time of the proceedings, provided the statement was made when the victim was under the age of 12 describing any act, attempted act, of child abuse or neglect. "Child abuse" and "child neglect," for purposes of this section, have the meanings provided in subdivision (c) of Section 1360. In addition, "child abuse" means any act proscribed by Chapter 5 (commencing with Section 281) of Title 9 of Part 1 of the Penal Code committed against a minor.

§ 1260. Statements concerning declarant's will or revocable trust

(a) Except as provided in subdivision (b), evidence of any of the following statements made by a declarant who is unavailable as a witness is not made inadmissible by the hearsay rule:

(1) That the declarant has or has not made a will or established or amended a revocable trust.

(2) That the declarant has or has not revoked his or her will, revocable trust, or an amendment to a revocable trust.

(3) That identifies the declarant's will, revocable trust, or an amendment to a revocable trust.

(b) Evidence of a statement is inadmissible under this section if the statement was made under circumstances that indicate its lack of trustworthiness.

§ 1350. Unavailable declarant; hearsay rule

(a) In a criminal proceeding charging a serious felony, evidence of a statement made by a declarant is not made inadmissible by the hearsay rule if the declarant is unavailable as a witness, and all of the following are true:

(1) There is clear and convincing evidence that the declarant's unavailability was knowingly caused by, aided by, or solicited by the party against whom the statement is offered for the purpose of preventing the arrest or prosecution of the party and is the result of the death by homicide or the kidnapping of the declarant.

(2) There is no evidence that the unavailability of the declarant was caused by, aided by, solicited by, or procured on behalf of, the party who is offering the statement.

(3) The statement has been memorialized in a tape recording made by a law enforcement official, or in a written statement prepared by a law enforcement official and signed by the declarant and notarized in the presence of the law enforcement official, prior to the death or kidnapping of the declarant.

(4) The statement was made under circumstances which indicate its trustworthiness and was not the result of promise, inducement, threat, or coercion.

(5) The statement is relevant to the issues to be tried.

(6) The statement is corroborated by other evidence which tends to connect the party against whom the statement is offered with the commission of the serious felony with which the party is charged. The corroboration is not sufficient if it merely shows the commission of the offense or the circumstances thereof.

(b) If the prosecution intends to offer a statement pursuant to this section, the prosecution shall serve a written notice upon the defendant at least 10 days prior to the hearing or trial at which the prosecution intends to offer the statement, unless the prosecution shows good cause for the failure to provide that notice. In the event that good cause is shown, the defendant shall be entitled to a reasonable continuance of the hearing or trial.

(c) If the statement is offered during trial, the court's determination shall be made out of the presence of the jury. If the defendant elects to testify at the hearing or motion brought pursuant to this section, the court shall exclude from the examination every person except the clerk, the court reporter, the bailiff, the prosecutor, the investigating officer, the defendant and his or her counsel, an investigator for the defendant, and the officer having custody of the defendant. Notwithstanding any other provision of law, the defendant's testimony at the hearing shall not be admissible in any other proceeding except the hearing brought on the motion pursuant to this section. If a transcript is made of the defendant's testimony, it shall be sealed and transmitted to the clerk of the court in which the action is pending.

(d) As used in this section, "serious felony" means any of the felonies listed in subdivision (c) of Section 1192.7 of the Penal Code or any violation of Section 11351, 11352, 11378, or 11379 of the Health and Safety Code.

(e) If a statement to be admitted pursuant to this section includes hearsay statements made by anyone other than the declarant who is unavailable pursuant to subdivision (a), those hearsay statements are inadmissible unless they meet the requirements of an exception to the hearsay rule.

§ 1390. Statements against parties involved in causing unavailability of declarant as witness

(a) Evidence of a statement is not made inadmissible by the hearsay rule if the statement is offered against a party that has engaged or aided and abetted in the wrongdoing that was intended to, and did, procure the unavailability of the declarant as a witness.

(b)(1) The party seeking to introduce a statement pursuant to subdivision (a) shall establish, by a preponderance of the evidence, that the elements of subdivision (a) have been met at a foundational hearing.

(2) The hearsay evidence that is the subject of the foundational hearing is admissible at the foundational hearing. However, a finding that the elements of subdivision (a) have been met shall not be based solely on the unconfronted hearsay statement of the unavailable declarant, and shall be supported by independent corroborative evidence.

(3) The foundational hearing shall be conducted outside the presence of the jury. However, if the hearing is conducted after a jury trial has begun, the judge presiding at the hearing may consider evidence already presented to the jury in deciding whether the elements of subdivision (a) have been met.

(4) In deciding whether or not to admit the statement, the judge may take into account whether it is trustworthy and reliable.

(c) This section shall apply to any civil, criminal, or juvenile case or proceeding initiated or pending as of January 1, 2011.

(d) This section shall remain in effect only until January 1, 2016, and as of that date is repealed, unless a later enacted statute, that is enacted before January 1, 2016, deletes or extends that date. If this section is repealed, the fact that it is repealed should it occur, shall not be deemed to give rise to any ground for an appeal or a postverdict challenge based on its use in a criminal or juvenile case or proceeding before January 1, 2016.

§ 1370. Threat of infliction of injury

(a) Evidence of a statement by a declarant is not made inadmissible by the hearsay rule if all of the following conditions are met:

(1) The statement purports to narrate, describe, or explain the infliction or threat of physical injury upon the declarant.

(2) The declarant is unavailable as a witness pursuant to Section 240.

(3) The statement was made at or near the time of the infliction or threat of physical injury. Evidence of statements made more than five years before the filing of the current action or proceeding shall be inadmissible under this section.

(4) The statement was made under circumstances that would indicate trustworthiness.

(5) The statement was made in writing, was electronically recorded, or made to a physician, nurse, paramedic, or to a law enforcement official.

(b) For purposes of paragraph (4) of subdivision (a), circumstances relevant to the issue of trustworthiness include, but are not limited to, the following:

(1) Whether the statement was made in contemplation of pending or anticipated litigation in which the declarant was interested.

(2) Whether the declarant has a bias or motive for fabricating the statement, and the extent of any bias or motive.

(3) Whether the statement is corroborated by evidence other than statements that are admissible only pursuant to this section.

(c) A statement is admissible pursuant to this section only if the proponent of the statement makes known to the adverse party the intention to offer the statement and the particulars of the statement sufficiently in advance of the proceedings in order to provide the adverse party with a fair opportunity to prepare to meet the statement.

§ 1380. Elder and dependent adults; statements by victims of abuse

(a) In a criminal proceeding charging a violation, or attempted violation, of Section 368 of the Penal Code, evidence of a statement made by a declarant is not made inadmissible by the hearsay rule if the declarant is unavailable as a witness, as defined by subdivisions (a) and (b) of Section 240, and all of the following are true:

(1) The party offering the statement has made a showing of particularized guarantees of trustworthiness regarding the statement, the statement was made under circumstances which indicate its trustworthiness, and the statement was not the result of promise, inducement, threat, or coercion. In making its determination, the court may consider only the circumstances that surround the making of the statement and that render the declarant particularly worthy of belief.

(2) There is no evidence that the unavailability of the declarant was caused by, aided by, solicited by, or procured on behalf of, the party who is offering the statement.

(3) The entire statement has been memorialized in a videotape recording made by a law enforcement official, prior to the death or disabling of the declarant.

(4) The statement was made by the victim of the alleged violation.

(5) The statement is supported by corroborative evidence.

(6) The victim of the alleged violation is an individual who meets both of the following requirements:

(A) Was 65 years of age or older or was a dependent adult when the alleged violation or attempted violation occurred.

(B) At the time of any criminal proceeding, including, but not limited to, a preliminary hearing or trial, regarding the alleged violation or attempted violation, is either deceased or suffers from infirmities of aging as manifested by advanced age or organic brain damage, or other physical, mental, or emotional dysfunction, to the extent that the ability of the person to provide adequately for the person's own care or protection is impaired.

(b) If the prosecution intends to offer a statement pursuant to this section, the prosecution shall serve a written notice upon the defendant at least 10 days prior to the hearing or trial at which the prosecution intends to offer the statement, unless the prosecution shows good cause for the failure to provide that notice. In the event that good cause is shown, the defendant shall be entitled to a reasonable continuance of the hearing or trial.

(c) If the statement is offered during trial, the court's determination as to the availability of the victim as a witness shall be made out of the presence of the jury. If the defendant elects to testify at the hearing on a motion brought pursuant to this section, the court shall exclude from the examination every person except the clerk, the court reporter, the bailiff, the prosecutor, the investigating officer, the defendant and his or her counsel, an investigator for the defendant, and the officer having custody of the defendant. Notwithstanding any other provision of law, the defendant's testimony at the hearing shall not be admissible in any other proceeding except the hearing brought on the motion pursuant to this section. If a transcript is made of the defendant's testimony, it shall be sealed and transmitted to the clerk of the court in which the action is pending.

FEDERAL RULES OF EVIDENCE

Rule 803.   Exceptions to the Rule Against Hearsay—Regardless of Whether the Declarant Is Available as a Witness

The following are not excluded by the rule against hearsay, regardless of whether the declarant is available as a witness:

(1) *Present Sense Impression.* A statement describing or explaining an event or condition, made while or immediately after the declarant perceived it.

(2) *Excited Utterance.* A statement relating to a startling event or condition, made while the declarant was under the stress of excitement that it caused.

(3) *Then–Existing Mental, Emotional, or Physical Condition.* A statement of the declarant's then-existing state of mind (such as motive, intent, or plan) or emotional, sensory, or physical condition (such as mental feeling, pain, or bodily health), but not including a statement of memory or belief to prove the fact remembered or believed unless it relates to the validity or terms of the declarant's will.

(4) *Statement Made for Medical Diagnosis or Treatment.* A statement that:

>   **(A)** is made for—and is reasonably pertinent to—medical diagnosis or treatment; and

>   **(B)** describes medical history; past or present symptoms or sensations; their inception; or their general cause.

Rule 804.   Exceptions to the Rule Against Hearsay—When the Declarant Is Unavailable as a Witness

* * *

(b) The Exceptions. The following are not excluded by the rule against hearsay if the declarant is unavailable as a witness:

>   * * *

>   **(2)** *Statement Under the Belief of Imminent Death.* In a prosecution for homicide or in a civil case, a statement that the declarant, while believing the declarant's death to be imminent, made about its cause or circumstances.

* * *

(6) *Statement Offered Against a Party That Wrongfully Caused the Declarant's Unavailability.* A statement offered against a party that wrongfully caused—or acquiesced in wrongfully causing—the declarant's unavailability as a witness, and did so intending that result.

CHAPTER 10

EXCEPTIONS TO THE HEARSAY RULE: BUSINESS AND OFFICIAL RECORDS

■ ■ ■

Table of Sections

§ 10.01 THE MAGIC OF BUSINESS AND OFFICIAL RECORDS

Assume a lawsuit in which the plaintiff sues the defendant for injuries the plaintiff claims she suffered when the defendant ran a light. A police officer who investigated the accident measured skid marks leading to the defendant's car which were 40 feet long. The investigating officer reported the skid measurements to his supervisor. If the supervisor attempts to inform the jury about the location and length of the skid marks by repeating the investigating officer's out of court statement, his testimony would violate the hearsay rule. Upon objection, it would be inadmissible. But if the investigating officer includes the information about the skid marks in his police report and the report is offered in evidence, then the entry regarding the length of the skidmarks can be received for the truth of the matter stated under either the business or official records exception to the hearsay rule if certain conditions are satisfied.[1]

The magic of business and official records extends even further. Assume that, after hearing from the investigating officer, the supervising

---

[1]. Gananian v. Zolin, 33 Cal.App.4th 634, 639, 39 Cal.Rptr.2d 384, 386–387 (1995).

officer includes the information about the skid marks in *his* report. If the supervisor's report, rather than his testimony, is offered in evidence, then the information about the skid marks can be received for the truth of the matter asserted. Again, if certain conditions relating to the admissibility of business and official records are satisfied, the report can be received to establish the length and location of the skid marks.[2]

Why should these exceptions allow the use of evidence that would otherwise be barred by the hearsay rule? The answer is rooted in the legal acceptance of business practice as well as in necessity. If businesses rely on business records "in the most important undertakings of mercantile and industrial life," then such records ought to be sufficiently reliable for use in court.[3] The basis for the exceptions is broad; as we shall see, however, case law and statutes limit the exceptions.[4]

§ 10.02 BUSINESS RECORDS AND THE BUSINESS DUTY RULE

Assume that in our example that the investigating officer interviewed a bystander at the accident scene who told the officer that he saw the defendant run the light. If the officer attempts to repeat the bystander's statement in court to prove that the defendant ran the light, the testimony would be barred by the hearsay rule. The bystander's declaration is an out of court statement offered to prove the truth of the matters asserted. But if the officer includes the bystander's statement in his report, may the bystander's statement be received for the truth of the matter stated? The answer in California and federal courts is "no".[1] The magic of business records does not generally extend that far. The reliability of business records derives only in part from the fact that they are prepared by individuals who have a duty to prepare them accurately.[2] Where the entry is based on information supplied by others, scrupulous accuracy in record-

---

2. Id. The first officer had first hand knowledge of the length of the skid marks and a duty to report that observation to the second officer who in turn had a duty to record the information and to do so accurately. See also McNary v. Department of Motor Vehicles, 45 Cal.App.4th 688, 695, 53 Cal.Rptr.2d 55, 59 (1996) and cases cited therein (applying the same requirement to official records).

3. Johnson v. Lutz, 253 N.Y. 124, 128, 170 N.E. 517, 518 (1930).

4. Documents offered under the exception for business records should be distinguished from documents that are admissible as nonhearsay. In a breach of contract action, for example, the plaintiff must offer the document that constitutes the contract as part of her prima facie case. The plaintiff does not have to resort to the hearsay exception for business records. The plaintiff is not offering the document for the "truth" of the assertions it contains. Rather, the plaintiff is offering the document as proof of the contract entered into between the parties. For a discussion of this point, see § 5.04, supra. See also Remington Investments, Inc. v. Hamedani, 55 Cal. App.4th 1033, 1042, 64 Cal.Rptr.2d 376, 382, cert. denied, 523 U.S. 1004, 118 S.Ct. 1185, 140 L.Ed.2d 316 (1998): "The Promissory Note document itself is not a business record as that term is used in the law of hearsay, but rather is an operative contractual document admissible merely upon adequate evidence of authenticity."

1. MacLean v. City & County of San Francisco, 151 Cal.App.2d 133, 143, 311 P.2d 158, 164 (1957); see also Federal Rule of Evidence 803(6) (Advisory Committee Note).

2. Johnson v. Lutz, 253 N.Y. 124, 128, 170 N.E. 517, 518 (1930).

ing the information cannot vouch for the reliability of the information.[3] In these circumstances, the proponent of the record must show that the information was imparted by persons with first hand knowledge who were under a duty to transmit their observations to the entrant.[4] The bystander had no such duty. In the absence of such a duty, the court may find that the information imparted to the entrant is unreliable.[5] The Code as well as the Rules empower the judge to exclude business records if the judge finds that the sources of the information used by the entrant fail to assure the record's "trustworthiness".[6]

Other hearsay exceptions, however, may supply the required reliability. If the bystander's statement, for example, qualifies as an excited utterance,[7] then the statement would be admissible in the report for the truth of the matter stated.[8] The police officer who overhears such a declaration has first hand knowledge of what the declarant said and a duty to report the declaration accurately. Likewise, the entrant has a duty to record the officer's report accurately.

QUESTIONS AND PROBLEMS

Over a hearsay or a lack of personal knowledge objection, determine whether the following evidence is admissible to establish that the defendant ran the light:

1. Bystander to officer: The red car ran the light.

Officer testifies: The bystander said to me, "The red car ran the light."

2. Bystander to officer: The red car ran the light.

Officer puts the bystander's statement into his report, and the report is offered in evidence.

---

3. Federal Rule of Evidence 803(6) (Advisory Committee Note).

4. West's Ann.California Evidence Code § 1271 (comment). See also Alvarez v. Jacmar Pacific Pizza Corp., 100 Cal.App.4th 1190, 1205, 122 Cal.Rptr.2d 890, 901 (2002) (holding that "911" reports could not be received to prove the crimes referred to in the reports because of the absence of evidence that the persons who imparted the crimes information to the "911" operators were under a duty to transmit the information); People v. Ayers, 125 Cal.App.4th 988, 994, 23 Cal.Rptr.3d 242, 245 (2005) (holding that reports prepared by domestic violence case workers were inadmissible to prove the victim's injuries, as the victim was not under a duty to describe her injuries to the case workers).

5. West's Ann.California Evidence Code § 1271 (comment).

6. West's Ann.California Evidence Code § 1271(d); Federal Rule of Evidence 803(6). The framers of the Code and the Federal Rules intended the business records exception to continue the law developed in the cases establishing the business duty rule. West's Ann.California Evidence Code § 1271(d) (comment); Federal Rule of Evidence 803(6) (Advisory Committee Note).

7. For an extended discussion of excited utterances, see § 9.04 supra.

8. The record and utterance satisfy the requirements for the admission of multiple hearsay. "A statement within the scope of an exception to the hearsay rule is not inadmissible on the ground that the evidence of such statement is hearsay evidence if such hearsay evidence consists of one or more statements each of which meets the requirements of an exception to the hearsay rule." West's Ann.California Evidence Code § 1201. Federal Rule of Evidence 805 is to the same effect. Cf. Rousseau v. West Coast House Movers, 256 Cal.App.2d 878, 886, 64 Cal.Rptr. 655, 661 (1967) (Statements in arrest reports that plaintiff had admitted drinking intoxicants could have been admitted as a party admission even though the reporting officers had not seen the plaintiff consume the liquor.). For an extended discussion of the multiple hearsay rule, see § 8.02 supra.

3.   Officer 1 sees the red car run the light.

Officer 1 testifies at the trial: The red car ran the light.

Adm

4.   Officer 1 tells Officer 2: I saw the red car run the light.

Officer 2 testifies at the trial: Officer 1 said to me, "I saw the red car run the light."

Not.

5.   Officer 1 tells Officer 2: I saw the red car run the light.

Officer 2 puts Officer 1's statement into his police report, and the report is offered in evidence.

Adm

6.   Bystander to Officer 1: Hey! The red car ran the light.

Officer 1 testifies: The bystander said to me, "Hey! The red car ran the light!"

Adm. exc. utt.

7.   Bystander to Officer 1: Hey! The red car ran the light.

Officer 1 puts the bystander's statement into his police report, and the report is offered in evidence.

Adm

8.   Bystander to Officer 1: Hey! The red car ran the light!

Officer 1 tells Officer 2. Officer 2 testifies: Officer 1 said to me, "The bystander said to me, 'Hey! The red car ran the light.' "

Not

9.   Bystander to Officer 1: Hey! The red car ran the light.

Officer 1 tells Officer 2. Officer 2 puts Officer 1's statement incorporating bystander's statement into his police report.

Adm

10.   Defendant to Officer 1: I ran the light.

Officer 1 testifies: The defendant said to me, "I ran the light."

Adm

11.   Defendant to Officer 1: I ran the light.

Officer 1 puts the defendant's statement into his police report, and the report is offered in evidence.

Adm

12.   Defendant to Bystander: I ran the light.

Bystander testifies: The defendant said to me, "I ran the light."

Adm

13.   Defendant to Bystander: I ran the light.

Bystander tells Officer 1. Officer 1 puts the bystander's statement incorporating the defendant's statement into his police report, and the report is offered in evidence.

Adm

§ 10.03   THE FORMAL EVIDENTIARY FOUNDATION FOR BUSINESS RECORDS

Under §§ 1270 and 1271, a writing prepared by a "business" as "a record of an act, condition, or event is not made inadmissible by the hearsay rule when offered to prove the act, condition, or event if: (a) [t]he writing was made in the regular course of a business; (b) [t]he writing was made at or near the time of the act, condition, or event; (c) [t]he custodian or other qualified witness testifies to its identity and the mode of its preparation; and (d) [t]he sources of information and method and time of preparation were such as to indicate its trustworthiness."[1] Each of the foundational elements is discussed separately.

Writing prepared by a business. As indicated, the use of business records as an exception to the hearsay rule stems from the recognition that businesses rely on such records in reaching important decisions.[2] Thus, it follows that if a given record was not made by a business, it would be inadmissible. But both the Code and the Federal Rules define businesses expansively. Under § 1270, a business includes "every kind of business, governmental activity, profession, occupation, calling, or operation of institutions, whether carried on for profit or not."[3] The Law Revision Commission stressed that the definition was designed "to encompass institutions not customarily thought of as businesses" and cited as examples the baptismal and wedding records of a church offered to prove the events recorded.[4]

Writing made in the regular course of business. For the record to qualify under the exception, it must have been made in the regular course of business. The Federal Rules of Evidence make the point more emphatically by requiring the proponent to show that "it was the regular practice" of the business to make the record.[5] Records that are not generated in the regular course of business are simply not reliable. They lack the systematic checking, regularity, continuity, and business reliance associated with business records.[6] For example, accident reports required by law to be filed with the Department of Motor Vehicles by persons involved in accidents are inadmissible under the exception: "Although it may be the regular course of business for the D.M.V. to receive the report, it undoubtedly is not in the regular course of business for the citizen author to make such a report."[7]

Writing made at or near the time of the act, condition, or event recorded. Business entries are only as good as the individuals who make them or the individuals who report the information to the entrant. Because human recall tends to deteriorate over time, both the Code and

---

1. West's Ann.California Evidence Code §§ 1270–1271. Federal Rule of Evidence 803(6) is to the same effect.

2. See § 10.01 supra.

3. West's Ann.California Evidence Code § 1270. Under the Federal Rules, a business includes "business, occupation, or calling, whether or not conducted for profit." Federal Rule of Evidence 803(6).

4. West's Ann.California Evidence Code § 1270 (comment).

5. Federal Rule of Evidence 803(6).

6. Id. (Advisory Committee Note).

7. Daniels v. Department of Motor Vehicles, 33 Cal.3d 532, 538, 189 Cal.Rptr. 512, 516, 658 P.2d 1313, 1317 (1983). Under the California Vehicle Code, a person involved in an automobile accident causing death or injury must file a report with the Highway Patrol or the police agency in which the accident occurred. West's Ann.California Vehicle Code § 20008. "No such accident report shall be used as evidence in any trial, civil or criminal, arising out of an accident * * *." Id. at § 20013.

the Federal Rules require the proponent to show that the entry was made at or near the time of the event or condition recorded.[8]

Given the diverse circumstances in which business records are generated, the drafters of the rules made no attempt to specify time limits. Whether the time of preparation is close enough to ensure accuracy is left instead to the discretion of the judge who is charged with considering the time of preparation in determining the record's trustworthiness.[9]

Custodian testifies to the record's identity and its mode of preparation. The rules of authentication require the proponent of a writing to produce evidence sufficient to sustain a finding that the writing is what the proponent claims it to be.[10] Thus, if in our example the plaintiff offers the police report, she must offer evidence that the record is in fact the police report.

In California, proof of foundational requirements must usually be made through admissible evidence.[11] Accordingly, the proponent must call knowledgeable witnesses to establish the mode and time of preparation of business records. This does not mean that the witness or "custodian" must have personal knowledge about the circumstances surrounding the creation of the particular record offered in evidence. Requiring the proponent to call all who participated in creating a given record would cripple the exception.[12] Thus, in our example, it would be enough for the witness to describe generally how police reports in the jurisdiction in question are made and to identify the report offered in evidence as one of those reports. Of course, the opponent is entitled to influence the weight which the fact finder may give to the report by exposing the witness's limited knowledge about how the report in question was prepared.

In California, it is possible to offer business records without calling a custodian or other knowledgeable witnesses. Section 1560 provides that when a party serves a subpoena duces tecum upon the custodian of records of a business in which the business is neither a party nor the place where any cause of action is alleged to have arisen, the custodian can comply by delivering a true, legible, and durable copy of all the records described in the subpoena to the clerk of the court or to the judge if there

---

8. West's Ann.California Evidence Code § 1271(b); Federal Rule of Evidence 803(6).

9. West's Ann.California Evidence Code § 1271(c); Federal Rule of Evidence 803(6). See also Gregory v. State Bd. of Control, 73 Cal.App.4th 584, 596–597, 86 Cal.Rptr.2d 575, 582 (1999) (holding that police reports prepared 11 and 20 months, respectively, after the events recorded were not prepared at or near the time of the events so as to qualify as business records).

10. West's Ann.California Evidence Code § 1400; Federal Rule of Evidence 901(a).

11. The Law Revision Commission recommended a rule permitting judges to consider inadmissible evidence in some circumstances in determining the existence of preliminary facts. 6 California Law Revision Commission, Reports, Recommendations, and Studies 19–21 (1964). The Legislature, however, retained the practice of requiring the use of admissible evidence to establish preliminary facts. See West's Ann.California Evidence Code §§ 400–406. Under the Federal Rules, the judge may consider nonprivileged inadmissible evidence in determining the existence of preliminary facts. See Federal Rule of Evidence 104(a).

12. People v. Williams, 36 Cal.App.3d 262, 274–275, 111 Cal.Rptr. 378, 385–386 (1973). See also Federal Rule of Evidence 803(6) (Advisory Committee Note). The same principle applies to the California hearsay exception for official records. See § 10.07 infra.

is no clerk.[13] Section 1561 provides that the records shall be accompanied by an affidavit in which the custodian states, among other matters, that the records are a true copy of the records described in the subpoena and that the originals were prepared by personnel of the business in the ordinary course of business at or near the time of the act, condition, or event described.[14] In addition, the custodian must identify the records as well as describe the mode by which the records were prepared. Section 1562 then provides that if the original records would have been admissible if the custodian (or other qualified witness) had appeared and testified to the matters stated in the affidavit "and if the requirements of Section 1271 have been met," the copies of the records are admissible in evidence.[15]

Section 1562 creates a hearsay exception for the matters the custodian states in the affidavit.[16] By providing that such matters are presumed to be true, the section also creates a presumption that places upon the opponent the burden of producing evidence disproving those matters.[17] But compliance with § 1561 does not ensure admissibility under § 1562. The requirements of the exception for business records must be met.[18] If the affidavit discloses, for example, that the person who prepared the records relied on information provided by an individual who had no business duty to impart the information, the judge can exclude the records.[19] Similarly, if the affidavit fails to disclose sufficiently the mode of preparation to enable the judge to determine the record's trustworthiness, the judge can exclude the record.[20]

The party serving the subpoena can defeat the procedures provided by §§ 1560–1562 and force the custodian of the records to appear at the hearing. The party can do so by simply stating in the subpoena that compliance with §§ 1560–1562 "will not be deemed sufficient compliance with this subpoena."[21]

Amendments to the Federal Rules now permit business records to be offered in evidence without the need to call a custodian. Rule 803(6) allows a party to offer a certification or declaration in lieu of the testimony of the custodian if the certification or declaration meets the requirements of

---

13. West's Ann.California Evidence Code § 1560. For other details, such as the time in which the subpoena is returnable, see § 1560.

14. West's Ann.California Evidence Code § 1561.

15. West's Ann.California Evidence Code § 1562.

16. Id.

17. Id. The presumption is one only "affecting the burden of producing evidence." Id. Consequently, the party offering the records still has the burden of persuading the judge that the records are trustworthy. See West's Ann.California Evidence Code §§ 603 and 405.

18. West's Ann.California Evidence Code § 1562.

19. See § 10.02 supra.

20. Taggart v. Super Seer Corp., 33 Cal.App.4th 1697, 1706, 40 Cal.Rptr.2d 56, 62 (1995) (Compliance with § 1561 will not assure admission of a business record where the custodian's declaration fails to disclose how the record was prepared or the sources used in its preparation.).

21. West's Ann.California Evidence Code § 1564.

Rule 902(11) on self-authentication.[22] Under Rule 902(11), extrinsic evidence of authentication is not required of domestic records of regularly conducted activity if the original or a copy of the domestic record "meets the requirements of Rule 803(6)(A)–(C), as shown by a certification of the custodian or another qualified person that complies with a federal statute or a rule prescribed by the Supreme Court. Before the trial or hearing, the proponent must give an adverse party reasonable written notice of the intent to offer the record—and must make the record and certification available for inspection—so that the party has a fair opportunity to challenge them."[23] Rule 803(6)(A)–(C) impose the following requirements: (A) the record was made at or near the time by—or from information transmitted by—someone with knowledge; (B) the record was kept in the course of a regularly conducted activity of a business, organization, occupation, or calling, whether or not for profit; and (C) making the record was a regular practice of that activity.[24]

The sources of information and method and time of preparation are such as to indicate trustworthiness. The judge is given broad discretion in determining whether the circumstances surrounding the creation of the record warrant its admission in evidence. It is this discretionary power that enables judges to exclude records based on information provided by individuals who had no business duty to impart the information.[25] It is also this power that authorizes judges to exclude records whose reliability is suspect because they were prepared with litigation in mind.

Chief among these are accident reports and hospital records. The classic case excluding accident reports is *Palmer v. Hoffman*,[26] where the United States Supreme Court upheld the exclusion of a report prepared in connection with a railroad accident on the ground that its principal use was in "litigating, not railroading."[27] *Palmer* has been followed in California,[28] but accident reports may nonetheless be admissible in the absence of evidence of self-serving motives.[29] Hospital and other medical records are less troubling, since the preparer is usually not a party to the suit. But even where the report was prepared at the request of a party, the report may be admitted if the judge finds that it is nonetheless trustworthy. A doctor's report evaluating the condition of the plaintiff's injuries and prepared at the plaintiff's request has been excluded when offered by the

---

22.   Federal Rule of Evidence 803(6).

23.   Federal Rule of Evidence 902(11).

24.   Federal Rule of Evidence 803(6).

25.   See § 10.02 supra.

26.   318 U.S. 109, 63 S.Ct. 477, 87 L.Ed. 645 (1943), reh'g denied, 318 U.S. 800, 63 S.Ct. 757, 87 L.Ed. 1163 (1943).

27.   Id. at 114, 63 S.Ct. at 481.

28.   See, e.g., Hoel v. Los Angeles, 136 Cal.App.2d 295, 309, 288 P.2d 989, 998 (1955); Reisman v. Los Angeles City School District, 123 Cal.App.2d 493, 503, 267 P.2d 36, 43 (1954).

29.   See County of Sonoma v. Grant W., 187 Cal.App.3d 1439, 1451, 232 Cal.Rptr. 471, 478 (1986); cf. Levy–Zentner Co. v. Southern Pacific Transp. Co., 74 Cal.App.3d 762, 783–786, 142 Cal.Rptr. 1, 15–17 (1977).

plaintiff because of its self-serving nature.[30] But similar reports offered by the plaintiff have been admitted when prepared at the request of the opposing party.[31]

The Code and the Federal Rules differ on how judges should exercise their discretion in ruling on the admissibility of business records. The Code proceeds from the assumption that it is the proponent who must convince the judge that the record is sufficiently trustworthy to be received in evidence.[32] The Rules, on the other hand, assume that records made in the course of regularly conducted activity will be taken as admissible unless the opponent convinces the judge that the sources of information or other circumstances "indicate a lack of trustworthiness."[33]

QUESTIONS AND PROBLEMS

1.   In order to assure the reliability of business records, the Code and the Rules require the proponent to call as the authenticating witnesses the persons who prepared the records. True or false?

2.   Because *Palmer* was a United States Supreme Court decision, neither California nor federal judges may allow the use of business records prepared by a party or at a party's direction in connection with the case in which they are offered. True or false?

3.   Because the hearsay exception for business records contemplates their creation by a business, records of non-profit organizations, such as religious institutions, do not qualify under the exception. True or false?

4.   Only records created in the regular course of business fall within the hearsay exception. Accordingly, accident reports required by law to filed with the California Department of Motor Vehicles are admissible under the exception. True or false?

5.   Both the Code and the Rules empower a judge to exclude a business record otherwise satisfying the conditions of admissibility if the judge finds that the sources of information and the method and time of preparation do not indicate trustworthiness. Under the Code, the proponent has the burden of persuading the judge of the record's trustworthiness. Under the Rules, the opponent has the burden of persuading the judge of the record's untrustworthiness. True or false?

§ 10.04 BUSINESS RECORDS
AND THE OPINION RULE

Whether opinions in business records can be received as part of the record depends initially on the application of the opinion rule. In California and federal courts, a lay witness may not testify in the form of an

---

30.   See Yates v. Bair Transport, Inc., 249 F.Supp. 681 (S.D.N.Y.1965) and cases cited therein.

31.   Id.

32.   West's Ann.California Evidence Code §§ 1271(d) and 405 (comment).

33.   Federal Rule of Evidence 803(6) and Advisory Committee Note.

opinion unless the opinion is rationally based on the witness's perception and is helpful to a clear understanding of the witness's testimony.[1] An officer's statement in a police report that "it was raining" would qualify. His conclusion would be based on his own perception and would surely help the fact finder understand the officer's perception of the weather conditions.

An expert, on the other hand, may not testify in the form of an opinion unless (1) the expert is qualified to give the opinion and (2) the fact finder needs the opinion in resolving important factual issues.[2] In a personal injury case, for example, an important question may be whether the injuries suffered by the plaintiff are permanent. It is unlikely that a jury listening to the plaintiff's complaints can resolve this issue. An opinion by a qualified physician would help. Accordingly, such an opinion in a medical report otherwise admissible under the exception would be admissible.

The point is that nothing in the exception for business records favors or disfavors opinions.[3] Whether a particular opinion is admissible depends on whether it would be admissible through the hearsay declarant if the declarant testified at the hearing.

The California courts, however, have taken a more restrictive approach. Opinions in business records should be limited to readily observable acts, events or conditions.[4] Thus, an opinion that the plaintiff suffered a broken leg should be admitted, but not an opinion that he suffers from a psychiatric condition.[5] The former opinion is a record of what the person making the diagnosis has observed while the latter is a conclusion reached by the psychiatrist after considering many factors.[6] The lengthier the thought process required to reach an opinion, the greater the need for cross examining the hearsay declarant.[7]

---

1. West's Ann.California Evidence Code § 800. Federal Rule of Evidence 701. Section 800 also permits lay witnesses to testify in the form of an opinion to the extent "permitted by law." West's Ann.California Evidence Code § 800.

2. West's Ann.California Evidence Code § 801. Federal Rule of Evidence 702. For a discussion of the admissibility of expert opinion and scientific evidence, see Chapter 16 infra.

3. Federal Rule of Evidence 803(6) includes an "opinion or diagnosis" among the matters that are admissible in business records. But the fact that they are admissible does not mean that in fact they must be admitted in a given record.

4. People v. Reyes, 12 Cal.3d 486, 502–504, 116 Cal.Rptr. 217, 227–228, 526 P.2d 225, 235–236 (1974). See also People v. Campos, 32 Cal.App.4th 304, 307–308, 38 Cal.Rptr.2d 113, 114–115 (1995) (holding that records containing opinions concerning the accused's mental state were not admissible as business or official records of acts, conditions, or events); Godfrey v. Steinpress, 128 Cal.App.3d 154, 184, 180 Cal.Rptr. 95, 111 (1982) (holding that a doctor's opinion regarding the cause of a patient's headaches was inadmissible under the business records exception to the hearsay rule).

5. People v. Reyes, 12 Cal.3d 486, 502–504, 116 Cal.Rptr. 217, 227–228, 526 P.2d 225, 235–236 (1974).

6. Id. See also People v. Beeler, 9 Cal.4th 953, 980–981, 39 Cal.Rptr.2d 607, 623 891 P.2d 153, 169 (1995), cert. denied, 516 U.S. 1053, 116 S.Ct. 723, 133 L.Ed.2d 675 (1996).

7. People v. Reyes, 12 Cal.3d 486, 502–504, 116 Cal.Rptr. 217, 227–228, 526 P.2d 225, 235–236 (1974).

The Federal Rules take a more expansive approach. Opinions may be admitted as part of business records if such opinions would be admissible through the hearsay declarant as a witness.[8]

QUESTIONS AND PROBLEMS

1.   Because Federal Rule of Evidence 803(6) expressly refers to opinions among the matters that are admissible in business records, such opinions are admissible in federal court. True or false?

2.   In the absence of judicial limitations, opinions in business records should be as admissible in California courts as they are in federal courts. True or false?

3.   Officer Jones investigated an accident occurring on Main Street. He measured skid marks left by Smith's car and found them to be 40 feet. In his report which he prepared shortly after the investigation, Jones made the following entries: "I measured the skid marks left by Smith's car and found them to be 40 feet. Since the posted speed limit on Main Street is 30 MPH, in my opinion Smith was speeding at the time of the accident." The plaintiff, who was injured when Smith hit him with his car, offers these portions of Jones' report in evidence. Smith objects on hearsay grounds and the opinion rule. How should a California or federal judge rule?

§ 10.05   BUSINESS RECORDS AND COMPUTER EVIDENCE

The same principles that govern the admissibility of business records apply to computer printouts and other computer generated information. Their reliability, too, stems from the sources of information used and the method and time of preparation.[1]

With respect to the method used, the California courts have rejected a "test requiring the proponent of computer evidence to introduce testimony on the acceptability and reliability of the particular hardware and

---

8.   Federal Rule of Evidence 803(6).

1.   In determining whether the entry in the computer printout was made at or near time of the event entered, the courts "consider the length of time between the act, condition, or event and the date of its recording, not the date of its eventual retrieval by computer printout." People v. Martinez, 22 Cal.4th 106, 126, 91 Cal.Rptr.2d 687, 702, 990 P.2d 563, 577 (2000).

Some computer generated documents are outside the scope of the hearsay rule. Computer generated records that fall within the verbal acts doctrine may be offered without violating the hearsay rule. In a breach of contract action, for example, the plaintiff may offer the contract entered into by the parties without violating the hearsay rule, even if a computer was used to generate the contract. See § 5.04 supra. Moreover, a record generated by a computer showing its internal operations (for example, when the computer was last accessed by a particular user) is not subject to a hearsay exception. Machine generated information is not hearsay. See § 5.06 supra. See also People v. Hawkins, 98 Cal.App.4th 1428, 1450, 121 Cal.Rptr.2d 627, 643 (2002): "As the trial judge in this case perceived, the true test for admissibility of a printout reflecting a computer's internal operations is not whether the printout was made in the regular course of business, but whether the computer was operating properly at the time of the printout. The trial court did not err in rejecting defendant's hearsay objection and admitting the printouts into evidence."

software, as well as internal maintenance and accuracy checks, as a prerequisite to admissibility under Evidence Code section 1271."[2] It is not necessary for the proponent to call as the custodian a computer expert who can personally perform the programming, inspect and maintain the software and hardware, and compare competing products.[3] Instead, it is enough for the proponent to call a "person who generally understands the system's operation and possesses sufficient knowledge and skill to properly use the system and explain the resultant data, even if unable to perform every task from initial design and programming to final printout * * *."[4]

The opposing party, however, may offer evidence of the unreliability of the hardware and software, as well as of its misuse, to prove the printout's untrustworthiness. Even where the opposing party is unsuccessful in barring the use of the printout, the evidence may be useful to the fact finder in assessing the weight to give to the printout.

Computers can be a powerful tool in gathering and assembling evidence. But as one commentator has noted, computer evidence can be unreliable:

> Computerized information is the product of a system that includes the people and the bureaucracy that gathers the information and runs the computers. The entire processing system, including not only the computer hardware and software but also the people and the agency involved, must be considered in evaluating the reliability of computerized information. Reliability problems may arise from many sources. Computerized information may be wrong, incomplete, or misleading due to mechanical failure, mistake, fraud, or bias. Ultimately, people are responsible for any errors, and there are infinite ways in which people can make mistakes, commit fraud or reflect bias. Broad discovery may be necessary to track down the reliability problems and evaluate the reliability of the computerized information.[5]

The exception for business records assumes that the record consists of a "writing".[6] Both the Code and the Rules define a writing broadly to embrace computer printouts and other representations.[7] As writings, computer printouts are subject in federal courts to the Best Evidence Rule, which requires the use of the original of a writing to prove the contents of the writing unless production of the original writing is excused,[8] and in California courts to the Secondary Evidence Rule, which

---

2. People v. Lugashi, 205 Cal.App.3d 632, 637, 252 Cal.Rptr. 434, 438 (1988).

3. Id. at 640, 252 Cal.Rptr. at 440.

4. Id.

5. Garcia, *"Garbage In, Gospel Out": Criminal Discovery, Computer Reliability, and the Constitution*, 88 UCLA Law Review 1043, 1073 (1991) (footnotes omitted). See also People v. Hernandez, 55 Cal.App.4th 225, 241, 63 Cal.Rptr.2d 769, 779 (1997): "In other words, the fact that hearsay evidence is put into a log and then again into a computer in the normal course of business does not render such evidence nonhearsay when it is retrieved from the computer even when most of the requirements of Evidence Code section 1271 are met."

6. West's Ann.California Evidence Code § 1271.

7. West's Ann.California Evidence Code §§ 250–251; Federal Rule of Evidence 1001(1).

8. Federal Rule of Evidence 1002.

allows the use of a true copy of a duly authenticated original to prove the contents of the original document.[9] The fact that a printout may be the output of diverse data fed into a computer can raise questions as to whether the printout is the "original". To minimize these concerns, in California § 1552 creates a presumption that "a printed representation of computer information or a computer program is presumed to be an accurate representation of the computer information or computer program it purports to represent."[10] Combined with § 255, which defines computer printouts as originals, these provisions satisfy the Secondary Evidence Rule and replace the requirements of authentication.[11] The presumption created by § 1552 affects only the burden of producing evidence. If the opposing party introduces evidence that the printed representation of the computer information or computer program is inaccurate or unreliable, the proponent must convince the judge by a preponderance of the evidence that the printed representation is an accurate representation of the existence and content of the computer information or computer program it purports to represent. Otherwise, the judge must exclude the exhibit.[12]

The Federal Rules provide that if data are stored in a computer or similar device, any printout or other output readable by sight, shown to reflect data accurately, is an "original."[13] The Rules also provide that the printout or other output can be authenticated by evidence describing the process or system used to produce the output and showing that the process or system produces an accurate result.[14]

§ 10.06 THE ABSENCE OF ENTRIES IN BUSINESS RECORDS

Just as entries in business records may be used to prove the occurrence of an act or event, or the existence of a condition, the absence of such entries may be offered to prove their nonoccurrence or nonexistence. A creditor, for example, may prove nonpayment by evidence that his records do not reflect that payment was received. The use of records for this purpose may not violate the hearsay rule. The creditor, for example, probably does not intend his failure to make a payment entry to substitute for the statement that the debtor has failed to make the payment.[1] Most likely, the creditor did not make the entry because no payment was received. But because the question has not been free of controversy, the Law Revision Commission opted for creating a hearsay exception for the absence of entries.[2]

---

9. West's Ann.California Evidence Code § 1520–1521. For an extended discussion of the Best Evidence and Secondary Evidence Rules, see § 13.05 infra.

10. West's Ann.California Evidence Code § 1552. There is no federal analogue to § 1552.

11. West' Ann.California Evidence Code § 255. For a discussion of these concepts, see § 13.07 infra.

12. Id.

13. Federal Rule of Evidence 1001(3).

14. Federal Rule of Evidence 901(b)(9).

1. For a discussion of when conduct constitutes hearsay, see § 5.05 supra.

2. West's Ann.California Evidence Code § 1271 and comment.

Section 1272 provides that evidence of the "absence from the records of a business of a record of an asserted act, condition, or event is not made inadmissible by the hearsay rule when offered to prove the nonoccurrence of the act or event, or the nonexistence of the condition, if: (a) [i]t was the regular course of that business to make records of all such acts, conditions, or events at or near the time of the act, condition, or event and to preserve them; and (b) [t]he sources of information and method and time of preparation of the records of that business were such that the absence of a record of an act, condition, or event is a trustworthy indication that the act or event did not occur or the condition did not exist."[3]

The Federal Rules of Evidence contain a similar provision.[4] Under the Federal Rules, testimony that a particular record does not contain an entry does not violate the Best Evidence Rule.[5] The Code is silent on this point. Since such evidence tends to prove the contents of the writing indirectly, an argument can be made that the evidence violates the rule.[6] Of course, proving the absence of the entry by offering the record is subject to the Secondary Evidence Rule in California and the Best Evidence Rule in federal courts.[7]

QUESTIONS AND PROBLEMS

Proving the nonoccurrence of an event through the absence of an appropriate entry in a business record violates the hearsay rule because such an offer is tantamount to the entrant's statement, "The event did not occur." Accordingly, both the Code and the Rules create a hearsay exception for such situations. Discuss.

§ 10.07 OFFICIAL RECORDS

Official records under the Code. Section 1280 creates a hearsay exception for official records.[1] It requires the same showing of trustworthiness that is required for business records under § 1271.[2] One of the justifications for the official records exception is similar to the one advanced for business records: to eliminate the need to call all of the

---

3. West's Ann.California Evidence Code § 1272.

4. Federal Rule of Evidence 803(7) and Advisory Committee Note.

5. Federal Rule of Evidence 1002 (Advisory Committee Note).

6. In California the Secondary Evidence Rule requires the proponent of a writing to prove the contents of the writing by the original of the writing or a duly authenticated copy unless production of the writing is excused. See West's Ann.California Evidence Code § 1520–1521. Oral proof of the contents of the writing is inadmissible unless certain conditions are satisfied. See West's Ann.California Evidence Code § 1523.

7. West's Ann.California Evidence Code § 1523; Federal Rule of Evidence 1002.

1. West's Ann.California Evidence Code § 1280.

2. Id. (comment).

witnesses who participated in the creation of the record.[3] The witnesses called to authenticate the record and to lay the foundation for the hearsay exception do not need to have personal knowledge of the facts contained in the record. Neither do the employees who make the entries. But the proponent does have to show that the entries offered are based on information supplied by public employees with first hand knowledge of the facts and a duty to report them accurately.[4] The proponent, moreover, must show that those making the entries had a duty to enter those facts and to do so accurately,[5] and that the entries were made at or near the time of the acts, conditions, or events recorded.[6]

Section 1280 differs from § 1271 in one significant respect. Where § 1271 requires that the record be made in the regular course of business,[7] § 1280 requires that the record be "made by and within the scope of duty of a public employee * * *."[8]

Evidence that is admissible under § 1280 may also be admissible as a business record under § 1271. But as the California Law Revision Commission pointed out:

> Section 1271 requires a witness to testify as to the identity of the record and its mode of preparation in every instance. In contrast, Section 1280 * * * permits the court to admit an official record or report without necessarily requiring a witness to testify as to its identity and mode of preparation if the court takes judicial notice or if sufficient independent evidence shows that the record or report was prepared in such a manner as to assure its trustworthiness.[9]

Amendments to the Code have overtaken this comment. Under some circumstances, business records may be admitted without calling a custodian or other qualified witness.[10] A sufficient affidavit can satisfy the

---

3. See Bhatt v. Department of Health Services for State, 133 Cal.App.4th 923, 929, 35 Cal.Rptr.3d 335, 339 (2005).

4. See People v. Flaxman, 74 Cal.App.3d Supp. 16, 20, 141 Cal.Rptr. 799, 801 (1977). A public employee can include the employees of a private firm acting as a fiscal agent for a public agency. See also Bhatt v. Department of Health Services for State, 133 Cal.App.4th 923, 929, 35 Cal.Rptr.3d 335, 340 (2005).

5. Gananian v. Zolin, 33 Cal.App.4th 634, 640, 39 Cal.Rptr.2d 384, 387 (1995).

6. West's Ann. California Evidence Code § 1280(b). If the entry is not timely, the court should reject the official record as untrustworthy. See Gregory v. State Bd. of Control, 73 Cal.App.4th 584, 597, 86 Cal.Rptr.2d 575, 582 (1999).

7. See § 10.03 supra.

8. West's Ann.California Evidence Code § 1280. A report prepared by a "forensic alcohol trainee" is not made by and within the scope of duty of a public employee where the applicable regulations require a forensic alcohol supervisor or analyst to supervise the tests performed by the trainee and the proponent fails to offer evidence of such supervision. Shea v. Department of Motor Vehicles, 62 Cal.App.4th 1057, 1060, 72 Cal.Rptr.2d 896, 897 (1998). Moreover, the results of an alcohol forensic analysis are not admissible as part of an official record, where the proponent fails to show that the technician doing the analysis was under a duty to perform the analysis or that the employee making the entry was under a duty to make the entry and to do so accurately. Furman v. Department of Motor Vehicles, 100 Cal.App.4th 416, 422–423, 122 Cal.Rptr.2d 520, 525 (2002).

9. West's Ann.California Evidence Code § 1280 (comment).

10. See § 10.03 supra.

evidentiary foundation.[11] Whether a judge can judicially notice the identity of an official record and its mode of preparation depends not on § 1280 but on the limits imposed by the Code on judicial notice.[12]

Because the same showing of trustworthiness is required of official records as of business records, the limitations imposed on business records apply to official ones as well. Official records are equally subject to the opinion rule[13] and the rule requiring those who impart information to the preparer to be under a duty to provide such information. In People v. Baeske,[14] for example, a police report offered to prove a license number was excluded because the individual who provided the number was "not a public employee with any duty either to observe facts correctly or to report her observations accurately to the police department."[15] But as in the case of business records, other hearsay exceptions may supply the required reliability. In Jackson v. Department of Motor Vehicles[16] the issue was the admissibility of a statement in a police report in which the plaintiff admitted driving a car. Although the officer who took the statement did not see who drove the car, the statement was nonetheless admitted for the truth of the matter stated. The plaintiff's statement fell within the admissions exception to the hearsay rule, and the officer had first hand knowledge of what the plaintiff said as well as a duty to record the information.[17] As in the case of business records, the entrant does not have to have first hand knowledge of the information contained in the official record. If the exception's other requirements are satisfied, the trustworthiness requirement can be established by showing that the official record is based upon the observations of public employees who have a duty to observe the facts recorded and to report their observations correctly.[18]

---

11. Id.

12. For a discussion of the limits of judicial notice, see § 19.01 infra. For a discussion of how judicial notice and presumptions established a traffic survey as an official record, see People v. Flaxman, 74 Cal.App.3d Supp. 16, 141 Cal.Rptr. 799 (1977); of how they established a California Law Enforcement Telecommunications System (CLETS) computer printout as an official record, see People v. Dunlap, 18 Cal.App.4th 1468, 23 Cal.Rptr.2d 204 (1993); of how an abstract of judgment, combined with the presumption that an official duty has been performed, supports the inference that the accused has served a prison term for purposes of sentence enhancement under California Penal Code § 667.5, see People v. Tenner, 6 Cal.4th 559, 24 Cal.Rptr.2d 840, 862 P.2d 840 (1993).

13. See § 10.04 supra.

14. 58 Cal.App.3d 775, 130 Cal.Rptr. 35 (1976).

15. Id. at 780, 130 Cal.Rptr. at 35. See also People v. Hernandez, 55 Cal.App.4th 225, 240–241, 63 Cal.Rptr.2d 769, 779 (1997) (A computer printout which was prepared by a crime analyst from police reports and which identified the accused as the probable perpetrator of the rapes being tried was inadmissible as an official or business record, as the persons who furnished the information contained in the reports were under no duty to do so.); Behr v. County of Santa Cruz, 172 Cal.App.2d 697, 704, 342 P.2d 987, 992 (1959); § 10.02 supra.

16. 22 Cal.App.4th 730, 27 Cal.Rptr.2d 712 (1994).

17. Id. at 739, 27 Cal.Rptr.2d at 718. See also Rupf v. Yan, 85 Cal.App.4th 411, 431, 102 Cal.Rptr.2d 157, 172 (2000) (A party's admissions to a police officer incorporated by the officer into his report are admissible if the report meets the requirements of the official record's exception to the hearsay rule.).

18. People v. Baeske, 58 Cal.App.3d 775, 780, 130 Cal.Rptr. 35, 39 (1976).

Official records under the Federal Rules. The federal approach to official records departs from that of the Code in two significant respects. First, the Rules limit the admissibility of such records when offered against the accused in criminal cases, and, second, the Rules expand the admissibility of reports containing opinions in civil cases and in criminal cases when offered against the government.

Criminal cases. Federal Rule of Evidence 803(8)(A)(ii) creates a hearsay exception for a record or statement of a public office if it sets out a matter observed while under a legal duty to report, but not including, in a criminal case, a matter observed by law-enforcement personnel and neither the source of information nor other circumstances indicate a lack of trustworthiness.[19] In United States v. Oates[20] the Second Circuit held that this provision required excluding a government chemist's report offered against the accused. Reasoning that the chemist was a member of the law enforcement team, the court concluded that the report fell within the prohibition of the rule.[21]

The government contended that the use of the report was proper because the report also satisfied the federal exception for business records.[22] While not denying that the report qualified as a business record,[23] the Second Circuit rejected the government's argument.[24] In the court's view, extensive amendments by Congress to the exception for official records evidenced Congress' concern with trying criminal defendants by police report. Though not holding that the use of the chemist's report would violate the accused's right of confrontation,[25] the court refused to permit the government to circumvent the balance struck by Congress in Rule 803(8) by allowing the government to resort to other hearsay exceptions.[26] Other circuits, though not all, have embraced *Oates*.[27]

Some circuits have drawn a distinction between reports prepared by law enforcement personnel who were in an adversarial position to the accused and those prepared by personnel who were indifferent to the accused. In United States v. Orozco,[28] for example, the Ninth Circuit

---

19. Federal Rule of Evidence 803(8)(A)(ii).

20. 560 F.2d 45 (2d Cir.1977), on remand, 445 F.Supp. 351 (E.D.N.Y.1978), aff'd, 591 F.2d 1332 (2d Cir.1978).

21. Id. at 67–68.

22. Id. at 74.

23. Id. at 75.

24. Id. at 78.

25. Id. at 80.

26. Id. at 84. The Second Circuit, however, has retreated somewhat from this position. In United States v. Yakobov, 712 F.2d 20 (2d Cir.1983), it held that *Oates* did not preclude the government from offering a record to prove the absence of an entry under Federal Rule of Evidence 803(10), even though the record was inadmissible as an official record. Id. at 25–27.

27. United States v. Cain, 615 F.2d 380 (5th Cir.1980). The Seventh Circuit agrees but would allow the use of another hearsay exception if the preparer of the record takes the stand. United States v. King, 613 F.2d 670 (7th Cir.1980). The Eighth Circuit allows the use of other hearsay exceptions. United States v. Baker, 855 F.2d 1353 (8th Cir.1988), cert. denied, 490 U.S. 1069, 109 S.Ct. 2072, 104 L.Ed.2d 636 (1989).

28. 590 F.2d 789 (9th Cir.1979), cert. denied, 439 U.S. 1049, 99 S.Ct. 728, 58 L.Ed.2d 709 (1978).

upheld the use of border crossing cards prepared by immigration officials to prove that a car registered to the accused had crossed from Mexico into the United States shortly before narcotics were found in the car. While conceding that the immigration officials could be deemed law enforcement personnel, the court nonetheless upheld the use of the cards on the ground that they were trustworthy.[29] The cards had been prepared as part of a routine practice and at a time when the government and its agents were not in an adversarial position vis-à-vis the accused.[30]

Civil cases. Federal Rule of Evidence 803(8)(A)(iii) creates a hearsay exception for a record or statement of a public office if it sets out in a civil case or against the government in a criminal case, factual findings from a legally authorized investigation and neither the source of information nor other circumstances indicate a lack of trustworthiness.[31] The broad scope of this exception was examined by the United States Supreme Court in Beech Aircraft Corp. v. Rainey,[32] a wrongful death action brought by the spouses of two pilots killed in an aircraft accident against the manufacturer of the plane. The plaintiffs' theory was that the accident had been caused by engine failure. The manufacturer countered that the accident had been caused by pilot error. The question before the Court was the admissibility of a Judge Advocate General's report in which the investigator concluded, among other matters, that the "most probable cause of the accident was the pilots [sic] failure to maintain proper interval."[33]

In upholding the admissibility of the report, the Court rejected the argument that the "factual findings" contemplated by the rule excluded factually based conclusions or opinions:[34] "portions of investigatory reports otherwise admissible under Rule (8)(C) are not inadmissible merely because they state a conclusion or opinion. As long as the conclusion is based on a factual investigation and satisfies the Rule's trustworthiness requirement, it should be admissible along with other portions of the report."[35]

The Advisory Committee lists four factors federal judges should consider in determining the reliability of investigative reports: (1) the timeliness of the investigation, (2) the investigator's skill or experience, (3) whether a hearing was held and the level at which conducted, and (4)

---

29. Id. at 793–794. This provision allows defendants in criminal cases to offer factual findings in investigative reports against the government. But it does not authorize the government to offer such findings against defendants in criminal cases. Accordingly, this provision was unavailable to the government in *Oates* to justify the admission of the chemist's report.

30. Id.

31. Federal Rule of Evidence 803(8).

32. 488 U.S. 153, 109 S.Ct. 439, 102 L.Ed.2d 445 (1988), on remand, 868 F.2d 1531 (11th Cir.1989).

33. Id. at 157, 109 S.Ct. at 443.

34. Id. at 164, 109 S.Ct. at 447.

35. Id. at 170, 109 S.Ct. at 450. The Court declined to rule on the admissibility of conclusions of law under the Rules. Id. at 170, note 13, 109 S.Ct. at 450, note 13. Note that former Rule 803(8)(C) is now Rule 803(8)(A)(ii).

possible bias when reports are prepared with a view to possible litigation.[36]

In reaching its decision, the Court was influenced by the Rules' approach to admissibility. Under the exceptions for business and official records, admissibility is assumed in the first instance unless the opponent raises serious questions of reliability.[37] Under the Code, it is the proponent who must satisfy the judge that the business or official record is trustworthy.[38]

Would such a report be admissible in California? In Elsworth v. Beech Aircraft Corp.[39] the judge admitted a report of a Congressional committee which in turn referred to a study prepared by an employee of the General Accounting Office. The study stated that the FAA had considered withdrawing Beech's authorization to participate in an airworthiness certification process because Beech had failed to comply with enumerated obligations imposed by the FAA. The California Supreme Court held that the study was inadmissible.[40] The holding, however, is not dispositive of the question. Because the court found, among other matters, that the proponent had failed to produce evidence of the author's identity,[41] it held that the judge lacked a basis for finding that the study was prepared from sources of information indicating trustworthiness.[42]

A better guide to the admissibility of "factual findings" in California can be found in the court's approach to the admissibility of opinions in business or official records. As has been discussed,[43] the court has taken a cautious approach. The court has not taken the unequivocal position that opinions in records should be admissible if the opinion satisfies the conditions of admissibility imposed by the opinion rule.[44] Rather, the court seems to favor a rule limiting opinions in records to readily observable acts, events, or conditions.[45] In People v. Reyes[46] the court suggested that an opinion that an individual suffered a broken leg should be admitted but not an opinion that he suffers from a psychiatric condition.[47] In the court's view, the lengthier the thought process required to reach an opinion or conclusion, the greater the need for cross examining the

---

36. Federal Rule of Evidence 803(8) (Advisory Committee Note); see also, Beech Aircraft Corp. v. Rainey, 488 U.S. 153, 168, note 11, 109 S.Ct. 439, 450, note 11, 102 L.Ed.2d 445 (1988), on remand, 868 F.2d 1531 (11th Cir.1989).

37. Federal Rule of Evidence 803(8) (Advisory Committee Note).

38. See West's Ann.California Evidence Code §§ 1271(d) and 1280(c) and 405.

39. 37 Cal.3d 540, 208 Cal.Rptr. 874, 691 P.2d 630 (1984), cert. denied, 471 U.S. 1110, 105 S.Ct. 2345, 85 L.Ed.2d 861 (1985).

40. Id. at 553, 208 Cal.Rptr. at 882, 691 P.2d at 638.

41. Id.

42. Id.

43. See § 10.04 supra.

44. Elsworth v. Beech Aircraft Corp., 37 Cal.3d 540, 553, 208 Cal.Rptr. 874, 882, 691 P.2d 630, 638 (1984), cert. denied, 471 U.S. 1110, 105 S.Ct. 2345, 85 L.Ed.2d 861 (1985).

45. Id.

46. 12 Cal.3d 486, 116 Cal.Rptr. 217, 526 P.2d 225 (1974).

47. Id. at 502–504, 116 Cal.Rptr. at 227–228, 526 P.2d at 235–236.

hearsay declarant.[48] Applying this test, a judge might well conclude that findings or opinions based on extensive investigations should not be received through an official or business record. Perhaps, this is why early cases expressed the view that " 'records of investigations and inquiries conducted either voluntarily or pursuant to requirement of law by public officers concerning causes and effects, and involving the exercise of judgment and discretion, expression of opinion, and the making of conclusions, are not admissible in evidence as public records.' "[49]

The type of hearing at which a written expert opinion is offered can make a difference with regard to the admissibility of the opinion. In *Gordon v. Havasu Palms, Inc.*[50] a pilot sued a runway owner for injuries he sustained when he crashed on the runway. In support of its motion for summary judgment, the runway owner submitted two affidavits from professional pilots with extensive backgrounds in light aircraft operations. The affiants concluded that the cause of the accident was pilot error. The plaintiff countered with a declaration by a similarly experienced pilot who concluded that the conditions of the runway contributed to the cause of the accident. Finding that the opinions of the experts complied with the rules regarding the use of expert testimony and raised a triable issue of fact, the appellate court reversed the order granting the motion for summary judgment.[51] Unlike *Ellsworth*, however, the written expert opinions were not offered at a trial but at a hearing on a motion (summary judgment) which expressly authorizes the use of affidavits and declarations. Presumably, at the trial, over a hearsay objection, the parties would be compelled in California to call the experts to the stand where they could be cross examined under oath before the trier of fact on their opinions.

Convictions. Sometimes a party has to prove that a particular person has suffered a conviction. Some crimes, for example, are punished more heavily if at the time the accused committed the crime charged, he had already been convicted of enumerated offenses. Under the California Penal Code, persons who commit misdemeanor petty theft can be charged with felony theft if at the time of the theft they had previously been convicted and served time for petty theft.[52] Where in addition to pleading not guilty a defendant denies the truth of the allegation charging the prior conviction, the prosecution is obligated to prove the conviction as well as the offense charged. In these circumstances, the prosecution may rely on the business or official records exception to the hearsay rule to prove the fact of conviction. The fact of conviction recited in the record is hearsay since the recitation is an out of court statement offered to prove the truth of the matter asserted, namely, that on a particular date and in a

---

48. Id.

49. See, e.g., Pruett v. Burr, 118 Cal.App.2d 188, 200, 257 P.2d 690, 698 (1953), quoting from 20 American Jurisprudence § 1027 at 866.

50. 93 Cal.App.4th 244, 112 Cal.Rptr.2d 816 (2001).

51. Id. at 252–254, 112 Cal.Rptr.2d at 822–824.

52. West's Ann. California Penal Code § 666.

particular court the person named in the recitation was convicted of the offense specified in the record.[53]

Some penal statutes call for an enhanced punishment if the accused is found to have served time for a previous conviction. In addition to the Evidence Code amendment, the Penal Code authorizes a prosecutor to prove the incarceration element by offering certified copies of the penal institutions' records.[54] However, the availability of this exception does not preclude the prosecution from relying on other hearsay exceptions, such as the official records exception, to prove the incarceration element.[55]

The use of records of convictions to prove the fact of conviction must be distinguished from the use of those records to prove the misconduct giving rise to the conviction. Neither the business nor official records exceptions to the hearsay rule can be used to the prove the misconduct that gave rise to the conviction.[56] Resort must be made to other hearsay exceptions that expressly allow the use of the records for that hearsay purpose. Both the Code and the Rules contain limited hearsay exceptions for judgments of conviction offered to prove the underlying misconduct.[57]

QUESTIONS AND PROBLEMS

1. Suppose that the expert in *Rainey* had concluded that the pilot had been negligent. Does the case approve of using such a finding under the Federal Rules?

2. As construed, the Rules take a more cautious approach to the admissibility of opinions in business and official records than does the Code as construed. True or false?

3. In a federal prosecution filed in the Second Circuit, may a prosecutor rely on the business records exception in offering a report prepared by a government chemist in the regular course of his duties stating that the substance removed from the accused was heroin?

---

53. In California an amendment to the Evidence Code expressly provides that an official record may include a certified copy of a conviction record that is offered "to prove the commission, attempted commission, or solicitation of a criminal offense, service of a prison term, or other act, condition or event recorded in the record." See West's Ann. California Evidence Code § 452.5. This provision can be used to prove the misconduct giving rise to the conviction where the prosecution must prove the misconduct and not just the fact of conviction. See § 7.09 supra.

54. West's Ann. California Penal Code § 969b.

55. People v. Martinez, 22 Cal.4th 106, 119, 91 Cal.Rptr.2d 687, 697, 990 P.2d 563, 573–574(2000) (holding that a CLETS printout offered met the official records requirements).

56. A conviction record that merely enumerates the Penal Code sections of which the accused has been convicted does not necessarily disclose whether the accused inflicted serious injury in the course of violating those sections. In these circumstances, even Evidence Code § 452.5 would not authorize the use of the record to prove that the accused inflicted such an injury. For a discussion of this point, see § 7.09 supra.

57. See, e.g., West's Ann. California Evidence Code §§ 452.5 and 1300; Federal Rule of Evidence 803(22). For a discussion of this point, see §§ 12.03 and 15.07 infra. See also People v. Duran, 97 Cal.App.4th 1448, 1461, 119 Cal.Rptr.2d 272, 282 (2002), holding that § 452.5 "creates a hearsay exception allowing admission of qualifying court records to prove not only the fact of conviction, but also that the offense reflected in the record occurred."

4.   In a similar case filed in the Ninth Circuit, may the prosecutor rely on the official records exception in offering a record prepared by U.S. Customs officers in the regular course of their duties stating that a car, other evidence shows was registered to the defendant, crossed the Mexico–U.S. border?

§ 10.08   BUSINESS AND OFFICIAL RECORDS AND THE CONFRONTATION CLAUSE

Forensic evidence. Crawford v. Washington[1] raises the question whether the prosecution's use of documentary forensic evidence violates the accused's confrontation rights. In *Crawford*, the United States Supreme Court held that, over a hearsay objection, testimonial hearsay may not be offered against the accused unless (1) the hearsay declarant is produced for cross-examination by the accused or (2) if not produced, unless the accused was given an opportunity prior to the trial to cross examine the hearsay declarant.[2] The Sixth Amendment issue arises whenever the prosecution offers fingerprint analysis reports, autopsy reports, serology reports, drug analysis reports, DNA reports, and the like to link the accused with the crime charged or to prove some other element of the offense. The classic example is the drug analysis report which is offered to prove that the substance taken from the accused is an illegal drug. Establishing that the substance is an illegal drug is one of the elements which the prosecution must prove in order to obtain a conviction. If the technician who performed the drug analysis is not produced at the trial for cross-examination and instead his report is offered in evidence, is the accused deprived of the opportunity to confront a key prosecution witness?

In Melendez–Diaz v. Massachusetts,[3] the Court held that the prosecution's use of affidavits by drug analysts to establish that material seized by the police and connected to the defendant was cocaine violated the defendant's confrontation rights.[4] Since the drug analysts' statements amounted to the kind of testimony they would have given against the defendant if called by the prosecution at the drug trial, the Court found that the affidavits comprised testimonial hearsay under *Crawford*. "Absent a showing that the analysts were unavailable to testify at trial *and* that petitioner had a prior opportunity to cross-examine them, petitioner was entitled to 'be confronted with' the analysts at trial."[5]

Prior to *Melendez–Diaz*, the lower courts, both state and federal, were divided over whether the use of forensic reports violated the accused's confrontation rights.[6] Some held that these reports were testimonial, since

---

1.   541 U.S. 36, 124 S.Ct. 1354, 158 L.Ed.2d 177 (2004).

2.   Id. at 1370.

3.   557 U.S. 305, 129 S.Ct. 2527, 174 L.Ed.2d 314 (2009).

4.   Id. at 2540.

5.   Id. at 2532 (emphasis in the original).

6.   See cases cited in People v. Geier, 41 Cal.4th 555, 598, 161 P.3d 104, 134, 61 Cal.Rptr.3d 580, 615 (2007).

the reports are prepared for possible use against the accused at the trial.[7] Others, including California's, did not consider these types of reports to be testimonial. These courts emphasized that reports that merely convey a scientific conclusion ("the substance tested turned out to be cocaine") and describe the steps taken to reach the conclusion are not the type of testimonial statements that concerned the Court in *Crawford*.[8] Some of these courts underscored that the preparer of the report is a neutral party who analyzes evidence but is not actively engaged in gathering evidence; these courts also pointed out that forensic reports can exonerate as well as incriminate the accused.[9] Some courts favoring admissibility worried about the practicable difficulties that would result if the forensic reports could be excluded on confrontation grounds. The prosecution would be forced to call as witnesses the person or persons who prepared the reports.[10]

In People v. Geier[11] the California Supreme Court aligned itself with those courts favoring the admissibility of forensic reports. At issue was the admissibility of the testimony of a DNA expert who testified that based on the genetic profiles generated by one of her firm's technicians, DNA samples extracted from the victim's vagina matched a sample of the defendant's DNA. The defendant was on trial for the rape and murder of the victim. In describing the procedures used to make the DNA match, the expert "relied entirely on [the technician's] forms, notes and report and at points quoted or paraphrased statements [the technician] had made in those written records, thus introducing them into evidence. * * * The prosecution thus introduced, through [the expert], hearsay statements of a declarant—[the technician]—who was not present at the trial and whom defendant had no prior opportunity to cross-examine."[12]

In holding that the technician's report was not testimonial, the court said that the report did not describe "a past fact related to criminal activity * * * for possible use at a later trial."[13]

> [The technician's observations constituted] a contemporaneous recordation of observable events rather than the documentation of past events. That is, she recorded her observations regarding the receipt of the DNA samples, her preparation of the samples for analysis, and the results of that analysis as she was actually performing those tasks. "Therefore, when [she] made those observations, [she]—like the de-

---

7. Id.

8. See Commonwealth v. Verde, 444 Mass. 279, 827 N.E.2d 701 (2005), as recounted in People v. Geier, supra note 6.

9. See State v. Forte, 360 N.C. 427, 629 S.E.2d 137 (2006), as recounted in People v. Geier, supra note 6.

10. See State v. Lackey, 280 Kan. 190, 120 P.3d 332 (2005), as recounted in People v. Geier, supra note 6.

11. 41 Cal.4th 555, 598, 161 P.3d 104, 134, 61 Cal.Rptr.3d 580, 615 (2007).

12. Id. at 621, 161 P.3d at 150, 61 Cal.Rptr.3d at 633 (Werdegar concurring opinion).

13. Id. at 605, 161 P.3d at 138, 61 Cal.Rptr.3d at 620.

clarant reporting an emergency in *Davis*—[was] 'not acting as [a] witness; and [was] not testifying.' "[14]

This holding is unlikely to withstand analysis under *Melendez–Diaz.* The United States Supreme Court rejected the dissent's claim that forensic analysts are disinterested unconventional witnesses who are not subject to confrontation.[15] Instead, the Court emphasized the need for the defense to cross examine seemingly neutral forensic experts.

> Forensic evidence is not uniquely immune from the risk of manipulation. According to a recent study conducted under the auspices of the National Academy of Sciences, "[t]he majority of [laboratories producing forensic evidence] are administered by law enforcement agencies, such as police departments, where the laboratory administrator reports to the head of the agency." National Research Council of the National Academies, Strengthening Forensic Science in the United States: A Path Forward 6–1 (Prepublication Copy Feb. 2009) (hereinafter National Academy Report). And "[b]ecause forensic scientists often are driven in their work by a need to answer a particular question related to the issues of a particular case, they sometimes face pressure to sacrifice appropriate methodology for the sake of expediency." *Id.,* at S–17. A forensic analyst responding to a request from a law enforcement official may feel pressure—or have an incentive—to alter the evidence in a manner favorable to the prosecution. Confrontation is one means of assuring accurate forensic analysis. While it is true, as the dissent notes, that an honest analyst will not alter his testimony when forced to confront the defendant, *post,* at 10, the same cannot be said of the fraudulent analyst. See Brief for National Innocence Network as *Amicus Curiae* 15–17 (discussing cases of documented "drylabbing" where forensic analysts report results of tests that were never performed); National Academy Report 1–8 to 1–10 (discussing documented cases of fraud and error involving the use of forensic evidence). Like the eyewitness who has fabricated his account to the police, the analyst who provides false results may, under oath in open court, reconsider his false testimony. See *Coy* v. *Iowa,* 487 U.S. 1012, 1019 (1988). And, of course, the prospect of confrontation will deter fraudulent analysis in the first place. Confrontation is designed to weed out not only the fraudulent analyst, but the incompetent one as well.[16]

In support of its *Grier* holding, the California Supreme Court emphasized that "the accusatory opinions—that defendant's DNA matched the DNA sample taken from the victim's vagina and that such a result was very unlikely unless defendant was the donor—were reached and conveyed, not through the nontestifying technician's laboratory notes and report but by

---

14. Id.

15. Melendez–Diaz v. Massachusetts, 557 U.S. 305, 129 S.Ct. 2527, 174 L.Ed.2d 314 (2009).

16. Id. at 2557.

the testifying [expert]."[17] This circumstance, however, may not withstand analysis under *Melendez–Diaz*. The defense has an interest in using cross-examination to explore, among other matters, whether the technicians who prepared the report were qualified to do their work and whether they followed appropriate protocols in performing it.

Significantly, in *Grier* the California Supreme Court observed that merely because a document qualifies as business record does not render it "nontestimonial since conceivably some such document could contain historical facts."[18] This view accords with that of the United States Supreme Court in *Melendez–Diaz*. The fact that documentary evidence offered by the prosecution qualifies under the forum's evidence rules as a business or official record does not foreclose an inquiry into whether the evidence constitutes testimonial hearsay under the Sixth Amendment.[19]

In *Melendez–Diaz* the Court also rejected the claim that no confrontation violation occurs where the defendant has the power to subpoena the hearsay declarant.

> [T]hat power—whether pursuant to state law or the Compulsory Process Clause—is no substitute for the right of confrontation. Unlike the Confrontation Clause, those provisions are of no use to the defendant when the witness is unavailable or simply refuses to appear. See, *e.g.*, *Davis*, 547 U. S., at 820 ("[The witness] was subpoenaed, but she did not appear at ... trial"). Converting the prosecution's duty under the Confrontation Clause into the defendant's privilege under state law or the Compulsory Process Clause shifts the consequences of adverse-witness no-shows from the State to the accused. More fundamentally, the Confrontation Clause imposes a burden on the prosecution to present its witnesses, not on the defendant to bring those adverse witnesses into court. Its value to the defendant is not replaced by a system in which the prosecution presents its evidence via *ex parte* affidavits and waits for the defendant to subpoena the affiants if he chooses.[20]

Witness statements. The U.S. Supreme Court has not yet ruled on whether statements by percipient witnesses offered against the accused through business or official records violate the accused's confrontation rights. In a related context, however, the Court has held that statements made by witnesses to 911 operators and to police officers at a crime scene may qualify as testimonial if the at the time the information was imparted no emergency existed.

> Statements are nontestimonial when made in the course of police interrogation under circumstances objectively indicating that the pri-

---

17. People v. Grier at 607, 161 P.3d at 140, 61 Cal.Rptr.3d at 621.

18. Id. at 606, note 12, 161 P.3d at 140, note 12, 61 Cal.Rptr.3d at 621, note 12.

19. "Whether or not they qualify as business or official records, the analysts' statements here—prepared specifically for use at petitioner's trial—were testimony against petitioner, and the analysts were subject to confrontation under the Sixth Amendment." Cite to Melendez.

20. Id. at 2540.

mary purpose of the interrogation is to enable police assistance to meet an ongoing emergency. They are testimonial when the circumstances objectively indicate that there is no such ongoing emergency, and that the primary purpose of the interrogation is to establish or prove past events potentially relevant to later criminal prosecution.[21]

Applying this test, the Court held that statements made by a crime victim to police called to the crime scene were testimonial."It is entirely clear from the circumstances that the interrogation was part of an investigation into possibly criminal past conduct. * * * There was no emergency in progress * * *. When the officer questioned [the victim] for the second time, and elicited the challenged statements, he was not seeking to determine (as in *Davis*) 'what is happening,' but rather 'what has happened.' "[22] If such statements qualify as testimonial when related to a police officer, their inclusion in a police report that qualifies as a business or official record would appear to be immaterial. Such statements would still be testimonial.

QUESTIONS AND PROBLEMS

1. In Crawford v. Washington the United States Supreme Court held that, over a confrontation objection, testimonial hearsay may not be offered against the accused unless (1) the hearsay declarant is produced for cross-examination by the accused or (2) if not produced, unless the accused was given an opportunity prior to the trial to cross examine the hearsay declarant. True or false?

2. In *Crawford* the Court also held that statements in business records do not generally qualify as testimonial statements. True or false?

3. Accordingly, if a police chemist's report qualifies as a business record under the California Evidence Code, the prosecution, over a confrontation objection, can offer that portion of the record in which the chemist wrote, "I tested the substance brought to me by the Officer Jones. It tested as heroin." True or false? In answering this question, assume that other evidence establishes that the substance given to the chemist was lawfully taken from the defendant, that the chemist was qualified to conduct the test, and that he performed the appropriate tests. In answering this question, assume also that the accused had not been given an opportunity prior to the trial to cross examine the chemist under oath.

§ 10.09   OTHER OFFICIAL WRITINGS

In addition to the general exception for official records, the Code contains exceptions for special kinds of public records and other official writings.

---

21. Davis v. Washington, 547 U.S. 813, 126 S.Ct. 2266, 2273–2274, 165 L.Ed.2d 224 (2006) (footnotes omitted).

22. Id. at 2278. For an extended discussion of when the use of witness statements violate the accused's confrontation rights, see § 6.06 supra.

Records of vital statistics. Section 1281 creates a hearsay exception for records of births, fetal deaths, deaths, or marriages if the maker is required by law to file the record in a designated public office and the record is made and filed as required by law.[1]

Findings of death under the Federal Missing Persons Act. Section 1282 provides a hearsay exception for written findings of death made by an employee of the United States who is authorized to make such findings under the Federal Missing Persons Act.[2] The findings may be received to establish the death of a person as well as the date, circumstances, and place of disappearance.[3]

Findings that a person is missing, captured or interned. Section 1283 creates a hearsay exception for official records which are made by an employee of the United States authorized to make such records and which state that a person is missing, missing in action, interned in a foreign country, captured by a hostile force, beleaguered by a hostile force, besieged by a hostile force, or detained in a foreign country against his or her will or is dead or alive.[4]

Statements that public records cannot be found. Section 1284 provides a hearsay exception for a written statement made by a public employee who is the official custodian of the records in a public office, reciting that diligent search failed to disclose a record, when offered to prove the absence of the record in that office.[5]

CALIFORNIA EVIDENCE CODE

§ 1270. "A business"

As used in this article, "a business" includes every kind of business, governmental activity, profession, occupation, calling, or operation of institutions, whether carried on for profit or not.

§ 1271. Business record

Evidence of a writing made as a record of an act, condition, or event is not made inadmissible by the hearsay rule when offered to prove the act, condition, or event if:

(a) The writing was made in the regular course of a business;

(b) The writing was made at or near the time of the act, condition, or event;

---

1. West's Ann.California Evidence Code § 1281.
2. West's Ann.California Evidence Code § 1282.
3. Id.
4. West's Ann.California Evidence Code § 1283.
5. West's Ann.California Evidence Code § 1284.

(c) The custodian or other qualified witness testifies to its identity and the mode of its preparation; and

(d) The sources of information and method and time of preparation were such as to indicate its trustworthiness.

§ 1272. Absence of entry in business records

Evidence of the absence from the records of a business of a record of an asserted act, condition, or event is not made inadmissible by the hearsay rule when offered to prove the nonoccurrence of the act or event, or the nonexistence of the condition, if:

(a) It was the regular course of that business to make records of all such acts, conditions, or events at or near the time of the act, condition, or event and to preserve them; and

(b) The sources of information and method and time of preparation of the records of that business were such that the absence of a record of an act, condition, or event is a trustworthy indication that the act or event did not occur or the condition did not exist.

§ 1280. Record by public employee

Evidence of a writing made as a record of an act, condition, or event is not made inadmissible by the hearsay rule when offered in any civil or criminal proceeding to prove the act, condition, or event if all of the following applies:

(a) The writing was made by and within the scope of duty of a public employee;

(b) The writing was made at or near the time of the act, condition, or event; and

(c) The sources of information and method and time of preparation were such as to indicate its trustworthiness.

§ 1560. Compliance with subpoena duces tecum for business records

(a) As used in this article:

(1) "Business" includes every kind of business described in Section 1270.

(2) "Record" includes every kind of record maintained by a business.

(b) Except as provided in Section 1564, when a subpoena duces tecum is served upon the custodian of records or other qualified witness of a business in an action in which the business is neither a party nor the place where any cause of action is alleged to have arisen, and the subpoena requires the production of all or any part of the records of the business, it is sufficient compliance therewith if the custodian or other qualified witness delivers by mail or otherwise a true, legible, and durable copy of all of the records described in the subpoena to the clerk of the court or to another person described in subdivision (d) of Section 2026.010

of the Code of Civil Procedure, together with the affidavit described in Section 1561, within one of the following time periods:

(1) In any criminal action, five days after the receipt of the subpoena.

(2) In any civil action, within 15 days after the receipt of the subpoena.

(3) Within the time agreed upon by the party who served the subpoena and the custodian or other qualified witness.

(c) The copy of the records shall be separately enclosed in an inner envelope or wrapper, sealed, with the title and number of the action, name of witness, and date of subpoena clearly inscribed thereon; the sealed envelope or wrapper shall then be enclosed in an outer envelope or wrapper, sealed, and directed as follows:

(1) If the subpoena directs attendance in court, to the clerk of the court.

(2) If the subpoena directs attendance at a deposition, to the officer before whom the deposition is to be taken, at the place designated in the subpoena for the taking of the deposition or at the officer's place of business.

(3) In other cases, to the officer, body, or tribunal conducting the hearing, at a like address.

(d) Unless the parties to the proceeding otherwise agree, or unless the sealed envelope or wrapper is returned to a witness who is to appear personally, the copy of the records shall remain sealed and shall be opened only at the time of trial, deposition, or other hearing, upon the direction of the judge, officer, body, or tribunal conducting the proceeding, in the presence of all parties who have appeared in person or by counsel at the trial, deposition, or hearing. Records that are original documents and that are not introduced in evidence or required as part of the record shall be returned to the person or entity from whom received. Records that are copies may be destroyed.

(e) As an alternative to the procedures described in subdivisions (b), (c), and (d), the subpoenaing party in a civil action may direct the witness to make the records available for inspection or copying by the party's attorney, the attorney's representative, or deposition officer as described in Section 2020.420 of the Code of Civil Procedure, at the witness' business address under reasonable conditions during normal business hours. Normal business hours, as used in this subdivision, means those hours that the business of the witness is normally open for business to the public. When provided with at least five business days' advance notice by the party's attorney, attorney's representative, or deposition officer, the witness shall designate a time period of not less than six continuous hours on a date certain for copying of records subject to the subpoena by the party's attorney, attorney's representative, or deposition officer. It shall be the responsibility of the attorney's representative to deliver any copy of the records as directed in the subpoena. Disobedience to the deposition subpoena issued pursuant to this subdivision is punishable as provided in Section 2020.240 of the Code of Civil Procedure.

§ 1561. Affidavit accompanying records

(a) The records shall be accompanied by the affidavit of the custodian or other qualified witness, stating in substance each of the following:

(1) The affiant is the duly authorized custodian of the records or other qualified witness and has authority to certify the records.

(2) The copy is a true copy of all the records described in the subpoena duces tecum, or pursuant to subdivision (e) of Section 1560 the records were delivered to the attorney, the attorney's representative, or deposition officer, for copying at the custodian's or witness' place of business, as the case may be.

(3) The records were prepared by the personnel of the business in the ordinary course of business at or near the time of the act, condition, or event.

(4) The identity of the records.

(5) A description of the mode of preparation of the records.

(b) If the business has none of the records described, or only part thereof, the custodian or other qualified witness shall so state in the affidavit, and deliver the affidavit and those records that are available in the manners provided in Section 1560.

(c) Where the records described in the subpoena were delivered to the attorney or his or her representative or deposition officer for copying at the custodian's or witness' place of business, in addition to the affidavit required by subdivision (a), the records shall be accompanied by an affidavit by the attorney or his or her representative or deposition officer stating that the copy is a true copy of all the records delivered to the attorney or his or her representative or deposition officer for copying.

§ 1562. Admissibility of affidavit and copy of records

If the original records would be admissible in evidence if the custodian or other qualified witness had been present and testified to the matters stated in the affidavit, and if the requirements of Section 1271 have been met, the copy of the records is admissible in evidence. The affidavit is admissible as evidence of the matters stated therein pursuant to Section 1561 and the matters so stated are presumed true. When more than one person has knowledge of the facts, more than one affidavit may be made. The presumption established by this section is a presumption affecting the burden of producing evidence.

§ 1564. Personal attendance of custodian and production of original records

The personal attendance of the custodian or other qualified witness and the production of the original records is not required unless, at the discretion of the requesting party, the subpoena duces tecum contains a clause which reads:

"The personal attendance of the custodian or other qualified witness and the production of the original records are required by this subpoena. The procedure authorized pursuant to subdivision (b) of Section 1560, and Sections 1561 and 1562, of the Evidence Code will not be deemed sufficient compliance with this subpoena."

FEDERAL RULES OF EVIDENCE

Rule 803. Exceptions to the Rule Against Hearsay—Regardless of Whether the Declarant Is Available as a Witness

The following are not excluded by the rule against hearsay, regardless of whether the declarant is available as a witness:

* * *

(6) *Records of a Regularly Conducted Activity.* A record of an act, event, condition, opinion, or diagnosis if:

> **(A)** the record was made at or near the time by—or from information transmitted by—someone with knowledge;

> **(B)** the record was kept in the course of a regularly conducted activity of a business, organization, occupation, or calling, whether or not for profit;

> **(C)** making the record was a regular practice of that activity;

> **(D)** all these conditions are shown by the testimony of the custodian or another qualified witness, or by a certification that complies with Rule 902(11) or (12) or with a statute permitting certification; and

> **(E)** neither the source of information nor the method or circumstances of preparation indicate a lack of trustworthiness.

(7) *Absence of a Record of a Regularly Conducted Activity.* Evidence that a matter is not included in a record described in paragraph (6) if:

> **(A)** the evidence is admitted to prove that the matter did not occur or exist;

> **(B)** a record was regularly kept for a matter of that kind; and

> **(C)** neither the possible source of the information nor other circumstances indicate a lack of trustworthiness.

(8) *Public Records.* A record or statement of a public office if:

> **(A)** it sets out:

>> **(i)** the office's activities;

(ii) a matter observed while under a legal duty to report, but not including, in a criminal case, a matter observed by law-enforcement personnel; or

(iii) in a civil case or against the government in a criminal case, factual findings from a legally authorized investigation; and

(B) neither the source of information nor other circumstances indicate a lack of trustworthiness.

(9) *Public Records of Vital Statistics.* A record of a birth, death, or marriage, if reported to a public office in accordance with a legal duty.

(10) *Absence of a Public Record.* Testimony—or a certification under Rule 902—that a diligent search failed to disclose a public record or statement if the testimony or certification is admitted to prove that:

(A) the record or statement does not exist; or

(B) a matter did not occur or exist, if a public office regularly kept a record or statement for a matter of that kind.

Rule 902.   Evidence That Is Self–Authenticating

The following items of evidence are self-authenticating; they require no extrinsic evidence of authenticity in order to be admitted:

* * *

(11) *Certified Domestic Records of a Regularly Conducted Activity.* The original or a copy of a domestic record that meets the requirements of Rule 803(6)(A)–(C), as shown by a certification of the custodian or another qualified person that complies with a federal statute or a rule prescribed by the Supreme Court. Before the trial or hearing, the proponent must give an adverse party reasonable written notice of the intent to offer the record—and must make the record and certification available for inspection—so that the party has a fair opportunity to challenge them.

(12) *Certified Foreign Records of a Regularly Conducted Activity.* In a civil case, the original or a copy of a foreign record that meets the requirements of Rule 902(11), modified as follows: the certification, rather than complying with a federal statute or Supreme Court rule, must be signed in a manner that, if falsely made, would subject the maker to a criminal penalty in the country where the certification is signed. The proponent must also meet the notice requirements of Rule 902(11).

CHAPTER 11

EXCEPTIONS TO THE HEARSAY RULE: FORMER TESTIMONY

■ ■ ■

Table of Sections

§ 11.01　FORMER TESTIMONY UNDER THE EVIDENCE CODE

The Evidence Code provides a hearsay exception for former testimony. The exception can best be understood through a series of examples.

Example One. Assume that in 1990, A is prosecuted for arson. In its case in chief the prosecution calls W who testifies as follows: "A said to me, 'I intend to defraud my insurer; help me burn my house.'"

A is convicted and appeals. In 1991, his conviction is reversed, and the case is remanded for a new trial. W fails to appear at the trial, so the prosecution offers the testimony that W gave at the first trial. A objects on hearsay grounds.

The objection should be overruled. Section 1291(a)(2) creates a hearsay exception for former testimony where (1) the declarant is unavailable as a witness and (2) the party against whom the testimony is now offered had the right and opportunity at the first trial to cross examine the declarant with an interest and motive similar to those which the party has at the current trial.[1] Here, W is unavailable;[2] moreover, A's interest in

---

1. West's Ann.California Evidence Code § 1291.

2. For a discussion of the unavailability requirement, see § 6.02 supra.

cross examining W at the second trial would be similar, if not identical, with the interest A had in the first trial—diverting fault from A. Actual cross-examination at the first trial is not required; the judge need only find that A had the right and opportunity to cross examine W.[3]

The justification for the exception is based upon need—the unavailability of the hearsay declarant—and partial satisfaction of the hearsay rule—the opponent was afforded an opportunity to cross examine the hearsay declarant with an interest and motive similar to those he has in the proceeding in which the testimony is offered. Though the opponent is deprived of the opportunity of cross examining the hearsay declarant in front of the present fact finder, partial satisfaction is believed to furnish the reliability necessary to justify the exception.

Suppose that in the first trial, W's testimony on direct had been given in response to the following question: "It's true, is it not, that A told you that he intended to defraud his insurer?" At the retrial, A objects to the introduction of W's testimony on the additional ground that the prosecution's question was leading. Though the question is leading, it must be overruled unless A raised a similar objection at the time the prosecution posed the question at the first trial.[4] When testimony is offered against a party who was a party to the action in which the testimony was given, objections to the form of the question are waived unless made in the earlier proceeding.[5]

Example Two. Assume that in the original prosecution A cross examined W. On cross W conceded that by the time he and A arrived at the house an electrical storm was taking place and the house was already on fire. At the second trial A offers the cross-examination after the judge allows the jury to hear W's direct examination. The prosecution objects on hearsay grounds and on the additional grounds of no opportunity to *cross examine* W at the first trial.

The objections should be overruled. It is true that the prosecution did not cross examine W at the first trial. But that was because, as the calling party, the prosecution was not entitled to cross examine W.[6] Not having had that right is immaterial, however, since the prosecution had the right and opportunity to redirect W at the first trial.[7] That opportunity is considered an adequate substitute for the prosecution's present right to examine W further at the retrial.[8]

---

3. West's Ann.California Evidence Code § 1291(a)(2).

4. It is immaterial that the judge who presided over the criminal trial overruled the leading question objection.

5. West's Ann.California Evidence Code § 1291(b)(1).

6. See West's Ann.California Evidence Code § 761.

7. West's Ann.California Evidence Code § 762.

8. A would be entitled to the same ruling even if A had offered W's cross-examination testimony in his own case, i.e., without the prosecution offering W's direct. The prosecution had an opportunity to redirect W at the criminal trial.

Example Three. Assume that A and B jointly owned the house that burned. After the criminal case was concluded against A, B sued their insurer for the value of the house. The policy contained the standard clause excusing liability when the insured intentionally destroys the insured property. At the trial, W fails to appear, so the insurer offers the testimony W gave at the criminal trial. B objects on hearsay grounds.

Although B was not a party in the criminal proceeding, B's objection nonetheless should be overruled. Section 1292(a)(3) creates a hearsay exception for testimony given in a former proceeding by a person who is now unavailable as a witness when such testimony is offered against a party who was not a party to the former proceeding but whose motive for cross-examination is similar to that of the party who had the right and opportunity to cross examine the declarant when the testimony was given.[9] Thus, to be admissible, the judge must find that in the criminal trial A had the right and opportunity to cross examine W with an interest and motive similar to the one B has in the suit against the insured. Since the standard clause regarding destruction by the insured places B in the shoes of A, B has the same interest in discrediting W that A had in the criminal trial, i.e., diverting fault from A.

Assume as in Example One that W's testimony on direct was given in response to the following question: "It's true, is it not, that A told you that he intended to defraud his insurer?" May B object on the grounds that the prosecution's question at the criminal trial was leading? Unlike the answer to the same question in Example One, the answer now is yes.[10] Since B was not a party to the former proceeding, B will not be penalized for A's failure to object. Accordingly, B's objection should be sustained.

Example Four. Assume that the first lawsuit is an action by A against the insurer for the value of the house that burned. W, who was called by the insurer, testifies that "A asked me to help him burn the house." After the suit is concluded, A is prosecuted for arson. Because W is unavailable to testify, the prosecution offers the testimony W gave in the suit against the insured. A objects on hearsay grounds.

A's objection should be overruled. Section 1291 does not distinguish between civil and criminal proceedings. So long as the testimony is offered against a party who was a party to the earlier proceeding and so long as that party had the right and opportunity to cross examine the declarant with a motive and interest similar to those the party has in the present action, the conditions of the exception are satisfied.[11]

Example Five. Suppose instead that the prosecution in Example Four is against B on the theory that A was acting as B's agent. Unlike the

---

Unlike the Code, the Federal Rules make it clear that the opportunity to develop testimony by "redirect examination" is an adequate substitute for examination at the proceeding at which the former testimony is offered. Federal Rule of Evidence 804(b)(1).

9.   West's Ann.California Evidence Code § 1292(a)(3).

10.   West's Ann.California Evidence Code § 1292(b).

11.   See West's Ann.California Evidence Code § 1291(a)(2).

outcome under Section 1291, under Section 1292, B's hearsay objection would have to be sustained. When the former testimony is offered against a party who was not a party to the original action, then the action at which the former testimony is offered must be a civil action.[12] As noted by the Assembly Committee:

> Section 1292 does not make former testimony admissible in a criminal case. This limitation preserves the right of a person accused of a crime to confront and cross-examine the witnesses against him. When a person's life or liberty is at stake—as it is in a criminal action—the defendant should not be compelled to rely on the fact that another has had an opportunity to cross-examine the witness.[13]

QUESTIONS AND PROBLEMS

Rule on the admissibility of the following evidence offered in a California court:

a. *People v. A.* In an arson prosecution against A, over A's hearsay objection W testifies that A said to him, "I intend to defraud my insurer; help me burn my house." Should the judge sustain A's hearsay objection?

b. *People v. A.* Assume that A is convicted and that his conviction is overturned. At the retrial, over A's hearsay objection, the prosecution offers W's direct at the first trial because W is unavailable to testify. Should the judge sustain A's hearsay objection?

c. *A v. Insurance Company.* Following his conviction for arson, A sues his insurance company to collect for the loss of the house. The insurer defends on the ground that under the insurance contract A may not recover for property which he deliberately burned. Because W is unavailable to testify, over A's hearsay objection the insurer offers W's direct from the first prosecution. Should the judge sustain A's hearsay objection?

Suppose that W's testimony in the first prosecution had been given in response to the following question by the prosecutor: "It's true, is it not, that A approached you and asked you to help him burn his house?" A objects at the trial against the insurer on the ground that the question is leading and that, therefore, the judge should not permit the question or the answer to be proved. The insurance company replies that the judge should overrule the objection because A failed to object on those grounds at the criminal trial. How should the judge rule?

d. *B v. Insurance Company.* Assume that B and A owned the house that burned. Assume that B alone sues the insurance company to collect for the loss of the house. The insurance company defends on the ground that under the insurance contract B may not recover for property which A deliberately burned. Because W is unavailable to testify, over B's hearsay objection the insurance company offers W's direct from the first prosecution. Should the judge sustain B's hearsay objection?

---

12. Id.

13. Id. (comment).

Suppose the question that the prosecutor asked W at the first prosecution is identical to the one in the preceding question and that B objects on the ground that the question is leading. The insurance company responds that the judge should overrule the objection because A failed to object on those grounds at the criminal trial. How should the judge rule?

e. *A & B v. Insurance Company*. Assume that after the first prosecution, both A and B sue the insurance company to collect for the loss of the house. The insurance company defends on the ground that under the insurance contract neither A nor B may recover if A deliberately burned the house. Assume that over A and B's hearsay objection the judge allows the insurance company to offer the testimony which W gave at the first prosecution. Now, over the insurance company's hearsay objection, A and B offer A's cross-examination of W at the first prosecution. On cross by A, W testified as follows: "By the time A and I arrived at the house, an electrical storm was in progress and the house was already on fire and was almost totally destroyed." Should the judge sustain the insurance company's hearsay objection?

f. *People v. A*. Assume that the first lawsuit is an action by A against the insurance company for the value of the house that burned. W, who was called by the insurance company, testifies that "A asked me to help him burn the house." After the suit is concluded, A is prosecuted for arson. Because W is unavailable to testify, the prosecution offers the testimony W gave in the suit against the insured. A objects on hearsay grounds. How should the judge rule?

g. *People v. B*. Assume instead that the prosecution is against B on the theory that A was acting as B's agent. Should the judge uphold B's hearsay objection?

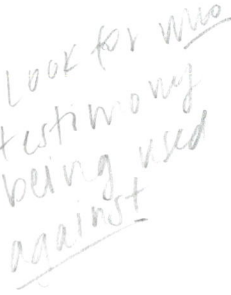

Look for who testimony being used against

§ 11.02 THE FORMAL EVIDENTIARY FOUNDATION FOR FORMER TESTIMONY

In order for testimony given in another action to be admissible, the testimony must satisfy a number of conditions, each of which is discussed below.

The kind of proceedings giving rise to former testimony. The testimony offered under the exception must have been given under oath in one of the proceedings listed in § 1290. The list includes a former trial of the same action (Example One) as well as of another action (Examples Three and Four).[1] It also includes a former hearing in the same action.[2] Thus, testimony given at a preliminary hearing can be offered at the trial if the other conditions of the exception are satisfied.

Court decisions have created two exceptions to these rules. A defendant's testimony at a probation revocation hearing may not be offered as

---

1. West's Ann.California Evidence Code § 1290.

2. Id.

former testimony at a subsequent trial of charges arising from the same transaction.[3] Neither may a defendant's testimony in support of a motion to suppress evidence be used by the prosecution as substantive evidence against the defendant at the trial.[4] Defendants should not be forced to give up such constitutional rights as taking the stand in their own behalf or asserting Fourth Amendment claims in order to preserve the privilege against self-incrimination.[5]

Arbitration proceedings are also among the proceedings included in § 1290, but the testimony must be proved through a verbatim transcript.[6]

Depositions taken in the action in which they are offered are not within the definition of former testimony. The admissibility of these depositions depends in the first instance on the Code of Civil Procedure.[7] Former testimony includes only depositions taken in an action *other* than the one in which the depositions are offered.[8] The admissibility of these depositions depends on the Evidence Code sections governing the use of former testimony.[9]

The unavailability of the hearsay declarant. A witness's former testimony is admissible only if the witness is unavailable to testify at the hearing at which the testimony is offered.[10] It is the witness's unavailability that creates the need for the exception. Section 240, which defines unavailability, is discussed in § 6.02.

---

3. People v. Coleman, 13 Cal.3d 867, 889, 120 Cal.Rptr. 384, 401, 533 P.2d 1024, 1041 (1975). It is immaterial whether the probationer's testimony is offered as former testimony or as an admission to prove the truth of the matter asserted.

4. Simmons v. United States, 390 U.S. 377, 394, 88 S.Ct. 967, 976, 19 L.Ed.2d 1247 (1968), on remand, 395 F.2d 769 (7th Cir.1968), appeal after remand, 424 F.2d 1235 (1970).

5. *Simmons* reached this conclusion on the basis of the Federal Constitution. Id. *Coleman* did so as an exercise of the California Supreme Court's supervisory powers. People v. Coleman, 13 Cal.3d 867, 889, 120 Cal.Rptr. 384, 401, 533 P.2d 1024, 1041 (1975). One consequence of Proposition 8 is the elimination of judicial barriers to the introduction of relevant evidence. See §§ 2.11 and 3.07 supra. Admissions made by probationers at revocation hearings are relevant. Since the use of these admissions is not barred by the Federal Constitution, Flint v. Mullen, 499 F.2d 100 (1st Cir.1974), cert. denied, 419 U.S. 1026, 95 S.Ct. 505, 42 L.Ed.2d 301 (1974), their use may now be mandated in California trials by Proposition 8. The California Supreme Court, however, has not decided this question.

Even if *Coleman* is still good law, *Coleman* nonetheless allows the prosecution to use the accused's probation hearing testimony "for purposes of impeachment or rebuttal where the probationer's revocation hearing testimony or evidence derived therefrom and his testimony on direct examination at the criminal proceeding are so clearly inconsistent as to warrant the trial court's admission of the revocation hearing testimony or its fruits in order to reveal to the trier of fact the probability that the probationer has committed perjury at either the trial or the revocation hearing." People v. Coleman, 13 Cal.3d 867, 889, 120 Cal.Rptr. 384, 401, 533 P.2d 1024, 1041 (1975).

6. West's Ann.California Evidence Code § 1290. Former testimony also includes testimony given under oath in a "proceeding to determine a controversy conducted by or under the supervision of an agency that has the power to determine such controversy and is an agency of the United States or a public entity in the United States." Id.

7. For a discussion of the admissibility of these depositions, see § 11.05 infra.

8. West's Ann.California Evidence Code § 1290(c).

9. For a discussion of the limitations on the use of these depositions, see § 11.03 infra.

10. See West's Ann.California Evidence Code §§ 1291(a) and 1292(a)(1).

The kind of party against whom former testimony can be offered. Former testimony can be offered against a party who was a party when the testimony was elicited in two circumstances. First, as described in Examples One and Four in § 11.01, former testimony can be offered against a party who had the right and opportunity to cross examine the declarant with an interest and motive similar to those which the party now has.[11] Having had that opportunity supplies the exception with the necessary reliability. In the Assembly Committee's view, whether the party against whom the former testimony is offered had that kind of opportunity calls for a practical, not a theoretical, assessment:

> The determination of similarity of interest and motive in cross-examination should be based on practical considerations and not merely on the similarity of the party's position in the two cases. For example, testimony contained in a deposition that was taken, but not offered in evidence at the trial, in a different action should be excluded if the judge determines that the deposition was taken for discovery purposes and that the party did not subject the witness to a thorough cross-examination because he sought to avoid a premature revelation of the weakness in the testimony of the witness or in the adverse party's case. In such a situation the party's interest and motive for cross-examination on the previous occasion would have been substantially different from his present interest and motive.[12]

Second, former testimony can also be offered against a party who was not a party at the time the testimony was given but whose motive and interest in crossing the hearsay declarant are similar to those of a party who did have the right and opportunity to cross examine the declarant.[13] Example Three in § 11.01 illustrates this exception. But, as demonstrated in Example Five, such former testimony can be offered only in a subsequent civil action.[14]

Third, former testimony can also be offered against the party who offered the evidence as well as against that party's successor in interest.[15]

---

11. See § 11.01 supra.

12. West's Ann.California Evidence Code § 1291 (comment). Accord: Wahlgren v. Coleco Industries, Inc., 151 Cal.App.3d 543, 198 Cal.Rptr. 715 (1984) (The party's motive and interest in crossing the deponent-declarant were dissimilar to the party's motive and interest in crossing the declarant at the trial.). See also People v. Sanders, 11 Cal.4th 475, 525–526, 46 Cal.Rptr.2d 751, 777, 905 P.2d 420, 446 (1995) (The prosecution's motive and interest in crossing a defense witness at a suppression hearing were dissimilar to those in crossing the witness at the trial, as the credibility of the witness was not a significant issue at the suppression hearing.).

13. West's Ann.California Evidence Code § 1292(a)(3). If the motive and interest are dissimilar, the testimony must be excluded. See Wahlgren v. Coleco Industries, Inc., 151 Cal.App.3d 543, 198 Cal.Rptr. 715 (1984) (holding that a party's interest and motive in crossing the deponent-declarant at the former hearing were dissimilar to the objecting party's interest and motive in crossing the declarant at the trial.); see also Gatton v. A.P. Green Services, Inc., 64 Cal.App.4th 688, 693, 75 Cal.Rptr.2d 523, 526 (1998) (holding that no party at the former hearing had an interest and motive in crossing the witness that were similar to those of the objecting party at the current trial.).

14. See § 11.01 supra.

15. West's Ann.California Evidence Code § 1291(a)(1). This section is limited to evidence which the party adduces on direct or redirect examination; it does not include evidence elicited by

It is immaterial that the offering party, as the calling party, could not cross the witness at the former hearing. The party's previous direct and redirect examination are considered an adequate substitute for that party's right to cross examine the declarant at the hearing at which the former testimony is offered.[16]

Grand jury testimony. Federal prosecutions for serious felonies are usually initiated by an indictment. In California, on the other hand, felony prosecutions frequently are initiated by a complaint that results in a preliminary hearing. Because California preliminary hearings are adversarial, the use of the transcript as former testimony does not raise as many questions as does the transcript of a grand jury proceeding.

Unlike the preliminary hearing, the accused is not entitled to be present at the time the government presents its evidence to the grand jurors. Since defendants do not have an opportunity to cross examine the government witnesses, the government may not offer a witness's grand jury testimony as former testimony against the accused. A different situation, however, is presented when the accused offers a witness's grand jury testimony against the government. It may qualify as former testimony if the trial judge finds that the government's motive and interest in eliciting the testimony are similar to the government's motive and interest at the trial.[17]

Two contrasting federal cases illustrate this point. In United States v. McFall,[18] the government convened a grand jury to consider evidence that the McFall had been engaged in an extortion scheme. The government called Sawyer as a witness with the apparent expectation that he would implicate McFall in the scheme. Sawyer, however, surprised the government by testifying that he and McFall had nothing to do with the scheme.

McFall was unable to call Sawyer at the subsequent trial because Sawyer was unavailable. Instead, McFall offered the Sawyer's grand jury testimony under the federal hearsay exception for former testimony. The trial judge excluded the testimony on the ground, among others, that the government's motive and interest in eliciting Sawyer's testimony before the grand jury were not similar to those the government had at the trial.

The Ninth Circuit held that the trial judge erred in excluding Sawyer's grand jury testimony. In reaching this holding, the court distinguished between the role of the government when it is using a grand jury as an investigative tool (to uncover evidence of a crime) as opposed to presenting evidence to the grand jury with the goal that it will move the grand jury to indict.

---

the opponent on cross-examination. People v. Rice, 59 Cal.App.3d 998, 1005, 131 Cal.Rptr. 330, 334 (1976).

16. West's Ann.California Evidence Code § 1291(a)(1) (comment).

17. See United States v. Salerno, 505 U.S. 317, 325, 112 S.Ct. 2503, 120 L.Ed.2d 255 (1992) (holding that whether under the Federal Rules of Evidence the government's motive and interest in eliciting testimony before the grand jury are similar to the government's interest at the trial depends on the particular circumstances of the case).

18. 558 F.3d 951 (9th Cir. 2009).

On balance, we agree with the D.C. Circuit's elaboration of the "similar motive" test and conclude that the government's fundamental objective in questioning Sawyer before the grand jury was to draw out testimony that would support its theory that McFall conspired with Sawyer to commit extortion-the same motive it possessed at trial. That motive may not have been as intense before the grand jury, but Rule 804(b)(1) does not require an identical quantum of motivation. Although McFall had already been indicted when Sawyer appeared before the grand jury, prosecutors did not obtain the final superseding indictment (which brought the total number of counts against McFall to twenty) until September 9, 2004, almost two years after Sawyer appeared before the grand jury. Moreover, Count 14 is a conspiracy charge, and thus depends on proof that McFall and Sawyer cooperated in a scheme to extort money from Digital Angel, providing prosecutors with ample incentive to develop testimony that would incriminate McFall.[19]

In United States v. DeNapoli[20] the Second Circuit held that the trial judge did not err in excluding grand juror testimony offered by the accused. The accused were on trial for rigging bids. At the hearing before the grand jury, a witness testified that he not aware of the existence of the bid rigging scheme. The witness was not available to testify at the subsequent trial, and the accused offered his grand jury testimony. In holding that the government's motive and interest in eliciting the witness's testimony before the grand jury were dissimilar to those of the government at the trial, the Second Circuit emphasized two factors. First, at the time the witness testified before the grand jury, the government was using the grand jury in its investigative role:

> [T]he defendants had already been indicted, and, as appellants' counsel conceded at argument, there existed no putative defendant as to whom probable cause was in issue. At most the Government had an interest in investigating further to see whether there might be additional defendants or additional projects within the criminal activity of the existing defendants. As to these matters, the prosecutor had no interest in showing that the denial of the [bid rigging scheme's] existence was false. The grand jury had already been persuaded, at least by the low standard of probable cause, to believe that the [scheme] existed and that the defendants had participated in it to commit crimes. It is fanciful to think that the prosecutor would have had any substantial interest in showing the falsity of the witnesses' denial of the [scheme's] existence just to persuade the grand jury to add one more project to the indictment.

Second, the grand jurors had indicated to the prosecutor that they did not believe the denial. * * * A prosecutor has no interest in showing

---

19. Id. at 558 F.3d 963.

20. 8 F.3d 909 (2d Cir.1993).

the falsity of testimony that a grand jury already disbelieves.[21]

When a federal prosecutor is presenting evidence to the grand jury in order to obtain an indictment, the prosecutor is acting like a California prosecutor who is presenting evidence of guilt before the magistrate presiding over the preliminary hearing. When a California prosecutor is surprised by a prosecution witness's testimony at a preliminary hearing, the prosecutor may well implement the strategy the prosecutor would have employed if the surprise had occurred at trial. That strategy would embrace one of two goals: (1) to try persuade the witness to recant his testimony and accept as true what the witness must have told the prosecution's investigators prior to the hearing; or (2) if the endeavor fails, to impeach the witness's credibility. Evidence that the prosecutor at the grand jury was acting in a role similar to that of a prosecutor at a preliminary hearing can help a judge discern the prosecutor's motive and interest. As a rule, California prosecutors do not use preliminary hearings as an investigative tool. The preliminary hearing is the place to determine whether the state possesses sufficient evidence to convince the magistrate that there is probable cause to believe that a felony has been committed and that the defendant is the person who committed the offense. If that is the prosecutor's purpose before the grand jury, then it is likely that a prosecutor's purpose in calling a witness is similar to the purpose the prosecutor would have in calling that witness at the trial.

QUESTIONS AND PROBLEMS

1.   Because the concerns of the hearsay rule are satisfied by the fact that the witness was previously examined under oath with an interest and motive similar to those of the party against whom the testimony is now offered, for purposes of the former testimony exception it is immaterial that the witness is available to testify at the hearing at which the testimony is offered. True or false?

2.   Under the Code, "former testimony" embraces deposition testimony that is offered in the case in which the deposition was taken. True or false?

3.   Former testimony is inadmissible under the hearsay exception for such testimony unless the party against whom offered or a predecessor in interest in fact cross examined the witness whose testimony is offered. True or false?

§ 11.03   OBJECTING TO SPECIFIC ITEMS OF FORMER TESTIMONY

Just because the former testimony of an unavailable witness satisfies the evidentiary foundation does not mean that the questions asked of the witness or the witness's answers may be proved. To begin with, the proponent need only offer those questions and answers which he or she

---

21.   Id. at 8 F.3d 915.

desires.[1] The opponent, moreover, retains the right to object to any question and answer to which the opponent could have objected if the hearsay declarant had appeared and taken the stand.[2] But where the former testimony is offered against a party who was a party to the former proceeding, objections to the form of the question are waived unless they were made at the time the former testimony was given.[3]

Example One in § 11.01 illustrates these limitations. In the first proceeding—the initial prosecution—the prosecutor called W who testified as follows: "A said to me, 'I intend to defraud my insurer; help me burn my house.'" At the retrial, W was unavailable to testify, so the prosecution offered the testimony W gave at the first trial. The testimony satisfies the foundational requirements because it is being offered against A who had the right and opportunity to cross examine W at the first trial with a motive and interest similar to those A has at the second trial. Nonetheless, A's statement regarding his plans to defraud his insurer is hearsay: his out of court statement is being offered to prove the truth of the matter stated, namely his plans to defraud his insurer.[4] Accordingly, at the retrial A may object to that portion of the testimony on hearsay grounds. Moreover, since his objection goes to the answer and not the form of the question, A may object at the retrial even if he failed to object to the answer at the first trial.[5]

But suppose that at the first trial W's testimony on direct had been given in response to the following question: "It's true, is it not, that A told you that he intended to defraud his insurer?" At the retrial, A objects to the question on the ground that the question is leading. Although the question is leading, the judge may not sustain the objection unless A objected on that ground at the first trial. A had an opportunity to object on that ground, and will not be permitted to raise this technical objection at the current trial. If A did object, it is immaterial that the judge at the first trial erroneously overruled the objection. A can still object to the form of the question at the second trial.

Objections based on the incompetence of the declarant or on privilege are to be determined by reference to the time when the former testimony was given.[6] A married person, for example, has a privilege to decline to answer questions if the answer disserves the interests of the witness's spouse. An objection on this ground at the present hearing will be sustained only if at the time the answer was sought at the former hearing the answer was protected by the privilege. Accordingly, the privilege claim

---

1. This right, however, does not include proving questions to which an objection was sustained at the former hearing. People v. Mayfield, 14 Cal.4th 668, 744, 60 Cal.Rptr.2d 1, 44, 928 P.2d 485, 528 (1997), cert. denied, 522 U.S. 839, 118 S.Ct. 116, 139 L.Ed.2d 68 (1997).

2. West's Ann.California Evidence Code §§ 1291(b) and 1292(b).

3. West's Ann.California Evidence Code § 1291(b)(1).

4. For a discussion of the definition of hearsay, see § 5.01 supra.

5. The hearsay objection would have to be overruled. B's statement regarding his plans falls into one of two hearsay objections: party admission or declaration of then existing state of mind. See §§ 7.01 and 9.08 supra.

6. West's Ann.California Evidence Code §§ 1291(b)(2) and 1292(b).

will be overruled if at the time the witness answered the question the witness was not married. In this instance, it is immaterial whether the objecting party was or was not a party in the earlier proceeding.[7]

§ 11.04   PROVING FORMER TESTIMONY

In theory, anyone who can remember the questions posed by the examiner and the answers given by the witness can be called to prove the witness's testimony. In practice, no one, not even the court reporter, is likely to remember the questions and answers. A convenient way to prove the testimony, then, is by offering the reporter's transcript of the questions and answers the proponent desires.[1]

Because a transcript is a writing,[2] its use requires compliance with authentication requirements as well as with the Secondary Evidence Rule. Section 1401 requires a writing to be authenticated before it may be received in evidence.[3] That means that the proponent must introduce "evidence sufficient to sustain a finding" that the transcript is what the proponent purports it to be.[4] In the case of transcripts of trials and related hearings and of depositions, judicial notice[5] and certain presumptions[6] can ease the task of authenticating the transcript.

At one time the California Best Evidence Rule required a party to prove the contents of a writing through the original of the writing unless production of the original was excused. Today, the Secondary Evidence Rule allows proof of an original writing by the original or a duly authenticated copy.[7] Accordingly, a copy of the original transcript will do as well as the original.[8] Doubts concerning the accuracy of copies of court transcripts can be removed by having the custodian of the original attach a certificate stating that the copy is a correct copy of the original.[9]

Once all foundational requirements have been complied with, the proponent may read the transcript to the fact finder. Some judges will allow the proponent to call a witness to read the hearsay declarant's answers to the questions, which in turn are read by the attorney. This procedure has the advantage of allowing the opposing party an opportunity to object to objectionable questions and answers where the parties have

---

7. Id.

1. A hearsay objection to the transcript can be met with the official records exception. See § 10.07 supra.

2. See West's Ann.California Evidence Code § 250.

3. West's Ann.California Evidence Code § 1401(a).

4. West's Ann.California Evidence Code § 1400.

5. A California judge may judicially notice the records of (1) any court of this state or (2) any court of the United States or of any state of the United States. West's Ann.California Evidence Code § 452.

6. See West's Ann.California Evidence Code §§ 1450–1454.

7. West's Ann.California Evidence Code § 1520–1521.

8. West's Ann.California Evidence Code § 1511.

9. West's Ann.California Evidence Code § 1531.

failed to agree on the portions of the transcript that ought to be admitted. Regardless of who reads the answers, jurors are routinely instructed to consider the former testimony as if it had been given by the unavailable witness at the trial.[10] If a transcript is used to prove the former testimony, the judge should edit out questions to which objections were sustained.[11] Moreover the judge should not give the jurors copies to help them follow the testimony; that would give undue weight to the testimony.[12]

Former testimony may also be proved by a videotape of the hearing at which the testimony was given.[13] The former testimony sections of the Code do not specify the form of evidence that must be offered to prove former testimony.[14] A tape is therefore admissible if it accurately depicts the events shown.[15] A videotape is a writing under the Code.[16] Accordingly, the requirements of the Secondary Evidence Rule and of authentication apply to videotapes.

§ 11.05   DEPOSITION TESTIMONY

The former testimony exception to the hearsay rule does not apply to depositions taken in the action in which they are offered.[1] The admissibility of these depositions is governed in the first instance by the Code of Civil Procedure.

Section 2025.620 of the Civil Procedure Code provides that at the trial or other hearing in the action, any part of a deposition may be used against any party "so far as admissible under the rules of evidence applied as though the deponent were then present and testifying as a witness * * *."[2] This provision allows the opponent to use the Evidence Code in opposing any part of the deposition that is offered. Two limitations, however, should be kept in mind.

First, the proponent can offer the deposition in the first place only for the purposes enumerated in the Civil Procedure Code. If the deponent testifies, a party may use the deposition to impeach the deponent's testimony or "for any other purpose permitted by the Evidence Code."[3] If the deposition is that of a party to the action, the adverse party may use the deposition for any purpose.[4] If the deponent resides more than 150 miles from the place of the trial or hearing or if the deponent is

---

10.   See CALJIC 2.12 (Fall 2006 Edition); BAJI 2.06 (Fall 2007 Edition).

11.   People v. Mayfield, 14 Cal.4th 668, 744, 60 Cal.Rptr.2d 1, 44, 928 P.2d 485, 528 (1997), cert. denied, 522 U.S. 839, 118 S.Ct. 116, 139 L.Ed.2d 68 (1997).

12.   People v. Stevenson, 79 Cal.App.3d 976, 990, 145 Cal.Rptr. 301, 309 (1978).

13.   People v. Moran, 39 Cal.App.3d 398, 411, 114 Cal.Rptr. 413, 420 (1974).

14.   An exception is testimony given at an arbitration proceeding. See § 11.02 supra.

15.   People v. Moran, 39 Cal.App.3d 398, 409, 114 Cal.Rptr. 413, 419 (1974).

16.   West's Ann.California Evidence Code § 250.

1.   West's Ann.California Evidence Code § 1290(c).

2.   West's Ann.California Civil Procedure Code § 2025.620.

3.   Id. § 2025.620(a).

4.   Id. § 2025.620(b).

unavailable under any of the grounds set out in § 240 of the Evidence Code, any party may use the deposition for any purpose.[5] Even if the distance or unavailability requirements are not met, the judge may nonetheless allow the use of a deposition if "[e]xceptional circumstances exist that make it desirable to allow [its use] in the interests of justice and with due regard to the importance of presenting the testimony of witnesses orally in court."[6]

Second, the broad right given to the opponent to rely on the Evidence Code in objecting to any part of a deposition can be illusory. Though Civil Procedure Code § 2025.460(c) reaffirms that "[o]bjections to the competency of the deponent, or to the relevancy, materiality, or admissibility at trial of the testimony * * * are unnecessary and are not waived by failure to make them before or during the deposition,"[7] this protection is undermined by another provision. Section 2025.460(b) provides that "[e]rrors and irregularities of any kind occurring at the oral examination that might be cured if promptly presented are waived unless a specific objection to them is timely made during the deposition. These errors and irregularities include, but are not limited to, those relating to the * * * form of any question or answer * * *."[8]

At the time a deposition is taken, it is difficult to forecast whether some future judge will find that an objectionable question or answer could have been cured if an objection had been promptly presented at the deposition. Consequently, the effect of the provision is to encourage lawyers to object specifically to such questions and answers, unless the parties have stipulated to preserving such objections.[9] "Usual stipulations" may not always preserve objections to the form of the question. Parties should not agree to the "usual stipulations" unless they know exactly which objections are preserved.

Objecting to a question does not mean that the deponent can decline to answer it. The Civil Procedure Code provides that the deposition must continue subject to the objection, unless the objecting party also demands that the taking of the deposition be suspended to allow for a motion for a protective order.[10] A party may instruct a deponent not to answer a question only if the question calls for the disclosure of privileged information.[11]

---

5. Id. §§ 2025.620(c)(1)–(2). The Civil Procedure Code no longer refers explicitly to California Evidence Code § 240. But the grounds of unavailability listed are identical to the grounds enumerated under § 240. Id.

6. West's Ann.California Civil Procedure Code § 2025.620(c)(3).

7. Id. § 2025.460(c).

8. Id. § 2025.460(b).

9. If the parties so stipulate in writing, depositions may be taken "in any manner and when so taken may be used like other depositions." Id. § 2016.030.

10. Id. at § 2025.460(b). Accord: Stewart v. Colonial Western Agency, Inc., 87 Cal.App.4th 1006, 1014–1015, 105 Cal.Rptr.2d 115, 120–121 (2001).

11. West's Ann. California Civil Procedure Code §§ 2017.010 and 2025.460(a). Accord: Stewart v. Colonial Western Agency, Inc., 87 Cal.App.4th 1006, 1014–1015, 105 Cal.Rptr.2d 115, 120–121 (2001).

§ 11.06   FORMER TESTIMONY UNDER THE FEDERAL RULES

Federal Rule of Evidence 804(b)(1) provides a hearsay exception for former testimony that in most ways is similar to the exception created by the Evidence Code. In addition to requiring the unavailability of the witness,[1] the central limitation is that the party against whom the testimony is offered (or in a civil case whose predecessor in interest) had "an opportunity and similar motive to develop [the testimony] by direct, cross-, or redirect examination."[2]

One difference is that the Rules do not attempt to specify which objections to former testimony are waived by failure to make the objection at the time the testimony was given.[3] Presumably, no such waiver takes place, except in the case of depositions. The Federal Rules of Civil Procedure governing the use of depositions contain waiver provisions that are similar to those found in the Code of Civil Procedure, and these would apply to depositions taken in the case offered.[4]

Another difference is that Congress amended the federal rule to encompass depositions taken in the action in which offered, as well as

---

1. Federal Rule of Evidence 804(a).

2. Federal Rule of Evidence 804(b)(1)(B).

3. For the Code's treatment of the waiver issue, see § 11.03 supra.

4. See Federal Rule of Civil Procedure 32(d)(3)(A)–(B). For a discussion of the California waiver rules governing the use of depositions offered in the action in which they are taken, see § 11.05 supra.

As noted, Federal Rule of Evidence 804(b)(1) is silent about whether parties opposing the former testimony must show that at the former hearing they objected on the same grounds to a question or answer the proponent seeks to prove at the current hearing. In the absence of stipulations, the Federal Rules of Civil Procedure impose this requirement to the extent that the defect in the question or answer could have been cured if promptly presented at the deposition. See Federal Rule of Civil Procedure 32(d)(3)(B).

The requirement imposes no additional burden on the proponent when the deposition was taken in the action offered. Even under the rule approved by the Supreme Court for former testimony, the proponent would have been subject to the limitations imposed by the Federal Rules of Civil Procedure. Those rules, not the exception for former testimony, would have governed the use of the deposition at trial. That, however, would not have been true in the case of depositions not taken in the action offered. Such a deposition would been governed exclusively by the federal rule on former testimony, not the Federal Rules of Civil Procedure. The federal exception for former testimony contains no waiver provisions. A question, then, is whether by subjecting both types of depositions to the exception for former testimony and subjecting one kind—those taken in the action offered—to the limitations of the procedural rules, Congress inadvertently opened the door to imposing the same limitations on the other kind as well.

The Federal Rules of Civil Procedure are not dispositive of the matter. The waiver provisions of Rule 32 apply to depositions offered "[a]t the trial." Federal Rule of Civil Procedure 32(a)(1). Whether "trial" refers only to the trial of the action in which the deposition was taken is not entirely clear. Some commentators believe that a deposition not taken in the action offered is admissible under Rule 32 if the testimony given was such "that the party-opponent in [the other action] had the same interest and motive in his cross-examination that the present opponent now has." Wright, Miller & Marcus, Federal Practice and Procedure § 2150 at 191 (West 1994). The question, however, is not whether such a deposition should be admissible under Rule 32 but whether its use should be governed exclusively by the federal former testimony exception to the hearsay rule. The Code avoids these uncertainties by exempting from the definition of former testimony those depositions offered in the action in which they are taken.

depositions taken in an action other than the one in which offered.[5] Under the Code, the use of the former depositions is governed by the Civil Procedure Code, not the former testimony sections of the Evidence Code.[6] A consequence is that the proponent of a deposition in federal court may have to comply with the requirements of the Federal Rules of Evidence as well as with those of the Federal Rules of Civil Procedure. The unavailability grounds prescribed by the Federal Rules of Evidence are not identical with the grounds enumerated in the Federal Rules of Civil Procedure. For example, under Federal Rule of Civil Procedure 32(a)(3) any party can use the deposition of a witness for any purpose if the witness is at a distance greater than 100 miles from the place of the trial or hearing.[7] No such "unavailability" is recognized under the Federal Rules of Evidence.[8] The definition of unavailability under the Federal Rule of Evidence is not exclusive, however. Presumably, a federal judge is authorized to consider other grounds of unavailability, such as the ones that appear only in the Federal Rules of Civil Procedure.

QUESTIONS AND PROBLEMS

1. Consider the admissibility of the following deposition testimony under the Federal Rules of Civil Procedure and the California Civil Procedure Code:

a. At the trial, Brown testifies on direct examination as follows:, "The defendant had the red light."On cross-examination, over the plaintiff's objection, may the defendant seek to prove that at his deposition Brown testified, "The plaintiff had the red light."

b. At the trial, the plaintiff testifies, "I had the green light." On cross-examination, over the plaintiff's objection, may the defendant seek to prove that at her deposition, the plaintiff testified, "I think that I may have had the green light; I am not 100% sure."

2. Consider the admissibility of the following deposition testimony under the Federal Rules of Civil Procedure and the California Civil Procedure Code:

Deposition of Tom Grey noticed by the plaintiff's lawyer:

Plaintiff's Counsel: You, of course, saw the defendant run the red light, did you not?

Tom Grey: Yes.

Grey dies before the trial, and the plaintiff offers Grey's deposition. The defendant objects on hearsay grounds and also on the ground that the question is leading. How should the judge rule?

3. A and B were injured when the bus they were riding in crashed. A sued the bus company to recover for his injuries. Prior to the trial, A took Grey's deposition as in (2) and shortly thereafter the bus company settled with A. Grey then dies.

---

5. Federal Rule of Evidence 804(b)(1).

6. See § 11.05 supra.

7. Federal Rule of Civil Procedure 32(a)(3)(B).

8. Federal Rule of Evidence 804(a).

B then sued the bus company and at the trial offered Grey's deposition. How should the judge rule on the defendant's objection that the question is leading under the former testimony exception of the Federal Rules of Evidence and the California Evidence Code?

4.   Suppose that at his deposition Grey had also testified as follows:

Plaintiff's Counsel: Did you and your wife discuss who had the red light?

Tom Grey: Yes.

Plaintiff's Counsel: What did she say?

Tom Grey: She said to me, "The defendant run the red light."

B also offers this portion of Grey's deposition. How should the judge rule on the defendant's hearsay objection under the former testimony exception of the Federal Rules of Evidence and the California Evidence Code?

5.   Suppose that A had not settled and at the trial had offered this portion of Grey's deposition. How should the judge rule on the defendant's hearsay objection under the Federal Rules of Civil Procedure and the California Civil Procedure Code?

Would you change your ruling if the parties had stipulated at the deposition that "all objections, except as to form of the question, are reserved until the time of trial"?

§ 11.07 FORMER TESTIMONY AND THE CONFRONTATION CLAUSE

Because the use of former testimony requires the unavailability of the witness, the use of former testimony against the accused deprives the accused of the opportunity to cross examine the declarant under oath in the presence of the fact finder. Nonetheless, in Ohio v. Roberts[1] the United States Supreme Court rejected the claim that the use against the accused of the preliminary hearing transcript of a witness who was unavailable to testify at the trial violated his right to confront his accusers.[2] In reaching its decision, the Court emphasized a number of factors.

First, there was a need for the evidence, the prosecution having established the witness's unavailability at the trial.[3] Second, the preliminary hearing testimony was reliable. Not only did the evidence fall within a "firmly rooted hearsay exception,"[4] but the lawyer for the accused cross examined the witness at the preliminary hearing with the "principal *purpose* of cross-examination"—challenging the declarant's sincerity, perception, recollection, and narration.[5] Finally, the Court could find no

---

1. 448 U.S. 56, 100 S.Ct. 2531, 65 L.Ed.2d 597 (1980).

2. Id. at 75.

3. Id.

4. Id. at 66.

5. Id. at 71 (emphasis in the original).

reason for distinguishing the use of "preliminary hearing testimony previously subjected to cross-examination from previously cross-examined prior-trial testimony, which the Court had deemed generally immune from subsequent confrontation attack."[6]

Crawford v. Washington[7] does not change the outcome in *Roberts*. Although *Crawford* disapproved of *Roberts'* holding that hearsay offered against the accused does not result in a confrontation violation if it falls within a firmly rooted hearsay exception,[8] *Crawford's* test for determining confrontation violations is consistent with *Roberts'* outcome. Under *Crawford*, over a confrontation objection, testimonial hearsay may not be offered against the accused unless (1) the hearsay declarant is produced for cross-examination by the accused or (2) if not produced, unless the accused was given an opportunity prior to the trial to cross examine the hearsay declarant.[9] Testimonial statements include testimony elicited at a preliminary hearing or a former trial.[10] Although the hearsay declarant did not appear at Roberts' trial, the prosecution demonstrated her unavailability as a witness and showed that at the preliminary hearing Roberts had been given an opportunity to cross examine her about the statements subsequently offered at the trial.[11]

Under the California Evidence Code and the Federal Rules of Evidence, testimony from a preliminary hearing or former trial may not be offered at the current trial as former testimony unless the declarant is unavailable to testify and the accused had an opportunity to cross examine the declarant at the earlier hearing with a motive and interest similar to the ones the accused has at the trial.[12] In the absence of exceptional circumstances, these statutory limitations alone should satisfy *Crawford's* requirements.[13]

The California courts have taken a cautious approach with respect to the unavailability requirement. The California Supreme Court has interpreted § 240 as requiring the prosecution to show, not only reasonable diligence in attempting to obtain the witness's attendance by the court's process, but also the use of reasonable means to prevent the witness from becoming "absent," at least where the witness is critical to the prosecu-

---

6.   Id. at 72–73. If the accused was not represented by counsel at the former hearing, then the Sixth Amendment requires exclusion of the former testimony, irrespective of whether the accused attempted to cross examine the declarant at the former hearing. Pointer v. Texas, 380 U.S. 400, 406–408, 85 S.Ct. 1065, 13 L.Ed.2d 923 (1965). However, ineffective assistance by counsel at the former hearing will not render the former testimony inadmissible unless the ineffective assistance affected the cross-examination of the declarant. Mancusi v. Stubbs, 408 U.S. 204, 216, 92 S.Ct. 2308, 33 L.Ed.2d 293 (1972).

7.   541 U.S. 36, 124 S.Ct. 1354, 158 L.Ed.2d 177 (2004).

8.   Id. at 61.

9.   Id. at 68.

10.   Id.

11.   For an extended discussion of hearsay and confrontation, see § 6.03 et seq., supra.

12.   West's Ann. California Evidence Code §§ 1290–1291; Federal Rule of Evidence 804(a)–(b)(1).

13.   See People v. Carter, 36 Cal.4th 1114, 1171, 117 P.3d 476, 515, 32 Cal.Rptr.3d 759, 804 (2005), cert. denied, 547 U.S. 1099, 126 S.Ct. 1881, 164 L.Ed.2d 570 (2006).

tion.[14] In People v. Louis[15] the prosecution failed to make the latter showing when it agreed to release a material witness under his own recognizance without verifying where the witness would be staying and without keeping the witness under surveillance.[16] The witness disappeared before the trial. Where an unavailable witness's testimony is largely cumulative, however, the failure to keep periodic tabs on the witness will not preclude the use of the witness's former testimony.[17] In the case of any witness, due diligence requires the prosecution to make timely efforts to secure the witness's appearance in court:

> Waiting until the morning a trial begins to try to locate a witness after being out of touch for several months is generally not prudent or reasonable, and certainly is not an untiring effort to secure a witness's presence at trial. * * * Witnesses have jobs, they plan vacations * * *, they have child care responsibilities, they leave town for a few days. A party who wanted to ensure a witness was available to testify would usually plan ahead, and not wait a day or two before the testimony was needed.[18]

The California courts have also excluded former testimony offered against the accused where the accused did not have a "meaningful opportunity"[19] to cross-examine the hearsay declarant at the proceeding in which the testimony was given. In People v. Brock,[20] for example, the court held that the victim's preliminary hearing testimony was improperly admitted against the accused where, due to the victim's medical condition, the magistrate restricted the accused's right to object and limited the accused to asking the victim only three questions on cross-examination.[21] And in People v. Johnson[22] the court held that the victim's preliminary hearing testimony had been improperly admitted against the accused where the interpreter for the victim made substantial errors in the translation.[23] In the court's view, such errors deny the accused the right to cross-examination contemplated by the former testimony exception to the hearsay rule and by the Confrontation Clause.[24] Similarly, a magis-

---

14. People v. Louis, 42 Cal.3d 969, 991, 232 Cal.Rptr. 110, 123, 728 P.2d 180, 193 (1986) (quoting from United States v. Mann, 590 F.2d 361, 368 (1st Cir.1978)).

15. Id.

16. Id. at 992, 232 Cal.Rptr. at 124, 728 P.2d at 194.

17. People v. Hovey, 44 Cal.3d 543, 563, 244 Cal.Rptr. 121, 132, 749 P.2d 776, 786 (1988), cert. denied, 488 U.S. 871, 109 S.Ct. 188, 102 L.Ed.2d 157 (1988).

18. People v. Avila, 131 Cal.App.4th 163, 169, 31 Cal.Rptr.3d 441, 445 (2005). See also People v. Wilson, 36 Cal.4th 309, 341, 114 P.3d 758, 781, 30 Cal.Rptr.3d 513, 540 (2005), cert. denied, 547 U.S. 1042, 126 S.Ct. 1617, 164 L.Ed.2d 336 (2006) (holding that whether due diligence has been met depends on "the timeliness of the search, the importance of the proffered testimony, and whether leads of the witness's possible location were competently explored.").

19. People v. Brock, 38 Cal.3d 180, 190, 211 Cal.Rptr. 122, 128, 695 P.2d 209, 215 (1985) and cases cited therein.

20. Id.

21. Id. at 197–198, 211 Cal.Rptr. at 132–133, 695 P.2d at 219–220.

22. 46 Cal.App.3d 701, 120 Cal.Rptr. 372 (1975).

23. Id. at 704, 120 Cal.Rptr. at 374.

24. Id. The fact that a party offers an interpreter's rendition of someone else's out of court statement does not add a "hearsay layer." Interpreters are but "conduits" and their rendition of

trate's failure to accord the accused's attorney adequate time to prepare for cross-examination denies the accused a meaningful opportunity to cross examine the hearsay declarant.[25]

Similarity, not identity, of motive and interest is all that is required. Learning information after the first proceeding that might have altered the examination of the witness will not necessarily lead to the exclusion of the witness's testimony. In People v. Harris,[26] for example, the accused objected to the use of a witness's preliminary hearing testimony on the ground that at the time his counsel cross examined the witness, he was not aware that the witness had been engaged in selling illegal drugs. The accused claimed that eliciting that information would have been critical to the jury in determining the witness's credibility. The appellate court upheld the use of the witness's preliminary hearing testimony: the accused's motive and interest in cross examining the witness at the preliminary hearing and the trial were similar—to challenge the credibility of the witness. Moreover, at the preliminary hearing, the defense succeeded during cross-examination in eliciting other evidence that impeached the witness's credibility—the witness conceded lying to the police on two occasions.[27]

Changes in the way preliminary hearings are conducted in California raise fresh questions about the admissibility of preliminary hearing testimony against the accused at a subsequent proceeding. In 1990, the California electorate approved Proposition 115. Among the changes made by the proposition is an amendment to the Evidence Code which permits the use of hearsay at a preliminary hearing[28] if offered through a law enforcement officer qualified by either five years of experience or completion of a class certified by the Commission of Peace Officer Standards and Training.[29] Clearly, statements by crime witnesses offered through the officer at the preliminary hearing cannot be offered as former testimony against the accused at subsequent proceedings.[30] Under these circumstances, the accused has no opportunity—much less a meaningful one—to cross examine the hearsay declarant.

The accused's inability to confront crime witnesses at preliminary hearings is compounded by another change effected by Proposition 115.

---

the out of court declarant's statement is to be considered the statement of the declarant so long as the interpreter is unbiased and skilled in interpreting accurately. Correa v. Superior Court, 27 Cal.4th 444, 448, 117 Cal.Rptr.2d 27, 29, 40 P.3d 739, 741 (2002).

25. People v. Gibbs, 255 Cal.App.2d 739, 745, 63 Cal.Rptr. 471, 475 (1967) (Five minutes is an inadequate time to prepare to cross examine a material witness.).

26. 37 Cal.4th 310, 118 P.3d 545, 33 Cal.Rptr.3d 509 (2005), cert. denied, 547 U.S. 1065, 126 S.Ct. 1655, 164 L.Ed.2d 411 (2006).

27. Id. at 333, note 4, 118 P.3d at 562, note 4, 33 Cal.Rptr.3d 509 at 529, note 4.

28. West's Ann.California Evidence Code § 1203.1.

29. West's Ann.California Penal Code § 872(b). In Whitman v. Superior Court, 54 Cal.3d 1063, 2 Cal.Rptr.2d 160, 820 P.2d 262 (1991), the California Supreme Court held that the testifying officer must have "sufficient knowledge of the crime or the circumstances under which the out-of-court statement was made so as to meaningfully assist the magistrate in assessing the reliability of the statement." Id. at 1079, 2 Cal.Rptr.2d at 167, 820 P.2d at 267.

30. People v. Best, 56 Cal.App.4th 41, 46, 64 Cal.Rptr.2d 809, 813 (1997).

This change strips the accused of the right to call and examine hearsay declarants as a matter of right. Upon request of the prosecution, the accused may not call any witnesses unless the accused first satisfies the magistrate through an offer of proof that the testimony of witnesses, if believed, "would be reasonably likely to establish an affirmative defense, negate an element of a crime charged, or impeach the testimony of a prosecution witness or the statement of a declarant testified to by a prosecution witness."[31]

QUESTIONS AND PROBLEMS

1.   In Crawford v. Washington, the U.S. Supreme Court held that testimonial hearsay offered against a criminal defendant offends the Confrontation Clause unless the prosecution produces the hearsay declarant for cross-examination or, if the declarant is unavailable to testify, unless the defendant had an opportunity prior to the trial to cross examine the declarant. True or false?

2.   In Roberts v. Ohio the defendant was prosecuted for using a credit card without the owner's permission. At the preliminary hearing, the prosecution called the victim who testified that she did not give the defendant permission to use her credit card. Because the victim was unavailable to testify at the trial, the prosecution offered the victim's preliminary hearing testimony under Ohio's hearsay exception for former testimony. The U.S. Supreme Court affirmed, holding that no confrontation violation occurred at the trial because the former testimony exception is a firmly rooted exception to the hearsay rule. But because *Crawford* supersedes *Roberts*, today the defendant's confrontation objection would have to be sustained. Discuss.

3.   The changes made by Proposition 115, as construed by the California Supreme Court in *Whitman*, dispel any concerns that the use of preliminary hearing testimony against defendants at trial will violate their right to confront their accusers. True or false?

4.   What advantages does a defendant lose at trial when the prosecution is allowed to offer the preliminary hearing testimony of the witnesses who testified against the defendant at the preliminary hearing?

§ 11.08   PRELIMINARY HEARING TESTIMONY OF MINOR VICTIMS

Ordinarily, the preliminary hearing testimony of a witness is admissible as former testimony at the trial only if the witness is unavailable to testify and the party against whom the testimony is offered had an opportunity to cross examine the witness at the preliminary hearing with a motive and interest similar to those which the party has at the trial.[1] Section 1293 creates a special hearsay exception for minors who are crime victims by deleting the requirement that the child witness be unavailable

---

31.   West's Ann.California Penal Code § 866(a).

1.   See § 11.01 supra.

at the trial.[2] However, the former testimony is admissible only in proceedings to declare the minor a dependent child of the court pursuant to § 300 of the Welfare and Institutions Code.[3]

The issues must be such that a defendant in the preliminary hearing had the right and opportunity to cross examine the minor with an interest and motive similar to that which the parent or guardian against whom the testimony is offered has at the proceeding to declare the minor a dependent child.[4] But the parent or guardian may challenge the admissibility of the former testimony on the ground that "new substantially different issues are present in the proceeding to declare the minor a dependent child than were present in preliminary examination."[5] The parent or guardian may also object to any portion of the former testimony that would be objectionable if the child witness had appeared and testified at the proceeding to declare the child a dependent.[6]

The California Penal Code also contains provisions protecting child witnesses. Chief among these are §§ 1346 and 1347. Section 1346 allows the videotaping of the preliminary examination of child witnesses under the age of 16 and the use of the tape at the trial as former testimony "[if] at the time of trial the court finds that further testimony would cause the victim emotional trauma so that the victim is medically unavailable or otherwise unavailable within the meaning of section 240 of the Evidence Code."[7] Section 1347 establishes a procedure similar to the Maryland procedure at issue in Maryland v. Craig.[8] It allows the judge to order that the testimony of children under 14 be taken out of the presence of the judge, jury, defendant, and attorneys by means of a two-way closed circuit television, if the judge finds by clear and convincing evidence that the impact of enumerated factors—including the conduct of the accused or his counsel during the trial—is so substantial as to render the minor unavailable as a witness unless the closed circuit procedure is used.[9]

CALIFORNIA EVIDENCE CODE

§ 1290. "Former testimony"

As used in this article, "former testimony" means testimony given under oath in:

---

2. West's Ann.California Evidence Code § 1293.

3. Id.

4. Id.

5. Id.

6. Id.

7. West's Ann. California Penal Code § 1346.

8. 497 U.S. 836, 110 S.Ct. 3157, 111 L.Ed.2d 666 (1990). For an extended discussion of this case, see § 14.05 infra.

9. West's Ann. California Penal Code § 1347. The procedure is available only if the child's testimony involves the recitation of facts relating to sexual offenses or violent felonies. Id.

(a) Another action or in a former hearing or trial of the same action;

(b) A proceeding to determine a controversy conducted by or under the supervision of an agency that has the power to determine such a controversy and is an agency of the United States or a public entity in the United States;

(c) A deposition taken in compliance with law in another action; or

(d) An arbitration proceeding if the evidence of such former testimony is a verbatim transcript thereof.

§ 1291.   Former testimony offered against party to former proceeding

(a) Evidence of former testimony is not made inadmissible by the hearsay rule if the declarant is unavailable as a witness and:

(1) The former testimony is offered against a person who offered it in evidence in his own behalf on the former occasion or against the successor in interest of such person; or

(2) The party against whom the former testimony is offered was a party to the action or proceeding in which the testimony was given and had the right and opportunity to cross-examine the declarant with an interest and motive similar to that which he has at the hearing.

(b) The admissibility of former testimony under this section is subject to the same limitations and objections as though the declarant were testifying at the hearing, except that former testimony offered under this section is not subject to:

(1) Objections to the form of the question which were not made at the time the former testimony was given.

(2) Objections based on competency or privilege which did not exist at the time the former testimony was given.

§ 1292.   Former testimony offered against person not a party to former proceeding

(a) Evidence of former testimony is not made inadmissible by the hearsay rule if:

(1) The declarant is unavailable as a witness;

(2) The former testimony is offered in a civil action; and

(3) The issue is such that the party to the action or proceeding in which the former testimony was given had the right and opportunity to cross-examine the declarant with an interest and motive similar to that which the party against whom the testimony is offered has at the hearing.

(b) The admissibility of former testimony under this section is subject to the same limitations and objections as though the declarant were testifying at the hearing, except that former testimony offered under this section is not subject to objections based on competency or privilege which did not exist at the time the former testimony was given.

§ 1293.   Former testimony made at a preliminary examination by a minor child as a complaining witness; admissibility

(a) Evidence of former testimony made at a preliminary examination by a minor child who was the complaining witness is not made inadmissible by the hearsay rule if:

(1) The former testimony is offered in a proceeding to declare the minor a dependent child of the court pursuant to Section 300 of the Welfare and Institutions Code.

(2) The issues are such that a defendant in the preliminary examination in which the former testimony was given had the right and opportunity to cross-examine the minor child with an interest and motive similar to that which the parent or guardian against whom the testimony is offered has at the proceeding to declare the minor a dependent child of the court.

(b) The admissibility of former testimony under this section is subject to the same limitations and objections as though the minor child were testifying at the proceeding to declare him or her a dependent child of the court.

(c) The attorney for the parent or guardian against whom the former testimony is offered or, if none, the parent or guardian may make a motion to challenge the admissibility of the former testimony upon a showing that new substantially different issues are present in the proceeding to declare the minor a dependent child than were present in the preliminary examination.

(d) As used in this section, "complaining witness" means the alleged victim of the crime for which a preliminary examination was held.

(e) This section shall apply only to testimony made at a preliminary examination on and after January 1, 1990.

FEDERAL RULES OF EVIDENCE

Rule 804.   Exceptions to the Rule Against Hearsay—When the Declarant Is Unavailable as a Witness

* * *

(b) The Exceptions. The following are not excluded by the rule against hearsay if the declarant is unavailable as a witness:

(1) *Former Testimony.* Testimony that:

(A) was given as a witness at a trial, hearing, or lawful deposition, whether given during the current proceeding or a different one; and

(B) is now offered against a party who had—or, in a civil case, whose predecessor in interest had—an opportunity and similar motive to develop it by direct, cross-, or redirect examination.

CHAPTER 12

EXCEPTIONS TO THE HEARSAY RULE: LEARNED TREATISES, COMMERCIAL LISTS, AND JUDGMENTS

■ ■ ■

Table of Sections

---

§ 12.01 LEARNED TREATISES

Section 1341 creates a hearsay exception for "[h]istorical works, books of science or art, and published maps or charts, made by persons indifferent between the parties, * * * when offered to prove facts of general notoriety and interest."[1] Though seemingly generous, the exception is of limited value because the general notoriety requirement has been construed to include only facts that are not subject to dispute.[2] Such facts include the definition of words found in dictionaries, life expectancies found in actuarial tables, and the information found in tables of weights and measures, and currency, annuity, and interest tables.[3] Facts of general notoriety do not include statements in medical treatises, as "medicine is not considered one of the exact sciences."[4] It is, instead, the kind of field in which knowledge changes; consequently, "if [medical] treatises were to be held admissible, the question at issue might be tried, not by testimony, but upon excerpts from works presenting partial views of variant and perhaps contradictory theories."[5]

---

1. West's Ann.California Evidence Code § 1341.

2. See Gallagher v. Market St. R. Co., 67 Cal. 13, 6 P. 869 (1885). Although *Gallagher* was decided 80 years before the adoption of the Code, it construed a provision virtually identical to § 1341.

3. Id. at 16, 6 P. at 871.

4. Id.

5. Id. at 16, 6 P. at 872.

The fact that experts can be cross examined about the content of learned treatises does not affect the hearsay limitations on the admissibility of statements in such works. Under the Code, expert witnesses, including medical experts, may be cross examined about the content or tenor of any scientific journal or treatise if at least one of three conditions is satisfied: (1) the expert referred to, considered, or relied upon the publication in arriving at or in forming the expert opinion; (2) the publication has been admitted in evidence; or (3) the publication has been established as a reliable authority by the testimony or admission of the expert or another expert, or by judicial notice.[6] But the right to conduct such a cross-examination does not mean that the portion of the publication used is in evidence for the truth of the matter stated.[7] The pertinent statements may not be read to the jury unless the publication has been admitted or qualifies for admission under a hearsay exception such as the one for learned treatises.[8]

The Federal Rules of Evidence take a more generous approach to the admissibility of information contained in learned treatises. Under Rule 803(18), statements contained in such treatises (including medical ones) may be admitted for the truth of the matter asserted if (1) such statements are established as reliable authority by expert testimony or judicial notice and (2) the treatise was relied upon by an expert witness on direct examination or was called to the expert's attention on cross-examination.[9] Thus, when a treatise has been established as authoritative, appropriate passages may be offered in evidence, so long as an expert is on the stand and available to explain and assist in applying the treatise.[10] If admitted, the passages may be read into evidence but may not be received as exhibits.[11] This limitation is designed "to prevent jurors from overvaluing the written word and from roaming at large through the treatise thereby forming conclusions not subjected to expert explanation and assistance."[12]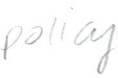

QUESTIONS AND PROBLEMS

1. The plaintiff sues the defendant, an obstetrician, for injuries sustained during childbirth. The defendant failed to perform a caesarian. The plaintiff previously had given birth by caesarian and claims that accepted medical practice requires that subsequent births be by caesarian. The plaintiff's expert has just testified on direct that "once a caesarian, always a caesarian." The defendant now cross examines the expert as follows; rule on the plaintiff's objections under the Code and the Rules:

     Defendant: You are familiar with the leading literature in this field?

---

6.   West's Ann.California Evidence Code § 721(b).

7.   Id. (comment).

8.   West's Ann. California Evidence Code § 721(b).

9.   Federal Rule of Evidence 803(18).

10.   Id. (Advisory Committee Note).

11.   Federal Rule of Evidence 803(18).

12.   M. Graham, Handbook of Federal Evidence § 803.18 (3d ed. 1991).

Expert: Of course.

Defendant: In reaching the opinion you gave on direct examination, you took that literature into account?

Expert: Yes.

Defendant: Including Dr. Michael Wald's 1987 article in the Old England Journal of Medicine?

Expert: Yes.

Defendant: You are aware, then, that Dr. Wald concludes, "Under some circumstances, natural childbirth can follow a caesarian."? I believe that's on page 19.

Expert: Yes.

Defendant: Do you agree with Dr. Wald?

Expert: Yes.

Plaintiff: Objection. Move to strike on grounds of hearsay.

Judge: ?

2. Suppose, instead, that the examination was as follows:

Defendant: Do you agree with Dr. Wald?

Expert: No.

Defendant: But you nonetheless regard Dr. Wald's work, including his article, as authoritative, do you not?

Expert: Yes.

Defendant: Your Honor, I ask the court's permission to read to the jury that portion of Dr. Wald's work to which I just referred.

Plaintiff: Objection. Calls for hearsay.

Judge: ?

§ 12.02   COMMERCIAL LISTS

Some of the examples listed by the California courts of facts of general notoriety that can be proved through learned treatises[1] are the kinds of matters that can be proved through lists and tabulations. Section 1340 creates a hearsay exception for "a statement, other than an opinion, contained in a tabulation, list, directory, register, or other published compilation * * * if the compilation is generally used and relied upon as accurate in the course of a business as defined in [the section creating a hearsay exception for business records]."[2] Examples cited by the Law Revision Commission include actuarial and annuity tables.[3] The Federal

---

1. See § 12.01 supra.

2. West's Ann.California Evidence Code § 1340. See People ex rel. Lockyer v. R.J. Reynolds Tobacco Co., 116 Cal.App.4th 1253, 1278, 11 Cal.Rptr.3d 317, 339 (2004) (approving of trial court's finding that a surveyor's data qualified under the hearsay exception because businesses generally use and rely on the data in the course of business).

3. Id. (comment).

Rules include market quotations as well and broaden the classes of individuals who rely on such compilations.[4] Under the Rules, such compilations are admissible if generally used and relied upon by the *public* as well as by persons in particular occupations.[5]

California judges have construed § 1340 to include the public, not just businesses, in defining the kinds of compilations that are admissible under the section. In **In re Michael G.**[6] the state sought to have a minor declared a ward of the court on the grounds that the minor possessed a can of spray paint containing toluene. To prove that the paint contained toluene, the prosecution offered the can taken from the minor. The label listed toluene as an ingredient and warned about its effects if the paint were swallowed. After taking judicial notice that the public uses and relies on labels for warnings, the judge received the label under § 1340. In upholding the judge's ruling, the reviewing court distinguished between labels that include a hazardous ingredient and those that do not. "A label *including* (rather than excluding) a hazardous substance is inherently trustworthy, in that a manufacturer would have no interest in proclaiming that the product contained such a substance if it did not."[7]

QUESTIONS AND PROBLEMS

Under the Code and the Rules, a party may prove a telephone number by offering in evidence the appropriate page from a telephone directory issued by one of the major telephone companies. True or false?

§ 12.03 JUDGMENTS

Judgments of conviction. Section 1300 creates a hearsay exception for final judgments "adjudging a person guilty of a crime punishable as a felony" when offered in a civil action to prove any fact essential to the judgment.[1] Such judgments are hearsay, since in effect they are statements by the pronouncing court that a particular individual stands convicted of a felony.[2] Indeed, multiple hearsay is involved, since the judgment is usually proved by a record reflecting the judge's oral pronouncement of sentence, which in turn is based on a finding of guilt, a guilty verdict, or a guilty plea.[3] Moreover, since the judgment is being offered as evidence that the accused engaged in the misconduct giving rise to the convicted offense, in the case of findings of guilt or guilty verdicts

---

4. Federal Rule of Evidence 803(17).

5. Id.

6. 19 Cal.App.4th 1674, 24 Cal.Rptr.2d 260 (1993).

7. Id. at 1678, 24 Cal.Rptr.2d at 262 (emphasis in the original). The court, however, limited its holding to proving the presence of the dangerous substance and not its quality or quantity. Id.

1. West's Ann.California Evidence Code § 1300.

2. Id. (comment).

3. West's Ann.California Penal Code §§ 1191 and 1200. "In a criminal case, judgment is rendered when the trial court orally pronounces sentence." People v. Ibanez, 76 Cal.App.4th 537, 543, 90 Cal.Rptr.2d 536, 540 (1999).

the hearsay rule is implicated even further. In effect, the judgment is being offered as proof of the minimum evidence the prosecution had to offer to make out a prima facie case. Thus, where a plaintiff sues to recover a reward offered by the defendant for the arrest and conviction of a person who committed a crime, § 1300 will allow the plaintiff to offer a judgment of conviction as evidence that the person committed the crime.[4]

Section 1300 is limited to judgments based on felony charges on the theory that only such judgments are sufficiently reliable to justify a hearsay exception. "The seriousness of the charge assures that the facts will be thoroughly litigated, and the fact that the judgment must be based upon a determination that there was no reasonable doubt concerning the defendant's guilt assures that the question of guilt will be thoroughly considered."[5] The section, however, does not limit judgments to those resulting only from a guilty verdict or a finding of guilt. Its terms do not exclude judgments based on guilty pleas. Presumably, the self-incrimination element inherent in guilty pleas lends such judgments the desired reliability.

Section 1300 applies to any offense punishable as a felony. "The fact that a misdemeanor sentence is imposed does not affect the admissibility of the judgment under this section."[6]

Section 1300 allows the use of judgments as evidence of material issues. Whether or not the judgment should have a conclusive effect depends on principles of collateral estoppel and not on the law of evidence.[7]

At one time, judgments based on pleas of nolo contendere were inadmissible under § 1300. The exclusion was based on the policy of encouraging such pleas. The section was amended in 1982 to include felony judgments based on nolo pleas among the judgments that can be offered under § 1300. The change was made to help crime victims "obtain compensation from the criminals who inflicted [their] injuries."[8]

Judgments of conviction that fail to satisfy the conditions of § 1300 may also be offered under other hearsay exceptions. Sometimes a party must prove the fact of a conviction. Whenever the prosecution, for example, seeks to enhance punishment by alleging a prior conviction, the prosecution is entitled to prove that fact. Such convictions can include misdemeanor convictions. In those circumstances, § 1300 is unavailable for the additional reason that it creates a hearsay exception only for judgments offered in civil cases. The prosecution, however, may rely on

---

4. West's Ann.California Evidence Code § 1300 (comment).

5. Id.

6. Id. But if the prosecution elects to treat the offense as a misdemeanor, then the conviction may not be offered under § 1300. County of Los Angeles v. Civil Service Commission, 39 Cal.App.4th 620, 631, 46 Cal.Rptr.2d 256, 264 (1995).

7. West's Ann.California Evidence Code § 1300 (comment).

8. West's Ann.California Penal Code § 1016 (legislative history).

the official records exception to the hearsay rule to prove judgments that are beyond the ambit of § 1300.[9]

Judgments of conviction have been used to disprove assertions made by witnesses. In Leader v. State[10] the plaintiff sued the defendants for injuries he suffered when arrested. On direct examination, the plaintiff testified that he had been beaten by one of the defendants, a CHP officer, even though he was not belligerent or resisting arrest.[11] The defendants then offered judgments adjudging the plaintiff guilty of the misdemeanor crimes of assaulting and resisting arrest by the CHP officer. The reviewing court held that it was error to exclude the judgments, since they could be used to contradict the plaintiff's testimony.[12] However, a subsequent case, People v. Wheeler,[13] holds that, in the absence of a special hearsay exception, misdemeanor conviction judgments may not be used over a hearsay objection to prove that the accused engaged in the misconduct giving rise to the convicted offense.[14]

Traditional hearsay exceptions are unavailing under these circumstances. Section 1300 cannot be used to prove the facts essential to the misdemeanor conviction because the section is limited to proving felony conviction judgments and then only when such judgments are offered in a *civil* action.[15] *Wheeler* was a criminal case. The exception for party admissions to the hearsay rule cannot be used, but for a different reason: asking the accused on cross whether he has been convicted of a misdemeanor would prove only the fact of conviction and not the misconduct giving rise to the conviction.[16] For the same reason, the business and official records exceptions cannot be used: those records would prove only the fact that the witness has been convicted of the misdemeanor enumerated in the records.[17] Consequently, in the absence of a new hearsay exception, over objection the proponent must offer the misconduct that gave rise to the misdemeanor conviction and not the judgment of conviction to disprove assertions made by witnesses, such as those made by the plaintiff in *Leader*.[18]

---

9. For a discussion of the official records exception to the hearsay rule, see § 10.07 supra.

10. 182 Cal.App.3d 1079, 226 Cal.Rptr. 207 (1986).

11. Id. at 1091, 226 Cal.Rptr. at 215.

12. Id. at 1092, 226 Cal.Rptr. at 215. Under § 780(i), a party is entitled to attack the credibility of a witness by proving the nonexistence of any fact testified to by a witness. West's Ann.California Evidence Code § 780(i). *Leader* is unclear as to the hearsay exception theory under which the convictions were offered. The defendants offered certified copies. Leader v. State, 182 Cal.App.3d 1079, 1082, 226 Cal.Rptr. 207, 208 (1986).

13. 4 Cal.4th 284, 14 Cal.Rptr.2d 418, 841 P.2d 938 (1992).

14. Id.

15. Section 788, which governs the use of convictions to impeach witnesses, cannot be used either, because this section creates a hearsay exception only for felony convictions and then only when the conviction is used as evidence of the accused's character for lack of veracity, not as evidence of contradiction. West's Ann.California Evidence Code § 788.

16. People v. Wheeler, 4 Cal.4th 284, 300, 14 Cal.Rptr.2d 418, 428, 841 P.2d 938, 948 (1992).

17. Id. at 300, note 13, 14 Cal.Rptr.2d at 428, note 13, 841 P.2d at 948, note 13.

18. Id. at 300, note 14, 14 Cal.Rptr.2d at 428, note 14, 841 P.2d at 948, note 14.

Section 452.5, which was added to the Evidence Code by the Legislature in 1996, has been construed as providing the needed exception. Section 452.5 provides that an "official record of conviction certified in accordance with subdivision (a) of Section 1530 is admissible pursuant to Section 1280 to prove the commission, attempted commission, or solicitation of a criminal offense, service of a prison term, or other act, condition or event recorded by the record."[19] Section 1280 creates a hearsay exception for official records, and § 1530 permits copies of records in the custody of a public entity to be offered without the need to call a custodian to authenticate the copy if attested or certified as a correct copy of the original record by a public employee having legal custody of the record.[20]

As a matter of statutory construction, it is not entirely clear whether § 452.5 can always be used to offer a conviction record as proof that the accused engaged in the misconduct giving rise to the conviction. Though the section does state that the record "is admissible" as an official record when offered to prove "the commission" of the offense, this provision is limited by the requirement that the record be offered to prove only those acts, conditions, or events recorded in the record. Thus, if the only event recorded is the fact of conviction, using that entry to prove that the accused engaged in the misconduct giving rise to the conviction would still appear to violate the hearsay rule. In People v. Duran,[21] however, the California Court of Appeal clarified this uncertainty by holding that § 452.5 "creates a hearsay exception allowing admission of qualifying court records to prove not only the fact of conviction, but also that the offense reflected in the record occurred."[22]

Without a special hearsay exception such as § 452.5, complying with *Wheeler* would be problematical. Proving, for example, that a witness, who denies resisting arrest, in fact resisted arrest would force the impeaching party to call witnesses with first hand knowledge of the witness's misconduct at the time of the arrest. Since the opposing party would be entitled to call witnesses who could give a different account of the events surrounding the arrest, evidence about the credibility of a witness could quickly degenerate into a hearing in which the witness's conduct at the time of arrest would be relitigated. The potential prejudice to the parties,

---

19. West's Ann. California Evidence Code § 452.5.

20. See West's Ann. California Evidence Code §§ 1280 and 1530.

21. 97 Cal.App.4th 1448, 119 Cal.Rptr.2d 272 (2002).

22. Id. at 1460, 119 Cal.Rptr.2d at 282. Under California's Sexually Violent Predator Act, sex offenders, who as a result of a mental impairment continue to present a danger of reoffending upon release from prison, may be committed to a treatment facility upon release. West's Ann. California Welfare & Institutions Code § 6600 et seq. To qualify for commitment, the state must show, among other matters, that the defendant has been convicted of a sexually violent offense against two or more persons. Id. § 6600(a)(1). The act specifically allows the use of probation and sentencing reports, among other documents, to prove that the defendant engaged in sexually violent acts in committing the predicate offenses. Id. § 6600(a)(3). Accordingly, these reports may be offered to prove as true the descriptions of attacks provided by victims to those preparing the reports. People v. Otto, 26 Cal.4th 200, 208, 109 Cal.Rptr.2d 327, 333–334, 26 P.3d 1061, 1065–1066 (2001).

the court, and the jurors is obvious, unless the trial judge firmly limits the evidence. The judge can do so by relying on § 352.[23]

Section 452.5 does not eliminate the prejudicial risk entirely, however. Records of conviction offered under the section are not, by virtue of the section, entitled to any special conclusive effect. The opposing party is still entitled to offer evidence contesting the existence of the facts essential to the judgment reflected in the conviction record. Thus, if a record of a misdemeanor conviction is offered to prove that the accused resisted arrest, the accused should be entitled to call witnesses with first hand knowledge to testify that the accused did not in fact resist the arrest. The judge, however, would still be empowered by § 352 to place some limits on the number of witnesses offered on this question.

Section 1300 is unavailable to prove that a witness has been convicted of a felony when offered to prove the witness's character for lack of veracity. But § 788, which governs the use of felony convictions to impeach witnesses, creates a hearsay exception for such judgments when offered for that purpose.[24]

The Federal Rules provide an exception similar to § 1300 for felony grade judgments. The Rules, however, make it clear that such judgments can be predicated upon a plea of guilty as well as upon a finding of guilt or a guilty verdict.[25] The Rules, moreover, still exclude judgments based upon a plea of nolo contendere.[26]

Civil judgments. "Where a judgment against an indemnitee or person protected by a warranty is not made conclusive on the indemnitor or warrantor, Section 1301 permits the judgment to be used as hearsay evidence in an action to recover on the indemnity or warranty."[27]

When the liability, obligation, or duty of a third person is an issue in a civil action, § 1302 provides a hearsay exception for final judgments against that person when offered to prove such liability, obligation, or duty.[28] The liability of a third person is an issue under § 1224. If, under the substantive law that applies to an action, the liability of the defendant depends in whole or in part upon the liability of a declarant, then under § 1224 evidence of a statement made by the declarant is as admissible against the defendant as it would be if offered against the declarant in an action involving that liability.[29]

---

23. Of course, if the evidence is also probative of the substantive issues to be decided in the case, the judge should admit the evidence. The evidence would then possess additional probative value, since it would not be limited to credibility. That would have been true in *Leader*, where the defendants had to prove that the plaintiff had resisted the arrest in question.

24. West's Ann.California Evidence Code § 788 and comment.

25. Federal Rule of Evidence 803(22).

26. Id.

27. West's Ann.California Evidence Code § 1301 (comment).

28. West's Ann.California Evidence Code § 1302.

29. For a discussion of § 1224, see § 7.03 supra.

1.The plaintiff sues to recover a reward which the defendant promised to anyone providing information leading to the arrest of the person who stole his car. The plaintiff testifies that he told the police that he saw Bob Jones driving the defendant's car. A police officer testifies that he arrested Jones on the basis of the plaintiff's report. To prove that Jones had stolen the car, the plaintiff offers the record of a judgment of conviction adjudging Bob Jones guilty of committing the felony of car theft. The plaintiff offers the record as an official or business record. The defendant objects on the ground that even admitting the record under either exception would still violate the hearsay rule. How should the judge rule?

If the judge sustains the objection, what other hearsay exceptions would you call to the plaintiff's attention in a California or federal court?

2. The defendant is prosecuted in California for making fraudulent promises. The chief witness for the prosecution is W. The defendant seeks to impeach W with the records of two judgments of conviction. The first conviction record is for perjury, a felony. The second is for the misdemeanor of taking an apple from a store without paying for it. The prosecutor concedes that under the Evidence Code, the defendant may use the felony judgment to impeach W's credibility, but he objects to the misdemeanor judgment on the ground that its use as proof that he stole the apple is inadmissible under the hearsay exceptions for official records under § 1280 and judgments under § 1300. How should the judge rule?

If the judge sustains the hearsay objection, what other exception would you call to the defendant's attention in a California court?

CALIFORNIA EVIDENCE CODE

§ 452.5. Criminal conviction records; computer-generated records; admissibility

(a) * * *

(b) An official record of conviction certified in accordance with subdivision (a) of Section 1530 is admissible pursuant to Section 1280 to prove the commission, attempted commission, or solicitation of a criminal offense, prior conviction, service of a prison term, or other act, condition, or event recorded by the record.

§ 1300. Judgment of conviction of crime punishable as felony

Evidence of a final judgment adjudging a person guilty of a crime punishable as a felony is not made inadmissible by the hearsay rule when offered in a civil action to prove any fact essential to the judgment whether or not the judgment was based on a plea of nolo contendere.

§ 1301. Judgment against person entitled to indemnity

Evidence of a final judgment is not made inadmissible by the hearsay rule when offered by the judgment debtor to prove any fact which was essential to the judgment in an action in which he seeks to:

(a) Recover partial or total indemnity or exoneration for money paid or liability incurred because of the judgment;

(b) Enforce a warranty to protect the judgment debtor against the liability determined by the judgment; or

(c) Recover damages for breach of warranty substantially the same as the warranty determined by the judgment to have been breached.

§ 1302. Judgment determining liability of third person

When the liability, obligation, or duty of a third person is in issue in a civil action, evidence of a final judgment against that person is not made inadmissible by the hearsay rule when offered to prove such liability, obligation, or duty.

§ 1340. Commercial lists and the like

Evidence of a statement, other than an opinion, contained in a tabulation, list, directory, register, or other published compilation is not made inadmissible by the hearsay rule if the compilation is generally used and relied upon as accurate in the course of a business as defined in Section 1270.

§ 1341. Publications concerning facts of general notoriety and interest

Historical works, books of science or art, and published maps or charts, made by persons indifferent between the parties, are not made inadmissible by the hearsay rule when offered to prove facts of general notoriety and interest.

§ 1530. Copy of writing in official custody

(a) A purported copy of a writing in the custody of a public entity, or of an entry in such a writing, is prima facie evidence of the existence and content of such writing or entry if:

(1) The copy purports to be published by the authority of the nation or state, or public entity therein in which the writing is kept;

(2) The office in which the writing is kept is within the United States or within the Panama Canal Zone, the Trust Territory of the Pacific Islands, or the Ryukyu Islands, and the copy is attested or certified as a correct copy of the writing or entry by a public employee, or a deputy of a public employee, having the legal custody of the writing; or

(3) The office in which the writing is kept is not within the United States or any other place described in paragraph (2) and the copy is attested as a correct copy of the writing or entry by a person having authority to make attestation. The attestation must be accompanied by a final statement certifying the genuineness of the signature and the official position of (i) the person who attested the copy as a correct copy or (ii) any

foreign official who has certified either the genuineness of the signature and official position of the person attesting the copy or the genuineness of the signature and official position of another foreign official who has executed a similar certificate in a chain of such certificates beginning with a certificate of the genuineness of the signature and official position of the person attesting the copy. Except as provided in the next sentence, the final statement may be made only by a secretary of an embassy or legation, consul general, consul, vice consul, or consular agent of the United States, or a diplomatic or consular official of the foreign country assigned or accredited to the United States. Prior to January 1, 1971, the final statement may also be made by a secretary of an embassy or legation, consul general, consul, vice consul, consular agent, or other officer in the foreign service of the United States stationed in the nation in which the writing is kept, authenticated by the seal of his office. If reasonable opportunity has been given to all parties to investigate the authenticity and accuracy of the documents, the court may, for good cause shown, (i) admit an attested copy without the final statement or (ii) permit the writing or entry in foreign custody to be evidenced by an attested summary with or without a final statement.

(b) The presumptions established by this section are presumptions affecting the burden of producing evidence.

FEDERAL RULES OF EVIDENCE

Rule 803.   Exceptions to the Rule Against Hearsay—Regardless of Whether the Declarant Is Available as a Witness

The following are not excluded by the rule against hearsay, regardless of whether the declarant is available as a witness:

* * *

(17) *Market Reports and Similar Commercial Publications.* Market quotations, lists, directories, or other compilations that are generally relied on by the public or by persons in particular occupations.

(18) *Statements in Learned Treatises, Periodicals, or Pamphlets.* A statement contained in a treatise, periodical, or pamphlet if:

(A) the statement is called to the attention of an expert witness on cross-examination or relied on by the expert on direct examination; and

(B) the publication is established as a reliable authority by the expert's admission or testimony, by another expert's testimony, or by judicial notice.

If admitted, the statement may be read into evidence but not received as an exhibit.

* * *

(22) *Judgment of a Previous Conviction.* Evidence of a final judgment of conviction if:

> **(A)** the judgment was entered after a trial or guilty plea, but not a nolo contendere plea;
>
> **(B)** the conviction was for a crime punishable by death or by imprisonment for more than a year;
>
> **(C)** the evidence is admitted to prove any fact essential to the judgment; and
>
> **(D)** when offered by the prosecutor in a criminal case for a purpose other than impeachment, the judgment was against the defendant.

The pendency of an appeal may be shown but does not affect admissibility.

(23) *Judgments Involving Personal, Family, or General History, or a Boundary.* A judgment that is admitted to prove a matter of personal, family, or general history, or boundaries, if the matter:

> **(A)** was essential to the judgment; and
>
> **(B)** could be proved by evidence of reputation.

CHAPTER 13

AUTHENTICATION AND THE BEST AND SECONDARY EVIDENCE RULES

■ ■ ■

Table of Sections

§ 13.01　THE REQUIREMENT OF AUTHENTICATION

Whenever a writing is offered in evidence, the proponent must also offer enough evidence to permit the judge to find that the writing is what the proponent claims it to be.[1] If, for example, the plaintiff offers a writing which he claims is the contract that he and the defendant entered into, then the plaintiff must offer some evidence indicating that the writing is indeed that contract. In the words of the Law Revision Commission, the plaintiff must show that the writing is "authentic," i.e., the contract entered into between the parties.[2] If the writing is not the contract, then the writing is irrelevant and inadmissible.

Because authentication is a form of relevance, the role of the judge is quite limited. If, viewing the evidence in the light most favorable to the

---

1.　West's Ann. California Evidence Code § 1400.

2.　Id. (comment).

plaintiff, the judge concludes that a reasonable jury could find the writing to be the contract, then the judge must let the issue of the contract's authenticity go to the jury.[3] The defendant is entitled to offer evidence disputing the writing's authenticity, but such evidence will not prevent the introduction of the writing so long as the plaintiff's evidence meets the sufficiency standard. It is up to the jury, not the judge, to decide from all of the evidence whether the writing is in fact the contract entered into by the parties. Indeed, if the writing is received, the defendant can require the judge to instruct the jurors to disregard the writing unless they first find that it is the contract.[4] The instruction, coupled with the limited power given to the judge to determine the writing's authenticity, assures that the parties will not be deprived of the right to have the jury pass on a material factual issue.[5]

Sometimes, evidence that an individual possessed a particular writing supplies the necessary connection with the case. In People v. Gibson[6] the defendant was prosecuted for pimping. The reviewing court approved the admission of two manuscripts taken from the defendant's home which described the operation of a prostitution enterprise. The manuscripts were probative of the knowledge the accused needed to run such an enterprise.[7] Because of the location where the manuscripts were recovered, it was immaterial that the prosecution was unable to tie the manuscripts to the accused by such evidence as fingerprints.[8] Occasionally, however, evidence in addition to location may be necessary to connect the writing with the case. In People v. Kraft[9] the accused was prosecuted for killing a number of young men. Over the accused's irrelevancy objection, the trial judge allowed the prosecution to introduce a document recovered from the accused's car bearing 61 "cryptic" entries. The prosecution maintained that the document was a list in "code" of the murder victims. The reviewing court upheld the trial judge's ruling. Combined with other evidence offered by the prosecution, a reasonable jury could find that the list referred to the young men the prosecution claimed had been murdered by the accused.[10]

Although authentication is usually associated with writings, the concept applies whenever any tangible object is offered in evidence.[11] Whether the object be the knife the prosecution believes the accused used to kill the victim or the ladder the plaintiff claims was defective, the proponent must connect the object with the case. Showing that the object is relevant to the issues to be decided will require some evidence that the object is what the

---

3. West's Ann. California Evidence Code §§ 403(a)(3) and 1400.

4. West's Ann. California Evidence Code § 403(c)(2).

5. Id. (comment).

6. 90 Cal.App.4th 371, 108 Cal.Rptr.2d 809 (2001).

7. Id. at 382–383, 108 Cal.Rptr.2d at 816–817.

8. Id.

9. 23 Cal.4th 978, 99 Cal.Rptr.2d 1, 5 P.3d 68 (2000), cert. denied 532 U.S. 908, 121 S.Ct. 1234, 149 L.Ed.2d 142 (2001).

10. Id. at 1033–1034, 99 Cal.Rptr.2d at 36–38, 5 P.3d at 100–101.

11. West's Ann. California Evidence Code § 1400 (comment).

proponent claims it is. For purposes of admissibility, the quantum of evidence, as in the case of writings, need satisfy only a sufficiency standard.[12]

Under the Evidence Code, a trial judge may admit evidence on the condition that the proponent supply the evidence connecting the item with the case before the close of the evidence.[13] Thus, a judge could admit the purported contract, knife, or ladder subject to a motion to strike if the proponent failed to furnish the connecting evidence.[14]

QUESTIONS AND PROBLEMS

1.   Plaintiff sues Steps, Inc. in a California court for injuries he claims he suffered when he fell from defendant's defective ladder. Plaintiff identifies a ladder, labeled as "Plaintiff's Exhibit A," as the ladder from which he fell, and then offers the ladder in evidence. Steps, Inc. objects on the ground of lack of authentication. How should the judge rule?

2.   In arguing for admissibility, over a hearsay objection may the plaintiff rely on a label that says, "Manufactured by Steps, Inc."?

3.   In support of its authentication objection, may Steps, Inc. tell the judge that it wishes to call Tom Jones, who the defendant claims is the employee who builds its ladders and who, according to the defendant, will testify that Plaintiff's Exhibit A was not manufactured by the defendant?

§ 13.02   AUTHENTICATING WRITINGS

The various Code provisions describing the manner in which the requirement of authentication can be satisfied assume that the object to be authenticated is a writing. The provisions are not exclusive; they are illustrative only, and the proponent is free to use any otherwise admissible evidence to identify a writing.[1]

A writing can be authenticated by anyone who saw the writing made or executed.[2] A writing can also be authenticated by evidence that the party against whom it is offered has at any time admitted its authenticity or has treated the writing as authentic.[3] A writing can be authenticated by

---

12.   West's Ann. California Evidence Code § 403(a)(1).

13.   West's Ann. California Evidence Code § 403(b).

14.   West's Ann. California Evidence Code § 403(b) does not empower judges to admit the testimony of a witness on the condition that the proponent later demonstrate the witness's personal knowledge of the subject matter of the testimony. Id. Against a lack of personal knowledge objection, the proponent must show the witness's personal knowledge before the witness can continue with the testimony. West's Ann. California Evidence Code § 702(a). Section 1401(a) provides that "[a]uthentication of a writing is required before it may be received in evidence." West's Ann. California Evidence Code § 1401(a). But since § 1401(a) is not exempted by § 403(b), presumably the requirement is not violated if the writing is received only conditionally.

1.   West's Ann. California Evidence Code § 1410.

2.   West's Ann. California Evidence Code § 1413.

3.   West's Ann. California Evidence Code § 1414. See also Ambriz v. Kelegian, 146 Cal.App.4th 1519, 1527, 53 Cal.Rptr.3d 700, 705 (2007) (holding that by seeking to offer portions of the same deposition offered by the proponent, the opponent authenticated the deposition).

evidence that the writing was received in response to a communication sent to the person who is claimed by the proponent to be the author of the writing.[4] A writing can also be authenticated by evidence that it refers to or states matters that are unlikely to be known to anyone other than the person claimed by the proponent to be the maker of the writing.[5]

A writing can be authenticated by evidence that the writing is in the handwriting of the maker or, if signed, that the signature is the maker's.[6] A lay witness who has personal knowledge of the maker's handwriting or signature can give an opinion on whether the handwriting or signature is the maker's.[7] The ways in which the witness acquires the personal knowledge include having seen the purported maker write or sign,[8] having seen a writing purporting to be in the handwriting of the supposed maker and upon which the supposed maker has acted,[9] or having received letters in the due course of mail purporting to be from the supposed maker in response to letters duly addressed and mailed by the witness to the supposed maker.[10]

An expert can give an opinion on the authenticity of a writing by comparing the writing with one that has been authenticated as having been prepared or signed by the purported maker.[11] This method applies to any form of writing, not just handwriting, since experts can now compare typewritten specimens and other forms of writing as accurately as they can compare handwriting specimens.[12]

A handwritten document can also be authenticated by providing the fact finder, whether judge or jury, with a specimen which the court finds was admitted or treated as authentic by the party against whom the handwritten document is offered.[13] A judge, for example, may allow a jury to compare signatures on insurance claim forms with the signature on the accused's driver's license where the accused concedes that the signature on the license is his.[14] In this case, it is the fact finder, rather than the expert, who makes the comparison. In all cases, however, it is up to the fact finder to determine whether the purported writing is in fact what the proponent claims it to be.

Acknowledged writings. The Civil Procedure Code provides for the "acknowledgment" of such instruments as conveyances.[15] An acknowledg-

---

4. West's Ann. California Evidence Code § 1420.

5. West's Ann. California Evidence Code § 1421. For a discussion of the relationship of this section to the Best Evidence Rule, see § 13.08 infra.

6. West's Ann. California Evidence Code § 1415.

7. West's Ann. California Evidence Code § 1416.

8. Id.

9. Id.

10. Id.

11. West's Ann. California Evidence Code § 1418.

12. Id. (comment).

13. West's Ann. California Evidence Code § 1417.

14. People v. Rodriguez, 133 Cal.App.4th 545, 554, 34 Cal.Rptr.3d 886, 893 (2005).

15. West's Ann. Code of Civil Procedure §§ 1180 et seq.

ment consists of a certificate in which a designated officer certifies that the person signing the instrument personally appeared before the officer and declared to the officer that he signed the instrument in his authorized capacity.[16] If the certificate meets the requirements of the Civil Code, then the Evidence Code provides that the certificate can be received as prima facie evidence of the facts recited in the certificate and of the authenticity of the signature of the person by whom the instrument purports to have been signed.[17] Since authenticity raises a sufficiency issue, the certificate should permit the proponent to get to the jury on the issue of whether the signature appearing in the instrument is that of the person who appeared before the officer. The Evidence Code, however, does not include wills among acknowledged writings.[18]

Official writings: seals. The presence of certain seals serves to designate the official status of some writings. Section 1452 provides that a seal is presumed to be genuine and its use authorized if it purports to be the seal of the United States, a public entity in the United States, a nation recognized by the United States, a public entity in a nation recognized by the United States, or a notary public within any state of the United States.[19] Accordingly, the presence of such a seal authenticates the writing as an official writing of the entity entitled to the use of the seal. But the presumption created by § 1452 is one affecting only the burden of producing evidence. If the party opposing the writing introduces evidence sufficient to sustain a finding that the seal is not genuine or its use is not authorized, then the fact finder will have to determine the authenticity of the writing, including the seal, without recourse to any presumption.[20] If, on the other hand, the opponent introduces no evidence challenging the genuineness of the seal or its use, then the fact finder will be required to find that the writing is authentic.[21]

Signatures can serve the same function as seals in designating certain writings as official. Section 1453 provides that a signature is presumed to be genuine and authorized if it purports to be the signature, affixed in an official capacity, of a public employee of the United States or any public

---

16. West's Ann. California Evidence Code § 1189.

17. West's Ann. California Evidence Code § 1451.

18. Id.

19. West's Ann. California Evidence Code § 1452.

20. West's Ann. California Evidence Code § 1450 (comment).

21. Id. In Jacobson v. Gourley, 83 Cal.App.4th 1331, 100 Cal.Rptr.2d 349 (2000), the Department of Motor Vehicles sought to suspend a motorist's license at an administrative hearing on the ground that the motorist had driven while intoxicated. The department offered a report indicating that a person bearing the motorist's name had tested positively for blood alcohol. The report was impressed with a stamped emblem of the San Bernardino County Sheriff's Department, together with the name and address of the sheriff's scientific investigation unit. The emblem was offered as a "seal" to authenticate the report as one emanating from the county's sheriff's department. The reviewing court upheld the exclusion of the report: the emblem could not be used as a seal to authenticate the report because it was not signed. According to the court, the provisions of the Code of Civil Procedure defining a seal contemplate the use of a seal to attest to the signature on a document. Id. at 1334–1335, 100 Cal.Rptr.2d at 351. Here, however, the seal was not offered to attest to a signature but to authenticate the document as one emanating from the sheriff's office.

entity in the United States, or of a notary public within any state of the United States.[22] Accordingly, the presence of such a signature will authenticate the writing as an official writing of the entity of the employee whose signature appears. The presumption created by § 1453 is the same as the presumption created by § 1452. If the party opposing the writing introduces evidence sufficient to sustain a finding that the signature is not genuine or not authorized, then the fact finder will have to determine the authenticity of the writing without recourse to the presumption.[23] If the opponent fails to challenge the genuineness of the signature or its use, then the fact finder must find that the document is authentic.[24]

Official writings: attestations and certifications. An official writing may be proved by a copy purporting to be published by the authority of the national, state, or public entity in which the writing is kept.[25] An official writing kept in the United States may also be proved by a copy if it is attested or certified as a correct copy of the official writing by a public employee having legal custody of the writing.[26] Although the attestation or certification is an out of court statement asserting the copy's authenticity, the attestation or certification may be received for the truth as an exception to the hearsay rule.[27]

§ 13.03   AUTHENTICATION UNDER THE FEDERAL RULES

Under the Federal Rules as under the Code, authentication is a sufficiency issue. "To satisfy the requirement of authenticating or identifying an item of evidence, the proponent must produce evidence sufficient to support a finding that the item is what the proponent claims it is."[1] The methods by which a writing can be authenticated are similar to those found in the Code.[2] The Rules, like the Code, provide that the methods enumerated are illustrative, not exclusive.[3] And like the Code, the Rules also allow the judge to admit an item of evidence subject to a motion to strike if the proponent fails to connect the item with the case before the close of the evidence.[4]

---

22.   West's Ann. California Evidence Code § 1453. Signatures of foreign nations or their public entities are dealt with in § 1454.

23.   West's Ann. California Evidence Code § 1450 (comment).

24.   Id.

25.   West's Ann. California Evidence Code § 1530(a)(1).

26.   West's Ann. California Evidence Code § 1530(a)(2). If the office in which the writing is kept is not within the United States, additional attestation requirements must be met. See West's Ann. California Evidence Code § 1530(a)(3).

27.   West's Ann. California Evidence Code § 1530 (comment). The hearsay exception is only for the attestation or certification. Whether or not the contents of the copy of the writing are admissible for the truth of the matters stated depends on the hearsay rule and its exceptions. Some courts still miss this point. See, e.g., In re Kirk, 74 Cal.App.4th 1066, 1075, 88 Cal.Rptr.2d 648, 654 (1999); People v. Torres, 71 Cal.App.4th 704, 716–717, 84 Cal.Rptr.2d 96, 104 (1999).

1.   Federal Rule of Evidence 901(a).

2.   See Federal Rule of Evidence 901(b).

3.   Id.

4.   Federal Rule of Evidence 104(b).

The Rules differ from the Code in two important respects. The requirement of authentication is not limited to writings. The Rules make explicit what is implicit in the Code: that the requirement of authentication applies to any tangible object that is offered in evidence.[5] Although no special rules are provided for authenticating chattels, the Rules do give special attention to voice identification and computer printouts. A voice can be identified by anyone who acquired the necessary knowledge by hearing the voice at any time under circumstances connecting the voice with the alleged speaker.[6] A computer printout can be authenticated by evidence describing the process or system used to produce the result and showing that the process or system produces an accurate result.[7]

Unlike the Code, the Rules also provide for the "self-authentication" of certain writings.[8] If a writing qualifies for self-authentication, no extrinsic evidence of authenticity is required as a condition of admissibility.[9] These writings include domestic public documents under seal, certified copies of public records, acknowledged documents, official publications, newspapers and periodicals, trade inscriptions, and commercial paper.[10]

Instead of self-authentication, the Code uses presumptions to favor the authentication of some writings. These presumptions favor the authentication of acknowledged documents,[11] some writings affecting interests in real or personal property,[12] documents bearing official seals,[13] and documents bearing official signatures.[14] In addition, under Code, a book purporting to be printed or published by public authority is presumed to have been so printed or published;[15] a book purporting to contain reports of cases adjudged in the tribunals of the state or nation where the book is published is presumed to contain correct reports of those cases;[16] and printed materials purporting to be a particular newspaper or periodical are presumed to be that newspaper or periodical if regularly issued at average intervals not exceeding three months.[17] These presumptions do not shift the burden of persuasion with regard to the existence of the

---

5. Whereas West's Ann. California Evidence Code § 1400 refers to the authentication of a "writing," Federal Rule of Evidence 901 refers to the authentication of "the item."

6. Federal Rule of Evidence 901(b)(5). For the requirements for identifying telephone conversations, see Federal Rule of Evidence 901(b)(6).

7. Federal Rule of Evidence 901(b)(9). For an extended discussion of the admissibility of computer printouts as an exception to the hearsay rule, see § 10.05 supra.

8. Federal Rule of Evidence 902.

9. Id.

10. Id.

11. West's Ann. California Evidence Code § 1451.

12. West's Ann. California Evidence Code § 643.

13. West's Ann. California Evidence Code § 1452.

14. West's Ann. California Evidence Code § 1453–1454.

15. West's Ann. California Evidence Code § 644.

16. West's Ann. California Evidence Code § 645.

17. West's Ann. California Evidence Code § 645.1.

presumed fact. If the opponent introduces some evidence contesting the authenticity of the book or periodical, the proponent must convince the fact finder of the document's authenticity by the appropriate persuasion standard without the aid of the presumption.[18]

Substantial overlap characterizes the Code's and the Rules' approaches to authentication. Except for the Rules' provision on self-identification, most differences appear to be the product of drafting choices and do not raise significant policy concerns.

QUESTIONS AND PROBLEMS

Plaintiff sues Green Giant for injuries allegedly caused by a piece of metal packed with peas from a Green Giant can. To prove that the piece of metal was contained in a Green Giant can of peas, plaintiff offers the can with the Green Giant label still attached. A federal judge should overrule Green Giant's lack of authentication objection. True or false?

§ 13.04 AUTHENTICATING PHOTOGRAPHS, MOVIES, AUDIO TAPES, VIDEO TAPES, MAPS, DIAGRAMS, AND COMPUTER RECONSTRUCTIONS

Writings are defined broadly under the Code and the Federal Rules.[1] Under the Code, for example, writings include "handwriting, typewriting, printing, photostating, photographing, photocopying, transmitting by electronic mail or facsimile, and every other means of recording upon any tangible thing any form of communication or representation, including letters, words, pictures, sounds, or symbols, or combinations thereof, and any record thereby created, regardless of the manner in which the record has been stored."[2] Accordingly, photographs, audio tapes, and video tapes, DVDs as well as movies, must be authenticated if offered in evidence.

Photographs. The same principles of authentication that apply to photographs apply to the other media as well. When a photograph is offered, the proponent must show that it correctly represents the matters depicted. To make this showing, the proponent must call a witness who is familiar with the matters depicted in the photograph. It is not necessary to call the person who took the photograph or to establish when the photograph was taken. What matters is that the photograph depict correctly the manner in which matters appeared at a time that is relevant to the case. For example, if in a personal injury action the plaintiff offers a photograph of the intersection where the collision took place, the photograph should show how the intersection appeared at the time of the collision.

18. West's Ann. California Evidence Code § 630.

1. West's Ann. California Evidence Code § 250; Federal Rule of Evidence 1001.

2. West's Ann. California Evidence Code § 250.

Changes in the matters portrayed affect the probative value of photographs and can be a ground for excluding them. If an issue is whether the defendant should have seen the plaintiff prior to the collision, a photograph taken in the fall when the leaves have fallen may give the fact finder a mistaken impression of the defendant's view if the accident took place in the spring, when trees and bushes have sprouted new leaves. If the lighting conditions are an important issue, then a photograph that incorrectly portrays the lighting conditions might mislead the fact finder.[3] Whether changed conditions should result in the exclusion of a photograph depends in part on the purpose for which the photograph is offered. If the purpose is merely to show the layout of streets, buildings, or stairwells, or the vantage point of a witness, then it may not matter that the photograph incorrectly portrays the lighting conditions.[4] But if the lighting conditions are also an issue in the case and the judge concludes that the jury might not abide by an instruction limiting their consideration of the photograph to the purposes identified by the proponent, the judge may exclude the photograph on the grounds that its probative value is outweighed by the risk that it might mislead the jury.[5]

The angle from which a photograph is taken can also affect its probative value. If a photograph is offered to show the view the defendant would have had if the defendant had stopped and looked left ten feet from the intersection, a photograph taken from another spot could mislead the fact finder. Similarly, the use of special lens may also distort the view available through normal eyesight.

Even if a photograph is relevant, it can nonetheless be excluded if its probative value is substantially outweighed by the risk that the jury may be moved to reach a verdict on an emotional basis rather than on a detached consideration of the evidence.[6] Whether or not a photograph should be excluded is committed to the trial judge's discretion in California under § 352 and in federal court under Rule 403. As a rule, appellate courts will not disturb a judge's ruling admitting a photograph that may be gruesome,[7] unless its probative value is quite slight and its prejudicial effect substantial.

In People v. Marsh[8] a major issue was whether a child died as a result of falling, as claimed by the accused, or of a beating, as contended by the

---

3. People v. Vaiza, 244 Cal.App.2d 121, 126, 52 Cal.Rptr. 733, 736 (1966) (It was an abuse of discretion for the judge to admit photographs taken at 7:30 p.m. to illustrate the lighting conditions that prevailed at 2:00 a.m.).

4. People v. Rodrigues, 8 Cal.4th 1060, 1114, 36 Cal.Rptr.2d 235, 260, 885 P.2d 1, 27 (1994), cert. denied 516 U.S. 851, 116 S.Ct. 147, 133 L.Ed.2d 93 (1995). The fact that a video of a crime scene was taken during the day when the crime occurred at night was irrelevant when the purpose of the video was to show that the height of walls and other structures had not changed since the time of the crime. People v. Mayfield, 14 Cal.4th 668, 746, 60 Cal.Rptr.2d 1, 46, 928 P.2d 485, 530 (1997), cert. denied 522 U.S. 839, 118 S.Ct. 116, 139 L.Ed.2d 68 (1997).

5. For a discussion of the judge's discretionary power to exclude relevant evidence on the grounds of unfair prejudice, see § 2.10 supra.

6. People v. Scheid, 16 Cal.4th 1, 65 Cal.Rptr.2d 348, 358, 939 P.2d 748, 757 (1997).

7. See, e.g., People v. Marsh, 175 Cal.App.3d 987, 998, 221 Cal.Rptr. 311, 319 (1985) and cases cited therein.

8. Id.

prosecution. To prove that the child's head injuries could only have been inflicted by force of a magnitude far in excess of any accident, the prosecution offered and the judge admitted seven autopsy photographs.

> The least gruesome [showed] an interior section of the victim's skull with the residue of heavy blood clots. * * * Another [showed] an almost full view of the victim's nude body the closeup portion of which is the exterior surface of the exposed brain below which dangles part of the bloody scalp and in the background of which is the child's blood-spattered torso "field dressed" with the ribcages rolled back to expose the bowels. Another [pictured] the victim's neck and head with half of the scalp drawn down over his face and the other half pealed [sic] rearward exposing the right hemisphere of the brain. Another [exhibited] the left brain hemisphere with massive blood clotting and a portion of the severed skull plate lying immediately behind the head. Another [showed] the top of the victims's head with the scalp removed and dangling but with the skull plate still intact, depicting extensive hemorrhaging in several areas. Another [was] of the right side of the head with the scalp pulled forward and backwards to expose the undersurfaces, showing extensive hemorrhaging. Yet another [showed] the left side of the head with similar hemorrhaging.[9]

Though the photographs were probative of the proposition that the child did not die accidentally, the reviewing court held that the judge abused his discretion in admitting the photographs. "[T]he jury was not enlightened one additional whit by viewing these seven gory photographs. The oral testimony of the autopsy surgeon describing his findings comprehensively advised the jury of his observations and why he concluded there were multiple fatal impact sites which could not have been caused by a fall * * *."[10] In addition to being cumulative, the photographs were gruesome "solely because of the autopsy surgeon's handiwork * * *. In other words, their inflammatory nature [was] greatly enhanced by the manner in which the surgeon chose to 'pose' the body portions."[11]

---

9. Id. at 996–997, 221 Cal.Rptr. at 318. Discretion to exclude photographs under Evidence Code § 352 is more limited at the penalty phase than at the guilt phase of a capital trial. "This is so because the prosecution has the right to establish the circumstances of the crime, including its gruesome consequences (§ 190.3, factor (a)), and because the risk of an improper guilt finding based on visceral reactions is no longer present." People v. Bonilla, 41 Cal.4th 313, 354, 60 Cal.Rptr.3d 209, 242, 160 P.3d 84, 111 (2007).

The fact that a photograph or an audio, video, or digital tape may be cumulative of testimony is not an automatic ground for excluding the photograph or tape. Though a judge should take cumulative effect into account in weighing the probative value of the photograph or tape against the policy of preventing the presentation of needless evidence, a judge will not abuse his or her discretion in admitting photographic evidence so long as it assists the jurors in evaluating or understanding other evidence. People v. Michaels, 28 Cal.4th 486, 532, 122 Cal.Rptr.2d 285, 319, 49 P.3d 1032, 1060 (2002), cert. denied, 538 U.S. 1058, 123 S.Ct. 2214, 155 L.Ed.2d 1109 (2003).

10. People v. Marsh, 175 Cal.App.3d 987, 998, 221 Cal.Rptr. 311, 319 (1985).

11. Id. at 999, 221 Cal.Rptr. at 320. Courts have also expressed reservations about admitting photographs of murder victims taken while they were alive. Unless they are probative of a material proposition, the photographs should be excluded because of the danger they will arouse the sympathies of the jurors. See People v. Osband, 13 Cal.4th 622, 676–677, 55 Cal.Rptr.2d 26, 61, 919 P.2d 640, 675 (1996) and cases cited therein. On the other hand, in California death penalty cases, courts have repeatedly approved the use of the photographs of the victim in the

Marsh should be contrasted with People v. Stitely,[12] where the California Supreme Court approved the admission of autopsy photographs of a victim that showed her dissected neck and anus. The neck photographs were not unduly prejudicial because they were needed to show why the victim's death by strangulation was the result of premeditation and not of a rash act.[13] The anal photographs were necessary to depict injuries that supported the prosecution's theory that the anal sex charged was forcible and not consensual.[14] In addition, the prosecution's medical expert needed to display the photographs to the jurors to explain his findings regarding the cause of death (prolonged strangulation) and sexual trauma (extensive tears and bleeding).[15]

Video tapes, movies, and DVDs. Video tapes and movies differ from photographs in that they capture much more information. Movies in particular can be conceptualized as a series of photographs. Differences in the quantum of information are generally immaterial, however.[16] Take, for example, the video tape of the accused robbing the bank. What matters is that the tape show the accused robbing the bank that gave rise to the prosecution. Consequently, the chief role of the authenticating witness is to identify the tape as depicting the accused in a particular bank on a particular date.[17] Much the same can be said of movies or video tapes depicting the effects of the injury on the plaintiff. What matters is that the "Day in the Life" video tape, DVD, or movie accurately portray the effects of the injury.[18] The task of the proponent is to establish that fact through a witness who is familiar with the effects of the injury on the plaintiff.[19]

---

penalty phase, since the circumstances attending the crime are a factor relevant to the issues of aggravation and penalty. People v. Smithey, 20 Cal.4th 936, 990, 86 Cal.Rptr.2d 243, 280, 978 P.2d 1171, 1205 (1999), cert. denied, 529 U.S. 1026, 120 S.Ct. 1435, 146 L.Ed.2d 324 (2000), and cases cited therein. Moreover, at the death penalty phase, "because the defendant has already been found guilty of the capital crime, the potential for prejudice on the issue of guilt is not present." People v. Anderson, 25 Cal.4th 543, 592, 106 Cal.Rptr.2d 575, 614, 22 P.3d 347, 380 (2001), cert. denied, 534 U.S. 1136, 122 S.Ct. 1082, 151 L.Ed.2d 982 (2002).

12. 35 Cal.4th 514, 26 Cal.Rptr.3d 1, 108 P.3d 182, cert. denied, 546 U.S. 865, 126 S.Ct. 164, 163 L.Ed.2d 151 (2005).

13. Id. at 545, 26 Cal.Rptr.3d at 25–26, 108 P.3d at 203.

14. Id.

15. Id.

16. A video recording is authenticated by testimony or other evidence that it accurately depicts what it purports to show. People v. Mayfield, 14 Cal.4th 668, 747, 60 Cal.Rptr.2d 1, 46, 928 P.2d 485, 530 (1997). For limitations on the use of video tapes, see generally People v. Rodrigues, 8 Cal.4th 1060, 1114–1115, 36 Cal.Rptr.2d 235, 260–261, 885 P.2d 1, 26–27 (1994).

17. See People v. Carpenter, 15 Cal.4th 312, 386, 63 Cal.Rptr.2d 1, 43, 935 P.2d 708, 750, cert. denied, 522 U.S. 1078, 118 S.Ct. 858, 139 L.Ed.2d 757 (1998) (holding that an authenticating witness's testimony that a video tape accurately depicted the crime scene was sufficient to authenticate the tape).

18. Jones v. City of Los Angeles, 20 Cal.App.4th 436, 440, note 5, 24 Cal.Rptr.2d 528, 530, note 5 (1993).

19. A judge should not exclude the video or movie on the grounds that the testimony of the plaintiff or the authenticating witness describing the effects of the injury necessarily renders the tape or movie cumulative. A video may well be the most effective way of conveying to the jurors the limitations imposed by the injuries as well as the kinds of assistance and medical attention required as a result of the injuries. See Jones v. City of Los Angeles, 20 Cal.App.4th 436, 444, 24 Cal.Rptr.2d 528, 533–534 (1993). Nor should a judge exclude a photograph as cumulative simply

Though "frame by frame" authentication is not required, the opponent should nonetheless be alert to distortions that can be produced by the camera angle used, the lens employed, and creative editing.[20] Distortions that might mislead the jurors can result in the exclusion of the exhibit. People v. Gonzalez[21] is illustrative. The reviewing court upheld the trial court's exclusion of a video tape offered to show the lighting conditions at the crime scene on the ground that the human eye can see much more than could be depicted by the type of camcorder used.[22]

Audio tapes and CDs. Audio tapes and CDs, like video tapes and movies, capture information over time. Their value stems from recording the voices of individuals who are connected with the case. A taped confession offered as a personal admission is of no value unless it is the confession of the accused. One way for the prosecution to connect the voice on the tape with that of the accused is through an authenticating witness. Anyone who is sufficiently familiar with the accused's voice to say that it is the accused on the tape can serve as the witness.[23]

In cases of taped confessions, the California decisions suggest that the proponent must demonstrate also that the tape is a faithful and complete reproduction of the confession.[24] This requirement calls for a witness who was present when the confession was made to vouch for the tape's accuracy and completeness. Most likely, the requirement stems from an implicit or explicit representation by the proponent that the tape contains "the accused's confession" as well as from concerns over the misleading effects of receiving only partial statements.

Audio tapes, like video tapes, can be challenged on the ground that their selective reproduction may mislead the trier of fact.[25] Moreover, if

---

because a witness has described the items depicted. See, e.g., People v. Box, 23 Cal.4th 1153, 1199, 99 Cal.Rptr.2d 69, 102, 5 P.3d 130, 160 (2000), cert. denied, 532 U.S. 963, 121 S.Ct. 1497, 149 L.Ed.2d 383 (2001); People v. Ibarra, 151 Cal.App.4th 1145, 1151, 61 Cal.Rptr.3d 22, 27 (2007). As the adage states, a picture is worth a thousand words.

20.　Harmon v. San Joaquin Light & Power Corp., 37 Cal.App.2d 169, 174, 98 P.2d 1064, 1067 (1940).

21.　38 Cal.4th 932, 44 Cal.Rptr.3d 237, 135 P.3d 649 (2006).

22.　Id. at 952, 44 Cal.Rptr.3d at 252, 135 P.3d at 662.

23.　Other means for authenticating the voice on the tape are available. The nature of the conversation may be such as to suggest that only the accused could have made the statements. See, e.g., People v. Fonville, 35 Cal.App.3d 693, 709, 111 Cal.Rptr. 53, 63 (1973).

24.　See, e.g., People v. Spencer, 60 Cal.2d 64, 77–78, 31 Cal.Rptr. 782, 790–791, 383 P.2d 134, 142–143 (1963), cert. denied, 377 U.S. 1007, 84 S.Ct. 1924, 12 L.Ed.2d 1055 (1964); see also People v. Ketchel, 59 Cal.2d 503, 518–519, 30 Cal.Rptr. 538, 544–545, 381 P.2d 394, 400–401 (1963), regarding the accuracy and completeness of the transcript of an audio tape.

25.　The judge's authority to exclude tapes that may mislead jurors is derived from West's Ann. California Evidence Code § 352. Federal Rule of Evidence 403 vests federal judges with a similar power. For an extended discussion of a judge's discretionary power to exclude relevant evidence, see § 2.10 supra.

Judges may allow jurors to hear taped confessions that are partially inaudible so long as the audible parts are relevant as well as substantially complete and correct. People v. Polk, 47 Cal.App.4th 944, 952–953, 54 Cal.Rptr.2d 921, 926 (1996). Moreover, judges may allow jurors to use a transcript as an aid to understanding the tape if the judges first find that the transcript is an accurate transcription of the audible portions of the tape. Id. at 953–954, 54 Cal.Rptr.2d at

the tape is received, the opponent is entitled to offer such other parts as may be available and necessary to make the part received understood.[26]

Some federal cases hold that it is error for a district court judge to allow jurors to replay tapes during their deliberations. Jurors might only replay some parts of the tapes, or the tapes, even if replayed in their entirety, might give some evidence undue emphasis.[27] In federal prosecutions, the replaying of the tapes by jurors is a violation of the Federal Rules of Criminal Procedure.[28] These rules require the presence of the accused at all stages of the trial.[29] Whether the replaying requires reversal of the judgment ordinarily depends on the application of the harmless error rule. But where the federal judge erroneously allows the jurors to replay tapes which have *not* been received in evidence, automatic reversal is required.[30] Such an error is deemed to be "structural" because of the appellate court's inability to determine the harm caused by the replaying.[31]

Maps, diagrams, and computer reconstructions. Maps and diagrams, whether prepared in advance of trial or during the trial, are like photographs. The matters depicted must be authenticated by a knowledgeable witness as a correct representation of those matters as they appeared at a time that is relevant to the case. Diagrams and maps do not have to be prepared to scale if relative sizes and distances are unimportant. If they are important, the judge may exclude the maps or diagrams if their rendition of the matters depicted would mislead the jury.

The use of computer reconstructions of crime and accident scenes present the same issues as diagrams and video tapes. The matters depicted in the reconstruction should be authenticated by a witness familiar with the scene as a correct representation of those matters at a time that is relevant to the case. Because of the novelty of computer reconstructions, the proponent should consider offering expert testimony explaining how the technology used reconstructs the matters depicted accurately.[32]

926–927. Judges, however, should not let jurors hear tapes that are so inaudible as to invite speculation as to their meaning. Id. at 954, 54 Cal.Rptr.2d at 927.

26. West's Ann. California Evidence Code § 365.

27. See United States v. Noushfar, 78 F.3d 1442, 1445 (9th Cir.1996) and cases cited therein.

28. Federal Rule of Criminal Procedure 43(a)(2).

29. Id.

30. United States v. Noushfar, 78 F.3d 1442, 1445 (9th Cir.1996).

31. Id.

32. The Federal Rules of Evidence may require the use of such testimony. Since the accuracy of computer generated results depends on the computer system used to produce them, the proponent should authenticate the results by evidence describing the system used and showing that the system produces accurate results. Federal Rule of Evidence 901(b)(9). Technically, such evidence is not indispensable in California so long as a knowledgeable witness vouches for the accuracy of the computer generated reconstruction. But the evidence may be useful in persuading the judge to accept results generated by novel methods.

For an analysis of the admissibility problems posed by computer generated evidence, see F. Galves, *Where the Not–So–Wild Things Are: Computers in the Courtroom, the Federal Rules of Evidence, and the Need for Institutional Reform and More Judicial Acceptance*, 13 Harv. J. of L. & Tech. 161 (2000).

QUESTIONS AND PROBLEMS

1. So long as a photograph is probative of the issues to be proved, the judge must admit it irrespective of its gruesome aspects. True or false?   *False*

2. Because the use of special lens and other techniques can distort the matters depicted in a photograph, both the Code and the Rules require the proponent of a photograph to produce the photographer for cross-examination by the adverse party. True or false?   *False*

§ 13.05   AUTHENTICATING REAL AND DEMONSTRATIVE EVIDENCE

Real evidence generally refers to tangible objects that played a part in the events that are the subject of a trial.[1] Examples include the gun or other instrument used in the crime, the ladder or other object the plaintiff claims was the cause of injury, as well as the computer or other object the plaintiff alleges failed to meet the contract specifications. Real evidence also includes the video tape of the defendant beating the victim or robbing the bank.

Demonstrative evidence, on the other hand, usually refers to visual aids which help the fact finder understand the evidence presented.[2] Demonstrative evidence can consist of models, maps, diagrams, charts, photographs, video tapes, and demonstrations. Demonstrative evidence can also include items resembling objects connected with the case when those objects are unavailable for use at the hearing. People v. Wiley,[3] for example, upheld the use of a baseball bat and a hammer which resembled those found at the crime scene but which could not be located for use at the trial.[4] But where the item offered does not resemble the object connected with the case, then the item should be excluded.[5]

The fact that demonstrative evidence is used to help illumine other evidence should not mislead the opponent into concluding that its use is not objectionable. Such evidence can be objected to on a number of grounds, including failing to aid, as well as misleading, the fact finder.

Admissibility in general. Two broad principles determine the admissibility of demonstrative and real evidence. One is that the evidence be relevant.[6] The other is that its probative value not be substantially

---

1. M. Graham, Handbook of Federal Evidence § 401.2 (3d ed. 1991). Neither the California Evidence Code nor the Federal Rules of Evidence defines demonstrative or real evidence.

2. Id.

3. 18 Cal.3d 162, 176, 133 Cal.Rptr. 135, 143, 554 P.2d 881, 889 (1976).

4. On the same principle, photographs of medical equipment, resembling equipment found in the defendant's office, were admissible to prove that the defendant possessed equipment similar to those in the photographs. People v. Slocum, 52 Cal.App.3d 867, 891–892, 125 Cal.Rptr. 442, 456 (1975), cert. denied, 426 U.S. 924, 96 S.Ct. 2635, 49 L.Ed.2d 379 (1976). The photographs were offered only as resembling the equipment. Id.

5. People v. Vaiza, 244 Cal.App.2d 121, 126, 52 Cal.Rptr. 733, 736 (1966).

6. Only relevant evidence is admissible. West's Ann. California Evidence Code § 350; Federal Rule of Evidence 402.

outweighed by the risks enumerated in § 352 and Rule 403.[7] These risks include the probability that the evidence might prejudice the opponent unfairly or mislead the jury.[8]

Complying with the requirements of authentication will usually demonstrate the relevance of real evidence. Although authentication is usually associated with writings,[9] the concept applies whenever any tangible object is offered in evidence.[10] The proponent must show that the object is what he claims it to be. If the prosecution, for example, offers a gun on the theory that it is the gun used by the accused, then it must offer some evidence connecting the gun with the accused.

In making this showing, the proponent need satisfy only a sufficiency standard.[11] If, viewing the evidence in the light most favorable to the proponent, the judge concludes that reasonable jurors could find that the gun offered is the one the accused used, then the judge must let the issue of the gun's authenticity go to the jury. The opponent may offer countervailing evidence. But such evidence will not prevent the introduction of the gun as long as the proponent's evidence satisfies the sufficiency standard. The jurors, of course, will have the last word. Upon request by the opponent, the judge must instruct them to disregard the gun, unless they first find that it is indeed the gun the accused used.[12]

Compliance with the requirements of authentication will also show the relevance of demonstrative evidence. If in a personal injury action the plaintiff offers a map, diagram, sketch, photograph, or video tape of an intersection to illustrate the intersection involved in the collision, none of these aids is admissible over objection unless the plaintiff first demonstrates that they correctly depict the intersection involved. The probative value of much demonstrative evidence is derived from the accuracy with which it illumines other evidence that is relevant to the case. If the visual aid is inaccurate, then it should be excluded.[13] In applying this principle, the judge should keep in mind the purpose for which the demonstrative evidence is offered. A video tape of a crime scene offered to show the layout of such items as buildings, streets, and stairwells or the vantage of a witness may be received even though the video was shot during the day and the crime occurred at night.[14] But if the lighting conditions are also an issue and the judge concludes that the jurors might not abide by an instruction limiting their consideration of the evidence to the purposes identified by the proponent, the judge may exclude the evidence on the

---

7. West's Ann. California Evidence Code § 352; Federal Rule of Evidence 403.

8. Id. For an extended discussion of a trial judge's power to exclude unduly prejudicial evidence, see § 2.10 supra.

9. See § 13.01 supra.

10. Id.

11. West's Ann. California Evidence Code §§ 403 and 1400.

12. West's Ann. California Evidence Code § 403(c).

13. For an extended discussion of the admissibility of photographs, movies, audio and video tapes, maps, diagrams, and computer reconstructions, see § 13.04 supra.

14. People v. Rodrigues, 8 Cal.4th 1060, 1114, 36 Cal.Rptr.2d 235, 260, 885 P.2d 1, 27 (1994).

ground that its probable value on permissible issues is outweighed by the risk that it might mislead the jurors.

Sometimes, the proponent may not offer in evidence an aid, such as a sketch drawn by a witness to explain her testimony. The fact that the aid is not offered should not lull the opponent into foregoing objections that can be made. If a sketch of an intersection is inadmissible because it misrepresents the layout of the streets, then its use is likewise objectionable even if the sketch is not offered in evidence. Whether or not offered, the risk that the aid might mislead the fact finder is the same.

When a misleading aid is offered in evidence, the opponent is at least afforded an opportunity to object to its introduction. But when no offer is made, no such opportunity exists. Since it is the use of misleading aids in front of the fact finder that gives rise to the harm, it is to the opponent's advantage to object to their use at the earliest possible time. When an aid has been prepared in advance of trial, the opponent should object to its use by any witness until the aid has been authenticated. When a witness attempts to prepare the aid at the hearing, the opponent should object on relevance grounds and take the witness on voir dire to determine the witness's ability to depict accurately the events the witness is attempting to describe.

Photographs, movies, audio and video tapes, maps, diagrams, and computer reconstructions. Since these types of demonstrative aids are writings, their admissibility is considered in § 13.04.

Demonstrations. Judges may permit the use of demonstrations when they help illustrate the testimony of witnesses. For example, in a prosecution for driving under the influence, the arresting officer may be allowed to show the jury how he demonstrated the field sobriety tests to the accused. If the officer can do so, he may even be permitted to show the jury how the accused performed on the tests. Since these demonstrations are based on the witness's personal knowledge, the judges' principal concern is whether the witness can reproduce the conduct at issue accurately.

Experiments. Experiments may attempt to reconstruct an event in dispute. The plaintiff, for example, may wish to demonstrate to the jury how far a mannequin the size of the plaintiff would be blown by an exploding tire. Since the value of the experiment depends on whether the experimental conditions were substantially similar to those in the actual case, the judge should exclude the results unless the proponent satisfies the similarity requirement.[15]

---

15. See, e.g., Hale v. Firestone Tire & Rubber Co., 820 F.2d 928, 931–932 (8th Cir.1987); People v. Terry, 38 Cal.App.3d 432, 444–445, 113 Cal.Rptr. 233, 241–242 (1974) (holding that the length of time it took a detective to travel between two points was admissible to prove the length of time it took to travel between the points on the date in question as long as traffic conditions on the two dates were similar). See also People v. Turner, 8 Cal.4th 137, 198, 32 Cal.Rptr.2d 762, 797, 878 P.2d 521, 556 (1994) (holding that for experimental evidence to be admissible, the experiment must have been conducted under substantially similar—although not necessarily identical—conditions as those of the actual occurrence); People v. Bonin, 47 Cal.3d 808, 847, 254 Cal.Rptr. 298, 321, 765 P.2d 460, 483 (1989) (holding that the trial court committed error in

Some experiments may not fall within the demonstrative evidence category. The experimental results may be offered as possessing relevance that is independent of their illuminating effect on evidence that has been presented.[16] An example is the testimony of a ballistics expert that tests performed with the gun seized from the accused produced grooves and landings identical with those found on a bullet removed from the victim. Because the value of the evidence depends on the soundness of the scientific theory involved as well as on the ability of the expert to apply the theory, the opponent should be prepared to object on these grounds.[17]

Chain of custody. Experimental or laboratory results are irrelevant if the object tested is unconnected with the case or has been tampered with. In cases involving controlled substances, for example, the prosecution must show that the results of the substance tested came from the substance taken from the accused. One way to authenticate the results is by evidence accounting for the location and condition of the substance from the time it was taken from the accused to the time the results are offered at the hearing. This method of authentication is known as chain of custody and is especially useful when the object offered is fungible.

While a perfect chain of custody is desirable, gaps will not result in the exclusion of the evidence, so long as the links offered connect the evidence with the case and raise no serious questions of tampering.[18] Questions regarding authenticity are governed by a sufficiency standard. Consequently, doubts should be resolved in favor of admissibility, since it is up to the jury to determine whether the tests indeed were performed on the substance taken from the accused.

The introduction of fungible objects does not always require the use of a chain of custody. Fungible items can be made unique. Police officers often mark items seized with their initials and the date and time of the seizure, markings which set the items apart from similar ones. For example, if the issue is whether the bottle of wine offered in evidence is the one removed from the defendant's car, the identifying witness can authenticate the bottle by the markings he made when he seized it.

QUESTIONS AND PROBLEMS

1. In an unlawful detainer action, the tenant claimed that she withheld rent because the premises had become uninhabitable. To prove uninhabitabili-

---

admitting a criminalist's testimony that the striations left on his arm by a towel were similar to the striations found on the victim's neck, in the absence of evidence that the experimental conditions were similar to those attending the strangulation of the victim).

16. The line between demonstrative evidence and other kinds of evidence is not bright. For example, the officer who is asked to demonstrate, rather than describe, how the accused performed on a field sobriety test is producing evidence that is as consequential as a verbal description of how the accused performed.

17. For a extended discussion of the admissibility of scientific evidence and expert testimony, see § 16.04 infra.

18. See, e.g., People v. Lewis, 191 Cal.App.3d 1288, 1298, 237 Cal.Rptr. 64, 71 (1987); People v. Lozano, 57 Cal.App.3d 490, 495, 127 Cal.Rptr. 204, 207 (1976).

ty, the tenant called a housing inspector who testified that he inspected the premises on June 1 and found ten housing code violations during his inspection. One violation resulted from the condition of an electrical outlet, which was missing the protective plate and hence exposed the occupants to "live" wires. The tenant then examined the inspector as follows:

Tenant: Your Honor, may I approach the witness?

The Court: You may.

Tenant: Inspector, I hand you Defense Exhibit 3 for Identification. Do you recognize what is depicted in that exhibit?

Inspector: Yes, this is a photo of the electrical outlet I described.

Tenant: Is Exhibit 3 for Identification a fair and accurate depiction of the outlet as you saw it on June 1?

Inspector: Yes, it is. It looks exactly the way the outlet looked to me on June 1.

Tenant: Move Defense Exhibit 3 for Identification in evidence.

The Court: Any objection?

Landlord: Yes, Your Honor, lack of authentication. May I take the witness on voir dire in aid of my objection?

The Court: You may.

Landlord: Inspector, this is the first time you have seen Defense Exhibit 3?

Inspector: Yes.

Landlord: You don't know who took this photograph?

Inspector: No.

Landlord: You don't even know when it was taken?

Inspector: No.

Landlord: Renew my objection.

Judge: ?

§ 13.06 THE BEST AND SECONDARY EVIDENCE RULES

Unless certain exceptional circumstances exist, the Best Evidence Rule requires the content of a writing to be proved by the original writing and not by testimony recounting its contents or by a copy of the writing.[1] A major purpose of the rule is to minimize the possibility of misinterpretation that could occur if the production of the original writing were not required to prove its contents.

Both the Code and the Rules define an original as the writing itself or any counterpart intended to have the same effect by a person who

---

1. Federal Rule of Evidence 1002.

executed or issued it.[2] Thus, if the parties to a contract intend for the pink copy to serve as the original, that is the original for purposes of the federal Best Evidence Rule and the California Secondary Evidence Rule. The "original" of a photograph includes the negative or any print from it.[3] For electronically stored information, "original" means any printout (or other output readable by sight) if it accurately reflects the information.[4]

Both the Code and the Rules also define writings broadly. Under the Code, for example, writings include "handwriting, typewriting, printing, photostating, photographing, photocopying, transmitting by electronic mail or facsimile, and every other means of recording upon any tangible thing any form of communication or representation, including letters, words, pictures, sounds, or symbols, or combinations thereof, and any record thereby created, regardless of the manner in which the record has been stored."[5] Accordingly, testimony describing X-rays violates the Best Evidence Rule unless the X-rays have been received in evidence.[6]

Since the concern "is with getting the words or other contents before the court with accuracy and precision, * * * a counterpart serves equally as well as the original, if the counterpart is the product of a method which insures accuracy and genuineness."[7] Accordingly, the Rules provide that a "duplicate" can be offered in lieu of the original, unless a genuine question is raised about the original's authenticity or in the circumstances it would be unfair to admit the duplicate.[8] Duplicates are admissible also in California but under a broader provision that subsumes the duplicate-original doctrine of the Rules by allowing a party in the first instance to offer secondary evidence (including a duplicate) of the original.[9]

The Code defines a duplicate as "a counterpart produced by the same impression as the original, or from the same matrix, or by means of photography, including enlargements and miniatures, or by mechanical or electronic re-recording, or by chemical reproduction, or by other equivalent technique(s) which accurately reproduces the original."[10] The Rules define a duplicate similarly: "a counterpart produced by a mechanical, photographic, chemical, electronic, or other equivalent process or technique that accurately reproduces the original."[11] Thus, a photograph of a police artist's sketch of a suspect can be offered in place of the sketch.[12]

2. West's Ann. California Evidence Code § 255; Federal Rule of Evidence 1001(3).

3. West's Ann. California Evidence Code § 255; Federal Rule of Evidence 1001(3).

4. West's Ann. California Evidence Code § 255; Federal Rule of Evidence 1001(3).

5. West's Ann. California Evidence Code § 250.

6. Sirico v. Cotto, 67 Misc.2d 636, 324 N.Y.S.2d 483 (1971).

7. Federal Rule of Evidence 1003 (Advisory Committee Note).

8. Federal Rule of Evidence 1003.

9. West's Ann.California Evidence Code § 1521.

10. West's Ann. California Evidence Code § 260.

11. Federal Rule of Evidence 1001(4).

12. People v. Garcia, 201 Cal.App.3d 324, 328, 247 Cal.Rptr. 94, 96–97 (1988).

Because of the possibility of error, manually produced copies, whether handwritten or typed, are not within the definition.[13]

Although the Federal Rules of Evidence continue to apply the classic formulation of the Best Evidence Rule,[14] in 1999 the California Legislature replaced the Best Evidence Rule with the Secondary Evidence Rule. Under the new rule, the proponent may prove the contents of a writing through the original of the writing[15] or by any otherwise admissible secondary evidence.[16] This means that, unless otherwise provided, the proponent may prove the contents of a writing through the original, a copy (including a duplicate as defined in § 260), testimony about the contents of the original, or a written or oral summary of the original. The judge, however, must exclude the secondary evidence if the judge determines that (1) a genuine dispute exists concerning material terms of the original writing and justice requires its exclusion, or (2) admission of the secondary evidence would be unfair.[17] The new rule, however, does not relax the requirements of authentication. Accordingly, a party offering a copy (as opposed to testimony) of the original must still produce evidence demonstrating that the copy is a true copy of a duly authenticated original.[18] Moreover, as will be explained, the Code places strict limits on the use of testimony to prove the contents of a writing.[19]

In determining whether it would be unfair to admit a copy, California judges "may consider a broad range of factors, for example: (1) whether the proponent attempts to use the writing in a manner that could not reasonably have been anticipated, (2) whether the original was suppressed in discovery, (3) whether discovery conducted in a reasonably diligent (as opposed to exhaustive) manner failed to result in production of the original, (4) whether there are dramatic differences between the original and the secondary evidence (e.g., the original but not the secondary evidence is in color and the colors provide significant clues to interpretation), (5) whether the original is unavailable and, if so, why, and (6) whether the writing is central to the case or collateral."[20]

Because discovery is narrower in California criminal cases than in civil cases, an additional hurdle must be cleared in criminal cases before secondary evidence can be admitted. Even if no genuine dispute exists about the terms of the original and even if it were fair to receive the secondary evidence, the trial judge nonetheless must exclude the evidence if the judge determines that the original is in the proponent's possession, custody, or control, and the proponent has not made the original reason-

---

13.   Federal Rule of Evidence 1001 (Advisory Committee Note).

14.   Federal Rule of Evidence 1002.

15.   West's Ann. California Evidence Code § 1520.

16.   West's Ann. California Evidence Code § 1521(a).

17.   Id.

18.   West's Ann.California Evidence Code § 1521(c).

19.   See § 13.07 infra.

20.   West's Ann.California Evidence Code § 1522 (comment).

ably available for inspection at or before the trial.[21] This limitation, however, does not apply if the proponent is offering a (1) a duplicate, (2) a writing that is not closely related to the controlling issues in the action, (3) a copy of a writing in the custody of a public entity, or (4) a copy of a writing that is recorded in the public records, if a statute makes the record or a certified copy of it evidence of the writing.[22]

A number of factors moved the California Legislature to give secondary evidence generally the same status as the original writing in satisfying the Secondary Evidence Rule. Broad pretrial discovery gives civil litigants an opportunity to inspect the originals, thereby reducing the need to produce the originals in court to assure accuracy. Technological developments, especially the rise of facsimile transmission and electronic mail, pose unanticipated difficulties in ascertaining which document is the "original." A party bent on creating fraudulent documents is not likely to be deterred by the rule. Insisting on the original increases litigation costs unnecessarily.[23]

The federal Best Evidence Rule and the California Secondary Evidence Rule apply only when the proponent seeks to prove the contents of a writing. They do not apply simply because the proponent seeks to prove conversations that may have also been recorded or reduced to writing.[24] For example, in Meyers v. United States[25] the prosecution sought to prove the testimony which a witness gave to a Congressional committee. The prosecution did so by calling the lawyer who examined the witness before the committee. The accused claimed that the lawyer's testimony violated the Best Evidence Rule because the witness's Congressional testimony had been taken down by a stenographer. The reviewing court rejected the accused's claim. The prosecution was seeking to prove not the contents of the stenographic record but the lawyer's recollection of what the witness had said before the committee.[26] Had the prosecution sought to prove the contents of the stenographic record, then the accused's objection would have been well taken.

The distinction drawn in *Meyers* applies to any stenographic record. So long as the proponent is not attempting to prove the contents of a deposition or of the record formed at a preliminary hearing, for example, the proponent may elicit testimony about what the deponent or the witness said without violating the Best or Secondary Evidence Rule. The distinction applies to other records as well: payment may be proved

---

21. West's Ann.California Evidence Code § 1522. This requirement is subject to a number of exceptions. The requirement does not apply to duplicate originals, writings that are not closely related to the controlling issues in the action, or a copy of a writing that is in the custody of a public entity or that is recorded in the public records. Id.

22. West's Ann.California Evidence Code § 1522(a).

23. Best Evidence Rule, 26 Cal. L. Revision Comm'n Reports 369 (1996).

24. People v. Johnson, 39 Cal.App.3d 749, 763, 114 Cal.Rptr. 545, 554 (1974) (A police officer may relate the accused's confession in court even though it had been recorded.).

25. 171 F.2d 800 (D.C.Cir.1948), cert. denied, 336 U.S. 912, 69 S.Ct. 602, 93 L.Ed. 1076 (1949).

26. Id. at 812.

without producing a written receipt, and earnings may be proved without producing the books of account, as long as the proponent is not seeking to prove the contents of the written record.[27]

Whether inscriptions on chattels should be subject to the Best Evidence Rule has been controversial. Over objection, should testimony be received that a shirt found in a stolen car had a laundry tag with the defendant's initials? Since such inscriptions are within the broad definition of a writing, compliance with the Best Evidence Rule would require the production of the shirt. In People v. Mastin[28] the court rejected such a strict reading of the Best Evidence Rule. Instead, the court opted for the federal practice of leaving the application of the rule to the discretion of the trial judge. In exercising discretion, the judge should consider:

> the importance of examining the original and the difficulties involved in its production—the more complex the inscription, the less reliable the secondary evidence. The more critical the fact to be proved by the inscription, and the lesser the quantity and quality of other evidence to prove that fact, the greater is the importance of the inscribed chattel's production. The more difficult the production or the more inconvenience to the owner by temporary loss of the chattel, the greater must be the importance of examining the original before production is required.[29]

As a practical matter, since duplicates produced by means of photography generally can be offered in lieu of the original in federal and California courts, the availability of photographs of inscribed chattels has dampened the debate.[30] In California photographs of graffiti are expressly admissible in vandalism actions to prove that the accused was the author.[31]

Under the Federal Rules, testimony that a writing does not contain any reference to designated matter does not violate the Best Evidence Rule.[32] But since such testimony proves the contents of a writing indirectly, in California the argument can be made that the testimony violates the Secondary Evidence Rule.[33]

QUESTIONS AND PROBLEMS

1. In an action for personal injuries the plaintiff claims she sustained at an intersection, the plaintiff testifies that she came to a complete stop before

---

27. Federal Rule of Evidence 1002 (Advisory Committee Note).

28. 115 Cal.App.3d 978, 171 Cal.Rptr. 780 (1981).

29. Id. at 985, 171 Cal.Rptr. at 783.

30. In California, resort to the duplicate-original doctrine is no longer necessary. As a general rule, secondary evidence (a photograph) is admissible as the original (the shirt). See West's Ann.California Evidence Code § 1521.

31. West's Ann. California Evidence Code § 1410.5.

32. Federal Rule of Evidence 1002 (Advisory Committee Note).

33. The Secondary Evidence Rule adopted in 1999 still places limits on the use of testimony to prove the contents of a writing. See § 13.07 infra.

proceeding through the intersection. On cross-examination, the defendant seeks to impeach the plaintiff through the plaintiff's deposition testimony.

Defendant: You recall being deposed in this case?

Plaintiff: Yes.

Defendant: At the time you gave your deposition you swore to tell the truth?

Plaintiff: Yes.

Defendant: And you told the truth?

Plaintiff: Yes.

Defendant: At your deposition I asked you, "Did you come to a complete stop at the sign?"

Plaintiff: If you say so.

Defendant: And you answered, "Almost"?

Plaintiff: Violates the Best [Secondary] Evidence Rule.

Judge: ?

2. Assume that the plaintiff answered "No" to the last question.

Defendant: Your Honor, may the record reflect that on page nineteen, line three the plaintiff answered "Almost" to my question?

Plaintiff: Violates the Best [Secondary] Evidence Rule.

Judge: ?

3. Suppose that the defendant's strategy calls for introducing a photograph of the stop sign he claims the plaintiff ran.

Defendant: Were you with the plaintiff when he ran the sign?

Witness: Yes.

Defendant: Your Honor, may I approach the witness?

Judge: Yes.

Defendant: I show you what has been marked as Defense Exhibit Number 3 for Identification. Can you tell us what that is?

Witness: Yes, that appears to be a photograph of the sign the plaintiff ran.

Defendant: Would you please describe the exhibit to the jury?

Witness: Yes, it shows a street with a stop sign, the sign is in red, and the word "stop" is in white.

Plaintiff: Objection. Move to strike on Best [Secondary] Evidence Rule grounds.

Judge: ?

§ 13.07 EXCEPTIONS TO THE BEST EVIDENCE RULE

Federal Rules. The original is not required if it has been lost or destroyed, unless the proponent lost or destroyed the original in bad faith.[1] The original is not required if it cannot be obtained by available judicial process or procedure.[2] The original is not required if at a time when the original was under the control of the opponent, the opponent was put on notice, by the pleadings or otherwise, that the contents would be a subject of proof at the hearing and the opponent does not produce the original at the hearing.[3] The original is not required if it is not closely related to the controlling issues.[4] As noted earlier, an original also is not required if the proponent offers a duplicate of the original.[5]

The Rules also provide that the contents of a writing may be proved by the testimony or deposition of the party against whom offered or by that party's written admission without accounting for the nonproduction of the original.[6]

The Rules do not express a preference for a copy of a private writing that is unavailable. They allow the proponent to prove the contents of the original by a copy or testimony if production of the original writing is excused.

The contents of an official record or of a document authorized to be recorded or filed and actually recorded or filed do not have to be proved by the original record or document.[7] In this instance, however, testimony is inadmissible and the proponent must offer a copy certified or testified to be correct, unless a copy cannot be obtained by the exercise of reasonable diligence.[8]

California Evidence Code. The 1999 amendment allowing a party to offer otherwise admissible secondary evidence to prove the contents of a writing eliminated the exceptions to the Best Evidence Rule.[9] The amendment, however, retains the Code's preference for copies as opposed to testimony except in the following situations: (1) where the proponent does not have possession or control of a copy and the original is lost or has been

---

1. Federal Rule of Evidence 1004(1).

2. Federal Rule of Evidence 1004(2).

3. Federal Rule of Evidence 1004(3).

4. West's Ann. California Evidence Code § 1504; Federal Rule of Evidence 1004(4).

5. See § 13.06 supra.

6. Federal Rule of Evidence 1007. The Code does not have an equivalent provision. Presumably, proof of the contents of the original by these methods could satisfy the requirements of the Secondary Evidence Rule. See West's Ann.California Evidence Code §§ 1521, 1523.

7. Federal Rule of Evidence 1005.

8. Id.

9. Indeed, the amendment repeals the "Best Evidence Rule." West's Ann.California Evidence Code § 1521 (Comment). The name is retained here for ease of analysis and comparison to the Federal Rules.

destroyed without fraudulent intent on the part of the proponent, and (2) where the proponent does not have possession or control of the original or a copy and (a) neither the original nor the copy was reasonably procurable by the proponent by use of the court's process or other reasonable means or (b) the original is not closely related to the controlling issues and it would be inexpedient to require its production.[10] Since copies of official records and documents authorized to be recorded or filed are generally available, copies, rather than testimony, must be offered to prove the contents of the originals.

If no copy of a lost document is available, must the proponent prove the contents of the original verbatim? The question arose in Dart Industries, Inc. v. Commercial Union Insurance Co.[11] Dart sued Commercial for a declaratory judgment establishing that Commercial, as Dart's insurer, was obligated to provide a defense against claims filed by women who had suffered injuries from the use of a pharmaceutical manufactured by Dart. Because the original insurance contract had been lost or destroyed and no copy existed, Dart offered to prove the contents through the testimony of an insurance broker. The broker, however, did not attempt to reconstruct the contents of the contract verbatim but testified only that the original contract contained a provision insuring Dart against injuries from the ingestion of dangerous drugs. The California Supreme Court upheld the use of the broker's testimony. Where testimony is admissible to prove the contents of a writing, the requirements for using secondary evidence are satisfied by testimony proving the substance of the document; verbatim proof is not required.[12]

Summaries. The admission of summaries of the contents of voluminous books, records, and other documents by definition violates the federal Best Evidence Rule and constitutes secondary evidence under the California Secondary Evidence Rule. This is the case irrespective of whether the summaries are written or oral, or in the form of charts and the like. Summaries, however, may be the only practicable way of making the contents of the original writings available to the fact finder.[13] Both the Code and the Rules permit the use of summaries, whether written or oral;[14] the judge, however, may order the production of the originals for inspection by the opposing party.[15] The authority to use summaries, however, does not in any way relax other conditions of admissibility. If the

---

10. West's Ann.California Evidence Code § 1523.

11. 28 Cal.4th 1059, 124 Cal.Rptr.2d 142, 52 P.3d 79 (2002).

12. Id. at 1069, 124 Cal.Rptr.2d at 150–151, 52 P.3d at 86. *Dart* was tried before California replaced the Best Evidence Rule with the Secondary Evidence Rule. The court's holding, however, would apply equally to a case arising under the Secondary Evidence Rule.

13. Federal Rule of Evidence 1006 (Advisory Committee Note).

14. West's Ann. California Evidence Code §§ 1521, 1523(d); Federal Rule of Evidence 1006. Under § 1521, an oral or written summary of documents is secondary evidence of the documents. In the absence of the concerns enumerated in § 1521, an oral or written summary is as admissible as the original documents. Section 1523(d) expressly allows the use of oral summaries. For additional discussion, see § 13.06 supra.

15. Federal Rule of Evidence 1006.

originals are inadmissible over a hearsay objection, for example, then the summaries are likewise inadmissible for the same reason.[16]

Copies of California business records. Section 1550 provides that a photographic copy of a business record can be offered in lieu of the original if the copy was made and preserved as part of the records of a business in the regular course of such business.[17] This section is designed to continue in effect the provisions of the Uniform Photographic Copies of Business and Public Records as Evidence Act.[18] In light of the generous treatment afforded duly authenticated copies of originals, the value of § 1550 as an exception to the Secondary Evidence Rule has diminished.

California computerized information. As writings, computer printouts are subject to the Secondary Evidence Rule. The fact that a printout may be the output of diverse data fed into a computer can raise questions about whether a particular printout is the "original." To eliminate these concerns, § 1552 provides that a "printed representation of computer information or a computer program is presumed to be an accurate representation of the computer information or computer program that it purports to represent."[19] Combined with § 255, which defines computer printouts as originals, these provisions satisfy the Secondary Evidence Rule and replace the requirements of authentication. The presumption created by § 1552 affects only the burden of producing evidence. If a party to the action introduces evidence that a printed representation is inaccurate or unreliable, the offering party must convince the judge by a preponderance of the evidence that the printed representation is an accurate representation of the existence and content of the computer information or computer program it purports to represent.[20]

Similarly, a printed representation of images stored on a video or digital medium is presumed to be an accurate representation of the images it purports to represent.[21] As in the case of printed representations of computer information or a computer program, this provision, together with § 255, satisfies the Secondary Evidence Rule and replaces the requirements of authentication. As in the case of § 1552, the presumption created by this section affects only the burden of production and imposes upon the offering party the same persuasion burden if a party to the

---

16. See, e.g., Pajaro Valley Water Management Agency v. McGrath, 128 Cal.App.4th 1093, 1107, 27 Cal.Rptr.3d 741, 751 (2005) (holding that a "summary calculation of damages" is inadmissible over a hearsay objection, unless the information used to make the calculation falls within an exception).

17. West's Ann. California Evidence Code § 1550. A photographic copy can include a "nonerasable optical image reproduction provided that additions, deletions, or changes to the original document are not permitted by the technology * * *." Id. The proviso would appear to exclude the use of copies generated by printers connected to computers, since the original in the computer's memory can be changed.

18. Id. (comment).

19. West's Ann.California Evidence Code § 1552.

20. Id.

21. West's Ann. California Evidence Code § 1553.

action introduces evidence that the printed representation of the images is inaccurate or unreliable.[22]

QUESTIONS AND PROBLEMS

1. The use of summaries provides the proponent with several advantages. One is that it permits the proponent to present the jurors with voluminous information in an accessible form. The other is that the use of summaries allows the proponent to circumvent difficult hearsay problems. True or false?

2. The opponent should insist on inspecting the original documents if she suspects that the summaries inaccurately reflect the content of the originals. True or false?

3. In the case of most writings, if the original is not produced, the Code prefers copies to testimony. The Rules, on the other hand, express such a preference only in the case of public records or recorded writings but not private writings. True or false?

4. Plaintiff sues Defendant for breach of contract. According to Plaintiff, the parties agreed to the terms of the contract by using Plaintiff's laptop computer. They remained at the keyboard until the parties agreed to the terms displayed on the monitor. At the trial Plaintiff offers in evidence a paper copy of the "contract" which, according to Plaintiff, was produced by a printer connected to the laptop. Plaintiff testifies that the paper copy is an accurate copy of the "contract" in his laptop's memory and that the version in the memory has not be altered since the parties agreed to the terms displayed on the monitor. Defendant objects on authentication and Best Evidence grounds in federal court. How should the judge rule?

Defendant objects on authentication and Secondary Evidence grounds in a California court. How should the judge rule?

§ 13.08   THE RELATIONSHIP OF THE BEST AND SECONDARY EVIDENCE RULES TO THE REQUIREMENT OF AUTHENTICATION

Under the Best Evidence Rule, a party must offer the original of a writing unless production of the original is excused.[1] In addition, the demands of authentication will force the party to offer evidence that the writing is what the party claims it to be.[2] For example, if in a contract

---

22. Id.

1. See § 13.06 supra. The 1999 amendment replacing California's Best Evidence Rule with the Secondary Evidence Rule allows a party to offer secondary evidence of the original in the first instance, unless a genuine dispute exists concerning the material terms of the original and justice requires exclusion of the secondary evidence, or it would be unfair to admit the secondary evidence. See § 13.06 supra. Accordingly, California parties may still be required to produce and offer the original writing.

2. See § 13.01 supra. The 1999 amendment replacing California's Best Evidence Rule with the Secondary Evidence Rule does not relax the requirements of authentication. West's Ann.California Evidence Code § 1521(c).

action the plaintiff offers the original of the contract he claims the defendant breached, the plaintiff must authenticate the contract as the contract entered into between the parties. If the plaintiff is permitted to offer a copy of the original, then the plaintiff must also authenticate the copy.[3] This means that the plaintiff must offer evidence showing that the copy is a correct copy of the original contract between the parties.

In the case of some public records and recorded writings, the Code provides for the simultaneous satisfaction of the requirements of authentication and the Secondary Evidence Rule. Section 1530(a)(1) provides that if a copy of a writing in the custody of a public entity purports to be published by the authority of the nation or state, or public entity therein in which the writing is kept, then the copy shall be prima facie evidence of the existence and content of the original.[4] In addition, Section 1530(a)(2) provides that if the office in which the original is kept is within the United States and the office certifies that a copy is a correct copy of the original, then the copy shall also be prima facie evidence of the existence and content of the original.[5] To facilitate the admission of these records, the certification of authenticity may be received for the truth of the matters stated.[6]

The presumptions created by Section 1530 affect only the burden of producing evidence.[7] If the opponent fails to introduce evidence challenging the correctness of the copy, then the fact finder must find that the copy is a faithful reproduction of the original. But if the opponent does offer such evidence, then the fact finder will have to determine the correctness of the copy without regard to the presumptions.[8]

Section 1560 permits the custodian of business records to supply copies of the originals in response to a subpoena duces tecum.[9] The copies may be offered in evidence in lieu of the original records.[10] In the affidavit accompanying the copies, the custodian must authenticate the originals as well as the copies.[11] The affidavit may be received for the truth of the matters stated.[12] Whether the copies of the records may be received under the hearsay exception for business records is discussed in § 10.03 of this treatise.

Under § 1421, a party may authenticate a writing by evidence that the writing refers to matters unlikely to be known by anyone other than

---

3. West's Ann. California Evidence Code § 1401(b).

4. West's Ann. California Evidence Code § 1530.

5. Id. The certifying office may also be located in enumerated U.S. possessions. Id. Section 1530 also provides for the authentication by attestation of copies of writings kept in offices outside of the United States and its possessions. See § 1530(a)(3).

6. Id. (comment).

7. Id.

8. West's Ann. California Evidence Code § 1530(b) and comment.

9. West's Ann. California Evidence Code § 1560.

10. West's Ann. California Evidence Code § 1562.

11. West's Ann. California Evidence Code § 1561(a).

12. West's Ann. California Evidence Code § 1562 (comment).

the person who the proponent claims is the author of the writing.[13] Since authentication by this means requires the disclosure of some of the contents of the writing, the use of § 1421 can violate the Secondary Evidence Rule. Accordingly, § 1421 must be viewed as an exception to the rule.

§ 13.09   THE RELATIONSHIP OF AUTHENTICATION AND THE BEST AND SECONDARY EVIDENCE RULES TO THE HEARSAY RULE

When a writing is moved in evidence, the opponent can object to its admissibility on at least three grounds. One is lack of authentication, another is violation of the Best or Secondary Evidence Rules, and a third is hearsay. The first objection will force the proponent to identify the document and show its connection to the issues in the case.[1] For purposes of admissibility, the proponent need produce only enough evidence to persuade the judge that a reasonable fact finder could find the document to be what the proponent claims it to be.[2] Because a sufficiency standard applies, the judge must view the evidence in the light most favorable to the proponent.[3]

Compliance with the Best and Secondary Evidence Rules calls for a higher standard. The proponent in federal court must persuade the judge by a preponderance of the evidence that the document offered is either the original or, if a copy, that the failure to produce the original is excused.[4] In California courts, over objection the proponent must persuade the judge by a preponderance of the evidence that no genuine dispute exists concerning the material terms of the original writing and that admission of the secondary evidence would not be unfair.[5] In making this determination, the judge may consider the evidence produced by the proponent as well as by the opponent, and may take into account the credibility of the witnesses called on the issue.[6]

If the judge overrules the authentication and Best or Secondary Evidence Rule objections, the proponent still may not disclose the contents of the document to the jury until the judge rules on the hearsay objection. If the objection is overruled on the ground that the document is not

---

13.   West's Ann. California Evidence Code § 1421.

1.   See § 13.01 supra.

2.   Id.

3.   Id.

4.   Federal Rule of Evidence 104(a).

5.   West's Ann. California Evidence Code § 405 (comment).

6.   But if the issue in a federal contract action, for example, is not just whether the original contract was lost but whether the contract was entered into in the first place, then the latter issue must be given to the jury. The judge cannot withdraw this issue from the jury by excluding the secondary evidence of the contract on the ground that the original was not lost. Federal Rule of Evidence 1008 and Advisory Committee Note.

hearsay or, if hearsay, falls within an exception, then the proponent may disclose the contents to the jury. The proponent may read the document or have the witness on the stand read it. The proponent may also request permission to pass copies to the jury. Once the document has been admitted in evidence, the Best and Secondary Evidence Rules no longer apply and the parties and witnesses are free to read from the parts admitted without violating the rules.

QUESTIONS AND PROBLEMS

1. Rule on the following objections in a California and federal court:

    Plaintiff: Doctor, did you bring the X-rays you took of my leg?

    Doctor: Yes, I did.

    Plaintiff: Your Honor, may we have this document marked as Plaintiff's Exhibit Number 1 for Identification?

    Judge: So marked.

    Plaintiff: May the record reflect that I am showing Plaintiff's Exhibit Number 1 for Identification to the opposing party?

    Judge: Yes.

    Plaintiff: May I approach the witness?

    Judge: Yes.

    Plaintiff: I show you what has been marked as Plaintiff's Exhibit Number 1 for Identification. Can you tell us what this is?

    Doctor: Yes, the X-rays I took of your leg.

    Plaintiff: Would you please tell the jury what they show?

    Defendant: Objection. Violates the Best [Secondary] Evidence Rule.

    Judge: ? → *Yes, violates the Rules. Unless received in evidence.*

2. Suppose that instead of asking the doctor what the exhibit showed, the plaintiff moved the exhibit in evidence. How would you rule on the defendant's objection that the exhibit was improperly authenticated?

3. How would you rule on the defendant's objection that receiving the exhibit would violate the hearsay rule?

4. Suppose that instead of the X-rays, the plaintiff offered a report by the radiologist stating that the plaintiff's leg was broken. Would you sustain Best [Secondary] Evidence Rule and hearsay objections to testimony about what the radiologist wrote?

§ 13.10   THE COMPLETENESS DOCTRINE

Whenever matters are taken out of context, misleading impressions can be created. To diminish this risk, § 356 provides that when "part of an act, declaration, conversation, or writing is given in evidence by one party, the whole on the same subject may be inquired into by an adverse party; when a letter is read, the answer may be given; and when a detached act, declaration, conversation, or writing is given in evidence, any other act, declaration, conversation, or writing which is necessary to make it understood may also be given in evidence."[1] The Federal Rules contain a similar provision, but it is limited to writings and recorded statements and does not apply to conversations.[2]

Rosenberg v. Wittenborn[3] illustrates the rule's application. Plaintiffs sued the defendant to recover for injuries they claimed they suffered when the defendant ran a light and struck their car. To prove that the defendant ran the light, the plaintiffs called the officer who investigated the accident. He testified that at the time he investigated the accident the defendant admitted he had the red light. Over the plaintiffs' objection, the officer was allowed on cross to testify that the defendant also told him that he ran the light because his brakes, which had just been repaired, failed unexpectedly. The appellate court upheld the use of the officer's cross-examination testimony:

> Plaintiffs' attorney was trying to leave the jury with the impression that defendant by way of admission had told the officer * * * that he entered the intersection against the red light,—that he said this and no more. These statements were in fact so qualified when made to the officer that they carried no implication (such as plaintiffs would have the jury draw) that defendant ran the light because he was going too fast to stop within the distance he had available. * * * Considerations of fair play demanded that the portion of the conversation placed in evidence by plaintiffs be supplemented by the qualifying and enlightening portions of the conversation which gave a very different complexion than that which plaintiffs' segregated passages bore.[4]

Rosenberg is instructive in another respect: the fact that the statements offered by the defendant through the officer were hearsay beyond the exception for party admissions was immaterial. Since the part offered by the plaintiffs was received for the truth of the matter asserted, the balance could also be received for that purpose. Under these circumstances, the hearsay rule does not bar the use of such statements.[5]

When the balance of a conversation or writing is offered to place the part received in context, the proffered evidence must relate to "the same

---

1. West's Ann. California Evidence Code § 356.

2. Federal Rule of Evidence 106. The rule does not extend to conversations for "practical reasons." Id. (Advisory Committee Note).

3. 178 Cal.App.2d 846, 3 Cal.Rptr. 459 (1960). *Rosenberg* construed § 356's predecessor, West's Ann. California Code of Civil Procedure § 1854. West's Ann. California Evidence Code § 356 (comment). Section 1854 was identical to § 356. Id.

4. Rosenberg v. Wittenborn, 178 Cal.App.2d at 851–852, 3 Cal.Rptr. at 463.

5. Id. at 852, 3 Cal.Rptr. at 462. See also People v. Williams, 13 Cal.3d 559, 565, 119 Cal.Rptr. 210, 213, 531 P.2d 778, 781 (1975). Occasionally, courts will avoid the hearsay issue by asserting that the balance of the statement or conversation was admitted only to place the previously admitted portion in context. See, e.g., People v. Harris, 37 Cal.4th 310, 335, 118 P.3d 545, 563, 33 Cal.Rptr.3d 509, 531 (2005), cert. denied 547 U.S. 1065, 126 S.Ct. 1655, 164 L.Ed.2d 411 (2006), and cases cited therein.

subject."[6] That clearly was the case in *Rosenberg*, where the part offered on cross-examination explained the part received on direct. In contrast, in Witt v. Jackson[7] the balance did not relate to the same subject. In that case, Witt, a police officer, sued the defendant for injuries he suffered when the defendant rammed the rear of Witt's car. At the time of the accident, Witt was in the process of pulling a Dodge over. Witt claimed that he turned his overhead lights on before stopping the Dodge. The defendant's theory was that Witt caused the accident by moving into the defendant's lane without first determining that it was safe to do so. In support of his theory, the defendant had the officer who investigated the accident testify that Witt had told the officer that he had not turned on his overhead lights until after he had driven alongside the Dodge. Witt then attempted to offer the balance of the conversation in which he told the officer that after turning on his overheads he looked in the rear-view mirror and saw a car approaching him at approximately 65 miles per hour. That car turned out to be the defendant's.

The appellate court upheld the exclusion of this part of the conversation. The balance of Witt's conversation with the officer was unnecessary to place the part received in context. Moreover, since the excluded part dealt with a different subject, it did not help explain the inconsistency between Witt's testimony that he turned his overheads on before pulling alongside the Dodge and his statement to the officer that he turned them on after pulling alongside the car.[8] As *Rosenberg* and *Witt* illustrate, judges should take a pragmatic approach in applying § 356. Although the remainder of a conversation is inadmissible under § 356 unless it "explains, modifies, qualifies, or has relevant reference to the part already introduced,"[9] judges should not draw "narrow lines" around the exact subject in applying § 356.[10]

By its terms, § 356 can apply to more than one conversation: "when a detached * * * conversation * * * is given in evidence, any other * * * conversation * * * which is necessary to make it understood may also be given in evidence."[11] But in People v. Barrick[12] the California Supreme Court cast doubts on the plain meaning of this provision. To prove that the accused had unlawfully taken a car, the prosecution called a police officer who testified that when he found the accused asleep in the car, the accused, upon awakening, said that he had become tired and pulled over.

6. West's Ann. California Evidence Code § 356.

7. 57 Cal.2d 57, 17 Cal.Rptr. 369, 366 P.2d 641 (1961). Like *Rosenberg*, *Witt* was decided before the Evidence Code was adopted. But like *Rosenberg*, *Witt* also construed the statute that was superseded by § 356. That statute was identical to § 356. See note 3 supra.

8. Witt v. Jackson, 57 Cal.2d at 67, 17 Cal.Rptr. at 374, 366 P.2d at 646.

9. Carson v. Facilities Development Co., 36 Cal.3d 830, 850, 206 Cal.Rptr. 136, 148, 686 P.2d 656, 668 (1984).

10. People v. Hamilton, 48 Cal.3d 1142, 1174, 259 Cal.Rptr. 701, 720, 774 P.2d 730, 749 (1989), cert. denied, 494 U.S. 1039, 110 S.Ct. 1503, 108 L.Ed.2d 638 (1990), reh'g denied, 495 U.S. 924, 110 S.Ct. 1961, 109 L.Ed.2d 323 (1990).

11. West's Ann. California Evidence Code § 356.

12. 33 Cal.3d 115, 187 Cal.Rptr. 716, 654 P.2d 1243 (1982).

On cross-examination, the accused attempted to get the officer to testify that he also told the officer that he did not know how he had gotten into the car, as all he could remember was attending a party. The trial judge excluded this conversation.[13]

The conversation elicited on direct occurred when the officer first found the accused in the car, before the officer had given the accused the *Miranda* warnings. The second took place after the officer learned over his radio that the car had been stolen and the officer returned to the car to place the accused under arrest. Although the court acknowledged that both conversations related to the same subject—explaining the accused's presence in the car[14]—the court nonetheless upheld the exclusion of the second conversation: "Whatever defendant said after the delay in arrest and after having been warned of his rights thus is not simply a continuation of the prior conversation, but a distinct and separate interrogation. We therefore conclude that the trial court did not err in excluding defendant's postarrest statement."[15]

It may be that given the circumstances, the court viewed the accused's postarrest statement with suspicion. But credibility normally is a question reserved for the jurors and not a ground for excluding evidence. In a later case, the California Supreme Court appears to have reaffirmed the plain meaning of the completeness doctrine. "It applies only to statements that have some bearing upon, or connection with, the portion of the conversation originally introduced.* * * Statements pertaining to other matters may be excluded."[16] Under this standard, the second conversation in *Barrick* would have qualified under the doctrine since it pertained to the same subject—the accused's presence in the car unlawfully taken. The fact that the accused's second conversation helped him would not have been a ground for excluding the second part of the conversation. Matters admissible under the doctrine may include self-serving statements.[17]

QUESTIONS AND PROBLEMS

Plaintiff sues defendant for personal injuries she suffered when the defendant allegedly ran a red light and struck her with his car. Plaintiff calls the officer who in the course of investigating the accident interviewed the defendant. Rule on the admissibility of the following evidence in a California court:

> Plaintiff's Counsel: Did you ask the defendant if he ran the light?
>
> Officer: Yes.

---

13. Id. at 131–132, 187 Cal.Rptr. at 726–727, 654 P.2d at 1253–1254.

14. Id.

15. Id.

16. People v. Samuels, 36 Cal.4th 96, 130, 30 Cal.Rptr.3d 105, 132, 113 P.3d 1125, 1148 (2005).

17. See People v. Arias, 13 Cal.4th 92, 156, 51 Cal.Rptr.2d 770, 812, 913 P.2d 980, 1021, cert. denied, 520 U.S. 1251, 117 S.Ct. 2408, 138 L.Ed.2d 175 (1997).

Plaintiff's Counsel: What, if anything, did the defendant say?

Officer: He said he ran the light. *admission*

* * *

Defense Counsel: My client also told you, did he not, why he ran the light? *leading allowed or x*

Officer: Yes, he said, "My brakes, which I just had fixed, failed unexpectedly."

Plaintiff's Counsel: Move to strike on grounds of hearsay.

Judge: ?

CALIFORNIA EVIDENCE CODE

§ 250. "Writing"

"Writing" means handwriting, typewriting, printing, photostating, photographing, photocopying, transmitting by electronic mail or facsimile, and every other means of recording upon any tangible thing any form of communication or representation, including letters, words, pictures, sounds, or symbols, or combinations thereof, and any record thereby created, regardless of the manner in which the record has been stored.

§ 255. "Original"

"Original" means the writing itself or any counterpart intended to have the same effect by a person executing or issuing it. An "original" of a photograph includes the negative or any print therefrom. If data are stored in a computer or similar device, any printout or other output readable by sight, shown to reflect the data accurately, is an "original."

§ 260. "Duplicate"

A "duplicate" is a counterpart produced by the same impression as the original, or from the same matrix, or by means of photography, including enlargements and miniatures, or by mechanical or electronic rerecording, or by chemical reproduction, or by other equivalent technique which accurately reproduces the original.

§ 356. Entire act, declaration, conversation, or writing may be brought out to elucidate part offered

Where part of an act, declaration, conversation, or writing is given in evidence by one party, the whole on the same subject may be inquired into by an adverse party; when a letter is read, the answer may be given; and when a detached act, declaration, conversation, or writing is given in evidence, any other act, declaration, conversation, or writing which is necessary to make it understood may also be given in evidence.

§ 630. Presumptions affecting the burden of producing evidence

The presumptions established by this article, and all other rebuttable presumptions established by law that fall within the criteria of Section 603, are presumptions affecting the burden of producing evidence.

§ 644. Book purporting to be published by public authority

A book, purporting to be printed or published by public authority, is presumed to have been so printed or published.

§ 645. Book purporting to contain reports of cases

A book, purporting to contain reports of cases adjudged in the tribunals of the state or nation where the book is published, is presumed to contain correct reports of such cases.

§ 645.1. Printed materials purporting to be particular newspaper or periodical

Printed materials, purporting to be a particular newspaper or periodical, are presumed to be that newspaper or periodical if regularly issued at average intervals not exceeding three months.

§ 1400. Authentication defined

Authentication of a writing means (a) the introduction of evidence sufficient to sustain a finding that it is the writing that the proponent of the evidence claims it is or (b) the establishment of such facts by any other means provided by law

§ 1401. Authentication required

(a) Authentication of a writing is required before it may be received in evidence.

(b) Authentication of a writing is required before secondary evidence of its content may be received in evidence.

§ 1402. Authentication of altered writing

The party producing a writing as genuine which has been altered, or appears to have been altered, after its execution, in a part material to the question in dispute, must account for the alteration or appearance thereof. He may show that the alteration was made by another, without his concurrence, or was made with the consent of the parties affected by it, or otherwise properly or innocently made, or that the alteration did not change the meaning or language of the instrument. If he does that, he may give the writing in evidence, but not otherwise.

§ 1410. Article not exclusive

Nothing in this article shall be construed to limit the means by which a writing may be authenticated or proved.

§ 1410.5. Graffiti constitutes a writing; admissibility

(a) For purposes of this chapter, a writing shall include any graffiti consisting of written words, insignia, symbols, or any other markings which convey a particular meaning.

(b) Any writing described in subdivision (a), or any photograph thereof, may be admitted into evidence in an action for vandalism, for the purpose of proving that the writing was made by the defendant.

(c) The admissibility of any fact offered to prove that the writing was made by the defendant shall, upon motion of the defendant, be ruled upon outside the presence of the jury, and is subject to the requirements of Sections 1416, 1417, and 1418.

§ 1411. Subscribing witness' testimony unnecessary

Except as provided by statute, the testimony of a subscribing witness is not required to authenticate a writing.

§ 1412. Use of other evidence when subscribing witness' testimony required

If the testimony of a subscribing witness is required by statute to authenticate a writing and the subscribing witness denies or does not recollect the execution of the writing, the writing may be authenticated by other evidence.

§ 1413. Witness to the execution of a writing

A writing may be authenticated by anyone who saw the writing made or executed, including a subscribing witness.

§ 1414. Authentication by admission

A writing may be authenticated by evidence that:

(a) The party against whom it is offered has at any time admitted its authenticity; or

(b) The writing has been acted upon as authentic by the party against whom it is offered.

§ 1415. Authentication by handwriting evidence

A writing may be authenticated by evidence of the genuineness of the handwriting of the maker.

§ 1416. Proof of handwriting by person familiar therewith

A witness who is not otherwise qualified to testify as an expert may state his opinion whether a writing is in the handwriting of a supposed writer if the court finds that he has personal knowledge of the handwriting of the supposed writer. Such personal knowledge may be acquired from:

(a) Having seen the supposed writer write;

(b) Having seen a writing purporting to be in the handwriting of the supposed writer and upon which the supposed writer has acted or been charged;

(c) Having received letters in the due course of mail purporting to be from the supposed writer in response to letters duly addressed and mailed by him to the supposed writer; or

(d) Any other means of obtaining personal knowledge of the hand-writing of the supposed writer.

§ 1417.   Comparison of handwriting by trier of fact

The genuineness of handwriting, or the lack thereof, may be proved by a comparison made by the trier of fact with handwriting (a) which the court finds was admitted or treated as genuine by the party against whom the evidence is offered or (b) otherwise proved to be genuine to the satisfaction of the court.

§ 1418.   Comparison of writing by expert witness

The genuineness of writing, or the lack thereof, may be proved by a comparison made by an expert witness with writing (a) which the court finds was admitted or treated as genuine by the party against whom the evidence is offered or (b) otherwise proved to be genuine to the satisfaction of the court.

§ 1419.   Exemplars when writing is 30 years old

Where a writing whose genuineness is sought to be proved is more than 30 years old, the comparison under Section 1417 or 1418 may be made with writing purporting to be genuine, and generally respected and acted upon as such, by persons having an interest in knowing whether it is genuine.

§ 1420.   Authentication by evidence of reply

A writing may be authenticated by evidence that the writing was received in response to a communication sent to the person who is claimed by the proponent of the evidence to be the author of the writing.

§ 1421.   Authentication by content

A writing may be authenticated by evidence that the writing refers to or states matters that are unlikely to be known to anyone other than the person who is claimed by the proponent of the evidence to be the author of the writing.

§ 1450.   Classification of presumptions in article

The presumptions established by this article [regarding acknowledged and official writings] are presumptions affecting the burden of producing evidence.

§ 1451.   Acknowledged writings

A certificate of the acknowledgment of a writing other than a will, or a certificate of the proof of such a writing, is prima facie evidence of the facts recited in the certificate and the genuineness of the signature of each person by whom the writing purports to have been signed if the certificate meets the requirements of Article 3 (commencing with Section 1180) of Chapter 4, Title 4, Part 4, Division 2 of the Civil Code.

§ 1452.   Official seals

A seal is presumed to be genuine and its use authorized if it purports to be the seal of:

(a) The United States or a department, agency, or public employee of the United States.

(b) A public entity in the United States or a department, agency, or public employee of such public entity.

(c) A nation recognized by the executive power of the United States or a department, agency, or officer of such nation.

(d) A public entity in a nation recognized by the executive power of the United States or a department, agency, or officer of such public entity.

(e) A court of admiralty or maritime jurisdiction.

(f) A notary public within any state of the United States.

§ 1453. Domestic official signatures

A signature is presumed to be genuine and authorized if it purports to be the signature, affixed in his official capacity, of:

(a) A public employee of the United States.

(b) A public employee of any public entity in the United States.

(c) A notary public within any state of the United States.

§ 1454. Foreign official signatures

A signature is presumed to be genuine and authorized if it purports to be the signature, affixed in his official capacity, of an officer, or deputy of an officer, of a nation or public entity in a nation recognized by the executive power of the United States and the writing to which the signature is affixed is accompanied by a final statement certifying the genuineness of the signature and the official position of (a) the person who executed the writing or (b) any foreign official who has certified either the genuineness of the signature and official position of the person executing the writing or the genuineness of the signature and official position of another foreign official who has executed a similar certificate in a chain of such certificates beginning with a certificate of the genuineness of the signature and official position of the person executing the writing. The final statement may be made only by a secretary of an embassy or legation, consul general, consul, vice consul, consular agent, or other officer in the foreign service of the United States stationed in the nation, authenticated by the seal of his office.

§ 1520. Content of writing; proof

The content of a writing may be proved by an otherwise admissible original.

§ 1521. Secondary evidence rule

(a) The content of a writing may be proved by otherwise admissible secondary evidence. The court shall exclude secondary evidence of the content of writing if the court determines either of the following:

(1) A genuine dispute exists concerning material terms of the writing and justice requires the exclusion.

(2) Admission of the secondary evidence would be unfair.

(b) Nothing in this section makes admissible oral testimony to prove the content of a writing if the testimony is inadmissible under Section 1523 (oral testimony of the content of a writing).

(c) Nothing in this section excuses compliance with Section 1401 (authentication).

(d) The section shall be known as the "Secondary Evidence Rule."

§ 1522. Additional grounds for exclusion of secondary evidence

(a) In addition to the grounds for exclusion authorized by Section 1521, in a criminal action the court shall exclude secondary evidence of the content of a writing if the court determines that the original is in the proponent's possession, custody, or control, and the proponent has not made the original reasonably available for inspection at or before trial. This section does not apply to any of the following:

(1) A duplicate as defined in Section 260.

(2) A writing that is not closely related to the controlling issues in the action.

(3) A copy of a writing in the custody of a public entity.

(4) A copy of a writing that is recorded in the public records, if the record or a certified copy of it is made evidence of the writing by statute.

(b) In a criminal action, a request to exclude secondary evidence of the content of a writing, under this section or any other law, shall not be made in the presence of the jury.

§ 1523. Oral testimony of the content of a writing; admissibility

(a) Except as otherwise provided by statute, oral testimony is not admissible to prove the content of a writing.

(b) Oral testimony of the content of a writing is not made inadmissible by subdivision (a) if the proponent does not have possession or control of a copy of the writing and the original is lost or has been destroyed without fraudulent intent on the part of the proponent of the evidence.

(c) Oral testimony of the content of a writing is not made inadmissible by subdivision (a) if the proponent does not have possession or control of the original or a copy of the writing and either of the following conditions is satisfied:

(1) Neither the writing nor a copy of the writing was reasonably procurable by the proponent by use of the court's process or by other available means.

(2) The writing is not closely related to the controlling issues and it would be inexpedient to require its production.

(d) Oral testimony of the content of a writing is not made inadmissible by subdivision (a) if the writing consists of numerous accounts or other writings that cannot be examined in court without great loss of time, and the evidence sought from them is only the general result of the whole.

§ 1530. Copy of writing in official custody

(a) A purported copy of a writing in the custody of a public entity, or of an entry in such a writing, is prima facie evidence of the existence and content of such writing or entry if:

(1) The copy purports to be published by the authority of the nation or state, or public entity therein in which the writing is kept;

(2) The office in which the writing is kept is within the United States or within the Panama Canal Zone, the Trust Territory of the Pacific Islands, or the Ryukyu Islands, and the copy is attested or certified as a correct copy of the writing or entry by a public employee, or a deputy of a public employee, having the legal custody of the writing; or

(3) The office in which the writing is kept is not within the United States or any other place described in paragraph (2) and the copy is attested as a correct copy of the writing or entry by a person having authority to make attestation. The attestation must be accompanied by a final statement certifying the genuineness of the signature and the official position of (i) the person who attested the copy as a correct copy or (ii) any foreign official who has certified either the genuineness of the signature and official position of the person attesting the copy or the genuineness of the signature and official position of another foreign official who has executed a similar certificate in a chain of such certificates beginning with a certificate of the genuineness of the signature and official position of the person attesting the copy. Except as provided in the next sentence, the final statement may be made only by a secretary of an embassy or legation, consul general, consul, vice consul, or consular agent of the United States, or a diplomatic or consular official of the foreign country assigned or accredited to the United States. Prior to January 1, 1971, the final statement may also be made by a secretary of an embassy or legation, consul general, consul, vice consul, consular agent, or other officer in the foreign service of the United States stationed in the nation in which the writing is kept, authenticated by the seal of his office. If reasonable opportunity has been given to all parties to investigate the authenticity and accuracy of the documents, the court may, for good cause shown, (i) admit an attested copy without the final statement or (ii) permit the writing or entry in foreign custody to be evidenced by an attested summary with or without a final statement.

(b) The presumptions established by this section are presumptions affecting the burden of producing evidence.

§ 1531. Certification of copy for evidence

For the purpose of evidence, whenever a copy of a writing is attested or certified, the attestation or certificate must state in substance that the copy is a correct copy of the original, or of a specified part thereof, as the case may be.

§ 1532. Official record of recorded writing

(a) The official record of a writing is prima facie evidence of the existence and content of the original recorded writing if:

(1) The record is in fact a record of an office of a public entity; and

(2) A statute authorized such a writing to be recorded in that office.

(b) The presumption established by this section is a presumption affecting the burden of producing evidence.

§ 1550. Types of evidence as writing admissible as the writing itself

(a) If made and preserved as part of the records of a business, as defined in Section 1270, in the regular course of that business, the following types of evidence of a writing are as admissible as the writing itself:

(1) A nonerasable optical image reproduction or any other reproduction of a public record by a trusted system, as defined in Section 12168.7 of the Government Code, if additions, deletions, or changes to the original document are not permitted by the technology.

(2) A photostatic copy or reproduction.

(3) A microfilm, microcard, or miniature photographic copy, reprint, or enlargement.

(4) Any other photographic copy or reproduction, or an enlargement thereof.

(b) The introduction of evidence of a writing pursuant to subdivision (a) does not preclude admission of the original writing if it is still in existence. A court may require the introduction of hard copy printout of the document.

§ 1551. Photographic copies where original destroyed or lost

A print, whether enlarged or not, from a photographic film (including a photographic plate, microphotographic film, photostatic negative, or similar reproduction) of an original writing destroyed or lost after such film was taken or a reproduction from an electronic recording of video images on magnetic surfaces is admissible as the original writing itself if, at the time of the taking of such film or electronic recording, the person under whose direction and control it was taken attached thereto, or to the sealed container in which it was placed and has been kept, or incorporated in the film or electronic recording, a certification complying with the provisions of Section 1531 and stating the date on which, and the fact that, it was so taken under his direction and control.

§ 1552. Printed representation of computer information or computer programs

(a) A printed representation of computer information or a computer program is presumed to be an accurate representation of the computer information or computer program that it purports to represent. This presumption is a presumption affecting the burden of producing evidence. If a party to an action introduces evidence that a printed representation of computer information or computer program is inaccurate or unreliable, the party introducing the printed representation into evidence has the burden of proving, by a preponderance of the evidence, that the printed representation is an accurate representation of the existence and content of the computer information or computer program that it purports to represent.

(b) Subdivision (a) shall not apply to computer-generated official records certified in accordance with Section 452.5 or 1530.

§ 1553. Printed representation of images stored on a video or digital medium

A printed representation of images stored on a video or digital medium is presumed to be an accurate representation of the images it purports to represent. This presumption is a presumption affecting the burden of producing evidence. If a party to an action introduces evidence that a printed representation of images stored on a video or digital medium is inaccurate or unreliable, the party introducing the printed representation into evidence has the burden of proving, by a preponderance of the evidence, that the printed representation is an accurate representation of the existence and content of the images that it purports to represent.

FEDERAL RULES OF EVIDENCE

Rule 106. Remainder of or Related Writings or Recorded Statements

If a party introduces all or part of a writing or recorded statement, an adverse party may require the introduction, at that time, of any other part—or any other writing or recorded statement—that in fairness ought to be considered at the same time.

Rule 901. Authenticating or Identifying Evidence

(a) In General. To satisfy the requirement of authenticating or identifying an item of evidence, the proponent must produce evidence sufficient to support a finding that the item is what the proponent claims it is.

(b) Examples. The following are examples only—not a complete list—of evidence that satisfies the requirement:

    (1) *Testimony of a Witness with Knowledge.* Testimony that an item is what it is claimed to be.

    (2) *Nonexpert Opinion About Handwriting.* A nonexpert's opinion that handwriting is genuine, based on a familiarity with it that was not acquired for the current litigation.

(3) *Comparison by an Expert Witness or the Trier of Fact.* A comparison with an authenticated specimen by an expert witness or the trier of fact.

(4) *Distinctive Characteristics and the Like.* The appearance, contents, substance, internal patterns, or other distinctive characteristics of the item, taken together with all the circumstances.

(5) *Opinion About a Voice.* An opinion identifying a person's voice—whether heard firsthand or through mechanical or electronic transmission or recording—based on hearing the voice at any time under circumstances that connect it with the alleged speaker.

(6) *Evidence About a Telephone Conversation.* For a telephone conversation, evidence that a call was made to the number assigned at the time to:

> **(A)** a particular person, if circumstances, including self-identification, show that the person answering was the one called; or

> **(B)** a particular business, if the call was made to a business and the call related to business reasonably transacted over the telephone.

(7) *Evidence About Public Records.* Evidence that:

> **(A)** a document was recorded or filed in a public office as authorized by law; or

> **(B)** a purported public record or statement is from the office where items of this kind are kept.

(8) *Evidence About Ancient Documents or Data Compilations.* For a document or data compilation, evidence that it:

> **(A)** is in a condition that creates no suspicion about its authenticity;

> **(B)** was in a place where, if authentic, it would likely be; and

> **(C)** is at least 20 years old when offered.

(9) *Evidence About a Process or System.* Evidence describing a process or system and showing that it produces an accurate result.

(10) *Methods Provided by a Statute or Rule.* Any method of authentication or identification allowed by a federal statute or a rule prescribed by the Supreme Court.

Rule 902.   Evidence That Is Self–Authenticating

The following items of evidence are self-authenticating; they require no extrinsic evidence of authenticity in order to be admitted:

(1) *Domestic Public Documents That Are Sealed and Signed.* A document that bears:

> **(A)** a seal purporting to be that of the United States; any state, district, commonwealth, territory, or insular possession of the United States; the former Panama Canal Zone; the Trust Territo-

ry of the Pacific Islands; a political subdivision of any of these entities; or a department, agency, or officer of any entity named above; and

(B) a signature purporting to be an execution or attestation.

(2) *Domestic Public Documents That Are Not Sealed but Are Signed and Certified.* A document that bears no seal if:

(A) it bears the signature of an officer or employee of an entity named in Rule 902(1)(A); and

(B) another public officer who has a seal and official duties within that same entity certifies under seal—or its equivalent—that the signer has the official capacity and that the signature is genuine.

(3) *Foreign Public Documents.* A document that purports to be signed or attested by a person who is authorized by a foreign country's law to do so. The document must be accompanied by a final certification that certifies the genuineness of the signature and official position of the signer or attester—or of any foreign official whose certificate of genuineness relates to the signature or attestation or is in a chain of certificates of genuineness relating to the signature or attestation. The certification may be made by a secretary of a United States embassy or legation; by a consul general, vice consul, or consular agent of the United States; or by a diplomatic or consular official of the foreign country assigned or accredited to the United States. If all parties have been given a reasonable opportunity to investigate the document's authenticity and accuracy, the court may, for good cause, either:

(A) order that it be treated as presumptively authentic without final certification; or

(B) allow it to be evidenced by an attested summary with or without final certification.

(4) *Certified Copies of Public Records.* A copy of an official record—or a copy of a document that was recorded or filed in a public office as authorized by law—if the copy is certified as correct by:

(A) the custodian or another person authorized to make the certification; or

(B) a certificate that complies with Rule 902(1), (2), or (3), a federal statute, or a rule prescribed by the Supreme Court.

(5) *Official Publications.* A book, pamphlet, or other publication purporting to be issued by a public authority.

(6) *Newspapers and Periodicals.* Printed material purporting to be a newspaper or periodical.

(7) *Trade Inscriptions and the Like.* An inscription, sign, tag, or label purporting to have been affixed in the course of business and indicating origin, ownership, or control.

(8) *Acknowledged Documents.* A document accompanied by a certificate of acknowledgment that is lawfully executed by a notary public or another officer who is authorized to take acknowledgments.

(9) *Commercial Paper and Related Documents.* Commercial paper, a signature on it, and related documents, to the extent allowed by general commercial law.

(10) *Presumptions Under a Federal Statute.* A signature, document, or anything else that a federal statute declares to be presumptively or prima facie genuine or authentic.

(11) *Certified Domestic Records of a Regularly Conducted Activity.* The original or a copy of a domestic record that meets the requirements of Rule 803(6)(A)–(C), as shown by a certification of the custodian or another qualified person that complies with a federal statute or a rule prescribed by the Supreme Court. Before the trial or hearing, the proponent must give an adverse party reasonable written notice of the intent to offer the record—and must make the record and certification available for inspection—so that the party has a fair opportunity to challenge them.

(12) *Certified Foreign Records of a Regularly Conducted Activity.* In a civil case, the original or a copy of a foreign record that meets the requirements of Rule 902(11), modified as follows: the certification, rather than complying with a federal statute or Supreme Court rule, must be signed in a manner that, if falsely made, would subject the maker to a criminal penalty in the country where the certification is signed. The proponent must also meet the notice requirements of Rule 902(11).

Rule 903. Subscribing Witness's Testimony

A subscribing witness's testimony is necessary to authenticate a writing only if required by the law of the jurisdiction that governs its validity.

Rule 1001. Definitions That Apply to This Article

In this article:

(a) A "writing" consists of letters, words, numbers, or their equivalent set down in any form.

(b) A "recording" consists of letters, words, numbers, or their equivalent recorded in any manner.

(c) A "photograph" means a photographic image or its equivalent stored in any form.

(d) An "original" of a writing or recording means the writing or recording itself or any counterpart intended to have the same effect by the person who executed or issued it. For electronically stored information, "original" means any printout—or other output readable by sight—if it accurately reflects the information. An "original" of a photograph includes the negative or a print from it.

(e) A "duplicate" means a counterpart produced by a mechanical, photographic, chemical, electronic, or other equivalent process or technique that accurately reproduces the original.

Rule 1002. Requirement of the Original

An original writing, recording, or photograph is required in order to prove its content unless these rules or a federal statute provides otherwise.

Rule 1003. Admissibility of Duplicates

A duplicate is admissible to the same extent as the original unless a genuine question is raised about the original's authenticity or the circumstances make it unfair to admit the duplicate.

Rule 1004. Admissibility of Other Evidence of Content

An original is not required and other evidence of the content of a writing, recording, or photograph is admissible if:

(a) all the originals are lost or destroyed, and not by the proponent acting in bad faith;

(b) an original cannot be obtained by any available judicial process;

(c) the party against whom the original would be offered had control of the original; was at that time put on notice, by pleadings or otherwise, that the original would be a subject of proof at the trial or hearing; and fails to produce it at the trial or hearing; or

(d) the writing, recording, or photograph is not closely related to a controlling issue.

Rule 1005. Copies of Public Records to Prove Content

The proponent may use a copy to prove the content of an official record—or of a document that was recorded or filed in a public office as authorized by law—if these conditions are met: the record or document is otherwise admissible; and the copy is certified as correct in accordance with Rule 902(4) or is testified to be correct by a witness who has compared it with the original. If no such copy can be obtained by reasonable diligence, then the proponent may use other evidence to prove the content.

Rule 1006. Summaries to Prove Content

The proponent may use a summary, chart, or calculation to prove the content of voluminous writings, recordings, or photographs that cannot be conveniently examined in court. The proponent must make the originals or duplicates available for examination or copying, or both, by other parties at a reasonable time and place. And the court may order the proponent to produce them in court.

Rule 1007. Testimony or Statement of a Party to Prove Content

The proponent may prove the content of a writing, recording, or photograph by the testimony, deposition, or written statement of the party against whom the evidence is offered. The proponent need not account for the original.

CHAPTER 14

COMPETENCY OF WITNESSES

■ ■ ■

Table of Sections

---

§ 14.01   GENERAL RULE OF COMPETENCY

The Code and the Rules provide a general rule of competency.[1] All persons, irrespective of age, are qualified to be witnesses unless disqualified by statute.[2] The Common Law disqualifications are eliminated. That a witness may be a party, a felon, or related to a party are now grounds for impeachment, not disqualification as a witness.[3]

Under the Code, individuals are disqualified if they cannot testify in a manner others can understand or if they cannot appreciate the duty of a witness to tell the truth.[4] Witnesses are required to testify under oath for two reasons. One is to impress upon them the significance of testifying truthfully. The other is to lay the foundation for a potential perjury prosecution in the event the witness knowingly states as true a material matter which the witness knows to be false.[5]

Whether or not a person can communicate or can understand the obligation to testify truthfully are matters for determination by the judge.[6] The party objecting to the witness must persuade the judge by a prepon-

---

1. West's Ann.California Evidence Code § 700; Federal Rule of Evidence 601.
2. West's Ann. California Evidence Code § 700.
3. Federal Rule of Evidence 601 (Advisory Committee Note).
4. West's Ann. California Evidence Code § 701.
5. See West's Ann.California Penal Code § 118.
6. West's Ann. California Evidence Code § 701 (comment).

514

derance of the evidence that the witness is not qualified to testify.[7] In proceedings held outside the presence of the jury, the judge may reserve challenges to the witness's competency until the conclusion of the direct examination.[8] If the jury is present, the judge must resolve the challenge before allowing the examination to proceed.

Under the Federal Rules, all persons are qualified to be witnesses unless otherwise provided by the Rules.[9] A requirement imposed by the Rules is that before testifying all witnesses must declare by oath or affirmation their intention to testify truthfully.[10] In diversity cases, however, the Rules provide that the competency of witnesses is to determined in accordance with state law.[11]

§ 14.02 COMPETENCY AND THE PERSONAL KNOWLEDGE REQUIREMENT

Unless a witness is testifying as an expert, a witness's testimony about a particular matter is inadmissible unless the witness has personal or first hand knowledge of the matter.[1] Against objection, the examining party must show the witness's personal knowledge before the witness may testify about the matter.[2]

Unlike challenges to the competency of a witness, whether the witness possesses the requisite personal knowledge presents only a sufficiency question. If, viewing the evidence in the light most favorable to the examining party, the judge concludes that a reasonable jury could find that the witness possesses the necessary knowledge, then the objection will be overruled.[3] A witness's personal knowledge may be shown by any otherwise admissible evidence, including the witness's testimony.[4]

Whether a witness possesses personal knowledge depends on the witness's ability to perceive and recall the subject matter of the testimony. Under the Code, a person "perceives" when he acquires knowledge through the use of the senses.[5]

§ 14.03 PERSONS DISQUALIFIED BY STATUTE OR RULE

Presiding judges. The Evidence Code restricts calling presiding judges as witnesses. Before the judge presiding over a trial can be called,

---

7. West's Ann. California Evidence Code § 405 and comment.
8. West's Ann. California Evidence Code § 701.
9. Federal Rule of Evidence 601.
10. Federal Rule of Evidence 603.
11. Federal Rule of Evidence 601.
1. West's Ann. California Evidence Code § 702; Federal Rule of Evidence 602.
2. West's Ann. California Evidence Code § 702; Federal Rule of Evidence 602.
3. West's Ann. California Evidence Code § 403(a)(2); Federal Rule of Evidence 602.
4. West's Ann. California Evidence Code § 702(b).
5. West's Ann. California Evidence Code § 170.

the judge must disclose to the parties, out of the presence of the jury, the information the judge has about the case.[1] If no party objects to the judge testifying, the judge may testify.[2] If a party objects, the judge must declare a mistrial and assign the action for trial before another judge.[3] In a criminal case, double jeopardy does not attach, as the defendant who calls or objects to the calling of the judge as a witness is deemed to have consented to the mistrial.[4]

The Federal Rules take a more restrictive approach. The judge presiding at the trial may not testify in that trial, and no objection need be made to preserve the point.[5] In California, the judge may testify if no party objects.

Non-presiding judges. The Code also restricts calling non-presiding judges to testify about matters occurring in proceedings over which they presided. Judges who preside over judicial and quasi-judicial proceedings are "incompetent to testify, in any subsequent civil proceedings, as to any statement, conduct, decision or ruling, occurring at or in conjunction with the prior proceeding, except as to a statement or conduct that could (a) give rise to civil or criminal contempt, (b) constitute a crime, (c) be the subject of investigation by the State Bar or Commission on Judicial Performance or (d) give rise to disqualification proceedings under paragraph (1) or (6) subdivision (a) of Section 170.1 of the Code of Civil Procedure."[6] Paragraphs (1) and (6) call for the disqualification of judges who have personal knowledge of disputed evidentiary facts or who ought to disqualify themselves in the interests of justice.[7]

The Federal Rules do not have an equivalent provision.

Mediators and arbitrators. The Code provides that "no arbitrator or mediator shall be competent to testify, in any subsequent civil proceeding, as to any statement, conduct, decision, or ruling, occurring at or in conjunction with the prior proceeding, except as to a statement or conduct that could (a) give rise to civil or criminal contempt, (b) constitute a crime, (c) be the subject of investigation by the State Bar or Commission on Judicial Performance, or (d) give rise to disqualification [of judges under] Section 170.1 of the Code of Civil Procedure. [The prohibition, however,] does not apply to a mediator [presiding over certain mediations authorized by] the Family Code."[8]

---

1. West's Ann. California Evidence Code § 703.

2. Id.

3. Id.

4. Id.

5. Federal Rule of Evidence 605.

6. West's Ann. California Evidence Code § 703.5.

7. West's Ann. California Code of Civil Procedure § 170.1.

8. West's Ann. California Evidence Code § 703.5. The prohibition prevents a mediator from reporting misconduct at the mediation and a court from considering the report in determining whether a party should be sanctioned for failing to participate in good faith in the mediation. Foxgate Homeowners' Ass'n, Inc. v. Bramalea California, Inc., 26 Cal.4th 1, 17, 108 Cal.Rptr.2d 642, 655, 25 P.3d 1117, 1128 (2001).

The Federal Rules do not have an equivalent provision.

Sitting jurors. The Evidence Code also limits calling jurors as witnesses. Before a juror can be called to testify in a civil or criminal action, the juror must disclose to the parties, out of the presence of the remaining jurors, the information the juror has concerning the case.[9] If no party objects to the juror testifying, the juror must testify.[10] If a party objects, the judge must declare a mistrial and order the action assigned for trial before another jury.[11] If a mistrial is declared, the defendant in a criminal case may not claim double jeopardy, as calling or objecting to the calling of the juror is deemed a consent to the mistrial.[12]

Over objection, a federal juror may not testify as witness in the trial of the case in which the juror is sitting.[13] If the juror is called, the court must allow the opposing party to object out of the presence of the jury.[14]

Jurors and post-verdict proceedings. In California post-verdict proceedings, jurors may be called to testify about "statements made, or conduct, conditions, or events occurring, either within or without the jury room, of such character as [are] likely to have influenced the verdict improperly."[15] But to protect jurors from harassment, jurors may not testify about the effect such statements, conduct, conditions, or events had in influencing the jurors to assent or dissent from the verdict or upon the mental processes by which the verdict was reached.[16] Thus, the Code permits evidence of misconduct by trial jurors to be received but forbids the receipt of evidence about the effect of such misconduct on the deliberations of the jurors.[17] Examples of permissible evidence include improper discussion by jurors of the accused's failure to testify as well as of the sentence the court might impose if they found the accused guilty.[18] Evidence may also be received to show that jurors read, watched, heard or

---

9. West's Ann. California Evidence Code § 704.

10. Id.

11. Id.

12. Id.

13. Federal Rule of Evidence 606(a).

14. Id.

15. West's Ann. California Evidence Code § 1150. A trial judge is not limited to considering declarations and affidavits in determining whether juror misconduct has occurred. The judge may hold an evidentiary hearing on the question of misconduct. However, the judge does not need to hold the hearing unless the party charging the misconduct convinces the judge that the hearing will be productive. Where the misconduct evidence to be produced at the hearing consists of inadmissible hearsay, the judge may decline to hold the hearing. People v. Hayes, 21 Cal.4th 1211, 1257, 91 Cal.Rptr.2d 211, 242, 989 P.2d 645, 673 (1999).

16. West's Ann. Evidence Code § 1150. Other goals include preserving the stability of verdicts, discouraging postverdict jury tampering, and protecting the privacy of jury deliberations. In re Hamilton, 20 Cal.4th 273, 297 note 18, 84 Cal.Rptr.2d 403, 416 note 18, 975 P.2d 600, 614 note 18 (1999).

17. West's Ann. Evidence Code § 1150 (comment). "However, the rule against proof of juror mental processes is subject to the well-established exception for claims that a juror's preexisting bias was concealed on voir dire." In re Hamilton, 20 Cal.4th 273, 298, note 19, 84 Cal.Rptr.2d 403, 419, note 19, 975 P.2d 600, 616, note 19 (1999).

18. People v. Hord, 15 Cal.App.4th 711, 19 Cal.Rptr.2d 55, 63 (1993).

discussed news accounts of the cases in which they are sitting,[19] or asked witnesses questions about any matter related to the case.[20] Evidence may also be received in capital cases to show that jurors improperly consulted their pastors regarding Biblical passages approving the death penalty.[21]

Once the complaining party has established a prima facie case of juror misconduct, the court must presume that the misconduct was prejudicial unless the opponent convinces the court that the misconduct was harmless.[22] A presumption of prejudice is justified because the Code prohibits the complaining party from offering evidence about the effect of the misconduct upon the juror.[23] In determining whether the opponent has rebutted the presumption, the court may consider the entire record of the case as well as the evidence produced by the parties.[24] If the evidence shows a substantial likelihood that at least one juror was impermissively influenced, then the court must find that the misconduct was prejudicial and must vacate the verdict.[25] It is immaterial whether the juror who was impermissively influenced sits on a civil or criminal case. Civil litigants are as entitled to trial by unbiased and unprejudiced jurors as are parties to criminal proceedings.[26]

Jurors are required to decide a case based on the law as given by the judge. Accordingly, it is permissible for a party to show that a juror gave wrong legal advice[27] or that a juror consulted an outside lawyer for advice regarding the applicable law.[28] Similarly, it is permissible for a party to prove a juror's efforts to substitute religious standards for the applicable legal standards.[29]

---

19. See Province (Cassandra) v. Center for Women's Health & Family Birth, 20 Cal.App.4th 1673, 1678, 25 Cal.Rptr.2d 667, 670–671 (1993) and cases cited therein. It is not necessary for the complaining party to show that the jurors discussed the news accounts. It is misconduct for jurors just to watch, hear, or read such accounts. Id.

20. Juror misconduct can also be predicated on the ground that the jurors considered in their deliberations opinions based not on the evidence presented but on the special knowledge a juror brought to the deliberations by virtue of special training and experience. For a discussion of the point, see § 19.03 infra.

21. People v. Danks, 32 Cal.4th 269, 307, 82 P.3d 1249, 1274, 8 Cal.Rptr.3d 767, 798, cert. denied, 543 U.S. 961, 125 S.Ct. 441, 160 L.Ed.2d 326 (2004). See also People v. Tafoya, 42 Cal.4th 147, 192, 164 P.3d 590, 625, 64 Cal.Rptr.3d 163, 204 (2007).

22. See Province (Cassandra) v. Center for Women's Health & Family Birth, 20 Cal.App.4th 1673, 1678, 25 Cal.Rptr.2d 667, 670–671 (1993) and cases cited therein.

23. In re Hamilton, 20 Cal.4th 273, 295, 975 P.2d 600, 613, 84 Cal.Rptr.2d 403, 417 (1999).

24. See Province (Cassandra) v. Center for Women's Health & Family Birth, 20 Cal.App.4th 1673, 1678, 25 Cal.Rptr.2d 667, 670–671 (1993) and cases cited therein.

25. Id.

26. Id. See also In re Carpenter, 9 Cal.4th 634, 675, 38 Cal.Rptr.2d 665, 675, 889 P.2d 985, 1011 (1995) (The standard for determining whether juror misconduct is prejudicial is less tolerant than the standard imposed by the harmless error doctrine.); People v. Nesler, 16 Cal.4th 561, 581, 66 Cal.Rptr.2d 454, 468, 941 P.2d 87, 101 (1997) (Whether prejudice arises from juror misconduct is a mixed question of law and fact subject to an appellate court's independent determination.).

27. In re Stankewitz, 40 Cal.3d 391, 399, 220 Cal.Rptr. 382, 386, 708 P.2d 1260, 1264 (1985).

28. People v. Honeycutt, 20 Cal.3d 150, 156, 141 Cal.Rptr. 698, 700, 570 P.2d 1050, 1052 (1977).

29. See, e.g., People v. Mincey, 2 Cal.4th 408, 467, 6 Cal.Rptr.2d 822, 858–859, 827 P.2d 388, 425 (1992), cert. denied, 506 U.S. 1014, 113 S.Ct. 637, 121 L.Ed.2d 567 (1992) (in a death penalty

Where the alleged misconduct consists of statements by jurors, courts must distinguish between admissible statements that themselves constitute misconduct, such as statement of wrong legal advice, and inadmissible statements that merely reflect the reasoning process of the jurors, for example, a juror's reasons for his or her vote based on the erroneous advice. People v. Steele[30] is an example of the latter. Following his conviction of murder with special circumstances, the accused moved for a new trial because of juror misconduct. In support of his motion, the accused presented the declarations of two jurors who stated that they would not have voted for death if they had accepted the judge's instructions that life without possibility of parole meant exactly that. The California Supreme Court held that the trial judge correctly rejected the declarations.[31] The accused did not offer to prove, for example, that the two jurors had shared a mistaken interpretation of the judge's instruction with their fellow jurors; instead, the two jurors focused on the effect that a correct interpretation of the instruction would have had upon them.

Federal Rule 606 takes a more restrictive approach. In addition to precluding a juror from testifying about the effect of anything on that juror's or another juror's vote, or any juror's mental processes concerning the verdict or indictment, the Rule also provides that a juror may not testify about any statement made or incident that occurred during the jury's deliberations.[32] A juror, however, may testify about whether extraneous prejudicial information was improperly brought to the jury's attention; an outside influence was improperly brought to bear on any juror; or a mistake was made in entering the verdict on the verdict form.[33]

Tanner v. United States[34] illustrates the differences between the Code and the Federal Rules. Tanner appealed his convictions for fraud on the ground that, after the verdict, the judge erroneously denied him the opportunity to call two jurors who would testify that some of their fellow jurors had ingested alcohol, marihuana, and cocaine during the trial. The United States Supreme Court upheld the judge's denial of a hearing on the alleged juror misconduct: under the Federal Rules, "juror intoxication is not an 'outside influence' about which jurors may testify to impeach their verdicts."[35]

Section 1150 of the Code would not have barred the jurors' testimony. Evidence of juror intoxication within or without the jury room may be

---

case, disapproving of a juror's reading of Biblical verses approving the imposition of the death penalty in certain circumstances).

30. 27 Cal.4th 1230, 120 Cal.Rptr.2d 432, 47 P.3d 225 (2002), cert. denied, 537 U.S. 1115, 123 S.Ct. 874, 154 L.Ed.2d 791 (2003).

31. Id. at 1260–1261, 120 Cal.Rptr.2d at 456–457,47 P.3d at 245–246.

32. Federal Rule of Evidence 606(b).

33. Id.

34. 483 U.S. 107, 107 S.Ct. 2739, 97 L.Ed.2d 90 (1987), on remand, 845 F.2d 266 (11th Cir.1988).

35. Id. at 125, 107 S.Ct. at 2750.

received if it is likely to have influenced the verdict improperly.[36] To protect the jurors, however, the Code would have prohibited the accused from asking the jurors about the effect that the intoxication had on their deliberations.

The Supreme Court recognized that Tanner had a Sixth Amendment right to an unimpaired jury.[37] In the Court's view, however, Tanner's right to a mentally competent jury was not violated by the limits the Federal Rules place on the use of juror testimony. Prior to being seated, the jurors were questioned about their suitability to serve; moreover, during the course of the trial the jurors were observable by each other and could have reported inappropriate behavior before they rendered a verdict; finally, the judge gave Tanner an opportunity to impeach the verdict by nonjuror evidence of misconduct.[38] Tanner, for example, could have called the waiters who served the alcohol to the jurors.

A 2006 amendment to Federal Rule 606 allows the use of juror testimony to prove that the verdict reported was the result of a mistake in entering the verdict on the verdict form.[39] According to the Advisory Committee, the amendment is limited to such cases as " 'where the jury foreperson wrote down, in response to an interrogatory, a number different from that agreed upon by the jury, or mistakenly stated that the defendant was "guilty" when the jury had actually agreed that the defendant was not guilty.' "[40] The amendment, however, still bans juror testimony to prove that the jurors were operating under a misunderstanding of the consequences of the result they agreed upon.[41]

Does the Right to Truth-in-Evidence provision of Proposition 8 repeal the Evidence Code provision prohibiting the use of any evidence to show the effect of misconduct on the jurors' deliberations? Subject to enumerated exceptions, the Right to Truth-in-Evidence provision gives both the prosecution and the accused the state constitutional right to offer relevant evidence.[42] Since the accused's goal in offering the evidence is to reverse an adverse verdict on the ground that at least one juror was impermissively biased, evidence of the effect of the misconduct would appear to be not only relevant, but essential in establishing bias. In People v. Steele,[43] however, the California Supreme Court rejected this construction of Proposition 8. The court saved the Code's prohibition by holding that § 1150 is a substantive, not an evidentiary, limitation. This construction

---

36. West's Ann. California Evidence Code § 1150.

37. Tanner v. United States, 483 U.S. 107, 126, 107 S.Ct. 2739, 97 L.Ed.2d 90 (1987), on remand, 845 F.2d 266 (11th Cir.1988).

38. Id.

39. Federal Rule of Evidence 606(b).

40. Id. (Advisory Committee Note) (quoting from Robles v. Exxon Corp., 862 F.2d 1201, 1208 (5th Cir. 1989)).

41. Id.

42. For an extended discussion of this provision, see § 15.01 infra.

43. 27 Cal.4th 1230, 47 P.3d 225, 247, 120 Cal.Rptr.2d 432 (2002), cert. denied, 537 U.S. 1115, 123 S.Ct. 874, 154 L.Ed.2d 791 (2003).

allowed the court to conclude that evidence of the effect of juror misconduct can be excluded because it is immaterial.[44] Evidence that is immaterial is irrelevant and therefore outside the purview of relevance provision of Proposition 8.[45]

Lawyers. Though lawyers are not disqualified from testifying, the California State Bar Rules of Professional Conduct place some limits on attorneys who testify on behalf of or against their clients. A lawyer "shall not act as an advocate before a jury which will hear testimony from the [lawyer] unless (A) [t]he testimony relates to an uncontested matter; or (B) [t]he testimony relates to the nature and value of legal services rendered in the case; or (C) [t]he [lawyer] has the informed, written consent of the client."[46] If the lawyer represents the People or a governmental entity, "the consent must be obtained from the head of the office or a designee of the head of the office by which the [lawyer] is employed and shall be consistent with the principles of recusal."[47]

The limitation does not apply to bench trials or non-adversarial proceedings, such as legislative hearings.[48] The limitation, moreover, does not apply "to circumstances in which a lawyer in an advocate's firm will be a witness."[49]

In contrast, Rule 3.7 of the American Bar Association's Model Rules of Professional Conduct prohibits attorneys from appearing as a witness in any case they are trying—whether it is before a judge or a jury—unless their testimony relates to an uncontested matter; or the nature and value of legal services rendered in the case; or disqualification would work substantial hardship on the client.[50]

In addition to the limitations placed by the Rules of Professional Conduct, the California courts discourage testimony by trial counsel, especially by prosecutors in criminal cases. Prosecutors should not testify in cases they are trying except in "extraordinary circumstances."[51] "If a lawyer is both counsel and witness, he becomes more easily impeachable for interest and thus may be a less effective witness. Conversely, an opposing counsel may be handicapped in challenging the credibility of the lawyer when the lawyer also appears as an advocate in the case. An advocate who becomes a witness is in the unseemly and ineffective position of arguing his own credibility. The roles of an advocate and of a witness are inconsistent; the function of an advocate is to advance or argue the cause of another, while that of a witness is to state facts

---

44. Id. at 1263, 47 P.3d at 247, 120 Cal.Rptr.2d 432 at 458.

45. For an extended discussion of this point, see § 2.01 supra.

46. Rule 5–210, Rules of Professional Conduct of the State Bar of California, California Rules of Court, State (West Group 2001).

47. Id.

48. Id. (discussion).

49. Id.

50. ABA Model Rules of Professional Conduct 3.7 (2006).

51. People v. Guerrero, 47 Cal.App.3d 441, 445, 120 Cal.Rptr. 732, 734 (1975).

objectively."[52] If the calling party is the accused, then the accused should not be allowed to call the prosecutor unless he or she first demonstrates that there is no other source for the evidence sought.[53]

Law enforcement personnel. Some statutes prevent witnesses from testifying unless enumerated conditions are first satisfied. For example, the California Vehicle Code prohibits the use of radar evidence to establish a speeding violation unless the prosecution proves that the posted speed is justified by an engineering and traffic survey conducted within five years of the alleged violation.[54] Unless the prosecution discharges this burden, a traffic officer may not testify about any matters involving the use of radar.[55]

QUESTIONS AND PROBLEMS

1.   In moving for a new trial on account of juror misconduct, a California judge may receive evidence from the jurors about taking drugs in the jury deliberation room but may not receive evidence about the effect the drugs had on the jurors' deliberations. A federal judge, on the other hand, may not receive evidence from the jurors about the use of drugs in the jury deliberation room. True or false?

2.   Often the question before a reviewing court is the impact which inadmissible evidence had on the jurors. Since the jurors are the best source of evidence about that impact, both the Code and the Rules encourage the use of evidence by jurors for that purpose. True or false?

3.   In a motion to set aside a guilty verdict, a California defendant is entitled to offer evidence that a juror consulted a pastor who told the juror that it would be "right" to impose the death penalty upon the accused. True or false?

Assume the answer is true. The Right to Truth-in-Evidence provision of Proposition 8 would entitle the accused to offer evidence about the effect the pastor's advice had on the juror. True or false?

4.   Both the Code and Rules disfavor judges testifying in trials over which they preside and jurors testifying in trials in which they sit. In California, however, a presiding judge may testify unless one of the parties objects. In federal court, no objection is necessary. True or false?

§ 14.04   HYPNOTIZED WITNESSES

In People v. Shirley[1] the California Supreme Court held that "the testimony of a witness who has undergone hypnosis for the purpose of

---

52.   Id. (quoting from Canon 5 of the American Bar Association's Code of Professional Responsibility).

53.   People v. Garcia, 84 Cal.App.4th 316, 332, 100 Cal.Rptr.2d 789, 800 (2000).

54.   West's Ann. California Vehicle Code § 40802.

55.   See People v. Goulet, 13 Cal.App.4th Supp. 1, 17 Cal.Rptr.2d 801, 806 (1992).

1.   31 Cal.3d 18, 181 Cal.Rptr. 243, 723 P.2d 1354 (1982), cert. denied, 459 U.S. 860, 103 S.Ct. 133, 74 L.Ed.2d 114 (1982).

restoring his memory of the events in issue is inadmissible as to all matters relating to those events, from the hypnotic session forward."[2] The court was not convinced that the use of hypnosis to restore the memory of a potential witness had been generally accepted as a reliable technique by the relevant scientific community.[3] On the contrary, the court was troubled that "[d]uring the hypnotic session, neither the subject nor the hypnotist [could] distinguish between memories and pseudo memories * * * and when the subject [repeated the] recall in a waking state (e.g., in a trial) neither an expert nor a lay observer (e.g., the judge or jury) [could] make a similar distinction."[4] The court was equally concerned with the ineffectiveness of cross-examination in exposing pseudo memories. Since a witness who has undergone hypnosis sincerely believes that his testimony on the stand is his true recall and not the product of deliberate or inadvertent suggestion during the hypnotic session, even the most vigorous cross-examination cannot expose pseudo memories.[5]

The court exempted criminal defendants from the disqualification announced in *Shirley* because of concerns over their right to testify in their own defense.[6] Exempting criminal defendants is consistent with federal constitutional law. In Rock v. Arkansas[7] the United States Supreme Court invalidated a state rule that precluded the use of a defendant's hypnotically refreshed testimony. In the Court's view, such a blanket prohibition violates the accused's right to present evidence in his own defense.[8] The accused's right to present relevant evidence is not unlimited, however. Even under *Rock*, a judge can exclude a defendant's posthypnotic testimony if the state can demonstrate its unreliability in the case at hand.[9]

Shortly after the *Shirley* decision was announced, the California electorate approved Proposition 8, the Victims Bill of Rights.[10] One of its provisions, the Right to Truth–in–Evidence, gives parties to criminal proceedings the state constitutional right not to have relevant evidence excluded.[11] Since barring the testimony of previously hypnotized witnesses can exclude relevant evidence, a literal application of Proposition 8 would overturn *Shirley*. Concerned that the proposition would permit previously hypnotized witnesses to testify in all criminal cases, the Legislature added

---

2. Id. at 66–67, 181 Cal.Rptr. at 272, 723 P.2d at 1383.

3. Id.

4. Id. at 65, 181 Cal.Rptr. at 271–272, 723 P.2d at 1382.

5. Id. at 65, 181 Cal.Rptr. at 272, 723 P.2d at 1383.

6. Id. at 67, 181 Cal.Rptr. at 273, 723 P.2d at 1384.

7. 483 U.S. 44, 107 S.Ct. 2704, 97 L.Ed.2d 37 (1987).

8. Id. at 61, 107 S.Ct. at 2714.

9. Id. In reaching its decision, the Court declined to pass on the constitutionality of rules barring the use of testimony of previously hypnotized witnesses other than criminal defendants. Id. at 58, note 15, 107 S.Ct. at 2712, note 15.

10. For a discussion of the effect of Proposition 8 on the rules of evidence that apply in criminal cases, see § 3.07 supra.

11. For the language of this provision, see § 3.07 supra.

§ 795 to the Evidence Code in 1984.[12] This section strikes a middle ground between Proposition 8 and the disqualification announced in *Shirley* by permitting a previously hypnotized witness to testify if the judge finds that strict guidelines have been followed. These guidelines are designed to prevent the hypnotic session from improperly contaminating the witness's recall.[13] As amended, § 795 permits the use of a previously hypnotized witness's testimony if the following conditions are met:

(1) The testimony is limited to those matters that the witness recalled and related prior to the hypnosis.

(2) The substance of the prehypnotic memory was preserved in writing, audio recording, or video recording prior to the hypnosis.

(3) The hypnosis was conducted in accordance with all of the following procedures:

(A) A written record was made prior to hypnosis documenting the subject's description of the event, and information which was provided to the hypnotist concerning the subject matter of the hypnosis.

(B) The subject gave informed consent to the hypnosis.

(C) The hypnosis session, including the pre-and post-hypnosis interviews, was videotape recorded for subsequent review.

(D) The hypnosis was performed by a licensed physician and surgeon, psychologist, licensed clinical social worker, licensed marriage and family therapist, or licensed professional clinical counselor experienced in the use of hypnosis and independent of and not in the presence of law enforcement, the prosecution, or the defense.

(4) Prior to admission of the testimony, the court holds a hearing pursuant to Section 402 at which the proponent of the evidence proves by clear and convincing evidence that the hypnosis did not so affect the witness as to render the witness' prehypnosis recollection unreliable or to substantially impair the ability to cross-examine the witness concerning the witness' prehypnosis recollection. At the hearing, each side shall have the right to present expert testimony and to cross-examine witnesses.

(b) Nothing in this section shall be construed to limit the ability of a party to attack the credibility of a witness who has undergone hypnosis, or to limit other legal grounds to admit or exclude the testimony of that witness.

Section 795 clarifies *Shirley* by permitting previously hypnotized witnesses to testify if their testimony is limited to those matters which

---

12. West's Ann. California Evidence Code § 795 (legislative history). The Right to Truth–in–Evidence provision can be amended by a super majority in each house of the Legislature. West's Ann. California Constitution Article I, § 28(f)(2). Section 795 complies with the super majority requirement. 2 Assembly Final History, A.B. 2669 (Nov. 30, 1984).

13. People v. Aguilar, 218 Cal.App.3d 1556, 1563, 267 Cal.Rptr. 879, 882 (1990).

they recalled and related prior to the hypnotic session and if the other conditions of the section are satisfied. The witnesses, however, may not testify about new matters which surfaced during the hypnotic session. Section 795 does not limit the right of a party to attack the credibility of a witness who has undergone hypnosis.[14] Neither does the section limit the use of other grounds to admit or exclude the testimony of such a witness.[15]

Unlike *Shirley*, § 795 does not expressly exempt the criminal defendant from its application. People v. Aguilar,[16] however, holds that *Shirley*, not § 795, governs the use of a criminal defendant's posthypnotic testimony.[17] Since *Shirley* places no restrictions on the use of such testimony, the fact that the accused was hypnotized under circumstances that violate the conditions of § 795 is not a ground for preventing the accused from testifying.[18]

Section 795 applies only to criminal proceedings. Since *Shirley* does not distinguish between criminal and civil proceedings, *Shirley* governs the use of a witness's posthypnotic testimony in civil proceedings. Accordingly, if a witness in a civil matter has been hypnotized for the purpose of restoring her memory of the events in issue, the witness's testimony is inadmissible as to all matters relating to those events from the hypnotic session forward.[19] *Shirley*, however, does not apply to prehypnotic evidence offered in a civil case. Thus, a civil "witness who has undergone hypnosis is not barred from testifying to events which the court finds were recalled and related prior to the hypnotic session."[20] However, because *Shirley* exempts only the accused from the testimonial disqualification, *Shirley* applies to the parties in civil proceedings.[21] Accordingly, a party in a civil case is barred from testifying if the party's recollection of the events in question first surfaced during the hypnotic session.

Truth serum. The use of truth serum (sodium amytal and sodium pentothal) has given rise to the same concerns as the use of hypnosis.

---

14. Id.

15. Id.

16. 218 Cal.App.3d 1556, 267 Cal.Rptr. 879 (1990).

17. Id. at 1563, 267 Cal.Rptr. at 883.

18. Applying § 795 to criminal defendants would not necessarily violate their right to present evidence in their own defense. In Rock v. Arkansas, the United States Supreme Court held that a state can bar an accused's posthypnotic testimony if the state can demonstrate its unreliability in a given case. See 483 U.S. 44, 107 S.Ct. 2704, 97 L.Ed.2d 37 (1987); text accompanying note 7 supra. Since § 795 is designed to prevent the hypnotic session from improperly contaminating the witness's recall, using the section to exclude a defendant's posthypnotic testimony may not be unconstitutional.

19. People v. Shirley, 31 Cal.3d 18, 66–67, 181 Cal.Rptr. 243, 272, 723 P.2d 1354, 1383 (1982), cert. denied, 459 U.S. 860, 103 S.Ct. 133, 74 L.Ed.2d 114 (1982).

20. People v. Hayes, 49 Cal.3d 1260, 1273, 265 Cal.Rptr. 132, 138, 783 P.2d 719, 725 (1989). Section 795 supersedes the *Shirley–Hayes* rule only in criminal cases. See Schall v. Lockheed Missiles & Space Co., 37 Cal.App.4th 1485, 1490, 44 Cal.Rptr.2d 191, 195 (1995). Accordingly, a witness in a civil case is barred from testifying if the witness's recollection of the events in question first surfaced during the hypnotic session.

21. See Schall v. Lockheed Missiles & Space Co., 37 Cal.App.4th 1485, 1490, 44 Cal.Rptr.2d 191, 195 (1995).

Because truth serum dispels inhibitions, it induces subjects to talk free-ly.[22] But a looser tongue is not necessarily a more truthful one.[23] What a person says under the influence of sodium amytal may be no more reliable than what he says under the influence of large amounts of bourbon.[24] Consequently, what a person says under the influence of sodium amytal is inadmissible in California under the *Kelly* test.[25] Under *Kelly*, expert testimony based on novel scientific principles or techniques is inadmissible unless the principle or technique has been generally accepted by the pertinent scientific community.[26] A witness, moreover, may not testify about incidents "recalled" while under the influence of sodium amytal, unless the witness can demonstrate that he or she had personal knowledge of such incidents before the administration of the drug.[27] In addition, a witness may not testify about incidents recalled *after* the administration of sodium amytal if they are of the same nature as the incidents recalled while under the influence of the drug.[28] Sodium amytal "is likely to forever distort the memory of the subject."[29] Accordingly, a woman who claimed to have repressed all memory of childhood sexual abuse until she underwent sodium amytal therapy was not allowed to testify about inci-dents she related while under the drug or incidents she recalled two years after the therapy.[30]

QUESTIONS AND PROBLEMS

1. Section 795 supersedes *Shirley* in all California proceedings. True or false?

2. Section 795 governs the use of the accused's posthypnotic testimony. True or false?

3. The United States Supreme Court has held that blanket rules prohib-iting the use of a criminal defendant's posthypnotic testimony are unconstitu-tional. True or false?

4. Tom is called by the prosecution to identify the accused as the person who robbed a convenience store. The defense moves to exclude Tom's testimo-ny on the basis of § 795. At the hearing on the objection, the prosecution offers evidence that at the crime scene Tom described the robber as "6 foot two, about 180 pounds, and 20 to 25 years of age." This description matches the accused. Additional evidence shows that during the hypnotic session Tom also described the robber as having a scar over the right eye. This description

---

22. Ramona v. Superior Court (Ramona), 57 Cal.App.4th 107, 116, note 10, 66 Cal.Rptr.2d 766, 773, note 10 (1997).

23. Id.

24. Id.

25. Id. at 116, 66 Cal.Rptr.2d at 773 and cases cited therein.

26. See § 16.04 infra for a discussion of the requirements of the *Kelly* test.

27. Ramona v. Superior Court, 57 Cal.App.4th 107, 122, 66 Cal.Rptr.2d 766, 777 (1997).

28. Id. at 123, 66 Cal.Rptr.2d at 778.

29. Id.

30. Id.

also matches the accused. Further evidence offered by the prosecution shows that all of the conditions of § 795 have been satisfied. At the conclusion of the hearing the defense moves again to exclude all of Tom's testimony. How should the judge rule?

§ 14.05   CHILD WITNESSES

Increases in child molestation prosecutions have rekindled questions about the competency of child witnesses. Under the Code and the Rules, being of tender years is not a disqualification if the child nonetheless appreciates the duty to tell the truth and can express himself in a manner that can be understood by the parties, the fact finder, and the judge.[1] As a concession to their age, however, children who appear as witnesses in California need promise only to tell the truth instead of taking the conventional oath.[2]

Whether a child can express himself in a manner that can be understood by others does not present unduly difficult questions. The judge can make that determination readily by having the child answer some preliminary questions. Whether a child understands the duty to tell the truth under oath is another matter. Voir dire generally focuses on a child's ability to distinguish between the truth and a lie, and on the importance of telling the truth. A child who cannot tell the difference between the truth and a lie is incompetent to testify,[3] but the fact that the child testifies inconsistently or in an exaggerated form goes to the child's credibility, not his competency.[4]

The Code expressly empowers the judge to protect child witnesses. If the child is permitted to testify and is under fourteen years of age, the judge is enjoined to take "special care" to protect the child from undue embarrassment and to restrict the unnecessary repetition of questions.[5] In addition, the judge has a duty to insure that questions are stated in a form that are appropriate to the age of the witness, and, upon objection, may forbid the asking of questions unlikely to be understood by a child.[6]

In prosecutions for child endangerment, cruelty to children, and lewd acts with children, California judges may permit the use of leading questions in the direct examination of children under ten years of age.[7]

---

1. West's Ann. California Evidence Code § 701; Federal Rule of Evidence 601. See In re Crystal J., 218 Cal.App.3d 596, 601, 267 Cal.Rptr. 105, 108 (1990) (Judge properly disqualified a seven year-old child who "repeatedly stated he did not know the difference between the truth and a lie."). The judge, however, must conduct a competency hearing before ruling on the objection. Accordingly, it is improper for a judge to rule a four year-old child incompetent without holding a hearing. See People v. Roberto V., 93 Cal.App.4th 1350, 1369, 113 Cal.Rptr.2d 804, 818 (2001).

2. West's Ann. California Evidence Code § 710.

3. In re Crystal J., 218 Cal.App.3d 596, 601, 267 Cal.Rptr. 105, 108 (1990).

4. Adamson v. Department of Social Services, 207 Cal.App.3d 14, 20, 254 Cal.Rptr. 667, 670–671 (1988).

5. West's Ann. California Evidence Code § 765(b).

6. Id.

7. West's Ann. California Evidence Code § 767(b).

The danger of improper suggestion may perhaps be greatest when leading questions are asked of children. By allowing such questions, the Legislature has signaled its willingness to modify conventional limits on witness examination to obtain the testimony of children. The problem is that accommodating the needs of child witnesses can conflict with the accused's Sixth Amendment right to confront his accusers.

It is unclear how far a state can go in protecting child witnesses. In Coy v. Iowa[8] the United States Supreme Court held that the Sixth Amendment was violated when a screen was placed between a child witness and the accused in a sexual assault prosecution. Stressing the importance of face-to-face confrontation, the Court observed: "It is more difficult to tell a lie about a person 'to his face' than behind his back. In the former context, even if the lie is told, it will often be told less convincingly."[9]

Trial lawyers would agree. Moreover, defense lawyers would condemn the screen for another reason: its use, like the use of shackles and chains, unfairly suggests that the accused is a bad person deserving of punishment and removal from society. Coy's vitality, however, was drawn into question in Maryland v. Craig.[10] In that case, the Court held that the Sixth Amendment did not prohibit a child witness in an abuse prosecution from testifying outside the defendant's physical presence.[11] Under Maryland procedure, the child was examined by the prosecution and the defendant's lawyer in a room separate from the courtroom. The defendant, judge, and jury remained in the courtroom where they watched the examination on a video monitor. In upholding the Maryland procedure, the Court emphasized a provision requiring the prosecution to persuade the judge that forcing the child to testify in the defendant's presence would cause such serious emotional distress as to prevent the child from communicating reasonably.[12]

California law protects child witnesses in other ways. These protections apply in child dependency hearings as well as in criminal cases.

Children's hearsay statements and the corpus delicti doctrine. California follows the corpus delicti doctrine. To protect a criminal defendant against the possibility of conviction upon a false confession, the doctrine provides that no person may be convicted of a criminal offense

---

8. 487 U.S. 1012, 108 S.Ct. 2798, 101 L.Ed.2d 857 (1988), on remand, 433 N.W.2d 714 (Iowa 1988).

9. Id. at 1019, 108 S.Ct. at 2801.

10. 497 U.S. 836, 110 S.Ct. 3157, 111 L.Ed.2d 666 (1990), on remand, 322 Md. 418, 588 A.2d 328 (1991).

11. Id. at 855, 110 S.Ct. at 3169.

12. Id. at 856, 110 S.Ct. at 3169. Prosecutors may sometimes position themselves so that a child witness does not have to see the accused during direct examination. The California courts are divided on whether this practice violates the accused's confrontation rights. Herbert v. Superior Court, 117 Cal.App.3d 661, 671, 172 Cal.Rptr. 850, 855 (1981), holds that confrontation requires the accused and the witness to view each other while testifying. People v. Sharp, 29 Cal.App.4th 1772, 1784, 36 Cal.Rptr.2d 117, 125 (1994), rejects this construction of the Sixth Amendment, holding instead that no violation occurs where the accused can see the witness and the prosecution demonstrates that the procedure affording less than literal face-to-face confrontation was necessary to obtain the child's testimony.

unless there is some proof of each element of the crime independent of any confession claimed to have been made by the defendant.[13] Combined with the hearsay rule, the corpus delicti doctrine typically requires prosecutors to call crime victims, if available, to establish the elements of the offense charged before offering confessions claimed to have been made by the accused.[14]

Section 1228 of the Evidence Code relaxes this requirement in the case of child witnesses who have been the victims of enumerated sexual abuse offenses.[15] This section empowers the trial judge to admit for the truth of the matter stated the extra-judicial statements of complaining witnesses under age twelve if they are unavailable and their statements describe the complaining witness as a victim of sexual abuse, were made prior to the defendant's confession, and possess circumstantial guarantees of trustworthiness. The hearsay exception created by § 1228 is a narrow one, however; the statement may be received only for the limited purpose of satisfying the corpus delicti doctrine. The statement may be considered by the judge in determining the admissibility of the defendant's confession but may not be heard or considered by the jurors in determining the defendant's guilt.[16]

Children's hearsay statements and child dependency hearings. If a minor child testifies as the complaining witness at a preliminary hearing, then the child's testimony is admissible for the truth of the matter stated in a proceeding to declare the child a dependent child of the court pursuant to § 300 of the Welfare and Institutions Code.[17] Since the state does not have to demonstrate the child's unavailability to testify, the child does not have to be produced for cross-examination by the parent or guardian at the dependency proceeding if certain other conditions are met.[18]

---

13. People v. Cullen, 37 Cal.2d 614, 624, 234 P.2d 1, 7 (1951); see also CALJIC 2.72 (Fall Edition 2006).

14. In People v. Alvarez, 27 Cal.4th 1161, 1178–1180, 119 Cal.Rptr.2d 903, 916–918, 46 P.3d 372, 382–384 (2002), the California Supreme Court held that the Right to Truth–in–Evidence provision of Proposition 8 abrogated that aspect of the corpus delicti doctrine which permits an accused to object to the introduction of his extrajudicial statements on the ground that independent evidence of the corpus delicti is lacking. The court, however, held that the initiative left undisturbed those aspects of the doctrine requiring the prosecution to prove the corpus delicti with evidence independent of the accused's extrajudicial admissions. Id. Accordingly, jurors may still be instructed that no person may be convicted absent evidence of the crime independent of his or her extrajudicial statements, and defendants may still raise on appeal the adequacy of the prosecution's independent showing. Id. Presumably, defendants may also move for a directed verdict of acquittal whenever the prosecution fails to offer evidence proving the corpus delicti independently of the their extrajudicial statements. For a discussion of the Proposition 8, see § 3.07 supra.

15. West's Ann. California Evidence Code § 1228.

16. Id. Section 1228 may be used only where the prosecution seeks to satisfy the corpus delicti rule in order to offer the accused's "confession." For pretrial admissions to qualify as a confession, they must encompass all of the elements of the crime charged. Ambiguous, equivocal, or incomplete self-inculpatory statements do not qualify as confessions under § 1228. Creutz v. Superior Court (People), 49 Cal.App.4th 822, 828–829, 56 Cal.Rptr.2d 870, 874–875 (1996).

17. West's Ann. California Evidence Code § 1293.

18. Id. For a list of the conditions, see West's Ann. California Evidence Code § 1293. See also § 11.08 supra.

Even statements which a child does not make under oath may be admissible for the truth of the matter stated at juvenile court hearings. The Welfare and Institutions Code authorizes the juvenile court judge in a dependency hearing to receive for the truth of the matter stated those statements made by a minor who is under the age of twelve and the subject of the hearing if the statements are contained in the written report prepared by the county welfare or probation department and the child is unavailable for cross-examination.[19] The court may exclude the statements only if the objecting party establishes that they are unreliable because they are the "product of fraud, deceit, or undue influence."[20] If the child is unavailable for cross-examination on grounds of incompetency, then the judge may not rely on the statement exclusively to sustain a finding of jurisdiction over the child unless the judge finds that " 'the time, content and circumstances of the statement provide sufficient indicia of reliability.' "[21]

Complaints by children about sexual abuse may be offered in dependency hearings for the truth of the matter stated even if they are not offered as part of a social studies report. Recognizing the need for such an exception, the court in In re Cindy L.[22] invoked its Common Law powers to create a hearsay exception for such statements. Calling it the "child dependency hearsay exception," the court held that a juvenile court judge may admit such statements for the truth if the judge first finds that (1) the time, content, and circumstances of the statement indicate that it is reliable, (2) the child is either available for cross-examination or, if unavailable, other evidence corroborates the child's statement, and (3) other interested parties have been given sufficient notice of the public agency's intention to introduce the statement so as to have an opportunity to contest it.[23] In determining the statement's reliability, the judge should consider such factors as the spontaneity of the statement and its consistent repetition, the mental state of the child declarant, the use of terminology unexpected of a child of a similar age, and the lack of motive to fabricate.[24] The child's incompetency as a witness does not render the out of court statement inadmissible. It is but a factor that the judge can take into account in determining the reliability of the statement.[25]

Children's hearsay statements regarding abuse or neglect and criminal cases. The Legislature in 1995 added a new hearsay exception to the Code. Section 1360 provides an exception for statements describing any act of child abuse or neglect made by a child-victim under twelve and

19. West's Ann. California Welfare and Institutions Code § 355.

20. Id.

21. In re Lucero L., 22 Cal.4th 1227, 1248, 96 Cal.Rptr.2d 56, 71, 998 P.2d 1019, 1033 (2000) (quoting from In re Cindy L., 17 Cal.4th 15, 29, 69 Cal.Rptr.2d 803, 812, 947 P.2d 1340, 1349 (1997)).

22. 17 Cal.4th 15, 69 Cal.Rptr.2d 803, 947 P.2d 1340 (1997).

23. Id. at 29, 69 Cal.Rptr.2d at 812, 947 P.2d at 1349.

24. Id. at 29–30, 69 Cal.Rptr.2d at 813, 947 P.2d at 1350.

25. Id. at 34, 69 Cal.Rptr.2d at 815–816, 947 P.2d at 1352–1353.

offered in a criminal prosecution while the child-victim is still a minor. To be admissible under § 1360, the court must find in a hearing conducted outside the presence of the jury that the time, content, and circumstances surrounding the statements provide sufficient indicia of reliability.[26] In addition, either the child must testify at the hearing or, if unavailable, other evidence corroborates the child's out of court statements.[27] Finally, the proponent of the statement must give notice to the adverse party sufficiently in advance of the proceeding as to provide the opponent with a fair opportunity to defend against the statement.[28] In the case of a jury trial, the notice must be given before the jurors have been sworn.[29]

Section 1360 does not supplant In re Cindy L. The latter applies only in child dependency proceedings while § 1360 is limited to criminal prosecutions.

When the child does not testify at the trial, the accused's right to confront the prosecution's witnesses is implicated. In Crawford v. Washington[30] the United States Supreme Court held that, over a confrontation objection, testimonial hearsay may not be offered against the accused unless (1) the hearsay declarant is produced for cross-examination by the accused or (2) if not produced, unless the accused was given an opportunity prior to the trial to cross examine the hearsay declarant.[31] Prior to *Crawford*, the California Court of Appeal had upheld § 1360 against the claim that its use violates the accused's right to confront his accuser where the child-victim does not testify.[32] But because § 1360 creates a new hearsay exception, the court held that a confrontation violation would occur only where the prosecution failed to show that the circumstances surrounding the making of the hearsay statements rendered the declarant particularly worthy of belief.[33] This type of analysis, however, is no longer pertinent if the hearsay offered against the accused qualifies as a "testimonial" statement.[34] If it does, then the hearsay must be excluded unless

---

26. West's Ann. California Evidence § 1360. Among the factors a judge should take into consideration in determining the reliability of a child's out of court statements are the following: (1) whether the statements were made spontaneously, (2) whether the statements are consistent, (3) whether the child's mental state at the time of the statements indicates lack of reliability, (4) whether the child's descriptions and language demonstrate knowledge of sexual matters beyond that normally expected of children of the declarant's age, and (5) whether the child had a motive to fabricate the accusations. People v. Brodit, 61 Cal.App.4th 1312, 1330, 72 Cal.Rptr.2d 154, 164 (1998).

27. West's Ann. California Evidence § 1360. It is error for a judge to rule a child unavailable as a witness on grounds of incompetency without first holding a hearing on the child's testimonial competence. People v. Roberto V., 93 Cal.App.4th 1350, 1369, 113 Cal.Rptr.2d 804, 818 (2001).

28. West's Ann. California Evidence Code § 1360.

29. People v. Roberto V., 93 Cal.App.4th 1350, 1372, 113 Cal.Rptr.2d 804, 820 (2001).

30. 541 U.S. 36, 124 S.Ct. 1354, 158 L.Ed.2d 177 (2004).

31. Id. at 68.

32. People v. Eccleston, 89 Cal.App.4th 436, 448–449, 107 Cal.Rptr.2d 440, 449–450 (2001).

33. People v. Roberto V., 93 Cal.App.4th 1350, 1374–1375, 113 Cal.Rptr.2d 804, 822–823 (2001).

34. In People v. Sisavath, 118 Cal.App.4th 1396, 13 Cal.Rptr.3d 753 (2004), the California Court of Appeal held that statements offered under § 1360 that were made to a police officer and

the accused is given an opportunity to cross-examine the child at the trial or was given that opportunity before the trial.[35]

The California Penal Code also contains provisions protecting child witnesses. Chief among these are §§ 1346 and 1347. Section 1346 allows the videotaping of the preliminary examination of child witnesses under the age of 16 and the use of the tape at the trial as former testimony "[if] at the time of trial the court finds that further testimony would cause the victim emotional trauma so that the victim is medically unavailable or otherwise unavailable within the meaning of section 240 of the Evidence Code."[36]

Section 1347 establishes a procedure similar to the Maryland procedure at issue in *Craig*. It allows the judge to order that the testimony of children under 14 be taken out of the presence of the judge, jury, defendant, and attorneys by means of a two-way closed circuit television, if the judge finds by clear and convincing evidence that the impact of enumerated factors—including the conduct of the accused or his counsel during the trial—is so substantial as to render the minor unavailable as a witness unless the closed circuit procedure is used.[37]

Child witnesses and support persons. The California Penal Code allows some witnesses to be accompanied to the witness stand by a support person of his or her choosing.[38] Though the penal code provision is not limited to child witnesses, it is designed especially to assist the young witness or the witness who is a victim of a sexual offense by reducing the psychological harm and trauma the witness might experience.[39] The witness is not automatically entitled to the presence of the support person. To diminish the risk of diluting the accused's right to confront his accusers, the witness's need for the presence of a support person must demonstrated at an evidentiary hearing.[40] Consistent with *Craig*, the prosecution must show that, unless accompanied by the support person, the accused's presence would so traumatize the witness as to impair the witness's ability to communicate.[41]

---

a county employee charged with interviewing victims of child abuse qualified as testimonial statements. Id. at 1402, 13 Cal.Rptr.3d at 757–758.

35. For an extended discussion of when hearsay offered against the accused can violate the accused's confrontation rights, see § 6.03 et seq., supra.

36. West's Ann. California Penal Code § 1346.

37. West's Ann. California Penal Code § 1347.

38. West's Ann. California Penal Code § 868.5.

39. People v. Lord, 30 Cal.App.4th 1718, 1721, 36 Cal.Rptr.2d 453, 455 (1994).

40. People v. Adams, 19 Cal.App.4th 412, 443–444, 23 Cal.Rptr.2d 512, 531 (1993).

41. Id. But see People v. Johns, 56 Cal.App.4th 550, 556, 65 Cal.Rptr.2d 434, 438 (1997) (holding that because the use of a support person does not deprive the accused of the opportunity to confront his accusers face to face, as a constitutional matter the prosecution does not have to demonstrate that the accused's presence would so traumatize the witness as to impair the witness's ability to communicate).

Questions and Problems

1.   Because very young children are incapable of understanding their duties as witnesses, both the Code and the Rules require that children at least be the age of eight before they can be offered as witnesses. True or false?

2.   Because the Sixth Amendment's right to confront one's accusers necessarily includes cross examining them face to face under oath in the presence of the fact finders, any procedure which detracts from this type of confrontation is unconstitutional. True or false?

3.   Under § 1360, the prosecution may under some circumstances offer for the truth of the matter stated a child's statement describing any act of child abuse or neglect in some criminal cases. Admitting the statement against the defendant in a child abuse prosecution would not violate the Confrontation Clause because under § 1360 the child must testify at the trial. True or false?

4.   Prior to the hearing, a child says, "The defendant molested me." At a hearing to determine whether a child should be declared a ward of a California juvenile court, the child's statement may be offered to prove the truth of the matter stated if:

a.   The child made the statement under oath at a preliminary hearing to determine whether the accused molested the child and certain other conditions are met. True or false?

b.   Or the statement is included in a report prepared by a county welfare or probation department officer and the child is unavailable for cross-examination and certain other conditions are met. True or false?

c.   Or the child made the statement to her mother and the juvenile court judge finds that the statement is reliable and that certain other conditions are met. True or false?

§ 14.06   COGNITIVELY AND PHYSICALLY IMPAIRED WITNESSES

No fixed standard of intelligence is required of witnesses.[1] Accordingly, the fact that a witness may suffer from a mental impairment will not in itself preclude the witness from testifying.[2] Neither will the fact that the witness has been committed for insanity.[3] The inquiry, as in the case of all witnesses, is whether the witness appreciates the duty to tell the truth and can express himself in a manner that can be understood by others.[4] If the witness can do so despite the mental impairment, the witness is

---

1.   People v. Manuel, 94 Cal.App.2d 20, 23, 209 P.2d 981, 983 (1949).

2.   See, e.g., In re S.C., 138 Cal.App.4th 396, 422, 41 Cal.Rptr.3d 453, 475 (2006) (upholding trial judge's finding that a 15–year–old minor with Down's Syndrome, an IQ of 44, and a functioning level of a six or seven year old child was competent to testify).

3.   People v. Horowitz, 70 Cal.App.2d 675, 696, 161 P.2d 833, 845 (1945).

4.   West's Ann. California Evidence Code §§ 700–701. Expert testimony that a witness suffers from dementia and other brain disorders can be probative of the witness's inability to understand

qualified to testify. But if the witness testifies, the fact finder may consider the witness's mental condition in assessing the witness's ability to perceive and recall accurately the subject matter of the testimony.[5]

The fact that expert testimony may be helpful in determining the competency or credibility of mentally impaired witnesses does not empower California trial judges to subject them to mental health evaluations as a matter of course. The privacy interests of witnesses and the policy of encouraging witnesses to come forward would be undermined if witnesses could be subjected to psychiatric evaluations in the absence of exceptional circumstances.[6] Even a delusional witness may not be subjected to a mental health evaluation in support of an incompetence motion if the evidence before the judge discloses that the witness is a coherent communicator and understands the duty to testify truthfully under oath.[7]

Physically impaired witnesses do not, as a rule, present competency questions. Unlike mental impairments, physical disabilities do not usually implicate these witnesses' abilities to appreciate their duty to tell the truth or to recall the subject matter of their testimony. Their disabilities, however, may so impair these witnesses' ability to communicate as to preclude the accused from conducting the kind of cross-examination contemplated by the Confrontation Clause. People v. Tran[8] is illustrative. As a result of an assault, the victim was rendered a quadriplegic who at the trial could answer questions only by tapping once for "yes" and twice for "no." The defendants, who were convicted of inflicting the injuries, asked for a reversal on the ground that being forced to ask only yes or no questions on cross-examination deprived them of their right to confront their accuser. In affirming the convictions, the reviewing court distinguished People v. Brock[9] where the magistrate had improperly limited the defense to three questions on cross-examination on account of the witness's poor physical condition. Unlike *Brock*, the defendants in *Tran* were allowed to conduct a complete examination. And while acknowledging the difficulties presented by having to ask only one kind of question, the court nonetheless concluded that the limitation did not prevent the defendants from eliciting evidence favorable to the defense.[10]

---

the duty to testify truthfully. Stanchfield v. Hamer Toyota, Inc., 37 Cal.App.4th 1495, 1507, 44 Cal.Rptr.2d 565, 571 (1995).

5. 6 California Revision Commission, Reports, Recommendations, and Studies 709 (1964). Though ordered depublished by the California Supreme Court, People v. Nandkeshwar is illustrative. A young woman suffering from Down's Syndrome claimed to have been raped by the accused. At the trial, the jurors were allowed to consider evidence about the effects of the syndrome on such mental functions as memory, susceptibility to suggestion, and the inclination to fantasize. 38 Cal.Rptr.2d 41, 46–47 (1995). For a discussion of the use of evidence of mental disorders to impeach a witness, see § 15.10 infra.

6. People v. Anderson, 25 Cal.4th 543, 576, 106 Cal.Rptr.2d 575, 602, 22 P.3d 347, 369 (2001), cert. denied, 534 U.S. 1136, 122 S.Ct. 1082, 151 L.Ed.2d 982 (2002).

7. Id.

8. 47 Cal.App.4th 759, 54 Cal.Rptr.2d 905 (1996).

9. 38 Cal.3d 180, 211 Cal.Rptr. 122, 695 P.2d 209 (1985).

10. People v. Tran, 47 Cal.App.4th 759, 770, 54 Cal.Rptr.2d 905, 912 (1996). The position of the defendants is difficult to understand from a trial advocacy perspective. As a rule, a party

Individuals who use substances that distort perception or impair recollection are not disqualified from testifying, unless the use of the substances precludes them from communicating or from understanding their duty to tell the truth.[11] If persons who use such substances are found competent, their drug use can be employed by the opposing party to impeach the witnesses' abilities to perceive or recall the subject matter of their testimony.

Questions and Problems

1. The fact that a witness may be under the influence of intoxicants at the time the witness testifies may be a basis for impeaching the witness but never for finding the witness incompetent. True or false?

2. Over a personal knowledge objection, a witness may not testify about matters over which she has no recollection on account of any reason, including the use of mind altering substances. True or false?

3. Physically impaired witnesses, unlike mentally impaired witnesses, may testify so long as they are able to communicate the subject matter of their testimony on direct and cross-examination and can appreciate their duty to testify truthfully under oath. True of false?

§ 14.07 COMPETENCY AND THE HEARSAY DECLARANT

Neither the Code nor the Rules has a general provision regarding the competency of the hearsay declarant.[1] The Code, however, does have one specific provision. It allows a party to challenge the competency of a hearsay declarant whenever the declarant's former testimony is offered as an exception to the hearsay rule.[2] Objections based on competency are determined by reference to the time when the former testimony was given.[3] If the witness was incompetent to testify at the former hearing, then that objection can be raised at the hearing at which the former testimony is offered. The Code, however, does not expressly require other hearsay declarants to have been competent at the time they made their extrajudicial statements.[4]

Dean Charles McCormick found uncertainty among courts with regard to whether hearsay declarations could be excluded on the ground of the declarant's incompetency at the time the declarations were made.[5]

---

should ask only leading questions (those requiring a "yes" or "no" answer) on cross-examination. See § 1.04 supra.

11. West's Ann. California Evidence Code § 701.

1. See West's California Evidence Code § 700; Federal Rule of Evidence 601.

2. West's Ann. California Evidence Code §§ 1291–1292. Federal Rule of Evidence 804(b)(1), governing the use of former testimony, is silent on this point.

3. Id.

4. The Rules are in accord.

5. C. McCormick, Evidence § 240 (1st ed. 1954).

Wigmore favored exclusion, arguing that the hearsay rule was merely an additional test to be applied to otherwise admissible evidence.[6] In re Basilio T.[7] adopts Wigmore's view but recognizes an exception for excited utterances.[8] In re Emilye A.[9], however, effectively rejects Wigmore's view by extending *Basilio*'s exception to declarations regarding physical sensations as well as all other declarations admissible under any " 'firmly rooted' exception to the hearsay rule."[10]

QUESTIONS AND PROBLEMS

1. In California and federal courts, a hearsay declaration falling within an exception cannot be offered through the hearsay declarant if the declarant is incompetent to testify at the time the declaration is offered. For example, a California prosecutor may not offer an excited utterance through the declarant if the declarant does not understand his duty to tell the truth under oath. True or false?

2. Moreover, a California prosecutor may not offer the same excited utterance through a competent source if at the time the declarant made the declaration he was incompetent to testify. True or false?

CALIFORNIA EVIDENCE CODE

§ 700. General rule as to competency

Except as otherwise provided by statute, every person, irrespective of age, is qualified to be a witness and no person is disqualified to testify to any matter.

§ 701. Disqualification of witness

6. 5 J. H. Wigmore, Evidence § 1424 (Chadbourne rev. 1974).

7. 4 Cal.App.4th 155, 5 Cal.Rptr.2d 450 (1992).

8. Id. at 166–167, 5 Cal.Rptr.2d at 457.

9. 9 Cal.App.4th 1695, 12 Cal.Rptr.2d 294 (1992).

10. Id. at 1712, 12 Cal.Rptr.2d at 305.

At California preliminary hearings, prosecutors may use hearsay in support of a probable cause finding if the out of court statements are offered through a law enforcement officer. See § 1107 supra. The fact that the hearsay declarant may be incompetent to testify at the preliminary hearing is not a ground for excluding the statements. People v. Daily, 49 Cal.App.4th 543, 551–552, 56 Cal.Rptr.2d 787, 792 (1996). On the other hand, at least in juvenile court hearings some courts will still exclude a hearsay declarant's statements even if admissible under an exception if the declarant was not competent to testify at the time the declarant made the statements. See, e.g., In re Nemis M., 50 Cal.App.4th 1344, 1353, 58 Cal.Rptr.2d 324, 329 (1996).

The exception used in juvenile court hearings can make a difference, however. Use of the "child dependency" exception does not require a showing that the child declarant was competent at the time he or she made the extrajudicial statements. Whether the child was competent is only one factor the judge is to consider in determining whether the statements are sufficiently reliable to qualify for admission under the exception. In re Cindy L., 17 Cal.4th 15, 34, 69 Cal.Rptr.2d 803, 816, 947 P.2d 1340, 1353 (1997). For a discussion of the "child dependency" exception to the hearsay rule, see § 14.05 supra.

(a) A person is disqualified to be a witness if he or she is:

(1) Incapable of expressing himself or herself concerning the matter so as to be understood, either directly or through interpretation by one who can understand him; or

(2) Incapable of understanding the duty of a witness to tell the truth.

(b) In any proceeding held outside the presence of a jury, the court may reserve challenges to the competency of a witness until the conclusion of the direct examination of that witness.

§ 702. Personal knowledge of witness

(a) Subject to Section 801, the testimony of a witness concerning a particular matter is inadmissible unless he has personal knowledge of the matter. Against the objection of a party, such personal knowledge must be shown before the witness may testify concerning the matter.

(b) A witness' personal knowledge of a matter may be shown by any otherwise admissible evidence, including his own testimony.

§ 703. Judge as witness

(a) Before the judge presiding at the trial of an action may be called to testify in that trial as a witness, he shall, in proceedings held out of the presence and hearing of the jury, inform the parties of the information he has concerning any fact or matter about which he will be called to testify.

(b) Against the objection of a party, the judge presiding at the trial of an action may not testify in that trial as a witness. Upon such objection, the judge shall declare a mistrial and order the action assigned for trial before another judge.

(c) The calling of the judge presiding at a trial to testify in that trial as a witness shall be deemed a consent to the granting of a motion for mistrial, and an objection to such calling of a judge shall be deemed a motion for mistrial.

(d) In the absence of objection by a party, the judge presiding at the trial of an action may testify in that trial as a witness.

§ 703.5. Judges, arbitrators or mediators as witnesses; subsequent civil proceeding

No person presiding at any judicial or quasi-judicial proceeding, and no arbitrator or mediator, shall be competent to testify in any subsequent civil proceeding as to any statement, conduct, decision or ruling occurring at or in conjunction with the prior proceeding, except as to a statement or conduct that could (a) give rise to civil or criminal contempt, (b) constitute a crime, (c) be the subject of investigation by the State Bar or Commission on Judicial Performance, or (d) give rise to disqualification proceedings under paragraph (1) or (6) of subdivision (a) of Section 170.1 of the Code of Civil Procedure. However, this section does not apply to a mediator with regard to any mediation under Chapter 11 (commencing with Section 3160) of Part 2 of Division 8 of the Family Code.

§ 704. Juror as witness

(a) Before a juror sworn and impaneled in the trial of an action may be called to testify before the jury in that trial as a witness, he shall, in proceedings conducted by the court out of the presence and hearing of the remaining jurors, inform the parties of the information he has concerning any fact or matter about which he will be called to testify.

(b) Against the objection of a party, a juror sworn and impaneled in the trial of an action may not testify before the jury in that trial as a witness. Upon such objection, the court shall declare a mistrial and order the action assigned for trial before another jury.

(c) The calling of a juror to testify before the jury as a witness shall be deemed a consent to the granting of a motion for mistrial, and an objection to such calling of a juror shall be deemed a motion for mistrial.

(d) In the absence of objection by a party, a juror sworn and impaneled in the trial of an action may be compelled to testify in that trial as a witness.

§ 710. Oath required

Every witness before testifying shall take an oath or make an affirmation or declaration in the form provided by law, except that a child under the age of 10 or a dependent person with a substantial cognitive impairment, in the court's discretion, may be required only to promise to tell the truth.

§ 711. Confrontation

At the trial of an action, a witness can be heard only in the presence and subject to the examination of all the parties to the action, if they choose to attend and examine.

§ 712. Blood samples; technique in taking; affidavits in criminal actions; service; objections

Notwithstanding Sections 711 and 1200, at the trial of a criminal action, evidence of the technique used in taking blood samples may be given by a registered nurse, licensed vocational nurse, or licensed clinical laboratory technologist or clinical laboratory bioanalyst, by means of an affidavit. The affidavit shall be admissible, provided the party offering the affidavit as evidence has served all other parties to the action, or their counsel, with a copy of the affidavit no less than 10 days prior to trial. Nothing in this section shall preclude any party or his counsel from objecting to the introduction of the affidavit at any time, and requiring the attendance of the affiant, or compelling attendance by subpoena.

§ 750. Rules relating to witnesses apply to interpreters and translators

A person who serves as an interpreter or translator in any action is subject to all the rules of law relating to witnesses.

§ 751.   Oath required of interpreters and translators

(a) An interpreter shall take an oath that he or she will make a true interpretation to the witness in a language that the witness understands and that he or she will make a true interpretation of the witness' answers to questions to counsel, court, or jury, in the English language, with his or her best skill and judgment.

(b) In any proceeding in which a deaf or hard-of-hearing person is testifying under oath, the interpreter certified pursuant to subdivision (f) of Section 754 shall advise the court whenever he or she is unable to comply with his or her oath taken pursuant to subdivision (a).

(c) A translator shall take an oath that he or she will make a true translation in the English language of any writing he or she is to decipher or translate.

(d) An interpreter regularly employed by the court and certified or registered in accordance with Article 4 (commencing with Section 68560) of Chapter 2 of Title 8 of the Government Code, or a translator regularly employed by the court, may file an oath as prescribed by this section with the clerk of the court. The filed oath shall serve for all subsequent court proceedings until the appointment is revoked by the court.

§ 765.   Court to control mode of interrogation

(a) The court shall exercise reasonable control over the mode of interrogation of a witness so as to make such interrogation as rapid, as distinct, and as effective for the ascertainment of the truth, as may be, and to protect the witness from undue harassment or embarrassment.

(b) With a witness under the age of 14 is a dependent person with a substantial cognitive impairment, the court shall take special care to protect him or her from undue harassment or embarrassment, and to restrict the unnecessary repetition of questions. The court shall also take special care to insure that questions are stated in a form which is appropriate to the age or cognitive level of the witness. The court may in the interests of justice, on objection by a party, forbid the asking of a question which is in a form that is not reasonably likely to be understood by a person of the age or cognitive level of the witness.

§ 766.   Responsive answers

A witness must give responsive answers to questions, and answers that are not responsive shall be stricken on motion of any party.

§ 767.   Leading questions

(a) Except under special circumstances where the interests of justice otherwise require:

(1) A leading question may not be asked of a witness on direct or redirect examination.

(2) A leading question may be asked of a witness on cross-examination or recross-examination.

(b) The court may in the interests of justice permit a leading question to be asked of a child under 10 years of age or a dependent person with a substantial cognitive impairment in a case involving a prosecution under Section 273a, 273d, 288.5 368, or any of the acts described in Section 11165.1 or 11165.2 of the Penal Code.

§ 795. Testimony of hypnosis subject; admissibility; conditions

(a) The testimony of a witness is not inadmissible in a criminal proceeding by reason of the fact that the witness has previously undergone hypnosis for the purpose of recalling events which are the subject of the witness' testimony, if all of the following conditions are met:

(1) The testimony is limited to those matters that the witness recalled and related prior to the hypnosis.

(2) The substance of the prehypnotic memory was preserved in writing, audio recording, or video recording prior to the hypnosis.

(3) The hypnosis was conducted in accordance with all of the following procedures:

(A) A written record was made prior to hypnosis documenting the subject's description of the event, and information which was provided to the hypnotist concerning the subject matter of the hypnosis.

(B) The subject gave informed consent to the hypnosis.

(C) The hypnosis session, including the pre-and post-hypnosis interviews, was videotape recorded for subsequent review.

(D) The hypnosis was performed by a licensed physician and surgeon, psychologist, licensed clinical social worker, licensed marriage and family therapist, or licensed professional clinical counselor experienced in the use of hypnosis and independent of and not in the presence of law enforcement, the prosecution, or the defense.

(4) Prior to admission of the testimony, the court holds a hearing pursuant to Section 402 at which the proponent of the evidence proves by clear and convincing evidence that the hypnosis did not so affect the witness as to render the witness' prehypnosis recollection unreliable or to substantially impair the ability to cross-examine the witness concerning the witness' prehypnosis recollection. At the hearing, each side shall have the right to present expert testimony and to cross-examine witnesses.

(b) Nothing in this section shall be construed to limit the ability of a party to attack the credibility of a witness who has undergone hypnosis, or to limit other legal grounds to admit or exclude the testimony of that witness.

§ 1150. Evidence to test a verdict

(a) Upon an inquiry as to the validity of a verdict, any otherwise admissible evidence may be received as to statements made, or conduct, conditions, or events occurring, either within or without the jury room, of such a character as is likely to have influenced the verdict improperly. No evidence is admissible to show the effect of such statement, conduct, condition, or event upon a juror either in influencing him to assent to or dissent from the verdict or concerning the mental processes by which it was determined.

(b) Nothing in this code affects the law relating to the competence of a juror to give evidence to impeach or support a verdict.

§ 1228. Admissibility of certain out-of-court statements of minors under the age of 12; establishing elements of certain sexually oriented crimes

Notwithstanding any other provision of law, for the purpose of establishing the elements of the crime in order to admit as evidence the confession of a person accused of violating Section 261, 264.1, 285, 286, 288, 288a, 289, or 647a of the Penal Code, a court, in its discretion, may determine that a statement of the complaining witness is not made inadmissible by the hearsay rule if it finds all of the following:

(a) The statement was made by a minor child under the age of 12, and the contents of the statement were included in a written report of a law enforcement official or an employee of a county welfare department.

(b) The statement describes the minor child as a victim of sexual abuse.

(c) The statement was made prior to the defendant's confession. The court shall view with caution the testimony of a person recounting hearsay where there is evidence of personal bias or prejudice.

(d) There are no circumstances, such as significant inconsistencies between the confession and the statement concerning material facts establishing any element of the crime or the identification of the defendant, that would render the statement unreliable.

(e) The minor child is found to be unavailable pursuant to paragraph (2) or (3) of subdivision (a) of Section 240 or refuses to testify.

(f) The confession was memorialized in a trustworthy fashion by a law enforcement official.

If the prosecution intends to offer a statement of the complaining witness pursuant to this section, the prosecution shall serve a written notice upon the defendant at least 10 days prior to the hearing or trial at which the prosecution intends to offer the statement.

If the statement is offered during trial, the court's determination shall be made out of the presence of the jury. If the statement is found to be admissible pursuant to this section, it shall be admitted out of the presence of the jury and solely for the purpose of determining the admissibility of the confession of the defendant.

§ 1293. Former testimony by minor child complaining witness at preliminary examination

(a) Evidence of former testimony made at a preliminary examination by a minor child who was the complaining witness is not made inadmissible by the hearsay rule if:

(1) The former testimony is offered in a proceeding to declare the minor a dependent child of the court pursuant to Section 300 of the Welfare and Institutions Code.

(2) The issues are such that a defendant in the preliminary examination in which the former testimony was given had the right and opportunity to cross-examine the minor child with an interest and motive similar to that which the parent or guardian against whom the testimony is offered has at the proceeding to declare the minor a dependent child of the court.

(b) The admissibility of former testimony under this section is subject to the same limitations and objections as though the minor child were testifying at the proceeding to declare him or her a dependent child of the court.

(c) The attorney for the parent or guardian against whom the former testimony is offered or, if none, the parent or guardian may make a motion to challenge the admissibility of the former testimony upon a showing that new substantially different issues are present in the proceeding to declare the minor a dependent child than were present in the preliminary examination.

(d) As used in this section, "complaining witness" means the alleged victim of the crime for which a preliminary examination was held.

(e) This section shall apply only to testimony made at a preliminary examination on and after January 1, 1990.

§ 1360. Statements describing an act or attempted act of child abuse or neglect; criminal prosecutions; requirements

(a) In a criminal prosecution where the victim is a minor, a statement made by the victim when under the age of 12 describing any act of child abuse or neglect performed with or on the child by another, or describing an attempted act of child abuse or neglect with or on the child by another, is not made inadmissible by the hearsay rule if all of the following apply:

(1) The statement is not otherwise admissible by statute or court rule.

(2) The court finds, in a hearing conducted outside the presence of the jury, that the time, content, and circumstances of the statement provide sufficient indicia of reliability.

(3) The child either:

(A) Testifies at the proceedings.

(B) Is unavailable as a witness, in which case the statement may be admitted only if there is evidence of the child abuse or neglect that corroborates the statement made by the child.

(b) A statement may not be admitted under this section unless the proponent makes known to the adverse party the intention to offer the statement and the particulars of the statement sufficiently in advance of the proceedings in order to provide the adverse party with a fair opportunity to prepare to meet the statement.

(c) For purposes of this section, "child abuse" means an act proscribed by Section 273a, 273d, or 288.5 of the Penal Code, or any of the acts described in Section 11165.1 of the Penal Code, and "child neglect" means any of the acts described in Section 11165.2 of the Penal Code.

FEDERAL RULES OF EVIDENCE

Rule 601.   Competency to Testify in General

Every person is competent to be a witness unless these rules provide otherwise. But in a civil case, state law governs the witness's competency regarding a claim or defense for which state law supplies the rule of decision.

Rule 602.   Need for Personal Knowledge

A witness may testify to a matter only if evidence is introduced sufficient to support a finding that the witness has personal knowledge of the matter. Evidence to prove personal knowledge may consist of the witness's own testimony. This rule does not apply to a witness's expert testimony under Rule 703.

Rule 603.   Oath or Affirmation to Testify Truthfully

Before testifying, a witness must give an oath or affirmation to testify truthfully. It must be in a form designed to impress that duty on the witness's conscience.

Rule 604.   Interpreter

An interpreter must be qualified and must give an oath or affirmation to make a true translation.

Rule 605.   Judge's Competency as a Witness

The presiding judge may not testify as a witness at the trial. A party need not object to preserve the issue.

Rule 606.   Juror's Competency as a Witness

(a) At the Trial. A juror may not testify as a witness before the other jurors at the trial. If a juror is called to testify, the court must give a party an opportunity to object outside the jury's presence.

(b) During an Inquiry into the Validity of a Verdict or Indictment.

(1) ***Prohibited Testimony or Other Evidence.*** During an inquiry into the validity of a verdict or indictment, a juror may not testify about any statement made or incident that occurred during the jury's deliberations; the effect of anything on that juror's or another juror's vote; or any juror's mental processes concerning the verdict or indictment. The court may not receive a juror's affidavit or evidence of a juror's statement on these matters.

(2) ***Exceptions.*** A juror may testify about whether:

(A) extraneous prejudicial information was improperly brought to the jury's attention;

(B) an outside influence was improperly brought to bear on any juror; or

(C) a mistake was made in entering the verdict on the verdict form.

CHAPTER 15

ATTACKING AND SUPPORTING THE CREDIBILITY OF WITNESSES

■ ■ ■

Table of Sections

§ 15.01 INTRODUCTION

Trial lawyers know that the outcome of a trial will be determined in almost all cases by which witnesses the jurors choose to believe and which ones they decide to ignore. Telling jurors which witnesses to believe or disbelieve is thus a crucial part of a closing argument. But such an appeal will not be persuasive unless the lawyer can give the jurors reasons rooted in the evidence about why a witness should be believed or disbelieved. This inescapable dynamic of jury trials encourages lawyers to produce the most favorable evidence about the credibility of their witnesses and the most unfavorable about their opponents'. As we shall see, however, the rules of evidence counter this inclination by placing strict limits on the use of evidence to support or attack the credibility of witnesses. Despite the unquestioned relevance of such evidence, the rules proceed on the assumption that the unrestrained use of evidence on witness credibility may

545

distract from and confuse jurors about the issues to be decided. In the memorable words of Dean Charles McCormick, without limitations, the "sideshow" on witness credibility would threaten to take over the "circus" on the disputed issues.[1]

The rules restrict the use of evidence on witness credibility in two ways. First, the rules limit the kind of evidence that can be used to support or attack the credibility of witnesses. Second, the rules limit the circumstances under which such evidence can be used. For example, evidence that a witness has made statements that are consistent with the witness's testimony on direct examination is generally inadmissible to support the witness unless the opposing party has first attacked the witness's credibility.[2] Since the rules sometimes require an attack before permitting the use of evidence supporting a witness's credibility,[3] the permissible ways of impeaching witnesses are considered first in this chapter.

Special attention is devoted to Proposition 8.[4] In June 1982, the California electorate approved this initiative. A key provision gives parties to California criminal proceedings the state constitutional right not to have relevant evidence excluded. Since evidence attacking or supporting the credibility of witnesses is obviously relevant, this provision threatens to repeal those sections of the Evidence Code that ban or limit the use of such evidence.[5] The initiative also threatens to overturn the decisional restraints on the use of such evidence. The effect of Proposition 8 is

---

1. C. McCormick, McCormick on Evidence § 41 (E. Cleary 2d ed. 1972). In deciding whether to go forward with a case, lawyers often take into account their assessment of the credibility of key witnesses. For example, a review of the forensic evidence for all sexual assault cases reported in Duval County, Florida during a two year period showed that prosecutors cited problems with the credibility of the complaining witness as the most common reason for dropping cases. See Gray–Enron, Seaberg & Wears, *The Prosecution of Sexual Assault Cases: Correlation With Forensic Evidence*, Annals of Emergency Medicine 39 (January 2002).

2. West's Ann. California Evidence Code § 791; Federal Rule of Evidence 801(d)(1)(B).

3. See, e.g., West's Ann. California Evidence Code § 791 (requiring that a witness first be impeached in specified fashions before the court may admit a prior consistent statement to support the witness's credibility); Federal Rule of Evidence 801(d)(1)(B) (same); West's Ann. California Evidence Code § 1102(a), (b) (requiring a court to exclude evidence of the accused's bad character unless offered by the prosecution to rebut evidence of his or her good character); Federal Rule of Evidence 404(a)(1) (same).

But see People v. Herring, 20 Cal.App.4th 1066, 1071, 25 Cal.Rptr.2d 213, 216 (1993), which upheld the use of expert testimony in the prosecution's case-in-chief that the complaining victim in an attempted rape prosecution was "in the borderline range of mental retardation." Although the court acknowledged the impropriety of allowing a party to support a witness's credibility in the absence of an attack, the court ruled that the expert testimony was nonetheless admissible for another purpose: to show the victim's capacity to withhold her consent to a sex act. Id.

The method employed to support a witness's credibility may not first require an attack. For example, a party may support the credibility of a witness by other evidence that tends to establish the existence of facts testified to by the witness. See West's Ann.California Evidence Code § 780(i).

4. For an extended discussion of the impact of Proposition 8 on witness credibility, see § 15.03 infra.

5. See People v. Stern, 111 Cal.App.4th 283, 296, 3 Cal.Rptr.3d 479, 489 (2003) (holding that the Evidence Code's ban on the use of prior bad acts to attack the credibility of witnesses has been abrogated by Proposition 8 in criminal cases). See also In re Freeman, 38 Cal.4th 630, 640, note 5, 42 Cal.Rptr.3d 850, 859, note 5, 133 P.3d 1013, 1020, note 5 (2006) (same).

discussed in connection with each method considered to impeach or support a witness's credibility.[6]

A unique feature of the Code is § 780. This section provides a nonexclusive list of the matters the fact finder can consider in assessing the credibility of witnesses. The list is technically unnecessary. Evidence bearing on credibility is relevant, and, unless otherwise provided, all relevant evidence is admissible.[7] The list is nonetheless invaluable because it enables judges and lawyers to grasp at a glance the broad spectrum of evidence that may be available to attack or support a witness's credibility. Section 780 provides as follows:

> Except as otherwise provided by statute, the court or jury may consider in determining the credibility of a witness any matter that has any tendency in reason to prove or disprove the truthfulness of his testimony at the hearing, including but not limited to any of the following:
>
> (a) His demeanor while testifying and the manner in which he testifies.
>
> (b) The character of his testimony.
>
> (c) The extent of his capacity to perceive, to recollect, or to communicate any matter about which he testifies.
>
> (d) The extent of his opportunity to perceive any matter about which he testifies.
>
> (e) His character for honesty or veracity or their opposites.
>
> (f) The existence or nonexistence of a bias, interest, or other motive.
>
> (g) A statement previously made by him that is consistent with his testimony at the hearing.
>
> (h) A statement made by him that is inconsistent with any part of his testimony at the hearing.
>
> (i) The existence or nonexistence of any fact testified to by him.
>
> (j) His attitude toward the action in which he testifies or toward the giving of testimony.
>
> (k) His admission of untruthfulness.[8]

---

6. Proposition 8 permits amendments to the initiative if approved by at least a two-thirds vote of each house. In People v. Ewoldt, 7 Cal.4th 380, 27 Cal.Rptr.2d 646, 867 P.2d 757 (1994), the California Supreme Court held that whatever repealing effects Proposition 8 had on California Evidence Code § 1101(a) had been superseded by an amendment which had the effect of reenacting the entire section by the required super majority. Section 1101(a) bans the use of evidence to prove conduct in conformity with a person's character. West's Ann. California Evidence Code § 1101(a). The reenactment of § 1101, however, leaves untouched the effects of the initiative on the Code sections governing the use of character evidence to attack or support the credibility of witnesses. Section 1101(c) provides that "[n]othing in this section affects the admissibility of evidence offered to support or attack the credibility of a witness." West's Ann. California Evidence Code § 1101(c).

7. West's Ann. California Evidence Code § 351.

8. West's Ann. California Evidence Code § 780.

The Federal Rules of Evidence do not contain an equivalent provision, but similar principles can be derived by applying Rule 401, which defines relevant evidence to include evidence that is probative of a witness's credibility,[9] and Rule 402, which declares that all relevant evidence is admissible unless otherwise excluded.[10]

QUESTIONS AND PROBLEMS

In People v. Ewoldt the California Supreme Court held that amendments to the Code had the effect of nullifying the consequences of Proposition 8 on those provisions of the Code governing the use of character evidence. As a result, Proposition 8 no longer overrides those Code provisions limiting the use of character evidence to support or attack the credibility of witnesses. True or false?

§ 15.02   IMPEACHING ONE'S OWN WITNESS

Both the Code and the Federal Rules repeal the Common Law rule prohibiting parties from impeaching their own witnesses. Both provide that the credibility of a witness may be attacked by any party, including the party calling the witness.[1] As the Law Revision Commission noted, "A party has no actual control over a person who witnesses an event and is required to testify to aid the trier of fact in its function of determining the truth. Hence, a party should not be 'bound' by the testimony of a witness produced by him and should be permitted to attack the credibility of the witness without anachronistic limitations."[2]

§ 15.03   IMPEACHMENT BY PRIOR INCONSISTENT STATEMENTS

Both the Code and the Federal Rules recognize that a witness's credibility can be impeached by evidence that the witness has made statements that are inconsistent with the witness's testimony at the trial.[1] However, only those out of court statements that are inconsistent with the witness's testimony are admissible. Other statements accompanying the inconsistent statements are not. In People v. Morgan[2] a witness denied

---

9.   Federal Rule of Evidence 401.

10.   Federal Rule of Evidence 402.

1.   West's Ann. California Evidence Code § 785; Federal Rule of Evidence 607. The Code and the Rules notwithstanding, some statutes prohibit a party from using a witness's prior statements for any purpose, including impeachment. For example, Rule 1616(c) of the California Rules of Court bans the use of statements made in arbitration proceedings for any purpose. The purpose of the rule is to encourage parties to rely on arbitration, rather than litigation, by privileging arbitration proceedings. See Jimena v. Alesso, 36 Cal.App.4th 1028, 1030, 43 Cal.Rptr.2d 18, 20 (1995).

2.   West's Ann. California Evidence Code § 785 (comment).

1.   West's Ann. California Evidence Code § 780(h); Federal Rule of Evidence 801 (Advisory Committee Note).

2.   87 Cal.App.3d 59, 150 Cal.Rptr. 712 (1978), overruled on other grounds, People v. Kimble, 44 Cal.3d 480, 244 Cal.Rptr. 148, 749 P.2d 803 (1988).

having seen the accused at the robbery scene. To impeach her credibility, the prosecution was permitted to play a tape recording in which the witness had informed police officers that she had seen the accused at the crime scene. The reviewing court held that it was error to admit that portion of the recording in which the witness acknowledged having heard the accused argue with his accomplice over the spoils taken in the robbery: "There is no justification for permitting a witness' prior inconsistent statement to make admissible *other* prior *statements* of the witness, even though made at the same time, that are *not* inconsistent with the witness' testimony and possess no more reliability than any other inadmissible hearsay statements."[3]

The Code and the Rules abandon the Common Law requirement that before a witness can be asked about his prior inconsistent statements, the examiner must disclose the contents of the statement to the witness.[4] Disclosure diminishes the effectiveness of the attack by removing the element of surprise and giving the dishonest witness an opportunity to reshape his testimony in conformity with his earlier statement.[5] But under the Federal Rules, upon request, the examiner must show or disclose the prior inconsistent statement to opposing counsel.[6] This provision is designed to discourage the examiner from insinuating that a statement has been made when the contrary is true.[7] Under the Code, the opposing party can invoke the judge's authority to control the mode of a witness's interrogation to prevent the examiner from falsely suggesting the existence of a prior inconsistent statement.[8]

Both the Code and the Rules also reject the Common Law requirement that a party confront the witness with the prior inconsistent statement before offering extrinsic evidence of the statement.[9] From an advocacy perspective, confronting the witness with the prior statement has advantages. The examiner may persuade the witness to acknowledge making the prior statement and to adopt it as reflecting the truth. If she fails in this endeavor, the examiner is still free to impeach the witness with the statement. If the witness admits making the statement, the witness will be placed in the unenviable position of trying to reconcile his testimony with the statement. If he denies making the statement, the examiner will be free to offer extrinsic evidence of the statement.[10]

---

3. Id. at 75–76, 150 Cal.Rptr. at 721 (quoting B. Jefferson, California Evidence Benchbook § 10.1, p. 128 (1978 Supp.)) (emphasis in the original).

4. West's Ann. California Evidence Code § 769; Federal Rule of Evidence 613(a).

5. West's Ann. California Evidence Code § 769 (comment).

6. Federal Rule of Evidence 613(a).

7. Id. (Advisory Committee Note).

8. West's Ann. California Evidence Code § 765.

9. West's Ann. California Evidence Code § 770; Federal Rule of Evidence 613(b). "Extrinsic" evidence refers to proving the prior statement through a source other than the declarant, for example, by a witness who overheard the declarant make the prior statement.

10. West's Ann. California Evidence Code § 770; Federal Rule of Evidence 613(b).

In some cases, however, the examiner may not want to confront the witness with his prior inconsistent statement. Disclosure may prevent the effective cross-examination of several collusive witnesses.[11] Accordingly, both the Code and the Rules permit the examiner to forego confronting the witness. The examiner will still be allowed to offer extrinsic evidence of the statement, so long as the witness has not been excused from giving further testimony in the action.[12] Since the witness remains subject to being recalled, the opposing party and the witness are afforded an opportunity to have the witness explain or deny the statement before the evidence is closed.[13]

It bears emphasizing that a judge may exclude extrinsic evidence of an inconsistent statement "only if the witness during his examination was not given an opportunity to explain or deny the statement *and* he has been unconditionally excused and is not subject to being recalled as a witness."[14] Some cases discussing the need for the examiner to give the witness an opportunity to explain or deny the statement during the examination miss the latter point.[15]

Sometimes the calling party is surprised by the witness who on direct examination testifies inconsistently with the statements the witness made prior to the trial. Since under the Code and the Rules, parties may impeach their own witnesses, the calling party is entitled to confront the witness with the out of court statement and to try to get the witness to accept the statement as true or, failing that, to impeach the witness with the statement. If the witness admits making the out of court statement but claims that it was a lie, may the calling party offer extrinsic proof of the statement? The calling party should be given the opportunity. Hearing other witnesses describe the circumstances attending the making the of the out court statement might help the jurors decide what weight, if any, to give to the witness's explanations.

The question arose, albeit in an odd posture, in People v. Brown.[16] In *Brown* the victim informed friends, police officers, and a doctor that the accused had hit and kicked her in the stomach when she was pregnant. But at the accused's trial for murdering the fetus, she changed her story and on direct examination testified that the injuries to her stomach resulted from the accused having fallen on her. The prosecution did not confront the witness with her out of court statements on direct. The defense did on cross, and the victim acknowledged having made the prior statements but claimed that they were lies. Later, the accused attempted to bar the victim's friends, police officers, and doctor from repeating her

---

11. West's Ann. California Evidence Code § 770 (comment); Federal Rule of Evidence 613(b) (Advisory Committee Note).

12. West's Ann. California Evidence Code § 770(b).

13. Federal Rule of Evidence 613(b).

14. West's Ann. California Evidence Code § 770 (comment) (emphasis in the original).

15. See, e.g., People v. Garcia, 224 Cal.App.3d 297, 273 Cal.Rptr. 666 (1990) and cases cited therein.

16. 35 Cal.App.4th 1585, 42 Cal.Rptr.2d 155 (1995).

out of court statements implicating the accused on the ground that her explanation that they were lies no longer made them inconsistent with her testimony on direct. The reviewing court upheld the trial judge's ruling allowing the introduction of the out of court statements.[17]

From the defense's perspective, the witness turned out to be a favorable witness on direct examination. The defense inquiry into the out of court statements on cross was designed to diminish the effect of the prosecution's use of the extrinsic evidence of the statements. To take the "sting" out of a prior inconsistent statement, some advocates will ask the witness about the out of court statement on direct examination. But affording the witness an opportunity to acknowledge and explain the statement on direct does not necessarily preclude the opponent from calling other witnesses to prove the statement and the circumstances in which it was made. The extrinsic proof is not necessarily cumulative, as hearing from other witnesses may help the jurors determine the weight, if any, to give to the declarant's explanation. Although the circumstances attending the examination of the witness in *Brown* were unusual, having been hurt by the witness's testimony on direct, the prosecution in effect became the witness's opponent and was entitled to offer the extrinsic proof of the statements in an effort to discredit the witness's explanation on cross. Since the extrinsic proof was still probative of the witness's lack of credibility, the extrinsic evidence was properly received for impeachment purposes and in California could be received as well as for the truth of the matters stated.

Where the interests of justice require, the judge may permit the introduction of extrinsic evidence of an inconsistent statement even though the witness has been excused and has not had an opportunity to explain or deny the statement.[18] "An absolute rule forbidding introduction of such evidence where the specified conditions are not met may cause hardship in some cases. For example, the party seeking to introduce the statement may not have learned of its existence until after the witness has left the court and is no longer available to testify."[19]

Prior inconsistent statements and Proposition 8. In June 1982, the California electorate approved Proposition 8, an initiative entitled "The Victims Bill of Rights." One of its provisions, "The Right to Truth–in–Evidence," transformed the rules of evidence applicable to criminal proceedings by amending the state constitution to give the parties a right *not* to have relevant evidence excluded.[20] This provision, in pertinent part, reads as follows:

> Except as provided by statute hereafter enacted by a two-thirds vote of the membership of each house of the Legislature, relevant evidence shall not be excluded in any criminal proceeding * * *. Nothing in

---

17.   Id. at 1596, 42 Cal.Rptr.2d at 162.

18.   West's Ann. California Evidence Code § 770; Federal Rule of Evidence 613(b).

19.   West's Ann. California Evidence Code § 770 (comment).

20.   West's Ann. California Constitution Article I, § 28(f)(2).

this section shall affect any existing statutory rule of evidence relating to privilege or hearsay, or Evidence Code Sections 352, 782, or 1103.[21]

A literal application of this provision would repeal all the Code sections that ban or limit evidence bearing on the credibility of witnesses.[22] Since such evidence is relevant, its admissibility would be governed instead by § 352, a section expressly exempted from the operation of the Right to Truth–in–Evidence provision. Under § 352, a judge can exclude relevant evidence if its probative value is substantially outweighed by enumerated trial concerns.[23] These include the risk that the evidence may consume too much time, unfairly prejudice the opposing party, confuse the issues, or mislead the jury.[24] A literal interpretation of the proposition would thus replace the certainty provided by specific rules governing credibility with the discretion accorded trial judges by § 352. Whether or not the initiative has repealed the restrictions on the use of extrinsic evidence of prior inconsistent statements has not been decided.[25]

Proposition 8, however, has been construed as overturning People v. Disbrow.[26] In *Disbrow* the California Supreme Court declined on state constitutional grounds to follow the lead established by the United States Supreme Court in Harris v. New York.[27] *Harris* holds that custodial confessions which are inadmissible as admissions because of failure to comply with *Miranda* can nonetheless be used to impeach the accused, as long as the confessions are not coerced or involuntary.[28] Confessions that are inconsistent with the accused's testimony obviously are probative of the accused's lack of veracity.[29] Thus, relying on the initiative, the California Supreme Court overturned *Disbrow* and conformed state with federal practice.[30]

Proposition 8 also modifies People v. Belleci,[31] which prohibits the use in subsequent proceedings of any evidence that has been suppressed pursuant to Penal Code § 1538.5. Before Proposition 8, *Belleci* prohibited

---

21. Id.

22. Section 782, however, would not be affected because it is expressly exempted from the operation of Proposition 8. Section 782 governs the use of a complaining witness's sexual conduct to attack her credibility in sex offense prosecutions. West's Ann. California Evidence Code § 782.

23. West's Ann. California Evidence Code § 352.

24. Id.

25. A post-Proposition 8 decision discussing the need to give the witness an opportunity to explain or deny the statement fails to mention the impact of Proposition 8 on this requirement. People v. Garcia, 224 Cal.App.3d 297, 303–306, 273 Cal.Rptr. 666, 669–670 (1990).

26. 16 Cal.3d 101, 127 Cal.Rptr. 360, 545 P.2d 272 (1976).

27. 401 U.S. 222, 91 S.Ct. 643, 28 L.Ed.2d 1 (1971).

28. Id. at 224–226, 91 S.Ct. at 645–646.

29. It is immaterial that the confession made by the defendant is untrue. What matters is that the defendant's confession is inconsistent with his trial testimony. People v. Gutierrez, 28 Cal.4th 1083, 1131–1132, 124 Cal.Rptr.2d 373, 408, 52 P.3d 572, 601 (2002), cert. denied, 538 U.S. 1001, 123 S.Ct. 1899, 155 L.Ed.2d 829 (2003). Confessions taken in violation of *Miranda* may not offered for the truth of the matter asserted but only to impeach the accused's veracity.

30. People v. May, 44 Cal.3d 309, 314–315, 243 Cal.Rptr. 369, 374–375, 748 P.2d 307, 309–310 (1988). For an extended discussion of this point, see § 8.03 supra.

31. 24 Cal.3d 879, 887–888, 157 Cal.Rptr. 503, 508–510, 598 P.2d 473, 479–480 (1979).

the prosecution from using a written prior inconsistent statement to impeach the accused at trial, if the statement previously had been suppressed under the Fourth Amendment. Since such a statement is probative of the accused's lack of veracity and since the United States Supreme Court has approved the use of evidence seized in violation of the Fourth Amendment to impeach the accused,[32] after Proposition 8 the accused can be impeached with such a statement.[33]

If, as federal constitutional matter, voluntary statements taken in violation of the Fourth and Fifth Amendments may be used to impeach the accused, may voluntary statements taken in violation of the Sixth Amendment's right to counsel also be used for that limited purpose? Although the United States Supreme Court has not decided the issue,[34] California has joined the majority of courts considering the issue by holding that protecting the truth-finding function of a criminal trial requires the use of the statements.[35]

Prior inconsistent statements and the hearsay rule. In California, a prior inconsistent statement can be received for the truth of the matter stated as well as to impeach the witness.[36] In federal court, however, the statement can be received for the truth of the matter asserted only if it was given under penalty of perjury at a trial, hearing, or other proceeding or in a deposition.[37] If the statement was not made under these circumstances, it can be used only to impeach the witness. These and other aspects of inconsistent statements, including the degree of inconsistency required, are discussed in §§ 8.02–8.04.

The failure to report exculpatory information to the authorities. In People v. Tauber[38] the accused was prosecuted for disobeying a protective order requiring him to stay away from his former girlfriend. The accused called three witnesses who testified that it was the girlfriend who had sought to get together with the accused. On cross-examination the prosecutor was allowed, over objection, to ask the witnesses why they had failed to report their observations to the police prior to the trial. The reviewing court upheld the use of the questions: the witnesses' failure to inform the authorities of the exculpatory information was akin to making statements that were inconsistent with their testimony.[39] The witnesses' failure to contact the authorities is regarded as evidence that their testimony on direct was a recent fabrication. As a foundational matter, however, the prosecution must produce some evidence showing that the

32.   United States v. Havens, 446 U.S. 620, 100 S.Ct. 1912, 64 L.Ed.2d 559 (1980), reh'g denied, 448 U.S. 911, 101 S.Ct. 25, 65 L.Ed.2d 1172 (1980).

33.   People v. Moore, 201 Cal.App.3d 877, 884, 247 Cal.Rptr. 353, 358 (1988).

34.   Michigan v. Harvey, 494 U.S. 344, 354, 110 S.Ct. 1176, 1182, 108 L.Ed.2d 293 (1990).

35.   People v. Brown, 42 Cal.App.4th 461, 474, 49 Cal.Rptr.2d 652, 660 (1996) and cases cited therein.

36.   West's Ann. California Evidence Code § 1235.

37.   Federal Rule of Evidence 801(d)(1)(A).

38.   49 Cal.App.4th 518, 56 Cal.Rptr.2d 656 (1996).

39.   Id. at 524–525, 56 Cal.Rptr.2d at 660.

witnesses were aware before the trial that the information they possessed tended to exculpate the accused.[40]

Prior inconsistent statements and former testimony. Sometimes, a witness who has given helpful information to the police recants when called to testify at the preliminary hearing. A witness, for example, who tells the police that the accused was the assailant may claim at the preliminary hearing that she did not see the assailant. Under those circumstances, the prosecution may call to the stand the officer who took the statement to repeat the witness's statement. In California, the statement can be received to impeach the witness and, more importantly, to prove that the accused was the assailant.[41]

If the witness then fails to appear at the trial, may the prosecution offer the witness's and the officer's preliminary hearing testimony as former testimony?[42] If at the preliminary hearing the witness had identified the accused as her assailant, then that portion of her testimony would be admissible against the accused at the trial under the former testimony exception to the hearsay rule. But where, as in the example, the witness recants her out of court identification at the preliminary hearing, then her out of court statement to the officer will not be admissible for the truth at the trial in the absence of a hearsay exception for that statement.[43] Since the witness does not appear at the trial, the use of the hearsay exception for prior inconsistent statements is problematical. Under §§ 770 and 1235, a prior inconsistent statement may be offered for the truth only if the witness is afforded an opportunity to explain or deny the statement before the close of the evidence.[44] A hearsay declarant who does not appear at the trial is not afforded such an opportunity.[45] To help solve this problem, § 1294 of the Evidence Code allows the prosecution at the trial to offer the witness's statement to the officer for the truth of the matter asserted after offering the witness's recantation at the preliminary hearing.[46]

At the trial, the prosecution is limited to proving the witness's former testimony by videotape or transcript. If at the preliminary hearing the inconsistent statement was offered through a videotape taken by the police, then the prosecution may offer the videotape at the trial. If the statement was offered through the testimony of the officer who took the

---

40. Id.

41. See § 8.02 supra.

42. For a discussion of the admissibility of former testimony, see § 11.01 supra.

43. A hearsay declarant may be impeached with a statement made by the declarant that is inconsistent with the hearsay declaration received in evidence. West's Ann. California Evidence Code § 1202. However, unless the declaration falls within an exception, it may not be received for the truth of the matter stated. For a discussion of this point, see § 15.13 infra.

44. West's Ann. California Evidence Code §§ 770 and 1235. Multiple hearsay is admissible if each hearsay statement meets the requirements of an exception to the hearsay rule. West's Ann. California Evidence Code § 1201. This rule is unavailable because the inconsistent statement does not meet the requirements of the exception for inconsistent statements.

45. To satisfy the inconsistency requirement of the exception, the prosecution first would have to offer that portion of the witness's preliminary hearing testimony at which the witness denied having seen the assailant.

46. West's Ann. California Evidence Code § 1294.

statement, then the prosecution may offer that portion of the transcript of the preliminary hearing containing the statement.[47]

The accused may object to the introduction of the inconsistent statement on the grounds that the statement to the officer was not properly received at the preliminary hearing as a prior inconsistent statement, or that the videotape or transcript does not qualify as former testimony.[48] If the statement is received at the trial, the accused retains the right to call and cross-examine the witnesses who testified about the witness's prior inconsistent statement.[49]

QUESTIONS AND PROBLEMS

1.   In California and federal courts, prior inconsistent statements are always admissible to impeach a witness as well as for the truth asserted in such statements. True or false?

2.   Because of considerations of fairness as well as logic, the Code and the Rules require that a party confront a witness with his prior inconsistent statements before offering extrinsic evidence of such statements. True or false?

3.   In California criminal proceedings why does Proposition 8 threaten to repeal most statutory limits on the use of evidence offered to support or attack the credibility of witnesses?

4.   The defendant is prosecuted for robbery. At the preliminary hearing, the prosecution called W who testified that she saw the defendant commit the robbery. At the trial, W surprises the prosecution by testifying that she did not see the defendant commit the robbery. In a California or federal prosecution, may the prosecution call the court reporter who was present at the preliminary hearing to testify that he heard W say under oath that she saw the defendant commit the robbery? May the reporter's testimony be received for impeachment as well as for the truth? In answering these questions, assume that W can be recalled to the stand before the close of the evidence at the trial.

5.   The defendant is prosecuted for robbery. At the preliminary hearing, the prosecution called W to testify that she saw the defendant commit the robbery. However, W surprised the prosecution by testifying that she did not see the defendant commit the robbery. W also denied that she told a police officer prior to the hearing that she had seen the defendant commit the robbery. In a California or federal prosecution, may the prosecution call a police officer who interviewed W prior to the preliminary hearing to testify that he heard W say that she saw the defendant commit the robbery? If so, may the officer's testimony be received for impeachment as well as for the truth? In answering these questions, assume that W can be recalled to the stand before the close of the evidence at the preliminary hearing.

---

47. Id.

48. Id.

49. Id.

6. The defendant is prosecuted for robbery in a California state court. At the preliminary hearing, the prosecution called W to testify that she saw the defendant commit the robbery. However, W surprised the prosecution by testifying that she did not see the defendant commit the robbery. W also denied that she told a police officer prior to the hearing that she had seen the defendant commit the robbery, so the judge allowed the prosecution to call the police officer who interviewed W to testify that he heard W say that she saw the defendant commit the robbery. The defendant was held to answer. At the trial on the robbery charge, W was unavailable to testify, so the prosecution offers W's testimony and the officer's testimony on direct at the preliminary hearing as former testimony. The defendant objects on the ground that the officer's testimony may not be received for the truth of the matter stated as a prior inconsistent statement. Because W is unavailable, the defendant claims that he would be deprived of the opportunity to have W explain or deny making the statement to the officer. How should the judge rule?

§ 15.04 SUPPORTING CREDIBILITY WITH PRIOR CONSISTENT STATEMENTS

Section 791 allows a party to support the credibility of a witness with statements by the witness that are consistent with the witness's testimony if one of two conditions is satisfied.[1] First, if the witness was impeached with a prior inconsistent statement, the witness can be rehabilitated with a consistent statement, if the statement was made before the alleged inconsistent statement.[2] Second, where the witness has been expressly or impliedly charged with fabricating his testimony or allowing bias or other improper motive to shape his testimony, the witness can be rehabilitated with a prior consistent statement if the statement was made before the motive to fabricate or other improper motive is alleged to have arisen.[3]

Establishing that the improper motive arose after the declarant made the consistent statement is crucial to admissibility. In making this determination, the trial judge should be guided by the time when the opponent claims the improper motive arose.[4] In People v. Andrews[5] the accused cross examined the chief prosecution witness extensively about a "deal" the witness made with the prosecution in exchange for his testimony.[6] Since the cross-examination suggested that the witness harbored a motive to testify falsely as a result of the plea bargain, the prosecution was entitled to rehabilitate the witness through a statement which was consistent with his testimony and which the witness had made to the police prior to entering into the plea bargain.[7] When the impeaching party

---

1. West's Ann. California Evidence Code § 791.

2. West's Ann. California Evidence Code § 791(a).

3. West's Ann. California Evidence Code § 791(b).

4. People v. Noguera, 4 Cal.4th 599, 629, 15 Cal.Rptr.2d 400, 416, 842 P.2d 1160, 1176 (1992).

5. 49 Cal.3d 200, 260 Cal.Rptr. 583, 776 P.2d 285 (1989), cert. denied, 494 U.S. 1060, 110 S.Ct. 1536, 108 L.Ed.2d 775 (1990).

6. Id. at 209–212, 260 Cal.Rptr. at 588–589, 776 P.2d at 289–291.

7. Id. Accord: People v. Hillhouse, 27 Cal.4th 469, 491–492, 117 Cal.Rptr.2d 45, 62, 40 P.3d 754, 769 (2002), cert. denied, 537 U.S. 1114, 123 S.Ct. 869, 154 L.Ed.2d 789 (2003); People v.

suggests that a witness had more than one motive for fabricating his testimony, the witness may be rehabilitated by any consistent statement that was made before any one of the improper motives arose.[8]

In determining whether the prior consistent statement antedated the improper motive, the judge should bear in mind that the determination calls for the application of a sufficiency standard. The proponent needs to show only that a reasonable fact finder could find that the consistent statement was made before the improper motive arose.[9] Since a sufficiency test governs the question, the judge should allow the jury to hear the consistent statement if the judge concludes that reasonable jurors could find the statement was made before the improper motive arose if the proponent's evidence is believed.[10]

The rules allowing the use of statements that are consistent with a witness's testimony presuppose that the witness to be rehabilitated appeared and testified at the trial. A declarant, however, does need to appear at a trial in order to serve as witness. A witness may appear as a "hearsay declarant" whenever his out of court declarations are offered under a hearsay exception. In the case of exceptions that do not require the production of the hearsay declarant, the declarant in fact serves as "witness" even though he never sets foot in the courtroom. The jurors, after all, are entitled to consider his hearsay declaration for the truth of the matters asserted.

Not surprisingly, both the Code and the Rules allow parties to impeach hearsay declarants in the same manner as if the declarants had appeared and testified at the hearing.[11] This allows the party opposing the hearsay declaration to offer any of the declarant's out of court statements that are inconsistent with the hearsay declaration.[12] If such impeachment occurs, then in California the party offering the hearsay declaration is entitled to rehabilitate the hearsay declarant by any of the declarant's out of court statements that are consistent with the hearsay declaration and that predate the inconsistent statements.[13]

Gurule, 28 Cal.4th 557, 620, 123 Cal.Rptr.2d 345, 397, 51 P.3d 224, 267 (2002), cert. denied, 538 U.S. 964, 123 S.Ct. 1754, 155 L.Ed.2d 517 (2003); People v. Kennedy, 36 Cal.4th 595, 616, 31 Cal.Rptr.3d 160, 181, 115 P.3d 472, 489, cert. denied, 547 U.S. 1076, 126 S.Ct. 1781, 164 L.Ed.2d 527 (2006).

8. People v. Noguera, 4 Cal.4th 599, 629, 15 Cal.Rptr.2d 400, 416, 842 P.2d 1160, 1176 (1992). Accord: People v. Hillhouse, 27 Cal.4th 469, 491, 117 Cal.Rptr.2d 45, 62, 40 P.3d 754, 769 (2002), cert. denied, 537 U.S. 1114, 123 S.Ct. 869, 154 L.Ed.2d 789 (2003).

9. West's Ann. California Evidence Code § 403 (comment).

10. Upon request, the judge should instruct the jury to disregard the consistent statement unless the jurors first find that the statement was made before the improper motive arose. West's Ann. California Evidence Code § 403(c)(1).

11. See § 15.13 infra.

12. Id.

13. In federal court the party offering the hearsay declaration can rehabilitate with a prior consistent statement only if offered to rebut an express or implied charge of recent fabrication or improper motive and the consistent statement antedates the improper influence. See Federal Rule of Evidence 801(d)(1)(B).

Alibi evidence. Not all out of court statements offered at a trial are offered for the truth. For example, the prosecution may offer the accused's alibi in the state's case-in-chief, not for the truth of the matter stated—such a use would exonerate the accused—but as evidence of the accused's consciousness of guilt whenever the prosecution can establish the falsity of the alibi. Where the accused does not take the stand, the California courts take the position that the accused is not entitled to offer evidence of other statements that are consistent with the alibi offered by the prosecution. People v. Hitchings[14] is illustrative. The accused was prosecuted for murder. At his first trial he testified that he did not believe that he murdered the victims because he had no recollection of entering their home. His convictions were subsequently overturned on appeal, and at his second trial the prosecution offered his testimony from the first trial as proof of consciousness guilt because of the implausibility of his claim. The accused then sought to offer a more detailed statement he had made to his girlfriend after his arrest explaining why he had no recollection of the killings. The reviewing court upheld the trial judge's exclusion of the statement. It did not qualify as a prior consistent statement because the accused had not appeared as a witness in the second trial. He did not take the stand; nor did he appear as a hearsay witness, because his testimony at the first trial was not offered at the second trial for the truth of the matters stated.[15]

Prior consistent statements and Proposition 8. As has been discussed, a literal interpretation of the Right to Truth–in–Evidence provision of Proposition 8 repeals almost all statutory barriers and limitations on the use of relevant evidence in criminal cases.[16] Evidence that a witness has made statements that are consistent with his testimony is as probative of the witness's credibility as is evidence that the witness has made statements that are inconsistent with his testimony. A witness's credibility, after all, becomes an issue the moment the witness takes the stand. Accordingly, a literal application of Proposition 8 would repeal

---

14. 59 Cal.App.4th 915, 69 Cal.Rptr.2d 484 (1997).

15. Id. at 921, 69 Cal.Rptr.2d at 488. In support of its holding, the reviewing court cited People v. Williams, 16 Cal.3d 663, 128 Cal.Rptr. 888, 547 P.2d 1000 (1976). In *Williams* a witness told a police officer that the accused had committed a robbery. At the preliminary hearing, the witness denied making the statement, and the police officer was permitted to report the witness's statement for the truth as well as to impeach the witness. At the trial the witness was declared unavailable, and the prosecution was allowed to offer the witness's testimony at the preliminary hearing as former testimony. The prosecution then had the police officer report the witness's out of court statement. The California Supreme Court held that receiving the officer's testimony was error because the prosecution was not entitled to impeach a witness who had not testified at the trial. Id. at 669, 128 Cal.Rptr. at 892, 547 P.2d at 1004. In *Williams* the declarant did not testify at the second trial as a live witness or as a hearsay declarant. As in *Hitchings*, he did not appear as a hearsay declarant because his out of court statement (what he said under oath at the preliminary hearing) was not offered to prove the truth of the matters stated.

West's Ann. California Evidence Code § 1294 now permits the prosecution to offer as former testimony a transcript or video tape of the portion of the preliminary hearing containing the witness's and the police officer's testimony. For an extended discussion of § 1294, see § 15.03 supra.

16. For an extended discussion of the effect of Proposition 8 on the rules governing credibility, see § 15.03 supra.

§ 791 and permit parties in criminal proceedings to offer prior consistent statements to support the witness's credibility even though the witness's credibility has not been attacked.

Under Proposition 8, a judge can still exclude relevant evidence under § 352 if its probative value is substantially outweighed by such concerns as waste of time.[17] A judge could thus find that the probative value of prior consistent statements that fail to satisfy the conditions of § 791 is so slight as not to justify the time needed to receive them. Whether a judge will use § 352 to exclude such statements in a given trial cannot be known. The judge's decision may well depend on her assessment of the need for the evidence and the time required to receive it. The point, though, is that the certainty provided by § 791 may now have been replaced by the necessarily imprecise standards of § 352. To be sure, neither the California Supreme Court nor the Court of Appeal has decided whether Proposition 8 repeals § 791, and cases decided since the adoption of the initiative in June 1982 assume the continuing validity of the section.[18]

Prior consistent statements and the hearsay rule. Prior consistent statements that are admissible under § 791 may also be received for the truth of the matter stated under § 1236.[19]

Prior consistent statements under the Federal Rules. Under the Federal Rules, prior consistent statements may also be received for the truth of the matter asserted.[20] A major difference between the Code and the Rules is that under the Rules a prior consistent statement may be received only to rebut an express or implied charge of recent fabrication or improper influence.[21] The Rules do not contain a provision equivalent to § 791(a) which permits the use of a prior consistent statement to rehabilitate a witness if the witness has been impeached by a prior inconsistent statement and the consistent statement was made before the inconsistent one. But an argument can be made that the Rules should permit such rehabilitation: offering a prior inconsistent statement necessarily implies that the witness has fabricated his testimony since the time he made the inconsistent statement.[22]

---

17. For an extended discussion of judicial discretion to exclude relevant evidence under § 352 after Proposition 8, see § 2.11 supra.

18. See, e.g., People v. Hayes, 52 Cal.3d 577, 609, 276 Cal.Rptr. 874, 892, 802 P.2d 376, 394 (1990), cert. denied, 502 U.S. 958, 112 S.Ct. 420, 116 L.Ed.2d 440 (1991); People v. Frank, 51 Cal.3d 718, 733, 274 Cal.Rptr. 372, 381, 798 P.2d 1215, 1224 (1990), cert. denied, 501 U.S. 1213, 111 S.Ct. 2816, 115 L.Ed.2d 988 (1991), reh'g denied, 501 U.S. 1270, 112 S.Ct. 15, 115 L.Ed.2d 1099 (1991); People v. Andrews, 49 Cal.3d 200, 209–212, 260 Cal.Rptr. 583, 588–589, 776 P.2d 285, 289–291 (1989), cert. denied, 494 U.S. 1060, 110 S.Ct. 1536, 108 L.Ed.2d 775 (1990).

19. West's Ann. California Evidence Code § 1236. For an extended discussion of prior consistent statements as an exception to the hearsay rule, see § 8.05 supra.

20. Federal Rule of Evidence 801(d)(1)(B). For an extended discussion of the hearsay aspects of prior consistent statements under the Federal Rules, see § 8.06 supra.

21. Federal Rule of Evidence 801(d)(1)(B).

22. West's Ann. California Evidence Code § 791 (comment).

Another difference between the Code and the Rules is that the Code makes it clear that, if offered to rebut an express or implied charge of recent fabrication or improper motive, the prior consistent statement can be received only if it was made before the improper motive arose. The Federal Rules are not explicit in this respect. The United States Supreme Court, however, has interpreted the federal rule as requiring the rehabilitating party to show that the declarant made the consistent statement before the alleged fabrication or improper motive arose.[23]

QUESTIONS AND PROBLEMS

Determine the admissibility of the following evidence in a personal injury case tried in a California or federal court:

> Plaintiff's Counsel: What happened on June 1?
>
> Plaintiff: I got hurt while jumping out of my burning truck.
>
> * * *
>
> Defense Counsel: But on August 1, you told your mother that you didn't get hurt?
>
> Plaintiff: But only because I didn't want to worry her.
>
> * * *
>
> Plaintiff's Counsel: Did you see your doctor on July 1?
>
> Plaintiff: Yes.
>
> Plaintiff's Counsel: What did you tell her?
>
> Plaintiff: I said, "Doctor, I got hurt while jumping out of my burning truck."
>
> Defense Counsel: Objection. Move to strike as improper rehabilitation. Also as hearsay.
>
> Judge: ?

Compare with:

> Plaintiff's Counsel: What happened on June 1?
>
> Plaintiff: I got hurt while jumping out of my burning truck.
>
> * * *
>
> Defense Counsel: You saw your boss later on that day?
>
> Plaintiff: Yes.
>
> Defense Counsel: But you didn't tell him that you had gotten hurt jumping out of your burning truck?
>
> Plaintiff: I did not tell him.
>
> Defense Counsel: The next day, on June 2, you had your annual company physical?
>
> Plaintiff: Yes.

---

23. Tome v. United States, 513 U.S. 150, 159–160, 115 S.Ct. 696, 702–703, 130 L.Ed.2d 574 (1995). See also § 8.06 supra.

Defense Counsel: But you didn't tell the doctor that you had gotten hurt jumping out of the truck?

Plaintiff: I did not tell him.

* * *

Plaintiff's Counsel: Before you saw your boss on June 1, did you call your wife?

Plaintiff: Yes.

Plaintiff's Counsel: What did you tell her?

Plaintiff: That I had gotten hurt while jumping out of my burning truck.

Defense Counsel: Objection. Move to strike as improper rehabilitation and hearsay.

Judge: ?

* * *

Plaintiff's Counsel: Did your husband call you on June 1?

Plaintiff's Wife: Yes.

Plaintiff's Counsel: What did he say?

Plaintiff's Wife: He said, "Honey, guess what? I got hurt while jumping out of my burning truck."

Defense Counsel: Objection. Improper rehabilitation and also hearsay.

Judge: ?

Compare with:

District Attorney: What did you see the defendant do?

Witness: Take a book from the Bookstore and leave without paying for it.

* * *

Defense Counsel: You were charged with helping the defendant steal the book from the Bookstore?

Witness: Yes.

Defense Counsel: And you offered to testify against my client if the District Attorney dropped the charges against you?

Witness: Yes.

Defense Counsel: And the District Attorney told you that he would drop the charges against you after you testified against my client?

Witness: Yes.

* * *

District Attorney: Prior to agreeing to testify against the defendant, did you tell anyone what you saw the defendant do at the Bookstore?

Witness: Yes, I told my best friend, "I saw the defendant take a book from the Bookstore and leave without paying for it."

Defense Counsel: Objection. Improper rehabilitation.

Judge: ?

§ 15.05   IMPEACHMENT BY CONTRADICTION

A witness may be impeached by evidence of the nonexistence of any fact testified to by the witness.[1] Known as impeachment by contradiction, this form of attack should be distinguished from impeachment by self-contradiction. The latter refers to impeachment by the witness's own inconsistent statements. For example, if a witness testifies that the light facing him was red, he can be impeached by his previous statements in which he claimed that the light was green. Even if the witness has not expressed a conflicting statement about the color of the light, he can still be impeached or contradicted by the testimony of other witnesses who, facing the same light, claim that it was green.[2]

The major problem facing trial judges is the degree to which they should permit parties to impeach witnesses through contradiction. Permitting parties to refute any and all assertions made by witnesses could consume too much time and risk confusing the jury about the issues to be decided. Accordingly, judges can use their discretionary power to exclude evidence of contradiction that is only marginally probative of a witness's lack of credibility.

At Common Law, judges could invoke the collateral evidence rule to limit evidence of contradiction. Under this rule, evidence attacking the credibility of a witness had to be excluded unless it was independently probative of the issues being tried.[3] The rule was especially useful in determining the admissibility of evidence to contradict statements made by a witness on cross-examination. People v. Lavergne[4] illustrates how courts applied the rule.

Lavergne was tried for robbery. A key witness for the prosecution testified on direct that the accused and the witness had used the witness's car in the robbery. In response to a question on cross-examination, the witness testified that the car, a 1968 Cadillac, was his. The accused then sought to impeach the witness by calling the car's owner to testify that the Cadillac was his and had been stolen shortly before the robbery. The collateral evidence rule called for the judge to consider the relevance of the

---

1. West's Ann. California Evidence Code § 780(i).

2. See, e.g., People v. Barnett, 17 Cal.4th 1044, 1129–1131, 74 Cal.Rptr.2d 121, 175–176, 954 P.2d 384, 439–440 (1998) where a murder defendant claimed that he left town to avoid the real killer, who he claimed had killed the victim to avenge the theft of methamphetamine oil by the defendant and the victim; to disprove the defendant's claim, the prosecution was entitled to offer evidence showing that the reason the defendant left town was to avoid the police who were seeking the defendant after he escaped from custody.

3. West's Ann. California Evidence Code § 780 (comment).

4. 4 Cal.3d 735, 94 Cal.Rptr. 405, 484 P.2d 77 (1971).

impeaching evidence without taking the answer on cross-examination into account. Since the car owner's testimony that the Cadillac was his and had been stolen would not have thrown any light on the identity of the robber, the rule called for the exclusion of the evidence. The impeaching evidence was inadmissible because it was directed at a "collateral" matter rather than at the issues being tried.

Neither the California Evidence Code nor the Federal Rules retains the collateral evidence rule as a distinct principle. Instead, the rule has been subsumed by the discretionary power given to judges to exclude relevant evidence whenever its probative value is substantially outweighed by such trial concerns as waste of time and confusion of issues.[5] Today, judges can exclude evidence of a collateral nature if they conclude that its impeaching effect is significantly outweighed by the costs of its admission. Thus, in ruling on the admissibility of evidence offered in *Lavergne*, the judge would have to weigh the value of the evidence on the witness's lack of veracity against the risk that a prosecution for robbery might be transformed into one for car theft.[6]

Impeachment by contradiction and the accused. Where the witness to be impeached by evidence of contradiction is the accused, a danger exists that jurors might misuse the impeaching evidence as bad character evidence. Under the Code, character evidence generally is inadmissible to prove the accused's guilt of the offense charged.[7] In a prosecution for defrauding an innkeeper, for example, evidence that the accused defrauded other innkeepers is inadmissible to prove that the accused is guilty of the offense because he is the kind of person who would defraud the victim. But if the accused takes the stand and on direct examination denies ever engaging in such misconduct, the prosecution may attempt to impeach the accused by evidence that he defrauded other innkeepers.[8]

Whether the judge allows the jurors to hear the impeaching evidence depends on how the judge weighs the probative value of the evidence against its prejudicial effects. Among the prejudicial effects would be the risk that the jurors would disregard the instruction limiting their consideration of the evidence to its impeachment value. Other concerns would be the time required and confusion that might result if one trial on one charge of defrauding a single innkeeper were transformed into multiple trials of defrauding a number of innkeepers.

---

5. West's Ann.California Evidence Code § 352; Federal Rule of Evidence 403.

6. In approving the exclusion of the evidence, the Lavergne court noted that evidence that the witness had stolen the car is the kind of specific bad act evidence barred by § 787 when offered to prove a character trait to impeach a witness's credibility. But today Proposition 8 authorizes the use of such evidence in criminal cases. See § 15.06 infra. Accordingly, whether the Lavergne evidence of contradiction should now be excluded presents a harder call.

7. West's Ann. California Evidence Code § 1101(a); Federal Rule of Evidence 404(a).

8. People v. Westek, 31 Cal.2d 469, 475–476, 190 P.2d 9, 13 (1948). See also People v. Coffman, 34 Cal.4th 1, 72, 96 P.3d 30, 86, 17 Cal.Rptr.3d 710 (2004), cert. denied, 544 U.S. 1063, 125 S.Ct. 2517, 161 L.Ed.2d 1114 (2005) (holding that where the accused, who was on trial for murder, took the stand and denied killing not only the victim but "anyone else," the prosecutor, in cross examining the accused, was entitled to ask questions regarding the accused's possible murder of another victim). Id. at 72, 96 P.3d at 86, 17 Cal.Rptr.3d 710 at 777.

After the enactment of Proposition 8, concerns were raised about the judge's role in assessing the admissibility of the impeaching evidence. Under the Right to Truth–in–Evidence provision, parties to a criminal proceeding have the state constitutional right not to have relevant evidence excluded.[9] Character evidence is relevant because it is believed to be probative of conduct. Accordingly, evidence that the accused defrauded other innkeepers on other occasions would be admissible: it helps prove that the accused defrauded the victim in question because he is the kind of person who defrauds innkeepers. A literal application of Proposition 8 would thus require the judge to admit the evidence for the purpose of establishing guilt as well as for impeachment, unless the judge concludes that its probative value is substantially outweighed by its prejudicial effects under § 352.

The concerns raised by Proposition 8 were dispelled in part by the California Supreme Court's *Ewoldt* decision. In *Ewoldt*[10] the court held that by amending Evidence Code § 1101(b) by the super majority required for amendments to the initiative, the California Legislature reenacted the section—including § 1101(a)—in its entirety.[11] Section 1101(a) bans the use of evidence of a person's character for the purpose of proving conduct in conformity with that character.[12] Thus, after *Ewoldt* the role of the judge is to determine only whether the probative value of the contradicting evidence on the accused's credibility substantially outweighs the risk that the jurors might be unable to limit their consideration of the evidence to its impeachment value. This is also the role of the federal judge, since there is no federal equivalent of Proposition 8.[13]

QUESTIONS AND PROBLEMS

1. In a prosecution for driving while under the influence of an intoxicating liquor, the accused testifies that he never drives after taking more than two drinks. Over a character evidence objection, it is proper for impeachment purposes for the prosecution to call a witness to testify that the previous year she saw the defendant take three drinks and then drive. True or false?

2. Assume that the judge overrules the objection. What arguments should the accused make to convince the judge to exclude the evidence under the judge's discretionary power to exclude otherwise admissible evidence?

3. Both the Code and the Rules expressly adopt the collateral evidence rule. True or false?

---

9. For an extended discussion of this provision, see § 15.03 supra.

10. People v. Ewoldt, 7 Cal.4th 380, 27 Cal.Rptr.2d 646, 867 P.2d 757 (1994).

11. Id. at 391, 27 Cal.Rptr.2d at 652, 867 P.2d at 762.

12. West's Ann. California Evidence Code § 1101(a).

13. Note, however, that after Proposition 8 the evidence that the accused defrauded other innkeepers would be admissible as prior bad acts to prove his character for lack of veracity. See § 15.06 infra. In making the § 352 ruling, the judge would have to weigh the probative value of the evidence on this proposition against the risk that the jurors might not be able to abide by a limiting instruction telling them not to consider the evidence as proof of the accused's propensity to commit the fraud charged.

§ 15.06   IMPEACHMENT BY CHARACTER OF THE WITNESS—PRIOR BAD ACTS

The Common Law allowed the cross examiner to impeach a witness by inquiring into acts of misconduct by the witness that were not the subject of a conviction.[1] An example would be asking the witness if he cheated on his latest income tax returns. The theory of impeachment is that jurors ought to question the veracity of witnesses who engage in "bad acts." The bad acts doctrine is based on a character theory of impeachment. The misdeeds are offered as evidence of the witness's predisposition to be untruthful under oath.

The Code rejects the prior bad acts doctrine.[2] Other than felony convictions, § 787 prohibits the use of specific instances of a witness's conduct to prove a character trait to attack (or support) the credibility of the witness.[3] In civil proceedings, the Code's ban on the use of prior bad acts continues in effect.

In criminal cases, however, Proposition 8 repeals § 787.[4] The Right to Truth–in–Evidence provision gives parties to criminal proceedings the state constitutional right not to have relevant evidence excluded.[5] Evidence that a witness has cheated on his income tax returns is probative of the witness's character for lack of veracity. The proposition that the witness is the kind of person who will not tell the truth under oath is rendered more likely by evidence that he lies on his income tax returns than the proposition would be without the evidence.[6] Accordingly, under Proposition 8 such evidence is admissible in criminal cases unless excluded by the judge under § 352. Misconduct that has been held to be probative of a witness's character for lack of veracity includes possessing drugs for sale,[7] brandishing a weapon while verbally threatening the victim,[8] engaging in acts of prostitution,[9] and making death threats.[10] These forms of

---

1. C. McCormick, Handbook of the Law of Evidence § 42 (E. Cleary 2d ed. 1972).

2. Even before the Evidence Code was adopted, California did not recognize the prior bad acts doctrine. See West's Ann. California C.C.P. § 2051 (repealed 1967), which excluded evidence of particular acts.

3. West's Ann. California Evidence Code § 787. Accordingly, evidence that a witness entered the U.S. illegally is inadmissible to prove his or her predisposition to lie under oath. See Hernandez v. Paicius, 109 Cal.App.4th 452, 460, 134 Cal.Rptr.2d 756, 761 (2003).

4. People v. Harris, 47 Cal.3d 1047, 1080–1083, 255 Cal.Rptr. 352, 373–374, 767 P.2d 619, 639–641 (1989); see also People v. Adams, 198 Cal.App.3d 10, 17, 243 Cal.Rptr. 580, 584 (1988) (Under Proposition 8 the accused was entitled to offer evidence that the complaining witness in a rape case had falsely accused others of rape.).

5. For an extended discussion of the impact of Proposition 8 on the limitations on evidence bearing on credibility, see § 15.03 supra.

6. For an extended discussion of the meaning of relevance, see § 2.01 supra.

7. People v. Harris, 37 Cal.4th 310, 365, 33 Cal.Rptr.3d 509, 532, 118 P.3d 545, 565 (2005).

8. People v. Lepolo, 55 Cal.App.4th 85, 88, 63 Cal.Rptr.2d 735, 737 (1997).

9. People v. Alvarez, 14 Cal.4th 155, 201, note 11, 58 Cal.Rptr.2d 385, 412, note 11, 926 P.2d 365, 392, note 11 (1996).

10. People v. Hill, 34 Cal.App.4th 727, 738, 41 Cal.Rptr.2d 39, 45 (1995) (holding that the accused was entitled to impeach a prosecution witness by evidence that the witness threatened to

misconduct evince "moral turpitude," a "readiness to do evil," which like acts of dishonesty evidence a witness's predisposition to lie under oath.[11]

The Common Law restricted the use of the prior bad acts doctrine by binding the cross examiner to the witness's answer.[12] If the witness, for example, denied having cheated on his taxes, the cross examiner could not call other witnesses to contradict the witness. Even if IRS witnesses were willing and available to testify, their testimony could not be received over objection. This limitation was designed to prevent the current trial from being converted into one on whether or not the witness engaged in the bad act, here, evasion of taxes.

But testimony by the IRS agents that the witness cheated on his taxes is as probative of the witness's character for lack of veracity as is the witness's admission that he evaded taxes. Under a literal application of Proposition 8, such testimony would be admissible, unless excluded by the trial judge under § 352.[13] Similarly, countervailing evidence that the witness did not cheat on his taxes would likewise be relevant and admissible. Thus, under Proposition 8, unless the judge firmly restricts the use of the prior bad acts doctrine, a lurking danger is that the doctrine will overwhelm the issues to be decided in the current trial. A trial over whether the accused drove while under the influence could become a trial over whether a defense or prosecution witness evaded income taxes.[14]

Under Proposition 8, the prior bad acts doctrine has a flip side. Evidence relevant to the credibility of witnesses includes evidence supporting as well as attacking their veracity. Accordingly, Proposition 8 also introduces a "prior good acts doctrine" which sanctions the use of specific instances of conduct to support the credibility of witnesses. In People v. Harris,[15] for example, the California Supreme Court held that Proposition 8 allowed the prosecution to support the credibility of a witness who had served as an informant by calling an officer who testified that the witness

---

kill a woman who had reported a criminal incident involving the witness's boyfriend to the police). For an extended discussion of the judge's discretion to exclude evidence that is admissible under Proposition 8, see § 2.11 supra.

11. See People v. Alvarez, 14 Cal.4th 155, 201, note 11, 58 Cal.Rptr.2d 385, 412, note 11, 926 P.2d 365, 392, note 11 (1996). See also § 15.07 infra.

12. C. McCormick, Handbook on the Law of Evidence § 42 (E. Cleary 2d ed. 1972).

13. See People v. Hill, 34 Cal.App.4th 727, 738, 41 Cal.Rptr.2d 39, 45 (1995) (allowing the accused to offer extrinsic evidence of the witness's prior bad act after the witness on cross-examination denied committing the act).

14. Id. (holding that although the accused could impeach a prosecution witness with evidence that she threatened to kill a woman who reported a "criminal incident" involving the witness's boyfriend to the police, the accused was not entitled to show that the incident concerned a charge of rape: "Although wide latitude should be given to cross-examination designed to test the credibility of a prosecution witness, the court retains discretion to exclude collateral matters."). Accord: People v. Box, 23 Cal.4th 1153, 1203, 99 Cal.Rptr.2d 69, 105, 5 P.3d 130, 163 (2000), cert. denied, 532 U.S. 963, 121 S.Ct. 1497, 149 L.Ed.2d 383 (2001) (holding that although the accused was entitled to impeach a mental health expert by evidence that the state had filed charges of unprofessional conduct that could result in the revocation of his license, the accused was not entitled to show that the charges stemmed from allegations of sexual misconduct with six patients).

15. 47 Cal.3d 1047, 255 Cal.Rptr. 352, 767 P.2d 619 (1989).

had proved reliable in past cases.[16] Prior to Proposition 8, § 787 would have prohibited the use of the witness's past reliability to prove that the witness should be believed because his behavior in the past made him worthy of belief.[17]

The prior bad acts doctrine under the Federal Rules. The Federal Rules of Evidence introduced the prior bad acts doctrine into federal practice for the first time.[18] The Rules permit the cross examiner to inquire into specific instances of misconduct by the witness that may be probative of the witness's bad character for truthfulness.[19] But to limit the doctrine, the Rules preserve the Common Law restriction binding the examiner to the witness's answer.[20] If the witness denies committing the act, the examiner is prohibited from proving it extrinsically. Moreover, federal judges have the discretionary power to prevent the examiner from inquiring into prior bad acts in the first place if their probative value on the witness's character for lack of veracity is outweighed by the concerns enumerated in Rule 403.[21] This rule, which is the federal equivalent of California Evidence Code § 352, allows a judge to take into account the prejudicial effects of the evidence. Unfair prejudice is likely to be highest when the cross examiner seeks to impeach a criminal defendant with an act of misconduct that is identical or similar to the charges against which the accused is defending.

The Federal Rules permit a party to inquire into specific instances of conduct that may be probative of the witness's good character for truthfulness.[22] The rule is oddly worded in that it limits such inquiry to the cross-examination of the witness.[23] Since it is unlikely that a cross examiner will seek to support the credibility of the witness, the framers may have had redirect, rather than cross-examination, in mind.[24]

QUESTIONS AND PROBLEMS   *(second time)*

1. In a California civil case, a party may impeach a witness by asking the witness if she cheated on law school examinations. True or false?

2. In a California criminal case, a party may impeach a witness by asking the witness if she cheated on law school examinations. True or false?

---

16. Id. at 1080–1083, 255 Cal.Rptr. at 373–374, 767 P.2d at 639–641.

17. West's Ann. California Evidence Code § 787.

18. See Orfield, *Impeachment and Support of Witnesses in Federal Criminal Cases*, 11 University of Kansas Law Review 447, 460–464 (1964) (maintaining that prior to the enactment of the Federal Rules, federal courts barred the use of prior bad acts to impeach witnesses).

19. Federal Rule of Evidence 608(b).

20. Id.

21. Id. (Advisory Committee Note).

22. Federal Rule of Evidence 608(b).

23. Id.

24. See Government of Virgin Islands v. Roldan, 612 F.2d 775, 778, note 2 (3d Cir.1979), cert. denied, 446 U.S. 920, 100 S.Ct. 1857, 64 L.Ed.2d 275 (1980) (holding that the party calling the witness may rehabilitate on redirect where the bad character evidence first surfaced on cross-examination).

3. In a case tried in federal court, a party may impeach a witness by asking the witness on cross-examination if she cheated on law school examinations. True or false?

4. In the federal case, if the witness denies cheating on the examinations, the impeaching party may call the witness's professors to testify that the witness cheated on law school examinations. True or false?

5. In the California criminal case, if the witness denies cheating on the examinations, the impeaching party may call the witness's professors to testify that the witness cheated on law school examinations. True or false?

6. Assume that in the federal case, on cross-examination the witness admits cheating on law school examinations. On redirect examination, the calling party may ask the witness if she reports all of her income on her tax returns. True or false?

7. In a California criminal case, on direct examination a party may support the credibility of the witness by asking if she abided by the Honor Code in taking examinations. True or false?

8. In a case tried in federal court, on direct examination a party may support the credibility of the witness by asking if she abided by the Honor Code in taking examinations. True or false?

9. In a California civil case or a case tried in federal court, a party may support the credibility of the witness in the preceding question by calling the witness's professors to testify that the witness abided by the Honor Code in taking her examinations. True or false?

§ 15.07 IMPEACHMENT BY CHARACTER OF THE WITNESS—CONVICTIONS

California Evidence Code § 788 embodies the Common Law rule that a witness's credibility can be attacked by evidence that the witness has been convicted of a crime.[1] Why witnesses who have been convicted of crimes should not be trusted to testify truthfully is not altogether clear. At Common Law, convicts were disqualified from testifying.[2] When the disability was removed, convicts could testify, but at a price: their convictions could be used to impeach them. Section 788 follows this tradition by allowing a party to impeach a witness by evidence that the witness has been convicted of a felony.[3]

---

1. West's Ann. California Evidence Code § 788. Where the witness to be impeached is the accused, it is immaterial that the conviction offered occurred after the conduct for which the accused is on trial. Since the issue is the accused's veracity as a witness, what matters is that the conviction occur prior to the time the accused takes the stand. People v. Halsey, 21 Cal.App.4th 325, 327, 26 Cal.Rptr.2d 701, 702 (1993). A qualifying conviction can be used to impeach even if sentence has not been imposed at the time the conviction is offered. See People v. Martinez, 62 Cal.App.4th 1454, 1456, 73 Cal.Rptr.2d 358, 359 (1998).

2. Persons convicted of any felony or misdemeanors involving dishonesty or obstruction of justice were incompetent to testify. See C. McCormick, McCormick on Evidence § 42 (4th ed. J. Strong 1992).

3. West's Ann. California Evidence Code § 788. The elimination of other grounds for disqualifying certain person as witnesses also led to the use of those grounds for impeachment once the

The California Evidence Code and the Federal Rules of Evidence justify the use of convictions to impeach witnesses on the basis of a character theory of relevance.[4] They allow the fact finders to consider the misconduct underlying the conviction as evidence of a flaw in the witness's character for truth-telling under oath. So viewed, convictions may be probative of a witness's character for lack of veracity in two circumstances. The first is where the witness committed a crime involving dishonesty or false statement. Most, if not all, legal commentators would agree that convictions based on deceitful misconduct might say something about the witness's predisposition to lie under oath.[5]

Although less plausible, the second circumstance is where the witness committed some other type of crime and the witness was aware that his conduct (1) violated the penal laws or (2) subjected others to harms the penal laws seek to avoid. Where the witness was unaware that he was breaking the law or exposing others to criminal harms, then a conviction for his misconduct would say nothing about his propensity to disregard his legal obligation to testify truthfully. Accordingly, in the absence of evidence that the witness was aware that he was violating the penal laws or subjecting others to the harms proscribed by the penal laws, convictions for negligence or strict liability offenses should be inadmissible to impeach. Only those who consciously break the penal laws can be said to be inclined to disregard their legal obligation to tell the truth under oath; only those who consciously subject others to criminal harms can be said to be inclined to injure others by lying under oath. The Code, however, does not distinguish between convictions predicated on negligence or strict liability and convictions based on a higher mens rea, such as recklessness, knowledge or purpose. Section 788 permits impeachment by any felony conviction.[6]

The flaw in the Code's structure becomes more apparent when another consideration is taken into account. The impeaching party is not allowed to bring out the details of the misconduct giving rise to the conviction.[7] The jurors are to infer from the judgment of conviction (or the witness's admission of the conviction) that the witness engaged in misconduct that is probative of his or her character for lack of veracity. How

---

disqualifications were removed. That a witness may be party or related to a party are now grounds of impeachment rather than disqualification. See § 14.01 supra.

4. West's Ann. California Evidence Code § 788 (Comment); Federal Rule of Evidence 609 (Advisory Committee Note).

5. Social scientists, however, disagree about the value of past misconduct in predicting future misconduct. The belief that "character traits" exert influence over time and across diverse situations has been challenged by some experimental psychologists, most notably Walter Mischel. See W. Mischel, Personality and Assessment 122 (1968). See also § 3.09 supra. Some legal scholars also question the predictive value of past misconduct. When Congress amended the Federal Rules of Evidence to include provisions allowing evidence of the accused's other sexual assaults as proof of the accused's propensity to commit the sexual assault charged, of the more than forty judges, practicing lawyers, and academics asked to review the amendments, only the representatives of the U.S. Department of Justice favored adopting the amendments. See § 3.14 supra.

6. West's Ann. California Evidence Code § 788.

7. People v. Terry, 38 Cal.App.3d 432, 446, 113 Cal.Rptr. 233, 242 (1974).

jurors can do this when the witness has been convicted of felonies based on strict liability or negligence is difficult to fathom.

These difficulties could have been avoided if the California Legislature had adopted the recommendation of Professor James H. Chadbourne who, at the request of the California Law Revision Commission, prepared the study that eventually gave rise to the Evidence Code. Professor Chadbourne recommended a rule that would have limited convictions offered to impeach a witness to those in which an essential element of the crime is dishonesty or false statement.[8] Perjury is a paradigmatic example of a crime involving both false statement and dishonesty. A violation requires proof that a person knowingly stated as true a material matter the person knew to be false.[9] Jurors would have few problems using a conviction of this crime as proof of the witness's predisposition to lie under oath. But in enacting § 788 the legislature rejected Professor Chadbourne's recommendation and instead opted to retain the approach formerly contained in the Code of Civil Procedure. That approach allows a witness to be impeached by any felony conviction.[10]

Section 788, however, does not strip California trial judges of discretion to exclude felony convictions when offered to impeach a witness. Because § 788 merely states that a party "may" show that the witness has been convicted of a felony,[11] the use of the permissive term, as we shall see, has enabled the California appellate courts in civil cases (and criminal cases until the enactment of Proposition 8) to develop rules disfavoring the use of convictions which say little or nothing about a witness's character for lack of veracity.

Section 788 prohibits the use of felony convictions in four circumstances. A felony conviction may not be used to impeach a witness where (1) a pardon based on the witness's innocence has been granted by the jurisdiction in which the witness was convicted, (2) a pardon has been granted on the basis of a certificate of rehabilitation, (3) the conviction has been set aside because the felon has fulfilled the conditions of probation, or (4) the witness has been convicted by another jurisdiction and the witness has been relieved of the penalties and disabilities arising from the conviction pursuant to procedures substantially equivalent to those described in (2) and (3).[12]

If the conviction qualifies for use, the impeaching party may prove it in one of two ways: by asking the witness to admit the conviction or by

---

8. California Law Revision Commission, Tentative Recommendation and A Study Relating To The Uniform Rules of Evidence, Article IV. Witnesses, at 715 (March 1964).

9. West's Ann. California Penal Code § 118.

10. California Law Revision Commission, Tentative Recommendation and A Study Relating To The Uniform Rules of Evidence, Article IV. Witnesses, at 716 (March 1964).

11. West's Ann. California Evidence Code § 788.

12. Id. A felony conviction does not need to be "final" to be used to impeach a witness. A verdict of guilty will suffice even if sentence has not been pronounced. People v. Martinez, 62 Cal.App.4th 1454, 1456, 73 Cal.Rptr.2d 358, 359 (1998). Moreover, the fact that the sentencing judge is authorized to reduce a felony conviction to a misdemeanor conviction at sentencing does not bar the use of the verdict to impeach until such time as the sentencing judge reduces the conviction to a misdemeanor. Id.

offering the record of the judgment of conviction.[13] If the impeaching party uses the record, the party must satisfy the requirements of authentication[14] and the Secondary Evidence Rule.[15] The party, however, can ignore the requirements either of the business or official records exceptions to the hearsay rule. Section 788 itself creates a hearsay exception for the record and allows the record to be used as proof that the witness engaged in the misconduct giving rise to the conviction.[16]

If the impeaching party seeks to prove the conviction through the witness, two limitations apply. First, the impeaching party may not ask about the conviction unless the party believes in good faith that the witness has been convicted of a felony.[17] Good faith can be demonstrated by possessing a copy of the judgment or other documentary evidence of the conviction.[18] Second, as has been noted, the party may not elicit the details that gave rise to the offense.[19] The impeaching party is limited to bringing out the nature and date of the offense and the convicting court.[20] The object is to impeach the witness, not to retry the case.[21]

Convictions that are constitutionally invalid may not be used to impeach a witness.[22] A party who challenges the validity of a conviction on constitutional grounds is entitled to a hearing outside the presence of the jury.[23] At the hearing, the impeaching party must come forward with evidence, as well as persuade the judge, of the constitutionality of the conviction.[24]

People v. Beagle and § 788. Beginning with People v. Beagle,[25] the California Supreme Court sought to limit impeachment to those felonies that tell the fact finder something about the witness's character for lack of veracity. *Beagle*, however, has had a curious history. Although widely heralded as imposing needed limitations on § 788, it was virtually overturned by Proposition 8 in criminal cases. This initiative amended the state constitution to provide that "[a]ny felony conviction of any person

---

13. Id.

14. For a discussion of the requirements of authentication, see § 13.01 supra.

15. For a discussion of the requirements of the Best Evidence Rule, see § 13.06 supra.

16. West's Ann. California Evidence Code § 788 (comment). Section 788 also creates a hearsay exception for the witness's admission of the conviction as proof that the witness engaged in the conduct giving rise to the conviction. Id.

17. People v. Perez, 58 Cal.2d 229, 239, 23 Cal.Rptr. 569, 574, 373 P.2d 617, 622 (1962).

18. Id.

19. People v. Terry, 38 Cal.App.3d 432, 446, 113 Cal.Rptr. 233, 242 (1974).

20. Id.

21. People v. Malloy, 41 Cal.App.3d 944, 952, 116 Cal.Rptr. 592, 596 (1974). Note should be taken that under the Code a party may not impeach a witness by proof of "bad acts" that are probative of a propensity to lie under oath. Consequently, in a California civil case, a party may not ask a witness whether the witness has lied under oath for the purpose of establishing the witness's bad character for veracity. For a discussion of the prior bad acts doctrine, see § 15.06 supra.

22. People v. Coffey, 67 Cal.2d 204, 218, 60 Cal.Rptr. 457, 466, 430 P.2d 15, 24 (1967).

23. Id. at 217, 60 Cal.Rptr. at 466, 430 P.2d at 24.

24. Id.

25. 6 Cal.3d 441, 99 Cal.Rptr. 313, 492 P.2d 1 (1972).

* * * shall subsequently be used without limitation for purposes of impeachment * * * in any criminal proceeding."[26]

This mandate notwithstanding, the *Beagle* limitations warrant examination for two reasons. First, despite the initiative's unequivocal language, the California Supreme Court has construed Proposition 8 as allowing trial judges to use the *Beagle* limitations as guidelines in determining the admissibility of felony convictions in criminal cases.[27] Second, Proposition 8 does not affect civil proceedings; accordingly, those aspects of *Beagle* that apply to witnesses in civil cases have survived the initiative.

In *Beagle*, the court held that felony convictions admissible under § 788 to impeach a witness could nonetheless be excluded under § 352 "when the probative value of such evidence is substantially outweighed by the risk of undue prejudice."[28] The court identified five circumstances when the risk of undue prejudice outweighs the probative value of the conviction. First, when the conviction has little or no direct bearing on the witness's lack of veracity, it should be excluded.[29] As a rule, the court held that only convictions involving dishonesty are probative of a witness's lack of veracity.[30] Second, even when the conviction involves dishonesty, the conviction should be excluded if it is remote in time and the witness has led a blameless life since the conviction.[31] Third, even when the conviction involves dishonesty, the conviction should be excluded if it is for conduct identical or substantially similar to that for which the witness is on trial.[32] Fourth, where the witness has many convictions, the convictions should be excluded even when they involve dishonesty and are dissimilar to the conduct for which the witness is on trial because of the prejudice inherent in their numbers.[33] Finally, even when the conviction involves dishonesty and is dissimilar to the conduct for which the witness is on trial, it should be excluded when its introduction would deter the witness from taking the stand, and the judge concludes that it is more important to let the jury have the benefit of the witness's testimony than to have the witness remain silent.[34]

In People v. Woodard[35] the California Supreme Court made it clear that *Beagle* applied to all witnesses, not just the accused, and in all trials, not just criminal cases. Applying *Beagle* to civil cases encourages the

---

26. West's Ann. California Constitution Article I, § 28(f)(4).

27. People v. Clair, 2 Cal.4th 629, 655, 7 Cal.Rptr.2d 564, 578, 828 P.2d 705, 719 (1992), cert. denied, 506 U.S. 1063, 113 S.Ct. 1006, 122 L.Ed.2d 155 (1993). As result of *Clair*'s mandate, appellate courts routinely hold that trial judges should apply the *Beagle* limitations in determining the admissibility of prior convictions to impeach witnesses. See, e.g., People v. Whitworth, 67 Cal.App.4th 516, 522, 79 Cal.Rptr.2d 106, 109–110 (1998).

28. People v. Beagle, 6 Cal.3d 441, 447, 99 Cal.Rptr. 313, 316, 492 P.2d 1, 4 (1972).

29. Id.

30. Id.

31. Id.

32. Id.

33. Id.

34. Id.

35. 23 Cal.3d 329, 152 Cal.Rptr. 536, 590 P.2d 391 (1979).

parties to call witnesses who possess relevant information but who otherwise might not be called if they could be impeached by convictions that do not involve dishonesty or that are remote. In addition to the harm suffered by the parties, "the search for truth in our system of justice is impeded when prior felony convictions are improperly admitted to impeach the credibility of a nonparty witness."[36] But which of the *Beagle* guidelines apply to witnesses in civil cases?[37]

The first rule—that the conviction involve dishonesty—is clearly applicable. If the conviction has little or no bearing on the witness's character for lack of veracity, its probative value is so slight that many of the trial concerns enumerated in § 352 should call for its exclusion. These concerns include waste of time as well as unfair prejudice to the opposing party.[38] The second rule is also applicable. Even if the conviction involves dishonesty, the conviction nonetheless should be excluded if the conviction is remote in time and the witness has led a blameless life since being convicted. Such a conviction says little about the witness's current character for lack of veracity.

The third rule conceivably could apply to a civil defendant or cross-defendant who is sued for misconduct similar to that which gave rise to the conviction. Excluding convictions for conduct identical or substantially similar to that for which the witness is on trial is obviously motivated by a fear that the fact finder may improperly consider the conviction as bad character evidence.[39] For example, where the defendant is sued for damages for fraud, impeaching the defendant with a fraud conviction raises the danger that the fact finder may return a verdict against the defendant because of a belief that the defendant is the kind of person who commits frauds. Character evidence is inadmissible in civil cases to prove that a person conformed his conduct to a character trait.[40]

The fourth rule could also apply to civil parties. Impeaching a party with multiple convictions creates the risk that the fact finder may find against that party because of the belief that the party is a bad person undeserving of relief. The solution is for the judge to limit the number of convictions a party may use to impeach the witness.[41]

---

36. Id. at 338, 152 Cal.Rptr. at 541, 590 P.2d at 396.

37. In Robbins v. Wong, 27 Cal.App.4th 261, 32 Cal.Rptr.2d 337 (1994), the Court of Appeal for the Sixth District correctly noted that Proposition 8 has no effect on the admissibility of felony convictions to impeach witnesses in civil cases. But the court also concluded that "the Supreme Court's decisions concerning felony impeachment in criminal decisions—whether decided before or after the adoption of section 28(f)(4)—may not be construed as direct holdings on felony impeachment in civil proceedings." Id. at 273, 32 Cal.Rptr.2d at 344. That holding ignores the California Supreme Court's pronouncement in *Woodard* that *Beagle* applies to all witnesses in all trials, not just criminal cases.

38. For an extended discussion of a judge's discretionary power to exclude relevant evidence under § 352, see § 2.10 supra.

39. For an extended discussion of the policies excluding the use of character evidence, see § 3.04 supra.

40. West's Ann.California Evidence Code § 1101(a).

41. People v. Holt, 37 Cal.3d 436, 453, 208 Cal.Rptr. 547, 556, 690 P.2d 1207, 1216 (1984) (The judge should assess the prejudicial effects of impeaching the witness with more than one conviction.).

The fifth rule may also apply to civil litigants. Fear of impeachment by conviction may discourage a civil litigant from taking the stand. Though life and liberty are not at stake, the costs of losing a party's testimony in a civil trial may be as great as in criminal cases: the jurors might be deprived of crucial evidence bearing on the truth.

Most California Supreme Court cases construing *Beagle* simply apply one of the *Beagle* rules. Two, however, extend *Beagle* in ways that may call for *Beagle*'s application in civil cases. In People v. Rollo[42] the court held that it was error for the prosecution to prove only the fact that the accused had suffered a felony conviction, leaving it up to the accused to disclose its nature.[43] The procedure improperly relieved the judge from engaging in the prescribed weighing under § 352 and invited the jury to speculate about the nature and seriousness of the conviction.[44] In People v. Barrick[45] the court held that it was error for the prosecution to circumvent *Beagle* by calling a prior conviction for car theft a felony involving theft where the accused was charged with car theft.[46] *Rollo* would seem to apply to any civil party, and *Barrick* to defendants who are sued for conduct similar to that which gave rise to the conviction.

Impeachment by felony convictions and Proposition 8. A literal application of Proposition 8's state constitutional mandate that in criminal proceedings any felony conviction be used to impeach a witness "without limitation" would not only overturn *Beagle* and its progeny but would suspend all statutory limitations on the use of convictions. Only the Federal Constitution would constrain the right of parties to criminal proceedings to impeach witnesses with their felony convictions.

Not surprisingly, the California Supreme Court relied on the Fourteenth Amendment to place limits on this provision of Proposition 8. In People v. Castro[47] the court held that due process requires the exclusion of felony convictions that do not involve moral turpitude.[48] In the court's view, the use of such convictions offends due process because they say nothing about the witness's lack of veracity.[49] Therefore, to permit the fact finder to consider convictions devoid of moral turpitude would deprive the accused of a fair trial in which the fact finder considers only relevant and competent evidence on the issue of guilt or innocence.[50]

Why are convictions involving moral turpitude probative of a witness's lack of veracity? Because "a witness's moral depravity of any kind has some 'tendency in reason' * * * to shake one's confidence in his

---

42. 20 Cal.3d 109, 141 Cal.Rptr. 177, 569 P.2d 771 (1977).

43. Id. at 118, 141 Cal.Rptr. at 181, 569 P.2d at 775.

44. Id. at 119–120, 141 Cal.Rptr. at 181–182, 569 P.2d at 776.

45. 33 Cal.3d 115, 187 Cal.Rptr. 716, 654 P.2d 1243 (1982).

46. Id. at 127, 187 Cal.Rptr. at 723, 654 P.2d at 1250.

47. 38 Cal.3d 301, 211 Cal.Rptr. 719, 696 P.2d 111 (1985).

48. Id. at 314, 211 Cal.Rptr. at 727, 696 P.2d at 118.

49. Id.

50. Id. at 314, 211 Cal.Rptr. at 726, 696 P.2d at 119.

honesty."[51] Which felonies involve moral turpitude? Clearly, felonies involving false statement—of which perjury is the paradigm—since these felonies say something about a witness's willingness to lie under oath.[52] But according to *Castro*, any crime evincing a "readiness to do evil" involves moral turpitude.[53] Presumably, witnesses with such a character trait might do mischief on the stand by disregarding their obligation to testify truthfully under oath.

What kinds of convictions show a readiness to do evil? Examples cited in *Castro* include "child molestation, crimes of violence, torture, [and] brutality."[54] Apparently, a readiness to harm others physically is probative of a predisposition to harm others by lying on the stand.

In determining whether a felony involves moral turpitude, the judge may not consider the evidence giving rise to the conviction. If moral turpitude "can only be established through extrinsic evidence, confusion of issues becomes inevitable and unfair surprise more than probable. Therefore, * * * a witness's prior conviction should only be admissible for impeachment if the least adjudicated elements of the conviction necessarily involve moral turpitude."[55] A trial judge, therefore, must determine whether a conviction qualifies from a facial assessment of the statute violated.[56]

In *Castro*, the issue was whether a felony conviction for possessing heroin was admissible to impeach under Proposition 8. The court held that it was not because such a conviction does not necessarily involve moral turpitude.[57] On the other hand, the court held that a conviction for possessing heroin for sale might be admissible. Though this felony does not necessarily involve dishonesty, it does involve an intent to corrupt others.[58] A person's willingness to corrupt others might say something about that person's willingness to injure others by lying under oath.

Other felonies held to involve moral turpitude include battery upon a peace officer,[59] false imprisonment,[60] transporting a controlled substance for sale,[61] committing lewd and lascivious acts on children,[62] pimping and

---

51. Id.

52. Id. at 315, 211 Cal.Rptr. at 727, 696 P.2d at 119.

53. Id.

54. Id.

55. Id. at 317, 211 Cal.Rptr. at 728, 696 P.2d at 120. To reconcile § 28(f)'s command that felony convictions be used without limitation to impeach witnesses with § 28(d)'s reaffirmation of the court's power to exclude relevant evidence under § 352, the *Castro* court interpreted Proposition 8 as restoring the kind of discretion judges had to exclude convictions under § 352 prior to *Beagle*. Id. at 312, 211 Cal.Rptr. at 725, 696 P.2d at 117. Thus, a trial judge still retains discretion under § 352 to exclude evidence of the circumstances underlying the conviction. Id.

56. See People v. Feaster, 102 Cal.App.4th 1084, 1091, 125 Cal.Rptr.2d 896, 900 (2002).

57. People v. Castro, 38 Cal.3d 301, 318, 211 Cal.Rptr. 719, 729, 696 P.2d 111, 121 (1985).

58. Id.

59. People v. Lindsay, 209 Cal.App.3d 849, 857, 257 Cal.Rptr. 529, 534 (1989).

60. People v. Cornelio, 207 Cal.App.3d 1580, 1583, 255 Cal.Rptr. 775, 776 (1989).

61. People v. Navarez, 169 Cal.App.3d 936, 949, 215 Cal.Rptr. 519, 528 (1985).

62. People v. Massey, 192 Cal.App.3d 819, 823, 237 Cal.Rptr. 734, 736–737 (1987).

pandering,[63] possessing marihuana for sale,[64] voluntary manslaughter,[65] assault with a deadly weapon,[66] rape,[67] robbery,[68] burglary,[69] simple kidnaping,[70] car theft[71], driving a car without the owner's consent,[72] forgery,[73] assaulting a noninmate,[74] assault with intent to commit rape,[75] escape without force,[76] aggravated assault,[77] assault with intent to commit murder,[78] arson,[79] receiving stolen property,[80] felony hit-and-run,[81] indecent exposure,[82] felony vandalism,[83] felony drunk-driving,[84] driving a vehicle in a willful or wanton disregard for the safety of others while fleeing or attempting to elude a pursuing peace officer,[85] maintaining a place for the purpose of selling, giving away, or using controlled substances,[86] attempting by threats or violence to prevent an officer from performing a duty or resisting by force or violence an officer in the performance of his or her duties,[87] making terrorist threats,[88] and murder, attempted murder, and assault with a firearm.[89]

In addition to simple possession of heroin, felonies held not to involve moral turpitude include statutory rape,[90] involuntary manslaughter,[91]

63. People v. Jaimez, 184 Cal.App.3d 146, 150, 228 Cal.Rptr. 852, 854 (1986).

64. People v. Standard, 181 Cal.App.3d 431, 435, 226 Cal.Rptr. 62, 64 (1986).

65. People v. Partner, 180 Cal.App.3d 178, 187, 225 Cal.Rptr. 502, 507 (1986).

66. People v. Means, 177 Cal.App.3d 138, 139, 222 Cal.Rptr. 735 (1986). See also People v. Gutierrez, 28 Cal.4th 1083, 1138–1139, 124 Cal.Rptr.2d 373, 413, 52 P.3d 572, 606 (2002) (assault with a deadly weapon on a peace officer).

67. People v. Mazza, 175 Cal.App.3d 836, 843, 221 Cal.Rptr. 640, 644 (1985).

68. People v. Jackson, 174 Cal.App.3d 260, 266, 220 Cal.Rptr. 39, 42 (1985).

69. People v. Statler, 174 Cal.App.3d 46, 54, 219 Cal.Rptr. 713, 718 (1985).

70. People v. Zataray, 173 Cal.App.3d 390, 400, 219 Cal.Rptr. 33, 39 (1985).

71. Id. at 399, 219 Cal.Rptr. at 38.

72. People v. Rogers, 173 Cal.App.3d 205, 211, 218 Cal.Rptr. 494, 498 (1985).

73. People v. Parrish, 170 Cal.App.3d 336, 350, 217 Cal.Rptr. 700, 709 (1985).

74. People v. Williams, 169 Cal.App.3d 951, 956, 215 Cal.Rptr. 612, 617 (1985).

75. People v. Bonilla, 168 Cal.App.3d 201, 206, 214 Cal.Rptr. 191, 193 (1985).

76. People v. Waldecker, 195 Cal.App.3d 1152, 1158, 241 Cal.Rptr. 650, 653 (1987).

77. People v. Elwell, 206 Cal.App.3d 171, 177, 253 Cal.Rptr. 480, 483 (1988).

78. People v. Olmedo, 167 Cal.App.3d 1085, 1098, 213 Cal.Rptr. 742, 749 (1985).

79. People v. Miles, 172 Cal.App.3d 474, 482, 218 Cal.Rptr. 378, 383 (1985).

80. People v. Rodriguez, 177 Cal.App.3d 174, 178–179, 222 Cal.Rptr. 809, 812 (1986).

81. People v. Bautista, 217 Cal.App.3d 1, 7, 265 Cal.Rptr. 661, 666 (1990).

82. People v. Ballard, 13 Cal.App.4th 687, 696, 16 Cal.Rptr.2d 624, 630 (1993).

83. People v. Campbell, 23 Cal.App.4th 1488, 1493, 28 Cal.Rptr.2d 716, 719–720 (1994).

84. People v. Forster, 29 Cal.App.4th 1746, 1757, 35 Cal.Rptr.2d 705, 712 (1994).

85. People v. Dewey, 42 Cal.App.4th 216, 222, 49 Cal.Rptr.2d 537, 541 (1996).

86. People v. Vera, 69 Cal.App.4th 1100, 1103, 82 Cal.Rptr.2d 128, 130 (1999).

87. People v. Williams, 72 Cal.App.4th 1460, 1463–1464, 86 Cal.Rptr.2d 62, 64 (1999).

88. People v. Thornton, 3 Cal.App.4th 419, 422, 4 Cal.Rptr.2d 519, 521 (1992).

89. People v. Hinton, 37 Cal.4th 839, 888, 38 Cal.Rptr.3d 149, 194, 126 P.3d 981, 1018, cert. denied 549 U.S. 1033, 127 S.Ct. 581, 166 L.Ed.2d 434 (2006).

90. People v. Flanagan, 185 Cal.App.3d 764, 774, 230 Cal.Rptr. 64, 69 (1986). But see People v. Fulcher, 194 Cal.App.3d 749, 753, 236 Cal.Rptr. 845, 848 (1987) (holding that convictions for statutory rape occurring after the 1964 People v. Hernandez decision are for crimes of moral

simple battery,[92] felony battery,[93] simple assault,[94] felony child endangerment,[95] and simple possession of marihuana.[96]

Despite holdings to the contrary,[97] felonies based on strict liability or negligence should not be classified as crimes involving moral turpitude. As the *Castro* court emphasized, "a readiness to do evil" is what distinguishes felonies involving moral turpitude from other felonies.[98] At the very least, then, felonies involving moral turpitude must require the prosecution to prove that the accused was aware that his contemplated course of conduct posed some risk of harm to others.[99] Obviously, no such showing needs to be made in negligence offenses, since the gravamen of the offense is not that the accused was aware but that he should have been aware of the risk. And, of course, no such showing needs to be made in strict liability offenses, since these offenses lack a mens rea. Whether or not the accused knew or should have known about the risk is simply immaterial.

Felony child endangerment, for example, is not a crime involving moral turpitude. A facial assessment of its least adjudicated elements discloses that the offense can be committed without an awareness of harming the victim.[100] "Because [the offense] can be [committed] by wholly passive conduct, free from any element of force, violence, threat, fraud, deceit, or stealth, even when motivated by a sincere, good faith but unreasonable belief the conduct is in the child's best interests, * * * conviction under the statute does not necessarily imply a general readiness to do evil or any moral depravity."[101]

Discretion to exclude convictions after Proposition 8. Proposition 8 contains two seemingly conflicting positions on a judge's discretionary power to exclude convictions. Section 28(f)(4) of Article 1 of the

---

turpitude since the prosecution must prove that the accused unreasonably believed that the victim was of the age of consent).

91. People v. Solis, 172 Cal.App.3d 877, 883, 218 Cal.Rptr. 469, 472 (1985).

92. People v. Mansfield, 200 Cal.App.3d 82, 88–89, 245 Cal.Rptr., 800, 802–803 (1988).

93. Id.

94. People v. Thomas, 206 Cal.App.3d 689, 694, 254 Cal.Rptr. 15, 18 (1988).

95. People v. Sanders, 10 Cal.App.4th 1268, 1273–1274, 13 Cal.Rptr.2d 205, 208–209 (1992).

96. People v. Valdez, 177 Cal.App.3d 680, 697, 223 Cal.Rptr. 149, 158 (1986).

97. See, e.g., People v. Feaster, 102 Cal.App.4th 1084, 1093, 125 Cal.Rptr.2d 896, 902 (2002) (holding that a conviction of discharging a firearm in a grossly negligent manner is a crime involving moral turpitude).

98. People v. Castro, 38 Cal.3d 301, 315, 211 Cal.Rptr. 719, 727, 696 P.2d 111, 119 (1985).

99. People v. Sanders, 10 Cal.App.4th 1268, 1273–1274, 13 Cal.Rptr.2d 205, 208–209 (1992).

100. Id.

101. Id. The fact that the prosecution is entitled to offer evidence of a higher mens rea to prove the elements of a strict liability or negligence offense is immaterial. *Castro* prohibits the prosecution from going behind the conviction to show that in a given case the accused intended to harm the victim. Instead, *Castro* requires the judge to determine whether the felony involves moral turpitude by examining only the "least adjudicated elements of the conviction." People v. Castro, 38 Cal.3d 301, 315, 211 Cal.Rptr. 719, 727, 696 P.2d 111, 119 (1985). Accordingly, it is immaterial that in a strict liability or negligence prosecution the state offered evidence that the accused intended to harm the victim.

California Constitution strips judges of any such discretion by requiring that felony convictions be used to impeach witnesses "without limitation." Section 28(f)(2), on the other hand, reaffirms a judge's power to exclude relevant evidence whenever its probative value is substantially outweighed by the concerns enumerated in § 352. To reconcile the two sections, *Castro* interpreted Proposition 8 as restoring the kind of discretion judges had to exclude convictions for undue prejudice prior to *Beagle*.[102] In exercising their discretion, judges are to be guided, but not bound, by the limitations set out in *Beagle*.[103] Applying these guidelines, the California Supreme Court has held that even a felony conviction involving moral turpitude (voluntary manslaughter) may be excluded under § 352 if it is remote in time (22 years) and the witness has led a blameless life since the conviction.[104]

Rehabilitating the impeached witness. If a witness is impeached by a conviction, the judge may allow the witness to be rehabilitated by evidence showing why the conviction says little or nothing about the witness's character for lack of veracity. In *People v. Visciotti*[105] the accused was allowed to mitigate the effect of a conviction for assault with a deadly weapon with evidence that he was forced to plead guilty even though he had acted in self-defense.[106] But if the witness offers extenuating evidence, the impeaching party may offer countervailing evidence. In *Visciotti*, for example, the prosecution was entitled to respond with evidence that in the course of the assault the accused stabbed an additional person.[107] How much evidence the parties may offer about the conduct giving rise to the conviction is committed to the judge's discretion under

---

102. People v. Castro, 38 Cal.3d 301, 314, 211 Cal.Rptr. 719, 726, 696 P.2d 111, 119 (1985).

103. People v. Clair, 2 Cal.4th 629, 655, 7 Cal.Rptr.2d 564, 578, 828 P.2d 705, 719 (1992), cert. denied, 506 U.S. 1063, 113 S.Ct. 1006, 122 L.Ed.2d 155 (1993) (applying *Beagle* to a witness who was not the accused); People v. Collins, 42 Cal.3d 378, 381, 392, 228 Cal.Rptr. 899, 901, 908, 722 P.2d 173, 175, 182 (1986) (applying *Beagle* to the accused).

104. People v. Clair, 2 Cal.4th 629, 655, 7 Cal.Rptr.2d 564, 578, 828 P.2d 705, 719 (1992), cert. denied, 506 U.S. 1063, 113 S.Ct. 1006, 122 L.Ed.2d 155 (1993). In determining whether the witness has led a blameless life since the conviction, the judge may disregard convictions which are remote. But in assessing whether the witness has led a blameless life for a time sufficiently long to render the conviction remote, the court may discount periods in which the witness was incarcerated. People v. Turner, 8 Cal.4th 137, 200, 32 Cal.Rptr.2d 762, 798, 878 P.2d 521, 557 (1994).

The California Court of Appeal has relied on the continued vitality of § 352 in holding that, even after Proposition 8, trial judges retain discretion to withhold from the jury the nature of a conviction offered to impeach the accused if the conviction is similar or identical to the charge filed against the accused. See People v. Ballard, 13 Cal.App.4th 687, 696–698, 16 Cal.Rptr.2d 624, 630–631 (1993). In these circumstances, a judge may simply tell the jurors that the accused has been convicted of a crime involving moral turpitude. Id.

105. 2 Cal.4th 1, 5 Cal.Rptr.2d 495, 825 P.2d 388 (1992), cert. denied, 506 U.S. 893, 113 S.Ct. 267, 121 L.Ed.2d 196 (1992), reh'g denied, 506 U.S. 1016, 113 S.Ct. 646, 121 L.Ed.2d 575 (1992).

106. Id. at 51, 5 Cal.Rptr.2d at 521, 825 P.2d at 414.

107. Id. See also People v. Shea, 39 Cal.App.4th 1257, 1268, 46 Cal.Rptr.2d 388, 394 (1995) (Where on cross-examination the witness denied having committed one of the felonies of which he had been convicted, claiming that the conviction was simply part of a "deal," the prosecution was entitled to call the victim of the felony to establish that the witness had indeed committed the offense.).

§ 352. To save time and avoid confusion of issues, no judge should permit the parties to retry the conviction.

Standing to complain about the use of convictions. Defense counsel usually move in limine for the exclusion of convictions they believe cannot be used to impeach the accused in the event the accused takes the stand. Where the defense motion to exclude is denied, the accused must decide whether to take the stand and be impeached with the convictions or decline to testify to avoid the prejudice that might flow from the impeaching evidence. Where the accused claims that the trial judge's in limine ruling allowing the use of the conviction was erroneous, the accused must take the stand to preserve the error for appellate review.[108] Without the accused's testimony, the reviewing court cannot weigh the probative value of the conviction against its prejudicial effects.[109] In California, when the motion to exclude is denied, defense counsel may seek to mitigate the damaging effects of the convictions by bringing them out in the direct examination of the accused without losing the right to complain of the in limine ruling on appeal. Federal practice is to the contrary.[110] In California the decision to bring out the conviction on direct examination of the witness is a tactical one and ordinarily will not result in a violation of the accused's right to the effective assistance of counsel.[111]

Impeachment by misdemeanor convictions and the Right to Truth-in-Evidence. Under the Evidence Code, misdemeanor convictions may not be used to establish a witness's character for lack of veracity. Only felony convictions may be used for this purpose.[112] Misdemeanor convictions, moreover, may not be used for this purpose in criminal cases under § 28(f)(4) of Proposition 8, since this section focuses exclusively on the use of felony convictions. Section 28(d)(2), however, vests parties to criminal proceedings with the state constitutional right not to have relevant evidence excluded.[113] Since misdemeanor convictions that are probative of a witness's character for lack of veracity are relevant, such convictions are now admissible under this provision of Proposition 8.[114] In

---

108. People v. Collins, 42 Cal.3d 378, 384, 228 Cal.Rptr. 899, 903, 722 P.2d 173, 177 (1986) (This requirement applies only to cases reviewed after *Collins*.).

109. Id. Where over the accused's objections the trial judge at a pretrial hearing rules the convictions admissible to impeach, the accused does not have to object to their use at the trial in order to preserve an objection to the judge's ruling. People v. Carpenter, 21 Cal.4th 1016, 1056, 90 Cal.Rptr.2d 607, 634, 988 P.2d 531, 556 (1999), cert. denied, 531 U.S. 838, 121 S.Ct. 99, 148 L.Ed.2d 58 (2000).

110. Ohler v. United States, 529 U.S. 753, 760, 120 S.Ct. 1851, 146 L.Ed.2d 826 (2000) (holding that in federal trials a defendant who introduces the conviction on direct examination loses his or her right to complain on appeal about the in limine ruling allowing the use of the conviction for impeachment purposes).

111. People v. Mendoza, 78 Cal.App.4th 918, 928, 93 Cal.Rptr.2d 216, 222 (2000).

112. West's Ann. California Evidence Code § 788.

113. For an extended discussion of § 28(d), see § 15.03 supra.

114. People v. Wheeler, 4 Cal.4th 284, 294, 14 Cal.Rptr.2d 418, 424, 841 P.2d 938, 944 (1992). A judge has a sua sponte duty to instruct the jurors that a misdemeanor conviction, like a felony conviction, can be considered only for its effect on the credibility of the witness. People v. Lomeli, 19 Cal.App.4th 649, 654, 24 Cal.Rptr.2d 5, 9 (1993). But no such duty arises unless the judge first

the absence of a special hearsay exception, however, misdemeanor convictions may not be received for this purpose.[115]

Impeachment by convictions implicate the hearsay rule because of their value as evidence of a witness's character for lack of veracity. Their probative value derives from the assumption that the witness engaged in the misconduct giving rise to the convicted offense. A theft conviction, for example, is relevant because of the belief that thieves may not abide by their sworn duty to testify truthfully. Jurors who accept this proposition may thus disbelieve a witness convicted of theft. Jurors, however, will not reach this conclusion unless they believe that the witness is in fact a thief, i.e., that the witness engaged in the misconduct giving rise to the conviction. Thus, when a conviction is used to impeach a witness, it is offered as evidence that the witness engaged in the misconduct underlying the conviction.

Using convictions as evidence that the accused engaged in the underlying misconduct violates the hearsay rule. Where a judgment of conviction is used, the entry reflects a judge's out of court pronouncement that a given individual stands convicted of a particular crime.[116] When the witness's answer is used to establish the conviction, the witness is simply acknowledging the judge's out of court statement pronouncing him guilty of the crime. In either case, the judge's pronouncement is but a ministerial act based on a finding of guilt, a guilty verdict, or a guilty plea.[117] In the case of convictions based on a finding of guilt or a guilty verdict, the hearsay rule is implicated even further: the judge's pronouncement is being offered as evidence that the witness engaged in the misconduct giving rise to the conviction. The judge's words, in effect, are being offered as a substitute for the minimum evidence the prosecution had to offer to make out a prima facie case and for the fact finders' acceptance of that evidence. People v. Wheeler[118] holds that, in the absence of a hearsay exception, a misdemeanor conviction may not be received as proof that the witness engaged in the misconduct underlying the conviction.[119]

---

determines that the misdemeanor conviction in question is probative of the witness's bad character for lack of veracity.

Only misdemeanor convictions evincing "moral turpitude" can be used for this purpose. People v. Wheeler, supra at 290, 14 Cal.Rptr.2d at 425, 841 P.2d at 945. Misdemeanor convictions qualifying as crimes of moral turpitude include: possessing a concealed handgun, People v. Robinson, 37 Cal.4th 592, 625, 36 Cal.Rptr.3d 760, 786, 124 P.3d 363, 385, cert. denied, ___ U.S. ___, 127 S.Ct. 381, 166 L.Ed.2d 269 (2006); embezzlement, People v. Martinez, 103 Cal.App.4th 1071, 1081, 127 Cal.Rptr.2d 305, 312 (2002); failing to appear in court, People v. Maestas, 132 Cal.App.4th 1552, 1556, 34 Cal.Rptr.3d 503, 506 (2005); and sexual battery. People v. Chavez, 84 Cal.App.4th 25, 29, 100 Cal.Rptr.2d 680, 682 (2000). But misdemeanor simple battery convictions do not qualify as crimes involving moral turpitude. People v. Lopez, 129 Cal.App.4th 1508, 1522, 29 Cal.Rptr.3d 586, 597 (2005).

115. 4 Cal.4th 284, 294, 300, 14 Cal.Rptr.2d 418, 428, 841 P.2d 938, 948 (1992). The Right to Truth–in–Evidence provision of Proposition 8 does not affect the hearsay rule. See West's Ann. California Constitution Article I, § 28(f)(2).

116. For a discussion of this point, see § 12.03 supra.

117. West's Ann. California Penal Code §§ 1191 and 1200.

118. 4 Cal.4th 284, 14 Cal.Rptr.2d 418, 841 P.2d 938 (1992).

119. Id. at 299, 14 Cal.Rptr.2d at 427, 841 P.2d at 947.

Traditional hearsay exceptions are unavailing. Evidence Code § 788 may not be invoked to prove the facts essential to a misdemeanor conviction because, as noted, § 788 authorizes only the use of felony convictions to impeach witnesses.[120] Section 1300 cannot be used for this purpose because it is limited to proving felony convictions and then only when the felony convictions are offered in a *civil* action.[121] If the witness to be impeached is the accused, the exception for party admissions is likewise unavailing, but for a different reason: asking the witness on cross whether he has been convicted of a misdemeanor would prove only the fact of conviction and not the misconduct giving rise to the convicted offense.[122] For the same reason, the business and official records exceptions cannot be used: those records would prove only the fact that the witness has been convicted of the misdemeanors enumerated in the records.[123] Consequently, in the absence of a new hearsay exception, the impeaching party must offer the misconduct giving rise to the misdemeanor conviction and not the conviction to prove that the witness engaged in misconduct that is probative of his character for lack of veracity.[124] In essence, the impeaching party must treat the misconduct giving rise to the conviction as a prior bad act.[125]

In 1996 the Legislature added § 452.5(b) to the Evidence Code. The amendment provides that an "official record of conviction certified in accordance with subdivision (a) of Section 1530 is admissible pursuant to Section 1280 to prove the commission, attempted commission, or solicitation of a criminal offense, service of a prison term, or other act, condition or event recorded by the record."[126] Section 1280 creates a hearsay exception for official records, and § 1530 permits copies of records in the custody of a public entity to be offered without the need to call a custodian to authenticate the copy if attested or certified as a correct copy of the original record by a public employee having legal custody of the record.[127]

---

120. West's Ann. California Evidence Code § 788.

121. West's Ann. California Evidence Code § 1300. See also § 12.03 supra.

122. People v. Wheeler, 4 Cal.4th 284, 294, 300, 14 Cal.Rptr.2d 418, 428, 841 P.2d 938, 948 (1992).

123. Id. at 300, note 13, 14 Cal.Rptr.2d at 428, note 13, 841 P.2d at 948, note 13.

124. Id. at 300, note 14, 14 Cal.Rptr.2d at 428, note 14, 841 P.2d at 948, note 14.

125. See, e.g., People v. Lepolo, 55 Cal.App.4th 85, 91, 63 Cal.Rptr.2d 735, 739 (1997) (holding that the prosecution was entitled to impeach the accused with evidence that he had once threatened a police officer with a machete). See also People v. Chavez, 84 Cal.App.4th 25, 29, 100 Cal.Rptr.2d 680, 682 (2000) (holding that the prosecution was entitled to impeach the accused with evidence that he had committed a sexual battery). For a discussion of the prior bad acts doctrine, see § 15.06 supra.

A distinction should be drawn between misconduct that is probative of lack of veracity and arrests for that conduct. Only the former should be admissible to impeach a witness. Arrests can viewed as merely opinions by the arresting officer that the person arrested violated a penal code provision. Arrests can be based on hearsay. This is why jurors are told not to be biased against criminal defendants simply because they have been arrested for the offense for which they are on trial. See CALJIC 1.00 (Fall 2006 Edition).

126. West's Ann. California Evidence Code § 452.5.

127. See West's Ann. California Evidence Code §§ 1280 and 1530.

As a matter of statutory construction, it is not entirely clear whether § 452.5(b) can be used to offer a conviction record as proof that the accused engaged in the misconduct giving rise to the conviction. Though the section does state that the record may be offered to prove "the commission" of the offense, this provision is limited by the requirement that the record be offered to prove only those acts, conditions or events recorded in the record. Thus, if the only event recorded is the fact of conviction, using that entry to prove that the accused engaged in the misconduct giving rise to the conviction would still appear to violate the hearsay rule. However, in People v. Duran[128] the California Court of Appeal dispelled this uncertainty by holding that § 452.5(b) "creates a hearsay exception allowing admission of qualifying court records to prove not only the fact of conviction, but also that the offense reflected in the record occurred."[129]

In the absence of a special hearsay exception such as § 452.5(b), complying with *Wheeler* would be no easy task. Proving, for example, that the witness embezzled funds from his employer would require the impeaching party to call the witnesses who saw the witness embezzle the funds if the witness denies embezzling them. Since the opposing party would be entitled to prove that the witness did not in fact embezzle the funds, that party could call witnesses to give an account that differs from the one given by the impeaching party's witnesses. The dangers inherent in this process are clear: unless the trial judge firmly limits the evidence offered by the parties, evidence of the witness's credibility could degenerate into a retrial of the misdemeanor embezzlement charge.[130]

Section 452.5(b) does not eliminate the risk entirely, however. Records of conviction offered under the section are not by virtue of the section entitled to any special effect. Under the Right to Truth-in-Evidence provision of Proposition 8, the opposing party is still entitled to offer evidence contesting the existence of the facts essential to the judgment reflected in the conviction record. Thus, if a record of a misdemeanor conviction is offered to prove that a witness embezzled funds, the opposing party should be entitled to call witnesses with first hand knowledge to testify that the witness did not in fact embezzle the funds. The judge, however, would still be empowered by § 352 to limit the number of witnesses called on the question.

---

128. 97 Cal.App.4th 1448, 119 Cal.Rptr.2d 272 (2002).

129. Id. at 1460, 119 Cal.Rptr.2d at 282. It is difficult to conclude that the legislature intended § 452.5(b) to create such a broad hearsay exception. Section 452.5 is not located in the chapter dealing with hearsay and its exceptions but in the chapter on judicial notice. More importantly, the broad construction the court gave to the Subsection (b) would render moot important hearsay exceptions, such as the exceptions for felony judgments offered in a civil case to prove any fact essential to the judgment (§ 1300) and for felony convictions offered to impeach a witness (§ 788). Section 452.5 is made up of two subsections. The comment is limited to describing the need for Subsection (a). It says nothing about Subsection (b).

130. Judges should use § 352 to avoid such an outcome. Section 352 is not affected by Proposition 8. The Right to Truth–in–Evidence provision expressly preserves the right of trial judges to exclude relevant evidence whenever its probative value is substantially outweighed by the concerns enumerated in § 352. See § 15.03 supra.

Juvenile adjudications and Proposition 8. The Evidence Code is silent on whether juvenile adjudications can be used to impeach witnesses. People v. Sanchez[131] holds that juvenile adjudications cannot be used to impeach witnesses because juvenile proceedings are not criminal proceedings and do not result in criminal convictions.[132] But relying on *Wheeler*, People v. Lee[133] holds that in California criminal cases the misconduct giving rise to juvenile adjudications may be used to impeach a witness if the misconduct evinces moral turpitude as required by *Castro* and the juvenile has not been released from the penalties and disabilities arising from the adjudication by having been discharged honorably by the California Youth Authority.[134]

Under *Lee* it is immaterial whether the juvenile adjudication is for misconduct that violates a felony or misdemeanor.[135] Thus in *Lee* the witness was impeached by evidence of misconduct giving rise to felony burglary as well as misdemeanor theft.[136]

Cannot use expunged convictions

Expungement and Proposition 8. As enacted, § 788 prohibits the use of felony convictions to impeach a witness where the conviction has been expunged.[137] Under California Penal Code § 1203.4, a defendant who has fulfilled the conditions of probation may move to set aside his guilty plea or guilty verdict and enter a plea of not guilty.[138] If the motion is granted, the court must dismiss the accusations against the defendant, thereby releasing the defendant "from all penalties and disabilities resulting from the offense of which he or she [had] been convicted * * *."[139] Since a conviction that is probative of a witness's lack of veracity is nonetheless legally relevant even if it has been expunged, one would expect the Right to Truth–in–Evidence provision of Proposition 8 to override § 788's expungement provisions in California criminal cases. People v. Field,[140] however, holds otherwise. Though expunged convictions say little about a witness's lack of credibility and should be excluded under a judge's § 352 authority to exclude evidence of dubious value, *Field* mistakenly holds that such convictions are inadmissible because they are *irrelevant*.[141]

---

131.   170 Cal.App.3d 216, 216 Cal.Rptr. 21 (1985).

132.   Id. at 218, 216 Cal.Rptr. at 23.

133.   28 Cal.App.4th 1724, 34 Cal.Rptr.2d 723 (1994).

134.   Id. at 1738–1740, 34 Cal.Rptr.2d at 730–731.

135.   Id.

136.   Id.

137.   West's Ann. California Evidence Code § 788.

138.   West's Ann. California Penal Code § 1203.4.

139.   Id. Expungement, however, will not preclude the use of the expunged conviction in limited circumstances. See id.

140.   31 Cal.App.4th 1778, 37 Cal.Rptr.2d 803 (1995).

141.   Id. at 1788, 37 Cal.Rptr.2d at 810. Evidence that a witness has been convicted of a crime of that is probative of the witness's character for lack of veracity is relevant irrespective of whether the conviction has been expunged. For an extended discussion of this point, see § 2.04 supra.

As we have seen, Proposition 8 also amended the California Constitution by calling for the unlimited use of felony convictions to impeach witnesses. The defendant in *Field* urged the appellate court to use this provision to authorize the use of expunged convictions to impeach a witness. But the court declined to do so. It held the provision inapplicable because "by virtue of expungement, there no longer is a prior conviction."[142]

Impeachment by conviction under the Federal Rules. As amended in 2006, Federal Rule of Evidence 609(a)(2) allows a party to impeach any witness with any timely misdemeanor or felony conviction "if the court can readily determine that establishing the elements of the crime required proving—or the witness's admitting—a dishonest act or false statement."[143] It is immaterial whether the case is civil or criminal or whether the witness to be impeached is the accused or some other witness. The judge has no discretion to exclude such convictions.[144]

The amendment's purpose was to resolve a conflict over how a federal judge should determine whether a conviction involves dishonesty or false statement. Although the statutory elements of the offense will ordinarily indicate whether the conviction involved these elements, the Advisory Committee declined to limit a federal judge to a facial analysis of the statute violated.[145] Instead, the Committee opted to allow the impeaching party to offer and a federal judge to consider such documents as the indictment, a statement of admitted facts, and jury instructions to determine whether the factfinder had to find or the witness had to admit an act of dishonesty or false statement in order for the witness to be convicted.[146]

If the conviction does not involve dishonesty or false statement and the witness to be impeached is not the accused, only felony grade convictions may be used if the judge finds that their probative value is not substantially outweighed by the concerns enumerated in Rule 403.[147] Rule 403 is the federal equivalent of California Evidence Code § 352 and includes unfair prejudice and waste of time among the enumerated grounds.[148] To be relevant, the conviction should be probative of the witness's character for lack of veracity.

---

   142. Id.

   143. Federal Rule of Evidence 609(a)(2).

   144. Id. Under Federal Rule 609(a)(2), as construed by the Ninth Circuit, convictions involving dishonesty or false statement include only those crimes that involve deceit. United States v. Brackeen, 969 F.2d 827, 830 (9th Cir.1992) (en banc) (per curiam). Shoplifting, burglary, grand theft, bank robbery, and receiving stolen property, while disrespectful of the property rights of others, do not involve deceit in the abstract. See United States v. Foster, 227 F.3d 1096, 1100 (2000) and cases cited therein. But *Brackeen* does not foreclose using convictions of these crimes under Rule 609(a)(1). This provision allows the use of felony convictions that do not involve an act of dishonesty or a false statement. See United States v. Alexander, 48 F.3d 1477, 1488 (1995).

   145. Id. (Advisory Committee Note).

   146. Id.

   147. Federal Rule of Evidence 609(a)(1).

   148. Federal Rule of Evidence 403.

If the conviction does not involve dishonesty or false statement and the witness to be impeached is the accused, only felony grade convictions may be used if the judge determines that their probative value outweigh their prejudicial effect to the accused.[149] Because of the risk that a jury might misuse convictions as evidence of the accused's guilt, the Rules require that in all cases the government show that the probative value of the convictions, as impeachment evidence, outweighs their prejudicial effect to the accused.[150] Thus, this test and not the test of Rule 403 is employed.

Under the Federal Rules, a conviction may not be used to attack the credibility of a witness if a period of more than ten years has passed since the witness's conviction or the release from the confinement for it, whichever is later, unless the court determines that the probative value of the conviction, supported by specific facts and circumstances, substantially outweighs its prejudicial effect.[151]

Juvenile adjudications are generally inadmissible to impeach witnesses. But the judge may in a criminal case allow evidence of a juvenile adjudication of a witness other than the accused if conviction of the offense would be admissible to attack the credibility of an adult and the court is satisfied that admitting the evidence is necessary to fairly determine guilt or innocence.[152]

A conviction may not be used to impeach if (1) the conviction has been the subject of a pardon, annulment, certificate of rehabilitation, or other equivalent procedure based on a finding that the person has been rehabilitated, and the person has not been convicted of a later felony grade crime, or (2) the conviction has been the subject of a pardon, annulment, or other equivalent procedure based on a finding of innocence.[153]

The pendency of an appeal from a conviction does not render evidence of the conviction inadmissible. But evidence of the pendency of an appeal is admissible.[154]

As has been noted, defense counsel routinely move in limine for the exclusion of convictions they believe cannot be used to impeach the accused if the accused takes the stand. Where the motion to exclude is denied, defense counsel may seek to mitigate the damaging effects of the convictions by bringing them out in the direct examination of the accused. In California courts, they can do so without losing the right to complain of

---

149. Federal Rule of Evidence 609(a)(1).

150. Id. (Advisory Committee Note).

151. Federal Rule of Evidence 609(b). In addition, the proponent must give any adverse party reasonable notice of the intent to use the conviction so that the party has a fair opportunity to contest it. Id.

152. Federal Rule of Evidence 609(d).

153. Federal Rule of Evidence 609(c).

154. Federal Rule of Evidence 609(e).

the in limine ruling on appeal.[155] The judge, after all, has ruled on the use of the conviction. But this is not the practice in federal courts. In Ohler v. United States[156] a sharply divided United States Supreme Court held that in federal courts bringing out the conviction on direct examination waives any claim by the accused that the judge's in limine ruling was in error.[157]

QUESTIONS AND PROBLEMS

1. Both the Code and the Rules permit impeachment by convictions on the theory that convictions are probative of a character for lack of veracity as a witness. Describe how, as a logical matter, convictions are probative of such a character trait.

2. As a matter of statutory construction, the California Supreme Court in *Beagle* relied on § 352 to limit the use of felony convictions to impeach witnesses. Explain why the *Beagle* rules are appropriate factors for a judge to take into account in determining whether or not a given conviction should be admitted over a § 352 objection.

3. Prior to Proposition 8, the *Beagle* rules applied only to California criminal defendants. True or false?

4. Prior to Proposition 8, the California Supreme Court held that *Beagle* should be applied to all witnesses in all cases. True or false?

5. Section 28(f)(4) of Proposition 8 provides that "[a] prior felony conviction of any person in any criminal proceeding * * * shall subsequently be used without limitation for purposes of impeachment." Accordingly, § 28(f) repeals § 788 in criminal cases but § 788 still applies in civil cases. True or false?

6. Section 28(f)(2), as construed by the California Supreme Court, still provides trial judges some discretion in admitting felony convictions to impeach witnesses. True or false?

7. Under §§ 28(f)(2) and (4), as construed by the California Supreme Court, trial judges in criminal cases must exclude felony convictions to impeach witnesses if the convictions do not involve moral turpitude. True or false?

8. According to the California Supreme Court, convictions involving moral turpitude are probative of a witness's lack of veracity. Why?

9. Under the California Supreme Court's formulation of moral turpitude, convictions based on negligence or strict liability should not be used to impeach witnesses. True or false?

10. In California, in determining whether a felony conviction may be used to impeach under *Castro*, the parties may offer and the judge may consider evidence regarding the circumstances attending the commission of the crime giving rise to the conviction. True or false?

---

155. People v. Mendoza, 78 Cal.App.4th 918, 928, 93 Cal.Rptr.2d 216, 222 (2000).

156. 529 U.S. 753, 120 S.Ct. 1851, 146 L.Ed.2d 826 (2000).

157. Id. at 759–760, 120 S.Ct. at 1855. *Ohler* was a 5–4 decision.

11. In a California criminal case, a judge may exclude a felony conviction involving moral turpitude if the judge concludes that its probative value on the witness's character for lack of veracity is substantially outweighed by its prejudicial effects. True or false?

Assume the answer to be true. In balancing the probative value of the conviction against its prejudicial effects, the judge can use the *Beagle* limitations as guidelines. True or false?

12. Under the Right to Truth-in-Evidence provision of Proposition 8, a misdemeanor conviction that is probative of a witness's lack of veracity may be offered over an irrelevance objection to impeach the witness in a criminal case. True or false?

13. But according to People v. Wheeler, such a conviction may not be used to impeach over a hearsay objection unless the conviction falls within an appropriate exception. True or false?

14. Prior to People v. Duran, over a hearsay objection even a qualifying misdemeanor conviction could not be offered in a California criminal case to impeach a witness. True or false?

Accordingly, the impeaching party was relegated to proving the conviction as a prior bad act. True or false?

People v. Duran holds that the impeaching party may rely on Evidence Code § 452.5(b) in offering a qualifying misdemeanor conviction as proof of the misconduct underlying the conviction. True or false?

15. Under the Rules, a judge has no discretion to exclude a timely felony conviction offered to impeach if the conviction involves dishonesty or false statement. True or false?

16. Under the Rules, a judge has no discretion to exclude a timely misdemeanor conviction offered to impeach if the conviction involves dishonesty or false statement. True or false?

17. Under the Rules, if a conviction does not involve dishonesty or false statement, then such a conviction may be used against the accused if it is of a felony grade and the conviction passes the probative/prejudicial tests of Rule 403. True or false?

18. Under the Rules, if a conviction does not involve dishonesty or false statement, then such a conviction may be used against a witness other than the accused if it is of a felony grade and the conviction passes the probative/prejudicial tests of Rule 403. True or false?

19. Under the Rules, only timely misdemeanor convictions involving dishonesty or false statement can be used to impeach a witness. Other misdemeanor convictions cannot be used. True or false?

20. In California if the judge denies the defense motion to exclude a conviction during the in limine hearing, the defendant must take the stand in order to preserve his claim that the judge erroneously ruled the conviction admissible. True or false?

21. If the defendant does take the stand and admits the conviction on direct examination, he still retains the right on appeal to complain about the judge's ruling in limine ruling. True or false?

22. In federal court if the defendant admits the conviction on direct examination, he loses his right on appeal to complain about the judge's ruling admitting the conviction. True or false?

23. In California juvenile adjudications are not considered convictions. Accordingly, over a hearsay objection, a juvenile adjudication cannot be offered to prove the misconduct underlying the adjudication. True or false?

24. In a California criminal case, however, the misconduct underlying the juvenile adjudication can be offered under the Right to Truth-in-Evidence provision as evidence of the juvenile's bad character for truthfulness, provided the misconduct qualifies as moral turpitude under *Castro*. True or false?

25. In federal court, a juvenile adjudication is not admissible to impeach a witness unless the judge determines that fairness requires its admission and the adjudication is offered in a criminal case, the adjudication is offered to impeach a witness other than the accused, and the adjudication is for an offense that would be admissible to attack the credibility of an adult. True or false?

§ 15.08 IMPEACHMENT BY CHARACTER OF THE WITNESS—REPUTATION AND OPINION CONCERNING VERACITY

California Evidence Code §§ 786–787 permit a party to impeach the credibility of a witness by opinion or reputation evidence impugning the witness's character for honesty or veracity.[1] The same sections also permit a party to rehabilitate a witness by opinion or reputation evidence supporting the witness's character for honesty or veracity.[2] But evidence of the witness's good character is inadmissible unless the witness's credibility has first been attacked[3] and then only if the attack takes one of two forms: by opinion or reputation evidence impugning the witness's character for honesty or veracity,[4] or by a felony conviction.[5] Unless one of these conditions is satisfied, the Code takes the position that evidence of a witness's good character for honesty and veracity merely introduces "collateral material that is unnecessary to a proper determination of any legitimate issue in the action."[6]

---

1. West's Ann. California Evidence Code §§ 786–787.

2. Id.

3. West's Ann. California Evidence Code § 790.

4. West's Ann. California Evidence Code § 786.

5. Convictions are admissible on the theory that they are probative of a witness's character for lack of honesty and veracity. See West's Ann. California Evidence Code § 788. Accordingly, their use permits a witness to be rehabilitated by good character evidence for honesty and veracity in the form of opinion or reputation evidence. West's Ann. California Evidence Code §§ 787 and 790 and comments.

6. West's Ann. California Evidence Code § 790 (comment).

Before a reputation witness can testify that another witness's reputation for honesty and veracity is poor in the community in which he resides or among those with whom he habitually associates, the judge must decide whether the character witness is qualified to state the reputation.[7] The witness can be qualified by evidence that the witness has been present when neighbors, business associates, co-workers, friends, and fraternal or religious associates have discussed the witness whose veracity is to be impeached.[8] Evidence that the character witness is not an acquaintance of the witness to be impeached is not a basis for disqualification.[9] The character witness is not testifying from personal observations of that person; rather, the character witness is providing a conclusion based on what he has heard others say about that person's lack of veracity.[10]

The testimony of an opinion witness, on the other hand, is based on his observations of the person whose character for honesty and veracity is to be attacked. To elicit the opinion, the proponent must show as a preliminary matter that the witness is sufficiently acquainted with the person to be attacked as to be qualified to form an opinion regarding that person's lack of veracity. The opinion witness can be qualified by evidence regarding the length of time the witness has known the subject and the number of opportunities the witness has had to observe the subject in contexts in which dishonesty likely would have been exhibited.

On direct examination, a bad reputation witness may not be asked to give examples of what others have said about the subject's lack of veracity. The examples would violate the Code's ban on the use of specific instances of conduct to prove a witness's character for dishonesty[11] and the hearsay rule.[12] Similarly, the bad opinion witness may not be asked on direct about specific instances of conduct by the subject which caused the witness to conclude that the subject is a dishonest person. Though such evidence would not violate the hearsay rule, it would violate the ban on using specific misdeeds to prove a witness's bad character for dishonesty.

If the judge allows the opponent to use bad character evidence to attack the credibility of the witness, the party calling the witness may rehabilitate the witness by offering good character evidence regarding the witness's veracity. But if the witness is rehabilitated through good character witnesses, the rehabilitating party is likewise precluded from eliciting on direct examination examples of the subject's honesty. But cross-examination is another matter. The cross examiner may ask the good reputation witness whether the witness has heard of specific misdeeds by the subject which indicate dishonesty. If the witness denies having heard

---

7. West's Ann. California Evidence Code § 405 and comment.

8. See People v. Workman, 136 Cal.App.2d 898, 901–903, 289 P.2d 514, 515–517 (1955).

9. Rios v. Chand, 130 Cal.App.2d 833, 838–840, 280 P.2d 47, 50–51 (1955).

10. The Code provides a hearsay exception for the witness's conclusion, West's Ann. California Evidence Code § 1324, although the conclusion may not be hearsay, since the witness is not repeating an out-of-court statement.

11. West's Ann. California Evidence Code § 787.

12. For a discussion of the hearsay aspects of the testimony, see § 5.01 supra.

about such acts, the examiner may ask the witness whether he would change his testimony in light of such misdeeds. The examiner, however, must believe in good faith that the subject has engaged in the acts. The examination does not violate the ban on the use of specific acts to establish a character trait for dishonesty. The examiner is not offering the acts for that purpose; rather, the examiner is using the acts to test the reputation witness's qualifications to state the subject's reputation for honesty.

A similar fate awaits the personal opinion witness. On direct, the rehabilitating party may not ask the witness to disclose deeds by the subject which caused the opinion witness to conclude that the subject is an honest person. But on cross, the examiner may ask the witness if he knows about specific acts by the subject suggesting dishonesty. If the witness denies knowing about such misdeeds, the examiner may ask whether the witness would change his opinion in light of the acts. Again, the cross examiner must have a good faith basis for believing that the subject engaged in the acts. Inquiring into the misdeeds does not violate the ban on specific acts evidence; the examiner is merely probing the witness's qualifications to give an opinion regarding the subject's honesty. The jurors, of course, must be alerted to this distinction. A standard instruction, for example, warns jurors to consider such acts only in determining the weight to be given to the testimony of the good character witnesses.[13]

If on cross the good reputation witness denies having heard or the opinion witness denies knowing about acts suggesting dishonesty, the cross examiner may not prove the acts through other evidence. The cross examiner's questions about the misdeeds were designed to test the qualifications of the good character witnesses, not to prove the existence of the acts. The witnesses' denials, moreover, were not received to disprove the existence of the misdeeds, but to demonstrate the limits of the witnesses' personal knowledge. Extrinsic proof of the acts would thus be irrelevant to the witnesses' qualifications and would violate the Code's prohibition on the use of specific acts to prove a witness's character for dishonesty.[14]

Reputation and opinion evidence and Proposition 8. In criminal cases, a literal application of Proposition 8 threatens to repeal the statutory and judicial restraints on the use of character evidence to attack and support the credibility of witnesses. Under the Right to Truth–in–Evidence provision of the initiative, parties to criminal proceedings have a state constitutional right to offer otherwise admissible relevant evidence, unless the judge determines that the probative value of the evidence is substantially outweighed by the costs of admitting it.[15] A strict interpretation of the proposition would have the following effects:

---

13. California Jury Instructions, Criminal (CALJIC) 2.42 (Fall 2006 Edition).

14. West's Ann. California Evidence Code § 787.

15. For an extended discussion of this provision, see § 15.03 supra.

First, it would repeal § 790, which prohibits the introduction of good character evidence until after the witness's character for honesty and veracity has been attacked. A witness's credibility becomes an issue the moment the witness takes the stand. Therefore, the calling party should be able to support the witness's credibility even though it has not been attacked. Accordingly, People v. Taylor[16] holds that, Proposition 8 having repealed § 790, a criminal defendant is entitled to offer good character evidence of his honesty and veracity even if the prosecution has not first attacked the defendant's character for veracity.[17]

Second, in proving a witness's character for honesty or dishonesty, the proponent is no longer limited to reputation or opinion evidence. A party may now offer specific instances of honesty to prove the witness's character for honesty and specific instances of dishonesty to prove the witness's character for dishonesty. People v. Harris,[18] for example, holds that the prosecution may offer evidence that an informant has proved reliable in the past to show his predisposition to testify honestly at the trial,[19] and People v. Adams[20] holds that in a rape prosecution the accused may prove the complaining witness's character for dishonesty by evidence that she has falsely accused others of rape.[21]

Third, since evidence of specific acts that are probative of honesty or dishonesty is now admissible, the rule barring the extrinsic proof of such acts is no longer applicable in criminal cases. The cross examiner may still inquire into such acts to test the qualifications of the reputation or opinion witness. But now, subject to § 352, the examiner may also prove such acts to establish the subject's character for honesty or dishonesty.

The use of character evidence—whether in the form of opinion, reputation, or specific acts—is still subject to discretionary exclusion under § 352 after Proposition 8.[22] A judge can exclude all or some of this evidence if its prejudicial effects substantially outweigh its probative value on the witness's honesty or dishonesty. Where the witness who is impeached by the character evidence is the accused, special concerns arise. A risk exists that the jury may convict the accused on account of his bad character rather than upon the evidence of his guilt.[23] The risk is especially pronounced when the prosecution seeks to impeach the accused with specific acts of dishonesty that are similar to the offenses charged against the accused.

---

16.   180 Cal.App.3d 622, 225 Cal.Rptr. 733 (1986).

17.   Id. at 622, 225 Cal.Rptr. at 738.

18.   47 Cal.3d 1047, 255 Cal.Rptr. 352, 767 P.2d 619 (1989).

19.   Id. at 1080–1083, 255 Cal.Rptr. at 373–374, 767 P.2d at 639–641.

20.   198 Cal.App.3d 10, 243 Cal.Rptr. 580 (1988).

21.   Id. at 17, 243 Cal.Rptr. at 584. The use of specific acts to prove a witness's character for honesty or dishonesty are examined in detail in § 15.06 supra.

22.   See § 15.03 supra.

23.   For an extended discussion of this point, see § 3.04 supra.

Reputation and opinion evidence under the Federal Rules.
The Federal Rules track the Common Law with respect to the admissibility of character evidence to attack or support the credibility of a witness. Rule 608(a) provides that a witness may be attacked or supported by character evidence in the form of opinion or reputation, provided the evidence refers only to "character for truthfulness or untruthfulness".[24] Like the Code, however, the Rules prohibit the use of good character evidence unless the witness's character for truthfulness has first been attacked.[25]

The original rule prohibited the use of good character evidence, unless the witness's character for truthfulness had been "attacked by opinion or reputation evidence or otherwise." The restyled rule simply prohibits the use of good character evidence unless the witness's character for truthfulness has first been attacked. Since the restyled rules are not intended to make any substantive changes, the restyled rule should be read as incorporating the language of the original rule. The Advisory Committee Note to the original rule, notes that the term "otherwise" includes impeachment by conviction as well as by prior bad acts, such as corruption, since these forms of impeachment impugn the witness's character for truthfulness.[26] Impeachment by bias or interest does not qualify as an attack; whether impeachment by contradiction qualifies as an attack on the character of the witness depends on the circumstances.[27] Where the contradicting evidence "amounts in net effect to an attack on character for truth," the judge may permit the witness to be rehabilitated through good character evidence for truthfulness.[28]

If a party calls a good character witness, the opposing party may cross examine the witness about specific instances of misconduct by the subject that are probative of untruthfulness.[29] This inquiry is permitted to test the witness's qualifications to provide accurate information about the subject's character for truthfulness. If the witness denies hearing or knowing about the specific acts, the cross examiner may not prove them extrinsically.[30] Moreover, the cross examiner's right to inquire into specific instances of misconduct in the first place is bounded by Rule 403 which empowers federal judges to exclude relevant evidence if its probative value is substantially outweighed by such concerns as unfair prejudice.[31]

QUESTIONS AND PROBLEMS

1. Consider the admissibility of the following evidence in an action for breach of contract:

---

24. Federal Rule of Evidence 608(a)(1).

25. Federal Rule of Evidence 608(a)(2).

26. Federal Rule of Evidence 608 (Advisory Committee Note).

27. Id.

28. C. McCormick, McCormick on Evidence § 49 (E. Cleary 2d ed. 1972).

29. Federal Rule of Evidence 608(b).

30. Id.

31. Federal Rule of Evidence 403.

(verbal act)

Plaintiff: I said to the defendant, "I'll give you $10.00 for your evidence book."

Plaintiff's Counsel: What, if anything, did the defendant say?

Plaintiff: "I accept your offer." *PPO & verbal act*

* * *

Plaintiff's Counsel: Do you know the plaintiff's reputation for truth and veracity in the Stanford community?

Witness: Yes.

Plaintiff's Counsel: What is her reputation?

Witness: That she is a truthful person.

Defense Counsel: Objection. Move to strike as improper rehabilitation.

Judge: ? *Sustain in Both*

Compare with:

Defense Counsel: Do you know the plaintiff's reputation for recalling events?

Witness: Yes.

Defense Counsel: What is her reputation?

Witness: That she has a poor memory.

Plaintiff's Counsel: Objection. Move to strike as improper impeachment.

Judge: ? *Overruled stays in! (EVID)*

Compare with:

verbal act

Plaintiff: I said to the defendant, "I'll give you $10.00 for your evidence book."

Plaintiff's Counsel: What, if anything, did the defendant say?

Plaintiff: "I accept your offer." *PPO / verbal act*

* * *

Defense Counsel: What did you say to the plaintiff?

Defendant: I said, "I reject your offer." *verbal act*

* * *

Defense Counsel: What, if anything, did you hear the defendant say to the plaintiff?

Witness: The defendant said, "I reject your offer."

* * *

Plaintiff's Counsel: Do you know the plaintiff's reputation for truth and veracity in the Stanford community?

Witness: Yes.

— ∆ Attack π's character

Plaintiff's Counsel: And what is her reputation?

— π is allowed to rebut character

Witness: That she is a truthful person.

Defense Counsel: Objection. Move to strike as improper rehabilitation.

Judge: ?

Assume that in a federal trial the trial judge correctly denied the defense motion to strike. Consider the following cross-examination of the good character witness:

Defense Counsel: Did you hear that in 1987 the plaintiff cheated on her evidence examination?

Witness: No.

Plaintiff's Counsel: Objection. Move to strike as improper impeachment of my client.

Judge: ?   → *Yes, overrule*

Defense Counsel: Well, having now heard that the plaintiff cheated on her evidence exam in 1987, do you still maintain that her reputation at Stanford is that of a truthful person?

Witness: Well. . . .

Defense Counsel: Isn't it a fact that you also cheated on that examination?

Plaintiff's Counsel: Objection. Improper impeachment.

Judge: ?   *overrule, you can XC in FRE*

2. Assume that the witness answered "No" to the last question. Over the plaintiff's counsel's objection, in a federal trial could the witness's law professor testify that the witness in fact cheated on the evidence exam?

No, cannot prove w/ Extrinsic Evid.

Would your rulings in California be different if the case being tried were a criminal case after the enactment of Proposition 8?

§ 15.09 EXPERT TESTIMONY AND CREDIBILITY

Prior to the adoption of the Evidence Code, California shared the Common Law's antipathy to the use of expert testimony to attack or support the credibility of witnesses. The reason given for rejecting "psychiatric testimony as to the mental or emotional condition of a witness for purposes of impeachment"[1] was that the law governing impeachment said nothing about the use of expert testimony.[2] More to the point were the policy concerns raised by the California Supreme Court in Ballard v. Superior Court:

We do not overlook Judge Jerome Frank's warning against needlessly embarking "on an amateur's voyage on the fog-enshrouded sea

---

1. Ballard v. Superior Court, 64 Cal.2d 159, 172, 49 Cal.Rptr. 302, 310, 410 P.2d 838, 846 (1966).

2. Id. at 173, 49 Cal.Rptr. at 311, 410 P.2d at 847.

of psychiatry." * * * A psychiatrist's testimony on the credibility of a witness may * * * not be relevant; the techniques used and theories advanced may not be generally accepted; the psychiatrist may not be in any better position to evaluate credibility than the juror; difficulties may arise in communication between the psychiatrist and the jury; too much reliance may be placed upon the testimony of the psychiatrist; partisan psychiatrists may cloud rather than clarify issues; the testimony may be distracting, time-consuming and costly.[3]

Since jurors were assumed to be as good as experts in assessing the credibility of witnesses, there simply was no need for expert testimony. The courts, for example, were unreceptive to expert testimony explaining why eyewitnesses, though honest, could be mistaken on account of stress and other factors.[4]

Only in one area were the California courts somewhat receptive to the use of expert testimony to assess a witness's credibility. In cases involving sexual assaults, especially on females, fear of psychotically induced false charges moved the courts to permit the use of expert testimony about the victim's mental and emotional instability.[5] Relying on its authority to promulgate rules of criminal procedure in the absence of legislation, the California Supreme Court gave trial judges discretion to "order a psychiatric examination of the complaining witness in [cases] involving a sex violation if the defendant [presented] a compelling reason for such an examination."[6] In 1980, however, the Legislature amended the Penal Code to eliminate this judicial discretion.[7] Concerns that Proposition 8 might repeal the amendment prompted the Legislature to reenact the amendment by the super majority required by the proposition.[8]

Rape trauma syndrome. Beginning in the mid–1980's, the California courts became more receptive to expert testimony on witness credibility where the testimony can be especially helpful to jurors. In opening the doors to this kind of evidence, the courts have been careful to distinguish the use of expert testimony to attack or support the credibility of a witness from expert testimony to prove an element of the cause of action. In People v. Bledsoe,[9] for example, the court held that expert testimony that the complaining witness suffered from rape trauma syndrome was inadmissible to prove that the victim had been raped.[10] Since the syndrome was developed by rape counselors as a therapeutic tool to help identify and treat the emotional problems experienced by their clients and

---

   3. Id. at 174, note 10, 49 Cal.Rptr. at 310, note 10, 410 P.2d at 848, note 10.

   4. People v. Guzman, 47 Cal.App.3d 380, 384–386, 121 Cal.Rptr. 69, 71–72 (1975).

   5. People v. Neely, 228 Cal.App.2d 16, 20, 39 Cal.Rptr. 251, 253 (1964).

   6. Ballard v. Superior Court, 64 Cal.2d 159, 176, 49 Cal.Rptr. 302, 313, 410 P.2d 838, 849 (1966).

   7. West's Ann. California Penal Code § 1112.

   8. Id. (legislative history). The Right to Truth–in–Evidence provision of Proposition 8 can be amended by a two-thirds majority of each house. See § 15.03 supra.

   9. 36 Cal.3d 236, 203 Cal.Rptr. 450, 681 P.2d 291 (1984).

   10. Id. at 251, 203 Cal.Rptr. at 460, 681 P.2d at 301.

not as a device to determine whether a rape in fact had occurred, the court held that the syndrome is not sufficiently reliable to prove that a rape occurred.[11]

The court, however, pointed out that evidence that the complaining witness suffered from rape trauma syndrome could nonetheless be received to help jurors understand why the behavior of rape victims might seem inconsistent with having been raped.

> In a number of cases in which the issue has arisen, the alleged rapist has suggested to the jury that some conduct of the victim after the incident—for example, a delay in reporting the sexual assault—is inconsistent with her claim of having been raped, and evidence of rape trauma syndrome has been introduced to rebut such an inference by providing the jury with recent findings or professional research on the subject of the victim's reaction to sexual assault. * * * As a number of decisions recognized, in such a context expert testimony on rape trauma syndrome may play a particularly useful role by disabusing the jury of some widely held misconceptions about rape and rape victims, so that [the jury] may evaluate the evidence free of the constraints of popular myths.[12]

Child sexual abuse accommodation syndrome. *Bledsoe*'s approval of the use of expert testimony to explain the behavior of rape victims has been extended to sexually abused children. Evidence of child sexual abuse accommodation syndrome, while not admissible to prove that a child has been sexually abused, may be received to explain why a child refrained or delayed in reporting the abuse, or recanted his story in whole or in part.[13] *Bledsoe* has also been extended to the parents of sexually abused children: expert testimony may be admitted to show why it is not unusual for a parent of a sexually abused child to refrain from reporting the abuse.[14] Moreover, expert testimony that a profile of a typical child molester does not exist may also be received to disabuse jurors of the widespread belief that a child molester is "an old man in shabby clothes who loiters in playgrounds or schoolyards and lures unsuspecting children into sexual contact by offering them candy or money."[15]

Limitations on rape trauma and child accommodation syndrome evidence. To establish the materiality of the expert evidence, the proponent must identify the specific myth or misconception that the expert testimony seeks to disprove.[16] If the evidence is received, the jury must be told to consider it only for its bearing on the victim's conduct and not as proof that the molestation or rape occurred.[17] The judge should

---

11. Id.

12. Id. at 247, 203 Cal.Rptr. at 457, 681 P.2d at 298.

13. People v. Bowker, 203 Cal.App.3d 385, 394–395, 249 Cal.Rptr. 886, 891 (1988).

14. People v. McAlpin, 53 Cal.3d 1289, 1302, 283 Cal.Rptr. 382, 389, 812 P.2d 563, 570 (1991).

15. Id.

16. People v. Bowker, 203 Cal.App.3d 385, 394–395, 249 Cal.Rptr. 886, 891 (1988).

17. Id. Where child sexual abuse accommodation syndrome evidence is received, the judge has a sua sponte duty to charge the jury of the limited purposes for which the evidence has been

emphasize that the evidence is admissible "solely to show" that the victim's *post*-abuse conduct is not inconsistent with the claims of abuse.[18]

Because the evidence is admissible only to bolster the victim's credibility and not to prove that the alleged sexual misconduct took place, the evidence may be offered after the accused has attacked the victim's credibility on cross-examination or in his case-in-chief. As a general rule, a party may not support the credibility of a witness unless the witness's credibility has first been attacked.[19] Courts, however, may allow the prosecution to offer the evidence in its case-in-chief, since the victim's conduct—delaying in reporting the abuse, for example—may cause the jurors to wonder why the misconduct was not immediately reported if it had really occurred.[20]

Intimate partner/battered women's syndrome. Where a woman is charged with murder or voluntary manslaughter, the woman may offer evidence of battered women's syndrome (BWS) to prove that she acted in self-defense.[21] Self-defense requires proof (1) that the accused honestly believed that deadly force was necessary to avoid death or great bodily harm and (2) that a reasonable person in the accused's situation would have reached the same conclusion.[22] To prove that she believed that deadly force was necessary, the accused is entitled to relate the thoughts that crossed her mind, including recollections of prior assaults and threats made by the victim.[23] BWS evidence consists of "a pattern of psychological symptoms that develop after somebody has lived in a battering relationship" and include "a greater sensitivity to danger."[24] BWS evidence is thus admissible to show why the accused believed that she was in imminent danger of death or great bodily harm and needed to kill.[25] Evidence Code § 1107 now codifies this principle by permitting an expert to tell the jury that, as a result of suffering from BWS, the accused actually perceived that she was in imminent danger and needed to kill in self-defense.[26]

---

received. People v. Housley, 6 Cal.App.4th 947, 957, 8 Cal.Rptr.2d 431, 438 (1992). See also California Jury Instructions, Criminal 10.64 (Fall 2006 Edition).

18. See People v. Housley, 6 Cal.App.4th 947, 957, 8 Cal.Rptr.2d 431, 438 (1992), and cases cited therein.

19. See, e.g., West's Ann. California Evidence Code § 790 (prohibiting the use of evidence of a witness's good character unless evidence of his bad character has been admitted to attack the witness's credibility) and § 791 (barring evidence of a witness's prior statement that is consistent with the witness's testimony unless the witness has been impeached with a prior inconsistent statement).

20. People v. Patino, 26 Cal.App.4th 1737, 1744–1745, 32 Cal.Rptr.2d 345, 349 (1994).

21. People v. Aris, 215 Cal.App.3d 1178, 1197–1198, 264 Cal.Rptr. 167, 179–180 (1989). See also West's Ann. California Evidence Code § 1107.

22. People v. Aris, supra note 21, at 1186, 264 Cal.Rptr. at 172 (1989).

23. Id. at 1191, 264 Cal.Rptr. at 175.

24. Id. at 1194, 264 Cal.Rptr. at 177.

25. Id. at 1197–1198, 264 Cal.Rptr. at 179–180.

26. West's Ann.California Evidence Code § 1107. Contrary to suggestions in *Aris,* supra note 21, § 29 of the Penal Code should not be triggered by the expert's testimony. Section 29 prohibits experts in the guilt phase from testifying whether a defendant's mental disorder precluded the

At one time, BWS evidence was inadmissible to prove that the accused acted reasonably. Some courts maintained that the issue with respect to the second prong was not what the accused thought but what a reasonable woman in the accused's situation would have thought.[27] That position, however, ignored the possibility of framing the issue differently: namely, whether a reasonable woman suffering from BWS would have acted as the accused did. Thus framed, it is obvious that BWS evidence could assist the jurors in determining whether the accused's decision to use deadly force was reasonable under the circumstances. In People v. Humphrey[28] the California Supreme Court disapproved of the cases limiting BWS evidence to proving the woman's honest belief in the need to use deadly force; instead, the court held that the evidence also could be offered to prove that her decision to use deadly force was reasonable.[29]

BWS evidence is likewise admissible to rehabilitate the accused whenever the prosecution seeks to impeach her credibility by evidence that the accused's conduct before and after the killing was inconsistent with her claim of having acted in self-defense.[30] As in the case of rape or molestation victims, the expert testimony may be received to dispel commonly held misconceptions about battered women that are inconsistent with trial claims. BWS evidence is admissible to disabuse the jury of the notion "that because a woman strikes back at her batterer, she is engaging in 'mutual combat,' "[31] that she is "free to leave at any time,"[32] that she

defendant from forming the mens rea of the offense charged. West's Ann.California Penal Code § 29. "The question as to whether the defendant had or did not have the required mental states shall be decided by the trier of fact." Id. In cases involving BWS, the defense expert is not claiming that the defendant lacked the mens rea (e.g., the intent to kill). Nor is the expert claiming that the defendant lacked the mens rea by reason of a mental illness, disorder, or defect. Self-defense is in the nature of confession and avoidance: the accused concedes, for example, that she intended to kill but for reasons which, under the substantive criminal law, justify or excuse the killing (i.e., to prevent her own death or serious bodily harm). Thus, the expert's testimony does not implicate § 29, since it is not offered to disprove the mens rea. This distinction, however, has escaped some courts. See, e.g., People v. Erickson, 57 Cal.App.4th 1391, 1401, 67 Cal.Rptr.2d 740, 746 (1997).

Moreover, even if the expert's testimony disproved the mens rea, § 1107 could be seen as creating an exception to § 29. Subsection (d) of § 1107 does not bar this construction. Subsection (d) provides that § 1107 is intended only "as rule of evidence" and not as a "substantive change" affecting the Penal Code. West's Ann.California Evidence Code § 1107. Section 29 of the Penal Code is not a substantive penal rule but a rule of evidence. It does not change the law of homicide with respect to mens rea or self-defense; § 29 merely restricts the kind of evidence (i.e., expert testimony) that can be received to prove or disprove the mens rea. Some courts, however, have failed to understand that § 29 is not a substantive penal provision. See, e.g., People v. Erickson, supra.

27. People v. Aris, 215 Cal.App.3d 1178, 1196, 264 Cal.Rptr. 167, 179 (1989).

28. 13 Cal.4th 1073, 56 Cal.Rptr.2d 142, 921 P.2d 1 (1996).

29. Id. at 1086, 56 Cal.Rptr.2d at 150, 921 P.2d at 8. "[T]he jury, in determining objective reasonableness, must view the situation from the *defendant's perspective.*" Id. (emphasis in the original). Since a battered person's assessment of the seriousness of the risk may differ from that of someone who has not experienced battering, the jurors should take the defendant's perspective into account in determining the reasonableness of the defendant's fear for her life. Id.

30. People v. Day, 2 Cal.App.4th 405, 416, 2 Cal.Rptr.2d 916, 922 (1992).

31. Id. at 416, 2 Cal.Rptr.2d at 923.

32. Id. at 417, 2 Cal.Rptr.2d at 923.

would have left much earlier "if the beatings were really that bad,"[33] that women are "masochistic and enjoy the beatings,"[34] and that because she flees after killing the batterer, she evinces "a consciousness of guilt" rather than an inability to appreciate her newly found safety.[35]

 Evidence that explains rape trauma syndrome, child sexual abuse accommodation syndrome and battered women's syndrome informs the finder of fact that how they think the average reasonable person would behave and/or how they think they personally would behave are not necessarily the same way that people who have been raped, molested or battered in fact behave. It bears repeating that we have difficulty accepting what we do not understand. Depriving the fact finder of such understanding may well lead to a conclusion based on misconceptions held in good faith. That such conceptions are held in good faith in no way lessens the magnitude of the error and the injustice that may result.[36]

The value of expert testimony on rape trauma syndrome, child sexual abuse syndrome, and intimate partner/battered women's syndrome depends on whether the witness, whose credibility is being supported or assailed, in fact is suffering from one of these syndromes. Otherwise, the testimony would be irrelevant. Accordingly, one would expect the courts to allow the party opposing the expert an opportunity to show that the witness does not suffer from one of these syndromes. The lower appellate courts, however, divided on this point.[37] In People v. Brown[38] the California Supreme Court resolved the controversy by holding that if the expert's testimony complies with the requirements for admitting expert opinion, the proponent does not have to offer additional evidence indicating that the witness suffers from one of the syndromes.[39]

Brown, however, should be read with care. An expert's opinion about the effects of the syndrome is inadmissible under the rules pertaining to expert testimony unless the expert bases his or her opinion on evidence that shows that the witness suffers from the pertinent syndrome. In *Brown*, for example, the expert's testimony about why victims tend to recant previous accusations of abuse was supported by evidence that the victim and the accused were engaged in a "cycle of violence" that often

---

33. Id.

34. Id. at 418, 2 Cal.Rptr.2d at 924.

35. Id.

36. Id. at 419, 2 Cal.Rptr.2d at 925. BWS evidence may also be used by the *prosecution* to rehabilitate an assault victim who has been impeached by the accused with evidence that the victim has recanted accusations of other attacks by the accused. An expert can help the jury understand why a battered woman recants accusations of abuse when she reconciles with her batterer. People v. Gadlin, 78 Cal.App.4th 587, 594, 92 Cal.Rptr.2d 890, 895–896 (2000).

37. Compare People v. Gomez, 72 Cal.App.4th 405, 411, 85 Cal.Rptr.2d 101, 108 (1999) (holding that one battering incident is insufficient to establish battered wife's syndrome) with People v. Williams, 78 Cal.App.4th 1118, 1129, 93 Cal.Rptr.2d 356, 363 (2000) (holding that Evidence Code § 1107 does not require a history of battering in order for expert testimony on battered women's syndrome to be admissible).

38. 33 Cal.4th 892, 94 P.3d 574, 16 Cal.Rptr.3d 447 (2004).

39. Id. at 904, 94 P.3d at 581, 16 Cal.Rptr.3d at 456.

characterizes abusive relationships.[40] As is explained in the chapter on expert testimony, even under *Brown*'s theory of admissibility, the party opposing the expert should be permitted to object to the expert's opinion on the ground that the expert failed to base his or her opinion upon the kind of data reasonably relied upon by experts in the field, that is, data indicating that the witness suffers from the pertinent syndrome.[41]

Impeaching witnesses with expert testimony. In approving the use of expert testimony, the courts have not limited the parties to evidence supporting the credibility of witnesses. Expert testimony may also be offered to attack their credibility. An eyewitness, for example, can be impeached by expert testimony showing why eyewitnesses, though honest, may nonetheless be mistaken.[42] Similarly, battered women can be impeached by expert testimony explaining why they often recant their accusations when they choose to reconcile with their batterers prior to the batterer's trial.[43] Even children who have been sexually abused can be impeached by expert testimony explaining why such children often recant their accusations.[44]

As in the case of expert testimony offered to support credibility, expert evidence offered to attack credibility is committed to the trial judge's discretion under § 352. That discretion is not unbridled, however. As the California Supreme Court emphasized in the case of eyewitnesses, "When an eyewitness identification of the defendant is a key element of the prosecution's case but is not substantially corroborated by evidence giving it independent reliability, and the defendant offers qualified expert testimony on specific psychological factors shown by the record that could have affected the accuracy of the identification but are not likely to be fully known to or understood by the jury, it will ordinarily be error to exclude that testimony."[45] Among the factors not fully known or appreciated by the jury are the pitfalls in cross-racial identification and the lack of correlation between a witness's self-confidence in his identification and the accuracy of his identification.[46]

Inadmissibility of expert testimony on veracity. The fact that courts today are more receptive to expert testimony concerning the credibility of witnesses should not mislead counsel into believing that all

---

40. Id. at 907, 94 P.3d at 583, 16 Cal.Rptr.3d at 458.

41. See § 16.03 infra.

42. People v. McDonald, 37 Cal.3d 351, 208 Cal.Rptr. 236, 690 P.2d 709 (1984), appeal after remand, 203 Cal.App.3d 925, 237 Cal.Rptr. 597 (1987).

43. See People v. Morgan, 58 Cal.App.4th 1210, 1214, 68 Cal.Rptr.2d 772, 774 (1997).

44. People v. Housley, 6 Cal.App.4th 947, 954, 8 Cal.Rptr.2d 431, 435 (1992) (holding that a prosecutor is entitled to call an expert on child sexual abuse accommodation syndrome to explain why a child may recant the initial description of the events he gave to the police).

45. People v. McDonald, 37 Cal.3d 351, 377, 208 Cal.Rptr. 236, 254, 690 P.2d 709, 727 (1984), appeal after remand, 203 Cal.App.3d 925, 237 Cal.Rptr. 597 (1987).

46. Id. at 368–369, 208 Cal.Rptr. at 247–248, 690 P.2d at 720–721. But where the eyewitness testimony is "strong and unequivocal," is not the "only" evidence linking the defendant to the crime, and is "corroborated by other independent evidence of the crime," it not error for a trial judge to exclude the expert testimony. People v. Sanders, 11 Cal.4th 475, 508–510, 46 Cal.Rptr.2d 751, 766–767, 905 P.2d 420, 435–436 (1995).

expert testimony is now admissible if probative of credibility. "[W]here the *sole* purpose of the psychiatric examination and testimony relates to the credibility of a witness, the psychiatrist may not testify to the ultimate question of whether the witness is telling the truth on a particular occasion."[47] An expert, for example, called to explain why women who reunite with their batterers often recant their accusations may not testify that the woman in question was truthful when she first reported her injuries.[48] Jurors do not need the expert's opinion in order to assess the credibility of the woman.

Courts take a similar approach with respect to lay witnesses. As a rule, a lay witness should not be permitted to tell the jury whether another witness was truthful. Jurors can make this determination on their own without the witness's help. A distinction, however, is drawn between questions asking witnesses to assess the veracity of another witness and questions asking witnesses if they know of reasons why other witnesses might have been mistaken or untruthful. "It [is] permissible to ask whether [the witness knows] of facts that would show [that another] witness's testimony might be inaccurate or mistaken, or whether he [knows] of any bias, interest, or motive for [the other] witness to be untruthful."[49] Care, however, should be taken to prevent a party from asking questions on cross-examination that are designed to impugn the credibility of the witness on the stand by asking the witness to speculate about the credibility of other witnesses who have testified. "Were the other witnesses lying" questions should not be permitted unless the examiner is asking in good faith whether the witness on the stand knows of reasons why the other witnesses might be mistaken or untruthful. Misconduct in this regard can be minimized by limiting the cross examiner to asking the witness the pertinent question, namely, whether the witness knows of reasons why the other witnesses might be mistaken or untruthful.

Cases approving the use of expert testimony to support or attack the credibility of witnesses favor the use of relevant evidence. To this extent, the cases are consistent with Proposition 8, an initiative which mandates the introduction of all relevant evidence in criminal cases as a matter of constitutional right.[50] Expert evidence on the credibility of witnesses

---

47. People v. Ainsworth, 45 Cal.3d 984, 1012, 248 Cal.Rptr. 568, 585, 755 P.2d 1017, 1034 (1988) (emphasis in the original). See also People v. Coffman, 34 Cal.4th 1, 81, 17 Cal.Rptr.3d 710, 784, 96 P.3d 30, 93 (2004), cert. denied, 544 U.S. 1063, 125 S.Ct. 2517, 161 L.Ed.2d 1114 (2005): "The general rule is that an expert may not give an opinion whether a witness is telling the truth, for the determination of credibility is not a subject sufficiently beyond common experience that the expert's opinion would assist the trier of fact; in other words, the jury generally is as well equipped as the expert to discern whether a witness is being truthful."

48. People v. Morgan, 58 Cal.App.4th 1210, 1215–1216, 68 Cal.Rptr.2d 772, 775 (1997).

49. People v. Chatman, 38 Cal.4th 344, 382–383, 42 Cal.Rptr.3d 621, 655, 133 P.3d 534, 562–563 (2006).

50. The right to introduce all relevant evidence is subject to enumerated exceptions. For an extended discussion of the effects of this provision on the credibility of witnesses, see § 15.03 supra.

nonetheless can be excluded by judges under § 352.[51] They retain discretion to exclude expert evidence that is relevant to credibility whenever its probative value is substantially outweighed by such countervailing concerns as undue prejudice, consumption of time, and confusion of issues.[52]

Polygraph evidence. Prior to the passage of Proposition 8, California courts excluded evidence based on polygraph examinations on the ground that the scientific principles underlying polygraphy had not been generally accepted by the relevant scientific community.[53] A literal application of the initiative would have overturned the judicially created exclusionary rule and committed the admissibility of the evidence to the judge's discretion, since the proposition favors the admissibility of all relevant evidence irrespective of whether it has the support of the scientific community.[54] A year after Proposition 8, the California Legislature amended the Code to ban "the results of a polygraph examination, the opinion of a polygraph examiner, or any reference to an offer to take, failure to take, or taking of a polygraph examination * * * in any criminal proceeding * * * unless all parties stipulate to the admission of such results."[55] Although the Code section is limited to criminal cases, the courts have extended the ban to proceedings before the State Bar Court[56] and civil matters in general.[57]

The due process right of the accused to use polygraph results or to obtain a polygraph examination of the prosecution's witnesses depends on whether the accused can persuade the trial judge that the technique

---

A literal application of Proposition 8 would also require the use of expert evidence on credibility to be admitted on guilt whenever the evidence is relevant to this issue. For example, evidence that a rape victim suffers from rape trauma syndrome may be probative of whether she was raped. For a discussion of the admissibility of expert evidence on the issue of guilt, see Clarke, *Making the Woman's Experience Relevant to Rape: The Admissibility of Rape Trauma Syndrome in California*, 39 U.C.L.A. Law Review 251 (1991).

51. Proposition 8 exempts § 352 from its operation.

52. For an extended discussion of the trial judge's discretionary powers after Proposition 8, see §§ 2.10–2.11 supra. The rubric that "the use of psychiatric testimony to impeach a witness is generally disfavored" is still cited by some courts. See, e.g., People v. Marshall, 13 Cal.4th 799, 834, 55 Cal.Rptr.2d 347, 365, 919 P.2d 1280, 1298 (1996) and cases cited therein. In contemporary terms, these courts seem to be saying that judges should exclude the evidence unless they find that its probative value substantially outweighs its prejudicial effects. This description of a trial judge's weighing role reverses the one assigned to them under California Evidence Code § 352: judges should admit the proffered evidence unless they find that its probative value is substantially outweighed by its prejudicial effects. West's Ann. California Evidence Code § 352. The juxtaposition of the judges' weighing role is clearly an invitation to the trial bench to approach the admissibility of impeaching psychiatric evidence with suspicion, an approach endorsed by the California Supreme Court in People v. Chatman, 38 Cal.4th 344, 376, 42 Cal.Rptr.3d 621, 650, 133 P.3d 534, 558 (2006).

53. People v. Wochnick, 98 Cal.App.2d 124, 127–128, 219 P.2d 70, 72 (1950), cert. denied, 342 U.S. 888, 72 S.Ct. 179, 96 L.Ed. 666 (1951).

54. For a discussion of the exceptions to Proposition 8, see § 15.03 supra.

55. West's Ann. California Evidence Code § 351.1. Merely mentioning that a key prosecution witness has agreed to take a polygraph examination can result in reversible error. See People v. Basuta, 94 Cal.App.4th 370, 390, 114 Cal.Rptr.2d 285, 300 (2001), where a police officer called by the prosecution testified that a critical state witness "agreed to take a polygraph examination."

56. Arden v. State Bar, 43 Cal.3d 713, 723–724, 239 Cal.Rptr. 68, 73, 739 P.2d 1236, 1241 (1987).

57. Rufo v. Simpson, 86 Cal.App.4th 573, 602–603, 103 Cal.Rptr.2d 492, 512 (2001).

employed in administering the test has been generally accepted by the relevant scientific community.[58] Because currently no scientific consensus exists on the reliability of polygraph evidence, the Code's categorical exclusion of evidence that the accused offered to take or passed a polygraph test does not violate the accused's right to due process.[59] Therefore, whether the accused is entitled to offer such evidence depends on its admissibility under the tests for admitting expert testimony.[60]

It is one matter to exclude polygraph evidence on unreliability grounds when offered to support or attack the credibility of a witness. It is quite another matter when evidence of the accused's willingness to take a polygraph is offered, not for these purposes, but to rebut the prosecution's evidence that the accused failed to cooperate in investigating the crime charged. The California Supreme, however, has held that § 351.1 of the Code bars the accused from offering the evidence even for this purpose.[61]

The federal courts have not been generally receptive to the use of polygraph evidence. As in California, much of their antipathy stems from concerns in the scientific community about the unreliability of the evidence.[62]

Expert testimony and credibility under the Federal Rules. The Federal Rules of Evidence do not have a specific provision on the use of expert evidence to support or attack the credibility of witnesses. The use of this type of proof is governed by the provisions on expert testimony and scientific evidence.[63]

QUESTIONS AND PROBLEMS

1. As will be explored in Chapter 16, an expert's opinion is inadmissible unless the jurors need the expert's help in resolving a contested issue. Judges can invoke this principle to exclude expert opinion on a witness's credibility. Why did California judges invoke this principle until recently to exclude expert testimony on credibility?

2. Many of the same statutory principles governing the use of expert testimony in California courts apply in federal trials. Thus, one can expect the kinds of issues that have arisen in California to arise in federal trials. Proposition 8, however, does not apply to federal cases. Does the initiative favor or disfavor the use of expert testimony on credibility in California criminal trials?

3. In rebuttal in a child abuse prosecution tried in California, the prosecutor may call a duly qualified expert on child accommodation syndrome

---

58. People v. Ayala, 23 Cal.4th 225, 264, 96 Cal.Rptr.2d 682, 706, 1 P.3d 3, 26 (2000), cert. denied, 532 U.S. 908, 121 S.Ct. 1235, 149 L.Ed.2d 143 (2001).

59. People v. Maury, 30 Cal.4th 342, 413, 133 Cal.Rptr.2d 561, 623, 68 P.3d 1, 53 (2003).

60. For extended discussion of this point, see § 16.04 infra.

61. People v. Samuels, 36 Cal.4th 96, 128, 30 Cal.Rptr.3d 105, 130, 113 P.3d 1125 (2005), cert. denied 547 U.S. 1073, 126 S.Ct. 1771, 164 L.Ed.2d 522 (2006).

62. See C. Fishman and A. McKenna, Jones on Evidence § 41:670 et seq. (Nov. 2010).

63. See Federal Rules of Evidence 702–705.

to explain to the jurors why the victim recanted his accusations against the accused prior to the trial. True or false?

4. In rebuttal in a child abuse prosecution tried in California, the prosecutor may call a duly qualified expert on child accommodation syndrome to explain to the jurors why the victim's parents waited two days before reporting the abuse to the police. True or false?

5. In rebuttal in a forcible rape prosecution tried in California, the prosecutor may call a duly qualified expert on rape trauma syndrome to explain to the jurors why the victim waited three days before reporting the rape to the police. True or false?

6. In problems 3 and 5, the prosecution may also ask the expert whether in her opinion the abuse or rape took place. True or false?

7. The accused is charged with murdering her boyfriend. The accused claims that she killed her boyfriend in self-defense. The prosecution's evidence shows that the boyfriend was asleep at the time of the killing. In her case-in-chief, the accused describes a long history of abuse. Accordingly, in a California prosecution the accused can call a duly qualified expert on intimate partner battering syndrome to explain to the jurors why she believed that she was in imminent danger of death or great bodily harm. True or false?

8. In problem 7, the accused may ask the expert, if qualified, whether a reasonable woman in the accused's situation would have been moved to kill. True or false?

9. "When an eyewitness identification of the defendant is a key element of the prosecution's case but is not substantially corroborated by evidence giving it independent reliability, and the defendant offers qualified expert testimony on specific psychological factors shown by the record that could have affected the accuracy of the identification but are not likely to be fully known to or understood by the jury, it will ordinarily be error to exclude that testimony." This statement by the California Supreme Court is especially pertinent in cases involving cross-racial identification. True or false?

10. Because today courts are more open to the use of expert testimony to support or attack the credibility of witnesses, parties may, as a general rule, ask a duly qualified expert whether a particular witness has or has not been truthful. True or false?

11. In some jurisdictions, including California, polygraph evidence is inadmissible unless it meets the jurisdiction's tests for the admission of expert testimony based on scientific principles. True or false?

12. Even if polygraph evidence is admissible as expert testimony, in California the Code specifically prohibits the introduction of the results of a polygraph examination, the opinion of the polygraph examiner, or any reference to an offer to take, failure to take, or taking of a polygraph examination in any criminal proceeding unless all of the parties stipulate to the admission of such results. True or false?

§ 15.10　IMPEACHMENT BY DEMONSTRATING AN IMPAIRED CAPACITY TO PERCEIVE, RECOLLECT OR COMMUNICATE

Whether or not a witness's testimony is an accurate reconstruction of what the witness observed depends on three factors: the witness's ability to perceive, recall, and relate the perception accurately. Not surprisingly, the chief justification for requiring witnesses to testify under oath is to afford the cross examiner an opportunity to expose imperfections in perception, memory, and narration.[1] Exposing flaws is not limited to cross-examination, however. The Code gives parties a general right to offer evidence of a witness's "capacity to perceive, to recollect, or to communicate any matter about which he testifies."[2] Since such evidence is probative of the credibility of witnesses, the Federal Rules also confer the same right on the parties. As a rule, then, any matter that impairs a witness's ability to perceive, recall, or relate is probative of the witness's lack of credibility and is therefore relevant.

The use of drugs and other substances that distort perception may be used to impeach a witness.[3] Judges, however, generally will not permit a party to show merely that a witness is addicted to such drugs. Since what matters is whether the witness was under the influence of mind distorting drugs when the witness perceived the events in question, judges may limit parties to showing the use of such drugs at that time.[4] Though evidence of drug use predating the witness's observations may be probative of whether the witness used drugs on the occasion in question, the use of the evidence for this purpose is barred by §§ 786–787. These sections allow only the use of reputation or opinion evidence to support or attack a witness's character for honesty and veracity.[5] They do not permit the use of other character traits.[6] Moreover, other than convictions, they do not permit the use of specific instances of conduct to support or attack a witness's credibility.[7] The Federal Rules take a similar approach. Under Rule 608, evidence of a witness's character may be used to attack or support a witness's credibility only if the evidence is probative of the

---

1. Federal Rules of Evidence, Article VIII, Hearsay (Advisory Committee Note).

2. West's Ann. California Evidence Code § 780(c).

3. See Grover v. Morrison, 47 Cal.App. 521, 530, 190 P. 1078, 1081 (1920) (intoxication at time of perception). Evidence that a witness is under the influence of a drug that impairs recollection at the time he testifies may also be used to impeach the witness. People v. Viniegra, 130 Cal.App.3d 577, 581, 181 Cal.Rptr. 848, 850 (1982).

4. People v. Stanley, 206 Cal.App.2d 795, 798, 24 Cal.Rptr. 128, 130 (1962) (holding that evidence that a witness was a "great drunkard" constituted improper impeachment).

5. West's Ann. California Evidence Code § 786. The evidence, however, may be admissible as evidence of a habit. Unlike character evidence, habit evidence is admissible to prove that the actor conformed his conduct to his habit. See § 3.18 supra.

6. West's Ann. California Evidence Code § 786.

7. West's Ann. California Evidence Code § 787.

witness's character for truthfulness or untruthfulness.[8] The Rules do permit the use of specific instances of misconduct to prove the witness's bad character for untruthfulness, but the right is of limited value. The impeaching party may inquire into the specific instance only while cross examining the witness and may not prove the instance extrinsically.[9] Accordingly, under the Code and the Rules, evidence of a witness's drug addiction is inadmissible to prove the witness's predisposition to be under the influence of mind distorting drugs, say, at the time the witness perceived the events litigated.[10]

Although the California Supreme Court has not decided the question, a literal application of the Right to Truth–in–Evidence provision of Proposition 8 would repeal §§ 786–787 in criminal cases and allow parties to offer evidence of a witness's prior drug use to prove the witness's predisposition to be under the influence of the drug on the occasion in question.[11] Subject to enumerated exceptions, this provision gives parties a state constitutional right to introduce all relevant evidence.[12] One exception is § 352, which empowers judges to exclude relevant evidence whenever its probative value is substantially outweighed by such countervailing concerns as undue prejudice.[13] Since evidence that a witness is an addict may cause jurors to disbelieve the witness just because he is an addict and not because they believe that his drug use impaired his ability to perceive the events in question, a judge may exclude the evidence of addiction even after Proposition 8. On the other hand, when the impairment in perception or recollection results from repeated drug use, that use may be offered in evidence[14] even in cases unaffected by Proposition 8. Sections 786–787 are not implicated because repeated use is offered to establish the cause of the impairment and not a character trait.

Mental disorders that impair cognition are no longer an automatic ground for disqualifying individuals from testifying.[15] But evidence of such

---

8. Federal Rule of Evidence 608.

9. Id.

10. But if evidence of repeated drug use is offered instead to prove the witness's habit for consuming drugs, then the evidence is admissible. Habit evidence may be offered in California and federal courts to prove that a person conformed his or her conduct to the habit. See § 3.20 supra.

11. In a related context, the court has held that Proposition 8 supersedes § 787. In People v. Harris, 47 Cal.3d 1047, 1080–1082, 255 Cal.Rptr. 352, 373, 767 P.2d 619, 640 (1989), the court held that under the initiative the prosecution could support an informant-witness's credibility by evidence that the informant-witness had proved reliable in the past. Section 786 was not implicated, since the prosecution offered the evidence to support the witness's character for honesty and veracity.

12. For an extended discussion of the effects of Proposition 8 on evidence affecting credibility, see § 15.03 supra.

13. For an extended discussion of a judge's discretionary power to exclude relevant evidence, see § 2.10 supra.

14. People v. Manson, 61 Cal.App.3d 102, 137, 132 Cal.Rptr. 265, 283 (1976), cert. denied, 430 U.S. 986, 97 S.Ct. 1686, 52 L.Ed.2d 382 (1977) (Witness's extended use of hallucinogenics was properly placed before the jury.).

15. See § 14.06 supra. See also People v. Anderson, 25 Cal.4th 543, 574, 106 Cal.Rptr.2d 575, 600–601, 22 P.3d 347, 368 (2001), cert. denied, 534 U.S. 1136, 122 S.Ct. 1082, 151 L.Ed.2d 982

disorders may be used to impeach their credibility.[16] Evidence that a
witness suffers from a disorder affecting perception is relevant to impeach
the witness's account on direct examination. Because of the risk that some
jurors may give undue weight to evidence of mental disorders, a judge may
not allow the impeaching party to show merely that a witness has been
committed to a mental institution or treated for a mental disorder.[17] As in
the case of mind distorting drugs, the central inquiry is whether the
disorder impaired the witness's capacity to perceive at the time the
witness observed the events in question. Evidence that a witness suffers
from a mental disorder affecting recollection or narration is likewise
probative of the witness's lack of credibility.[18]

"Factors a court should consider in [determining the admissibility of
evidence of the mental disorder include] the nature of the psychological
problem, the temporal recency or remoteness of the condition, and whether the witness suffered from the condition at the time of the events to
which she is to testify."[19] "[A] mental illness that causes hallucinations or
delusions is generally more probative of credibility than a condition
causing only depression, irritability, impulsivity or anxiety."[20]

Evidence, for example, that a witness suffers from a mental disorder
that causes her to hallucinate or fantasize is not inadmissible character
evidence. The evidence is not offered to prove that the witness imagined

_____

(2002) (holding that a delusional witness was nonetheless competent to testify because she
understood her duty to tell the truth, could testify in a form understood by the jurors, and
reasonable jurors could find that she had personal knowledge of the subject matter of her
testimony). See also People v. Lewis, 26 Cal.4th 334, 354–362, 110 Cal.Rptr.2d 272, 291–297, 28
P.3d 34, 49–55 (2001), cert. denied, 535 U.S. 1019, 122 S.Ct. 1610, 152 L.Ed.2d 624 (2002)
(holding that an adult witness, who as a result of numerous mental disorders—including
psychosis, paranoia, schizophreniform disorder, and confabulation—had the mental age of a seven
year old, was nonetheless competent to testify but her disorders were admissible to impeach his
credibility).

   16. See People v. Anderson, 25 Cal.4th 543, 574, 106 Cal.Rptr.2d 575, 600–601, 22 P.3d 347,
368 (2001), cert. denied, 534 U.S. 1136, 122 S.Ct. 1082, 151 L.Ed.2d 982 (2002). See also People v.
Russel, 69 Cal.2d 187, 197, 70 Cal.Rptr. 210, 217–218, 443 P.2d 794, 801–802 (1968), cert. denied,
393 U.S. 864, 89 S.Ct. 145, 21 L.Ed.2d 132 (1968); People v. Neely, 228 Cal.App.2d 16, 20, 39
Cal.Rptr. 251, 253 (1964).

   17. While early cases permitted such an inquiry on cross-examination, see, e.g., People v.
Newton, 244 Cal.App.2d 82, 88, 52 Cal.Rptr. 727, 732 (1966), later cases insist that the
impeaching party show how the disorder impairs perception, recollection, or narration. See, e.g.,
People v. Cooks, 141 Cal.App.3d 224, 302–303, 190 Cal.Rptr. 211, 268 (1983), cert. denied, 464
U.S. 1046, 104 S.Ct. 718, 79 L.Ed.2d 180 (1984); People v. Pack, 201 Cal.App.3d 679, 686, 248
Cal.Rptr. 240, 244 (1988), reversed on other grounds by People v. Hammon, 15 Cal.4th 1117,
1123, 65 Cal.Rptr.2d 1, 4, 938 P.2d 986, 990 (1997), cert. denied, 522 U.S. 1125, 118 S.Ct. 1071,
140 L.Ed.2d 130 (1998) ("A person's credibility is not in question merely because he or she is
receiving treatment for a mental health problem.").

   18. See People v. Anderson, 25 Cal.4th 543, 574, 106 Cal.Rptr.2d 575, 600–601, 22 P.3d 347,
368 (2001), cert. denied, 534 U.S. 1136, 122 S.Ct. 1082, 151 L.Ed.2d 982 (2002). See also People v.
Neely, 228 Cal.App.2d 16, 20, 39 Cal.Rptr. 251, 253 (1964).

   19. Boggs v. Collins, 226 F.3d 728, 742 (6th Cir.2000). See also People v. Ledesma, 39 Cal.4th
641, 705, 47 Cal.Rptr.3d 326, 384, 140 P.3d 657, 706 (2006) (holding that a witness's hospitalization in a mental institution was inadmissible to impeach the witness where the hospitalization
occurred16 years before the trial).

   20. People v. Anderson, 25 Cal.4th 543, 608, 106 Cal.Rptr.2d 575, 628, 22 P.3d 347, 391
(2001), cert. denied, 534 U.S. 1136, 122 S.Ct. 1082, 151 L.Ed.2d 982 (2002) (Justice Kennard,
concurring).

the incident she related on the stand because she is the kind of person who imagines such incidents. Rather, the evidence is offered to prove that she imagined the incident in question because of his or her mental disorder.[21]

To ensure that developmentally disabled persons are treated fairly by the criminal justice system, California Penal Code § 1127g requires judges, upon request, to give the following jury instruction whenever a person with a developmental disability, or cognitive, mental, or communication impairment testifies as a witness:

> In evaluating the testimony of a person with a developmental disability, or cognitive, mental, or communication impairment, you should consider all of the factors surrounding the person's testimony, including their level of cognitive development. Although, because of his or her level of cognitive development, a person with a developmental disability, or cognitive, mental, or communication impairment may perform differently as a witness, that does not mean that a person with a developmental disability, or cognitive, mental, or communication impairment is any more or less credible a witness than another witness. You should not discount or distrust the testimony of a person with a developmental disability, or cognitive, mental, or communication impairment solely because he or she is a person with a developmental disability, or cognitive, mental, or communication impairment.[22]

The Penal Code does not define a "developmental disability" or a "cognitive, mental, or communication impairment". After reviewing § 1127g's legislative history, the court in People v. Keeper[23] held that the terms apply to persons whose disability or impairment causes them to be dependent on others for care.[24]

Judges who preside over prosecutions involving sexual offenses no longer have discretion to order a psychiatric examination of the complaining witness.[25] But the opposing party retains the right to impeach the complaining witness on account of mental disorders. Expert testimony may be received to inform the jurors about the effect of certain medical conditions upon the complaining witness's ability to tell the truth; the expert, however, may not tell the jurors whether the complaining witness told the truth.[26] That is a question on which jurors do not need expert help.

Inquiries into how drug use or mental disorders affect perception, recollection, or narration usually will require expert testimony.[27] In addi-

---

21. See People v. Long, 126 Cal.App.4th 865, 871, 24 Cal.Rptr.3d 654, 658 (2005).

22. West's Ann. California Penal Code § 1127g.

23. 192 Cal.App.4th 511, 121 Cal.Rptr.3d 451 (2011).

24. Id. at 520–521, 121 Cal.Rptr.3d at 457–458.

25. See West's Ann. California Penal Code § 1112; see also § 15.09 supra.

26. People v. Castro, 30 Cal.App.4th 390, 395–396, 35 Cal.Rptr.2d 839, 842 (1994).

27. The fact that expert testimony might be of some help does not empower trial judges to subject witnesses to psychiatric evaluations as a matter of course. The privacy interests of

tion to the risk that some jurors may unfairly discount the testimony of drug users and mentally impaired people, such inquiries pose the risk that considerable time will have to be devoted to proving the drug use or mental disorder and their effects. Careful weighing by the judge under § 352 is called for.[28]

To impeach a witness's capacity to perceive, it is not necessary to show that the impairment results from drug use or a mental disorder. Poor eyesight, the existence of obstructions, poor lighting conditions, the failure to wear corrective glasses, and the like will also do. The impairment may also result from the effect upon the witness of the very events he perceives. In People v. McDonald,[29] for example, the California Supreme Court approved the use of expert testimony showing why the stress experienced by crime eyewitnesses can cause them to mistakenly identify the perpetrator despite their best efforts to testify truthfully.[30]

Some early cases permitted a party to impeach a witness on the basis of the witness's poor memory.[31] The attack usually consisted of questions on cross-examination designed to show the witness's inability to remember other events.[32] Especially where such events are unconnected with the ones surrounding the trial, they are simply specific examples of forgetfulness on the witness's part. In effect, the cross examiner seeks to use those instances to prove the witness's character for forgetfulness and then to use that character to impeach the witness's credibility. The early cases did not survive the adoption of the Code. Under § 786 only character traits for honesty or veracity or their opposites are admissible to support or attack the credibility of witnesses, and under § 788 the only specific instances that may be used for this purpose are felony convictions.[33] In criminal cases, however, the use of specific instances is no longer limited by per se rules but is committed to the judge's discretion. Specific

---

witnesses as well as the policy of encouraging witnesses to come forward would be undermined if they could be subjected to psychiatric evaluations in the absence of exceptional circumstances. Moreover, in some circumstances trial judges might not need the expert help in determining the competency of witnesses or jurors in determining their credibility. People v. Anderson, 25 Cal.4th 543, 576, 106 Cal.Rptr.2d 575, 602, 22 P.3d 347, 369 (2001), cert. denied, 534 U.S. 1136, 122 S.Ct. 1082, 151 L.Ed.2d 982 (2002).

28. For a discussion of the judge's discretionary power to exclude relevant evidence under West's Ann. California Evidence Code § 352, see § 2.10 supra.

As a general rule, a criminal defendant does not have a Sixth Amendment right to move for the discovery of the psychiatric records of the prosecution's witnesses until the trial has commenced. See People v. Hammon, 15 Cal.4th 1117, 1127, 65 Cal.Rptr.2d 1, 7, 938 P.2d 986, 992 (1997). For discussion of this and related points, see § 23.03 infra.

29. 37 Cal.3d 351, 208 Cal.Rptr. 236, 690 P.2d 709 (1984), appeal after remand, 203 Cal.App.3d 925, 237 Cal.Rptr. 597 (1987).

30. But where the eyewitness testimony is strong and unequivocal and corroborated by independent evidence, a trial judge may exclude the expert's testimony. See People v. Sanders, 11 Cal.4th 475, 509, 46 Cal.Rptr.2d 751, 766, 905 P.2d 420, 436 (1995), cert. denied 519 U.S. 838, 117 S.Ct. 115, 136 L.Ed.2d 66 (1996). For an extended discussion on the use of expert testimony to support or impeach the credibility of witnesses, see § 15.09 supra.

31. See, e.g., Davis v. California Powder Works, 84 Cal. 617, 24 P. 387 (1890), appeal dism'd, 151 U.S. 389, 14 S.Ct. 350, 38 L.Ed. 206 (1894).

32. Id. at 625, 24 P. at 390.

33. West's Ann. California Evidence Code §§ 786 and 788.

instances of conduct that are probative of a witness's credibility are relevant, and, as has been noted, the Right to Truth–in–Evidence provision of Proposition 8 gives parties to criminal proceedings the state constitutional right to introduce all otherwise admissible relevant evidence.

QUESTIONS AND PROBLEMS

1. Because evidence showing an impaired capacity to perceive, recollect, and communicate is probative of a witness's lack of credibility, both the Code and the Rules allow a party to offer such evidence, including evidence, for example, that the witness is a forgetful person. True or false?

2. Under the Code and the Rules, evidence that a witness was a repeated drug user is probative of the witness's predisposition be under the influence of the drug. True or false?

But the witness's predisposition may not be offered to prove that he was under the influence of drugs on the occasion in question. True or false?

The witness's repeated drug use, however, may be offered to prove that on the occasion in question the witness was suffering from a condition impairing his perception. For example, a party may offer evidence of a witness's repeated use of hallucinogenics to prove that the repeated use impaired her ability to perceive the identity of the killer on the occasion in question. True or false?

Suppose that you offered the evidence of repeated drug use as evidence of the witness's habit. Assuming that you convinced the judge that such use would constitute a habit, would the evidence then be admissible to prove that the witness was under the influence of the drug on the occasion in question?

3. Evidence that a witness was committed to a mental hospital for a condition impairing her perception may always be used to prove that the witness was suffering from that condition on the occasion in question. Discuss.

§ 15.11   IMPEACHMENT BY EVIDENCE OF BIAS OR INTEREST

A witness can be impeached by evidence that the witness harbors a bias, interest, or other motive that casts doubts on the accuracy of the witness's testimony.[1] Examples of bias include a familial[2] or employment[3]

---

1. West's Ann. California Evidence Code § 780(f). Since bias is probative of a witness's lack of credibility, the relevance provisions of the Federal Rules authorize the use of bias evidence. See Federal Rules of Evidence 401–402.

2. People v. Pierce, 269 Cal.App.2d 193, 200, 75 Cal.Rptr. 257, 261 (1969), appeal after remand, 11 Cal.App.3d 313, 89 Cal.Rptr. 751 (1970) (Demonstration of familial bias was proper where the defense witnesses were related to the accused.).

3. People v. Burch, 46 Cal.App. 391, 396, 189 P. 716, 719 (1920) (holding that the accused was entitled to show that certain prosecution witnesses had been compensated for gathering evidence against the accused). In People v. Carpenter, 21 Cal.4th 1016, 90 Cal.Rptr.2d 607, 988 P.2d 531 (1999), cert. denied, 531 U.S. 838, 121 S.Ct. 99, 148 L.Ed.2d 58 (2000), a defense witness testified

relationship with a party, payment to the witness by a party of claims arising from the same transaction,[4] having a financial stake in the outcome of the case,[5] and providing special assistance or favors to a party.[6] Experts can be forced to disclose their fees for testifying[7] as well as their willingness to testify for only one side, such as the defense or the prosecution in criminal cases.[8]

The fact that a witness and a party belong to the same social organizations can be probative of bias.[9] However, the California courts have expressed reservations about the use of gang membership to impeach a witness.[10] One risk is that jurors might be unduly prejudiced against

---

that the accused was at work about the time the killer had been seen at the crime scene. On cross-examination, the prosecution was allowed to impeach the witness by evidence that the witness and the accused had invested in the witness's business. Impeachment on account of bias stemming from a business relationship is proper. Over objection, however, the trial judge then allowed the prosecution to introduce a letter in which the accused threatened to charge the witness a loan sharking interest rate unless the witness repaid the investment by a certain date. A witness who testifies for a party after having been threatened by that party is presumably a fairly reliable witness. Since the prosecution was not interested in bolstering the credibility of a defense witness, the accused claimed that the prosecutor's real purpose was to place before the jury inadmissible bad character evidence. The California Supreme Court disagreed, holding that the evidence of the threat was relevant to the witness's credibility on grounds of "bias and prejudice." Id. at 1054, 90 Cal.Rptr.2d at 633, 988 P.2d at 555. How the court reached this conclusion is unclear.

The court also justified the use of the letter as corroborating the testimony of a witness called earlier by the prosecution. Id. This witness testified that at the accused's request she purchased the gun which other evidence showed was the weapon used in the killings for which the accused was on trial. On cross-examination, the defense got the witness to concede that the accused told the witness that he wanted the gun "to move" money for the Mafia. Since the victims had nothing to do with the Mafia, the accused wanted to show that his ownership of the gun had nothing to do with killings. How the accused's threat to charge loan sharking interest rates corroborated the testimony of the prosecution witness is not explained by the court.

4. Zelayeta v. Pacific Greyhound Lines, 104 Cal.App.2d 716, 728, 232 P.2d 572, 580 (1951) (holding that the plaintiff was entitled to show that a witness called by the defendant had settled a claim against the defendant arising out of the same accident in which the plaintiff claimed he was injured).

5. H. W. Smith, Inc. v. Swenson, 105 Cal.App. 60, 65, 286 P. 1050, 1052 (1930) (holding that the defendant was entitled to show that a key witness for the plaintiff had assigned to the plaintiff on a fifty-fifty basis the notes upon which the plaintiff sued the defendant).

6. People v. Johnson, 47 Cal.3d 576, 591, 253 Cal.Rptr. 710, 722, 764 P.2d 1087, 1099 (1988), cert. denied, 493 U.S. 829, 110 S.Ct. 98, 107 L.Ed.2d 62 (1989) (holding that the prosecution was entitled to show that a witness, who testified for the accused in a murder case, had assisted the accused in escaping from a state hospital).

7. West's Ann. California Evidence Code § 722(b) ("The compensation and expenses paid or to be paid to an expert witness by the party calling him is a proper subject of inquiry by any adverse party as relevant to the credibility of the witness and the weight of his testimony."). See also Brokopp v. Ford Motor Co., 71 Cal.App.3d 841, 849, 139 Cal.Rptr. 888, 893 (1977).

8. People v. Rich, 45 Cal.3d 1036, 1088, 248 Cal.Rptr. 510, 543, 755 P.2d 960, 993, cert. denied, 488 U.S. 1051, 109 S.Ct. 884, 102 L.Ed.2d 1006 (1989).

9. In re Wing Y., 67 Cal.App.3d 69, 76, 136 Cal.Rptr. 390, 394 (1977). The Code as well as the Federal Rules prohibit using a witness's religious beliefs to support or attack the witness's credibility. ("As a practicing Presbyterian, do you believe in telling the truth under oath?") West's Ann. California Evidence Code § 789; Federal Rule of Evidence 610. Neither, however, precludes using a witness's religious beliefs or affiliations for the purpose of showing bias or interest. ("You and the plaintiff belong to the same church, do you not?") See, e.g., Federal Rule of Evidence 610 (Advisory Committee Note).

10. See People v. Cardenas, 31 Cal.3d 897, 904–906, 184 Cal.Rptr. 165, 168–169, 647 P.2d 569, 572–573 (1982) and cases cited therein.

witnesses who belong to gangs.[11] Another is that widespread reports on the growth and dangerousness of gangs in the state might improperly induce jurors to convict the accused on the basis of gang membership.[12] Though prosecutors should avoid eliciting information about gang activities, they are still free to establish that a witness and the accused live in the same neighborhood and belong to the same neighborhood groups.[13] Because of its inflammatory and prejudicial nature, judges should exclude gang membership evidence where other evidence shows the witness's association with the defendant.[14]

The California courts also disfavor the use of arrests to prove a defense witness's bias against police officers or the prosecution in a criminal case:

> We recognize that, even if the commission of a battery does not prove the batterer has a disposition to lie, an arrest for battery might suggest a reason for the batterer to be biased against the arresting officers or agency. * * * But it is established that evidence of mere arrests is inadmissible because it is more prejudicial than probative. * * * Against this serious prejudice, it is a weak "thread of inferences from past arrests by the police, to hostility against police in general, to a willingness to distort testimony." (Grudt v. City of Los Angeles, supra, 2 Cal.3d at p. 592, 86 Cal.Rptr. 465, 468 P.2d 825.)[15]

Criminal cases provide fertile ground for demonstrating a motive by some witnesses to slant their testimony in order to curry favor with the authorities. The classic example is the witness who agrees to testify against the accused in exchange for some benefit, ranging from immunity from prosecution to pleading to reduced charges to recommendations for leniency at sentencing. An agreement between the prosecution and the witness is not essential, however. The fact that a witness is on probation or parole,[16] or is facing unresolved charges can also be shown.[17] Such

---

11. Id. Because of its potential to prejudice the accused, "the use at trial of cumulative evidence of bias in the form of gang-affiliation evidence constitutes an abuse of discretion." People v. Davis, 42 Cal.App.4th 806, 813, 49 Cal.Rptr.2d 890, 895 (1996).

12. See People v. Cardenas, 31 Cal.3d 897, 904–906, 184 Cal.Rptr. 165, 168–169, 647 P.2d 569, 572–573 (1982) and cases cited therein.

13. People v. Munoz, 157 Cal.App.3d 999, 1012, 204 Cal.Rptr. 271, 278–279 (1984). For a discussion of how gang membership can be used to establish the accused's motive for committing the offense charged, see § 3.15 supra.

Although the courts have expressed reservations about the use of gang membership to prove bias, they have allowed the prosecution to show that the accused and a witness had been crime partners to impeach the credibility of the witness. See, e.g., People v. Freeman, 8 Cal.4th 450, 493, 34 Cal.Rptr.2d 558, 582, 882 P.2d 249, 273 (1994). When used in this manner, the jurors must be told not to consider the evidence as proof of the accused's predisposition to commit the crime charged. Id.

14. People v. Bojorquez, 104 Cal.App.4th 335, 342, 128 Cal.Rptr.2d 411, 415 (2002).

15. People v. Lopez, 129 Cal.App.4th 1508, 1523, 29 Cal.Rptr.3d 586, 597 (2005).

16. People v. Brown, 13 Cal.App.3d 876, 883, 91 Cal.Rptr. 904, 908 (1970), cert. denied, 404 U.S. 835, 92 S.Ct. 120, 30 L.Ed.2d 66 (1971).

17. People v. Blackwell, 81 Cal.App. 417, 419, 253 P. 964, 965 (1927).

witnesses can have a motive to please the prosecution, even if their hopes for favorable treatment are unfounded.[18]

Federal due process requires prosecutors to disclose to the defense exculpatory evidence that is material to guilt or punishment, irrespective of the whether the defense has requested such evidence.[19] The duty to disclose favorable evidence extends to evidence that bears on the credibility of material witnesses[20] and includes any inducements made to prosecution witnesses for favorable testimony.[21] A prosecutor's failure to disclose the benefits offered in exchange for testimony can result in the reversal of a conviction and in extreme cases in outright dismissal with prejudice.[22]

The right of criminal defendants to impeach prosecution witnesses on account of bias is protected by the Confrontation Clause of the Sixth Amendment.[23] State rules that prevent such impeachment must yield to the defendant's constitutional right to cross examine a witness for bias.[24] In Davis v. Alaska, for example, the United States Supreme Court held that Alaska's interest in protecting the confidentiality of a juvenile offender's record had to yield to the accused's interest in showing that the juvenile, who testified against the accused, was on probation for a juvenile offense.[25]

The impeaching party is not limited to showing why a witness may be biased in favor of the opposing party. The impeaching party may also demonstrate why a witness is hostile to its position. In In re Anthony P.,[26]

---

18. People v. Pantages, 212 Cal. 237, 258, 297 P. 890, 900 (1931). Just as evidence that a witness expects to receive something of value in exchange for testimony may be considered in evaluating his or her credibility, so may evidence that a witness declined an offer of financial gain in exchange for his or her silence. Both items of evidence are probative of the witness's credibility and are therefore relevant. See People v. Guerra, 37 Cal.4th 1067, 1142, 40 Cal.Rptr.3d 118, 184, 129 P.3d 321 (2006).

19. United States v. Agurs, 427 U.S. 97, 110–111, 96 S.Ct. 2392, 2401, 49 L.Ed.2d 342 (1976).

20. Giglio v. United States, 405 U.S. 150, 154, 92 S.Ct. 763, 766, 31 L.Ed.2d 104 (1972); People v. Ruthford, 14 Cal.3d 399, 406, 121 Cal.Rptr. 261, 265–266, 534 P.2d 1341, 1345–1346 (1975), overruled on other grounds, In re Sassounian, 9 Cal.4th 535, 545–546, note 7, 37 Cal.Rptr.2d 446, 452, note 7, 887 P.2d 527, 533, note 7 (1995).

21. People v. Westmoreland, 58 Cal.App.3d 32, 43, 129 Cal.Rptr. 554, 561 (1976).

22. People v. Kasim, 56 Cal.App.4th 1360, 1387, 66 Cal.Rptr.2d 494, 511 (1997).

23. Davis v. Alaska, 415 U.S. 308, 315–316, 94 S.Ct. 1105, 1110, 39 L.Ed.2d 347 (1974).

24. Id. at 320, 94 S.Ct. at 1112.

25. Id. In People v. Carpenter, 21 Cal.4th 1016, 90 Cal.Rptr.2d 607, 988 P.2d 531 (1999), cert. denied, 531 U.S. 838, 121 S.Ct. 99, 148 L.Ed.2d 58 (2000), the accused, citing *Davis*, sought to impeach a prosecution witness by asking on cross-examination whether she was on probation on a juvenile matter when she spoke to law enforcement personnel about the crime charged against the accused. The trial judge ruled that the accused could not ask the witness whether she had been on probation but could ask her "whether she had a juvenile case, and could 'develop with her whether she thought in any aspect of that juvenile case she was going to get any benefit in this case or anybody made any promises to her about any aspects of the juvenile case.'" Id. at 1050, 90 Cal.Rptr.2d at 630, 988 P.2d at 552. The California Supreme Court found no confrontation violation under *Davis*: the defense was not precluded "from presenting evidence she *did* receive any promises or benefits.... Moreover, the defense did not claim, and the record does not indicate, that the witness was on probation when she testified several years later." Id. at 1051, 90 Cal.Rptr.2d at 631, 988 P.2d at 553. The accused, however, had been precluded in the first place from inquiring about the witness's probationary status.

26. 167 Cal.App.3d 502, 213 Cal.Rptr. 424 (1985).

for example, a juvenile accused of molesting the complaining witness was entitled to show that the witness was prejudiced against him on account of his race.[27] In Anderson v. Southern Pac. Co.[28] the defendant was likewise entitled to show that the plaintiff's expert witness was biased because the witness had been discharged from employment on account of information furnished by the defendant.[29]

Cases like *Anderson* raise difficult questions for the trial judge. To what extent should the judge permit the parties to prove or disprove the event allegedly giving rise to the bias? To prevent an action, say, for wrongful death, from becoming an action, say, for the wrongful discharge of a witness, the Common Law relied on rules of thumb.[30] Some prevented extrinsic proof of bias, unless the witness was first asked about the bias on cross-examination. If the witness admitted the bias, no extrinsic proof was permitted.[31] Others permitted the fact of bias to be shown but not the reasons for it.[32] These rules of thumb have been superseded by § 352 and Federal Rule of Evidence 403, which vest judges with discretion to exclude relevant evidence whenever its probative value is substantially outweighed by such countervailing concerns as undue consumption of time and confusion of issues.[33] Section 352 and Rule 403 call for a flexible response tailored by the judge to the circumstances presented by the case being tried. If the witness sought to be impeached on the grounds of bias is a key witness and no other significant ground of impeachment is available, the judge may permit extended inquiry into the existence of, as well as the reasons for, the bias.[34]

Religious affiliations. Both the California Evidence Code and the Federal Rules of Evidence prohibit the use of a witness's religious beliefs or opinions to show that a witness's credibility is impaired or enhanced.[35] Evidence, for example, that a witness belongs to a religious sect that imposes a duty to tell the truth may not be offered to prove that the

---

27. Id. at 509–510, 213 Cal.Rptr. at 428–429.

28. 129 Cal.App. 206, 18 P.2d 703 (1933).

29. Id. at 212, 18 P.2d at 706.

30. See C. McCormick, McCormick on Evidence § 41 (E. Cleary 2d ed. 1972).

31. Id.

32. Eye v. Kafer, Inc., 202 Cal.App.2d 449, 456, 20 Cal.Rptr. 841, 845 (1962), quoting from Richardson v. Gage, 28 S.D. 390, 133 N.W. 692 (1911).

33. For an extended discussion on a judge's power to exclude relevant evidence under § 352, see § 2.10 supra.

34. Prior to the adoption of the Evidence Code, California followed the Common Law rule prohibiting the calling party from inquiring on redirect about a witness's reasons for being biased where the witness admitted the bias on cross-examination. See People v. Zemavasky, 20 Cal.2d 56, 63, 123 P.2d 478, 478 (1942). Rather than relying on § 352, some California courts have continued to rely on the Common Law rule in criminal cases even after the Legislature adopted the Code. See, e.g. People v. Morris, 46 Cal.3d 1, 36, 249 Cal.Rptr. 119, 141, 756 P.2d 843, 865 (1988), disapproved on other grounds, In re Sassounian, 9 Cal.4th 535, 545, 37 Cal.Rptr.2d 446, 452, 887 P.2d 527, 533 (1995); other courts seem to balance the reasons for the bias against their prejudicial effects. See, e.g., People v. Feagin, 34 Cal.App.4th 1427, 1433–1434, 40 Cal.Rptr.2d 918, 921 (1995).

35. West's Ann. California Evidence Code § 789; Federal Rule of Evidence 610.

witness told the truth. Conversely, a witness's refusal to belong to such a sect may not be offered as evidence that the witness was dishonest.

The state and federal provisions are merely a specific formulation of the general rule that, unless otherwise provided, a witness's character for truth-telling or its opposite is inadmissible in proving or disproving the witness's veracity as a witness.[36] Accordingly, a witness's affiliations— from membership in a gang to membership in the Presbyterian Church— are inadmissible for the purpose of showing a witness's character for veracity or lack of veracity. But disclosure of an affiliation with a gang or a church is admissible for the purpose of showing bias and interest.[37] A prosecutor, for example, is free to establish that a witness and the accused belong to the same neighborhood groups,[38] including the same religious organizations.

In California criminal cases, a literal application of the Right to Truth–in–Evidence provision of Proposition 8 would repeal the Code's ban of the use of a witness's religious beliefs or opinions to show that the witness's credibility is impaired or enhanced. This provision gives parties to criminal proceedings a state constitutional right not to have relevant evidence excluded.[39] Evidence that, on account of religious convictions, a witness is the kind of person who would tell the truth is probative of the proposition that the witness was truthful in his testimony. Since the concept of relevance includes evidence that is probative of a witness's veracity,[40] evidence of a witness's religious beliefs or opinions would thus be relevant and admissible under Proposition 8.[41]

Intimidation of witnesses. Sometimes parties are surprised by the reluctance of witnesses to testify in the manner they indicated prior to the trial. A prosecutor, for example, who expects a witness to place the accused at the crime scene, may learn for the first time on direct examination that the witness now claims an imperfect recollection of the events in question. It is useful in these circumstances for the prosecutor to expose some threat as the cause of the witness's difficulties. As a general matter, evidence that a witness is afraid to testify is probative of the witness's credibility and is therefore relevant.[42]

---

36. See West's Ann. California Evidence Code §§ 786 and 1101(a); Federal Rules of Evidence 404(a) and 608.

37. See People v. Munoz, 157 Cal.App.3d 999, 1012, 204 Cal.Rptr. 271, 278–279 (1984) (gang membership); Drake v. Dean, 15 Cal.App.4th 915, 19 Cal.Rptr.2d 325, 336 (1993) (religious affiliation); Federal Rule of Evidence 610 (Advisory Committee Note) (church affiliation).

38. See People v. Munoz, 157 Cal.App.3d 999, 1012, 204 Cal.Rptr. 271, 278–279 (1984).

39. For an extended discussion of the Right to Truth–in–Evidence provision, see § 15.03 supra.

40. West's Ann. California Evidence Code § 210.

41. A judge, however, may still exclude the evidence under the discretionary powers given judges by § 352. See § 15.03 supra.

42. People v. Gutierrez, 23 Cal.App.4th 1576, 1587, 28 Cal.Rptr.2d 897, 904 (1994). Accord: People v. Box, 23 Cal.4th 1153, 1205–1206, 99 Cal.Rptr.2d 69, 107, 5 P.3d 130, 165 (2000), cert. denied, 532 U.S. 963, 121 S.Ct. 1497, 149 L.Ed.2d 383 (2001).

A witness who testifies despite fear of recrimination of *any* kind by *anyone* is more credible because of his or her personal stake in the testimony. Just as the fact a witness expects to receive something in exchange for testimony may be considered in evaluating his or her credibility * * *, the fact a witness is testifying despite fear of recrimination is important to fully evaluating his or her credibility. For this purpose, it matters not the source of the threat. It could come from a friend of the defendant, or it could come from a stranger who merely approves of the defendant's conduct or disapproves of the victim. It could come from a person who perceives a social or political agenda to have been advanced by the defendant's actions. It could come from a member of the witness' profession, religion, or subculture, who disapproves of the witness' involvement for some reason. It could come from a zealot of any stripe, large groups of whom seem ready to rally to virtually any cause these days.[43]

Intimidation evidence, however, is inadmissible against the accused as proof of consciousness of guilt unless the prosecution offers some evidence connecting the accused with the intimidation.[44] Whether or not the prosecution has satisfied this condition calls for a sufficiency analysis. When the witness claims that someone other than the accused intimidated him, the question for the judge is whether reasonable jurors could find that the accused authorized the intimidation if the prosecutor's evidence is believed.[45] Although only a sufficiency analysis is called for, judges should nonetheless exclude the evidence under their discretionary authority if the probative value of the evidence is substantially outweighed by the risk that the jurors might misuse the evidence as proof that the accused is a bad person deserving of punishment or that he is the kind of person who would commit the offense charged.

In some instances it is the accused who wishes to show that an adverse witness's testimony has been improperly influenced by the prosecution. In People v. Badgett,[46] for example, the accused attempted to exclude a witness's testimony on the ground that, in exchange for immunity from prosecution, the witness had agreed to testify consistently with

---

43. People v. Olguin, 31 Cal.App.4th 1355, 1368–1369, 37 Cal.Rptr.2d 596, 601 (1994) (emphasis in the original). Sometimes witnesses claim to have been intimidated by violent gangs. In the absence of evidence linking the accused with the threats, trial judges should take steps to assure that the jurors do not unfairly associate the accused with the gangs. Such steps can include referring to the gangs by euphemisms. See People v. Ayala, 23 Cal.4th 225, 276–277, 96 Cal.Rptr.2d 682, 715–716, 1 P.3d 3, 34 (2000), cert. denied, 532 U.S. 908, 121 S.Ct. 1235, 149 L.Ed.2d 143 (2001).

44. See People v. Olguin, 31 Cal.App.4th 1355, 1368–1369, 37 Cal.Rptr.2d 596, 601 (1994). See also People v. Williams, 16 Cal.4th 153, 155, 66 Cal.Rptr.2d 123, 155, 940 P.2d 710, 742 (1997), cert. denied, 522 U.S. 1150, 118 S.Ct. 1169, 140 L.Ed.2d 179 (1998). For a discussion of whether a party's conduct, including intimidating witnesses, constitutes an admission, see § 7.06 supra.

45. See West's Ann. California Evidence Code § 403 and comment. See also Federal Rule of Evidence 104(b). Upon request the judge must instruct the jurors to disregard the evidence of intimidation unless they first find that the accused authorized the intimidating acts. West's Ann. California Evidence Code § 403. For a discussion of when sufficiency standards govern the determination of preliminary facts, see § 17.02 infra.

46. 10 Cal.4th 330, 41 Cal.Rptr.2d 635, 895 P.2d 877 (1995).

a statement she had given police. That statement, according to the accused, had been taken in violation of the witness's Fifth Amendment rights. A criminal defendant, however, lacks standing to object to a witness's testimony on the ground that the testimony is the fruit of involuntary statements made to the police.[47] That right is personal to the witness and may not be asserted by another.[48] But a criminal defendant does have standing to exclude testimony if its use violates the *defendant's* due process right to a fair trial.[49] A defendant is denied a fair trial if the prosecution's case depends substantially upon the testimony of a witness whose testimony has been rendered unreliable by coercive tactics employed by the prosecution or its agents.[50] "An immunity agreement that requires the witness to testify consistently with a previous statement to the police is deemed coercive and testimony produced by such an agreement is subject to exclusion from evidence."[51] So is an agreement that requires a witness's testimony to result in a conviction.[52] Of course, any plea agreement or grant of immunity has some coercive effect upon a witness. But an agreement or grant of immunity which requires the witness to testify only truthfully and fully will not violate the accused's right to a fair trial.[53] So long as the witness understands that his or her only obligation is to testify truthfully, it is immaterial that the agreement calls for the witness to plead guilty and the imposition of sentence after the witness has testified.[54] Even in these circumstances, however, the accused is entitled to inform the jurors that the witness is testifying pursuant to an agreement with the prosecution or as a result of a grant of immunity.[55]

QUESTIONS AND PROBLEMS

1. Though a party may always try to show that a witness is biased against him, neither the Code nor the Rules permit a party to show the reasons why the witness is biased. A party, for example, may show that an opposing witness had been fired by him but not the reasons for firing the witness. True or false?

---

47. Id. at 343, 41 Cal.Rptr.2d at 642, 895 P.2d at 883.

48. Id.

49. Id.

50. Id.

51. Id. at 357, 41 Cal.Rptr.2d at 651, 895 P.2d at 892.

52. People v. Gurule, 28 Cal.4th 557, 615, 123 Cal.Rptr.2d 345, 393, 51 P.3d 224, 264 (2002), cert. denied, 538 U.S. 964, 123 S.Ct. 1754, 155 L.Ed.2d 517 (2003).

53. People v. Badgett, 10 Cal.4th 330, 358, 41 Cal.Rptr.2d 635, 651, 895 P.2d 877, 892 (1995) (quoting from People v. Allen, 42 Cal.3d 1222, 232 Cal.Rptr. 849, 729 P.2d 115 (1986)). "Granting benefits, reduced sentences, or even immunity to secure a witness's testimony is commonplace and would not constitute such 'outrageous' conduct as to justify suppression or outright dismissal." People v. Ervin, 22 Cal.4th 48, 85–86, 91 Cal.Rptr.2d 623, 645, 990 P.2d 506, 526 (2000), cert. denied, 531 U.S. 842, 121 S.Ct. 107, 148 L.Ed.2d 65 (2000).

54. People v. Riel, 22 Cal.4th 1153, 1179–1180, 96 Cal.Rptr.2d 1, 22, 998 P.2d 969, 988 (2000), cert. denied, 531 U.S. 1087, 121 S.Ct. 803, 148 L.Ed.2d 690 (2001).

55. For an example of such an instruction, see People v. Avila, 38 Cal.4th 491, 596, note 17, 43 Cal.Rptr.3d 1, 87, note 17, 133 P.3d 1076, 1148, note 17 (2006).

Similarly, in a criminal case the defendant may offer evidence showing that a prosecution witness agreed to testify against him pursuant to an agreement reached with the prosecution. The defendant, however, may not offer evidence of the details of the agreement. True or false?

2. Evidence that a witness and the accused belong to the same social organization is probative of whether the witness was truthful when the witness testified on behalf of the accused. A prosecutor, for example, may show that a defense witness and the accused bowl in the same league and belong to the same country club. True or false?

3. Evidence that the organization to which the witness and the accused belong requires its members to lie for each other is probative of whether the witness was truthful when the witness testified on behalf of the accused. True or false? *May not nec. be adm.*

4. Under California Evidence Code § 787, however, such evidence is inadmissible in California if offered to prove the witness's character for lack of veracity. Other than prior convictions, § 787 prohibits the use of specific instances of conduct to establish a character trait to attack or support the veracity of a witness. True or false?

5. If offered as a prior bad act, such evidence is admissible under Federal Rule of Evidence 608 if the evidence is elicited on the cross-examination of the witness. True or false?

6. If in federal court the witness denies belonging to any such organization, the impeaching party may not prove his membership in such an organization extrinsically. True or false?

7. Suppose that instead of offering the evidence as a prior bad act the prosecution offers it as evidence of the witness's motive to lie on direct examination. In a California or federal court, would you allow the prosecution to prove the witness's membership and the organization's tenets extrinsically?

8. Though the Code and the Rules permit a party to show that a witness and the opposing party belong to the same religious organization as proof of the witness's bias, neither allows the calling party to offer the witness's religious affiliation as proof of the witness's good character for veracity. For example, the calling party may not offer evidence that the witness's religious tenets prohibit adherents from "bearing false witness against one's neighbors" as proof of the witness's good character for veracity. True or false?

9. In a California criminal case, would you allow the defendant to offer evidence that his key witness belongs to a religious organization that requires its members to testify truthfully?

That a key prosecution witness does not belong to such an organization?

10. Evidence that a witness was threatened with harm if she testified is probative of the witness's credibility. Accordingly, if admitted, the jury may consider the evidence of the threat in evaluating the witness's testimony. True or false?

But the judge should not allow the jury to consider the threat as evidence of the defendant's guilt unless the prosecution offers some evidence linking the threat with the defendant. True or false?

§ 15.12 IMPEACHING THE COMPLAINING WITNESS IN SEX OFFENSE PROSECUTIONS

California's rape shield law. California's rape shield provisions affect defense evidence in two ways. First, § 1103(c) prohibits the use of evidence of the victim's sexual relations with others to prove that the victim consented to having sexual relations with the accused because she is the kind of person who engages in consensual sex.[1] The defense is limited to offering only the victim's sexual conduct with the accused in proving the victim's predisposition to engage in consensual sex with the accused.[2] Second, § 782 prohibits the use of otherwise admissible evidence of the complaining witness's "sexual conduct" when offered under § 780 to attack her credibility, unless at a separate hearing the judge concludes that the probative value of the evidence is not substantially outweighed by the concerns enumerated in § 352.[3] Unless otherwise provided, § 780 allows the fact finder to consider in determining the credibility of a witness any evidence that "has a tendency in reason to prove or disprove the truthfulness of the witness's testimony."[4]

It is important to understand why § 782 was enacted. Without it, evidence of the victim's sexual conduct that appears to violate the rape shield law (e.g., the victim's relations with others) might be admissible, not as evidence of victim's predisposition to consent, but to "impeach" the victim. Rather than rely just on § 352 to screen the evidence, § 782 requires the judge to hold an evidentiary hearing to determine whether to admit otherwise admissible evidence of the victim's sexual conduct when offered to impeach the victim.[5] At the conclusion of the hearing, the judge, acting under § 352, can exclude the evidence, allow the defendant to offer the evidence to the jury, or allow the defendant to offer only part of the evidence.[6] How the judge rules depends on the judge's assessment of the importance of the evidence to the defendant and its prejudice to the

---

1. West's Ann. California Evidence Code § 1103(c). For an extended discussion of this provision, see § 3.12 supra.

2. West's Ann. California Evidence Code § 1103(c).

3. West's Ann. California Evidence Code § 782. For an extended discussion of a judge's power to exclude relevant evidence under § 352, see § 2.10 supra.

The term "sexual conduct" is not limited to the sexual conduct of rape victims. It includes also the sexual conduct of victims of any sexually related crimes, including the offenses of committing lewd and lascivious acts upon children and exhibiting pornographic material to children.

In prosecutions for committing lewd and lascivious acts upon children, defendants will sometimes seek to impeach the credibility of the complaining witness by offering evidence that the child learned about the acts from another source and not from the act alleged. The admissibility of such evidence is subject to a § 782 hearing. See People v. Woodward, 116 Cal.App.4th 821, 831, 10 Cal.Rptr.3d 779, 786 (2004).

4. West's Ann. California Evidence Code § 780.

5. West's Ann. California Evidence Code § 782.

6. Id.

victim, within the context of case being tried.[7] For example, if the judge has already allowed the defendant to impeach the victim through other evidence (e.g., prior inconsistent statements), the judge may find that the prejudice to the victim substantially outweighs the probative value of the evidence to the defendant.

The term "sexual conduct" encompasses any behavior that reflects the actor's or speaker's willingness to engage in sexual activity.[8] Though the term should not be narrowly construed, evidence that a witness has falsely accused others of engaging in sexual misconduct with the witness is not subject to a § 782 hearing. "Even though the content of the [accusation] has to do with sexual conduct, the sexual conduct is not the fact from which the jury is asked to draw an inference about the witness's credibility. The jury is asked to draw an inference about the witness's credibility from the fact that she stated as true something that was false."[9]

Additionally, some evidence offered under § 1103(c)(4) appears to be outside the ambit of § 782. Subsection (4) provides that if the prosecutor in a sexual assault prosecution "introduces evidence * * * or the complaining witness as a witness gives testimony, and that evidence or testimony relates to the complaining witness' sexual conduct, the defendant may cross-examine the witness who gives the testimony and offer relevant evidence limited specifically to the rebuttal of the evidence introduced by the prosecutor or given by the complaining witness."[10] Thus, if the victim on direct examination testifies that she did not have consensual sex with the accused because she opposes premarital sex, that testimony would allow the accused on cross to ask the victim whether she had consensual sex with, say, Harry, and to call Harry to testify to having had consensual sex with the victim in the event the victim denies having had consensual sex with him. Although evidence of having had consensual sex with Harry may not be received to prove the victim's predisposition to engage in consensual sex with the accused (the use of the evidence for that purpose is banned by the rape shield provision), the Code's express authorization of the use of the evidence for impeachment purposes under § 1103(c)(4) appears to subject its admissibility only to § 352 and not the more stringent requirements of § 782.[11] Admittedly, the evidence meets the relevance test of evidence offered on credibility under the definition provided by § 780. But the evidence is not offered under § 780 but under § 1103.

7. Id.

8. People v. Franklin, 25 Cal.App.4th 328, 334, 30 Cal.Rptr.2d 376, 380 (1994).

9. Id. at 335, 30 Cal.Rptr.2d at 380. Such evidence is admissible under Proposition 8 to impeach witnesses in criminal cases. For an extended discussion of the use of prior bad acts to attack the credibility of witnesses, see § 15.06 supra.

10. West's Ann. California Evidence Code § 1103(c)(4).

11. Section 1103 expressly provides that nothing in the "subdivision" is to be construed as making inadmissible evidence offered to attack the credibility of the complaining witness under § 782. West's Ann. California Evidence Code § 1103(c)(5). But here the opposite question is presented: whether evidence expressly made admissible by § 1103 to attack the credibility of the victim can be excluded under § 782.

The § 782 hearing is governed by an elaborate procedure, including the filing by the accused of a written motion and offer of proof.[12] Failure to comply with the procedural requirements will preclude the accused from raising the trial judge's error in excluding evidence of the complaining witness's sexual conduct that is offered to attack her credibility.[13]

To obtain a hearing on the admissibility of the impeaching evidence, the accused must persuade the judge that the proposed evidence is "sufficient."[14] Presumably, the proffer is sufficient if it is probative of a proposition discrediting the complaining witness's credibility and the use of the proffered evidence for that purpose is not barred by the Evidence Code. Since § 782 calls for the application of a sufficiency standard, in assessing the sufficiency of the proffered evidence the judge should assume that the testimony of the proposed witness is true.[15] The proffered evidence may be insufficient where its relevance depends on an answer which the accused hopes to elicit from the victim. For example, in People v. Jordan[16] the accused sought to attack the credibility of the victim by evidence that, contrary to her anticipated testimony, the victim had not had sexual relations with others.[17] A major flaw of the accused's offer of proof was the failure to allege a basis for believing that the victim would testify to having had sexual relations with others.[18]

Even if the evidence produced at the hearing is probative of the victim's lack of credibility and its use is not barred by the Code, the judge may still exclude the evidence if its probative value is substantially outweighed by the concerns enumerated in § 352. In People v. Casas,[19] for

---

12. Id.

13. People v. Sims, 64 Cal.App.3d 544, 554, 134 Cal.Rptr. 566, 572 (1976) (holding that the accused's failure to comply with the statutory requirements precluded his raising as error the trial judge's exclusion of evidence that the complaining witness was pregnant at the time of the alleged rape in order to prove that she had a motive to concoct the rape). Precluding the accused from offering evidence of his sexual conduct with the victim for failing to comply with the notice requirements will not automatically result in a Sixth Amendment violation of the right to produce defense evidence. See Michigan v. Lucas, 500 U.S. 145, 152, 111 S.Ct. 1743, 1748, 114 L.Ed.2d 205 (1991), on remand, 193 Mich.App. 298, 484 N.W.2d 685 (1992).

14. West's Ann. California Evidence Code § 782.

15. See People v. Chandler, 56 Cal.App.4th 703, 711, 65 Cal.Rptr.2d 687, 692 (1997).

16. 142 Cal.App.3d 628, 191 Cal.Rptr. 218 (1983).

17. Id. at 633, 191 Cal.Rptr. at 220.

18. Id. at 635, note 2, 191 Cal.Rptr. at 222, note 2. It is unclear how the accused could have adduced evidence that the victim had sex with others in the first place. Section 1103(c) prohibits the accused from offering evidence of the victim's sexual conduct with others to prove that the victim consented to the sexual encounter with the accused. West's Ann. California Evidence Code § 1103(c). If adduced for the sole purpose of disproving her testimony through extrinsic evidence, the judge could exclude the question under § 352. See discussion in text following note 21 infra.

Apparently, the accused's theory was that the victim should have been disbelieved because she had falsely accused others of having had sex with her. But the use of the evidence for this purpose is barred by § 787 which prohibits the use of specific instances of conduct to prove a character trait (falsely accusing others) to attack the credibility of a witness. At the time of Jordan's hearing, the Right to Truth-in-Evidence provision of Proposition 8 had not yet taken effect. Accordingly, § 787 applied to the hearing. For an extended discussion of this point, see § 15.06 supra.

19. 181 Cal.App.3d 889, 226 Cal.Rptr. 285 (1986), cert. denied, 479 U.S. 1010, 107 S.Ct. 652, 93 L.Ed.2d 707 (1986).

example, the accused admitted having had intercourse with the victim but claimed that she had agreed to the act for money.[20] In support of his position, the accused offered to call a witness who would testify that the victim also offered to have sex with the witness for money shortly before the accused encountered the victim.[21] At the § 782 hearing, the victim testified that she had never offered to have sex with the witness for money and that she had never been arrested or convicted of prostitution.[22] In upholding the trial judge's exclusion of the witness's testimony, the court said:

> The issues before the trial court were whether [the witness's] testimony that [the victim] had offered him sex for money shortly before defendant appeared * * * was relevant to attack [the victim's] credibility and whether it was more prejudicial than probative. Both *Varona* and *Rioz* suggest the trial court may weight [sic] the proffered evidence in light of all the evidence which has been received at the trial. Here, unlike *Varona*, the only evidence the victim was a prostitute consisted of defendant's and his friend's testimony. Further, defendant's account of his encounters with [the victim] verges on the improbable. More importantly, however, [the victim] had been beaten shortly after she left Ms. S's room and before she reported the incident to the police. In our view, the trial judge's determination [that] her injuries were inconsistent with the proffered evidence was entirely proper. Thus, defendant's offer of proof was only slightly relevant to attack [the victim's] credibility. Accordingly, we find no abuse of discretion by the trial court in excluding this evidence.[23]

It may be that the proposed witness's testimony of having been solicited by the victim was not convincing in light of the evidence of the victim's injuries. But the question was not whether the trial judge or two of the appellate judges found the evidence unpersuasive. Rather, the question was whether in weighing the probative value of the evidence against its prejudicial effects the trial judge should have taken the proposed witness's credibility into account. Federal appellate courts that have considered the question say that the judge may not do so.

> "Rule 403 [the federal equivalent of California Evidence Code § 352] does not permit exclusion of evidence because the judge does not find it credible." United States v. Thompson, 615 F.2d 329, 333 (5th Cir.1980). "Weighing probative value against unfair prejudice under [Rule] 403 means probative value with respect to a material fact *if the evidence is believed, not the degree the court finds it believable.*" Bowden v. McKenna, 600 F.2d 282, 284–85 (1st Cir.1979), cert. denied, 444 U.S. 899, 100 S.Ct. 208, 62 L.Ed.2d 135 (1979), (footnote omitted and emphasis added). See also 22 C. Wright & K.

---

20. Id. at 894, 226 Cal.Rptr. at 288–289.

21. Id.

22. Id.

23. Id. at 897, 226 Cal.Rptr. at 290–291.

Graham, Federal Practice & Procedure: Evidence § 5214, at 265–66 (1978). Rather than discounting the probative value of the [proffered evidence] on the basis of its perception of the degree to which the evidence was worthy of belief, the district court should have determined the probative value of the [proffered evidence] if true, and weighed that probative value against the danger of unfair prejudice, leaving to the jury the difficult choice of whether to credit the evidence.[24]

Tradition as well as constitutional concerns justify the federal approach. Credibility is a question for the jury;[25] moreover, to allow judges to exclude evidence which they consider unbelievable may violate the right to trial by jury.[26] Thus, in *Casas* the question should have been whether the probative value of the proposed witness's testimony on the victim's lack of credibility, if believed, was substantially outweighed by the prejudice to the *victim* of admitting the evidence.[27] The purpose of the rape shield laws, after all, is to encourage victims of sex offenses to come forward by protecting them from extensive questioning about their sexual history in open court.[28] Without considering the credibility of the proposed witness's testimony in *Casas*, the judge could have concluded that the costs to the victim would have been too high. Some jurors might have been tempted to disregard the complaining witness's testimony because they disapproved of her sexual conduct. Others might have been unable to abide by the instruction limiting the evidence to the victim's credibility. They might have misused the witness's testimony as evidence that the victim consented to the act with the accused because she was the kind of person who would do so for money.[29]

---

24. Ballou v. Henri Studios, Inc., 656 F.2d 1147, 1154 (5th Cir.1981) (emphasis in the original).

25. C. Wright & K. Graham, Federal Practice & Procedure—Evidence § 5214 (1978). See also People v. Cudjo, 6 Cal.4th 585, 608–609, 25 Cal.Rptr.2d 390, 404–405, 863 P.2d 635, 649–650 (1993) (Whether or not the witness reporting the hearsay declaration is credible is a question reserved for the jury; accordingly, trial judges may not exclude the declaration under § 352 on the grounds that they find the reporting witness unworthy of belief.).

26. See People v. Cudjo, 6 Cal.4th 585, 608–609, 25 Cal.Rptr.2d 390, 404–405, 863 P.2d 635, 649–650 (1993).

27. A California trial judge should not pass on the credibility of the witness in assessing the probative value of the witness's testimony under §§ 352 and 782. See People v. Chandler, 56 Cal.App.4th 703, 711, 65 Cal.Rptr.2d 687, 692 (1997) and cases cited therein.

28. People v. Jordan, 142 Cal.App.3d 628, 632, 191 Cal.Rptr. 218, 220 (1983).

29. Another aspect of *Casas* is troubling. The admissibility of the witness's testimony to impeach the victim's credibility is problematical in the first place. The evidence could not have been offered to prove that, because the victim offered to have sex with the witness for money, the victim offered to have sex with the accused for money because she was the kind of person who had sex for money. In a rape prosecution, evidence of the complaining witness's sexual conduct with other persons is not admissible to prove the complaining witness's predisposition to consent to the sexual encounter with the accused. West's Ann. California Evidence Code § 1103(c). Theoretically, the impeaching evidence could have been offered to disprove evidence by the victim that she had never offered to have sex with anyone for money. But nothing in the opinion suggests that at the trial the victim somehow volunteered such a statement. Also theoretically, evidence of sex for money with others could have been offered as proof of a plan by the victim to have sex with others, including the accused, for money. But, again, nothing in the opinion suggests that the accused urged this non-character purpose at the § 782 hearing.

Cases, such as *Casas*, where the accused seeks to impeach the complaining witness with a history of prostitution have posed serious problems for the California courts. Prostitutes are as entitled to the protection of the rape laws as anyone else. They too have the right to decline any sexual contact they consider unwelcome. Moreover, where the accused claims that the sexual encounter in question was simply an exchange of sex for money or drugs, the Evidence Code, as noted, precludes the accused from offering the victim's history as a prostitute as evidence of her predisposition to engage in consensual commercial transactions involving sex.[30] The accused must advance other theories of admissibility. One that appears to be gaining currency is that the victim's history as a prostitute is being offered as a prior bad act that is probative of the victim's character for lack of veracity.[31] As has been discussed, in California criminal cases Proposition 8 now allows the parties to impeach a witness by evidence that the witness has engaged in misdeeds that are probative of the witness's character for lack of veracity.[32] The theory of impeachment is that the misconduct indicates that the witness is the kind of person who cannot be trusted to tell the truth under oath.[33] Engaging in prostitution is considered by some California courts as evidencing a predisposition to lie under oath.[34] Of course, relying on this theory will not guarantee that the evidence will be admitted. The accused must still convince the judge at the § 782 hearing that the probative value of the evidence is not substantially outweighed by the countervailing concerns, including the impact on the victim, that have been discussed.

The trial judge's discretion to exclude defense evidence impeaching the complaining witness in sex offense prosecutions has been upheld as constitutional.[35] But that discretion in not unlimited. In Olden v. Kentucky[36] the accused sought to impeach the complaining witness by evidence that she had a motive to accuse him falsely of rape. It was the accused's contention that the complaining witness lied about their consensual acts out of fear of jeopardizing her relationship with another man. The trial judge, however, refused to allow the accused to offer evidence of the victim's relationship with the other man because of "its possibility for prejudice."[37] The victim was white and the other man black. Because under the circumstances the evidence would have been highly probative of the victim's lack of credibility, the United States Supreme Court held that

---

30. Id.

31. People v. Chandler, 56 Cal.App.4th 703, 708, 65 Cal.Rptr.2d 687, 691 (1997).

32. See § 15.06 supra.

33. Id.

34. People v. Chandler, 56 Cal.App.4th 703, 708, 65 Cal.Rptr.2d 687, 691 (1997) and cases cited therein (noting that California courts consider prostitution a crime involving moral turpitude).

35. People v. Blackburn, 56 Cal.App.3d 685, 691–692, 128 Cal.Rptr. 864, 867 (1976).

36. 488 U.S. 227, 109 S.Ct. 480, 102 L.Ed.2d 513 (1988).

37. Id. at 230, 109 S.Ct. at 482.

the trial judge's ruling deprived the accused of his right to confront the witnesses against him.[38]

The federal rape shield law. The Federal Rules also contain a rape shield provision. Rule 412 permits the accused to offer evidence of specific instances of his own sexual conduct with the victim to prove consent, if the judge first determines at a separate hearing that the probative value of the evidence outweighs its prejudice to the victim.[39] The rule also allows the accused to offer evidence of specific instances of the victim's specific sexual conduct with others to prove that someone other than the accused is responsible for the assault charged.[40] The use of the evidence for this purpose is also subject to a finding at a separate hearing that its probative value outweighs its prejudice to the victim.[41] Rule 412, however, does not authorize the use of evidence of the victim's sexual conduct for impeachment purposes.[42]

QUESTIONS AND PROBLEMS

1. In a rape prosecution tried in a California or federal court, the accused in his case in chief may prove the victim's predisposition to engage in consensual sex by evidence that he and the victim engaged in consensual sex on other occasions. True or false?

2. But the accused may not establish the victim's predisposition to engage in consensual sex by evidence that she had consensual sex with others. True or false?

3. Consider the admissibility of the following evidence in a rape prosecution tried in a California court:

 a. On direct the complaining witness testifies that she did not consent to having sex with the accused. To impeach the witness, may the accused ask the victim on cross-examination whether she had consensual sex with Tom, Dick, and Harry prior to the date of the alleged rape without complying with the procedural requirements of § 782?

---

38. Id. at 232, 109 S.Ct. at 483. The Court described the impeaching evidence as having a "strong potential to demonstrate the falsity of [the complaining witness's] testimony." Id.

39. Federal Rule of Evidence 412 and Advisory Committee Note.

40. Id.

41. Id.

42. Rule 412 as originally enacted barred the use of the evidence for impeaching the victim by failing to authorize its use for this purpose. The rule proceeded from the assumption that evidence of the victim's predisposition to engage in sex acts was inadmissible in a criminal case for any purpose unless otherwise authorized by the rule. See the Committee Note of the Standing Committee on Rules of Practice and Procedure of the Judicial Conference of the United States accompanying a proposed amendment to Rule 412; Weinstein, Mansfield, Abrams & Berger, Evidence: 1993 Rules, Statute and Case Supplement, at 47.

As part of the Violent Crime Control and Law Enforcement Act of 1994, Congress amended Rule 412 to authorize in a civil case the use of the victim's sexual behavior in certain circumstances. The amended rule, however, continues to bar evidence "relating to the alleged victim's sexual behavior or alleged sexual predisposition, whether offered as substantive evidence or *impeachment*," unless otherwise authorized. Federal Rule of Evidence 412 (Advisory Committee Note) (emphasis added). No express authorization of the use of the evidence for impeachment is contained in the amended rule.

b. On direct the complaining witness testifies that she did not consent to have sex with the accused and would never have consented because premarital sex violates her beliefs. May the accused offer evidence that the victim had consensual sex with Harry to contradict the victim without complying with § 782?

If the judge allows the accused to offer the evidence, what limiting instruction should the judge give the jurors?

c. In the prosecution's case in chief, the victim testifies that the accused had sex with her against her will. On cross-examination, may the defense lawyer ask the following question without first complying with § 782: "Isn't is a fact that on the occasion in question you agreed to have sex with my client for $100.00?"

d. Assume that the witness answers "no" to the preceding question. On the same cross-examination, for impeachment may the defense lawyer ask the following question without first complying with § 782: "Isn't is a fact that the day before the occasion in question, you agreed to have sex with Harry for $100.00?"

e. Suppose that instead the defense lawyer claims that the question seeks to adduce evidence that the victim engaged in consensual commercial sex with the accused on the occasion in question as part of a common plan or scheme to engage in consensual commercial sex. Would you admit the evidence for this purpose without first requiring a § 782 hearing?

f. In his case-in-chief the accused testifies that the victim consented to the sexual transaction and that it is not true that he raped her. The accused then calls Bob to testify that the victim falsely accused him of having raped her after they had consensual sex. The accused offers Bob's testimony, not as evidence that the victim is the kind of person who consents to sex, but as evidence that the victim falsely accused him of raping her as part of a common plan or scheme to accuse others of falsely raping her.

May the accused offer this evidence without complying with § 782? See People v. Franklin, discussed in the materials.

If the judge allows the accused to offer the evidence, what limiting instruction should the judge give the jurors?

Suppose that the accused offers Bob's testimony as a prior bad act under Proposition 8. Would that change your ruling on the applicability of § 782?

g. The accused intends to testify in his case-in-chief that the victim consented to the sexual transaction and that it is not true that he raped her. Over the prosecutor's objection that the accused failed to comply with the notice and hearing requirements of § 782, on cross-examination may the accused attempt to elicit testimony from the victim (1) that at the time of the alleged rape the victim was living with Joe and (2) that she feared that Joe might leave her if he found out that she was "running around?" In answering this question, assume that the evidence about the victim's relationship with Joe qualifies as evidence of the complaining witness's "sexual conduct" under § 782.

Assume that the evidence about the victim's relationship with Joe relates to her sexual conduct and falls within the category defined as "evidence offered to prove that any alleged victim engaged in other sexual behavior." Under Federal Rule of Evidence 412 such evidence is inadmissible unless offered for the limited purposes set out in the Rule. Those purposes do not include using the evidence to impeach the rape victim.

What arguments would you make to persuade the judge to receive the evidence despite Rule 412? See Olden v. Kentucky, discussed in the materials.

§ 15.13   IMPEACHING THE HEARSAY DECLARANT

When a hearsay declaration is received under an exception, the hearsay declarant in effect has testified even though the declarant may not have appeared as a witness. The jurors, after all, are entitled to consider the hearsay declaration for the truth of the matter asserted. As a rule, then, both the Code and the Federal Rules permit the party opposing the hearsay declaration to impeach the hearsay declarant in the same manner as if the declarant had appeared and testified.[1]

Inconsistent statements. In the case of declarants who do testify, any statements they have made that are inconsistent with their testimony can be offered to impeach them.[2] Moreover, their statements can be offered to prove the truth of the matters stated so long as the declarants are given an opportunity to explain or deny their statements under oath and in the presence of the fact finder before the close of the evidence.[3] But when the "witness" to be impeached is a hearsay declarant who does not appear as a witness, two problems arise when the impeaching party seeks to discredit the declarant with statements by the declarant that are inconsistent with the hearsay declaration that has been received in evidence.

One is that the inconsistent statement may not be a *prior* inconsistent statement but a *subsequent* one: the declarant may have made the inconsistent statement after making the hearsay declaration that was received in evidence. Assume that the hearsay declaration received was an excited utterance in which the declarant was overheard saying, "The green car is running the light!" After making that declaration, the declarant tells his girlfriend, "I am no longer sure that it was the green car that ran the light." If the party opposing the excited utterance is allowed to call the girlfriend to offer the inconsistent statement which the declarant made to her, that party in effect would be permitted to impeach the hearsay

---

1. West's Ann. California Evidence Code § 1202; Federal Rule of Evidence 806. In California, for example, a hearsay declarant may be impeached by felony convictions related to theft. People v. Jacobs, 78 Cal.App.4th 1444, 1452, 93 Cal.Rptr.2d 783, 789 (2000).

2. See § 15.03 supra.

3. Id. The Federal Rules impose additional limits on inconsistent statements offered for the truth of the matter asserted. See id.

declarant through a *subsequent* inconsistent statement. Both the Code and the Rules nonetheless allow the impeaching party to use the statement.[4] Since the declarant did not appear as a witness, the impeaching party did not have an opportunity to examine the declarant about the nature or the circumstances surrounding the making of the excited utterance. Therefore, the Code and the Rules recognize that fairness requires allowing the impeaching party to use the inconsistent statement even if the declarant made the statement after making the hearsay declaration that has been received in evidence.

The other problem concerns the interests of the party who offered the hearsay declaration in the first place. When, as in the example, the hearsay declarant does not appear as a witness, the proponent of the hearsay declaration is deprived of an opportunity to have the declarant explain or deny the inconsistent statement attributed by the opponent's witnesses to the declarant. Under the rules governing the use of conventional inconsistent statements, the absence of such an opportunity would be fatal to the introduction of the inconsistent statement.[5] But that is not the case when the inconsistent statement is offered to impeach a hearsay declarant. Since the proponent has benefitted from the introduction of the absent declarant's hearsay declaration, the opponent will be permitted to use the inconsistent statement even though the proponent will be deprived of the opportunity to have the declarant explain or deny the inconsistent statement.[6] Under the Code, however, the proponent is entitled to some consolation: unless the impeaching statement falls within a recognized exception to the hearsay rule, the inconsistent statement may be received only for impeachment and not for the truth of the matter stated.[7] The Federal Rules are silent on this point. But one can expect the same outcome. Unless the inconsistent statement falls within a recognized exception or exemption to the federal hearsay rule, the statement may be received only to impeach the hearsay declarant. Although the Code and the Rules focus on the use of inconsistent statements to impeach the hearsay declarant, both permit the use of any impeaching evidence that would have been admissible if the declarant had appeared and testified.[8]

---

4. West's Ann. California Evidence Code § 1202; Federal Rule of Evidence 806. The impeaching party, however, must be the party against whom the hearsay declaration was offered, People v. Beyea, 38 Cal.App.3d 176, 193, 113 Cal.Rptr. 254, 264 (1974), even though § 1202 does not contain such a limitation and § 785 allows the calling party to impeach his own witnesses. For a judicial explanation of the purposes of § 1202, see generally People v. Corella, 122 Cal.App.4th 461, 469, 18 Cal.Rptr.3d 770, 777 (2004).

5. See § 15.03 supra.

6. West's Ann. California Evidence Code § 1202; Federal Rule of Evidence 806.

7. West's Ann. California Evidence Code § 1202 and comment. In the example, the inconsistent statement would not qualify under the prior inconsistent statement exception to the hearsay rule of § 1235, as the statement was made after the making of the hearsay declaration that was received in evidence. A provision added to the Code in 1996 creates a new hearsay exception for inconsistent statements used to impeach witnesses who appear at preliminary hearings but who fail to appear at the trial. See West's Ann. California Evidence Code § 1294. For a discussion of this exception, see § 15.03 supra.

8. West's Ann. California Evidence Code § 1202; Federal Rule of Evidence 806. See, e.g., People v. Stevenson, 79 Cal.App.3d 976, 989, 145 Cal.Rptr. 301, 309 (1978) (The party opposing

Moreover, both also allow the credibility of the hearsay declarant to be supported by any evidence that would have been admissible for that purpose if the declarant had testified as a witness.[9]

Convictions. Because both the Code and the Federal Rules permit the party opposing the hearsay declaration to impeach the hearsay declarant in the same manner as if the declarant had appeared and testified,[10] the impeaching party may use convictions to discredit the hearsay declarant.[11] The convictions offered must, of course, satisfy the conditions for the use of convictions to impeach witnesses.

In an unusual case, the California Court of Appeal allowed the prosecution to use convictions to impeach the accused, even though he did not testify. In People v. Jacobs[12] the accused and a codefendant were tried for receiving stolen property. The evidence showed that Jacobs and his codefendant were attempting to sell property that had been stolen. The codefendant offered a portion of a statement Jacobs made to a police officer in which Jacobs acknowledged owning the car in which the stolen property was found.[13] Jacobs then moved in evidence another portion of his statement to the officer.[14] In this portion, Jacobs claimed to have bought the stolen property from a man named "Will." Even though Jacobs did not testify at the trial, the reviewing court upheld the use of convictions to impeach his credibility. By moving in evidence the balance of his statement to the police officer, Jacobs in effect became a hearsay declarant and could therefore be impeached under § 1202 with his convictions.[15]

Preliminary hearings and hearsay declarants. Until 1990, California prosecutors who chose to proceed against felony suspects by way of a complaint and a preliminary hearing instead of an indictment had to comply with the rules of evidence at the hearing. That year, Proposition 115 amended the Penal Code to allow prosecutors to offer hearsay in support of the probable cause finding at the preliminary hearing if offered

---

the hearsay statement may impeach the hearsay declarant with a felony conviction involving dishonesty.). Accord: People v. Jacobs, 78 Cal.App.4th 1444, 1452, 93 Cal.Rptr.2d 783, 789 (2000).

9.   West's Ann. California Evidence Code § 1202.

10.   West's Ann. California Evidence Code § 1202; Federal Rule of Evidence 806. In California, for example, a hearsay declarant may be impeached by felony convictions related to theft. People v. Jacobs, 78 Cal.App.4th 1444, 1452, 93 Cal.Rptr.2d 783, 789 (2000).

11.   See, e.g., People v. Jacobs, 78 Cal.App.4th 1444, 1449, 93 Cal.Rptr.2d 783, 786 (2000).

12.   Id.

13.   Apparently, the codefendant offered this portion of Jacob's statement as a party admission.

14.   Apparently, Jacobs relied on California Evidence Code § 356 to offer the balance of his statement to the officer. Section 356 provides that where "part of an act, declaration, conversation, or writing is given in evidence by one party, the whole on the same subject may be inquired into by an adverse party; when a letter is read, the answer may be given; and when a detached act, declaration, conversation, or writing is given in evidence, any other act, declaration, conversation, or writing which is necessary to make it understood may also be given in evidence." Since the portion offered by the codefendant was offered for the truth, the portion offered by Jacobs could also be offered for the truth, even though this portion was a self-serving statement. For a discussion of this point, see § 13.10 supra.

15.   People v. Jacobs, 78 Cal.App.4th 1444, 1449, 93 Cal.Rptr.2d 783, 786 (2000).

through a law enforcement officer who meets enumerated criteria.[16] Section 1203, which gives adverse parties the right to call and cross-examine hearsay declarants, no longer applies to preliminary hearings by virtue of the proposition.[17] Thus, by using the officer, prosecutors can offer the statements of complaining witnesses without exposing them to cross-examination.

Proposition 115 also altered the rights of defendants to offer evidence at preliminary hearings. At the request of the prosecution, the magistrate may not allow the accused to call witnesses unless the accused convinces the magistrate through an offer of proof that their testimony, "if believed, would be reasonably likely to establish an affirmative defense, negate an element of a crime charged, or impeach the testimony of a prosecution witness or the statement of a declarant testified to by a prosecution witness."[18] In People v. Erwin[19] the accused relied on this provision for permission to call the victim whose statements had been received through a law enforcement officer. The magistrate denied the request on the ground that the intent of Proposition 115 was to prohibit the defense from calling declarants of the hearsay statements offered by the prosecution. The Court of Appeal disagreed with the magistrate's construction of the initiative and upheld the Superior Court's order directing the magistrate to exercise his discretion in determining whether the accused should be permitted to call the complaining witness.[20] In reaching this conclusion, the reviewing court emphasized that this provision of the proposition was independent of the one granting prosecutors the right to use hearsay in support of the probable cause finding.[21]

QUESTIONS AND PROBLEMS

1. The plaintiff offers in evidence an excited utterance in which the declarant stated, "The defendant is running the light!" To impeach the declarant, may the defendant offer a declaration made later in the day by the declarant in which he stated to a friend, "I'm not so sure that the defendant was the person whom I saw running the light."? In answering the question, assume that the hearsay declarant did not appear as a witness.

2. Assume that the judge allows the use of the statement. May the statement be received for the truth of the matter asserted in a federal or California court?

16. See West's Ann. California Penal Code § 872. In Whitman v. Superior Court, 54 Cal.3d 1063, 2 Cal.Rptr.2d 160, 820 P.2d 262 (1991), the California Supreme Court held that the testifying officer must have "sufficient knowledge of the crime or the circumstances under which the out-of-court statement was made so as to meaningfully assist the magistrate in assessing the reliability of the statement." Id. at 1079, 2 Cal.Rptr.2d at 167, 820 P.2d at 267.

17. West's Ann. California Evidence Code §§ 1203–1203.1.

18. West's Ann. California Penal Code § 866.

19. 20 Cal.App.4th 1542, 25 Cal.Rptr.2d 348 (1993).

20. Id. at 1549–1551, 25 Cal.Rptr.2d at 352–353.

21. Id.

§ 15.14   ETHICAL CONSTRAINTS ON WITNESS EXAMINATIONS

The adversarial nature of trials invites the parties to do all they can to support the credibility of their own witnesses and to discredit their opponents'. As we have seen in this chapter, the rules of evidence place strict limits on these efforts. In addition, the rules of professional responsibility impose restrictions on what lawyers can do.

A common limitation is that a lawyer should not knowingly adduce perjury. ABA Model Rule of Professional Conduct 3.3(a)(4) prohibits a lawyer from offering evidence the lawyer knows to be false and Rule 3.4(b) prohibits a lawyer from assisting a witness to testify falsely.[1] California Rule of Professional Conduct 5–200(A) requires lawyers to use only those means in representing clients as are consistent with the truth.[2]

The duty to refrain from presenting evidence the lawyer knows to be false does not extend to evidence the attorney suspects but does not know to be false.[3] A " 'lawyer should not conclude that testimony is or will be false unless there is a firm factual basis for doing so. Such a basis exists when facts known to the lawyer or the client's own statements indicate to the lawyer that the testimony is false.' * * * [But] counsel's belief in their client's guilt certainly cannot create an ethical bar against introduction of exculpatory evidence."[4] Judges and jurors, not counsel, are charged with the responsibility of determining the facts.[5]

The ethical constraints on a lawyer on cross-examination stem from case law as well as the professional rules. Case law, for example, prohibits a lawyer from asking a witness about prior bad acts unless the lawyer in good faith believes that the witness has engaged in such acts.[6] Similarly, a lawyer may not ask a character witness whether he has heard of conduct on the part of the subject that is at variance with the subject's reputation unless the lawyer believes in good faith that the subject engaged in such conduct.[7]

Although most ethical constraints apply to the lawyers for both sides, sometimes they are directed at prosecutors. Most appeals involving evidentiary issues are criminal in nature and only defendants can appeal from guilty verdicts. Thus, it is criminal defendants, as opposed to prosecutors, who on appeal complain about misconduct in the examination of witnesses. Though appellate judges review the misconduct claims from this

---

1.   American Bar Association Model Rules of Professional Conduct 3.3(a)(4) and 3.4(b).

2.   California Rule of Professional Conduct 5–200(A).

3.   People v. Riel, 22 Cal.4th 1153, 1217, 96 Cal.Rptr.2d 1, 49, 998 P.2d 969, 1013 (2000), cert. denied, 531 U.S. 1087, 121 S.Ct. 803, 148 L.Ed.2d 690 (2001).

4.   Lord v. Wood, 184 F.3d 1083, 1095, note 9 (9th Cir.1999).

5.   United States ex rel. Wilcox v. Johnson, 555 F.2d 115, 122 (3d Cir.1977).

6.   See § 15.06 supra.

7.   See § 15.08 supra.

perspective, it is nonetheless apparent that most of their admonitions should apply to all lawyers, irrespective of whom they represent or the nature of the proceeding.

Among the appellate admonitions worth noting are the following: (1) Prosecutors have a duty to guard against statements by witnesses containing inadmissible matter; if prosecutors believe that a witness may give an inadmissible answer, they must warn the witness not to give the answer.[8] (2) Prosecutors also have a duty to refrain from asking questions that suggest facts harmful to the accused unless they have a good faith belief that such facts exist.[9] (3) In federal courts, prosecutors may not call a witness to the stand where the primary purpose is to impeach the witness with prior inconsistent statements that otherwise would not be admissible as substantive evidence against the accused.[10]

ARTICLE 1 OF THE CALIFORNIA CONSTITUTION

§ 28. Findings and declarations; rights of victims; enforcement

* * *

(f) In addition to the enumerated rights provided in subdivision (b) that are personally enforceable by victims as provided in subdivision (c), victims of crime have additional rights that are shared with all of the People of the State of California. These collectively held rights include, but are not limited to, the following:

* * *

(2) **Right to Truth–in–Evidence.** Except as provided by statute hereafter enacted by two-thirds vote of the membership in each house of the Legislature, relevant evidence shall not be excluded in any criminal proceeding, including pretrial and post conviction motions and hearings, or in any trial or hearing of a juvenile for a criminal offense, whether heard in juvenile or adult court. Nothing in this section shall affect any existing statutory rule of evidence relating to privilege or hearsay, or Evidence Code, Sections 352, 782 or 1103. Nothing in this section shall affect any existing statutory or constitutional right of the press.

* * *

(4) **Use of Prior Convictions.** Any prior felony conviction of any person in any criminal proceeding, whether adult or juvenile, shall subsequently be used without limitation for purposes of impeachment or enhancement of sentence in any criminal proceeding. When a prior felony

---

8. People v. Warren, 45 Cal.3d 471, 481–482, 247 Cal.Rptr. 172, 178, 754 P.2d 218, 224–225 (1988), and cases cited therein.

9. Id. at 480–481, 247 Cal.Rptr. at 177, 754 P.2d at 224, and cases cited therein.

10. See United States v. Hogan, 763 F.2d 697, 701 (5th Cir.1985) and cases cited therein.

conviction is an element of any felony offense, it shall be proven to the trier of fact in open court.

CALIFORNIA EVIDENCE CODE

§ 351.1. Polygraph examinations; results, opinion of examiner or reference; exclusion

(a) Notwithstanding any other provision of law, the results of a polygraph examination, the opinion of a polygraph examiner, or any reference to an offer to take, failure to take, or taking of a polygraph examination, shall not be admitted into evidence in any criminal proceeding, including pretrial and post conviction motions and hearings, or in any trial or hearing of a juvenile for a criminal offense, whether heard in juvenile or adult court, unless all parties stipulate to the admission of such results.

(b) Nothing in this section is intended to exclude from evidence statements made during a polygraph examination which are otherwise admissible.

§ 452.5. Criminal conviction records; computer-generated records; admissibility

(a) The official acts and records specified in subdivisions (c) and (d) of Section 452 include any computer-generated official court records, as specified by the Judicial Council which relate to criminal convictions, when the record is certified by a clerk of the municipal or superior court pursuant to Section 69844.5 or 71280.5 of the Government Code at the time of computer entry.

(b) An official record of conviction certified in accordance with subdivision (a) of Section 1530 is admissible pursuant to Section 1280 to prove the commission, attempted commission, or solicitation of a criminal offense, prior conviction, service of a prison term, or other act, condition, or event recorded by the record.

§ 765. Court to control mode of interrogation

(a) The court shall exercise reasonable control over the mode of interrogation of a witness so as to make such interrogation as rapid, as distinct, and as effective for the ascertainment of the truth, as may be, and to protect the witness from undue harassment or embarrassment.

(b) With a witness under the age of 14, the court shall take special care to protect him or her from undue harassment or embarrassment, and to restrict the unnecessary repetition of questions. The court shall also take special care to insure that questions are stated in a form which is appropriate to the age of the witness. The court may in the interests of justice, on objection by a party, forbid the asking of a question which is in a form that is not reasonably likely to be understood by a person of the age of the witness.

§ 766. Responsive answers

A witness must give responsive answers to questions, and answers that are not responsive shall be stricken on motion of any party.

§ 767. Leading questions

(a) Except under special circumstances where the interests of justice otherwise require:

(1) A leading question may not be asked of a witness on direct or redirect examination.

(2) A leading question may be asked of a witness on cross-examination or recross-examination.

(b) The court may in the interests of justice permit a leading question to be asked of a child under 10 years of age in a case involving a prosecution under Section 273a, 273d, 288, or 288.5 of the Penal Code.

§ 768. Writings

(a) In examining a witness concerning a writing, it is not necessary to show, read, or disclose to him any part of the writing.

(b) If a writing is shown to a witness, all parties to the action must be given an opportunity to inspect it before any question concerning it may be asked of the witness.

§ 769. Inconsistent statement or conduct

In examining a witness concerning a statement or other conduct by him that is inconsistent with any part of his testimony at the hearing, it is not necessary to disclose to him any information concerning the statement or other conduct.

§ 770. Evidence of inconsistent statement of witness

Unless the interests of justice otherwise require, extrinsic evidence of a statement made by a witness that is inconsistent with any part of his testimony at the hearing shall be excluded unless:

(a) The witness was so examined while testifying as to give him an opportunity to explain or to deny the statement; or

(b) The witness has not been excused from giving further testimony in the action.

§ 771. Production of writing used to refresh memory

(a) Subject to subdivision (c), if a witness, either while testifying or prior thereto, uses a writing to refresh his memory with respect to any matter about which he testifies, such writing must be produced at the hearing at the request of an adverse party and, unless the writing is so produced, the testimony of the witness concerning such matter shall be stricken.

(b) If the writing is produced at the hearing, the adverse party may, if he chooses, inspect the writing, cross-examine the witness concerning it, and introduce in evidence such portion of it as may be pertinent to the testimony of the witness.

(c) Production of the writing is excused, and the testimony of the witness shall not be stricken, if the writing:

(1) Is not in the possession or control of the witness or the party who produced his testimony concerning the matter; and

(2) Was not reasonably procurable by such party through the use of the court's process or other available means.

§ 772. Order of examination

(a) The examination of a witness shall proceed in the following phases: direct examination, cross-examination, redirect examination, re-cross-examination, and continuing thereafter by redirect and recross-examination.

(b) Unless for good cause the court otherwise directs, each phase of the examination of a witness must be concluded before the succeeding phase begins.

(c) Subject to subdivision (d), a party may, in the discretion of the court, interrupt his cross-examination, redirect examination, or recross-examination of a witness, in order to examine the witness upon a matter not within the scope of a previous examination of the witness.

(d) If the witness is the defendant in a criminal action, the witness may not, without his consent, be examined under direct examination by another party.

§ 773. Cross-examination

(a) A witness examined by one party may be cross-examined upon any matter within the scope of the direct examination by each other party to the action in such order as the court directs.

(b) The cross-examination of a witness by any party whose interest is not adverse to the party calling him is subject to the same rules that are applicable to the direct examination.

§ 774. Re-examination

A witness once examined cannot be reexamined as to the same matter without leave of the court, but he may be reexamined as to any new matter upon which he has been examined by another party to the action. Leave may be granted or withheld in the court's discretion.

§ 775. Court may call witnesses

The court, on its own motion or on the motion of any party, may call witnesses and interrogate them the same as if they had been produced by a party to the action, and the parties may object to the questions asked and the evidence adduced the same as if such witnesses were called and examined by an adverse party. Such witnesses may be cross-examined by all parties to the action in such order as the court directs.

§ 776. Examination of adverse party or witness

(a) A party to the record of any civil action, or a person identified with such a party, may be called and examined as if under cross-examination by any adverse party at any time during the presentation of evidence by the party calling the witness.

(b) A witness examined by a party under this section may be cross-examined by all other parties to the action in such order as the court directs; but, subject to subdivision (e), the witness may be examined only as if under redirect examination by:

(1) In the case of a witness who is a party, his own counsel and counsel for a party who is not adverse to the witness.

(2) In the case of a witness who is not a party, counsel for the party with whom the witness is identified and counsel for a party who is not adverse to the party with whom the witness is identified.

(c) For the purpose of this section, parties represented by the same counsel are deemed to be a single party.

(d) For the purpose of this section, a person is identified with a party if he is:

(1) A person for whose immediate benefit the action is prosecuted or defended by the party.

(2) A director, officer, superintendent, member, agent, employee, or managing agent of the party or of a person specified in paragraph (1), or any public employee of a public entity when such public entity is the party.

(3) A person who was in any of the relationships specified in paragraph (2) at the time of the act or omission giving rise to the cause of action.

(4) A person who was in any of the relationships specified in paragraph (2) at the time he obtained knowledge of the matter concerning which he is sought to be examined under this section.

(e) Paragraph (2) of subdivision (b) does not require counsel for the party with whom the witness is identified and counsel for a party who is not adverse to the party with whom the witness is identified to examine the witness as if under redirect examination if the party who called the witness for examination under this section:

(1) Is also a person identified with the same party with whom the witness is identified.

(2) Is the personal representative, heir, successor, or assignee of a person identified with the same party with whom the witness is identified.

§ 777. Exclusion of witness

(a) Subject to subdivisions (b) and (c), the court may exclude from the courtroom any witness not at the time under examination so that such witness cannot hear the testimony of other witnesses.

(b) A party to the action cannot be excluded under this section.

(c) If a person other than a natural person is a party to the action, an officer or employee designated by its attorney is entitled to be present.

§ 778. Recall of witness

After a witness has been excused from giving further testimony in the action, he cannot be recalled without leave of the court. Leave may be granted or withheld in the court's discretion.

§ 780. General rule as to credibility

Except as otherwise provided by statute, the court or jury may consider in determining the credibility of a witness any matter that has any tendency in reason to prove or disprove the truthfulness of his testimony at the hearing, including but not limited to any of the following:

(a) His demeanor while testifying and the manner in which he testifies.

(b) The character of his testimony.

(c) The extent of his capacity to perceive, to recollect, or to communicate any matter about which he testifies.

(d) The extent of his opportunity to perceive any matter about which he testifies.

(e) His character for honesty or veracity or their opposites.

(f) The existence or nonexistence of a bias, interest, or other motive.

(g) A statement previously made by him that is consistent with his testimony at the hearing.

(h) A statement made by him that is inconsistent with any part of his testimony at the hearing.

(i) The existence or nonexistence of any fact testified to by him.

(j) His attitude toward the action in which he testifies or toward the giving of testimony.

(k) His admission of untruthfulness.

§ 782. Sexual offenses; evidence of sexual conduct of complaining witness; procedure for admissibility; treatment of resealed affidavits

(a) If in any of the circumstances described in subdivision (c), if evidence of sexual conduct of the complaining witness is offered to attack the credibility of the complaining witness under Section 780, the following procedure shall be followed:

(1) A written motion shall be made by the defendant to the court and prosecutor stating that the defense has an offer of proof of the relevancy

of evidence of the sexual conduct of the complaining witness proposed to be presented and its relevancy in attacking the credibility of the complaining witness.

(2) The written motion shall be accompanied by an affidavit in which the offer of proof shall be stated. The affidavit shall be filed under seal and only unsealed by the court to determine if the offer of proof is sufficient to order a hearing pursuant to paragraph (3). After that determination, the affidavit shall be resealed by the court.

(3) If the court finds that the offer of proof is sufficient, the court shall order a hearing out of the presence of the jury, if any, and at the hearing allow the questioning of the complaining witness regarding the offer of proof made by the defendant.

(4) At the conclusion of the hearing, if the court finds that evidence proposed to be offered by the defendant regarding the sexual conduct of the complaining witness is relevant pursuant to Section 780, and is not inadmissible pursuant to Section 352 of this code, the court may make an order stating what evidence may be introduced by the defendant, and the nature of the questions to be permitted. The defendant may then offer evidence pursuant to the order of the court.

(5) An affidavit resealed by the court pursuant to paragraph (2) shall remain sealed, unless the defendant raises an issue on appeal or collateral review relating to the offer of proof contained in the sealed document. If the defendant raises that issue on appeal, the court shall allow the Attorney General and appellate counsel for the defendant access to the sealed affidavit. If the issue is raised on collateral review, the court shall allow the district attorney and defendant's counsel access to the sealed affidavit. The use of the information contained in the affidavit shall be limited solely to the pending proceeding.

(b) As used in this section, "complaining witness" means:

(1) The alleged victim of the crime charged, the prosecution of which is subject to this section, pursuant to paragraph (1) of subdivision (c).

(2) An alleged victim offering testimony pursuant to paragraph (2) or paragraph (3) of subdivision (c).

(c) The procedure provided by subdivision (a) shall apply in any of the following:

(1) In a prosecution under Section 261, 262, 264.1, 286, 288, 288a, 288.5, or 289 of the Penal Code, or for assault with intent to commit, attempt to commit, or conspiracy to commit any crime defined in any of those sections, except if the crime is alleged to have occurred in a local detention facility, as defined in Section 6031.4, or in a state prison, as defined in Section 4504.

(2) When an alleged victim testifies pursuant to subdivision (b) of Section 1101 as a victim of a crime listed in Section 243.4, 261, 261.5, 269, 285, 286, 288, 288a, 288.5, 289, 314, or 647.6 of the Penal Code, except if

the crime is alleged to have occurred in a local detention facility, as defined in Section 6031.4 of the Penal Code, or in a state prison, as defined in Section 4504 of the Penal Code.

(3) When an alleged victim of a sexual offense testifies pursuant to Section 1108, except if the crime is alleged to have occurred in a local detention facility, as defined in Section 6031.4 of the Penal Code, or in a state prison, as defined in Section 4504 of the Penal Code.

§ 783. Sexual harassment, sexual assault, or sexual battery cases; admissibility of evidence of plaintiff's sexual conduct; procedure

In any civil action alleging conduct which constitutes sexual harassment, sexual assault, or sexual battery, if evidence of sexual conduct of the plaintiff is offered to attack credibility of the plaintiff under Section 780, the following procedures shall be followed:

(a) A written motion shall be made by the defendant to the court and the plaintiff's attorney stating that the defense has an offer of proof of the relevancy of evidence of the sexual conduct of the plaintiff proposed to be presented.

(b) The written motion shall be accompanied by an affidavit in which the offer of proof shall be stated.

(c) If the court finds that the offer of proof is sufficient, the court shall order a hearing out of the presence of the jury, if any, and at the hearing allow the questioning of the plaintiff regarding the offer of proof made by the defendant.

(d) At the conclusion of the hearing, if the court finds that evidence proposed to be offered by the defendant regarding the sexual conduct of the plaintiff is relevant pursuant to Section 780, and is not inadmissible pursuant to Section 352, the court may make an order stating what evidence may be introduced by the defendant, and the nature of the questions to be permitted. The defendant may then offer evidence pursuant to the order of the court.

§ 785. Parties may attack or support credibility

The credibility of a witness may be attacked or supported by any party, including the party calling him

§ 786. Character evidence generally

Evidence of traits of his character other than honesty or veracity, or their opposites, is inadmissible to attack or support the credibility of a witness.

§ 787. Specific instances of conduct

Subject to Section 788, evidence of specific instances of his conduct relevant only as tending to prove a trait of his character is inadmissible to attack or support the credibility of a witness.

§ 788. Prior felony conviction

For the purpose of attacking the credibility of a witness, it may be shown by the examination of the witness or by the record of the judgment that he has been convicted of a felony unless:

(a) A pardon based on his innocence has been granted to the witness by the jurisdiction in which he was convicted.

(b) A certificate of rehabilitation and pardon has been granted to the witness under the provisions of Chapter 3.5 (commencing with Section 4852.01) of Title 6 of Part 3 of the Penal Code.

(c) The accusatory pleading against the witness has been dismissed under the provisions of Penal Code Section 1203.4, but this exception does not apply to any criminal trial where the witness is being prosecuted for a subsequent offense.

(d) The conviction was under the laws of another jurisdiction and the witness has been relieved of the penalties and disabilities arising from the conviction pursuant to a procedure substantially equivalent to that referred to in subdivision (b) or (c).

§ 789. Religious belief

Evidence of his religious belief or lack thereof is inadmissible to attack or support the credibility of a witness.

§ 790. Good character of witness

Evidence of the good character of a witness is inadmissible to support his credibility unless evidence of his bad character has been admitted for the purpose of attacking his credibility.

§ 791. Prior consistent statement of witness

Evidence of a statement previously made by a witness that is consistent with his testimony at the hearing is inadmissible to support his credibility unless it is offered after:

(a) Evidence of a statement made by him that is inconsistent with any part of his testimony at the hearing has been admitted for the purpose of attacking his credibility, and the statement was made before the alleged inconsistent statement; or

(b) An express or implied charge has been made that his testimony at the hearing is recently fabricated or is influenced by bias or other improper motive, and the statement was made before the bias, motive for fabrication, or other improper motive is alleged to have arisen.

§ 1103. Character evidence of crime victim to prove conduct; evidence of defendant's character or trait for violence; evidence of manner of dress of victim; evidence of complaining witness' sexual conduct

* * *

(c) (1) Notwithstanding any other provision of this code to the contrary, and except as provided in this subdivision, in any prosecution under Section 261, 262, or 264.1 of the Penal Code, or under Section 286, 288a, or 289 of the Penal Code, or for assault with intent to commit, attempt to commit, or conspiracy to commit a crime defined in any of those sections, except where the crime is alleged to have occurred in a local detention facility, as defined in Section 6031.4, or in a state prison, as defined in Section 4504, opinion evidence, reputation evidence, and evidence of specific instances of the complaining witness' sexual conduct, or any of that evidence, is not admissible by the defendant in order to prove consent by the complaining witness.

(2) Notwithstanding paragraph (3), evidence of the manner in which the victim was dressed at the time of the commission of the offense shall not be admissible when offered by either party on the issue of consent in any prosecution for an offense specified in paragraph (1), unless the evidence is determined by the court to be relevant and admissible in the interests of justice. The proponent of the evidence shall make an offer of proof outside the hearing of the jury. The court shall then make its determination and at that time, state the reasons for its ruling on the record. For the purposes of this paragraph, "manner of dress" does not include the condition of the victim's clothing before, during, or after the commission of the offense.

(3) Paragraph (1) shall not be applicable to evidence of the complaining witness' sexual conduct with the defendant.

(4) If the prosecutor introduces evidence, including testimony of a witness, or the complaining witness as a witness gives testimony, and that evidence or testimony relates to the complaining witness' sexual conduct, the defendant may cross-examine the witness who gives the testimony and offer relevant evidence limited specifically to the rebuttal of the evidence introduced by the prosecutor or given by the complaining witness.

(5) Nothing in this subdivision shall be construed to make inadmissible any evidence offered to attack the credibility of the complaining witness as provided in Section 782.

(6) As used in this section, "complaining witness" means the alleged victim of the crime charged, the prosecution of which is subject to this subdivision.

§ 1107. Intimate partner battering and its effects; expert testimony in criminal actions; sufficiency of foundation; abuse and domestic violence; applicability to Penal Code; impact on decisional law

(a) In a criminal action, expert testimony is admissible by either the prosecution or the defense regarding intimate partner battering and its effects, including the nature and effect of physical, emotional, or mental abuse on the beliefs, perceptions, or behavior of victims of domestic violence, except when offered against a criminal defendant to prove the occurrence of the act or acts of abuse which form the basis of the criminal charge.

(b) The foundation shall be sufficient for admission of this expert testimony if the proponent of the evidence establishes its relevancy and the proper qualifications of the expert witness. Expert opinion testimony on intimate partner battering and its effects shall not be considered a new scientific technique whose reliability is unproven.

(c) For purposes of this section, "abuse" is defined in Section 6203 of the Family Code and "domestic violence" is defined in Section 6211 of the Family Code and may include acts defined in Section 242, subdivision (e) of Section 243, Section 262, 273.5, 273.6, 422 or 653m of the Penal Code.

(d) This section is intended as a rule of evidence only and no substantive change affecting the Penal Code is intended.

(e) This section shall be known, and may be cited as, the Expect Witness Testimony on Intimate Partner Battering and its Effects Section of the Evidence Code.

(f) The changes in this section that become effective on January 1, 2005, are not intended to impact any existing decisional law regarding this section, and that decisional law should apply equally to this section as it refers to "intimate partner battering and its effects" in place of "battered women's syndrome."

§ 1202. Credibility of hearsay declarant

Evidence of a statement or other conduct by a declarant that is inconsistent with a statement by such declarant received in evidence as hearsay evidence is not inadmissible for the purpose of attacking the credibility of the declarant though he is not given and has not had an opportunity to explain or to deny such inconsistent statement or other conduct. Any other evidence offered to attack or support the credibility of the declarant is admissible if it would have been admissible had the declarant been a witness at the hearing. For the purposes of this section, the deponent of a deposition taken in the action in which it is offered shall be deemed to be a hearsay declarant.

§ 1235. Inconsistent statement

Evidence of a statement made by a witness is not made inadmissible by the hearsay rule if the statement is inconsistent with his testimony at the hearing and is offered in compliance with Section 770.

§ 1236. Prior consistent statement

Evidence of a statement previously made by a witness is not made inadmissible by the hearsay rule if the statement is consistent with his testimony at the hearing and is offered in compliance with Section 791.

§ 1294. Unavailable witnesses; prior inconsistent statements; preliminary hearing or prior proceeding

(a) The following evidence of prior inconsistent statements of a witness properly admitted in a preliminary hearing or trial of the same criminal matter pursuant to Section 1235 is not made inadmissible by the hearsay rule if the witness is unavailable and former testimony of the witness is admitted pursuant to Section 1291:

(1) A video recorded statement introduced at a preliminary hearing or prior proceeding concerning the same criminal matter.

(2) A transcript, containing the statements, of the preliminary hearing or prior proceeding concerning the same criminal matter.

(b) The party against whom the prior inconsistent statements are offered, at his or her option, may examine or cross-examine any person who testified at the preliminary hearing or prior proceeding as to the prior inconsistent statements of the witness.

FEDERAL RULES OF EVIDENCE

Rule 607.   Who May Impeach a Witness

Any party, including the party that called the witness, may attack the witness's credibility.

Rule 608.   A Witness's Character for Truthfulness or Untruthfulness

(a) Reputation or Opinion Evidence. A witness's credibility may be attacked or supported by testimony about the witness's reputation for having a character for truthfulness or untruthfulness, or by testimony in the form of an opinion about that character. But evidence of truthful character is admissible only after the witness's character for truthfulness has been attacked.

(b) Specific Instances of Conduct. Except for a criminal conviction under Rule 609, extrinsic evidence is not admissible to prove specific instances of a witness's conduct in order to attack or support the witness's character for truthfulness. But the court may, on cross-examination, allow them to be inquired into if they are probative of the character for truthfulness or untruthfulness of:

(1) the witness; or

(2) another witness whose character the witness being cross-examined has testified about.

By testifying on another matter, a witness does not waive any privilege against self-incrimination for testimony that relates only to the witness's character for truthfulness.

Rule 609.   Impeachment by Evidence of a Criminal Conviction

(a) In General. The following rules apply to attacking a witness's character for truthfulness by evidence of a criminal conviction:

(1) for a crime that, in the convicting jurisdiction, was punishable by death or by imprisonment for more than one year, the evidence:

    (A) must be admitted, subject to Rule 403, in a civil case or in a criminal case in which the witness is not a defendant; and

    (B) must be admitted in a criminal case in which the witness is a defendant, if the probative value of the evidence outweighs its prejudicial effect to that defendant; and

(2) for any crime regardless of the punishment, the evidence must be admitted if the court can readily determine that establishing the elements of the crime required proving—or the witness's admitting— a dishonest act or false statement.

(b) Limit on Using the Evidence After 10 Years.

This subdivision (b) applies if more than 10 years have passed since the witness's conviction or release from confinement for it, whichever is later. Evidence of the conviction is admissible only if:

    (1) its probative value, supported by specific facts and circumstances, substantially outweighs its prejudicial effect; and

    (2) the proponent gives an adverse party reasonable written notice of the intent to use it so that the party has a fair opportunity to contest its use.

(c) Effect of a Pardon, Annulment, or Certificate of Rehabilitation. Evidence of a conviction is not admissible if:

    (1) the conviction has been the subject of a pardon, annulment, certificate of rehabilitation, or other equivalent procedure based on a finding that the person has been rehabilitated, and the person has not been convicted of a later crime punishable by death or by imprisonment for more than one year; or

    (2) the conviction has been the subject of a pardon, annulment, or other equivalent procedure based on a finding of innocence.

(d) Juvenile Adjudications. Evidence of a juvenile adjudication is admissible under this rule only if:

    (1) it is offered in a criminal case;

    (2) the adjudication was of a witness other than the defendant;

    (3) an adult's conviction for that offense would be admissible to attack the adult's credibility; and

    (4) admitting the evidence is necessary to fairly determine guilt or innocence.

(e) Pendency of an Appeal. A conviction that satisfies this rule is admissible even if an appeal is pending. Evidence of the pendency is also admissible.

Rule 610.   Religious Beliefs or Opinions

Evidence of a witness's religious beliefs or opinions is not admissible to attack or support the witness's credibility.

Rule 611.   Mode and Order of Examining Witnesses and Presenting Evidence

(a) Control by the Court; Purposes. The court should exercise reasonable control over the mode and order of examining witnesses and presenting evidence so as to:

> **(1)** make those procedures effective for determining the truth;
>
> **(2)** avoid wasting time; and
>
> **(3)** protect witnesses from harassment or undue embarrassment.

(b) Scope of Cross–Examination. Cross-examination should not go beyond the subject matter of the direct examination and matters affecting the witness's credibility. The court may allow inquiry into additional matters as if on direct examination.

(c) Leading Questions. Leading questions should not be used on direct examination except as necessary to develop the witness's testimony. Ordinarily, the court should allow leading questions:

> **(1)** on cross-examination; and
>
> **(2)** when a party calls a hostile witness, an adverse party, or a witness identified with an adverse party.

Rule 612.   Writing Used to Refresh a Witness's Memory

(a) Scope. This rule gives an adverse party certain options when a witness uses a writing to refresh memory:

> **(1)** while testifying; or
>
> **(2)** before testifying, if the court decides that justice requires the party to have those options.

(b) Adverse Party's Options; Deleting Unrelated Matter. Unless 18 U.S.C. § 3500 provides otherwise in a criminal case, an adverse party is entitled to have the writing produced at the hearing, to inspect it, to cross-examine the witness about it, and to introduce in evidence any portion that relates to the witness's testimony. If the producing party claims that the writing includes unrelated matter, the court must examine the writing in camera, delete any unrelated portion, and order that the rest be delivered to the adverse party. Any portion deleted over objection must be preserved for the record.

(c) Failure to Produce or Deliver the Writing. If a writing is not produced or is not delivered as ordered, the court may issue any appropriate order. But if the prosecution does not comply in a criminal case, the court must strike the witness's testimony or—if justice so requires— declare a mistrial.

Rule 613. Witness's Prior Statement

(a) Showing or Disclosing the Statement During Examination. When examining a witness about the witness's prior statement, a party need not show it or disclose its contents to the witness. But the party must, on request, show it or disclose its contents to an adverse party's attorney.

(b) Extrinsic Evidence of a Prior Inconsistent Statement. Extrinsic evidence of a witness's prior inconsistent statement is admissible only if the witness is given an opportunity to explain or deny the statement and an adverse party is given an opportunity to examine the witness about it, or if justice so requires. This subdivision (b) does not apply to an opposing party's statement under Rule 801(d)(2).

Rule 614. Court's Calling or Examining a Witness

(a) Calling. The court may call a witness on its own or at a party's request. Each party is entitled to cross-examine the witness.

(b) Examining. The court may examine a witness regardless of who calls the witness.

(c) Objections. A party may object to the court's calling or examining a witness either at that time or at the next opportunity when the jury is not present.

Rule 615. Excluding Witnesses

At a party's request, the court must order witnesses excluded so that they cannot hear other witnesses' testimony. Or the court may do so on its own. But this rule does not authorize excluding:

(a) a party who is a natural person;

(b) an officer or employee of a party that is not a natural person, after being designated as the party's representative by its attorney;

(c) a person whose presence a party shows to be essential to presenting the party's claim or defense; or

(d) a person authorized by statute to be present.

Rule 806. Attacking and Supporting the Declarant's Credibility

When a hearsay statement—or a statement described in Rule 801(d)(2)(C), (D), or (E)—has been admitted in evidence, the declarant's credibility may be attacked, and then supported, by any evidence that would be admissible for those purposes if the declarant had testified as a witness. The court may admit evidence of the declarant's inconsistent statement or conduct, regardless of when it occurred or whether the declarant had an opportunity to explain or deny it. If the party against whom the statement was admitted calls the declarant as a witness, the party may examine the declarant on the statement as if on cross-examination.

CHAPTER 16

EXPERT TESTIMONY AND
THE OPINION RULE

■ ■ ■

Table of Sections

§ 16.01   THE OPINION RULE

The American system of proof discourages the giving of opinions.[1] It proceeds on the assumption that the fact finder can resolve factual disputes on the basis of the information presented by the parties. If the issue is whether the defendant was negligent, then the jurors can decide that question on the basis of the evidence that was received. The jurors do not need a witness to tell them whether in the witness's opinion the defendant was negligent.

Observations, however, are often expressed in the form of opinions or conclusions. When we say that it is raining or it is cold, those observations are really deductions or conclusions based on our experience with weather conditions. Though the law of evidence disfavors opinions, it recognizes that forcing witnesses to describe their observations without using conclusions would make for awkward, time-consuming testimony. Both the Code and the Federal Rules allow lay witnesses to testify in the form of an

---

1. Holland v. Zollner, 102 Cal. 633, 635, 36 P. 930, 931 (1894), aff'd, 102 Cal. 633, 37 P. 231 (1894).

opinion if the opinion is rationally based on the perception of the witness and is helpful to a clear understanding of the witness's testimony.[2]

At times, the fact finder, whether judge or juror, is incapable of resolving a factual issue because the knowledge needed is beyond the fact finder's experience. An issue in a personal injury case, for example, may be whether the plaintiff's back injury is permanent. Jurors hearing the plaintiff's description of her injuries and even her doctor's diagnosis of the injuries will probably be unable to decide this issue without expert help. Accordingly, the law of evidence will permit an expert to tell the jurors whether in the expert's opinion the plaintiff's injuries are permanent.[3] Of course, the expert will not be allowed to provide the jurors with the opinion or prognosis, unless the expert is qualified to do so.[4] The jurors, however, do not need to be "wholly ignorant" of the subject to which the expert opinion is directed. Expert opinion should be excluded only when it

---

2. West's Ann. California Evidence Code § 800; Federal Rule of Evidence 701. The Federal Rule was amended to exclude lay opinions which are based on scientific, technical, or other specialized knowledge and which would otherwise be governed by the limitations imposed on expert testimony by Rule 702. See Federal Rule of Evidence 701. The amendment is designed "to eliminate the risk that the reliability requirements set forth in Rule 702 will be evaded through the simple expedient of proffering an expert in lay witness clothing. Under the amendment, a witness' testimony must be scrutinized under the rules regulating expert opinion to the extent that the witness is providing testimony based on scientific, technical, or other specialized knowledge within the scope of Rule 702." Id. (Advisory Committee Note).

3. West's Ann. California Evidence Code § 801; Federal Rule of Evidence 702. See, e.g., Betterton v. Leichtling, 101 Cal.App.4th 749, 756, 124 Cal.Rptr.2d 644, 649 (2002) ("Here, the effect of Betterton's aspirin use on the risk of surgical complications was a subject beyond the general knowledge of lay people. Therefore, the jury should have relied only on expert testimony when it determined whether the use of aspirin causes significant risks in surgery.").

But where the jury does not need the expert's help, the expert should not be permitted to testify. See, e.g., Westbrooks v. State, 173 Cal.App.3d 1203, 1209–1210, 219 Cal.Rptr. 674, 678 (1985) (Expert opinion could not be received on whether safety measures eliminated dangerous conditions at a collapsed bridge as the jurors could determine that issue from the evidence without expert help.); Laurie S. v. Superior Court, 26 Cal.App.4th 195, 201, 31 Cal.Rptr.2d 506, 510 (1994) (Expert opinion on whether a parent's mental illness subjected a child to the risk of harm or neglect was unnecessary where the fact finder could make that determination from evidence of the parent's conduct toward the child.); People v. Brandon, 32 Cal.App.4th 1033, 1049, 38 Cal.Rptr.2d 751, 761 (1995) (Expert opinion on whether a photo array was impermissibly suggestive was unnecessary where the jurors could decide for themselves whether the photos had been fairly selected.); People v. Torres, 33 Cal.App.4th 37, 47–48, 39 Cal.Rptr.2d 103, 108–109 (1995) (Expert opinion on whether the accused is guilty of the offense charged or whether a crime has been committed is likewise inadmissible as the jurors can resolve those issues from the evidence without expert help.); Loth v. Truck–A–Way Corp., 60 Cal.App.4th 757, 767, 70 Cal.Rptr.2d 571, 578 (1998) (Expert opinion on damages for loss of enjoyment of life—"hedonic" damages—is inadmissible as the jurors do not need an expert's help in determining such damages.); People v. Son, 79 Cal.App.4th 224, 240–241, 93 Cal.Rptr.2d 871, 883 (2000) (Expert opinion on coerced confessions was inadmissible in the absence of evidence that the accused's confession was coerced.); Piscitelli v. Friedenberg, 87 Cal.App.4th 953, 970–971, 105 Cal.Rptr.2d 88, 100–102 (2001) (In a legal malpractice case, expert opinion was inadmissible on whether the plaintiff would have prevailed in an arbitration proceeding that did not take place as a result of the lawyer's alleged negligence; it was up to the jurors, not the expert, to make this determination based on the evidence that would have been presented at the arbitration.); People v. Smith, 30 Cal.4th 581, 628, 134 Cal.Rptr.2d 1, 39, 68 P.3d 302, 333, cert. denied, 540 U.S. 1163, 124 S.Ct. 1169, 157 L.Ed.2d 1208 (2004) (Jurors do not generally need expert help in determining the credibility of a witness.); Kotla v. Regents of the University of California, 115 Cal.App.4th 283, 293, 8 Cal.Rptr.3d 898, 905 (2004) (In a wrongful termination case, expert opinion on whether an employer's actions manifested a motive to retaliate against the employee was inadmissible, as the jurors could make that determination from the evidence.).

4. West's Ann. California Evidence Code § 801; Federal Rule of Evidence 702.

would add nothing to the jurors' common fund of knowledge.[5]

To ensure the reliability of the expert opinion, the proponent also must satisfy the judge that, in reaching the opinion, the expert relied on matters of a type reasonably relied upon by experts in the field.[6] Sometimes the proponent must clear an additional hurdle. If the expert's testimony is based on a novel scientific principle or technique, the proponent may also have to demonstrate that the principle or technique has been generally accepted as valid by the relevant scientific community.[7]

This chapter examines the limitations imposed on lay and expert opinion.

§ 16.02 LAY OPINION

Despite the general proscription against opinions, lay witnesses have been permitted to give a variety of opinions. An old case, Holland v. Zollner,[1] lists some of the opinions that have been received from lay witnesses: to estimate quantity, value, weight, measure, time, distance, and velocity; to describe such emotions as anger, fear, excitement, love, hatred, sorrow, and joy; to describe character traits, such as truthfulness and mendacity; to describe aspects of appearance, such as age, manner of walking, and type of hair; to relate whether others appeared to be sick, well, intoxicated, or even irrational.[2]

Some of these deductions resemble observations that for convenience's sake are expressed in the form of a shorthand opinion or conclusion, for example, describing others as angry, happy, or sad. Others imply greater deliberation in reaching the characterization, for example, describ-

---

5. People v. McDonald, 37 Cal.3d 351, 367, 208 Cal.Rptr. 236, 246, 690 P.2d 709, 719 (1984). See, e.g., People v. Prince, 40 Cal.4th 1179, 1223, 156 P.3d 1015, 1047, 57 Cal.Rptr.3d 543, 581 (2007): "Notwithstanding the ability of jurors to review the evidence before them and draw commonsense inferences, it may aid them to learn from a person with extensive training in crime scene analysis, who has examined not only the evidence in the particular case but has in mind his or her experience in analyzing hundreds of other cases, whether certain features that appear in all the charged crimes are comparatively rare, and therefore suggest in the expert's opinion that the crimes were committed by the same person."

6. West's Ann. California Evidence Code § 801; Federal Rule of Evidence 702.

7. People v. Kelly, 17 Cal.3d 24, 30, 130 Cal.Rptr. 144, 148, 549 P.2d 1240, 1244 (1976). For a discussion of the federal treatment of this additional requirement, see § 16.05 infra.

1. 102 Cal. 633, 36 P. 930 (1894), aff'd, 102 Cal. 633, 37 P. 231 (1894).

2. Id. 635–636, 36 P. at 931. A lay witness may also give an opinion based on comparing a shoe with a shoe print. People v. Lucero, 64 Cal.App.4th 1107, 1111, 75 Cal.Rptr.2d 806, 809 (1998).

Courts, however, draw a distinction between lay testimony describing someone's behavior as a manifestation of his state of mind and lay testimony describing that person's state of mind directly. "Generally, a lay witness may not give an opinion about another's state of mind. However, a witness may testify about objective behavior and describe behavior as being consistent with a state of mind." People v. Chatman, 38 Cal.4th 344, 397, 42 Cal.Rptr.3d 621, 667, 133 P.3d 534, 572 (2006), cert. denied, 549 U.S. 1120, 127 S.Ct. 938, 166 L.Ed.2d 718 (2007). Accordingly, a witness may testify that the accused "seemed to enjoy kicking the custodian" because, as a percipient witness, the witness spoke from personal observation and was thus "competent to testify that defendant's behavior and demeanor were consistent with enjoyment" where a history of enjoying inflicting pain was relevant at the penalty phase of a murder trial. Id.

ing someone as irrational. The witness who provides this opinion can probably describe a number of specific acts which prompted the witness to characterize the conduct as irrational.[3] Yet, both characterizations—angry and irrational—are offered by the California Law Revision Commission as examples of permissible lay opinions.[4] The examples underscore the modern approach to lay opinions. The question is not whether the witness can describe the observations underlying an opinion but whether the opinion is helpful to a clear understanding of the witness's testimony.[5] If, in the exercise of discretion, the judge finds that the opinion is helpful, the judge will permit the jurors to hear the opinion if it is rationally based on the witness's perception.[6] Of course, if the witness's opinion or conclusion is not rationally based, it is inadmissible. A witness, for example, may not offer an opinion that someone appeared to be under the influence of cocaine unless the witness is familiar with the effects of cocaine.[7]

QUESTIONS AND PROBLEMS

1. A lay witness should not be permitted to describe another person as "seeming confused" because, unless the witness is an expert on psychological moods, such testimony would be sheer speculation. True or false?

2. A witness should not be permitted to estimate the speed of a car unless the witness has some basis in personal experience (such as having driven motor vehicles for a considerable period of time) for arriving at the estimate. True or false?

3. A witness should not be permitted to estimate the speed of a car because the law of evidence favors precision and not estimates which may mislead the fact finder about the true speed of the car. True or false?

§ 16.03 EXPERT OPINION

Expert testimony and the personal knowledge requirement. Experts differ from lay witnesses in one important respect: their opinions do not have to be based on their personal observations. Their opinions can

---

3. See, e.g., Holland v. Zollner, 102 Cal. 633, 36 P. 930 (1894), aff'd, 102 Cal. 633, 37 P. 231 (1894).

4. 6 California Law Revision Commission, Reports, Recommendations, and Studies 931–935 (1964). See also People v. Farnam, 28 Cal.4th 107, 153, 121 Cal.Rptr.2d 106, 147, 47 P.3d 988, 1023 (2002), cert. denied, 537 U.S. 1124, 123 S.Ct. 861, 154 L.Ed.2d 806 (2003) (approving the admission of a police officer's opinion that the defendant appeared "very defiant"); People v. Gurule, 28 Cal.4th 557, 621, 123 Cal.Rptr.2d 345, 397, 51 P.3d 224, 268 (2002) (approving a police officer's testimony that he had not heard or observed "any delusional or hallucinatory speech or conduct on the part of a [subject]"); People v. Hinton, 37 Cal.4th 839, 889, 38 Cal.Rptr.3d 149, 195, 126 P.3d 981, 1019, cert. denied, 549 U.S. 1033, 127 S.Ct. 581, 166 L.Ed.2d 434 (2006) (approving a witness's testimony that it appeared to him that the defendant was directing a drug transaction).

5. 6 California Law Revision Commission, Reports, Recommendations, and Studies 933 (1964).

6. As a matter of effective advocacy, a good lawyer will usually ask a witness who testifies in a conclusionary form to explain how the witness arrived at the conclusion.

7. See People v. Navarette, 30 Cal.4th 458, 494, 133 Cal.Rptr.2d 89, 114, 66 P.3d 1182, 1203 (2003), cert. denied 540 U.S. 1151, 124 S.Ct. 1149, 157 L.Ed.2d 1045 (2004).

be based on matters or data made known to them at or before the hearing.[1] An example helps illustrate this important difference.

Assume a personal injury case in which one of the issues is whether the plaintiff's back injury will be permanent. A jury hearing the plaintiff's description of her injuries will probably be unable to answer this question without expert help. Jurors simply do not have the background necessary to draw the inference one way or another from the plaintiff's testimony. In theory, the plaintiff can have an expert draw the necessary inference in one of three ways.

One is to have the expert draw the inference on the basis of the evidence available to the jury. A qualified medical doctor may be able to arrive at the prognosis by watching the plaintiff in court and hearing her description of the injuries.[2] If the doctor was not present during the plaintiff's testimony, he might still be permitted to supply the prognosis on the basis of a hypothetical question. Hypothetical questions allow experts to furnish opinions based on matters which are beyond their personal knowledge but which are supported by the evidence.[3] In our example, the plaintiff's lawyer could frame a hypothetical question in which he would ask the doctor to assume the existence of certain symptoms which the lawyer in turn would take from the plaintiff's description of her injuries on her direct examination.

A third and more likely way is to have the doctor provide the prognosis on the basis of the information experts in the field use in reaching the kind of prognosis the plaintiff desires. The information could include the plaintiff's medical history, as well as the doctor's examination of the plaintiff, and the results of tests ordinarily performed to determine the severity of injuries, such as the plaintiff's. Thus, much of the information the doctor might rely on might be beyond the doctor's personal knowledge. But under the Code and the Rules, experts do not have to base

---

1. West's Ann. California Evidence Code § 801; Federal Rule of Evidence 703. An exception to this rule is made in California where a medical doctor who testifies as a percipient witness has not been retained under the procedural rules as an expert witness. As a percipient witness, the doctor may testify only about the "prognosis, diagnosis, causation of injuries, duration or necessity of medical expenses" but not about such matters as the standard of care that should apply in the case. Paxton v. Stewart, 68 Cal.App.4th 331, 341, 80 Cal.Rptr.2d 179, 186 (1998).

2. An expert may base an opinion on testimony he hears or reads. Estate of Collin, 150 Cal.App.2d 702, 712–714, 310 P.2d 663, 670–672 (1957).

3. It is up to the jury to determine whether the assumed facts have been proved by the standard appropriate to the proceeding. See, e.g., CALJIC 2.82 (Fall 2006 Edition). Judges, however, should not allow an expert to answer a hypothetical question unless some evidence has been or will be received to support the existence of each assumed fact. See People v. Gardeley, 14 Cal.4th 605, 618, 59 Cal.Rptr.2d 356, 364, 927 P.2d 713, 721(1996), cert. denied, 522 U.S. 854, 118 S.Ct. 148, 139 L.Ed.2d 94 (1997); Hyatt v. Sierra Boat Co., 79 Cal.App.3d 325, 339, 145 Cal.Rptr. 47, 55 (1978). Neither should judges permit an expert to answer a hypothetical question which omits a material fact whose existence has been conceded by the parties. Coe v. State Farm Mutual Auto. Ins. Co., 66 Cal.App.3d 981, 994–995, 136 Cal.Rptr. 331, 338 (1977).

In ruling on a motion for summary judgment, a judge may disregard declarations by doctors whose opinions are not supported by the evidence. See People v. Bushling v. Fremont Medical Center, 117 Cal.App.4th 493, 510, 11 Cal.Rptr.3d 653, 665 (2004). (" '[A]n expert's opinion that something could be true if certain assumed facts are true, without any foundation for concluding those assumed facts exist' * * * has no evidentiary value.").

their opinion on their own observations. Their opinions can be based on information that is made known to them at the hearing (e.g., through a hypothetical question) or before the hearing (e.g., the plaintiff's recital of her medical history).[4]

The inadmissibility of the information upon which the expert opinion is based. It is immaterial that the data on which the expert relies are inadmissible.[5] So long as the data are of the type reasonably relied upon by experts in the field, the expert may base his opinion on that data.[6] For example, if in reaching a particular prognosis, doctors routinely rely on radiologists' reports, an expert may base an opinion on such a report even if the report has not been, or cannot be, received in evidence. The expert, moreover, is entitled to tell the jury that he relied on a radiologist's report in reaching his opinion.[7]

Permitting experts to base opinions on data that are of the type reasonably relied upon by experts in the field conforms evidentiary practice with the customs and practices of experts themselves. If sound medical practices allow doctors to reach important health decisions on information provided by patients and specialists, such as radiologists, then those decisions should be sufficiently reliable to be used in court. But the latitude accorded to experts to rely on matters that may not be admissible should not lull the opponent into foregoing hearsay, Best Evidence Rule, and other objections. It is one matter for an expert to tell the jury that he relied on a radiologist's report in reaching his prognosis. It is quite another for the expert to disclose the contents of the report in his testimony. Such a disclosure would violate the Best Evidence Rule[8] as well as the hearsay rule if the radiologist's findings are related by the expert for the truth of the matter stated.[9]

---

4. West's Ann. California Evidence Code § 801; Federal Rule of Evidence 703.

5. West's Ann. California Evidence Code § 801; Federal Rule of Evidence 703.

6. West's Ann. California Evidence Code § 801; Federal Rule of Evidence 703. See, e.g., Brown v. Colm, 11 Cal.3d 639, 644, 114 Cal.Rptr. 128, 130, 522 P.2d 688, 690 (1974) (A doctor may rely on medical literature in reaching an opinion so long as the literature is of the type reasonably relied upon by experts in the field.); People v. Miller, 25 Cal.App.4th 913, 917, 31 Cal.Rptr.2d 423, 425 (1994) (In a mentally disordered offender proceeding, a mental health expert may rely on a probation report in determining whether the offender is mentally disordered since such reports are reasonably relied upon by experts in the field.). But expert opinions that are based in part or in whole on matter that is not a proper basis for such opinions may be excluded. West's Ann. California Evidence Code § 803. The basis of the opinion may be improper as a matter of law. See, e.g., Spencer v. G. A. MacDonald Const. Co., 63 Cal.App.3d 836, 857–859, 134 Cal.Rptr. 78, 92 (1976) (Labor Code precluded an expert from basing opinions on violation of safety rules.). The opinion may also be excluded because the expert relied on matters experts in the field would have ignored. See, e.g., Board of Trustees v. Porini, 263 Cal.App.2d 784, 793–794, 70 Cal.Rptr. 73, 79–80 (1968) (In forming an opinion whether a teacher was suffering from mental illness, it was improper for a psychiatrist to consider information supplied by lay persons and contained in a dossier on the teacher.). See generally § 16.04 infra.

7. West's Ann. California Evidence Code § 802; Federal Rule of Evidence 705.

8. The Best Evidence Rule requires a party to prove the contents of a writing through the writing itself and not through a secondary source, such as testimony about the contents of the writing. California has relaxed this requirement much more than the Federal Rules by the replacing the state's Best Evidence Rule with the Secondary Evidence Rule. See § 13.06 supra.

9. See, e.g., People v. Coleman, 38 Cal.3d 69, 92, 211 Cal.Rptr. 102, 116, 695 P.2d 189, 203 (1985); Genrich v. State, 202 Cal.App.3d 221, 229, 248 Cal.Rptr. 303, 308 (1988); Mosesian v.

Jurors may consider the basis of an expert's opinion in assessing the weight, if any, they should give to the expert's testimony. Upon request, the opposing party is entitled to have the jurors instructed to consider the evidence only for this limited purpose.[10] But the fact that the opponent is entitled to a limiting instruction does not authorize the proponent to disclose the contents of reports and other hearsay which the expert took into account in reaching his opinion. The value of the disclosure to the expert's credibility may be too slight when compared with the risk that the jurors might be unable to abide by the instruction directing them not to consider the matters disclosed for the truth of the matter stated.[11] The risk varies with the amount of details disclosed. The greater the details, the greater the risk that jurors will be unable to abide by the instruction.

Federal Rule of Evidence 703 was amended in 2000 to make clear that the proponent of the expert opinion should not disclose to the jurors facts or data that are otherwise inadmissible unless the court determines that their probative value in assisting the jury to evaluate the expert's opinion substantially outweighs their prejudicial effect.[12] Disclosure to the jury must, of course, be accompanied by a limiting instruction. As noted, under Rule 703, the judge may not allow the proponent to disclose the inadmissible matter unless the judge finds that the evaluative value of the evidence substantially outweighs its prejudicial effects.[13] Under the California approach, the traditional balancing rule requires the judge to allow disclosure of the inadmissible matter unless its evaluative value is substantially outweighed by its prejudicial effects.[14]

Expert opinion on ultimate issues. It is also immaterial that the

Pennwalt Corp., 191 Cal.App.3d 851, 860, 236 Cal.Rptr. 778, 782 (1987); accord: People v. Catlin, 26 Cal.4th 81, 137, 109 Cal.Rptr.2d 31, 73–74, 26 P.3d 357, 393 (2001). See also People v. Gardeley, 34 Cal.App.4th 1614, 1624, 36 Cal.Rptr.2d 136, 142 (1994) (Although a qualified expert may testify that a predicate crime was an act in furtherance of gang activities under penal provisions punishing gang activities, unless the expert had first-hand knowledge of the activities giving rise to the crime, over a hearsay objection his testimony could not be received as proof of the predicate crime.).

When a California defendant pleads not guilty by reason of insanity, the prosecution is entitled to have its mental health experts examine the defendant. At the trial, the prosecution may call its experts and ask them whether they took into account any statements made by the defendant in reaching their diagnosis. Ordinarily, any admissions made by the defendant to the mental health experts may be offered by the prosecution for the truth of the matter stated under the party admissions exception to the hearsay rule. See generally § 7.01 supra. But, as an accommodation to the defendant's right against self-incrimination, a California judge must instruct the jurors not to consider any incriminating statements made by the defendant to the mental health experts for the truth of the matter stated. See People v. Jantz, 137 Cal.App.4th 1283, 1293, 40 Cal.Rptr.3d 875, 882 (2006).

10. A California trial judge does not have a sua sponte duty to give the limiting instruction. See People v. Boyer, 38 Cal.4th 412, 464, 42 Cal.Rptr.3d 677, 722, 133 P.3d 581, 619 (2006).

11. People v. Coleman, 38 Cal.3d 69, 92, 211 Cal.Rptr. 102, 116, 695 P.2d 189, 203 (1985). See also People v. Bell, 40 Cal.4th 582, 607, 151 P.3d 292, 309, 54 Cal.Rptr.3d 453, 473 (2007) (holding that the trial judge did not abuse his discretion in excluding the basis of the expert's opinion where the judge concluded that the jurors could not abide by the limiting instruction instructing them not to consider the basis for the truth of the matters stated).

12. Federal Rule of Evidence 703.

13. Id.

14. See West's Ann. California Evidence Code § 352.

expert's opinion embraces ultimate factual issues.[15] The question for the judge is whether the opinion would help the jurors decide an issue that is beyond their competence. Among the examples cited in the Advisory Committee Note to Federal Rule 704 are opinions about the cause of a landslide and whether an abortion was necessary to save the life of a patient.[16] Special statutes, however, prevent experts in California and federal prosecutions from stating whether the accused harbored the mens rea of the offense charged.[17]

Expert testimony directed at ultimate factual issues must be distinguished from expert testimony directed at legal questions. As a rule, expert testimony is inadmissible in resolving questions of law. Accordingly, expert testimony may not be received to determine whether probable cause existed as a defense to a malicious prosecution claim[18] or whether police officers responding to a crisis involving a person threatening suicide have a legal duty under the tort law that exposes them to liability if they fail to prevent the suicide.[19] Likewise, an expert may not testify whether a party owes a nondelegable duty to another party, whether certain contracts are illegal, or whether a party is required to be registered as a contract carrier.[20] Nor may a linguist or other expert testify about the proper interpretation of an insurance contract.[21] Neither may a securities expert give an opinion whether a broker breached a duty to supervise sales by one of its registered representatives.[22] On the other hand, personal injury claims arising out of sports settings sometimes raise difficult questions of whether a defendant owed the plaintiff a duty not to increase the risk of harm inherent in the sport. In determining whether the defendant owed the plaintiff such a duty, a judge may seek the advice of

---

15. West's Ann. California Evidence Code § 805; Federal Rule of Evidence 704. See also People v. Valdez, 58 Cal.App.4th 494, 507, 68 Cal.Rptr.2d 135, 143 (1997) and cases cited therein. Experts, however, may not give opinions on pure questions of law. Devin v. United Services Auto. Ass'n, 6 Cal.App.4th 1149, 1157, note 5, 8 Cal.Rptr.2d 263, 268, note 5 (1992). For example, a witness may not define offenses for the jury since that responsibility is committed to the trial judge. People v. Torres, 33 Cal.App.4th 37, 39 Cal.Rptr.2d 103, 107 (1995).

16. Federal Rule of Evidence 704 (Advisory Committee Note).

17. West's Ann. California Penal Code § 29; Federal Rule of Evidence 704(b). The Federal Rule also precludes an expert from stating whether the accused entertained the mental state required for a defense to the crime charged. Federal Rule of Evidence 704(b). The California statute has been upheld against the claim that excluding the expert's opinion violates due process. See, e.g., People v. Jackson, 152 Cal.App.3d 961, 199 Cal.Rptr. 848, 852 (1984). Although the Right to Truth–in–Evidence provision of Proposition 8 may have repealed § 29, the section was subsequently reenacted by the super majority required to override Proposition 8. See People v. Whitler, 171 Cal.App.3d 337, 342, 214 Cal.Rptr. 610, 613–614 (1985).

18. Williams v. Coombs, 179 Cal.App.3d 626, 638, 224 Cal.Rptr. 865, 873 (1986), reversed on other grounds, Sheldon Appel Co. v. Albert & Oliker, 47 Cal.3d 863, 254 Cal.Rptr. 336, 765 P.2d 498 (1989).

19. Adams v. City of Fremont, 68 Cal.App.4th 243, 266, 80 Cal.Rptr.2d 196, 209 (1998).

20. Summers v. A.L. Gilbert Co., 69 Cal.App.4th 1155, 1185, 82 Cal.Rptr.2d 162, 180 (1999). Federal courts likewise disfavor the use of experts on questions of law. See, e.g., Nieves–Villanueva v. Soto–Rivera, 133 F.3d 92, 100 (1st Cir. 1997).

21. Industrial Indem. Co. v. Apple Computer, Inc., 79 Cal.App.4th 817, 835, note 4, 95 Cal.Rptr.2d 528, 539, note 4 (1999).

22. Asplund v. SIFE, 86 Cal.App.4th 26, 49, 103 Cal.Rptr.2d 34, 49 (2000).

experts.[23]

Qualifying the expert. The expert, of course, must be qualified to provide the jury with the help it needs. An expert may be qualified by virtue of special knowledge, experience, skill, training, and education.[24] Against the opponent's objection, the proponent must persuade the judge by a preponderance of the evidence that the witness possesses the necessary expertise before the witness provides the expert opinion.[25]

The opponent does not have to rest on the expert's answers on direct to challenge the expert's qualifications. The opponent may request permission to take the expert on *voir dire* in aid of the objection. *Voir dire* is a limited form of cross-examination. It provides the opponent with an opportunity to elicit testimony from the witness that may indicate to the judge that the expert is not qualified to give the opinions sought by the proponent.

Voir dire is preferable to waiting for cross-examination. If after the *voir dire* the judge sustains the opponent's objection, the jurors will not hear the expert opinion. If the opponent waits until cross-examination to challenge the expert's qualifications and the challenge is granted, the opponent will be in the unhappy position of having to ask the judge to instruct the jury to disregard the inadmissible opinions. *Voir dire,* however, should be undertaken with care. Unless the opponent has grounds for believing that the witness will provide the evidence he seeks, the opponent risks convincing the jury, as well as the judge, of the expert's undoubted credentials to provide the desired opinions.

---

23. American Golf Corp. v. Superior Court, 79 Cal.App.4th 30, 37, 93 Cal.Rptr.2d 683, 689 (2000).

24. West's Ann. California Evidence Code §§ 720 and 802; Federal Rule of Evidence 702. "Error regarding a witness's qualifications as an expert will be found only if the evidence shows that the witness '*clearly lacks* qualification as an expert.' " People v. Farnam, 28 Cal.4th 107, 162, 121 Cal.Rptr.2d 106, 154, 47 P.3d 988, 1028 (2002), cert. denied, 537 U.S. 1124, 123 S.Ct. 861, 154 L.Ed.2d 806 (2003) (quoting People v. Chavez, 39 Cal.3d 823, 828, 218 Cal.Rptr. 49, 52, 705 P.2d 372, 376 (1985)) (emphasis in the original).

The fact that the expert has not testified as an expert is not a basis for precluding his testimony. At some point, experts qualify to testify for the first time. McCleery v. City of Bakersfield, 170 Cal.App.3d 1059, 1066, 216 Cal.Rptr. 852, 856 (1985). But if the expert is not qualified to give the opinion sought, he may not give it irrespective of his professional achievements in other fields. Putensen v. Clay Adams, Inc., 12 Cal.App.3d 1062, 1081, 91 Cal.Rptr. 319, 331 (1970).

Special statutes may impose additional requirements for the qualification of some expert witnesses. For example, the California Health and Safety Code requires experts testifying about the standard of care physicians should observe in medical emergencies to have had "substantial professional experience within the last five years while assigned to provide emergency medical coverage in a general acute care hospital emergency department." West's Ann. Health and Safety Code § 1799.110.

25. West's Ann. California Evidence Code §§ 405 (comment) and 720 and comment. See also People v. Ashmus, 54 Cal.3d 932, 970, 2 Cal.Rptr.2d 112, 132, 820 P.2d 214, 234 (1991), cert. denied, 506 U.S. 841, 113 S.Ct. 124, 121 L.Ed.2d 79 (1992), reh'g denied, 506 U.S. 1015, 113 S.Ct. 641, 121 L.Ed.2d 571 (1992). Neither the Code nor the Federal Rules requires the proponent "to tender" the witness as an expert before asking the witness for expert opinions. Where no such tender is made, a party challenging the expert's qualifications should object at the conclusion of a question asking for the expert's opinion.

An opponent can attempt to diminish the impact of the expert's qualifications by offering to stipulate to the expert's expertise. The opponent should avoid over stipulating; he should specify with particularity the areas in which he concedes the expert to be qualified. The proponent can resist the offer, especially if the stipulation fails to include all areas in which expert opinions will be elicited. But even if the offer is not deficient in this respect, the proponent is entitled to have the fact finder consider the expert's qualifications in determining how much weight, if any, to give to the expert's testimony. If the circumstances attending the hearing make it unwise to resist the offer, the proponent should make sure that the stipulation includes the expert's qualifications as well as a clear understanding of the areas in which the expert is qualified to offer opinions.

Disclosing the basis of the expert opinion. Although most experts do so in order to be persuasive witnesses, experts do not have to disclose the bases of their opinions on direct examination.[26] A judge, however, may require such disclosure.[27] The cross examiner, of course, may always require the expert to disclose the bases for his opinions, including the matters on which the expert relied.[28]

Inadmissible expert opinion. Just because the fact finder needs expert help and an expert is qualified to provide that help does not mean that the expert's opinion will be admitted. Some rules may bar the use of the expert evidence even if the evidence meets all tests for the use of expert opinion. California Evidence Code § 1157, for example, prohibits the discovery of a hospital's peer review committee's records.[29] As a result, expert testimony based on such records is inadmissible, irrespective of whether the testimony otherwise meets the tests for admitting expert testimony. Exclusion is required in order to enforce the privilege.[30] Also, California Evidence Code § 1101(a) bans the use of character evidence to prove that the accused is guilty of the offense charged because the accused is the kind of person who would commit the offense.[31] Accordingly, evidence by a qualified expert that the accused's performance on standardized psychological tests revealed that he possessed the characteristics of fathers who abuse their children would be inadmissible to prove that the accused abused his daughter.[32] The expert testimony is inadmissible not

---

26.   West's Ann. California Evidence Code § 802; Federal Rule of Evidence 705.

27.   Id.

28.   West's Ann. California Evidence Code § 721(a); Federal Rule of Evidence 705.

29.   West's Ann. California Evidence Code § 1157.

30.   Fox v. Kramer, 22 Cal.4th 531, 541, 93 Cal.Rptr.2d 497, 503, 994 P.2d 343, 349 (2000).

31.   West's Ann. California Evidence Code § 1101(a). For an extended discussion of this rule, see § 3.04 supra.

32.   See, e.g., In re Cheryl H., 153 Cal.App.3d 1098, 1123–1124, 200 Cal.Rptr. 789, 805–806 (1984). A subsequent amendment to the Code allowing the prosecution to offer evidence of other sexual assaults as evidence of the defendant's propensity to commit the sexual assault charged, does not change this outcome. Under the amended section, the prosecution is limited to offering only evidence of specific instances of sexual misconduct. It may not offer opinion evidence. See West's Ann. California Evidence Code § 1108. On the use of expert evidence to attack or support the credibility of witnesses, see § 15.09 supra.

because of its expert nature but because it falls within the prohibition of § 1101(a).

The ban on the use of character evidence has serious implications for the admissibility of "profile" evidence. As underscored by the California Court of Appeal:

> [P]rofile evidence is inherently prejudicial because it requires the jury to accept an erroneous starting point in its consideration of the evidence. We illustrate the problem by examining the syllogism underlying profile evidence: criminals act in a certain way; the defendant acted that way; therefore the defendant is a criminal. Guilt flows ineluctably from the major premise through the minor one to the conclusion. The problem is the major premise is faulty. It implies that criminals, and only criminals, act in a given way. In fact, certain behavior may be consistent with both innocent and illegal behavior, as the People's expert conceded here.[33]

While the similarities between those fitting a profile and a potential defendant may be a proper consideration for law enforcement in investigating criminal activity, "they are inappropriate for consideration on the issue of guilt or innocence for the very reason given in the drug courier profile cases: the potential of including innocent people as well as the guilty."[34]

Accordingly, the prosecution may not offer evidence that the accused fit the "profile" of an Hispanic drug dealer in order to prove that the accused, an Hispanic, was guilty of possessing a controlled substance[35] or that the accused behaved in ways characteristic of some rapists in order to prove that the accused was guilty of rape.[36] The federal courts are in accord with respect to the use of profile evidence in drug prosecutions.[37]

"Profile" evidence, however, is not inadmissible expert character evidence when offered to prove some relevant proposition other than the accused's predisposition to commit the crime charged. In a prosecution for conspiring to manufacture and distribute drugs the jurors may need help in understanding the roles that different conspirators or materials play in order to appreciate the significance of the prosecution's evidence. Jurors, for example, may not understand the importance of the presence of a small quantity of cocaine, together with a large number of plastic baggies, unless they are told that cocaine is sold in small quantities in plastic baggies. When offered for this background purpose, expert testimony regarding the methods employed to market a drug may be received with the appropriate limiting instructions.[38]

---

33. People v. Robbie, 92 Cal.App.4th 1075, 1085, 112 Cal.Rptr.2d 479, 486–487 (2001).

34. People v. Martinez, 10 Cal.App.4th 1001, 1006, 12 Cal.Rptr.2d 838, 841 (1992).

35. Id.; People v. Castaneda, 55 Cal.App.4th 1067, 1071–1072, 64 Cal.Rptr.2d 395, 398 (1997).

36. People v. Robbie, 92 Cal.App.4th 1075, 1085, 112 Cal.Rptr.2d 479, 486–487 (2001).

37. See, e.g., United States v. Beltran–Rios, 878 F.2d 1208, 1210 (9th Cir. 1989).

38. People v. Lopez, 21 Cal.App.4th 1551, 1554–1555, 26 Cal.Rptr.2d 741, 743–744 (1994). See also People v. Singh, 37 Cal.App.4th 1343, 1380, 44 Cal.Rptr.2d 644, 664 (1995) (In a prosecution

On occasion, however, expert opinion is excluded because it fails to satisfy the tests for admissible expert evidence. The expert, for example, may not be qualified to provide the opinion or the opinion may be based on unreliable or improper matter. These issues are explored in the next section.

QUESTIONS AND PROBLEMS

1. Expert testimony should be admissible only when the fact finder needs expert help in resolving contested factual issues and the witness is qualified to provide the expert help. For example, if the issue is whether the plaintiff's injuries are permanent, the judge should allow a duly qualified expert to offer the jury his opinion on this question. True or false?

2. Before rendering their opinions, experts must first disclose the basis of their opinions. For example, if in reaching his opinion that the plaintiff's injuries are permanent the expert relied on a report by a radiologist who examined the plaintiff, the expert must tell the jurors that he relied on the radiologist's report before offering his opinion to the jurors. True or false?

3. Because experts are used to help jurors draw inferences that may be beyond their competence, experts must necessarily base their opinions on evidence that has been or will be admitted. For example, over objection an expert will not be allowed to tell the jurors that in his opinion the plaintiff's injuries are permanent if the expert's opinion is based in part on the radiologist's report and the report has not been offered or over objection cannot be received in evidence. True or false?

4. In telling the jurors that his opinion is based in part on the radiologist's report, the expert is entitled to tell the jurors that he paid particular attention to that portion of the report where the radiologist said, "The plaintiff's leg is broken in three places." A hearsay objection by the defendant would have to be overruled because of the need to provide the jurors with the information on which the expert relied. True or false? *doesn't have to admit but can.*

5. In a federal or California court, the judge may allow the expert to disclose to the jurors information that he took into account in reaching his opinion even if the information is not admissible, provided the judge instructs the jurors to consider the evidence only for the limited purpose for which it was received. True or false?

6. In exercising discretion, the role of the federal judge differs from that of the California judge. A federal judge should not allow the expert to share inadmissible information with the jurors unless the judge finds that the evaluative value of the information outweighs it prejudicial effects. A California judge, on the other hand, may allow the expert to share the information with the jurors if the judge concludes that its probative value is not substantially outweighed by its prejudicial effects. True or false?

for fraudulently causing car accidents for the purpose of filing false insurance claims, it was proper for the prosecution to offer expert testimony explaining why "the relationship [among] the various pieces of evidence, e.g., the extent of damage, type and extent of injuries, number of passengers in the car, use of common caregiver or attorney" suggested that the collisions had been staged.).

7. Accordingly, a federal judge is more likely than a California judge to let the expert inform the jurors that he paid particular attention to that portion of the report where the radiologist said, "The plaintiff's leg is broken in three places." Truc or false?

8. A party is entitled to strike responses to hypothetical questions that are based on matter that has not been or cannot be admitted in evidence. True or false?

9. Since jurors must decide ultimate issues, over objection an expert cannot give an opinion that embraces most such issues. To permit such opinions would invade the province of the jurors. Accordingly, in a personal injury case an expert on "accidentology" should not be allowed to testify that in her opinion the defendant was negligent. Discuss.

Likewise, in a medical malpractice case, a medical expert should not be allowed to testify that in her opinion the defendant's conduct fell below the standard of care observed by doctors in the pertinent medical community. True or false?

10. It is preferable to challenge an expert's qualifications to give enumerated opinions on *voir dire* than to wait for cross-examination. True or false?

§ 16.04   EXPERT OPINION AND THE *KELLY* TEST

Expert opinion will not help jurors resolve factual issues that are beyond their competence unless the opinion is validly drawn from appropriate data.[1] The Code attempts to assure the reliability of expert opinions by requiring not only that the expert be qualified to give the opinion but also by limiting experts to giving only those opinions which are based on matter "that is of a type that reasonably may be relied upon" by experts in the field.[2] If the judge concludes that the opinion is based on matters that experts in the field would not use, then the judge should exclude the opinion. Such opinions would hardly help the jurors and, worse, could mislead them.[3] This is why the Code expressly empowers California judges to exclude on their own motion or upon objection "testimony in the form of an opinion that is based in whole or in part on matter that is not a proper basis for such an opinion."[4]

---

1. See, e.g., Nelson v. County of Los Angeles, 113 Cal.App.4th 783, 792, 6 Cal.Rptr.3d 650, 658 (2003) (In a wrongful death action, the plaintiff's expert properly based his opinion on the cause of death "on the videotape of [the deceased's] death, the coroner's autopsy reports and photographs, the report of another pathologist who performed a post-mortem examination of [the deceased] at the [plaintiffs's] request, [the deceased's] records from the Department of Corrections, and the deposition testimony given by several of the deputies. No more was required.").

2. West's Ann. California Evidence Code § 801.

3. See, e.g., Stephen v. Ford Motor Co., 134 Cal.App.4th 1363, 1371, 37 Cal.Rptr.3d 9, 15 (2005) (approving trial judge's exclusion of a tire expert's opinion on the ground that the expert based his opinion on matter—amateur photographs—experts in the field would have ignored).

4. West's Ann. California Evidence Code § 803. See also, People v. Murtishaw, 29 Cal.3d 733, 175 Cal.Rptr. 738, 758, 767, 631 P.2d 446, 466 (1981), cert. denied, 455 U.S. 922, 102 S.Ct. 1280, 71 L.Ed.2d 464 (1982), disapproved on other grounds, People v. Boyd, 38 Cal.3d 762, 773, 700

California courts have used the reasonable reliance test to exclude expert opinions which in their view were based on inappropriate matters. For example, in Isaacs v. Huntington Memorial Hospital[5] expert testimony that Pasadena had the second highest crime rate in Los Angeles County was properly excluded because the expert relied on statistics provided by a contact in the police department rather than on official information prepared by the California Department of Justice.[6] Similarly, in Board of Trustees v. Porini[7] expert testimony that a teacher was mentally ill was excluded because the expert improperly relied on opinions by lay persons contained in a dossier on the teacher.[8] In Smith v. ACandS, Inc.[9] expert testimony regarding the quantity of asbestos at a job site based on photographs was held inadmissible because the correct method for measuring asbestos levels requires filtering air through a membrane and then using an electron microscope to magnify the membrane and count the retained asbestos fibers.[10]

Sometimes an expert opinion will be excluded because the expert failed to take into account factors the expert was legally required to consider. In City of San Diego v. Sobke[11] expert testimony regarding the goodwill value of a condemned property was excluded because the expert's valuation methods did not include matters that had to be considered under California law.[12] On some occasions, expert opinion will also be excluded because it fails to satisfy a legal standard that applies to the case. For example, in a medical malpractice case, a doctor's opinion on causation-in-fact is inadmissible unless the doctor explains how the defendant's negligent act was the cause of the plaintiff's injuries.[13]

The Code's reasonable reliance test is the principal test the California courts employ to exclude unreliable expert opinions. It is the test the

---

P.2d 782, 790, 215 Cal.Rptr. 1, 9 (1985) (disapproving the use of prosecution experts to predict a murder defendant's dangerousness in the penalty phase of the trial where the empirical studies show such predictions to be unreliable); but see People v. Jones, 29 Cal.4th 1229, 1260, 131 Cal.Rptr.2d 468, 492, 64 P.3d 762, 782, cert. denied, 540 U.S. 952, 124 S.Ct. 395, 157 L.Ed.2d 286 (2003) ("While the prosecution is prohibited from offering expert testimony predicting future dangerousness in its case-in-chief, * * * it may explore the issue on cross-examination or in rebuttal if defendant offers expert testimony predicting good prison behavior in the future.").

  5.   38 Cal.3d 112, 211 Cal.Rptr. 356, 695 P.2d 653 (1985).

  6.   Id. at 134, 211 Cal.Rptr. at 367, 695 P.2d at 664.

  7.   263 Cal.App.2d 784, 70 Cal.Rptr. 73 (1968).

  8.   Id. at 793–794, 70 Cal.Rptr. at 79–80.

  9.   31 Cal.App.4th 77, 37 Cal.Rptr.2d 457 (1994).

  10.   Id. at 92, 37 Cal.Rptr.2d at 465.

  11.   65 Cal.App.4th 379, 76 Cal.Rptr.2d 9 (1998).

  12.   Id. at 396, 76 Cal.Rptr.2d at 20.

  13.   See Jennings v. Palomar Pomerado Health Systems, Inc., 114 Cal.App.4th 1108, 1114, 8 Cal.Rptr.3d 363, 367 (2003). For similar reasons, expert declarations may likewise be excluded if the expert fails to disclose valid grounds for his or her opinion. See, e.g., Johnson v. Superior Court, 143 Cal.App.4th 297, 306, 49 Cal.Rptr.3d 52, 58 (2006) ("The crucial issue was whether too many radioactive seeds were implanted into plaintiff's prostate. Dr. Wallner's declaration does not explain how the number of seeds to be implanted is usually determined, or what is the recognized standard for making the determination. He says no more than what was done was within the standard of care.").

courts will use unless in their view the expert opinion is predicated on some novel scientific principle or technique.

The *Kelly* Test. When the expert opinion is based on novel scientific principles or techniques, the California courts use the *Kelly* test to determine the admissibility of the opinion. Adopting the approach taken in Frye v. United States,[14] the California Supreme Court held in People v. Kelly[15] that the proponent must persuade the judge that the novel scientific principle or technique " 'has been sufficiently established to have gained general acceptance in the particular field in which it belongs.' "[16] General acceptance, not just reasonable reliance, is the test.

Critics of the *Kelly* approach emphasize the difficulties of distinguishing expert testimony based on novel scientific principles from other expert testimony, of deciding in which particular field the principle belongs, and of determining whether it has been generally accepted by the appropriate members of that field.[17] The California Supreme Court has nonetheless upheld the use of the general acceptance test.[18] In the court's view, the test promotes a degree of uniformity with respect to the admissibility of evidence based on scientific principles: "Individual judges whose particular conclusions may differ regarding the reliability of particular scientific evidence, may discover substantial agreement and consensus in the scientific community."[19] Of greater importance, the test is designed "to interpose a substantial obstacle to the unrestrained admission of evidence based upon new scientific principles."[20] In the court's view, caution is called for because of the risk that jurors might give unwarranted weight to " 'scientific' evidence when presented by 'experts' with impressive credentials."[21] Finally, the court favors applying stringent standards to the use of scientific evidence based upon a new scientific technique because "once a trial court has admitted evidence based upon a new scientific technique, and that decision is affirmed on appeal by a published appellate decision, the precedent so established may control subsequent trials, at least until

---

14. 54 App.D.C. 46, 293 F. 1013 (1923).

15. 17 Cal.3d 24, 130 Cal.Rptr. 144, 549 P.2d 1240 (1976).

16. Id. at 30, 130 Cal.Rptr. at 148, 549 P.2d at 1244, quoting Frye v. United States, 54 App.D.C. 46, 293 F. 1013, 1014 (1923). In some instances, however, the courts will decline to apply *Kelly* to evidence involving a novel scientific technique. Where jurors are as capable as experts in understanding and evaluating the reliability of the technique used, there is no need to apply *Kelly*. Examples include expert testimony based on shoe print, fingerprint, and bullet comparisons. See People v. DePriest, 42 Cal.4th 1, 40, 163 P.3d 896, 924, 63 Cal.Rptr.3d 896, 930 (2007) and cases cited therein.

17. See, e.g., C. McCormick, Handbook of the Law of Evidence § 203 (E. Cleary 2d ed. 1972).

18. In People v. Leahy, 8 Cal.4th 587, 34 Cal.Rptr.2d 663, 882 P.2d 321 (1994), the California Supreme Court reaffirmed its adherence to the *Kelly* test. The court refused to follow the lead of the United States Supreme Court, which in Daubert v. Merrell Dow Pharmaceuticals, Inc., 509 U.S. 579, 113 S.Ct. 2786, 125 L.Ed.2d 469 (1993), held that the adoption of the Federal Rules of Evidence superseded the use of the *Frye* test in federal courts. For a discussion of the federal approach to the use of scientific evidence, see § 16.05 infra.

19. People v. Kelly, 17 Cal.3d 24, 31, 130 Cal.Rptr. 144, 149, 549 P.2d 1240, 1245 (1976).

20. Id.

21. Id.

new evidence is presented reflecting a change in the attitude of the scientific community.''[22]

The court's defense notwithstanding, the use of the *Kelly* test does pose some problems. As the critics maintain, at times it calls for the difficult task of distinguishing novel scientific evidence from other expert testimony. In People v. Stoll,[23] for example, the California Supreme Court was called upon to determine whether the reasonable reliance test or *Kelly* applied to a clinical psychologist's opinion that a defendant charged with committing lewd and lascivious acts upon children displayed no signs of deviance or abnormality. In holding that *Kelly* did not apply, the court discerned two "themes" that should guide judges and lawyers in determining which of the two tests applies.[24]

First, the court emphasized that *Kelly* is limited "to that class of expert testimony which is based, in whole or in part, on a technique, process, or theory which is *new* to science and, even more so, the law."[25] Until the courts are reasonably certain the pertinent scientific community no longer views such techniques as "experimental or of dubious validity", the courts should forego the use of the evidence.[26] Upon objection, then, the proponent must persuade the judge that the principle

---

22. Id. at 32, 130 Cal.Rptr. at 149, 549 P.2d at 1245. It is not altogether clear why an appellate opinion upholding the use of particular scientific principle or technique should be given an estoppel effect. Traditional principles of res judicata and collateral estoppel simply do not apply because the parties to the appellate case approving the use of the evidence at the trial level are not the parties in the subsequent suit in which the admissibility of the evidence is contested. The doctrine of stare decisis may likewise be unavailable. It provides that a point of law determined by an appellate court should be followed by the lower courts within the jurisdiction. Auto Equity Sales, Inc. v. Superior Court, 57 Cal.2d 450, 455, 20 Cal.Rptr. 321, 323, 369 P.2d 937, 939 (1962). Thus, the California Supreme Court's determination in *Kelly* that evidence based on novel scientific principles or techniques must pass the general acceptance test is binding on the lower courts. But an appellate determination that a particular principle or technique passes the test may be no more than an appellate assessment that the trial judge's ruling admitting the evidence over objection was not incorrect. In essence, the appellate court is merely rejecting the appealing party's claim that the trial judge's assessment of the evidence presented by the opposing parties, including the credibility of the witnesses, was in error.

Irrespective of whether conventional doctrine supports the court's statement in *Kelly*, lower courts must now resolve which aspects of a favorable *Kelly* appellate determination are entitled to an estoppel effect. The consensus appears to be that only the first determination—that a particular principle or technique has been generally accepted by the pertinent scientific community—is entitled to this effect. See People v. Morganti, 43 Cal.App.4th 643, 658, 50 Cal.Rptr.2d 837, 846 (1996) and cases cited therein. Whether correct procedures were used in the case at hand and whether the expert called to relate the findings is qualified to give them are not entitled to an estoppel effect. Id. at 660–663, 50 Cal.Rptr.2d at 848–849 and cases cited therein. *Morganti* has been cited with approval by the California Supreme Court. People v. Venegas, 18 Cal.4th 47, 78, 74 Cal.Rptr.2d 262, 282, 954 P.2d 525, 545 (1998).

23. 49 Cal.3d 1136, 265 Cal.Rptr. 111, 783 P.2d 698 (1989).

24. Id. at 1156, 265 Cal.Rptr. at 123, 783 P.2d at 710.

25. Id. (emphasis in the original). "In determining whether a scientific technique is 'new' for *Kelly* purposes, long-standing use by police officers seems less significant a factor than repeated use, study, testing, and confirmation by scientists or trained technicians. * * * To hold that a scientific technique could become immune from *Kelly* scrutiny merely by reason of long-standing and persistent use by law enforcement *outside* the laboratory or the courtroom, seems unjustified." People v. Leahy, 8 Cal.4th 587, 606, 34 Cal.Rptr.2d 663, 674, 882 P.2d 321, 332 (1994) (emphasis in the original).

26. People v. Stoll, 49 Cal.3d 1136, 1157, 265 Cal.Rptr. 111, 124, 783 P.2d 698, 711 (1989).

or technique either is not new to science or law or, if it is, that it satisfies the *Kelly* test.

Second, the court underscored that *Kelly* should be applied to expert evidence that carries a "misleading aura of scientific infallibility."[27] The court's concern is with "the unproven technique or procedure" which threatens to mislead jurors because they appear "both in name and description to provide some definitive truth which the expert need only accurately recognize and relay to the jury. The most obvious examples are machines or procedures which analyze physical data."[28] Other examples cited by the court include expert opinions based on polygraphs, truth serum, Nalline tests, human bite marks, microscopic identification of gunshot residue particles, electrophoretic testing of body fluid and blood stains, the hemostick method of presumptive testing for the presence of blood,[29] and penile plethysmographs.[30]

Kelly is not limited "to techniques analyzing 'physical evidence.' "[31] It can embrace also expert opinion based on social science research. Given the test's aim of barring the use of evidence based on techniques "which carry an undeserved aura of certainty",[32] the test applies as well to "less tangible new procedures",[33] such as " 'a new scientific process operating on purely psychological evidence.' "[34] As an example, the court cited hypnotically refreshed testimony. In People v. Shirley the court held that hypnotically refreshed testimony should be excluded because its use did not satisfy the *Kelly* test.[35]

Expert opinions beyond the reach of *Kelly*. *Kelly* does not apply to expert testimony that employs methods that "are not new" to science or the law and that "carry no misleading aura of scientific infallibility."[36] Sometimes, however, it is difficult to distinguish expert opinions subject to *Kelly* from opinions that are not. Before *Stoll*, for example, reasonable people could disagree on whether *Kelly* applied to an opinion that a person

---

27. Id. at 1157, 265 Cal.Rptr. at 124, 783 P.2d at 711.

28. Id.

29. Id.

30. Id. at 1160, note 21, 265 Cal.Rptr. at 126, note 21, 783 P.2d at 713, note 21.

31. Id. at 1156, 265 Cal.Rptr. at 123, 783 P.2d at 710.

32. Id.

33. Id.

34. Id. (quoting People v. Shirley, 31 Cal.3d 18, 181 Cal.Rptr. 243, 723 P.2d 1354 (1982)).

35. Id. Likewise, what a person says under the influence of sodium amytal (truth serum) is inadmissible under the *Kelly* test. See Ramona v. Superior Court (Ramona), 57 Cal.App.4th 107, 116, 66 Cal.Rptr.2d 766, 773 (1997) and cases cited therein. What a person says under the influence of sodium amytal may be no more reliable than what he says under the influence of large amounts of bourbon. Id. at 116, note 10, 66 Cal.Rptr.2d at 773, note 10. Moreover, a person may not testify about incidents "recalled" while under the influence of sodium amytal, unless that person can demonstrate that he or she had personal knowledge of such incidents before the administration of the drug. Id. at 121, 66 Cal.Rptr.2d at 777. In addition, a person may not testify about incidents recalled after the administration of sodium amytal if they are of the same nature as the incidents recalled while under the influence of the drug. Id. at 123, 66 Cal.Rptr.2d at 778.

36. People v. Stoll, 49 Cal.3d 1136, 1157, 265 Cal.Rptr. 111, 124, 783 P.2d 698, 711 (1989).

charged with committing lewd and lascivious acts did not exhibit signs of deviance or abnormality.

Occasionally, the courts have expressly held that the admissibility of certain expert opinions is governed by the reasonable reliance test derived from the Code and not by *Kelly*. In *Stoll*, the court provided examples of some of these opinions. Among them are expert testimony on why eyewitness identification may be mistaken, on why the personality of the accused is inconsistent with committing the offense charged, on why the accused did not harbor the mens rea of the offense charged,[37] and on why rape victims often do or say things that are inconsistent with their trial claims.[38] In these cases, the question is not whether the opinion is based on principles that have been generally accepted by the relevant scientific community, but whether the opinion is based on matters of the type that reasonably may be relied upon by experts in the field.

Other cases holding expert opinions only to the standards of the reasonable reliance test include People v. Bledsoe,[39] which approved the use of rape trauma syndrome to explain why rape victims sometimes act inconsistently with their claims of rape;[40] People v. Bowker,[41] which upheld the use of child sexual abuse accommodation syndrome to explain why child abuse victims refrain or delay in reporting abuse or recant their stories in whole or in part;[42] People v. McAlpin,[43] which upheld the use of expert testimony to explain why parents of sexually abused children refrain from reporting the abuse[44] and to disabuse jurors of the myth that child molesters fit a narrow profile;[45] People v. Stoll,[46] which upheld the use of a psychologist's testimony based in part on test results to show that a defendant charged with committing lewd and lascivious acts upon children displayed no signs of deviance or abnormality;[47] People v. McDonald,[48] which approved the use of expert testimony to demonstrate why eyewitness identification can be mistaken;[49] People v. Cegers,[50] which

---

37. Id. at 1157–1158, 265 Cal.Rptr. at 124, 783 P.2d at 711.

38. Id. at 1160–1161, 265 Cal.Rptr. at 126–127, 783 P.2d at 713.

39. 36 Cal.3d 236, 203 Cal.Rptr. 450, 681 P.2d 291 (1984).

40. Id. at 247, 203 Cal.Rptr. at 457, 681 P.2d at 298. For an extended discussion of *Bledsoe*, see § 15.09 supra.

41. 203 Cal.App.3d 385, 249 Cal.Rptr. 886 (1988).

42. Id. at 394–395, 249 Cal.Rptr. at 891. For a discussion of whether California judges should use the reasonable reliance or the *Kelly* test in determining the admissibility of expert opinion based on child sexual abuse accommodation syndrome, see Linda E. Carter, *Admissibility of Expert Testimony in Child Sexual Abuse Cases in California: Retire* Kelly–Frye *and Return to A Traditional Analysis,* 22 Loyola of Los Angeles Law Review 1103 (1989).

43. 53 Cal.3d 1289, 283 Cal.Rptr. 382, 812 P.2d 563 (1991).

44. Id. at 1302, 283 Cal.Rptr. at 389, 812 P.2d at 570.

45. Id.

46. 49 Cal.3d 1136, 265 Cal.Rptr. 111, 783 P.2d 698 (1989).

47. Id. at 1161, 265 Cal.Rptr. at 127, 783 P.2d at 714.

48. 37 Cal.3d 351, 208 Cal.Rptr. 236, 690 P.2d 709 (1984), appeal after remand, 203 Cal.App.3d 925, 237 Cal.Rptr. 597 (1987).

49. Id. at 368–369, 208 Cal.Rptr. at 247–248, 690 P.2d at 720–721.

50. 7 Cal.App.4th 988, 9 Cal.Rptr.2d 297 (1992).

approved the use of "confusional arousal syndrome" to show why people who suffer from sleep apnea can engage in violent behavior while mentally asleep;[51] People v. Pride,[52] which upheld the use of hair comparison analysis to identify a class of possible donors of the hair;[53] People v. Clark,[54] which upheld the use of opinions based on "blood spatter" evidence;[55] People v. Webb,[56] which approved the use of fingerprint analysis based on laser procedures;[57] People v. Peneda,[58] which upheld an opinion that testing of samples taken from stashes of cocaine showed that each stash contained over 100 pounds of cocaine;[59] People v. Bury,[60] which upheld the use of the results of a preliminary alcohol screening test (PAS) performed on an Alco–Sensor device as proof of the accused's intoxication;[61] People v. Hood,[62] which upheld the use of a computer animation of a crime scene;[63] Texaco Producing, Inc. v. County of Kern,[64] which upheld a valuation opinion based on appraisal methods used in the oil and gas industry;[65] Wilson v. Phillips,[66] which upheld a psychologist's opinion that the plaintiffs suffered from dissociative amnesia, a condition which causes especially children to repress memories of sexual abuse until their recall is triggered by some unanticipated event;[67] People v. Bui,[68] which upheld a forensic toxicologist's opinion that the use of methamphetamine in greater than therapeutic dosages results in impaired driving;[69] People v. Ayala,[70] which upheld a radiologist's opinion that a bullet depicted on an X-ray was the same size as a bullet taped on the victim's neck;[71] People v. Hill,[72] which upheld the use of the Profiler Plus DNA test kit without first requiring proof that its reliability had been generally accepted by the

---

51.　Id. at 999–1000, 9 Cal.Rptr.2d at 304–305.

52.　3 Cal.4th 195, 10 Cal.Rptr.2d 636, 833 P.2d 643 (1992), cert. denied, 507 U.S. 935, 113 S.Ct. 1323, 122 L.Ed.2d 709 (1993).

53.　Id. at 239, 10 Cal.Rptr.2d at 661, 833 P.2d at 669.

54.　5 Cal.4th 950, 22 Cal.Rptr.2d 689, 857 P.2d 1099 (1993).

55.　Id. at 1017, 22 Cal.Rptr.2d at 732, 857 P.2d at 1142–1143.

56.　6 Cal.4th 494, 24 Cal.Rptr.2d 779, 862 P.2d 779 (1993).

57.　Id. at 523, 24 Cal.Rptr.2d at 798, 862 P.2d at 797.

58.　32 Cal.App.4th 1022, 38 Cal.Rptr.2d 312 (1995).

59.　Id. at 1024, 38 Cal.Rptr.2d at 316.

60.　41 Cal.App.4th 1194, 49 Cal.Rptr.2d 107 (1996).

61.　Id. at 1200–1202, 49 Cal.Rptr.2d at 110–111.

62.　53 Cal.App.4th 965, 62 Cal.Rptr.2d 137 (1997), cert. denied, 522 U.S. 1093, 118 S.Ct. 886, 139 L.Ed.2d 873 (1998).

63.　Id. at 969–970, 62 Cal.Rptr.2d at 140.

64.　66 Cal.App.4th 1029, 78 Cal.Rptr.2d 433 (1998).

65.　Id. at 1048–49, 78 Cal.Rptr.2d at 445.

66.　73 Cal.App.4th 250, 86 Cal.Rptr.2d 204 (1999).

67.　Id. at 252–253, 86 Cal.Rptr.2d at 206.

68.　86 Cal.App.4th 1187, 103 Cal.Rptr.2d 908 (2001).

69.　Id. at 1195, 103 Cal.Rptr.2d at 914.

70.　24 Cal.4th 243, 99 Cal.Rptr.2d 532, 6 P.3d 193 (2000), cert. denied, 532 U.S. 1029, 121 S.Ct. 1978, 149 L.Ed.2d 770 (2001).

71.　Id. at 281, 99 Cal.Rptr.2d at 557, 6 P.2d at 215–216.

72.　89 Cal.App.4th 48, 107 Cal.Rptr.2d 110 (2001).

pertinent scientific community;[73] People v. Farnam,[74] which upheld the use of expert testimony based on the CAL–ID system for matching fingerprints;[75] and People v. Nolan,[76] which upheld the use the ADX Abbott machine to determine the presence of drugs in urine without requiring proof that its reliability had been generally accepted by the relevant scientific community.[77]

The reasonable reliance test and not the general acceptance test has also been used by courts to justify the use of medical opinions, especially with respect to the cause of an injury.[78] Examples include opinions that the cause of death resulted from strangulation,[79] that rectal abrasions indicated anal intercourse without the use of lubricants,[80] that death was caused by a blunt instrument,[81] that a child's injuries were not caused accidentally,[82] that genital injuries were consistent with sexual abuse,[83] that the absence of genital trauma is not necessarily inconsistent with forcible sexual intercourse,[84] and that the pesticide Dursban caused the plaintiff's autism.[85] The same test has been used to justify using medical opinions about mental illnesses, including some as "esoteric" as "Munchausen's syndrome,"[86] and defining a defendant as a sexually violent predator subject to confinement under the Sexually Violent Predators Act.[87]

In California, expert testimony on "hedonic" damages, although based on relatively new theories, does not raise *Kelly* issues. The testimony is excluded on another ground: jurors do not need expert help in determining this loss. "No amount of expert testimony on the value of life could possibly help a jury decide that difficult question. A life is not a

---

73. Id. at 58, 107 Cal.Rptr.2d at 118.

74. 28 Cal.4th 107, 121 Cal.Rptr.2d 106, 47 P.3d 988 (2002), cert. denied, 537 U.S. 1124, 123 S.Ct. 861, 154 L.Ed.2d 806 (2003).

75. Id. at 159–160, 121 Cal.Rptr.2d at 152, 47 P.3d at 1026–1027.

76. 95 Cal.App.4th 1210, 116 Cal.Rptr.2d 331 (2002).

77. Id. at 1213–1214, 116 Cal.Rptr.2d at 334–335.

78. For medical opinions to be admissible, it is not necessary for the opinion to be based on certainty. Recognizing the realities attending medicine, a medical diagnosis may be based on probabilities. Absolute scientific certainty is not required. See People v. Mendibles, 199 Cal. App.3d 1277, 1293, 245 Cal.Rptr. 553, 562 (1988).

79. People v. Memro, 38 Cal.3d 658, 692, 214 Cal.Rptr. 832, 855, 700 P.2d 446, 469 (1985).

80. People v. Stanley, 36 Cal.3d 253, 256, 203 Cal.Rptr. 461, 463, 681 P.2d 302, 304 (1984).

81. People v. Wiley, 18 Cal.3d 162, 166, 133 Cal.Rptr. 135, 137, 554 P.2d 881, 883 (1976).

82. People v. Jackson, 18 Cal.App.3d 504, 507, 95 Cal.Rptr. 919, 921 (1971).

83. People v. Mendibles, 199 Cal.App.3d 1277, 1295, 245 Cal.Rptr. 553, 563 (1988).

84. People v. Rowland, 4 Cal.4th 238, 266, 14 Cal.Rptr.2d 377, 395, 841 P.2d 897, 915 (1992), cert. denied, 510 U.S. 846, 114 S.Ct. 138, 126 L.Ed.2d 101 (1993).

85. Roberti v. Andy's Termite & Pest Control, Inc., 113 Cal.App.4th 893, 901, 6 Cal.Rptr.3d 827, 832 (2003).

86. People v. Phillips, 122 Cal.App.3d 69, 87, 175 Cal.Rptr. 703, 714 (1981). Individuals suffering from this syndrome injure themselves to draw attention to themselves.

87. People v. Ward, 71 Cal.App.4th 368, 373–373, 83 Cal.Rptr.2d 828, 831 (1999). Confinement under the act requires expert proof that the defendant is likely to engage in sexually violent criminal behavior unless confined. West's Ann. California Welfare and Institutions Code § 6600(a).

stock, car, home, or other such item bought and sold in some market-place."[88]

California plaintiffs in personal injury actions are entitled to recover for the loss of enjoyment of life as part of the damages for pain and suffering.[89] But to prevent jurors from awarding double damages for the same injury, California jurors may not be given separate instructions on pain and suffering, and on the loss of enjoyment of life.[90] Plaintiffs, however, are free to inform the jurors about how an injury has impaired their enjoyment of life. But, as noted, they may not offer expert testimony on "hedonic" damages to establish this loss.

Expert opinions excluded by *Kelly*. In addition to the examples cited by the court in *Stoll*, a number of expert opinions have been excluded on the ground that the scientific principle or technique involved failed to pass the *Kelly* test. Opinions excluded on this basis include opinions that a child could not have died from falling down stairs based on tests conducted with a dummy,[91] that a child had been molested based on observations of how the child played with anatomically correct dolls,[92] that the complaining witness had been raped because she exhibited symptoms of rape trauma syndrome,[93] and that a child had been molested because the child exhibited symptoms of child sexual abuse accommodation syndrome.[94] In addition, a police officer's opinion about a suspect's intoxication based on a nystagmus test may not be received in the absence of evidence showing that the pertinent scientific community has generally accepted the test as a reliable indicator of intoxication.[95] Nor may an expert testify about the presence of benzene based on the results of a "syncrometer" in the absence of evidence that the pertinent scientific community has generally accepted syncrometers as reliable detectors of benzene.[96] Neither may an expert testify that a dog matched a scent on an object with a scent captured on a "scent transfer unit" in the absence of evidence that experts in the field have generally accepted such units as

---

88. Loth v. Truck–A–Way Corp., 60 Cal.App.4th 757, 767, 70 Cal.Rptr.2d 571, 578 (1998). Others courts, including Illinois, Louisiana, Nebraska, and the Seventh Circuit, also disapprove of the use of expert testimony on hedonic damages. See id.

89. Id. at 763, 70 Cal.Rptr.2d at 575 (1998).

90. Id. at 766, 70 Cal.Rptr.2d at 577.

91. People v. Dellinger, 163 Cal.App.3d 284, 293–295, 209 Cal.Rptr. 503, 508–510 (1984), appeal after remand, 214 Cal.App.3d 1198, 247 Cal.Rptr. 527 (1988).

92. In re Amber B., 191 Cal.App.3d 682, 691, 236 Cal.Rptr. 623, 629 (1987); In re Christine C., 191 Cal.App.3d 676, 680, 236 Cal.Rptr. 630, 632 (1987).

93. People v. Bledsoe, 36 Cal.3d 236, 251, 203 Cal.Rptr. 450, 460, 681 P.2d 291, 301 (1984). The evidence, however, may be admissible to support the credibility of the complaining witness. See § 15.09 supra.

94. People v. Jeff, 204 Cal.App.3d 309, 333, 251 Cal.Rptr. 135, 149 (1988); In re Sara M., 194 Cal.App.3d 585, 593, 239 Cal.Rptr. 605, 610 (1987). The evidence, however, may be admissible to support the credibility of the victim. See § 15.09 supra.

95. People v. Leahy, 8 Cal.4th 587, 610, 34 Cal.Rptr.2d 663, 677, 882 P.2d 321, 325 (1994). See also People v. Joehnk, 35 Cal.App.4th 1488, 1505, 42 Cal.Rptr.2d 6, 15 (1995) which holds that the relevant scientific community has accepted HGN evidence "as useful, when viewed with other relevant indications, in deciding whether a subject is under the influence of alcohol."

96. Melaleuca, Inc. v. Clark, 66 Cal.App.4th 1344, 1357–58, 78 Cal.Rptr.2d 627, 635 (1998).

reliable,[97] or offer an opinion on the presence of toxigenic mold in the absence of evidence that experts in the field have generally accepted as valid the results from the "Immunosciences Mycotoxin Antibody Test" and the "IBT Blood Serology Test."[98]

Kelly can also preclude an ordinary witness from testifying when the testimony stems from the use of techniques that fail to satisfy *Kelly*'s reliability standards. In Ramona v. Superior Court[99] the plaintiff sued her father for sexual abuse. The father moved for summary judgment on the ground that *Kelly* precluded the introduction of evidence of repressed memories recalled by the plaintiff while under the influence of sodium amytal. The reviewing court agreed and ordered the trial court to grant the father's motion: the plaintiff had failed to produce any evidence indicating a shift from the scientific consensus that sodium amytal is an unreliable truth serum.[100]

Expert opinions satisfying *Kelly*. Expert opinions held to satisfy the *Kelly* test include opinions based on footprint analysis,[101] dentition analysis,[102] as well as on electrophoretic analyses of semen,[103] blood stains,[104] and saliva,[105] nystagmus tests to determine intoxication,[106] the agglutination inhibition process used to detect the presence of specific genetic markers in the bloodstream,[107] segmentation to enhance the clarity of photographic images,[108] and gamma marker blood analysis.[109] In addition, the Legislature has declared that expert testimony regarding battered women's syndrome may be offered by the prosecution or the defense without the need to show compliance with *Kelly*.[110] In determin-

---

97. People v. Willis, 115 Cal.App.4th 379, 385–386, 9 Cal.Rptr.3d 235, 240–241 (2004). For other admissibility requirements of scent evidence, see § 5.06 note 3, supra.

98. Geffcken v. D'Andrea, 137 Cal.App.4th 1298, 1309, 41 Cal.Rptr.3d 80, 88 (2006).

99. 57 Cal.App.4th 107, 66 Cal.Rptr.2d 766 (1997).

100. Id. at 121–122, 66 Cal.Rptr.2d at 777. The reviewing court also found that the prevailing scientific consensus likewise rejected the reliability of repressed memories recalled *after* a sodium amytal interview. Id. at 123, 66 Cal.Rptr.2d at 778.

101. People v. Knights, 166 Cal.App.3d 46, 52–53, 212 Cal.Rptr. 307, 311–312 (1985).

102. People v. Slone, 76 Cal.App.3d 611, 625, 143 Cal.Rptr. 61, 69 (1978).

103. People v. Ashmus, 54 Cal.3d 932, 971–972, 2 Cal.Rptr.2d 112, 133, 820 P.2d 214, 234–235 (1991), cert. denied, 506 U.S. 841, 113 S.Ct. 124, 121 L.Ed.2d 79 (1992), reh'g denied, 506 U.S. 1015, 113 S.Ct. 641, 121 L.Ed.2d 571 (1992). The court distinguished People v. Brown, 40 Cal.3d 512, 230 Cal.Rptr. 834, 726 P.2d 516 (1985), rev'd on other grounds sub nom. California v. Brown, 479 U.S. 538, 107 S.Ct. 837, 93 L.Ed.2d 934 (1987), which held that in that case the proponent had failed to satisfy the *Kelly* test with regard to similar evidence.

104. People v. Morris, 53 Cal.3d 152, 206–208, 279 Cal.Rptr. 720, 751–752, 807 P.2d 949, 980–981 (1991), cert. denied, 502 U.S. 959, 112 S.Ct. 421, 116 L.Ed.2d 441 (1991).

105. People v. Cooper, 53 Cal.3d 771, 813, 281 Cal.Rptr. 90, 113, 809 P.2d 865, 888 (1991), cert. denied, 502 U.S. 1016, 112 S.Ct. 664, 116 L.Ed.2d 755 (1991).

106. People v. Joehnk, 35 Cal.App.4th 1488, 1505, 42 Cal.Rptr.2d 6, 15 (1995).

107. People v. Morganti, 43 Cal.App.4th 643, 658, 50 Cal.Rptr.2d 837, 847 (1996).

108. People v. Williams, 46 Cal.App.4th 1767, 1778–1779, 54 Cal.Rptr.2d 521, 527 (1996).

109. People v. Riel, 22 Cal.4th 1153, 1191–1192, 96 Cal.Rptr.2d 1, 31, 998 P.2d 969, 996–997 (2000), cert. denied, 531 U.S. 1087, 121 S.Ct. 803, 148 L.Ed.2d 690 (2001).

110. West's Ann. California Evidence Code § 1107. The evidence, however, may not be offered "against a criminal defendant to prove the occurrence of the act or acts of abuse which form the basis of the criminal charge." Id.

ing admissibility, judges may *not* consider the evidence as "a new scientific technique whose reliability is unproven."[111]

For a number of years, the California courts were divided on whether DNA analysis or fingerprinting satisfies the *Kelly* test. People v. Axell[112] upheld the use of DNA analysis.[113] People v. Barney,[114] citing scientific evidence that came to light after *Axell*, found no general acceptance of the statistical methods used to determine the significance of a DNA match.[115] Accordingly, *Barney* held that it was error to admit the DNA evidence.[116]

At issue in *Barney* was the general acceptance of a particular statistical method used to calculate the probability that a person selected randomly from the general population would match the accused's DNA. Known as the unmodified product rule, *Barney* held that the method was not generally accepted by the pertinent scientific community.[117] *Barney*, however, did not rule out the possibility that another method, known as the modified ceiling approach, might satisfy the general acceptance test.[118] Noting that the latter method has gained general acceptance in the scientific community nationwide, in People v. Venegas[119] the California

---

111. Id.

112. 235 Cal.App.3d 836, 1 Cal.Rptr.2d 411 (1991).

113. Id. at 862, 1 Cal.Rptr.2d at 427. "When a sample of DNA—usually in the form of hair, blood, saliva, or semen—is left at the crime scene by a perpetrator, a forensic genetic analysis is conducted. First, DNA analysts create a genetic 'profile' or 'type' of the perpetrator's DNA by determining which variants or alleles exist at several variable loci. Second, the defendant's DNA is analyzed in exactly the same manner to create a profile for comparison with the perpetrator's profile. If the defendant's DNA produces a different profile than the perpetrator's, even by only one allele, the defendant could not have been the source of the crime scene DNA, and he or she is absolutely exonerated. If, on the other hand, the defendant's DNA produces exactly the same genetic profile, the defendant could have been the source of the perpetrator's DNA—but so could any other person with the same genetic profile. Third, when the perpetrator's and defendant's profiles are found to match, the statistical significance of the match must be explained in terms of the rarity or commonness of that profile within a particular population[,] that is, the number of people within a population expected to possess that particular genetic profile, or, put another way, the probability that a randomly chosen person in that population possesses that particular genetic profile. Only then can the jury weigh the value of the profile match." People v. Brown, 91 Cal.App.4th 623, 628–629, 110 Cal.Rptr.2d 750, 754–755 (2001) (footnotes omitted).

For a more detailed but equally lucid explanation of the probative value of DNA evidence, see People v. Pizarro, 110 Cal.App.4th 530, 3 Cal.Rptr.3d 21 (2003).

For a discussion of the appropriate population database that should be used for estimating the statistical match, as well of the relevance of the perpetrator's genotype, see id. at 623–634, 3 Cal.Rptr.3d at 97–105. In determining compliance with *Kelly*, the court can consider whether it is the generally accepted practice by the pertinent scientific community to take into account laboratory error rates in arriving at the statistical match. People v. Reeves, 91 Cal.App.4th 14, 43–44, 109 Cal.Rptr.2d 728, 751 (2001). But even if taking such errors into account is not the generally accepted practice, the opponent may still offer evidence showing how such errors might have affected the statistical match in his or her case in order to assist the fact finder in assessing the weight to be given to the match. Id.

114. 8 Cal.App.4th 798, 10 Cal.Rptr.2d 731 (1992).

115. Id. at 821, 10 Cal.Rptr.2d at 744.

116. Id. at 822, 10 Cal.Rptr.2d at 747. The court also held that it was error to admit the evidence without requiring the proponent to prove that correct procedures were used in performing the DNA analysis. Id.

117. Id. at 814–15, 10 Cal.Rptr.2d at 740.

118. Id. at 821–822, 10 Cal.Rptr.2d at 745.

119. 18 Cal.4th 47, 74 Cal.Rptr.2d 262, 954 P.2d 525 (1998).

Supreme Court held that the modified method met the *Kelly* test.[120]

Barney illustrates another point. The fact that an opinion has been found to satisfy *Kelly* does not preclude the opponent from challenging that finding with evidence that the relevant scientific community no longer accepts the principle or technique involved. Science, after all, is dynamic; what makes for sound science on one occasion may not on another.

Similarly, the fact that an opinion has been excluded for failing to satisfy *Kelly* does not preclude the proponent from attempting to satisfy the test in another case. Seven years after *Barney*, the California Supreme Court reviewed the scientific literature on the unmodified product rule that had been published since *Barney* and concluded that the published literature, as well as the clear weight of judicial authority, showed that the rule had gained general acceptance in the relevant scientific community.[121] People v. Ashmus[122] also illustrates this point. In that case, the California Supreme Court upheld the use of electrophoretic analysis to link the accused with the crime even though in People v. Brown,[123] the court had approved the exclusion of evidence based on the same test. In *Ashmus*, unlike *Brown*, the court found that the proponent had produced the evidence necessary to support the trial court's determination that electrophoretic testing had been generally accepted as reliable by the pertinent scientific community.[124]

The *Kelly* Rule and Proposition 8. Subject to enumerated exceptions, the Right to Truth–in–Evidence provision of Proposition 8 gives parties to criminal proceedings the state constitutional right not to have

---

120. Id. at 88–89, 74 Cal.Rptr.2d at 289. In addition, DNA analysis based on a polymerase chain reaction (PCR) has also been upheld as complying with *Kelly.* People v. Morganti, 43 Cal.App.4th 643, 671, 50 Cal.Rptr.2d 837, 855 (1996). The PCR method is used whenever the DNA sample is too small or degraded for use in the more common RFLP DNA analysis. Id. at 662, 50 Cal.Rptr.2d at 849. DNA analysis based on a PCR method involving short tandem repeats or STRs has also been upheld as complying with *Kelly.* People v. Allen, 72 Cal.App.4th 1093, 1098–1100, 85 Cal.Rptr.2d 655, 658–660 (1999). In reaching this conclusion, the reviewing court relied in part on out of state appellate opinions approving the use of method. Id.

In general, "California courts have recognized that two methodologies are widely used in forensic DNA testing: restriction fragment length polymorphism (RFLP) and PCR [polymerase chain reaction]. * * * There are three subtypes of PCR testing: DQ–Alpha, which tests a single genetic marker; Polymarker, which tests five genetic markers; and the STR [Short Tandem Repeat Test], which tests three or more genetic markers. * * * The RFLP and PCR methodologies, including the PCR subtypes, have acquired general acceptance in the scientific community." People v. Hill, 89 Cal.App.4th 48, 57, 107 Cal.Rptr.2d 110, 117 (2001).

121. People v. Soto, 21 Cal.4th 512, 541, 88 Cal.Rptr.2d 34, 55, 981 P.2d 958, 977 (1999).

122. 54 Cal.3d 932, 2 Cal.Rptr.2d 112, 820 P.2d 214 (1991), cert. denied, 506 U.S. 841, 113 S.Ct. 124, 121 L.Ed.2d 79 (1992), reh'g denied, 506 U.S. 1015, 113 S.Ct. 641, 121 L.Ed.2d 571 (1992).

123. 40 Cal.3d 512, 230 Cal.Rptr. 834, 726 P.2d 516 (1985), rev'd on other grounds sub nom. California v. Brown, 479 U.S. 538, 107 S.Ct. 837, 93 L.Ed.2d 934 (1987).

124. People v. Ashmus, 54 Cal.3d 932, 971, 2 Cal.Rptr.2d 112, 133, 820 P.2d 214, 235 (1991), cert. denied, 506 U.S. 841, 113 S.Ct. 124, 121 L.Ed.2d 79 (1992), reh'g denied, 506 U.S. 1015, 113 S.Ct. 641, 121 L.Ed.2d 571 (1992). See also People v. Venegas, 18 Cal.4th 47, 94, 74 Cal.Rptr.2d 262, 293, 954 P.2d 525, 556 (1998), where the California Supreme Court expressly left open the question of whether the use of the unmodified product rule to calculate DNA matches can satisfy the *Kelly* test.

relevant evidence excluded.[125] Since the California Supreme Court has acknowledged that the *Kelly* rule excludes unquestionably relevant evidence that fails to meet the general acceptance test,[126] a literal application of Proposition 8 would overturn the rule. Indeed, such an interpretation would also repeal the Evidence Code limitations on the use of expert opinion in criminal cases since the limitations are not among the enumerated exceptions.

In People v. Harris[127] the California Supreme Court rejected the claim that Proposition 8 mandated the use of polygraph evidence that failed the *Kelly* test. Mistakenly assuming that unreliable evidence is irrelevant, the court held that judges may still use § 352 to exclude scientific evidence that fails the *Kelly* test.[128] Section 352 is expressly exempted from the operation of the Right to Truth–in–Evidence provision. In the court's view, this section incorporates § 350 which mandates the exclusion of irrelevant evidence.[129]

Though reliability and relevance are different concepts, the court still could utilize § 352 to exclude some forms of scientific evidence. Section 352 was enacted in part to give judges the power to exclude evidence that is unduly prejudicial.[130] Surely evidence that carries an undeserved and misleading aura of scientific infallibility falls within that classification. The court, however, has not adopted this construction. Instead, in People v. Leahy[131] the court reaffirmed *Harris*, holding that Proposition 8 left undisturbed the court's power under § 352 to exclude unreliable scientific evidence on the grounds of irrelevance.[132]

QUESTIONS AND PROBLEMS

1.   Describe the two tests used in California to determine the admissibility of expert opinions.

2.   What guidelines has the California Supreme Court provided to trial judges to help them determine whether *Kelly* should apply?

3.   In California, the prosecution is entitled to offer evidence from a duly qualified expert explaining why women suffering from rape trauma syndrome sometimes delay in reporting a rape and why children suffering from child sexual abuse accommodation syndrome sometimes refrain from reporting the abuse or recant their stories. According to the California appellate courts, whether the expert may testify should be resolved by the trial judge under the reasonable reliance standard of the Code. True or false?

---

125.   For an extended discussion of Proposition 8, see §§ 2.11 and 15.03 supra.

126.   People v. Kelly, 17 Cal.3d 24, 30, 130 Cal.Rptr. 144, 148, 549 P.2d 1240, 1244 (1976).

127.   47 Cal.3d 1047, 255 Cal.Rptr. 352, 767 P.2d 619 (1989).

128.   Id. at 1094, 255 Cal.Rptr. at 382, 767 P.2d at 649.

129.   Id.

130.   West's Ann. California Evidence Code § 353 and comment.

131.   8 Cal.4th 587, 34 Cal.Rptr.2d 663, 882 P.2d 321 (1994).

132.   Id. at 598, 34 Cal.Rptr.2d at 669, 882 P.2d at 327.

4. The California appellate courts preclude a duly qualified expert from telling the jurors that victims suffering from these syndromes have in fact been raped or abused. The ground given is that the proponent of the opinion has failed to persuade the trial judge that experts in these syndromes have generally accepted the existence of the syndrome as proof that the rape or abuse took place. True or false?

5. California person injury plaintiffs are entitled to recover for the loss of the enjoyment of life as part of the damages for pain and suffering. To prove damages for the loss of enjoyment of life, plaintiffs are entitled to call an expert on "hedonic" damages. True or false?

6. At a California trial, the judge overrules the defendant's objections and allows the prosecution to offer DNA evidence linking the defendant with material found at the crime scene. The judge also overrules the defendant's objection that the expert called by the prosecution was not qualified to testify. On appeal, the California Court of Appeal affirms the defendant's conviction of the crime charged, holding that the trial judge properly overruled the defense objections to the expert qualifications and the use of DNA evidence. In subsequent California prosecutions, may the prosecutor cite the appellate opinion in asking the trial judge to overrule the defense objection that DNA evidence is not admissible?

In subsequent California prosecutions, may the prosecutor cite the appellate opinion in overruling the defense objection that the expert called by the prosecution is unqualified to testify about DNA and its implications?

7. Does the fact that an appellate court has decided that a given technique satisfies *Kelly* preclude a trial judge from finding otherwise if that finding is justified by the evidence presented to the judge?

8. Why does a literal application of Proposition 8 overturn the *Kelly* rule?

§ 16.05   THE FEDERAL APPROACH

As originally enacted, Federal Rule of Evidence 703 provided that facts or data used by an expert in reaching an opinion did not have to be admissible if "of a type reasonably relied upon by experts in the particular field in forming opinions or inferences."[1] Although the rule focused on dispensing with the admissibility of the underlying data, the Advisory Committee's note suggests that the quoted language might have had another purpose as well—to assure the reliability of the opinion. In its note, the Advisory Committee cites the California Law Revision Commission's comment to Evidence Code § 801.[2] Section 801 limits expert opinions to those based on matter "that is of a type that reasonably may be relied upon by an expert in forming an opinion upon the subject to which his testimony relates * * *."[3] In its comment the Law Revision Commis-

---

1. Federal Rule of Evidence 703 (West 1975).

2. Federal Rule of Evidence 801 (advisory committee note).

3. West's Ann. California Evidence Code § 801(b).

sion stresses that "[i]n large measure, this [limitation] assures the reliability and trustworthiness of the information used by experts in forming their opinions."[4] If this was the construction the Advisory Committee intended to give to Rule 703, then the rule provided federal judges with a basis for excluding unreliable expert testimony, including opinions based on novel scientific principles or techniques not generally accepted by the pertinent scientific community.

Whatever the intention of the Advisory Committee, in its 1993 *Daubert v. Merrell Dow Pharmaceuticals, Inc.*[5] decision, the U.S. Supreme Court defined the role of federal judges in screening expert testimony. The issue in *Daubert* was whether the trial judge had properly excluded an expert opinion that failed to meet *Frye*'s general acceptance test.[6] The proponents claimed that the adoption of the Federal Rules of Evidence had displaced *Frye*. The Court agreed. Noting sharp divisions among the circuits on the proper standards for admitting expert testimony, the Court held that under the Federal Rules of Evidence federal trial judges must ensure "that any and all scientific testimony or evidence is not only relevant, but reliable."[7]

The Court laid down four guidelines to help federal judges assess the evidence's scientific validity. One is whether the evidence is based on theories or techniques that can be or have been tested.[8] In the Court's view, the testing of hypotheses is what distinguishes science from other fields.[9] Another guideline is whether the theory or technique has been subjected to peer review and publication.[10] Though publication is not a sine qua non of admissibility (some propositions may be too new or of limited interest to be published), publication "in a peer-reviewed journal" is a relevant consideration "in assessing the scientific validity of a particular technique or methodology on which an opinion is premised."[11] A judge should also consider the known or potential rate of error as well as the existence and maintenance of standards controlling a technique's operation.[12] Finally, a judge should consider whether the techniques or theories employed have been generally accepted or rejected by the pertinent scientific community.[13] Though a finding that the proffered evidence is scientifically valid does not require that the techniques or theories sup-

---

4. Id. (comment).

5. 509 U.S. 579, 113 S.Ct. 2786, 125 L.Ed.2d 469 (1993).

6. Id. at 585.

7. Id. at 589. At the time, Rule 702 provided that "[i]f scientific, technical, or other specialized knowledge will assist the trier of fact to understand the evidence or to determine a fact in issue, a witness qualified as an expert by knowledge, skill, experience, training, or education, may testify thereto in the form of an opinion or otherwise." Federal Rule of Evidence 702 (West 1975).

8. Daubert v. Merrell Dow Pharmaceuticals, Inc., 509 U.S. 579, 593, 113 S.Ct. 2786, 125 L.Ed.2d 469 (1993).

9. Id.

10. Id. at 593–594.

11. Id.

12. Id.

13. Id.

porting it be generally accepted, widespread acceptance or rejection "can be an important factor" in ruling the evidence admissible.[14]

The Court did not intend the *Daubert* guidelines to be exclusive. Lower federal courts are free to consider other factors in determining the reliability of expert testimony. Examples include whether the expert is proposing to testify on the basis of research conducted independently of the litigation, whether the expert has adequately accounted for obvious alternative explanations, whether the expert has unjustifiably extrapolated from an accepted premise to an unfounded conclusion, and whether the field of expertise claimed by the expert is known to reach reliable results.[15] The last factor is important because it is designed to foreclose testimony by "experts" who uncritically find that a principle or technique is generally accepted because the experts in the field depend for their living on the viability of the contested principle or technique.

To help ensure that unreliable scientific evidence is withheld from the jurors, Federal Rule of Evidence 702 was amended after *Daubert* to exclude expert opinion based on scientific, technical or other specialized knowledge unless the judge finds that "(b) the testimony is based on sufficient facts or data; (c) the testimony is the product of reliable principles and methods; and (d) the expert has reliably applied the principles and methods to the facts of the case."[16] In the opinion of the Advisory Committee, the "standards set forth in the amendment are broad enough to require consideration of any or all of the specific *Daubert* factors where appropriate."[17] In its note, the Advisory Committee makes clear that, as in California, the proponent must establish the admissibility requirements of expert testimony and other scientific evidence by a preponderance of the evidence.[18]

Has *Daubert* promoted or discouraged the use of expert testimony in federal trials? Thus far, *Daubert* appears to have restrained the use of expert testimony in federal civil cases.

> A Rand Institute report released early in 2002 concludes that for several years after *Daubert*, challenges to expert evidence in federal civil actions prevailed more often than before. Focusing on cases from the Third Circuit, the authors found that among those cases in which expert evidence was challenged, "the exclusion rate ... for evidence based on physical science in a product liability case jumped from 53 percent during the two years before *Daubert* to 70 percent between mid–1995 and mid–1996"—though the rate subsided after that. LLOYD DIXON & BRIAN GILL, CHANGES IN THE STANDARDS FOR ADMITTING EXPERT EVIDENCE IN FEDERAL CIVIL CASES SINCE THE *DAUBERT* DECISION XVI (2001).

---

14.   Id. The Court underscored that in assessing the reliability of scientific evidence the judge should also apply other rules, such as Rule 703. Id.

15.   See generally, Federal Rule 702 (Advisory Committee Note).

16.   Federal Rule of Evidence 702.

17.   Id. (Advisory Committee Note).

18.   Id.

A tangible result of this increasing scrutiny of expert evidence appears to have been an increase in both summary judgment motions and their success rate. "[S]ummary judgments were granted in 21 percent of challenges during the four years preceding *Daubert*, compared to 48 percent between July 1995 and June 1997." *Id.* at xvi, 56. Noting that the success rate of *Daubert* challenges declined after 1997, the authors speculate that litigants "either did not propose . . . [expert] evidence not meeting the new standards, or better tailored the evidence they did propose to fit the new standards." *Id.* at xvii.

The Rand study's most surprising discovery is how little *Daubert* seems to have changed the significance of *Frye*'s old "general acceptance" test. Before *Daubert* a judge's finding that an expert's methods were generally accepted always or almost always assured a judgment that the evidence was reliable. After *Daubert* a favorable finding on general acceptance secured such a judgment ninety percent of the time. Conversely, an *unfavorable* finding on general acceptance resulted in a finding of unreliability in an overwhelming majority of cases before *Daubert*—and if anything made exclusion of the evidence even more certain afterward. *See id.* at 44.[19]

Is *Daubert* limited to "scientific" testimony? In Kumho Tire Co. Ltd. v. Carmichael[20] the United States Supreme Court answered this question in the negative. The Court held that the federal judiciary's obligation to ensure that all scientific testimony is not only relevant but reliable extends to all "expert" testimony. Emphasizing the inclusion in Federal Rule of Evidence 702 of such categories as "technical" and "other specialized knowledge" in addition to "scientific knowledge," the Court held that *Daubert* applied to the testimony of a tire failure expert called by the plaintiffs to establish that their injuries were caused by a defective tire manufactured by the defendant.[21]

In discharging their gatekeeping function to ensure the relevance and reliability of expert testimony, federal trial judges are accorded some protection. In reviewing the propriety of a trial judge's ruling admitting or excluding scientific evidence, federal appellate courts must apply the abuse of discretion standard.[22]

QUESTIONS AND PROBLEMS

1.   In *Daubert* the United States Supreme Court held that under the Federal Rules of Evidence federal judges no longer could consider the general acceptance test. True or false?

---

19.   Fisher, Evidence, Chapter 9 (Foundation Press 2002) (emphasis in the original). Cf. Advisory Committee Note, Federal Rule of Evidence 702 ("A review of the caselaw after *Daubert* shows that the rejection of expert testimony is the exception rather than the rule.").

20.   526 U.S. 137, 119 S.Ct. 1167, 143 L.Ed.2d 238 (1999).

21.   Id. at 141, 119 S.Ct. at 1171143 L.Ed. at 246.

22.   General Electric Co. v. Joiner, 522 U.S. 136, 146, 118 S.Ct. 512, 519, 139 L.Ed.2d 508, 519 (1997).

2. The *Daubert* guidelines federal judges are to apply in determining the admissibility of expert testimony are exclusive. True or false?

3. According to the Advisory Committee, Federal Rule of Evidence 702 was amended after *Daubert* to conform the rule to reflect the *Daubert* guidelines. Explain.

§ 16.06 SATISFYING THE *KELLY* TEST

In all cases in which expert opinion is offered, the proponent must convince the judge that the expert testimony would be helpful to the jury and that the expert is qualified to give them that help.[1] If *Kelly* applies, the proponent must also persuade the judge that the scientific principles underlying the expert testimony meet the general acceptance test.[2] Moreover, if the expert testimony is predicated on the application of specific protocols or methodologies, the proponent must satisfy the judge that the correct procedures were followed.[3]

Since *Kelly* is designed to withhold expert testimony that is too unreliable to be evaluated properly, the question whether the underlying scientific principle or technique has been generally accepted by the relevant scientific community is governed by § 405.[4] Under § 405, the judge should exclude the expert testimony unless the proponent convinces the judge by a preponderance of the evidence that the principle or technique in question meets the *Kelly* standards of acceptance.[5] If after the hearing it is unclear to the judge whether the required scientific consensus has developed, the judge should exclude the expert evidence.[6]

Moreover, the question whether specific protocols or methodologies have been followed also should be governed by § 405. The failure to follow correct procedures in applying the novel principle or technique involved could give rise to opinions that are as unreliable as opinions based on principles and techniques rejected by the relevant scientific community.[7] Accordingly, the failure to follow the appropriate procedures can result in the exclusion of the expert opinion even if the proponent has demonstrat-

---

1. See § 16.01 supra.

2. People v. Kelly, 17 Cal.3d 24, 30, 130 Cal.Rptr. 144, 148, 549 P.2d 1240, 1244 (1976).

3. Id. The California Supreme Court has characterized the *Kelly* test as consisting of three prongs. The first is whether the principle or technique underlying the expert opinion has been generally accepted by the relevant scientific community; the second is whether the expert is qualified to testify about the principle's or technique's general acceptance by the pertinent scientific community; the third is whether the expert opinion offered was the result of following correct scientific procedures. People v. Venegas, 18 Cal.4th 47, 78, 74 Cal.Rptr.2d 262, 282, 954 P.2d 525, 545 (1998).

4. West's Ann. California Evidence Code § 405 and comment; see also People v. Ashmus, 54 Cal.3d 932, 971, 2 Cal.Rptr.2d 112, 132, 820 P.2d 214, 235 (1991), cert. denied, 506 U.S. 841, 113 S.Ct. 124, 121 L.Ed.2d 79 (1992), reh'g denied, 506 U.S. 1015, 113 S.Ct. 641, 121 L.Ed.2d 571 (1992).

5. West's Ann. California Evidence Code §§ 115 and 405. See also People v. Brown, 40 Cal.3d 512, 533, 230 Cal.Rptr. 834, 843, 726 P.2d 516, 525 (1985).

6. People v. Brown, 40 Cal.3d 512, 535, 230 Cal.Rptr. 834, 845, 726 P.2d 516, 527 (1985).

7. People v. Axell, 235 Cal.App.3d 836, 862, 1 Cal.Rptr.2d 411, 427 (1991).

ed the general acceptance by the pertinent scientific community of the scientific principles or techniques underlying the opinion.[8]

Confusion surrounding this prong of the *Kelly* test stems from the courts' failure to distinguish between evidence attacking the expert opinion once it has been admitted and evidence offered to prevent the admission of the expert opinion. Sometimes, the evidence attacking the methods of gathering, preserving, or testing the data used to formulate the expert opinion is offered, not at the hearing to determine compliance with the *Kelly*, but after the court has held that the *Kelly* standards have been satisfied.[9] Obviously, in such a situation whether or not the appropriate protocols or methodologies have been followed goes to weight and should be considered by the trier of fact.[10] But where the attacking evidence has been offered at the hearing to determine whether the *Kelly* standards have been met, then the court cannot escape its duty to take the evidence into account in making its *Kelly* ruling.[11] Such a duty is consistent with California Evidence Code § 801(b). This provision requires judges to exclude expert opinion unless based on matter "that is of the type that reasonably may be relied upon" by experts in the field.[12] Obviously, whether or not a *Kelly* issue is involved, this command calls for the exclusion of expert opinion whenever based on matter that is inappropriate because of the failure to abide by the protocols or methodologies experts in the field would observe.

Kelly does not require the judge to determine whether the novel scientific principles underlying the expert testimony are "reliable as a matter of scientific fact".[13] Rather, *Kelly* merely requires the judge to determine "from the professional literature and expert testimony whether * * * the new scientific technique is accepted as reliable in the relevant scientific community [or] whether ' "scientists significant either in number or expertise publicly oppose [a technique] as unreliable." ' "[14] *Kelly*, moreover, "does not demand the impossible—proof of an absolute unanimity of views in the scientific community before a new technique will be

---

8. People v. Venegas, 18 Cal.4th 47, 78, 74 Cal.Rptr.2d 262, 282, 954 P.2d 525, 545 (1998). See also People v. Pizarro, 110 Cal.App.4th 530, 558, note 29, 3 Cal.Rptr.3d 21, 43, note 29 (2003) (quoting with approval from Méndez, *Expert Testimony and the Opinion Rule: Conforming the Evidence Code to the Federal Rules*, 37 U.S.F. L.Rev. 411, 426 (2003)).

9. See, e.g., People v. Wright, 62 Cal.App.4th 31, 41, 72 Cal.Rptr.2d 246, 252 (1998).

10. Presumably, this is what the California Supreme Court had in mind when it declared, "Careless testing affects the weight of the evidence and not its admissibility, and must be attacked on cross-examination or by other expert testimony." People v. Farmer, 47 Cal.3d 888, 913, 254 Cal.Rptr. 508, 524, 765 P.2d 940, 956 (1989), cert. denied, 490 U.S. 1107, 109 S.Ct. 3158, 104 L.Ed.2d 1021 (1989). For a discussion of which factors of DNA analysis go to weight and which go to admissibility, see People v. Brown, 91 Cal.App.4th 623, 654, 110 Cal.Rptr.2d 750, 775 (2001); People v. Pizarro, 110 Cal.App.4th 530, 554–558, 3 Cal.Rptr.3d 21, 41–43 (2003).

11. People v. Venegas, 18 Cal.4th 47, 78–79, 74 Cal.Rptr.2d 262, 282, 954 P.2d 525, 545 (1998).

12. West's Ann. California Evidence Code § 801(b).

13. People v. Axell, 235 Cal.App.3d 836, 854, 1 Cal.Rptr.2d 411, 421 (1991). In federal courts, however, *Daubert* imposes this role on the judge. See § 16.04 supra.

14. People v. Axell, 235 Cal.App.3d 836, 854, 1 Cal.Rptr.2d 411, 421 (1991) (quoting People v. Brown, 40 Cal.3d 512, 230 Cal.Rptr. 834, 726 P.2d 516 (1985)).

deemed reliable; any such unanimity would be highly unusual * * *. Rather, the test is met if use of the technique is supported by a clear majority of the members of that community."[15] " 'General acceptance' under *Kelly* means a consensus drawn from a typical cross-section of the relevant, qualified scientific community."[16]

The California Supreme Court has provided trial judges with guidelines in evaluating evidence on whether a novel scientific principle or technique meets the general acceptance test. First, judges should weigh the relative qualifications of the experts called to testify on the question.[17] Since the court wants scientists to speak for themselves in determining the position of the scientific community, judges should consider whether the expert qualifies "as a scientist" and not merely as a technician or law enforcement officer.[18] The field in question may well be one in which only a scientist, "in regular communication with other colleagues in the field," is competent to say whether a novel scientific principle or technique has attained the necessary acceptance.[19]

Second, judges should hesitate before accepting the testimony of a single witness that a novel scientific principle or technique has been generally accepted by the relevant scientific community. In the court's view, it is "questionable whether the testimony of a single witness alone is ever sufficient to represent, or attest to, the views of an entire scientific community regarding the reliability of a new technique. Ideally, resolution of the general acceptance issue [will] require consideration of the views of a typical cross-section of the scientific community, including representatives, if there are such, of those who oppose or question the new technique."[20]

Third, judges should avoid giving too much weight to the testimony of experts whose close identification with a principle or technique prevents them from assessing "fairly and impartially the nature and extent of any opposing scientific views."[21] That an expert is a leading proponent of a particular technique or has built a career on the reliability of the technique are factors a judge should take into account in assessing the weight to give to the expert's testimony.[22] Judges, however, must tolerate a certain degree of interest "if scientists familiar with the theory and practice of a new technique are to testify at all."[23]

---

15. People v. Guerra, 37 Cal.3d 385, 418, 208 Cal.Rptr. 162, 183, 690 P.2d 635, 656 (1984).

16. People v. Leahy, 8 Cal.4th 587, 612, 34 Cal.Rptr.2d 663, 679, 882 P.2d 321, 337 (1994).

17. People v. Kelly, 17 Cal.3d 24, 40, 130 Cal.Rptr. 144, 154, 549 P.2d 1240, 1250 (1976).

18. Id. at 40, 130 Cal.Rptr. at 154, 549 P.2d at 1250.

19. Id.

20. Id. at 27, 130 Cal.Rptr. at 152, 549 P.2d at 1248.

21. Id. at 38, 130 Cal.Rptr. at 153, 549 P.2d at 1249.

22. Id.

23. People v. Reilly, 196 Cal.App.3d 1127, 1140, 242 Cal.Rptr. 496, 504 (1987), quoting from People v. Young, 425 Mich. 470, 391 N.W.2d 270 (1986).

In deciding whether a technique is generally accepted, judges are not limited to the evidence produced by the parties. They may consider "decisions from other jurisdictions and relevant scientific literature".[24] In considering decisions from other jurisdictions, judges should bear in mind that the relevant "consensus is that of scientists, not courts."[25] Similarly, in reviewing the relevant scientific literature, judges should view "such writings as 'evidence,' not of the actual reliability of the new scientific technique, but of its acceptance *vel non* in the scientific community. * * * [I]f a fair overview of the literature discloses that scientists significant either in number or expertise publicly oppose [the technique], the court can safely conclude there is no such consensus at the present time."[26]

A trial judge need not hold a *Kelly* hearing if an appellate court has endorsed the reliability of the principle or technique involved.[27] "[O]nce a trial court has admitted evidence based upon a new scientific technique, and that decision is affirmed on appeal by a published appellate decision, the precedent so established may control subsequent trials, at least until new evidence is presented reflecting a change in the attitude of the scientific community."[28] Judges, moreover, may take judicial notice of *Kelly* hearings and their results held within their jurisdiction.[29]

Questions and Problems

1.　In California, the proponent of expert testimony must convince the judge that the jury needs the expert help and that the expert is qualified to give it. Moreover, if the *Kelly* test applies to the testimony, the proponent must convince the judge by a preponderance of the evidence that the testimony satisfies the general acceptance test. True or false?

2.　California Evidence Code § 405 requires the proponent to convince the judge by a preponderance of the evidence that in reaching her opinion, the expert followed correct scientific procedures. True or false?

3.　In federal cases, *Daubert* forces judges to determine the scientific validity of expert testimony grounded in science. *Kelly*, on the other hand, merely requires judges to determine whether the contested technique has been accepted as reliable by the relevant scientific community. True or false?

4.　Because the answer to the preceding question is "true", California judges have to find only by a sufficiency standard that the relevant community has accepted the contested technique as reliable. True or false?

24.　People v. Axell, 235 Cal.App.3d 836, 854, 1 Cal.Rptr.2d 411, 422 (1991).

25.　People v. Reilly, 196 Cal.App.3d 1127, 1135, 242 Cal.Rptr. 496, 500 (1987).

26.　Id. (quoting from People v. Shirley, 31 Cal.3d 18, 181 Cal.Rptr. 243, 723 P.2d 1354 (1982)).

27.　People v. Brown, 40 Cal.3d 512, 530, 230 Cal.Rptr. 834, 841, 726 P.2d 516, 523 (1985).

28.　People v. Kelly, 17 Cal.3d 24, 32, 130 Cal.Rptr. 144, 149, 549 P.2d 1240, 1245 (1976).

29.　People v. Smith, 215 Cal.App.3d 19, 26, 263 Cal.Rptr. 678, 681 (1989).

§ 16.07 *DAUBERT v. KELLY*

In People v. Leahy[1] the California Supreme Court declined to adopt *Daubert* as the standard to be used to determine the admissibility of expert testimony in California. Instead, the court chose to adhere to the *Kelly* test.[2] Although the court conceded that the Evidence Code sections governing expert testimony do not expressly sanction the use of the general acceptance test, the court found the test compatible with those provisions.[3] More importantly, the court concluded that, despite its weaknesses, *Kelly* was effective in excluding expert opinion based on novel scientific principles or techniques not generally accepted by the pertinent scientific community.[4]

California's rejection of *Daubert* should not be overstated, however. *Kelly* is of limited application. California judges are required to apply *Kelly* only when the admissibility of an expert's opinion is challenged on the ground that it is based on novel scientific principles or techniques that lack the required acceptance by experts in the field. Still, a California judge's screening role can differ sharply from a federal judge's when *Kelly* does apply. While *Daubert* forces federal judges to determine the scientific validity of all expert testimony grounded in science, *Kelly* merely requires California judges to determine whether the contested principle or technique has been accepted as reliable by the relevant scientific community. The role of the California judge is not to determine reliability as a scientific matter but only whether the relevant scientific community has reached the prescribed consensus. The head counting obligation *Kelly* imposes on California judges is obviously much less onerous than the burden *Daubert* places on federal judges.

On the other hand, California judges do play a role similar to that of federal judges when expert opinion is challenged on non-*Kelly* grounds. Over objection the proponent must still persuade the judge by preponderance of the evidence that (1) the expert's opinion is based on the type of matter relied upon by experts in the field and (2) the expert followed accepted protocols or methodologies in reaching his or her opinion. Opinions based on matter experts would ignore or on incorrect procedures are unlikely to produce valid conclusions. Accordingly, ruling on these objections requires California judges to assess the scientific validity of the proffered opinion.

Does *Kelly* really matter? It is impossible to determine whether California trial judges are called upon to decide *Kelly* challenges more often than other challenges to the introduction of expert testimony. Trial courts are not required to keep these data. Moreover, appellate opinions disposing of expert testimony claims may not be representative. Still, appellate decisions do shed some light on the kinds of challenges Califor-

---

1. 8 Cal.4th 587, 34 Cal.Rptr.2d 663, 882 P.2d 321 (1994).

2. Id. at 599–604, 34 Cal.Rptr.2d at 670–673, 882 P.2d at 328–331.

3. Id.

4. Id. The court was also impressed by the California Legislature's failure to abrogate the general acceptance test despite ample opportunity to so. Id.

nia trial judges have to resolve. In the last 20 or so years, of about 30 cases presenting expert questions on appeal, 15 raised *Kelly* issues.[5] The figure suggests that in a substantial number of cases California judges are relieved from determining the scientific validity of the principle or technique underlying expert opinion.

Daubert's re-examination of the role of judges in screening expert evidence offers an opportunity to reconsider the role judges should play. Should judges be empowered to withhold the opinion from the jury unless they are satisfied by a preponderance of the evidence that the opinion satisfies the reasonable reliance, general acceptance or other tests? Or should judges let the jury evaluate the worth of the opinion once they find that the proponent's evidence satisfies the applicable test by a sufficiency standard? Under the latter standard, judges would let the jury hear the expert testimony if judges conclude that a reasonable jury could find that the opinion satisfies the pertinent test if the proponent's evidence is believed. Although a reconsideration of the judge's screening role raises important fundamental questions about the proper allocation of power between judge and jury, the history of the rules of evidence as enacted and interpreted suggests a continuing commitment to retaining the present balance. As some judges have stressed, jurors are not to be trusted to evaluate the validity of expert evidence, especially when the evidence appears to judges to carry "an undeserved aura of scientific infallibility".[6]

Nonetheless, something can be learned from *Daubert*. Precisely because *Kelly* is limited to assessing the admissibility of evidence based on novel scientific principles or techniques, California trial judges, like their federal counterparts, must determine the validity of other expert testimony. In discharging this function, it would be more useful to provide California judges and practitioners with the kind of checklist provided by amended Federal Rule 702 than the simple and somewhat incomplete principle of § 801(b). Limiting expert opinions to those based on matter "that is of a type that reasonably may be relied upon by an expert in forming an opinion upon the subject to which his testimony relates" does not embrace the universe of objections that could be raised. It would be much more useful if § 801(b) were rewritten to include also challenges to the validity of the principles as well as the propriety of the methods experts use in reaching their opinions.

The 1999 version of Uniform Rule of Evidence 702 includes these grounds as well as challenges to the need for the expert testimony, the qualifications of the witness to provide the evidence, and the propriety of the data used by the expert in his or her testimony.[7] Grouping the most common objections in one section would help judges and lawyers grasp quickly the standards for admitting expert testimony in California.

---

5. See § 16.04 supra.

6. People v. Stoll, 49 Cal.3d 1136, 1157, 265 Cal.Rptr. 111, 124, 783 P.2d 698, 711 (1989).

7. Uniform Rule of Evidence 702, Federal Rules of Evidence (West Group 2001–2002 ed.).

The amended section or its comment should make clear that the grounds listed are not exclusive.[8] Scientific and technical knowledge is dynamic, and it would be unwise to attempt to include all possible substantive objections to expert evidence in a single rule.[9] Moreover, to dispel confusion about the burden the proponent must discharge, the comment should be rewritten to clarify that objections based on the use of inappropriate matter, invalid principles, or incorrect methods should be determined under § 405.[10]

The limited applicability of *Kelly* also needs to be reconsidered. Despite its flaws, its saving virtue is that it precludes saddling judges—many of whom have no scientific training—with the difficult burden of determining the scientific validity of opinions in those instances where the opponent merely claims rejection by the pertinent scientific community of the principle or technique underlying the opinion. Head counting might be a better way of excluding unreliable expert evidence contested on this ground than an individual judge's determination of the scientific validity of the principle or technique involved. But there appears to be no convincing reason for limiting *Kelly* to those cases in which the principle or technique is "novel". While *Kelly* might be especially useful in those cases, any expert opinion predicated on principles or techniques rejected by experts in the field should likewise be excluded. The Federal Rules, as amended, and the Uniform Rules of Evidence do not limit the general acceptance test to novel scientific principles or techniques.[11] The comment to an amended § 801(b) should make this clear.

QUESTIONS AND PROBLEMS

1. In assessing the screening role of the judge, the fundamental question is whether judges should apply a sufficiency test or some higher test in determining whether jurors should consider expert testimony challenged on reliability grounds. True or false?

2. The head counting burden imposed by *Kelly* on California judges is just as onerous as the burden *Daubert* places on federal judges. Discuss.

3. As a normative matter, *Kelly* should be applied only to expert opinions that rely on novel principles or techniques. Discuss.

---

8. For an example of how this can be accomplished, see Uniform Rule of Evidence 702(e): "In determining the reliability of a principle or method, the court shall consider all relevant additional factors, which may include: * * *." Id.

9. As the California Law Revision Commission observed, "It is not practical to formulate a detailed statutory rule that lists all of the matters upon which an expert may properly base his opinion, for it would be necessary to prescribe specific rules applicable to each field of expertise. This is clearly impossible; the subjects upon which expert opinion may be received are too numerous to make statutory prescriptions of applicable rules a feasible venture." West's Ann. California Evidence Code § 801 (comment).

10. The comment to § 405 already provides that this section governs whether an expert is qualified to testify. See West's Ann. California Evidence Code § 405 (comment).

11. Federal Rule of Evidence 702; Uniform Rule of Evidence 702, Federal Rules of Evidence (West Group 2001–2002 ed.).

§ 16.08   CROSS EXAMINING THE EXPERT WITNESS

An expert may be cross examined to the same extent as any other witness.[1] In addition, an expert "may be cross examined as to (1) his qualifications, (2) the subject to which his expert testimony relates, and (3) the matter upon which his opinion is based and the reasons for his opinion."[2] An expert, moreover, may be cross examined about the compensation and expenses paid to him by the calling party.[3]

The Code, however, prohibits cross examining an expert about the content or tenor of any scientific, technical, or professional text, treatise, journal or similar publication unless one of three conditions is satisfied: (1) the expert referred to, considered, or relied upon the publication in arriving at or in forming the expert opinion; (2) the publication has been admitted in evidence; or (3) the publication has been established as a reliable authority by the testimony or admission of the expert or another expert, or by judicial notice.[4] The Law Revision Commission justifies the limitations on the following grounds:

> If an expert witness has relied on a particular publication in forming his opinion, it is necessary to permit cross-examination in regard to that publication in order to show whether the expert correctly read, interpreted, and applied the portions he relied on. Similarly, it is important to permit an expert witness to be cross-examined concerning those publications referred to or considered by him in forming his opinion. An expert's reasons for not relying on particular publications that were referred to or considered by him while forming his opinion may reveal important information bearing upon the credibility of his testimony. However, a rule permitting cross-examination on technical treatises not considered by the expert witness would permit the cross-examiner to utilize this opportunity not for its ostensible purpose—to test the expert's opinion—but to bring before the trier of fact the opinion of absentee authors without the safeguard of cross-examination. * * * [T]he statements in the text might be based on inadequate background research, might be subject to unexpressed qualifications that would be applicable to the case before the court, or might be unreliable for some other reason that could be revealed if the author were subject to cross-examination.[5]

Despite these admonitions, the California Supreme Court has overlooked the Code's prohibition on crossing examining experts on treatises

---

1. West's Ann. California Evidence Code § 721(a).

2. Id. The Federal Rules contain no equivalent provision, but such cross-examination is proper in federal court because it is relevant as it pertains to matters affecting the expert's credibility.

3. West's Ann. California Evidence Code § 722.

4. West's Ann.California Evidence Code § 721(b). Even then, the pertinent statements may not be read to the jury unless the publication has been admitted or qualifies for admission under a hearsay exception such as the one for learned treatises. See § 12.01 supra.

5. West's Ann.California Evidence Code § 721(b) (comment).

they did not consider. According to the court, "[A] party seeking to attack the credibility of [an] expert may bring to the attention of the jury material relevant to the issue on which the expert has offered an opinion [and] of which the expert was *unaware* or which he did *not* consider."[6]

Though the material may be called to the expert's attention on cross-examination, upon request the jury must be told not to consider the material for the truth of the matter asserted unless it has been received in evidence or qualifies under a hearsay exception such as the one for learned treatises.[7] Thus, while a mental health expert may be asked whether he is aware that a particular researcher has found that "psychiatrists are unable to accurately diagnose schizophrenia and paranoia"[8], the jurors should be warned not to consider the researcher's finding for the truth of the matter asserted.[9] In framing the questions, moreover, the cross examiner should avoid insinuating as true the matter asserted. A party, after all, "may not by its questions testify regarding the content of that material."[10]

The right to cross examine an expert even on matters relied on or considered in reaching an opinion is not limitless. The right is subject to § 352: if disclosure of the matters would be unduly prejudicial, the judge may halt the examination.[11] People v. Coleman[12] is illustrative. A husband accused of murdering his wife called several mental health experts to establish that he was either insane or suffering from diminished capacity at the time he killed her. Over his objection, the prosecution was allowed

---

6. People v. Bell, 49 Cal.3d 502, 532, 262 Cal.Rptr. 1, 17, 778 P.2d 129, 145 (1989), cert. denied, 495 U.S. 963, 110 S.Ct. 2576, 109 L.Ed.2d 757 (1990) (emphasis added).

In criminal cases, the Right to Truth–in–Evidence provision of Proposition 8, if literally construed, would repeal the Code limitation on crossing experts. Evidence that an expert is unaware of important works in his field of expertise is relevant to the expert's lack of credibility. But *Bell* did not rely on Proposition 8 to defend the departure from the Code. For an extended discussion of the effects of Proposition 8 on evidence attacking or supporting the credibility of witnesses, see § 15.03 supra.

Perhaps what the *Bell* court had in mind is the distinction between identity and substance. It is one matter to ask an expert on cross to identify those publications the expert did not consider or rely on; it is quite another to use the expert to get the substance of those publications before the fact finder.

7. As a practical matter, such cross-examination is not fruitful unless the expert concedes that the author of the material is an expert in the area in which the testifying expert offered an opinion. If the testifying expert refuses to concede the author's expertise, the cross-examiner will have to establish it through some other source.

The hearsay problem will disappear if the testifying expert adopts the assertions in the material as his or her own. This can be done by asking the testifying expert if he or she agrees with the assertions in the material. If the expert declines to adopt the assertions, then the cross examiner will have to rely on a hearsay exception. For a discussion of the learned treatise exception to the hearsay rule, see § 12.01 supra.

8. People v. Visciotti, 2 Cal.4th 1, 80–81, 5 Cal.Rptr.2d 495, 541–542, 825 P.2d 388, 434 (1992), cert. denied, 506 U.S. 893, 113 S.Ct. 267, 121 L.Ed.2d 196 (1992), reh'g denied, 506 U.S. 1016, 113 S.Ct. 646, 121 L.Ed.2d 575 (1992).

9. Id.

10. Id.

11. People v. Coleman, 38 Cal.3d 69, 92, 211 Cal.Rptr. 102, 117, 695 P.2d 189, 204 (1985) and cases cited therein.

12. Id.

to cross examine the experts about the contents of letters written by the wife in which she accused the defendant of having hurt her and of threatening to kill her and the children. Because the experts had considered the letters in forming their opinion, the judge permitted the cross-examination for the limited purpose of attacking their credibility. The California Supreme Court held that the judge abused his discretion:

> Accusatory statements "from the grave" such as these have so great a potential to unfairly prejudice the defendant that the courts have long recognized that a limiting instruction will be insufficient to prevent improper use. * * * Here the letters were only a small portion of the material on which the psychiatrists based their opinions and were not cited by them as items of major significance in their evaluation of the defendant's mental capacity. * * * Finally, those portions of the letters which the prosecutor legitimately offered to challenge the psychiatric opinions could have been selected and presented in a fashion which would have lessened their emotional impact and would have avoided the improper inference that the victim's accusations were true.[13]

The limits on the cross examiner are inapplicable if the publication has been received in evidence.[14] No risk then exists that inadmissible evidence will be brought before the jury.[15] The problem is getting such publications into evidence. Judicial notice is unlikely to help since statements in technical treatises are hardly the kind of "universally known" facts and propositions within the grasp of persons of average intelligence.[16] The hearsay exception for learned treatises is likewise unavailing; it provides an exception only for "facts of general notoriety and interest,"[17] that is, facts and propositions that are not subject to dispute.[18]

The Federal Rules are more generous than the Code with respect to the cross-examination of experts. First, they permit the cross examiner to inquire about statements in treatises, irrespective of whether the expert relied on them or considers them authoritative.[19] The Rules are designed to avoid "the possibility that the expert may at the outset block cross-examination by refusing to concede reliance or authoritativeness."[20] Second, the Rules provide that the statements may be admitted for the truth of the matter asserted if (1) the statements are established as reliable authority by expert testimony or judicial notice and (2) the treatise was relied upon by an expert witness on direct examination or was called to the expert's attention on cross-examination.[21] Thus, when a treatise has

---

13. Id. at 93, 211 Cal.Rptr. at 117, 695 P.2d at 204.

14. West's Ann. California Evidence Code § 721(b) and comment.

15. Id. (comment).

16. West's Ann. California Evidence Code § 451(f) and comment.

17. West's Ann. California Evidence Code § 1341.

18. See § 12.01 supra.

19. Federal Rule of Evidence 803(18) (Advisory Committee Note).

20. Id.

21. Federal Rule of Evidence 803(18).

been established as authoritative, appropriate passages may be offered in evidence, so long as an expert is on the stand and available to explain and assist in applying the treatise.[22]

QUESTIONS AND PROBLEMS

1. As a general matter, both the Code and the Rules allow a party to cross examine an expert to the same extent as any other witness. Thus, an expert can be impeached with his prior inconsistent statements as well as with evidence that he testifies only for one side in criminal cases. True or false?

2. Suppose that in a California medical malpractice case the defendant wants to get before the jury a statement in a medical journal that says, "Under some circumstances, natural childbirth can follow an earlier delivery by Caesarian." The author is unavailable to testify, and the defendant concedes that the statement is inadmissible under the hearsay exception for learned treatises. In light of the limitations imposed by § 721, over a hearsay objection how can the defendant take advantage of the plaintiff's expert to try to introduce the statement on cross-examination?

3. Would the defendant have an easier time in federal court? In answering the last two questions, review the problem following § 12.01 supra.

§ 16.09 ETHICAL AND CONSTITUTIONAL CONSTRAINTS ON THE USE OF EXPERT TESTIMONY BY PROSECUTORS

The California courts have imposed both ethical and constitutional constraints on the use of expert witnesses by prosecutors. Although attorneys may ethically present evidence they suspect but do not personally know is false, prosecutors, as the representatives of a sovereign whose interest in a criminal proceeding is not that "it shall win a case, but that justice shall be done" may not become the architects of a proceeding that fails to comport with the standards of justice.[1] Accordingly, a "prosecutor who, before trial, seriously doubts the accuracy of an expert witness's testimony should not present that evidence to a jury, especially in a capital case."[2]

Moreover, "[d]ue process requires the prosecution to disclose exculpatory evidence that is material to the defendant's guilt or innocence, or to punishment. * * * This duty includes disclosure of material evidence impeaching prosecution witnesses. * * * Exculpatory evidence is material if it creates a reasonable probability that the outcome of the trial would

---

22. Id. (Advisory Committee Note).

1. People v. Seaton, 26 Cal.4th 598, 650, 110 Cal.Rptr.2d 441, 476, 28 P.3d 175, 205 (2001), cert. denied, 535 U.S. 1036, 122 S.Ct. 1794, 152 L.Ed.2d 652 (2002) (quoting from Kyles v. Whitley, 514 U.S. 419, 439, 115 S.Ct. 1555, 131 L.Ed.2d 490 (1995)).

2. Id.

have been different had the evidence been disclosed."[3] Accordingly, if "the prosecution becomes aware of information that casts doubt on the accuracy of the testimony of one of its expert witnesses, it must disclose that evidence if it is material."[4]

§ 16.10   COURT APPOINTED EXPERTS

Federal Rule 706 and Evidence Code § 730 allow judges to appoint experts on their own or a party's motion if in the judge's discretion expert assistance is necessary.[1] Section 730 authorizes judges to appoint experts to investigate and report as well as to testify. Rule 706 is not as specific; it simply requires the judge to inform the experts of their duties. Experts appointed by federal judges, however, are required to inform the parties of their findings, if any.[2] The Code is silent on this point, but nothing in the Code precludes a California judge from ordering court appointed experts to disclose their findings to the parties.

Rule 706 expressly allows the parties to depose a court appointed expert. The Code does not contain an equivalent provision. In California, deposing experts is generally governed by the Civil Procedure Code.[3]

Rule 706(b) and Evidence Code § 731(c) empower the judge to fix the compensation to be paid to court appointed experts and, in civil actions, to apportion the cost of the compensation among the parties.

Rule 706(a) allows each party (including the calling party) to cross-examine a court appointed expert. In California, each party may cross-examine the court appointed expert if the court calls and examines the expert.[4] But if a party calls the court appointed expert, the calling party may not examine the expert as if on cross-examination.[5]

Both the Code and the Rules allow the judge to inform the jurors of the fact that an expert witness was appointed by the court.[6] It is improper, however, for a judge to vouch for the credibility of court appointed experts.[7] In both jurisdictions, the calling of court appointed experts does not preclude the parties from calling their own experts to testify on the same matters.[8]

---

3. Id. at 648, 110 Cal.Rptr.2d at 474–475, 28 P.3d at 204.

4. Id.

1. West's Ann. California Evidence Code § 730; Federal Rule of Evidence 706.

2. Federal Rule of Evidence 706.

3. West's Ann. Civil Procedure Code § 2034.010 et seq.

4. West's Ann. California Evidence Code § 732.

5. Id.

6. West's Ann. California Evidence Code § 722; Federal Rule of Evidence Rule 706(c).

7. See, e.g., People v. Coddington, 23 Cal.4th 529, 97 Cal.Rptr.2d 528, 603, 616, 2 P.3d 1081, 1149 (2000), cert. denied 531 U.S. 1195, 121 S.Ct. 1199, 149 L.Ed.2d 113 (2001).

8. West's Ann. California Evidence Code § 733; Federal Rule of Evidence 706(d).

CALIFORNIA EVIDENCE CODE

§ 720. Qualification as an expert witness

(a) A person is qualified to testify as an expert if he has special knowledge, skill, experience, training, or education sufficient to qualify him as an expert on the subject to which his testimony relates. Against the objection of a party, such special knowledge, skill, experience, training, or education must be shown before the witness may testify as an expert.

(b) A witness' special knowledge, skill, experience, training, or education may be shown by any otherwise admissible evidence, including his own testimony.

§ 721. Cross-examination of expert witness

(a) Subject to subdivision (b), a witness testifying as an expert may be cross-examined to the same extent as any other witness and, in addition, may be fully cross-examined as to (1) his or her qualifications, (2) the subject to which his or her expert testimony relates, and (3) the matter upon which his or her opinion is based and the reasons for his or her opinion.

(b) If a witness testifying as an expert testifies in the form of an opinion, he or she may not be cross-examined in regard to the content or tenor of any scientific, technical, or professional text, treatise, journal, or similar publication unless any of the following occurs:

(1) The witness referred to, considered, or relied upon such publication in arriving at or forming his or her opinion.

(2) The publication has been admitted in evidence.

(3) The publication has been established as a reliable authority by the testimony or admission of the witness or by other expert testimony or by judicial notice.

If admitted, relevant portions of the publication may be read into evidence but may not be received as exhibits.

§ 722. Credibility of expert witness

(a) The fact of the appointment of an expert witness by the court may be revealed to the trier of fact.

(b) The compensation and expenses paid or to be paid to an expert witness by the party calling him is a proper subject of inquiry by any adverse party as relevant to the credibility of the witness and the weight of his testimony.

§ 723. Limit on number of expert witnesses

The court may, at any time before or during the trial of an action, limit the number of expert witnesses to be called by any party.

§ 730. Appointment of expert by court

When it appears to the court, at any time before or during the trial of an action, that expert evidence is or may be required by the court or by any party to the action, the court on its own motion or on motion of any party may appoint one or more experts to investigate, to render a report as may be ordered by the court, and to testify as an expert at the trial of the action relative to the fact or matter as to which the expert evidence is or may be required. The court may fix the compensation for these services, if any, rendered by any person appointed under this section, in addition to any service as a witness, at the amount as seems reasonable to the court.

Nothing in this section shall be construed to permit a person to perform any act for which a license is required unless the person holds the appropriate license to lawfully perform that act.

§ 731. Payment of court-appointed expert

(a) In all criminal actions and juvenile court proceedings, the compensation fixed under Section 730 shall be a charge against the county in which such action or proceeding is pending and shall be paid out of the treasury of such county on order of the court.

(b) In any county in which the board of supervisors so provides, the compensation fixed under Section 730 for medical experts in civil actions in such county shall be a charge against and paid out of the treasury of such county on order of the court.

(c) Except as otherwise provided in this section, in all civil actions, the compensation fixed under Section 730 shall, in the first instance, be apportioned and charged to the several parties in such proportion as the court may determine and may thereafter be taxed and allowed in like manner as other costs.

§ 732. Calling and examining court-appointed expert

Any expert appointed by the court under Section 730 may be called and examined by the court or by any party to the action. When such witness is called and examined by the court, the parties have the same right as is expressed in Section 775 to cross-examine the witness and to object to the questions asked and the evidence adduced.

§ 733. Right to produce other expert evidence

Nothing contained in this article shall be deemed or construed to prevent any party to any action from producing other expert evidence on the same fact or matter mentioned in Section 730; but, where other expert witnesses are called by a party to the action, their fees shall be paid by the party calling them and only ordinary witness fees shall be taxed as costs in the action.

§ 800. Opinion testimony by lay witness

If a witness is not testifying as an expert, his testimony in the form of an opinion is limited to such an opinion as is permitted by law, including but not limited to an opinion that is:

(a) Rationally based on the perception of the witness; and

(b) Helpful to a clear understanding of his testimony.

§ 801.   Opinion testimony by expert witness

If a witness is testifying as an expert, his testimony in the form of an opinion is limited to such an opinion as is:

(a) Related to a subject that is sufficiently beyond common experience that the opinion of an expert would assist the trier of fact; and

(b) Based on matter (including his special knowledge, skill, experience, training, and education) perceived by or personally known to the witness or made known to him at or before the hearing, whether or not admissible, that is of a type that reasonably may be relied upon by an expert in forming an opinion upon the subject to which his testimony relates, unless an expert is precluded by law from using such matter as a basis for his opinion.

§ 802.   Statement of basis of opinion

A witness testifying in the form of an opinion may state on direct examination the reasons for his opinion and the matter (including, in the case of an expert, his special knowledge, skill, experience, training, and education) upon which it is based, unless he is precluded by law from using such reasons or matter as a basis for his opinion. The court in its discretion may require that a witness before testifying in the form of an opinion be first examined concerning the matter upon which his opinion is based.

§ 803.   Opinion based on improper matter

The court may, and upon objection shall, exclude testimony in the form of an opinion that is based in whole or in significant part on matter that is not a proper basis for such an opinion. In such case, the witness may, if there remains a proper basis for his opinion, then state his opinion after excluding from consideration the matter determined to be improper.

§ 804.   Opinion based on opinion or statement of another

(a) If a witness testifying as an expert testifies that his opinion is based in whole or in part upon the opinion or statement of another person, such other person may be called and examined by any adverse party as if under cross-examination concerning the opinion or statement.

(b) This section is not applicable if the person upon whose opinion or statement the expert witness has relied is (1) a party, (2) a person identified with a party within the meaning of subdivision (d) of Section 776, or (3) a witness who has testified in the action concerning the subject matter of the opinion or statement upon which the expert witness has relied.

(c) Nothing in this section makes admissible an expert opinion that is inadmissible because it is based in whole or in part on the opinion or statement of another person.

(d) An expert opinion otherwise admissible is not made inadmissible by this section because it is based on the opinion or statement of a person who is unavailable for examination pursuant to this section.

§ 805.   Opinion on ultimate issue

Testimony in the form of an opinion that is otherwise admissible is not objectionable because it embraces the ultimate issue to be decided by the trier of fact.

FEDERAL RULES OF EVIDENCE

Rule 701.   Opinion Testimony by Lay Witnesses

If a witness is not testifying as an expert, testimony in the form of an opinion is limited to one that is:

(a) rationally based on the witness's perception;

(b) helpful to clearly understanding the witness's testimony or to determining a fact in issue; and

(c) not based on scientific, technical, or other specialized knowledge within the scope of Rule 702.

Rule 702.   Testimony by Expert Witnesses

A witness who is qualified as an expert by knowledge, skill, experience, training, or education may testify in the form of an opinion or otherwise if:

(a) the expert's scientific, technical, or other specialized knowledge will help the trier of fact to understand the evidence or to determine a fact in issue;

(b) the testimony is based on sufficient facts or data;

(c) the testimony is the product of reliable principles and methods; and

(d) the expert has reliably applied the principles and methods to the facts of the case.

Rule 703.   Bases of an Expert's Opinion Testimony

An expert may base an opinion on facts or data in the case that the expert has been made aware of or personally observed. If experts in the particular field would reasonably rely on those kinds of facts or data in forming an opinion on the subject, they need not be admissible for the opinion to be admitted. But if the facts or data would otherwise be inadmissible, the proponent of the opinion may disclose them to the jury only if their probative value in helping the jury evaluate the opinion substantially outweighs their prejudicial effect.

Rule 704. Opinion on an Ultimate Issue

(a) In General—Not Automatically Objectionable. An opinion is not objectionable just because it embraces an ultimate issue.

(b) Exception. In a criminal case, an expert witness must not state an opinion about whether the defendant did or did not have a mental state or condition that constitutes an element of the crime charged or of a defense. Those matters are for the trier of fact alone.

Rule 705. Disclosing the Facts or Data Underlying an Expert's Opinion

Unless the court orders otherwise, an expert may state an opinion—and give the reasons for it—without first testifying to the underlying facts or data. But the expert may be required to disclose those facts or data on cross-examination.

Rule 706. Court–Appointed Expert Witnesses

(a) Appointment Process. On a party's motion or on its own, the court may order the parties to show cause why expert witnesses should not be appointed and may ask the parties to submit nominations. The court may appoint any expert that the parties agree on and any of its own choosing. But the court may only appoint someone who consents to act.

(b) Expert's Role. The court must inform the expert of the expert's duties. The court may do so in writing and have a copy filed with the clerk or may do so orally at a conference in which the parties have an opportunity to participate. The expert:

(1) must advise the parties of any findings the expert makes;

(2) may be deposed by any party;

(3) may be called to testify by the court or any party; and

(4) may be cross-examined by any party, including the party that called the expert.

(c) Compensation. The expert is entitled to a reasonable compensation, as set by the court. The compensation is payable as follows:

(1) in a criminal case or in a civil case involving just compensation under the Fifth Amendment, from any funds that are provided by law; and

(2) in any other civil case, by the parties in the proportion and at the time that the court directs—and the compensation is then charged like other costs.

(d) Disclosing the Appointment to the Jury. The court may authorize disclosure to the jury that the court appointed the expert.

(e) Parties' Choice of Their Own Experts. This rule does not limit a party in calling its own experts.

UNIFORM RULES OF EVIDENCE (1999)

Rule 701.   Opinion Testimony by Lay Witnesses.

If a witness's testimony is not based on scientific, technical, or other specialized knowledge within the scope of Rule 702, the witness's testimony in the form of opinions or inferences is limited to those opinions or inferences that are rationally based on the perception of the witness, and helpful to a clear understanding of the witness's testimony or the determination of a fact in issue.

Rule 702.   Testimony by Experts.

(a) General rule. If a witness's testimony is based on scientific, technical, or other specialized knowledge, the witness may testify in the form of opinion or otherwise if the court determines the following are satisfied:

(1) the testimony will assist the trier of fact to understand evidence or determine a fact in issue;

(2) the witness is qualified by knowledge, skill, experience, training, or education as an expert in the scientific, technical, or other specialized field;

(3) the testimony is based upon principles or methods that are reasonably reliable, as established under subdivision (b), (c), (d), or (e);

(4) the testimony is based upon sufficient and reliable facts or data; and

(5) the witness has applied the principles or methods reliably to the facts of the case.

(b) Reliability deemed to exist. A principle or method is reasonably reliable if its reliability has been established by controlling legislation or judicial decision.

(c) Presumption of reliability. A principle or method is presumed to be reasonably reliable if it has substantial acceptance within the relevant scientific, technical, or specialized community. A party may rebut the presumption by proving that it is more probable than not that the principle or method is not reasonably reliable.

(d) Presumption of unreliability. A principle or method is presumed not to be reasonably reliable if it does not have substantial acceptance within the relevant scientific, technical, or specialized community. A party may rebut the presumption by proving that it is more probable than not that the principle or method is reasonably reliable.

(e) Other reliability factors. In determining the reliability of a principle or method, the court shall consider all relevant additional factors, which may include:

(1) the extent to which the principle or method has been tested;

(2) the adequacy of research methods employed in testing the principle or method;

(3) the extent to which the principle or method has been published and subjected to peer review;

(4) the rate of error in the application of the principle or method;

(5) the experience of the witness in the application of the principle or method;

(6) the extent to which the principle or method has gained acceptance within the relevant scientific, technical, or specialized community; and

(7) the extent to which the witness's specialized field of knowledge has gained acceptance within the general scientific, technical, or specialized community.

CHAPTER 17

THE ROLE OF JUDGE AND JURY

■ ■ ■

Table of Sections

§ 17.01 ALLOCATING POWER BETWEEN JUDGE AND JURY

The California Evidence Code and the Federal Rules of Evidence have much in common in defining the respective roles of judges and jurors. Their differences, while significant in some instances, are few in number.

The California provisions begin by defining as preliminary facts those facts upon whose existence or nonexistence depends the admissibility or inadmissibility of other evidence offered by the parties to prove their contentions.[1] Questions regarding the admissibility of evidence are classified by the Code as questions of law to be decided by the judge.[2] The Federal Rules of Evidence are in accord,[3] and both the Code and Rules specify the procedure the judge is to follow in determining the existence or nonexistence of disputed preliminary facts.[4]

The Code expressly commits all "questions of fact" to the jurors, including questions regarding the credibility of witnesses and hearsay

---

1. West's Ann. California Evidence Code § 400 and comment.

2. West's Ann. California Evidence Code § 310.

3. Federal Rule of Evidence 104(a).

4. West's Ann. California Evidence Code § 402; Federal Rule of Evidence 104(c).

declarants.[5] The Rules do not have an analogous provision. A specific rule, however, may be unnecessary as under the Common Law tradition judges determine the admissibility of the evidence and jurors the weight of the admitted evidence.[6]

Useful as the rubric may be—that judges determine the admissibility of the evidence[7] while jurors find the "facts" from that evidence[8]—it does not answer all questions that might arise in the course of a trial. One reason is that judges often have to make fact determinations in ruling on the admissibility of evidence. Another is that judges play two distinct roles in making their admissibility rulings. One role calls for the judge to screen the proffered evidence on a sufficiency basis; the other role by a higher standard, usually by a preponderance of the evidence.[9] An example helps illustrate the differences in the two roles:

The accused is prosecuted for murder. The prosecution calls Witness A to testify that the accused told her that he killed the victim. The accused objects to the testimony on the ground that he made no such statement and offers to testify to that effect. The prosecution responds that the jury is entitled to hear Witness A's testimony irrespective of the accused's testimony and that, as a result, the accused must wait until his case-in-chief to offer his testimony. On what basis should the judge rule on the objection?

When the opponent claims that a declarant did not make a statement attributed to him, the objection is one of irrelevancy. In our example, if the accused was not the one who confessed killing the victim, the declaration would be immaterial and therefore not probative of a proposition that is properly provable in the action.[10] That objection is determined by the judge under the sufficiency standard in § 403. It provides that when the proffered evidence is the statement of a particular person and the preliminary fact question is whether that person made the statement, the judge should exclude the proffered evidence unless the proponent produces "evidence sufficient to sustain a finding of the existence of the preliminary fact * * *."[11]

---

5. West's Ann. California Evidence Code § 312.

6. C. McCormick, McCormick on Evidence § 53 (West 4th ed. 1992).

7. Questions of law, including questions regarding the admissibility of evidence, are for the court. West's Ann. California Evidence Code § 310. Other questions of law include the construction of statutes, Florio v. Lau, 68 Cal.App.4th 637, 641, 80 Cal.Rptr.2d 409, 411 (1998); of written contracts, Heppler v. J.M. Peters Co., 73 Cal.App.4th 1265, 1285, 87 Cal.Rptr.2d 497, 515 (1999); whether a plaintiff in a defamation action is a public figure, Khawar v. Globe Intern., Inc., 19 Cal.4th 254, 264, 79 Cal.Rptr.2d 178, 183, 965 P.2d 696, 701 (1998), cert. denied, 526 U.S. 1114, 119 S.Ct. 1760, 143 L.Ed.2d 791 (1999); whether a corporate veil should be pierced, Rosales v. Thermex–Thermatron Inc., 67 Cal.App.4th 187, 196, 78 Cal.Rptr.2d 861, 866 (1998); whether it is fair to impose successor liability on a corporation, id; and whether a legal duty exists. Johnson v. United Services Auto. Ass'n., 67 Cal.App.4th 626, 636, 79 Cal.Rptr.2d 234, 240 (1998), overruled on other grounds, Lueter v. California, 94 Cal.App.4th 1285, 1289, 115 Cal.Rptr.2d 68, 71 (2002).

8. West's Ann. California Evidence Code § 312.

9. West's Ann. California Evidence Code § 403 (comment).

10. For an extended discussion of relevance, see § 2.01 supra.

11. West's Ann. California Evidence Code § 403(a)(2).

The sufficiency standard of § 403 places strict limits on the role of the judge. The judge must let the jurors hear the declaration if the judge concludes that reasonable jurors *could* find that the accused made the statement. In making this assessment, the judge cannot pass on the credibility of the witnesses; that responsibility is assigned to the jury. The sole question for the judge is whether a reasonable jury *could* find the preliminary fact if the proponent's evidence is believed. Since Witness A is prepared to testify that he heard the accused confess killing the victim, that evidence alone satisfies the sufficiency standard of § 403. Accordingly, the judge must overrule the accused's objection and deny his request to take the stand to testify that he did not make the statement. The accused must wait until his case-in-chief. If at that time the accused denies having told Witness A that he killed the victim and the judge finds the accused to be more credible than Witness A, the judge nonetheless must let Witness A's account stand. It is up to the jurors, not the judge, to determine whether to believe Witness A or the accused. Empowering the judge to withhold this kind of evidence from the jury on the judge's assessment of who is telling the truth would deprive the prosecution of the right to have the jury determine an important factual question.

Section 403 provides the losing party some consolation. Upon request, the judge must instruct the jurors to disregard the proffered evidence unless they first find the preliminary fact.[12] In our example, they would be told to disregard the confession unless they first found that indeed the accused made the statement. But the Code, as we shall see, is silent on the standard by which the jurors must find that the accused made the statement.

A federal judge would make the same rulings under Rule 104(b). The relevance of A's testimony depends on whether the accused made the admission A attributes to him. In the language of Rule 104(b), "the relevance of [the] evidence depends on whether a fact exists," namely whether the accused made the admission.[13] In determining whether to let the jurors hear A's testimony, the federal judge is directed by the rule to apply a sufficiency standard.[14] The principal difference between the Code and Rules in this respect is that the Code explicitly informs the judge and the litigants that the question whether the accused made the admission is to be governed by the standards set out in § 403. As will be shown, the Code expressly identifies the preliminary fact questions that are impliedly embraced by Rule 104(b). Providing the judge and the parties and their lawyers with this kind of information is useful to trial planning and management. Section 403 is superior to the Rule 104(b) in this respect.

Upon request, a federal judge would also give the jurors a limiting instruction telling them to disregard the A's testimony unless they first find that the accused made the admission. But giving such an instruction

---

12. West's Ann. California Evidence Code § 403(c)(1).

13. Federal Rule of Evidence 104(b).

14. Id.

upon request would be the product of established practice and not the result of a directive under the Federal Rules. The Rules do not contain a provision equivalent to § 403(c)(1) which requires the judge upon request to instruct the jurors to disregard the proffered evidence unless they find that the preliminary fact in issue exists.[15] The California provision provides useful guidance to judges, litigants and their lawyers.

Assume that the prosecution calls a second witness, Officer B, to testify that the accused confessed killing the victim. The accused objects to the introduction of the confession on the ground that the confession was coerced and requests permission to produce evidence to that effect. Must the judge grant the accused's request? The answer is yes. Federal constitutional considerations aside, the questions raised by the accused's objection are governed by § 405. This section "deals with evidentiary rules designed to withhold evidence from the jury because it is too unreliable to be evaluated properly * * *."[16] Section 405 proceeds on the assumption that it is unrealistic to expect a jury to disregard a confession which it finds to be involuntary, especially when parts of the confession are corroborated by other evidence.[17] Accordingly, § 405 entitles the opponent to a hearing on the existence or nonexistence of the preliminary facts, which in this case center on the voluntariness of the confession.

Assume that at the hearing the accused testifies that Officer B promised him leniency in return for the confession and that Officer B denies having made any such promises. By what standard must the judge resolve the conflict in the evidence? Unless the rule of law applicable to the preliminary fact dispute states otherwise, the proponent must convince the judge by a preponderance of the evidence that the proffered evidence meets the required standards of trustworthiness,[18] in our case that the accused confessed voluntarily. Under § 405, the judge sits as a jury of one, and like jurors is entitled to consider the evidence pro and con, including the credibility of the witnesses. If at the conclusion of the § 405 hearing the judge believes Officer B, he will let the jury hear the confession. If he believes the accused, he will withhold the confession from the jury. If the judge cannot decide whom to believe, he will also withhold the confession, since the prosecution has the burden of persuasion.

Section 405 hearings differ from § 403 hearings in three important respects. First, unless the proponent stipulates to the opponent's evidence, the judge must allow the opponent to offer evidence of the nonexistence of the preliminary fact before ruling on the objection. Second, in ruling on whether the proponent has carried the burden of persuasion, the judge can consider the evidence produced by each side, as well as the credibility of the witnesses. Third, if the judge overrules the objection and admits the

---

15. West's Ann. California Evidence Code § 403(c)(1).

16. Id.

17. West's Ann. California Evidence Code § 405 (comment).

18. Id. Unless the rule of law governing the preliminary fact determination under § 405 specifies a higher burden of persuasion, the applicable standard is proof by a preponderance of the evidence. West's Ann. California Evidence Code § 115.

proffered evidence, the opponent is not entitled to an instruction telling the jurors to disregard the evidence unless they first find the preliminary fact,[19] in our case that the confession was voluntary. The opponent is not given a "second bite" at the apple, i.e., to have the jurors, as well as the judge, consider the admissibility of the evidence. That power is delegated exclusively to the judge by § 405. But the jury still retains the power to accept or reject the confession, since the jury ultimately decides what weight, if any, to give to the testimony of any witness.[20] In deciding the weight to give to the confession, the jurors may consider both the officer's and the accused's testimony.

A federal judge should behave exactly as a California judge in determining the admissibility of the confession. However, this would not be readily apparent to California practitioners reading Federal Rule 104(a) and its accompanying Advisory Committee Note. As will be seen, the Code has default provisions allocating and defining the production and persuasion burdens when those burdens are unascertainable under the "rule of law" governing the specific question arising under § 405. The Federal Rules do not. The United States Supreme Court has filled this gap by holding that the proponent of the evidence should be required to prove preliminary fact questions arising under Rule 104(a) by a preponderance of the evidence.[21] As will be explained, this holding is inconsistent with the role of the California judge when ruling on some aspects of hearsay declarations which in California are governed by § 403. In general, §§ 403 and 405 represent a better thought out approach to preliminary fact questions.

QUESTIONS AND PROBLEMS

1. The defendant is prosecuted for murder. Rule on the following objections in a California and federal court:

DA: What did the defendant say to you?

W: He said, "I want to come clean. I'm the one who stabbed the victim."

Defendant: Objection. Hearsay.

Judge: Overruled.

Defendant: Move to strike on the ground that I did not say that to W. Request permission to take the stand to testify to that effect.

Judge: ?

If the judge denies the defendant's request to offer countervailing evidence until he opens up his case-in-chief, upon request what limiting instruction, if any, should the judge give to the jurors?

---

19.   West's Ann. California Evidence Code § 405(b)(2).

20.   West's Ann. California Evidence Code §§ 405 (comment) and 406.

21.   Bourjaily v. United States, 483 U.S. 171, 175, 107 S.Ct. 2775, 97 L.Ed.2d 144 (1987). See also Huddleston v. United States, 485 U.S. 681, 685, 108 S.Ct. 1496, 99 L.Ed.2d 771 (1988).

Compare with:

DA: What did the defendant say to you?

Officer: He said, "I want to come clean. I'm the one who stabbed the victim."

Defendant: Objection. Hearsay.

Judge: Overruled.

Defendant: Move to strike on the ground that my statement to the officer was coerced. Request a hearing outside the presence of the jury to offer evidence in support of my motion to strike.

Judge: ?

Assume the judge grants the defendant's request for an evidentiary hearing. At the hearing, defense counsel examines the defendant as follows:

Defense Counsel: Did you tell the officer it was you who stabbed the victim?

Defendant: Yes.

Defense Counsel: Why?

Defendant: Because the officer said that if I didn't confess he would arrest my son for the stabbing.

At the hearing, the prosecution then examines the officer as follows:

DA: Did the defendant tell you that he stabbed the victim?

Officer: Yes.

DA: Did you threaten him in any way?

Officer: No. After placing him in the rear of my patrol car, without my asking him anything, he said, "I want to come clean; I am the one who stabbed the victim."

Defense counsel: Move to suppress my client's confession on the ground that it was coerced.

Judge: ?

If the judge denies the defense motion to strike the confession and allows the jury to hear it, upon the defendant's request, may the judge instruct the jurors to disregard the confession unless they first find that it was not coerced?

Why is sufficiency the appropriate standard when the relevancy of proffered evidence is disputed?

2.   Under § 403, when an issue is governed by a sufficiency standard, the jury is invited to determine the existence or nonexistence of the preliminary fact in dispute. Why?

3.   Why is the jury precluded from making the same determination with respect to preliminary fact disputes governed by § 405?

§ 17.02 PRELIMINARY MATTERS GOVERNED BY § 403

Scholars disagree on when judges should use a sufficiency standard, as contemplated in § 403, or a higher standard, as is usually the case under § 405, in ruling on the admissibility of evidence.[1] The Code avoids the controversy by describing with particularity the kinds of preliminary fact issues governed by § 403 and relegating all other issues for determination under § 405.[2] Moreover, to eliminate uncertainties, various Code sections specifically state that admissibility depends on satisfying a sufficiency standard.[3] Finally, the comment to § 403 provides a useful commentary on the kinds of preliminary fact determinations that fall under the section.

Rule 104(b), on the other hand, does not specify the preliminary fact questions that fall within its ambit. Although the term "conditional relevancy" used in the Advisory Committee Note probably embraces the kinds of preliminary fact questions listed under § 403,[4] Rule 104(b) does not provide judges and litigants or their lawyers with the same kind of detailed guidance as do § 403 and its comment.

The preliminary fact issues listed in § 403 "are not finally decided by the judge because they have been traditionally regarded as jury questions. They involve the credibility of testimony or the probative value of evidence that is admitted on the ultimate issues."[5] To preserve the jury's right to determine factual issues,[6] § 403 limits judges to employing a sufficiency standard in screening the admissibility of evidence subject to the section. Federal Rule 104(b) likewise achieves the same goal by requiring the judge to use a sufficiency test in screening the admissibility of evidence falling within the rule's ambit.[7]

The preliminary facts subject to resolution under the standards of § 403 are as follows:

Relevance of the proffered evidence. Section 403 governs when the relevance of the proffered evidence depends on the existence of a preliminary fact.[8] As the Assembly Committee notes, "[I]f P sues D upon an alleged agreement, evidence of negotiations with A is inadmissible

---

1. West's Ann. California Evidence Code § 403 (comment).

2. See West's Ann. California Evidence Code §§ 403 and 405. A separate section, § 404, governs the question whether the judge should sustain a claim of privilege under the self-incrimination clause. West's Ann. California Evidence Code § 404.

3. See, e.g., West's Ann. California Evidence Code §§ 1222, 1223, and 1400.

4. See text accompanying note 26 infra. Professor John Kaplan questions whether Rule 104(b) embraces all of the situations enumerated by Evidence Code § 403. See Kaplan, *Of Mabrus and Zorgs*, 66 California Law Review 987, 995 (1978).

5. West's Ann. California Evidence Code § 403 (comment).

6. West's Ann. California Evidence Code § 312.

7. Federal Rule of Evidence 104(b).

8. West's Ann. California Evidence Code § 404(a)(1).

because irrelevant unless A is shown to be D's agent; but the evidence of the negotiations with A is admissible if there is evidence sufficient to sustain a finding of the agency."[9]

Personal knowledge of a witness. Section 702 provides that the testimony of a lay witness concerning a particular matter is inadmissible unless the witness has personal knowledge of the matter.[10] Against objection, personal knowledge must be shown before the witness may testify about the matter.[11] Section 403 governs when the personal knowledge of a witness is contested.[12]

Section 800 permits lay witnesses to testify in the form of an opinion if it is rationally based on the perception of the witness and the opinion is helpful to a clear understanding of the witness's testimony.[13] Whether or not the opinion is based on the witness's perception is governed by § 403, as the limitation is merely "a specific application" of the personal knowledge requirement.[14]

Authenticity of writings. When a writing is offered in evidence, the proponent must also offer evidence that the writing is what the proponent claims it to be.[15] If in a contract dispute the plaintiff offers a writing which she claims is the contract she and the defendant entered into, then the plaintiff must offer some evidence indicating that the writing is indeed that contract. Whether or not the writing is the contract is governed by § 403.[16] To eliminate any uncertainty about the point, § 1400, which defines authentication, imposes the same requirement.[17]

Although authentication is usually associated with writings, the concept applies whenever any tangible object is offered in evidence.[18] Whether the object be the knife the prosecution believes the accused used to kill the victim or the ladder the plaintiff claims was defective, the proponent must connect the object with the case. Showing that the object is relevant to the issues to be decided will require some evidence that the object is what the proponent claims it to be. For purposes of admissibility, the quantum of evidence, as in the case of writings, need satisfy only § 403's sufficiency standard.

Identity of the actor or declarant. Section 403 governs when "the proffered evidence is of a statement or other conduct of a particular person and the preliminary fact is whether that person made the state-

---

9. Id.

10. West's Ann. California Evidence Code § 702.

11. Id.

12. West's Ann. California Evidence Code § 403(a)(2).

13. West's Ann. California Evidence Code § 800.

14. West's Ann. California Evidence Code § 403 (comment).

15. West's Ann. California Evidence Code § 1400.

16. West's Ann. California Evidence Code § 403(a)(3).

17. West's Ann. California Evidence Code § 1400.

18. Id. (comment).

ment or so conducted himself."[19] Impeaching a witness through a prior conviction assumes that the witness was the person who was convicted. If the identity of the person convicted is disputed, the judge must permit the use of the conviction if the proponent demonstrates by a sufficiency of the evidence that the person convicted was the witness.[20] The same principle applies when the preliminary issue is whether a particular person engaged in other conduct, including the making of statements.

Earlier we saw that, when the identity of a declarant is contested, the declaration may be received if the proponent establishes the identity of the declarant by a sufficiency of the evidence.[21] The same standard applies to the identity of hearsay declarants.[22] Thus, any evidence that the statement was made by the claimed declarant is sufficient to warrant the introduction of admissions by parties under § 1220, of previous statements by witnesses under §§ 1235–1236, as well as of the statements by the declarants who are described in §§ 1224–1227 and whose liability, breach of duty, or right is in issue.[23]

Whether a party has authorized or adopted an admission is also governed by § 403.[24] Since the admission of a coconspirator is a form of an authorized admission, the admission is admissible upon the introduction of evidence sufficient to sustain a finding of the conspiracy.[25]

Section 403 and the doctrine of conditional relevance. A review of the kinds of preliminary facts governed by § 403 reveals that most involve some aspect of relevance. A writing or other tangible object is irrelevant unless it is what the proponent claims it to be; the statement of a declarant is irrelevant unless the declarant made the statement; similarly, a person's conduct is irrelevant unless it is the conduct of that person. In each instance the evidence is irrelevant unless some condition is fulfilled. For this reason, some scholars view these preliminary fact determinations as calling for a special relevance analysis known as "conditional relevancy."[26] This is the approach taken by the Federal Rules of Evidence to these kinds of preliminary fact determinations.[27] The Rules, like the Code, condition the admission of the proffered evidence upon proof of the preliminary facts by a sufficiency standard.[28]

---

19. West's Ann. California Evidence Code § 403(a)(4).

20. Id. (comment).

21. See § 17.01 supra.

22. West's Ann. California Evidence Code § 403 (comment).

23. Id. For a description of the declarants in §§ 1224–1227, see § 7.03 supra.

24. West's Ann. California Evidence Code § 403 (comment).

25. Id. For a discussion of the foundational requirements for admitting coconspirators' declarations, see § 7.04 supra. Federal requirements differ from those imposed by the Code. See id.

26. See the authorities listed in Federal Rule of Evidence 104 (Advisory Committee Note).

27. Federal Rule of Evidence 104(b). The restyled rule substitutes the reference to "condition of fact" with "depends on whether a fact exists".

28. Id.

The personal knowledge requirement does not rest upon concepts of relevance, special or otherwise. Requiring lay witnesses to testify on the basis of first hand knowledge has more to do with using the most reliable sources of information than with relevance.[29] But even in this instance the use of a sufficiency standard is justified: jurors are as capable as judges in ascertaining whether a witness acquired his knowledge through the use of the senses.[30]

QUESTIONS AND PROBLEMS

1. The kinds of preliminary fact determinations listed under § 403 fall within the relevance approach of the Federal Rules. True or false?

2. Questions regarding the personal knowledge requirement are resolved under a sufficiency standard because such questions raise issues of relevance. True or false?

§ 17.03 PRELIMINARY MATTERS GOVERNED BY § 405

Section 405 is designed as a default provision. If a preliminary issue is not governed by § 403, it will be determined under § 405.[1] Despite the simplicity of this approach, uncertainty about the scope of § 403 led the drafters of the Code to list in the accompanying comment some of the preliminary fact issues governed by § 405.

Competency of witnesses. Whether a witness is capable of expressing himself in a manner that can be understood or is capable of understanding the duty to tell the truth are matters to be resolved by the judge under § 405.[2] But, as has been noted,[3] whether a witness possesses the requisite personal knowledge is decided by the judge under § 403. Under Rule 104(a), the questions concerning the qualification of a person to be a witness are to be determined by the judge.[4]

Qualification of experts. Whether a witness is qualified to provide the fact finder with an expert opinion is determined by the judge under § 405.[5] Accordingly, the judge's determination that the witness is qualified is binding on the fact finder, but the fact finder may consider the witness's qualifications in deciding what weight, if any, to give to the

---

29. C. McCormick, McCormick on Evidence § 10 (J. Strong 4th ed. 1991).

30. The Federal Rules, like the Code, impose a sufficiency standard on the question of whether a witness is testifying on the basis of first hand knowledge. Federal Rule of Evidence 602.

1. West's Ann. California Evidence Code § 405. A separate section, § 404, governs claims of privilege under the self-incrimination clause. West's Ann. California Evidence Code § 404.

2. West's Ann. California Evidence Code § 701 (comment).

3. See § 17.02 supra.

4. Federal Rule of Evidence 104(a).

5. West's Ann. California Evidence Code § 405 (comment).

opinion.[6] Moreover, whether the expert's opinion is based on matters of a type reasonably relied upon by experts in the field or on scientific principles and techniques generally accepted by the pertinent scientific community are questions to be decided by the judge under § 405. The proponent must convince the judge by a preponderance of the evidence that expert evidence meets these tests.[7]

Under Rule 104(a), whether a person qualifies as an expert is to be determined by the judge.[8]

Section 405 also governs whether a witness is sufficiently acquainted with a person to give an opinion on that person's sanity[9] or with a person's handwriting to give an opinion on whether a writing is in that person's handwriting.[10]

Writings. Although the authenticity of a writing presents a § 403 issue, whether a writing offered for comparison is "genuine" must be determined by the judge under § 405 before admitting the writing for comparison with other writings whose authenticity is in dispute.[11] For example, if the plaintiff attempts to authenticate the signature on Exhibit A as Smith's through a signature purporting to be Smith's on Exhibit B, before Exhibit B can be received for comparison purposes the plaintiff must convince the judge by a preponderance of the evidence that the signature on Exhibit B is Smith's. Only then may the jury be allowed to compare the signature on Exhibit B with the signature on Exhibit A to determine if the signature on Exhibit A is Smith's. One would expect a similar role for a federal judge if the writing offered for comparison does not raise a conditional relevancy question. Rule 104(a), like § 405, is a default provision. It is generally applicable unless the preliminary question at issue is to be decided under the conditional relevancy provision of Rule 104(b).[12]

Under the California Secondary Evidence Rule, a party may prove the contents of a writing by offering the original writing or secondary evidence of the original.[13] The proponent, however, must offer the original if a genuine dispute exists concerning the material terms of the original and justice requires excluding the secondary evidence, or if admitting the secondary evidence would be unfair.[14] Presumably, upon objection the proponent must convince the judge under § 405 either that no genuine

---

6. West's Ann. California Evidence Code § 720 (comment).

7. See People v. Brown, 40 Cal.3d 512, 535, 230 Cal.Rptr. 834, 845, 726 P.2d 516, 527 (1985).

8. Federal Rule of Evidence 104(a) and Advisory Committee Note.

9. West's Ann. California Evidence Code § 405 (comment).

10. Id.

11. Id.

12. Federal Rule of Evidence 104(a)–(b) and Advisory Committee Note. ("[Rule 104(a)] is of general application. It must, however, be read as subject to the special provisions for 'conditional relevancy' in subdivision (b) * * *."). Id. (Advisory Committee Note).

13. West's Ann. California Evidence Code §§ 1521–1522.

14. West's Ann. California Evidence Code § 1522.

dispute exists concerning the material terms of the original writing or that admission of the secondary evidence would be not be unfair.[15]

The Federal Rules of Evidence retain the traditional Best Evidence Rule. Proof of the contents of a writing must be made through the original of the writing unless nonproduction of the original writing is excused.[16] As in California, most questions regarding the satisfaction of the rule's requirements are for the judge under the standards of Rule 104(a).[17]

Privileges. The party objecting on the grounds of privilege must establish the privileged nature of the matter under § 405.[18] Moreover, the party claiming an exception to the privilege must establish the preliminary facts under the same standard.[19] These rules are consistent with one of the goals of § 405: to withhold evidence from the fact finder because public policy requires its exclusion.

The Federal Rules do not contain equivalent provisions. Congress rejected the Rules' article on privileges and substituted a provision that leaves the development of privileges in federal question cases to the Common Law as interpreted by the federal courts.[20] State privilege law applies only in those cases where state law supplies the rule of decision with respect to an element of a claim or defense.[21]

The policy of withholding evidence from the fact finder because public policy justifies its exclusion also requires the objecting party to convince the judge under § 405 that admissions should be excluded because they were made in the course of compromise negotiations.[22] The same result should also obtain in federal court under Rule 104(a).

Witness unavailability. The proponent of evidence requiring the unavailability of the declarant has the burden of persuading the judge of the declarant's unavailability as a witness under § 405.[23] If the opponent objects to the evidence on the ground that the proponent procured the declarant's unavailability to prevent the declarant from testifying, the opponent must establish that claim under § 405.[24]

---

15. This was the practice under the Best Evidence Rule. West's Ann. California Evidence Code § 405 (comment). For an extended discussion of the requirements of the Best Evidence and Secondary Evidence Rules, see § 13.06 supra.

16. Federal Rule of Evidence 1002.

17. Federal Rule of Evidence 1008 (Advisory Committee Note).

18. Id. Most privileges for confidential communications create a presumption that the communications protected by these privileges were made in confidence. See § 20.04 infra.

19. West's Ann. California Evidence Code § 405 (comment).

20. Federal Rule of Evidence 501 and Advisory Committee Note. Professors Mueller and Kirkpatrick maintain that the federal common law places upon the party opposing the privilege the burden of showing that an exception applies. Mueller & Kirkpatrick, Evidence § 1.12 at 44 (Aspen 2d ed. 1999).

21. Federal Rule of Evidence 501 and Advisory Committee Note.

22. West's Ann. California Evidence Code § 405 (comment).

23. Id.

24. Id.

The Rules and Advisory Committee Notes are silent on these points. Presumably, these questions are committed to the judge for resolution under the standards of Rule 104(a). However, neither this rule nor its note indicates which party should have the production and persuasion burdens. The federal approach to hearsay is that of the Common Law, that is, a general rule of exclusion with exceptions.[25] Under this approach, the burden of proof on preliminary matters relating to admissibility is usually on the proponent.[26] Thus, upon objection the proponent of the evidence would have to persuade the judge of the declarant's unavailability. Because of the Rules' silence, resort to the federal common law is necessary to determine whether the opponent has the burden of proof on the question of whether the proponent procured the declarant's unavailability.

Hearsay evidence. "When hearsay evidence is offered, two preliminary fact questions may be raised. The first question relates to the authenticity of the proffered declaration—was the statement actually made by the person alleged to have made it? The second question relates to the existence of those circumstances that make the hearsay sufficiently trustworthy to be received—e.g., was the declaration spontaneous, the confession voluntary, the business record trustworthy? Under [the Code], questions relating to authenticity of the proffered declaration are decided under Section 403. * * * But other preliminary fact questions are decided under Section 405."[27]

Section 405, not § 403, thus governs whether a declaration, when made, was so far contrary to the declarant's interests that a reasonable person in the declarant's position would not have made the statement unless he believed it to be true; whether a statement previously made by a witness is inconsistent with the witness's testimony and complies with the requirements of § 770; whether a statement previously made by a witness is consistent with the witness's testimony and complies with the requirements of § 791; whether a statement previously made by a witness qualifies as past recollection recorded; whether a statement previously made by a witness qualifies as a statement of prior identification; whether a declaration qualifies as an excited utterance or as a contemporaneous statement; whether a declaration qualifies as a statement of a present or past mental state; whether certain writings meet the requirements for business and official records; and whether testimony given in another action qualifies as former testimony.

The use of § 405 to determine the existence of these kinds of preliminary facts is justified. Section 405 is designed in part to withhold evidence from the jury that is too unreliable for proper jury evaluation.[28] Hearsay is the classic example of untrustworthy evidence. The judge should not expose the jury to it unless the judge is satisfied that the

---

25. Federal Rules of Evidence, ARTICLE VIII. HEARSAY. (Advisory Committee Note—INTRODUCTORY NOTE: THE HEARSAY PROBLEM).

26. Mueller & Kirkpatrick, Evidence § 1.12 at 44 (Aspen 2d ed. 1999).

27. Id.

28. Id.

circumstances justifying its admission as an exception have been demonstrated under the tough standards of § 405.

The language of Federal Rule of Evidence 104 and its accompanying Advisory Committee Note would support a similar construction in the case of hearsay and its exceptions. To the extent that the relevance of the hearsay declaration depends on the existence of the preliminary fact in dispute, the question would call for the application of the sufficiency standard of Rule 104(b). Preliminary fact disputes relating to the circumstances justifying the hearsay exception would fall within Rule 104(a). But this is not the construction given to Rule 104 by the United States Supreme Court. In California, for example, the Code requires the prosecution to prove the foundational facts of the hearsay exception for coconspirators' declarations by the sufficiency standard of § 403. The California approach is predicated on the theory that coconspirators' admissions are a form of authorized admissions, and the question of authority is governed by § 403.[29] But in Bourjaily v. United States[30] the Supreme Court held that under the Federal Rules the proponent must establish the foundational facts of the coconspirators' hearsay exception by a preponderance of the evidence.[31]

Reasonable people might differ on whether the foundational facts for this hearsay exception should be proved by a sufficiency or higher standard.[32] The point, though, is that the United States Supreme Court felt free to require proof by the more likely than not standard because of the failure of Rule 104 and its note to specify the appropriate standard as clearly as do § 403 and its accompanying comment.

In ruling on the admissibility of hearsay under an exception to the hearsay rule, may the judge exclude the statement if the judge finds the witness reporting the statement to be incredible? In People v. Cudjo[33] the trial judge excluded a declaration against penal interest offered by the accused in exculpation on the ground that the reporting witness was unworthy of belief. But because credibility is a question for the jury, the California Supreme Court held that it is error for trial judges to exclude hearsay declarations on this ground.[34] Whether the declaration was sufficiently against interest to qualify under the exception was a question for the judge under § 405; whether the declarant made the statement was a question for the jury under § 403; whether the judge should have let the

---

29. West's Ann. California Evidence Code § 403 (comment).

30. 483 U.S. 171, 107 S.Ct. 2775, 97 L.Ed.2d 144 (1987).

31. Id. at 175.

32. See Kaplan, *Of Mabrus and Zorgs*, 66 California Law Review 987, 997 (1978) (arguing that the foundational facts of the hearsay exception for coconspirators' statements should be governed by § 405 since jurors are unlikely to engage in the required fact finding before considering the statement).

33. 6 Cal.4th 585, 25 Cal.Rptr.2d 390, 863 P.2d 635 (1993).

34. Id. at 607–608, 25 Cal.Rptr.2d at 404–405, 863 P.2d at 649–650. See also Vorse v. Sarasy, 53 Cal.App.4th 998, 1011–1012, 62 Cal.Rptr.2d 164, 172–173 (1997) (holding that a judge may not strike a witness's testimony on the ground that the witness's testimony is not credible as witness credibility is a jury question).

jury decide this question was governed by the sufficiency standards of § 403. In this regard, the reporting witness's testimony that he heard the declarant make the statement was sufficient evidence to take the question of its making to the jury.[35]

QUESTIONS AND PROBLEMS

1.   As a general rule, under the Code those aspects of a hearsay exception justifying the creation of the exception, if contested, are decided by the judge under the standards of § 405. Other questions, however, such as the identity of the hearsay declarant or whether the declarant made the statement, are decided by the judge under the standards of § 403. True or false?

2.   Where the witness reporting the hearsay declaration is not the declarant, then a judge may exclude the declaration if the judge has good grounds for disbelieving the reporting witness. True or false?

3.   Whether or not matter is privileged or falls within an exception to a privilege are decided under § 405 because this section favors withholding information from the fact finder that is either unreliable or whose exclusion is favored by public policy. True or false?

§ 17.04   THE BURDEN OF PROOF IN § 405 DETERMINATIONS

Section 405 does not prescribe the burden of proof that applies to the determination of the preliminary facts governed by the section. Instead, § 405 directs the judge to "the rule of law" under which the issue arises in allocating the burden of producing evidence and determining the burden of persuasion.[1]

Confessions provide a good example of how § 405 works. At one time, the California courts required the prosecution to prove beyond a reasonable doubt that the accused had properly waived his *Miranda* rights or had confessed voluntarily.[2] Accordingly, the "rule of law under which the issue" arose required the prosecution to meet this standard if the accused challenged a confession on *Miranda* or involuntariness grounds.

The standard of proof changed with the advent of Proposition 8's Right to Truth–in–Evidence provision. This provision gives parties to criminal proceedings the state constitutional right not to have relevant

---

35. Whether a judge should consider the hearsay declarant's motivation or that of the reporting witness in ruling on a hearsay objection is controversial. A few hearsay exceptions expressly authorize the judge to consider motivation. See § 9.01 supra. Most are silent on this point, and in the case of declarations against interest, the cases seem to be at odds with the Evidence Code. See id.

1.   West's Ann. California Evidence Code § 405.

2.   See People v. Stroud, 273 Cal.App.2d 670, 678, 78 Cal.Rptr. 270, 275 (1969) (holding that the prosecution must prove compliance with *Miranda* beyond a reasonable doubt); People v. Jimenez, 21 Cal.3d 595, 606, 147 Cal.Rptr. 172, 178, 580 P.2d 672, 678 (1978) (holding that the prosecution must prove voluntariness beyond a reasonable doubt).

evidence excluded.[3] Since a confession is legally relevant irrespective of whether it was taken in compliance with *Miranda* or given involuntarily, Proposition 8 overturned the cases requiring the preliminary facts to be proven beyond a reasonable doubt.[4]

Proposition 8, of course, cannot diminish federal constitutional rights. Today, the admissibility of evidence over a federal constitutional objection is determined by the standards the United States Supreme Court laid down in Lego v. Twomey.[5] In that case, the Court held that the accused is entitled to a "clear-cut" determination that his constitutional rights have been observed.[6] That demand can be met only by requiring the prosecution to prove compliance with the constitutional standards at least by a preponderance of the evidence.[7]

Proposition 8 also changed the burden of persuasion that applies when the accused challenges the legality of a pretrial identification. Prior to the initiative, the courts required the prosecution to prove by clear and convincing evidence that the in-court identification was free from the taint of any illegal pretrial identification.[8] Since federal standards now govern this question, the prosecution need prove only by a preponderance of the evidence that federal constitutional identification requirements were observed.

The "rule of law" applicable to a given preliminary fact dispute governed by § 405 may be silent with respect to the burdens of producing evidence and of persuasion. The Code provides two default positions on these questions. Section 115 provides that, unless otherwise provided by law, the burden of persuasion requires "proof by a preponderance of the evidence."[9] Section 550 in turn places the burden of producing evidence on a particular issue on the party with the burden of persuasion on that issue.[10] As a rule, then, unless the applicable rule of law states otherwise, the proponent must convince the judge by a preponderance of the evidence of the existence of the preliminary facts governed by § 405.

---

3. For an extended discussion of the Right to Truth–in–Evidence provision of Proposition 8, see § 15.03 supra.

4. People v. Kelly, 51 Cal.3d 931, 972, note 1, 275 Cal.Rptr. 160, 186, note 1, 800 P.2d 516, 541, note 1 (1990) (Mosk, J. concurring), cert. denied, 502 U.S. 842, 112 S.Ct. 134, 116 L.Ed.2d 101 (1991), reh'g denied, 502 U.S. 1000, 112 S.Ct. 624, 116 L.Ed.2d 646 (1991) (holding that compliance with *Miranda* need be shown only by a preponderance of the evidence); People v. Markham, 49 Cal.3d 63, 71, 260 Cal.Rptr. 273, 278, 775 P.2d 1042, 1047 (1989) (holding that voluntariness need be shown only by a preponderance of the evidence).

5. 404 U.S. 477, 92 S.Ct. 619, 30 L.Ed.2d 618 (1972).

6. Id. at 489, 92 S.Ct. at 627.

7. Id. See also Colorado v. Connelly, 479 U.S. 157, 168, 107 S.Ct. 515, 93 L.Ed.2d 473 (1986) (waiver of *Miranda* rights); United States v. Matlock, 415 U.S. 164, 177, 94 S.Ct. 988, 39 L.Ed.2d 242 (1974) (suppression motions raising Fourth Amendment questions). For a discussion of whether proof beyond a reasonable doubt should apply in determining the admissibility of confessions, dying declarations, and some declarations against interest, see Saltzburg, *Standards of Proof and Preliminary Questions of Fact*, 27 Stanford Law Review 271 (1975).

8. People v. Martin, 2 Cal.3d 822, 832, 87 Cal.Rptr. 709, 717, 471 P.2d 29, 37 (1970).

9. West's Ann. California Evidence Code § 115.

10. West's Ann. California Evidence Code § 550(b).

The Rules do not contain similar default provisions with respect to the allocation of the production and persuasion burdens governing preliminary fact determinations under Rule 104(a).[11] In the case of hearsay, however, the Rules place upon the objecting party the burden of persuading the judge that the proffered evidence is assertive and therefore hearsay.[12] Despite claims to the contrary, placing the burden of persuasion on the opponent is achieved by directive of the of Advisory Committee in its note and not by the language of Rule 801(a). The Code is silent on this point. Presumably, in California the proponent would have the burden of persuading the judge that the evidence is not assertive.[13]

Questions and Problems

1. At one time the California courts required the prosecution to prove beyond a reasonable doubt that the police complied with *Miranda* when the accused objected to the introduction of his confession on *Miranda* grounds. However, the Right-to-Truth in Evidence provision of Proposition 8 overturned these cases. Why?

But even after Proposition 8, the standard of proof for preliminary fact determinations governed by federal constitutional standards must at least comply with the federal standards. Accordingly, today California prosecutors must persuade a judge at least by a preponderance of the evidence that the officer complied with *Miranda* before interrogating the defendant. True or false?

2. When the "rule of law" applicable to a preliminary fact governed by § 405 is silent with respect to the burden of proof, how does a judge determine and allocate the burdens of producing evidence and persuasion?

§ 17.05 THE RULES OF EVIDENCE AND §§ 403 AND 405 DETERMINATIONS

The rules of evidence apply to hearings on the admissibility of evidence under §§ 403 and 405. The Law Revision Commission initially recommended that the rules not apply to determinations made under § 405.[1] That position, however, was not adopted by the Legislature.[2]

---

11. Professors Mueller and Kirkpatrick maintain that these burdens are generally on the proponent in federal court. "Aside from tradition and ease in application, there seem to be three reasons for this allocation. First, usually the offering party is best situated to explain and justify the evidence it chooses to present and can best aid the court in applying the rule in question. Second, the standard allocation is simply an outgrowth or particular application of the broader idea that a party who asks a court to do anything usually bears the burden of explaining and justifying the request. Third, this allocation is an aspect of the adversary system in which parties gather and present evidence, and part of the necessary burden is explaining and justifying consideration of the evidence." Mueller & Kirkpatrick, Evidence § 1.12 at 44 (Aspen 2d ed. 1999).

12. Federal Rule of Evidence 801 (Advisory Committee Note).

13. See text accompanying note 7, supra, in Méndez, *I. Hearsay and Its Exceptions: Conforming the Evidence Code to the Federal Rules*, 37 U.S.F. Law Review 351, 353 (2003).

1. 6 California Law Revision Commission, Reports, Recommendations, and Studies 19 (1964).

2. See the wording of West's Ann. California Evidence Code § 405.

The Commission was concerned that applying the rules could result in the exclusion of reliable hearsay statements:

> For example, if witness *W* hears *X* shout, "Help! I'm falling down the stairs!", the statement is admissible only if the judge finds that *X* actually was falling down the stairs while the statement was being made. If the only evidence that he was falling down the stairs is the statement itself, or the statements of bystanders who no longer can be identified, the statement must be excluded. Although the statement is admissible as a substantive matter under the hearsay rule, it must be held inadmissible if the formal rules of evidence are rigidly applied during the judge's preliminary inquiry.[3]

In the Commission's view, the rules of evidence were developed largely to protect jurors untrained in the law from weak and unreliable evidence.[4] Judges need no such protection. The Legislature, however, declined to adopt the Commission's recommendation.

The drafters of the Federal Rules of Evidence adopted the position espoused by the Commission and others. The Rules provide that in determining preliminary questions concerning the admissibility of evidence, the judge "is not bound by the evidence rules, except those on privilege."[5] The federal approach allows the judge to consider a hearsay declaration as proof of the foundation elements of a hearsay exception. But whether the declaration alone should suffice as proof of the foundational facts has been controversial. In 1997 Congress amended Rule 801(d)(2) to provide that "the statement must be considered but does not by itself establish the declarant's authority under (C), the existence or scope of the relationship under (D), or the existence of the conspiracy or participation in it under (E)."[6] These subdivisions refer to the hearsay exemptions for authorized admissions, admissions by agents and servants, and coconspirators' admissions.[7]

QUESTIONS AND PROBLEMS

Reconsider your answers to the problems following § 7.04, supra, in light of this section.

§ 17.06 CONDITIONAL ADMISSIBILITY

Sometimes the relevance of an item of evidence depends on the proof of other facts. For example, in an action for breach of a written contract, the relevance of a contract tendered by the plaintiff will depend on whether it was the contract entered into by the defendant. If the contract

---

3. 6 California Law Revision Commission, Reports, Recommendations, and Studies 20 (1964).

4. Id.

5. Federal Rule of Evidence 104(a).

6. Federal Rule of Evidence 801(d)(2).

7. Id.

was signed by someone other than the defendant, then the relevance of the contract will depend on whether the person signing was authorized to do so by the defendant.[1] Absent evidence that the defendant entered into the contract or that it was signed by an agent authorized to do so, the contract would be irrelevant. It would be wholly unconnected with the defendant and, therefore, immaterial.

Section 403 of the Evidence Code places upon the proponent of the evidence (the plaintiff in our example) the burden of producing evidence of the facts connecting the contract with the defendant.[2] Against the objection of the opposing party, the proponent of the proffered evidence must usually produce the evidence of the preliminary facts (the connecting evidence) before the proffered evidence (the contract) can be received in evidence.[3] However, the trial judge may admit the proffered evidence on the condition that the proponent supply the evidence of the preliminary or connecting facts before the close of the evidence.[4]

If the proffered evidence is received, the judge may, and upon request of the opposing party, must instruct the jury to disregard the proffered evidence unless the jury first finds the preliminary facts.[5] The instruction insures that the judge's conclusion about the existence of the preliminary fact will not deprive the opponent of a jury determination of the issue.

The Federal Rules also permit the judge to receive evidence on a conditional basis.[6] Like § 403, the Federal Rules impose a sufficiency test. Upon the opponent's motion, the judge must strike the evidence unless the proponent introduces evidence "sufficient to support a finding that the fact does exist."[7] The major difference between the Rules and the Code is that the Rules do not contain a provision regarding the limiting instruction. Giving such an instruction is the product of federal trial practice.

Questions and Problems

1. A judge has discretion to admit an item of evidence subject to a motion to strike if the proponent fails to introduce evidence showing the item's relevance before the close of the evidence. In a breach of contract action, for example, a judge may admit the document the plaintiff claims is the contract, subject to a motion to strike the document from the evidence if before the close of the evidence the plaintiff fails to offer evidence that the

---

1. Brown v. Spencer, 163 Cal. 589, 126 P. 493 (1912).

2. West's Ann. California Evidence Code § 403(a).

3. Id.

4. West's Ann. California Evidence Code § 403(b). No such discretion exists when the opposing party objects to evidence on the ground that the witness does not possess the requisite personal knowledge. Against such an objection, the proponent must show that the witness possesses the required personal knowledge before the witness may continue with his testimony. West's Ann. California Evidence Code § 702; Federal Rule of Evidence 602.

5. West's Ann. California Evidence Code § 403(c)(1).

6. Federal Rule of Evidence 104(b).

7. Id. For a discussion of the special meaning given to the term "conditional relevance" under the Federal Rules, see § 17.02 supra.

document received in evidence is the contract signed by the parties. True or false?

2. The judge's discretion extends to objections protesting a witness's lack of personal knowledge. True or false?

§ 17.07 PRELIMINARY FACT DETERMINA-TIONS INVOLVING ULTIMATE ISSUES

Section 405 allows judges to withhold evidence from the jury based on their resolution of conflicts in the evidence of the preliminary facts and on their assessment of the credibility of the witnesses called to prove or disprove the preliminary facts.[1] The judges' broad powers to pass on preliminary fact questions governed by § 405 are justified by the purposes of the section. Section 405 is "designed to withhold evidence from the jury because it is too unreliable or because public policy requires its exclusion."[2]

These broad powers sometimes can threaten a party's right to jury determinations of factual issues whenever the preliminary fact issue is also an issue involved in the merits of the case. In a contract action, for example, one of the issues may be the existence of the contract. The defendant's position might be that the signature on the contract is not his. Whether or not the signature on the contract is the defendant's calls for § 403 determination.[3] The judge's role in deciding the question will not threaten the parties' right to a jury decision on the issue because § 403 requires the judge to apply a sufficiency standard in ruling on the admissibility of the contract.[4]

Suppose, however, that the plaintiff offers in evidence, not the original contract, but a copy authenticated as a true copy of the original on the theory that the original was lost through no fault of the plaintiff. Under the California Secondary Evidence Rule, the plaintiff may offer a copy, unless the defendant disputes the existence of the original.[5] Whether the original was lost as claimed by the plaintiff or never existed as claimed by the defendant is governed by § 405. A ruling in favor of the plaintiff could imply a finding of the existence of the contract. To avoid contaminating the jurors with his ruling, the Code prohibits the judge from informing them about the basis of his or her ruling.[6]

But a ruling in favor of the defendant would result in a verdict in the defendant's favor without the question of the existence or nonexistence of the contract ever getting to the jury. To avoid this outcome, the Federal Rules provide that "in a jury trial, the jury determines—in accordance

---

1. See § 17.01 supra.
2. West's Ann. California Evidence Code § 405 (comment).
3. See § 17.02 supra.
4. Id.
5. West's Ann. California Evidence Code §§ 1520–1521.
6. West's Ann. California Evidence Code § 405(b)(1).

with Rule 104(b)—any issue about whether: (a) an asserted writing, recording, or photograph ever existed; (b) another one produced at the trial or hearing is the original; or (c) other evidence of content accurately reflects the content."[7]

The Code does not have a similar provision. Instead, the California Secondary Evidence Rule empowers judges to exclude secondary evidence of the content of a writing if the judge concludes that a genuine dispute exists concerning the material terms of the writing and justice requires its exclusion.[8] Since exclusion of secondary evidence could result in a directed verdict in favor of the objecting party whenever a disputed material term is dispositive, consideration should be given to adopting the federal approach.[9]

Judges have discretion to hold hearings on the admissibility of evidence out of the presence or hearing of the jury.[10] But challenges to the admissibility of confessions and admissions in criminal cases must be held out of the jury's presence if requested by any party.[11] The purpose is to avoid prejudicing the accused in the event the confession or admission is excluded. The Federal Rules go farther. The presence of the jurors does not depend on a request by party. Hearings on the admissibility of confessions in all cases must be conducted out of the hearing of the jury.[12]

Holding hearings out of the presence of the jury can result in the duplication of evidence. Take a confession which the accused claims was coerced. If the judge rules against the accused at the § 402 hearing[13] and admits the confession, the accused is still entitled to urge the jury to give little or no weight to the confession because it was coerced.[14] To make that argument in summation, the accused must be given an opportunity to produce the evidence of coercion before the jury.[15] The parties will have to reproduce before the jury much of the evidence they produced before the judge.

QUESTIONS AND PROBLEMS

1. The plaintiff sues the defendant in federal court for breach of contract. At the trial, the plaintiff offers as an exhibit what she claims is a

7. Federal Rule of Evidence 1008.

8. West's Ann. California Evidence Code § 1521.

9. See Kaplan, *Of Mabrus and Zorgs*, 66 California Law Review 987, 995 (1978) (pointing out that, under California's old Best Evidence Rule, the Code failed to confer upon California jurors the powers given by the Rule 1008 to federal jurors).

10. West's Ann. California Evidence Code § 402(b); Federal Rule of Evidence 104(c).

11. West's Ann. California Evidence Code § 402(b); Federal Rule of Evidence 104(c). No request is necessary under the Federal Rules. Federal Rule of Evidence 104(c).

12. Federal Rule of Evidence 104(c).

13. Hearings on the admissibility of evidence under §§ 403 and 405 are sometimes denominated "402 hearings" because it is § 402 which authorizes the use of hearings on admissibility to take place out of the presence of the jury. West's Ann. California Evidence Code § 402.

14. West's Ann. California Evidence Code § 406.

15. Id.

true copy of the contract the defendant breached. The plaintiff justifies the use of a copy on the ground that the original contract was lost through no fault on her part. The defendant objects to the copy on the ground that there was never "an original" contract. The judge must exclude the copy unless the plaintiff persuades the judge by a preponderance of the evidence of the existence of the original contract. True or false?

2. If a judge rules a confession voluntary and thus admissible in a hearing outside the presence of the jurors, the judge must give the accused an opportunity to present evidence to the jurors about why the confession is unreliable. True or false?

3. Assume that the answer to the preceding question is "true". Since in effect the jurors are given an opportunity to redetermine the admissibility of the confession, they should be told by the judge to disregard such a confession unless they first find it to have been given voluntarily. True or false?

§ 17.08 LIMITING INSTRUCTIONS AND § 403 DETERMINATIONS

If the judge admits the proffered evidence under § 403, the judge "may, and on request shall, instruct the jury" to disregard the proffered evidence unless the jury first finds the preliminary fact.[1] Section 403, however, is silent on two important questions: (1) Must all the jurors agree on the existence or nonexistence of the preliminary fact? (2) By what standard of persuasion must the jurors find the existence or nonexistence of the preliminary fact?

Since jury unanimity is not required in California civil cases,[2] presumably jury unanimity is not required in finding preliminary facts in civil matters. The same number needed to return a verdict should suffice in finding preliminary facts. And since jurors can return verdicts based on the preponderance of the evidence in most civil proceedings,[3] presumably that standard applies in those proceedings at least with respect to preliminary facts that are also elements of the claim or defense.

In California, jury unanimity is required in criminal cases.[4] Presumably, then, jury unanimity is also required in finding preliminary facts in such cases. In California, as elsewhere, jurors can return a guilty verdict only if they find the accused guilty beyond a reasonable doubt.[5] Presumably, that standard of persuasion applies to preliminary facts that are also elements of the offense. But the standard may apply to other preliminary facts. At least where circumstantial evidence has been received, jurors are told that "each fact which is essential to complete a set of circumstances necessary to establish guilt must be proved beyond a reasonable doubt. In

1. West's Ann. California Evidence Code § 403(c)(1).
2. West's Ann. California Constitution Article 1, § 16.
3. West's Ann. California Evidence Code § 115.
4. West's Ann. California Constitution Article 1, § 16.
5. West's Ann. California Penal Code § 1096.

other words, before an inference essential to establish guilt may be found to have been proved beyond a reasonable doubt, each fact or circumstance upon which such inference necessarily rests must be proved beyond a reasonable doubt."[6]

But some California cases suggest that facts found and used by jurors in a chain of reasoning leading to a guilty verdict can be found by a preponderance of the evidence. For example, California jurors are routinely told to disregard evidence of uncharged misdeeds unless they first find by a preponderance of the evidence that the misdeed was committed.[7] In its note, the Committee on Standard Jury Instructions, Criminal, acknowledges a conceivable conflict between this instruction and the one requiring jurors to find beyond a reasonable doubt each circumstance upon which inferences rest.[8] Other cases hold that in screening the evidence under § 403, a judge should withhold the evidence from the jury unless the judge finds that a reasonable jury could find the preliminary fact in issue by a preponderance of the evidence.[9] Under this standard, a judge would withhold a co-conspirator's declaration from the jury unless the proponent proffers "sufficient evidence to allow the trier of fact to determine that the conspiracy exists by a preponderance of the evidence."[10] This is the sufficiency test which federal judges must employ.[11]

The addition of the more likely than not standard probably adds little to the traditional sufficiency test since the test is still heavily tilted in favor of admissibility. For purposes of admissibility, the question for California trial judges under Proposition 8 would appear to be whether a reasonable juror could find that a conspiracy existed if the proponent's evidence is believed. Subject to certain exceptions, Proposition 8 requires the admission of relevant evidence as a matter of state constitutional right in California criminal cases.[12] Whether jurors should be instructed to disregard the evidence *after* it has been admitted unless they find the conspiracy or other preliminary fact by some higher standard is a separate question and presumably not one governed by Proposition 8.

The Federal Rules contain no general provisions on limiting instructions.[13] Federal judges gives these as a result of established practice and not as a result of a specific rule.

---

6. CALJIC 2.01 (Fall 2006 Edition).

7. See CALJIC 2.50.1 (Fall 2006 Edition).

8. Id.

9. See, e.g., People v. Simon, 184 Cal.App.3d 125, 132, 228 Cal.Rptr. 855, 860 (1986) and cases cited therein.

10. See People v. Herrera, 83 Cal.App.4th 46, 64, 98 Cal.Rptr.2d 911, 922 (2000) and cases cited therein.

11. See Huddleston v. United States, 485 U.S. 681, 687, 108 S.Ct. 1496, 99 L.Ed.2d 771 (1988).

12. For a discussion of Proposition 8, see § 3.07 supra.

13. The Federal Rules contain a specific provision concerning the limited admissibility of evidence. Federal Rule of Evidence 105, like California Evidence Code § 355, provides that "if the court admits evidence that is admissible against a party or for a purpose—but not against another

§ 17.09   OTHER PROVISIONS RELATING TO ADMISSIBILITY

Under the Code, questions of law, including questions concerning the admissibility of evidence and other rules of evidence, are for the court.[1] Federal Rule of Evidence 104(a) captures this principle. Under the Code, questions of fact are to be decided by the jury, including the effect and value of the evidence addressed to it and the credibility of witnesses and hearsay declarants.[2] The Rules do not have an analogous provision, but an explicit rule is unnecessary because, as has been noted, the Common Law preserves fact questions for determination by jurors.

Under the Code, a person claiming the federal or state self-incrimination privilege has the burden of showing that the proffered evidence might tend to incriminate him or her.[3] The proffered evidence is inadmissible unless "it clearly appears to the court that the proffered evidence cannot possibly have a tendency to incriminate the person claiming the privilege."[4] The Rules do not have an equivalent provision. Presumably, in federal court the privilege claimant would rely federal cases defining the witness privilege under the Self–Incrimination Clause of the Fifth Amendment.

Under the Code and the Rules, judges have discretion to determine whether hearings on preliminary fact questions should be conducted out of the presence or hearing of the jury.[5] But the Rules mandate all hearings on the admissibility of confessions to be held outside the hearing of the jury.[6] The Code requires such a hearing only upon request by a party.[7] The Rules provide that the "[b]y testifying on a preliminary question, a defendant in a criminal case does not become subject to cross-examination on other issues in the case."[8] The Code is silent on this point.

Both the Code and the Rules specify that the provisions governing preliminary fact questions do not limit the right of a party to introduce before the jury evidence relevant to weight or credibility.[9] As has been noted, the admission of proffered evidence often requires the parties at trial to offer much of the same evidence received at the admissibility hearing in order to afford the jurors a basis for determining the weight to be given to the evidence.[10]

---

party or for another purpose—the court, on timely request, must restrict the evidence to its proper scope and instruct the jury accordingly."

1. West's Ann. California Evidence Code § 310.

2. West's Ann. California Evidence Code § 312.

3. West's Ann. California Evidence Code § 404.

4. Id.

5. West's Ann. California Evidence Code § 402; Federal Rule of Evidence 104(c).

6. Federal Rule of Evidence 104 (c).

7. West's Ann. California Evidence Code § 402(b).

8. Federal Rule of Evidence 104(d).

9. West's Ann. California Evidence Code § 406; Federal Rule of Evidence 104(e).

10. See text accompanying note 13, § 17.07 supra.

§ 17.10 PRELIMINARY FACT DETERMINATIONS UNDER THE FEDERAL RULES OF EVIDENCE

As has been highlighted in the previous sections, the Code and the Federal Rules differ in some important respects with regard to the role of the judge in admitting evidence. Both the Code and Rules agree that judges should exercise different screening powers in determining the admissibility of evidence. To preserve the jury's fact finding function, both require judges to use a sufficiency standard in determining the admissibility of certain kinds of evidence. By specifying the kinds of preliminary fact disputes subject to this standard, § 403 provides judges and parties greater guidance than does Rule 104(b)'s conditional relevance approach.

To assure the exclusion of evidence disfavored by the rules, both the Code and the Rules give judges greater screening powers. The Code achieves this goal by making § 405 a default provision. If the preliminary fact dispute is not governed by § 403, it falls within the ambit of § 405. If the "rule of law" governing the § 405 dispute does not specify the burden of proof, other Code default provisions require the proponent to come forward with proof that convinces the judge by a preponderance of the evidence of the existence or nonexistence of the disputed preliminary fact.

Rule 104(a) is also a default provision. In determining the admissibility of evidence, the federal judge is to exercise the powers conferred by this subdivision unless the preliminary fact question is governed by Rule 104(b)'s conditional relevancy provision. While § 405 does not attempt to specify the kinds of preliminary fact questions falling within the section, Rule 104(a) expressly provides that preliminary questions concerning the qualification of a person to be a witness, the existence of a privilege, or the admissibility of evidence are to be determined under subdivision (a) unless the question is governed by Rule 104(b).

The Code makes up for § 405's lack of specificity by extensive discussion in the comments to §§ 403 and 405 about the kinds of preliminary facts falling within each section. The detailed comments provide judges and parties with greater guidance than do Rule 104 and its note. Although reasonable people can differ about whether the foundational facts for some hearsay exceptions should be proved only by a sufficiency standard or by a higher standard, in their comments the drafters of the Code make clear their election to treat some of these facts as raising only a sufficiency issue.

The Rules do not specify which burden of persuasion applies when the preliminary fact question is not governed by the sufficiency standard. The

United States Supreme Court, however, has "traditionally required that these matters be established by a preponderance of proof."[1]

The Code and the Rules are at odds with respect to the kind of evidence that can be received to prove the existence or nonexistence of preliminary facts when the judge is asked to make the admissibility determinations contemplated by § 405 and Rule 104(a). Under the Rules, the judge "is not bound by evidence rules, except those on privilege."[2] Under the Code, the rules of evidence apply.

Section 403 of the Code requires judges to give jurors limiting instructions when jurors are asked to redetermine the existence of preliminary facts. The Rules do not have an equivalent provision; federal judges, however, customarily give such instructions.

Finally, the Rules provide that in the case of some Best Evidence Rule objections, the judge must allow the disputed preliminary fact to go to the jury under a sufficiency standard when the issue is also a question in the merits of the case. The related California provision does not go this far with respect to similar questions raised under California's Secondary Evidence Rule.

§ 17.11 JURY INSTRUCTIONS: ALLOCATING POWER BETWEEN JUDGE AND JURY

Judges are charged with the task of instructing the jurors on the law that governs the case.[1] If requested by either party, the judge must instruct the jury on any pertinent points of law.[2] Judges, however, may refuse to give instructions that are not supported by the evidence.[3] But unless this discretion is circumscribed, withholding an instruction may deprive a party of the right to have the jurors determine the issue.

The California Supreme Court explored the problem in People v. Flannel.[4] In a murder prosecution, the accused requested the judge to instruct the jury on the effects of intoxication. The accused asked the

---

1. Bourjaily v. United States, 483 U.S. 171, 175, 107 S.Ct. 2775, 97 L.Ed.2d 144 (1987).

2. Federal Rule of Evidence 104(a).

1. West's Ann. California Penal Code § 1093(f); West's Ann. California Civil Procedure Code § 607(9); Federal Rule of Civil Procedure 51; Federal Rule of Criminal Procedure 30.

In California, a judge must instruct the jurors sua sponte on the "general principles of law that are closely and openly connected with the facts presented at trial." People v. Lopez, 19 Cal.4th 282, 287, 79 Cal.Rptr.2d 195, 197–98, 965 P.2d 713, 715–16 (1998). In criminal cases, the sua sponte obligation extends to instructing on lesser included offenses, even over the accused's objection. Id.

An offense is a lesser included offense if it meets one of two tests: (1) when all of the elements of the lesser are included in the definition of the charged offense or (2) when the charging allegations of the accusatory pleading include language describing the charged offense in such a way that if committed as specified the lesser offense is necessarily committed. Id.

2. West's Ann. California Penal Code § 1093(f); West's Ann. California Civil Procedure Code § 607(9); Federal Rule of Civil Procedure 51; Federal Rule of Criminal Procedure 30.

3. People v. Brown, 40 Cal.3d 512, 533, 230 Cal.Rptr. 834, 843, 726 P.2d 516, 525 (1985).

4. 25 Cal.3d 668, 160 Cal.Rptr. 84, 603 P.2d 1 (1979).

judge to tell the jurors to acquit him of murder and voluntary manslaughter if the evidence of intoxication raised a reasonable doubt about his ability to harbor the mens rea of either offense by reason of his having been intoxicated at the time he delivered the lethal blow.[5] In reviewing the trial judge's refusal to give the requested instruction, the California Supreme Court set out the standard judges are to use in ruling on instructions that must be supported by the evidence:

> If defendant proffers evidence enough to deserve consideration by the jury, i.e., "evidence from which a jury composed of reasonable men could have concluded that there was diminished capacity sufficient to negate the requisite criminal intent" * * *, the trial court must so instruct. A trial court should not, however, measure the substantiality of the evidence by undertaking to weigh the credibility of the witnesses, a task exclusively relegated to the jury. If the evidence should prove minimal and insubstantial, however, the court need not instruct on its effect. * * * In other words, "[t]he court should instruct the jury on every theory of the case, but only to the extent each is supported by substantial evidence." * * * We likewise note that "[d]oubts as to the sufficiency of the evidence to warrant instructions should be resolved in favor of the accused."[6]

The court is correct in pointing out that trial judges should employ a sufficiency test. Giving judges greater power would risk depriving parties of their right to a jury determination of contested factual matters. This is why preliminary fact disputes governed by § 403[7] and motions for directed verdicts[8] are determined by a sufficiency standard. Indeed, this is also why appellate judges apply a sufficiency standard in determining whether a verdict is supported by the evidence.[9] Giving judges the power to decide these issues by a higher standard would overturn the traditional allocation of power between judge and jury, and raise serious constitutional questions.

The difficulty with *Flannel* stems from the court's departure from the traditional formulation of the sufficiency test. In the context of jury instructions, the sufficiency standard requires the judge to view the evidence in the light most favorable to the party requesting the instruc-

---

5. Id. at 685, 160 Cal.Rptr. at 94, 603 P.2d at 11.

6. Id. at 684–685, 160 Cal.Rptr. at 93, 603 P.2d at 10 (footnotes omitted).

7. See § 17.01 supra.

8. See § 18.04 infra.

9. See § 18.09 infra. "To determine whether there is substantial evidence to support a conviction we must view the record in a light most favorable to conviction, resolving all conflicts in the evidence and drawing all reasonable inferences in support of conviction. We may conclude that there is no substantial evidence in support of conviction only if it can be said that on the evidence presented no reasonable factfinder could find the defendant to be guilty on the theory presented." People v. Nguyen, 21 Cal.App.4th 518, 528–529, 26 Cal.Rptr.2d 323, 329 (1993).

Jeopardy attaches to an order dismissing a prosecution on the basis of insufficiency of evidence. It is immaterial whether the order of dismissal is granted explicitly by the trial court during the course of the trial or implicitly by the appellate court in its order reversing the judgment of conviction for insufficiency of evidence. See Burks v. United States, 437 U.S. 1, 16, 98 S.Ct. 2141, 2150, 57 L.Ed.2d 1 (1978).

tion.[10] This means that the judge must accept the evidence most favorable to the requesting party as true and must disregard conflicting evidence.[11] It also means that the judge can draw only those inferences from the evidence which are most favorable to the requesting party.[12] The question for the judge is whether a reasonable jury could find the desired fact if the evidence of the party requesting the instruction is believed. If, after considering the evidence in this light, the judge believes that a reasonable jury could find the desired fact or is unsure whether the jury could find the fact, the judge must let the issue go the jury. Under those circumstances, it is up to the jury to determine the existence of the facts upon which jury instructions are given.

In *Flannel*, however, the court introduced the concept that the trial judge can withhold an instruction from the jury if the judge concludes that the evidence is "minimal and insubstantial". How a judge can do that without weighing the evidence of the desired fact against the evidence contradicting the fact is a mystery. Indeed, in *Flannel* the court engaged in the very weighing it said was improper. It found the accused's evidence of intoxication insubstantial when weighed against the conflicting testimony of other witnesses and the accused's own "equivocal" testimony about his state of sobriety.[13] The undiluted sufficiency test would have required the court to disregard the conflicting evidence and to assume the truth of the accused's testimony. Perhaps, the jury would have convicted Mr. Flannel in any event. But he should not have been deprived of the opportunity to have the jury determine whether his intoxication raised a reasonable doubt about his guilt of the offenses charged.

Flannel's departure from the traditional sufficiency standard is wrong. Judges who follow this aspect of *Flannel* risk denying parties the right to have a jury determine material factual issues. Fortunately, since its *Flannel* decision, the California Supreme Court has reaffirmed the rule that in evaluating the evidence to determine whether a requested instruction should be given, the trial judge should not measure the substantiality of the evidence by weighing the credibility of the witnesses.[14]

---

10. See, e.g., Campbell v. General Motors Corp., 32 Cal.3d 112, 118, 184 Cal.Rptr. 891, 894, 649 P.2d 224, 227 (1982) and cases cited therein. See also Maxwell v. Powers, 22 Cal.App.4th 1596, 1607, 28 Cal.Rptr.2d 62, 68 (1994) ("Parties have the 'right to have the jury instructed as to the law applicable to all their theories of the case which [are] supported by the pleadings and the evidence, whether or not that evidence [is] considered persuasive by the trial court.' ") (quoting from Fish v. Los Angeles Dodgers Baseball Club, 56 Cal.App.3d 620, 633, 128 Cal.Rptr. 807, 817 (1976), disapproved on other grounds, Soule v. General Motors Corp., 8 Cal.4th 548, 34 Cal.Rptr.2d 607, 882 P.2d 298 (1994)).

11. See, e.g., Campbell v. General Motors Corp., 32 Cal.3d 112, 118, 184 Cal.Rptr. 891, 894, 649 P.2d 224, 227 (1982) and cases cited therein.

12. Id.

13. People v. Flannel, 25 Cal.3d 668, 685–689, 160 Cal.Rptr. 84, 91, 603 P.2d 1, 11 (1979).

14. See People v. Tufunga, 21 Cal.4th 935, 944, 90 Cal.Rptr.2d 143, 149, 987 P.2d 168, 173 (1999). Some divisions of the California Court of Appeal have also followed suit. See, e.g., People v. Lee, 131 Cal.App.4th 1413, 1426, 32 Cal.Rptr.3d 745, 754 (2005) (holding that trial judges should disregard the opponent's evidence in determining whether the proponent's evidence warrants the giving of an instruction).

QUESTIONS AND PROBLEMS

Explain why *Flannel*'s deviation from the classical formulation of the sufficiency standard threatens to deprive parties of their right to a jury determination of contested material factual issues.

§ 17.12   WITNESS EXAMINATION: ALLOCATING POWER BETWEEN COUNSEL AND JURY

The rules of evidence do not operate in a vacuum. They operate in an adversarial system which is dependent on party initiative. By calling and examining the witnesses, the parties by and large determine who will testify and what the witnesses will say on the stand.[1] The parties and their lawyers are the activists in Common Law trials; their actions are the key determinants in how trials unfold.

Jurors, on the other hand, are passive observers. Although they are the judges of the facts, their role in the production of evidence has been nonexistent until recent times. Their cognitive needs are the subject of the lawyers' speculations. Though counsel structure their examinations with the jurors' needs in mind, they must necessarily guess, since jurors are not encouraged to make their needs known. This state of affairs is now beginning to change.

Many jurisdictions, including California[2] and the Ninth Circuit,[3] permit jurors to ask witnesses questions.[4]

> There is nothing improper about the practice of allowing occasional questions from jurors to be asked of witnesses. If a juror is unclear as to a point in the proof, it makes good sense to allow questions to be asked about it. If nothing else, the question should alert trial counsel that a particular factual issue may need more extensive development. Trials exist to develop truth. It may sometimes be that counsel are so familiar with a case that they fail to see problems that would naturally bother a juror who is presented with the facts the first time.[5]

---

1. Judges can also call and interrogate witnesses, West's Ann. California Evidence Code § 775, and question witnesses called by the parties. See also Federal Rule of Evidence 610. But judges usually do not exercise these powers; they leave the calling and interrogation of witnesses to the parties. Judges may interrogate witness to aid in eliciting the truth, in preventing misunderstandings, in clarifying testimony, and covering omissions. In doing so, judges must be temperate and scrupulously fair, and must not distort the record or expressly or impliedly direct a verdict. See People v. Harris, 37 Cal.4th 310, 349, 33 Cal.Rptr.3d 509, 541, 118 P.3d 545, 572 (2005), cert. denied 547 U.S. 1065, 126 S.Ct. 1655, 164 L.Ed.2d 411 (2006).

2. People v. McAlister, 167 Cal.App.3d 633, 644, 213 Cal.Rptr. 271, 276 (1985).

3. United States v. Gonzales, 424 F.2d 1055, 1056 (9th Cir.1970).

4. For a list of these jurisdictions, see Allen v. State, 807 S.W.2d 639, 640–641 (Tex.App.1991) rev'd, 845 S.W.2d 907 (Tex.Crim.App.1993).

5. United States v. Callahan, 588 F.2d 1078, 1086 (5th Cir.1979), cert. denied, 444 U.S. 826, 100 S.Ct. 49, 62 L.Ed.2d 33 (1979).

California courts, while permitting the practice, do not encourage it because of the risks it poses.[6] These include placing counsel in the "intolerable position" of offending a juror by objecting to his questions or permitting improper and possibly prejudicial testimony to be received without objection,[7] lessening a juror's objectivity because of the juror's involvement in the examination of witnesses,[8] and producing tension or actual antagonism in the juror as a result of the interaction between the juror and the witnesses.[9]

To diminish these risks, the trial judge should have the jurors write down their questions.[10] At a hearing out of the presence of the jurors and witnesses, the judge and counsel should screen the questions.[11] Only those questions found to be proper should be asked of the witness,[12] and the judge, not the jurors, should pose the questions to the witness.[13] Following the witness's answer, the parties should be allowed to ask follow-up questions.[14]

CALIFORNIA EVIDENCE CODE

§ 400. "Preliminary fact"

As used in this article, "preliminary fact" means a fact upon the existence or nonexistence of which depends the admissibility or inadmissibility of evidence. The phrase "the admissibility or inadmissibility of evidence" includes the qualification or disqualification of a person to be a witness and the existence or nonexistence of a privilege.

§ 401. "Proffered evidence"

As used in this article, "proffered evidence" means evidence, the admissibility or inadmissibility of which is dependent upon the existence or nonexistence of a preliminary fact.

---

6. People v. McAlister, 167 Cal.App.3d 633, 645, 213 Cal.Rptr. 271, 277 (1985).

7. Id.

8. Id.

9. Id.

10. Id. at 644, 213 Cal.Rptr. at 276.

11. Allen v. Texas, 807 S.W.2d 639, 641 (Tex.App.1991) rev'd, 845 S.W.2d 907 (Tex.Crim.App. 1993) (holding that only the Texas Court of Criminal Appeals and the Legislature have competence to adopt a rule allowing jurors to ask witnesses questions in criminal cases).

12. People v. McAlister, 167 Cal.App.3d 633, 644, 213 Cal.Rptr. 271, 276 (1985). If the judge permits the jurors to ask questions without first screening them, at least in a criminal case a party may complain on appeal about the impropriety of the questions even though the party did not object at the time the question was asked. Id.

13. Some California cases have approved of a procedure allowing the lawyers to ask the questions that have been screened by the judge and counsel. The lawyer for the party calling the witness gets to ask the questions. See People v. Majors, 18 Cal.4th 385, 407, 75 Cal.Rptr.2d 684, 699, 956 P.2d 1137, 1152 (1998) and cases cited therein.

14. People v. McAlister, 167 Cal.App.3d 633, 645, 213 Cal.Rptr. 271, 277 (1985).

§ 402. Procedure for determining foundational and other preliminary facts

(a) When the existence of a preliminary fact is disputed, its existence or nonexistence shall be determined as provided in this article.

(b) The court may hear and determine the question of the admissibility of evidence out of the presence or hearing of the jury; but in a criminal action, the court shall hear and determine the question of the admissibility of a confession or admission of the defendant out of the presence and hearing of the jury if any party so requests.

(c) A ruling on the admissibility of evidence implies whatever finding of fact is prerequisite thereto; a separate or formal finding is unnecessary unless required by statute.

§ 403. Determination of foundational and other preliminary facts where relevancy, personal knowledge, or authenticity is disputed

(a) The proponent of the proffered evidence has the burden of producing evidence as to the existence of the preliminary fact, and the proffered evidence is inadmissible unless the court finds that there is evidence sufficient to sustain a finding of the existence of the preliminary fact, when:

(1) The relevance of the proffered evidence depends on the existence of the preliminary fact;

(2) The preliminary fact is the personal knowledge of a witness concerning the subject matter of his testimony;

(3) The preliminary fact is the authenticity of a writing; or

(4) The proffered evidence is of a statement or other conduct of a particular person and the preliminary fact is whether that person made the statement or so conducted himself.

(b) Subject to Section 702, the court may admit conditionally the proffered evidence under this section, subject to evidence of the preliminary fact being supplied later in the course of the trial.

(c) If the court admits the proffered evidence under this section, the court:

(1) May, and on request shall, instruct the jury to determine whether the preliminary fact exists and to disregard the proffered evidence unless the jury finds that the preliminary fact does exist.

(2) Shall instruct the jury to disregard the proffered evidence if the court subsequently determines that a jury could not reasonably find that the preliminary fact exists.

§ 404. Determination of whether proffered evidence is incriminatory

Whenever the proffered evidence is claimed to be privileged under Section 940, the person claiming the privilege has the burden of showing that the proffered evidence might tend to incriminate him; and the proffered evidence is inadmissible unless it clearly appears to the court that the proffered evidence cannot possibly have a tendency to incriminate the person claiming the privilege.

§ 405. Determination of foundational and other preliminary facts in other cases

With respect to preliminary fact determinations not governed by Section 403 or 404:

(a) When the existence of a preliminary fact is disputed, the court shall indicate which party has the burden of producing evidence and the burden of proof on the issue as implied by the rule of law under which the question arises. The court shall determine the existence or nonexistence of the preliminary fact and shall admit or exclude the proffered evidence as required by the rule of law under which the question arises.

(b) If a preliminary fact is also a fact in issue in the action:

(1) The jury shall not be informed of the court's determination as to the existence or nonexistence of the preliminary fact.

(2) If the proffered evidence is admitted, the jury shall not be instructed to disregard the evidence if its determination of the fact differs from the court's determination of the preliminary fact.

§ 406. Evidence affecting weight or credibility

This article does not limit the right of a party to introduce before the trier of fact evidence relevant to weight or credibility.

FEDERAL RULES OF EVIDENCE

Rule 104. Preliminary Questions

(a) In General. The court must decide any preliminary question about whether a witness is qualified, a privilege exists, or evidence is admissible. In so deciding, the court is not bound by evidence rules, except those on privilege.

(b) Relevance That Depends on a Fact. When the relevance of evidence depends on whether a fact exists, proof must be introduced sufficient to support a finding that the fact does exist. The court may admit the proposed evidence on the condition that the proof be introduced later.

(c) Conducting a Hearing So That the Jury Cannot Hear It. The court must conduct any hearing on a preliminary question so that the jury cannot hear it if:

(1) the hearing involves the admissibility of a confession;

(2) a defendant in a criminal case is a witness and so requests; or

(3) justice so requires.

(d) Cross–Examining a Defendant in a Criminal Case. By testifying on a preliminary question, a defendant in a criminal case does not become subject to cross-examination on other issues in the case.

(e) Evidence Relevant to Weight and Credibility. This rule does not limit a party's right to introduce before the jury evidence that is relevant to the weight or credibility of other evidence.

CHAPTER 18

PRESUMPTIONS AND BURDEN OF PROOF

■ ■ ■

Table of Sections

§ 18.01 BURDEN OF PROOF

The term "burden of proof" refers to two distinct burdens: the burden of producing evidence[1] and the burden of persuasion.[2] In a criminal case, for example, the prosecution has both burdens. To avoid a directed verdict of acquittal, the prosecution must initially produce some evidence in its case-in-chief of each element of the offense; to avoid an acquittal or hung jury, the prosecution must also persuade the jurors beyond a reasonable doubt of the existence of each element. Since the prosecution runs the risk of losing its case if it does not discharge its persuasion burden, sometimes this burden is referred to as the risk of non-persuasion.

Under the Code, the burden of producing evidence "as to a particular fact" is initially on the party with the burden of persuasion on that fact.[3] In a criminal case, for example, the prosecution must establish the

---

1. West's Ann. California Evidence Code § 110.

2. West's Ann. California Evidence Code § 115. The Code uses the term "burden of proof" to refer to the persuasion burden. Id. To avoid confusion, "persuasion burden," "burden of persuasion," and "risk of non-persuasion" is used in this work whenever the Code employs "burden of proof" in this sense.

3. West's Ann. California Evidence Code § 550(b).

perpetrator's identity beyond a reasonable doubt. Accordingly, the prosecution has the burden of producing evidence of the perpetrator's identity in its case-in-chief. As will be seen, however, presumptions can shift both the production and persuasion burdens on some issues. The Code thus provides that ultimately the burden of producing evidence "as to a particular fact is on the party against whom a finding on that fact would be required in the absence of further evidence."[4]

§ 18.02   THE STANDARDS OF PERSUASION

The Code recognizes three persuasion standards: in descending order they are proof beyond a reasonable doubt, by clear and convincing evidence, and by a preponderance of the evidence.[1]

Proof beyond a reasonable doubt is the highest standard known to American law. As matter of federal due process, it is the standard that applies in all criminal trials. As the United States Supreme Court held in In re Winship, "Lest there remain any doubt about the constitutional stature of the reasonable-doubt standard, we explicitly hold that the Due Process Clause protects the accused against conviction except upon proof beyond a reasonable doubt of every fact necessary to constitute the crime with which he is charged."[2]

In California, Penal Code § 1096 defines proof beyond a reasonable doubt:

> A defendant in a criminal action is presumed to be innocent until the contrary is proved, and in case of a reasonable doubt whether his or her guilt is satisfactorily shown, he or she is entitled to an acquittal, but the effect of this presumption is only to place upon the state the burden of proving him or her guilty beyond a reasonable doubt. Reasonable doubt is defined as follows: "It is not a mere possible doubt; because everything relating to human affairs is open to some possible or imaginary doubt. It is that state of the case, which, after the entire comparison and consideration of all the evidence, leaves the minds of jurors in that condition that they cannot say they feel an abiding conviction of the truth of the charge."[3]

In charging the jury, the judge may read § 1096 to the jury; if the judge does so, the judge does not need to instruct the jury further on the meaning of reasonable doubt.[4]

Proof by a preponderance of the evidence is the easiest to quantify. It requires the proponent to convince the jury that the existence of a particular fact is more probable than its nonexistence.[5] If, after reviewing

---

4.   West's Ann. California Evidence Code § 550(a).

1.   West's Ann. California Evidence Code § 115.

2.   397 U.S. 358, 364, 90 S.Ct. 1068, 1072, 25 L.Ed.2d 368 (1970).

3.   West's Ann. California Penal Code § 1096.

4.   West's Ann. California Penal Code § 1096a.

5.   West's Ann. California Evidence Code § 500 (comment).

the evidence, the jury is at equipoise on a particular issue, the jury must decide that issue against the party having the persuasion burden on that issue. In the words of the standard jury instruction, "If the evidence is so evenly balanced that you are unable to say that the evidence on either side of an issue preponderates, your finding on that issue must be against the party who had the burden of proving it."[6]

The clear and convincing standard falls somewhere between the reasonable doubt and the more-likely-than-not standards. It is the applicable standard when greater confidence in a civil verdict is desired. The standard jury instruction defines clear and convincing as "evidence of such convincing force that it demonstrates, in contrast to the opposing evidence, a high probability of the truth of the fact[s] for which it is offered as proof. Such evidence requires a higher standard of proof than proof by a preponderance of the evidence."[7]

The clear and convincing standard applies when civil proceedings can result in the impairment of significant interests. Unless otherwise required by statute or the state or federal constitutions, it up to the courts to determine whether the interests at stake require the imposition of the more rigorous standard.[8] As a matter of federal due process, the United States Supreme Court has held that a state may not strip an individual of his liberty interests through civil commitment proceedings unless the state demonstrates by clear and convincing evidence that the individual is mentally ill and dangerous.[9]

California cases requiring proof by clear and convincing evidence include Conservatorship of Sanderson[10] (establishing a conservatorship under the Probate Code); In re Angelia P.[11] (terminating a parent's interest in a child); In re Robert P.[12] (removing a child from parental

---

6. BAJI 2.60 (Fall 2007 Edition).

7. BAJI 2.62 (Fall 2007 Edition). See also In re David C., 152 Cal.App.3d 1189, 1208, 200 Cal.Rptr. 115, 127 (1984): " 'Clear and convincing' evidence requires a finding of high probability. The evidence must be so clear as to leave no substantial doubt. It must be sufficiently strong to command the unhesitating assent of every reasonable mind."

8. Baxter Healthcare Corp. v. Denton, 120 Cal.App.4th 333, 365, 15 Cal.Rptr.3d 430, 451 (2004). Evidence Code § 524 is an example of a statute imposing the clear and convincing persuasion standard. It provides that "in a civil proceeding in which the State Board of Equalization is a party, that board shall have the burden of proof by clear and convincing evidence in sustaining its assertion of a penalty for intent to evade or fraud against a taxpayer, with respect to any factual issue relevant to ascertaining the liability of the a taxpayer." West's Ann. California Evidence Code § 524.

9. Addington v. Texas, 441 U.S. 418, 431, 99 S.Ct. 1804, 1812, 60 L.Ed.2d 323 (1979), on remand, 588 S.W.2d 569 (Tex.1979). California goes further. It requires proof beyond a reasonable doubt. Conservatorship of Roulet, 23 Cal.3d 219, 234, 152 Cal.Rptr. 425, 434–435, 590 P.2d 1, 11 (1979).

10. 106 Cal.App.3d 611, 620, 165 Cal.Rptr. 217, 222 (1980).

11. 28 Cal.3d 908, 919, 171 Cal.Rptr. 637, 643, 623 P.2d 198, 203 (1981). But once a court has determined a parent's unfitness by clear and convincing evidence, it need apply only a preponderance standard in determining whether the child should be placed in a permanent alternative family. Cynthia D. v. Superior Court, 5 Cal.4th 242, 256, 19 Cal.Rptr.2d 698, 706, 851 P.2d 1307, 1315 (1993). See also Guardianship of Diana B., 30 Cal.App.4th 1766, 1777, 36 Cal.Rptr.2d 447, 453 (1994) (Orders granting a guardianship petition need be supported only by a preponderance of the evidence.).

12. 61 Cal.App.3d 310, 318, 132 Cal.Rptr. 5, 10 (1976).

custody); Field Research Corp. v. Patrick[13] (proving malice in defamation actions); In re Marriage of Weaver[14] (proving oral transmutation of separate property into community property); Davies Machinery Co. v. Pine Mountain Club, Inc.[15] (establishing that a novation extinguished an existing obligation and created a new one); Crail v. Blakely[16] (establishing an oral agreement to make mutual wills); People v. Mitchell Bros.' Santa Ana Theater[17] (proving obscenity in a public nuisance abatement action); Wilks v. Mouton[18] (setting aside elections on grounds of irregularities); and People v. Englebrecht (enjoining a public nuisance arising from noncriminal gang related activities).[19] In addition, the punitive damages section of the Civil Code requires the plaintiff to prove by clear and convincing evidence that the defendant was guilty of oppression, fraud, or malice.[20]

QUESTIONS AND PROBLEMS

1.   Describe the three standards of persuasion. Of the three, how many can be quantified?

2.   If a party must prove an element by a preponderance of the evidence, what should the jurors be told to do if they find themselves in "equipoise" on that element?

3.   What is the justification for using the intermediate clear and convincing evidence standard?

§ 18.03   ALLOCATING THE PRODUCTION AND PERSUASION BURDENS

The burden of producing evidence on a particular issue is usually on the party having the persuasion burden on that issue.[1] As a rule, a party has the burden of persuasion on "each fact the existence or nonexistence of which is essential to the claim for relief or defense that he is assert-

---

13.   30 Cal.App.3d 603, 608, 106 Cal.Rptr. 473, 476 (1973), cert. denied, 414 U.S. 922, 94 S.Ct. 218, 38 L.Ed.2d 157 (1973). See also Planned Protective Services, Inc. v. Gorton, 200 Cal.App.3d 1, 8–9, 245 Cal.Rptr. 790, 793 (1988).

14.   224 Cal.App.3d 478, 487, 273 Cal.Rptr. 696, 701 (1990).

15.   39 Cal.App.3d 18, 25, 113 Cal.Rptr. 784, 788 (1974) ("The intention of the parties to extinguish the prior obligation and to substitute a new agreement in its place must 'clearly appear.'").

16.   8 Cal.3d 744, 749, 106 Cal.Rptr. 187, 191, 505 P.2d 1027, 1031 (1973).

17.   128 Cal.App.3d 937, 940, 180 Cal.Rptr. 728, 730 (1982), appeal after remand, 165 Cal.App.3d 378, 211 Cal.Rptr. 501 (1985), cert. denied, 474 U.S. 948, 106 S.Ct. 347, 88 L.Ed.2d 293 (1985), reh'g denied, 474 U.S. 1077, 106 S.Ct. 841, 88 L.Ed.2d 811 (1986).

18.   42 Cal.3d 400, 404, 229 Cal.Rptr. 1, 3, 722 P.2d 187, 190 (1986), cert. denied, 479 U.S. 1066, 107 S.Ct. 953, 93 L.Ed.2d 1002 (1987).

19.   88 Cal.App.4th 1236, 1254–1255, 106 Cal.Rptr.2d 738, 751–752 (2001). *Englebrecht* includes a useful list of cases requiring proof by clear and convincing evidence. See id. at note 5.

20.   West's Ann. California Civil Code § 3294(a).

1.   West's Ann. California Evidence Code § 550.

ing."[2] With few exceptions, however, the Evidence Code "does not attempt to indicate what facts may be essential to a particular party's claim for relief or defense. The facts that must be shown to establish a cause of action or defense are determined by the substantive law [governing the case], not the law of evidence."[3]

Courts, as well as the Legislature, play a role in allocating the persuasion burdens. "In determining whether the normal allocation of the burden of [persuasion] should be altered, the courts consider a number of factors: the knowledge of the parties concerning the particular fact, the availability of the evidence to the parties, the most desirable result in terms of public policy in the absence of proof of the particular fact, and the probability of the existence or nonexistence of the fact."[4] In Webster v. Trustees of California State University,[5] for example, the court found that the university's greater access to the evidence, as well as public policy, justified placing on the university the burden of persuading a faculty hearing committee of the plaintiff's incapacity to continue teaching.[6] Normally, the plaintiff, as the party seeking relief from the termination of his employment, would have had the burden of establishing his job competence.

As has been noted, in criminal cases the prosecution has the burden of persuasion.[7] In addition, the Code imposes the burden of persuasion on the party claiming that a person did not exercise the requisite degree of care[8] or that any person, including himself, was insane.[9] The Code also imposes the persuasion burden on the state on all issues relating to the historic locations of rivers, streams, and other water bodies and the authority of the state in issuing a patent or grant in any action in which the state is a party "where (a) the boundary of land patented or otherwise granted by the state is in dispute, or (b) the validity of any state patent or grant dated prior to 1950 is in dispute."[10] In all other cases, the general rule applies unless special statutes or decisions state otherwise.

---

2. West's Ann. California Evidence Code § 500.

3. Id. (comment).

4. Id. Accord: Sargent Fletcher, Inc. v. Able Corp., 110 Cal.App.4th 1658, 1670, 3 Cal.Rptr.3d 279, 287 (2003).

5. 19 Cal.App.4th 1456, 24 Cal.Rptr.2d 150 (1993). See also Wolf v. Superior Court, 107 Cal.App.4th 25, 35, 130 Cal.Rptr.2d 860, 867 (2003) ("In cases where the financial records essential to proving the contingent compensation owed are in the exclusive control of the defendant, fundamental fairness * * * requires shifting the burden of proof to the defendant.").

6. Webster v. Trustees of California State University, supra note 5 at 1464, 24 Cal.Rptr.2d at 155. For a list of cases where the courts have shifted the element of causation from the plaintiff to the defendant, see Sargent Fletcher, Inc. v. Able Corp., 110 Cal.App.4th 1658, 1670, 3 Cal.Rptr.3d 279, 287 (2003).

7. See § 18.02 supra.

8. West's Ann. California Evidence Code § 521.

9. West's Ann. California Evidence Code § 522.

10. West's Ann. California Evidence Code § 523.

1. As a general rule, the substantive law that governs an action determines which party has the burdens of production and persuasion on the issues raised by the pleadings. True or false?

2. But in criminal cases, the prosecution must always prove each element of the offense charged beyond a reasonable doubt. True or false?

§ 18.04 PRESUMPTIONS AND INFERENCES

Referring to the law of presumptions, Judge Learned Hand once remarked, "Judges have mixed it up until nobody can tell what on earth it means and the important thing is to get something which is workable and which can be understood and I don't much care what it is."[1] This section and others that follow attempt to satisfy Judge Hand's demand by clarifying the law of presumptions through examples.

Example 1—Inferences. Assume a breach of contract action in which the plaintiff claims that the defendant failed to perform as promised. The defendant's position is that no contract existed because the plaintiff failed to accept the defendant's offer.

To prevail, the plaintiff must prove, among other matters, the existence of the contract. Since the existence of the contract is essential to his breach claim, the plaintiff has the burden of persuasion on this issue.[2] In the end, he must persuade the jurors of the existence of the contract by a preponderance of the evidence.[3] Moreover, the plaintiff also has the burden of producing evidence on the existence of the contract. Under the Code, the production burden is initially on the party having the persuasion burden on a given issue.[4]

The production burden imposes upon the plaintiff "the obligation * * * to introduce evidence sufficient to avoid a ruling against him on the issue."[5] To avoid an adverse directed verdict at the conclusion of his case-in-chief, the plaintiff must introduce some evidence of the contract's existence. Under the sufficiency standard, the judge must deny the defendant's motion for a directed verdict and let the issue of the contract's existence go to the jury if the judge concludes that a reasonable jury could find the contract from the plaintiff's evidence *if believed*. A sufficiency standard is used in ruling on motions for directed verdicts in order to vouchsafe a party's right to jury determinations of material factual issues.[6]

---

1. ALI Proceedings 217–218 (1940–41).

2. West's Ann. California Evidence Code § 500.

3. West's Ann. California Evidence Code § 115.

4. West's Ann. California Evidence Code § 550.

5. West's Ann. California Evidence Code § 110.

6. West's Ann. California Code Civil Procedure Code § 581c;. Salomons v. Lumsden, 95 Cal.App.2d Supp. 924, 926, 213 P.2d 132, 133 (1949). For the same reason, the role of the judge in screening evidence under West's Ann. California Evidence Code § 403 is similarly circumscribed. See § 17.01 supra.

Assume that the defendant's position that no contract existed is based on never having received the plaintiff's written acceptance. In his case-in-chief the plaintiff produces evidence that he prepared a written acceptance of the defendant's offer and asked his secretary to mail it to the defendant at the address on the defendant's written offer. The plaintiff's secretary testifies that he copied the defendant's name and address from the offer and, after affixing the correct postage, dropped the acceptance in the mailbox outside the office. Assume finally that the law of contracts provides that an offer is not accepted unless the acceptance is received by the offeror. At the conclusion of the plaintiff's case-in-chief, should the judge grant the defendant's motion for a directed verdict on the ground that the plaintiff failed to produce any evidence that the defendant received the acceptance?

The judge should deny the defendant's motion. In applying the sufficiency standard, the judge must view the evidence in the light most favorable to the party against whom the motion is directed.[7] The standard requires the judge to accept not only the evidence most favorable to the plaintiff as true but to disregard conflicting evidence; it also requires the judge to draw only those inferences from the evidence which are most favorable to the plaintiff.[8] Here, the plaintiff has failed to produce any direct evidence showing that the defendant received the acceptance. But an inference that can be drawn from the evidence is that the defendant received the acceptance because the acceptance letter was correctly addressed, had the appropriate postage, and was deposited in the U.S. mails. Since a reasonable jury could draw this inference, the plaintiff is entitled to get to the jury on the question of whether the defendant received the acceptance.

Defeating the motion does not mean that the plaintiff will win. In his case-in-chief, the defendant will be entitled to produce evidence that he did not receive the acceptance. Since the plaintiff has the burden of persuasion on the contract's existence, the judge must tell the jury to return a verdict for the defendant unless the plaintiff convinces them by a preponderance of the evidence that the defendant received the acceptance. Whether or not the jury will find for the plaintiff on this issue will depend on their willingness to draw the very inference the judge drew when ruling on the defendant's motion for a directed verdict. Their willingness to do so will in turn depend on their assessment of all of the evidence, including the credibility of the witnesses.

Much has been made of inferences. Simply put, they are the kinds of conclusions we draw in everyday problem solving. Technically, they are deductions "of fact that may logically and reasonably be drawn from

---

7. Campbell v. General Motors Corp., 32 Cal.3d 112, 118, 184 Cal.Rptr. 891, 894, 649 P.2d 224, 227 (1982); Ewing v. Cloverleaf Bowl, 20 Cal.3d 389, 395, 143 Cal.Rptr. 13, 15, 572 P.2d 1155, 1157 (1978).

8. Campbell v. General Motors Corp., 32 Cal.3d 112, 118, 184 Cal.Rptr. 891, 894, 649 P.2d 224, 227 (1982); Ewing v. Cloverleaf Bowl, 20 Cal.3d 389, 395, 143 Cal.Rptr. 13, 15, 572 P.2d 1155, 1157 (1978).

another fact or groups of facts found or otherwise established in the action.''[9]

Thus far, the resolution of the plaintiff's breach action has not involved presumptions. Presumptions, however, can alter both the production and persuasion burdens in a given action. To explore the effects of presumptions let us apply one to the plaintiff's case.

Example 2—Thayer Presumptions. In ruling on the defendant's motion for a directed verdict, the judge was faced with the question of whether she should rule in the defendant's favor in light of the plaintiff's failure to produce any direct evidence that the defendant had received the plaintiff's acceptance. Because of the strict limits which the sufficiency standard imposes, the judge had no choice but to deny the defendant's motion: a reasonable jury could find that the defendant received the acceptance if the plaintiff's evidence was believed. The judge's task would have been substantially eased if the plaintiff had called to the judge's attention a presumption created by the Evidence Code: "A letter correctly addressed and properly mailed is presumed to have been received in the ordinary course of mail."[10]

Analysis shows that this presumption, like all presumptions, consists of two elements: the basic facts and the presumed facts. The basic facts are correctly addressing and properly mailing a letter. The presumed fact is that such a letter is received in the ordinary course of mail. In our example, the plaintiff offered evidence of the basic facts. Since, in passing on the defendant's motion for a directed verdict, the judge had to assume the truth of the plaintiff's evidence, the judge would have no choice but to assume the existence of the presumed fact, namely, that the defendant received the plaintiff's acceptance in the ordinary course of mail. Since the presumed fact supplies the very evidence the defendant claims is missing from the plaintiff's case-in-chief, the judge would have to deny the defendant's motion for a directed verdict.

Presumptions, however, can have a life that extends beyond motions for directed verdicts. They can alter a jury's fact finding function. Their effect depends on the kind of presumption involved and can best be seen by comparing life without presumptions with life with presumptions. Take the breach of contract case in which the plaintiff offered no direct evidence that the defendant received the plaintiff's acceptance. If in a world without presumptions the defendant offers no evidence that he failed to receive the plaintiff's acceptance, the plaintiff would win only if the jury believed by a preponderance of the evidence that the defendant received the acceptance. That would depend on the jury's willingness to draw the necessary inference from the plaintiff's evidence. But in a world with presumptions, that mode of fact finding can change. In such a world, the judge would now instruct the jury to find the presumed fact (that the defendant received the acceptance in the ordinary course of mail) if the

---

9.   West's Ann. California Evidence Code § 600(b).

10.   West's Ann. California Evidence Code § 641.

jury first found the basic facts (that the acceptance was correctly addressed and properly mailed).[11] Only if the defendant produced some evidence that he did not receive the acceptance would the world revert to one without presumptions. In that world, the judge would say nothing about the presumption and the jury would be free to draw whatever inferences it wished from all of the evidence.[12]

It is crucial to note that the presumption we have been considering did not alter the burden of persuasion. To prevail, the plaintiff must still persuade the jurors by a preponderance of the evidence that the defendant received the acceptance. But the presumption assisted the plaintiff in two respects. It helped him get by the defendant's motion for a directed verdict by relieving him of the need to produce evidence of the presumed fact. Moreover, where the defendant produced no evidence that he failed to receive the acceptance, the plaintiff got the benefit of having the jurors instructed to find the presumed fact if they found the basic facts. But because the presumed fact (that the acceptance was received in the ordinary course of mail) is one of the elements the plaintiff must prove by a preponderance of the evidence, the judge would have to instruct the jurors to find the presumed fact only if they first found the basic facts by that standard.

Some presumptions, however, do more than just affect the burden of producing evidence. They can shift the burden of persuasion on the existence of the presumed fact. An example illustrates this important point.

Example 3—Morgan Presumptions. Assume a personal injury action in which the plaintiff seeks to recover for injuries she suffered when the defendant allegedly hit her while driving a car at an excessive speed. To recover, the plaintiff must prove, among other matters, that the defendant did not exercise the degree of care required under the circumstances. Ordinarily, the plaintiff would have both the production and persuasion burdens on this issue.[13] Assume that to avoid an adverse directed verdict on this issue the plaintiff offers evidence in her case-in-chief that the defendant was driving in excess of the speed limit posted by a city ordinance. That evidence, as we have seen, would get the plaintiff to the jury on that issue under the directed verdict standard. In a world without presumptions, the judge would simply tell the jury to return a verdict for the defendant unless the plaintiff convinced them by a preponderance of the evidence that the defendant failed to exercise the degree of care required under the circumstances.

Enter now the concept of negligence per se. The Evidence Code provides that the failure to exercise due care is "presumed" if the person violated an ordinance which, among other matters, was designed to

---

11. West's Ann. California Evidence Code § 604 and comment.

12. Id. Accord: Craig v. Brown & Root, Inc., 84 Cal.App.4th 416, 421, 100 Cal.Rptr.2d 818, 821 (2000).

13. West's Ann. California Evidence Code §§ 521 and 550.

prevent the kind of injuries suffered by the plaintiff.[14] Unlike the earlier presumption, this one alters the burden of persuasion.[15] It shifts to the defendant the burden of convincing the jury by a preponderance of the evidence that he exercised due care, i.e., that his violation of the ordinance was reasonable and justified under the circumstances.[16]

The presumption does not alter the plaintiff's burden in proving the basic facts.[17] Since the presumed fact is one of the elements of the plaintiff's cause of action, the plaintiff must still establish the basic facts at least by a preponderance of the evidence. At the close of the evidence, the jurors would be told to find the presumed fact (that the defendant was negligent) if they first found the basic facts by this standard. In addition, they would be told to find for the plaintiff on this issue unless persuaded by the defendant of the nonexistence of the presumed fact by a preponderance of the evidence.[18]

The effects of the two presumptions can be summarized as follows in an action in which the plaintiff must prove element B by a preponderance of the evidence and in which B is also a presumed fact:

Example 2 (Thayer) presumption. (1) If the plaintiff establishes the basic facts by a sufficiency standard, the defendant's motion for a directed verdict based on the absence of evidence of B must be denied. (2) If the defendant fails to introduce any evidence disproving B, then the judge will tell the jurors to find B if they first find the basic facts by the appropriate standard. (3) But if the defendant disproves B by a sufficiency standard, the judge will say nothing to the jurors about the presumption.

Example 3 (Morgan) presumption. (1) If the plaintiff establishes the basic facts by a sufficiency standard, the defendant's motion for a directed verdict based on the absence of evidence of B must be denied. (2) If the defendant fails to introduce any evidence disproving B, then the judge will tell the jurors to find B if they first find the basic facts by the appropriate standard. (3) But if the defendant disproves B by a sufficiency standard, the judge will tell the jurors to find B if they first find the basic facts by the appropriate standard, unless the defendant persuades them of B's nonexistence by the appropriate standard.

---

14. West's Ann. California Evidence Code § 669. In addition to the statutory doctrine of § 669, the California courts have created a judicial doctrine of negligence per se which does not rely on the existence of an ordinance or statute. For a specification of the requirements of the judicial doctrine, see Elcome v. Chin, 110 Cal.App.4th 310, 316–317, 1 Cal.Rptr.3d 631, 636 (2003). In general, the plaintiff must offer evidence that (1) the injury is of a kind that ordinarily does not occur in the absence of someone's negligence; (2) the injury was caused by an instrumentality in the exclusive control of the defendant; and (3) the injury was not due to any voluntary action or contribution on the part of the plaintiff. Id.

15. Id.

16. Id. (comment).

17. These are whether the defendant violated the ordinance and whether the violation contributed or caused the plaintiff's injuries. West's Ann. California Evidence Code § 669 (comment). Whether the ordinance was designed to prevent the injury the plaintiff complains of and whether the plaintiff was among the class of persons for whose protection the ordinance was adopted are questions for the judge, not the jury. Id.

18. West's Ann. California Evidence Code § 606 and comment.

Both presumptions are advantageous to the party in whose favor they operate. The second is more beneficial, since it shifts to the opposing party the burden of disproving the presumed fact. Since their effects are different, it is important to tell whether a given presumption is of the first or second kind. The first kind is derived from Evidence Code §§ 603 and 604; the second, from §§ 606 and 607. Understanding the origin of these code sections will aid in distinguishing between the two kinds of presumptions.

QUESTIONS AND PROBLEMS

1.   Assume a California action in which the plaintiff has to allege and prove B by a preponderance of the evidence. If the plaintiff fails to offer any direct or circumstantial evidence of B in her case-in-chief, then the defendant is entitled to a directed verdict. True or false?

2.   Assume that California has a presumption that states that proof of B will be presumed from proof of A. If the plaintiff offers evidence of A in her case-in-chief, then the judge should deny the defense motion for a directed verdict. True or false?

3.   Assume that California defines the presumption as one affecting only the burden of producing evidence.

(a) If the defendant offers no evidence disproving B, then the judge should instruct the jurors to find B if they find A by a preponderance of the evidence. True or false?

(b) If the defendant offers some evidence disproving B, then the judge should say nothing to the jurors about the presumption. True or false?

4.   Assume, instead, that California defines the presumption as one also affecting the burden of persuasion.

(a) If the defendant offers no evidence disproving B, then the judge should instruct the jurors to find B if they find A by a preponderance of the evidence. True or false?

(b) If the defendant offers some evidence disproving B, then the judge should instruct the jurors to find B if they find A by a preponderance of the evidence, unless the defendant persuades them by a preponderance of the evidence of the nonexistence of B. True or false?

§ 18.05   DISTINGUISHING BETWEEN REBUTTABLE PRESUMPTIONS

The two kinds of presumptions described in the previous section are known as rebuttable presumptions. The opposing party is entitled to introduce evidence "rebutting" the presumed facts. The opposing party can do this by offering evidence disproving the presumed facts. Returning to the second example in the previous section, the defendant could attack the presumed fact (that he received the plaintiff's acceptance in the ordinary course of mail) by evidence that he did not receive the acceptance.[1]

Over one-hundred years ago, Professor James Thayer described the first kind of presumption, the one found in §§ 603 and 604. His view was that a presumption merely shifted to the opposing party the burden of producing evidence rebutting the presumed fact.[2] If the opposing party produced some evidence of the nonexistence of the presumed fact, then the presumption would "burst" and the judge would tell the jury nothing about the presumption. Half a century later, Professor Edmund Morgan challenged Thayer's view of presumptions. Professor Morgan believed that presumptions should also shift to the opposing party the burden of persuading the jurors of the nonexistence of the presumed fact.[3] Producing some evidence of the nonexistence of the presumed fact was not enough; the jury was to be instructed to find the presumed fact unless persuaded otherwise by the opposing party under the appropriate standard.

Unlike Professor Thayer, who saw presumptions mainly as a device for allocating the burden of producing evidence on the existence or nonexistence of the presumed fact, Professor Morgan recognized that presumptions often reflect the considerations of fairness, policy, and probability that in the first place allocate the various elements of any case between the plaintiff's prima facie case and the defendant's affirmative defenses.[4] In his view, if these considerations warrant imposing the risk of nonpersuasion on the party with the burden of producing evidence on a given element, then those same considerations should place the risk of nonpersuasion on the party with the burden of producing evidence rebutting the presumed fact.[5] Dean Charles McCormick in particular noted that the kinds of presumptions Professor Morgan had in mind often advance desirable social goals, irrespective of whether the presumed fact has an underlying basis in probability and logical inference.[6] An example is the presumption that a person not heard from in five years is dead.[7] Though the presumption of death from five years' absence may conflict with the inference that life continues for its normal expectancy, the policies favor-

---

1. The opponent can also attack the basic facts by evidence of their nonexistence. In the example, the defendant could challenge the basic facts by evidence, for instance, that the plaintiff's secretary admitted prior to the trial to having no recollection of having mailed the acceptance. As will be seen, however, introducing evidence of the nonexistence of the basic facts does not dispel (rebut) the presumed fact. Such evidence simply places upon the jury the burden of determining the existence of the basic facts. See United Sav. & Loan Ass'n v. Reeder Dev. Corp., 57 Cal.App.3d 282, 300, 129 Cal.Rptr. 113, 124 (1976).

2. J. Thayer, A Preliminary Treatise on Evidence at Common Law 346 (1898). See also C. McCormick, McCormick on Evidence § 344 (J. Strong 4th ed. 1992).

3. E. Morgan, Some Problems of Proof under the Anglo–American System of Litigation 80–81 (1956).

4. Id.

5. Id.

6. C. McCormick, Handbook of the Law of Evidence § 345 (E. Cleary 2d ed. 1972).

7. West's Ann. California Evidence Code § 667.

ing distributing estates, settling titles, and permitting life to proceed normally justify the presumption.[8]

Faced with two opposing views of presumptions, the framers of the Code opted for both. Sections 603–604 describe Thayer presumptions while §§ 606–607 describe Morgan ones. Presumptions, however, whether created by statute or case law, do not usually indicate whether they come within Thayer's or Morgan's view. In the absence of an explicit classification, the judge must decide whether a given presumption is designed to promote some social policy (and hence is governed by §§ 606–607) or merely to facilitate the allocation of the production burden with respect to the existence or nonexistence of the presumed fact (and hence is governed by §§ 603–604). According to the Law Revision Commission, § 603.

> presumptions are designed to dispense with unnecessary proof of facts that are likely to be true if not disputed. Typically, such presumptions are based on an underlying logical inference. In some cases, the presumed fact is so likely to be true and so little likely to be disputed that the law requires it to be assumed in the absence of contrary evidence. In other cases, evidence of the nonexistence of the presumed fact, if there is any, is so much more readily available to the party against whom the presumption operates that he is not permitted to argue that the presumed fact does not exist unless he is willing to produce such evidence. In still other cases, there may be no direct evidence of the existence or nonexistence of the presumed fact; but, because the case must be decided, the law requires a determination that the presumed fact exists in light of common experience indicating that it usually exists in such cases. * * * Typical of such presumptions are the presumption that a mailed letter was received * * * and presumptions relating to the authenticity of documents * * *.[9]

Section 605 presumptions, on the other hand, are established to effectuate some public policy other than, or in addition to, facilitating the trial of actions.[10]

> What makes a presumption one affecting the burden of [persuasion] is the fact that there is always some further reason of policy for the establishment of the presumption. It is the existence of this further basis in policy that distinguishes a presumption affecting the burden of [persuasion] from a presumption affecting the burden of producing evidence. * * * Frequently, too, a presumption affecting the burden of [persuasion] will have an underlying basis in probability and logical inference. For example, the presumption of the validity of a ceremonial marriage may be based in part on the probability that most marriages are valid. However, an underlying logical inference is not essential. In fact, the lack of underlying inference is a strong indication that the presumption affects the burden of [persuasion]. Only the

---

8. Id. (comment).

9. West's Ann. California Evidence Code § 603 (comment).

10. West's Ann. California Evidence Code § 605 and comment.

needs of public policy can justify the direction of a particular presumption that is not warranted by the application of probability and common experience to the known facts.[11]

To help parties and judges distinguish between § 603 (Thayer) and § 605 (Morgan) presumptions, the Code provides a list of common presumptions. Section 603 presumptions include the following: money delivered by one to another is presumed to have been due to the latter;[12] a thing delivered to another is presumed to have belonged to the latter;[13] an obligation delivered up to the debtor is presumed to have been paid;[14] a person in possession of an order on himself for the payment of money, or delivery of a thing, is presumed to have paid the money or delivered the thing accordingly;[15] an obligation possessed by the creditor is presumed not to have been paid;[16] the payment of earlier rent or installments is presumed from a receipt for the later rent or installments;[17] the things which a person possesses are presumed to be owned by him;[18] a person who exercises acts of ownership over property is presumed to be the owner of it;[19] a judgment, when not conclusive, is presumed to correctly determine or set forth the rights of the parties, but there is no presumption that the facts essential to the judgment have been correctly determined;[20] a writing is presumed to have been truly dated;[21] a letter correctly addressed and properly mailed is presumed to have been received in the ordinary course of mail;[22] a trustee or other person, whose duty it was to convey real property to a particular person, is presumed to have actually conveyed to him when such presumption is necessary to perfect title of such person or his successor in interest;[23] a deed or will or other writing purporting to create, terminate, or affect an interest in real or personal property is presumed to be authentic if it is at least 30 years old, is in such condition as to create no suspicion concerning its authenticity, was kept, or if found was found, in a place where such writing, if authentic, would be likely to be kept or found, and has been generally acted upon as authentic by persons having an interest in the matter;[24] a book, purporting to be printed or published by public authority, is presumed to have been so printed or published;[25] a book, purporting to contain reports of

---

11. Id. (comment).

12. West's Ann. California Evidence Code § 631.

13. West's Ann. California Evidence Code § 632.

14. West's Ann. California Evidence Code § 633.

15. West's Ann. California Evidence Code § 634.

16. West's Ann. California Evidence Code § 635.

17. West's Ann. California Evidence Code § 636.

18. West's Ann. California Evidence Code § 637.

19. West's Ann. California Evidence Code § 638.

20. West's Ann. California Evidence Code § 639.

21. West's Ann. California Evidence Code § 640.

22. West's Ann. California Evidence Code § 641.

23. West's Ann. California Evidence Code § 642.

24. West's Ann. California Evidence Code § 643.

25. West's Ann. California Evidence Code § 644.

cases adjudged in the tribunals of the state or nation where the book is published, is presumed to contain correct reports of such cases;[26] printed materials, purporting to be a particular newspaper or periodical, are presumed to be that newspaper or periodical if regularly issued at average intervals not exceeding three months;[27] the defendant in a personal injury action is presumed to have been negligent if the plaintiff establishes the conditions giving rise to the doctrine of res ipsa loquitur;[28] and the facts stated by a registered process server in his return are presumed to be true.[29]

Section 605 (Morgan) presumptions include the following: the owner of the legal title to property is presumed to be the owner of the full beneficial title;[30] a ceremonial marriage is presumed to be valid;[31] official duties are presumed to have been regularly performed;[32] a person is presumed to intend the ordinary consequences of his voluntary act;[33] any California or federal court or any court of general jurisdiction, acting as such, is presumed to have acted in the lawful exercise of its jurisdiction when the act of the court is under collateral attack;[34] a person not heard from in five years is presumed to be dead;[35] an unlawful intent is presumed from the doing of an unlawful act;[36] the defendant in a personal injury action is presumed to have been negligent if the plaintiff establishes the conditions giving rise to the doctrine of negligence per se;[37] any ordinance enacted by local government entities limiting the number of building permits for residential construction or changing the standard of residential development on vacant land is presumed to have an impact on the supply of residential units,[38] and payment by check is presumed by

---

26. West's Ann. California Evidence Code § 645.

27. West's Ann. California Evidence Code § 645.1.

28. West's Ann. California Evidence Code § 646.

29. West's Ann. California Evidence Code § 647.

30. West's Ann. California Evidence Code § 662. This presumption can be rebutted only by clear and convincing evidence. Id.

31. West's Ann. California Evidence Code § 663.

32. West's Ann. California Evidence Code § 664. This presumption does not apply to the lawfulness of an arrest if it is found or otherwise established that the arrest was made without a warrant. Id.

33. West's Ann. California Evidence Code § 665. The United States Supreme Court has stricken a similar presumption as unconstitutional. Sandstrom v. Montana, 442 U.S. 510, 99 S.Ct. 2450, 61 L.Ed.2d 39 (1979), on remand, 184 Mont. 391, 603 P.2d 244 (1979). See also § 18.07 infra. This presumption is inapplicable in a criminal action to prove the specific intent of the accused where specific intent is an element of the offense charged. West's Ann. California Evidence Code § 665.

34. West's Ann. California Evidence Code § 666.

35. West's Ann. California Evidence Code § 667.

36. West's Ann. California Evidence Code § 668. For a discussion of the constitutionality of this presumption, see § 18.07 infra. This presumption is inapplicable in a criminal action to establish the accused's specific intent where that intent is an element of the crime charged. West's Ann. California Evidence Code § 668.

37. West's Ann. California Evidence Code § 669. For additional limitations on this presumption, see West's Ann. California Evidence Code § 669.1.

38. West's Ann. California Evidence Code § 669.5. See § 669.5 for additional limitations on the presumption.

proof of a copy of the check produced in accordance with § 1550 of the Evidence Code, together with the original bank statement reflecting payment of the check by the bank on which it was drawn or a copy of the bank statement produced in accordance with § 1550.[39]

In addition, the courts have construed some presumptions found in other codes as presumptions shifting the burden of persuasion. Among these are the following: a deed absolute in form is presumed to convey a fee simple interest in property;[40] real property acquired by spouses as joint tenants is presumed to be the community property of the spouses;[41] a worker is presumed to have been discharged for reasons other than misconduct and not to have left his employment voluntarily unless his employer gives contrary written notice to the Department of Human Resources within five days of termination;[42] an employment contract in which the only consideration is the services to be performed and which is silent as to duration is presumed to be terminable at will upon reasonable notice;[43] heart trouble which develops or manifests itself while certain state employees are in the service of the state is presumed to arise out of and in the course of their employment;[44] a non-citizen defendant is presumed not to have been advised that a plea of guilty or nolo contendere could result in deportation, exclusion from admission to the United States, or denial of naturalization in the absence of a court record indicating that he was so advised prior to the entry of the plea.[45]

QUESTIONS AND PROBLEMS

1. California recognizes only Thayer presumptions. True or false?

2. California recognizes both Thayer and Morgan presumptions. True or false?

3. A difference between Thayer and Morgan presumptions is that the latter seek to further some social policy, such as the early distribution of estates and the protection of the marital relationship. True or false?

39. West's Ann. California Evidence Code § 670. Section 1550 allows for the introduction of copies of certain types of business records.

40. Develop–Amatic Engineering v. Republic Mortgage Co., 12 Cal.App.3d 143, 148, 91 Cal.Rptr. 193, 195 (1970) (construing West's Ann. California Civil Code § 1105).

41. Baron v. Baron, 9 Cal.App.3d 933, 938–939, 88 Cal.Rptr. 404, 407 (1970) (construing West's Ann. California Civil Code § 5110).

42. Miranda v. Department of Human Resources Dev., 33 Cal.App.3d 314, 319, 109 Cal.Rptr. 35, 38 (1973), appeal after remand, 47 Cal.App.3d 434, 120 Cal.Rptr. 855 (1975) (construing West's Ann. California Unemployment Insurance Code § 1256).

43. Haycock v. Hughes Aircraft Co., 22 Cal.App.4th 1473, 1488, 28 Cal.Rptr.2d 248, 257 (1994).

44. Reeves v. W.C.A.B., 80 Cal.App.4th 22, 95 Cal.Rptr.2d 74, 78–80 (2000).

45. People v. Dubon, 90 Cal.App.4th 944, 108 Cal.Rptr.2d 914, 921–922 (2001).

§ 18.06 CONCLUSIVE PRESUMPTIONS

The Code also recognizes the existence of conclusive presumptions.[1] These differ from rebuttable presumptions in two crucial respects. The judge must tell the jurors that if they find the basic facts by the requisite standard, they must find the presumed fact "irrespective of the strength of the opposing evidence."[2] In addition, the judge upon objection must bar the party opposing a conclusive presumption from offering evidence that rebuts the presumed fact.[3]

In rare instances, however, courts will decline to apply conclusive presumptions where their application would defeat the policies behind them. An example is the presumption that, subject to certain limitations, the issue of a wife cohabiting with her husband, who is not impotent or sterile, is conclusively presumed to be the child of the marriage.[4] In County of Orange v. Leslie B.[5] a biological father sought to use this presumption to avoid supporting his child. At the time he fathered the child, the mother was married to and living with another man who subsequently divorced her. Since the policies underlying the presumption—to preserve the integrity of the family unit, protect children from the legal and social stigma of illegitimacy, and promote individual rather than state responsibility for child support—would not be served by applying the presumption, the court declined to do so.[6]

Among the conclusive presumptions listed in the Code are the following: the facts recited in a written instrument are conclusively presumed to be true as between the parties thereto, or their successors in interest, but not facts in the recital of consideration;[7] whenever a party has, by his own

---

1. See West's Ann. California Evidence Code §§ 601 and 620.

2. West's Ann. California Evidence Code § 601 (comment). In People v. Forrester, 30 Cal.App.4th 1697, 1701–1702, 37 Cal.Rptr.2d 19, 21 (1994), the court struck as unconstitutional a conclusive presumption which required the jurors to find that a defendant who fails to appear within 14 days of the date assigned for his or her appearance intends to evade the process of the court. See also People v. Vanegas, 115 Cal.App.4th 592, 601, 9 Cal.Rptr.3d 398, 405 (2004), where the court struck as unconstitutional a conclusive presumption that instructed the jurors that a violation of the basic speed law was an act inherently dangerous to human life in a prosecution where the charge of implied malice murder required the prosecution to prove that the defendant had engaged in an intentional act the natural consequences of which were dangerous to human life.

3. See Melendrez v. D & I Investment, Inc.,127 Cal.App.4th 1238, 1250, note 17, 26 Cal.Rptr.3d 413, 424, note 17 (2005). The party opposing the conclusive presumption, however, is still entitled to offer evidence disputing the existence of the basic facts.

4. California Evidence Code § 621 created this exception. It was repealed in 1994 and placed in the Family Code without substantive change. See West's Ann. California Family Code §§ 7540–7541.

5. 14 Cal.App.4th 976, 17 Cal.Rptr.2d 797 (1993).

6. Id. at 983, 17 Cal.Rptr.2d at 800. See also Comino v. Kelley, 25 Cal.App.4th 678, 684–685, 30 Cal.Rptr.2d 728, 731 (1994), where the mother sought to have the presumption applied against her husband in order to defeat the claims of the biological father who was the only father the child knew; the court refused to apply the presumption.

7. West's Ann. California Evidence Code § 622. Estoppel certificates qualify as "written instruments." Plaza Freeway L.P. v. First Mountain Bank, 81 Cal.App.4th 616, 96 Cal.Rptr.2d 865, 867 (2000). On the other hand, void agreements do not qualify as "written agreements" under the Evidence Code; neither do agreements offered "on a take-it-or-leave-it" basis, City of Santa Cruz v. Pacific Gas & Electric Co., 82 Cal.App.4th 1167, 1176–1177, 99 Cal.Rptr.2d 198,

statement or conduct, intentionally and deliberately led another to believe that a particular thing is true and to act upon such belief, he is not, in any litigation arising out of such statement or conduct, permitted to contradict it;[8] and a tenant is not permitted to deny title of his landlord at the time of the commencement of the relation.[9]

The last two examples aptly illustrate the California Law Revision Commission's observation about conclusive presumptions: they "are not evidentiary rules so much as they are rules of substantive law."[10] As substantive law rules, conclusive presumptions in civil cases will not be set aside as violative of due process unless no rational connection exists between the basic and presumed facts.[11] An example of such a presumption can be found in Griffiths v. Superior Court where the court upheld as rational a statutory presumption that conviction of two or more alcohol related offenses is conclusive evidence of unprofessional medical conduct.[12]

§ 18.07　PRESUMPTIONS IN CRIMINAL CASES

When the United States Supreme Court held in In re Winship[1] that due process requires the prosecution to prove the accused's guilt beyond a reasonable doubt, the Court laid the basis for a constitutional attack on any presumption that threatens to lighten the prosecution's burden of proof. Thus far, the Court has stricken two kinds of presumptions as unconstitutional—conclusive presumptions and rebuttable presumptions of the Morgan variety.[2]

Conclusive presumptions are unconstitutional because they relieve the prosecution from having to prove the presumed fact beyond a reason-

---

205 (2000), or medical consent forms. Quintanilla v. Dunkelman, 133 Cal.App.4th 95, 117, 34 Cal.Rptr.3d 557, 573 (2005).

8. West's Ann. California Evidence Code § 623. The term "equitable estoppel" is sometimes used to describe the misconduct encompassed by § 623. See Schnyder v. State Bd. of Equalization, 101 Cal.App.4th 538, 550, 124 Cal.Rptr.2d 571, 580 (2002). The equitable estoppel doctrine applies to the government as well as to private parties. See Emma Corp. v. Inglewood Unified School Dist., 114 Cal.App.4th 1018, 1029, 8 Cal.Rptr.3d 213, 221 (2004). For a discussion of the elements of equitable estoppel, see State Water Resources Control Bd. Cases, 136 Cal.App.4th 674, 819, 39 Cal.Rptr.3d 189, 304 (2006).

Equitable estoppel under § 623 must be distinguished from judicial estoppel. Judicial estoppel is a judicial remedy designed to prevent abuse of judicial proceedings by prohibiting a party from taking inconsistent positions in the same or different judicial proceedings. See M. Perez Co. v. Base Camp Condominiums Ass'n No. One, 111 Cal.App.4th 456, 463, 3 Cal.Rptr.3d 563, 568 (2003).

9. West's Ann. California Evidence Code § 624. Non-statutory conclusive presumptions also exist in California. See, e.g., Parkinson v. Johnson, 160 Cal. 756, 761, 117 P. 1057, 1059 (1911) (holding that where a bill is "properly enrolled, authenticated, and deposited in the office of the Secretary of State, it is conclusive evidence of the legislative will, and courts will not look into the journals of the Legislature, or permit any other evidence to be submitted, to determine whether or how a bill passed.").

10. West's Ann. California Evidence Code § 620.

11. Griffiths v. Superior Court, 96 Cal.App.4th 757, 779, 117 Cal.Rptr.2d 445, 461 (2002).

12. Id.

1. 397 U.S. 358, 364, 90 S.Ct. 1068, 1072, 25 L.Ed.2d 368 (1970).

2. For a discussion of the nature of conclusive presumptions, see § 18.06 supra; of Morgan presumptions, § 18.05 supra.

able doubt.[3] They impermissibly withdraw the issue of the existence of the presumed fact from the jury[4] and prevent the accused from raising a reasonable doubt about the existence of the presumed fact. Assume that an offense consists of elements A and B. If the judge instructs the jurors that if they find A, they must find B, the prosecution is relieved of its *Winship* obligation of having to prove B beyond a reasonable doubt. The jurors are not given an opportunity to determine the existence of B, and the accused is prevented from winning an acquittal by raising a reasonable doubt about the existence of B. Instructing the jurors that they must first find A beyond a reasonable doubt will not cure the constitutional infirmity. The prosecution is still relieved of its *Winship* burden of proving B beyond a reasonable doubt; the jurors are still denied a chance to consider the existence of B, and the accused is still deprived of an opportunity to raise a reasonable doubt about the existence of a fact essential to conviction.[5]

Rebuttable presumptions of the Morgan variety have also been declared unconstitutional by the Court.[6] Assume again that an offense consists of elements A and B. If the judge instructs the jurors that if they find A, they must find B unless the accused disproves B at least by a preponderance of the evidence, the presumption shifts to the accused the burden of disproving an element of the offense. As the Court held in Sandstrom v. Montana,[7] In re Winship is violated because the prosecution is relieved of proving B beyond a reasonable doubt.[8] In re Winship is also violated because the accused is burdened with disproving B by a standard higher than that of merely raising a reasonable doubt about the existence of the presumed fact.

So long as the presumption requires the accused to disprove B at least by a preponderance of the evidence, telling the jurors that they must find B beyond a reasonable doubt will not remedy the problem. Such instructions would be hopelessly conflicting. Belief beyond a reasonable doubt

---

3. Sandstrom v. Montana, 442 U.S. 510, 523, 99 S.Ct. 2450, 2458, 61 L.Ed.2d 39 (1979), on remand, 184 Mont. 391, 603 P.2d 244 (1979). The presumption stricken in *Sandstrom* provided that "the law presumes that a person intends the ordinary consequences of his voluntary acts." Id. at 512, 99 S.Ct. at 2453. Compare West's Ann. California Evidence Code § 668 which provides that a "person is presumed to intend the ordinary consequences of his voluntary act."

4. Id.

5. For an example of a conclusive presumption stricken as unconstitutional, see People v. Forrester, 30 Cal.App.4th 1697, 1701–1702, 37 Cal.Rptr.2d 19, 21 (1994), where the court disapproved a presumption which required the jurors to find that a defendant who fails to appear within 14 days of the date assigned for his or her appearance intends to evade the process of the court.

6. Sandstrom v. Montana, 442 U.S. 510, 523, 99 S.Ct. 2450, 2458, 61 L.Ed.2d 39 (1979), on remand, 184 Mont. 391, 603 P.2d 244 (1979). In *Sandstrom*, the Court referred to Morgan-type presumptions as "mandatory presumptions." Id. at 515, 99 S.Ct. at 2454. In Francis v. Franklin, 471 U.S. 307, 105 S.Ct. 1965, 85 L.Ed.2d 344 (1985), the Court used "mandatory presumptions" to refer to Morgan-type and conclusive presumptions. Id. at 314, note 2, 105 S.Ct. at 1971, note 2.

7. Sandstrom v. Montana, 442 U.S. 510, 523, 99 S.Ct. 2450, 2458, 61 L.Ed.2d 39 (1979), on remand, 184 Mont. 391, 603 P.2d 244 (1979).

8. Id. at 524, 99 S.Ct. at 2459.

necessarily vanishes when the fact finder entertains a reasonable doubt about the matter.

The U.S. Supreme Court's presumptions analysis applies to criminal contempt proceedings as well as to traditional prosecutions. As a constitutional matter, a person may not be adjudged guilty of criminal contempt unless his or her guilt is found beyond a reasonable doubt.[9] Contempt is civil for federal constitutional purposes when the contempt order allows the contemnor to purge the contempt by performing an act completely within the contemnor's control, e.g., answering a question. Contempt is criminal when the contemnor does not have the power to purge the contempt, i.e., when the penalty is unconditional.[10]

The California Supreme Court has applied *Sandstrom* broadly. Even telling the jurors that the accused's only obligation is to raise a reasonable doubt about the existence of the presumed fact will not save the presumption.[11] Jurors might construe such an instruction as compelling them to find the presumed fact as a matter of law when the accused fails to offer evidence rebutting the presumed fact and, as a logical matter, the basic facts do not compel the finding of the presumed fact.[12] As the California Supreme Court stressed in People v. Roder, "If that was the jury's understanding, the presumption would not have operated merely as a permissive inference."[13]

In *Roder* the court in effect construed Evidence Code § 607 as creating merely permissive inferences.[14] Section 607 provides that "[w]hen a presumption affecting the burden of [persuasion] operates in a criminal action to establish presumptively any fact that is essential to the defendant's guilt, the presumption operates only if the facts that give rise to the presumption have been found or otherwise established beyond a reasonable doubt and, in such case, the defendant need only raise a reasonable doubt as to the existence of the presumed fact."[15] To prevent jurors from being compelled to find the presumed fact as a matter of law if the accused fails to introduce evidence disproving the presumed fact, the judge should tell the jurors only that, if they wish, they *may* find the presumed fact from the basic facts.[16] The permissive language would thus reduce the presumption to a permissive inference, which in the court's view is constitutional.[17]

---

9. Hicks on Behalf of Feiock v. Feiock, 485 U.S. 624, 632, 108 S.Ct. 1423, 1429, 99 L.Ed.2d 721 (1988).

10. Id.

11. People v. Roder, 33 Cal.3d 491, 189 Cal.Rptr. 501, 658 P.2d 1302 (1983).

12. Id. at 504, 189 Cal.Rptr. at 510, 658 P.2d at 1311.

13. Id. The use of conclusive or rebuttable presumptions to prove an element against a cotemner in criminal contempt proceedings is also unconstitutional. See In re Ivey, 85 Cal. App.4th 793, 802–803, 102 Cal.Rptr.2d 447, 454 (2000).

14. People v. Roder, 33 Cal.3d 491, 506–507 and note 11, 189 Cal.Rptr. 501, 508 and note 11, 658 P.2d 1302, 1309 and note 11 (1983)

15. West's Ann. California Evidence Code § 607.

16. See Matter of Ivey, 85 Cal.App.4th 793, 804, 102 Cal.Rptr.2d 447, 455 (2000).

17. Instructions on permissive inferences must also meet due process standards. See § 18.09 infra.

The issue of what constitutes impermissible presumptions in criminal cases still haunts some California courts. An example is the court that decided People v. Pinkston, 112 Cal.App.4th 387, 5

The United States Supreme Court has not passed directly on the constitutionality of Thayer-type presumptions.[18] These require the judge to instruct the jurors to find the presumed fact if they find the basic facts but only if the opponent fails to introduce any evidence contradicting the presumed fact.[19] Though the matter was not presented in these terms in *Roder*, the court's language embraces this kind of presumption. Such a presumption could compel the jurors to find the presumed fact as a matter of law even if the basic facts do not compel a finding of the presumed fact beyond a reasonable doubt. Clearly, such a presumption would not operate "merely as a permissive inference."

Affirmative defenses. Presumptions are not the only threat to *Winship*. Affirmative defenses pose the same risk to the extent that their proof in effect requires the accused to disprove some of the elements of the offense. Assume again that the elements of an offense are A and B. If affirmative defense C is really non-B, then requiring the accused to prove C at least by a preponderance of the evidence would necessarily relieve the prosecution of having to prove B beyond a reasonable doubt.

The United States Supreme Court considered the effect of affirmative defenses on *Winship* in Martin v. Ohio.[20] In that case, the accused was

---

Cal.Rptr.3d 274 (2003). Under California law, it is a crime for a person who is eluding or attempting to elude a police officer to drive his or her vehicle in a "willful or wanton disregard for the safety of persons or property," a state of mind that requires proof of the defendant's awareness of the risks posed by his manner of driving. Another provision of the statute provides that for "purposes of this section, a willful or wanton disregard for the safety of persons or property includes, but is not limited to, driving while fleeing or attempting to elude a pursuing peace officer during which time either three or more violations that are assigned a traffic violation point count under [Vehicle Code] Section 12810 occur, or damage to property occurs." Id. at 393, 5 Cal.Rptr.3d at 279. In *Pinkston* the accused claimed that an instruction based on this statute relieved the prosecution of having to prove that he drove with a willful or wanton disregard for the safety of persons or property. The Court of Appeal rejected this claim, holding that the statute merely defined "in precise terms, one way in which the People may prove the element of willful or wanton disregard for the safety of persons or property." Id. at 394, 5 Cal.Rptr.3d at 280. Justice Anthony Kline dissented. If "willful or wanton disregard for the safety of persons or property" requires proof of recklessness (and it does), then in his view an instruction based on the second provision necessarily creates a conclusive presumption. Id. at 396, 5 Cal.Rptr.3d at 281. In effect, the jurors are told that if they find beyond a reasonable doubt that the accused drove in a manner which violated three or more provisions assigned a traffic point violation or damaged property, they must find that the accused drove with a reckless state of mind. Under such a construction of the statute, evidence that the defendant, for example, was unaware that he damaged property while eluding the police would be immaterial and therefore inadmissible. A party opposing a conclusive presumption may not offer evidence that rebuts the presumed fact. See Melendrez v. D & I Investment, Inc.,127 Cal.App.4th 1238, 1250, note 17, 26 Cal.Rptr.3d 413, 424, note 17 (2005).

18. In *Sandstrom*, the Court found it unnecessary to pass on Thayer-type presumptions. Sandstrom v. Montana, 442 U.S. 510, 515, 99 S.Ct. 2450, 2455, 61 L.Ed.2d 39 (1979), on remand, 184 Mont. 391, 603 P.2d 244 (1979). But language in *Francis* could be construed to prohibit instructing juries on Thayer-type presumptions where the accused fails to rebut the presumed fact: "A mandatory presumption instructs the jury that it must infer the presumed fact if the State proves certain predicate facts." Francis v. Franklin, 471 U.S. 307, 314, 105 S.Ct. 1965, 1971, 85 L.Ed.2d 344 (1985) (footnotes omitted).

19. If the opponent introduces evidence contradicting the presumed fact, then the judge will say nothing to the jury about the presumption. For an extended discussion of Thayer presumptions, see § 18.02 supra.

20. 480 U.S. 228, 107 S.Ct. 1098, 94 L.Ed.2d 267 (1987), reh'g denied, 481 U.S. 1024, 107 S.Ct. 1913, 95 L.Ed.2d 519 (1987).

prosecuted for murder under an Ohio statute that defined the offense as "purposely, and with prior calculation and design, caus[ing] the death of another."[21] The accused relied on self-defense. In the instructions, the jurors were told that they could acquit the accused if they found by a preponderance of the evidence that she believed herself to be "in imminent danger of death or great bodily harm" at the time she delivered the lethal blow.[22] As Justice Powell pointed out, the proposition that the accused believed herself to be in imminent danger when delivering the lethal blow was inconsistent with the proposition that she killed the victim as a result of prior calculation and design.[23] In his view, compelling the accused to prove the affirmative defense by a preponderance of the evidence necessarily relieved the prosecution of the obligation to prove the element of prior calculation and design beyond a reasonable doubt.[24]

The majority disagreed, however. The jurors had been instructed that to convict they had to find that the prosecution had proven each element of the offense, including prior calculation and design, beyond a reasonable doubt and that in making this determination the jurors were to consider all of the evidence, including the accused's evidence of self-defense.[25] In light of these instructions, the majority concluded that the jury must have rejected the defendant's version of the killing. Ohio, therefore, did "not shift to the defendant the burden of disproving any element of the state's case."[26]

The Justices' disagreement[27] about the outcome of the case may be less important than their agreement about the fundamental controlling principles. *Martin* did not purport to diminish *Winship* in any respect. Both the majority and the dissenters agreed that the constitutionality of the Ohio law, as given in the jury instructions, was to be determined by *Winship*'s mandate that "due process protects the accused against conviction except upon proof beyond a reasonable doubt of every fact necessary to constitute the crime with which he is charged."[28]

Affirmative defenses have not proved as troublesome in California. The California courts recognize that any defense that requires the defendant to disprove any element of the offense contravenes the requirement that the prosecution prove each element beyond a reasonable doubt.[29]

---

21.   Id. at 230, 107 S.Ct. at 1100.

22.   Id. at 233, 107 S.Ct. at 1101.

23.   Id. at 238–239, 107 S.Ct. at 1104 (Justice Powell dissenting).

24.   Id.

25.   Id. at 233, 107 S.Ct. at 1101.

26.   Id. at 234, 107 S.Ct. at 1102.

27.   The Court split 5 to 4 on whether the conviction should be affirmed.

28.   Martin v. Ohio, 480 U.S. 228, 231–232, 107 S.Ct. 1098, 1100–1101, 94 L.Ed.2d 267 (1987), reh'g denied, 481 U.S. 1024, 107 S.Ct. 1913, 95 L.Ed.2d 519 (1987) (quoting In re Winship, 397 U.S. 358, 364, 90 S.Ct. 1068, 1072, 25 L.Ed.2d 368 (1970)).

29.   See People v. Mower, 28 Cal.4th 457, 479–480, 122 Cal.Rptr.2d 326, 343–344, 49 P.3d 1067, 1080–1081 (2002) and cases cited therein. Unfortunately, *Mower* is not a model of clarity. What the California Supreme Court meant to say is that if a defendant introduces evidence in support of a defense that has the effect of disproving an element the prosecution must prove

Unlike the federal courts, however, the California courts do not have to reach for the Federal Constitution to support their position. The Evidence Code incorporates § 1096 of the Penal Code which places upon the prosecution the burden of proving each element of the offense beyond a reasonable doubt.[30] Once criminal defendants avail themselves of a defense to introduce evidence that disproves an element of the offense, the jurors must be instructed to acquit unless they find the element beyond a reasonable doubt.[31] Examples include evidence that a defendant possessed a drug with a physician's prescription when charged with unlawfully possessing a dangerous or restricted drug, lawfully acquired a hypodermic needle when charged with unlawfully possessing such a needle, lawfully prescribed narcotics when charged with unlawfully prescribing narcotics to an addict, and qualified as designated caregiver or patient when charged with unlawfully possessing or cultivating marihuana.[32]

Presumptions, competency to stand trial, and insanity. Under the Penal Code, a person who is "mentally incompetent" cannot be tried on a criminal charge.[33] A person is mentally incompetent "if, as a result of mental disorder or developmental disability, the defendant is unable to understand the nature of the criminal proceedings or to assist counsel in the conduct of a defense in a rational manner."[34] The burden of persuasion on the issue of competency is placed on the defendant: "It shall be presumed that the defendant is mentally competent unless it is proved by a preponderance of the evidence that the defendant is mentally incompetent."[35]

In Medina v. California[36] the United States Supreme Court upheld the constitutionality of this presumption. Since the issues decided at a competency hearing are separate from those determined at the trial on guilt, the concerns raised by *Winship* and *Sandstrom* are not implicated. The focus is not on whether the procedures governing competency hearings relieve the prosecution from proving the elements of the offense beyond a reasonable doubt but on whether the procedures satisfy due process. Because the California procedures entitle the defendant to the assistance of counsel and require the use of psychiatric evidence to

---

beyond a reasonable doubt, then the jury should be instructed that the prosecution has the burden of disproving the defense beyond a reasonable doubt or, alternatively, of proving the disputed element beyond a reasonable doubt. Only when the offense requires proof of a fact "collateral" to the defendant's guilt (i.e., a fact that does not disprove an element of the offense), may the accused be required to prove that fact at least by a preponderance of the evidence. Id.

30. See West's Ann. California Evidence Code § 501; West's Ann. California Penal Code § 1096.

31. See People v. Mower, 28 Cal.4th 457, 479–480, 122 Cal.Rptr.2d 326, 343–344, 49 P.3d 1067, 1080–1081 (2002) and cases cited therein.

32. Id. For other offenses having a similar effect, see id. at note 7.

33. West's Ann. California Penal Code § 1367.

34. Id.

35. West's Ann. California Penal Code § 1369(f).

36. 505 U.S. 437, 112 S.Ct. 2572, 120 L.Ed.2d 353 (1992), reh'g denied 505 U.S. 1244, 113 S.Ct. 19, 120 L.Ed.2d 946 (1992).

determine the defendant's mental condition,[37] the Court found that the Penal Code provisions were "constitutionally adequate" to guard against trying an incompetent defendant.[38]

The Evidence Code places upon the "party claiming that any person, including himself, is or was insane * * * the burden of proof on that issue."[39] The Penal Code in turn places upon the accused the burden of proving his or her insanity by a preponderance of the evidence.[40] Placing the burden of persuasion on the accused does not violate due process so long as the jury first finds that all of the elements of the offense have been proved beyond a reasonable doubt.[41] The Penal Code provides that, during the guilt phase, the accused is to be "conclusively presumed" to have been sane at the time the offense was allegedly committed.[42] The presumption does not violate *Winship* because it does not relieve the prosecution from proving the mens rea of the offense beyond a reasonable doubt and does not preclude the accused from offering evidence of mental disorders to disprove the existence of the mens rea.[43]

QUESTIONS AND PROBLEMS

Thayer: producing en
Morgan: shifts burd. of persuasion
shifts burd. of

Assume a prosecution for possessing stolen property. The prosecution must prove beyond a reasonable doubt that, in addition to possessing the property, the defendant was aware that it was stolen. The owner testifies that the property is his and that he never gave it to the defendant. The defendant testifies that he bought the property from a migrant worker and had no idea that it was stolen.

Determine the constitutionality of the following jury instructions:

If you find beyond a reasonable doubt that the defendant was a dealer in second-hand merchandise, that he bought stolen property, and that he bought such property under circumstances which should have caused him to make reasonable inquiry that the person from whom the defendant bought the property had the legal right to sell it, and that the defendant did not make such reasonable inquiry,

(a) Then you shall presume that the defendant bought such property knowing that it was stolen. *conclusive*

(b) Then you shall presume that the defendant bought such property knowing that it was stolen unless the defendant persuades you by a preponderance of the evidence that he did not know it was stolen.

Morgan

---

37. Id. at 450, 112 S.Ct. at 2580.

38. Id. at 452, 112 S.Ct. at 2581.

39. West's Ann. California Evidence Code § 522.

40. West's Ann. California Penal Code § 25(b).

41. Leland v. Oregon, 343 U.S. 790, 792, 72 S.Ct. 1002, 1004–1005, 96 L.Ed. 1302 (1952), reh'g denied, 344 U.S. 848, 73 S.Ct. 4, 97 L.Ed. 659 (1952).

42. West's Ann. California Penal Code § 1026(a).

43. People v. Wetmore, 22 Cal.3d 318, 326, note 6, 149 Cal.Rptr. 265, 271, note 6, 583 P.2d 1308, 1314, note 6 (1978). An amendment to the Penal Code now limits the evidence to disproving only the mens rea of specific intent crimes. West's Ann. California Penal Code § 28(a).

Morgan

Inference

(c) Then you shall presume that the defendant bought such property knowing that it was stolen unless the defendant raises a reasonable doubt about whether he knew that it was stolen.

(d) Then you may, if you wish, infer that the defendant knew that the property was stolen, unless from all of the evidence you have a reasonable doubt whether the defendant knew that the property was stolen.

§ 18.08 LEGISLATIVE REALLOCATION OF THE BURDEN OF PROOF IN CRIMINAL CASES

As the previous section makes clear, a state may not, in the guise of jury instructions, shift to the accused the burden of disproving elements which under *Winship*[1] the state must prove beyond a reasonable doubt. But may a state effect the prohibited shift by redefining the offense? Speaking for a Court with no dissenters, Justice Powell said that the answer to that question is no:

> [I]f *Winship* were limited to those facts that constitute a crime as defined by state law, a State could undermine many of the interests that decision sought to protect without effecting any substantive change in its law. It would only be necessary to redefine the elements that comprise different crimes * * *. *Winship* is concerned with substance rather than this kind of formalism.[2]

But Justice Powell's unqualified answer is no longer the prevailing view. Over his vigorous dissent, a majority held in Patterson v. New York[3] that all that *Winship* requires is that the prosecution prove each element of the offense as defined by the state.[4] In *Patterson* the accused was convicted of murder under a New York law that defined murder as causing the death of a person with the intent to do so.[5] It was an affirmative defense that at the time the accused delivered the lethal blow he was acting "under the influence of extreme emotional disturbance for which there was a reasonable explanation or excuse."[6] Prior to reforming its criminal laws, New York used the Common Law definition of murder. Common Law murder required proof of malice aforethought, which in turn required the state to prove that the accused did not kill in the heat of passion.[7] Under the new statute, malice aforethought was eliminated, and heat of passion became "extreme emotional disturbance." This element was then made into an affirmative defense, which, like heat of passion,

---

1. 397 U.S. 358, 90 S.Ct. 1068, 25 L.Ed.2d 368 (1970).

2. Mullaney v. Wilbur, 421 U.S. 684, 698–699, 95 S.Ct. 1881, 1889, 44 L.Ed.2d 508 (1975).

3. 432 U.S. 197, 97 S.Ct. 2319, 53 L.Ed.2d 281 (1977).

4. Id. at 205–206, 97 S.Ct. at 2324.

5. Id. at 198, 97 S.Ct. at 2319.

6. Id.

7. Id. at 217–220, 97 S.Ct. at 2330–2332 (Justice Powell, dissenting).

reduced what would otherwise be murder to manslaughter.[8] The majority of the justices held that the new statute did not violate *Winship;* as enacted the statute did not require the state to prove that the accused did not kill while under the influence of an extreme emotional disturbance.[9]

§ 18.09 INFERENCES IN CRIMINAL CASES

Inferences differ from presumptions in that they are simply the kind of deductions or conclusions jurors draw from the evidence in much the same way that they draw deductions or conclusions from a given piece of information in everyday problem solving. For example, earlier we saw that a jury could infer that a letter was received from evidence that the letter was mailed with the correct address and proper postage.[1] Inferences differ from presumptions in one important respect: they are permissive. Jurors are told only that they may draw a particular inference from a given item or items of evidence *if they wish.*

Though less likely to do so than presumptions, inferences can also deprive the accused of due process. The problem is most acute when the judge instructs the jury on inferences that happen to coincide with the facts the prosecution must prove beyond a reasonable doubt under *Winship.*[2] For example, assume that an offense requires the prosecution to prove that the accused possessed checks stolen from the mails knowing the checks to have been stolen from the mails; may the judge tell the jurors that they may infer from the unexplained possession of recently stolen mail that the accused possessed the mail with knowledge that it was stolen?

According to the United States Supreme Court, the judge may do so if the "inference submitted to the jury as sufficient to support conviction satisfies the reasonable doubt standard (that is, the evidence necessary to invoke the inference is sufficient for a rational juror to find the inferred fact beyond a reasonable doubt) as well as the more-likely-than-not standard * * *."[3]

Although the Court's test is not a model of clarity, the Court seems to be saying that the judge should apply a sufficiency standard in determining the constitutionality of an instruction on an inference. The judge should instruct on the inference only if the judge concludes that the prosecution's evidence, if believed, could move a reasonable juror to find the inference beyond a reasonable doubt. Such an instruction would accord with due process because a challenge to the conviction on insufficiency of evidence would have to be rejected. In reviewing the challenge,

---

8. Id.

9. Id. at 205–206, 97 S.Ct. at 2324.

1. See § 18.04 supra.

2. 397 U.S. 358, 90 S.Ct. 1068, 25 L.Ed.2d 368 (1970). For an extended discussion of In re Winship, see §§ 18.02 and 18.07 supra.

3. Barnes v. United States, 412 U.S. 837, 843, 93 S.Ct. 2357, 2361, 37 L.Ed.2d 380 (1973).

the appellate court would have to employ the very sufficiency standard used by the trial judge in deciding whether to instruct on the inference.[4]

QUESTIONS AND PROBLEMS

1. Unlike presumptions, instructions on permissive inferences do not violate the accused's right to a trial that comports with due process. True or false?

2. The defendant is charged with possessing mail which he knew was stolen from the US mails. Assume that the addressee testifies that he never received the letter taken from the defendant and that he never authorized the defendant to remove the letter from her mailbox. The prosecution requests the judge to instruct the jury according to the following statutory inference: "You may infer from the unexplained possession of recently stolen mail that the accused possessed the mail with knowledge that it was stolen." According to *Barnes*, what test should the judge employ in determining whether to grant the prosecution's request? What would you call this test? Why is this test the proper one? In answering the last question, consider the test the appellate court would employ in determining whether to affirm or reverse the defendant's conviction if the defendant predicates his appeal on the ground that the evidence adduced at the trial was insufficient to support the jury's finding that he knew that the mail he possessed was stolen.

§ 18.10 PRESUMPTIONS UNDER THE FEDERAL RULES

As submitted by the United States Supreme Court, the Federal Rules adopted Morgan's view of presumptions in civil cases. The original rule placed on "the opposing party the burden of establishing the nonexistence of the presumed fact, once the party invoking the presumption established the basic facts giving rise to it."[1] The Advisory Committee that formulated the Rules favored Morgan over Thayer presumptions on the ground that Thayer presumptions accorded "presumptions too 'slight and evanescent' an effect."[2] But Congress changed the recommended rule and, instead, adopted Thayer's view of presumptions. Rule 301 provides that "[i]n a civil case, unless a federal statute or these rules provide otherwise, the party against whom a presumption is directed has the burden of producing evidence to rebut the presumption. But this rule does not shift the burden of persuasion, which remains on the party who had it originally."[3]

But the instructions given to a federal jury about the effect of the presumption differ from those given under the Code with respect to

---

4. People v. Johnson, 26 Cal.3d 557, 577–578, 162 Cal.Rptr. 431, 433–444, 606 P.2d 738, 750–751 (1980).

1. Federal Rule of Evidence 301 (Report of the Senate Committee on the Judiciary).

2. Federal Rule of Evidence 301 (Advisory Committee Note), Deleted and Superseded Materials (West 2002–2003 ed.).

3. Federal Rule of Evidence 301.

Thayer presumptions. In California, if the opponent disproves the presumed fact by a sufficiency standard, the presumption disappears, and the judge will tell the jury nothing about the presumption.[4] But under the Federal Rules, the judge may "instruct the jury that it may infer the existence of the presumed fact from proof of the basic facts."[5] In effect, the judge is permitted to treat a rebutted presumption as an inference.[6] Where the opponent fails to produce evidence rebutting the presumption, California judges will instruct the jurors to find the presumed fact if they first find the basic facts by the appropriate persuasion standard.[7] Federal judges, however, give a more limited instruction. They will tell the jurors that they "may presume the existence of the presumed fact" if they find the basic facts.[8] The use of the permissive "may" might suggest to some that an inference is intended and not a Thayer presumption, despite the use of the term "presume".

Rule 301 presumptions apply in all civil actions and proceedings unless a different presumption is prescribed by an Act of Congress or the Rules.[9] An Act of Congress can include presumptions created by courts construing federal statutes.[10] Rule 301 presumptions may not apply to cases governed by *Erie*.[11] Rule 302 provides that "[i]n a civil case, state law governs the effect of a presumption regarding a claim or defense for which state law supplies the rule of decision."[12]

QUESTIONS AND PROBLEMS

1. Although the United States Supreme Court recommended a rule on presumptions adopting Morgan's view, Congress replaced the rule with one essentially adopting Thayer's view. True or false?

2. Some observers believe that Rule 301 tracks Professor Thayer's view of presumptions. Would Thayer agree? If not, why?

CALIFORNIA EVIDENCE CODE

§ 110.   "Burden of producing evidence"

"Burden of producing evidence" means the obligation of a party to introduce evidence sufficient to avoid a ruling against him on the issue.

---

4.   See § 18.04 supra.

5.   Federal Rule of Evidence 301 (Conference Report).

6.   For an discussion of inferences, see § 18.09 supra.

7.   See § 18.04 supra.

8.   Federal Rule of Evidence 301 (Conference Report).

9.   Federal Rule of Evidence 301.

10.   An example is the Morgan-type presumption the United States Supreme Court created in disparate impact cases brought under Title VII of the 1964 Civil Rights Act. See Griggs v. Duke Power Co., 401 U.S. 424, 432, 91 S.Ct. 849, 854, 28 L.Ed.2d 158 (1971).

11.   Erie Railroad Co. v. Tompkins, 304 U.S. 64, 58 S.Ct. 817, 82 L.Ed. 1188 (1938).

12.   Federal Rule of Evidence 302.

§ 115.   "Burden of proof"

"Burden of proof" means the obligation of a party to establish by evidence a requisite degree of belief concerning a fact in the mind of the trier of fact or the court. The burden of proof may require a party to raise a reasonable doubt concerning the existence or nonexistence of a fact or that he establish the existence or nonexistence of a fact by a preponderance of the evidence, by clear and convincing proof, or by proof beyond a reasonable doubt.

Except as otherwise provided by law, the burden of proof requires proof by a preponderance of the evidence.

§ 600.   Presumption and inference defined

(a) A presumption is an assumption of fact that the law requires to be made from another fact or group of facts found or otherwise established in the action. A presumption is not evidence.

(b) An inference is a deduction of fact that may logically and reasonably be drawn from another fact or group of facts found or otherwise established in the action.

§ 601.   Classification of presumptions

A presumption is either conclusive or rebuttable. Every rebuttable presumption is either (a) a presumption affecting the burden of producing evidence or (b) a presumption affecting the burden of proof.

§ 602.   Statute making one fact prima facie evidence of another fact

A statute providing that a fact or group of facts is prima facie evidence of another fact establishes a rebuttable presumption.

§ 603.   Presumption affecting the burden of producing evidence defined

A presumption affecting the burden of producing evidence is a presumption established to implement no public policy other than to facilitate the determination of the particular action in which the presumption is applied.

§ 604.   Effect of presumption affecting burden of producing evidence

The effect of a presumption affecting the burden of producing evidence is to require the trier of fact to assume the existence of the presumed fact unless and until evidence is introduced which would support a finding of its nonexistence, in which case the trier of fact shall determine the existence or nonexistence of the presumed fact from the evidence and without regard to the presumption. Nothing in this section shall be construed to prevent the drawing of any inference that may be appropriate.

§ 605. Presumption affecting the burden of proof defined

A presumption affecting the burden of proof is a presumption established to implement some public policy other than to facilitate the determination of the particular action in which the presumption is applied, such as the policy in favor of establishment of a parent and child relationship, the validity of marriage, the stability of titles to property, or the security of those who entrust themselves or their property to the administration of others.

§ 606. Effect of presumption affecting burden of proof

The effect of a presumption affecting the burden of proof is to impose upon the party against whom it operates the burden of proof as to the nonexistence of the presumed fact.

§ 607. Effect of certain presumptions in a criminal action

When a presumption affecting the burden of proof operates in a criminal action to establish presumptively any fact that is essential to the defendant's guilt, the presumption operates only if the facts that give rise to the presumption have been found or otherwise established beyond a reasonable doubt and, in such case, the defendant need only raise a reasonable doubt as to the existence of the presumed fact.

FEDERAL RULES OF EVIDENCE

Rule 301.   Presumptions in Civil Cases Generally

In a civil case, unless a federal statute or these rules provide otherwise, the party against whom a presumption is directed has the burden of producing evidence to rebut the presumption. But this rule does not shift the burden of persuasion, which remains on the party who had it originally.

Rule 302.   Applying State Law to Presumptions in Civil Cases

In a civil case, state law governs the effect of a presumption regarding a claim or defense for which state law supplies the rule of decision.

CHAPTER 19

JUDICIAL NOTICE

■ ■ ■

Table of Sections

§ 19.01   JUDICIAL NOTICE UNDER THE EVIDENCE CODE

In general. When a judge "notices" a fact, the party with the burden of proving that fact is relieved of the obligation of introducing evidence establishing the fact. Judicial notice is thus a substitute for evidence. Judicial notice confers an additional benefit on the party with the obligation of establishing the noticed fact: matters judicially noticed are binding on the jury and preclude the opponent from offering evidence disputing the noticed fact.[1] But judicial notice generally does not replace the need to produce evidence because the matters a judge can notice are few.[2]

The Code divides these matters into two categories. One—mandatory judicial notice—consists of matters which the judge must notice, whether or not the judge has been requested to notice them.[3] The other—permissive judicial notice—consists of matters which the judge may notice on his or her own motion but which the judge must notice if notice is requested and certain procedural requirements are met.[4]

Mandatory judicial notice. The mandatory category recognizes that courts must be free to discover and apply the law applicable to the case. Though the category includes matters both of law and fact, many of

---

1. West's Ann. California Evidence Code § 457 ("[T]he trial court may, and upon request shall, instruct the jury to accept as a fact the matter noticed.").

2. "Judicial notice may not be taken of any matter unless authorized or required by law." West's Ann. California Evidence Code § 450.

3. West's Ann. California Evidence Code § 451 (comment).

4. West's Ann. California Evidence Code §§ 452–453.

the matters in this category that must be judicially noticed are legal in nature. These include the decisional, constitutional, and public statutory law of California and the United States; regulations of California and federal agencies, including documents published in the Federal Register; California and federal rules of court, including rules of pleading, practice and procedure; and the state bar rules of professional conduct.[5] Factual matters a court must notice include the true "signification" of all English words and phrases and of all legal expressions; and, perhaps most importantly, universally known facts.[6]

Permissive judicial notice. The permissive category also includes matters both of law and fact. Sometimes, matters of law or fact necessary to the resolution of the case may be known neither to the court nor easily discoverable by the court because the sources of information are not readily available. If the party requesting judicial notice of matters in this category furnishes the court with adequate information for the court to

---

5. West's Ann. California Evidence Code § 451 and comment. The power to notice federal decisional law includes noticing decisions that do not appear in West's Federal Reporter and Federal Supplement. See Boghos v. Certain Underwriters at Lloyd's of London, 36 Cal.4th 495, 502, note 3, 30 Cal.Rptr.3d 787, 792, note 3, 115 P.3d 68, 72, note 3 (2005). The power also includes noticing unpublished opinions of the California Court of Appeal. See People v. Hill, 17 Cal.4th 800, 847, note 9, 72 Cal.Rptr.2d 656, 683, note 9, 952 P.2d 673, 700, note 9 (1998).

The power to notice the statutory law of California includes the power to notice materials comprising the law's legislative history, Planning and Conservation League v. DWR, 17 Cal.4th 264, 271, note 4, 70 Cal.Rptr.2d 635, 640, note 4, 949 P.2d 488, 493, note 4 (1998), including reports of the California Law Revision Commission. Estate of Joseph, 17 Cal.4th 203, 210, note 1, 70 Cal.Rptr.2d 619, 623, note 1, 949 P.2d 472, 476, note 1 (1998) and analyses by legislative committees. In re Devon C., 79 Cal.App.4th 929, 933, note 6, 94 Cal.Rptr.2d 513, 516, note 6 (2000). In determining the meaning of initiatives, courts may notice the ballot arguments and legislative materials, People v. Snyder, 22 Cal.4th 304, 309, note 5, 92 Cal.Rptr.2d 734, 737, note 5, 992 P.2d 1102, 1105, note 5 (2000), including printed discussions by the Legislative Analyst. Apartment Ass'n of L.A. County, Inc. v. City of L.A., 24 Cal.4th 830, 837, note 1, 102 Cal.Rptr.2d 719, 723, note 1, 14 P.3d 930, 935, note 1 (2001).

For a description of the types of documents that can be judicially noticed as comprising legislative history, see People v. Patterson, 72 Cal.App.4th 438, 442–443, 84 Cal.Rptr.2d 870, 872–873 (1999); Hoechst Celanese Corp. v. Franchise Tax Bd., 25 Cal.4th 508, 519, note 5, 106 Cal.Rptr.2d 548, 557, note 5, 22 P.3d 324, 332, note 5, cert. denied, 534 U.S. 1040, 122 S.Ct. 614, 151 L.Ed.2d 537 (2001). As a rule, documents containing the views of individual legislators, including a bill's author, cannot be judicially noticed; neither may the analyses or opinions concerning the meaning of legislation prepared by executive branch agencies be noticed. People v. Patterson, supra. Moreover, "[p]ost enrollment documents are not a proper indicia of legislative intent because it is not reasonable to infer that they were ever read or considered by the Legislature." Whaley v. Sony Computer Entertainment America, Inc., 121 Cal.App.4th 479, 488, Note 4, 17 Cal.Rptr.3d 88, 95, note 4 (2004). Unpassed bills generally may not be noticed since they are of "little value" as evidence of legislative intent. People v. Baniqued, 85 Cal.App.4th 13, 27–28, 101 Cal.Rptr.2d 835, 845 (2000).

Letters expressing the opinions of individual legislators are usually inadmissible in assessing the meaning of a statute because the meaning depends on the intent of the entire California Legislature, not of individual legislators. In some circumstances, however, such letters might be relevant. In City of Brentwood v. Central Valley Regional Water Quality Control Bd., 123 Cal.App.4th 714, 20 Cal.Rptr.3d 322 (2004), the reviewing court took judicial notice of a letter sent by several legislators to the Board protesting its interpretation of a time period for imposing penalties. The issue before the court was the correct interpretation of the time period, and the Board's response to the letter in turn prompted the Legislature to amend the statutory language. The letter was thus essential to understanding the Legislature's goal in approving the amendment. Id. at 728, 20 Cal.Rptr.3d at 322.

6. West's Ann. California Evidence Code § 451 and comment.

notice the matter, then the court must do so if proper notice has been given to each adverse party.[7]

Matters which may be judicially noticed under the permissive category include the decisional, constitutional, and statutory law of sister states and of the territories and possessions of the United States; regulations of sister states and of the territories and possessions of the United States; official acts of the legislative, executive, and judicial departments of the United States, or of any state, territory, or possession of the United States; court records and rules of any California court, federal court, or any state, territory, or possession of the United States; the law of organizations of nations, foreign nations, and public entities in foreign nations; and, again, perhaps most importantly, locally known and easily verifiable facts.[8]

Universally and locally known facts and easily verifiable facts. These facts are singled out for special treatment for two reasons. First, under the view reflected in the Federal Rules, these are the only facts that are the proper subject of judicial notice.[9] Second, the other essentially legal matters alluded to in the mandatory and permissive categories of the Code are considered by some commentators as an inappropriate subject of judicial notice.[10]

Universally and locally known facts and easily verifiable facts are "adjudicative facts" in the sense that they comprise the kind of propositions which must be proved in any lawsuit.[11] Jurisdictional requirements, for example, may require a party to establish that a cause of action arose in a particular geographical area at a particular time.[12] In the absence of judicial notice, the party would have to introduce evidence establishing these facts.

---

7. West's Ann. California Evidence Code § 452 and comment. Where a party claims that an ordinance creates a duty designed to protect against the kind of injury the party complains he suffered, the court must examine the ordinance to determine the validity of the party's claim. In such a situation, the court must notice the ordinance if the party provides the court with a copy and gives proper notice to the adverse parties. See Haggis v. City of Los Angeles, 22 Cal.4th 490, 501, note 3, 93 Cal.Rptr.2d 327, 334, note 3, 993 P.2d 983, 989, note 3 (2000).

8. West's Ann. California Evidence Code § 452 and comment. Official acts and records that may be noticed under the permissive category include computer generated official records, as specified by the California Judicial Council, relating to criminal convictions when the records are certified by the Superior Court clerk at the time of the computer entry. See West's Ann. California Evidence Code § 452.5. California courts can also take judicial notice of records posted by the California State Bar on its website, including records indicating when an attorney was admitted to practice law. See In re White, 121 Cal.App.4th 1453, 1469, note 14, 18 Cal.Rptr.3d 444, 456, note 14 (2004). But official acts and records do not include materials prepared by private parties and merely filed with a state agency. Such materials are not the "acts" of the agency. See Stevens v. Superior Court, 75 Cal.App.4th 594, 608, 89 Cal.Rptr.2d 370, 380 (1999).

9. See Federal Rule of Evidence 201(a) and Advisory Committee Note.

10. See id. (Advisory Committee Note).

11. Id.

12. See, e.g., People v. Posey, 32 Cal.4th 193, 216, 8 Cal.Rptr.3d 551, 568, 82 P.3d 755, 770, cert. denied 542 U.S. 909, 124 S.Ct. 2848, 159 L.Ed.2d 276 (2004), where the reviewing court took judicial notice that Santa Rosa is in Marin County in an appeal in which the accused challenged the jury's venue findings.

The other matters alluded to in the mandatory and permissive categories of the Code are classified by some commentators as "legislative facts."[13] These commentators believe that judges should be free to consult pertinent data to determine the content or applicability of a rule of law.[14] While parties and their counsel may be consulted on these matters, these commentators emphasize that whether a particular rule of law governs a case is not normally a matter determined by resort to evidentiary sources, such as witnesses.[15] The Federal Rules of Evidence adopt this view and limit judicial notice to adjudicative facts.[16] The Code does not. But as a practical matter, most controversies surrounding judicial notice involve adjudicative facts, i.e., matters a party would be expected to prove in the absence of judicial notice. Thus, the usual question presented is whether a particular matter falls within the categories created for noticing universally known facts, locally known facts, and easily verifiable facts.

The term "universally known facts" is something of a misnomer. The term does not require a showing that "every man on the street has knowledge of such facts. A fact known among persons of reasonable and average intelligence and knowledge will satisfy the 'universally known' requirement."[17] "Persons", moreover, means Americans. Thus, who won the last U.S. Presidential election may be a universally known fact but not who was last elected president in France. The judge's knowledge is not determinative. A judge who knows who won the last French presidential election may not notice that fact unless it is widely enough known to qualify as a universally known fact.[18]

The term "locally known facts" refers to matters of "such common knowledge within the territorial jurisdiction of the court that they cannot reasonably be the subject of dispute."[19] Territorial "refers to the county in which a superior court is located or the judicial district in which a municipal or justice court is located."[20] But the fact judicially noticed need

---

13. See, e.g., Federal Rule of Evidence 201 and Advisory Committee Note.

14. Id. (Advisory Committee Note).

15. Id.

16. Federal Rule of Evidence 201.

17. West's Ann. California Evidence Code § 451 (comment). Among the universally known facts noticed by courts are "(1) that street gangs generally claim a 'home territory' and attempt to prohibit rival gang members from entering the area upon threat of severe physical injury and (2) that gang activity spawns violence." Medina v. Hillshore Partners, 40 Cal.App.4th 477, 481, 46 Cal.Rptr.2d 871, 873–874 (1995). See also People v. McDonald, 137 Cal.App.4th 521, 538, 40 Cal.Rptr.3d 422, 436 (2006), where the court relied in part on § 451(f) to notice that urinating in public is unpleasant and, therefore, constitutes a criminal public nuisance.

18. West's Ann. California Evidence Code § 451 (comment).

19. West's Ann. California Evidence Code § 452(g). See also Federal Rule of Evidence 201(b) ("generally known within the territorial jurisdiction of the trial court"). California courts have relied on § 452(g) to notice the banks' custom of sending customers monthly statements with cancelled checks. See Roy Supply, Inc. v. Wells Fargo Bank, 39 Cal.App.4th 1051, 1074, 46 Cal.Rptr.2d 309, 323 (1995), and cases cited therein. When the issue arises, one would expect the courts to notice the emerging banks' practice of sending monthly "paperless" statements over the internet.

20. West's Ann. California Evidence Code § 452 (comment). As a result of court consolidation, municipal and justice courts no longer exist in California.

not be something physically located within the court's territorial jurisdiction so long as common knowledge of the fact exists within the court's territorial jurisdiction.[21] The Golden Gate Bridge is not in Santa Clara County, but a judge in that county can take judicial notice that it is located in San Francisco and Marin Counties. Santa Clara County residents know where the Golden Gate Bridge is located.

The term "easily verifiable facts" refers to facts that are not widely known but can be readily ascertained by "resort to sources of reasonably indisputable accuracy."[22] The fact that Christmas 1942 fell on a Wednesday is not widely known. But that fact can be readily ascertained by consulting a calendar. On the other hand, the link between exposure to electric and magnetic fields and cancer is "far from indisputable" and therefore cannot be readily ascertained by resort to sources of reasonably indisputable accuracy.[23] For the same reason, the harmlessness of marihuana cannot be readily established by resort to such sources.[24]

Sources of indisputable accuracy are not limited to calendars and almanacs, and the like; they can also include treatises and encyclopedias, persons learned in the subject matter,[25] as well as agency documents

---

21. Id. See, e.g., People v. Bhakta, 135 Cal.App.4th 631, 641, 37 Cal.Rptr.3d 652, 659 (2006), where the reviewing court for the judicial district in which Los Angeles is located took judicial notice that Los Angeles is a city whose population exceeds 750,000 in an action allowing a city attorney to prosecute a violation of the state's unfair competition law in the name of the people of California only if the city's population exceeds that figure.

22. West's Ann. California Evidence Code § 452(h). See Federal Rule of Evidence 201(b) ("can be accurately and readily determined from sources whose accuracy cannot reasonably be questioned").

23. See Ford v. Pacific Gas and Elec. Co., 60 Cal.App.4th 696, 706, 70 Cal.Rptr.2d 359, 367 (1997).

24. Comings v. State Bd. Of Education, 23 Cal.App.3d 94, 101–102, 100 Cal.Rptr. 73, 78–79 (1972).

25. West's Ann. California Evidence Code § 454 (a)(1). A judge may take judicial notice of the content of an assessor's handbook in determining the propriety of an assessor's action, Hunt–Wesson Foods, Inc. v. Alameda County, 41 Cal.App.3d 163, 179, 116 Cal.Rptr. 160, 171 (1974), and may use a death certificate in determining the date of death. People v. Terry, 38 Cal.App.3d 432, 439–440, 113 Cal.Rptr. 233, 238 (1974). A judge may also take judicial notice of facts found in highly regarded studies of reasonably indisputable accuracy. In Gavin W. v. YMCA of Metropolitan Los Angeles, 106 Cal.App.4th 662, 131 Cal.Rptr.2d 168 (2003), the reviewing court used such a study to notice that "55 percent of children ages 13 and under live in families with two employed parents or an employed single head of household of a person." Id. at 672, 131 Cal.Rptr.2d at 175.

But where a party claims that he was employed pursuant to an oral contract while the other claims the employment resulted from a written contract, a judge may not judicially notice the written contract as the contract between the parties. Gould v. Maryland Sound Industries, Inc., 31 Cal.App.4th 1137, 1145–1146, 37 Cal.Rptr.2d 718, 722 (1995). Neither may a court take judicial notice of statements in a police report as such reports are "reasonably subject to dispute." People v. Jones, 15 Cal.4th 119, 172, note 17, 61 Cal.Rptr.2d 386, 418, note 17, 931 P.2d 960, 992, note 17 (1997), cert. denied, 522 U.S. 955, 118 S.Ct. 381, 139 L.Ed.2d 297 (1997), overruled on other grounds, People v. Hill, 17 Cal.4th 800, 72 Cal.Rptr.2d 656, 952 P.2d 673 (1998). A court may not take judicial notice of articles discussing problems with computers as proof that reliance on computers is misplaced. The information in the articles does not qualify as easily verifiable facts. People v. Martinez, 22 Cal.4th 106, 132–133, 91 Cal.Rptr.2d 687, 707, 990 P.2d 563, 582 (2000).

Where the advice of learned persons is required to take judicial notice, the court on its own motion or on motion of any party may appoint one or more persons to provide the advice. West's Ann. California Evidence Code § 460.

describing how the agency applies statutory mandates.[26] But the fact that the court and parties may resort to such sources does not mean that the sources must be received as evidence or sent to the jury room as exhibits. Their use is limited "to consultation by the judge and the parties" in determining whether the judge should take judicial notice.[27] Indeed, in determining the propriety of taking judicial notice, the judge can consider information that may be inadmissible. Except for § 352[28] and the rules of privilege, the exclusionary rules of evidence do not apply to judicial notice.[29]

Noticing court records. The permissive category allows judges to notice the records of any California court or of any court of record of the United States or sister state.[30] But the authority to do so extends generally to noticing only the existence of the record. It does not empower judges to notice as true, assertions contained in the records.[31] The transcript of a preliminary hearing, for example, is a court record. If relevant, a judge may notice the transcript as the transcript of a particular preliminary hearing and may even notice it as the original transcript. The judge, however, may not circumvent the hearsay rule by noticing as true the complaining witness's testimony.

Whether or not the judge can consider the facts noticed for the truth of the matter stated depends on the hearsay rule and its exceptions. A judge, for example, may notice an answer given by an adverse party in response to an interrogatory as that party's response to the interrogatory. But the judge may not consider the answer for the truth of the matter stated unless it falls within a hearsay exception, for example, the excep-

---

26. In re Cervera, 24 Cal.4th 1073, 1082, note 3, 103 Cal.Rptr.2d 762, 768, note 3, 16 P.3d 176, 181, note 3 (2001) (noticing California Department of Corrections documents).

27. West's Ann. California Evidence Code § 452 (comment).

28. Section 352 empowers judges to exclude relevant evidence whenever its probative value is substantially outweighed by other concerns, such as undue prejudice to the opposing party. West's Ann. California Evidence Code § 352. For an extended discussion of § 352, see § 2.10 supra.

29. West's Ann. California Evidence Code § 454(a)(2).

30. West's Ann. California Evidence Code § 452(d). Court records can include opinions ordered "depublished" by the California Supreme Court. People v. Hill, 17 Cal.4th 800, 848, note 9, 72 Cal.Rptr.2d 656, 683, note 9, 952 P.2d 673, 700, note 9 (1998). Generally, the California Rules of Court prohibit the citation of such opinions. But the rules do not bar a court from noticing an unpublished opinion if the court does not cite it for its precedential value. Id.

31. Whitehouse v. Six Corp., 40 Cal.App.4th 527, 537, 48 Cal.Rptr.2d 600, 606 (1995) (Over a hearsay objection, a judge may not notice an appraiser's assessment of the value of a property even though the assessment was contained in declarations which in turn were part of the court's file.); Garcia v. Sterling, 176 Cal.App.3d 17, 22, 221 Cal.Rptr. 349, 352 (1985) (A judge may notice the existence of statements in a deposition but may not notice them for the truth of the matters asserted.). But see Sebago, Inc. v. City of Alameda, 211 Cal.App.3d 1372, 1380, 259 Cal.Rptr. 918, 921 (1989) (In a motion on the pleadings a judge may notice the contents of an answer to an interrogatory in which the answering party stated its reasons for believing that adult entertainment downgrades neighborhoods.).

The same principle applies to official acts of executive agencies noticed under the permissive category. For example, a judge may notice an official document as a letter by the California Secretary of Resources certifying that an agency's actions satisfy environmental requirements. The hearsay rule is not implicated because the letter is noticed only for the limited purpose of proving the act of certification. Cf. San Mateo County Coastal Landowners' Ass'n v. County of San Mateo et al., 38 Cal.App.4th 523, 552, 45 Cal.Rptr.2d 117, 134 (1995).

tion for party admissions.[32] But merely considering the answer for the truth is not the same as noticing as true the propositions asserted in the answer. As has been noted, the fact finder must accept as established any matter properly notice by the judge.[33] A judge, therefore, may not notice as true, propositions contained in matter noticed unless those propositions fall into such categories of judicial notice as universally or locally known facts or easily verifiable facts. Conversely, just because an item of evidence falls within a hearsay exception does not mean that a court can notice as true the matter asserted.[34] It simply means that the jurors may consider the item of evidence for the truth of the matter asserted.

Where the contents of the court record are offered for a nonhearsay purpose, the court may notice the record if it otherwise qualifies for judicial notice. A judge, for example, may notice the contents of a complaint filed in another action to prove that homeowners were on notice of housing defects but not to prove the existence of the defects.[35] Similarly, a judge may notice a letter in its files for the nonhearsay purpose of showing that a lawyer had been put on notice of the date of a court hearing.[36] A judge may also notice a prior judgment and other court records in determining whether to sustain a demurrer on res judicata grounds,[37] and may also notice another judge's factual findings in determining the res judicata or collateral estoppel effects of those findings in a subsequent action.[38]

The decisions are in conflict on whether a judge can notice findings made by other judges. In re David C.,[39] for example, holds that a judge can notice facts asserted in findings and orders in prior juvenile court proceedings in determining whether to declare the minor free of parental custody and control.[40] People v. Tolbert,[41] on the other hand, holds that in ruling

---

32. See Rodas v. Spiegel, 87 Cal.App.4th 513, 517, 104 Cal.Rptr.2d 439, 442 (2001) (holding that a court may notice for the truth admissions in a party's opposition to a demurrer).

33. See text accompanying note 1, supra.

34. See Big Valley Band of Pomo Indians v. Superior Court, 133 Cal.App.4th 1185, 1192, 35 Cal.Rptr.3d 357, 363 (2005).

35. Magnolia Square Homeowners Ass'n v. Safeco Ins. Co. of America, 221 Cal.App.3d 1049, 1056, 271 Cal.Rptr. 1, 4 (1990). In a similar vein, a judge may notice briefs filed by parties in another action to determine whether they are inconsistent with the party's claims in the present action. State Farm v. Quackenbush, 77 Cal.App.4th 65, 77, note 3, 91 Cal.Rptr.2d 381, 389, note 3 (1999).

36. People v. Jimenez, 38 Cal.App.4th 795, 802, note 11, 45 Cal.Rptr.2d 466, 470, note 11 (1995).

37. Dunkin v. Boskey, 82 Cal.App.4th 171, 180, note 4, 98 Cal.Rptr.2d 44, 49, note 4 (2000).

38. Kilroy v. State, 119 Cal.App.4th 140, 148, 14 Cal.Rptr.3d 109, 115 (2004). Under California's sham pleading doctrine, plaintiffs are precluded from amending complaints to omit harmful allegations, unless they explain the omissions. A court may take judicial notice of the superseded pleadings to determine whether in the amended pleadings the plaintiff failed to explain any harmful omissions. Deveny v. Entropin, Inc., 139 Cal.App.4th 408, 425, 42 Cal. Rptr.3d 807, 819 (2006).

39. 152 Cal.App.3d 1189, 200 Cal.Rptr. 115 (1984).

40. Id. at 1204–1205, 200 Cal.Rptr. at 125. See also People v. Smith, 215 Cal.App.3d 19, 26, 263 Cal.Rptr. 678, 681 (1989) (A judge may take judicial notice of *Kelly* findings made by other judges of the same court.).

41. 176 Cal.App.3d 685, 222 Cal.Rptr. 313 (1986).

on a demurrer to the information a Superior Court judge may not notice the magistrate's factual findings in support of the magistrate's order dismissing the complaint.[42] A judge, however, may take judicial notice of findings of other judges in order to determine if estoppel prevents the relitigation of an issue previously litigated.[43]

Some cases hold that a California judge may notice a judicial finding that is the product of an adversarial hearing in which the parties had an opportunity to present evidence on the existence or nonexistence of the finding.[44] But as the court aptly observed in Sosinsky v. Grant,[45] allowing judicial notice on this basis is "tantamount to taking judicial notice that the judge's factual finding must necessarily have been correct and the judge is therefore infallible."[46] Moreover, the fact that the judicial finding was the subject of conflicting evidence is persuasive proof that the matter to which the finding relates is not the kind of universally or locally known or easily verifiable fact that is the proper subject of judicial notice.

A California judge, however, may notice the results (as opposed to findings) reached in court records. A judge, for example, may notice an appellate court's affirmance of a defendant's convictions, including the number and type of convictions,[47] as well as a trial court's order adjudicating interests in land.[48]

Noticing agency records. The permissive category also allows judges to notice the official acts of the executive departments of the United States or of any state, including California.[49] As in the case of court records, the authority given to judges extends only to noticing the existence of the act or record. It does not empower the judges to notice as true the assertions contained in such acts. A judge, for example, may notice a report as a 1994 Report of the United States Surgeon General entitled, "Preventing Tobacco Use Among Young People." But the judge may not notice the truth of the matters asserted in the report, except to the extent such matters fall within the judicial notice categories for factual matters—universally or locally known facts or easily verifiable facts.[50]

---

42. Id. at 690, 222 Cal.Rptr. at 315–316 (In dismissing kidnaping charges, the magistrate found that the victim had voluntarily accompanied the defendant.). See also Gilmore v. Superior Court (Schmidt), 230 Cal.App.3d 416, 418, 281 Cal.Rptr. 343, 344–345 (1991) (A judge may not take judicial notice of the statement of facts in an appellate opinion.); Sosinsky v. Grant, 6 Cal.App.4th 1548, 1563–1564, 8 Cal.Rptr.2d 552, 561 (1992) (A judge may not take judicial notice of findings of other judges for the truth of the matter asserted.).

43. Western Mut. Ins. Co. v. Yamamoto, 29 Cal.App.4th 1474, 1485, 35 Cal.Rptr.2d 698, 704 (1994).

44. See, e.g., Lockley v. Law Office of Cantrell, 91 Cal.App.4th 875, 881–883, 110 Cal.Rptr.2d 877, 882–883 (2001) and cases cited therein.

45. 6 Cal.App.4th 1548, 1563–1564, 8 Cal.Rptr.2d 552, 561 (1992).

46. Id. at 1568, 8 Cal.Rptr.2d at 564. Accord: Kilroy v. State, 119 Cal.App.4th 140, 148, 14 Cal.Rptr.3d 109, 115 (2004).

47. People v. Harbolt, 61 Cal.App.4th 123, 71 Cal.Rptr.2d 459 (1997).

48. People v. Crusilla, 77 Cal.App.4th 141, 147, 91 Cal.Rptr.2d 415, 419 (1999).

49. West's Ann. California Evidence Code § 452(c).

50. Mangini v. R.J. Reynolds Tobacco Co., 7 Cal.4th 1057, 1063–1064, 31 Cal.Rptr.2d 358, 362, 875 P.2d 73 (1994). In People v. Crusilla, 77 Cal.App.4th 141, 147, 91 Cal.Rptr.2d 415, 419 (1999),

A court, however, may notice as official acts the regulations and orders issued by administrative agencies when the existence and effect of such regulations and orders are an issue. For example, under California's primary jurisdiction doctrine, a court is required to stay a claim when enforcement of the claim requires the resolution of issues which have been committed to the special competence of an administrative body.[51] In order to determine whether the stay should be lifted, the court must ascertain whether the administrative agency has passed on the matters within its competence. In making this determination, the court may notice those agency records that reflect the agency's action.[52]

Official acts of the executive departments of the United States and of the states do not include papers filed with these agencies. For example, the contents of applications, including supporting documents, filed with the California Department of Insurance may not be judicially noticed under this category.[53]

Requesting permissive judicial notice. The court must take judicial notice of any matter that may be noticed if a party requests that such notice be taken and meets certain procedural requirements.[54] The requesting party must furnish the court with sufficient information to enable it to take judicial notice and give each adverse party sufficient notice of the request to prepare to meet it.[55] But the party's failure to satisfy these

---

the court noticed a publication prepared by the California Attorney General's Office discussing jurisdictional issues over the US–Mexico point of entry at San Ysidro. An issue in the case was whether California had jurisdiction over crimes committed at the point of entry. By considering the contents of the publication, the court went beyond merely noticing the publication as an official act of a California agency. The propriety of noticing the contents most likely would not have been an issue in federal court, as the matters discussed in the publication would have fallen into the "legislative facts" category. Under the federal judicial notice doctrine, judges are free to consult pertinent data to determine the content or applicability of a rule of law. The California doctrine, however, is otherwise and, hence, the problem raised in *Crusilla*.

51. Wise v. Pacific Gas & Electric Co., 77 Cal.App.4th 287, 295–296, 91 Cal.Rptr.2d 479, 484 (1999).

52. Id. at 297, 91 Cal.Rptr.2d at 485 (approving judicial notice of the records of Public Utilities Commission reflecting the commission's adjudication of a complaint). See also County of Amador v. El Dorado County Water Agency, 76 Cal.App.4th 931, 949, 91 Cal.Rptr.2d 66, 77 (1999) (taking judicial notice of a water rights order issued by the State Water Resources Control Board); Etcheverry v. Tri–Ag Serv., 22 Cal.4th 316, 330–331, 93 Cal.Rptr.2d 36, 45, 993 P.2d 366, 374 (2000) (taking judicial notice of the existence and content of an EPA regulation); Vedanta Society of Southern California v. California Quartet, 84 Cal.App.4th 517, 522, note 2, 100 Cal.Rptr.2d 889, 894, note 2 (2000) (taking judicial notice of County of Orange Planning and Development Services Department documents showing that the public had been given advance notice of a board's consideration of an appeal.). *County of Orange* did not implicate the hearsay rule since the documents judicially noticed constituted the notice and thus fell within the verbal acts doctrine. For a discussion of this doctrine, see § 5.94 supra. See also California School of Culinary Arts v. Lujan, 112 Cal.App.4th 16, 26, 4 Cal.Rptr.3d 785, 793 (2003) (taking judicial notice of an agency's minutes, orders, and findings to help determine whether the agency meant to exclude trade school teachers from its definition of "teachers").

53. Stevens v. Superior Court, 75 Cal.App.4th 594, 608, 89 Cal.Rptr.2d 370, 380 (1999).

54. West's Ann. California Evidence Code § 453 and comment.

55. Id. See also Ross v. Creel Printing & Publishing Co., 100 Cal.App.4th 736, 743, 122 Cal.Rptr.2d 787, 792 (2002) (declining to take judicial notice of a Nevada district attorney's handbook in a debtor's action against a creditor where the party requesting judicial notice failed to supply the court with information about the source, purpose, or official ratification of the handbook).

requirements will not preclude the judge from noticing the matter if the matter can otherwise be noticed under the permissive section.[56]

A judge may decline to take permissive judicial notice if the requesting party fails to meet the notice requirement.[57] Complying with the requirement is important because judicial notice is binding on the jury and precludes the opponent from offering evidence disputing the noticed fact.[58] Notice may be given through the pleadings or otherwise.[59] Flexibility is called for because the need for judicial notice may not be readily apparent: "In many cases, it will be reasonable to expect the notice to be given at or before the time of the pretrial conference. In other cases, matters of fact or law of which the court should take judicial notice may come up at the trial. [The Code] merely requires reasonable notice, and the reasonableness of the notice given will depend upon the circumstances of the particular case."[60]

A judge may also decline to take permissive judicial notice if the requesting party fails to provide the court with "sufficient information" to enable it to notice the requested fact.[61] The Code does not define "sufficient information," as the requirement will necessarily vary from case to case.[62] The Code proceeds on the assumption that the requesting party will use the best evidence available.[63] The Code, however, permits the judge to consult or use any source of pertinent information, including the advice of experts, whether or not furnished by the parties.[64] Except for § 352 and the rules of privilege, the exclusionary rules of evidence do not apply to the information the parties may offer or the court may consider in determining the propriety of taking judicial notice.[65]

A judge may take judicial notice of matters within the permissive category without the request of the parties if the judge complies with certain procedural requirements. Before instructing the jury on the effect of judicial notice, the judge must afford the parties a reasonable opportunity to present information on the propriety of taking judicial notice and

---

56. West's Ann. California Evidence Code § 453 (comment). The requirements imposed on the requesting party are "intended as a safeguard and not as a rigid limitation on the court's power to take judicial notice. * * * [W]here the party requesting that judicial notice be taken fails to give the requisite notice * * * or fails to furnish sufficient information * * *, the judge may [still] take judicial notice [of the matters in the permissive section] and may consult and use any source of pertinent information, whether or not furnished by the parties." Id.

57. Id.

58. Id. See also West's Ann. California Evidence Code § 457 and comment.

59. West's Ann. California Evidence Code § 453.

60. Id. (comment).

61. West's Ann. California Evidence Code § 453 and comment.

62. Id. (comment).

63. Id. "[W]hen a party desires the appellate court to take judicial notice of a document or record on file in the court below[,] the parties should furnish the appellate court with a copy of such document or record certified by its custodian." People v. Preslie, 70 Cal.App.3d 486, 495, 138 Cal.Rptr. 828, 833 (1977). The certification requirement applies also to out of state court records. Ross v. Creel Printing & Pub. Co., 100 Cal.App.4th 736, 743, 122 Cal.Rptr.2d 787, 792 (2002).

64. West's Ann. California Evidence Code § 454.

65. Id.

the tenor of the matter to be noticed, if the matter is of substantial consequence to the determination of the action.[66] The same procedural requirements apply if the judge seeks to notice a universally known fact under the mandatory category.[67] If the judge resorts to any source of information not received in open court, the information and its source must be made part of the record, and the judge must give each party a reasonable opportunity to meet the information before noticing the matter.[68]

Instructing the jury on judicial notice. If the court notices a matter that otherwise would have been for determination by the jury, the court may, and upon request must, instruct the jury to accept the noticed matter as a fact.[69] Because of its conclusive effect, the opponent is not permitted to introduce evidence disputing the noticed fact.[70] The conclusive nature of judicially noticed facts can pose problems in criminal cases. Judges may not notice facts which the prosecution must prove under In re Winship.[71] *Winship*[72] requires the state to prove beyond a reasonable doubt "every fact necessary to constitute the crime with which [the accused] is charged."[73]

Denying a request to take judicial notice. If the trial judge denies a request to take judicial notice of any matter—whether listed under the mandatory or permissive sections—the court must advise the parties of its decision at the earliest practicable time and indicate for the record that the request has been denied.[74] The requirement is designed to provide the parties with an adequate opportunity to submit evidence on the matter on which judicial notice was anticipated but not taken.[75]

The trial judge's refusal or failure to take judicial notice does not become the law of the case. It will not preclude that judge or another trial judge from judicially noticing the same matter in a subsequent proceeding of the same action.[76]

---

66. West's Ann. California Evidence Code § 455. See In re Estate of Nicholas, 177 Cal.App.3d 1071, 1090, 223 Cal.Rptr. 410, 420 (1986) (holding that a judge must comply with the procedural requirements of § 455 before noticing matters within the permissive category). The requirements of § 455 presumably are satisfied when a party properly requests judicial notice of matters within the permissive category. As has been noted, the party must furnish the court with sufficient information to permit the judge to take judicial notice and must give the opponent sufficient notice to enable the opponent to meet the request. West's Ann. California Evidence Code § 453.

67. West's Ann. California Evidence Code § 455.

68. Id.

69. West's Ann. California Evidence Code § 457.

70. Id. (comment).

71. People v. Barre, 11 Cal.App.4th 961, 965, 14 Cal.Rptr.2d 307, 310 (1992).

72. 397 U.S. 358, 90 S.Ct. 1068, 25 L.Ed.2d 368 (1970).

73. Id. at 364, 90 S.Ct. at 1072. Accord: Dillard v. Roe, 244 F.3d 758, 769 (9th Cir.), cert. denied, 534 U.S. 905, 122 S.Ct. 238, 151 L.Ed.2d 172 (2001) (holding that a criminal defendant's California right to trial by jury on whether he had previously been convicted of felony offenses was not violated where the trial judge judicially noticed the convictions but refrained from instructing the jurors that the defendant was the person named in the conviction records).

74. West's Ann. California Evidence Code § 456.

75. Id. (comment).

76. West's Ann. California Evidence Code § 458.

Judicial notice by reviewing courts. A reviewing court must take judicial notice of any matter that the trial court properly noticed.[77] In addition, a reviewing court must notice those matters the trial court was required but failed to notice.[78] Matters a trial court is obligated to notice include those within the mandatory category[79] and those within the permissive category if a proper request is made.[80]

A reviewing court may notice for the first time matters within the permissive category.[81] In determining whether to take judicial notice, the reviewing court, like the trial court, may use or consult any pertinent information.[82] Except for § 352 and the rules of privilege, in selecting the information the reviewing court is not constrained by the exclusionary rules of evidence.[83]

Even at the appellate level, the parties are entitled to procedural protections. When noticing universally known facts or matters within the permissive category, the court must afford each party a reasonable opportunity to present information relevant to the propriety of taking judicial notice and the tenor of the matter to be noticed.[84] In addition, if the appellate court resorts to any source of information not received in open court, the information and its source must be made part of the record and the court must give each party an opportunity to meet the information before taking judicial notice.[85]

Reviewing courts are not required to apply the matters they notice. Whether a reviewing court applies a noticed fact depends on the rules and principles governing appellate review and not on the law of evidence.[86] The California Supreme Court has laid down one such principle: as a general rule, a reviewing court should not apply a noticed fact if the record discloses that the matter was not presented to and considered by the trial court in the first instance.[87] The rule is designed to prevent the

---

77. West's Ann. California Evidence Code § 459 and comment.

78. Id.

79. West's Ann. California Evidence Code § 451.

80. West's Ann. California Evidence Code §§ 452–453.

81. West's Ann. California Evidence Code § 459(a) and comment.

82. West's Ann. California Evidence Code § 459(b) and comment.

83. Id.

84. West's Ann. California Evidence Code § 459(c).

85. West's Ann. California Evidence Code § 459(d).

86. West's Ann. California Evidence Code § 459 (comment). See also People v. Jackson, 7 Cal.App.4th 1367, 10 Cal.Rptr.2d 5 (1992), in which the reviewing court refused to notice that a burglary was of an inhabited dwelling house on the ground that to do so "would do 'violence to the elementary principle that the function of the appellate court, in reviewing a trial court judgment on direct appeal is limited to matters contained in the record of the trial proceedings.'" Id. at 1373, 10 Cal.Rptr.2d at 9 (citing People v. Pena, 25 Cal.App.3d 414, 101 Cal.Rptr. 804 (1972)). Accord: People v. Amador, 24 Cal.4th 387, 394, 100 Cal.Rptr.2d 617, 622, 9 P.3d 993, 998 (2000) (holding that in reviewing a trial court's denial of a motion to suppress, the reviewing court would not notice matters that should have been presented to the trial court, since the reviewing court was limited to reviewing the trial court's denial order on the basis of the record before the trial court.).

87. People v. Hardy, 2 Cal.4th 86, 134, 5 Cal.Rptr.2d 796, 820, 825 P.2d 781, 805 (1992), cert. denied, 506 U.S. 987, 113 S.Ct. 498, 121 L.Ed.2d 435 (1992). See also People v. Sakarias, 22

unfairness that would flow from permitting one side to press an issue or theory on appeal that was not raised in the trial court.[88] A reviewing court, however, may apply the noticed fact where no such unfairness results, for example, where the opposing party does not oppose the taking of judicial notice.[89]

QUESTIONS AND PROBLEMS

1.   Under the Code and the Rules, a trial judge sitting in San Francisco may notice the following facts: that President Nixon resigned his presidency, that Stanford University is located in Santa Clara County, and that the dean of Stanford Law School can be reached by telephone at (650) 723–4455. True or false?

2.   Judicial notice under the Federal Rules is limited to adjudicative facts; the Code, on the other hand, extends judicial notice to legislative facts. True or false?

3.   Under the Code and the Rules, a trial judge may notice that the deposition offered by a party is the deposition of the opposing party and that the copy offered is the original copy. In addition, the judge probably can notice the answers contained in the deposition for the truth of the matters asserted. True or false?

§ 19.02 JUDICIAL NOTICE UNDER THE FEDERAL RULES

As mentioned in the previous section, the Federal Rules of Evidence limit judicial notice to "adjudicative facts," those a party would normally be expected to prove in the absence of judicial notice.[1] These are the matters which the Code denominates universally known facts, locally known facts, and easily verifiable facts.[2]

Federal judges have discretion to take judicial notice of adjudicative facts on their own motion.[3] They must, however, notice these facts if requested by a party and if supplied with the necessary information.[4] But

---

Cal.4th 596, 635, 94 Cal.Rptr.2d 17, 44, 995 P.2d 152, 176 (2000), cert. denied, 531 U.S. 947, 121 S.Ct. 347, 148 L.Ed.2d 279 (2000) (holding that in determining whether a prosecutor impermissibly argued inconsistent factual theories in two trials in violation of due process, the reviewing court would not notice the transcript of the other trial since the inconsistencies were not raised in the trial court and could better be explored by way of an evidentiary hearing in a habeas corpus proceeding).

88.   People v. Hardy, 2 Cal.4th 86, 134, 5 Cal.Rptr.2d 796, 820, 825 P.2d 781, 805 (1992), cert. denied, 506 U.S. 987, 113 S.Ct. 498, 121 L.Ed.2d 435 (1992).

89.   Id.

1.   Federal Rule of Evidence 201(a). For a discussion of how the jurors' conception of evidence embraces matter that is outside the information formally received at the trial, see Scott W. Howe, *Untangling Competing Conceptions of Evidence,* 30 Loyola of Los Angeles Law Review 1199 (1977).

2.   See § 19.01; see also Federal Rule of Evidence 201(b).

3.   Federal Rule of Evidence 201(c).

4.   West's Ann. California Evidence Code § 201(d).

before taking judicial notice, federal judges upon request must accord the parties an opportunity to be heard on the propriety of taking judicial notice and the tenor of the matter to be noticed.[5]

The power to take judicial notice is not limited to the federal trial bench or the trial phase of a case. Like California judges, federal judges may take judicial notice at any stage of the proceeding, including the appeal.[6]

The major difference between the Code and the Federal Rules is that judicially noticed facts are not binding on the jury in federal criminal cases. In such cases, the judge must instruct the jury "that it may or may not accept the noticed fact as conclusive."[7] By converting such facts into permissive inferences, the Rules reduce possible conflicts with the constitutional requirement that the prosecution prove beyond a reasonable doubt "every fact necessary to constitute the crime with which [the accused] is charged."[8] In California, case law prohibits judges from giving a conclusive effect to judicially noticed facts which the prosecution must prove beyond a reasonable doubt.[9]

§ 19.03 JURY NOTICE

Accepting jury service does not require jurors to leave their common sense or experience at the courthouse door. Jurors, collectively, bring a common fund of information to the jury box which does not have to be proved or disproved by the parties. Matters falling within this fund are used by jurors to assess the evidence that is presented; strictly speaking, these matters are not "adjudicative facts" but an aspect of legal reasoning.[1]

It is one matter for jurors to draw upon their common fund of knowledge in evaluating the evidence. It is quite another for a juror to use his or her "special knowledge" in deciding an issue in controversy. For example, in a prosecution for driving while under the influence, it would be improper for a juror who is an engineer to tell his fellow jurors that the device used to determine the accused's blood alcohol content is infallible, where the reliability of the device is contested. The jurors should determine that issue on the basis of the evidence presented by the parties.[2]

---

5. Federal Rule of Evidence 201(e).

6. Federal Rule of Evidence 201(f).

7. Federal Rule of Evidence 201(g).

8. In re Winship, 397 U.S. 358, 364, 90 S.Ct. 1068, 1072, 25 L.Ed.2d 368 (1970).

9. People v. Barre, 11 Cal.App.4th 961, 966, 14 Cal.Rptr.2d 307, 310 (1992).

1. Federal Rule of Evidence 201 (Advisory Committee Note).

2. In re Malone, 12 Cal.4th 935, 963, 50 Cal.Rptr.2d 281, 299, 911 P.2d 468, 486 (1996) (holding that it was misconduct for a juror to express reservations about the reliability of polygraph evidence based on the juror's study of polygraphy in psychology). Accord: McDonald v. Southern Pacific Trans. Co., 71 Cal.App.4th 256, 263–264, 83 Cal.Rptr.2d 734, 738 (1999) (holding that it was misconduct for a juror who was a transportation consultant to express his opinion on whether it was feasible to place crossing arms at a railroad grade crossing). See also People v. Barton, 37 Cal.App.4th 709, 715, 43 Cal.Rptr.2d 671, 674 (1995) ("It is misconduct for a jury 'to

Of course, it is not always easy to distinguish between the jurors' common knowledge and their special knowledge. Moreover, even the improper use of special knowledge, when known, may not lead to a new trial or a reversal. Both the California Evidence Code and the Federal Rules of Evidence place strict limits on the admissibility of evidence of jury misconduct.[3] Still, parties can try to protect themselves by reminding the jurors of their oath to decide the case on the basis of the evidence presented.

Requiring jurors to decide the case on the basis of the evidence presented preserves important values. Confidence in the outcome produced by the adversary system assumes that the parties will challenge and test the information upon which the jury will rely. Jurors who use information "outside the record" become essentially untested evidentiary sources. This is why judges routinely instruct jurors to avoid news accounts of the trial and to refrain from discussing the case with anyone until they begin their deliberations and even then are told to discuss the case only with their fellow jurors. In addition, if they have heard about the case prior to the trial, they are instructed to set aside any preformed impressions about the case.

Jurors should avoid gathering information on their own. They should not go to the crime or accident scene to conduct their own, unsupervised investigations.[4] In assessing the evidence, they may, of course, examine the exhibits that have been received, but they should be discouraged from conducting their own experiments with the exhibits, especially if those experiments do not take place in the jury deliberation room.[5]

---

obtain information from outside sources either as to factual matters or for guidance on the law.'") (quoting from People v. Karis, 46 Cal.3d 612, 250 Cal.Rptr. 659, 758 P.2d 1189 (1988)). But see Iwekaogwu v. City of Los Angeles, 75 Cal.App.4th 803, 820, 89 Cal.Rptr.2d 505, 517 (1999) (holding that in an employment discrimination case it was not misconduct for a juror to inform the other jurors of instances of discrimination he had witnessed while a reserve police officer: "A juror does not commit misconduct merely by describing a personal experience in the course of deliberations."). Accord: People v. Steele, 27 Cal.4th 1230, 1266–1267, 120 Cal.Rptr.2d 432, 461, 47 P.3d 225, 249 (2002), cert. denied, 537 U.S. 1115, 123 S.Ct. 874, 154 L.Ed.2d 791 (2003) (holding, over Chief Justice Ronald George's strong dissent, that in a murder prosecution, it was not misconduct for some jurors with medical knowledge to inform the others that the results of a brain electrical activity mapping test were unreliable because, contrary to the expert's testimony, the control groups used to determine its validity were too small).

3. See § 14.03 supra. Moreover, although the improper use of special knowledge can give rise to a presumption of prejudice, the complaining party is not entitled to a new trial if the presumption is rebutted. See People v. Barton, 37 Cal.App.4th 709, 715, 43 Cal.Rptr.2d 671, 674 (1995), and authorities cited therein.

4. The California Penal Code expressly authorizes trial judges to allow jurors to view "the place in which the offense is charged to have been committed, or in which any other material fact occurred, or any personal property which has been referred to in the evidence and cannot conveniently be brought into the courtroom * * *." West Ann. California Penal Code § 1119. The jurors must be supervised by a person appointed by the court who must be sworn "to suffer no person to speak or communicate with the jury * * *." Id. This provision notwithstanding, a judge may allow jurors to pose questions if the answers are needed to understand the objects viewed. People v. Bolin, 18 Cal.4th 297, 323, 75 Cal.Rptr.2d 412, 431, 956 P.2d 374, 393 (1998).

5. See Bell v. State of California, 63 Cal.App.4th 919, 931, 74 Cal.Rptr.2d 541, 549 (1998) and cases cited therein. In People v. Bogle, 41 Cal.App.4th 770, 48 Cal.Rptr.2d 739 (1995), the accused

CALIFORNIA EVIDENCE CODE

§ 450. Judicial notice may be taken only as authorized by law

Judicial notice may not be taken of any matter unless authorized or required by law.

§ 451. Matters which must be judicially noticed

Judicial notice shall be taken of the following:

(a) The decisional, constitutional, and public statutory law of this state and of the United States and the provisions of any charter described in Section 3, 4, or 5 of Article XI of the California Constitution.

(b) Any matter made a subject of judicial notice by Section 11343.6, 11344.6, or 18576 of the Government Code or by Section 1507 of Title 44 of the United States Code.

(c) Rules of professional conduct for members of the bar adopted pursuant to Section 6076 of the Business and Professions Code and rules of practice and procedure for the courts of this state adopted by the Judicial Council.

(d) Rules of pleading, practice, and procedure prescribed by the United States Supreme Court, such as the Rules of the United States Supreme Court, the Federal Rules of Civil Procedure, the Federal Rules of Criminal Procedure, the Admiralty Rules, the Rules of the Court of Claims, the Rules of the Customs Court, and the General Orders and Forms in Bankruptcy.

(e) The true signification of all English words and phrases and of all legal expressions.

(f) Facts and propositions of generalized knowledge that are so universally known that they cannot reasonably be the subject of dispute.

§ 452. Matters which may be judicially noticed

Judicial notice may be taken of the following matters to the extent that they are not embraced within Section 451:

(a) The decisional, constitutional, and statutory law of any state of the United States and the resolutions and private acts of the Congress of the United States and of the Legislature of this state.

---

identified the lock which each key on his keychain purported to open. He did not include among the locks a safe found in his room. The keychain as well as the safe were given to the jurors as exhibits. The jurors then determined that one of the keys on the keychain opened the safe. On appeal the reviewing court held that, given the accused's testimony, the use of the key by the jurors to open the safe did not constitute an impermissible experiment. Id. at 780, 48 Cal.Rptr.2d at 744. As the *Bogle* court emphasized, jurors may only conduct experiments " '*within the lines of offered evidence*, but if their experiments shall *invade new fields* and they shall be influenced in their verdict by discoveries from such experiments which will not fall fairly within the scope and purview of the evidence, then, manifestly, the jury has been itself taking evidence without the knowledge of either party, evidence which it is not possible for the party injured to meet, answer, or explain.' " Id. at 778–779, 48 Cal.Rptr.2d at 743 (quoting from Higgins v. Los Angeles Gas & Electric Co., 159 Cal. 651, 656–657, 115 P. 313, 315 (1911)) (emphasis in the original).

(b) Regulations and legislative enactments issued by or under the authority of the United States or any public entity in the United States.

(c) Official acts of the legislative, executive, and judicial departments of the United States and of any state of the United States.

(d) Records of (1) any court of this state or (2) any court of record of the United States or of any state of the United States.

(e) Rules of court of (1) any court of this state or (2) any court of record of the United States or of any state of the United States.

(f) The law of an organization of nations and of foreign nations and public entities in foreign nations.

(g) Facts and propositions that are of such common knowledge within the territorial jurisdiction of the court that they cannot reasonably be the subject of dispute.

(h) Facts and propositions that are not reasonably subject to dispute and are capable of immediate and accurate determination by resort to sources of reasonably indisputable accuracy.

§ 452.5. Criminal conviction records; computer-generated records; admissibility

(a) The official acts and records specified in subdivisions (c)and (d) of Section 452 include any computer-generated official records, as specified by the Judicial Council which relate to criminal convictions, when the record is certified by the clerk of the superior court pursuant to Section 69844.5 of the Government Code at the time of the computer entry.

(b) An official record of conviction certified in accordance with subdivision (a) of Section 1530 is admissible pursuant to Section 1280 to prove the commission, attempted commission, or solicitation of a criminal offense, prior conviction, service of a prison term, or other act, condition, or event recorded by the record.

§ 453. Compulsory judicial notice upon request

The trial court shall take judicial notice of any matter specified in Section 452 if a party requests it and:

(a) Gives each adverse party sufficient notice of the request, through the pleadings or otherwise, to enable such adverse party to prepare to meet the request; and

(b) Furnishes the court with sufficient information to enable it to take judicial notice of the matter.

§ 454. Information that may be used in taking judicial notice

(a) In determining the propriety of taking judicial notice of a matter, or the tenor thereof:

(1) Any source of pertinent information, including the advice of persons learned in the subject matter, may be consulted or used, whether or not furnished by a party.

(2) Exclusionary rules of evidence do not apply except for Section 352 and the rules of privilege.

(b) Where the subject of judicial notice is the law of an organization of nations, a foreign nation, or a public entity in a foreign nation and the court resorts to the advice of persons learned in the subject matter, such advice, if not received in open court, shall be in writing.

§ 455.   Opportunity to present information to court

With respect to any matter specified in Section 452 or in subdivision (f) of Section 451 that is of substantial consequence to the determination of the action:

(a) If the trial court has been requested to take or has taken or proposes to take judicial notice of such matter, the court shall afford each party reasonable opportunity, before the jury is instructed or before the cause is submitted for decision by the court, to present to the court information relevant to (1) the propriety of taking judicial notice of the matter and (2) the tenor of the matter to be noticed.

(b) If the trial court resorts to any source of information not received in open court, including the advice of persons learned in the subject matter, such information and its source shall be made a part of the record in the action and the court shall afford each party reasonable opportunity to meet such information before judicial notice of the matter may be taken.

§ 456.   Noting for record denial of request to take judicial notice

If the trial court denies a request to take judicial notice of any matter, the court shall at the earliest practicable time so advise the parties and indicate for the record that it has denied the request.

§ 457.   Instructing jury on matter judicially noticed

If a matter judicially noticed is a matter which would otherwise have been for determination by the jury, the trial court may, and upon request shall, instruct the jury to accept as a fact the matter so noticed.

§ 458.   Judicial notice by trial court in subsequent proceedings

The failure or refusal of the trial court to take judicial notice of a matter, or to instruct the jury with respect to the matter, does not preclude the trial court in subsequent proceedings in the action from taking judicial notice of the matter in accordance with the procedure specified in this division.

§ 459.   Judicial notice by reviewing court

(a) The reviewing court shall take judicial notice of (1) each matter properly noticed by the trial court and (2) each matter that the trial court was required to notice under Section 451 or 453. The reviewing court may take judicial notice of any matter specified in Section 452. The reviewing court may take judicial notice of a matter in a tenor different from that noticed by the trial court.

(b) In determining the propriety of taking judicial notice of a matter, or the tenor thereof, the reviewing court has the same power as the trial court under Section 454.

(c) When taking judicial notice under this section of a matter specified in Section 452 or in subdivision (f) of Section 451 that is of substantial consequence to the determination of the action, the reviewing court shall comply with the provisions of subdivision (a) of Section 455 if the matter was not theretofore judicially noticed in the action.

(d) In determining the propriety of taking judicial notice of a matter specified in Section 452 or in subdivision (f) of Section 451 that is of substantial consequence to the determination of the action, or the tenor thereof, if the reviewing court resorts to any source of information not received in open court or not included in the record of the action, including the advice of persons learned in the subject matter, the reviewing court shall afford each party reasonable opportunity to meet such information before judicial notice of the matter may be taken.

§ 460. Appointment of expert by court

Where the advice of persons learned in the subject matter is required in order to enable the court to take judicial notice of a matter, the court on its own motion or on motion of any party may appoint one or more such persons to provide such advice. If the court determines to appoint such a person, he shall be appointed and compensated in the manner provided in Article 2 (commencing with Section 730) of Chapter 3 of Division 6.

FEDERAL RULES OF EVIDENCE

Rule 201. Judicial Notice of Adjudicative Facts

(a) Scope. This rule governs judicial notice of an adjudicative fact only, not a legislative fact.

(b) Kinds of Facts That May Be Judicially Noticed. The court may judicially notice a fact that is not subject to reasonable dispute because it:

    (1) is generally known within the trial court's territorial jurisdiction; or

    (2) can be accurately and readily determined from sources whose accuracy cannot reasonably be questioned.

(c) Taking Notice. The court:

    (1) may take judicial notice on its own; or

    (2) must take judicial notice if a party requests it and the court is supplied with the necessary information.

(d) Timing. The court may take judicial notice at any stage of the proceeding.

(e) Opportunity to Be Heard. On timely request, a party is entitled to be heard on the propriety of taking judicial notice and the nature of the fact to be noticed. If the court takes judicial notice before notifying a party, the party, on request, is still entitled to be heard.

(f) Instructing the Jury. In a civil case, the court must instruct the jury to accept the noticed fact as conclusive. In a criminal case, the court must instruct the jury that it may or may not accept the noticed fact as conclusive.

CHAPTER 20

PRIVILEGES: AN INTRODUCTION

■ ■ ■

Table of Sections

§ 20.01 AN OVERVIEW

The Code assumes that the search for the truth will best be served by imposing upon all persons a general duty to give evidence when they are required to do so.[1] Unless otherwise provided by statute, the Code provides that no person has the right to refuse to testify, to prevent another from testifying, to refuse to disclose any matter, or to prevent another from disclosing any matter that may be helpful to the resolution of the case.[2]

Privileges, as the California Law Revision Commission notes, necessarily handicap the court or jury in reaching just results because they withhold relevant information.[3] By enacting privileges, the California Legislature has determined that the needs for justice should be subordinated to personal, professional, and institutional interests that are best served by protecting certain information from disclosure or by exempting certain persons from their duty to give evidence.[4]

The investigation of truth and the dispensation of justice, however, demand restricting the privileges that are granted within the narrow-

---

1. 6 California Law Revision Commission, Reports, Recommendations, and Studies 207 (1964).

2. West's Ann. California Evidence Code § 911.

3. 6 California Law Revision Commission, Reports, Recommendations, and Studies 207 (1964).

4. Id. Statutory privileges are subject to a criminal defendant's Sixth and Eighth Amendments rights. Accordingly, a client's assertion of the attorney-client privilege must yield when disclosure of the protected communications is essential to showing the client's bias against the accused in a capital case. People v. Mincey, 2 Cal.4th 408, 463, 6 Cal.Rptr.2d 822, 856, 827 P.2d 388, 422 (1992), cert. denied, 506 U.S. 1014, 113 S.Ct. 637, 121 L.Ed.2d 567 (1992). See generally § 21.06 infra.

est limits required by the purposes they serve; every step beyond these limits provides an obstacle to the administration of justice. On the other hand, when it is necessary to grant a privilege, the privilege granted must be broad enough to accomplish its purpose—it must not be subject to exceptions that strike at the very interest the privilege is created to protect.[5]

The Code attempts to strike this balance by describing with particularity the kinds of information that are privileged, the individuals who are entitled to claim the privilege, the fora in which the privilege can be asserted, and the circumstances in which the privilege can be waived or in which an exception applies.

The Code establishes three kinds of privileges. One exempts certain persons from their duty to give evidence. Examples include the privilege of a spouse not to be called as witness by an adverse party in any proceeding in which the other spouse is a party[6] and the privilege of the accused not to be called as witness by the prosecution.[7] Another type of privilege exempts a witness from having to provide certain kinds of testimony. A married person, for example, has a privilege not to testify *against* the other spouse,[8] and any witness has a right not to answer any question if the answer might tend to incriminate him or her.[9] The third kind of privilege protects from disclosure information that has been conveyed in confidence in the context of enumerated professional relationships. Examples include the attorney-client, psychotherapist-patient, and clergy member-penitent privileges.

Some of the Code's provisions apply to all three kinds of privileges. An example is § 913 which prohibits the judge or counsel from commenting on the exercise of a privilege.[10] Others apply only to some kinds of privileges. For example, whether disclosing a confidential communication to third persons waives the protection accorded to such communications is governed by § 912. By definition, this provision can apply only to those privileges protecting confidential communications conveyed in the context of certain professional relationships. The Code expressly limits the operation of § 912 to communications between attorneys and clients, physicians and patients, psychotherapists and patients, members of the clergy and penitents, sexual assault counselors and victims, domestic violence counselors and victims, and communications between spouses.[11]

The Code strips California judges of their Common Law power to create new privileges. "Courts may not add to the statutory privileges

---

5. 6 California Law Revision Commission, Reports, Recommendations, and Studies 207 (1964).

6. West's Ann. California Evidence Code § 971.

7. West's Ann. California Evidence Code § 930.

8. West's Ann. California Evidence Code § 970.

9. West's Ann. California Evidence Code § 940.

10. West's Ann. California Evidence Code § 913.

11. West's Ann. California Evidence Code § 912. The privilege for marital communications is not based on a professional relationship. But to be privileged, marital communications must be made in confidence. Accordingly, the waiver provisions of § 912 apply to these communications.

except as required by state or federal constitutional law * * *; nor may courts imply unwritten exceptions to existing statutory privileges."[12] Only privileges created by statute are recognized under the Code.[13] Accordingly, communications by probationers to probation officers,[14] by children to parents,[15] by inmates to "jailhouse lawyers,"[16] and by patients to psychiatric social workers[17] and others not specified in the statutes defining privileges for confidential communications are not protected.[18] Treaties are considered statutes.[19] California, for example, recognizes the privilege that the Vienna Convention on Consular Relations gives to members of a consular post to refuse to give evidence about matters connected with their functions.[20] In addition to federal treaties, California courts may rely on federal statutes that create privileges. In Union Bank of California, N.A. v. Superior Court[21] the reviewing court held that a California judge could not compel a national bank to disclose banking information which was protected from disclosure by a federal statute.[22] California courts, moreover, may rely on the state constitutional right of privacy to protect from disclosure communications that are not the subject of a statutory privilege.[23]

The Code's treatment of privileges is divided into two parts. The first sets out general provisions that apply to all or most privileges, for example, the provision describing the fora in which the privileges apply.[24]

---

12. Roberts v. City of Palmdale, 5 Cal.4th 363, 373, 20 Cal.Rptr.2d 330, 335, 853 P.2d 496, 501 (1993).

13. West's Ann. California Evidence Code § 911 and comment. Some cases mistakenly claim that "the privileges contained in the Evidence Code are *exclusive* * * *." See, e.g., Garstang v. Superior Court, 39 Cal.App.4th 526, 532, 46 Cal.Rptr.2d 84, 87 (1995) (quoting from Valley Bank of Nevada v. Superior Court, 15 Cal.3d 652, 125 Cal.Rptr. 553, 542 P.2d 977 (1975)) (emphasis in the original). That claim is true only to the extent that all statutory privileges happen to be in the Evidence Code. The code, however, does not preclude the Legislature from enacting and placing privileges in other codes. Moreover, even as *Garstang* acknowledges, the state constitutional right of privacy may supply a privilege where no statutory privilege exists. Id.

14. People v. Carter, 34 Cal.App.3d 748, 751, 110 Cal.Rptr. 324, 326 (1973), cert. denied, 419 U.S. 846, 95 S.Ct. 81, 42 L.Ed.2d 75 (1974).

15. In re Terry W., 59 Cal.App.3d 745, 747, 130 Cal.Rptr. 913, 914 (1976).

16. People v. Velasquez, 192 Cal.App.3d 319, 328, 237 Cal.Rptr. 366, 371 (1987).

17. Belmont v. California State Personnel Bd., 36 Cal.App.3d 518, 522, 111 Cal.Rptr. 607, 609 (1974).

18. There is no California "self-critical analysis" privilege protecting from disclosure assessments of affirmative action plans undertaken by federal contractors pursuant to requirements imposed by federal law. Cloud v. Superior Court (Western Atlas), 50 Cal.App.4th 1552, 1558, 58 Cal.Rptr.2d 365, 369 (1996). Some, though not all, federal courts recognize this privilege. See id. at 1557, 58 Cal.Rptr.2d at 368.

19. West's Ann. California Evidence Code § 230.

20. People v. Corona, 211 Cal.App.3d 529, 538, 259 Cal.Rptr. 524, 530 (1989).

21. 130 Cal.App.4th 378, 29 Cal.Rptr.3d 894 (2005).

22. Id. at 389, 29 Cal.Rptr.3d at 901.

23. Valley Bank of Nevada v. Superior Court, 15 Cal.3d 652, 658, 125 Cal.Rptr. 553, 555, 542 P.2d 977, 979 (1975) (holding that bank customers may rely on the state constitutional right of privacy to object to disclosure to third persons of confidential information furnished to their banks).

24. West's Ann. California Evidence Code §§ 901 and 910.

These provisions are examined in this chapter. The second part describes each of the statutory privileges in detail.

The Code establishes fifteen privileges.[25] In addition, the Code protects from disclosure information contained in in-hospital studies,[26] medical and psychiatric studies,[27] and the records of quality assurance committees in diverse health fields.[28] A detailed examination of each Code privilege is beyond the scope of this work. Consideration is limited to the principal privileges: those that protect communications between attorneys and clients, psychotherapists and patients, physicians and patients, sexual assault counselors and victims, domestic violence counselors and victims, human trafficking caseworkers and victims, members of the clergy and penitents, and spouses. In addition, two other marital privileges are considered: the privilege of a spouse not to be called by an adverse party in any proceeding in which the other spouse is a party and the privilege of a spouse not to testify against the other spouse. The work product doctrine is also examined. This doctrine protects from disclosure memoranda and other writings generated by lawyers in the course of representing clients. The work product doctrine is established by the Civil Procedure Code and not the Evidence Code.

Privileges and the Federal Rules of Evidence. As proposed by the Advisory Committee and prescribed by the United States Supreme Court, the Federal Rules of Evidence established nine privileges, including the attorney-client, psychotherapist-patient, husband-wife, and clergyman-penitent privileges.[29] But the committee's attempt to create a uniform federal law of privileges was rejected by Congress which, instead, adopted a rule which left the Common Law privileges in their present state and relegated their future development to federal judges "in light of reason and experience."[30]

In civil actions and proceedings, in which state law supplies the rule of decision, Congress mandated that state, not federal, law determine the applicability of privileges.[31] Thus, lawyers who try matters in federal courts in which California law supplies the rule of decision must turn to the California Evidence Code to determine the law of privileges. But lawyers who try matters in federal courts that are governed by federal substantive law must turn to federal case law to determine the existence and application of privileges. The federal law of privileges is beyond the scope of this work.

Federal and California constitutional right of privacy. Some of the privileges established by the Evidence Code protect from disclosure

---

25. For a list of these privileges, see § 20.02 infra.
26. West's Ann. California Evidence Code § 1156.
27. West's Ann. California Evidence Code § 1156.1.
28. See West's Ann. California Evidence Code § 1157–1157.7.
29. Federal Rules of Evidence for United States Courts and Magistrates 192–211 (West 1979).
30. Federal Rule of Evidence 501 and Advisory Committee Note.
31. Id.

not only information that is transmitted in confidence in context of specified relationships but also information which is private in nature. For example, both the psychotherapist-patient and physician-patient privileges protect communications exchanged between patients and their psycho-therapists or physicians. Although the contents of the communications do not have to relate to private matters in order to be privileged, if they do include such matters, the communications may also be protected from disclosure by the Federal and California Constitutions. In Griswold v. Connecticut[32] the United States Supreme Court declared that various guarantees of the Bill of Rights create zones of privacy.[33] In In re Lifschutz[34] the California Supreme Court held that the confidentiality of the psychotherapeutic session falls within one such zone.[35] Since *Lifschutz*, the California Constitution has been amended to include among the inalienable rights of all people the right to pursue and obtain privacy.[36] Accordingly, even if a judge finds that one of the Code privileges does not protect a particular communication from disclosure, the party objecting on privilege grounds should consider objecting also on privacy grounds. The scope of the federal and state privacy rights are beyond the scope of this work.

privilege AND privacy

QUESTIONS AND PROBLEMS

1. Describe the three kinds of privileges established by the Code.

2. Only privileges created by statutes are recognized under the Code. True or false?

3. The Federal Rules of Evidence, as enacted, contain a number of privileges, some of which are similar to those established by the Code. True or false?

§ 20.02 APPLICABILITY OF PRIVILEGES

The Code establishes fifteen privileges: the privilege of the accused not to be called as a witness,[1] the privilege of any person to refuse to disclose any matter that may be incriminating,[2] the attorney-client privilege,[3] the privilege not to testify against a spouse and to decline to be called as a witness by the adverse party in any proceeding in which the spouse is a party,[4] the privilege for confidential marital communications,[5]

---

32. 381 U.S. 479, 85 S.Ct. 1678, 14 L.Ed.2d 510 (1965).

33. Id. at 484.

34. 2 Cal.3d 415, 85 Cal.Rptr. 829, 467 P.2d 557 (1970).

35. Id. at 432, 85 Cal.Rptr. at 839, 467 P.2d at 567.

36. See West's Ann. California Constitution, Article I, § 1.

1. West's Ann. California Evidence Code § 930.

2. West's Ann. California Evidence Code § 940.

3. West's Ann. California Evidence Code § 950.

4. West's Ann. California Evidence Code § 970.

5. West's Ann. California Evidence Code § 980.

the physician-patient privilege,[6] the psychotherapist-patient privilege,[7] the clergyman-penitent privilege,[8] the sexual assault victim-counselor privilege,[9] the domestic violence victim-counselor privilege,[10] the human trafficking caseworker-victim privilege,[11] the privilege for official information and the identity of informers,[12] and the privileges for secret ballot votes,[13] trade secrets,[14] and a newsman's refusal to disclose news sources.[15]

These privileges apply in all proceedings in which testimony can be compelled by law.[16] Accordingly, the privileges cannot be invoked to restrain the dissemination of protected information outside of a litigation context.[17] For example, over objection the physician-patient privilege prevents confidential communications between doctors and their patients from being disclosed in proceedings in which testimony can be compelled.[18] The privilege, however, cannot be used to restrain a newspaper from disclosing the information: "[T]he physician-patient privilege is a rule of evidence concerning the admissibility of evidence in court and is not a substantive rule regulating the conduct of physicians."[19]

An exception is made in the case of the attorney-client privilege. An attorney who is suspected of engaging in criminal activity has a duty to assert the attorney-client privilege to prevent the disclosure pursuant to a search warrant of materials protected by the privilege, even though there may be no pending proceeding in which testimony may be compelled. As the California Supreme Court explained in People v. Superior Court (Laff),[20] "Permitting unfettered access to attorney-client communications, simply because there is no pending proceeding at which testimony can be compelled, would violate the policies supporting the privilege as well as the statutory and ethical obligations of attorneys to maintain client confidences."[21]

Proceedings in which testimony can be compelled include civil and criminal actions, coroners' inquests, legislative hearings, administrative hearings, grand jury proceedings, and arbitration proceedings.[22] "Statutes

---

6. West's Ann. California Evidence Code § 990.

7. West's Ann. California Evidence Code § 1010.

8. West's Ann. California Evidence Code § 1030.

9. West's Ann. California Evidence Code § 1035.

10. West's Ann. California Evidence Code § 1037.

11. West's Ann. California Evidence Code § 1038.

12. West's Ann. California Evidence Code § 1040.

13. West's Ann. California Evidence Code § 1050.

14. West's Ann. California Evidence Code § 1060.

15. West's Ann. California Evidence Code § 1070.

16. West's Ann. California Evidence Code §§ 901 and 910 (comment).

17. Hurvitz v. Hoefflin, 84 Cal.App.4th 1232, 1243, 101 Cal.Rptr.2d 558, 566 (2000).

18. See § 24.01 infra.

19. Hurvitz v. Hoefflin, 84 Cal.App.4th 1232, 1243, 101 Cal.Rptr.2d 558, 566 (2000).

20. 25 Cal.4th 703, 107 Cal.Rptr.2d 323, 23 P.3d 563 (2001).

21. Id. at 715,107 Cal.Rptr.2d at 333, 23 P.3d at 571.

22. West's Ann. California Evidence Code § 901 and comment.

that relax the rules of evidence in particular proceedings do not have the effect of making privileges inapplicable in such proceedings. For example, Labor Code Section 5708, which provides that the officer conducting an Industrial Accident Commission proceeding 'shall not be bound by the common law or statutory rules of evidence,' does not make privileges inapplicable in such proceedings. * * * On the other hand, * * * other statutes provide exceptions to particular privileges for particular types of proceedings. E.g., Evidence Code § 998 (physician-patient privilege inapplicable in criminal proceedings); Labor Code §§ 4055, 6407, 6408 (testimony by physician and certain reports of physicians admissible as evidence in Industrial Accident Commission proceedings)."[23]

QUESTIONS AND PROBLEMS

1. With the exception of the attorney-client privilege, the privileges established by the Code apply only to those proceedings in which testimony can be compelled. True or false?

2. Some statutes, however, may exempt privileges from proceedings in which they would normally apply. True or false?

§ 20.03 PRIVILEGE CLAIMS AND BURDEN OF PROOF

The person objecting on the ground of privilege must establish the privileged nature of the matter by a preponderance of the evidence.[1] "Thus, if the disputed preliminary fact is whether a person is married to a party and, hence whether their confidential communications are privileged under [the privilege for marital communications], the burden * * * is on the party asserting the privilege to persuade the judge of the existence of the marriage."[2]

The attorney-client, physician-patient, psychotherapist-patient, clergyman-penitent, sexual assault counselor-victim, domestic violence counselor-victim, and marital communications privileges require that the communications be made in confidence in order for the communications to be privileged. This does not mean that the subject matter of the communication must be "confidential" in nature. It means simply that the communicant intended the communication to be confidential.[3] A client, for example, who tells her lawyer in confidence that she ran a light is entitled to have her communication protected by the attorney-client privilege even if numerous spectators saw her run the light and even if before consulting her lawyer she told others that she ran the light.[4] The private nature of a

---

23. West's Ann. California Evidence Code § 910 (comment).

1. West's Ann. California Evidence Code §§ 115 and 405 and comment.

2. West's Ann. California Evidence Code § 405 (comment).

3. Menendez v. Superior Court, 3 Cal.4th 435, 446, 11 Cal.Rptr.2d 92, 99, 834 P.2d 786, 793 (1992).

4. Lohman v. Superior Court, 81 Cal.App.3d 90, 97, 146 Cal.Rptr. 171, 175 (1978).

communication, however, may help establish the communicant's intent that the communication be kept secret.[5]

Each of the privileges for confidential communications specifies the criteria which must be met in order for the communication to qualify for protection as a confidential communication.[6] But under the Code, the communications embraced by these privileges are presumed to have been made in confidence.[7] The effect of the presumption is to shift to the party opposing the privilege the burden of persuading the judge by a preponderance of the evidence that the communication was not made in confidence.[8] The presumption is necessary to protect the privileged matter. "If the privilege claimant were required to show that the communication was made in confidence, he would be compelled, in many cases, to reveal the subject matter of the communication in order to establish his right to the privilege."[9]

The party seeking disclosure of the privileged communication can overcome the presumption by evidence that the parties to the communication did not intend to keep it confidential.[10] Evidence "that the communication was made under circumstances where others could easily overhear is a strong indication that the communication was not intended to be confidential."[11] People v. Boothe[12] is illustrative: the presence of a stepdaughter was sufficient to overcome the presumption that a communication by one spouse to another was protected by the privilege for confidential marital communications.[13]

Even if the communication was made in confidence, the party opposing the privilege is entitled to show that the holder has waived the privilege.[14] Again, it is the privilege opponent and not the privilege claimant who has the burden of persuading the judge by a preponderance of the evidence that the holder has waived the privilege.[15]

Some privileged communications must be disclosed even if the holder has not waived the privilege. Disclosure can be compelled whenever the privileged information falls within an exception.[16] As in the case of a

---

5. C. McCormick, McCormick on Evidence § 80 (J. Strong 4th ed. 1992).

6. The criteria are reviewed under each privilege.

7. West's Ann. California Evidence Code § 917.

8. Id.

9. Id. (comment).

10. Id.

11. Id.

12. 65 Cal.App.3d 685, 135 Cal.Rptr. 570 (1977).

13. Id. at 691, 135 Cal.Rptr. at 574.

14. See Roman Catholic Archbishop of Los Angeles v. Superior Court, 131 Cal.App.4th 417, 442, 32 Cal.Rptr.3d 209, 228 (2005), cert. denied, 547 U.S. 1071, 126 S.Ct. 1783, 164 L.Ed.2d 518 (2006). For actions constituting waiver, see § 20.05 infra.

15. West's Ann. California Evidence Code § 405 (comment).

16. See, e.g., § 21.06 infra.

waiver claim, the privilege opponent, not the privilege claimant, has the burden of persuading the judge that an exception applies.[17]

QUESTIONS AND PROBLEMS

1. Ordinarily, the party objecting to the introduction of evidence on the grounds of privilege must establish the privileged nature of the evidence by a preponderance of the evidence. True or false?

2. The privileges protecting confidential communications require the party objecting to the introduction of such communications to establish that the communication was confidential in nature. Thus, a client's disclosure to her lawyer that she ran a light is not protected by the attorney-client privilege if prior to meeting with her lawyer the client told others that she ran the light. True or false?

3. With respect to privileges for confidential communications, the Code provides that such communications are presumed to have been made in confidence. The effect of this presumption is to shift to the party opposing the privilege claim the burden of persuading the judge that the communication was not made in confidence. True or false?

4. The party opposing a privilege claim has the burden of persuading the judge by a preponderance of the evidence that the information claimed to be privileged must be disclosed because it falls within an exception to the privilege. True or false?

§ 20.04 RULING ON PRIVILEGE CLAIMS

In ruling on most privilege objections, the judge, as a general rule, may not require the privilege holder to disclose even in camera the matter claimed to be privileged.[1] In determining whether disclosure should be compelled, the courts have not always distinguished between (1) claims by the privilege opponent that no privilege exists (no in camera disclosure

---

17. See Geilim v. Superior Court, 234 Cal.App.3d 166, 174, 285 Cal.Rptr. 602, 607 (1991); OXY Resources California LLC v. Superior Court, 115 Cal.App.4th 874, 894, 9 Cal.Rptr.3d 621, 639 (2004). See also West's Ann. California Evidence Code § 405 (comment).

1. West's Ann. California Evidence Code § 915(a) and comment. See also Doe 2 v. Superior Court, 132 Cal.App.4th 1504, 1517, 34 Cal.Rptr.3d 458, 466 (2005) (holding that a judge may not compel disclosure of a confidential communication protected by the clergy-penitent privilege even if the disclosure is to be made under a protective order). Where the privileged matter has already been disclosed, the judge may compel in camera disclosure to rule on the privilege claim. In Klang v. Shell Oil Co., 17 Cal.App.3d 933, 95 Cal.Rptr. 265 (1971), the plaintiff's attorney informed a police officer of the circumstances surrounding a traffic accident involving the plaintiff. At the trial for damages for the injuries he suffered, the plaintiff sought to prevent the defendant from using his attorney's statement to the officer on the ground that the communication was protected from disclosure by the attorney-client privilege. At an in camera hearing to determine the admissibility of the communication, the judge took evidence of the statement. The reviewing court upheld the in camera disclosure: it was not the type of disclosure prohibited by the Code because "the disclosure had already occurred without action of any kind by the court." Id. at 938, 95 Cal.Rptr. at 268.

Often, privilege claims arise when a party files a motion to quash a subpoena for privileged information. A judge ordinarily should not rule on the motion until after granting the parties an oral hearing on the motion to quash. Titmas v. Superior Court, 87 Cal.App.4th 738, 745 104 Cal.Rptr.2d 803, 809 (2001) (motion to quash based on the attorney-client privilege).

permitted) and (2) claims by the privilege opponent that the holder has waived the privilege or that the privileged matter falls within an exception (in camera disclosure permitted).[2] Today, the California courts distinguish between these claims in determining whether in camera disclosure of the privileged material should be compelled to enable the judge to rule on the privilege claim:

> The rule against in camera review, however, is not absolute. (See Cornish v. Superior Court (1989) 209 Cal.App.3d 467, 480, 257 Cal. Rptr. 383.) "The rule is based on the notion that when there is a claim of attorney client privilege, for example, it is neither customary nor necessary to review the contents of the communication in order to determine whether the privilege applies as the court's factual determination does not involve the nature of the communications or the effect of disclosure but rather the existence of the relationship at the time the communication was made, the intent of the client and whether the communication emanates from the client. [Citation.]" (Ibid.) "[C]ourts have recognized [that], if necessary to determine whether an exception to the privilege applies, the court may conduct an in camera hearing notwithstanding section 915. [Citation.]" (Ibid., italics added.) Generally, in camera hearings should be limited to a determination whether there is an exception to, or waiver of, the privilege, and "whether the exception or waiver depends on the content of the communication. [Citation.]" (People v. Manago (1990) 220 Cal.App.3d 982, 990, fn. 4, 269 Cal.Rptr. 819.) "[W]here an exception to a privilege depends upon the content of a communication, the court may require disclosure in camera in making its ruling." (Mavroudis v. Superior Court (1980) 102 Cal.App.3d 594, 606, 162 Cal.Rptr. 724.)[3]

In criminal cases a judge may order in chambers disclosure of privileged information when necessary to rule on the accused's claim that the information is essential to the constitutional right "to matters reasonably required to permit a full and fair cross-examination" of the witnesses who testify against him.[4] Moreover, where a judge is asked to rule on a claim that the information sought is protected by the privileges for confidential communications between victims and sexual assault or domestic counselors, the privilege for official information and the identity of informers, or is a trade secret, the court may require the person from whom disclosure is sought or the person authorized to claim the privilege to disclose the

---

2. See, e.g., State Farm Fire & Cas. v. Superior Court, 54 Cal.App.4th 625, 645, 62 Cal.Rptr.2d 834, 848 (1997) (barring disclosure of privileged information in camera for purposes of ruling on the application of the crime/fraud exception to the attorney-client privilege). A party, however, may consent to in camera disclosure of the information claimed to be privileged in order to facilitate a ruling on the privilege claim. Wellpoint Health Networks v. Superior Court, 59 Cal.App.4th 110, 121, 68 Cal.Rptr.2d 844, 851 (1997).

3. OXY Resources California LLC v. Superior Court, 115 Cal.App.4th 874, 896, 9 Cal.Rptr.3d 621, 640 (2004).

4. Vela v. Superior Court, 208 Cal.App.3d 141, 151, 255 Cal.Rptr. 921, 926 (1989).

information in chambers.[5] An exception is made for these privileges because the court may sustain the privilege claim only if the court finds that the need to maintain secrecy outweighs the need for disclosure in the case before the court.[6]

Sometimes the issue is not whether a privilege applies but only the extent to which it applies to portions of documents that otherwise are discoverable. Lipton v. Superior Court[7] holds that a judge may order in camera review of the documents where such a review is essential to the court's determinations of the privilege claims.[8] In a criminal case, however, a judge may not compel in camera disclosure of client communications in ruling on a defense attorney's motion for withdrawal on the ground that the client's communications revealed a conflict of interest.[9]

Under California Penal Code § 1524(c), a lawyer, physician, psychotherapist, or member of the clergy, who is not reasonably suspected of engaging in criminal activity, may object to the issuance of a search warrant for documentary evidence in their possession on the ground it contains privileged information.[10] If a privilege claim is raised, any items seized must be sealed and a hearing must be held to determine the applicability of the privilege.[11] Section 915(a) allows in camera disclosure of privileged matter that is subject to a Penal Code § 1524 proceeding if there is no other feasible means to rule on the validity of the privilege claim.[12]

Lawyers who are suspected of engaging in criminal activity may not rely on § 1524 to prevent disclosure of client files seized pursuant to a search warrant. But these lawyers nonetheless are entitled to have a court seal the files seized from their offices until a hearing can be conducted to

---

5. For a discussion of the privileges for confidential communications between victims and sexual assault and domestic violence counselors, see Chapters 25–26 infra. For a discussion of the privilege for official information and identity of informers, and trade secrets, see West's Ann. California Evidence Code § 915(b). This exception applies only when a court is ruling on the privilege claim. It does not apply, for example, in an administrative hearing. Id. (comment).

6. West's Ann. California Evidence Code § 915(b) (comment). Disclosure may be required only if the court is unable to rule on the privilege claim without the information. The disclosure in chambers must be in confidence. All persons must be excluded except the person disclosing the information, the person authorized to claim the privilege, and such other persons as the person authorized to claim the privilege is willing to have present. If the judge determines that the information is privileged, neither the judge nor any other person "may ever disclose, without the consent of a person authorized to permit disclosure, what was disclosed in the course of the proceedings in chambers." West's Ann. California Evidence Code § 915(b).

In criminal cases, a judge may not rule on a claim that an informer's identity is privileged solely on the basis of the in camera hearing. The judge's ruling must be based on the in camera proceedings as well as on a hearing in which the accused is entitled to be heard. West's Ann. California Evidence Code § 1042.

7. 48 Cal.App.4th 1599, 56 Cal.Rptr.2d 341 (1996).

8. Id. at 1620, 56 Cal.Rptr.2d at 353.

9. See Aceves v. Superior Court (People), 51 Cal.App.4th 584, 595, 59 Cal.Rptr.2d 280, 286 (1996).

10. West's Ann. California Penal Code § 1524(c).

11. Id.

12. West's Ann. California Evidence Code § 915(a).

determine any privilege claims.[13] Since the court may order the hearing to be held in camera,[14] presumably the court can rely on Evidence Code § 915(a) to compel the disclosure of the information claimed to be privileged in order to rule on the privilege claims.[15]

Effects of ruling errors. If a judge erroneously overrules a privilege claim and compels disclosure of the privileged information, the person authorized to claim the privilege may still assert the privilege in a subsequent proceeding.[16] Erroneous coerced disclosures do not operate as a waiver; evidence of the erroneous disclosure is therefore inadmissible.[17] Moreover, neither the failure to resist an erroneous order to disclose privileged information nor the failure to seek review of the order constitutes a waiver of the privilege.[18] The person authorized to claim the privilege may still claim it in a later stage of the same proceeding or in a subsequent proceeding.[19]

Sometimes, no party to a proceeding is authorized to claim a privilege and the person from whom the information is sought is likewise not authorized to claim the privilege. In these circumstances, the court, on its own motion or the motion of any party, must exclude the privileged matter.[20] If the judge fails to do so, the person authorized to claim the privilege may still claim it in a subsequent proceeding.[21]

The Code requires lawyers,[22] physicians,[23] psychotherapists,[24] sexual assault counselors,[25] and domestic assault counselors[26] to claim the privilege on behalf of their clients or patients if present when disclosure of the privileged communication is sought. If the holder is not present, their failure to claim the privilege will not preclude the holder from claiming the privilege in a subsequent proceeding.[27] Neither will their failure excuse the court's obligation to exclude the privileged information on its

---

13. People v. Superior Court (Bauman & Rose), 37 Cal.App.4th 1757, 1767, 44 Cal.Rptr.2d 734, 740 (1995).

14. Id.

15. By its express terms, California Evidence Code § 915(a) allows in camera disclosure of the information claimed to be privileged only if the hearing into the privilege claim is held pursuant to Penal Code § 1524.

16. West's Ann. California Evidence Code § 919(a)(1).

17. Id. (comment).

18. West's Ann. California Evidence Code § 919(b).

19. Id. and comment.

20. West's Ann. California Evidence Code § 916.

21. West's Ann. California Evidence Code § 919(a)(2). The judge's obligation to exclude the privileged matter includes the duty to inform a witness of the availability of the privilege. People v. Flores, 71 Cal.App.3d 559, 564, 139 Cal.Rptr. 546, 548 (1977).

22. West's Ann. California Evidence Code § 955.

23. Id.

24. West's Ann. California Evidence Code § 1015.

25. West's Ann. California Evidence Code § 1036.

26. West's Ann. California Evidence Code § 1037.6.

27. People v. Vargas, 53 Cal.App.3d 516, 527, 126 Cal.Rptr. 88, 95–96 (1975).

own motion or the motion of any party.[28]

Standing to raise ruling errors. A party may predicate error on a ruling erroneously sustaining a claim of privilege. As a litigant, a party is injured by the exclusion of the matter erroneously ruled as privileged.

A party, however, may predicate error on a ruling disallowing a claim of privilege only if the party is the holder of the privilege.[29] A party who is not the holder is not harmed by the erroneous admission of information that is otherwise admissible. That party's only grievance is that "the overriding of the outsider's rights has resulted in a fuller fact-disclosure than the party desires."[30] The Code, however, provides an exception for a party who is a spouse and who predicates error on a ruling disallowing a claim of privilege by the other spouse under the marital privileges established by §§ 970–971.[31] These sections give a married person the privilege not testify against a spouse in any proceeding and to decline to be called as a witness by the adverse party in any proceeding in which the spouse is a party. The complaining spouse, though not the holder of these privileges, is nonetheless harmed by an erroneous ruling disallowing the privileges; these privileges are designed to protect the marital relationship from the disruption that might be occasioned if a spouse testifies against the spouse-party.[32]

Commenting on the exercise of privileges. If judges and parties were permitted to comment on the exercise of a privilege and if jurors were permitted to draw adverse inferences from the its exercise, a party would be under great pressure to forego the privilege, and its protection could be largely lost.[33] Accordingly, the Code prohibits any comment on the exercise of a privilege as well as the drawing of any adverse inference from its exercise.[34] Moreover, the Code provides that, upon request, the court must instruct the jurors not to draw any adverse inferences from the exercise of the privilege.[35]

The no comment rule applies only if the witness claims a privilege and the claim is sustained. It does not apply to potential witnesses who are not called because a party believes they will claim a privilege. Thus, a party may comment on the adverse party's failure to call corroborating witnesses even if they might have claimed a privilege if called.[36]

When the accused exercises the right under the Fifth Amendment not to take the stand, the Constitution prohibits the judge and the prosecutor

---

28. Id.

29. West's Ann. California Evidence Code § 918.

30. C. McCormick, Handbook of the Law of Evidence § 73.1 (J. Strong 4th ed. 1992).

31. West's Ann. California Evidence Code § 918.

32. West's Ann. California Evidence Code § 970 (comment).

33. West's Ann. California Evidence Code § 913(a) and comment.

34. Id.

35. West's Ann. California Evidence Code § 913(b).

36. People v. Ford, 45 Cal.3d 431, 448–449, 247 Cal.Rptr. 121, 131–133, 754 P.2d 168, 178–180 (1988).

from commenting adversely on the witness's refusal to testify.[37] Such comment is unconstitutional because it cuts down on the privilege against self-incrimination by making its assertion costly.[38] Upon request, the judge must instruct the jurors not to draw any adverse inference from the accused's failure to testify.[39]

QUESTIONS AND PROBLEMS

1. Except in criminal cases where the accused's right to confront his accusers is implicated, as a general rule a judge may not require disclosure of matter the opponent claims to be privileged in order to rule on the privilege claim. True or false?

2. If a judge erroneously overrules a privilege claim and compels disclosure of the privileged information, the holder may still assert the privilege in a subsequent proceeding because erroneously compelled disclosures do not operate as a waiver. True or false?

3. A party may predicate error on a ruling erroneously sustaining a claim of privilege. A party, however, generally may not predicate error on a ruling erroneously disallowing a claim of privilege if the party is not the holder of the privilege. True or false?

4. Parties as well as judges are permitted to comment on the exercise of a privilege. True or false?

§ 20.05 WAIVER OF PRIVILEGES

As has been noted, privileges exist because the California Legislature has determined that in some instances the need for relevant information should be subordinated to personal, professional, and institutional interests that are best served by withholding certain information. An attorney, for example, can best serve her client if she has all relevant information which the client possesses. To encourage full disclosure, the attorney-client privilege entitles the client and the attorney to refuse to disclose confidential communications transmitted between the client and the attorney in the course of the attorney-client relationship.[1] Obviously, the holder of the privilege—the client in this instance—can waive the protection afforded by the privilege. In such a circumstance, the confidential information can be received if it is otherwise admissible under the rules of the forum.

Conscious relinquishment. The holder can consciously waive the protection afforded by the privilege by electing to disclose or permitting another to disclose the privileged information.[2] A married person, for

---

37. Griffin v. California, 380 U.S. 609, 614, 85 S.Ct. 1229, 1232, 14 L.Ed.2d 106 (1965), reh'g denied, 381 U.S. 957, 85 S.Ct. 1797, 14 L.Ed.2d 730 (1965).

38. Id.

39. Carter v. Kentucky, 450 U.S. 288, 303, 101 S.Ct. 1112, 1120, 67 L.Ed.2d 241 (1981).

1. West's Ann. California Evidence Code §§ 952 and 954.

2. West's Ann. California Evidence Code § 912(a).

example, has a privilege not to be called as a witness by the adverse party in any proceeding in which the spouse is a party.[3] As the holder of the privilege, a married person with information that may be especially helpful to her spouse may elect to waive the privilege and appear as a witness.

Negligent waivers. An intent to waive the privilege is not required. The holder can waive the privilege simply by failing to claim it in any proceeding in which the holder has the legal standing and opportunity to claim the privilege.[4] This rule is simply a specialized formulation of the established rule that the failure to object to the introduction of inadmissible evidence waives the error.[5] Thus, negligence, as well as conscious relinquishment, can result in waiver. But the holder does not waive the privilege by failing to appear to assert the privilege in proceedings to which the holder is not a party.

Negligent disclosures of privileged information often occur in a discovery context. The California Discovery Act provides that the failure of a party to object to the disclosure of privileged matter waives the privilege. This rule applies to various discovery modes, including demands for the inspection or production of documents,[6] depositions by written questions,[7] oral depositions,[8] interrogatories,[9] and requests for admissions.[10] The failure to object waives any objection based on the traditional privileges, such as the attorney-client privilege, as well as those based on the work product doctrine. This doctrine, which is discussed in Chapter 22, protects from disclosure certain memoranda generated by lawyers in the course of representing a client.

Imposing a waiver penalty may appear to be unduly harsh in a discovery context where voluminous documents often are involved. This is especially the case where the penalized party was *not* even negligent in failing to assert the privilege.[11] Even in this situation, however, strictly applying the waiver rule is consistent with the general principle embodied in the Evidence Code: consent to disclosure of a privileged communication can be inferred from "the failure to claim the privilege in any proceeding in which the holder has the legal standing and opportunity to claim the privilege."[12] As will be seen, however, the courts have begun to place some

---

3. See § 28.01 infra.

4. West's Ann. California Evidence Code § 912(a).

5. West's Ann. California Evidence Code § 353.

6. West's Ann. California Civil Procedure Code § 2031.300(a).

7. Id. § 2028.050(a).

8. Id. § 2025.460(a).

9. Id. § 2030.290(a).

10. Id. § 2033.280(a).

11. See, e.g., O'Mary v. Mitsubishi Electronics America, 59 Cal.App.4th 563, 577, 69 Cal. Rptr.2d 389, 399 (1997)

12. West's Ann. California Evidence Code § 912(a).

limits on the unrestrained application of this principle in the discovery context.[13]

Waiver by voluntary disclosure of confidential communications to third persons. Some privileges give the holder the right to decline to testify. A married person, for example, has a privilege not to be called as a witness by an adverse party in an action in which a spouse is a party.[14] Others exempt a person from having to give certain types of testimony. A married person, for example, has a privilege not to testify against the other spouse.[15] Still others give the holder only the right to refuse to disclose and to prevent another from disclosing *confidential communications* made in the context of specified professional relationships.[16] Examples include the privileges for lawyers and clients, physicians and patients, psychotherapists and patients, members of the clergy and penitents, sexual abuse and domestic abuse counselors and victims, and the privilege for confidential marital communications.[17]

Privileges protecting confidential communications from disclosure can be waived if the holder discloses, without coercion, a significant part of the protected communication to a third person.[18] If a client, for example, tells his best friend that he told his lawyer that he ran the light, the privilege protecting the client's communication with the lawyer from disclosure is lost. Both the client and the attorney can be compelled to disclose the privileged communication. On the other hand, if the client merely tells his friend that he discussed the accident with his lawyer, the privilege is not waived. Merely acknowledging the existence of a confidential communication or disclosing the topic of a confidential communication does not waive the privilege.[19] In this regard, San Diego Trolley, Inc. v. Superior Court[20] is especially instructive. The court held that the psychotherapist-patient privilege was not waived by a patient's disclosure at a deposition that she was being treated for anxiety by a psychiatrist, that she was taking medications for her condition, and that she had informed her employer of her treatment. Moreover, the court held that the privilege was not waived by the patient's filing of a related workers' compensation claim unless the privilege opponent could demonstrate that a significant part of the confidential communications with the psychiatrist was disclosed in the course

---

13. See O'Mary v. Mitsubishi Electronics America, 59 Cal.App.4th 563, 577, 69 Cal.Rptr.2d 389, 399 (1997) (holding that inadvertent disclosures during discovery do not waive the privilege). It is unclear, however, whether the court's use of "inadvertent" includes negligent disclosures or is limited to those occurring without fault.

14. West's Ann. California Evidence Code § 971.

15. West's Ann. California Evidence Code § 970.

16. See, e.g., West's Ann. California Evidence Code § 954.

17. Though the privilege for marital communications does not involve a professional relationship, the privilege protects confidential spousal communications. The Code's provisions for waiver by voluntary disclosure of confidential communications thus apply to this privilege as well. See West's Ann. California Evidence Code § 912.

18. West's Ann. California Evidence Code § 912(a).

19. See San Diego Trolley, Inc. v. Superior Court, 87 Cal.App.4th 1083, 1094, 105 Cal.Rptr.2d 476, 483 (2001).

20. Id.

of those proceedings.[21] Waiver requires the disclosure of a significant part of the communications exchanged in confidence by the parties in their relationship.[22]

As long as the holder's disclosure was not coerced, the holder's state of mind is generally immaterial. The party claiming waiver does not have to show that the holder intended to waive the privilege. Neither does that party have to show that the holder was aware or, if unaware, should have been aware that waiver could result from the disclosure. Indeed, under the Code the party claiming waiver does not even have to show that the holder was aware that he or she was disclosing confidential information protected by a privilege. All that party has to show is that the holder's disclosure was not coerced.[23] Thus, a form of strict liability, in addition to negligence and conscious relinquishment, can furnish a basis for waiving a privilege.[24]

In the discovery context, however, strict liability will not result in the loss of the attorney-client privilege in some circumstances.[25] Where during discovery counsel mistakenly but in good faith voluntarily discloses information protected by the privilege, the privilege is not waived. "An honest mistake of law, where the law is unsettled and debatable, both militates against a finding of waiver * * * and offers a possible basis for relief from actions taken in connection with pretrial discovery."[26]

Lawyers who receive privileged information through the opponent's inadvertence are under an ethical obligation to refrain from examining the information and to notify the opponent of the error: "When a lawyer who receives materials that obviously appear to be subject to an attorney-client privilege or otherwise clearly appear to be confidential and privileged and

---

21. Id.

22. People v. Hayes, 21 Cal.4th 1211, 1265, note 14, 91 Cal.Rptr.2d 211, 248, note 14, 989 P.2d 645, 679, note 14 (1999), cert. denied, 531 U.S. 980, 121 S.Ct. 431, 148 L.Ed.2d 438 (2000). Although Congress declined to enact the privileges recommended by the Advisory Committee appointed by the United States Supreme Court, the committee's note to Rule 511 provides that a client does not waive the attorney-client privilege merely by disclosing a subject he discussed with his attorney; "he would have to make disclosure of the communication itself in order to effect a waiver."

23. West's Ann. California Evidence Code § 912.

24. Of course, the party claiming waiver is always free to try to show that the holder intended to waive the privilege, or was aware that disclosing the confidential information would waive the privilege, or was negligent in disclosing the privileged information, or was aware that he was disclosing information protected by a privilege.

25. Inadvertent disclosure during discovery "by no stretch of the imagination shows *consent* to the disclosure: It merely demonstrates that the poor paralegal or junior associate who was lumbered with the tedious job of going through voluminous files and records in preparation for a document production may have missed something." O'Mary v. Mitsubishi Electronics America, 59 Cal.App.4th 563, 577, 69 Cal.Rptr.2d 389, 399 (1997) (emphasis in the original). Such inadvertent disclosures cannot be viewed as voluntary; under the Code; only noncoerced disclosures lose the protection of the privilege. Accord: State Compensation Ins. Fund v. WPS, Inc., 70 Cal.App.4th 644, 654, 82 Cal.Rptr.2d 799, 805 (1999) ("Based on the language of Evidence Code section 912, we hold that 'waiver' does not include accidental, inadvertent disclosure of privileged information by the attorney.").

26. Wells Fargo Bank v. Superior Court, 22 Cal.4th 201, 211–212, 91 Cal.Rptr.2d 716, 724, 990 P.2d 591, 597 (2000) (Counsel for the trustee mistakenly disclosed to the beneficiary information pertaining to the administration of the trust.).

where it is reasonably apparent that the materials were provided or made available through inadvertence, the lawyer receiving such materials should refrain from examining the materials any more than is essential to ascertain if the materials are privileged, and shall immediately notify the sender that he or she possesses material that appears to be privileged."[27] Lawyers who ignore this ethical constraint and make use of the privileged information can be disqualified from representing their clients.[28]

The California Law Revision Commission justifies the loss of the privilege on a strict liability basis on the grounds that "the seal of secrecy has in fact been broken and [that] the holder did not himself consider the matter sufficiently confidential to keep it secret. If the holder does not think it important to keep the matter secret, there is then no reason to permit him to exclude the communication when it is needed in order to do justice."[29]

The Commission's position is persuasive when the holder reveals to others what he said in confidence to his lawyer, spouse, physician, psychotherapist, clergyman, sexual assault counselor and domestic violence counselor.[30] Then, as Professor John H. Wigmore advocated, "[F]airness requires that his privilege shall cease whether he intended that result or not," for the holder "cannot be allowed, after disclosing as much as he pleases, to withhold the remainder."[31]

The Commission's position is less convincing, however, when the holder does not disclose the actual confidential communication but merely makes statements to third persons that happen to have the same subject matter as the confidential communication. There is a difference between telling your friend that you ran the light and revealing to your friend that you told your lawyer that you ran the light. People v. Tamborrino[32] rejects the view that a privilege is waived by the holder's voluntary disclosure to third persons of information that happens to have the same subject matter as the confidential communication.

In *Tamborrino* the client testified at his trial on a robbery charge that the victim had a motive to frame him because he had sold her fake cocaine. Over the client's objection, the trial judge asked the client whether he had related this information to his lawyer. The appellate court held that the client's testimony did not waive the protection which the

---

27. State Compensation Ins. Fund v. WPS, Inc., 70 Cal.App.4th 644, 656, 82 Cal.Rptr.2d 799, 807 (1999). Accord: Rico v. Mitsubishi Motors Corp., 42 Cal.4th 807, 817, 171 P.3d 1092, 1099, 68 Cal.Rptr.3d 758, 766 (2007) (applying the ethical constraint where the information was protected from disclosure by the work product doctrine).

28. See Rico v. Mitsubishi Motors Corp., 42 Cal.4th 807, 817, 171 P.3d 1092, 1099, 68 Cal.Rptr.3d 758, 767 (2007). In *Rico*, the privileged information was protected from disclosure by the work product doctrine. Id.

29. 6 California Law Revision Commission, Reports, Recommendations, and Studies 262 (1964).

30. Waiver by disclosure affects only confidential communications with these advisors and counselors. West's Ann. California Evidence Code § 912.

31. 8 Wigmore, Evidence § 2327 (McNaughton Rev. 1961).

32. 215 Cal.App.3d 575, 263 Cal.Rptr. 731 (1989).

attorney-client privilege conferred on his communications with his lawyer: "Defendant's testimony concerning facts that might have been previously related by him to his counsel is not equivalent to disclosure by him of the actual content of an attorney-client communication, and does not constitute a waiver of the privilege."[33] To waive the privilege, the holder must reveal a substantial portion of the actual communications.[34]

The fact that a holder can lose the privilege by disclosing a significant part of the privileged communications to a third person does not strip the holder of all protection. A patient, for example, does not waive her entire medical history by revealing information about her use of a particular drug. Only those confidential communications with her doctor relating to the drug's use and its effects can be disclosed.[35] Nor does a patient waive her entire psychiatric history by disclosing as a witness, pursuant to an in camera review, that she is under psychiatric care and is taking medication for her condition.[36]

---

33. Id. at 582, 263 Cal.Rptr. at 734–735.

34. See Maas v. Municipal Court, 175 Cal.App.3d 601, 606, 221 Cal.Rptr. 245, 248 (1985) (holding that a client's testimony against an accomplice pursuant to a plea agreement did not waive the client's privilege protecting confidential communications with her attorney).

The rule that voluntary disclosure of a significant part of a confidential communication to third persons waives the privilege irrespective of the holder's intentions makes some sense when the information disclosed is private in nature. Most people regard information about venereal diseases or investments as private. If, after telling your doctor that you may have venereal disease or your lawyer that some investments may be illegal, you then tell your best friend about your illness or your crime, some justification exists for the rule: you can hardly claim a privilege for information which is no longer private by virtue of your actions. In the case of the attorney-client privilege, moreover, the rule makes even more sense if the client's revelation to a third person was in disregard of the lawyer's advice not to talk to anyone about the investment.

But even this defense of the waiver rule is problematic. The California Supreme Court recognizes that the privileges for confidential communications do not require the information to be "confidential" in nature. Menendez v. Superior Court, 3 Cal.4th 435, 446, 11 Cal.Rptr.2d 92, 99, 834 P.2d 786, 793 (1992). All that is required is that the information be transmitted in confidence. Id. Doctors, moreover, do not typically warn patients not to talk about their illnesses with a third person. Even limiting the rule to the attorney-client relationship has its difficulties. Clients consult lawyers on many matters that do not necessarily have a private aspect. The 1980s mergers and acquisitions madness was widely reported in the media both before and after the deals were consummated. Statements by the bidding parties often were the heart of the stories. Surely, the publicity given these matters did not strip bidders of the protection afforded by the attorney-client privilege to their consultations with their lawyers after some losers sued. If holders do not lose the privilege when they disclose their problems before consulting a lawyer or health practitioner, why should they lose the privilege by disclosing the same information after the consultation?

Upholding the privilege in these circumstances would not necessarily entail intolerable costs. Telling your friend that you invested funds illegally or that you had a pre-existing injury are party admissions. They are admissible as an exception to the hearsay rule irrespective of whether the revelations to your friend came before or after your disclosures to your lawyer or doctor. Privileges do not bar the use of all admissions. They prohibit only the use of admissions you make to your lawyer or doctor or other specified individuals. And, as noted, even then privileges do not bar the use of these statements if you reveal to a third person what you told your lawyer or doctor or other specified individuals.

35. Jones v. Superior Court, 119 Cal.App.3d 534, 551, 174 Cal.Rptr. 148, 155 (1981).

36. See People v. Webb, 6 Cal.4th 494, 517, note 16, 24 Cal.Rptr.2d 779, 793, note 16, 862 P.2d 779, 793, note 16 (1993). See also San Diego Trolley, Inc. v. Superior Court, 87 Cal.App.4th 1083, 1094, 105 Cal.Rptr.2d 476, 483 (2001) (The psychotherapist-patient privilege is not waived by a patient's disclosure at a deposition that she was being treated for anxiety by a psychiatrist, that she was taking medications for her condition, and that she had informed her employer of her treatment; moreover, neither is the privilege waived by the patient's filing of a related workers'

Waiver by disclosing confidential communications to third persons will not occur in some situations. One is where the information disclosed is not a significant part of the privileged communication. For example, telling a third person that you have communicated with an attorney does not waive the privilege protecting the content of communications with the attorney.[37] Neither will denying that you discussed certain subjects with a psychiatrist waive the privilege protecting the content of communications with the psychiatrist.[38] Moreover, even disclosing a significant part of a privileged communication to third persons will not result in waiver when the disclosure is reasonably necessary for accomplishing the purpose for which the lawyer, physician, psychotherapist, sexual assault counselor, or domestic violence counselor was consulted.[39]

> For example, where a confidential communication from a client is related by his attorney to a physician, appraiser, or other expert in order to obtain that person's assistance so that the attorney will better be able to advise his client, the disclosure is not a waiver of the privilege, even though the disclosure is made with the client's knowledge and consent. Nor would a physician's or psychotherapist's keeping of confidential records necessary to diagnose or treat a patient, such as confidential hospital records, be a waiver of the privilege, even though other authorized persons have access to the records. Similarly, the patient's presentation of a physician's prescription to a registered pharmacist would not constitute a waiver of the physician-patient privilege because such disclosure is reasonably necessary for the accomplishment of the purpose for which the physician is consulted.[40]

Disclosing confidential communications to third persons when the disclosure is itself privileged will also not result in waiver.[41]

> [A person, for example,] does not waive his attorney-client privilege by telling his wife in confidence what it was that he told his lawyer. Nor does a person waive the marital communication privilege by telling his attorney in confidence in the course of the attorney-client relationship what it was that he told his wife. And a person does not waive the lawyer-client privilege as to a communication by relating it to another attorney in the course of a separate relationship. A privileged communication does not cease to be privileged merely because it has been related in the course of another privileged communication. The

compensation claim unless a significant part of the confidential communications with the psychiatrist is disclosed in the course of those proceedings.).

37. People v. Gardner, 106 Cal.App.3d 882, 887, 165 Cal.Rptr. 415, 417–418 (1980).

38. People v. Perry, 7 Cal.3d 756, 783, 103 Cal.Rptr. 161, 178, 499 P.2d 129, 146 (1972).

39. West's Ann. California Evidence Code § 912(a) and comment. See also West's Ann. California Evidence Code § 1037.2.

40. Id. (comment). The privilege will not be waived when lawyers representing a set of plaintiffs or defendants circulate confidential communications among themselves if the "mutual disclosures were reasonably necessary to accomplish the purpose for which [the] attorneys were consulted." Raytheon Co. v. Superior Court (Renault), 208 Cal.App.3d 683, 687, 256 Cal.Rptr. 425, 429 (1989).

41. West's Ann. California Evidence Code § 912(c).

theory underlying the concept of waiver is that the holder of the privilege has abandoned the secrecy to which he is entitled under the privilege. Where the revelation of the privileged matter takes place in another privileged communication, there has not been such an abandonment.[42]

Waiver by consent of the holder. Waiver may occur if the holder consents to disclosure by a third person of a significant part of the privileged communications.[43] A patient, for example, waives the psychotherapist-patient privilege by calling the psychotherapist as a witness and eliciting information disclosing a significant part of the privileged communications.[44] Such a disclosure will also preclude the holder from claiming the privilege to prevent the disclosure of those communications in subsequent proceedings.[45] But the holder may still claim the privilege to prevent the disclosure of privileged communications made after the waiver.[46]

Waiver by one of several joint holders. Where two or more persons are the joint holders of the attorney-client privilege, the physician-patient privilege, the psychotherapist-patient privilege, the sexual assault victim-counselor privilege, or the domestic violence victim-counselor privilege, waiver by one of the holders does not preclude the others from claiming the privilege.[47] Moreover, a waiver by one spouse of the privilege for confidential marital communications does not prevent the other spouse from claiming the privilege.[48]

Waiver by contract. The California Law Revision Commission rejected the view that waiver of a privilege can be implied from a contractual agreement by the holder to waive the privilege.[49] Applications for health or life insurance, for example, typically require the applicant to waive the physician-patient privilege. The Commission's position was that disclosure pursuant to the provision, rather than the provision itself, gave rise to the waiver.[50] The Commission's position is reflected in § 912(a) which pro-

---

42. Id. (comment).

43. Id.

44. People v. Garaux, 34 Cal.App.3d 611, 613, 110 Cal.Rptr. 119, 120 (1973).

45. Id. It is immaterial whether the subsequent proceedings are related to the proceeding in which the waiver took place. Id.

46. People v. Superior Court (Broderick), 231 Cal.App.3d 584, 590, 282 Cal.Rptr. 418, 422 (1991).

47. West's Ann. California Evidence Code § 912(b). An insurer who retains an attorney to defend the insured against malpractice actions is a joint holder with the insured of the attorney-client privilege. American Mut. Liability Ins. Co. v. Superior Court, 38 Cal.App.3d 579, 591, 113 Cal.Rptr. 561, 571 (1974). Consequently, the insured's waiver of the attorney-client privilege does not preclude the insurer from claiming the privilege. Id.

48. West's Ann. California Evidence Code § 912(b).

49. 6 California Law Revision Commission, Reports, Recommendations, and Studies 262 (1964). Waiver by contract was advocated in the 1953 version of the Uniform Rules of Evidence. Id.

50. Id.

vides that a privilege is waived if the holder, without coercion, consents to a significant disclosure of the privileged matter.[51]

Courts nonetheless look to releases in determining some privilege claims. Insurance agreements typically require the beneficiary to file a proof of claim in order to collect the benefits under a life insurance policy. These claims may require the beneficiary to authorize health providers to release the insured's medical records to the insurer. In Grey v. Superior Court[52] the insurer relied on the authorization to ask that the insured's psychiatric records be produced for inspection. The court upheld the beneficiary's claim that the records were protected from disclosure by the psychotherapist-patient privilege.[53] The beneficiary had not included the psychiatrist among the health providers authorized to release medical records to the insurer. The court, therefore, held that the beneficiary had not waived the privilege with respect to the psychiatric records.[54]

Insurance liability policies often contain a standard cooperation clause requiring the insured to cooperate with the carrier in the event the insured is sued. Jurisdictions have split over whether the clause waives the attorney-client privilege for confidential communications between the insured and their lawyers arising from the suit against the insured. In Rockwell International Corp. v. Superior Court[55] California rejected the view that such clauses waive the privilege in a suit by the insured against the carrier for breach of contract.[56]

Disclosure of confidential information pursuant to a contractual obligation is not necessarily a voluntary disclosure resulting in the waiver of the privilege when the information is sought by third parties. In Pollock v. Superior Court[57] the plaintiff sued an insurance company for breach of contract and breach of the implied covenant of good faith and fair dealing on the ground that the company had wrongfully terminated the payments due him under a disability income policy. As part of discovery, the plaintiff asked the company for the names and addresses of insureds who, like plaintiff, had received and then were denied disability payments. When the insurance company refused to supply the names and addresses, the plaintiff moved the court for an order compelling their disclosure. The appellate court upheld the trial court's refusal to grant the motion: "The names of [the company's] claimants are not discoverable because the disclosure would reveal not only the identity of the claimants but also the nature of their ailments ('psychiatric disability'). The submission of a claim to [the company] is a condition precedent to coverage under a policy purchased by the claimant and, therefore, a necessity. For this reason, the

---

51. West's Ann. California Evidence Code § 912(a).

52. 62 Cal.App.3d 698, 133 Cal.Rptr. 318 (1976).

53. Id. at 703, 133 Cal.Rptr. at 320.

54. Id.

55. 26 Cal.App.4th 1255, 32 Cal.Rptr.2d 153 (1994).

56. Id. at 1261–1265, 32 Cal.Rptr.2d at 157–159.

57. 93 Cal.App.4th 817, 113 Cal.Rptr.2d 453 (2001).

psychotherapist-patient privilege is not waived by the claimant, and it cannot be waived by the insurer."[58]

Waiver by refreshing recollection with privileged matter. Witnesses do not always recall the details of the testimony the examiner wishes to elicit. Sometimes, witnesses refresh their recollection prior to testifying or even while testifying by referring to notes and other memoranda. If a witness uses confidential information, such as a transcript of her interview with the attorney, to refresh her recollection, is the opposing party entitled to inspect and introduce the memorandum used by the witness?

Evidence Code § 771 provides that if a witness uses a writing to refresh her recollection prior to or while testifying, the writing must be produced at the request of the adverse party and, unless produced, the testimony of the witness must be stricken.[59] Section 771 also provides that if the writing is produced, the adverse party may inspect it, cross examine the witness about it, and introduce any part that is pertinent to the witness's testimony.[60] The Code is silent on the conflict between the privileges and § 771. Most major privileges, however, provide that the holder may claim the privilege unless it has been waived.[61] Thus, courts have attempted to resolve the conflict between the privileges and § 771 by determining whether the use of confidential information to refresh recollection amounts to a waiver of the privilege.

When the holder uses a privileged memorandum to refresh her recollection *while* testifying, the holder is testifying from a refreshed recollection and is not just indirectly reading the memorandum into the record.[62] Since the holder is not offering the confidential communications contained in the memorandum, the use of the memorandum to refresh recollection should not be viewed as a waiver of the privilege. Quite simply, the holder is not disclosing the contents of the memorandum. The courts, however, do not appear to agree. Fairness, in their view, requires finding a waiver: "It would be unconscionable to allow a rule of evidence that a witness can testify to material contained in a report, though not verbatim, and then prevent disclosure of the reports."[63]

The courts use the same approach when the witness who uses privileged information to refresh recollection *while* testifying is not the holder, but the holder is present and can claim the privilege.[64] Where the holder fails to object to questions calling for the witness to disclose the privileged information in the refreshing memorandum, the privilege is

---

58. Id. at 821, 113 Cal.Rptr.2d at 457.

59. West's Ann. California Evidence Code § 771.

60. Id.

61. See, e.g., West's Ann. California Evidence Code §§ 954 (attorney-client privilege), 980 (marital communications privilege), 994 (physician-patient privilege), 1014 (psychotherapist-patient privilege), 1033–1034 (clergyman-penitent privilege).

62. For a discussion of the rules pertaining to refreshing recollection, see § 8.09 supra.

63. Kerns Const. Co. v. Superior Court, 266 Cal.App.2d 405, 414, 72 Cal.Rptr. 74, 79 (1968).

64. Id.

deemed to have been waived. Such an outcome is not surprising, for, as we have seen, the failure to claim the privilege waives it in any proceeding in which the holder has the legal standing and opportunity to claim the privilege. But where the questions call only for the witness to answer from his recollection, albeit refreshed, the courts still use a waiver approach if the holder claims the privilege.[65] The use of this approach is questionable: the witness who testifies on the basis of a refreshed recollection is not reading the memorandum into the record. Moreover, merely testifying about matters which also happen to be the subject of a privileged communication does not waive the privilege.[66] But the courts nonetheless justify finding a waiver in these circumstances on fairness to the adverse party rather than on logic.[67]

If the holder uses a memorandum with privileged information—a transcript, for example, of the holder's consultation with the lawyer—to refresh her recollection *prior* to testifying, then the adverse party may not compel its production under § 771.[68] To the courts, such writings are indistinguishable from an attorney's confidential oral statements reminding the witness of what the witness, as a client, originally told the attorney, and oral statements are beyond the reach of § 771.[69] The question, though, is not whether such memoranda are the functional equivalent of oral reminders but whether their use prior to testifying waives the privilege. No waiver should occur because the holder is testifying on the basis of present recollection, albeit refreshed, and is not disclosing the contents of the privileged communications.

The effect of waiver in other proceedings. The Evidence Code does not have a provision addressing the effect in unrelated proceedings of waiver by disclosure of the privileged information. In the absence of such a provision, one would expect the judge in the unrelated proceeding to overrule the privilege claim in the case of confidential communications made in the course of specified professional relationships, such as the attorney-client relationship. Under the Code, the holder waives the privilege whenever the holder discloses without coercion a significant part of the communication.[70] The California courts, however, have expressed discomfort with this outcome. In San Diego Trolley, Inc. v. Superior Court[71] an issue was whether the driver of a trolley that injured the plaintiff had waived the protection accorded her confidential communications with her psychiatrist under the psychotherapist-patient privilege because she had filed a stress-related workers' compensation claim against the trolley company.

65. Id.

66. People v. Tamborrino, 215 Cal.App.3d 575, 582, 263 Cal.Rptr. 731, 734–735 (1989).

67. Kerns Const. Co. v. Superior Court, 266 Cal.App.2d 405, 414, 72 Cal.Rptr. 74, 79 (1968).

68. Sullivan v. Superior Court, 29 Cal.App.3d 64, 72–73, 105 Cal.Rptr. 241, 246–247 (1972).

69. Id.

70. See West's Ann. California Evidence Code § 912.

71. 87 Cal.App.4th 1083, 105 Cal.Rptr.2d 476 (2001).

[A]ny waiver of the psychotherapist-patient privilege which has occurred in one proceeding must be carefully limited with respect to its later use in entirely unrelated proceedings. * * * Because among other reasons nontestimonial pretrial disclosures of privileged communications are not usually made in a public setting, are not otherwise widely disseminated and in fact may be subject to judicial protection from wide dissemination, a pretrial disclosure of such a communication may not suggest to a patient the possibility that the information disclosed will be available to anyone who, at anytime in the future, believes he needs the information. Of concern here also is the impact the uncontrolled use of information disclosed in one setting might have on a litigant's behavior: in the absence of some limitation as to later use of confidential information[,] psychotherapeutic patients will be unnecessarily discouraged from asserting compensation for emotional injuries for fear that any disclosure needed to obtain compensation will haunt them in perpetuity.[72]

In holding that the holder had not "knowingly" waived the psychotherapist-patient privilege, the court emphasized two considerations. First, there was no evidence that the patient had any reason for anticipating that the information she imparted in the workers' compensation proceedings would be available to anyone other than those considering her claims; second, there was no evidence that she had in fact disclosed a significant part of her confidential communications in those proceedings.[73] This holding of *San Diego Trolley* must be cited with care, however. As has been explained, under Code conscious relinquishment is not required for a waiver to be effective. Accordingly, the court should have limited its holding to the ground specified in the Code: no waiver occurred because the patient did not voluntarily disclose a significant part of her communications with her psychiatrist in the workers' compensation proceedings.[74]

The eavesdropper doctrine. The Code rejects the eavesdropper doctrine. This doctrine permits individuals who overhear confidential communications to reveal them despite the desire of the communicants to keep them confidential.[75] Instead, the Code protects against disclosure by eavesdroppers and other wrongful interceptors of confidential information by permitting the holder of the privilege to assert the privilege against anyone, including the eavesdropper, who acquires the information without the holder's consent.[76]

Under the Code, it is immaterial that a reasonable person in the communicant's situation would have been aware of the eavesdropper's presence. What matters is the communicant's belief that the means used

---

72. Id. at 1093, 105 Cal.Rptr.2d at 482.

73. Id. at 1094, 105 Cal.Rptr.2d at 483.

74. See West's Ann. California Evidence Code § 912(a).

75. 6 California Law Revision Commission, Reports, Recommendations, and Studies 398 (1964).

76. See West's Ann. California Evidence Code § 954 (comment) relating to the attorney-client privilege.

does not disclose the information to a third person. But if the communicant is aware that the means chosen for transmitting the information discloses it to third persons who are not authorized to be present, the communication is not deemed confidential and acquires no protection.[77] The communicant, as well as anyone who overhears the communication, can be compelled to disclose it. Transmitting the information under circumstances where others can easily overhear it is evidence that the communicant did not intend the information to be confidential.[78] However, confidential communications do not lose their privileged character simply because they are communicated by electronic means or because persons involved in the delivery, facilitation, or storage of electronic communications might have access to their content.[79] Moreover, under the Code, communications between attorneys and clients, physicians and patients, psychotherapists and patients, members of the clergy and penitents, husbands and wives, sexual assault victims and their counselors, and domestic violence victims and their counselors are presumed to be confidential.[80] The effect of the presumption is to shift to the party opposing the claim of privilege the burden of persuading the judge that the communication was not made in confidence.[81]

QUESTIONS AND PROBLEMS

1. A holder of a privilege may choose to forego the protection afforded by the privilege. The accused, for example, can waive her privilege against self-incrimination and take the stand as witness in her own case-in-chief. True or false?

2. A holder of privilege can waive it by failing to claim it in any proceeding in which the holder has the legal standing and opportunity to claim the privilege. Thus, the failure by a party to object to a question calling for the disclosure of information he provided in confidence to his lawyer can waive the attorney-client privilege. True or false?

3. Disclosing without coercion a significant part of a protected communication will waive the privilege protecting confidential communications from disclosure. Accordingly, telling your best friend what you told your lawyer in confidence can waive the attorney-client privilege even if you intended your communication to your friend to be confidential. True or false?

4. But the mere fact that conversations with others may involve the same subject matter as your confidential communications with your lawyer will not necessarily result in the waiver of the attorney-client privilege. True or false?

---

77. Id.

78. Id.

79. West's Ann. California Evidence Code § 917(b).

80. Id.

81. Id. and comment. For a discussion of presumptions which shift the burden of persuasion, see § 20.03 supra.

5. Moreover, merely telling your friend that you have discussed your case with your lawyer will not waive the privilege protecting confidential communications between clients and their lawyers. True or false?

6. Disclosing significant parts of privileged communications to third persons will not result in waiver if the disclosure was reasonably necessary for accomplishing the purpose for which the lawyer was consulted. For example, if at the request of your lawyer you tell his paralegal about the circumstances attending the accident about which you consulted the lawyer, that disclosure should not result in the waiver of the attorney-client privilege. True or false?

7. The California Law Revision Commission rejected the view that waiver of a privilege can be implied from a contractual agreement by the holder to waive the privilege. Courts nonetheless look to such "releases" in determining some privilege claims. True or false?

8. Under the Code as construed, the use of privileged information to refresh a witness's recollection during the trial should not waive the privilege protecting such information from disclosure since the witness is testifying from a refreshed recollection and is not disclosing the contents of the writing containing the privileged information. True or false?

9. Under the Code as construed, the use of privileged information to refresh a witness's recollection prior to the trial does not give the adverse party the right to compel the production of the writing containing the privileged information under § 771. True or false?

10. The Code rejects the eavesdropper doctrine. Under this doctrine, wrongful interceptors of privileged information may disclose such information irrespective of the communicants' desire to keep their communications confidential. True or false?

11. Instead, the Code permits the holder to assert the privilege against anyone who acquires the information without the holder's consent. True or false?

12. But if the holder is aware that the means chosen for transmitting the privileged information discloses it to third persons who are not authorized to be present, the communication will not be deemed to be confidential and can be disclosed over objection. True or false?

13. Transmitting confidential communications by electronic means results in the loss of the privileges for such communications because today everyone is aware that persons involved in the delivery, facilitation, or storage of electronic communications might have access to their content. True or false?

CALIFORNIA EVIDENCE CODE

§ 900. Application of definitions

Unless the provision or context otherwise requires, the definitions in this chapter govern the construction of this division. They do not govern the construction of any other division.

§ 901.   Proceeding

"Proceeding" means any action, hearing, investigation, inquest, or inquiry (whether conducted by a court, administrative agency, hearing officer, arbitrator, legislative body, or any other person authorized by law) in which, pursuant to law, testimony can be compelled to be given.

§ 902.   Civil proceeding

"Civil proceeding" means any proceeding except a criminal proceeding.

§ 903.   Criminal proceeding

"Criminal proceeding" means:

(a) A criminal action; and

(b) A proceeding pursuant to Article 3 (commencing with Section 3060) of Chapter 7 of Division 4 of Title 1 of the Government Code to determine whether a public officer should be removed from office for willful or corrupt misconduct in office.

§ 905.   Presiding officer

"Presiding officer" means the person authorized to rule on a claim of privilege in the proceeding in which the claim is made.

§ 910.   Applicability of division

Except as otherwise provided by statute, the provisions of this division apply in all proceedings. The provisions of any statute making rules of evidence inapplicable in particular proceedings, or limiting the applicability of rules of evidence in particular proceedings, do not make this division inapplicable to such proceedings.

§ 911.   Refusal to be or have another as witness, or disclose or produce any matter

Except as otherwise provided by statute:

(a) No person has a privilege to refuse to be a witness.

(b) No person has a privilege to refuse to disclose any matter or to refuse to produce any writing, object, or other thing.

(c) No person has a privilege that another shall not be a witness or shall not disclose any matter or shall not produce any writing, object, or other thing.

§ 912.   Waiver of privilege

(a) Except as otherwise provided in this section, the right of any person to claim a privilege provided by Section 954 (lawyer-client privilege), 980 (privilege for confidential marital communications), 994 (physician-patient privilege), 1014 (psychotherapist-patient privilege), 1033 (privilege of penitent), 1034 (privilege of clergyman), or 1035.8 (sexual assault counselor-victim privilege), or 1037.5 (domestic violence counselor-victim privilege) is waived with respect to a communication protected by such privilege if any holder of the privilege, without coercion, has disclosed a significant part of the communication or has consented to such disclosure made by anyone. Consent to disclosure is manifested by any statement or other conduct of the holder of the privilege indicating consent to the disclosure, including failure to claim the privilege in any proceeding in which the holder has the legal standing and opportunity to claim the privilege.

(b) Where two or more persons are joint holders of a privilege provided by Section 954 (lawyer-client privilege), 994 (physician-patient privilege), 1014 (psychotherapist-patient privilege), or 1035.8 (sexual assault counselor-victim privilege), or 1037.5 (domestic violence counselor-victim privilege), a waiver of the right of a particular joint holder of the privilege to claim the privilege does not affect the right of another joint holder to claim the privilege. In the case of the privilege provided by Section 980 (privilege for confidential marital communications), a waiver of the right of one spouse to claim the privilege does not affect the right of the other spouse to claim the privilege.

(c) A disclosure that is itself privileged is not a waiver of any privilege.

(d) A disclosure in confidence of a communication that is protected by a privilege provided by Section 954 (lawyer-client privilege), 994 (physician-patient privilege), 1014 (psychotherapist-patient privilege), or 1035.8 (sexual assault counselor-victim privilege), or 1037.5 (domestic violence counselor-victim privilege), when such disclosure is reasonably necessary for the accomplishment of the purpose for which the lawyer, physician, psychotherapist, or sexual assault counselor was consulted, is not a waiver of the privilege.

§ 913. Comment on, and inferences from, exercise of privilege

(a) If in the instant proceeding or on a prior occasion a privilege is or was exercised not to testify with respect to any matter, or to refuse to disclose or to prevent another from disclosing any matter, neither the presiding officer nor counsel may comment thereon, no presumption shall arise because of the exercise of the privilege, and the trier of fact may not draw any inference therefrom as to the credibility of the witness or as to any matter at issue in the proceeding.

(b) The court, at the request of a party who may be adversely affected because an unfavorable inference may be drawn by the jury because a privilege has been exercised, shall instruct the jury that no presumption arises because of the exercise of the privilege and that the jury may not draw any inference therefrom as to the credibility of the witness or as to any matter at issue in the proceeding.

§ 914. Determination of claim of privilege; limitation on punishment for contempt

(a) The presiding officer shall determine a claim of privilege in any proceeding in the same manner as a court determines such a claim under Article 2 (commencing with Section 400) of Chapter 4 of Division 3.

(b) No person may be held in contempt for failure to disclose information claimed to be privileged unless he has failed to comply with an order of a court that he disclose such information. This subdivision does not apply to any governmental agency that has constitutional contempt power, nor does it apply to hearings and investigations of the Industrial Accident Commission, nor does it impliedly repeal Chapter 4 (commencing with Section 9400) of Part 1 of Division 2 of Title 2 of the Government Code. If no other statutory procedure is applicable, the procedure prescribed by Section 1991 of the Code of Civil Procedure shall be followed in seeking an order of a court that the person disclose the information claimed to be privileged.

§ 915. Disclosure of privileged information in ruling on claim of privilege

(a) Subject to subdivision (b), the presiding officer may not require disclosure of information claimed to be privileged under this division or attorney work product under subdivision (a) of Section 2018.030 of the Code of Civil Procedure in order to rule on the claim of privilege; provided, however, that in any hearing conducted pursuant to subdivision (c) of Section 1524 of the Penal Code in which a claim of privilege is made and the court determines that there is no other feasible means to rule on the validity of the claim other than to require disclosure, the court shall proceed in accordance with subdivision (b).

(b) When a court is ruling on a claim of privilege under Article 9 (commencing with Section 1040) of Chapter 4 (official information and identity of informer) or under Section 1060 (trade secret) or under subdivision (b) of Section 2018.030 of the Code of Civil Procedure (attorney work product) and is unable to do so without requiring disclosure of the information claimed to be privileged, the court may require the person from whom disclosure is sought or the person authorized to claim the privilege, or both, to disclose the information in chambers out of the presence and hearing of all persons except the person authorized to claim the privilege and any other persons as the person authorized to claim the privilege is willing to have present. If the judge determines that the information is privileged, neither the judge nor any other person may ever disclose, without the consent of a person authorized to permit disclosure, what was disclosed in the course of the proceedings in chambers.

§ 916. Exclusion of privileged information where persons authorized to claim privilege are not present

(a) The presiding officer, on his own motion or on the motion of any party, shall exclude information that is subject to a claim of privilege under this division if:

(1) The person from whom the information is sought is not a person authorized to claim the privilege; and

(2) There is no party to the proceeding who is a person authorized to claim the privilege.

(b) The presiding officer may not exclude information under this section if:

(1) He is otherwise instructed by a person authorized to permit disclosure; or

(2) The proponent of the evidence establishes that there is no person authorized to claim the privilege in existence.

§ 917. Presumption that certain communications are confidential; privileged character of electronic communications

(a) If a privilege is claimed on the ground that the matter sought to be disclosed is a communication made in confidence in the course of the lawyer-client, physician-patient, psychotherapist-patient, clergy-penitent, husband-wife, sexual assault counselor-victim, or domestic violence counselor-victim relationship, the communication is presumed to have been made in confidence and the opponent of the claim of privilege has the burden of proof to establish that the communication was not confidential.

(b) A communication between persons in a relationship listed in subdivision (a) does not lose its privileged character for the sole reason that it is communicated by electronic means or because persons involved in the delivery, facilitation, or storage of electronic communication may have access to the content of the communication.

(c) For purposes of this section, "electronic" has the same meaning provided in Section 1633.2 of the Civil Code.

§ 918. Error in overruling claim of privilege

A party may predicate error on a ruling disallowing a claim of privilege only if he is the holder of the privilege, except that a party may predicate error on a ruling disallowing a claim of privilege by his spouse under Section 970 or 971.

§ 919. Admissibility where disclosure erroneously compelled; claim of privilege; coercion

(a) Evidence of a statement or other disclosure of privileged information is inadmissible against a holder of the privilege if:

(1) A person authorized to claim the privilege claimed it but nevertheless disclosure erroneously was required to be made; or

(2) The presiding officer did not exclude the privileged information as required by Section 916.

(b) If a person authorized to claim the privilege claimed it, whether in the same or a prior proceeding, but nevertheless disclosure erroneously was required by the presiding officer to be made, neither the failure to refuse to disclose nor the failure to seek review of the order of the presiding officer requiring disclosure indicates consent to the disclosure or constitutes a waiver and, under these circumstances, the disclosure is one made under coercion.

§ 920. Implied repeal of other statutes related to privileges

Nothing in this division shall be construed to repeal by implication any other statute relating to privileges.

FEDERAL RULES OF EVIDENCE

Rule 501. Privileges Recognized Only as Provided [Not enacted.]

Except as otherwise required by the Constitution of the United States or provided by Act of Congress, and except as provided in these rules or in other rules adopted by the Supreme Court, no person has a privilege to:

(1) Refuse to be a witness; or

(2) Refuse to disclose any matter; or

(3) Refuse to produce any object or writing; or

(4) Prevent another from being a witness or disclosing any matter of producing any object or writing.

ADVISORY COMMITTEE'S NOTE

No attempt is made in these rules to incorporate the constitutional provisions which relate to the admission and exclusion of evidence, whether denominated as privileges or not. The grand design of these provisions does not readily lend itself to codification. The final reference must be the provisions themselves and the decisions construing them. Nor is formulating a rule an appropriate means of settling unresolved constitutional questions.

Similarly, privileges created by act of Congress are not within the scope of these rules. These privileges do not assume the form of broad principles; they are the product of resolving particular problems in particular terms. Among them are included such provisions as 13 U.S.C. § 9, generally prohibiting official disclosure of census information and conferring a privileged status on retained copies of census reports; 42 U.S.C. § 2000e–5(a), making inadmissible in evidence anything said or done during Equal Employment Opportunity conciliation proceeding; 42 U.S.C. § 2240, making required reports of incidents by nuclear facility licensees inadmissible in actions for damages; 45 U.S.C. §§ 33, 41, similarly as to reports of accidents by railroads; 49 U.S.C. § 1441(e), declaring C.A.B. accident investigation reports inadmissible in actions for damages. The rule leaves them undisturbed.

The reference to other rules adopted by the Supreme Court makes clear that provisions relating to privilege in those rules will continue in operation. See, for example, the "work product" immunity against discovery spelled out under the Rules of Civil Procedure in Hickman v. Taylor, 329 U.S. 495, 67 S.Ct. 385, 91 L.Ed. 451 (1947), now formalized in revised Rule 26(b)(3) of the Rules of Civil Procedure, and the secrecy of grand jury proceedings provided by Criminal Rule 6.

With respect to privileges created by state law, these rules in some instances grant them greater status than has heretofore been the case by according them recognition in federal criminal proceedings, bankruptcy, and federal question litigation. See Rules 502 and 510. There is, however, no provision generally adopting state-created privileges.

In federal criminal prosecutions the primacy of federal law as to both substance and procedure has been undoubted. See, for example, United States v. Krol, 374 F.2d 776 (7th Cir.1967), sustaining the admission in a federal prosecution of evidence obtained by electronic eavesdropping, despite a state statute declaring the use of these devices unlawful and evidence obtained therefrom inadmissible. This primacy includes matters of privilege. As stated in 4 Barron, Federal Practice and Procedure § 2151, p. 175 (1951):

"The determination of the question whether a matter is privileged is governed by federal decisions and the state statutes or rules of evidence have no application."

In Funk v. United States, 290 U.S. 371, 54 S.Ct. 212, 78 L.Ed. 369 (1933), the Court had considered the competency of a wife to testify for her husband and concluded that, absent congressional action or direction, the federal courts were to follow the common law as they saw it "in accordance with present day standards of wisdom and justice." And in Wolfle v. United States, 291 U.S. 7, 54 S.Ct. 279, 78 L.Ed. 617 (1934), the Court said with respect to the standard appropriate in determining a claim of privilege for an alleged confidential communication between spouses in a federal criminal prosecution:

"So our decision here, in the absence of Congressional legislation on the subject, is to be controlled by common law principles, not by local statute." *Id.,* 13, 54 S.Ct. at 280.

On the basis of *Funk* and *Wolfle,* the Advisory Committee on Rules of Criminal Procedure formulated Rule 26, which was adopted by the Court. The pertinent part of the rule provided:

"The ... privileges of witnesses shall be governed, except when an act of Congress or these rules otherwise provide, by the principles of the common law as they may be interpreted ... in the light of reason and experience."

As regards bankruptcy, section 21(a) of the Bankruptcy Act provides for examination of the bankrupt and his spouse concerning the acts, conduct, or property of the bankrupt. The Act limits examination of the spouse to business transacted by her or to which she is a party but provides "That the spouse may be so examined, any law of the United States or of any State to the contrary notwithstanding." 11 U.S.C. § 44(a). The effect of the quoted language is clearly to override any conflicting state rule of incompetency or privilege against spousal testimony. A fair reading would also indicate an overriding of any contrary state rule of privileged confidential spousal communications. Its validity has never been questioned and seems most unlikely to be. As to other privileges, the suggestion has been made that state law applies, though with little citation of authority, 2 Moore's Collier on Bankruptcy ¶ 21.13, p. 297 (14th ed. 1961). This position seems to be contrary to the expression of the Court in McCarthy v. Arndstein, 266 U.S. 34, 39, 45 S.Ct.

16, 69 L.Ed. 158 (1924), which speaks in the pattern of Rule 26 of the Federal Rules of Criminal Procedure:

"There is no provision [in the Bankruptcy Act] prescribing the rules by which the examination is to be governed. These are, impliedly, the general rules governing the admissibility of evidence and the competency and compellability of witnesses."

With respect to federal question litigation, the supremacy of federal law may be less clear, yet indications that state privileges are inapplicable preponderate in the circuits. In re Albert Lindley Lee Memorial Hospital, 209 F.2d 122 (2d Cir.1953), cert. denied Cincotta v. United States, 347 U.S. 960, 74 S.Ct. 709, 98 L.Ed. 1104; Colton v. United States, 306 F.2d 633 (2d Cir.1962); Falsone v. United States, 205 F.2d 734 (5th Cir.1953); Fraser v. United States, 145 F.2d 139 (6th Cir.1944), cert. denied 324 U.S. 849, 65 S.Ct. 684, 89 L.Ed. 1409; United States v. Brunner, 200 F.2d 276 (6th Cir.1952). *Contra,* Baird v. Koerner, 279 F.2d 623 (9th Cir.1960). Additional decisions of district courts are collected in Annot., 95 A.L.R.2d 320, 336. While a number of the cases arise from administrative income tax investigations, they nevertheless support the broad proposition of the inapplicability of state privileges in federal proceedings.

In view of these considerations, it is apparent that, to the extent that they accord state privileges standing in federal criminal cases, bankruptcy, and federal question cases, the rules go beyond what previously has been thought necessary or proper.

On the other hand, in diversity cases, or perhaps more accurately cases in which state law furnishes the rule of decision, the rules avoid giving state privileges the effect which substantial authority has thought necessary and proper. Regardless of what might once have been thought to be the command of Erie R. Co. v. Tompkins, 304 U.S. 64, 58 S.Ct. 817, 82 L.Ed. 1188 (1938), as to observance of state created privileges in diversity cases, Hanna v. Plumer, 380 U.S. 460, 85 S.Ct. 1136, 14 L.Ed.2d 8 (1965), is believed to locate the problem in the area of choice rather than necessity. Wright, Procedural Reform: Its Limitations and Its Future, 1 Ga.L.Rev. 563, 572–573 (1967). Contra, Republic Gear Co. v. Borg–Warner Corp., 381 F.2d 551, 555, n. 2 (2d Cir.1967), and see authorities there cited. Hence all significant policy factors need to be considered in order that the choice may be a wise one.

The arguments advanced in favor of recognizing state privileges are: a state privilege is an essential characteristic of a relationship or status created by state law and thus is substantive in the *Erie* sense; state policy ought not to be frustrated by the accident of diversity; the allowance or denial of a privilege is so likely to affect the outcome of litigation as to encourage forum selection on that basis, not a proper function of diversity jurisdiction. There are persuasive answers to these arguments.

(1) As to the question of "substance," it is true that a privilege commonly represents an aspect of a relationship created and defined by a State. For example, a confidential communications privilege is often an incident of marriage. However, in litigation involving the relationship itself, the privilege is not ordinarily one of the issues. In fact, statutes frequently make the communication privilege inapplicable in cases of divorce. McCormick § 88, p.

177. The same is true with respect to the attorney-client privilege when the parties to the relationship have a falling out. The reality of the matter is that privilege is called into operation, not when the relation giving rise to the privilege is being litigated, but when the litigation involves something substantively devoid of relation to the privilege. The appearance of privilege in the case is quite by accident, and its effect is to block off the tribunal from a source of information. Thus its real impact is on the method of proof in the case, and in comparison any substantive aspect appears tenuous.

(2) By most standards, criminal prosecutions are attended by more serious consequences than civil litigation, and it must be evident that the criminal area has the greatest sensitivity where privilege is concerned. Nevertheless, as previously noted, state privileges traditionally have given way in federal criminal prosecutions. If a privilege is denied in the area of greatest sensitivity, it tends to become illusory as a significant aspect of the relationship out of which it arises. For example, in a state having by statute an accountant's privilege, only the most imperceptible added force would be given the privilege by putting the accountant in a position to assure his client that, while he could not block disclosure in a federal criminal prosecution, he could do so in diversity cases as well as in state court proceedings. Thus viewed, state interest in privilege appears less substantial than at first glance might seem to be the case.

Moreover, federal interest is not lacking. It can scarcely be contended that once diversity is invoked the federal government no longer has a legitimate concern in the quality of judicial administration conducted under its aegis. The demise of conformity and the adoption of the Federal Rules of Civil Procedure stand as witness to the contrary.

(3) A large measure of forum shopping is recognized as legitimate in the American judicial system. Subject to the limitations of jurisdiction and the relatively modest controls imposed by venue provisions and the doctrine of forum non conveniens, plaintiffs are allowed in general a free choice of forum. Diversity jurisdiction has as its basic purpose the giving of a choice, not only to plaintiffs but, in removal situations, also to defendants. In principle, the basis of the choice is the supposed need to escape from local prejudice. If the choice were tightly confined to that basis, then complete conformity to local procedure as well as substantive law would be required. This, of course, is not the case, and the choice may in fact be influenced by a wide range of factors. As Dean Ladd has pointed out, a litigant may select the federal court "because of the federal procedural rules, the liberal discovery provisions, the quality of jurors expected in the federal court, the respect held for federal judges, the control of federal judges over a trial, the summation and comment upon the weight of evidence by the judge, or the authority to grant a new trial if the judge regards the verdict against the weight of the evidence." Ladd, Privileges, 1969 Ariz.St.L.J. 555, 564. Present Rule 43(a) of the Civil Rules specifies a broader range of admissibility in federal than in state courts and makes no exception for diversity cases. Note should also be taken that Rule 26(b)(2) of the Rules of Civil Procedure, as revised, allows discovery to be had of liability insurance, without regard to local state law upon the subject.

When attention is directed to the practical dimensions of the problem, they are found not to be great. The privileges affected are few in number. Most states provide a physician-patient privilege; the proposed rules limit the privilege to a psychotherapist-patient relationship. See Advisory Committee's Note to Rule 504. The area of marital privilege under the proposed rules is narrower than in most states. See Rule 505. Some states recognize privileges for journalists and accountants; the proposed rules do not.

Physician-patient is the most widely recognized privilege not found in the proposed rules. As a practical matter it was largely eliminated in diversity cases when Rule 35 of the Rules of Civil Procedure became effective in 1938. Under that rule, a party physically examined pursuant to court order, by requesting and obtaining a copy of the report or by taking the deposition of the examiner, waives any privilege regarding the testimony of every other person who has examined him in respect of the same condition. While waiver may be avoided by neither requesting the report nor taking the examiner's deposition, the price is one which most litigant-patients are probably not prepared to pay.

Rule 511. Waiver of Privilege by Voluntary Disclosure [Not enacted.]

A person upon whom these rules confer a privilege against disclosure of the confidential matter or communication waives the privilege if he or his predecessor while holder of the privilege voluntarily discloses or consents to disclosure of any significant part of the matter or communication. This rule does not apply if the disclosure is itself a privileged communication.

ADVISORY COMMITTEE'S NOTE

The central purpose of most privileges is the promotion of some interest or relationship by endowing it with a supporting secrecy or confidentiality. It is evident that the privilege should terminate when the holder by his own act destroys this confidentiality. McCormick §§ 87, 97, 106; 8 Wigmore §§ 2242, 2327–2329, 2374, 2389–2390 (McNaughton Rev.1961).

The rule is designed to be read with a view to what it is that the particular privilege protects. For example, the lawyer-client privilege covers only communications, and the fact that a client has discussed a matter with his lawyer does not insulate the client against disclosure of the subject matter discussed, although he is privileged not to disclose the discussion itself. See McCormick § 93. The waiver here provided for is similarly restricted. Therefore a client, merely by disclosing a subject which he had discussed with his attorney, would not waive the applicable privilege; he would have to make disclosure of the communication itself in order to effect a waiver.

By traditional doctrine, waiver is the intentional relinquishment of a known right. Johnson v. Zerbst, 304 U.S. 458, 464, 58 S.Ct. 1019, 82 L.Ed. 1461 (1938). However, in the confidential privilege situations, once confidentiality is destroyed through voluntary disclosure, no subsequent claim of privilege can restore it, and knowledge or lack of knowledge of the existence of the privilege appears to be irrelevant. California Evidence Code § 912; 8 Wigmore § 2327 (McNaughton Rev.1961).

Rule 512. Privileged Matter Disclosed Under Compulsion or Without Opportunity to Claim Privilege [Not enacted.]

Evidence of a statement or other disclosure of privileged matter is not admissible against the holder of the privilege if the disclosure was (a) compelled erroneously or (b) made without opportunity to claim the privilege.

ADVISORY COMMITTEE'S NOTE

Ordinarily a privilege is invoked in order to forestall disclosure. However, under some circumstances consideration must be given to the status and effect of a disclosure already made. Rule 511, immediately preceding, gives voluntary disclosure the effect of a waiver, while the present rule covers the effect of disclosure made under compulsion or without opportunity to claim the privilege.

Confidentiality, once destroyed, is not susceptible of restoration, yet some measure of repair may be accomplished by preventing use of the evidence against the holder of the privilege. The remedy of exclusion is therefore made available when the earlier disclosure was compelled erroneously or without opportunity to claim the privilege.

With respect to erroneously compelled disclosure, the argument may be made that the holder should be required in the first instance to assert the privilege, stand his ground, refuse to answer, perhaps incur a judgment of contempt, and exhaust all legal recourse, in order to sustain his privilege. See Fraser v. United States, 145 F.2d 139 (6th Cir.1944), cert. denied 324 U.S. 849, 65 S.Ct. 684, 89 L.Ed. 1409; United States v. Johnson, 76 F.Supp. 538 (M.D.Pa.1947), aff'd 165 F.2d 42 (3d Cir.1947), cert. denied 332 U.S. 852, 68 S.Ct. 355, 92 L.Ed. 422, reh. denied 333 U.S. 834, 68 S.Ct. 457, 92 L.Ed. 1118. However, this exacts of the holder greater fortitude in the face of authority than ordinary individuals are likely to possess, and assumes unrealistically that a judicial remedy is always available. In self-incrimination cases, the writers agree that erroneously compelled disclosures are inadmissible in a subsequent criminal prosecution of the holder, Maguire, Evidence of Guilt 66 (1959); McCormick § 127; 8 Wigmore § 2270 (McNaughton Rev.1961), and the principle is equally sound when applied to other privileges. The modest departure from usual principles of res judicata which occurs when the compulsion is judicial is justified by the advantage of having one simple rule, assuring at least one opportunity for judicial supervision in every case.

The second circumstance stated as a basis for exclusion is disclosure made without opportunity to the holder to assert his privilege. Illustrative possibilities are disclosure by an eavesdropper, by a person used in the transmission of a privileged communication, by a family member participating in psychotherapy, or privileged data improperly made available from a computer bank.

Rule 513. Comment Upon or Inference From Claim of Privilege; Instruction [Not enacted.]

(a) Comment or inference not permitted. The claim of a privilege, whether in the present proceeding or upon a prior occasion, is not a proper subject of comment by judge or counsel. No inference may be drawn therefrom.

(b) Claiming privilege without knowledge of jury. In jury cases, proceedings shall be conducted, to the extent practicable, so as to facilitate the making of claims of privilege without the knowledge of the jury.

(c) Jury instruction. Upon request, any party against whom the jury might draw an adverse inference from a claim of privilege is entitled to an instruction that no inference may be drawn therefrom.

ADVISORY COMMITTEE'S NOTE

Subdivision (a). In Griffin v. California, 380 U.S. 609, 614, 85 S.Ct. 1229, 14 L.Ed.2d 106 (1965), the Court pointed out that allowing comment upon the claim of a privilege "cuts down on the privilege by making its assertion costly." Consequently it was held that comment upon the election of the accused not to take the stand infringed upon his privilege against self-incrimination so substantially as to constitute a constitutional violation. While the privileges governed by these rules are not constitutionally based, they are nevertheless founded upon important policies and are entitled to maximum effect. Hence the present subdivision forbids comment upon the exercise of a privilege, in accord with the weight of authority. Courtney v. United States, 390 F.2d 521 (9th Cir.1968); 8 Wigmore §§ 2243, 2322, 2386; Barnhart, Privilege in the Uniform Rules of Evidence, 24 Ohio St.L.J. 131, 137–138 (1963). Cf. McCormick § 80.

Subdivision (b). The value of a privilege may be greatly depreciated by means other than expressly commenting to a jury upon the fact that it was exercised. Thus, the calling of a witness in the presence of the jury and subsequently excusing him after a sidebar conference may effectively convey to the jury the fact that a privilege has been claimed, even though the actual claim has not been made in their hearing. Whether a privilege will be claimed is usually ascertainable in advance and the handling of the entire matter outside the presence of the jury is feasible. Destruction of the privilege by innuendo can and should be avoided. Tallo v. United States, 344 F.2d 467 (1st Cir.1965); United States v. Tomaiolo, 249 F.2d 683 (2d Cir.1957); San Fratello v. United States, 343 F.2d 711 (5th Cir.1965); Courtney v. United States, 390 F.2d 521 (9th Cir.1968); 6 Wigmore § 1808, pp. 275–276; 6 U.C.L.A.Rev. 455 (1959). This position is in accord with the general agreement of the authorities that an accused cannot be forced to make his election not to testify in the presence of the jury. 8 Wigmore § 2268, p. 407 (McNaughton Rev.1961).

Unanticipated situations are, of course, bound to arise, and much must be left to the discretion of the judge and the professional responsibility of counsel.

Subdivision (c). Opinions will differ as to the effectiveness of a jury instruction not to draw an adverse inference from the making of a claim of privilege. See Bruton v. United States, 389 U.S. 818, 88 S.Ct. 126, 19 L.Ed.2d

70 (1968). Whether an instruction shall be given is left to the sound judgment of counsel for the party against whom the adverse inference may be drawn. The instruction is a matter of right, if requested. This is the result reached in Bruno v. United States, 308 U.S. 287, 60 S.Ct. 198, 84 L.Ed. 257 (1939), holding that an accused is entitled to an instruction under the statute (now 18 U.S.C. § 3481) providing that his failure to testify creates no presumption against him.

The right to the instruction is not impaired by the fact that the claim of privilege is by a witness, rather than by a party, provided an adverse inference against the party may result.

CHAPTER 21

THE ATTORNEY–CLIENT PRIVILEGE

■ ■ ■

Table of Sections

§ 21.01 NATURE OF THE PRIVILEGE

The attorney-client privilege is designed to promote effective representation by encouraging clients to disclose all pertinent information, favorable as well as unfavorable, without fear that others may be informed.[1] The Code achieves this goal by providing clients and other holders of the privilege, such as a client's guardian, conservator, or personal representative if the client is dead, with the right to refuse to disclose and to prevent another from disclosing a confidential communication between the client and the attorney.[2] Though not a holder, the attorney who was the lawyer at the time the confidential communication was made may also assert the privilege on behalf of the client.[3] The privilege, however, belongs to the client and not to the attorney.[4]

---

1. West's Ann. California Evidence Code § 950 (comment); see also Greyhound Corp. v. Superior Court, 56 Cal.2d 355, 396, 15 Cal.Rptr. 90, 112, 364 P.2d 266, 288 (1961). For a critique of government efforts to monitor communications between lawyers and their clients since the September 2001 attacks on the World Trade Center, see Marjorie Cohn, *The Evisceration of the Attorney–Client Privilege in the Wake of September 11, 2001*, 71 Fordham Law Review 1233 (2003).

2. West's Ann. California Evidence Code § 954. The California Supreme Court has found a privilege analogous to the attorney-client privilege between recipients of Aid to Families with Dependent Children and their lay advocates in administrative hearings. Welfare Rights Organization v. Crisan, 33 Cal.3d 766, 772, 190 Cal.Rptr. 919, 923, 661 P.2d 1073, 1076 (1983).

3. West's Ann. California Evidence Code § 954(c).

The attorney-client privilege must be distinguished from a lawyer's professional obligation to maintain secret the communications imparted by the client. Except "in those rare instances when disclosure is explicitly permitted or mandated by statute, it is never the business of the lawyer to disclose publicly the secrets of the client."[5] The California Business and Professions Code requires a lawyer to "maintain inviolate the confidence, and at every peril to himself or herself to preserve the secrets, of his or her clients."[6] This duty is broader than the duty imposed upon lawyers by the attorney-client privilege. The privilege applies only in proceedings in which testimony can be compelled.[7] The duty established by the Business and Professions Code applies in private settings as well.

Nonetheless, the attorney-client privilege is a broad one. "[U]nder the Evidence Code, the attorney-client privilege applies to confidential communications within the scope of the attorney-client privilege even if the communication does not relate to pending litigation; the privilege applies not only to communications made in anticipation of litigation, but also to legal advice when no litigation is threatened."[8] Moreover, "[t]he privilege is absolute and disclosure may not be ordered, without regard to relevance, necessity or any particular circumstances peculiar to the case."[9]

Matters unprotected by the privilege—in general. Not all matters the client discloses to a lawyer in confidence are protected. For example, if the lawyer is consulted to enable the client to commit a crime or a fraud, the client's communications fall within an exception to the privilege and are not protected from disclosure.[10] As is discussed in § 21.06, the Evidence Code provides a number of exceptions to the attorney-client privilege.

The privilege, moreover, does not immunize the subject matter of the communication conveyed to the lawyer. Assume, for example, that following an accident a client tells his lawyer, "I ran the light." Though the client's statement to his lawyer is a party admission,[11] over a privilege claim the adverse party may not compel disclosure of the communication. But the privilege will not preclude the adverse party from calling the

---

4. HLC Properties, Ltd. v. Superior Court, 35 Cal.4th 54, 62, 24 Cal.Rptr.3d 199, 204, 105 P.3d 560, 565 (2005).

5. General Dynamics Corp. v. Superior Court, 7 Cal.4th 1164, 1190, 32 Cal.Rptr.2d 1, 17, 876 P.2d 487, 503 (1994).

6. West's Ann. California Business and Professions Code § 6068(e)(1). There are some exceptions to this duty. For example, an in-house counsel "may disclose ostensible employer-client confidences to her own attorneys to the extent they may be relevant to the preparation and prosecution of her wrongful termination action against her former client-employer." Fox Searchlight Pictures, Inc. v. Paladino, 89 Cal.App.4th 294, 310, 106 Cal.Rptr.2d 906, 920 (2001).

7. See § 20.02 supra.

8. Roberts v. City of Palmdale, 5 Cal.4th 363, 371, 20 Cal.Rptr.2d 330, 333, 853 P.2d 496, 499 (1993).

9. Gordon v. Superior Court, 55 Cal.App.4th 1546, 1557, 65 Cal.Rptr.2d 53, 59 (1997).

10. See § 21.06 infra.

11. For a detailed discussion of party admissions, see § 7.01 supra.

client as an adverse witness and asking him whether he ran the light. It is the communication and not the subject matter that is protected.[12]

The same principle extends to information which others furnish the client and which the client in turn supplies to the lawyer. Assume, for example, that in addition the client tells the lawyer, "The day before I ran the light my mechanic warned me that, unless replaced, the brakes might fail." Again, the client's statement to the lawyer is a party admission. Over a privilege claim, however, the adverse party may not compel disclosure of the communication. But the privilege will not preclude the adverse party from calling the client or the mechanic to establish the mechanic's warning.

The same principle applies to tangible items which the client furnishes the lawyer. Assume that, in addition, the client gives the lawyer a written report in which the mechanic warns the client that the brakes might fail unless replaced. The adverse party may not only compel production of the report but may offer it in evidence to the extent that it is admissible under the rules of evidence. Tangible items, including documents, that exist prior to the formation of the attorney-client relationship do not acquire the protection afforded by the privilege simply because the client transfers them to the attorney.[13] A contrary rule would encourage the suppression of unfavorable evidence. Accordingly, tangible items transferred to an attorney may be produced and offered in evidence to the same extent as if they had remained in the client's hands.

> [A] document, report, or photograph that would otherwise be admissible in evidence does not become privileged merely because the client delivers it to his attorney. Unless a report or photograph is created for the purpose of communicating information to the attorney, it cannot have the character of a privileged communication when it comes into existence and accordingly cannot become privileged if it is later delivered to the attorney.[14]

Matters unprotected by the privilege—criminal cases. A criminal defense lawyer has an affirmative duty to inform the court whenever the lawyer removes, alters, or comes into possession of physical evidence relating to the crime.[15] The physical evidence is not limited to weapons and the like but can include incriminatory writings. In People v. San-

---

12. "Nor does the attorney-client privilege protect independent facts related to a communication; that a communication took place, the time, date and participants in the communication." State Farm Fire & Cas. v. Superior Court, 54 Cal.App.4th 625, 639, 62 Cal.Rptr.2d 834, 844 (1997).

13. Jasper Constr., Inc. v. Foothill Jr. College Dist., 91 Cal.App.3d 1, 17, 153 Cal.Rptr. 767, 776 (1979) (holding that an engineer's report prepared at the plaintiff's request did not become privileged just because the plaintiff subsequently had the engineer provide a copy to plaintiff's attorney); Green & Shinee v. Superior Court, 88 Cal.App.4th 532, 537, 105 Cal.Rptr.2d 886, 889 (2001) (holding that reports which police officers had a duty to prepare did not become privileged by virtue of having been provided to their lawyer).

14. Holm v. Superior Court, 42 Cal.2d 500, 511, 267 P.2d 1025, 1031 (1954), reh'g denied, 42 Cal.2d 500, 268 P.2d 722 (1954) (concurring and dissenting opinion).

15. People v. Superior Court (Fairbank), 192 Cal.App.3d 32, 39–40, 237 Cal.Rptr. 158, 163 (1987). For an extended discussion of this obligation, see § 21.04 infra.

chez,[16] for example, the evidence consisted of notes prepared by the accused in which he described plans to kill the victim. The notes were found by the accused's sister who gave them to a lawyer who in turn gave them to the investigator for the defense who then gave them to defense counsel. The appellate court held that the defense lawyer's minimum obligation was to turn over the notes to the trial court.[17]

Requiring the defense lawyer to turn over incriminating evidence does not necessarily violate the accused's privilege against self-incrimination. In *Sanchez* no violation of the privilege occurred because the accused was not compelled to create the notes or to authenticate them as his at the trial.[18]

Special limits on the privilege—the Brown and Public Records Acts. Special statutes governing public entities do not necessarily call for the loss of the attorney-client privilege. The Brown Act, for example, which requires all meetings of local legislative bodies to be open to the public,[19] calls for the abrogation of the attorney-client privilege except for legal advice regarding "pending litigation."[20] In Roberts v. City of Palmdale[21] a taxpayer sought the disclosure of a letter in which the city attorney advised city council members about matters of interest to the taxpayer. The court rejected the taxpayer's claim that the letter should be disclosed because it did not relate to pending litigation. The letter simply was not subject to the Brown Act because its receipt by individual board members did not constitute a "meeting" involving the kind of "collective action" contemplated by the act.[22] Of course, if the letter had been but a subterfuge "to engage in collective deliberation on public business through a series of letters or telephone calls passing from one member of the governing body to the next," the open meeting requirement would have been violated and the letter would have been subject to disclosure.[23]

The court also rejected the taxpayer's claim that the letter was subject to disclosure under the Public Records Act. This act mandates the inspection of any public record,[24] unless the record pertains "to pending litigation."[25] The court, however, construed the act as exempting public records protected by the attorney-client privilege even if the attorney's communication pertains to matters that are not in litigation.[26]

---

16.   24 Cal.App.4th 1012, 30 Cal.Rptr.2d 111 (1994).

17.   Other courts have held that the defense lawyer has a duty to turn over to the prosecution such instrumentalities of a crime as the murder weapon. See, e.g., People v. Lee, 3 Cal.App.3d 514, 83 Cal.Rptr. 715 (1970).

18.   People v. Sanchez, 24 Cal.App.4th 1012, 1024, 30 Cal.Rptr.2d 111, 119 (1994).

19.   West's Ann. California Government Code § 54953(a).

20.   West's Ann. California Government Code § 54956.9.

21.   5 Cal.4th 363, 20 Cal.Rptr.2d 330, 853 P.2d 496 (1993).

22.   Id. at 376, 20 Cal.Rptr.2d at 337, 853 P.2d at 503.

23.   Id.

24.   West's Ann. California Government Code § 6250.

25.   West's Ann. California Government Code § 6254(b).

26.   Roberts v. City of Palmdale, 5 Cal.4th 363, 372–373, 20 Cal.Rptr.2d 330, 334–335, 853 P.2d 496, 500–501 (1993).

Special limits on the privilege—suits by beneficiaries against trustees. In some jurisdictions, trustees may resist disclosing confidential communications with lawyers they retain to defend against claims of breach of fiduciary duties made by the beneficiaries. To protect the beneficiaries' right to information regarding the trust, however, the privilege will not be sustained when the communications relate only to matters pertaining to the administration of the trust.[27] In the latter situation, the attorney is viewed as acting on behalf of the beneficiaries. California, however, does not follow this rule. In California, an attorney retained by the trustee is the trustee's attorney, and the trustee may refuse to disclose confidential communications with the attorney regardless of whether they relate to trust administration or claims of breach of the trustee's fiduciary duties.[28] The fact that the trust pays for the trustee's attorney fees is immaterial.[29]

A different situation is presented when a successor trustee seeks to compel the predecessor trustee to disclose information protected by the attorney-client privilege. In Moeller v. Superior Court[30] a successor trustee, who was also a beneficiary, raised objections to the trustee's final accounting and sought redress for the trustee's alleged breach of fiduciary duties. The predecessor trustee resisted producing some documents for inspection on the ground that the documents were protected by the attorney-client privilege. The court rejected the predecessor trustee's claims: "[W]hen a successor trustee takes office it assumes all of the powers of trustee, including the power to assert the privilege with respect to confidential communications between a predecessor trustee and an attorney on matters of trust administration."[31] Ensuring that a trust continues to operate smoothly when a change in trustee takes place requires that the power to assert the attorney-client privilege pass from the predecessor trustee to the successor.[32] *Moeller*, however, does not compel a predecessor trustee to disclose advice of counsel which the predecessor obtained while trustee to protect against charges of misconduct.[33]

Elements of the privilege. To be privileged from disclosure, the attorney-client communication must meet a number of tests: first, the communication must have been made between a client and an attorney; second, the communication must have been made in the course of the attorney-client relationship; and, third, the communication must have

---

27.　See authorities cited in Wells Fargo Bank v. Superior Court, 22 Cal.4th 201, 208, 91 Cal.Rptr.2d 716, 721, 990 P.2d 591, 595 (2000).

28.　Wells Fargo Bank v. Superior Court, 22 Cal.4th 201, 208, 91 Cal.Rptr.2d 716, 721, 990 P.2d 591, 595 (2000).

29.　Id. at 213, 91 Cal.Rptr.2d at 725, 990 P.2d at 595–599.

30.　16 Cal.4th 1124, 69 Cal.Rptr.2d 317, 947 P.2d 279 (1997).

31.　Id. at 1131, 69 Cal.Rptr.2d at 321, 947 P.2d at 283.

32.　Id. at 1133, 69 Cal.Rptr.2d at 322, 947 P.2d at 284.

33.　Id. at 1134, 69 Cal.Rptr.2d at 323, 947 P.2d at 285.

been transmitted in confidence. Each of these requirements is considered separately.

QUESTIONS AND PROBLEMS

The attorney-client privilege is designed to protect from disclosure confidential communications transmitted by a client to her attorney. Over a privilege claim, may the client or her lawyer prevent the disclosure of the following communications?

a. Client: "I have been charged with stealing an examination from the registrar's office. At my arraignment, I asked for permission to consult a lawyer. That's why I'm here. I did take the examination. It was a mistake. I don't want the incident to affect my taking the bar. Can you help me?"

b. Suppose that after consulting the attorney, the client confesses to her best friend that she took the examination. Would that admission be protected from disclosure by the attorney-client privilege on the grounds that disclosure would reveal the substance of the client's communication with the lawyer?

c. Suppose that the client turned over the stolen examination to the lawyer. Would the lawyer have a duty to inform the court of the location of the examination?

§ 21.02   THE COMMUNICATION MUST BE BETWEEN AN ATTORNEY AND A CLIENT

In order for the communication to be protected from disclosure, it must qualify as one between an attorney and the client.[1] An attorney is defined as "a person authorized, or reasonably believed by the client to be authorized, to practice law in any state or nation."[2] Since the privilege is intended to encourage full disclosure, the client's reasonable but mistaken belief that the person he is consulting is an attorney is sufficient to justify application of the privilege.[3]

A client's failure to inquire whether the attorney is licensed to practice law will not defeat the privilege if the attorney was not licensed. "A client should not be forced to inquire about the jurisdictions where the lawyer is entitled to practice and whether such jurisdictions recognize the

---

1. West's Ann. California Evidence Code § 954. Sending a letter to a friend, with the uncommunicated "expectation" that it will be shared with an attorney, does not, without more, qualify as a communication between a client and an attorney. See Doe 2 v. Superior Court, 132 Cal.App.4th 1504, 1521, 34 Cal.Rptr.3d 458, 470 (2005).

2. West's Ann. California Evidence Code § 950. A lawyer may also include a law corporation. West's Ann. California Evidence Code § 954.

3. West's Ann. California Evidence Code § 950 (comment). Whether a "jailhouse lawyer" is within the definition depends on whether the client honestly and reasonably believed the inmate to be a lawyer. People v. Velasquez, 192 Cal.App.3d 319, 328, 237 Cal.Rptr. 366, 371 (1987).

lawyer-client relationship before he may safely communicate with the lawyer."[4] But if the person the client consults warns the client that she is no longer licensed to practice law, then the client's disclosures to that person are not privileged.[5]

A district attorney is not an "attorney" who represents a "client." A district attorney is a public officer who, under the direct supervision of the Attorney General, represents the sovereign power of the people of the state and by whose authority and in whose name all prosecutions must be conducted.[6]

Because the district attorney does not have a client, confidentiality regarding the fruits of investigations by a public prosecutor are governed, not by the attorney-client privilege, but by Evidence Code § 1040.[7] This section sets out a privilege for official information, which is defined as "information acquired in confidence by a public employee in the course of his or her duty and not open, or officially disclosed, to the public prior to the time the claim of privilege is made."[8] It allows a public entity to resist disclosing official information, unless a court determines that the necessity for preserving the confidentiality of the information is outweighed by the need for disclosure in the interest of justice.[9]

In California criminal cases, the reciprocal discovery chapter enacted as part of Proposition 115 does not affect either the attorney-client privilege or the work product doctrine. Section 1054.6 of the Penal Code provides that "[n]either the defendant nor the prosecuting attorney is required to disclose any materials or information which are work product as defined in subdivision (a) of Section 2018.030 of the Code of Civil Procedure, or which are privileged pursuant to an express statutory provision, or are privileged as provided by the Constitution of the United States."[10] The term "express statutory provision" includes the attorney-client privilege.[11] Section 2018.030 defines the absolute work product privilege. It provides that "[a]ny writing that reflects an attorney's impressions, conclusions, opinions, or legal research or theories shall not be discoverable under any circumstances."[12]

---

4. Id.

5. People v. Klvana, 11 Cal.App.4th 1679, 1723, 15 Cal.Rptr.2d 512, 539 (1992).

6. Shepherd v. Superior Court, 17 Cal.3d 107, 122, 130 Cal.Rptr. 257, 265, 550 P.2d 161, 169 (1976).

7. Id. at 122–123, 130 Cal.Rptr. at 265–266, 550 P.2d at 169–170. See also People ex rel. Lockyer v. Superior Court, 83 Cal.App.4th 387, 399–400, 99 Cal.Rptr.2d 646, 655 (2000) (holding that assistant district attorneys may not claim the attorney-client or work product privileges for any materials generated as assistant district attorneys, as they are not the holders of these privileges, and reaffirming the rule that to the extent that materials prepared by assistant district attorneys are entitled to confidentiality, protection of such materials can be invoked only by the district attorney pursuant to Evidence Code § 1040).

8. West's Ann. California Evidence Code § 1040.

9. Id.

10. West's Ann. California Penal Code § 1054.6.

11. See, e.g., Roland v. Superior Court, 124 Cal.App.4th 154, 168, 21 Cal.Rptr.3d 151, 159 (2004).

12. West's Ann. Civil Procedure Code § 2018(c). For discussion of the work product doctrine, see Chapter 22 infra.

A client is defined as "a person who, directly or through an authorized representative, consults a lawyer for the purpose of retaining the lawyer or securing legal service or advice from him in his professional capacity * * *."[13] A client is not limited to natural persons. The term includes corporations, public entities, and such unincorporated organizations as labor unions, social clubs, and fraternal societies when the organization is the client.[14] A client also includes successors;[15] for example, a successor corporation becomes the holder of the attorney-client privileged held by the predecessor corporation.[16]

A "client," however, does not include the beneficiaries of a trust when the lawyer serves only as the attorney for the trustee.[17] Nor does a "client" include the shareholders of a corporation. Accordingly, in the absence of an independent attorney-client relationship with corporate counsel, shareholders are not entitled to access to communications between the corporation and its lawyers falling within the ambit of the attorney-client privilege.[18] Neither does a "client" include the members of an unincorporated association, when the association brings suit on its own behalf.[19] In these circumstances, the association, not its members, is the holder of the attorney-client privilege.

When a client who is not a natural person claims the privilege, the court must determine whether the persons who supplied the information to the attorney are within the privilege. In D.I. Chadbourne v. Superior Court[20] the California Supreme Court held that "the public policy behind the attorney-client privilege requires that an artificial person be given equal opportunity with a natural person to communicate with its attorney, within the professional relationship, without fear that its communication will be made public."[21] But the court also stressed that a corporation should not be given "greater privileges than are enjoyed by a natural

---

13. West's Ann. California Evidence Code § 951. A "client" also includes an incompetent who consults a lawyer as well as a guardian or conservator who consults the lawyer on behalf of the incompetent. Id.

14. West's Ann. California Evidence Code §§ 175 and 951 (comment).

15. West's Ann. California Evidence Code § 953(d).

16. See, e.g., Venture Law Group v. Superior Court, 118 Cal.App.4th 96, 103, 12 Cal.Rptr.3d 656, 661 (2004).

17. Fletcher v. Alameda County Superior Court, 44 Cal.App.4th 773, 777, 52 Cal.Rptr.2d 65, 67 (1996).

18. NFLP v. Superior Court, 65 Cal.App.4th 100, 111, 75 Cal.Rptr.2d 893, 900 (1998).

19. Smith v. Laguna Sur Villas Community Ass'n, 79 Cal.App.4th 639, 643, 94 Cal.Rptr.2d 321, 323 (2000). In State Comp. Ins. Fund v. Superior Court, 91 Cal.App.4th 1080, 111 Cal.Rptr.2d 284 (2001), the state seized files belonging to an insurance company in connection with its investigation of employee compensation claims filed by an employee of an employer insured by the insurance company. The insurance company claimed that some of the documents seized by the state were protected by the attorney-client privilege. The state sought to defeat the privilege claim with a declaration in which the employer waived the privilege with regard to the documents. The reviewing court held that the employer-insured had no standing to waive the privilege; the privilege existed between the insurance company and its lawyers and, as a result, the insurance company, not the insured, was the holder of the privilege. Id. at 1087, 111 Cal.Rptr.2d at 288–289.

20. 60 Cal.2d 723, 36 Cal.Rptr. 468, 388 P.2d 700 (1964).

21. Id. at 736–738, 36 Cal.Rptr. at 477–478, 388 P.2d at 709–710.

person merely because it must utilize a person in order to speak."[22] The court then listed eleven principles to guide trial judges in determining whether a communication by a corporate agent to a lawyer is protected by the privilege:

1. When the employee of a defendant corporation is also a defendant in his own right (or is a person who may be charged with liability), his statement regarding the facts with which he or his employer may be charged, obtained by a representative of the employer and delivered to an attorney who represents (or will represent) either or both of them, is entitled to the attorney-client privilege on the same basis as it would be entitled thereto if the employer-employee relationship did not exist;

2. When such an employee is not a codefendant (or person who may be charged with liability), his communication should not be so privileged unless, under all of the circumstances of the case, he is the natural person to be speaking for the corporation; that is to say, that the privilege will not attach in such case unless the communication constitutes information which emanates from the corporation (as distinct from the nonlitigant employee), and the communicating employee is such a person who would ordinarily be utilized for communication to the corporation's attorney;

3. When an employee has been a witness to matters which require communication to the corporate employer's attorney, and the employee has no connection with those matters other than as a witness, he is an independent witness; and the fact that the employer requires him to make a statement for transmittal to the latter's attorney does not alter his status or make his statement subject to the attorney-client privilege;

4. Where the employee's connection with the matter grows out of his employment to the extent that his report or statement is required in the ordinary course of the corporation's business, the employee is no longer an independent witness, and his statement or report is that of the employer;

5. If, in the case of the employee last mentioned, the employer requires (by standing rule or otherwise) that the employee make a report, the privilege of that report is to be determined by the employer's purpose in requiring the same; that is to say, if the employer directs the making of the report for confidential transmittal to its attorney, the communication may be privileged;

6. When the corporate employer has more than one purpose in directing such an employee to make such report or statement, the dominant purpose will control, unless the secondary use is such that confidentiality has been waived;

---

22. Id.

7. If otherwise privileged under the rules stated above, a communication does not lose its privilege merely because it was obtained, with the knowledge and consent of the employer, by an agent of the employer acting under such agency;

8. For such purpose an insurance company with which the employer carries indemnity insurance, and its duly appointed agents, are agents of the employer corporation; but the extent to which this doctrine may be carried, and the number of hands through which the communication may travel without losing confidentiality must always depend on reason and the particular facts of the case;

9. And in all corporate employer-employee situations it must be borne in mind that it is the intent of the person from whom the information emanates that originally governs its confidentiality (and hence its privilege); thus where the employee who has not been expressly directed by his employer to make a statement, does not know that his statement is sought on a confidential basis (or knowing that fact does not intend it to be confidential), the intent of the party receiving and transmitting that statement cannot control the question of privilege;

10. Similarly, where the corporate employer directs the employee, at the request of its insurance carrier, to make such a statement, the intent of the employer controls; and unless the insurance carrier (or its agent) has advised the employer that the employee's statement is to be obtained and used in such manner, it cannot be said that the corporation intended the statement to be made as a confidential communication from client to attorney;

11. Finally, no greater liberality should be applied to the facts which determine privilege in the case of a corporation than would be applied in the case of a natural person (or association of persons), except as may be necessary to allow the corporation to speak.[23]

Two cases illustrate how courts have applied the *Chadbourne* principles to communications by corporate agents. In *Chadbourne* the plaintiff sued the corporation for injuries she suffered when she fell on a sidewalk allegedly as a result of the corporation's negligence. In response to interrogatories, the corporation admitted that it had in its possession a written report by an employee who had worked on the sidewalk. The corporation, however, refused to produce the report for inspection by the plaintiff on the ground that it was protected by the attorney-client privilege. The report had been taken by an adjuster for the corporation's insurer at the request of the insurer's attorneys who also served as the corporation's attorneys in the lawsuit. In rejecting the corporation's privilege claim, the court pointed out that, since the employee had not been charged with liability, the report was not entitled to protection under the first *Chadbourne* principle.[24] Moreover, the report was not entitled to

---

23. Id.

24. Id.

protection under the second *Chadbourne* principle, since there was no evidence that the employee who provided the report was the natural person to be speaking for the corporation.[25] Finally, the report was not entitled to protection under the ninth *Chadbourne* principle because there was no evidence that the employee intended that his report be transmitted in confidence to the corporation's lawyers.[26] Under this principle, the adjuster's intent in receiving and transmitting the employee's report was not controlling.[27]

In contrast, in Sierra Vista Hospital v. Superior Court[28] an accident report which was prepared by a corporate employee at the request of the corporation on a form supplied by the corporation's insurer and which was transmitted to the corporation's lawyers was held to be within the privilege. *Sierra Vista* differs from *Chadbourne* in important respects. First, the employee who prepared the report was the head of the nursing services. Since the accident involved a patient falling from a bed, the head of the nursing services was the logical person to investigate the accident and to supply the results of the investigation to the corporation's attorneys.[29] Under the second *Chadbourne* principle, the employee was thus the natural person to be speaking for the hospital. Second, the form used by the employee warned the employee that the report was to be confidential and for the use of the hospital's attorneys.[30] Thus, as required by the ninth *Chadbourne* principle, there was evidence that the employee intended the report to be transmitted in confidence to the corporation's lawyers. Finally, the fifth *Chadbourne* requirement was also satisfied: the report was prepared at the hospital's request and the warning on the form indicated that the hospital had directed the employee to make the report for confidential transmittal to its attorneys.[31]

May a shareholder compel a corporation to disclose communications between the corporation and its lawyers when those communications are protected by the attorney-client privilege? In California, the answer is "no." Although California law gives shareholders the right to inspect some corporate records, there is no "shareholder exception" to the protection accorded by the attorney client privilege to confidential communications between a corporation and its lawyers.[32] In this respect, it is immaterial

---

25. Id.

26. Id.

27. Id.

28. 248 Cal.App.2d 359, 56 Cal.Rptr. 387 (1967).

29. Id. at 366–368, 56 Cal.Rptr. at 391–392.

30. Id.

31. Other cases applying the *Chadbourne* principles include Martin v. W.C.A.B., 59 Cal. App.4th 333, 69 Cal.Rptr.2d 138 (1997); Soltani–Rastegar v. Superior Court, 208 Cal.App.3d 424, 256 Cal.Rptr. 255 (1989); Vela v. Superior Court, 208 Cal.App.3d 141, 255 Cal.Rptr. 921 (1989); Alpha Beta Co. v. Superior Court, 157 Cal.App.3d 818, 203 Cal.Rptr. 752 (1984); Payless Drug Stores, Inc. v. Superior Court, 54 Cal.App.3d 988, 127 Cal.Rptr. 4 (1976); and People v. Glen Arms Estate, 230 Cal.App.2d 841, 41 Cal.Rptr. 303 (1964).

32. NFLP v. Superior Court, 65 Cal.App.4th 100, 107, 75 Cal.Rptr.2d 893, 897 (1998) (holding that, while a corporate director may have the right to inspect corporate records, the corporation, as the holder of the attorney-client privilege, may assert the privilege in a suit by the director against the corporation).

whether the shareholders action is a derivative suit[33] or against a closely held corporation.[34]

California shareholders have standing to bring a derivative action against an extracorporate third party to enforce the rights of the corporation provided certain prerequisites are satisfied.[35] But where the extracorporate third party defendant is the corporation's counsel and the derivative action is for legal malpractice, the trial court must dismiss the suit unless the corporation, as the privilege holder, waives the attorney-client privilege.[36] To allow the suit to go forward would put the attorney defendant in an untenable position: the privilege would preclude the lawyer from mounting a defense to the claims of breach of duty to the corporate client unless the corporation allowed the lawyer to disclose the communications alleged to constitute the breach of duty.[37]

QUESTIONS AND PROBLEMS

1. The attorney-client privilege attaches to confidential communications between a client and someone who is not licensed to practice law so long as the client reasonably believes that the person the client consulted was licensed to practice law. True or false?

2. For purposes of the privilege, a client can include natural persons and such entities as corporations. When a corporation is the client, communications to the corporation's attorneys by corporate agents who are the natural persons to be speaking for the corporation are protected by the privilege. True or false?

3. When a corporate employee has been a witness to matters which require communicating to the corporate employer's attorney and the employee has no connection with those matters other than as a witness, the employee's communications are not protected by the privilege. True or false?

§ 21.03 INFORMATION MUST BE TRANSMITTED BETWEEN CLIENT AND LAWYER IN THE COURSE OF ATTORNEY–CLIENT RELATIONSHIP[1]

Although actual employment is not essential,[2] to be privileged the information must be transmitted in the course of retaining a lawyer or

---

33. McDermott, Will & Emery v. Superior Court, 83 Cal.App.4th 378, 385, 99 Cal.Rptr.2d 622, 626 (2000) (holding that corporations, not their shareholders, are the holders of the privilege).

34. Smith v. Laguna Sur Villas Community Assn., 79 Cal.App.4th 639, 644, 94 Cal.Rptr.2d 321, 324 (2000).

35. McDermott, Will & Emery v. Superior Court, 83 Cal.App.4th 378, 382–383, 99 Cal.Rptr.2d 622, 625 (2000).

36. Id. at 383–384, 99 Cal.Rptr.2d at 626.

37. Id.

1. West's Ann. California Evidence Code § 952.

2. People v. Canfield, 12 Cal.3d 699, 705, 117 Cal.Rptr. 81, 84–85, 527 P.2d 633, 636–637 (1974).

securing a lawyer's legal services or advice in his or her professional capacity.[3] The privilege "applies not only to communications made in anticipation of litigation, but also to [those made while securing] legal advice when no litigation is threatened."[4] If employment does result, its termination does not affect the privilege.[5] The protection against disclosure afforded by the privilege lasts until the privilege itself ends.[6]

If the client uses the attorney in a nonlegal capacity—as a business agent, for example—then the information transmitted between the client and the attorney is not protected by the privilege.[7] If the client uses the attorney both in a legal and nonlegal capacity—for example, as a lawyer and labor negotiator—then the communications between the client and the attorney are not protected unless their "dominant purpose" was "in furtherance of the attorney-client relationship."[8] Accordingly, communications stemming principally from the lawyer's role as labor negotiator are not within the privilege.[9]

Disclosures made by a client to an attorney after the attorney has declined employment are not protected by the privilege.[10] A client cannot have a "reasonable expectation of being represented by an attorney after the attorney's explicit refusal to undertake representation."[11] "Moreover evidence of an attorney's express refusal of representation may give rise to

---

3. West's Ann. California Evidence Code § 951. Even a letter in which the writer seeks legal advice and which is seized by the police prior to delivery is protected by the privilege so long as the writer had a reasonable expectation of being represented by the lawyer to whom the letter is addressed. People v. Gardner, 106 Cal.App.3d 882, 887, 165 Cal.Rptr. 415, 418 (1980).

The rationale for not requiring actual employment to protect the client's disclosures is compelling: "no person could ever safely consult an attorney for the first time with a view to his employment if the privilege depended on the chance of whether the attorney after hearing his statement of the facts decided to accept the employment or decline it." Estate of Dupont, 60 Cal.App.2d 276, 288–289, 140 P.2d 866, 873 (1943).

4. Roberts v. City of Palmdale, 5 Cal.4th 363, 371, 20 Cal.Rptr.2d 330, 334, 853 P.2d 496, 500 (1993).

5. People v. Singh, 123 Cal.App. 365, 369, 11 P.2d 73, 74 (1932).

6. For a discussion on how the privilege can be terminated, see § 21.05 infra.

7. Chicago Title Ins. Co. v. Superior Court, 174 Cal.App.3d 1142, 1151, 220 Cal.Rptr. 507, 514 (1985) and cases cited therein.

8. Montebello Rose Co. v. Agricultural Labor Relations Board, 119 Cal.App.3d 1, 31, 173 Cal.Rptr. 856, 873 (1981).

9. Id. When an lawyer acts both in an attorney and non-attorney capacity, a judge may not order in camera disclosure of each communication sought to determine whether the dominant purpose of the communication was the furtherance of the attorney-client relationship. Communications with such a purpose are protected from disclosure by the privilege. See Costco Wholesale Corp. v. Superior Court, 47 Cal.4th 725, 739, 219 P.3d 736, 746, 101 Cal.Rptr.3d 758, 769 (2009). However, to assist the judge the party claiming the privilege may consent to an in camera review of the communications. Id.

10. People v. Gionis, 9 Cal.4th 1196, 1210, 40 Cal.Rptr.2d 456, 464, 892 P.2d 1199, 1207 (1995).

11. Id. at 1211, 40 Cal.Rptr.2d at 464–465, 892 P.2d at 1207–1208.

a reasonable inference that, in continuing to speak to the attorney, the person is not thereafter consulting with the attorney for advice 'in his professional capacity.' "[12] Under such circumstances, a finding that the client consulted the attorney in his capacity as a friend and not as an attorney is fatal to the client's privilege claim.[13]

The privilege is not limited to the client's oral disclosures. It can include nonverbal acts, such as displaying a scar, intended by the client as a means of communicating.[14] It can include also photographs of the client taken by the attorney's agents for the purpose of communicating information to the attorney.[15] The privilege, moreover, protects the legal opinions and advice given by the lawyer in the course of the relationship[16] and includes such uncommunicated legal opinions as the attorney's impressions and conclusions.[17] The privilege extends to warnings given by the lawyer to the client[18] and embraces even an attorney's nonverbal acts, such as displaying police reports to the client.[19]

To be privileged, the information does not have to be "confidential" in nature.[20] Though the private nature of a communication may help establish the client's intent to convey the communication in confidence,[21] the Code does not require the information to be "private." A client, for example, who tells her lawyer that she ran a light may claim the privilege even though before consulting the lawyer she told others that she ran the light.[22] Moreover, neither the lawyer nor the client can be compelled to disclose the information the attorney uses in advising the client even though the information may come from such "public" sources as law review articles and newspapers.[23]

Information which an attorney acquires in ways that do not involve a communication by the client is not privileged. Examples include an

---

12. Id. at 1211, 40 Cal.Rptr.2d at 465, 892 P.2d at 1208.

13. Id. at 1212, 40 Cal.Rptr.2d at 465, 892 P.2d at 1208.

14. City and County of San Francisco v. Superior Court, 37 Cal.2d 227, 235, 231 P.2d 26, 30 (1951).

15. People v. Gillard, 57 Cal.App.4th 136, 163, 66 Cal.Rptr.2d 790, 807 (1997).

16. West's Ann. California Evidence Code § 952.

17. Id. (comment).

18. Mitchell v. Superior Court, 37 Cal.3d 591, 600–601, 208 Cal.Rptr. 886, 891, 691 P.2d 642, 647 (1984) (holding that an attorney's warning to the clients about the dangers of a fumigant was protected by the privilege in a suit in which the clients claimed emotional distress over learning that the fumigant had contaminated areas near their homes).

19. In re Navarro, 93 Cal.App.3d 325, 329, 155 Cal.Rptr. 522, 524 (1979) (holding that an attorney could not be held in contempt for refusing to disclose whether she had shown her client a robbery arrest report).

20. Menendez v. Superior Court, 3 Cal.4th 435, 447, 11 Cal.Rptr.2d 92, 99, 834 P.2d 786, 793 (1992).

21. Cf. Solon v. Lichtenstein, 39 Cal.2d 75, 80, 244 P.2d 907, 910 (1952) (holding that client's disclosure of information to others indicated that the client did not intend to convey the same information to his lawyer in confidence).

22. See § 20.03 supra.

23. In re Jordan, 12 Cal.3d 575, 580, 116 Cal.Rptr. 371, 374, 526 P.2d 523, 526 (1974).

attorney's impressions of a client's mental condition.[24] And even though a client imparts his identity to the lawyer, the identity is not protected,[25] unless disclosure would tend to incriminate the client[26] or reveal the nature of the client's problem.[27] An attorney, for example, may not be compelled to identify a client on whose behalf the attorney mailed a check for back taxes to the IRS.[28] Similarly, the fee arrangement is not protected by the privilege, unless disclosure would tend to incriminate the client or reveal the nature of the client's problem.[29] The privilege, moreover, does not include "independent facts" related to a communication, such as the facts that a communication took place, and the time and date it took place.[30]

QUESTIONS AND PROBLEMS

1.   Only those communications in which a client seeks the lawyer's legal services or advice are protected by the privilege. If the client uses the lawyer in a nonlegal capacity—for example, as business consultant—then the information which the client imparts to the lawyer is not protected by the privilege. True or false?

2.   The attorney-client privilege is not limited to the client's oral disclosures. Nonverbal acts—such as displaying a scar—intended by the client to convey information are also protected by the privilege. True or false?

3.   The privilege protects only those communications imparted by the client to the lawyer. The lawyer's responses, including her legal advice, are outside the privilege. True or false?

4.   The privilege protects only confidential communications between the client and her attorney. To be confidential, the information conveyed must be private in nature. Accordingly, a client's revelation to her lawyer that she ran a stop light in broad daylight in the presence of many witnesses is not privileged. True or false?

5.   Even though a client imparts his identity to his lawyer in confidence, that communication is not normally privileged unless disclosure would tend to

---

24.   Oliver v. Warren, 16 Cal.App. 164, 168, 116 P. 312, 314 (1911).

25.   Willis v. Superior Court, 112 Cal.App.3d 277, 291, 169 Cal.Rptr. 301, 308 (1980). See also Tien v. Superior Court, 139 Cal.App.4th 528, 537, 43 Cal.Rptr.3d 121, 127 (2006).

26.   Id.

27.   Rosso, Johnson, Rosso & Ebersold v. Superior Court, 191 Cal.App.3d 1514, 1519, 237 Cal.Rptr. 242, 244 (1987).

28.   Baird v. Koerner, 279 F.2d 623, 635 (9th Cir.1960) (applying California law). The California constitutional right of privacy may prevent the disclosure of the clients' identities in some circumstances where disclosure is not barred by the attorney-client privilege. See Hooser v. Superior Court, 84 Cal.App.4th 997, 1003–1004, 101 Cal.Rptr.2d 341, 346 (2000).

29.   Willis v. Superior Court, 112 Cal.App.3d 277, 291, 169 Cal.Rptr. 301, 308 (1980). However, that counsel is advancing litigation expenses is protected from disclosure by the attorney-client privilege. See DeBlase v. Superior Court, 41 Cal.App.4th 1279, 1285, 49 Cal.Rptr.2d 229, 233 (1996).

30.   2,022 Ranch, L.L.C. v. Superior Court, 113 Cal.App.4th 1377, 1388, 7 Cal.Rptr.3d 197, 205 (2003).

incriminate the client or reveal the nature of the client's problem. True or false?

§ 21.04 INFORMATION MUST BE TRANSMITTED IN CONFIDENCE

The privilege protects only information transmitted "in confidence by a means which, so far as the client is aware, discloses the information to no third persons other than those who are present to further the interest of the client in the consultation or those to whom disclosure is reasonably necessary for the transmission of the information or the accomplishment of the purpose for which the lawyer is consulted * * *."[1] The Code rejects the eavesdropper doctrine, which permits individuals who overhear attorney-client communications to reveal them despite the desire of the attorney and client to keep the communications confidential.[2] Clients are protected against the risk of disclosure by eavesdroppers and other wrongful interceptors of confidential information transmitted between clients and lawyers by permitting the holder of the privilege to assert the privilege against anyone, including an eavesdropper, who acquires the information without the client's consent.[3]

Means of transmission. If the client is aware that the means chosen for transmission discloses the information to third persons who are not authorized to be present, the communication is not confidential.[4] Such a communication acquires no protection and can be disclosed by anyone who overhears it. Because such a communication is beyond the privilege, the client and the lawyer can also be compelled to disclose it over a privilege claim. Transmitting information under circumstances where others can easily overhear the communication is evidence that the client did not intend the communication to be confidential.[5] Under the Code, however, communications between attorney and client are presumed to be confiden-

---

1. West's Ann. California Evidence Code § 952.

2. For a detailed discussion of the eavesdropper doctrine, see § 20.05 supra.

3. West's Ann. California Evidence Code § 952.

4. West's Ann. California Evidence Code § 954 (comment).

5. Id. See, e.g., People v. Urbano, 128 Cal.App.4th 396, 404, 26 Cal.Rptr.3d 871, 876 (2005), where the reviewing court upheld a trial judge's ruling allowing the prosecution to offer a statement made by the accused to his lawyer. The reporting witness who overheard the statement was one of several attorneys in the courtroom while the court was in recess and was seated in the row of seats closest to the back of the courtroom. The client was speaking with his lawyer in the jury box. By way of contrast, the reviewing court approved the trial judge's ruling preventing the prosecution from offering a statement overheard by the prosecutor's investigating officer which the defendant made to his lawyer at counsel's table while a witness was testifying. Counsel and their clients, the court reasoned, should be able to communicate during court proceedings without fear that their communications can be used against them if they happen to speak too loudly. Id. at 401, 26 Cal.Rptr.3d at 874. The reviewing court, however, acknowledged that People v. Poulin, 27 Cal.App.3d 54, 64–65, 103 Cal.Rptr. 623, 630 (1972), is to the contrary. There, the reviewing court approved the use of a statement overheard by the bailiff which the client made to his attorney at counsel's table while a witness was testifying. Unlike the *Urbano* court, the *Poulin* court does not discuss the need to grant special consideration to conversations between lawyers and their clients during court proceedings.

tial.[6] The effect of the presumption is to shift to the party opposing the claim of privilege the burden of persuading the judge that the communication was not made in confidence.[7]

The increasing use of electronic communications has raised concerns about the confidentiality of communications between attorneys and their clients. Evidence Code § 917 now provides that confidential communications do not lose their privileged character simply because they are communicated by electronic means or because persons involved in the delivery, facilitation, or storage of electronic communications might have access to their content.[8] However, email communications between clients and their attorneys may fail to achieve the status of protected confidential communications when the client uses an employer's computer after the employer has alerted the client that (1) communications using the employer's electronic means are not private, may be monitored, and may be used only for business purposes; and (2) the client is aware of and agrees to these conditions.[9]

Presence of third persons. The presence of third persons who can overhear the communication does not always strip the communication of protection. Third persons may be present to further the interests of the client in the consultation.[10] Examples include spouses, parents, business associates, joint clients, interpreters, experts and others the client needs in consulting a lawyer or in securing the lawyer's advice or services.[11]

---

6. West's Ann. California Evidence Code § 917.

7. Id. For a detailed discussion of this presumption, see § 20.04 supra.

8. West's Ann. California Evidence Code § 917(b). Section 917(b) is not limited to the attorney-client privilege. It applies as well to the physician-patient, psychotherapist-patient, clergy-penitent, husband-wife, sexual assault counselor-victim and domestic violence counselor-victim privileges. Id.

9. See Holmes v. Petrovich Development Co., 191 Cal.App.4th 1047, 1068, 119 Cal.Rptr.3d 878, 895–96 (2011). "When Holmes e-mailed her attorney, she did not use her home computer to which some unknown persons involved in the delivery, facilitation, or storage may have access. Had she done so, that would have been a privileged communication unless Holmes allowed others to have access to her e-mails and disclosed their content. Instead, she used defendants' computer, after being expressly advised this was a means that was not private and was accessible by Petrovich, the very person about whom Holmes contacted her lawyer and whom Holmes sued. This is akin to consulting her attorney in one of defendants' conference rooms, in a loud voice, with the door open, yet unreasonably expecting that the conversation overheard by Petrovich would be privileged." Id.

10. West's Ann. California Evidence Code § 952.

11. Id. (comment). See also Insurance Co. of North America v. Superior Court, 108 Cal.App.3d 758, 771, 166 Cal.Rptr. 880, 888 (1980) (holding that business associates include the officers of a client who is not a natural person as well as officers and employees of parent and subsidiary companies). A client can share copies of legal memoranda prepared by his or her counsel with an outside party without waiving the attorney-client privilege if such sharing is reasonably necessary to accomplish the purpose for which the client consulted the attorney. For example, in STI Outdoor v. Superior Court, 91 Cal.App.4th 334, 109 Cal.Rptr.2d 865 (2001), the appellate court held that such sharing of memoranda did not waive the privilege because the memoranda were prepared to help the client and the outside party finalize a license agreement. Id. at 340, 109 Cal.Rptr.2d at 869.

The presence of a supervisor who can initiate disciplinary proceedings against a police officer is not in the interests of the officer. Accordingly, the presence of the supervisor will prevent the officer's disclosures to his lawyer from acquiring the protection accorded by the attorney-client privilege. Gonzales v. Municipal Court, 67 Cal.App.3d 111, 119, 136 Cal.Rptr. 475, 480 (1977).

Confidential communications are not limited to those that take place between the lawyer and the client. They also include communications by the client to third persons—such as the lawyers' secretary, guardians ad litem, as well as doctors and other experts employed by the lawyers to examine the client—who serve as conduits for the communication from the client to the attorney.[12] These communications are considered confidential because they are "reasonably necessary for the transmission of the information"[13] from the client to the attorney. The same principle applies to targets of a government investigation who share privileged information. They "may share information with each other without waiving the attorney-client privilege if cooperation is reasonably necessary for counsel to provide representation in the investigation. In other words parties aligned on the same side in an investigation or litigation may, in some circumstances, share privileged documents without waiving the attorney-client privilege."[14]

Although information exchanged in confidence between clients and their lawyers does not lose its confidentiality because of the use of conduits, the attorney-client privilege does not prevent conduits from *voluntarily* disclosing information they learn in their roles.[15] If willingly to cooperate, former officers and employees often are the best available sources of information against corporations.[16] But voluntary disclosure by conduits does not necessarily result in the loss of the attorney-client privilege. The client or lawyer retains the right to prevent the conduit from disclosing the information protected by the privilege in any proceeding in which testimony can be compelled.[17] Even in such a proceeding, however, a conduit can be compelled to disclose nonprivileged information. For example, in a suit by an insured against the insurance company, a conduit employed by the company and its lawyers can testify about her knowledge of the company's practices and procedures, and of the existence of claims manuals and other documents normally used by the company in the operation of its business.[18] Moreover, such a conduit may disclose

---

12. West's Ann. California Evidence Code § 952 (comment). See also City and County of San Francisco v. Superior Court, 37 Cal.2d 227, 236, 231 P.2d 26, 29 (1951) (doctors); Ex parte Ochse, 38 Cal.2d 230, 232, 238 P.2d 561, 562 (1951) (psychiatrists); De Los Santos v. Superior Court, 27 Cal.3d 677, 682–686, 166 Cal.Rptr. 172, 176, 613 P.2d 233, 237 (1980) (guardians ad litem); People v. Clark, 50 Cal.3d 583, 621, 268 Cal.Rptr. 399, 424, 789 P.2d 127, 152 (1990), cert. denied, 498 U.S. 973, 111 S.Ct. 442, 112 L.Ed.2d 425 (1990) (court appointed psychologist); People v. Aguilar, 218 Cal.App.3d 1556, 1564–1565, 267 Cal.Rptr. 879, 883 (1990) (hypnotist).

13. West's Ann. California Evidence Code § 952 (comment).

14. McKesson HBOC, Inc. v. Superior Court, 115 Cal.App.4th 1229, 1238, 9 Cal.Rptr.3d 812, 818 (2004).

15. See State Farm Fire & Cas. v. Superior Court, 54 Cal.App.4th 625, 637–638, 62 Cal. Rptr.2d 834, 843 (1997). Interpreters, however, have a duty not to disclose information they obtain in the course of transmitting information between clients and their lawyers. See People v. Alvarez, 14 Cal.4th 155, 235, 58 Cal.Rptr.2d 385, 435, 926 P.2d 365, 415 (1996), cert. denied, 522 U.S. 829, 118 S.Ct. 94, 139 L.Ed.2d 50 (1997) (citing California Standards of Judicial Administration § 18.3(c)).

16. See State Farm Fire & Cas. v. Superior Court, supra note 15.

17. West's Ann. California Evidence Code §§ 901, 954.

18. See State Farm Fire & Cas. v. Superior Court, 54 Cal.App.4th 625, 639, 62 Cal.Rptr.2d 834, 844 (1997).

whether the company failed to produce such documents despite a request for their production by the insured.[19]

Ethical constraints, however, limit the right of lawyers to contact the opposing party or its employees when the opposing party is represented by an attorney. Rule 2–100(A) of the California Rules of Professional Conduct prohibits an attorney from communicating directly or indirectly with a party the attorney knows is represented by a lawyer. When the opposing party is a corporation, the prohibition includes ex parte contact with officers, directors, managing agents as well as some current employees.

An employee may not be contacted if "the subject of the communication is any act or omission of such person in connection with the matter which may be binding upon or imputed to the organization for purposes of civil or criminal liability or whose statement may constitute an admission on the part of the organization."[20] An attorney, however, does not violate the prohibition unless the attorney has actual knowledge that the employee interviewed is represented by the corporation's attorney. Knowledge that the corporation is represented by in-house counsel is not sufficient to trigger the rule.[21]

Although the prohibition does not include former employees,[22] an attorney nonetheless should refrain from asking former employees about "privileged communications."[23] To ensure former employees do not divulge privileged information, the opposing party may seek a protective order.[24]

Expert investigations and reports. Confidential communications also embrace revelations by the client or by the attorney to experts whom the attorney desires to use in advising or serving the client.[25] Such disclosures are entitled to protection because they are reasonably necessary for accomplishing the purpose for which the lawyer is consulted.[26] But the fact that revelations to experts may be protected does not mean that the expert's investigations or reports to the lawyer are necessarily privileged.

Assume that a client tells his lawyer that he ran a light because his brakes failed. The lawyer asks a mechanic to inspect the brakes, and the mechanic provides the lawyer with an oral and written report indicating that the brakes failed because they needed to be replaced. Over a privilege claim, may the mechanic be asked (1) to describe his inspection and

---

19. Id.

20. See California Rule of Professional Conduct 2–100(B).

21. Truitt v. Superior Court (A, T & SF Ry. Co.), 59 Cal.App.4th 1183, 1188, 69 Cal.Rptr.2d 558, 561 (1997).

22. Continental Ins. Co. v. Superior Court, 32 Cal.App.4th 94, 119, 37 Cal.Rptr.2d 843, 858 (1995).

23. Bobele v. Superior Court, 199 Cal.App.3d 708, 714–715, 245 Cal.Rptr. 144, 148 (1988).

24. Id.

25. West's Ann. California Evidence Code § 952 (comment).

26. Id.

findings and (2) to disclose the contents of his oral and written reports to the lawyer?

Investigations. The mechanic may be compelled to describe his tests and findings so long as the information requested does not call for disclosing confidential information which the client or attorney may have provided to the mechanic. In the leading case, Grand Lake Drive In v. Superior Court,[27] the plaintiff's attorney hired an engineer to inspect and conduct tests on a sidewalk on which the plaintiff was injured. Over the plaintiff's privilege objection, the engineer was required to answer questions regarding his observations of the sidewalk and the results of his tests.[28] His answers were not privileged; they called for knowledge which the engineer acquired in the course of his investigation and not for confidential information which the attorney or client may have given him.[29]

Sometimes, the knowledge which an expert acquires as a result of his investigations cannot be divorced from the confidential information which the attorney or the client furnished him. Under these circumstances, the attorney-client privilege is not limited to protecting communications but extends to the "observations made as a consequence of protected communications."[30] In People v. Meredith[31] the client informed his lawyer that he had retrieved and attempted to burn a wallet belonging to the crime victim. The client also told the lawyer that he had placed the burned remnants in a plastic bag and placed the bag in a trash can behind his house. The lawyer had an investigator look for the wallet. The investigator found the wallet in the place described by the client and gave it to the attorney. After determining that it contained credit cards with the victim's name, the attorney turned the wallet over to the police, stating only that the wallet belonged to the victim. Over the client's privilege claim, the trial judge allowed the investigator to describe the location where he found the wallet.

The court agreed that if the defense had left the wallet where it was discovered, the investigator's testimony about the wallet's location would have been barred as "observations derived from privileged communications."[32] The court, however, refused to extend the privilege to cases in which counsel has removed or altered evidence.

---

27. 179 Cal.App.2d 122, 3 Cal.Rptr. 621 (1960).

28. Id. at 126, 3 Cal.Rptr. at 624.

29. Id. See also People v. Bolden, 29 Cal.4th 515, 551, 127 Cal.Rptr.2d 802, 829, 58 P.3d 931, 954 (2002), cert. denied, 538 U.S. 1016, 123 S.Ct. 1935, 155 L.Ed.2d 854 (2003). In this case, the prosecution offered evidence that a defense expert had been present and participated in tests conducted by a prosecution expert. "Because there is no evidence that [the defense expert's] observations during the testing or his opinions concerning the validity of the testing were the product of a privileged communication, admission of [his] testimony and other evidence concerning his role in the testing of the dried stain material did not violate defendant's attorney-client privilege."

30. People v. Meredith, 29 Cal.3d 682, 692, 175 Cal.Rptr. 612, 618, 631 P.2d 46, 52 (1981).

31. Id.

32. Id. at 695, 175 Cal.Rptr. at 620, 631 P.2d at 53.

When defense counsel alters or removes physical evidence, he necessarily deprives the prosecution of the opportunity to observe that evidence in its original condition or location. * * * [T]o bar admission of testimony concerning the original condition and location of the evidence in such a case permits the defense in effect to "destroy" critical information; it is as if * * * the wallet in this case bore a tag bearing the words "located in the trash can by [the client's] residence," and the defense, by taking the wallet, destroyed the tag. To extend the attorney-client privilege to a case in which the defense removed evidence might encourage defense counsel to race the police to seize critical evidence.[33]

Meredith is not inconsistent with *Grand Lake*. *Meredith* reiterates the principle that observations derived from privileged communications should be barred if the observations might disclose information conveyed in confidence. In *Meredith* the risk was substantial that the investigator's observations would lead the jurors to conclude that the wallet's location was originally provided by the client to the lawyer. That is why the investigator's observations about the wallet's location would have been barred by the attorney-client privilege if the defense had not removed the wallet.

Meredith simply creates an exception to the privilege whenever counsel or their agents remove or alter evidence. The exception, moreover, does not call for the unfettered receipt of the observations. *Meredith* prohibits the prosecution from disclosing the contents of the attorney-client communication or the original source of the information in offering physical evidence the defense has removed or altered.[34] If necessary, the prosecution must accept a stipulation simply informing the jury of the location or condition of the evidence.[35]

Reports. Whether the expert's oral or written report to the attorney is protected by the attorney-client privilege is another matter. As a general rule, reports provided by experts to lawyers at their request are not protected by the attorney-client privilege.[36] Whether such reports are entitled to protection depends on whether their disclosure would reveal information which the client transmitted to the lawyer in confidence. An example of a report that would not compromise confidential communications between a client and the attorney can be found in San Diego Professional Ass'n v. Superior Court.[37] In that case the plaintiff sued the defendant for the balance due on a contract requiring the plaintiffs to plan and supervise the construction of a building. The defendant cross-complained, claiming, among other matters, that the plaintiff designed the building improperly. To identify possible defects in the plans, the defen-

---

33. Id. at 694, 175 Cal.Rptr. at 619, 631 P.2d at 53.

34. Id. at 695, note 8, 175 Cal.Rptr. at 620, note 8, 631 P.2d at 54, note 8.

35. Id.

36. San Diego Professional Ass'n v. Superior Court, 58 Cal.2d 194, 204, 23 Cal.Rptr. 384, 389, 373 P.2d 448, 453 (1962).

37. Id.

dant's attorney retained an engineering firm to review the architectural designs and building specifications. The plaintiff then sought to inspect the firm's report to the defendant's attorney. In upholding the trial judge's inspection order, the court observed that

> neither the client's body, mind, nor private and confidential papers were submitted to the engineers for examination and report. They were handed the "contract documents." In other words, their primary duty was not to examine and assess the client's building, but to evaluate and report any errors found in certain architectural designs, building specifications and contracts, all of which were part of the documents which constituted the contract between the parties to the lawsuit. Such documents were not private to the client, but were equally available to both parties, both before and during the pendency of the action. * * * [T]he proper rule is, that if the facts and circumstances surrounding the creation of the agency indicate that the agent was retained to evaluate and pass on to the attorney matters which emanate in confidence from the client, both his opinions and his report are clothed with the privilege. But where, as here, the facts and circumstances indicate that the expert is to examine, evaluate, and subsequently to testify as to matters which are not in the nature of a confidential communication from client to attorney, then the letter of transmittal (report) is not privileged simply because it is reduced to writing and is delivered to an attorney.[38]

On the other hand, reports in which the expert serves as a conduit for confidential information from the client to the attorney are protected from disclosure.[39] The expert is simply providing the attorney information which the client would have furnished if the client had been qualified to do so. Examples include reports by medical and mental experts on the client's physical or mental condition,[40] as well as evaluations by engineers of information supplied in whole or in part by the client at the attorney's request.[41]

Returning to our example, the attorney-client privilege would not preclude the disclosure of the mechanic's oral and written reports to the attorney. Neither report would betray any communications transmitted in confidence by the client to the lawyer. A different case would be presented if the client had informed the lawyer that pressing the brake produced a grinding noise. If the lawyer had asked the mechanic to take that into account in assessing the condition of the brakes, then that disclosure as well as the reports would be protected by the privilege.

In determining whether the attorney-client privilege protects expert reports, care must be taken to distinguish reports prepared at the lawyer's

38. Id. at 201, 23 Cal.Rptr. at 388, 373 P.2d at 452.

39. West's Ann. California Evidence Code § 952.

40. Cf. Torres v. Municipal Court, 50 Cal.App.3d 778, 785, 123 Cal.Rptr. 553, 557 (1975).

41. National Steel Products Co. v. Superior Court, 164 Cal.App.3d 476, 484, 210 Cal.Rptr. 535, 538 (1985).

request from reports that existed before the creation of the attorney-client relationship. As we have seen, pre-existing reports and other tangible items do not become privileged simply because the client delivers them to the attorney.[42] If a client gives his lawyer the murder weapon, for example, the fact that the lawyer possesses the weapon is not protected by the privilege.[43] A privilege claim will not entitle the lawyer to decline to answer questions regarding the weapon's location. The lawyer, moreover, has an obligation to inform the court whenever the lawyer removes, alters, or takes possession of physical evidence pertaining to the crime.[44] The court must give the prosecution timely access to the evidence, including information about its alteration.[45] The court, however, must take steps to ensure that privileged information is not disclosed.[46] A court, for example, may permit the prosecution to inspect and offer the murder weapon, but it may preclude the prosecution from revealing that it was the defense lawyer who brought the weapon to the court's attention or that it was the client who told the lawyer that the weapon was the murder weapon.

Expert reports and the work product doctrine. Expert reports that are not protected from disclosure by the attorney-client privilege nonetheless may be protected by the attorney work product doctrine. To encourage attorneys to investigate the favorable as well as the unfavorable aspects of cases, the doctrine entitles lawyers to withhold some of the materials they prepare in the course of representing clients. These materials can include reports prepared by experts at the attorney's request to assist the attorney in evaluating evidence. Unlike the attorney-client privilege, the protection afforded by the work product doctrine does not depend on whether the expert report discloses confidential communications.

We have seen that a mechanic's report to a lawyer on the conditions of a client's brakes is not protected by the attorney-client privilege if disclosure of the report would not betray any confidential communications. That report, however, can be withheld under the work product doctrine if the report was commissioned by the lawyer to help evaluate evidence. The work product doctrine is examined in Chapter 22.

The use of experts and waiver. We have seen that a holder can waive the privilege for attorney-client communications by disclosing to a third person a significant part of the protected information without coercion.[47] In the absence of a special rule, this waiver principle could force disclosure of confidential information transmitted to an expert. Assume that the client tells the lawyer that pressing the brake produced a grinding noise and that the lawyer asks the mechanic to take that

---

42. See § 21.01 supra.

43. People v. Superior Court (Fairbank), 192 Cal.App.3d 32, 35, 237 Cal.Rptr. 158, 159 (1987).

44. Id. at 39–40, 237 Cal.Rptr. at 163.

45. Id.

46. Id.

47. See § 20.05 supra.

condition into account in assessing the condition of the brakes. Such a disclosure could amount to a waiver of the confidential communication, and over a privilege claim the attorney as well as the client could be compelled to disclose the client's communication with lawyer. But, as we have also seen, the provisions relating to waiver provide that disclosures to third persons will not waive the privilege if the disclosure is reasonably necessary for accomplishing the purpose for which the lawyer is consulted.[48] Since the attorney cannot represent the client adequately without the mechanic's assistance, the disclosure will not waive the privilege.

It is immaterial that the client may have provided the same information to the mechanic at the attorney's request. That disclosure is likewise protected for the same reason. Moreover, the client's testimony about her knowledge of the brakes, including hearing the grinding noise, will not waive the privilege for the communications with her attorney or with the attorney's mechanic. Unless the client reveals the contents of these communications, merely disclosing on the stand information which the client may have also transmitted in confidence does not waive the privilege.[49]

The attorney-client privilege will protect disclosures made to experts even if the they are not retained. Disclosures made to experts in a retention interview are protected "as long as there was a reasonable expectation of * * * confidentiality."[50] The opposing lawyer may not communicate with the expert, whether or not retained, without the consent of the lawyer who initially consulted the expert. If the opposing lawyer violates this rule and becomes privy to information protected by the privilege, the offending lawyer and even his entire firm can be prohibited from participating further in the action giving rise to the violation.[51]

Waiver of the privilege, however, will occur when the client calls an expert as a witness to testify about matters which the expert could have learned only in the course of the attorney-client relationship.[52] "[T]he

---

48. West's Ann. California Evidence Code § 912.

49. People v. Tamborrino, 215 Cal.App.3d 575, 582, 263 Cal.Rptr. 731, 734–735 (1989). See also § 20.05 supra. Compare People v. Barnett, 17 Cal.4th 1044, 74 Cal.Rptr.2d 121, 954 P.2d 384 (1998), where the holder of the privilege not only failed to object to disclosing conversations he had with his own expert about the location of methamphetamine oil but even "blurted out" on cross-examination that the expert must have been incompetent when he failed to locate it; held: the holder waived the privilege by disclosing without coercion a significant part of his conversations with the expert. Accordingly, the opposing party was entitled to call the expert to explain his efforts to find the oil. Id. at 1124, 74 Cal.Rptr.2d at 172, 954 P.2d at 435.

50. Shadow Traffic Network v. Superior Court, 24 Cal.App.4th 1067, 1080, 29 Cal.Rptr.2d 693, 700 (1994) (footnotes omitted). Although the absence of a confidentiality agreement between the consulting lawyer and the expert is not fatal to a privilege claim, the "better practice" is for the consulting lawyer to insist on such an agreement. Id. at 1083, 29 Cal.Rptr.2d at 702.

51. Id. at 1088, 29 Cal.Rptr.2d at 705. "[D]efense counsel's hiring of an expert who ha[s] been exposed to plaintiff's confidential information in a retention interview [gives] rise to a *rebuttable presumption* that the expert shared plaintiff's confidential information with the defense counsel." Western Digital Corp. v. Superior Court, 60 Cal.App.4th 1471, 1480, 71 Cal.Rptr.2d 179, 184 (1998) (emphasis in the original).

52. Shadow Traffic Network v. Superior Court, 24 Cal.App.4th 1067, 1078, 29 Cal.Rptr.2d 693, 699 (1994) (footnotes omitted).

confidential nature of the communication is gone once it is determined that the expert is to be a witness—the client having impliedly, if not actually, consented to the disclosure of the information given to the attorney by way of the expert."[53] But merely designating an expert as a witness does not necessarily result in the waiver of the privilege:

> The rule we deduce from the cases is this: The designation of a party as an expert trial witness is not in itself an implied waiver of the party's attorney-client privilege because his initial status is that of a possible expert witness. If the designation is withdrawn before the party discloses a significant part of a privileged communication * * * or before it is known with reasonable certainty that the party will actually testify as an expert, the privilege is secure; if the party provides privileged documents or testifies as an expert (such as by stating his opinion in a declaration or at a deposition) the privilege is waived. (Sanders v. Superior Court (1973) 34 Cal.App.3d 270, 279, 109 Cal.Rptr. 770; County of Los Angeles v. Superior Court, supra, 222 Cal.App.3d at pp. 654–655, 271 Cal.Rptr. 698; Tennenbaum v. Deloitte & Touche (1996) 77 F.3d 337, 341 [in determining whether the privilege has been waived, the "triggering event is disclosure, not a promise to disclose"].)[54]

In one situation neither the attorney-client privilege nor the work product doctrine will protect from disclosure reports prepared by an expert commissioned by an attorney, even if the expert is not designated or called as a witness. Where the attorney calls other experts who rely on the non-testifying expert's report in reaching their opinions, the opposing party is entitled to cross examine the testifying experts about the matters, including the privileged information, contained in the report.[55] The Evidence Code expressly provides that an expert may be fully cross examined about "the matter upon which his or her opinion is based and the reasons for his or her opinion."[56] Indeed, the opposing party may even call the non-testifying expert as a rebuttal witness and ask him about his report.[57]

In criminal cases the defense obligation to designate experts as witnesses does not waive the attorney-client privilege. Proposition 115 requires the defense to provide the prosecution at least 30 days prior to the trial with the names and addresses of defense witnesses, "including any reports or statements of experts made in connection with the case, including the results of physical or mental examinations, scientific tests,

---

53. National Steel Products Co. v. Superior Court, 164 Cal.App.3d 476, 484, 210 Cal.Rptr. 535, 539 (1985). Under the Code, authorizing another to disclose confidential information operates as a waiver of the privilege for such information. West's Ann. California Evidence Code § 912.

54. Shooker v. Superior Court, 111 Cal.App.4th 923, 930, 4 Cal.Rptr.3d 334, 340 (2003) (holding that the attorney-client privilege was not waived where the designation of the expert as a witness was withdrawn before the expert disclosed any significant confidential information during his deposition).

55. People v. Ledesma, 39 Cal.4th 641, 695, 47 Cal.Rptr.3d 326, 376, 140 P.3d 657, 698 (2006).

56. West's Ann. California Evidence Code § 721.

57. See People v. Combs, 34 Cal.4th 821, 864, 22 Cal.Rptr.3d 61, 96, 101 P.3d 1007, 1036 (2004), cert. denied, 545 U.S. 1107, 125 S.Ct. 2549, 162 L.Ed.2d 281 (2005).

experiments, or comparisons which the defendant intends to offer in evidence * * *."[58] Another provision, however, exempts "any materials or information which are * * * privileged pursuant to an express statutory provision * * *."[59] Rodriguez v. Superior Court[60] holds that, while the first provision requires the defense to identify the experts it plans to call, the second entitles the defense to withhold expert reports which are protected by the attorney-client privilege.[61] Whether such reports are protected from disclosure depends on the privilege and not on the proposition. As has been noted, designating or calling an expert as a witness to testify about matters which the expert could have learned only in the course of the attorney-client relationship will waive the privilege. Thus, if pursuant to Proposition 115 the defense designates as a witness a psychologist who tested the accused to evaluate his propensity for sexual violence, the court can compel the defense to disclose the psychologist's report to the prosecution.[62] As construed, however, the disclosure obligation includes more: in these circumstances the defense must also disclose the accused's answers to the questions posed by the psychologist in administering the tests as well as the raw test results.[63] "Requiring pretrial disclosure of the raw results of standardized psychological and intelligence tests administered and relied upon by an expert the defense intends to call at trial allows access to information necessary to prepare the case, reduces the chance of surprise at trial, furthers the attainment of truth and lessens the risk of a judgment based on incomplete testimony."[64]

QUESTIONS AND PROBLEMS

1. The Code adopts the eavesdropper doctrine. Thus, if an eavesdropper wrongfully intercepts confidential communications between a client and his

---

58. West's Ann. California Penal Code § 1054.3. This section does not apply to the accused. Id.

59. West's Ann. California Penal Code § 1054.6.

60. 14 Cal.App.4th 1260, 18 Cal.Rptr.2d 120 (1993).

61. Id. at 1268, 18 Cal.Rptr.2d at 125. The second provision also includes expert reports protected by the psychotherapist-patient privilege, the work product doctrine, and the Fifth Amendment. Andrade v. Superior Court (People), 46 Cal.App.4th 1609, 1611–1612, 54 Cal.Rptr.2d 504, 506 (1996).

62. Some courts, however, maintain that it is the calling of the expert and not his designation as a witness under Proposition 115 that may result in the waiver of the attorney-client or psychotherapist-patient privilege. See, e.g., Andrade v. Superior Court (People), 46 Cal.App.4th 1609, 1614, 54 Cal.Rptr.2d 504, 508 (1996).

63. Woods v. Superior Court (People), 25 Cal.App.4th 178, 183, 30 Cal.Rptr.2d 182, 184 (1994). Reports prepared by experts at the request of a lawyer lose the protection afforded by the work product doctrine once the lawyer designates or calls the expert as a witness. See § 22.02 infra.

The production of raw notes is not limited to those prepared by experts. Raw notes of witness interviews, whether prepared by investigators or lawyers, must also be produced under Proposition 115, unless they fall within the absolute privilege of the work product doctrine. Thompson v. Superior Court (People), 53 Cal.App.4th 480, 487, 61 Cal.Rptr.2d 785, 789 (1997). This rule applies to the defense as well as to the prosecution. Id. For a discussion of the work product doctrine, see Chapter 22 infra.

64. Woods v. Superior Court (People), 25 Cal.App.4th 178, 184, 30 Cal.Rptr.2d 182, 185 (1994).

lawyer, the eavesdropper may reveal the communications in court. True or false?

2.   If a client knowingly discloses information to a lawyer in the presence of third persons who are not entitled to be present at the interview, that information is not privileged even though it might otherwise be protected from disclosure. True or false?

3.   The presence of some third persons does not destroy the privilege if they are present to further the interests of the client. Such third persons can include interpreters as well as others the client needs in consulting the lawyer. True or false?

4.   The client tells his lawyer in confidence that the reason he ran the light is that his brakes failed. The lawyer engages a mechanic to inspect the brakes. Over an attorney-client privilege objection:

   a.   The opposing party can compel the mechanic to describe the condition in which he found the brakes.

   b.   The opposing party can compel the mechanic to reveal what he told the client's lawyer about the condition of the brakes.

   c.   The opposing party can compel the mechanic to disclose that the lawyer told him that the client told the lawyer that the reason the client ran the light was that the brakes failed.

   d.   The opposing party can compel the mechanic to disclose his report to the lawyer about the condition of the brakes even though the report states that it is based in part on the lawyer's representation that the client told the lawyer that the brakes made a grinding noise.

5.   A client can waive the attorney-client privilege by disclosing without coercion a significant part of the protected information to third persons. But this rule does not apply to third persons to whom the disclosure is reasonably necessary for accomplishing the purpose for which the client consulted the lawyer. Thus, the waiver the rule does not apply to (4)(d). True or false?

6.   But if the client calls the mechanic as an expert witness, then over a privilege objection the opposing party can compel the expert to disclose what the attorney told him about the condition of the brakes, including the fact that the client said that the brakes made a grinding noise. True or false?

§ 21.05   CLAIMING THE PRIVILEGE

A client, whether or not a party, has a privilege to refuse to disclose and to prevent another from disclosing a confidential communication between the client and lawyer if the privilege is claimed by (1) the holder of the privilege, (2) a person authorized by the holder to claim the privilege, or (3) the person who was the lawyer at the time the confidential communication was made.[1] A client may appear and claim the privi-

---

1.   West's Ann. California Evidence Code § 954. A third party may not vicariously claim the privilege for the holder. People v. Barnett, 17 Cal.4th 1044, 1137, 74 Cal.Rptr.2d 121, 181, 954 P.2d 384, 444 (1998). Like the privilege against self-incrimination, the attorney-client privilege is personal and may be claimed only by the holder or other persons designated in the statute. Id.

lege even if the client is not a party or intervenor in the action in which the privilege is claimed.[2] A client has "standing" to assert the privilege simply by virtue of the fact that the client is the holder.[3] The lawyer not only has the right to assert the privilege but has an obligation to do so if present when disclosure of the communication is sought.[4]

A holder is (1) the client when the client has no guardian or conservator,[5] (2) the guardian or conservator of the client when the client has a guardian or conservator,[6] (3) the personal representative of the client if the client is dead,[7] or (4) in the case of a client who is not a natural person, a successor, assignee, trustee in dissolution or any similar representative of a firm, association, organization, partnership, business trust, corporation, or public entity that is no longer in existence.[8]

The privilege may be claimed only if a holder of the privilege is in existence.[9] The privilege terminates when the client's estate is finally distributed and his personal representative is discharged.[10] In most jurisdictions, the privilege survives the death of the client.[11] The Code's position only partially aligns California with the majority.[12] In California the privilege ceases to exist once the client's estate is wound up. Though good reasons exist for maintaining the privilege while the estate is being administered, especially if the estate is involved in litigation, the Law Revision Commission saw "little reason to preserve secrecy at the expense

---

2. Mylan Laboratories, Inc. v. Soon–Shiong, 76 Cal.App.4th 71, 80, 90 Cal.Rptr.2d 111, 117 (1999).

3. Id.

4. West's Ann. California Evidence Code § 955. The lawyer, however, may not claim the privilege if no holder is in existence or if instructed not to do so by a person who is authorized to permit disclosure. Id. As a general rule, "the custodian of materials protected by an evidentiary privilege owes a duty to the holder of the privilege to claim the privilege and to take actions necessary to ensure that the materials are not disclosed improperly." People v. Superior Court (Laff), 25 Cal.4th 703, 713, 107 Cal.Rptr.2d 323, 330, 23 P.3d 563, 569 (2001).

5. West's Ann. California Evidence Code § 953(a).

6. West's Ann. California Evidence Code § 953(b).

7. West's Ann. California Evidence Code § 953(c).

8. West's Ann. California Evidence Code § 953(d). A receiver appointed pursuant to Civil Procedure Code § 564 may also claim the attorney-client privilege. Shannon v. Superior Court, 217 Cal.App.3d 986, 995, 266 Cal.Rptr. 242, 247 (1990).

9. West's Ann. California Evidence Code § 954 (comment).

10. Id. See also HLC Properties, Ltd. v. Superior Court, 35 Cal.4th 54, 66, 24 Cal.Rptr.3d 199, 207, 105 P.3d 560, 567 (2005).

11. C. McCormick, McCormick on Evidence § 94 (4th ed. J. Strong 1992).

12. West's Ann. California Evidence Code § 954 (comment). Other jurisdictions, including the federal courts, hold that the attorney-client privilege is not terminated at the time the client's estate is wound up. The privilege continues after the client's death unless the privileged communications are sought in litigation between the client's heirs. Swidler & Berlin v. United States, 524 U.S. 399, 404–405 and note 2, 118 S.Ct. 2081, 2085 and note 2, 141 L.Ed.2d 379, 385 and note 2 (1998).

The issue arose in federal courts when the Office of Independent Counsel sought notes which a lawyer made while interviewing Vincent W. Foster, Deputy White House Counsel. Mr. Foster consulted the lawyer in connection with Congressional and other investigations regarding the 1993 dismissal of employees from the White House Travel Office. Mr. Foster died a few days after the interview. The United States Supreme Court held that the federal attorney-client privilege barred the production of the notes. Id. at 410, 118 S.Ct. at 2088, 141 L.Ed.2d at 388–389.

of excluding relevant evidence after the estate is wound up and the representative is discharged."[13] However, unlike the attorney-client privilege, a lawyer's ethical obligation to maintain inviolate a client's confidences and secrets survives the death of the client even after the estate is wound up and the representative is discharged. Subject to some exceptions, a "lawyer is forever [ethically] precluded from disclosing a client's confidential information or using that information against a client's wishes."[14]

The client as the holder can waive the privilege.[15] Waiver will occur if the client discloses a significant part of the privileged communication without coercion.[16] However, a similar disclosure by the attorney will not result in a waiver of the privilege unless the client consents to the attorney's disclosure.[17]

QUESTIONS AND PROBLEMS

1. A client may claim the privilege to prevent disclosure of confidential communications only if the client is a party to the case in which the privilege is claimed. True or false?

2. Unless otherwise instructed by the holder, a lawyer has an obligation to claim the privilege if present when disclosure is sought. True or false?

3. The attorney-client privilege terminates after the client's estate is wound up and the representative is discharged. True or false?

§ 21.06   EXCEPTIONS

Communications that otherwise would be privileged are not protected from disclosure if they fall within the following exceptions:

1. No privilege exists if the services of the lawyer were sought or obtained to enable or aid anyone to commit or plan to commit a crime or fraud.[1] A distinction is made between disclosures that merely reveal a plan to commit a crime or fraud and disclosures that are made for the purpose of obtaining the lawyer's help in aiding or enabling someone to commit or plan to commit a crime or fraud. Only the latter disclosures fall within the exception.[2]

When a client merely discloses a plan that may involve a crime or fraud, the lawyer is placed in the position of dissuading the client from

---

13. Id.

14. Lamport, "Ethics Issues Finding Way Into Court," MCLE SELF–STUDY, *California Bar Journal,* January 1998, p. 22, 24. The ethical duty to maintain a client's confidences inviolate is imposed by West's Ann. California Business and Professions Code § 6068(e)(1).

15. For a discussion of how the privilege can be waived, see § 20.05.

16. West's Ann. California Evidence Code § 912.

17. Id.

1. West's Ann. California Evidence Code § 956.

2. People v. Clark, 50 Cal.3d 583, 622, 268 Cal.Rptr. 399, 425, 789 P.2d 127, 153 (1990), cert. denied, 498 U.S. 973, 111 S.Ct. 442, 112 L.Ed.2d 425 (1990).

following through on the plans. Such revelations should be protected, since the purpose of the privilege is to protect client disclosures made in the course of seeking legal advice.[3] But when a client reveals a plan to commit a crime or fraud to obtain the lawyer's help in committing the crime or fraud, the client is not consulting the lawyer for a proper purpose; instead, the client is abusing the attorney-client relationship.[4] Accordingly, what a client tells a lawyer whom the client consults to promote an extortion scheme is not protected by the privilege.[5] But only those communications that are reasonably related to the crime or fraud are discoverable.[6] A finding that the crime-fraud exception applies does not open all of the client's files or communications with his or her attorney to inspection.[7]

It is immaterial whether the client or lawyer instigated the crime or fraud which the client then joins. "Where the entire attorney-client relationship is embarked upon in furtherance of criminal activity, and the relationship is permeated by criminal activity and the client takes an active part in it, the crime-fraud exception is satisfied notwithstanding that it may have been the attorney who originally conscripted the client for the illegal purpose."[8]

The crime-fraud exception is narrower than a similar exception to the physician-patient and the psychotherapist-patient privileges. No privilege exists if the services of a physician or psychotherapist are sought or obtained to enable or aid anyone to commit a crime or a *tort*.[9] People seldom consult their physicians or psychotherapists about matters that might subsequently be determined to be a tort, but people do consult lawyers about these matters. The narrower exception for communications between clients and lawyers is designed to encourage clients to discuss potential torts with lawyers.[10]

The crime exception embraces "inchoate" offenses, such as solicitation and conspiracy, as well as "substantive" offenses. A client who requests a lawyer's aid in committing enumerated crimes is guilty of solicitation.[11] If the lawyer agrees to aid in the commission of the crime,

---

3. West's Ann. California Evidence Code § 951.

4. Glade v. Superior Court, 76 Cal.App.3d 738, 746, 143 Cal.Rptr. 119, 124 (1978).

5. People v. Pic'l, 114 Cal.App.3d 824, 881, 171 Cal.Rptr. 106, 139 (1981), disapproved on other grounds, People v. Kimble, 44 Cal.3d 480, 244 Cal.Rptr. 148, 749 P.2d 803 (1988). For the exception to apply, the attorney does not need to be aware of the client's wrongful purposes. See People v. Clark, 50 Cal.3d 583, 622, 268 Cal.Rptr. 399, 425, 789 P.2d 127, 153, cert. denied, 498 U.S. 973, 111 S.Ct. 442, 112 L.Ed.2d 425 (1990).

6. BP Alaska Exploration, Inc. v. Superior Court, 199 Cal.App.3d 1240, 1268, 245 Cal.Rptr. 682, 701 (1988).

7. Id.

8. People v. Superior Court (Bauman & Rose), 37 Cal.App.4th 1757, 1768, note 4, 44 Cal.Rptr.2d 734, 740, note 4 (1995).

9. West's Ann. California Evidence Code §§ 997 and 1018.

10. West's Ann. California Evidence Code § 997 (comment).

11. West's Ann. California Penal Code § 653f. Perjury and subornation of perjury are among the enumerated offenses that can be solicited. Id.

both the lawyer and the client are guilty of conspiracy if either commits the necessary overt acts.[12] If the client commits the offense, the lawyer is also guilty as an accomplice if, with the purpose of facilitating the commission of the crime, the lawyer aided the client in planning or committing the offense.[13]

2. No privilege exists for communications between a deceased client and her lawyer when those communications are relevant to an issue between parties all of whom claim through the deceased client, regardless of whether the claims are by testate or intestate succession or by inter vivos transaction.[14] "The traditional exception for litigation between claimants by testate or intestate succession is based on the theory that claimants in privity with the estate claim *through* the client, not adversely, and the deceased client presumably would want his communications [with his lawyer] disclosed in litigation between such claimants so that his desires in regard to the disposition of his estate might be correctly ascertained and carried out. This rationale is equally applicable where one or more of the parties is claiming by inter vivos transaction as, for example, in an action between a party who claims under a deed (executed by a client in full possession of his faculties) and a party who claims under a will executed while the client's mental stability was dubious."[15]

3. No privilege exists for communications relevant to an issue of breach, by the lawyer or by the client, of a duty arising out of the attorney-client relationship.[16] "It would be unjust to permit a client either to accuse his attorney of a breach of duty and to invoke the privilege to prevent the attorney from bringing forth evidence in defense of the charge or to refuse to pay his attorney's fee and invoke the privilege to defeat the attorney's claim. * * * The duty involved must, of course, be one arising out of the lawyer-client relationship, e.g., the duty of the lawyer to exercise reasonable diligence on behalf of his client, the duty of the lawyer to care faithfully and account for his client's property, or the client's duty to pay for the lawyer's service."[17] Accordingly, an attorney may reveal communications with his client when the client charges the attorney with misrepresenting the consequences of entering a guilty plea.[18] An attorney also may disclose pertinent client communications when the client charges

---

12. West's Ann. California Penal Code §§ 182 and 184.

13. People v. Beeman, 35 Cal.3d 547, 199 Cal.Rptr. 60, 674 P.2d 1318 (1984).

14. West's Ann. California Evidence Code § 957. This exception is limited to communications between the deceased client and her lawyer and does not extend to communications between that lawyer and one of the parties claiming through the deceased client. See Fletcher v. Alameda County Superior Court, 44 Cal.App.4th 773, 779, 52 Cal.Rptr.2d 65, 68 (1996).

15. West's Ann. California Evidence Code § 957 (comment).

16. West's Ann. California Evidence Code § 958.

17. Id. (comment). The exception created by § 958 is sometimes referred to as "the in issue doctrine" which is said to create an "implied waiver" when the privilege holder tenders an issue involving the substance or content of a protected communication. See Eisendrath v. Superior Court, 109 Cal.App.4th 351, 363, 134 Cal.Rptr.2d 716, 724 (2003). No implied waiver is necessary, however, as tendering such an issue triggers the exception.

18. People v. Morris, 20 Cal.App.3d 659, 664, 97 Cal.Rptr. 817, 819 (1971).

the attorney with malpractice[19] or with ineffective assistance of counsel.[20] A successful challenge to a conviction on ineffectiveness grounds, however, does not necessarily mean that the confidential communications disclosed at the ineffectiveness hearing will be admissible against the defendant as admissions in a subsequent retrial.

In People v. Ledesma[21] the accused successfully overturned his conviction on the ground of ineffective assistance of counsel. At the habeas hearing on his ineffectiveness claim, the accused maintained that his attorney had failed to investigate a diminished capacity defense adequately. At the hearing, over the accused's objection a mental health expert testified that the accused had told him that he had committed the offense charged. Prior to the first trial, the mental health expert had been appointed to assist the accused's attorney evaluate his mental health. Because the accused's confidential communications to the expert were pertinent at the ineffectiveness hearing, the accused's objection was properly overruled at that hearing.

At the retrial, the prosecution, over the accused's objection, was allowed to call the mental health expert to testify that the accused had told him that he had committed the offense charged. On appeal, the California Supreme Court rejected the prosecution's claim that the accused had waived both the psychotherapist-patient and attorney-client privileges.

> The purpose of the exception to the attorney-client privilege established by Evidence Code section 958 is to avoid the injustice of permitting "a client either to accuse his attorney of a breach of duty and to invoke the privilege to prevent the attorney from bringing forth evidence in defense of the charge or to refuse to pay his attorney's fee and invoke the privilege to defeat the attorney's claims." (7 Cal. Law Revision. Com. Rep., supra, p. 176.) That purpose was fully met when [the mental health expert] was permitted to testify for the prosecution at the habeas corpus hearing. To interpret section 958 as abolishing the privilege for all purposes in this context would raise serious questions as to whether section 958 conflicts with the defendant's Sixth Amendment right to counsel, a right that the [attorney-client] privilege is intended to promote.
>
> Furthermore, in a case such as this, in which the defendant successfully established that his previous attorney provided constitutionally ineffective assistance, the disclosure of confidential communications at the habeas corpus hearing can be attributed to the attorney's ineffective assistance. The admission of those communications at a retrial may be viewed as a further consequence of the violation of the defendant's right to effective assistance of counsel. * * * In light

---

19. Smith, Smith & Kring v. Superior Court, 60 Cal.App.4th 573, 580, 70 Cal.Rptr.2d 507, 511 (1997).

20. Durdines v. Superior Court, 76 Cal.App.4th 247, 255, 90 Cal.Rptr.2d 217, 223 (1999).

21. 39 Cal.4th 641, 47 Cal.Rptr.3d 326, 140 P.3d 657 (2006).

of these serious constitutional concerns, we conclude the attorney-client privilege continues to apply for purposes of retrial after otherwise privileged matters have been disclosed in connection with habeas corpus proceedings, under Evidence Code section 958.[22]

In Solin v. O'Melveny & Myers[23] Solin represented clients who were under investigation for criminal conduct. To protect himself from possible criminal exposure, Solin sought the advice of an attorney with O'Melveny & Myers. Solin concluded that the advice was deficient and sued O'Melveny & Myers for malpractice. Solin's client intervened, asking that Solin's malpractice action to be dismissed to avoid the disclosure of their confidential conversations with Solin. Solin claimed that it would be unnecessary for him or O'Melveny & Myers to disclose those client communications he shared with O'Melveny. The appellate court disagreed and affirmed the trial court's dismissal, holding that it would be "fundamentally unfair for a client [Solin] to sue a law firm for the advice obtained and then seek to forbid the attorney [O'Melveny & Myers] who gave that advice from reciting verbatim, as nearly as memory permits, the words spoken by his accuser during the consultation."[24]

In California, shareholders have the right to bring a derivative malpractice action against the corporation's outside counsel.[25] The corporation, not the shareholders, is the client, however.[26] Because the attorney-client privilege exists only between the corporation and its outside counsel, the exception allowing counsel to disclose confidential client communications in malpractice suits would be inapplicable to shareholder derivative malpractice suits. In McDermott, Will & Emery v. Superior Court the California Court of Appeal responded to this quandary by prohibiting shareholder derivative malpractice actions.[27] The court felt compelled to issue the prohibition because under the Evidence Code California courts have no Common Law power to create the needed exception in shareholder derivative malpractice actions.[28]

A less stringent limitation applies to suits by in-house counsel for wrongful termination of employment. Such suits pose the risk of disclosure of confidential information acquired by the attorney-plaintiff in the course of the employment relationship. Accordingly, such a suit can be maintained only if "it can be established without breaching the attorney-client privilege or unduly endangering the values lying at the heart of the professional relationship."[29]

---

22. Id. at 694–695, 47 Cal.Rptr.3d at 375, 140 P.3d at 698 (2006).

23. 89 Cal.App.4th 451, 107 Cal.Rptr.2d 456 (2001).

24. Id. at 465–466, 107 Cal.Rptr.2d at 466–467.

25. McDermott, Will & Emery v. Superior Court, 83 Cal.App.4th 378, 382, 99 Cal.Rptr.2d 622, 624 (2000).

26. Id. at 383, 99 Cal.Rptr.2d at 626.

27. Id. at 385, 99 Cal.Rptr.2d at 627.

28. Id.

29. General Dynamics Corp. v. Superior Court, 7 Cal.4th 1164, 1169, 32 Cal.Rptr.2d 1, 4, 876 P.2d 487, 490 (1994).

4. No privilege exists for communications relevant to an issue concerning the intention or competence of a client executing an attested document in which the lawyer serves as the attesting witness, or concerning the execution or attestation of such a document.[30] "The mere fact that an attorney acts as an attesting witness should not destroy the lawyer-client privilege as to all statements made concerning the document attested; but the privilege should not prohibit the lawyer from performing the duties expected of an attesting witness."[31]

5. No privilege exists for communications relevant to an issue regarding a deceased client's intentions with respect to a deed of conveyance, will or other writing executed by the client purporting to affect an interest in property.[32] This exception allows an attorney to disclose a client's true intentions with regard to dispositive instruments even if the attorney was not an attesting witness.[33]

6. No privilege exists for communications relevant to an issue regarding the validity of a deed of conveyance, will, or other writing executed by a deceased client purporting to affect an interest in property.[34] As in the case of the fifth exception, an attorney may disclose communications pertaining to the validity of such instruments even if the attorney was not an attesting witness.[35]

7. No privilege exists for communications offered in a civil proceeding between one or more clients or their successors in interest where the clients retained or consulted a lawyer upon a matter of common interest.[36]

8. No privilege exists for communications which the lawyer reasonably believes must be disclosed to prevent a criminal act which the lawyer reasonably believes is likely to result in death or substantial bodily harm to an individual.[37] This exception, which was added in 1993, parallels the exception for communications between a psychotherapist and a patient

---

30. West's Ann. California Evidence Code § 959.

31. Id. (comment).

32. West's Ann. California Evidence Code § 960.

33. Id. (comment).

34. West's Ann. California Evidence Code § 961.

35. West's Ann. California Evidence Code § 960 (comment).

36. West's Ann. California Evidence Code § 962. By its terms, this exception applies only to clients who sue each other and who seek to use the communications they made to their joint lawyer. It does not apply to clients who had separate counsel. As a rule, however, privileged information shared by parties represented by separate counsel will result in the waiver of the privilege unless the "common interest doctrine" applies. This doctrine is derived from California Civil Code § 47(c), which provides that certain communications between parties who have shared interests are subject to a qualified privilege. See OXY Resources California LLC v. Superior Court, 115 Cal.App.4th 874, 891, 9 Cal.Rptr.3d 621, 636 (2004). Under the doctrine, sharing information protected under the attorney-client privilege will not result in waiver of the privilege if the court finds that the participants in the exchange had a reasonable expectation that the information would remain confidential and that the disclosure was reasonably necessary to accomplish the purpose for which the lawyers were consulted. Id. If the court finds that the information shared does not qualify for protection under the common interest doctrine, then the objecting party's privilege objection must be overruled.

37. West Ann. California Evidence Code § 956.5.

which the psychotherapist reasonably believes should be disclosed to prevent the patient from endangering himself or another.[38]

In People v. Dang[39] the accused, among other crimes, was prosecuted for assaulting his spouse and for dissuading a witness from testifying by force or threat. At the trial his former attorney testified that the accused told him that if the witnesses to the assault refused to accept a bribe to refrain from testifying, he would "whack" them. The appellate court held that the trial judge had correctly overruled the accused's claim that his statements to the lawyer were protected from disclosure under the attorney-client privilege.[40] The accused's statements fell within the exception when made because a reasonable lawyer would have concluded that disclosure would have been necessary to prevent the client from committing a criminal act which the lawyer believed was likely to result in death or substantial bodily harm.

Although the attorney reported the client's threats to the district attorney, disclosure under the analogous exception to the psychotherapist-patient privilege is not required for the communication to lose its privileged status. The test under the psychotherapist-patient privilege is whether at the time the threats were made a reasonable psychotherapist would have known that disclosure was necessary to prevent the threatened danger.[41] It is the making of a credible threat, not its disclosure by the psychotherapist, that triggers the exception. The same test should apply to the loss of the attorney-client privilege.

The exceptions for the attorney-client privilege differ from those for the physician-patient and the psychotherapist-patient privileges in an important respect. The latter two privileges do not exist in any proceeding in which issues concerning the medical, mental or emotional condition of the patient have been tendered by the patient.[42] As was emphasized in Miller v. Superior Court,[43] no such exception applies to the attorney-client privilege. In *Miller* the plaintiff brought a malpractice suit against the lawyer who represented her in dissolution proceedings. The defendant lawyer claimed that the plaintiff's action was barred by the statute of limitations. To prove that the plaintiff had been aware of her potential malpractice claim prior to the time claimed by the plaintiff, the defendant sought an order compelling the plaintiff to produce letters and memoranda she had received from several lawyers she had consulted after the dissolution. The trial judge granted the order on the ground that the letters and memoranda from the other lawyers were not privileged.[44] The reviewing court held that the trial judge erred. Though the client had put

---

38. For a discussion of this exception, see § 23.03 infra.

39. 93 Cal.App.4th 1293, 113 Cal.Rptr.2d 763 (2001).

40. Id. at 1297–1298, 113 Cal.Rptr.2d at 766–767.

41. See § 23.03 infra.

42. West's Ann. California Evidence Code §§ 966 and 1016.

43. 111 Cal.App.3d 390, 168 Cal.Rptr. 589 (1980).

44. Id. at 394, 168 Cal.Rptr. at 591.

in issue her state of mind regarding when she first learned about her malpractice claim, tendering that issue neither waived the privilege protecting the communications with the other lawyers nor fell within the exceptions for attorney-client communications enumerated in the Code.[45] It is only when the client places in issue the decisions, conclusions, and mental state of his or her lawyer that the privilege no longer applies.[46]

Merritt v. Superior Court[47] illustrates this point. The plaintiff brought a claim of bad faith refusal to settle an action against an insurer. The plaintiff claimed that the insurer's actions prevented his lawyers from making a settlement offer. When the insurer attempted to discover how its actions had prevented the plaintiff's lawyers from making an offer, the plaintiff asserted the attorney-client privilege. The court affirmed the overruling of the privilege: litigants waive their privilege when they place their attorney's state of mind in issue.[48]

A related issue is whether defending on the basis of advice given by a lawyer strips the attorney-client communications of protection. Some federal cases hold that the "defense" has that effect.[49] The California courts are in agreement where it can be shown that the client is defending on the basis of the lawyer's advice.[50]

The due process exception. Criminal defendants have urged courts to create an exception for communications protected by the attorney-client privilege when offered to impeach a client who appears as a prosecution witness or to establish the client's guilt of the offense charged against the accused. In People v. Godlewski[51] the accused was prevented from offering a codefendant's communications with his lawyer to prove that it was the codefendant who had killed the victim. In upholding the codefendant's privilege claim, the court rejected the accused's claim that the right to a fair trial guaranteed by due process entitled him to "a per se right" to breach the privilege.[52] Instead, the court adopted a balancing approach used by the federal courts. To override the privilege, the accused must demonstrate (1) that the communications sought are probative of a proposition that is essential to the defense, (2) that the communications

---

45. Id.

46. Mitchell v. Superior Court, 37 Cal.3d 591, 605, 208 Cal.Rptr. 886, 894, 691 P.2d 642, 649 (1984) and cases cited therein.

47. 9 Cal.App.3d 721, 88 Cal.Rptr. 337 (1970).

48. Id. at 730, 88 Cal.Rptr. at 342. See also Steiny & Co. v. California Elec. Supply Co., 79 Cal.App.4th 285, 292, 93 Cal.Rptr.2d 920, 925 (2000) (Where a party asserting a claim invokes a privilege that withholds crucial information, fundamental fairness requires overruling the privilege claim.). *Steiny* involved a trade secret. Id.

49. See, e.g., Handgards, Inc. v. Johnson & Johnson, 413 F.Supp. 926 (N.D.Cal.1976).

50. Transamerica Title Ins. Co. v. Superior Court 188 Cal.App.3d 1047, 1053, 233 Cal.Rptr. 825, 829 (1987); Southern California Gas Co. v. Public Utilities Comm'n, 50 Cal.3d 31, 42, 265 Cal.Rptr. 801, 807, 784 P.2d 1373, 1379 (1990) (The attorney-client privilege is not waived unless the client claims reliance on the advice of counsel.).

51. 17 Cal.App.4th 940, 21 Cal.Rptr.2d 796 (1993).

52. Id. at 948, 21 Cal.Rptr.2d at 801.

are highly probative of that proposition, and (3) that the accused has no recourse to other evidence for establishing that proposition.[53]

In *Godlewski* the accused failed the last two tests: although the proffered testimony was directed at a significant issue, it did not prove that the codefendant was the killer; moreover, the accused had access to other evidence showing that the codefendant was the killer.[54] By contrast, in People v. Mincey[55] the California Supreme Court upheld the accused's confrontation right to pierce a witness's privilege claim. The defense sought on cross-examination to elicit the witness's bias against the accused by evidence that the witness's lawyer had informed her that cooperation with the prosecution might result in leniency in her own case. The court held that the trial judge erred in upholding the witness's attorney-client claim since the evidence was essential to establishing her bias.[56]

QUESTIONS AND PROBLEMS

1. A prosecutor is less likely to compel the disclosure of a client's statements to a lawyer the client sees for help in drafting a contract to set prices among competitors if that client did not know that such a contract was illegal under the penal code than if the client knew such contracts were illegal at the time of the consultation. True or false?

2. A prosecutor can probably compel the disclosure of a statement by a client to his lawyer in which the client threatens to kill another, even though the client made the statement in an interview otherwise protected by the attorney-client privilege. True or false?

3. According to the United States Supreme Court, to obtain a conviction for tax evasion the government must prove that the accused was aware of his duty to pay the tax. Cheek v. United States, 498 U.S. 192, 201, 111 S.Ct. 604, 112 L.Ed.2d 617 (1991). Smith was prosecuted for tax evasion. In his case-in-chief, he testified that his lawyer told him that he didn't have to pay the tax. The prosecution in rebuttal called the lawyer to ask her what she told the Smith. Smith objects on the ground that the communications between him and his lawyer are protected by the attorney-client privilege. How should the court rule?

4. Because the accused if convicted risks loss of liberty or life, the accused is automatically entitled to pierce the attorney-client privilege in order to prove that the client committed the offense for which the accused is on trial. True or false?

---

53. Id. at 948–949, and note 27, 21 Cal.Rptr.2d at 801–802 and note 27.

54. Id.

55. 2 Cal.4th 408, 6 Cal.Rptr.2d 822, 827 P.2d 388 (1992).

56. Id. at 463, 6 Cal.Rptr.2d at 856, 827 P.2d at 423. But see People v. Gurule, 28 Cal.4th 557, 594, 123 Cal.Rptr.2d 345, 376, 51 P.3d 224, 250 (2002), cert. denied, 538 U.S. 964, 123 S.Ct. 1754, 155 L.Ed.2d 517 (2003), where the California Supreme Court observed that the accused does not have the general right to invade another person's attorney-client privilege.

§ 21.07 CONFIDENTIALITY AND CONFLICTS OF INTEREST

The codes of professional responsibility, including California's, prohibit an attorney from representing more than one client in matters in which the interests of the clients conflict.[1] Where the potential conflict arises from the successive representation of clients with potentially adverse interests, the need to preserve the confidentiality of the communications of the first client requires that the attorney and his firm be disqualified from representing the second client.[2]

Where the first client seeks to have the attorney and his firm disqualified, the client must demonstrate a substantial relationship between the subjects of the antecedent and current representation. If such a relationship is demonstrated, access to the first client's confidential information is presumed and the attorney and his firm must desist from representing the second client.[3]

§ 21.08 SEARCH WARRANTS AND CONFIDENTIAL CLIENT FILES

The issuance of a valid search warrant for the seizure of client files which the lawyer claims are privileged does not substitute for a hearing to determine whether the files fall within the crime-fraud exception to the attorney-client privilege.[1] The showing required for issuing a search warrant is lower than the showing necessary to establish the crime-fraud exception. A valid search warrant may be issued on the basis of a probability based on the evidence presented to the issuing judge; in contrast, a party opposing the privilege claim must not only establish a prima facie case of crime or fraud,[2] but must also persuade the judge by a preponderance of the evidence of the facts establishing the crime or fraud.[3] The procedure, moreover, for issuing a search warrant is ex parte; rulings on privilege claims presuppose an adversarial evidentiary hearing.[4]

---

1. Rule 3–310(C)(1), Rules of Professional Conduct of the State Bar of California. See also Rule 1.7, American Bar Association Model Rules of Professional Conduct.

2. Flatt v. Superior Court, 9 Cal.4th 275, 283, 36 Cal.Rptr.2d 537, 541, 885 P.2d 950, 954 (1994). An attorney who is of counsel to a firm will be treated as a member of the firm for the purpose of determining whether the firm should be disqualified from representing the second client. People v. SpeeDee Oil Change Systems, Inc., 20 Cal.4th 1135, 1155, 86 Cal.Rptr.2d 816, 830–831, 980 P.2d 371, 384–385 (1999).

3. Flatt v. Superior Court, 9 Cal.4th 275, 283, 36 Cal.Rptr.2d 537, 541, 885 P.2d 950, 954 (1994).

1. People v. Superior Court (Bauman & Rose), 37 Cal.App.4th 1757, 1769, 44 Cal.Rptr.2d 734, 741 (1995).

2. Id.

3. See West's Ann. California Evidence Code § 405 (comment).

4. People v. Superior Court (Bauman & Rose), 37 Cal.App.4th 1757, 1769, 44 Cal.Rptr.2d 734, 741 (1995).

An attorney, as the custodian of client files protected by the attorney-client privilege, owes the client a duty to claim the privilege and take actions necessary to ensure that the privileged matter is not disclosed improperly.[5] Accordingly, even before any charges have been filed, an attorney suspected of engaging in criminal activity may assert the attorney-client privilege to protect from disclosure materials seized from the attorney pursuant to a search warrant.[6] The attorney, moreover, may also assert the work product doctrine to prevent disclosure of material that qualifies for protection under this doctrine.[7] Where appropriate, a court has the inherent authority to appoint a special master at court expense to determine the validity of the claims of privilege asserted by the attorney.[8]

§ 21.09 FEDERAL RULES OF EVIDENCE

As has been noted, Congress declined to enact the privileges article recommended by the United States Supreme Court. Instead, Congress substituted a provision, Rule 501,[1] that leaves the development and determination of federal privilege law to the federal Common Law. In 2008, however, Congress enacted Federal Rule of Evidence 502, relating to the attorney-client privilege and the work product doctrine. According to the Advisory Committee Note, the rule has two purposes: "It resolves some longstanding disputes in the courts about the effect of certain disclosures of communications or information protected by the attorney-client privilege or as work product—specifically those disputes involving inadvertent disclosure and subject matter waiver." It also "responds to the widespread complaint that litigation costs necessary to protect against waiver of attorney-client privilege or work product have become prohibitive due to the concern that any disclosure (however innocent or minimal) will operate as a subject matter waiver of all protected communications or information."[2] The new Rule and its Note are set out in the statutory section at the end of this chapter.

CALIFORNIA EVIDENCE CODE

§ 950. Lawyer

As used in this article, "lawyer" means a person authorized, or reasonably believed by the client to be authorized, to practice law in any state or nation.

---

5. People v. Superior Court (Laff), 25 Cal.4th 703, 713, 107 Cal.Rptr.2d 323, 330, 23 P.3d 563, 569 (2001).

6. Id. at 716, 107 Cal.Rptr.2d at 334, 23 P.3d at 572.

7. Id. at 718–719, 107 Cal.Rptr.2d at 335–336, 23 P.3d at 573–574. For a discussion of the work product doctrine, see Chapter 22 infra.

8. People v. Superior Court (Laff), 25 Cal.4th 703, 736, 107 Cal.Rptr.2d 323, 350,. Trial judges have no general duty to exclude evidence on their own motion. People v. Carpenter, 15 Cal.4th 312, 411, 63 Cal.Rptr.2d 1, 60, 935 P.2d 708, 767 (1997), cert. denied, 522 U.S. 1078, 118 S.Ct. 858, 139 L.Ed.2d 757 (1998).

1. See Federal Rule of Evidence 501.

2. Federal Rule of Evidence 502 (Advisory Committee Note).

§ 951. Client

As used in this article, "client" means a person who, directly or through an authorized representative, consults a lawyer for the purpose of retaining the lawyer or securing legal service or advice from him in his professional capacity, and includes an incompetent (a) who himself so consults the lawyer or (b) whose guardian or conservator so consults the lawyer in behalf of the incompetent.

§ 952. Confidential communication between client and lawyer

As used in this article, "confidential communication between client and lawyer" means information transmitted between a client and his or her lawyer in the course of that relationship and in confidence by a means which, so far as the client is aware, discloses the information to no third persons other than those who are present to further the interest of the client in the consultation or those to whom disclosure is reasonably necessary for the transmission of the information or the accomplishment of the purpose for which the lawyer is consulted, and includes a legal opinion formed and the advice given by the lawyer in the course of that relationship. A communication between a client and his or her lawyer is not deemed lacking in confidentiality solely because the communication is transmitted by facsimile, cellular telephone, or other electronic means between the client and his or her lawyer.

§ 953. Holder of the privilege

As used in this article, "holder of the privilege" means:

(a) The client, if the client has no guardian or conservator.

(b) A guardian or conservator of the client, if the client has a guardian or conservator.

(c) The personal representative of the client if the client is dead, including a personal representative appointed pursuant to Section 12252 of the Probate Code.

(d) A successor, assign, trustee in dissolution, or any similar representative of a firm, association, organization, partnership, business trust, corporation, or public entity that is no longer in existence.

§ 954. Lawyer-client privilege

Subject to Section 912 and except as otherwise provided in this article, the client, whether or not a party, has a privilege to refuse to disclose, and to prevent another from disclosing, a confidential communication between client and lawyer if the privilege is claimed by:

(a) The holder of the privilege;

(b) A person who is authorized to claim the privilege by the holder of the privilege; or

(c) The person who was the lawyer at the time of the confidential communication, but such person may not claim the privilege if there is no holder of the privilege in existence or if he is otherwise instructed by a person authorized to permit disclosure.

The relationship of attorney and client shall exist between a law corporation as defined in Article 10 (commencing with Section 6160) of Chapter 4 of Division 3 of the Business and Professions Code and the persons to whom it renders professional services, as well as between such persons and members of the State Bar employed by such corporation to render services to such persons. The word "persons" as used in this subdivision includes partnerships, corporations, limited liability companies, associations and other groups and entities.

§ 955. When lawyer required to claim privilege

The lawyer who received or made a communication subject to the privilege under this article shall claim the privilege whenever he is present when the communication is sought to be disclosed and is authorized to claim the privilege under subdivision (c) of Section 954.

§ 956. Exception: Crime or fraud

There is no privilege under this article if the services of the lawyer were sought or obtained to enable or aid anyone to commit or plan to commit a crime or a fraud.

§ 956.5. Reasonable belief that disclosure of confidential communication relating to representation of client is necessary to prevent criminal act that lawyer reasonably believes likely to result in death of, or substantial bodily harm to, an individual; exception to privilege

There is no privilege under this article if the lawyer reasonably believes that disclosure of any confidential communication relating to representation of a client is necessary to prevent a criminal act that the lawyer reasonably believes is likely to result in the death of, or substantial bodily harm to, an individual.

§ 957. Exception: Parties claiming through deceased client

There is no privilege under this article as to a communication relevant to an issue between parties all of whom claim through a deceased client, regardless of whether the claims are by testate or intestate succession, nonprobate transfer, or inter vivos transaction.

§ 958. Exception: Breach of duty arising out of lawyer-client relationship

There is no privilege under this article as to a communication relevant to an issue of breach, by the lawyer or by the client, of a duty arising out of the lawyer-client relationship.

§ 959. Exception: Lawyer as attesting witness

There is no privilege under this article as to a communication relevant to an issue concerning the intention or competence of a client executing an attested document of which the lawyer is an attesting witness, or concerning the execution or attestation of such a document.

§ 960. Exception: Intention of deceased client concerning writing affecting property interest

There is no privilege under this article as to a communication relevant to an issue concerning the intention of a client, now deceased, with respect to a deed of conveyance, will, or other writing, executed by the client, purporting to affect an interest in property.

§ 961. Exception: Validity of writing affecting property interest

There is no privilege under this article as to a communication relevant to an issue concerning the validity of a deed of conveyance, will, or other writing, executed by a client, now deceased, purporting to affect an interest in property.

§ 962. Exception: Joint clients

Where two or more clients have retained or consulted a lawyer upon a matter of common interest, none of them, nor the successor in interest of any of them, may claim a privilege under this article as to a communication made in the course of that relationship when such communication is offered in a civil proceeding between one of such clients (or his successor in interest) and another of such clients (or his successor in interest).

FEDERAL RULES OF EVIDENCE

Rule 502. Attorney–Client Privilege and Work Product; Limitations on Waiver

The following provisions apply, in the circumstances set out, to disclosure of a communication or information covered by the attorney-client privilege or work-product protection.

(a) Disclosure Made in a Federal Proceeding or to a Federal Office or Agency; Scope of a Waiver. When the disclosure is made in a federal proceeding or to a federal office or agency and waives the attorney-client privilege or work-product protection, the waiver extends to an undisclosed communication or information in a federal or state proceeding only if:

   (1) the waiver is intentional;

   (2) the disclosed and undisclosed communications or information concern the same subject matter; and

   (3) they ought in fairness to be considered together.

(b) Inadvertent Disclosure. When made in a federal proceeding or to a federal office or agency, the disclosure does not operate as a waiver in a federal or state proceeding if:

(1) the disclosure is inadvertent;

(2) the holder of the privilege or protection took reasonable steps to prevent disclosure; and

(3) the holder promptly took reasonable steps to rectify the error, including (if applicable) following Federal Rule of Civil Procedure 26(b)(5)(B).

(c) Disclosure Made in a State Proceeding. When the disclosure is made in a state proceeding and is not the subject of a state-court order concerning waiver, the disclosure does not operate as a waiver in a federal proceeding if the disclosure:

(1) would not be a waiver under this rule if it had been made in a federal proceeding; or

(2) is not a waiver under the law of the state where the disclosure occurred.

(d) Controlling Effect of a Court Order. A federal court may order that the privilege or protection is not waived by disclosure connected with the litigation pending before the court—in which event the disclosure is also not a waiver in any other federal or state proceeding.

(e) Controlling Effect of a Party Agreement. An agreement on the effect of disclosure in a federal proceeding is binding only on the parties to the agreement, unless it is incorporated into a court order.

(f) Controlling Effect of this Rule. Notwithstanding Rules 101 and 1101, this rule applies to state proceedings and to federal court-annexed and federal court-mandated arbitration proceedings, in the circumstances set out in the rule. And notwithstanding Rule 501, this rule applies even if state law provides the rule of decision.

(g) Definitions. In this rule:

(1) "attorney-client privilege" means the protection that applicable law provides for confidential attorney-client communications; and

(2) "work-product protection" means the protection that applicable law provides for tangible material (or its intangible equivalent) prepared in anticipation of litigation or for trial.

ADVISORY COMMITTEE'S NOTE

This new rule has two major purposes:

1) It resolves some longstanding disputes in the courts about the effect of certain disclosures of communications or information protected by the attorney-client privilege or as work product—specifically those disputes involving inadvertent disclosure and subject matter waiver.

2) It responds to the widespread complaint that litigation costs necessary to protect against waiver of attorney-client privilege or work product have become prohibitive due to the concern that any disclosure (however innocent

or minimal) will operate as a subject matter waiver of all protected communications or information. This concern is especially troubling in cases involving electronic discovery. *See, e.g., Hopson v. City of Baltimore,* 232 F.R.D. 228, 244 (D. Md. 2005) (electronic discovery may encompass "millions of documents" and to insist upon "record-by-record pre-production privilege review, on pain of subject matter waiver, would impose upon parties costs of production that bear no proportionality to what is at stake in the litigation").

The rule seeks to provide a predictable, uniform set of standards under which parties can determine the consequences of a disclosure of a communication or information covered by the attorney-client privilege or work product protection. Parties to litigation need to know, for example, that if they exchange privileged information pursuant to a confidentiality order, the court's order will be enforceable. Moreover, if a federal court's confidentiality order is not enforceable in a state court then the burdensome costs of privilege review and retention are unlikely to be reduced.

The rule makes no attempt to alter federal or state law on whether a communication or information is protected under the attorney-client privilege or work product immunity as an initial matter. Moreover, while establishing some exceptions to waiver, the rule does not purport to supplant applicable waiver doctrine generally.

The rule governs only certain waivers by disclosure. Other common-law waiver doctrines may result in a finding of waiver even where there is no disclosure of privileged information or work product. *See, e.g., Nguyen v. Excel Corp.,* 197 F.3d 200 (5th Cir. 1999) (reliance on an advice of counsel defense waives the privilege with respect to attorney-client communications pertinent to that defense); *Byers v. Burleson,* 100 F.R.D. 436 (D.D.C. 1983) (allegation of lawyer malpractice constituted a waiver of confidential communications under the circumstances). The rule is not intended to displace or modify federal common law concerning waiver of privilege or work product where no disclosure has been made.

Subdivision (a). The rule provides that a voluntary disclosure in a federal proceeding or to a federal office or agency, if a waiver, generally results in a waiver only of the communication or information disclosed; a subject matter waiver (of either privilege or work product) is reserved for those unusual situations in which fairness requires a further disclosure of related, protected information, in order to prevent a selective and misleading presentation of evidence to the disadvantage of the adversary. *See, e.g., In re United Mine Workers of America Employee Benefit Plans Litig.,* 159 F.R.D. 307, 312 (D.D.C. 1994) (waiver of work product limited to materials actually disclosed, because the party did not deliberately disclose documents in an attempt to gain a tactical advantage). Thus, subject matter waiver is limited to situations in which a party intentionally puts protected information into the litigation in a selective, misleading and unfair manner. It follows that an inadvertent disclosure of protected information can never result in a subject matter waiver. *See* Rule 502(b). The rule rejects the result in *In re Sealed Case,* 877 F.2d 976 (D.C. Cir. 1989), which held that inadvertent disclosure of documents during discovery automatically constituted a subject matter waiver.

The language concerning subject matter waiver—"ought in fairness"—is taken from Rule 106, because the animating principle is the same. Under both Rules, a party that makes a selective, misleading presentation that is unfair to the adversary opens itself to a more complete and accurate presentation.

To assure protection and predictability, the rule provides that if a disclosure is made at the federal level, the federal rule on subject matter waiver governs subsequent state court determinations on the scope of the waiver by that disclosure.

Subdivision (b). Courts are in conflict over whether an inadvertent disclosure of a communication or information protected as privileged or work product constitutes a waiver. A few courts find that a disclosure must be intentional to be a waiver. Most courts find a waiver only if the disclosing party acted carelessly in disclosing the communication or information and failed to request its return in a timely manner. And a few courts hold that any inadvertent disclosure of a communication or information protected under the attorney-client privilege or as work product constitutes a waiver without regard to the protections taken to avoid such a disclosure. *See generally Hopson v. City of Baltimore,* 232 F.R.D. 228 (D. Md. 2005), for a discussion of this case law.

The rule opts for the middle ground: inadvertent disclosure of protected communications or information in connection with a federal proceeding or to a federal office or agency does not constitute a waiver if the holder took reasonable steps to prevent disclosure and also promptly took reasonable steps to rectify the error. This position is in accord with the majority view on whether inadvertent disclosure is a waiver.

Cases such as *Lois Sportswear, U.S.A., Inc. v. Levi Strauss & Co.,* 104 F.R.D. 103, 105 (S.D.N.Y. 1985), and *Hartford Fire Ins. Co. v. Garvey,* 109 F.R.D. 323, 332 (N.D. Cal. 1985), set out a multi-factor test for determining whether inadvertent disclosure is a waiver. The stated factors (none of which is dispositive) are the reasonableness of precautions taken, the time taken to rectify the error, the scope of discovery, the extent of disclosure and the overriding issue of fairness. The rule does not explicitly codify that test, because it is really a set of non-determinative guidelines that vary from case to case. The rule is flexible enough to accommodate any of those listed factors. Other considerations bearing on the reasonableness of a producing party's efforts include the number of documents to be reviewed and the time constraints for production. Depending on the circumstances, a party that uses advanced analytical software applications and linguistic tools in screening for privilege and work product may be found to have taken "reasonable steps" to prevent inadvertent disclosure. The implementation of an efficient system of records management before litigation may also be relevant.

The rule does not require the producing party to engage in a post-production review to determine whether any protected communication or information has been produced by mistake. But the rule does require the producing party to follow up on any obvious indications that a protected communication or information has been produced inadvertently.

The rule applies to inadvertent disclosures made to a federal office or agency, including but not limited to an office or agency that is acting in the course of its regulatory, investigative or enforcement authority. The consequences of waiver, and the concomitant costs of pre-production privilege review, can be as great with respect to disclosures to offices and agencies as they are in litigation.

Subdivision (c). Difficult questions can arise when 1) a disclosure of a communication or information protected by the attorney-client privilege or as work product is made in a state proceeding, 2) the communication or information is offered in a subsequent federal proceeding on the ground that the disclosure waived the privilege or protection, and 3) the state and federal laws are in conflict on the question of waiver. The Committee determined that the proper solution for the federal court is to apply the law that is most protective of privilege and work product. If the state law is more protective (such as where the state law is that an inadvertent disclosure can never be a waiver), the holder of the privilege or protection may well have relied on that law when making the disclosure in the state proceeding. Moreover, applying a more restrictive federal law of waiver could impair the state objective of preserving the privilege or work-product protection for disclosures made in state proceedings. On the other hand, if the federal law is more protective, applying the state law of waiver to determine admissibility in federal court is likely to undermine the federal objective of limiting the costs of production.

The rule does not address the enforceability of a state court confidentiality order in a federal proceeding, as that question is covered both by statutory law and principles of federalism and comity. *See* 28 U.S.C. § 1738 (providing that state judicial proceedings "shall have the same full faith and credit in every court within the United States ... as they have by law or usage in the courts of such State ... from which they are taken."). *See also Tucker v. Ohtsu Tire & Rubber Co.,* 191 F.R.D. 495, 499 (D. Md. 2000) (noting that a federal court considering the enforceability of a state confidentiality order is "constrained by principles of comity, courtesy, and ... federalism"). Thus, a state court order finding no waiver in connection with a disclosure made in a state court proceeding is enforceable under existing law in subsequent federal proceedings.

Subdivision (d). Confidentiality orders are becoming increasingly important in limiting the costs of privilege review and retention, especially in cases involving electronic discovery. But the utility of a confidentiality order in reducing discovery costs is substantially diminished if it provides no protection outside the particular litigation in which the order is entered. Parties are unlikely to be able to reduce the costs of pre-production review for privilege and work product if the consequence of disclosure is that the communications or information could be used by non-parties to the litigation.

There is some dispute on whether a confidentiality order entered in one case is enforceable in other proceedings. *See generally Hopson v. City of Baltimore,* 232 F.R.D. 228 (D. Md. 2005), for a discussion of this case law. The rule provides that when a confidentiality order governing the consequences of disclosure in that case is entered in a federal proceeding, its terms are enforceable against non-parties in any federal or state proceeding. For example, the court order may provide for return of documents without waiver irrespective of the care taken by the disclosing party; the rule contemplates enforcement of "claw-back" and "quick peek" arrangements as a way to avoid the excessive costs of pre-production review for privilege and work product. *See Zubulake v. UBS Warburg LLC,* 216 F.R.D. 280, 290 (S.D.N.Y. 2003) (noting that parties may enter into "so-called 'claw-back' agreements that allow the parties to forego privilege review altogether in favor of an agreement to return inadvertently produced privilege documents"). The rule provides a party with a predictable protection from a court order—predictability that is needed to allow the party to plan in advance to limit the prohibitive costs of privilege and work product review and retention.

Under the rule, a confidentiality order is enforceable whether or not it memorializes an agreement among the parties to the litigation. Party agreement should not be a condition of enforceability of a federal court's order.

Under subdivision (d), a federal court may order that disclosure of privileged or protected information "in connection with" a federal proceeding does not result in waiver. But subdivision (d) does not allow the federal court to enter an order determining the waiver effects of a separate disclosure of the same information in other proceedings, state or federal. If a disclosure has been made in a state proceeding (and is not the subject of a state-court order on waiver), then subdivision (d) is inapplicable. Subdivision (c) would govern the federal court's determination whether the state-court disclosure waived the privilege or protection in the federal proceeding.

Subdivision (e). Subdivision (e) codifies the well-established proposition that parties can enter an agreement to limit the effect of waiver by disclosure between or among them. Of course such an agreement can bind only the parties to the agreement. The rule makes clear that if parties want protection against non-parties from a finding of waiver by disclosure, the agreement must be made part of a court order.

Subdivision (f). The protections against waiver provided by Rule 502 must be applicable when protected communications or information disclosed in federal proceedings are subsequently offered in state proceedings. Otherwise the holders of protected communications and information, and their lawyers, could not rely on the protections provided by the Rule, and the goal of limiting costs in discovery would be substantially undermined. Rule 502(f) is intended to resolve any potential tension between the provisions of Rule 502 that apply to state proceedings and the possible limitations on the applicability of the Federal Rules of Evidence otherwise provided by Rules 101 and 1101.

The rule is intended to apply in all federal court proceedings, including court-annexed and court-ordered arbitrations, without regard to any possible limitations of Rules 101 and 1101. This provision is not intended to raise an inference about the applicability of any other rule of evidence in arbitration proceedings more generally.

The costs of discovery can be equally high for state and federal causes of action, and the rule seeks to limit those costs in all federal proceedings, regardless of whether the claim arises under state or federal law. Accordingly, the rule applies to state law causes of action brought in federal court.

Subdivision (g). The rule's coverage is limited to attorney-client privilege and work product. The operation of waiver by disclosure, as applied to other evidentiary privileges, remains a question of federal common law. Nor does the rule purport to apply to the Fifth Amendment privilege against compelled self-incrimination.

The definition of work product "materials" is intended to include both tangible and intangible information. *See In re Cendant Corp. Sec. Litig.*, 343 F.3d 658, 662 (3d Cir. 2003) ("work product protection extends to both tangible and intangible work product").

RULE 503. LAWYER–CLIENT PRIVILEGE
[NOT ENACTED.]

(a) Definitions. As used in this rule:

(1) A "client" is a person, public officer, or corporation, association, or other organization or entity, either public or private, who is rendered professional legal services by a lawyer, or who consults a lawyer with a view to obtaining professional legal services from him.

(2) A "lawyer" is a person authorized, or reasonably believed by the client to be authorized, to practice law in any state or nation.

(3) A "representative of the lawyer" is one employed to assist the lawyer in the rendition of professional legal services.

(4) A communication is "confidential" if not intended to be disclosed to third persons other than those to whom disclosure is in furtherance of the rendition of professional legal services to the client or those reasonably necessary for the transmission of the communication.

(b) General rule of privilege. A client has a privilege to refuse to disclose and to prevent any other person from disclosing confidential communications made for the purpose of facilitating the rendition of professional legal services to the client, (1) between himself or his representative and his lawyer or his lawyer's representative, or (2) between his lawyer and the lawyer's representative, or (3) by him or his lawyer to a lawyer representing another in a matter of common interest, or (4) between representatives of the client or between the client and a representative of the client, or (5) between lawyers representing the client.

(c) Who may claim the privilege. The privilege may be claimed by the client, his guardian or conservator, the personal representative of a deceased client, or the successor, trustee, or similar representative of a corporation, association, or other organization, whether or not in existence. The person who was the lawyer at the time of the communication may claim the privilege but only on behalf of the client. His authority to do so is presumed in the absence of evidence to the contrary.

(d) Exceptions. There is no privilege under this rule:

(1) Furtherance of crime or fraud. If the services of the lawyer were sought or obtained to enable or aid anyone to commit or plan to commit what the client knew or reasonably should have known to be a crime or fraud; or

(2) Claimants through same deceased client. As to a communication relevant to an issue between parties who claim through the same deceased client, regardless of whether the claims are by testate or intestate succession or by *inter vivos* transaction; or

(3) Breach of duty by lawyer or client. As to a communication relevant to an issue of breach of duty by the lawyer to his client or by the client to his lawyer; or

(4) Document attested by lawyer. As to a communication relevant to an issue concerning an attested document to which the lawyer is an attesting witness; or

(5) Joint clients. As to a communication relevant to a matter of common interest between two or more clients if the communication was made by any of them to a lawyer retained or consulted in common, when offered in an action between any of the clients.

Advisory Committee's Note

Subdivision (a). (1) The definition of "client" includes governmental bodies, Connecticut Mutual Life Ins. Co. v. Shields, 18 F.R.D. 448 (S.D.N.Y. 1955); People ex rel. Department of Public Works v. Glen Arms Estate, Inc., 230 Cal.App.2d 841, 41 Cal.Rptr. 303 (1964); Rowley v. Ferguson, 48 N.E.2d 243 (Ohio App.1942); and corporations, Radiant Burners, Inc. v. American Gas Assn., 320 F.2d 314 (7th Cir.1963). *Contra,* Gardner, A Personal Privilege for Communications of Corporate Clients—Paradox or Public Policy, 40 U.Det.L.J. 299, 323, 376 (1963). The definition also extends the status of client to one consulting a lawyer preliminarily with a view to retaining him, even though actual employment does not result. McCormick, § 92, p. 184. The client need not be involved in litigation; the rendition of legal service or advice under any circumstances suffices. 8 Wigmore § 2294 (McNaughton Rev.1961). The services must be professional legal services; purely business or personal matters do not qualify. McCormick § 92, p. 184.

The rule contains no definition of "representative of the client." In the opinion of the Advisory Committee, the matter is better left to resolution by decision on a case-by-case basis. The most restricted position is the "control group" test, limiting the category to persons with authority to seek and act upon legal advice for the client. See, *e.g.,* City of Philadelphia v. Westinghouse Electric Corp., 210 F.Supp. 483 (E.D.Pa.1962), mandamus and prohibition denied *sub nom.* General Electric Co. v. Kirkpatrick, 312 F.2d 742 (3d Cir.), cert. denied 372 U.S. 943, 83 S.Ct. 937, 9 L.Ed.2d 969; Garrison v. General Motors Corp., 213 F.Supp. 515 (S.D.Cal.1963); Hogan v. Zletz, 43 F.R.D. 308 (N.D.Okla.1967), aff'd *sub nom.* Natta v. Hogan, 392 F.2d 686 (10th Cir.1968); Day v. Illinois Power Co., 50 Ill.App.2d 52, 199 N.E.2d 802 (1964). Broader formulations are found in other decisions. See, *e.g.,* United States v. United

Shoe Machinery Corp., 89 F.Supp. 357 (D.Mass.1950); Zenith Radio Corp. v. Radio Corp. of America, 121 F.Supp. 792 (D.Del.1954); Harper & Row Publishers, Inc. v. Decker, 423 F.2d 487 (7th Cir.1970), aff'd without opinion by equally divided court 400 U.S. 955, 91 S.Ct. 351, 27 L.Ed.2d 263 (1971), reh. denied 401 U.S. 950, 91 S.Ct. 917, 28 L.Ed.2d 234; D.I. Chadbourne, Inc. v. Superior Court, 60 Cal.2d 723, 36 Cal.Rptr. 468, 388 P.2d 700 (1964). Cf. Rucker v. Wabash R. Co., 418 F.2d 146 (7th Cir.1969). See generally, Simon, The Attorney–Client Privilege as Applied to Corporations, 65 Yale L.J. 953, 956–966 (1956); Note, Attorney–Client Privilege for Corporate Clients: The Control Group Test, 84 Harv.L.Rev. 424 (1970).

The status of employees who are used in the process of communicating, as distinguished from those who are parties to the communication, is treated in paragraph (4) of subdivision (a) of the rule.

(2) A "lawyer" is a person licensed to practice law in any state or nation. There is no requirement that the licensing state or nation recognize the attorney-client privilege, thus avoiding excursions into conflict of laws questions. "Lawyer" also includes a person reasonably believed to be a lawyer. For similar provisions, see California Evidence Code § 950.

(3) The definition of "representative of the lawyer" recognizes that the lawyer may, in rendering legal services, utilize the services of assistants in addition to those employed in the process of communicating. Thus the definition includes an expert employed to assist in rendering legal advice. United States v. Kovel, 296 F.2d 918 (2d Cir.1961) (accountant). Cf. Himmelfarb v. United States, 175 F.2d 924 (9th Cir.1949). It also includes an expert employed to assist in the planning and conduct of litigation, though not one employed to testify as a witness. Lalance & Grosjean Mfg. Co. v. Haberman Mfg. Co., 87 F. 563 (S.D.N.Y.1898), and see revised Civil Rule 26(b)(4). The definition does not, however, limit "representative of the lawyer" to experts. Whether his compensation is derived immediately from the lawyer or the client is not material.

(4) The requisite confidentiality of communication is defined in terms of intent. A communication made in public or meant to be relayed to outsiders or which is divulged by the client to third persons can scarcely be considered confidential. McCormick § 95. The intent is inferable from the circumstances. Unless intent to disclose is apparent, the attorney-client communication is confidential. Taking or failing to take precautions may be considered as bearing on intent.

Practicality requires that some disclosure be allowed beyond the immediate circle of lawyer-client and their representatives without impairing confidentiality. Hence the definition allows disclosure to persons "to whom disclosure is in furtherance of the rendition of professional legal services to the client," contemplating those in such relation to the client as "spouse, parent, business associate, or joint client." Comment, California Evidence Code § 952.

Disclosure may also be made to persons "reasonably necessary for the transmission of the communication," without loss of confidentiality.

Subdivision (b) sets forth the privilege, using the previously defined terms: client, lawyer, representative of the lawyer, and confidential communication.

Substantial authority has in the past allowed the eavesdropper to testify to overheard privileged conversations and has admitted intercepted privileged letters. Today, the evolution of more sophisticated techniques of eavesdropping and interception calls for abandonment of this position. The rule accordingly adopts a policy of protection against these kinds of invasion of the privilege.

The privilege extends to communications (1) between client or his representative and lawyer or his representative, (2) between lawyer and lawyer's representative, (3) by client or his lawyer to a lawyer representing another in a matter of common interest, (4) between representatives of the client or the client and a representative of the client, and (5) between lawyers representing the client. All these communications must be specifically for the purpose of obtaining legal services for the client; otherwise the privilege does not attach.

The third type of communication occurs in the "joint defense" or "pooled information" situation, where different lawyers represent clients who have some interests in common. In Chahoon v. Commonwealth, 62 Va. 822 (1871), the court said that the various clients might have retained one attorney to represent all; hence everything said at a joint conference was privileged, and one of the clients could prevent another from disclosing what the other had himself said. The result seems to be incorrect in overlooking a frequent reason for retaining different attorneys by the various clients, namely actually or potentially conflicting interests in addition to the common interest which brings them together. The needs of these cases seem better to be met by allowing each client a privilege as to his own statements. Thus if all resist disclosure, none will occur. Continental Oil Co. v. United States, 330 F.2d 347 (9th Cir.1964). But, if for reasons of his own, a client wishes to disclose his own statements made at the joint conference, he should be permitted to do so, and the rule is to that effect. The rule does not apply to situations where there is no common interest to be promoted by a joint consultation, and the parties meet on a purely adversary basis. Vance v. State, 190 Tenn. 521, 230 S.W.2d 987 (1950), cert. denied 339 U.S. 988, 70 S.Ct. 1010, 94 L.Ed. 1389. Cf. Hunydee v. United States, 355 F.2d 183 (9th Cir.1965).

Subdivision (c). The privilege is, of course, that of the client, to be claimed by him or by his personal representative. The successor of a dissolved corporate client may claim the privilege. California Evidence Code § 953; New Jersey Evidence Rule 26(1). *Contra,* Uniform Rule 26(1).

The lawyer may not claim the privilege on his own behalf. However, he may claim it on behalf of the client. It is assumed that the ethics of the profession will require him to do so except under most unusual circumstances. American Bar Association, Canons of Professional Ethics, Canon 37. His authority to make the claim is presumed unless there is evidence to the contrary, as would be the case if the client were now a party to litigation in which the question arose and were represented by other counsel. Ex parte Lipscomb, 111 Tex. 409, 239 S.W. 1101 (1922).

Subdivision (d) in general incorporates well established exceptions.

(1) The privilege does not extend to advice in aid of future wrongdoing. 8 Wigmore § 2298 (McNaughton Rev.1961). The wrongdoing need not be that of the client. The provision that the client knew or reasonably should have known of the criminal or fraudulent nature of the act is designed to protect the client who is erroneously advised that a proposed action is within the law. No preliminary finding that sufficient evidence aside from the communication has been introduced to warrant a finding that the services were sought to enable the commission of a wrong is required. Cf. Clark v. United States, 289 U.S. 1, 15–16, 53 S.Ct. 465, 77 L.Ed. 993 (1933); Uniform Rule 26(2)(a). While any general exploration of what transpired between attorney and client would, of course, be inappropriate, it is wholly feasible, either at the discovery stage or during trial, so to focus the inquiry by specific questions as to avoid any broad inquiry into attorney-client communications. Numerous cases reflect this approach.

(2) Normally the privilege survives the death of the client and may be asserted by his representative. Subdivision (c), *supra*. When, however, the identity of the person who steps into the client's shoes is in issue, as in a will contest, the identity of the person entitled to claim the privilege remains undetermined until the conclusion of the litigation. The choice is thus between allowing both sides or neither to assert the privilege, with authority and reason favoring the latter view. McCormick § 98; Uniform Rule 26(2)(b); California Evidence Code § 957; Kansas Code of Civil Procedure § 60–426(b)(2); New Jersey Evidence Rule 26(2)(b).

(3) The exception is required by considerations of fairness and policy when questions arise out of dealings between attorney and client, as in cases of controversy over attorney's fees, claims of inadequacy of representation, or charges of professional misconduct. McCormick § 95; Uniform Rule 26(2)(c); California Evidence Code § 958; Kansas Code of Civil Procedure § 60–426(b)(3); New Jersey Evidence Rule 26(2)(c).

(4) When the lawyer acts as attesting witness, the approval of the client to his so doing may safely be assumed, and waiver of the privilege as to any relevant lawyer-client communications is a proper result. McCormick § 92, p. 184; Uniform Rule 26(2)(d); California Evidence Code § 959; Kansas Code of Civil Procedure § 60–426(b)(d) [*sic*].

(5) The subdivision states existing law. McCormick § 95, pp. 192–193. For similar provisions, see Uniform Rule 26(2)(e); California Evidence Code § 962; Kansas Code of Civil Procedure § 60–426(b)(4); New Jersey Evidence Rule 26(2). The situation with which this provision deals is to be distinguished from the case of clients with a common interest who retain different lawyers. See subdivision (b)(3) of this rule, *supra*.

CHAPTER 22

THE WORK PRODUCT DOCTRINE

■ ■ ■

Table of Sections

§ 22.01   NATURE OF THE DOCTRINE

In the course of representing clients, attorneys generate numerous and diverse memoranda. These range from notes on witness interviews to memos on the strengths and weaknesses of the case. Memoranda assessing witnesses are common as are reports on investigations and instructions to paralegals on matters needing further investigation. To encourage attorneys to prepare for trial thoroughly, to investigate the favorable as well as the unfavorable aspects of cases, and to prevent opponents from taking undue advantage of their adversary's industry and efforts, many of these memoranda are protected from disclosure by the work product doctrine.[1] As adopted in the Civil Procedure Code, the work product doctrine achieves these goals by creating two privileges. One, an absolute privilege, provides that "any writing that reflects an attorney's impressions, conclusions, opinions, or legal research or theories shall not be discoverable under any circumstances."[2] The other, a qualified privilege, provides that

---

1. West's Ann. California Civil Procedure Code § 2018.020. Professor Fred C. Zacharias identifies two additional justifications for the work product doctrine: (1) encouraging litigants to confide in their lawyers and to participate in the preparation of legal materials, and (2) limiting the possibility that lawyers will routinely be called to testify, an eventuality that could lead to disqualification and result in delay and expense. Fred C. Zacharias, *Who Owns Work Product?,* 2006 Univ. of Illinois L. Rev. 127, 132–133 (2006).

2. West's Ann. California Civil Procedure Code § 2018.030(a). Courts have construed the work product doctrine to embrace opinions formed by lawyers even if they have not reduced the opinions to writing. A contrary rule would encourage lawyers to document their opinions at great cost to their clients in order to avail themselves of the protection afforded by the doctrine. See Fireman's Fund Ins. Co. v. Superior Court, 196 Cal.App.4th 1263, 1281, 127 Cal.Rptr.3d 768, 782 (2011).

other matter constituting an attorney's work product "is not discoverable unless the court determines that denial of discovery will unfairly prejudice the party seeking discovery in preparing his claim or defense or will result in an injustice."[3]

The Civil Procedure Code does not define "work product." The material embraced by the term is left to judicial determination.[4] Materials of a derivative nature, such as "diagrams prepared for trial, audit reports, appraisals, and other expert opinions, developed as a result of the initiative of counsel in preparing for trial" fall within the definition.[5] Materials outside the doctrine include "(1) the identity or location of evidentiary matter, such as material objects; (2) material objects themselves that constitute admissible evidence; (3) information about prospective or potential witnesses, such as their names, phone numbers, addresses, and occupations; (4) written or recorded statements of prospective witnesses."[6]

The work product doctrine is not limited to writings prepared by an attorney in anticipation of a lawsuit. The doctrine applies as well to writings an attorney prepares in a nonlitigation capacity.[7] The doctrine, moreover, is not limited to materials prepared by the attorney in the course of representing the client. It can include materials prepared by paralegals, such as investigators, at the attorney's request,[8] as well as reports prepared by experts for use by the attorney.[9]

Propria persona litigants, not just lawyers, can claim the work product.[10] Litigants who represent themselves are as entitled as lawyers to protection against attempts by opponents to take undue advantage of their trial preparation efforts.[11] Deputy District Attorneys, however, can not claim the work product doctrine for materials they generate in their official capacity. The holder of the privilege for those materials is the District Attorney.[12]

---

3. West's Ann. California Civil Procedure Code § 2018.030(b).

4. City of Long Beach v. Superior Court, 64 Cal.App.3d 65, 71, 134 Cal.Rptr. 468, 472 (1976).

5. Mack v. Superior Court, 259 Cal.App.2d 7, 10, 66 Cal.Rptr. 280, 283 (1968).

6. Fellows v. Superior Court, 108 Cal.App.3d 55, 69, 166 Cal.Rptr. 274, 283 (1980), quoting B. Jefferson, California Evidence Benchbook § 41.2 (1972).

7. "Neither the text of the statute nor the policy underlying the creation of the absolute privilege warrants a class distinction between the lawyer-negotiator and the lawyer-litigator. There is also no valid reason to differentiate between the writings reflecting the private thought processes of a lawyer acting on behalf of a client at the beginning of a business deal and the thoughts of a lawyer when that business deal goes sour with resultant litigation." Rumac v. Bottomley, 143 Cal.App.3d 810, 812, 192 Cal.Rptr. 104, 105 (1983).

8. Insurance Co. of North America v. Superior Court, 108 Cal.App.3d 758, 771, 166 Cal.Rptr. 880, 888 (1980).

9. See § 22.02 infra.

10. Dowden v. Superior Court, 73 Cal.App.4th 126, 128, 86 Cal.Rptr.2d 180, 182 (1999).

11. Id. at 134, 86 Cal.Rptr.2d at 186. In addition, *Dowden* stresses that the statute creating the doctrine does not limit its benefits to attorneys. Id. But see West's Ann. California Code of Civil Procedure § 2018.020 emphasizing "the rights of attorneys" to prepare cases.

12. People ex rel. Lockyer v. Superior Court, 83 Cal.App.4th 387, 399, 99 Cal.Rptr.2d 646, 654 (2000).

Like the attorney-client privilege, the work product doctrine does not immunize from disclosure tangible items which the client furnishes to the lawyer.[13] Thus, reports prepared by the client or at the client's request before retaining the attorney and subsequently provided to the attorney cannot be excluded under the work product doctrine.[14] A contrary rule would encourage the suppression of unfavorable evidence.[15] On the other hand, materials of a "derivative" or "interpretative" nature, such as the attorney's impressions of the legal significance of such reports, are protected from disclosure by the doctrine.[16]

Although the work product doctrine is framed in terms of materials that are not "discoverable," the doctrine's application is not limited to the discovery stage of a proceeding. An attorney can claim the work product privilege at trial.[17] The doctrine can be claimed also in criminal proceedings.[18] The doctrine, moreover, survives the proceeding for which the work product was prepared[19] and can be claimed in subsequent suits.[20]

Since the work product doctrine was created to protect the attorney, it is the lawyer and not the client who holds the privilege and can claim or waive it.[21] A client, however, may claim the work product privilege if the attorney is not present to claim it.[22] If the material falls within the absolute privilege, the attorney may refuse to disclose it even if the client does not object to the material's disclosure.[23] Indeed, the lawyer may assert the doctrine "even against the client in the context of litigation where adversaries of the client seek discovery [of the work product] for use against the client."[24] The doctrine, however, applies only to the product the attorney generates as a counselor or litigator.[25] Materials

---

13. See § 21.01 supra. See also Jasper Const., Inc. v. Foothill Jr. College Dist., 91 Cal.App.3d 1, 16, 153 Cal.Rptr. 767, 776 (1979).

14. Wilson v. Superior Court, 226 Cal.App.2d 715, 724, 38 Cal.Rptr. 255, 261 (1964). See also Jasper Const., Inc. v. Foothill Jr. College Dist., 91 Cal.App.3d 1, 16, 153 Cal.Rptr. 767, 776 (1979); Bank of the Orient v. Superior Court, 67 Cal.App.3d 588, 598, 136 Cal.Rptr. 741, 747 (1977).

15. See § 21.01 supra.

16. Mack v. Superior Court, 259 Cal.App.2d 7, 10, 66 Cal.Rptr. 280, 283 (1968).

17. Rodriguez v. McDonnell Douglas Corp., 87 Cal.App.3d 626, 648, 151 Cal.Rptr. 399, 410 (1978).

18. People v. Williams, 93 Cal.App.3d 40, 63–64, 155 Cal.Rptr. 414, 427 (1979). By statute, only material falling within the absolute privilege is protected in criminal cases. See West's California Penal Code § 1054.6; Izazaga v. Superior Court, 54 Cal.3d 356, 382, note 19, 815 P.2d 304, 321, note 19, 285 Cal.Rptr. 231, 248, note 19 (1991).

19. Popelka, Allard, McCowan & Jones v. Superior Court, 107 Cal.App.3d 496, 502, 165 Cal.Rptr. 748, 752 (1980).

20. Fellows v. Superior Court, 108 Cal.App.3d 55, 62–63, 166 Cal.Rptr. 274, 278–279 (1980).

21. Lohman v. Superior Court, 81 Cal.App.3d 90, 101, 146 Cal.Rptr. 171, 177–178 (1978).

22. Mack v. Superior Court, 259 Cal.App.2d 7, 10, 66 Cal.Rptr. 280, 282 (1968).

23. Lasky, Haas, Cohler & Munter v. Superior Court, 172 Cal.App.3d 264, 279, 218 Cal.Rptr. 205, 214 (1985).

24. Id. There is no work product doctrine, however, in an action between an attorney and the client if the work product is relevant to an issue of breach arising out of the attorney-client relationship. See § 22.03 infra.

25. Aetna Cas. & Sur. Co. v. Superior Court, 153 Cal.App.3d 467, 478–479, 200 Cal.Rptr. 471, 478 (1984).

prepared by an attorney while acting in other capacities, such as a business agent, do not fall within the doctrine.[26] When a lawyer acts both in an attorney and non-attorney capacity, a judge must review each communication sought to determine whether the material was generated in the attorney capacity. If so, the material falls within the work product doctrine.[27]

A conflict exists between an attorney's duty to release to a client all client papers and property after representation has ended and the attorney's right to refuse to disclose materials protected by the work product doctrine. Rule 3–700 (D) of the Rules of Professional Conduct provides that an attorney "whose employment has been terminated shall * * * promptly release to the client, at the request of the client, all the client papers and property."[28] Relying on this rule, the plaintiff in Metro–Goldwyn–Mayer v. Superior Court[29] asked the judge to order its former attorney to release all papers relating to a merger which had become the subject of the lawsuit. The judge refused on the grounds that the papers were protected from disclosure by the absolute privilege of the work product doctrine, since they contained the attorney's thoughts and impressions. The appellate court reversed. The court noted but refused to resolve the conflict between a lawyer's duties under the rules of professional conduct and the lawyer's rights under the work product doctrine. Instead, the court held that under the circumstances of the case the former attorney had waived his rights under the work product doctrine.[30] The attorney had undertaken to represent the defendants in a separate but related action. Since those clients would have the benefit of the work product the attorney generated while representing the plaintiff, the court held that it would be unconscionable to give them that benefit while denying it to the former client.[31]

QUESTIONS AND PROBLEMS

1. The work product doctrine consists of two privileges. One, an absolute one, protects from disclosure an attorney's impressions, conclusions, opinions, or legal research or theories. The other, a qualified one, protects from disclosure all other matters prepared by an attorney or by others at her direction in the course of representing a client unless a court determines that

---

26. Watt Industries, Inc. v. Superior Court, 115 Cal.App.3d 802, 805, 171 Cal.Rptr. 503, 504 (1981).

27. Wellpoint Health Networks v. Superior Court, 59 Cal.App.4th 110, 123, 68 Cal.Rptr.2d 844, 852 (1997). Accord: 2,022 Ranch, L.L.C. v. Superior Court, 113 Cal.App.4th 1377, 1398, 7 Cal.Rptr.3d 197, 213 (2003).

28. Rule 3–700 (D), Rules of Professional Conduct of the State Bar of California <www.calbar. ca.gov/state/calbar/calbar_generic.jsp?sImagePath=Current_Rules.gif & sCategoryPath=/Home/ Attorney% 20Resources/Rules% 20% 26% 20Regulations/Rules% 20of% 20Professional% 20Con-duct&sFileType=HTML&sCatHtmlPath=html/RPC_Current-Rules-3-700.html> (January 2008).

29. 25 Cal.App.4th 242, 30 Cal.Rptr.2d 371 (1994).

30. Id. at 249, 30 Cal.Rptr.2d at 376.

31. Id.

denial of discovery would unfairly prejudice the party seeking discovery. True or false?

2.　Describe the kinds of materials held to be outside the work product doctrine.

3.　Unlike the attorney-client privilege, the work product doctrine does immunize from discovery tangible items which the client furnishes to the attorney. Accordingly, a mechanic's report prepared before the client's consultation with the lawyer warning the client that the brakes could fail is immunized from discovery if the client gives the report to the lawyer. True or false?

4.　The work product doctrine is not limited to the discovery stage of a proceeding. It can be claimed at trial in both civil and criminal cases. True or false?

§ 22.02　PARTICULAR APPLICATIONS

Witness statements. Statements by percipient witnesses are not protected by the attorney-client privilege because that privilege protects only confidential communications between the client and the attorney.[1] Nor are such statements protected by the work product doctrine if they merely reflect what a person said during an interview.[2] To be protected under the doctrine, witness statements must be "derivative" or "interpretative" in nature.[3] They must include the attorney's impressions, including the legal significance, of a percipient witness's statement.[4] Those impressions, however, are absolutely privileged.[5] Thus, even the opponent's claim of "unfair prejudice" or "injustice" will not override an attorney's right to decline answering interrogatories asking her to describe "the nature and extent of the testimony" of the witnesses the attorney plans to call.[6]

Witness lists. Compelling an attorney to disclose the identity and location of persons who possess relevant information does not violate the work product doctrine.[7] Persons who possess relevant knowledge do not belong to a party, and their disclosure will not reveal the lawyer's

---

1.　See § 21.01 supra.

2.　People ex rel. Lockyer v. Superior Court, 83 Cal.App.4th 387, 398, 99 Cal.Rptr.2d 646, 654 (2000).

3.　Rodriguez v. McDonnell Douglas Corp., 87 Cal.App.3d 626, 647–648, 151 Cal.Rptr. 399, 410 (1978).

4.　Id.

5.　City of Long Beach v. Superior Court, 64 Cal.App.3d 65, 80, 134 Cal.Rptr. 468, 478 (1976).

6.　Id. Whether witness statements that are prepared by a lawyer but that do not include the lawyer's assessment of the witnesses should be protected from disclosure by the qualified privilege is unsettled. In Coito v. Superior Court, 106 Cal.Rptr.3d 342 (2010), a majority of the California Court of Appeal declined to extend the qualified privilege to these statements. Id. at 351. The dissenter, however, would extend the privilege to such statements because their very existence is due to "the attorney's initiative and efforts." Id. at 361. Whether the majority or the dissenter is right will be decided by the California Supreme Court which in June 2010 granted the petition to review the case. 110 Cal.Rptr.3d 462, 232 P.3d 97 (2010).

7.　City of Long Beach v. Superior Court, 64 Cal.App.3d 65, 73, 134 Cal.Rptr. 468, 473 (1976).

strategy. However, compelling a lawyer to disclose the identity of witnesses the lawyer intends to call at trial violates the qualified privilege of the work product doctrine.[8] "The decision to call or not to call a witness is made after consideration of the strengths and weaknesses of a case and the legal theory chosen by the attorney. Selection of the witnesses through whom the attorney wishes to present his or her case is an intimate part of the attorney's mental processes."[9] A court, however, may order the parties to exchange witness lists in a trial setting conference.[10] Because discovery has ended by that time, such an order does not undermine the goal of encouraging lawyers to prepare for trial thoroughly and is necessary for the efficient management of the court's calendar.[11]

Compelling a lawyer to disclose during discovery the identity of potential witnesses interviewed by the lawyer also violates the qualified work product privilege.[12] Such a disclosure would "necessarily reflect counsel's evaluation of the case by revealing which witnesses or persons who claimed knowledge of the [case] counsel deemed important enough to interview."[13] Moreover, compelling the lawyer to disclose the notes the lawyer took during the witness interviews would violate the absolute work product privilege, if the notes would reveal the lawyer's " 'impressions, conclusions, opinions, or legal research or theories.' "[14] On the other hand, forcing the lawyer to disclose statements independently prepared by potential witnesses would not violate the work product or attorney-client privileges, as merely turning over such statements to a lawyer does not bring them within the privileges.[15]

Expert reports. Earlier, we saw that, as a rule, expert reports prepared at counsel's request are not protected from disclosure by the attorney-client privilege.[16] Whether such reports are entitled to protection under this privilege depends on whether disclosing the report would reveal information the client transmitted to the lawyer in confidence.[17] Such

---

8. Id. at 80, 134 Cal.Rptr. at 477.

9. In re Jeanette H., 225 Cal.App.3d 25, 32, 275 Cal.Rptr. 9, 13 (1990).

10. Id. at 36, 275 Cal.Rptr. at 16.

11. Id.

12. Nacht & Lewis Arch. v. Superior Court, 47 Cal.App.4th 214, 217, 54 Cal.Rptr.2d 575, 576–577 (1996).

13. Id.

14. Id. (quoting from the Civil Procedure Code § 2018.030(a)). But see Coito v. Superior Court, 106 Cal.Rptr.3d 342 (2010), where the court held that witness statements taken by an attorney are not protected from disclosure by the work product doctrine unless the statements reveal something significant about the attorney's impressions, conclusions or opinions about the case. The court, however, would permit the objecting attorney to request "an in camera hearing before the superior court * * * to convince [the] court that the [witness] interview or some portion of it should be protected as qualified work product." Id. at 351. Why those portions of a witness statement revealing the attorney's impressions should not be protected by the absolute privilege, as provided by the Civil Procedure Code, is left unclear by the Coito court. The California Supreme Court may resolve this question. In June 2010 it granted the petition to review the decision. 110 Cal.Rptr.3d 462, 232 P.3d 97 (2010).

15. Id. and note 2.

16. See § 21.04 supra.

17. Id.

reports are protected only if disclosure would betray a confidential communication.[18]

The work product doctrine affords expert reports greater protection. Reports prepared by an expert at the behest of an attorney in preparation for trial are part of the attorney's work product[19] even if their disclosure would not reveal any confidential communications. Reports in which experts assist attorneys in preparing pleadings, evaluating evidence, cross examining opposing experts, and other matters that reflect an attorney's mental processes are protected by the absolute privilege of the doctrine.[20] Reports in which experts describe their qualifications and give their opinions on contested issues as experts are protected only by the qualified privilege of the doctrine.[21]

In ruling on a claim that an expert report is protected from disclosure by the work product doctrine, a judge must first determine whether the report falls within the absolute or the qualified privilege. If the report falls within the former category, the claim must be sustained. If it falls within the latter, the claim must be sustained unless the party seeking disclosure satisfies the judge that sustaining the claim will unfairly prejudice the party in preparing a claim or defense or will result in injustice.[22] In ruling on the privilege claim, the judge may order in camera inspection of the report only if the privilege claimant is relying on the qualified privilege.[23] Disclosure is prohibited if the claimant is relying on the absolute privilege.[24]

If, after receiving the report, the attorney designates or calls the expert as a witness, then the work product privilege is lost, and the opposing party is entitled to discover the expert's knowledge and opinions,

---

18. Id.

19. County of Los Angeles v. Superior Court, 222 Cal.App.3d 647, 656, 271 Cal.Rptr. 698, 703 (1990).

20. National Steel Products Co. v. Superior Court, 164 Cal.App.3d 476, 489, 210 Cal.Rptr. 535, 543 (1985).

21. Id.

22. Id. See also In re Tabatha G., 45 Cal.App.4th 1159, 1167–68, 53 Cal.Rptr.2d 93, 98 (1996), a parental termination proceeding in which a psychological study ordered by a mother's attorney to determine how well the child had bonded with the mother was held to be discoverable because withholding the study under the work product doctrine would have subjected the child to the potential trauma of a new study.

23. West's Ann. California Evidence Code § 915(b). For a discussion of the in camera procedures to be followed by the judge in ruling whether material protected by the qualified privilege should be disclosed, see id.

24. West's Ann. California Evidence Code § 915(a). Where a party claims that the information sought is protected from disclosure by both the work product doctrine and the attorney-client privilege, a judge may not compel in camera disclosure of the information in order to determine whether it is protected by attorney-client privilege. See West's Ann. California Evidence Code § 915. Because of this prohibition, the judge should first rule on the attorney-client privilege claim. If the judge sustains the claim, then it may not order in camera disclosure to determine whether the information is discoverable under the qualified privilege of the work product doctrine. See Costco Wholesale Corp. v. Superior Court, 47 Cal.4th 725, 737, note 4, 219 P.3d 736, 743, note 4, 101 Cal.Rptr.3d 758, 767, note 4 (2009). Only if the judge overrules the attorney-client privilege claim may the judge order in camera disclosure of the information to determine whether it is protected under the qualified privilege of the work product doctrine. Id.

including the report.[25] Once the opposing party has undertaken discovery of the expert, the attorney employing the expert cannot revive the work product doctrine and bar unfavorable expert testimony by informing the opposing party that the expert will not be called as a witness after all.[26] But if discovery has not yet been undertaken, the attorney may withdraw the designation of the expert as a witness and reassert the work product doctrine.[27] Moreover, if the expert is withdrawn and continues as a consultant to the attorney, the opposing lawyer may not communicate with the expert or retain the expert as a witness or as a consultant.[28] If the opposing lawyer violates this rule and becomes privy to the other attorney's work product, the offending lawyer must recuse himself, as "there is no way the offending attorney could separate that knowledge from his or her preparation of the case."[29]

In one situation, however, the work product doctrine will not protect from disclosure reports prepared by an expert commissioned by an attorney, even if the expert is not designated or called as a witness. Where the attorney calls other experts who rely on the expert's report in reaching their opinions, the opposing party is entitled to cross examine the testifying experts about the matters, including the privileged information, contained in the report.[30] The Evidence Code expressly provides that an expert may be fully cross examined about "the matter upon which his or her opinion is based and the reasons for his or her opinion."[31]

The provisions of the Civil Procedure Code defining the work product doctrine do not expressly provide for its loss when an attorney designates or calls an expert as a witness. Its loss is nonetheless consistent with the

---

25. Sanders v. Superior Court, 34 Cal.App.3d 270, 277, 109 Cal.Rptr. 770, 776 (1973). Under California law, a party to a civil proceeding may demand an exchange of expert witness information. West's Ann. California Civil Procedure Code § 2034.290. The exchange requires a party to provide the name and address of any expert the party plans to call at the trial. Id. Moreover, the party must include an expert witness declaration if the expert was retained for the purpose of "forming and expressing an opinion in anticipation of the litigation or in preparation of the trial." Id. Failure to include the declaration may result in the exclusion of the expert's testimony. Id.

The declaration must include a summary of the expert's qualifications and of the testimony he or she is expected to give, a representation that the expert will testify, and a representation that the expert will be sufficiently prepared to submit to a meaningful oral deposition regarding his or her testimony. Id. No declaration needs to be filed if the expert is also a percipient witness, such as a treating physician. However, even percipient expert witnesses must be listed in the exchange. Schreiber v. Estate of Kiser, 22 Cal.4th 31, 36, 91 Cal.Rptr.2d 293, 297, 989 P.2d 720, 723 (1999).

A party, however, does not have to list an expert the party does not plan to call at the trial. Id. at 37, 91 Cal.Rptr.2d at 298, 989 P.2d at 724. In effect, by deciding not to call the expert, a party can "bury" the identity and opinion of an expert who does not support the party's position. Id. By contrast, a federal litigant can be required to identify such an expert in limited circumstances. See § 22.04 infra.

26. Lunghi v. Clark Equipment Co., 153 Cal.App.3d 485, 489–491, 200 Cal.Rptr. 387, 388–389 (1984).

27. County of Los Angeles v. Superior Court, 222 Cal.App.3d 647, 656, 271 Cal.Rptr. 698, 704 (1990).

28. Id. at 657–658, 271 Cal.Rptr. at 705.

29. Id.

30. People v. Ledesma, 39 Cal.4th 641, 695, 47 Cal.Rptr.3d 326, 376, 140 P.3d 657, 698 (2006).

31. West's Ann. California Evidence Code § 721.

waiver doctrine for privileges established by the Evidence Code. Waiver of the privileges protecting confidential communications from disclosure will occur under the Evidence Code once the holder irretrievably designates an expert as a witness or calls the expert to testify about matters about which the expert could have learned only in the course of the confidential relationship.[32] However, the work product doctrine is not lost if the expert is not designated or called as a witness. "The opinions of experts who have not been designated as trial witnesses are protected by the attorney work-product rule."[33] Even the expert's identity remains privileged until the expert is designated.[34] "An expert's identity and opinions are discoverable prior to designation only so long as it has become reasonably certain that the expert will testify at trial * * * or if fairness requires it."[35]

Retention of an expert is not indispensable to the doctrine's application. The work product doctrine is not lost even if the expert is not retained, provided the lawyer consulted the expert with the expectation that their communications would remain confidential.[36]

A lawyer's decision not to call as witnesses experts retained to help prepare the case is protected from disclosure by the work product doctrine. In People v. Coddington[37] the defense chose to call only three of seven psychiatrists retained by the defense to help assess the defendant's sanity. Over objection, the trial judge permitted the prosecution to ask the experts whether they were aware that the defense had also asked the other four psychiatrists to evaluate the defendant. The appellate court held that the question was improper: "Work product encompasses the investigation of defendant's mental state to assess both the favorable and the unfavorable aspects of the case. It also encompasses counsel's impressions and conclusions regarding witnesses who would be favorable and those who would not be so. * * * It follows that [a] party's decision that an expert who has been consulted should not be called to testify is within the privilege."[38]

QUESTIONS AND PROBLEMS

1. Witness statements are not protected under the work product doctrine unless they are "derivative" or "interpretative." Accordingly, a witness's statement that contains the attorney's impressions of the value of the witness is protected under the absolute privilege. True or false?

---

32. See § 21.04 supra.

33. Armenta v. Superior Court, 101 Cal.App.4th 525, 535, 124 Cal.Rptr.2d 273, 280 (2002).

34. Hernandez v. Superior Court, 112 Cal.App.4th 285, 297, 4 Cal.Rptr.3d 883, 893 (2003).

35. Id.

36. Armenta v. Superior Court, 101 Cal.App.4th 525, 535, 124 Cal.Rptr.2d 273, 280 (2002).

37. 23 Cal.4th 529, 97 Cal.Rptr.2d 528, 2 P.3d 1081 (2000), cert. denied 531 U.S. 1195, 121 S.Ct. 1199, 149 L.Ed.2d 113, overruled on other grounds, Price v. Superior Court, 25 Cal.4th 1046, 108 Cal.Rptr.2d 409, 25 P.3d 618 (2001).

38. Id. at 606, 97 Cal.Rptr.2d at 596, 2 P.3d at 1142. The court noted that the prosecutor's questions did not violate the attorney-client privilege because the prosecutor did not ask for any confidential communications between the client and the nontestifying experts. Id. at 605, 97 Cal.Rptr.2d at 595, 2 P.3d at 1142.

2.   The attorney-client privilege protects from disclosure expert reports prepared at counsel's request if disclosure would reveal information which the client gave to the lawyer in confidence. The work product doctrine is broader. It protects such reports even if their disclosure would not reveal confidential communications. True or false?

3.   If after receiving the report the lawyer designates the expert as a witness, the work product doctrine is lost and the opposing party can discover the report. True or false?

§ 22.03   WAIVER, EXCEPTIONS, SEARCH WARRANTS, AND BURDEN OF PROOF

Waiver. As we have seen, reports prepared by experts for attorneys in preparation of trial are protected from disclosure by the work product doctrine.[1] The protection, however, is lost if after receiving the report the attorney designates or calls the expert as a witness.[2]

Like privileges for confidential communications, the work product doctrine can also be waived if the attorney, who is the holder, voluntarily discloses or permits another to disclose the contents of a writing protected by the doctrine to persons who have no interest in maintaining the confidentiality of the writing.[3] But where parties or their counsel collaborate on work product, "waiver of [the] privilege by one of the joint holders does not bar the other joint holder from asserting [the privilege]."[4]

Waiver, moreover, will not occur if the attorney discloses the writing to the client in confidence.[5] Because the attorney is the holder, the attorney may assert the doctrine even if the client does not object to disclosing the writing.[6]

Responses by employers to some employment discrimination claims can result in the loss of the work product doctrine as well as the attorney-client privilege. California employment law, like federal employment law, allows employers to respond to claims of a hostile work environment by proof that the employer undertook a timely investigation of the complaints

---

1.   See § 22.02 supra.

2.   Id.

3.   BP Alaska Exploration, Inc. v. Superior Court, 199 Cal.App.3d 1240, 1260–1261, 245 Cal.Rptr. 682, 695 (1988). Although there is no statutory provision governing waiver of work product, the California courts have recognized that the waiver doctrine is applicable to the work product doctrine as well as to the attorney-client privilege. An attorney may waive the work product doctrine by disclosing or consenting to disclosure of a significant part of the work product to a person, other than the client, who has no interest in maintaining the confidentiality accorded by the doctrine. OXY Resources California LLC v. Superior Court, 115 Cal.App.4th 874, 891, 9 Cal.Rptr.3d 621, 636 (2004).

4.   Armenta v. Superior Court, 101 Cal.App.4th 525, 533, 124 Cal.Rptr.2d 273, 278 (2002), quoting from American Mut. Liab. Ins. Co. v. Superior Court, 38 Cal.App.3d 579, 591, 113 Cal.Rptr. 561, 570 (1974).

5.   BP Alaska Exploration, Inc. v. Superior Court, supra note 3, at 1253, 245 Cal.Rptr. at 690.

6.   Id. at 1260–1261, 245 Cal.Rptr. at 695.

and any necessary corrective action.[7] When an employer uses a lawyer to undertake the investigation and then asserts a defense based on the advice given by the lawyer, the employer puts the "adequacy of the investigation directly at issue, and cannot stand on the attorney-client privilege or the work product doctrine to preclude a thorough examination of its adequacy. The defendant cannot have it both ways. If it chooses this course, it does so with the understanding that the attorney-client privilege and the work product doctrine are thereby waived."[8] But where an employer uses a nonattorney to conduct the investigation, the employer does not waive the protections which the attorney-client privilege and the work product doctrine accord to communications between the investigator and the employer's attorney. These communications are entitled to protection from disclosure to the extent they fall within the attorney-client privilege or the work product doctrine.[9]

Like the holders of other privileges, the holder of the work product privilege can also waive it by consciously relinquishing its protection or by failing to claim the privilege when the holder has the legal standing and opportunity to claim it.[10] The Civil Procedure Code specifically provides that a party's failure to respond timely to an inspection demand waives any objection to the demand, including objections based on privileges or the work product doctrine.[11]

Waiver, however, will not occur when counsel inadvertently disclose information protected by the work product doctrine. In Rico v. Mitsubishi Motors Corp.[12] the plaintiff's lawyers, during the course of a deposition, came to possess a document prepared by one of the defendant's lawyers. Because the document contained the lawyer's assessment of the defense expert witnesses, the document was protected from disclosure by the absolute privilege of the work product doctrine. Although it was unclear how the plaintiffs' lawyers came to possess the document (the plaintiffs' lawyers claimed that the court reporter provided them with the document; the defendant's lawyer claimed that the document was removed from his briefcase while he was out of the room where the deposition took place), the California Supreme Court proceeded on the assumption that the document had been inadvertently disclosed. In these circumstances, the court held, the lawyer receiving the privileged materials has an ethical obligation to refrain from examining the materials more than is necessary to establish their confidential nature and to notify opposing counsel that he or she possesses the materials.[13] Lawyers who violate this ethical

---

7. Wellpoint Health Networks v. Superior Court, 59 Cal.App.4th 110, 125–126, 68 Cal.Rptr.2d 844, 854–855 (1997).

8. Id. at 128–129, 68 Cal.Rptr.2d at 856.

9. Kaiser Foundation Hosp. v. Superior Court, 66 Cal.App.4th 1217, 1228, 78 Cal.Rptr.2d 543, 550 (1998).

10. Id. See also West's Ann. California Evidence Code § 20.05.

11. See West's Ann. California Civil Procedure Code § 2031.300.

12. 42 Cal.4th 807, 171 P.3d 1092, 68 Cal.Rptr.3d 758 (2007).

13. "When a lawyer who receives materials that obviously appear to be subject to an attorney-client privilege or otherwise clearly appear to be confidential and privileged and where it is

constraint and use the confidential information may be disqualified from continuing to represent their clients.[14]

Exceptions. The Civil Procedure Code provides three exceptions to the work product doctrine. "In an action between an attorney and his or her client or former client, no work product privilege * * * exists if the work product is relevant to an issue of breach by the attorney of a duty to the attorney's client arising out of the attorney-client relationship."[15] This exception complements the provision which creates an exception to the attorney-client privilege for a communication "relevant to an issue of breach, by the lawyer or by the client, of a duty arising out of the lawyer-client relationship."[16]

Second, the state bar may discover the work product of an attorney against whom disciplinary charges are pending when the product is relevant to issues of breach of duty by the lawyer.[17] The client, however, must approve the discovery by the state bar.[18] Client approval is deemed to have been granted whenever the client has initiated a complaint against the attorney.[19]

Third, "when a lawyer is suspected of knowingly participating in a crime or fraud, there is no protection of work product under [the provision creating the working product doctrine] in any official investigation by a law enforcement agency or proceeding or action brought by a public prosecutor in the name of the People of California if the services of the lawyer were sought or obtained to enable or aid anyone to commit or plan to commit a crime or fraud."[20] This exception complements the exception to the attorney-client privilege for confidential communications between clients and attorneys if the services of the lawyer were sought or obtained to enable or aid anyone to commit or plan to commit a crime or a fraud.[21]

---

reasonably apparent that the materials were provided or made available through inadvertence, the lawyer receiving such materials should refrain from examining the materials any more than is essential to ascertain if the materials are privileged, and shall immediately notify the sender that he or she possesses material that appears to be privileged." Id. at 817, 171 P.3d at 1099, 68 Cal.Rptr.3d at 766 (quoting from State Comp. Ins. Fund v. WPS, Inc., 70 Cal.App.4th 644, 82 Cal.Rptr.2d 799 (1999)).

14. Id.

15. West's Ann. California Civil Procedure Code § 2018.080.

16. West's Ann. California Evidence Code § 958.

17. West's Ann. California Civil Procedure Code § 2018.070(a).

18. Id.

19. Id. § 2018.070(c). The state bar's right of discovery is also subject to a protective order, where requested and for good cause, to ensure the confidentiality of the work product except for its use by the state bar in disciplinary investigations and its consideration under seal in State Bar Court proceedings. Id.

20. West's Ann. California Civil Procedure Code § 2018.050. The addition of this exception is not intended to limit an attorney's right to request an in camera hearing as provided in People v. Superior Court (Laff), 25 Cal.4th 703, 716, 107 Cal.Rptr.2d 323, 334, 23 P.3d 563, 572 (2001), to determine whether the materials sought are privileged. West's Ann. California Civil Procedure Code § 2018.060. For a discussion of the *Laff* in camera procedures, see text accompanying note 25 infra.

21. West's Ann. California Evidence Code § 956.

Search Warrants. The issuance of a valid search warrant for the seizure of client files which the lawyer claims are privileged does not substitute for a hearing to determine whether the files fall within the work product doctrine or the attorney-client privilege.[22] The showing required for issuing a search warrant is lower than the showing that is necessary to establish exceptions to the doctrine or the privilege. A valid search warrant may be issued on the basis of a probability, not a prima facie showing, of criminal activity; in contrast, a party opposing the privilege claim must establish a prima facie case of crime or fraud.[23] Moreover, the procedure for issuing a search warrant is ex parte; rulings on privilege claims presuppose an adversarial evidentiary hearing.[24] Accordingly, even before any charges have been filed, an attorney suspected of engaging in criminal activity may assert the attorney-client privilege[25] and the work product doctrine[26] to protect from disclosure materials seized from the attorney pursuant to a search warrant. Where appropriate, a court may use its inherent authority to appoint a special master at court expense to determine the claims of privilege asserted by the attorney.[27]

Burden of persuasion. The attorney claiming the work product privilege has the burden of persuading the judge by a preponderance of the evidence that the material sought falls within the doctrine.[28] In ruling on the claim, the judge may conduct an in camera inspection of the material claimed to be privileged only if it falls within the qualified privilege and the judge is unable to rule on the privilege claim without requiring disclosure of the material.[29]

The party claiming that matter falling within the qualified privilege should be disclosed has the burden of persuading the judge that denial of discovery will unfairly prejudice the party in preparing his claim or defense or will result in an injustice.[30] In ruling on the claim, the judge may conduct an in camera inspection of the material claimed to be

---

22. People v. Superior Court (Bauman & Rose), 37 Cal.App.4th 1757, 1769, 44 Cal.Rptr.2d 734, 741 (1995).

23. Id. In addition to making out a prima facie case showing the facts necessary to demonstrate that the material falls within an exception to the work product doctrine, the party seeking to discover the material must persuade the judge by preponderance of the evidence of the existence of those facts. This is the standard of persuasion that applies when a party claims that material protected from disclosure under the attorney-client privilege falls within an exception to the privilege. See West's Ann. California Evidence Code § 405 (comment).

24. People v. Superior Court (Bauman & Rose), 37 Cal.App.4th 1757, 1769, 44 Cal.Rptr.2d 734, 741 (1995).

25. People v. Superior Court (Laff), 25 Cal.4th 703, 716, 107 Cal.Rptr.2d 323, 334, 23 P.3d 563, 572 (2001).

26. Id. at 718–719, 107 Cal.Rptr.2d at 335–336, 23 P.3d at 573–574.

27. Id. at 736, 742, 107 Cal.Rptr.2d at 350, 355, 23 P.3d at 585, 589.

28. BP Alaska Exploration, Inc. v. Superior Court, 199 Cal.App.3d 1240, 1261, 245 Cal.Rptr. 682, 696 (1988) and cases cited therein.

29. West's Ann. California Evidence Code § 915(b).

30. Fellows v. Superior Court, 108 Cal.App.3d 55, 57, 166 Cal.Rptr. 274, 281 (1980), quoting from B. Jefferson, California Evidence Benchbook § 41.1 (1972).

privileged if the judge is unable to rule on the privilege claim without requiring disclosure of the material.[31]

The party claiming that matter otherwise privileged under the work product doctrine falls within an exception has the burden of persuading the judge by a preponderance of the evidence that the matter is within an exception.[32]

QUESTIONS AND PROBLEMS

1.   The protection afforded by the work product doctrine will be lost if the attorney, who is the holder, voluntarily discloses the contents of the writings protected by the doctrine to persons who have no interest in maintaining the confidentiality of the writings. True or false?

2.   The crime-fraud exception to the attorney-client privilege does not apply to the work product doctrine. True or false?

3.   In ruling on work product privilege claims, the judge may conduct an in camera inspection of the material claimed to be privileged only if the material is protected by the qualified privilege and the disclosure is necessary for the judge to rule on the privilege claim. True or false?

§ 22.04   THE FEDERAL WORK PRODUCT DOCTRINE

Rule 26(b)(3) of the Federal Rules of Civil Procedure provides that a party may not ordinarily discover documents and tangible things that are prepared in anticipation of litigation or for trial by or for another party or its representative (including the other party's attorney, consultant, surety, indemnitor, insurer, or agent).[1] But, those materials may be discovered if they are otherwise discoverable under Rule 26(b)(1) and the party shows that it has substantial need for the materials to prepare its case and cannot, without undue hardship, obtain their substantial equivalent by other means.[2] This provision is similar to the California qualified privilege which permits discovery of an attorney's work product only upon a showing of special need.[3] Under Rule 26(b)(1), parties may obtain discovery of any matter, not privileged, which is relevant to the subject matter involved in the pending action, even if the information sought is inadmissible at the trial, as long as the information appears reasonably calculated to lead to the discovery of admissible evidence.[4]

---

31.   West's Ann. California Evidence Code § 915(b).

32.   Imposing the burden of persuasion on the party claiming the applicability of an exception is consistent with those provisions of the Evidence Code imposing that burden on the party claiming that matter protected under the attorney-client privilege falls within an exception. See West's Ann. California Evidence Code § 405 (comment).

1.   Federal Rule of Civil Procedure 26(b)(3)(A).

2.   Id.

3.   See § 22.01 supra.

4.   Federal Rule of Civil Procedure 26(b)(1).

The Federal Rule also contains an absolute privilege: "If the court orders discovery of those materials, it must protect against disclosure of the mental impressions, conclusions, opinions, or legal theories of a party's attorney or other representative concerning the litigation."[5]

Testifying experts. Separate rules govern the discovery of facts known and opinions held by experts and acquired or developed in anticipation of litigation or for trial.

Mandatory disclosures. Without awaiting a discovery request, a party must disclose to other parties the identity of any expert who may be used at the trial.[6] The disclosure must be accompanied by a written report prepared and signed by the expert containing a complete statement of all opinions to be expressed and the basis and reasons therefor; the data or other information considered by the witness in forming the opinions; any exhibits to be used as a summary of or support for the opinions; the qualifications of the witness, including a list of all publications authored by the witness within the preceding ten years; the compensation to be paid for the study and testimony; and a list of any other cases in which the witness has testified as an expert at trial or by deposition within the preceding four years.[7]

Depositions. A party may depose any person identified as an expert whose opinions may be presented at trial.[8] The deposition, however, may not be conducted until after the written report has been provided to the deposing party, if such a report is required.[9]

Nontestifying experts. If the expert has been retained in anticipation of litigation or preparation for trial but is not expected to be called as a witness, then the facts and opinions held by the expert may not be discovered by deposition or interrogatories, unless the party seeking discovery makes a showing of exceptional circumstances under which it is impracticable to obtain facts or opinions on the same subject by other means.[10]

This provision is "concerned only with experts retained or specially consulted in relation to trial preparation."[11] Accordingly, the provision "precludes discovery against experts who were informally consulted in preparation for trial, but not retained or specially employed."[12]

California practice contrasted. California takes a different approach to the discovery of facts and opinions held by experts. If the expert is irretrievably designated as a witness or called as a witness, both the attorney-client privilege and the work product doctrine are waived.

---

5. Federal Rule of Civil Procedure 26(b)(3)(B).

6. Federal Rule of Civil Procedure 26(a)(2)(A).

7. Federal Rule of Civil Procedure 26(a)(2)(B).

8. Federal Rule of Civil Procedure 26(b)(4)(A).

9. Id.

10. Federal Rule of Civil Procedure 26(b)(4)(B).

11. Id. (Advisory Committee Note).

12. Id.

If the expert is not designated or called as a witness, then discovery of the facts and opinions held by the expert can be resisted to the extent that disclosure would also disclose confidential communications exchanged by the attorney and the client.[13] Discovery also can be resisted under the work product doctrine. In assessing this claim, the judge must distinguish between work product falling within the absolute and qualified privileges. If the former applies, then disclosure of the work product may not be compelled. If the latter applies, disclosure can be compelled only upon a showing of special need.[14]

Nothing in the Federal Rules of Civil Procedure or the California Civil Procedure or Evidence Codes prevents parties from using both testifying and nontestifying experts in preparing their cases. Use of nontestifying experts can afford greater protection to sensitive information. In California this is especially the case where the information falls within the absolute privilege of the work product doctrine, and in federal court where the expert used was not specially retained in anticipation of litigation or trial preparation but was consulted only on an informal basis.

§ 22.05   TREATING EXPERTS LIKE PERCIPIENT WITNESSES

For discovery purposes, should experts be treated differently from ordinary "fact" or percipient witnesses? Assume a case in which Witness A sees the defendant run a red light and strike the plaintiff while he was in the cross-walk. The attorney for the plaintiff interviews Witness A. Nothing in the rules of evidence or professional responsibility would preclude the attorney for the defendant from contacting Witness A ex parte and interviewing her. In the interview, the defendant's attorney would be free to ask Witness A about the information the plaintiff's attorney gave her and about the information she gave to the plaintiff's lawyer. The professional responsibility rules would preclude the defendant's attorney only from contacting the plaintiff without first securing the plaintiff's attorney's permission. Moreover, nothing in the procedural or evidence rules would preclude the defendant's attorney from noticing and taking Witness A's deposition and asking Witness A to disclose the information she and the plaintiff's attorney exchanged in the interview. The defendant's lawyer would also be free to call Witness A in the defense case-in-chief if the plaintiff did not call her.

Experts, as we have seen, are treated differently. For example, California's attorney-client privilege is not limited to confidential exchanges of information between the client and the lawyer. Disclosing such communications to an expert will not result in the loss of the privilege if the disclosure is reasonably necessary to accomplishing the purpose for which

---

13.   See § 21.04 supra.

14.   See § 22.02 supra.

the lawyer was consulted.[1] Accordingly, if the opposing party notices the expert's deposition, the party retaining the expert is entitled to raise the attorney-client privilege to bar the expert from answering any question that would disclose any confidential information transmitted between the client and the attorney. The opposing lawyer may not circumvent the privilege claim by seeking merely to interview the expert. California case law prohibits a party's lawyer from contacting and interviewing an expert who has been consulted by the opposing party lawyer, even if the expert was not retained.[2] A violation of this prohibition can result in disqualifying the offending lawyer and his firm from continuing to represent their client.[3]

California's work product doctrine provides even greater protection to parties and their lawyers who retain experts.[4] The doctrine is not limited to protecting from disclosure confidential exchanges between the attorneys and clients and their experts. Reports prepared by an expert at the behest of an attorney in preparation for trial are part of the attorney's work product even if their disclosure would not reveal any confidential communications.[5] Accordingly, if the opposing party takes the expert's deposition, the lawyer for the retaining party may interpose the work product doctrine to bar the expert from answering any question that would disclose matter protected by the doctrine. As in the case of the attorney-client privilege, the opposing party's lawyer may not circumvent the work product claim by simply seeking to interview the expert. A party is barred from communicating with or retaining the opposing party's experts.[6] Lawyers who violate this prohibition can be disqualified from continuing to represent their clients.[7]

Sound policies justify these limitations. Occasionally, lawyers must disclose to experts information which they have received in confidence from their clients in order to better represent them. A rule that called for the loss of the attorney-client privilege in these circumstances would undermine rather than promote the attorney-client relationship. The work product doctrine promotes similar values. To encourage attorneys to prepare for trial thoroughly and to investigate the favorable as well as the unfavorable aspects of cases, the doctrine protects from disclosure many of the memoranda prepared by lawyers.[8] Both privileges encourage lawyers to consult experts when necessary to represent their clients adequately.

---

1. See West's California Evidence Code § 952.

2. Shadow Traffic Network v. Superior Court, 24 Cal.App.4th 1067, 1080, 29 Cal.Rptr.2d 693, 700 (1994): "We therefore conclude that communications made to a potential expert in a retention interview can be considered confidential and therefore subject to protection from subsequent disclosure even if the expert is not thereafter retained as long as there was a reasonable expectation of such confidentiality."

3. Id. at 1087, 29 Cal.Rptr.2d at 705.

4. See § 22.02 supra.

5. Id.

6. County of Los Angeles v. Superior Court, 222 Cal.App.3d 647, 657, 271 Cal.Rptr. 698, 704 (1990).

7. Id.

8. See § 22.01 supra.

At some point, however, these protections should yield to countervailing policies. The adversarial system is predicated on the assumption that jurors are most likely to reconstruct a past event accurately if the parties are given an opportunity to demonstrate to the jurors why the evidence presented by the other side should be rejected. The tool given to opponents is the right to cross examine their adversaries' witnesses. But the value of cross-examination depends on the information the examiner possesses. As a general rule, cross examiners will not ask important questions unless they know the answers.[9] So unless the cross examiner is given an opportunity to discover formally or informally the information the expert considered or relied upon in reaching an opinion given on direct examination, the value of the cross-examination is seriously diminished. California law strikes a balance between the policies favoring the use of experts as consultants, on the one hand, and as witnesses, on the other. In California both the attorney-client and work product privileges are waived if the privileged information is supplied to an expert who is subsequently irretrievably designated as a witness or called as a witness.[10] It is at this point that an expert is generally treated like an ordinary percipient witness.

A percipient witness can generally be called by any party.[11] If a party designates a percipient witness as a witness but declines to call the witness, the opponent is not precluded from calling the witness. No one "owns" percipient witnesses. In California, the same result obtains when the witness called is an expert. Once the retaining party has irretrievably designated the expert as a witness, the retaining party may no longer rely on the attorney-client privilege or the work product doctrine to bar unfavorable expert testimony.[12] As Professor Steven Easton emphasizes, by designating the expert as a witness, the retaining party has assured the court that the expert has information that can help the fact finders resolve important evidentiary issues.[13] The opponent, therefore, is allowed to offer the information to the fact finders by calling the expert if the retaining party decides not to call the expert after all. In California, however, there is an exception to this rule. If the opponent has not undertaken discovery of the expert, the lawyer for the retaining party may withdraw the designation of the expert as a witness and reassert the work product doctrine[14] as well as the attorney-client privilege if the expert has not

---

9. See Miguel A. Méndez, *Crawford v. Washington: A Critique*, 57 Stanford L. Rev. 569, 570 (2004).

10. See §§ 21.04, 22.01, and 22.02 supra.

11. Some privileges prevent the calling of some percipient witnesses. California examples include the privilege of a married person not to be called as a witness by the adverse party in any proceeding in which the other spouse is a party, and the privilege of the accused not to be called as witness by the prosecution. See § 20.01 supra.

12. See § 22.02 supra.

13. Steven D. Easton, *"Red Rover, Red Rover, Send That Expert Right Over": Clearing the Way for Parties to Introduce the Testimony of Their Opponents' Expert Witnesses*, 55 SMU L. Rev. 1427, 1462 (2002).

14. See § 22.01 supra.

disclosed any privileged information.[15] In these circumstances, the expert reverts to the status of a consultant, and the opponent may not communicate with the expert or retain the expert as a witness or as a consultant.[16] This outcome contrasts sharply with the manner in which percipient witnesses are treated. A party may not prevent the opponent from contacting, deposing, or calling a percipient witness by withdrawing the witness's designation as a witness.[17] The fact the witness might provide damaging testimony is not a ground for preventing the witness from being contacted or deposed, or from testifying. Why experts should be treated differently when their designation as witnesses has been withdrawn prior to discovery by the opponent is not clear. By designating the expert as a witness, the retaining party has in effect vouched for the expert's usefulness in resolving important evidentiary issues. Unfortunately, the retaining party's reliance on the expert turned out to be misplaced. But that party, and not the opponent, should pay the price of miscalculation. That party should be precluded from raising objections based on the attorney-client privilege or the work product doctrine to withhold potentially damaging but helpful evidence from the court.

Federal practice in this area is not uniform. Circuits disagree about the extent to which experts should be treated like ordinary percipient witnesses once they have been designated as witnesses. In his work, Professor Easton surveys the federal decisions and examines the pertinent federal statutes.[18] His recommendations for reform mirror California practice in almost all respects. However, Professor Easton would go further and prohibit a party from reasserting the attorney-client privilege and the work product doctrine simply by withdrawing the expert's designation as a witness.[19]

CALIFORNIA CIVIL PROCEDURE CODE

§ 2018.010. "Client" defined

For purposes of this chapter, "client" means a "client" as defined in Section 951 of the Evidence Code.

---

15. See § 21.04 supra.

16. See § 22.01 supra.

17. Clients are treated differently. The rules of professional responsibility prohibit a lawyer from contacting the opposing party if the party is represented by an attorney. The Fifth Amendment prohibits a prosecutor from calling the accused in the state's case-in-chief or in rebuttal, unless the accused has waived his or her right not to be called as witness.

18. Stephen D. Easton, *Ammunition for the Shoot–Out with Hired Gun's Hired Gun: A Proposal for Full Expert Witness Disclosure*, 32 Arizona L. J. 465 (2000); *Can We Talk? Removing Counterproductive Ethical Restraints Upon Ex Parte Communication Between Attorneys and Adverse Expert Witnesses*, 73 Indiana L. J. 647 (2001); *"Red Rover, Red Rover, Send that Expert Right Over": Clearing the Way for Parties to Introduce the Testimony of Their Opponents' Expert Witnesses*, 55 SMU L. Rev. 1427 (2002).

19. See Stephen D. Easton, *"Red Rover, Red Rover, Send that Expert Right Over": Clearing the Way for Parties to Introduce the Testimony of Their Opponents' Expert Witnesses*, 55 SMU L. Rev. 1427, 1478 (2002).

§ 2018.020.   Policy of the state

It is the policy of the state to do both of the following:

(a) Preserve the rights of attorneys to prepare cases for trial with that degree of privacy necessary to encourage them to prepare their cases thoroughly and to investigate not only the favorable but the unfavorable aspects of those cases.

(b) Prevent attorneys from taking undue advantage of their adversary's industry and efforts.

§ 2018.030.   Writings and written documentation

(a) A writing that reflects an attorney's impressions, conclusions, opinions, or legal research or theories is not discoverable under any circumstances.

(b) The work product of an attorney, other than a writing described in subdivision (a), is not discoverable unless the court determines that denial of discovery will unfairly prejudice the party seeking discovery in preparing that party's claim or defense or will result in an injustice.

§ 2018.040.   Restatement of existing law

This chapter is intended to be a restatement of existing law relating to protection of work product. It is not intended to expand or reduce the extent to which work product is discoverable under existing law in any action.

§ 2018.050.   Participation in crime or fraud

Notwithstanding Section 2018.040, when a lawyer is suspected of knowingly participating in a crime or fraud, there is no protection of work product under this chapter in any official investigation by a law enforcement agency or proceeding or action brought by a public prosecutor in the name of the people of the State of California if the services of the lawyer were sought or obtained to enable or aid anyone to commit or plan to commit a crime or fraud.

§ 2018.060.   In camera hearings

Nothing in this chapter is intended to limit an attorney's ability to request an in camera hearing as provided for in People v. Superior Court (Laff)(2001) 25 Cal.4th 703, [107 Cal.Rptr.2d 328].

§ 2018.070.   Disciplinary proceedings

(a) The State Bar may discover the work product of an attorney against whom disciplinary charges are pending when it is relevant to issues of breach of duty by the lawyer and requisite client approval has been granted.

(b) Where requested and for good cause, discovery under this section shall be subject to a protective order to ensure the confidentiality of the work product except for its use by the State Bar in disciplinary investigations and its consideration under seal in State Bar Court proceedings.

(c) For purposes of this chapter, whenever a client has initiated a complaint against an attorney, the requisite client approval shall be deemed to have been granted.

§ 2018.080. Breach of duty; actions against attorney by client or former client

In an action between an attorney and a client or a former client of the attorney, no work product privilege under this chapter exists if the work product is relevant to an issue of breach by the attorney of a duty to the client arising out of the attorney-client relationship.

FEDERAL RULES OF CIVIL PROCEDURE

Rule 26. Duty to Disclose; General Provisions Governing Discovery

(a) Required Disclosures.

(1) * * *

(2) *Disclosure of Expert Testimony.*

(A) *In General.* In addition to the disclosures required by Rule 26(a)(1), a party must disclose to the other parties the identity of any witness it may use at trial to present evidence under Federal Rule of Evidence 702, 703, or 705.

(B) *Witnesses Who Must Provide a Written Report.* Unless otherwise stipulated or ordered by the court, this disclosure must be accompanied by a written report—prepared and signed by the witness—if the witness is one retained or specially employed to provide expert testimony in the case or one whose duties as the party's employee regularly involve giving expert testimony. The report must contain:

(i) a complete statement of all opinions the witness will express and the basis and reasons for them;

(ii) the facts or data considered by the witness in forming them;

(iii) any exhibits that will be used to summarize or support them;

(iv) the witness's qualifications, including a list of all publications authored in the previous 10 years;

(v) a list of all other cases in which, during the previous 4 years, the witness testified as an expert at trial or by deposition; and

(vi) a statement of the compensation to be paid for the study and testimony in the case.

(C) *Witnesses Who Do Not Provide a Written Report.* Unless otherwise stipulated or ordered by the court, if the witness is not required to provide a written report, this disclosure must state:

> **(i)** the subject matter on which the witness is expected to present evidence under Federal Rule of Evidence 702, 703, or 705; and

> **(ii)** a summary of the facts and opinions to which the witness is expected to testify.

(D) Time to Disclose Expert Testimony. A party must make these disclosures at the times and in the sequence that the court orders. Absent a stipulation or a court order, the disclosures must be made:

> **(i)** at least 90 days before the date set for trial or for the case to be ready for trial; or

> **(ii)** if the evidence is intended solely to contradict or rebut evidence on the same subject matter identified by another party under Rule 26(a)(2)(B) or (C), within 30 days after the other party's disclosure.

* * *

(b) Discovery Scope and Limits.

(1) Scope in General. Unless otherwise limited by court order, the scope of discovery is as follows: Parties may obtain discovery regarding any nonprivileged matter that is relevant to any party's claim or defense—including the existence, description, nature, custody, condition, and location of any documents or other tangible things and the identity and location of persons who know of any discoverable matter. For good cause, the court may order discovery of any matter relevant to the subject matter involved in the action. Relevant information need not be admissible at the trial if the discovery appears reasonably calculated to lead to the discovery of admissible evidence. All discovery is subject to the limitations imposed by Rule 26(b)(2)(C).

* * *

(3) *Trial Preparation: Materials.*

(A) *Documents and Tangible Things.* Ordinarily, a party may not discover documents and tangible things that are prepared in anticipation of litigation or for trial by or for another party or its representative (including the other party's attorney, consultant, surety, indemnitor, insurer, or agent). But, subject to Rule 26(b)(4), those materials may be discovered if:

> **(i)** they are otherwise discoverable under Rule 26(b)(1); and

> **(ii)** the party shows that it has substantial need for the materials to prepare its case and cannot, without undue hardship, obtain their substantial equivalent by other means.

(B) *Protection Against Disclosure.* If the court orders discovery of those materials, it must protect against disclosure of the mental impressions, conclusions, opinions, or legal theories of a party's attorney or other representative concerning the litigation.

* * *

(4) *Trial Preparation: Experts.*

(A) *Deposition of an Expert Who May Testify.* A party may depose any person who has been identified as an expert whose opinions may be presented at trial. If Rule 26(a)(2)(B) requires a report from the expert, the deposition may be conducted only after the report is provided.

(B) *Trial–Preparation Protection for Draft Reports or Disclosures.* Rules 26(b)(3)(A) and (B) protect drafts of any report or disclosure required under Rule 26(a)(2), regardless of the form in which the draft is recorded.

(C)*Trial–Preparation Protection for Communications Between a Party's Attorney and Expert Witnesses.* Rules 26(b)(3)(A) and (B) protect communications between the party's attorney and any witness required to provide a report under Rule 26(a)(2)(B), regardless of the form of the communications, except to the extent that the communications:

> **(i)** relate to compensation for the expert's study or testimony;

> **(ii)** identify facts or data that the party's attorney provided and that the expert considered in forming the opinions to be expressed; or

> **(iii)** identify assumptions that the party's attorney provided and that the expert relied on in forming the opinions to be expressed.

(D) *Expert Employed Only for Trial Preparation.* Ordinarily, a party may not, by interrogatories or deposition, discover facts known or opinions held by an expert who has been retained or specially employed by another party in anticipation of litigation or to prepare for trial and who is not expected to be called as a witness at trial. But a party may do so only:

> **(i)** as provided in Rule 35(b); or

> **(ii)** on showing exceptional circumstances under which it is impracticable for the party to obtain facts or opinions on the same subject by other means.

(E) *Payment.* Unless manifest injustice would result, the court must require that the party seeking discovery:

> **(i)** pay the expert a reasonable fee for time spent in responding to discovery under Rule 26(b)(4)(A) or (D); and

> **(ii)** for discovery under (D), also pay the other party a fair portion of the fees and expenses it reasonably incurred in obtaining the expert's facts and opinions.

(5) *Claiming Privilege or Protecting Trial–Preparation Materials.*

(A) *Information Withheld.* When a party withholds information otherwise discoverable by claiming that the information is privileged or subject to protection as trial-preparation material, the party must:

> **(i)** expressly make the claim; and

> **(ii)** describe the nature of the documents, communications, or tangible things not produced or disclosed—and do so in a manner that, without revealing information itself privileged or protected, will enable other parties to assess the claim.

(B) *Information Produced.* If information produced in discovery is subject to a claim of privilege or of protection as trial-preparation material, the party making the claim may notify any party that received the information of the claim and the basis for it. After being notified, a party must promptly return, sequester, or destroy the specified information and any copies it has; must not use or disclose the information until the claim is resolved; must take reasonable steps to retrieve the information if the party disclosed it before being notified; and may promptly present the information to the court under seal for a determination of the claim. The producing party must preserve the information until the claim is resolved.

CHAPTER 23

THE PSYCHOTHERAPIST-
PATIENT PRIVILEGE

■ ■ ■

Table of Sections

---

§ 23.01 NATURE OF THE PRIVILEGE

The psychotherapist-patient privilege is designed to promote effective diagnosis and treatment by psychotherapists by encouraging full disclosure by patients. It is also designed to enhance research on mental and emotional problems by encouraging full disclosure by research subjects.

> Psychoanalysis and psychotherapy are dependent upon the fullest revelation of the most intimate and embarrassing details of the patient's life. Research on mental or emotional problems requires similar disclosure. Unless a patient or research subject is assured that such information can and will be held in utmost confidence, he will be reluctant to make the full disclosure upon which diagnosis and treatment or complete and accurate research depends.[1]

Accordingly, the Code provides patients and research subjects with a privilege to refuse to disclose and to prevent another from disclosing a confidential communication between the patient or research subject and the psychotherapist.[2] To be privileged, the communication must meet a number of tests.

First, the communication must be between a patient and a psychotherapist in the course of the psychotherapist-patient relationship.[3] A

---

1. West's Ann. California Evidence Code § 1014 (comment). The privilege also protects the patient's right of privacy. Menendez v. Superior Court (People), 3 Cal.4th 435, 448, 11 Cal. Rptr.2d 92, 100, 834 P.2d 786, 794 (1992).

2. West's Ann. California Evidence Code § 1014.

3. West's Ann. California Evidence Code § 1012.

patient is defined as a person who consults a psychotherapist or submits to an examination by a psychotherapist for the purpose of securing a diagnosis or preventive, palliative, or curative treatment of his mental or emotional condition.[4] A person who seeks the help of a psychotherapist to avoid a prison or jail sentence is not a patient.[5] For example, a person who seeks the help of a psychotherapist to obtain probation and thereby avoid a jail term is not a patient; his dominant purpose is neither diagnostic nor therapeutic.[6] In contrast, a person who seeks the help of a psychotherapist as a condition of probation is a patient.[7] "The dominant purpose of probation-conditioned psychotherapy must always be therapeutic, regardless of defendant's motive, because the Penal Code expressly provides that the general purpose of all probation conditions is 'the reformation and rehabilitation of the probationer.' "[8]

Neither is a patient someone who consults a psychotherapist principally for reasons other than the diagnosis or treatment of a mental or emotional condition. Unless the dominant purpose is to seek diagnosis or treatment for a mental or emotional condition, the disclosures a person makes to a psychotherapist are not protected by the privilege.[9] Similarly, a person who is interviewed by a prosecution psychiatrist after having been warned that anything he says can be used against him is simply not consulting the psychotherapist for the purposes contemplated by the privilege. Since he is not a patient, the privilege will not protect his statements to the psychiatrist.[10] A patient, however, can include persons who do not seek diagnosis or treatment but who submit to examination for psychiatric or psychological research purposes.[11]

A psychotherapist is defined broadly. The term includes:

---

4. West's Ann. California Evidence Code § 1011. The physician-patient privilege is broader than the psychotherapist-patient privilege. In addition to embracing a patient's mental or emotional condition, the former also includes the patient's physical condition. See West's Ann. California Evidence Code § 991.

5. People v. Cabral, 12 Cal.App.4th 820, 827, 15 Cal.Rptr.2d 866, 870 (1993) (holding that the accused's letter to a psychotherapist, admitting that he had sexually molested his daughter and requesting admission to a sex offenders' treatment program, was not protected by the psychotherapist-patient privilege because the defendant admitted in the letter that his purpose was to obtain probation).

6. Id.

7. Story v. Superior Court, 109 Cal.App.4th 1007, 1016, 135 Cal.Rptr.2d 532, 539 (2003).

8. Id. In addition, the court stressed that the patient's motive in seeking psychotherapy is not always dispositive. "As a general matter, the dispositive fact is *what* the participants do, not *why*." Id. (emphasis in the original).

9. Id. In In re Tabatha G., 45 Cal.App.4th 1159, 53 Cal.Rptr.2d 93 (1996), a parent opposing the termination of her parental rights had a psychologist determine the extent to which the child had bonded with her. The County Social Services Department then sought to discover the psychologist's study. The parent resisted on the ground the study was protected by the psychotherapist-patient privilege. The reviewing court upheld the juvenile court's ruling that the study did not fall with the privilege. "Here the purpose of the bonding study was to obtain evidence of the existence and nature of a relationship between [the mother and daughter] * * *. In this regard, [the mother] was not a 'patient' for purposes of the privilege because she was not seeking a diagnosis or treatment of a mental or emotional condition nor was any scientific research involved." Id. at 1161, 53 Cal.Rptr.2d at 99.

10. Cf. People v. Henderson, 19 Cal.3d 86, 98, 137 Cal.Rptr. 1, 8, 560 P.2d 1180, 1187 (1977).

11. West's Ann. California Evidence Code § 1011 and comment.

(a) A person authorized, or reasonably believed by the patient to be authorized, to practice medicine in any state or nation who devotes, or is reasonably believed by the patient to devote, a substantial portion of his or her time to the practice of psychiatry. (b) A person licensed as a psychologist under Chapter 6.6 (commencing with Section 2900) of Division 2 of the Business and Professions Code. (c) A person licensed as a clinical social worker under Article 4 (commencing with Section 4996) of Chapter 14 of Division 2 of the Business and Professions Code, when he or she is engaged in applied psychotherapy of a nonmedical nature. (d) A person who is serving as a school psychologist and holds a credential authorizing that service issued by the state. (e) A person licensed as a marriage, family, and child counselor under Chapter 13 (commencing with Section 4980) of Division 2 of the Business and Professions Code. (f) A person registered as a psychological assistant who is under the supervision of a licensed psychologist or board certified psychiatrist as required by Section 2913 of the Business and Professions Code, or a person registered as a marriage, family, and child counselor intern who is under the supervision of a licensed marriage, family, and child counselor, a licensed clinical social worker, a licensed psychologist, or a licensed physician and surgeon certified in psychiatry, as specified in Section 4980.44 of the Business and Professions Code. (g) A person registered as an associate clinical social worker who is under supervision as specified in Section 4996.23 of the Business and Professions Code. (h) A person exempt from the Psychology Licensing Law pursuant to subdivision (d) of Section 2909 of the Business and Professions Code who is under the supervision of a licensed psychologist or board certified psychiatrist. (i) A psychological intern as defined in Section 2911 of the Business and Professions Code who is under the supervision of a licensed psychologist or board certified psychiatrist. (j) A trainee, as defined in subdivision (c) of Section 4980.03 of the Business and Professions Code, who is fulfilling his or her supervised practicum required by subparagraph (B) of paragraph (1) of subdivision (d) of Section 4980.36 of, or subdivision (c) of Section 4980.37 of, the Business and Professions Code and is supervised by a licensed psychologist, a board certified psychiatrist, a licensed clinical social worker, a licensed marriage and family therapist, or a licensed professional clinical counselor. (k) A person licensed as a registered nurse pursuant to Chapter 6 (commencing with Section 2700) of Division 2 of the Business and Professions Code, who possesses a master's degree in psychiatric mental health nursing. (*l*) An advanced practice registered nurse who is certified as a clinical nurse specialist pursuant to Article 9 (commencing with Section 2828) of Chapter 6 of Division 2 of the Business and Professions Code and who participates in expert clinical practice in the specialty of psychiatric-mental health nursing. (m) A person rendering mental health treatment or counseling services as authorized pursuant to Section 6924 of the Family Code. (n) A person licensed as a professional clinical counselor under Chapter 16 (commencing with Section 4999.10) of Division 2 of the Business and Professions Code. (o) A person registered as a clinical counselor intern who is under the supervision of a licensed professional clinical counselor, a licensed marriage and family therapist, a licensed clinical social worker, a licensed psychologist, or a licensed physician and surgeon certified in psychiatry, as specified in Sections 4999.42 to 4999.46, inclusive, of the Business and Professions Code. (p) A clinical counselor trainee, as defined in subdivision (g) of Section 4999.12 of the Business and Professions Code, who is fulfilling his or her supervised practicum required by paragraph (3) of subdivision (c) of Section 4999.32 of, or paragraph (3) of subdivision (c) of Section 4999.33 of, the Business and Professions Code, and is supervised by a licensed psychologist, a board-certified psychiatrist, a licensed clinical social worker, a licensed marriage and family therapist, or a licensed professional clinical counselor.[12]

The psychotherapist-patient relationship is not limited to individual psychotherapists. The relationship can exist between a psychological corporation, a marriage, family, and child counseling corporation, or a licensed clinical social workers' corporation and the patients to whom they render professional services, as well as between those patients and the psychotherapists employed by those corporations.[13]

Second, to be protected, the communication must consist of information, including information obtained by an examination of the patient, that is transmitted between the patient and the psychotherapist in the course of the psychotherapist relationship.[14] The protected information includes the fact of consultation,[15] as well as the patient's identity,[16] as disclosure would identify the patient as having mental or emotional difficulties. Disclosure of a patient's identity can nonetheless be ordered where withholding the identity would deprive a party of her day in court. In Alameda County v. Superior Court[17] the plaintiff sued a county hospital for personal injuries she suffered when allegedly raped by a patient confined in the psychiatric wing. The plaintiff claimed that she was forced by the patient into a men's bathroom where the patient raped her. Because she did not know the identity of the rapist, the plaintiff sought to compel the defendant hospital to provide her with the name of the man found in the bathroom with her at the time of the alleged rape. The reviewing court upheld the trial court's order requiring the disclosure of the patient's identity: no alternative means existed for learning the identity of the man the plaintiff claimed raped her.[18] But even then the

---

12. West's Ann. California Evidence Code § 1010.

13. West's Ann. California Evidence Code § 1014.

14. West's Ann. California Evidence Code § 1012.

15. Alhambra v. Superior Court, 110 Cal.App.3d 513, 518, 168 Cal.Rptr. 49, 52 (1980).

16. Smith v. Superior Court, 118 Cal.App.3d 136, 141, 173 Cal.Rptr. 145, 148 (1981).

17. 194 Cal.App.3d 254, 239 Cal.Rptr. 400 (1987).

18. Id. at 261, 239 Cal.Rptr. at 404.

judge must take steps to minimize the invasion of the patient's privacy interests, for example, by limiting the disclosure only to the parties.[19]

The privilege is not limited to disclosures made by the patient. It includes also the diagnosis made and the advice given by the psychotherapist in the course of the relationship.[20] The privilege, however, does not cover warnings by psychotherapists about a patient's condition when the substantive law governing the case makes such warnings a material issue. In San Diego Trolley, Inc. v. Superior Court[21] the plaintiff sought to recover for injuries she sustained when one of the defendant's trolleys ran over her. At her deposition, the trolley operator admitted that at the time of the accident she had been under psychiatric care for anxiety. Although the psychotherapist-patient privilege protected the patient's communications from disclosure, it did not prevent the plaintiff from discovering whether the psychotherapist had warned the defendant about whether the operator's medical condition impaired her ability to operate the trolley. Under the substantive law governing the personal injury action, such a warning and its disregard would constitute a ground of liability.[22]

Third, under § 1012, the information must be transmitted "in confidence by a means which, so far as the patient is aware, discloses the information to no third persons other than those who are present to further the interest of the patient in the consultation, or those to whom disclosure is reasonably necessary for the transmission of the information or the accomplishment of the purpose for which the psychotherapist is consulted * * *."[23] If the information is shared with persons to whom disclosure is not reasonably necessary to accomplish the purpose for which the psychotherapist is consulted, the information lacks the confidentiality required by the privilege. A number of examples can be found in Roman Catholic Archbishop of Los Angeles v. Superior Court,[24] an action to recover for clerical sexual abuse. The reviewing court upheld most of the referee's findings that communications among church staff members were not within the privilege even when they contained psychological information about some of the priests charged with sexual abuse. Typical of these communications was a memo to the file by the Vicar for Clergy reporting on the treatment recommendations transmitted by a priest's psychotherapist: "This communication does not fall within the 'furtherance of the purpose' rule of Evidence Code section 1012 because the Vicar was not involved in rendering psychotherapy to the priest, nor was he being supervised by a treating psychotherapist."[25]

---

19. Id. at 254, 239 Cal.Rptr. at 406.

20. West's Ann. California Evidence Code § 1012.

21. 87 Cal.App.4th 1083, 105 Cal.Rptr.2d 476 (2001).

22. Id. at 1096, 105 Cal.Rptr.2d at 485.

23. West's Ann. California Evidence Code § 1012.

24. 131 Cal.App.4th 417, 32 Cal.Rptr.3d 209 (2005), cert. denied, 547 U.S. 1071, 126 S.Ct. 1783, 164 L.Ed.2d 518 (2006).

25. 131 Cal.App.4th 417, 454, 32 Cal.Rptr.3d 209, 237.

Under § 1012, information exchanged in confidence between patients and their psychotherapists does not lose its confidential nature simply because it is shared with others to whom disclosure is reasonably necessary to accomplish the purpose for which the psychotherapist is consulted. The information remains protected by the privilege. An example is information provided by the patient which the psychotherapist then shares with a specialist who might be of help in diagnosing or treating the patient. In juvenile cases, however, the courts have been willing to require the limited disclosure of information protected by the privilege. While this might be sound policy, the courts have turned § 1012 on its head by citing the section in support of their holdings.

In Christopher M.[26] is illustrative. A juvenile court referee, as part one of the conditions of probation, ordered the juvenile to turn over to the court all records relating to his medical and psychological treatment. The juvenile objected on the ground that the condition would violate his psychotherapist-patient privilege. The reviewing court disagreed, holding that § 1012 codified "an express exception to the psychotherapist-patient privilege that permits disclosure of otherwise privileged communications between patient and psychotherapist to third persons to whom disclosure is reasonably necessary to accomplish the purpose for which the psychotherapist is consulted."[27] Section 1012, however, is simply inapplicable. The section seeks to retain the protected status of communications between patients and psychotherapist when the communications are shared with third persons to whom disclosure is reasonably necessary to accomplish the purpose of which the patient consulted the psychotherapist. Thus, the question in *In re Christopher M.* was not whether turning over the information to the juvenile court would strip it of its confidential nature but whether the court could compel the disclosure of the information.[28]

The Code rejects the eavesdropper doctrine, which permits individuals who overhear psychotherapist-patient communications to reveal them despite the desire of the patient and the psychotherapist to keep the communications confidential.[29] Patients are protected against the risk of disclosure by eavesdroppers and other wrongful interceptors of confidential information transmitted between patients and psychotherapists by permitting the holder of the privilege to assert it against anyone, including the eavesdropper, who acquires the information without the patient's consent.[30]

If the patient is aware that the means chosen for transmission discloses the information to third persons who are not authorized to be

---

26. 127 Cal.App.4th 684, 696, 26 Cal.Rptr.3d 61, 70 (2005).

27. Id. at 696, 26 Cal.Rptr.3d at 70.

28. Other courts agree with In re Christopher M. "exception." See, e.g., In re Pedro M., 81 Cal.App.4th 550, 554, 96 Cal.Rptr.2d 839, 841 (2000), and cases cited therein.

29. See West's Ann. California Evidence Code § 952, relating to the attorney-client privilege, and comment.

30. Id.

present, the communication is not confidential.[31] Such a communication acquires no protection and can be disclosed by those who overhear it. Since such a communication is beyond the privilege, the patient and the psychotherapist can be compelled to disclose it over a privilege claim. Transmitting the information under circumstances where others could easily overhear it is evidence that the patient did not intend the communication to be confidential.[32] Under the Code, however, communications between psychotherapists and patients are presumed to be confidential.[33] The effect of the presumption is to shift to the party opposing the claim of privilege the burden of persuading the judge that the communication was not made in confidence.[34]

The presence of third persons to further the interest of the patient in the consultation does not strip the information of its confidential nature.[35] Spouses, parents, and others who the patient needs in consulting the psychotherapist or in securing his services may be present. Moreover, disclosing information in the presence of members of a therapy group does not defeat the privilege.[36] " 'Group therapy' is designed to provide comfort and revelation to the patient who shares similar experiences and or difficulties with other like persons within the group. The presence of each person is for the benefit of the others * * * and is designed to facilitate the patient's treatment."[37]

Confidential communications are not limited to those that take place between the patient and the psychotherapist. They also include communications made to third persons—such as the psychotherapist's secretary or a physician or clinical social worker—who serve as conduits for the communication from the patient to the psychotherapist.[38] These communications are confidential because they are reasonably necessary for the transmission of the information.[39]

Confidential communications also embrace revelations by the patient to experts the psychotherapist wishes to use in diagnosing or treating the patient's condition. These disclosures are entitled to protection because

---

31. See West's Ann. California Evidence Code § 954 (comment) relating to the attorney-client privilege.

32. Id. However, confidential communications do not lose their privileged character simply because they are communicated by electronic means or because persons involved in the delivery, facilitation, or storage of electronic communications might have access to their content. West's Ann. California Evidence Code § 917.

33. West's Ann. California Evidence Code § 917.

34. Id. For a discussion of this presumption, see § 20.03 supra.

35. West's Ann. California Evidence Code § 1012.

36. Farrell L. v. Superior Court, 203 Cal.App.3d 521, 527, 250 Cal.Rptr. 25, 28–29 (1988).

37. Id.

38. See West's Ann. California Evidence Code § 952 and comment relating to the attorney-client privilege. With regard to clinical social workers and others used to gather and transmit information from the patient to the psychotherapist, see Luhdorff v. Superior Court, 166 Cal.App.3d 485, 489, 212 Cal.Rptr. 516, 518 (1985).

39. West's Ann. California Evidence Code § 1012.

they are reasonably necessary for accomplishing the purpose for which the psychotherapist is consulted.[40]

Confidential communications also include information provided to the psychotherapist by the patient's immediate family. In Grosslight v. Superior Court[41] the plaintiff sued the parents of a young girl for injuries inflicted by the girl. The plaintiff's theory was that the parents were liable for the injuries because they were aware of the girl's dangerous propensities and had failed to control her behavior. To prove the parents' knowledge, the plaintiff sought to inspect the girl's psychiatric records. The court held that the parents' statements to the girl's psychotherapists were privileged because they were made for the purpose of facilitating her diagnosis and treatment.[42]

QUESTIONS AND PROBLEMS

1. The psychotherapist-patient privilege promotes effective diagnosis and treatment by encouraging full disclosure by patients without fear that their confidential communications with their therapists will be revealed. The privilege, however, is broader and includes communications by research subjects as well as patients in order to enhance research on mental and emotional problems. True or false?

2. For the patient's communications to be protected, the patient must make them in the course of seeking a diagnosis or treatment of a mental or emotional problem. If the dominant purpose is not to seek such diagnosis or treatment, the communications are not protected. True or false?

3. The confidential information protected by the privilege includes the fact of consultation as well as the patient's identity, unless disclosure is necessary to give a party her day in court. True or false?

4. The physician-patient privilege is broader than the psychotherapist-patient privilege because the former includes a patient's physical condition as well as his mental and emotional condition. True or false?

5. The privilege, however, does not include warnings by psychotherapists when the substantive law makes such warnings a material issue. For example, in a personal injury suit a plaintiff may ask a psychotherapist whether she warned the defendant, the owner of a cab that injured the plaintiff, that the cab driver could should not operate the cab while taking tranquilizers the psychotherapist prescribed for a nervous condition. True or false? *goes to notice — patient can't prevent disclosure*

---

40. Id.

41. 72 Cal.App.3d 502, 140 Cal.Rptr. 278 (1977).

42. Id. at 506–507, 140 Cal.Rptr. at 281. Accord: Roman Catholic Archbishop of Los Angeles v. Superior Court, 131 Cal.App.4th 417, 455, 32 Cal.Rptr.3d 209, 238 (2005), cert. denied, 547 U.S. 1071, 126 S.Ct. 1783, 164 L.Ed.2d 518 (2006) (holding that in an action for damages for sexual abuse, a memorandum from a member of the Vicar for Clergy's staff to a priest's psychotherapists containing information about a troubled priest's personal history was "appropriately shielded by the psychotherapist-patient privilege because it was a disclosure reasonably necessary to accomplish the purpose for which the psychotherapist was consulted, namely, diagnosis and treatment of the patient.").

§ 23.02　CLAIMING THE PRIVILEGE

A patient, whether or not a party, has a privilege to refuse to disclose and to prevent another from disclosing a confidential communication between the patient and the psychotherapist if the privilege is claimed by (1) the holder of the privilege, (2) a person authorized by the holder to claim the privilege, or (3) the person who was the psychotherapist at the time the confidential communication was made.[1] The psychotherapist not only has the right to claim the privilege, but is under an obligation to do so if present when disclosure of the communication is sought.[2]

A holder is (1) the patient when he has no guardian or conservator, (2) the guardian or conservator when the patient has a guardian or conservator, or (3) the personal representative of the patient if the patient is dead.[3] If the patient has separate guardians of the estate and of the person, either may claim the privilege.[4] The privilege also may be claimed by a mental health expert who treats or counsels a minor pursuant to Civil Code § 25.9.[5]

The privilege may be claimed only if a holder of the privilege is in existence.[6] Once the patient's estate has been distributed and the representative discharged, the privilege terminates.[7] At that point, "the importance of providing complete access to information relevant to a particular proceeding should prevail over whatever remaining interest the decedent may have had in secrecy."[8]

The holder can waive the privilege.[9]

QUESTIONS AND PROBLEMS

1. The patient, as the holder of the privilege, has standing to claim it whether or not she is a party to the proceeding in which the privilege is claimed. True or false?

2. Unless otherwise instructed by the patient, the psychotherapist has an obligation to claim the privilege if present when disclosure of a protected communication is sought. True or false?

---

1. West's Ann. California Evidence Code § 1014.

2. West's Ann. California Evidence Code § 1015. The psychotherapist, however, may not claim the privilege if no holder is in existence or if instructed not to do so by a person authorized to permit disclosure. West's Ann. California Evidence Code § 1014.

3. West's Ann. California Evidence Code § 1013.

4. See West's Ann. California Evidence Code § 993 (comment) relating to the physician-patient privilege.

5. West's Ann. California Evidence Code § 1014.5.

6. See West's Ann. California Evidence Code § 954 (comment) relating to the attorney-client privilege.

7. See West's Ann. California Evidence Code § 993 (comment) relating to the physician-patient privilege.

8. Id.

9. For a discussion of how the privilege can be waived, see § 20.05.

§ 23.03 EXCEPTIONS

Communications that otherwise would be privileged are not protected from disclosure if they fall within the following exceptions. In construing these exceptions, the California Supreme Court has provided two guidelines. First, the psychotherapist privilege should be construed liberally in favor of the patient,[1] and, second, exceptions to the privilege should be construed narrowly.[2]

1. No privilege exists for communications relevant to an issue concerning the mental or emotional condition of the patient if such issue has been tendered by (1) the patient; (2) any party claiming through or under the patient; (3) any party claiming as a beneficiary of the patient through a contract to which the patient is or was a party; or (4) a plaintiff in an action for the wrongful death of the patient or the parent in an action for injury to a child-patient.[3] If the patient or a party claiming through or under the patient tenders the mental or emotional condition of the patient, fairness requires giving the opposing party information that is relevant to that condition but that otherwise would be shielded by the privilege.[4]

The patient-litigant exception limits the usefulness of the psychotherapist-patient privilege in many cases in which the privilege could otherwise be claimed. A patient's mental or emotional condition is most likely to arise in personal injury actions alleging emotional distress or in criminal cases where the accused relies on such concepts as diminished capacity to disprove the mens rea of the offense charged.[5] Because of the patient-litigant exception, the privilege cannot be claimed in these kinds of proceedings.

The exception does not apply unless the patient tenders a specific mental or emotional condition. A claim for damages for physical injuries does not fall within the exception just because such injuries give rise to pain and other discomforts experienced at a mental level.[6] On the other hand, a claim for damages for emotional distress can tender the patient's mental or emotional condition.[7] In addition, a wrongful death action on

---

1. Roberts v. Superior Court, 9 Cal.3d 330, 337, 107 Cal.Rptr. 309, 313, 508 P.2d 309, 313 (1973).

2. People v. Stritzinger, 34 Cal.3d 505, 513, 194 Cal.Rptr. 431, 436, 668 P.2d 738, 743 (1983).

3. West's Ann. California Evidence Code § 1016. See generally §§ 1016–1027 for the exceptions to the privilege.

4. See West's Ann. California Evidence Code § 996 (comment) relating to the physician-patient privilege.

5. People v. Arcega, 32 Cal.3d 504, 523, note 8, 186 Cal.Rptr. 94, 104, note 8, 651 P.2d 338, 348, note 8 (1982). Unlike the physician-patient privilege, the psychotherapist-patient privilege applies to criminal proceedings. For the reasons why the two privileges are treated differently in this respect, see § 24.03 infra.

6. Roberts v. Superior Court, 9 Cal.3d 330, 339, 107 Cal.Rptr. 309, 314, 508 P.2d 309, 314 (1973).

7. In re Lifschutz, 2 Cal.3d 415, 435, 85 Cal.Rptr. 829, 842, 467 P.2d 557, 570 (1970).

behalf of a patient who kills himself at a mental facility tenders the patient's mental condition, since, among other matters, the medical facility may defend on the ground that the suicide was inevitable given the patient's mental condition.[8]

The patient or party claiming the privilege through or under the patient must be the party who tenders the mental or emotional condition. In Simek v. Superior Court[9] a mother sought the father's psychiatric records in an action to terminate the father's visitation rights. Although the father's emotional stability was relevant in determining his fitness to have visitation rights, the court held that the patient-litigant exception did not apply. By merely resisting the mother's petition to terminate his visitation rights, the father did not tender his mental or emotional condition.[10]

2. No privilege exists for communications between a patient and a psychotherapist appointed by order of a court to examine the patient.[11]

> Generally, where the relationship of psychotherapist and patient is created by court order, there is not a sufficiently confidential relationship to warrant extending the privilege to communications made in the course of that relationship. Moreover, when the psychotherapist is appointed by the court, it is most often for the purpose of having the psychotherapist testify concerning his conclusions as to the patient's condition. It would be inappropriate to have the privilege apply in this situation.[12]

In a criminal case, however, the defendant's disclosures to a court appointed psychotherapist may not be offered through the psychotherapist for the truth of the matters asserted if the defendant's counsel was not present at the time of the disclosures.[13] In re Spencer[14] holds that to allow the jurors to consider the defendant's disclosures for the truth would raise

---

8. Patterson v. Superior Court, 147 Cal.App.3d 927, 931, 193 Cal.Rptr. 99, 101 (1983).

9. 117 Cal.App.3d 169, 172 Cal.Rptr. 564 (1981).

10. Id. at 176, 172 Cal.Rptr. at 568. See also In re Daniel C. H., 220 Cal.App.3d 814, 829, 269 Cal.Rptr. 624, 631 (1990) (Child did not tender his mental condition in a juvenile dependency action by complaining about the father's acts.).

11. West's Ann. California Evidence Code § 1017(a).

12. Id. (comment). But the privilege does apply to communications made by parents to counselors when the counseling stems from a Juvenile Court referral. Eduardo A. v. Juan A., 209 Cal.App.3d 1038, 1041, 261 Cal.Rptr. 68, 69 (1989). Such counseling is not considered to be within the exception. Id.

Moreover, the privilege also applies to communications made by juveniles to therapists as part of a treatment plan ordered by the Juvenile Court. In re Pedro M., 81 Cal.App.4th 550, 554–555, 96 Cal.Rptr.2d 839, 841 (2000). But in assessing the juvenile's compliance with the plan, the therapist may testify about the juvenile's performance so long as care is taken to prevent disclosure of "the details of the therapeutic session * * *." Id. See also In re Mark L., 94 Cal.App.4th 573, 114 Cal.Rptr.2d 499 (2001), where the court held that in a hearing to determine whether a child should be reunited with his parents, over the child's privilege objection, the child's psychotherapist may testify about the progress the child has made while under therapy, so long as the therapist does not disclose the child's communications or the details of the therapy. Id. at 584, 114 Cal.Rptr.2d at 506.

13. In re Spencer, 63 Cal.2d 400, 412, 46 Cal.Rptr. 753, 761, 406 P.2d 33, 41 (1965).

14. Id.

the concerns that moved the U.S. Supreme Court in Massiah v. United States[15] to hold that a defendant's guarantee of counsel was violated when the prosecution was allowed to offer "against him at his trial evidence of his incriminating words, which federal agents had deliberately elicited from him after he had been indicted and in the absence of his counsel."[16]

In addition, in a criminal case a defendant's disclosures to a psychotherapist may not be disclosed over objection when the psychotherapist was appointed under § 1017 to provide information needed to advise the defendant on entering or withdrawing an insanity plea or on presenting a defense based on a mental or emotional condition.[17] If the defendant decides not to tender his mental or emotional condition, the privilege will protect the confidentiality of the communications between him and his court-appointed psychotherapist. But if the defendant does tender the issue—by a plea of insanity, by presenting evidence of his mental or emotional condition, or by raising the question of sanity at the time of the trial—then the communications between the defendant and the court-appointed psychotherapist will lose the protection afforded by the privilege.[18]

A criminal defendant cannot avert waiving the privilege protecting his communications with a psychotherapist appointed under § 1017 by tendering his mental state through other mental health experts. A psychotherapist appointed under § 1017 can be called as a rebuttal witness by the prosecution when the accused tenders his mental state through other mental health experts who rely on the psychotherapist's report to defense counsel.[19]

In one circumstance a criminal defendant's tender of his emotional or mental condition will not result in the disclosure of communications with his psychotherapist. He can prevent disclosure by claiming the attorney-client privilege. When lawyers ask psychotherapists to examine their clients, their clients' revelations to the psychotherapist are protected by the attorney-client privilege, where the psychotherapist's services are reasonably necessary for accomplishing the purpose for which the client consulted the lawyer.[20] Unlike the psychotherapist-patient and the physician-patient privileges, the attorney-client privilege does not include a client-litigant exception.[21] A client-litigant can thus raise questions about

---

15. 377 U.S. 201, 84 S.Ct. 1199, 12 L.Ed.2d 246 (1964).

16. Id. at 206.

17. West's Ann. California Evidence Code § 1017(a). The privilege, however, does not apply when the court, at the request of the defense, appoints an expert in Sexually Violent Predator Act (SVPA) proceedings. The limitation in § 1017(a) is limited to criminal proceedings. SVPA proceedings are considered civil in nature. See People v. Angulo, 129 Cal.App.4th 1349, 1367, 30 Cal.Rptr.3d 189, 201 (2005).

18. Id.

19. See People v. Combs, 34 Cal.4th 821, 863, 22 Cal.Rptr.3d 61, 95–96, 101 P.3d 1007, 1036 (2004).

20. See § 21.04.

21. People v. Lines, 13 Cal.3d 500, 511, 119 Cal.Rptr. 225, 232, 531 P.2d 793, 800 (1975).

his mental capacity to commit the offense charged without losing his attorney-client privilege.[22]

The attorney-client privilege protects not only revelations by clients to experts, such as psychotherapists, whom the attorney desires to use in advising and serving the client, but also the expert's reports to the attorney.[23] But if the defendant calls the psychotherapist as a witness, he waives the attorney-client privilege, and his revelations to the psychotherapist can be received over a privilege claim.[24] Waiver will occur irrespective of whether the psychotherapist is called at the trial or at a pretrial hearing in the same case.

People v. Clark[25] illustrates this point. The judge appointed a psychiatrist named Mayland to assist the defense in ascertaining the accused's mental state at the time the offenses were committed. At a pretrial hearing to suppress the accused's confession, the defense called Mayland to testify about the accused's inability to waive his *Miranda* rights voluntarily. In his testimony Mayland related the accused's accounts to him of how the crimes were committed. At the trial the defense called other psychiatrists to establish the accused's inability to form the mens rea of the offense charged. Over the accused's attorney-client privilege, the prosecution was permitted to cross examine these experts by referring to the statements the accused had made to Mayland. "By calling Mayland to the stand during the suppression hearing, defendant manifested an intent that his communications with Mayland be revealed to third parties and that the attorney-client privilege be waived."[26]

In one situation, neither the attorney-client privilege nor the work product doctrine will protect from disclosure reports prepared by an expert commissioned by an attorney, even if the expert is not designated as a witness or called as a witness. Where the attorney calls other experts who rely on the expert's report in reaching their opinions, the opposing party is entitled to cross examine the testifying experts about the matters, including the privileged information, contained in the report.[27] The Evidence Code expressly provides that an expert may be fully cross examined about "the matter upon which his or her opinion is based and the reasons for his or her opinion."[28]

In addition to the attorney-client privilege, the work product doctrine can be invoked to prevent the disclosure of patient communications to a psychotherapist, including the fact that, at the attorney's request, the

---

22. Id.

23. See § 21.04 supra.

24. Calling the expert is viewed as consenting to disclosure by the expert of the confidential communications. Finley v. Superior Court, 29 Cal.App.3d 342, 347, 104 Cal.Rptr. 699, 702 (1972). See also National Steel Products Co. v. Superior Court, 164 Cal.App.3d 476, 484, 210 Cal.Rptr. 535, 539 (1985).

25. 5 Cal.4th 950, 22 Cal.Rptr.2d 689, 857 P.2d 1099 (1993).

26. Id. at 1066, 22 Cal.Rptr.2d at 724, 857 P.2d at 1134.

27. People v. Ledesma, 39 Cal.4th 641, 695, 47 Cal.Rptr.3d 326, 376, 140 P.3d 657, 698 (2006).

28. West's Ann. California Evidence Code § 721.

patient consulted the psychotherapist. In People v. Coddington[29] the accused called a number of psychiatrists to testify at the sanity phase of his trial. Over objection, the prosecutor was allowed on cross-examination to show that the experts were unaware that the accused also had consulted three other mental health experts the defense had chosen not to call. In summation, the prosecutor invited the jurors to infer that the other experts were not called because their testimony would not have been favorable. The reviewing court held that the prosecutor's cross-examination and argument violated defense counsel's work product privilege: "Work product encompasses the investigation of defendant's mental state to assess both the favorable and the unfavorable aspects of the case. It also encompasses counsel's impressions and conclusions regarding witnesses who would be favorable and those who would not be so. * * * It follows that the party's decision that an expert who has been consulted should not be called to testify is within the privilege."[30]

3. Under § 1017(b), no privilege exists for communications between a patient and a psychotherapist appointed by the Board of Prison Terms to examine the patient pursuant to the Penal Code provisions requiring the evaluation of prisoners for severe mental disorders.[31] Accordingly, the psychotherapist-patient privilege does not apply if the psychotherapist was appointed by the court in proceedings to determine whether the patient is a Mentally Disordered Sexual Offender. Section 1017(b), however, does not address the admissibility of testimony by psychotherapists called to determine whether the patient is a Sexually Violent Predator. An SVP is defined as someone who (1) suffers from "a diagnosed mental disorder that makes the person a danger to the health and safety of others in that it is likely that he or she will engage in sexually violent criminal behavior" and (2) has been "convicted of a sexually violent offense against two or more victims."[32] People v. Martinez[33] holds that the psychotherapist-patient privilege does not apply to SVP proceedings.[34]

4. No privilege exists for communications between a patient and psychotherapist if the services of the psychotherapist were sought or obtained to enable or aid anyone to commit or plan to commit a crime or a tort or to escape detection or apprehension after committing a crime or a tort.[35] This exception is broader than the one which provides that the

29. 23 Cal.4th 529, 97 Cal.Rptr.2d 528, 2 P.3d 1081 (2000), cert. denied, 531 U.S. 1195, 121 S.Ct. 1199, 149 L.Ed.2d 113, overruled on other grounds, Price v. Superior Court, 25 Cal.4th 1046, 108 Cal.Rptr.2d 409, 25 P.3d 618 (2001).

30. Id. at 606, 97 Cal.Rptr.2d at 596, 2 P.3d at 1142. The work product privilege would have been lost, however, if the accused had called the three experts. See § 22.02.

31. West's Ann. California Evidence Code § 1017(b).

32. West's Ann. California Welf. & Inst. Code section 6600 et seq.

33. 88 Cal.App.4th 465, 483, 105 Cal.Rptr.2d 841, 853 (2001).

34. The California Supreme Court has construed amendments to the SVPA statute as permitting the attorney petitioning for the commitment to have access to otherwise confidential information regarding the alleged SVP's treatment for mental disorders. See Albertson v. Superior Court, 25 Cal.4th 796, 805–806, 107 Cal.Rptr.2d 381, 389, 23 P.3d 611, 618 (2001).

35. West's Ann. California Evidence Code § 1018.

attorney-client privilege does not apply when the communication was made to enable someone to commit or plan to commit a crime or a fraud.[36] "People seldom, if ever, consult their [psychotherapists] in regard to matters which might subsequently be determined to be a tort, and there is no desirable end to be served by encouraging such communications. On the other hand, people often consult lawyers about matters which may later turn out to be torts and it is desirable to encourage discussion of such matters with lawyers."[37]

In determining whether the services of the psychotherapist were sought for therapy or to enable the commission of a crime or a tort, the patient's motive may be immaterial.

> It appears that in virtually all psychotherapy, what motivates the participants is *not* psychotherapy for its own sake. For example, the psychotherapist is sometimes motivated by self-interest, as when he earns his living solely through his practice. For his part, the patient is sometimes motivated by self-preservation, as when he struggles to resist the temptation of suicide or antisocial conduct. As a general matter, the dispositive fact is *what* the participants do, not *why*.[38]

5. No privilege exists for communications relevant to an issue between parties, all of whom claim through the deceased patient, regardless of whether the claims are by testate or intestate succession or by inter vivos transaction.[39] "The traditional exception for litigation between claimants by testate or intestate succession is based on the theory that claimants in privity with the estate claim *through* the [patient], not adversely, and the deceased [patient] presumably would want his communications disclosed in litigation between such claimants so that his desires in regard to the disposition of his estate might be correctly ascertained and carried out. This rationale is equally applicable where one or more of the parties is claiming by inter vivos transaction, as for example, in an action between a party who claims under a deed (executed by a [patient] in full possession of his faculties) and a party who claims under a will executed while the [patient's] mental stability was dubious."[40]

6. No privilege exists for communications relevant to an issue of breach, by the psychotherapist or by the patient, of a duty arising out of the psychotherapist-patient relationship.[41]

7. No privilege exists for communications relevant to an issue concerning the intention of a patient, now deceased, with regard to a deed of conveyance, will, or other writing, executed by the patient, purporting to

---

36. See § 21.06 supra.

37. See West's Ann. California Evidence Code § 997 (comment) relating to the physician-patient privilege.

38. Menendez v. Superior Court (People), 3 Cal.4th 435, 452–455, 11 Cal.Rptr.2d 92, 103–104, 834 P.2d 786, 797–798 (1992) (emphasis in the original).

39. West's Ann. California Evidence Code § 1019.

40. See West's Ann. California Evidence Code § 957 (comment) (emphasis in the original) relating to the attorney-client privilege.

41. West's Ann. California Evidence Code § 1020.

affect an interest in property.[42] This exception permits the psychotherapist to disclose the patient's true intentions regarding dispositive instruments.[43]

8. Similarly, no privilege exists for communications relevant to an issue concerning the validity of a deed of conveyance, will, or other writing, executed by the patient, now deceased, purporting to affect an interest in property.[44]

9. No privilege exists for communications offered in proceedings initiated at the request of the accused under the Penal Code to determine his sanity in a criminal action.[45] "The psychotherapist-patient privilege does not apply when the defendant raises the issue of his sanity at the time of trial."[46]

10. No privilege exists for communications "when the psychotherapist has reasonable cause to believe that the patient is in such mental or emotional condition as to be dangerous to himself or to the person or property of another and that disclosure of the communication is necessary to prevent the threatened danger."[47] "Although this exception might inhibit the relationship between the patient and his psychotherapist to a limited extent, it is essential that appropriate action be taken if the psychotherapist becomes convinced during the course of treatment that the patient is a menace to himself or others, and the patient refuses to permit the psychotherapist to make the disclosure necessary to prevent the threatened danger."[48] In ruling on whether the communications fall within the privilege, the judge may order in camera disclosure.[49]

Because this exception focuses on the need to protect the intended victim from potential danger, the exception seemingly applies only if, at

---

42. West's Ann. California Evidence Code § 1021.

43. See California Evidence Code § 960 (comment) regarding the attorney-client relationship.

44. West's Ann. California Evidence Code § 1022.

45. West's Ann. California Evidence Code § 1023.

46. Id. (comment).

47. West's Ann. California Evidence Code § 1024. Under California law, law enforcement personnel may confiscate any firearm from a person who has been detained for examination of his mental condition. West's Ann. Welfare and Institutions Code § 8102. Upon the release of the person detained, the confiscating agency has 30 days to petition for a hearing to determine whether the return of the firearm would be likely to result in the endangering of the person detained or others. Id. Psychiatric testimony that the person detained continues to be a danger to himself or others is admissible at the hearing under the exception created by California Evidence Code § 1024. People v. One Ruger .22–Caliber Pistol, 84 Cal.App.4th 310, 315, 100 Cal.Rptr.2d 780, 784 (2000).

48. West's Ann. California Evidence Code § 1024 (comment). In California, it is crime to threaten another with death or great bodily harm with the intent that the threat be taken seriously. West's Ann. California Penal Code § 422. Statements by patients to psychotherapists threatening others may qualify as an exception to the privilege. But whether those statements alone qualify as a threat under the Penal Code depends on whether they disclose the required intent. The Penal Code does not punish emotional outbursts but only those whose purpose is to instill fear in others. People v. Felix, 92 Cal.App.4th 905, 913, 112 Cal.Rptr.2d 311, 318–319 (2001).

49. Mavroudis v. Superior Court, 102 Cal.App.3d 594, 606, 162 Cal.Rptr. 724, 733 (1980). Disclosure does not contravene § 915, since the disclosure is not to determine the applicability of the privilege but of the exception. Id.

the time disclosure of the patient's threats is sought, disclosure is necessary to prevent the threatened danger. The courts, however, have rejected this construction and have applied the exception even if the threatened harm has occurred.[50] When the holder claims the privilege to prevent disclosure of threats he communicated to his psychotherapist, the only question is whether the threats fell within the exception *when made*. If, at the time the threats are made, the psychotherapist has or should have reasonable cause to believe that disclosure is necessary to prevent the threatened danger, the threats lose the protection afforded by the privilege, and the psychotherapist can be compelled to disclose the threats in subsequent proceedings.[51] It is thus immaterial whether the psychotherapist takes any steps to protect the intended victim or whether the victim has already been harmed by the time disclosure of the threats is sought.[52]

In determining whether at the time the threats were made the psychotherapist should have known that disclosure was necessary to prevent the threatened danger, the judge must take into account the standards of the psychotherapeutic community.[53] If necessary, expert testimony on the relevant standard may be received.[54] But even though the exception calls for an objective standard, the judge should nonetheless accord broad discretion to the psychotherapist's judgment about the need to disclose the threats in order to prevent the threatened danger.[55] The fact that the accused has been charged with crimes against the victim in the trial at which disclosure of the threats is sought is insufficient to show that the psychotherapist should have known about the need to disclose the threats to avert the threatened danger at the time the threats were made.[56]

Only those communications giving rise to the psychotherapist's reasonable belief that the patient is dangerous to others fall within the exception.[57] Other communications remain privileged.

People v. Clark[58] holds that, once the psychotherapist discloses the patient's threats, they lose their confidentiality and can be offered over a privilege claim.[59] *Clark*'s holding is based on the belief that the psycho-

---

50. See People v. Wharton, 53 Cal.3d 522, 557, 280 Cal.Rptr. 631, 651, 809 P.2d 290, 310 (1991) and cases cited therein.

51. Id. at 558, 280 Cal.Rptr. at 652, 809 P.2d at 311.

52. Id.

53. Mavroudis v. Superior Court, 102 Cal.App.3d 594, 599, 162 Cal.Rptr. 724, 729 (1980). Expert testimony may be received on the question whether the psychotherapist should have known of the threatened danger. Id. at 605, 162 Cal.Rptr. at 733. See also Menendez v. Superior Court (People), 3 Cal.4th 435, 449, 11 Cal.Rptr.2d 92, 101, 834 P.2d 786, 795 (1992).

54. Menendez v. Superior Court (People), 3 Cal.4th 435, 452–455, 11 Cal.Rptr.2d 92, 103–104, 834 P.2d 786, 797–798 (1992)

55. Id.

56. Luhdorff v. Superior Court, 166 Cal.App.3d 485, 493–494, 212 Cal.Rptr. 516, 520–521 (1985).

57. People v. Wharton, 53 Cal.3d 522, 561, 280 Cal.Rptr. 631, 654, 809 P.2d 290, 313 (1991).

58. 50 Cal.3d 583, 268 Cal.Rptr. 399, 789 P.2d 127 (1990), cert. denied, 498 U.S. 973, 111 S.Ct. 442, 112 L.Ed.2d 425 (1990).

59. Id. at 620, 268 Cal.Rptr. at 423, 789 P.2d at 151.

therapist's disclosure of the patient's threats destroys the therapeutic relationship.[60] That holding, however, conflicts with those provisions of the Code which provide that, once a communication is privileged, it loses its protection only if the holder waives the protection afforded by the privilege or the communication falls within an exception to the privilege.[61] Waiver can occur when the holder consents to disclosure by a third person of a significant part of the privileged communication.[62] But since a patient does not ordinarily consent to the psychotherapist's disclosure of his threats, no basis exists for finding a waiver. The psychotherapist can nonetheless be compelled to disclose the threats over a privilege claim, but this is so because the threats fall within the exception and not because they have already been disclosed by the psychotherapist. In Menendez v. Superior Court[63] the California Supreme Court attempted to place some limits on *Clark's* expansive language. It reiterated the principle that because "only the patient has the power to waive the privilege in any part * * * only the patient has the power to cause the privilege to go out of existence in its entirety."[64]

Though the exception overrides the privilege, the exception does not require the psychotherapist to disclose the threatening communication or even to issue a warning.[65] But in Tarasoff v. Regents of the University of California,[66] the California Supreme Court held that a psychotherapist has a Common Law duty to use reasonable care to protect the intended victim of a patient who presents a serious danger of violence. The failure to discharge this duty can give rise to an action in negligence against the psychotherapist.[67]

> When a therapist determines, or pursuant to the standards of his profession should determine, that his patient presents a serious danger of violence to another, he incurs an obligation to use reasonable care to protect the intended victim against such danger. The discharge of this duty may require the therapist to take one or more of various steps, depending upon the nature of the case. Thus it may call for him to warn the intended victim or others likely to apprise the victim of the danger, to notify the police, or to take whatever other steps are reasonably necessary under the circumstances.[68]

---

60. Id. at 620, 268 Cal.Rptr. at 424, 789 P.2d at 152.

61. See § 20.05 supra.

62. Id.

63. 3 Cal.4th 435, 11 Cal.Rptr.2d 92, 834 P.2d 786 (1992).

64. Id. at 449, 11 Cal.Rptr.2d at 100, 834 P.2d at 794.

65. Id. at 451, 11 Cal.Rptr.2d at 102, 834 P.2d at 796.

66. 17 Cal.3d 425, 131 Cal.Rptr. 14, 551 P.2d 334 (1976).

67. Id. at 431, 131 Cal.Rptr. at 20, 551 P.2d at 340.

68. Id. *Tarasoff* is now codified in California Civil Procedure Code § 43.92 which provides that

"(a) There shall be no monetary liability on the part of, and no cause of action shall arise against, any person who is a psychotherapist as defined in Section 1010 of the Evidence Code in failing to warn of and protect from a patient's threatened violent behavior or failing to predict and warn of and protect from a patient's violent behavior except where the patient has communicated to the psychotherapist a serious threat of physical violence against a reasonably

If the psychotherapist in fact gives the intended victim a *Tarasoff* warning, then, according to the California Supreme Court, "the disclosed threat is not covered by the privilege."[69] By so holding, the court in effect created an additional exception to the psychotherapist-patient privilege. Under the Code, it is the making of a credible threat, not its disclosure by the psychotherapist, that triggers the exception.

The duty to protect foreseeable victims from potential harm does not displace all of the obligations the psychotherapist owes the patient. In discharging the duty, the psychotherapist should choose means that "preserve the privacy of the patient to the fullest extent compatible with the prevention of the threatened danger."[70] Moreover, disclosing the patient's threats pursuant to the duty owed potential victims does not strip other communications between the patient and the psychotherapist of protection.[71] If a particular communication does not give the psychotherapist reasonable cause to believe that the patient is dangerous and that disclosure is necessary to prevent harm, that communication remains protected if it otherwise meets the tests for privileged communications.[72]

Because the nature of appeals have forced the appellate courts to deal with the exceptions to the psychotherapist-patient privilege on a piecemeal basis, the relationship between some of the exceptions is not always clear. An example, however, helps clarify some of these relationships. Assume that a patient makes the following statement to his psychotherapist: "Doctor, I'm feeling a great dealing of anxiety. I want your help in escaping detection for killing my parents. Would you say that I was with you here at 10 PM on Thursday, December 1st?"

In a prosecution for murdering his parents, a psychotherapist-patient privilege claim must be overruled and the psychotherapist compelled to disclose the patient's statement. Even though the patient made the statement in part for a therapeutic purpose (to relieve stress over killing his parents) and communicated the statement in confidence, it is not privileged. Under the fourth exception, no privilege exists for communications made by a patient to a psychotherapist to enlist the psychotherapist's help in escaping detection or apprehension after committing a crime.

---

identifiable victim or victims." and "(b) There shall be no monetary liability on the part of, and no cause of action shall arise against, a psychotherapist who, under the limited circumstances specified above, discharges his or her duty to warn and protect by making reasonable efforts to communicate the threat to the victim or victims and to a law enforcement agency."

Under § 43.92, the threat does not have to be communicated by the patient to the psychotherapist. It can be communicated also by family members. See Ewing v. Goldstein, 120 Cal.App.4th 807, 818, 15 Cal.Rptr.3d 864, 872 (2004).

69. Menendez v. Superior Court (People), 3 Cal.4th 435, 447, 11 Cal.Rptr.2d 92, 99, 834 P.2d 786, 793 (1992).

70. Tarasoff v. Regents of University of California, 17 Cal.3d 425, 441, 131 Cal.Rptr. 14, 27, 551 P.2d 334, 347 (1976).

71. Menendez v. Superior Court (People), 3 Cal.4th 435, 454, 11 Cal.Rptr.2d 92, 104, 834 P.2d 786, 798 (1992).

72. Id.

Assume that, instead, the patient said, "Doctor, I am feeling a great deal of anxiety. I killed my parents, and I am afraid that I may kill my sister too." Again, in a prosecution for murdering the parents, a psychotherapist–patient privilege must be overruled and the psychotherapist compelled to disclose the statement. Although the patient made the statement in part for a therapeutic purpose and communicated the statement in confidence, it is not privileged. Under the tenth exception, no privilege exists for communications if the psychotherapist has reasonable cause to believe that the patient is in such a mental condition as to be dangerous to others and disclosure is necessary to prevent the threatened danger. Even if the psychotherapist has not disclosed the statement to anyone, a judge could find that at the time the patient made the statement a reasonable psychotherapist would have believed that the patient was a danger to his sister and that disclosure was necessary to prevent the threatened danger.

That the part relating to the parents can be severed from the part relating to the sister does not necessarily mean that only the part relating to the sister falls within the exception. It was clearly against the patient's interests to admit killing his parents. This admission makes his threat to kill his sister credible. Consequently, it is the entire communication that should cause the psychotherapist to conclude that disclosure of the communication is necessary to prevent the threatened danger to the sister.

If pursuant to *Tarasoff* the psychotherapist warns the sister of the danger, the judge can overrule the psychotherapist–patient claim on the additional ground that the psychotherapist's disclosure is not covered by the privilege.[73]

11. No privilege exists in a proceeding brought by the patient to establish his or her competence.[74] "When a patient has placed his mental condition in issue by instituting a proceeding to establish his competence, he should not be permitted to withhold the most vital evidence relating thereto."[75]

12. No privilege exists for information that the psychotherapist or the patient is required to report to a public employee or for information required to be recorded in a public office, if such report or record is open to public inspection.[76] "[N]o valid purpose is served by preventing the use of relevant information when the law requiring the information to be reported to a public office does not restrict disclosure."[77] In the absence of

---

73. It is not clear whether the "disclosed threat" referred to by the court is the psychotherapist's statement to the victim relating the patient's threat or the threatening statement made by the patient to the psychotherapist. Some courts take the position that psychotherapists may disclose to potential victims only the "fact" that the patient poses a serious danger of violence. See, e.g., Pettus v. Cole, 49 Cal.App.4th 402, 447, 57 Cal.Rptr.2d 46, 76 (1996) and cases cited therein.

74. West's Ann. California Evidence Code § 1025.

75. See West's Ann. California Evidence Code § 1005 (comment) relating to the physician-patient privilege.

76. West's Ann. California Evidence Code § 1026.

77. See West's Ann. California Evidence Code § 1006 (comment) relating to the physician-patient privilege.

an indication that psychiatric evaluations of police officers are open to the public, their production cannot be compelled under this exception.[78]

13. No privilege exists if the patient is under the age of sixteen and the psychotherapist has reasonable cause to believe that the patient has been the victim of a crime and that disclosure of the communication is in the best interests of the child.[79] This exception "is necessary to permit court disclosure of communications to a psychotherapist by a child who has been the victim of a crime (such as child abuse) in a proceeding in which the commission of such crime is a subject of inquiry. Although the exception * * * might inhibit the relationship between the patient and his psychotherapist to a limited extent, it is essential that appropriate action be taken if the psychotherapist becomes convinced during the course of treatment that the patient is the victim of a crime and that disclosure of the communication would be in the best interest of the child."[80]

The effect of the exception is to make the psychotherapist, not the child, the holder of the privilege. If the child is the victim of a crime, disclosure will be precluded only if the psychotherapist claims that revealing the communication would not be in the best interest of the child.[81] Disclosure is in the best interest of the child if it is designed to enable others to ascertain how the child can best be treated.[82]

The Child Abuse and Neglect Reporting Act requires a health practitioner to report to a child protective agency any instance of suspected or known child abuse.[83] Since a health practitioner includes psychiatrists and psychologists,[84] they must report the abuse even if they learned about it in the course of the psychotherapist-patient relationship. People v. John B.[85] holds that, while the act creates an exception to the psychotherapist-patient privilege, it does so only for the information which the psychotherapist reports to the child protective agency.[86] Unreported information remains privileged.

Exceptions to the privilege and the constitutional right of privacy. The availability of an exception for communications otherwise protected by the psychotherapist-patient privilege does not always require the disclosure of the privileged information. The state constitutional right to privacy[87] can be invoked to bar the disclosure, since communications

---

78. Lemelle v. Superior Court of Orange County, 77 Cal.App.3d 148, 158, note 2, 143 Cal.Rptr. 450, 456, note 2 (1978).

79. West's Ann. California Evidence Code § 1027. The exception does not apply if the psychotherapist does not believe that the child has been the victim of a crime. People v. Castro, 30 Cal.App.4th 390, 397, 35 Cal.Rptr.2d 839, 843 (1994).

80. West's Ann. California Evidence Code § 1027. (comment).

81. People v. Caplan, 193 Cal.App.3d 543, 556, 238 Cal.Rptr. 478, 486 (1987).

82. Id.

83. West's Ann. California Penal Code § 11166.

84. West's Ann. California Penal Code § 11165.8.

85. 192 Cal.App.3d 1073, 237 Cal.Rptr. 659 (1987).

86. Id. at 1078, 237 Cal.Rptr. at 662.

87. West's Ann. California Constitution Article 1, § 1.

between a patient and a psychotherapist are protected by this right.[88] The right to privacy is not absolute, however, and must yield to a compelling state interest.[89] To protect children, for example, the state can require psychotherapists to report known or suspected child abuse, even though the reporting requirement invades the patient's privacy interests in maintaining the confidentiality of revelations disclosed during therapy.[90] Similarly, to protect potential victims from threatened harm, the state can require psychotherapists to warn the victims, even though warning them may reveal the threats the patient made during therapy.[91]

Confrontation, due process, and privilege claims. Claims of privilege can conflict with the accused's right to a fair trial and to confront witnesses. The accused, for example, may wish to attack a witness's credibility by exposing the witness's mental or emotional disorders.[92] Inquiry into a witness's emotional or psychiatric history is often met with a claim that the information is protected from disclosure by the psychotherapist-patient privilege. Where such information is in the state's possession, federal due process requires the prosecution to disclose it to the accused if it is material as well as exculpatory, even if the information is protected by a qualified privilege.[93]

Drawing on federal precedents, the California courts have held that the accused is entitled to have the trial judge review material on the witness's mental health in camera to determine whether it is privileged and, if so, whether it is so essential to the defense as to override the privilege and warrant its disclosure.[94] The accused, however, is not entitled to the in camera review unless he describes the material requested with reasonable specificity and provides a plausible justification for its use.[95] Moreover, the accused may not request the in camera review until after the trial has commenced.[96] In the view of the California Supreme

---

88. Roe v. Superior Court, 229 Cal.App.3d 832, 837, 280 Cal.Rptr. 380, 382 (1991).

89. Id. and cases cited therein.

90. Id. at 838–839, 280 Cal.Rptr. at 381–382.

91. People v. Wharton, 53 Cal.3d 522, 561, 280 Cal.Rptr. 631, 654, 809 P.2d 290, 313–314 (1991).

92. For a discussion of the use of a witness's mental disorders to impeach the witness's credibility, see § 15.10 supra.

93. Pennsylvania v. Ritchie, 480 U.S. 39, 57, 107 S.Ct. 989, 1001, 94 L.Ed.2d 40 (1987) (In a prosecution for raping his minor daughter, the accused was entitled to an in camera review of the minor's records compiled by a state agency charged with protecting children even if under state law those records were confidential.). The United States Supreme Court expressed no opinion on whether the information would have to be disclosed if protected by an absolute privilege. Id. at note 14. See also People v. Webb, 6 Cal.4th 494, 518, 24 Cal.Rptr.2d 779, 794, 862 P.2d 779, 794 (1993).

94. People v. Reber, 177 Cal.App.3d 523, 532, 223 Cal.Rptr. 139, 146 (1986). See also Farrell L. v. Superior Court, 203 Cal.App.3d 521, 527, 250 Cal.Rptr. 25, 29 (1988); People v. Boyette, 201 Cal.App.3d 1527, 1533, 247 Cal.Rptr. 795, 797 (1988).

95. People v. Pack, 201 Cal.App.3d 679, 687, 248 Cal.Rptr. 240, 243 (1988). The right of the accused to discover the mental health records of a witness applies only to witnesses the prosecution plans to call. It does not necessarily apply to codefendants the accused believes might take the stand and offer evidence that is adverse to the accused. Nielsen v. Superior Court, 55 Cal.App.4th 1150, 1156 and note 2, 64 Cal.Rptr.2d 566, 570 and note 2 (1997).

96. People v. Hammon, 15 Cal.4th 1117, 1127, 65 Cal.Rptr.2d 1, 7, 938 P.2d 986, 993 (1997).

Court, there is no Sixth Amendment right to pretrial discovery of privileged information.[97]

QUESTIONS AND PROBLEMS

1. The psychotherapist-patient privilege does not apply to communications that are relevant to an issue concerning the patient's mental or emotional condition if the patient tendered the issue. True or false?

2. A claim by a patient for damages for physical injuries does not exempt his confidential communications with his psychotherapist from the privilege under the patient-litigant exception unless the patient also claims damages for emotional distress. True or false?

3. Unless the patient is the party tendering his emotional or mental condition, his confidential communications with his psychotherapist do not necessarily fall within the patient-litigant exception. For example, a parent does not tender his mental condition in an action to terminate his visitation rights by simply resisting the action. True or false?

4. The psychotherapist-patient privilege does not apply to communications made by the patient to a psychotherapist appointed by a court to examine the patient, for example, one appointed pursuant to conservatorship proceedings. But this exception does not apply where the therapist is appointed at the request of defense to advise the lawyer on whether the accused should present an insanity plea or present a defense based on a mental condition. True or false?

5. No privilege exists for communications between a patient and a psychotherapist if the services of the psychotherapist were sought to enable the patient to commit or plan to commit a crime or tort. The crime-fraud exception to the attorney-client privilege is narrower, since confidential consultations with a lawyer about matters subsequently determined to be a tort are privileged. True or false?

6. No privilege exists for patient threats if the psychotherapist has reasonable cause to believe that the patient is in such mental or emotional condition as to be dangerous to others and that disclosure of the threat is necessary to prevent the threatened danger. True or false?

7. In determining whether to uphold the privilege claim to prevent the disclosure of threats, the question for the judge is whether the threats fell within the exception when made. The question is not whether disclosure is necessary to prevent the threatened danger at the time that disclosure in sought in court. True or false?

8. The Evidence Code does not compel a psychotherapist to disclose patient threats. But under *Tarasoff* a psychotherapist has a duty to use reasonable care to protect the intended victim of a patient who presents a serious danger of violence. Breach of this duty can give rise to a negligence action. True or false?

---

97. Id.

9. If pursuant to *Tarasoff* the psychotherapist does warn the intended victim, a privilege objection to the disclosure of the threat must be overruled on the ground, among others, that the privilege does not cover what the psychotherapist told the victim. Discuss.

10. In criminal cases, the accused may wish to attack a witness's credibility by exposing the witness's emotional or mental disorders. Because such cross-examination may be vital to the accused's right to confront his accusers, the accused may always discover a witness's psychiatric history irrespective of the witness's privilege claims. True or false?

CALIFORNIA EVIDENCE CODE

§ 1010. Psychotherapist

As used in this article, "psychotherapist" means:

(a) A person authorized, or reasonably believed by the patient to be authorized, to practice medicine in any state or nation who devotes, or is reasonably believed by the patient to devote, a substantial portion of his or her time to the practice of psychiatry.

(b) A person licensed as a psychologist under Chapter 6.6 (commencing with Section 2900) of Division 2 of the Business and Professions Code.

(c) A person licensed as a clinical social worker under Article 4 (commencing with Section 4996) of Chapter 14 of Division 2 of the Business and Professions Code, when he or she is engaged in applied psychotherapy of a nonmedical nature.

(d) A person who is serving as a school psychologist and holds a credential authorizing that service issued by the state.

(e) A person licensed as a marriage, family, and child counselor under Chapter 13 (commencing with Section 4980) of Division 2 of the Business and Professions Code.

(f) A person registered as a psychological assistant who is under the supervision of a licensed psychologist or board certified psychiatrist as required by Section 2913 of the Business and Professions Code, or a person registered as a marriage, family, and child counselor intern who is under the supervision of a licensed marriage, family, and child counselor, a licensed clinical social worker, a licensed psychologist, or a licensed physician and surgeon certified in psychiatry, as specified in Section 4980.44 of the Business and Professions Code.

(g) A person registered as an associate clinical social worker who is under supervision as specified in Section 4996.23 of the Business and Professions Code.

(h) A person exempt from the Psychology Licensing Law pursuant to subdivision (d) of Section 2909 of the Business and Professions Code who is under the supervision of a licensed psychologist or board certified psychiatrist.

(i) A psychological intern as defined in Section 2911 of the Business and Professions Code who is under the supervision of a licensed psychologist or board certified psychiatrist.

(j) A trainee, as defined in subdivision (c) of Section 4980.03 of the Business and Professions Code, who is fulfilling his or her supervised practicum required by subparagraph (B) of paragraph (1) of subdivision (d) of Section 4980.36 of, or subdivision (c) of Section 4980.37 of, the Business and Professions Code and is supervised by a licensed psychologist, a board certified psychiatrist, a licensed clinical social worker, a licensed marriage and family therapist, or a licensed professional clinical counselor.

(k) A person licensed as a registered nurse pursuant to Chapter 6 (commencing with Section 2700) of Division 2 of the Business and Professions Code, who possesses a master's degree in psychiatric mental health nursing.

(*l*) An advanced practice registered nurse who is certified as a clinical nurse specialist pursuant to Article 9 (commencing with Section 2828) of Chapter 6 of Division 2 of the Business and Professions Code and who participates in expert clinical practice in the specialty of psychiatric-mental health nursing.

(m) A person rendering mental health treatment or counseling services as authorized pursuant to Section 6924 of the Family Code.

(n) A person licensed as a professional clinical counselor under Chapter 16 (commencing with Section 4999.10) of Division 2 of the Business and Professions Code.

(o) A person registered as a clinical counselor intern who is under the supervision of a licensed professional clinical counselor, a licensed marriage and family therapist, a licensed clinical social worker, a licensed psychologist, or a licensed physician and surgeon certified in psychiatry, as specified in Sections 4999.42 to 4999.46, inclusive, of the Business and Professions Code.

(p) A clinical counselor trainee, as defined in subdivision (g) of Section 4999.12 of the Business and Professions Code, who is fulfilling his or her supervised practicum required by paragraph (3) of subdivision (c) of Section 4999.32 of, or paragraph (3) of subdivision (c) of Section 4999.33 of, the Business and Professions Code, and is supervised by a licensed psychologist, a board-certified psychiatrist, a licensed clinical social worker, a licensed marriage and family therapist, or a licensed professional clinical counselor.

§ 1010.5. Privileged communication between patient and educational psychologist

A communication between a patient and an educational psychologist, licensed under Article 5 (commencing with Section 4986) of Chapter 13 of Division 2 of the Business and Professions Code, shall be privileged to the same extent, and subject to the same limitations, as a communication between a patient and a psychotherapist described in subdivisions (c), (d), and (e) of Section 1010.

§ 1011. "Patient"

As used in this article, "patient" means a person who consults a psychotherapist or submits to an examination by a psychotherapist for the purpose of securing a diagnosis or preventive, palliative, or curative treatment of his mental or emotional condition or who submits to an examination of his mental or emotional condition for the purpose of scientific research on mental or emotional problems.

§ 1012. "Confidential communication between patient and psychotherapist"

As used in this article, "confidential communication between patient and psychotherapist" means information, including information obtained by an examination of the patient, transmitted between a patient and his psychotherapist in the course of that relationship and in confidence by a means which, so far as the patient is aware, discloses the information to no third persons other than those who are present to further the interest of the patient in the consultation, or those to whom disclosure is reasonably necessary for the transmission of the information or the accomplishment of the purpose for which the psychotherapist is consulted, and includes a diagnosis made and the advice given by the psychotherapist in the course of that relationship.

§ 1013. "Holder of the privilege"

As used in this article, "holder of the privilege" means:

(a) The patient when he has no guardian or conservator.

(b) A guardian or conservator of the patient when the patient has a guardian or conservator.

(c) The personal representative of the patient if the patient is dead.

§ 1014. Psychotherapist-patient privilege; application to individuals and entities

Subject to Section 912 and except as otherwise provided in this article, the patient, whether or not a party, has a privilege to refuse to disclose, and to prevent another from disclosing, a confidential communication between patient and psychotherapist if the privilege is claimed by:

(a) The holder of the privilege.

(b) A person who is authorized to claim the privilege by the holder of the privilege.

(c) The person who was the psychotherapist at the time of the confidential communication, but such person may not claim the privilege if there is no holder of the privilege in existence or if he or she is otherwise instructed by a person authorized to permit disclosure.

The relationship of a psychotherapist and patient shall exist between a psychological corporation as defined in Article 9 (commencing with Section 2995) of Chapter 6.6 of Division 2 of the Business and Professions Code, a marriage and family corporation as defined in Article 6 (commencing with Section 4987.5) of Chapter 13 of Division 2 of the Business and Professions Code, a licensed clinical social workers corporation as defined in Article 5 (commencing with Section 4998) of Chapter 14 of Division 2 of the Business and Professions Code, or a professional clinical counselor corporation as defined in Article 7 (commencing with Section 4999.123) of Chapter 16 of Division 2 of the Business and Professions Code, and the patient to whom it renders professional services, as well as between those patients and psychotherapists employed by those corporations to render services to those patients. The word "persons" as used in this subdivision includes partnerships, corporations, limited liability companies, associations and other groups and entities.

§ 1015. When psychotherapist required to claim privilege

The psychotherapist who received or made a communication subject to the privilege under this article shall claim the privilege whenever he is present when the communication is sought to be disclosed and is authorized to claim the privilege under subdivision (c) of Section 1014.

§ 1016. Exception: Patient-litigant exception

There is no privilege under this article as to a communication relevant to an issue concerning the mental or emotional condition of the patient if such issue has been tendered by:

(a) The patient;

(b) Any party claiming through or under the patient;

(c) Any party claiming as a beneficiary of the patient through a contract to which the patient is or was a party; or

(d) The plaintiff in an action brought under Section 376 or 377 of the Code of Civil Procedure for damages for the injury or death of the patient.

§ 1017. Exception: Psychotherapist appointed by court or board of prison terms

(a) There is no privilege under this article if the psychotherapist is appointed by order of a court to examine the patient, but this exception does not apply where the psychotherapist is appointed by order of the court upon the request of the lawyer for the defendant in a criminal proceeding in order to provide the lawyer with information needed so that he or she may advise the defendant whether to enter or withdraw a plea based on insanity or to present a defense based on his or her mental or emotional condition.

(b) There is no privilege under this article if the psychotherapist is appointed by the Board of Prison Terms to examine a patient pursuant to the provisions of Article 4 (commencing with Section 2960) of Chapter 7 of Title 1 of Part 3 of the Penal Code.

§ 1018. Exception: Crime or tort

There is no privilege under this article if the services of the psychotherapist were sought or obtained to enable or aid anyone to commit or plan to commit a crime or a tort or to escape detection or apprehension after the commission of a crime or a tort.

§ 1019. Exception: Parties claiming through deceased patient

There is no privilege under this article as to a communication relevant to an issue between parties all of whom claim through a deceased patient, regardless of whether the claims are by testate or intestate succession or by inter vivos transaction.

§ 1020. Exception: Breach of duty arising out of psychotherapist-patient relationship

There is no privilege under this article as to a communication relevant to an issue of breach, by the psychotherapist or by the patient, of a duty arising out of the psychotherapist-patient relationship.

§ 1021. Exception: Intention of deceased patient concerning writing affecting property interest

There is no privilege under this article as to a communication relevant to an issue concerning the intention of a patient, now deceased, with respect to a deed of conveyance, will, or other writing, executed by the patient, purporting to affect an interest in property.

§ 1022. Exception: Validity of writing affecting property interest

There is no privilege under this article as to a communication relevant to an issue concerning the validity of a deed of conveyance, will, or other writing, executed by a patient, now deceased, purporting to affect an interest in property.

§ 1023. Exception: Proceeding to determine sanity of criminal defendant

There is no privilege under this article in a proceeding under Chapter 6 (commencing with Section 1367) of Title 10 of Part 2 of the Penal Code initiated at the request of the defendant in a criminal action to determine his sanity.

§ 1024. Exception: Patient dangerous to himself or others

There is no privilege under this article if the psychotherapist has reasonable cause to believe that the patient is in such mental or emotional condition as to be dangerous to himself or to the person or property of another and that disclosure of the communication is necessary to prevent the threatened danger.

§ 1025. Exception: Proceeding to establish competence

There is no privilege under this article in a proceeding brought by or on behalf of the patient to establish his competence.

§ 1026. Exception: Required report

There is no privilege under this article as to information that the psychotherapist or the patient is required to report to a public employee or as to information required to be recorded in a public office, if such report or record is open to public inspection.

§ 1027. Exception: Child under 16 victim of crime

There is no privilege under this article if all of the following circumstances exist:

(a) The patient is a child under the age of 16.

(b) The psychotherapist has reasonable cause to believe that the patient has been the victim of a crime and that disclosure of the communication is in the best interest of the child.

FEDERAL RULES OF EVIDENCE

Rule 504. Psychotherapist–Patient Privilege [Not enacted.]

(a) Definitions.

(1) A "patient" is a person who consults or is examined or interviewed by a psychotherapist.

(2) A "psychotherapist" is (A) a person authorized to practice medicine in any state or nation, or reasonably believed by the patient so to be, while engaged in the diagnosis or treatment of a mental or emotional condition, including drug addiction, or (B) a person licensed or certified as a psychologist under the laws of any state or nation, while similarly engaged.

(3) A communication is "confidential" if not intended to be disclosed to third persons other than those present to further the interest of the patient in the consultation, examination, or interview, or persons reasonably necessary for the transmission of the communication, or persons who are participating in the diagnosis and treatment under the direction of the psychotherapist, including members of the patient's family.

(b) General rule of privilege. A patient has a privilege to refuse to disclose and to prevent any other person from disclosing confidential communications, made for the purposes of diagnosis or treatment of his mental or emotional condition, including drug addiction, among himself, his psychotherapist, or persons who are participating in the diagnosis or treatment under the direction of the psychotherapist, including members of the patient's family.

(c) Who may claim the privilege. The privilege may be claimed by the patient, by his guardian or conservator, or by the personal representative of a deceased patient. The person who was the psychotherapist may claim the privilege but only on behalf of the patient. His authority so to do is presumed in the absence of evidence to the contrary.

(d) Exceptions.

(1) Proceedings for hospitalization. There is no privilege under this rule for communications relevant to an issue in proceedings to hospitalize the patient for mental illness, if the psychotherapist in the course of diagnosis or treatment has determined that the patient is in need of hospitalization.

(2) Examination by order of judge. If the judge orders an examination of the mental or emotional condition of the patient, communications made in the course thereof are not privileged under this rule with respect to the particular purpose for which the examination is ordered unless the judge orders otherwise.

(3) Condition an element of claim or defense. There is no privilege under this rule as to communications relevant to an issue of the mental or emotional condition of the patient in any proceeding in which he relies upon the condition as an element of his claim or defense, or, after the patient's death, in any proceeding in which any party relies upon the condition as an element of his claim or defense.

ADVISORY COMMITTEE'S NOTE

The rules contain no provision for a general physician-patient privilege. While many states have by statute created the privilege, the exceptions which have been found necessary in order to obtain information required by the public interest or to avoid fraud are so numerous as to leave little if any basis for the privilege. Among the exclusions from the statutory privilege, the following may be enumerated; communications not made for purposes of diagnosis and treatment; commitment and restoration proceedings; issues as to wills or otherwise between parties claiming by succession from the patient; actions on insurance policies; required reports (venereal diseases, gunshot wounds, child abuse); communications in furtherance of crime or fraud; mental or physical condition put in issue by patient (personal injury cases); malpractice actions; and some or all criminal prosecutions. California, for example, excepts cases in which the patient puts his condition in issue, all criminal proceedings, will and similar contests, malpractice cases, and disciplinary proceedings, as well as certain other situations, thus leaving virtually nothing covered by the privilege. California Evidence Code §§ 990–1007. For other illustrative statutes see Ill.Rev.Stat.1967, c. 51, § 5.1; N.Y.C.P.L.R. § 4504; N.C.Gen.Stat.1953, § 8–53. Moreover, the possibility of compelling gratuitous disclosure by the physician is foreclosed by his standing to raise the question of relevancy. See Note on "Official Information" Privilege following Rule 509, *infra*.

The doubts attendant upon the general physician-patient privilege are not present when the relationship is that of psychotherapist and patient. While the common law recognized no general physician-patient privilege, it had indicated a disposition to recognize a psychotherapist-patient privilege, Note, Confidential Communications to a Psychotherapist: A New Testimonial Privilege, 47 Nw.U.L.Rev. 384 (1952), when legislatures began moving into the field.

The case for the privilege is convincingly stated in Report No. 45, Group for the Advancement of Psychiatry 92 (1960):

"Among physicians, the psychiatrist has a special need to maintain confidentiality. His capacity to help his patients is completely dependent upon their willingness and ability to talk freely. This makes it difficult if not impossible for him to function without being able to assure his patients of confidentiality and, indeed, privileged communication. Where there may be exceptions to this general rule * * *, there is wide agreement that confidentiality is a *sine qua non* for successful psychiatric treatment. The relationship may well be likened to that of the priest-penitent or the lawyer-client. Psychiatrists not only explore the very depths of their patients' conscious, but their unconscious feelings and attitudes as well. Therapeutic effectiveness necessitates going beyond a patient's awareness and, in order to do this, it must be possible to communicate freely. A threat to secrecy blocks successful treatment."

A much more extended exposition of the case for the privilege is made in Slovenko, Psychiatry and a Second Look at the Medical Privilege, 6 Wayne L.Rev. 175, 184 (1960), quoted extensively in the careful Tentative Recommendation and Study Relating to the Uniform Rules of Evidence (Article V. Privileges), Cal.Law Rev.Comm'n, 417 (1964). The conclusion is reached that Wigmore's four conditions needed to justify the existence of a privilege are amply satisfied.

Illustrative statutes are Cal.Evidence Code §§ 1010–1026; Ga.Code § 38–418 (1961 Supp.); Conn.Gen.Stat., § 52–146a (1966 Supp.); Ill.Rev.Stat.1967, c. 51, § 5.2.

While many of the statutes simply place the communications on the same basis as those between attorney and client, 8 Wigmore § 2286, n. 23 (McNaughton Rev.1961), basic differences between the two relationships forbid resorting to attorney-client save as a helpful point of departure. Goldstein and Katz, Psychiatrist–Patient Privilege: The GAP Proposal and the Connecticut Statute, 36 Conn.B.J. 175, 182 (1962).

Subdivision (a). (1) The definition of patient does not include a person submitting to examination for scientific purposes. Cf. Cal.Evidence Code § 1101. Attention is directed to 42 U.S.C. 242a(2), as amended by the Drug Abuse and Control Act of 1970, P.L. 91–513, authorizing the Secretary of Health, Education, and Welfare to withhold the identity of persons who are the subjects of research on the use and effect of drugs. The rule would leave this provision in full force. See Rule 501.

(2) The definition of psychotherapist embraces a medical doctor while engaged in the diagnosis or treatment of mental or emotional conditions,

including drug addiction, in order not to exclude the general practitioner and to avoid the making of needless refined distinctions concerning what is and what is not the practice of psychiatry. The requirement that the psychologist be in fact licensed, and not merely be believed to be so, is believed to be justified by the number of persons, other than psychiatrists, purporting to render psychotherapeutic aid and the variety of their theories. Cal.Law Rev.Comm'n, *supra,* at pp. 434–437.

The clarification of mental or emotional condition as including drug addiction is consistent with current approaches to drug abuse problems. See, *e.g.,* the definition of "drug dependent person" in 42 U.S.C. 201(q), added by the Drug Abuse Prevention and Control Act of 1970, P.L. 91–513.

(3) Confidential communication is defined in terms conformable with those of the lawyer-client privilege. Rule 503(a)(4), *supra,* with changes appropriate to the difference in circumstance.

Subdivisions (b) and (c). The lawyer-client rule is drawn upon for the phrasing of the general rule of privilege and the determination of those who may claim it. See Rule 503(b) and (c).

The specific inclusion of communications made for the diagnosis and treatment of drug addiction recognizes the continuing contemporary concern with rehabilitation of drug dependent persons and is designed to implement that policy by encouraging persons in need thereof to seek assistance. The provision is in harmony with Congressional actions in this area. See 42 U.S.C. § 260, providing for voluntary hospitalization of addicts or persons with drug dependence problems and prohibiting use of evidence of admission or treatment in any proceeding against him, and 42 U.S.C. § 3419 providing that in voluntary or involuntary commitment of addicts the results of any hearing, examination, test, or procedure used to determine addiction shall not be used against the patient in any criminal proceeding.

Subdivision (d). The exceptions differ substantially from those of the attorney-client privilege, as a result of the basic differences in the relationships. While it has been argued convincingly that the nature of the psychotherapist-patient relationship demands complete security against legally coerced disclosure in all circumstances, Louisell, The Psychologist in Today's Legal World: Part II, 41 Minn.L.Rev. 731, 746 (1957), the committee of psychiatrists and lawyers who drafted the Connecticut statute concluded that in three instances the need for disclosure was sufficiently great to justify the risk of possible impairment of the relationship. Goldstein and Katz, Psychiatrist–Patient Privilege: The GAP Proposal and the Connecticut Statute, 36 Conn.B.J. 175 (1962). These three exceptions are incorporated in the present rule.

(1) The interests of both patient and public call for a departure from confidentiality in commitment proceedings. Since disclosure is authorized only when the psychotherapist determines that hospitalization is needed, control over disclosure is placed largely in the hands of a person in whom the patient has already manifested confidence. Hence damage to the relationship is unlikely.

(2) In a court ordered examination, the relationship is likely to be an arm's length one, though not necessarily so. In any event, an exception is necessary for the effective utilization of this important and growing procedure. The exception, it will be observed, deals with a court ordered examination rather than with a court appointed psychotherapist. Also, the exception is effective only with respect to the particular purpose for which the examination is ordered. The rule thus conforms with the provisions of 18 U.S.C. § 4244 that no statement made by the accused in the course of an examination into competency to stand trial is admissible on the issue of guilt and of 42 U.S.C. § 3420 that a physician conducting an examination in a drug addiction commitment proceeding is a competent and compellable witness.

(3) By injecting his condition into litigation, the patient must be said to waive the privilege, in fairness and to avoid abuses. Similar considerations prevail after the patient's death.

CHAPTER 24

THE PHYSICIAN–PATIENT PRIVILEGE

■ ■ ■

Table of Sections

§ 24.01 NATURE OF THE PRIVILEGE

Like the psychotherapist-patient privilege, the physician-patient privilege seeks to promote effective diagnosis and treatment by encouraging full disclosure by patients.[1] The privilege also seeks to protect the patient from the humiliation that might follow from the disclosure of the patient's ailments.[2] The Code seeks to achieve this goal by giving patients, whether or not a party, a privilege to refuse to disclose and to prevent another from disclosing a confidential communication between the patient and the physician.[3] To be privileged, the communication must meet a number of criteria:

First, the communication must be one made between the patient and the physician in the course of the physician-patient relationship. Second, only those aspects of the communication transmitted in the course of the physician-patient relationship are protected from disclosure And, third, the communication must be transmitted in a way intended to keep the communication confidential. Each of these criteria is examined separately.

To be protected from disclosure, the communication must be one made between the patient and the physician in the course of the physician-patient relationship.[4] However, neither a contract to treat nor payment of the fees is necessary to the existence of the privilege.[5]

---

1. See § 23.01 supra. See also California Evidence Code §§ 991–992 (West 1966).

2. Board of Medical Quality Assurance v. Gherardini, 93 Cal.App.3d 669, 679, 156 Cal.Rptr. 55, 61 (1979).

3. West's Ann. California Evidence Code § 994.

4. West's Ann. California Evidence Code § 992.

5. Kramer v. Policy Holders' Life Ins. Assn., 5 Cal.App.2d 380, 386, 42 P.2d 665, 668 (1935).

A patient is defined as someone "who consults a physician or submits to an examination by a physician for the purpose of securing a diagnosis or preventive, palliative, or curative treatment of his physical or mental or emotional condition."[6] No distinction is made between consultations for diagnosis and consultations for treatment.

> Persons do not ordinarily consult physicians from idle curiosity. They may be sent by their attorney to obtain a diagnosis in contemplation of some legal proceeding * * *. They may submit to an examination for insurance purposes * * *. They may seek diagnosis from one physician to check the diagnosis made by another. They may seek diagnosis from one physician in contemplation of seeking treatment from another. Communications made under such circumstances are as deserving of protection as are communications made to a treating physician.[7]

Not all persons who see a doctor are protected by the privilege. A sperm donor, for example, whose sole purpose is to sell his sperm does not qualify as a "patient" even though he was interviewed by medical personnel as part of the process of donating his sperm.[8] Moreover, individuals who participate in health studies may not always qualify as "patients" under the privilege. In Kizer v. Sulnick[9] the Department of Health Services sought the production of a study of the effects of a waste disposal facility on the residents living near the facility. In ordering the production of the study, the court held that the privilege claimants had failed to demonstrate that the participants came within the privilege.[10] Though the court conceded that participation by the residents "might constitute consultation with a physician,"[11] the claimants failed to produce evidence "that the purpose [of the consultation] was to obtain a diagnosis of the [participants'] condition. It appears more likely that the purpose was to determine whether a statistically significant portion of the residents * * * shared similar medical complaints in order to determine whether the presence of the waste facility was the cause of these symptoms. Participation in such a group study does not invoke the same considerations of confidentiality as an individual's communication with his or her doctor."[12]

---

6.   West's Ann. California Evidence Code § 991.

7.   Id. (comment).

8.   Johnson v. Superior Court, 80 Cal.App.4th 1050, 1063, 95 Cal.Rptr.2d 864, 872 (2000).

9.   202 Cal.App.3d 431, 248 Cal.Rptr. 712 (1988).

10.   Id. at 439, 248 Cal.Rptr. at 716.

11.   Id.

12.   Id. Many of the participants had sued the waste facility for injuries resulting from the presence of the facility. Id. No privilege applies in suits in which the patient tenders a medical issue. See § 24.03 infra. Tort actions for personal injuries are a classic example. Accordingly, the court held that even if the privilege applied to the study, it did not apply to the participants who were plaintiffs in the suit. Id. The participants, however, were not parties to the administrative proceeding in which the medical records were sought and, thus, did not tender their medical condition in that proceeding. A better explanation of the court's holding is that by tendering the medical issue in the lawsuit, the participants waived the privilege in the administrative proceeding. For a discussion of how privileges can be waived, see § 20.05 supra.

A physician is defined as "a person authorized, or reasonably believed by the patient to be authorized, to practice medicine in any state or nation."[13] The privilege thus protects patients from reasonable mistakes about the licensing status of the "physician" they consult and entitles patients to assume that communications with out-of-state "physicians" will be given the same protection as communications with California physicians. "A patient should not be forced to inquire about the jurisdictions where the physician is authorized to practice medicine and whether such jurisdictions recognize the physician-patient privilege before he may safely communicate with the physician."[14]

Second, the privilege protects from disclosure only those communications between the patient and physician transmitted in the course of the physician-patient relationship.[15] The privilege protects the patient's verbal disclosures as well as the nonverbal information which the physician obtains by examining the patient.[16] Photographs and videotapes taken by a physician of a patient's condition are entitled to the same protection as the physicians's observations of the condition.[17] The physician's diagnosis and advice are also within the privilege.[18]

Whether or not a patient's identity is protected by the privilege depends upon whether disclosure would reveal confidential information, such as the reasons why the patient consulted the physician. In Marcus v. Superior Court[19] the plaintiff sued a physician for medical malpractice in the administration of an angiogram. In his deposition, the physician claimed the physician-patient privilege in refusing to identify other patients to whom he had administered angiograms. In upholding the privilege claim, the court stressed that, under the circumstances, disclosing the patients' names was tantamount to revealing their reasons for consulting the physician.[20]

Third, the information must be transmitted "in confidence by a means which so far as the patient is aware, discloses the information to no third persons other than those who are present to further the interest of the patient in the consultation or those to whom disclosure is reasonably necessary for the transmission of the information or the accomplishment

---

13. West's Ann. California Evidence Code § 990.

14. Id. (comment). The physician-patient relationship also exists between a medical or podiatry corporation, as defined in the Medical Act, and the patient to whom it renders professional services, as well as between the licensed physicians and surgeons employed by the corporation and the patients to whom they render the professional services. West's Ann. California Evidence Code § 994(c).

15. West's Ann. California Evidence Code § 992.

16. Id.

17. Binder v. Superior Court, 196 Cal.App.3d 893, 897, 242 Cal.Rptr. 231, 234 (1987). Disclosing medical records, such as photographs of the patient's condition, may also violate the state constitutional right to privacy. Id. at 899, 242 Cal.Rptr. at 235.

18. Id.

19. 18 Cal.App.3d 22, 95 Cal.Rptr. 545 (1971).

20. Id. at 25, 95 Cal.Rptr. at 547.

of the purpose for which the physician is consulted * * *."[21] The Code rejects the eavesdropper doctrine, which permits individuals who overhear physician-patient communications to reveal them despite the desire of the patient and the physician to keep them confidential.[22] Patients are protected against the risk of disclosure by eavesdroppers and other wrongful interceptors of confidential information by permitting the holder of the privilege to assert it against anyone, including the eavesdropper, who acquires the information without the patient's consent.[23]

If the patient is aware that the means chosen for transmitting the information discloses it to third persons who are not authorized to be present, the communication is not deemed confidential.[24] Such a communication acquires no protection and those who overhear it, as well as the patient and the physician, can be compelled to disclose the communication. Transmitting the information under circumstances where others can easily overhear it is evidence that the patient did not intend the communication to be confidential.[25] Under the Code, however, communications between physicians and patients are presumed to be confidential.[26] The effect of the presumption is to place on the party opposing the claim of privilege the burden of persuading the judge that the communication was not made in confidence.[27]

The presence of third persons to further the interest of the patient in the consultation does not strip the information of its confidential nature.[28] Spouse, parents, nurses, technicians, and others the patient needs in consulting the physician or in securing his or her services may be present.

Confidential communications are not limited to those that take place between the patient and the physician. They also include communications made to third persons—such as the physician's secretary or nurse or another physician—who serve as conduits for the communication from the patient to the physician.[29] These communications are confidential because they are reasonably necessary for the transmission of the information.[30]

Confidential communications also embrace revelations by the patient or the physician to experts whom the physician wishes to use in diagnos-

---

21. Id.

22. See West's Ann. California Evidence Code § 952 and (comment), relating to the attorney-client privilege.

23. Id.

24. See West's Ann. California Evidence Code § 954 (comment) relating to the attorney-client relationship.

25. Id. However, confidential communications do not lose their privileged character simply because they are communicated by electronic means or because persons involved in the delivery, facilitation, or storage of electronic communications might have access to their content. West's Ann. California Evidence Code § 917.

26. West's Ann. California Evidence Code § 917.

27. Id. For a discussion of this presumption, see § 20.03 supra.

28. West's Ann. California Evidence Code § 992.

29. See West's Ann. California Evidence Code § 952 and comment relating to the attorney-client relationship.

30. West's Ann. California Evidence Code § 992.

ing or treating the patient's condition. These disclosures are entitled to protection because they are reasonably necessary for accomplishing the purpose for which the physician is consulted.[31] These disclosures include also the information a physician provides a patient's health insurer to obtain payment of the physician's fees.[32]

The physician-patient privilege does not necessarily preclude a doctor from testifying for the defense in a personal injury action even though the physician has treated the plaintiff. Only if the doctor considers or discloses information obtained in the course of the physician-patient relationship will the privilege claim prevent the doctor from testifying.[33]

QUESTIONS AND PROBLEMS

1.   The physician-patient privilege seeks to promote effective diagnosis and treatment by encouraging full disclosure by patients. True or false?

2.   Only those communications which a patient makes while seeking a diagnosis are protected. Communications made while merely consulting the physician about a possible course of treatment are not protected. True or false?

3.   The physician-patient privilege is broader than the psychotherapist-patient privilege because the former includes mental as well as physical conditions. True or false?

4.   If the "physician" was not authorized to practice medicine, then the privilege does not apply even if the patient reasonably believed that the physician was authorized to practice. True or false?

5.   Whether or not a patient's name is privileged depends on whether disclosure would reveal confidential information, such as the reasons the patient consulted the physician. True or false?

6.   The privilege protects the doctor's diagnosis and advice as well as the patient's revelations. True or false?

7.   The privilege also protects disclosures which the patient or the doctor makes to third persons whom the doctor wishes to use in diagnosing or treating the patient. True or false?

8.   The third persons can include the information a doctor provides a patient's health insurer to obtain payment of the doctor's fees. True or false?

§ 24.02 CLAIMING THE PRIVILEGE

A patient, whether or not a party, has a privilege to refuse to disclose or to prevent another from disclosing a confidential communication between the patient and the physician if the privilege is claimed by (1) the

---

31. Id.

32. Blue Cross v. Superior Court, 61 Cal.App.3d 798, 801, 132 Cal.Rptr. 635, 637 (1976). An insurer is deemed to be authorized by the patient or other holder to claim the privilege when disclosure of the information is sought. Id. at 800, 132 Cal.Rptr. at 636.

33. Torres v. Superior Court, 221 Cal.App.3d 181, 187, 270 Cal.Rptr. 401, 404 (1990).

holder of the privilege, (2) a person authorized by the holder to claim the privilege, or (3) the person who was the physician at the time the confidential communication was made.[1] The physician not only has the right to claim the privilege but has an obligation to do so if present when disclosure of the communication is sought.[2]

A holder is defined as (1) the patient when he has no guardian or conservator, (2) the guardian or conservator when the patient has a guardian or conservator, or (3) the personal representative if the patient is dead.[3] If the patient has separate guardians of his estate and of his person, either may claim the privilege.[4]

A drug manufacturer can be among the persons authorized by the holder to claim the privilege. In Rudnick v. Superior Court[5] the plaintiff sued a drug manufacturer for injuries allegedly sustained from taking an unsafe drug. The manufacturer resisted producing records from doctors reporting adverse reactions to the drug on the ground that revealing the records would violate the physician-patient privilege. The court held that the manufacturer was entitled to a hearing to determine whether the physicians' disclosure of the adverse reactions was reasonably necessary to accomplish the purpose for which the patients consulted their physicians.[6] If so, then the manufacturer would be among the persons implicitly authorized by the holders to claim the privilege.[7]

Disclosures of confidential information by physicians to a patient's health insurer to obtain payment of the physician's fees are protected by the physician-patient privilege.[8] These disclosures have been held to be reasonably necessary to accomplishing the purpose for which the physician is consulted.[9] Like the drug manufacturer, the health insurer is deemed to have been authorized by the patient to claim the privilege when disclosure of this information is sought from the insurer.[10]

The privilege may be claimed only if a holder is in existence.[11] Once the patient's estate has been distributed and the representative discharged, the privilege terminates. At that point, "the importance of providing complete access to information relevant to a particular proceed-

---

1. West's Ann. California Evidence Code § 994.

2. West's Ann. California Evidence Code § 995. The physician, however, may not claim the privilege if the holder is no longer in existence or if a person authorized to claim the privilege has instructed the physician not to claim it. West's Ann. California Evidence Code §§ 994–995.

3. West's Ann. California Evidence Code § 993. The personal representative of the patient has the right "to freely communicate with [the patient's] doctors, thoroughly investigate [the patient's] condition, and assert the privilege to the extent it is appropriate." Hale v. Superior Court, 28 Cal.App.4th 1421, 1424, 34 Cal.Rptr.2d 279, 280 (1994).

4. West's Ann. California Evidence Code § 993 (comment).

5. 11 Cal.3d 924, 114 Cal.Rptr. 603, 523 P.2d 643 (1974).

6. Id. at 933–934, 114 Cal.Rptr. at 610–611, 523 P.2d at 650–651.

7. Id.

8. Blue Cross v. Superior Court, 61 Cal.App.3d 798, 801, 132 Cal.Rptr. 635, 636 (1976).

9. Id.

10. Id.

11. West's Ann. California Evidence Code § 993 (comment).

ing should prevail over whatever remaining interest the decedent may have had in secrecy."[12]

The privilege may be waived by the holder.[13]

QUESTIONS AND PROBLEMS

1. The patient, as a holder of the privilege, may claim it to prevent the disclosure of confidential communications. His physician has an obligation to do so if present when disclosure is sought unless instructed otherwise by the patient or the patient's representative. True or false?

2. Drug manufacturers who receive confidential patient information from doctors can claim the privilege if the doctors furnished the manufacturers with the information to seek help in diagnosing or treating the patient's conditions. True or false?

§ 24.03 EXCEPTIONS

Communications that would otherwise be privileged are not protected if they fall within the following exceptions:

1. No privilege exists for communications relevant to an issue concerning the condition of the patient if the issue has been tendered by (1) the patient, (2) a party claiming through or under the patient, (3) a party claiming as a beneficiary of the patient through a contract to which the patient is or was a party, or (4) a plaintiff who brings an action under the Civil Procedure Code for damages for injury to or the death of the patient.[1] If the patient or a party claiming through or under the patient tenders the physical, mental or emotional condition of the patient, fairness requires giving the opposing party information that is relevant to that condition but that otherwise would be shielded by the privilege.[2] The same policy requires a like result when a survivor sues for the wrongful death of the patient or a parent sues for injuries to a child.[3] As was stated by Justice Traynor:

> The patient-litigant exception precludes one who has placed in issue his physical condition from invoking the privilege on the ground that disclosure of his condition would cause him humiliation. He cannot have his cake and eat it too.[4]

The patient-litigant exception limits the usefulness of the privilege in many cases in which the privilege otherwise could be claimed. A party's physical, mental, or emotional condition is most likely to arise in personal

---

12. Id.

13. For a discussion of how the privilege can be waived, see § 20.05 supra.

1. West's Ann. California Evidence Code § 996.

2. Id. (comment).

3. Id.

4. City and County of San Francisco v. Superior Court, 37 Cal.2d 227, 232, 231 P.2d 26, 28 (1951).

injury claims. By filing such a claim, a plaintiff tenders at least one of these conditions and thereby loses the privilege.

The exception does not apply unless the party tendering the issue is the patient or a party claiming through or under the patient. Carlton v. Superior Court[5] underscores this point. In that case, a passenger sued a driver on the ground that the driver was intoxicated at the time of the accident. To prove the driver's intoxication, the passenger offered a medical record of an examination taken shortly after the accident showing that the driver was intoxicated. The court upheld the driver's physician-patient claim. By denying his intoxication, the driver did not tender his physical or mental condition at the time of the accident.[6]

The exception, moreover, applies only to the conditions tendered by the patient or the parties claiming through or under him. Claims of hearing loss and emotional distress on account of jet noise or of arm and shoulder injuries from a car accident do not entitle the opposing party to all of the patient's medical history.[7] Only the medical history that is pertinent to the conditions tendered by the patient fall within the exception.[8]

In one instance the pertinent medical history may embrace not just that of the patient tendering the issue but of a nonparty as well. In Palay v. Superior Court[9] a child sued the Harbor–UCLA Medical Center on the grounds that the center and its attending physicians were negligent in failing to diagnose and treat a cardiac disease detected at birth. The center sought to discover the mother's medical records for the period when she was pregnant with the child. The mother resisted on the ground that her medical history was protected from disclosure by the physician-patient privilege.

The court conceded that the mother's privilege was separate from the child's and that only the child's medical history fell within the patient-litigant exception, since, as the plaintiff, only the child had tendered his medical condition.[10] The court nonetheless held that mother's privilege had to yield to the patient-litigant exception: "The medical histories of a mother and her child, while the infant [is] *in utero* are inextricably related. [D]uring pregnancy the mother and the fetus are one indivisible

---

5. 261 Cal.App.2d 282, 67 Cal.Rptr. 568 (1968).

6. Id. at 290, 67 Cal.Rptr. at 573. In such a situation, the injured party should move for discovery of the medical records under § 999. This section exempts from the privilege communications relevant to an issue concerning the condition of the patient in a proceeding to recover damages on account of the conduct of the patient. See text accompanying note 17 infra.

7. Britt v. Superior Court, 20 Cal.3d 844, 863–864, 143 Cal.Rptr. 695, 707–708, 574 P.2d 766, 778–779 (1978); Hallendorf v. Superior Court, 85 Cal.App.3d 553, 556, 149 Cal.Rptr. 564, 566 (1978). The same principle applies to waiver of the privilege by disclosing a significant part of the privileged communication. See § 20.05 supra.

8. Britt v. Superior Court, 20 Cal.3d 844, 863–864, 143 Cal.Rptr. 695, 707–708, 574 P.2d 766, 778–779 (1978). See also Allison v. Workers' Comp. Appeals Bd., 72 Cal.App.4th 654, 659, 84 Cal.Rptr.2d 915, 919 (1999) (holding that an action to recover for a wrist injury does not entitle the defendant to discover all of the plaintiff's medical history).

9. 18 Cal.App.4th 919, 22 Cal.Rptr.2d 839 (1993).

10. Id. at 927, 22 Cal.Rptr.2d at 843.

unit. Therefore, we find that, under a theory of inseparability, during the period Mother was pregnant with Child, the privilege as to her prenatal medical records must yield to * * * the patient-litigant exception * * *.''[11]

2.   No privilege exists if the services of the physician were sought or obtained to enable or aid any one to commit or plan to commit a crime or a tort or to escape detection or apprehension after committing a crime or tort.[12] "This [exception] is broader in scope than [the one providing] that the lawyer-client privilege does not apply when the communication was made to enable anyone to commit or plan to commit a crime or a *fraud*. * * * People seldom, if ever, consult their physicians in regard to matters which might subsequently be determined to be a tort, and there is no desirable end to be served by encouraging such communications. On the other hand, people often consult lawyers about matters which may later turn out to be torts, and it is desirable to encourage discussion of such matters with lawyers."[13]

3.   No privilege exists if disclosure is sought in a criminal proceeding.[14] In contrast, the psychotherapist-patient privilege applies in all proceedings.[15] While the Law Revision Commission was advised that patients may not talk freely with psychotherapists unless assured that their communications will remain confidential in criminal proceedings, the Commission received no such information about patients who consult doctors for medical advice or treatment.[16]

4.   No privilege exists for communications relevant to an issue concerning the condition of the patient in a proceeding to recover damages on account of the conduct of the patient if good cause for disclosure of the communications is shown.[17] In John B. v. Superior Court[18] the plaintiff sued her husband for allegedly infecting her with AIDS. She sought to discover, among other matters, the results of her husband's HIV and

---

11.   Id. at 930, 22 Cal.Rptr.2d at 846.

12.   West's Ann. California Evidence Code § 997.

13.   Id. (comment) (emphasis in the original).

14.   West's Ann. California Evidence Code § 998. Section 5328 of the Welfare and Institutions Code protects some medical records from disclosure in criminal proceedings. "All information and records obtained in the course of providing services under [various provisions of the Welfare and Institutions Code] to either voluntary or involuntary recipients of services shall be confidential." West's Ann. Welfare and Institutions Code § 5328.

15.   West's Ann. California Evidence Code § 1014 (comment). But under the psychotherapist-patient privilege, no privilege exists for communications relevant to an issue concerning the mental or emotional conditions of the patient if the issue is tendered by the patient. California Evidence Code § 1016 (West 1966); see also § 23.03 supra. Thus, the psychotherapist-patient privilege will not afford the accused protection in criminal cases when the accused relies on such concepts as diminished capacity to disprove the mens rea of the offense charged. See, e.g., People v. Arcega, 32 Cal.3d 504, 523, note 8, 186 Cal.Rptr. 94, 104, note 8, 651 P.2d 338, 348, note 8 (1982).

16.   West's Ann. California Evidence Code § 1014 (comment).

17.   West's Ann. California Evidence Code § 999. As originally enacted, § 999 applied only in proceedings to recover damages arising out of the criminal conduct of the patient. Id. (comment). As amended, the party claiming the exception does not need to show that the conduct of the patient would constitute a crime. Id. The good cause requirement is designed to protect the patient against "fishing expeditions" into his medical records. Id.

18.   38 Cal.4th 1177, 45 Cal.Rptr.3d 316, 137 P.3d 153 (2006).

AIDS tests, and the medical treatment he received for these conditions and all sexually transmitted diseases. The reviewing court approved the issuance of a subpoena for these matters.[19]

This exception applies even where the plaintiff is the patient. In Slagle v. Superior Court (Maryon)[20] the plaintiff sued for injuries he claimed he suffered when the defendant hit him with her car. The defendant claimed contributory negligence and sought medical records showing that the plaintiff had suffered from impaired vision for several months prior to the accident. The plaintiff contended that the medical records did not fall within the exception for communications relevant to an issue tendered by the patient because the plaintiff was not seeking to recover for injury to his eyes. The court affirmed the trial court's order requiring production of the records: it was immaterial that the plaintiff was not seeking to recover for injury to his eyes; the defendant was relying on a different exception, one that "permits disclosure *not only* where the patient is a party to the action *but also* in a case where a party's liability is based on the conduct of the patient."[21]

5. No privilege exists in administrative proceedings brought by a public entity to determine whether a right, authority, license, or privilege (including the right or privilege to be employed by the public entity or to hold a public office) should be revoked, suspended, terminated, limited, or conditioned.[22] A distinction must be made between the medical records, say, of a licensee and those of the licensee's patients. For example, an administrative investigation of the competency of a doctor does not automatically entitle the investigative body to the medical records of the doctor's patients. Since these records are protected by the state's constitutional right of privacy, the investigative body must at least demonstrate "the relevance or materiality" of the patients' medical records before disclosure can be compelled.[23] The right to privacy, however, does not cover medical records sought by administrative agencies if the identities of the patients are not disclosed.[24] Deleting the information identifying the patients will satisfy the constitutional requirements.[25]

6. No privilege exists for communications relevant to an issue between parties all of whom claim through a deceased patient, regardless of whether the claims are by testate or intestate succession or by inter vivos transaction.[26] "The traditional exception for litigation between claimants

---

19. Id. at 1202, 45 Cal.Rptr.3d at 335, 137 P.3d at 169.

20. 211 Cal.App.3d 1309, 260 Cal.Rptr. 122 (1989).

21. Id. at 1314, 260 Cal.Rptr. at 125 (quoting from the comment to California Evidence Code § 999) (emphasis in the original).

22. West's Ann. California Evidence Code § 1007.

23. Board of Medical Quality Assurance v. Gherardini, 93 Cal.App.3d 669, 681, 156 Cal.Rptr. 55, 62 (1979).

24. Board of Medical Quality Assurance v. Hazel Hawkins Memorial Hospital, 135 Cal.App.3d 561, 565, 185 Cal.Rptr. 405, 408 (1982).

25. Kizer v. Sulnick, 202 Cal.App.3d 431, 439, 248 Cal.Rptr. 712, 716 (1988).

26. West's Ann. California Evidence Code § 1000.

by testate or intestate succession is based on the theory that claimants in privity with the estate claim *through* the [patient], not adversely, and the deceased [patient] presumably would want his communications disclosed in litigation between such claimants so that his desires in regard to the disposition of his estate might be correctly ascertained and carried out. This rationale is equally applicable where one or more of the parties is claiming by inter vivos transaction, as for example, in an action between a party who claims under a deed (executed by a [patient] in full possession of his faculties) and a party who claims under a will executed while the [patient's] mental stability was dubious."[27]

7. No privilege exists for communications relevant to an issue of breach, by the physician or by the patient, of a duty arising out of the physician-patient relationship.[28]

8. No privilege exists for communications relevant to an issue concerning the intention of the patient, now deceased, with respect to a deed of conveyance, will, or other writing executed by the patient purporting to affect an interest in property.[29] This exception allows the physician to disclose the patient's true intentions regarding dispositive instruments.[30]

9. Similarly, no privilege exists for communications relevant to an issue concerning the validity of a deed of conveyance, will, or other writing executed by a patient, now deceased, purporting to affect an interest in property.[31]

10. No privilege exists for communications offered in proceedings to commit the patient or otherwise place him or his property, or both, under the control of another because of the patient's alleged mental or physical condition.[32] "This exception covers not only commitments of mentally ill persons, but also such cases as the appointment of a conservator under the Probate Code over the patient's person or property. In these cases, the proceedings are being conducted for the benefit of the patient and he should not have a privilege to withhold evidence that the court needs in order to act properly for his welfare."[33] The exception also embraces proceedings under the Welfare and Institutions Code to declare a minor a dependent child of the court.[34]

The exception is considerably broader than the analogous exception provided under the psychotherapist-patient privilege.[35] A psychotherapist

---

27. See West's Ann. California Evidence Code § 957 (comment) (emphasis in the original) relating to the attorney-client privilege.

28. West's Ann. California Evidence Code § 1001.

29. West's Ann. California Evidence Code § 1002.

30. West's Ann. California Evidence Code § 960 (comment) relating to the attorney-client privilege.

31. West's Ann. California Evidence Code § 1003.

32. West's Ann. California Evidence Code § 1004.

33. Id. (comment).

34. In re Jeannie Q., 32 Cal.App.3d 288, 304, 107 Cal.Rptr. 646, 658 (1973).

35. West's Ann. California Evidence Code § 1014 (comment).

may disclose a privileged communication only if the psychotherapist has reasonable cause to believe that the patient is in such mental or emotional condition as to be dangerous to himself or to the person or property of another that disclosure is necessary to prevent the threatened danger.[36]

11. No privilege exists for communications offered in proceedings brought by or on behalf of the patient to establish his competence.[37] "When a patient has placed his mental condition in issue by instituting a proceeding to establish his competence, he should not be permitted to withhold the most vital evidence relating thereto."[38]

12. No privilege exists for information that the physician or the patient is required to report to a public employee or that is required to be recorded in a public office, if such report or record is open to public inspection.[39] "[N]o valid purpose is served by preventing the use of relevant information when the law requiring the information to be reported to a public office does not restrict disclosure."[40]

QUESTIONS AND PROBLEMS

1. The physician-patient privilege does not apply to communications that are relevant to an issue concerning the patient's mental, emotional or physical condition if tendered by the patient. True or false?

2. The patient must tender the condition for the exception to apply. A patient does not tender a medical condition simply by denying that he was intoxicated at the time of the accident. True or false?

3. But if the discovering party's theory is that the patient's conduct was the cause of the accident, then the party can discover that portion of the patient's medical history describing medical conditions that are probative of the patient's conduct. For example, if the defendant's theory is that the plaintiff was contributorily negligent on account of impaired vision, then the defendant is entitled to discover those portions of the plaintiff's medical records relating to her vision even if the plaintiff did not claim damages for injuries to her eyes and hence did not tender that medical condition. True or false?

4. The physician-patient privilege does not apply to commitment proceedings where the patient is the object of a petition to place the patient under a conservatorship because he can no longer take care of himself by reason of a mental disorder. True or false?

5. The physician-patient privilege, like the psychotherapist-patient privilege, can be claimed in criminal proceedings. True or false?

---

36. West's Ann. California Evidence Code § 1024.
37. West's Ann. California Evidence Code § 1005.
38. Id. (comment).
39. West's Ann. California Evidence Code § 1006.
40. Id. (comment).

CALIFORNIA EVIDENCE CODE

§ 990. Physician

As used in this article, "physician" means a person authorized, or reasonably believed by the patient to be authorized, to practice medicine in any state or nation.

§ 991. Patient

As used in this article, "patient" means a person who consults a physician or submits to an examination by a physician for the purpose of securing a diagnosis or preventive, palliative, or curative treatment of his physical or mental or emotional condition.

§ 992. Confidential communication between patient and physician

As used in this article, "confidential communication between patient and physician" means information, including information obtained by an examination of the patient, transmitted between a patient and his physician in the course of that relationship and in confidence by a means which, so far as the patient is aware, discloses the information to no third persons other than those who are present to further the interest of the patient in the consultation or those to whom disclosure is reasonably necessary for the transmission of the information or the accomplishment of the purpose for which the physician is consulted, and includes a diagnosis made and the advice given by the physician in the course of that relationship.

§ 993. Holder of the privilege

As used in this article, "holder of the privilege" means:

(a) The patient when he has no guardian or conservator.

(b) A guardian or conservator of the patient when the patient has a guardian or conservator.

(c) The personal representative of the patient if the patient is dead.

§ 994. Physician-patient privilege

Subject to Section 912 and except as otherwise provided in this article, the patient, whether or not a party, has a privilege to refuse to disclose, and to prevent another from disclosing, a confidential communication between patient and physician if the privilege is claimed by:

(a) The holder of the privilege;

(b) A person who is authorized to claim the privilege by the holder of the privilege; or

(c) The person who was the physician at the time of the confidential communication, but such person may not claim the privilege if there is no holder of the privilege in existence or if he or she is otherwise instructed by a person authorized to permit disclosure.

The relationship of a physician and patient shall exist between a medical or podiatry corporation as defined in the Medical Practice Act and the patient to whom it renders professional services, as well as between such patients and licensed physicians and surgeons employed by such corporation to render services to such patients. The word "persons" as used in this subdivision includes partnerships, corporations, limited liability companies, associations, and other groups and entities.

§ 995. When physician required to claim privilege

The physician who received or made a communication subject to the privilege under this article shall claim the privilege whenever he is present when the communication is sought to be disclosed and is authorized to claim the privilege under subdivision (c) of Section 994.

§ 996. Patient-litigant exception

There is no privilege under this article as to a communication relevant to an issue concerning the condition of the patient if such issue has been tendered by:

(a) The patient;

(b) Any party claiming through or under the patient;

(c) Any party claiming as a beneficiary of the patient through a contract to which the patient is or was a party; or

(d) The plaintiff in an action brought under Section 376 or 377 of the Code of Civil Procedure for damages for the injury or death of the patient.

§ 997. Exception: Crime or tort

There is no privilege under this article if the services of the physician were sought or obtained to enable or aid anyone to commit or plan to commit a crime or a tort or to escape detection or apprehension after the commission of a crime or a tort.

§ 998. Exception: Criminal proceeding

There is no privilege under this article in a criminal proceeding.

§ 999. Communication relating to patient condition in proceeding to recover damages; good cause

There is no privilege under this article as to a communication relevant to an issue concerning the condition of the patient in a proceeding to recover damages on account of the conduct of the patient if good cause for disclosure of the communication is shown.

§ 1000. Parties claiming through deceased patient

There is no privilege under this article as to a communication relevant to an issue between parties all of whom claim through a deceased patient, regardless of whether the claims are by testate or intestate succession or by inter vivos transaction.

§ 1001. Breach of duty arising out of physician-patient relationship

There is no privilege under this article as to a communication relevant to an issue of breach, by the physician or by the patient, of a duty arising out of the physician-patient relationship.

§ 1002. Intention of deceased patient concerning writing affecting property interest

There is no privilege under this article as to a communication relevant to an issue concerning the intention of a patient, now deceased, with respect to a deed of conveyance, will, or other writing, executed by the patient, purporting to affect an interest in property.

§ 1003. Validity of writing affecting property interest

There is no privilege under this article as to a communication relevant to an issue concerning the validity of a deed of conveyance, will, or other writing, executed by a patient, now deceased, purporting to affect an interest in property.

§ 1004. Commitment or similar proceeding

There is no privilege under this article in a proceeding to commit the patient or otherwise place him or his property, or both, under the control of another because of his alleged mental or physical condition.

§ 1005. Proceeding to establish competence

There is no privilege under this article in a proceeding brought by or on behalf of the patient to establish his competence.

§ 1006. Required report

There is no privilege under this article as to information that the physician or the patient is required to report to a public employee, or as to information required to be recorded in a public office, if such report or record is open to public inspection.

§ 1007. Exception—Proceeding to terminate right, license or privilege

There is no privilege under this article in a proceeding brought by a public entity to determine whether a right, authority, license, or privilege (including the right or privilege to be employed by the public entity or to hold a public office) should be revoked, suspended, terminated, limited, or conditioned.

CHAPTER 25

THE SEXUAL ASSAULT COUNSELOR–VICTIM PRIVILEGE

■ ■ ■

Table of Sections

§ 25.01 NATURE OF THE PRIVILEGE

A victim of a sexual assault, whether or not a party, has a privilege to refuse to disclose and to prevent another from disclosing a confidential communication between the victim and a sexual assault counselor.[1] The purpose of the privilege is to promote effective counseling by encouraging full disclosure by victims. To be privileged, the communication must satisfy a number of tests.

First, the communication must be between the victim of a sexual assault and a sexual assault counselor in the course of the victim-sexual assault counselor relationship.[2]

A sexual assault is defined broadly, ranging from various forms of rape to unlawful sexual intercourse and from various forms of lewd and lascivious conduct with children to molesting or annoying children.[3] The term includes as well attempts to commit the enumerated offenses.[4]

A victim is anyone who consults a sexual assault victim counselor for the purpose of securing advice or assistance concerning a mental, physical, or emotional condition caused by a sexual assault.[5] A sexual assault victim counselor is someone whose primary purpose is to render advice or

---

1. West's Ann. California Evidence Code § 1035.8. The privilege is a qualified, not an absolute, privilege. See § 25.03 infra.

2. West's Ann. California Evidence Code § 1037.2.

3. For a list of the enumerated offenses, see West's Ann. California Evidence Code § 1036.2.

4. Id.

5. West's Ann. California Evidence Code § 1035.

assistance to sexual assault victims and who is qualified to do so by reason of training and experience.[6]

Second, the privilege extends only to information transmitted between the victim and the sexual assault counselor in the course of their relationship.[7] The privilege includes all the facts and circumstances involved in the alleged sexual assault as well as all information regarding the victim's prior or subsequent sexual conduct and opinions regarding the victim's sexual conduct or reputation in sexual matters.[8] The privilege, however, protects only the information transmitted between the victim and the counselor. It does not prevent disclosing the fact that the victim attended a sexual abuse presentation.[9] But to encourage victims to seek advice and assistance, the privilege prevents disclosing the fact that the victim sought the help of a sexual abuse counselor.[10]

Third, the information must be transmitted "in confidence by a means which, so far as the victim is aware, discloses the information to no third persons other than those who are present to further the interests of the victim in the consultation or those to whom disclosures are reasonably necessary for the transmission of the information or an accomplishment of the purposes for which the sexual assault counselor is consulted."[11] The Code rejects the eavesdropper doctrine, which allows individuals who overhear victim-sexual assault counselor communications to reveal them despite the desire of the victim and the counselor to keep them confidential.[12] Victims are protected against the risk of disclosure by eavesdroppers and other wrongful interceptors by permitting the holder of the privilege to assert it against anyone, including eavesdroppers, who acquires the information without the victim's consent.[13]

If the victim is aware that the means chosen for transmitting the information discloses it to third persons who are not authorized to be present, the communication is not deemed confidential.[14] Such a communication acquires no protection and can be disclosed by those who overhear it. Transmitting the information under circumstances where others can easily overhear it is evidence that the victim did not intend the communication to be confidential.[15] Under the Code, however, communi-

---

6. For details regarding the qualifications of sexual assault victim counselors, see West's Ann. California Evidence Code § 1035.2.

7. West's Ann. California Evidence Code § 1035.4.

8. Id.

9. People v. Gilbert, 5 Cal.App.4th 1372, 1391, 7 Cal.Rptr.2d 660, 672 (1992).

10. Id.

11. West's Ann. California Evidence Code § 1035.2.

12. See West's Ann. California Evidence Code § 952 and comment relating to the attorney-client privilege.

13. Id.

14. See West's Ann. California Evidence Code § 954 (comment) relating to the attorney-client privilege.

15. Id. However, confidential communications do not lose their privileged character simply because they are communicated by electronic means or because persons involved in the delivery,

cations between victims and their counselors are presumed to be confidential.[16] Consequently, the person opposing the privilege has the burden of persuading the judge that the communication was not made in confidence.

The presence of third persons to further the interests of the victim in the consultation does not strip the information of its confidential nature.[17] Spouses, parents, and others the victim needs in consulting the counselor may be present.

Confidential communications are not limited to those that take place between the victim and the counselor. They can also include communications made to third persons who serve as conduits for the communication from the victim to the counselor.[18] Examples include revelations by the victim to others whom the counselor wishes to use in counseling the victim. These disclosures are protected because they are reasonably necessary for accomplishing the purposes for which the counselor is consulted.[19]

QUESTIONS AND PROBLEMS

1.   A victim of a sexual assault has a privilege to refuse to disclose and to prevent another from disclosing a confidential communication between the victim and a sexual assault counselor. True or false?

2.   A sexual assault is not limited to rape but may include unlawful sexual intercourse (statutory rape) as well as lewd and lascivious conduct with children. True or false?

3.   To qualify as "victim," the victim must consult a sexual assault counselor for the purpose of securing advice or assistance regarding mental, physical, or emotional conditions caused by a sexual assault. True or false?

4.   The information protected from disclosure by the privilege is limited to the facts and circumstances surrounding the alleged sexual assault. True or false?

5.   Communications between a victim and a sexual assault counselor are not presumed to be confidential. Consequently, the party claiming the privilege must persuade the judge that the communications in question were made in confidence. True or false?

6.   The privilege protects from disclosure revelations by the victim to others whom the counselor wishes to use in counseling the victim. True or false?

§ 25.02   CLAIMING THE PRIVILEGE

A victim of sexual assault, whether or not a party, has a privilege to refuse to disclose and prevent another from disclosing a confidential

---

facilitation, or storage of electronic communications might have access to their content. West's Ann. California Evidence Code § 917.

16.   West's Ann. California Evidence Code § 917.

17.   West's Ann. California Evidence Code § 1035.4.

18.   Id.

19.   Id.

communication between the victim and a sexual assault victim counselor if the privilege is claimed by (1) the holder of the privilege, (2) a person authorized by the holder to claim the privilege, or (3) the person who was the counselor at the time the communication was made.[1] The counselor not only has the right to claim the privilege, but has an obligation do so if present when disclosure of the communication is sought.[2]

A holder is (1) the victim when such person has no guardian or conservator, (2) the guardian or conservator when the victim has a guardian or conservator, or (3) the personal representative of the victim if the victim is dead.[3]

The privilege may be claimed only if a holder is in existence.[4] The privilege can be waived by the holder.[5]

QUESTIONS AND PROBLEMS

1. The victim of a sexual assault, as the holder of the privilege, may claim the privilege whether or not the victim is a party to the proceeding in which the privilege is claimed. True or false?

2. The counselor, however, has no obligation to claim the privilege even if present when disclosure of a protected communication is sought. True or false?

§ 25.03 COMPELLED DISCLOSURES

A court in the exercise of its discretion may compel disclosure of information received by the sexual assault counselor if certain conditions are met.[1]

First, the judge must find that the information received by the counselor "constitutes relevant evidence of the facts and circumstances involving an alleged sexual assault about which the victim is complaining and which is the subject of a criminal proceeding * * *."[2] Second, the judge must find that the probative value of the evidence outweighs the prejudicial effects that disclosure of the information might have on the victim, the treatment relationship, and the treatment services.[3]

In ruling on the claim of privilege, the judge "may require the person from whom disclosure is sought or the person authorized to claim the

---

1. West's Ann. California Evidence Code § 1035.8.

2. West's Ann. California Evidence Code § 1036.

3. West's Ann. California Evidence Code § 1035.6.

4. West's Ann. California Evidence Code § 1035.8(c).

5. For a discussion of how the privilege can be waived, see § 20.05 supra.

1. West's Ann. California Evidence Code § 1035.4.

2. Id.

3. Id. A judge may also compel disclosure in child abuse proceedings if the judge determines that the probative value of the information outweighs the effect that disclosure will have on the child, the treatment relationship, and the treatment services. Id.

privilege, or both, to disclose the information in chambers out of the presence and hearing of all persons except the person authorized to claim the privilege and such other persons as the person authorized to claim the privilege is willing to have present."[4] If the judge determines that the information is privileged, neither the judge nor any other person may disclose the information revealed in chambers, unless authorized to do so by a person authorized to permit disclosure.[5]

If the judge determines that particular information may be subject to disclosure pursuant to the balancing test, the judge must follow a pre-scribed procedure before ordering the information disclosed:

One, the judge must inform the defendant of the nature of the information which may be subject to disclosure.[6]

Two, the judge must hold a hearing out of the presence of the jury, if any, to allow the questioning of the sexual assault counselor about the information which the judge has determined may be subject to disclosure.[7]

Three, at the conclusion of the hearing the judge must determine which items of information should be disclosed. The judge's order must specify the evidence that may be offered by the defendant and the nature of the questions that will be permitted. The defendant may then offer the evidence pursuant to the judge's order.[8]

The sexual assault victim-counselor privilege does not mandate the receipt of the evidence. Whether evidence of the victim's sexual conduct is admissible to prove that the victim consented to the acts or to attack the credibility of the victim is governed by §§ 782 and 1103.[9]

QUESTIONS AND PROBLEMS

1. Unlike the major privileges, the privilege protecting the confidential communications of sexual assault victims does not contain exceptions. Instead, the privilege allows for the discretionary disclosure of the communications if certain conditions are met. True or false?

2. Among the conditions that must be met are a finding by the judge that the probative value of the communications on relevant issues outweighs their prejudicial effects on the victim, the treatment relationship, and the treatment services. True or false?

3. If the judge orders disclosure, the evidence may be offered over a privilege objection. But whether the fact finder hears the evidence depends on whether it is admissible under §§ 782 and 1102 of the Code, among others. True or false?

---

4. Id.

5. Id.

6. Id.

7. Id.

8. Id.

9. Id. For a discussion of §§ 782 and 1102, see §§ 3.12 and 15.12 of this treatise.

CALIFORNIA EVIDENCE CODE

§ 1035. Victim

As used in this article, "victim" means a person who consults a sexual assault counselor for the purpose of securing advice or assistance concerning a mental, physical, or emotional condition caused by a sexual assault.

§ 1035.2. Sexual assault counselor

As used in this article, "sexual assault counselor" means any of the following:

(a) A person who is engaged in any office, hospital, institution, or center commonly known as a rape crisis center, whose primary purpose is the rendering of advice or assistance to victims of sexual assault and who has received a certificate evidencing completion of a training program in the counseling of sexual assault victims issued by a counseling center that meets the criteria for the award of a grant established pursuant to Section 13837 of the Penal Code and who meets one of the following requirements:

(1) Is a psychotherapist as defined in Section 1010; has a master's degree in counseling or a related field; or has one year of counseling experience, at least six months of which is in rape crisis counseling.

(2) Has 40 hours of training as described below and is supervised by an individual who qualifies as a counselor under paragraph (1). The training, supervised by a person qualified under paragraph (1), shall include, but not be limited to, the following areas:

(A) Law.

(B) Medicine.

(C) Societal attitudes.

(D) Crisis intervention and counseling techniques.

(E) Role playing.

(F) Referral services.

(G) Sexuality.

(b) A person who is employed by any organization providing the programs specified in Section 13835.2 of the Penal Code, whether financially compensated or not, for the purpose of counseling and assisting sexual assault victims, and who meets one of the following requirements:

(1) Is a psychotherapist as defined in Section 1010; has a master's degree in counseling or a related field; or has one year of

counseling experience, at least six months of which is in rape assault counseling.

(2) Has the minimum training for sexual assault counseling required by guidelines established by the employing agency pursuant to subdivision (c) of Section 13835.10 of the Penal Code, and is supervised by an individual who qualifies as a counselor under paragraph (1). The training, supervised by a person qualified under paragraph (1), shall include, but not be limited to, the following areas:

(A) Law.

(B) Victimology.

(C) Counseling.

(D) Client and system advocacy.

(E) Referral services.

§ 1035.4. Confidential communication between the sexual assault counselor and the victim; disclosure

As used in this article, "confidential communication between the sexual assault counselor and the victim" means information transmitted between the victim and the sexual assault counselor in the course of their relationship and in confidence by a means which, so far as the victim is aware, discloses the information to no third persons other than those who are present to further the interests of the victim in the consultation or those to whom disclosures are reasonably necessary for the transmission of the information or an accomplishment of the purposes for which the sexual assault counselor is consulted. The term includes all information regarding the facts and circumstances involving the alleged sexual assault and also includes all information regarding the victim's prior or subsequent sexual conduct, and opinions regarding the victim's sexual conduct or reputation in sexual matters.

The court may compel disclosure of information received by the sexual assault counselor which constitutes relevant evidence of the facts and circumstances involving an alleged sexual assault about which the victim is complaining and which is the subject of a criminal proceeding if the court determines that the probative value outweighs the effect on the victim, the treatment relationship, and the treatment services if disclosure is compelled. The court may also compel disclosure in proceedings related to child abuse if the court determines the probative value outweighs the effect on the victim, the treatment relationship, and the treatment services if disclosure is compelled.

When a court is ruling on a claim of privilege under this article, the court may require the person from whom disclosure is sought or the person authorized to claim the privilege, or both, to disclose the information in chambers out of the presence and hearing of all persons except the person authorized to claim the privilege and such other persons as the person authorized to claim the privilege is willing to have present. If the judge determines that the information is privileged and must not be disclosed, neither he or she nor any other person may ever disclose, without the consent of a person authorized to permit disclosure, what was disclosed in the course of the proceedings in chambers.

If the court determines certain information shall be disclosed, the court shall so order and inform the defendant. If the court finds there is a reasonable likelihood that particular information is subject to disclosure pursuant to the balancing test provided in this section, the following procedure shall be followed:

(1) The court shall inform the defendant of the nature of the information which may be subject to disclosure.

(2) The court shall order a hearing out of the presence of the jury, if any, and at the hearing allow the questioning of the sexual assault counselor regarding the information which the court has determined may be subject to disclosure.

(3) At the conclusion of the hearing, the court shall rule which items of information, if any, shall be disclosed. The court may make an order stating what evidence may be introduced by the defendant and the nature of questions to be permitted. The defendant may then offer evidence pursuant to the order of the court. Admission of evidence concerning the sexual conduct of the complaining witness is subject to Sections 352, 782, and 1103.

§ 1035.6. Holder of the privilege

As used in this article, "holder of the privilege" means:

(a) The victim when such person has no guardian or conservator.

(b) A guardian or conservator of the victim when the victim has a guardian or conservator.

(c) The personal representative of the victim if the victim is dead.

§ 1035.8. Sexual assault counselor privilege

A victim of a sexual assault, whether or not a party, has a privilege to refuse to disclose, and to prevent another from disclosing, a confidential communication between the victim and a sexual assault counselor if the privilege is claimed by any of the following:

(a) The holder of the privilege;

(b) A person who is authorized to claim the privilege by the holder of the privilege; or

(c) The person who was the sexual assault counselor at the time of the confidential communication, but that person may not claim the privilege if there is no holder of the privilege in existence or if he or she is otherwise instructed by a person authorized to permit disclosure.

§ 1036. Claim of privilege by sexual assault counselor

The sexual assault counselor who received or made a communication subject to the privilege under this article shall claim the privilege if he or she is present when the communication is sought to be disclosed and is authorized to claim the privilege under subdivision (c) of Section 1035.8.

§ 1036.2. Sexual assault

As used in this article, "sexual assault" includes all of the following:

(a) Rape, as defined in Section 261 of the Penal Code.

(b) Unlawful sexual intercourse, as defined in Section 261.5 of the Penal Code.

(c) Rape in concert with force and violence, as defined in Section 264.1 of the Penal Code.

(d) Rape of a spouse, as defined in Section 262 of the Penal Code.

(e) Sodomy, as defined in Section 286 of the Penal Code, except a violation of subdivision (e) of that section.

(f) A violation of Section 288 of the Penal Code.

(g) Oral copulation, as defined in Section 288a of the Penal Code, except a violation of subdivision (e) of that section.

(h) Penetration of the genital or anal openings of another person with a foreign object, substance, instrument, or device, as specified in Section 289 of the Penal Code.

(i) Annoying or molesting a child under 18, as defined in Section 647a of the Penal Code.

(j) Any attempt to commit any of the above acts.

CHAPTER 26

THE DOMESTIC VIOLENCE COUNSELOR–VICTIM PRIVILEGE

■ ■ ■

Table of Sections

§ 26.01 NATURE OF THE PRIVILEGE

A victim of domestic violence, whether or not a party, has a privilege to refuse to disclose and to prevent another from disclosing a confidential communication between the victim and a domestic violence counselor.[1] The purpose of the privilege is to promote effective counseling by encouraging full disclosure by the victim. To be privileged, the communication must meet a number of tests.

First, the communication must be between the victim of domestic violence and a domestic violence counselor in the course of the domestic violence victim-counselor relationship.[2]

Domestic violence is defined as abuse perpetrated against a family or household member.[3] A family or household member means "a spouse, former spouse, parent, child, any other adult person related by consanguinity or affinity within the second degree, or any other person who regularly resides in the household, or who within the last six months regularly resided in the household."[4]

Domestic violence also includes abuse against a person who is in, or has been in, a dating, courtship, or engagement relationship by a person with whom they have had a dating, courtship, or engagement relation-

---

1. West's Ann. California Evidence Code § 1037.5. The privilege is a qualified, not an absolute, privilege.

2. West's Ann. California Evidence Code § 1037.2.

3. West's Ann. Family Law § 6211.

4. Id.

950

ship.[5] The term also includes abuse against the mother of a minor child who under the Uniform Parentage Act is presumed to be the child of the male parent.[6] Finally, the term embraces abuse by one parent against the other parent.[7]

Abuse means "intentionally or recklessly causing or attempting to cause bodily injury, or placing another person in reasonable apprehension of imminent serious bodily injury to herself, himself, or another."[8]

A victim is anyone who suffers domestic violence as that term is defined.[9] A domestic violence counselor is a person employed for the purpose of rendering advice or assistance to victims of domestic violence and who is qualified to do so by reason of training and experience.[10]

Second, the privilege extends only to information transmitted between the victim and the counselor in the course of their relationship.[11] The privilege includes "all information regarding the facts and circumstances involving all incidences of domestic violence, as well as all information about the children or the victim or abuser and the relationship of the victim with the abuser."[12]

Third, to be privileged, the information must be transmitted "in confidence by a means which so far as the victim is aware, discloses the information to no third persons other than those who are present to further the interests of the victim in the consultation or those to whom disclosures are reasonably necessary for the transmission of the information or an accomplishment of the purposes for which the domestic violence counselor is consulted."[13] The Code rejects the eavesdropper doctrine, which permits individuals who overhear domestic violence victim-counselor communications to reveal them despite the desire of the victim and the counselor to maintain them confidential.[14] Victims are protected against the risk of disclosure by eavesdroppers and other wrongful interceptors by permitting the holder of the privilege to assert it against anyone, including the eavesdropper, who acquires the information without the victim's consent.[15]

If the victim is aware that the means chosen for transmitting the information discloses it to third persons who are not authorized to be

---

5. Id.

6. Id.

7. Id.

8. Id.

9. West's Ann. California Evidence Code § 1037.

10. For details regarding the qualifications of domestic violence counselors, see West's Ann. California Evidence Code § 1037.1.

11. West's Ann. California Evidence Code § 1037.2.

12. Id.

13. Id.

14. See West's Ann. California Evidence Code § 952 and comment relating to the attorney-client privilege.

15. Id.

present, the communication is not confidential.[16] Such a communication acquires no protection, and those who overhear it, as well as the victim and the counselor, can be compelled to disclose the communication. Transmitting the information under circumstances where others can easily overhear it is evidence that the victim did not intend the communication to be confidential.[17] Under the Code, communications between domestic violence victims and their counselors are presumed to be confidential.[18] Thus, the person opposing the privilege has the burden of persuading the judge that the communication was not made in confidence.

The presence of third persons to further the interests of the victim in the consultation does not strip the information of its confidential nature.[19] Spouses, parents, and others the victim needs in consulting the counselor may be present.

Confidential communications are not limited to those that take place between the victim and the counselor. They can also embrace communications made to third persons who serve as conduits for the communication from the victim to the counselor.[20] Examples include revelations by the victim to others whom the counselor wishes to use in counseling the victim. These disclosures are protected because they are reasonably necessary for accomplishing the purposes for which the counselor is consulted.[21]

QUESTIONS AND PROBLEMS

1.   The purpose of the domestic violence victim-counselor privilege is to promote effective counseling by encouraging full disclosure by the victim. True or false?

2.   For purposes of the privilege, a victim is anyone who suffers domestic violence. Domestic violence consists of abuse which is perpetrated against a household member, among others. True or false?

3.   The privilege, however, does not include nonfamily members, such as girlfriends and boyfriends, even if the victim resides with the abuser. True or false?

§ 26.02   CLAIMING THE PRIVILEGE

The domestic violence victim, whether or not a party, has a privilege to refuse to disclose or to prevent another from disclosing a confidential

---

16.   See West's Ann. California Evidence Code § 954 (comment) relating to the attorney-client privilege.

17.   Id. However, confidential communications do not lose their privileged character simply because they are communicated by electronic means or because persons involved in the delivery, facilitation, or storage of electronic communications might have access to their content. West's Ann. California Evidence Code § 917.

18.   West's Ann. California Evidence Code § 917.

19.   West's Ann. California Evidence Code § 1037.2.

20.   Id.

21.   Id.

communication between the victim and the domestic violence counselor if the privilege is claimed by (1) the holder of the privilege, (2) a person authorized by the holder to claim the privilege, or (3) the person who was the counselor at the time the communication was made.[1] The counselor has the right as well as the obligation to claim the privilege if present when disclosure of the communication is sought.[2]

A holder is (1) the victim when he or she has no guardian or conservator or (2) the guardian or conservator when the victim has a guardian or conservator.[3]

The privilege may be claimed only if a holder is in existence.[4] The privilege can be waived by the holder.[5]

QUESTIONS AND PROBLEMS

1. A domestic violence victim may not claim the privilege unless she is a party to the proceeding in which the privilege is claimed. True or false?

2. The counselor has no obligation to the claim the privilege for the victim, even if present when disclosure of the privileged communication is sought. True or false?

3. May the victim, as the holder, waive the privilege?

§ 26.03 COMPELLED DISCLOSURES

The court in the exercise of its discretion may compel disclosure of information received by a domestic violence counselor if certain conditions are satisfied.[1]

First, the judge must find that information received by the counselor "constitutes relevant evidence of the facts and circumstances involving a crime [which was] allegedly perpetrated against the victim or another household member and which is the subject of a criminal proceeding * * *."[2] Second, the judge must find that the probative value of the evidence outweighs the prejudicial effects that disclosure of the information may have on the victim, the counseling relationship, and the counseling services.[3] The judge may compel disclosure without the required balancing if the victim is dead or is not the complaining witness in a criminal action against the perpetrator.[4]

---

1. West's Ann. California Evidence Code § 1037.5.

2. West's Ann. California Evidence Code § 1037.6.

3. West's Ann. California Evidence Code § 1037.4.

4. West's Ann. California Evidence Code § 1037.5.

5. For a discussion of how the privilege can be waived, see § 20.05 supra.

1. West's Ann. California Evidence Code § 1037.2. A domestic counselor has a statutory duty to warn the victim of "any applicable" limitations on the confidentiality of their communications. West's Ann. California Evidence Code § 1037.8.

2. West's Ann. California Evidence Code § 1037.2.

3. Id.

4. Id.

In ruling on the claim of privilege, the judge "may require the person from whom disclosure is sought or the person authorized to claim the privilege, or both, to disclose the information in chambers outside the presence and hearing of all persons except the person authorized to claim the privilege and such other persons as the person authorized to claim the privilege consents to have present."[5] If the judge determines that the information is privileged, neither the judge nor any other person may disclose the information revealed in chambers, unless authorized to do so by a person authorized to permit disclosure.[6]

If the judge determines that particular information may be subject to disclosure pursuant to the balancing test, the judge must follow a pre-scribed procedure before ordering the information disclosed:

One, the judge must inform the defendant of the nature of the information which may be subject to disclosure.[7]

Two, the judge must hold a hearing out of the presence of the jury, if any, to allow the questioning of the domestic violence counselor about the information which the judge has determined may be subject to disclosure.[8]

Three, at the conclusion of the hearing the judge must determine which items of information should be disclosed. The judge's order must specify the evidence that may be offered by the defendant and the nature of the questions that will be permitted. The defendant may then offer the evidence pursuant to the judge's order.[9]

The domestic violence victim-counselor privilege does not mandate the receipt of the evidence. Whether the evidence is admissible depends on the rules of evidence.[10] Moreover, the privilege does not limit any obligation to report instances of child abuse required by the Penal Code.[11]

QUESTIONS AND PROBLEMS

1. Unlike the major privileges, the privilege protecting the confidential communications of domestic violence victims does not contain exceptions. Instead, the privilege allows for discretionary disclosure of the communications if certain conditions are met. True or false?

2. Among the conditions that must be met are a finding by the judge that the information received by the counselor would be probative of the facts and circumstances involving a crime which was allegedly perpetrated against the victim and which is the subject of a criminal proceeding. True or false.

3. In addition, the judge must find that the probative value of the communications on the issues to which the evidence can be directed out-

---

5. Id.

6. Id.

7. See id. and West's Ann. California Evidence Code § 1035.4.

8. West's Ann. California Evidence Code §§ 1037.2 and 1035.4.

9. Id.

10. Id.

11. West's Ann. California Evidence Code § 1037.3.

weighs the prejudicial effects which disclosure of the information might have on the victim, the counseling relationship, and the counseling services. True or false?

4. If the judge overrules the privilege objection, the objecting party may still raise other objections to the admissibility of the evidence. True or false?

CALIFORNIA EVIDENCE CODE

§ 1037. Victim

As used in this article, "victim" means any person who suffers domestic violence, as defined in Section 1037.7.

§ 1037.1. Domestic violence counselor; qualifications; domestic violence victim service organization

(a)(1) As used in this article, "domestic violence counselor" means a person who is employed by a domestic violence victim service organization, as defined in this article, whether financially compensated or not, for the purpose or rendering advice or assistance to victims of domestic violence and who has at least 40 hours of training as specified in paragraph (2).

(2) The 40 hours of training shall be supervised by an individual who qualifies as a counselor under paragraph (1), and who has at least one year of experience counseling domestic violence victims for the domestic violence victim service organization. The training shall include, but need not be limited to, the following areas: history of domestic violence, civil and criminal law as it relates to domestic violence, the domestic violence victim-counselor privilege and other laws that protect the confidentiality of victim records and information, societal attitudes towards domestic violence, peer counseling techniques, housing, public assistance and other financial resources available to meet the financial needs of domestic violence victims, and referral services available to domestic violence victims.

(3) A domestic violence counselor who has been employed by the domestic violence victim service organization for a period of less than six months shall be supervised by a domestic violence counselor who has at least one year of experience counseling domestic violence victims for the domestic violence victim service organization.

(b) As used in this article, "domestic violence victim service organization" means a nongovernmental organization or entity that provides shelter, programs, or services to victims of domestic violence and their children, including, but not limited to, either of the following:

(1) Domestic violence shelter-based programs, as described in Section 18294 of the Welfare and Institutions Code.

(2) Other programs with the primary mission to provide services to victims of domestic violence whether or not that program exists in an agency that provides additional services.

§ 1037.2. Confidential communication; compulsion of disclosure by court; claim of privilege

(a) As used in this article, "confidential communication" means any information, including, but not limited to, written or oral communication, transmitted between the victim and the counselor in the course of their relationship and in confidence by a means which, so far as the victim is aware, discloses the information to no third persons other than those who are present to further the interests of the victim in the consultation or those to whom disclosures are reasonably necessary for the transmission of the information or an accomplishment of the purposes for which the domestic violence counselor is consulted. The term includes all information regarding the facts and circumstances involving all incidences of domestic violence, as well as all information about the children of the victim or abuser and the relationship of the victim with the abuser.

(b) The court may compel disclosure of information received by a domestic violence counselor which constitutes relevant evidence of the facts and circumstances involving a crime allegedly perpetrated against the victim or another household member and which is the subject of a criminal proceeding, if the court determines that the probative value of the information outweighs the effect of disclosure of the information on the victim, the counseling relationship, and the counseling scrvices. The court may compel disclosure if the victim is either dead or not the complaining witness in a criminal action against the perpetrator. The court may also compel disclosure in proceedings related to child abuse if the court determines that the probative value of the evidence outweighs the effect of the disclosure on the victim, the counseling relationship, and the counseling services.

(c) When a court rules on a claim of privilege under this article, it may require the person from whom disclosure is sought or the person authorized to claim the privilege, or both, to disclose the information in chambers out of the presence and hearing of all persons except the person authorized to claim the privilege and such other persons as the person authorized to claim the privilege consents to have present. If the judge determines that the information is privileged and shall not be disclosed, neither he nor she nor any other person may disclose, without the consent of a person authorized to permit disclosure, any information disclosed in the course of the proceedings in chambers.

(d) If the court determines that information shall be disclosed, the court shall so order and inform the defendant in the criminal action. If the court finds there is a reasonable likelihood that any information is subject to disclosure pursuant to the balancing test provided in this section, the procedure specified in subdivisions (1), (2), and (3) of Section 1035.4 shall be followed.

§ 1037.3. Child abuse; reporting

Nothing in this article shall be construed to limit any obligation to report instances of child abuse as required by Section 11166 of the Penal Code.

§ 1037.4. Holder of the privilege

As used in this article, "holder of the privilege" means:

(a) The victim when he or she has no guardian or conservator.

(b) A guardian or conservator of the victim when the victim has a guardian or conservator, unless the guardian or conservator is accused of perpetrating domestic violence against the victim.

§ 1037.5. Privilege of refusal to disclose communication; claimants

A victim of domestic violence, whether or not a party to the action, has a privilege to refuse to disclose, and to prevent another from disclosing, a confidential communication between the victim and a domestic violence counselor in any proceeding specified in Section 901 if the privilege is claimed by any of the following persons:

(a) The holder of the privilege.

(b) A person who is authorized to claim the privilege by the holder of the privilege.

(c) The person who was the domestic violence counselor at the time of the confidential communication. However, that person may not claim the privilege if there is no holder of the privilege in existence or if he or she is otherwise instructed by a person authorized to permit disclosure.

§ 1037.6. Claim of privilege by counselor

The domestic violence counselor who received or made a communication subject to the privilege granted by this article shall claim the privilege whenever he or she is present when the communication is sought to be disclosed and he or she is authorized to claim the privilege under subdivision (c) of Section 1037.5.

§ 1037.7. Domestic violence

As used in this article, "domestic violence" means "domestic violence" as defined in Section 6211 of the Family Code.

CHAPTER 27

PRIVILEGE FOR CONFIDENTIAL MARITAL COMMUNICATIONS

■ ■ ■

Table of Sections

§ 27.01 NATURE OF THE PRIVILEGE

A person, whether or not a party, has a privilege to refuse to disclose and to prevent another from disclosing a communication which was made in confidence between that person and his or her spouse while they were husband and wife.[1] Since the purpose of the privilege is to encourage free and open communication between spouses,[2] the privilege may be claimed to protect confidential communications made during a marriage even though the marriage has been terminated by the time the privilege is claimed.[3]

As in the case of the other privileges for confidential communications, this privilege seeks to protect only the communications from disclosure. The subject matter of the communication is not privileged. For example, if the privilege prevents a party from using marital communications to prove the sex practices of a couple, that party is still free to use other nonprivileged evidence to prove their practices.[4]

To be privileged, the communication must meet a number of tests. First, the communication must have been made "during the marital relationship".[5] That requires a showing that the communication was made

---

1. West's Ann. California Evidence Code § 980.

2. Id. (comment).

3. Id.

4. See, e.g., Pearce v. Club Med Sales, Inc., 172 F.R.D. 407, 409 (1997) (applying the California Evidence Code to a diversity case). For an extended discussion of this point, see § 21.01 supra.

5. California Evidence Code § 980 (West 1966).

while the spouses were legally married. Communications between spouses of a voidable marriage are protected,[6] but not communications between spouses of a void marriage[7] or between unmarried individuals who live together.[8]

California does not recognize Common Law marriages entered into within the state. Under the Family Code, consent alone will not constitute a marriage.[9] California, however, does recognize Common Law marriages entered into in a state where such marriages are valid.[10] Spouses legally married under the laws of such a state may claim the California privilege for confidential marital communications.[11]

Second, the privilege protects only communications between the spouses. The privilege, for example, will not prevent a wife from testifying about noncommunicative acts the husband performed in her presence.[12] In People v. Bradford[13] the accused was prosecuted for killing a victim with sulphuric acid. The privilege did not prevent his wife from testifying that she retrieved tags which the accused had placed in a trash barrel and which bore the legend, "Sulphuric Acid," that the accused had given her jewelry that had belonged to the victim, and that shoes with acid burns belonged to the accused.[14] Nor will the privilege prevent one spouse from identifying handwriting as the other spouse's.[15]

On the other hand, the contents of writings between the spouses will be protected from disclosure if they otherwise qualify as confidential marital communications. Depictions of private acts in videotapes of the spouses are likewise protected. An example is Rubio v. Superior Court,[16] where the reviewing court analogized a video tape of the spouses committing sex acts to a writing between the spouses describing the sex acts.[17]

A spousal writing will not be protected if it is not communicated to the spouse. In People v. Bogle[18] the accused was tried for murder. Over his objection, the prosecution was allowed to introduce a suicide note

---

6. People v. Godines, 17 Cal.App.2d, 721, 727, 62 P.2d 787, 790 (1936).

7. People v. Gallego, 52 Cal.3d 115, 176, 276 Cal.Rptr. 679, 709, 802 P.2d 169, 199 (1990), cert. denied, 502 U.S. 924, 112 S.Ct. 337, 116 L.Ed.2d 277 (1991).

8. People v. Delph, 94 Cal.App.3d 411, 416, 156 Cal.Rptr. 422, 425 (1979).

9. West's Ann. California Family Code § 300.

10. West's Ann. California Family Code § 308.

11. People v. Badgett, 10 Cal.4th 330, 363, 41 Cal.Rptr.2d 635, 655, 895 P.2d 877, 897 (1995).

12. People v. Bradford, 70 Cal.2d 333, 342 and note 2, 74 Cal.Rptr. 726, 730 and note 2, 450 P.2d 46, 50 and note 2 (1969), cert. denied, 399 U.S. 911, 90 S.Ct. 2204, 26 L.Ed.2d 566 (1970).

13. Id.

14. Id. at 338, 74 Cal.Rptr. at 728, 450 P.2d at 48. Accord: People v. Cleveland, 32 Cal.4th 704, 743, 11 Cal.Rptr.3d 236, 267, 86 P.3d 302, 328 (2004), cert. denied, 543 U.S. 1058, 125 S.Ct. 867, 160 L.Ed.2d 784 (2005) (holding that the wife was not precluded from testifying that on the night of the murders she had seen her husband, the defendant, return to their home wearing a watch and possessing cocaine).

15. People v. Saidi–Tabatabai, 7 Cal.App.3d 981, 986, 86 Cal.Rptr. 866, 869 (1970).

16. 202 Cal.App.3d 1343, 249 Cal.Rptr. 419 (1988).

17. Id. at 1348, 249 Cal.Rptr. at 421.

18. 41 Cal.App.4th 770, 48 Cal.Rptr.2d 739 (1995).

written by the accused and addressed to his wife. Receiving the note did not violate the privilege for confidential marital communications. Since the accused admitted that he never sent the suicide note to his wife, the note never attained the status of a communication between the spouses.[19]

Third, the communication must have been "made in confidence".[20] If the communicating spouse is aware that the means chosen for transmitting the information discloses it to third persons, the communication is not confidential.[21] Transmitting the information under circumstances where third persons can easily overhear it is evidence that the communicating spouse did not intend the communication to be confidential.[22] For example, jailhouse conversations between spouses are not protected if the spouses know that the conversations might be monitored by the jailers.[23] Nor are letters from an inmate to his spouse protected if the inmate believes that the jailers are intercepting and reading his mail.[24] But where the jailers lead the spouses to believe that their conversations will be confidential, the communications will be protected.[25]

Under the Code, communications between spouses are presumed to be confidential.[26] The effect of the presumption is to place on the party opposing the claim of privilege the burden of persuading the judge that the communication was not made in confidence.[27]

Even if the communication is protected by the privilege, a spouse can waive its protection. Waiver will occur if the spouse voluntarily discloses a significant part of the communication or consents to its disclosure by someone else.[28]

The Code rejects the eavesdropper doctrine, which permits individuals who overhear confidential communications between spouses to reveal them despite the desire of the spouses to keep them confidential.[29] The

---

19. Id. at 784, 48 Cal.Rptr.2d at 747.

20. West's Ann. California Evidence Code § 980.

21. Id.

22. See West's Ann. California Evidence Code § 954 (comment) relating to the attorney-client privilege. However, confidential communications do not lose their privileged character simply because they are communicated by electronic means or because persons involved in the delivery, facilitation, or storage of electronic communications might have access to their content. West's Ann. California Evidence Code § 917.

23. People v. Santos, 26 Cal.App.3d 397, 402, 102 Cal.Rptr. 678, 681 (1972). See also People v. Hill, 12 Cal.3d 731, 764–765, 117 Cal.Rptr. 393, 418, 528 P.2d 1, 26 (1974) (Inmates and their visitors have no reasonable expectation of privacy in ordinary jailhouse conversations.).

24. People v. Mickey, 54 Cal.3d 612, 654, 286 Cal.Rptr. 801, 819, 818 P.2d 84, 102 (1991), cert. denied, 506 U.S. 819, 113 S.Ct. 65, 121 L.Ed.2d 32 (1992).

25. North v. Superior Court, 8 Cal.3d 301, 311, 104 Cal.Rptr. 833, 839, 502 P.2d 1305, 1311 (1972).

26. West's Ann. California Evidence Code § 917.

27. Id. For a discussion of this presumption, see § 20.03 supra.

28. See West's Ann. California Evidence Code § 912. See also People v. Cleveland, 32 Cal.4th 704, 743, 11 Cal.Rptr.3d 236, 267, 86 P.3d 302, 328 (2004), cert. denied, 543 U.S. 1058, 125 S.Ct. 867, 160 L.Ed.2d 784 (2005).

29. See West's Ann. California Evidence Code §§ 952 and comment (relating to the attorney-client privilege) and 980 (comment).

Code protects spouses against the risk of disclosure by eavesdroppers and other wrongful interceptors of confidential information by permitting the spouses to assert the privilege against anyone, including the eavesdropper, who acquires the information without the spouses' consent.[30]

QUESTIONS AND PROBLEMS

1. The privilege for confidential marital communications is designed to encourage open communications between spouses. True or false?

2. To be privileged, the communications must have been made during the marital relationship. Accordingly, communications between unmarried people who live together are not protected by this privilege. True or false?

3. The privilege protects only communicative acts. It will not prevent a spouse from testifying that she saw her husband shoot the victim in a homicide prosecution. True or false?

4. Under the Code, communications between spouses are presumed to be confidential. True or false?

§ 27.02   CLAIMING THE PRIVILEGE

Both spouses are the holders of the privilege, and either may claim it.[1] In addition, a spouse's guardian or conservator may claim the privilege on behalf of the spouse.[2] The personal representative, however, may not claim the privilege, as no one can claim the privilege for a dead spouse.[3] The privilege can be claimed only by the surviving spouse or that spouse's guardian or conservator.[4]

Since both spouses are holders, a spouse can claim the privilege even if the other has waived it.[5] Thus, if a spouse waives the privilege by disclosing the confidential communication to a third person, the non-waiving spouse can prevent that person from revealing the communication.[6] However, if a spouse who is a party fails to object to the introduction of a confidential marital communication, that spouse may not complain on appeal about the admission of the communication.[7]

---

30. Id.

1. West's Ann. California Evidence Code § 980 and comment.

2. Id.

3. Id.

4. Id.

5. Id.

6. Id. For a discussion of how the privilege can be waived, see § 20.05 supra.

7. People v. Cleveland, 32 Cal.4th 704, 743, 11 Cal.Rptr.3d 236, 267, 86 P.3d 302, 328 (2004), cert. denied, 543 U.S. 1058, 125 S.Ct. 867, 160 L.Ed.2d 784 (2005). See also West's Ann. California Evidence Code § 912: "Consent to disclosure is manifested by * * * conduct of the holder of the privilege * * *, including failure to claim the privilege in any proceeding in which the holder has the legal standing and opportunity to claim the privilege."

QUESTIONS AND PROBLEMS

Since both spouse are the holders of the privilege for marital communications, over a spouse's objection such communications cannot be revealed even if the other spouse wishes to waive the privilege. Accordingly, even if a spouse is willing to testify that her husband told her he shot the victim, over the husband's objection she may not do so. True or false?

§ 27.03 EXCEPTIONS

Communications that would otherwise be privileged are not protected if they fall within the following exceptions:

1. No privilege exists for communications made in whole or part to enable or aid anyone to commit or plan to commit a crime or fraud.[1]

> It is important to note that the exception * * * is quite limited. It does not permit disclosure of communications that merely reveal a plan to commit a crime or fraud; it permits disclosure only of communications made to *enable* or *aid* anyone to commit or plan to commit a crime or fraud. Thus, unless the communication is for the purpose of obtaining assistance in the commission of the crime or fraud or in furtherance thereof, it is not made admissible by the exception * * *.[2]

Accordingly, a husband's statements to his wife before the alleged offense "as to what he intended to do or why he intended to do it or how he intended to do it, or after the alleged commission of the crime as to what he had done, why he had done it or how he had done it" were not within the exception.[3] On the other hand, statements by the accused urging his wife to dispose of letters and other matters related to his crimes were within the exception.[4] The accused was not merely revealing a plan to commit a crime or fraud but was enabling his wife to commit obstruction of justice.[5]

2. No privilege exists for communications offered in a proceeding "to commit either spouse or otherwise place him or his property, or both, under the control of another because of his alleged mental or physical condition."[6]

> Commitment and competency proceedings are undertaken for the benefit of the subject person. Frequently, much or all of the evidence bearing on a spouse's competency or lack of competency will consist of communications to the other spouse. It would be undesirable to permit either spouse to invoke a privilege to prevent the presentation of this vital information inasmuch as these proceedings are of such

---

1. West's Ann. California Evidence Code § 981.

2. Id. (comment) (emphasis in the original).

3. People v. Dorsey, 46 Cal.App.3d 706, 718, 120 Cal.Rptr. 508, 515 (1975).

4. People v. Von Villas, 11 Cal.App.4th 175, 15 Cal.Rptr.2d 112 (1992).

5. Id. at 222, 15 Cal.Rptr.2d at 140.

6. West's Ann. California Evidence Code § 982.

vital importance both to society and to the spouse who is the subject of the proceedings.[7]

3. For similar reasons, no privilege exists for communications offered in proceedings brought by or on behalf of either spouse to establish his or her competency.[8]

4. No privilege exists for communications offered in a proceeding brought by or on behalf of one spouse against the other spouse or between a surviving spouse and a person who claims through the deceased spouse, regardless of whether such claim is by testate or intestate succession or by inter vivos transaction.[9] This exception applies to litigation between spouses as well as to litigation between a surviving spouse and the successor to a deceased spouse.[10]

5. No privilege exists for communications offered in a criminal proceeding in which one spouse is charged with committing a crime at any time against the person or property of the other spouse or of a child of either spouse.[11] Neither does the privilege apply where one spouse is charged with committing a crime at any time against the person or property of a third person where the crime is committed in the course of committing a crime against the person or property of the other spouse.[12] Nor does the privilege apply where one spouse is charged with committing bigamy or with neglecting or abandoning a child or spouse under the Penal Code.[13]

6. No privilege exists for communications offered in juvenile court proceedings brought under Chapter 2 of the Welfare and Institutions Code.[14] This chapter deals with the removal of minors from parental custody, the treatment of minors in need of protective services, and the

---

7. Id. (comment).

8. West's Ann. California Evidence Code § 983.

9. West's Ann. California Evidence Code § 984.

10. Id. (comment).

11. West's Ann. California Evidence Code § 985. "Child" as used in the statute can include the adult child of one of the spouses, People v. McGraw, 141 Cal.App.3d 618, 621–622, 190 Cal.Rptr. 461, 463 (1983), as well as a foster child. Dunn v. Superior Court (People), 21 Cal.App.4th 721, 723, 26 Cal.Rptr.2d 365, 366 (1993).

In People v. Johnson, 233 Cal.App.3d 425, 284 Cal.Rptr. 579 (1991), cert. denied, 503 U.S. 963, 112 S.Ct. 1568, 118 L.Ed.2d 213 (1992), the accused was charged in one count with murdering his girlfriend and in another count with attempting to murder his wife. At the preliminary hearing, the wife testified that in the course of assaulting her the accused threatened to do to her what he had done to his girlfriend. That statement was admissible under the exception for confidential marital communications offered in a criminal proceeding in which one spouse is charged with a crime against the person of the other spouse. But the count charging the accused with attempting to murder his wife was dismissed before trial. At the murder trial, over the accused's privilege claim, the judge nonetheless allowed the wife to repeat the statement she made at the preliminary hearing. The appellate court upheld the use of the statement: after the statement was made public at the preliminary hearing, it lost its "confidential character." Id. at 437, 284 Cal.Rptr. at 584.

12. Id.

13. Id.

14. West's Ann. California Evidence Code § 986.

duty of parents to support their minor children.[15]

7. No privilege exists for communications offered in a criminal proceeding when offered by a defendant who is one of the spouses between whom the communications were made.[16] "When a married person is the defendant in a criminal proceeding and seeks to introduce evidence which is material to his defense, his spouse (or his former spouse) should not be privileged to withhold the information."[17]

The exceptions for confidential marital communications do not override the privileges a married person has (1) not to testify against the other spouse and (2) not to be called as a witness by the adverse party in any proceeding in which the other spouse is a party.[18] Thus, a married person may assert these privileges if called by the prosecution to relate communications falling within the crime-fraud exception for confidential marital communications.[19] In the case of exceptions two through six, however, the privileges accorded married persons are not a bar to disclosure, since those privileges are subject to similar exceptions.[20] Moreover, disclosure under the seventh exception—communications offered by a criminal defendant who was one of the spouses between whom the communications were made—is not barred by the privileges accorded to married persons: the spouse is asked to testify *for*, not *against*, the accused, and it is the spouse and not the adverse party who is the calling party.

QUESTIONS AND PROBLEMS

1. The privilege for confidential marital communications does not apply to communications made in whole or in part to enable or aid someone in committing or planning to commit a crime or fraud. Accordingly, a statement by the wife to her husband describing how she committed a theft is protected but not a statement asking her husband to help her "fence" the fruits of the theft. True or false?

2. The privilege, however, does apply to communications offered in a criminal proceeding in which one spouse is charged with assaulting the other spouse. Thus, the wife's statement to her husband, "You deserved that punch I gave you." is protected by the privilege. Otherwise, the use of such statements would undermine the marital relationship. True or false?

3. Husband is prosecuted for murder. At the trial, he wants his wife to testify that he told her that the killing was an accident. The judge should overrule the wife's claim that the husband's statement is protected from disclosure by the privilege for marital communications. True or false?

---

15. West's Ann. California Welfare and Institutions Code § 202.

16. West's Ann. California Evidence Code § 987.

17. Id. (comment).

18. West's Ann. California Evidence Code § 981 (comment).

19. Id.

20. Compare West's Ann. California Evidence Code §§ 982–986 with § 972(a)–(d).

4. In the above example, the judge should also overrule the wife's additional claim that she cannot be compelled to provide the testimony under the spousal privileges. True or false?

CALIFORNIA EVIDENCE CODE

§ 980. Confidential marital communication privilege

Subject to Section 912 and except as otherwise provided in this article, a spouse (or his guardian or conservator when he has a guardian or conservator), whether or not a party, has a privilege during the marital relationship and afterwards to refuse to disclose, and to prevent another from disclosing, a communication if he claims the privilege and the communication was made in confidence between him and the other spouse while they were husband and wife.

§ 981. Exception: Crime or fraud

There is no privilege under this article if the communication was made, in whole or in part, to enable or aid anyone to commit or plan to commit a crime or a fraud.

§ 982. Commitment or similar proceeding

There is no privilege under this article in a proceeding to commit either spouse or otherwise place him or his property, or both, under the control of another because of his alleged mental or physical condition.

§ 983. Competency proceedings

There is no privilege under this article in a proceeding brought by or on behalf of either spouse to establish his competence.

§ 984. Proceeding between spouses

There is no privilege under this article in:

(a) A proceeding brought by or on behalf of one spouse against the other spouse.

(b) A proceeding between a surviving spouse and a person who claims through the deceased spouse, regardless of whether such claim is by testate or intestate succession or by inter vivos transaction.

§ 985. Criminal proceedings

There is no privilege under this article in a criminal proceeding in which one spouse is charged with:

(a) A crime committed at any time against the person or property of the other spouse or of a child of either.

(b) A crime committed at any time against the person or property of a third person committed in the course of committing a crime against the person or property of the other spouse.

(c) Bigamy.

(d) A crime defined by Section 270 or 270a of the Penal Code.

§ 986. Juvenile court proceedings

There is no privilege under this article in a proceeding under the Juvenile Court Law, Chapter 2 (commencing with Section 200) of Part 1 of Division 2 of the Welfare and Institutions Code.

§ 987. Exception—Communication offered by spouse who is criminal defendant

There is no privilege under this article in a criminal proceeding in which the communication is offered in evidence by a defendant who is one of the spouses between whom the communication was made.

CHAPTER 28

THE SPOUSAL PRIVILEGES

■ ■ ■

Table of Sections

§ 28.01 NATURE OF THE PRIVILEGES

A married person has a privilege not to be called as a witness by the adverse party in any proceeding in which the other spouse is a party.[1] The privilege is similar to the privilege given to the accused not to be called as a witness.[2] Thus, unless the wife waives the privilege, a prosecutor may not call her to testify against her husband in a prosecution against the husband. Exempting a spouse from the duty to give evidence is based on the need to avoid the prejudicial effect of forcing the witness-spouse to decline to take the stand in the presence of the fact finder.[3]

In addition, a married person has a privilege not to testify against a spouse in any proceeding irrespective of whether the spouse is a party.[4] This privilege does not entitle a married person to decline to take the stand. It simply permits a married person to refuse to answer any question that would compel her to testify against her spouse. A criminal defendant, for example, may call a witness to establish that it was the witness's husband who committed the offense charged. In these circumstances, the witness can be compelled to take the stand since her husband is not a party, but she can refuse to answer any question that would compel her to testify against her husband.[5] The privilege is designed to protect the marital relationship. Compelling one spouse to testify against

---

1. West's Ann. California Evidence Code § 971.

2. Id. (comment). See also West's Ann. California Evidence Code § 930.

3. West's Ann. California Evidence Code § 971 (comment).

4. West's Ann. California Evidence Code § 970.

5. Sustaining the spouse-witness's privilege not to testify against her spouse may violate the accused's Sixth Amendment right to produce evidence that is reliable and critical to the defense. See Chambers v. Mississippi, 410 U.S. 284, 93 S.Ct. 1038, 35 L.Ed.2d 297 (1973).

the other spouse "would seriously disturb or disrupt the marital relationship. Society stands to lose more from such disruption than it stands to gain from testimony which would be available if the privilege did not exist."[6]

The interrelationship between the spousal privileges can confuse courts. People v. Lucas[7] is illustrative. At the preliminary hearing, the prosecution sought to call the accused's wife. She did not have to take the stand, however, because she asserted her privilege not to be called as witness by the adverse party. At the trial, the accused called her as a witness. The trial judge excused her from testifying because she asserted her privilege not to testify *against* her husband. The trial judge, however, wrongly assumed that this privilege entitled the witness to decline taking the stand, instead of merely entitling her to refuse to answer any question calling for her to testify against her husband.[8] Of course, if the witness had testified favorably toward her spouse, then she would have waived her privilege on cross-examination to decline answering any question calling for her to testify against him. But, as Justice Kennard pointed out in her dissent, that potential outcome did not entitle her to decline to take the stand when called by her husband.[9] If the accused wanted her testimony, then he had to run the risk that her claim of privilege would be overruled on cross-examination. Still, that possibility was enough to move the California Supreme Court to approve the trial judge's ruling.[10]

A valid marriage is essential to both privileges. The marriage, however, does not have to be "viable."[11] Accordingly, Jurcoane v. Superior Court held it was immaterial that at the time the objecting spouse asserted the marital privilege she had not seen her husband for 17 years.[12] This holding is in obvious conflict with the rationale of a privilege which seeks to prevent disruption in the marital relationship. But as the reviewing court noted, California courts do not have authority to create or modify the privileges enacted by the legislature.[13] Since the legislature did not create an exception to the privilege for failed marriages, the spouse's privilege claim had to be sustained.[14]

A "married person" does not include unmarried persons who live together[15] or persons whose marriages have been dissolved at the time the privilege is claimed.

---

6.   West's Ann. California Evidence Code § 970 (comment).

7.   12 Cal.4th 415, 48 Cal.Rptr.2d 525, 907 P.2d 373 (1995).

8.   See West's Ann. California Evidence Code § 971 (comment).

9.   People v. Lucas, 12 Cal.4th 415, 501, 48 Cal.Rptr.2d 525, 581, 907 P.2d 373, 429 (1995).

10.   Id. at 490, 48 Cal.Rptr.2d at 574, 907 P.2d at 373.

11.   Jurcoane v. Superior Court, 93 Cal.App.4th 886, 889, 113 Cal.Rptr.2d 483, 485 (2001).

12.   Id.

13.   Id. at 895, 113 Cal.Rptr.2d at 490.

14.   Id. at 900, 113 Cal.Rptr.2d at 494.

15.   People v. Delph, 94 Cal.App.3d 411, 415, 156 Cal.Rptr. 422, 425 (1979).

The two privileges may not apply in the same proceeding. For example, "a married [woman] may be called as a witness in a grand jury proceeding because [her] spouse is not a party to that proceeding, but the witness may claim the privilege * * * to refuse to answer a question that would compel [her] to testify *against* [her] spouse."[16]

The privilege of a married person to decline to testify against the other spouse should not be confused with the privilege for confidential marital communications. The latter privilege is designed to encourage free and open communications between spouses by protecting their confidential communications from disclosure.[17] On the other hand, the privilege of a married person to decline to testify against the other spouse is designed to protect the marriage from the disruption that could occur if spouses could be compelled to testify against each other. This privilege can be invoked irrespective of whether the testimony would disclose confidential communications. Thus, a spouse may refuse to answer any question that would compel her to testify against the other spouse even if the testimony sought is not protected by the privilege for confidential marital communications. But if the spouse chooses to testify, the other spouse may still claim the privilege for marital communications to prevent the disclosure of communications protected by this privilege.

QUESTIONS AND PROBLEMS

1. Husband is prosecuted for theft. Over Wife's spousal privilege objection, may the prosecution call Wife in its case-in-chief to testify that she saw Husband commit the theft?

2. A prosecutor convenes a grand jury to consider whether Wife committed a robbery. Over Husband's spousal privilege objection, may the prosecution compel Husband to testify that he saw Wife commit the robbery?

3. Assume that Wife is indicted. At the trial, Husband waives his privileges not to be called as a witness against his spouse and not to testify against his spouse, and testifies that he saw Wife commit the robbery. Over Wife's marital communications privilege objection, may Husband testify that Wife said to him, "I'm sorry that I committed the robbery"?

4. In order for spouses to claim the spousal privileges, they must be validly married at the time the privileges are claimed. In contrast, spouses claiming the privilege for confidential marital communications do not have to be married to each other at the time the privilege is claimed, so long as the communications were made at a time when they were legally married. True or false?

§ 28.02 CLAIMING THE SPOUSAL PRIVILEGES

The privilege to decline answering any question compelling a spouse to testify against a spouse can be claimed only by the spouse whose

---

16. West's Ann. California Evidence Code § 971 (comment) (emphasis in the original).

17. See § 27.01 supra.

testimony is sought against the other spouse.[1] Because the privilege belongs only to the witness-spouse, the other spouse cannot claim the privilege.[2] The witness-spouse, however, can claim the privilege only when asked to testify *against,* not *for,* the other spouse.[3] Testimony that does not disserve the interests of the other spouse is not barred by the privilege.[4]

This limitation does not apply to a married person's privilege not to be called as a witness by the adverse party in an action in which the other spouse is a party. The spouse whose testimony is sought can claim the privilege even if the testimony would serve the interests of the other spouse. The privilege belongs only to the spouse whose testimony is sought. The other spouse cannot claim it.[5]

Waiver. Because the spousal privileges are not designed to encourage free and open communication between the spouses, the Code's general waiver provisions relating to confidential communications do not apply to the spousal privileges.[6] Instead, the Code provides special rules pertaining to the waiver of the spousal privileges.

Express waivers. Married persons, like other privilege holders, can expressly waive their privileges.[7] Accordingly, a married person can waive the privilege not to testify against his or her spouse as well as the privilege not to be called as a witness by the adverse party in a proceeding to which the spouse is a party. A wife may thus waive both privileges and agree to testify against her husband at his preliminary hearing and criminal trial. A married person may also waive the privilege not to testify against a spouse in a proceeding in which the spouse is not a party.[8] A criminal defendant, for example, can call a witness to testify that it was the witness's spouse and not the defendant who committed the crime charged. The witness can waive her privilege not to answer any question that calls for her testifying against her husband and provide the testimony desired by the defendant.

---

1. West's Ann. California Evidence Code § 970 and (comment).

2. Id. (comment).

3. Id.

4. Troy v. Superior Court, 186 Cal.App.3d 1006, 1013, 231 Cal.Rptr. 108, 112 (1986).

5. West's Ann. California Evidence Code § 971.

6. See West's Ann. California Evidence Code § 912. Under the general waiver provisions, the privilege for confidential communications will be lost if the holder voluntarily discloses significant part of the communications to a third person. Id. Thus, telling your friend that you told your lawyer that you committed the crime charged will waive the protection which the attorney-client privilege accords to your confidential communications with your lawyer. But telling your friend that you saw your spouse commit an offense will not preclude you from claiming the privilege prohibiting the prosecution from calling you as a witness in a prosecution charging your spouse with the offense.

7. See § 20.05 supra.

8. Id.

Implied waivers. Unless erroneously compelled to do so, a married person who testifies in a proceeding to which his spouse is a party, or who testifies against his spouse in any proceeding, loses both spousal privileges in the proceeding in which the testimony is given.[9] Accordingly, if a wife testifies on behalf of her husband at his preliminary hearing, on cross-examination the wife may not assert the privilege to decline to answer any question that calls for her to testify against her husband. She waived that privilege by testifying in favor of her husband. In addition, if the prosecution calls the wife to testify at the trial, the wife may not assert the privilege not to be called as a witness by the adverse party. She waived that privilege by testifying on behalf of her husband at the preliminary hearing, since preliminary hearings and trials are simply different phases of the same proceeding.

As has been noted, a married person does not have a privilege to decline to take the stand in a proceeding to which the spouse is not a party. But a married person who is compelled to testify in such a proceeding may still decline to answer any question that would require testifying against the spouse.[10] In these circumstances, the privilege not to testify against a spouse will be waived as to all matters only if the witness-spouse does testify against the spouse on some matter.[11]

The waiver provisions apply to any proceeding, whether civil or criminal.[12] "Hence, the privilege is waived for all purposes in an action if the spouse entitled to claim the privilege testifies at any time during the action. For example, if a civil action involves issues being separately tried, a wife whose husband is a party to the litigation may not testify for her husband at one trial and invoke the privilege in order to avoid testifying against him at a separate trial of a different issue. Nor may a wife testify against her husband at a preliminary hearing of a criminal action and refuse to testify against him at the trial."[13]

The waiver provisions do not apply if the spouse was erroneously compelled to testify against the other spouse.[14] For example, a spouse who testifies against her husband at a preliminary hearing may not decline to testify against her husband at the trial unless her testimony at the preliminary hearing was erroneously compelled.[15] Since the spouse-witness is the privilege claimant, she must persuade the judge that she was erroneously compelled to testify against her husband at the preliminary hearing.[16] Simply asserting that "they told me I had to" will not discharge the burden of persuasion.[17] The privilege claimant must produce evidence

---

9.   West's Ann. California Evidence Code § 973.

10.   Id.

11.   Id.

12.   Id.

13.   Id.

14.   West's Ann. California Evidence Code § 973.

15.   Id. (comment).

16.   People v. Resendez, 12 Cal.App.4th 98, 107, 15 Cal.Rptr.2d 575, 579 (1993).

17.   Id. at 105–108, 15 Cal.Rptr.2d at 578–580.

"demonstrating *who* it was who told her that she had to testify at defendant's preliminary hearing and *how* that statement to her, absent other surrounding circumstances, truly compelled her to testify during defendant's preliminary hearing."[18]

The waiver provisions apply even if the witness was not warned by the court or counsel that testifying could result in the loss of the spousal privileges.[19] In fact, the privileges are lost even if the claimant did not know that by testifying at the earlier hearing she would waive the protection accorded by the privileges at a subsequent hearing.[20] Thus, by testifying at a preliminary hearing, a spouse waives the spousal privileges even if she was unaware that she could assert the privileges at the hearing or that by failing to assert them at the hearing she could lose the privileges at the trial.[21]

The Code precludes married persons from taking unfair advantage of their marital status to escape their duty to testify when their legal interests coincide. The privilege not to be called by the adverse party in an action in which the spouse is a party and the privilege not to testify against a spouse are waived whenever a civil proceeding is brought or defended by a married person "for the immediate benefit of his spouse or himself and his spouse."[22] Examples include tort actions in which both spouses are joined as plaintiffs or defendants.[23] They can also include some tort actions in which only one spouse sues. Damages for personal injuries to a married person are considered community property.[24] Such an action by a married person is thus for his immediate benefit as well as that of his spouse.[25] In such actions, the nonsuing spouse cannot claim either privilege.

QUESTIONS AND PROBLEMS

1. Husband is prosecuted for robbery. Husband calls Wife to testify that Husband was home at the time the victim claims she was robbed. Over Wife's spousal privilege objection, on cross-examination may Wife decline to testify that Husband gave her a watch which the victim has identified as the watch taken in the robbery?

2. The state convenes a grand jury to inquire whether Wife stole a dress from a store. Husband, who is subpoenaed as a witness, testifies that he drove Wife to the store. Over a spousal privilege objection, may Husband be compelled to testify that Wife returned to the car with the dress identified as the one stolen from the store?

---

18.   Id. at 108, 15 Cal.Rptr.2d at 580.

19.   Id.

20.   Id.

21.   Id.

22.   West's Ann. California Evidence Code § 973(b).

23.   Id.

24.   Hand v. Superior Court, 134 Cal.App.3d 436, 440, 184 Cal.Rptr. 588, 590 (1982).

25.   Id. at 441–442, 184 Cal.Rptr. at 591.

3.   Assume that Husband testifies that Wife returned to the car with the dress identified as the one taken from the store. Wife is indicted and the case proceeds to trial. Over a spousal privilege objection, may the state call Husband in its case-in-chief?

4.   Assume, instead, that Husband provided the testimony at a preliminary hearing held to determine whether Wife should be held to answer for stealing the dress. Wife is held to answer for the theft. At the trial, over a spousal privilege objection, may the state call Husband in its case-in-chief?

5.   Assume that the judge rules that Husband can be called by the prosecution in its case-in-chief. Over a spousal privilege objection, may Husband decline to testify that Wife returned to the car with the dress?

6.   In support of his objection in (5), may Husband argue that neither the magistrate presiding at the preliminary hearing nor the lawyers for the state or the defense warned him that by testifying against Wife he might be compelled to testify against her at the trial?

§ 28.03   EXCEPTIONS

The privilege not to testify against a spouse does not apply in the following proceedings:

1.   A proceeding brought by or on behalf of one spouse against the other spouse.[1]

2.   A proceeding to commit or otherwise place the other spouse or that spouse's property, or both, under the control of another because of the spouse's alleged mental or physical condition.[2]

3.   A proceeding brought by or on behalf of a spouse to establish the spouse's competence.[3]

4.   A juvenile court proceeding brought under Chapter 2 of the Welfare and Institutions Code.[4] This chapter is concerned with the removal of minors from parental control, the treatment of minors in need of protective services, and the duty of parents to support their minor children.[5]

5.   A criminal proceeding in which one spouse is charged with a crime against the person or property of the other spouse or of a child, parent, relative, or cohabitant of either, whether or not committed before or during the marriage.[6] A cohabitant includes a spouse's housemate.[7] A cohabitant also includes those with whom a person lives in exchange for

---

1. West's Ann. California Evidence Code § 972.

2. Id.

3. Id.

4. Id.

5. West's Ann. California Welfare and Institutions Code § 202.

6. West's Ann. California Evidence Code § 972.

7. People v. Siravo, 17 Cal.App.4th 555, 562–563, 21 Cal.Rptr.2d 350, 353 (1993).

helping care for the home and yard.[8]

6. A criminal proceeding in which one spouse is charged with a crime against the person or property of a third person committed in the course of committing a crime against the person or property of the other spouse, whether or not committed before or during the marriage.[9] The exception does not apply if the crime against the third person is committed merely in the presence of the other spouse.[10] The crime against the third person must be committed in the course of committing a crime against the person or property of the other spouse.[11]

For the exception to apply, it is not indispensable that the nontestifying spouse be charged with an offense against the testifying spouse. In People v. Sinohui[12] the accused was charged with kidnaping and murdering his wife's boyfriend. The evidence at the trial showed that in committing these crimes against the victim, the accused falsely imprisoned his wife. The California Supreme Court upheld the trial judge's ruling compelling the wife to testify against the accused: a court may compel a spouse to testify under the exception even if the defendant is not charged with committing a crime against his or her spouse if the crimes against the third person and the testifying spouse are "part of continuous course of criminal conduct and have some logical relationship to each other."[13]

7. A criminal proceeding in which one spouse is charged with bigamy or with neglecting or abandoning a child or spouse under Penal Code §§ 270–270a.[14]

8. A proceeding "resulting from a criminal act which occurred prior to legal marriage of the spouses to each other regarding knowledge acquired prior to that marriage if prior to the legal marriage the witness spouse was aware that his or her spouse had been arrested for or had been formally charged with the crime or crimes about which the spouse is called to testify."[15]

9. A proceeding "brought against the spouse by a former spouse so long as the property and debts of the marriage have not been adjudicated, or in order to establish, modify, or enforce a child, family, or spousal support obligation arising from the marriage to the former spouse; * * * a proceeding brought against a spouse by the other parent in order to

---

8. People v. Bogle, 41 Cal.App.4th 770, 782, 48 Cal.Rptr.2d 739, 745 (1995).

9. West's Ann. California Evidence Code § 972.

10. People v. Resendez, 12 Cal.App.4th 98, 110, 15 Cal.Rptr.2d 575, 581 (1993) (holding that the exception did not apply where the accused was charged with attempting to murder a third person in his wife's presence).

11. West's Ann. California Evidence Code § 972.

12. 28 Cal.4th 205, 120 Cal.Rptr.2d 783, 47 P.3d 629 (2002).

13. Id. at 212, 120 Cal.Rptr.2d at 788, 47 P.3d at 633. In support of its construction of the exception, the court noted that whether or not the accused is charged with committing a crime against the testifying spouse, committing a crime against the testifying spouse disrupts the very marital harmony which the marital privileges seek to protect. Id. at 213–214, 120 Cal.Rptr.2d at 790, 47 P.3d at 634.

14. West's Ann. California Evidence Code § 972.

15. Id.

establish, modify, or enforce a child support obligation for a child of a nonmarital relationship of the spouse; or * * * a proceeding brought against a spouse by the guardian of a child of that spouse in order to establish, modify, or enforce a child support obligation of the spouse.''[16] In these proceedings, a married person does not have the privilege to refuse to provide information "relating to issues of income, expenses, assets, debts, and employment of either spouse, but may assert the privilege * * * if other information is requested by the former spouse, guardian, or other parent of the child.''[17] Moreover, any person, who demands otherwise privileged information that is made available in these proceedings and who has an obligation to support the child for whom an order to establish, modify, or enforce child support is sought, waives his or her marital privilege to the same extent as the spouse in these proceedings.[18]

QUESTIONS AND PROBLEMS

1. The spousal privileges do not apply in a proceeding brought by one spouse against the other spouse. Accordingly, the privileges do not apply in divorce proceedings. True or false?

2. The spousal privileges do not apply in civil commitment proceedings. True or false?

3. The spousal privileges do not apply in a prosecution in which one spouse is charged with assaulting the other spouse. True or false?

4. Husband is prosecuted for a theft that occurred prior to his marriage to Wife. Wife was aware that the theft charge was pending against Husband prior to marriage. May Wife claim the spousal privileges if called by the prosecution to testify that she saw Husband commit the theft? *N- know w gained before marriage*

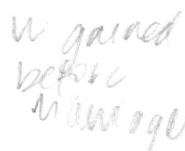

Assume that Wife is compelled to testify that she saw Husband commit the theft. After their marriage, Wife saw Husband conceal the fruits of the theft. May Wife claim the privilege not to testify against Husband to avoid providing this information? *y - after marriage*

CALIFORNIA EVIDENCE CODE

§ 970. Spouse's privilege not to testify against spouse; exception

Except as otherwise provided by statute, a married person has a privilege not to testify against his spouse in any proceeding.

§ 971. Privilege not to be called as a witness against spouse

Except as otherwise provided by statute, a married person whose spouse is a party to a proceeding has a privilege not to be called as a

---

16. Id.

17. Id.

18. Id.

witness by an adverse party to that proceeding without the prior express consent of the spouse having the privilege under this section unless the party calling the spouse does so in good faith without knowledge of the marital relationship.

§ 972. Exceptions to privilege

A married person does not have a privilege under this article in:

(a) A proceeding brought by or on behalf of one spouse against the other spouse.

(b) A proceeding to commit or otherwise place his or her spouse or his or her spouse's property, or both, under the control of another because of the spouse's alleged mental or physical condition.

(c) A proceeding brought by or on behalf of a spouse to establish his or her competence.

(d) A proceeding under the Juvenile Court Law, Chapter 2 (commencing with Section 200) of Part 1 of Division 2 of the Welfare and Institutions Code.

(e) A criminal proceeding in which one spouse is charged with:

(1) A crime against the person or property of the other spouse or of a child, parent, relative, or cohabitant of either, whether committed before or during marriage.

(2) A crime against the person or property of a third person committed in the course of committing a crime against the person or property of the other spouse, whether committed before or during marriage.

(3) Bigamy.

(4) A crime defined by Section 270 or 270a of the Penal Code.

(f) A proceeding resulting from a criminal act which occurred prior to legal marriage of the spouses to each other regarding knowledge acquired prior to that marriage if prior to the legal marriage the witness spouse was aware that his or her spouse had been arrested for or had been formally charged with the crime or crimes about which the spouse is called to testify.

(g) A proceeding brought against the spouse by a former spouse so long as the property and debts of the marriage have not been adjudicated, or in order to establish, modify, or enforce a child, family or spousal support obligation arising from the marriage to the former spouse; in a proceeding brought against a spouse by the other parent in order to establish, modify, or enforce a child support obligation for a child of a nonmarital relationship of the spouse; or in a proceeding brought against a spouse by the guardian of a child of that spouse in order to establish, modify, or enforce a child support obligation of the spouse. The married person does not have a privilege under this subdivision to refuse to provide information relating to the issues of income, expenses, assets, debts, and employment of either spouse, but may assert the privilege as otherwise provided in this article if other information is requested by the former spouse, guardian, or other parent of the child.

Any person demanding the otherwise privileged information made available by this subdivision, who also has an obligation to support the child for whom an order to establish, modify, or enforce child support is sought, waives his or her marital privilege to the same extent as the spouse as provided in this subdivision.

§ 973. Waiver of privilege

(a) Unless erroneously compelled to do so, a married person who testifies in a proceeding to which his spouse is a party, or who testifies against his spouse in any proceeding, does not have a privilege under this article in the proceeding in which such testimony is given.

(b) There is no privilege under this article in a civil proceeding brought or defended by a married person for the immediate benefit of his spouse or of himself and his spouse.

FEDERAL RULES OF EVIDENCE

Rule 505. Husband–Wife Privilege [Not enacted.]

(a) General rule of privilege. An accused in a criminal proceeding has a privilege to prevent his spouse from testifying against him.

(b) Who may claim the privilege. The privilege may be claimed by the accused or by the spouse on his behalf. The authority of the spouse to do so is presumed in the absence of evidence to the contrary.

(c) Exceptions. There is no privilege under this rule (1) in proceedings in which one spouse is charged with a crime against the person or property of the other or of a child of either, or with a crime against the person or property of a third person committed in the course of committing a crime against the other, or (2) as to matters occurring prior to the marriage, or (3) in proceedings in which a spouse is charged with importing an alien for prostitution or other immoral purpose in violation of 8 U.S.C. § 1328, with transporting a female in interstate commerce for immoral purposes or other offense in violation of 18 U.S.C. §§ 2421–2424, or with violation of other similar statutes.

ADVISORY COMMITTEE'S NOTE

Subdivision (a). Rules of evidence have evolved around the marriage relationship in four respects: (1) incompetency of one spouse to testify for the other; (2) privilege of one spouse not to testify against the other; (3) privilege of one spouse not to have the other testify against him; and (4) privilege against disclosure of confidential communications between spouses, sometimes extended to information learned by virtue of the existence of the relationship. Today these matters are largely governed by statutes.

With the disappearance of the disqualification of parties and interested persons, the basis for spousal incompetency no longer existed, and it, too, virtually disappeared in both civil and criminal actions. Usually reached by statute, this result was reached for federal courts by the process of decision. Funk v. United States, 290 U.S. 371, 54 S.Ct. 212, 78 L.Ed. 369 (1933). These rules contain no recognition of incompetency of one spouse to testify for the other.

While some 10 jurisdictions recognize a privilege not to testify against one's spouse in a criminal case, and a much smaller number do so in civil cases, the great majority recognizes no privilege on the part of the testifying spouse, and this is the position taken by the rule. Compare Wyatt v. United States, 362 U.S. 525, 80 S.Ct. 901, 4 L.Ed.2d 931 (1960), a Mann Act prosecution in which the wife was the victim. The majority opinion held that she could not claim privilege and was compellable to testify. The holding was narrowly based: The Mann Act presupposed that the women with whom it dealt had no independent wills of their own, and this legislative judgment precluded allowing a victim-wife an option whether to testify, lest the policy of the statute be defeated. A vigorous dissent took the view that nothing in the Mann Act required departure from usual doctrine, which was conceived to be one of allowing the injured party to claim or waive privilege.

About 30 jurisdictions recognize a privilege of an accused in a criminal case to prevent his or her spouse from testifying. It is believed to represent the one aspect of marital privilege the continuation of which is warranted. In Hawkins v. United States, 358 U.S. 74, 79 S.Ct. 136, 3 L.Ed.2d 125 (1958) it was sustained. Cf. McCormick § 66; 8 Wigmore § 2228 (McNaughton Rev. 1961): Comment, Uniform Rule 23(2).

The rule recognizes no privilege for confidential communications. The traditional justifications for privileges not to testify against a spouse and not to be testified against by one's spouse have been the prevention of marital dissension and the repugnancy of requiring a person to condemn or be condemned by his spouse. 8 Wigmore §§ 2228, 2241 (McNaughton Rev.1961). These considerations bear no relevancy to marital communications. Nor can it be assumed that marital conduct will be affected by a privilege for confidential communications of whose existence the parties in all likelihood are unaware. The other communication privileges, by way of contrast, have as one party a professional person who can be expected to inform the other of the existence of the privilege. Moreover, the relationships from which those privileges arise are essentially and almost exclusively verbal in nature, quite unlike marriage. See Hutchins and Slesinger, Some Observations on the Law of Evidence: Family Relations, 13 Minn.L.Rev. 675 (1929). Cf. McCormick § 90; 8 Wigmore § 2337 (McNaughton Rev.1961).

The parties are not spouses if the marriage was a sham, Lutwak v. United States, 344 U.S. 604, 73 S.Ct. 481, 97 L.Ed. 593 (1953), or they have been divorced, Barsky v. United States, 339 F.2d 180 (9th Cir.1964), and therefore the privilege is not applicable.

Subdivision (b). This provision is a counterpart of Rules 503(c), 504(c), and 506(c). Its purpose is to provide a procedure for preventing the taking of the spouse's testimony notably in grand jury proceedings, when the accused is absent and does not know that a situation appropriate for a claim of privilege is presented. If the privilege is not claimed by the spouse, the protection of Rule 512 is available.

Subdivision (c) contains three exceptions to the privilege against spousal testimony in criminal cases.

(1) The need of limitation upon the privilege in order to avoid grave injustice in cases of offenses against the other spouse or a child of either can scarcely be denied. 8 Wigmore § 2239 (McNaughton Rev.1961). The rule therefore disallows any privilege against spousal testimony in these cases and in this respect is in accord with the result reached in Wyatt v. United States, 362 U.S. 525, 80 S.Ct. 901, 4 L.Ed.2d 931 (1960), a Mann Act prosecution, denying the accused the privilege of excluding his wife's testimony, since she was the woman who was transported for immoral purposes.

(2) The second exception renders the privilege inapplicable as to matters occurring prior to the marriage. This provision eliminates the possibility of suppressing testimony by marrying the witness.

(3) The third exception continues and expands established Congressional policy. In prosecutions for importing aliens for immoral purposes, Congress has specifically denied the accused any privilege not to have his spouse testify against him. 8 U.S.C. § 1328. No provision of this nature is included in the Mann Act, and in Hawkins v. United States, 358 U.S. 74, 79 S.Ct. 136, 3 L.Ed.2d 125 (1958), the conclusion was reached that the common law privilege continued. Consistency requires similar results in the two situations. The rule adopts the Congressional approach, as based upon a more realistic appraisal of the marriage relationship in cases of this kind, in preference to the specific result in *Hawkins*. Note the common law treatment of pimping and sexual offenses with third persons as exceptions to marital privilege. 8 Wigmore § 2239 (McNaughton Rev.1961).

With respect to bankruptcy proceedings, the smallness of the area of spousal privilege under the rule and the general inapplicability of privileges created by state law render unnecessary any special provision for examination of the spouse of the bankrupt, such as that now contained in section 21(a) of the Bankruptcy Act. 11 U.S.C. § 44(a).

For recent statutes and rules dealing with husband-wife privileges, see California Evidence Code §§ 970–973, 980–987; Kansas Code of Civil Procedure §§ 60–423(b), 60–428; New Jersey Evidence Rules 23(2), 28.

CHAPTER 29

THE CLERGY-PENITENT PRIVILEGE

■ ■ ■

Table of Sections

---

§ 29.01   NATURE OF THE PRIVILEGE

A penitent, whether or not a party, has a privilege to refuse to disclose, and to prevent another from disclosing, a penitential communication if the penitent claims the privilege.[1] A member of the clergy has a more limited privilege. Whether or not a party, a member of the clergy has a privilege only to refuse to disclose a penitential communication if he or she claims the privilege.[2] Unlike the penitent, a member of the clergy cannot prevent another from disclosing a penitential communication.

A penitent is a person who has made a penitential communication to a member of the clergy.[3] A penitent, however, "is not required to be a member of any particular church or of the faith of the clergy member to whom he or she makes the penitential communication."[4] Thus, the clergy-penitent privilege may apply to communications made to a member of the clergy by persons who are not members of his or her religious organization.

A religious organization, however, can require that a penitent be a member by limiting the clergy member's authority to receive penitential communications to church members.[5] A member of the clergy is "a priest, minister, religious practitioner, or similar functionary of a church or religious denomination or religious organization."[6]

---

1.   West's Ann. California Evidence Code § 1033.

2.   West's Ann. California Evidence Code § 1034.

3.   West's Ann. California Evidence Code § 1031.

4.   Doe 2 v. Superior Court, 132 Cal.App.4th 1504, 1517, 34 Cal.Rptr.3d 458, 467 (2005) (quoting B. Jefferson, 2 Cal. Evidence Benchbook, (Cont.Ed.Bar 3d ed. 2005) § 39.5, p. 884).

5.   Id.

6.   West's Ann. California Evidence Code § 1030.

A penitential communication is "a communication made in confidence, in the presence of no third person so far as the penitent is aware, to a member of the clergy who, in course of the discipline or practice of his or her church, denomination, or organization, is authorized or accustomed to hear such communications and, under the discipline or tenets of his or her church, denomination, or organization, has a duty to keep such communications secret."[7] Whether communications made in a group setting qualify as confidential depends on the circumstances. In its remand of Doe 2 v. Superior Court,[8] the reviewing court invited the trial court to take evidence about the circumstances attending a church retreat that was limited to individuals who claimed to have been the victims of sexual abuse. The court was concerned that the presence of third persons might have prevented the victims' communications to a pastor from attaining the confidentiality required for protected penitential communications.[9]

Penitential communications are not limited to confessions.[10] "[T]here is no requirement that a communication have as its purpose the confession of a 'flawed act' to 'receive religious consolation and guidance in return' in order to be privileged."[11] Whether a particular communication qualifies as a penitential communication depends on whether the member of the clergy who receives it is authorized or accustomed to hear such communications and on whether the member of the clergy has a duty to keep the communication secret under the discipline or tenets of his or her church, denomination, or organization. In People v. Edwards[12] an accused's admission of a crime to a member of the clergy was held to be outside the privilege because under the tenets of the clergyman's church such admissions were not entitled to secrecy.[13]

A penitential communication is not made in confidence if the penitent is aware that the means chosen for transmission discloses the communication to third persons.[14] Such a communication does not acquire protection and can be disclosed by anyone having first-hand knowledge of the communication. Transmitting the information under circumstances where third persons can easily overhear the communication is evidence that the penitent did not intend the communication to be confidential.[15] Under the

---

7. West's Ann. California Evidence Code § 1032.

8. Doe 2 v. Superior Court, 132 Cal.App.4th 1504, 1517, 34 Cal.Rptr.3d 458, 467 (2005) (quoting B. Jefferson, 2 Cal. Evidence Benchbook, (Cont.Ed.Bar 3d ed. 2005) § 39.5, p. 884).

9. Id. at 1518, 34 Cal.Rptr.3d at 467.

10. California Evidence Code § 1032 (comment).

11. Doe 2 v. Superior Court, 132 Cal.App.4th 1504, 1518, 34 Cal.Rptr.3d 458, 468 (2005).

12. 203 Cal.App.3d 1358, 248 Cal.Rptr. 53 (1988), cert. denied, 489 U.S. 1027, 109 S.Ct. 1158, 103 L.Ed.2d 217 (1989).

13. Id. at 1364–1365, 248 Cal.Rptr. at 56–57.

14. West's Ann. California Evidence Code § 1032. See also Roman Catholic Archbishop of Los Angeles v. Superior Court, 131 Cal.App.4th 417, 445, 32 Cal.Rptr.3d 209, 230 (2005), cert. denied, 547 U.S. 1071, 126 S.Ct. 1783, 164 L.Ed.2d 518 (2006) ("The fact both parties to the original communication [the priest and the archbishop] knew it likely would be transmitted to a third person vitiated ab initio any privilege under Evidence Code section 1032 * * *.").

15. See West's Ann. California Evidence Code § 954 (comment) relating to the attorney-client privilege. However, confidential communications do not lose their privileged character simply

Code, however, communications between penitents and members of the clergy are presumed to be confidential.[16] The effect of the presumption is to place on the party opposing the claim of privilege the burden of persuading the judge that the communication was not made in confidence.[17]

The Code rejects the eavesdropper doctrine, which permits individuals who overhear confidential communications between penitents and members of the clergy to reveal them despite their desire to keep the communications confidential.[18] Penitents are protected against the risk of disclosure by eavesdroppers and other wrongful interceptors of confidential information by permitting them to assert the privilege against anyone, including the eavesdropper, who acquires the information without the penitent's consent.[19] Member of the clergy, however, cannot object to disclosure by eavesdroppers. Under their privilege, they cannot prevent another from disclosing a penitential communication.[20]

QUESTIONS AND PROBLEMS

1. A penitent has a privilege to refuse to disclose and to prevent another from disclosing a penitential communication. True or false?

2. A member of the clergy has a more limited privilege. While a member of the clergy has a privilege to refuse to disclose a penitential communication, she does not have a privilege to prevent another from disclosing such a communication. True or false?

3. Whether or not a confidential communication from a penitent qualifies under the privilege depends in part on whether the clergyperson's religious institution authorized her to hear the communication and the clergyperson has a duty under the tenets of the religious institution to keep such a communication secret. True or false?

4. Penitential communications are limited to confessions. True or false?

§ 29.02 CLAIMING THE PRIVILEGE

By claiming the privilege, the penitent, whether or not a party, can refuse to disclose or prevent another from disclosing a penitential communication.[1] The penitent is entitled to prevent others from disclosing a penitential communication because the penitent's privilege is designed to

---

because they are communicated by electronic means or because persons involved in the delivery, facilitation, or storage of electronic communications might have access to their content. West's Ann. California Evidence Code § 917.

16. West's Ann. California Evidence Code § 917.

17. Id. For a discussion of the presumption, see § 20.03 supra.

18. See West's Ann. California Evidence Code §§ 1033 (comment) and 952 (comment) relating to the attorney-client privilege.

19. Id.

20. West's Ann. California Evidence Code § 1034.

1. West's Ann. California Evidence Code § 1033.

protect the confidentiality of the penitent's communications. A member of the clergy, on the other hand, can refuse only to disclose a penitential communication by claiming the privilege.[2] The clergyperson's privilege is designed to protect members of the clergy only from violating religious tenets that prohibit disclosing penitential communications.[3] But a member of the clergy is not required to claim the privilege.[4] Whether the privilege should be claimed is left to the clergyperson's discretion and the discipline of the religious body of which the clergyperson is a member.[5]

Both the penitent and member of the clergy can waive their respective privileges.[6] But each can claim the privilege even if the other has waived.[7] A penitent, however, can prevent a member of the clergy from revealing the penitential communication even if the member of the clergy waives his or her privilege.[8] A member of the clergy does not have the same right, since a member of the clergy can refuse only to disclose a penitential communication.

The Code provides no exceptions to the clergy-penitent privilege.

QUESTIONS AND PROBLEMS

1. Adam tells his minister in confidence that he stole a painting. Under the tenets of the minister's church, the confession qualifies as a penitential communication. Adam is then prosecuted for the theft. Over a penitential communication objection, both Adam and the minister can refuse to reveal the confession. True or false?

2. Upon the advice of his bishop, the minister decides to waive his privilege. Over Adam's penitential communication objection, the minister may not reveal the confession. True or false?

3. Suppose that, instead, Adam decides to waive his privilege. Must the judge sustain the minister's privilege to decline to disclose the communication?

CALIFORNIA EVIDENCE CODE

§ 1030. Member of the clergy

As used in this article, "member of the clergy" means a priest, minister, religious practitioner, or similar functionary of a church or of a religious denomination or religious organization.

---

2. West's Ann. California Evidence Code § 1034.

3. Id. (comment).

4. The Code does impose such a duty upon lawyers, physicians, psychotherapists, sexual assault counselors, and domestic violence counselors. See West's Ann. California Evidence Code §§ 955, 995, 1015, 1035.8, and 1037.5.

5. West's Ann. California Evidence Code § 1034 (comment).

6. West's Ann. California Evidence Code §§ 1033–1034. For a discussion of how the privileges can be waived, see § 20.05 supra.

7. West's Ann. California Evidence Code § 1034 (comment).

8. West's Ann. California Evidence Code § 1033.

§ 1031. Penitent

As used in this article, "penitent" means a person who has made a penitential communication to a clergyman.

§ 1032. Penitential communication

As used in this article, "penitential communication" means a communication made in confidence, in the presence of no third person so far as the penitent is aware, to a clergyman who, in the course of the discipline or practice of his church, denomination, or organization, is authorized or accustomed to hear such communications and, under the discipline or tenets of his church, denomination, or organization, has a duty to keep such communications secret.

§ 1033. Privilege of penitent

Subject to Section 912, a penitent, whether or not a party, has a privilege to refuse to disclose, and to prevent another from disclosing, a penitential communication if he claims the privilege.

§ 1034. Privilege of clergy

Subject to Section 912, a clergyman, whether or not a party, has a privilege to refuse to disclose a penitential communication if he claims the privilege.

FEDERAL RULES OF EVIDENCE

Rule 506. Communications to Clergymen [Not enacted.]

(a) Definitions. As used in this rule:

(1) A "clergyman" is a minister, priest, rabbi, or other similar functionary of a religious organization, or an individual reasonably believed so to be by the person consulting him.

(2) A communication is "confidential" if made privately and not intended for further disclosure except to other persons present in furtherance of the purpose of the communication.

(b) General rule of privilege. A person has a privilege to refuse to disclose and to prevent another from disclosing a confidential communication by the person to a clergyman in his professional character as spiritual adviser.

(c) Who may claim the privilege. The privilege may be claimed by the person, by his guardian or conservator, or by his personal representative if he is deceased. The clergyman may claim the privilege on behalf of the person. His authority so to do is presumed in the absence of evidence to the contrary.

ADVISORY COMMITTEE'S NOTE

The considerations which dictate the recognition of privileges generally seem strongly to favor a privilege for confidential communications to clergymen. During the period when most of the common law privileges were taking shape, no clear-cut privilege for communications between priest and penitent emerged. 8 Wigmore § 2394 (McNaughton Rev.1961). The English political climate of the time may well furnish the explanation. In this country, however, the privilege has been recognized by statute in about two-thirds of the states and occasionally by the common law process of decision. *Id.,* § 2395; Mullen v. United States, 105 U.S.App.D.C. 25, 263 F.2d 275 (1958).

Subdivision (a). Paragraph (1) defines a clergyman as a "minister, priest, rabbi, or other similar functionary of a religious organization." The concept is necessarily broader than that inherent in the ministerial exemption for purposes of Selective Service. See United States v. Jackson, 369 F.2d 936 (4th Cir.1966). However, it is not so broad as to include all self-denominated "ministers." A fair construction of the language requires that the person to whom the status is sought to be attached be regularly engaged in activities conforming at least in a general way with those of a Catholic priest, Jewish rabbi, or minister of an established Protestant denomination, though not necessarily on a full-time basis. No further specification seems possible in view of the lack of licensing and certification procedures for clergymen. However, this lack seems to have occasioned no particular difficulties in connection with the solemnization of marriages, which suggests that none may be anticipated here. For similar definitions of "clergyman" see California Evidence Code § 1030; New Jersey Evidence Rule 29.

The "reasonable belief" provision finds support in similar provisions for lawyer-client in Rule 503 and for psychotherapist-patient in Rule 504. A parallel is also found in the recognition of the validity of marriages performed by unauthorized persons if the parties reasonably believed them legally qualified. Harper and Skolnick, Problems of the Family 153 (Rev.Ed.1962).

(2) The definition of "confidential" communication is consistent with the use of the term in Rule 503(a)(5) for lawyer-client and in Rule 504(a)(3) for psychotherapist-patient, suitably adapted to communications to clergymen.

Subdivision (b). The choice between a privilege narrowly restricted to doctrinally required confessions and a privilege broadly applicable to all confidential communications with a clergyman in his professional character as spiritual adviser has been exercised in favor of the latter. Many clergymen now receive training in marriage counseling and the handling of personality problems. Matters of this kind fall readily into the realm of the spirit. The same considerations which underlie the psychotherapist-patient privilege of Rule 504 suggest a broad application of the privilege for communications to clergymen.

State statutes and rules fall in both the narrow and the broad categories. A typical narrow statute proscribes disclosure of "a confession * * * made

* * * in the course of discipline enjoined by the church to which he belongs." Ariz.Rev.Stats.Ann.1956, § 12–2233. See also California Evidence Code § 1032; Uniform Rule 29. Illustrative of the broader privilege are statutes applying to "information communicated to him in a confidential manner, properly entrusted to him in his professional capacity, and necessary to enable him to discharge the functions of his office according to the usual course of his practice or discipline, wherein such person so communicating * * * is seeking spiritual counsel and advice," Fla.Stats.Ann.1960, § 90.241, or to any "confidential communication properly entrusted to him in his professional capacity, and necessary and proper to enable him to discharge the functions of his office according to the usual course of practice or discipline," Iowa Code Ann.1950, § 622.10. See also Ill.Rev.Stats.1967, c. 51, § 48.1; Minn.Stats.Ann.1945, § 595.02(3); New Jersey Evidence Rule 29.

Under the privilege as phrased, the communicating person is entitled to prevent disclosure not only by himself but also by the clergyman and by eavesdroppers. For discussion see Advisory Committee's Note under lawyer-client privilege, Rule 503(b).

The nature of what may reasonably be considered spiritual advice makes it unnecessary to include in the rule a specific exception for communications in furtherance of crime or fraud, as in Rule 503(d)(1).

Subdivision (c) makes clear that the privilege belongs to the communicating person. However, a prima facie authority on the part of the clergyman to claim the privilege on behalf of the person is recognized. The discipline of the particular church and the discreetness of the clergyman are believed to constitute sufficient safeguards for the absent communicating person. See Advisory Committee's Note to the similar provision with respect to attorney-client in Rule 503(c).

CHAPTER 30

THE HUMAN TRAFFICKING CASEWORKER-VICTIM PRIVILEGE

■ ■ ■

Table of Sections

§ 30.01 NATURE OF THE PRIVILEGE

Under the Code, a trafficking victim, whether or not a party to the action, has a privilege to refuse to disclose, and to prevent another from disclosing, a confidential communication between the victim and a human trafficking caseworker.[1]

A "victim" means any person who is a "trafficking victim" as defined in California Penal Code § 236.1.[2] This section punishes any person who deprives or violates the personal liberty of another with the intent to effect or maintain a felony violation of enumerated offenses, including prostitution, or to obtain forced labor or services.[3]

A human trafficking caseworker is defined as a person who is employed by any organization providing the programs specified in § 18294 of the Welfare and Institutions Code, whether financially compensated or not, for the purpose of rendering advice or assistance to victims of human trafficking, who has received specialized training in the counseling of human trafficking victims, and who meets at least one additional enumerated criterion.[4]

A "confidential communication" is defined as information transmitted between the victim and the caseworker in the course of their relationship and in confidence by a means which, so far as the victim is aware,

---

1. West's Ann. California Evidence Code § 1038.

2. West's Ann. California Evidence Code § 1038.2(a).

3. See West's Ann. California Penal Code § 236.1.

4. West's Ann. California Evidence Code § 1038.2(b).

discloses the information to no third persons other than those who are present to further the interests of the victim in the consultation or those to whom disclosures are reasonably necessary for the transmission of the information or an accomplishment of the purposes for which the human trafficking counselor is consulted. It includes all information regarding the facts and circumstances involving all incidences of human trafficking.[5]

§ 30.02 CLAIMING THE PRIVILEGE

As the holder of the privilege, a trafficking victim, whether or not a party to the action, has a privilege to refuse to disclose, and to prevent another from disclosing, a confidential communication between the victim and a human trafficking caseworker.[1] The human trafficking caseworker who received or made a communication subject to the privilege has the obligation to claim the privilege whenever he or she is present when the communication is sought to be disclosed and he or she is authorized to claim the privilege.[2]

§ 30.03 COMPELLED DISCLOSURES

The court may compel disclosure of information received by a human trafficking caseworker if it constitutes relevant evidence of the facts and circumstances involving a crime allegedly perpetrated against the victim and is the subject of a criminal proceeding, provided the court determines that the probative value of the information outweighs the effect of disclosure of the information on the victim, the counseling relationship, and the counseling services.[1] In ruling on the claim of privilege, the judge may hold an in camera hearing in which disclosure of the privileged information may be compelled.[2] If the judge determines that particular information may be subject to disclosure pursuant to the balancing test, the judge must follow a prescribed procedure before ordering the information disclosed.[3] At the conclusion of the hearing the judge must determine which items of information should be disclosed.[4]

CALIFORNIA EVIDENCE CODE

§ 1038. Privilege

(a) A trafficking victim, whether or not a party to the action, has a privilege to refuse to disclose, and to prevent another from disclosing, a

---

5. West's Ann. California Evidence Code § 1038.2(b)(2)(B).

1. West's Ann. California Evidence Code § 1038(a).

2. West's Ann. California Evidence Code § 1038(a)(3).

1. West's Ann. California Evidence Code § 1038.1(a).

2. West's Ann. California Evidence Code § 1038.1(b).

3. West's Ann. California Evidence Code § 1038.1(c).

4. Id.

confidential communication between the victim and a human trafficking caseworker if the privilege is claimed by any of the following persons:

(1) The holder of the privilege.

(2) A person who is authorized to claim the privilege by the holder of the privilege.

(3) The person who was the human trafficking caseworker at the time of the confidential communication. However, that person may not claim the privilege if there is no holder of the privilege in existence or if he or she is otherwise instructed by a person authorized to permit disclosure. The human trafficking caseworker who received or made a communication subject to the privilege granted by this article shall claim the privilege whenever he or she is present when the communication is sought to be disclosed and he or she is authorized to claim the privilege under this section.

(b) A human trafficking caseworker shall inform a trafficking victim of any applicable limitations on confidentiality of communications between the victim and the caseworker. This information may be given orally.

§ 1038.1. Compulsion of disclosure by court

(a) The court may compel disclosure of information received by a human trafficking caseworker that constitutes relevant evidence of the facts and circumstances involving a crime allegedly perpetrated against the victim and that is the subject of a criminal proceeding, if the court determines that the probative value of the information outweighs the effect of disclosure of the information on the victim, the counseling relationship, and the counseling services. The court may compel disclosure if the victim is either dead or not the complaining witness in a criminal action against the perpetrator.

(b) When a court rules on a claim of privilege under this article, it may require the person from whom disclosure is sought or the person authorized to claim the privilege, or both, to disclose the information in chambers out of the presence and hearing of all persons except the person authorized to claim the privilege and those other persons that the person authorized to claim the privilege consents to have present.

(c) If the judge determines that the information is privileged and shall not be disclosed, neither he nor she nor any other person may disclose, without the consent of a person authorized to permit disclosure, any information disclosed in the course of the proceedings in chambers. If the court determines that information shall be disclosed, the court shall so order and inform the defendant in the criminal action. If the court finds there is a reasonable likelihood that any information is subject to disclosure pursuant to the balancing test provided in this section, the procedure specified in paragraphs (1), (2), and (3) of Section 1035.4 shall be followed.

§ 1038.2. Definitions

(a) As used in this article, "victim" means any person who is a "trafficking victim" as defined in Section 236.1.[1]

(b) As used in this article, "human trafficking caseworker" means any of the following:

(1) A person who is employed by any organization providing the programs specified in Section 18294 of the Welfare and Institutions Code, whether financially compensated or not, for the purpose of rendering advice or assistance to victims of human trafficking, who has received specialized training in the counseling of human trafficking victims, and who meets one of the following requirements:

(A) Has a master's degree in counseling or a related field; or has one year of counseling experience, at least six months of which is in the counseling of human trafficking victims.

(B) Has at least 40 hours of training as specified in this paragraph and is supervised by an individual who qualifies as a counselor under subparagraph (A), or is a psychotherapist, as defined in Section 1010. The training, supervised by a person qualified under subparagraph (A), shall include, but need not be limited to, the following areas: history of human trafficking, civil and criminal law as it relates to human trafficking, societal attitudes towards human trafficking, peer counseling techniques, housing, public assistance and other financial resources available to meet the financial needs of human trafficking victims, and referral services available to human trafficking victims. A portion of this training must include an explanation of privileged communication.

(2) A person who is employed by any organization providing the programs specified in Section 13835.2 of the Penal Code, whether financially compensated or not, for the purpose of counseling and assisting human trafficking victims, and who meets one of the following requirements:

(A) Is a psychotherapist as defined in Section 1010, has a master's degree in counseling or a related field, or has one year of counseling experience, at least six months of which is in rape assault counseling.

(B) Has the minimum training for human trafficking counseling required by guidelines established by the employing agency pursuant to subdivision (c) of Section 13835.10 of the Penal Code, and is supervised by an individual who qualifies as a counselor under subparagraph (A). The training, supervised by a person qualified under subparagraph (A), shall include, but not be limited to, law, victimology, counseling techniques, client and system advocacy, and referral services. A portion of this training must include an explanation of privileged communication.

---

1. See Penal Code § 236.1.

(c) As used in this article, "confidential communication" means information transmitted between the victim and the caseworker in the course of their relationship and in confidence by a means which, so far as the victim is aware, discloses the information to no third persons other than those who are present to further the interests of the victim in the consultation or those to whom disclosures are reasonably necessary for the transmission of the information or an accomplishment of the purposes for which the human trafficking counselor is consulted. It includes all information regarding the facts and circumstances involving all incidences of human trafficking.

(d) As used in this article, "holder of the privilege" means the victim when he or she has no guardian or conservator, or a guardian or conservator of the victim when the victim has a guardian or conservator.

TABLE OF CASES

D

E

Eccleston, People v., 107 Cal.Rptr.2d 440 (Cal. App. 1 Dist.2001)—§ **14.05, n. 32.**

Edelbacher, People v., 254 Cal.Rptr. 586, 766 P.2d 1 (Cal.1989)—§ **2.02, n. 4.**

Eduardo A., In re, 209 Cal.App.3d 1038, 261 Cal.Rptr. 68 (Cal.App. 2 Dist.1989)— § **23.03, n. 12.**

Edwards, People v., 203 Cal.App.3d 1358, 248 Cal.Rptr. 53 (Cal.App. 1 Dist.1988)— § **29.01, n. 12.**

Eid, People v., 36 Cal.Rptr.2d 835 (Cal.App. 2 Dist.1994)—§ **1.03, n. 37.**

Eisendrath v. Superior Court, 134 Cal.Rptr.2d 716 (Cal.App. 2 Dist.2003)—§ **21.06, n. 17.**

Elcome v. Chin, 1 Cal.Rptr.3d 631 (Cal.App. 4 Dist.2003)—§ **18.04, n. 14.**

Elliot, People v., 35 Cal.Rptr.3d 759, 122 P.3d 968 (Cal.2005)—§ **9.01, n. 2.**

Elsey, People v., 97 Cal.Rptr.2d 269 (Cal.App. 3 Dist.2000)—§ **1.03, n. 45.**

Elsworth v. Beech Aircraft Corp., 208 Cal.Rptr. 874, 691 P.2d 630 (Cal.1984)—§ **10.07;** § **10.07, n. 39, 44.**

Elwell, People v., 206 Cal.App.3d 171, 253 Cal. Rptr. 480 (Cal.App. 5 Dist.1988)—§ **15.07, n. 77.**

Emilye A., In re, 12 Cal.Rptr.2d 294 (Cal.App. 4 Dist.1992)—§ **14.07, n. 8.**

Emma Corp. v. Inglewood Unified School Dist., 8 Cal.Rptr.3d 213 (Cal.App. 2 Dist.2004)— § **18.06, n. 8.**

Englebrecht, People v., 106 Cal.Rptr.2d 738 (Cal.App. 4 Dist.2001)—§ **18.02, n. 19.**

Epps, People v., 104 Cal.Rptr.2d 572, 18 P.3d 2 (Cal.2001)—§ **7.09, n. 8.**

Erickson, People v., 67 Cal.Rptr.2d 740 (Cal. App. 5 Dist.1997)—§ **15.09, n. 26.**

Erie R. Co. v. Tompkins, 304 U.S. 64, 58 S.Ct. 817, 82 L.Ed. 1188 (1938)—§ **4.02, n. 11;** § **18.10, n. 11.**

Ervin, People v., 91 Cal.Rptr.2d 623, 990 P.2d 506 (Cal.2000)—§ **8.02, n. 10;** § **15.11, n. 53.**

Erving, People v., 73 Cal.Rptr.2d 815 (Cal.App. 2 Dist.1998)—§ **3.15, n. 37.**

Erwin, People v., 25 Cal.Rptr.2d 348 (Cal.App. 2 Dist.1993)—§ **15.13, n. 19.**

Escobar, People v., 55 Cal.Rptr.2d 883 (Cal. App. 2 Dist.1996)—§ **1.03, n. 24;** § **3.15, n. 93.**

Escobar, People v., 98 Cal.Rptr.2d 696 (Cal. App. 1 Dist.2000)—§ **3.14, n. 47;** § **9.12, n. 17.**

Estate of (see name of party)

Estelle v. McGuire, 502 U.S. 62, 112 S.Ct. 475, 116 L.Ed.2d 385 (1991)—§ **3.10, n. 2.**

Etcheverry v. Tri–Ag Service, Inc., 93 Cal. Rptr.2d 36, 993 P.2d 366 (Cal.2000)— § **19.01, n. 52.**

Evans, People v., 31 Cal.Rptr.2d 20 (Cal.App. 1 Dist.1994)—§ **7.02, n. 13.**

Evers, People v., 12 Cal.Rptr.2d 637 (Cal.App. 4 Dist.1992)—§ **3.15, n. 75.**

Ewing v. Cloverleaf Bowl, 143 Cal.Rptr. 13, 572 P.2d 1155 (Cal.1978)—§ **18.04, n. 7, 8.**

Ewing v. Goldstein, 15 Cal.Rptr.3d 864 (Cal. App. 2 Dist.2004)—§ **23.03, n. 68.**

Ewoldt, People v., 27 Cal.Rptr.2d 646, 867 P.2d 757 (Cal.1994)—§ **3.07, n. 5;** § **3.08, n. 2;** § **3.16, n. 12, 26, 28, 33;** § **3.17, n. 3;** § **15.01, n. 6;** § **15.05, n. 10.**

Ex parte (see name of party)

Eye v. Kafer, Inc., 202 Cal.App.2d 449, 20 Cal.Rptr. 841 (Cal.App. 2 Dist.1962)— § **15.11, n. 32.**

F

Fair, People v., 203 Cal.App.3d 1303, 250 Cal. Rptr. 486 (Cal.App. 5 Dist.1988)—§ **8.08, n. 12, 15.**

Falsetta, People v., 89 Cal.Rptr.2d 847, 986 P.2d 182 (Cal.1999)—§ **3.14, n. 32;** § **3.16, n. 43.**

Farmer, People v., 254 Cal.Rptr. 508, 765 P.2d 940 (Cal.1989)—§ **9.04;** § **9.04, n. 9, 11, 12, 40, 43;** § **16.06, n. 10.**

Farnam, People v., 121 Cal.Rptr.2d 106, 47 P.3d 988 (Cal.2002)—§ **7.06, n. 5;** § **16.02, n. 4;** § **16.03, n. 24;** § **16.04, n. 74.**

Farr, People v., 255 Cal.App.2d 679, 63 Cal. Rptr. 477 (Cal.App. 2 Dist.1967)—§ **9.08, n. 5.**

Farrell L. v. Superior Court, 203 Cal.App.3d 521, 250 Cal.Rptr. 25 (Cal.App. 5 Dist. 1988)—§ **23.01, n. 49;** § **23.03, n. 94.**

Fasanaro v. Mooney Aircraft Corp., 687 F.Supp. 482 (N.D.Cal.1988)—§ **4.02, n. 13.**

Fassberg Const. Co. v. Housing Authority of City of Los Angeles, 60 Cal.Rptr.3d 375 (Cal.App. 2 Dist.2007)—§ **7.07, n. 16.**

Fauber, People v., 9 Cal.Rptr.2d 24, 831 P.2d 249 (Cal.1992)—§ **1.03, n. 36;** § **7.02, n. 9.**

Feagin, People v., 40 Cal.Rptr.2d 918 (Cal.App. 2 Dist.1995)—§ **15.11, n. 34.**

Feaster, People v., 125 Cal.Rptr.2d 896 (Cal. App. 2 Dist.2002)—§ **15.07, n. 56, 97.**

Feist v. Feist, 236 Cal.App.2d 433, 46 Cal.Rptr. 93 (Cal.App. 4 Dist.1965)—§ **3.05, n. 7.**

Felix, People v., 82 Cal.Rptr.2d 701 (Cal.App. 4 Dist.1999)—§ **3.03, n. 4.**

Felix, People v., 28 Cal.Rptr.2d 860 (Cal.App. 4 Dist.1994)—§ **3.15, n. 58.**

Felix, People v., 112 Cal.Rptr.2d 311 (Cal.App. 2 Dist.2001)—§ **5.04, n. 28;** § **23.03, n. 48.**

Fellows v. Superior Court, 108 Cal.App.3d 55, 166 Cal.Rptr. 274 (Cal.App. 2 Dist.1980)— § **22.01, n. 6, 20;** § **22.03, n. 30.**

Field, People v., 37 Cal.Rptr.2d 803 (Cal.App. 4 Dist.1995)—§ **15.07, n. 140.**

Field Research Corp. v. Patrick, 30 Cal.App.3d 603, 106 Cal.Rptr. 473 (Cal.App. 1 Dist. 1973)—§ **18.02, n. 13.**

Fields, People v., 72 Cal.Rptr.2d 255 (Cal.App. 2 Dist.1998)—§ **5.05, n. 21.**

Fieldson Associates, Inc. v. Whitecliff Labora- tories, Inc., 276 Cal.App.2d 770, 81 Cal.

H

K

M

Mickey, People v., 286 Cal.Rptr. 801, 818 P.2d 84 (Cal.1991)—§ **27.01, n. 24.**

Miles, People v., 172 Cal.App.3d 474, 218 Cal. Rptr. 378 (Cal.App. 2 Dist.1985)—§ **15.07, n. 79.**

Miller, People v., 31 Cal.Rptr.2d 423 (Cal.App. 2 Dist.1994)—§ **16.03, n. 6.**

Miller, People v., 97 Cal.Rptr.2d 684 (Cal.App. 6 Dist.2000)—§ **3.15, n. 16.**

Miller v. Superior Court, 111 Cal.App.3d 390, 168 Cal.Rptr. 589 (Cal.App. 1 Dist.1980)— § **21.06, n. 43.**

Millwee, People v., 74 Cal.Rptr.2d 418, 954 P.2d 990 (Cal.1998)—§ **5.04, n. 55; § 9.12, n. 17.**

Milner, People v., 246 Cal.Rptr. 713, 753 P.2d 669 (Cal.1988)—§ **3.18, n. 1.**

Mincey, People v., 6 Cal.Rptr.2d 822, 827 P.2d 388 (Cal.1992)—§ **14.03, n. 29; § 20.01, n. 4; § 21.06, n. 55.**

Minifie, People v., 56 Cal.Rptr.2d 133, 920 P.2d 1337 (Cal.1996)—§ **3.12, n. 21.**

Miranda v. Department of Human Resources Dev., 33 Cal.App.3d 314, 109 Cal.Rptr. 35 (Cal.App. 2 Dist.1973)—§ **18.05, n. 42.**

Miranda, People v., 96 Cal.Rptr.2d 758, 1 P.3d 73 (Cal.2000)—§ **6.10, n. 2; § 9.01, n. 27.**

Miron, People v., 210 Cal.App.3d 580, 258 Cal. Rptr. 494 (Cal.App. 5 Dist.1989)—§ **9.04, n. 32.**

Mitcham, People v., 5 Cal.Rptr.2d 230, 824 P.2d 1277 (Cal.1992)—§ **6.10, n. 5.**

Mitchell v. Superior Court, 208 Cal.Rptr. 886, 691 P.2d 642 (Cal.1984)—§ **21.03, n. 18; § 21.06, n. 46.**

Mitchell, United States v., 172 F.3d 1104 (9th Cir.1999)—§ **3.15, n. 55.**

Mitchell Brothers' Santa Ana Theater, People ex rel. Cooper v., 128 Cal.App.3d 937, 180 Cal.Rptr. 728 (Cal.App. 4 Dist.1982)— § **18.02, n. 17.**

Moccia, United States v., 681 F.2d 61 (1st Cir.1982)—§ **3.04, n. 8.**

Moe v. Avions Marcel Dassault–Breguet Aviation, 727 F.2d 917 (10th Cir.1984)—§ **4.02, n. 13.**

Moeller v. Superior Court, 69 Cal.Rptr.2d 317, 947 P.2d 279 (Cal.1997)—§ **21.01, n. 29.**

Montebello Rose Co. v. Agricultural Labor Relations Bd., 119 Cal.App.3d 1, 173 Cal.Rptr. 856 (Cal.App. 5 Dist.1981)—§ **21.03, n. 8.**

Monterroso, People v., 22 Cal.Rptr.3d 1, 101 P.3d 956 (Cal.2004)—§ **9.03, n. 23.**

Moody v. Peirano, 4 Cal.App. 411, 88 P. 380 (Cal.App. 1 Dist.1906)—§ **3.25; § 3.25, n. 5, 6.**

Moore, People v., 201 Cal.App.3d 877, 247 Cal. Rptr. 353 (Cal.App. 2 Dist.1988)—§ **8.03, n. 16; § 15.03, n. 33.**

Morales, People v., 257 Cal.Rptr. 64, 770 P.2d 244 (Cal.1989)—§ **9.10, n. 10.**

Morales, People v., 263 Cal.App.2d 368, 69 Cal.Rptr. 402 (Cal.App. 4 Dist.1968)— § **7.04, n. 22.**

Moran, People v., 39 Cal.App.3d 398, 114 Cal. Rptr. 413 (Cal.App. 1 Dist.1974)—§ **11.04, n. 13, 15.**

Morehouse v. Taubman Co., 5 Cal.App.3d 548, 85 Cal.Rptr. 308 (Cal.App. 1 Dist.1970)— § **4.03, n. 3.**

Morgan, People v., 68 Cal.Rptr.2d 772 (Cal. App. 1 Dist.1997)—§ **15.09, n. 43, 48.**

Morgan, People v., 87 Cal.App.3d 59, 150 Cal. Rptr. 712 (Cal.App. 2 Dist.1978)—§ **15.03, n. 2.**

Morgan, People v., 23 Cal.Rptr.3d 224 (Cal. App. 3 Dist.2005)—§ **5.04, n. 42; § 5.05, n. 24.**

Morgan v. Regents of University of Cal., 105 Cal.Rptr.2d 652 (Cal.App. 1 Dist.2000)— § **7.03, n. 3.**

Morganti, People v., 50 Cal.Rptr.2d 837 (Cal. App. 1 Dist.1996)—§ **16.04, n. 22, 107, 120.**

Morris, People v., 279 Cal.Rptr. 720, 807 P.2d 949 (Cal.1991)—§ **1.03, n. 15; § 16.04, n. 104.**

Morris, People v., 249 Cal.Rptr. 119, 756 P.2d 843 (Cal.1988)—§ **15.11, n. 34.**

Morris, People v., 20 Cal.App.3d 659, 97 Cal. Rptr. 817 (Cal.App. 1 Dist.1971)—§ **21.06, n. 18.**

Mosesian v. Pennwalt Corp., 191 Cal.App.3d 851, 236 Cal.Rptr. 778 (Cal.App. 5 Dist. 1987)—§ **16.03, n. 9.**

Mower, People v., 122 Cal.Rptr.2d 326, 49 P.3d 1067 (Cal.2002)—§ **18.07, n. 29, 31, 32.**

M. Perez Co. v. Base Camp Condominiums Ass'n No. One, 3 Cal.Rptr.3d 563 (Cal.App. 3 Dist.2003)—§ **18.06, n. 8.**

Mullaney v. Wilbur, 421 U.S. 684, 95 S.Ct. 1881, 44 L.Ed.2d 508 (1975)—§ **18.08, n. 2.**

Mullen v. United States, 263 F.2d 275, 105 U.S.App.D.C. 25 (D.C.Cir.1958)—§ **29.02.**

Mullens, People v., 14 Cal.Rptr.3d 534 (Cal. App. 4 Dist.2004)—§ **3.14, n. 30.**

Muniz, People v., 213 Cal.App.3d 1508, 262 Cal.Rptr. 743 (Cal.App. 4 Dist.1989)— § **4.08, n. 23.**

Munoz, People v., 157 Cal.App.3d 999, 204 Cal.Rptr. 271 (Cal.App. 4 Dist.1984)— § **15.11, n. 13, 37, 38.**

Murphy v. Davids, 181 Cal. 706, 186 P. 143 (Cal.1919)—§ **3.05, n. 9.**

Murphy Auto Parts Co. v. Ball, 249 F.2d 508, 101 U.S.App.D.C. 416 (D.C.Cir.1957)— § **9.04, n. 5.**

Murtishaw, People v., 175 Cal.Rptr. 738, 631 P.2d 446 (Cal.1981)—§ **16.04, n. 4.**

Muscato, United States v., 534 F.Supp. 969 (E.D.N.Y.1982)—§ **5.04, n. 44.**

Mutual Life Ins. Co. of New York v. Hillmon, 145 U.S. 285, 12 S.Ct. 909, 36 L.Ed. 706 (1892)—§ **9.10, n. 1.**

Muzquiz v. City of Emeryville, 94 Cal.Rptr.2d 579 (Cal.App. 1 Dist.2000)—§ **3.19, n. 25.**

Mylan Laboratories Inc. v. Soon–Shiong, 90 Cal.Rptr.2d 111 (Cal.App. 2 Dist.1999)— § **21.05, n. 2.**

Q

R

Y

Z

TABLE OF STATUTES

TABLE OF RULES

MODEL CODE OF EVIDENCE RULES

INDEX

References are to Sections

References are to Sections

WRONGFUL DEATH—Cont'd
Pleading,
    Admissions, § 7.07

X RAYS
Best evidence, § 13.06

†

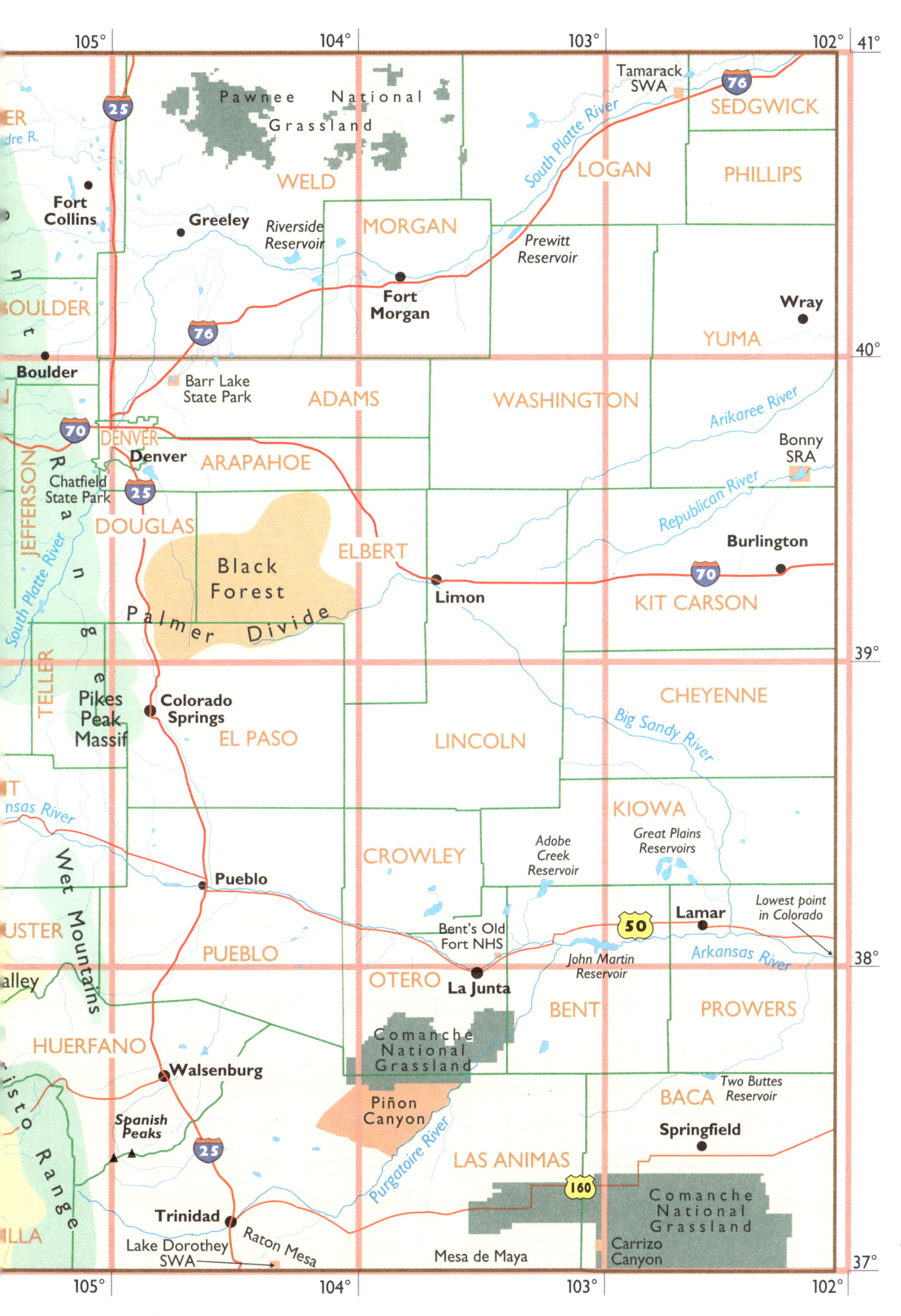